EVERYTHING You Were Taught About American Slavery Is Wrong

Ask a Southerner!

THE LOCHLAINN SEABROOK COLLECTION

Everything You Were Taught About the Civil War is Wrong, Ask a Southerner!
Everything You Were Taught About American Slavery is Wrong, Ask a Southerner!
Give This Book to a Yankee! A Southern Guide to the Civil War For Northerners
Honest Jeff and Dishonest Abe: A Southern Children's Guide to the Civil War
Confederacy 101: Amazing Facts You Never Knew About America's Oldest Political Tradition
The Great Yankee Coverup: What the North Doesn't Want You to Know About Lincoln's War!
A Rebel Born: A Defense of Nathan Bedford Forrest - Confederate General, American Legend (winner of the 2011 Jefferson Davis Historical Gold Medal)
A Rebel Born: The Screenplay
Nathan Bedford Forrest: Southern Hero, American Patriot - Honoring a Confederate Icon and the Old South
The Quotable Nathan Bedford Forrest: Selections From the Writings and Speeches of the Confederacy's Most Brilliant Cavalryman
Give 'Em Hell Boys! The Complete Military Correspondence of Nathan Bedford Forrest
Forrest! 99 Reasons to Love Nathan Bedford Forrest
Saddle, Sword, and Gun: A Biography of Nathan Bedford Forrest For Teens
The Quotable Jefferson Davis: Selections From the Writings and Speeches of the Confederacy's First President
The Quotable Alexander H. Stephens: Selections From the Writings and Speeches of the Confederacy's First Vice President
The Alexander H. Stephens Reader: Excerpts From the Works of a Confederate Founding Father
The Quotable Robert E. Lee: Selections From the Writings and Speeches of the South's Most Beloved Civil War General
The Old Rebel: Robert E. Lee As He Was Seen By His Contemporaries
The Articles of Confederation Explained: A Clause-by-Clause Study of America's First Constitution
The Constitution of the Confederate States of America Explained: A Clause-by-Clause Study of the South's Magna Carta
The Quotable Stonewall Jackson: Selections From the Writings and Speeches of the South's Most Famous General
Abraham Lincoln: The Southern View - Demythologizing America's Sixteenth President
The Unquotable Abraham Lincoln: The President's Quotes They Don't Want You To Know!
Lincolnology: The Real Abraham Lincoln Revealed in His Own Words - A Study of Lincoln's Suppressed, Misinterpreted, and Forgotten Writings and Speeches
The Great Impersonator! 99 Reasons to Dislike Abraham Lincoln
The Quotable Edward A. Pollard: Selections From the Writings of the Confederacy's Greatest Defender
Encyclopedia of the Battle of Franklin - A Comprehensive Guide to the Conflict that Changed the Civil War
Carnton Plantation Ghost Stories: True Tales of the Unexplained from Tennessee's Most Haunted Civil War House!
The McGavocks of Carnton Plantation: A Southern History - Celebrating One of Dixie's Most Noble Confederate Families and Their Tennessee Home
Jesus and the Law of Attraction: The Bible-Based Guide to Creating Perfect Health, Wealth, and Happiness Following Christ's Simple Formula
The Bible and the Law of Attraction: 99 Teachings of Jesus, the Apostles, and the Prophets
Christ Is All and In All: Rediscovering Your Divine Nature and the Kingdom Within
Jesus and the Gospel of Q: Christ's Pre-Christian Teachings As Recorded in the New Testament
The Way of Holiness: The Story of Religion and Myth From the Cave Bear Cult to Christianity
Christmas Before Christianity: How the Birthday of the "Sun" Became the Birthday of the "Son"
Britannia Rules: Goddess-Worship in Ancient Anglo-Celtic Society - An Academic Look at the United Kingdom's Matricentric Spiritual Past
The Book of Kelle: An Introduction to Goddess-Worship and the Great Celtic Mother-Goddess Kelle, Original Blessed Lady of Ireland
The Goddess Dictionary of Words and Phrases: Introducing a New Core Vocabulary for the Women's Spirituality Movement
Princess Diana: Modern Day Moon-Goddess - A Psychoanalytical and Mythological Look at Diana Spencer's Life, Marriage, and Death (with Dr. Jane Goldberg)
Aphrodite's Trade: The Hidden History of Prostitution Unveiled
UFOs and Aliens: The Complete Guidebook
The Caudills: An Etymological, Ethnological, and Genealogical Study - Exploring the Name and National Origins of a European-American Family
The Blakeneys: An Etymological, Ethnological, and Genealogical Study - Uncovering the Mysterious Origins of the Blakeney Family and Name

It's a Matter of Historical Record That . . .

- slavery is a universal institution that was once found in every known society.
- Africa has been practicing slavery longer than any other region on earth.
- Africans were selling and exporting their own people as slaves as early as 500 BC.
- Africans were the only people who engaged continually in the African-European-American slave trade for its full 424 years.
- before 1820 no free blacks ever came to the U.S. from Africa. All were imported as slaves—that is, already enslaved by fellow Africans in their native country.
- without Africa's encouragement, commitment, participation, and collusion there would have been no black slavery in America.
- there were once so many white slaves in Africa that a series of wars were fought and an abolition society was formed to rescue and emancipate them.
- Africa's black slave owners treated both their black and white slaves with absolute savagery, daily subjecting them to horrific forms of abuse and even torture that included whipping, branding, starvation, exposure, and beheading.
- the transatlantic slave trade benefitted Africa in at least one way: by increasing the monetary value of African slaves, it greatly reduced instances of their abuse, torture, murder, and sacrifice by fellow Africans.
- American white slavery laid the groundwork for American black slavery.
- in early America a white slave was worth less than half that of a black slave.
- American black slavery got its start in the North.
- the American black slave trade began in the North.
- the American abolition movement was launched in the South.
- America's first known official slave owner was a black man, Angolan-born Anthony Johnson, who became a wealthy Virginia planter and owned both black and white slaves.
- New York was founded to serve as a slave state and New York City was founded to serve as a slave port.
- New York City was America's slaving capital for over a century.
- New York practiced slavery for 239 years, longer than any other state, making not the South, but the North America's one and only true slavocracy or "slave regime."
- one early historian referred to New York as a slave "regime never paralleled in equal volume elsewhere."
- in the 1700s emancipating slaves in New England was illegal, and in most Northern states slaves were made slaves for life.
- from slavery's first appearance in the Southern states, black servants could purchase their freedom any time they wished.
- in 1776 the Northern states had far more slaves than the South did.
- in some Northern towns 100 percent of the adult males were slave owners; in most Southern towns none of the adult males were slave owners.
- Northern slaves were registered as part of their owner's "livestock," Southern slaves were registered as members of their owner's family.
- in 1787, at the Constitutional Convention in Philadelphia, Pennsylvania, the New England states voted to keep the African slave trade open for as long as possible, at least until 1808.

- in the 1800s many Northern states banned black suffrage.
- Massachusetts was the first state to legalize, legitimize, and monetize slavery, and the first to ban interracial marriage.
- in the Old North there were few laws protecting black slaves. Yankee slave owners had complete freedom to discipline their chattel in any manner they saw fit, and various barbarities—from whipping and branding, to public torture and burning slaves at the stake—were legal, routine, and socially accepted.
- in the Old South black slaves were protected by a myriad of stringent rules and regulations, crimes against slaves were punishable by law, cruel slaveholders were rare and when caught harshly penalized, and the vast majority of slaves lived lives of comfort, safety, health, and security from birth to death.
- this is one of the many reasons black American slaves, when given a choice, preferred to be owned by Southern slaveholders rather than Northern ones.
- Britons who visited the Old South testified that the living and working conditions of free English laborers was at least five times worse than what was experienced by black Southern slaves.
- antiliteracy laws, meant to prevent both black slaves and free blacks from learning to read and write, were first invented in the puritanical North, where they were strictly and sometimes violently enforced.
- when antiliteracy-laws arose decades later in the far more lenient South, they were routinely ignored by servant owners, the constabulary, and the judicial system.
- Jim Crow laws were "universal" in all of the Northern states, but rare and "unusual" in the Old South.
- segregation was the norm in the Old North, but unknown in the antebellum South.
- in the mid 1800s in a number of Northern states, in particular Illinois, blacks who tried to move or work there were arrested and enslaved.
- in Massachusetts blacks who "intermingled" with white women were sold into permanent slavery and deported to West Indian plantations.
- authentic slavery was never practiced in the South.
- so-called "Southern slavery" was absolutely benign, a form of "mild servitude," compared to indigenous African slavery—which included some of the most cruel, uncivilized, and inhumane forms of bondage ever recorded.
- Southern black servants were treated better than servants in any other part of the New World.
- Dixie's African servants were so heavily indulged by their owners that being a "slave" came to be an enviable status symbol among Southern blacks.
- 18th-Century American slave traders said that imported Irish slaves were treated far worse than imported African slaves.
- the majority of Confederate generals did not own slaves, and most, like Robert E. Lee, were abolitionists.
- many Union generals, like Ulysses S. Grant, owned slaves and said they would not fight for abolition.
- according to the 1860 U.S. Census a mere 4.8 percent of Southerners owned slaves, 95.2 percent did not.
- prior to the formation of the Confederacy, Yankees viewed slavery as the "cornerstone

of the Union."

- the North practiced slavery for over a century longer than the South did: the North for 239 years, the South for only 116 years.
- the South was never directly involved in the American slave trade.
- the American slave trade was exclusively a Yankee enterprise.
- the Middle Passage was not the most hazardous or unpleasant leg of an African slave's journey through the notorious Slave Triangle. It was the harrowing Beginning Passage (the land route from Africa's interior to the coast), where three times as many slaves died as on the Middle Passage. The Beginning Passage was part of the domestic African slavery system, a system in which non-Africans (that is, white Europeans and Americans) played no role.
- Yankee slave ships were still sailing to and from Africa and the West Indies, purchasing black human cargo, right into the Civil War period.
- U.S. President Abraham Lincoln was a white racist, supremacist, and separatist whose plans for African-Americans included corralling them in their own all-black state and deporting the rest back "to their own native land," as he phrased it.
- C.S. President Jefferson Davis adopted a black boy during the Civil War and banned the foreign slave trade in the South before the North did.
- both Davis and Lincoln said that the Civil War was not fought over slavery.
- the North declared that it fought to "preserve the Union," not to abolish slavery.
- the South declared that it fought to "uphold the Constitution," not to maintain slavery.
- the Confederacy enlisted black soldiers long before the Union did.
- the Northern armies were racially segregated, the Southern armies were racially integrated.
- as many as 1 million African-Americans fought for the Confederacy, five times more than fought for the Union.
- in 1862, fearing that a "negro influx" would jeopardize his chances of reelection in 1864, Lincoln issued a "human blockade" to prevent freed Southern blacks from migrating into the Northern states.
- the Northern states never actually officially abolished slavery, but slowly and methodically emancipated their slaves over a 100 year period.
- the North refused to grant the South the same time frame to abolish slavery in her own region.
- the North only began gradually abolishing its own slavery system when it became unprofitable, and because most white Yankees could not abide the presence of African-Americans, not because of concerns over black civil rights.
- the South earnestly wanted to end slavery, and was working on plans to do so when Lincoln illegally and unnecessarily invaded Dixie.
- the American South was the last region in the West to practice slavery and the first one to try to abolish it.
- according to hundreds of eyewitness accounts, both domestic and foreign, the Old North was far more racist than the Old South.
- there were tens of thousands of both African-American and Native-American slave owners.
- in January 1865, four months before the end of the Civil War, and almost a year before

the U.S. abolished slavery under the Thirteenth Amendment, the Confederacy was planning complete emancipation across the South.

- Lincoln was not against slavery, he was against the spread of slavery, and he was only against its extension because he did not like the fact that slavery forced whites and blacks to "intermingle."
- Lincoln stalled emancipation, blocked black civil rights, promoted American apartheid, and spent his entire adult life pushing for black deportation. For these reasons alone Lincoln should not be called the "Great Emancipator."
- like Lincoln, the great majority of Northerners, including the Union armies, were anti-abolition and did not support the idea of nationwide emancipation.
- after nearly three years in office, President Lincoln only finally issued the Emancipation Proclamation for political and military purposes, not to help African-Americans themselves.
- Lincoln's Emancipation Proclamation did not free a single slave—and was not intended to.
- when asked what was to become of Southern slaves after they were "freed" by his Emancipation Proclamation, Lincoln compared them to wild hogs, and said: "Let 'em root, pig, or perish!"—and that is exactly what occurred.
- after the issuance of the Emancipation Proclamation, only three things happened immediately: Union recruitment plummeted, Union desertion skyrocketed, and the quality of life for blacks sank to an all time low, remaining far beneath even slavery levels for the next 100 years.
- after emancipation 95 percent of all blacks voluntarily remained in the South, and many of those who moved north were treated so poorly that they later quickly returned to Dixie.
- by 1867, just two years after the Emancipation Proclamation was issued, 1 million, or 25 percent, of all Southern blacks had perished from starvation, neglect, infanticide, corruption, and disease.
- Lincoln never once referred to his Emancipation Proclamation as either a "black civil rights measure" or "humanitarian emancipation"; instead he revealingly called it a "war measure" and a "military emancipation."
- the Emancipation Proclamation was truly a national disaster, prompting Lincoln to later declare that it was "the greatest folly of my life."
- it would have cost ten times less to simply free America's slaves than to go to war—more proof that the Civil War was not over slavery.
- slavery is still being vigorously practiced around the world, including in Africa and the United States.

These and a thousand other well documented facts utterly decimate the mainstream's pro-North, liberal view of American slavery. And you will find these facts only in this book: *Everything You Were Taught About American Slavery is Wrong, Ask a Southerner!* Read on and discover for yourself the many truths that the anti-South movement would rather you not know. Help save genuine Southern culture, society, tradition, and history: educate yourself, then recommend our books to your family members, friends, and work associates. It is a great cause to preserve Southern Truth for future generations.

EVERYTHING
You Were Taught About American Slavery Is Wrong

Ask a Southerner!

LOCHLAINN SEABROOK
JEFFERSON DAVIS HISTORICAL GOLD MEDAL WINNER

LAVISHLY ILLUSTRATED

Foreword by Barbara G. Marthal, B.A., M.Ed.

Author of "Fighting for Freedom: A Documented Story"

SEA RAVEN PRESS, NASHVILLE, TENNESSEE, USA

EVERYTHING YOU WERE TAUGHT ABOUT
AMERICAN SLAVERY IS WRONG, ASK A SOUTHERNER!

Published by
Sea Raven Press, Cassidy Ravensdale, President
PO Box 1484, Spring Hill, Tennessee 37174-1484 USA
SeaRavenPress.com • searavenpress@gmail.com

First Sea Raven Press Edition: December 2014
ISBN: 978-0-9913779-3-0
Library of Congress Control Number: 2014955209

Everything You Were Taught About American Slavery is Wrong, Ask a Southerner!, by Lochlainn Seabrook. Foreword by Barbara G. Marthal. Includes endnotes, bibliographical references, and an index. Portions of this book have been adapted from the author's other works.

Front and back cover design and art, book design, layout, and interior art by Lochlainn Seabrook
Typography: Sea Raven Press Book Design
All images, graphic design, graphic art, and illustrations copyright © Lochlainn Seabrook
Front cover image: 16th-Century English slave galleon

The views on the American "Civil War" documented in this book *are* those of the publisher.

The paper used in this book is acid-free and lignin-free. It has been certified by the Sustainable Forestry Initiative and the Forest Stewardship Council and meets all ANSI standards for archival quality paper.

PRINTED & MANUFACTURED IN OCCUPIED TENNESSEE, FORMER CONFEDERATE STATES OF AMERICA

Dedication

To the world's white, red, brown, yellow, and black slaves. You helped develop human civilization, and we are your grateful descendants.

REBECCA, CHARLEY and ROSA.
Slave Children from New Orleans.
PHOTOGRAPHED BY KIMBALL, 477 BROADWAY, N. Y.
Ent'd, according to act of Congress, in the year [illegible], by P. BACON, in the Clerk's Office of the U. S. for the So. Dist. of N. Y.

Epigraph

"The exact contrary of what is generally believed is often the truth."

Jean De La Bruyère (1645-1696)

CONTENTS

SEA RAVEN PRESS
THE WORLD'S #1 SOUTH-FRIENDLY BOOK PUBLISHER
Restoring Dixie's honor
Defending traditional Southern culture
Preserving authentic Confederate history
One book at a time!
Nashville, Tennessee
SeaRavenPress.com

Notes to the Reader

THE TWO MAJOR POLITICAL PARTIES IN VICTORIAN AMERICA

☛ In any study of America's antebellum, bellum, and postbellum periods, it is vitally important to understand that in 1860 the two major political parties—the Democrats and the newly formed Republicans—were the opposite of what they are today. In other words, the Democrats of the mid 19th Century were Conservatives, akin to the Republican Party of today, while the Republicans of the mid 19th Century were Liberals, akin to the Democratic Party of today. Thus the Confederacy's Democratic president, Jefferson Davis, was a Conservative (with libertarian leanings); the Union's Republican president, Abraham Lincoln, was a Liberal (with socialistic leanings).[1]

ON THE PHRASE "CIVIL WAR"

☛ I heartily dislike the phrase American "Civil War," for it is a false description, one invented by the North to disguise the Truth about the conflict of 1861. So my occasional use of this term, in this work and others, deserves an explanation.

Webster's definition of civil war, "a battle between regions or states belonging to the same country," clearly does not fit the reality of Lincoln's War, which pitted the United States of America against the Confederate States of America—the latter being a separate and legally created sovereignty; an autonomous republic formed under the well accepted constitutional guarantee of states' rights (see Amendments Nine and Ten)—which tacitly allows both the accession and secession of individual states in and out of the Union.[2]

My infrequent use of the phrase "Civil War" then is merely due to space requirements, poetic license, literary aesthetics, and momentary idiosyncratic taste, and is not meant to be a reflection of my actual view of the conflict. I use the dastardly term in the titles and subtitles of some of my books because most works on this topic today are not only searched for online, but are searched for using "Civil War." If I were to use the "War for Southern Independence," the "War Against Northern Aggression," or my personally preferred phrase, "Lincoln's War," my books would never be found by the very people I primarily write them for: those who were brought up on the pro-North version of the conflict. For these terms are almost wholly unknown north of the Mason-Dixon

Line.

One should bear in mind that while today educated persons, particularly educated Southerners, all share an abhorrence for the phrase "Civil War," it was not always so. Confederates who lived through and even fought in the conflict, regularly used the term throughout the 1860s, and even long after. Among them were Confederate generals such as Nathan Bedford Forrest,[3] Richard Taylor,[4] and Joseph E. Johnston,[5] not to mention the Confederacy's vice president, Alexander H. Stephens.[6] Even the Confederacy's highest leader, President Jefferson Davis, used the term "Civil War,"[7] and in one case at least, as late as 1881—the year he wrote his brilliant exposition, *The Rise and Fall of the Confederate Government*.[8]

ON THE WORD "YANKEE"

☛ Though this word carries a wide variety of meanings and definitions around the world and even in the United States, I use it in the Civil War era sense to signify an American Northerner; or more specifically, anyone from one of the states that formed the U.S. Union (as contrasted with the states of the Southern Confederacy) after Abraham Lincoln's election in November 1860.

ON THE WORD "RACE"

☛ As with the phrase "Civil War," I use the word "race" only as a concession to popular culture. As genetic studies have repeatedly shown, there is no such thing as a separate or "pure" race of people. In other words, there is no gene that makes one "red" (Indian), "yellow" (Asian), "white" (European), "black" (African), or "brown" (Hispanic). All living humans are simply "varieties" that descend from a single ancestor, belong to a single race, derive their genes from a single source, and form a single species: *Homo sapiens sapiens*.[9]

More scientifically, every member of our species shares the same number of chromosomes, is inter-fertile with all others, and has blood that is constructed of the identical pattern of agglutinins and antigens—which is what makes blood transfusions between *all* humans possible.[10] Even many of our more enlightened ancient predecessors understood this, one of whom was Saint Paul, who said:

> God that made the world and all things therein . . . hath made of one blood all nations of men for to dwell on all the face of the earth.[11]

The widely varied appearances of humans stem not only from heredity (our ancestors), but also from geographic, that is, environmental, conditions. Thus physically speaking we are primarily the products of that part of the world in which our ancestors lived. This means, in turn, that there are no "superior" or "inferior" races, as individuals such as Yankee President Abraham Lincoln and

Yankee Generals Ulysses S. Grant and William T. Sherman believed.[12]

For example, prehistoric people who lived in cold dark climates tended to have short stocky bodies, straight hair, small narrow noses, blue eyes, and light skin, all physical adaptations to cool temperatures, low humidity, upper elevations, and decreased sunlight—that is, boreal environments. Prehistoric people who lived in warm sunny climates tended to have tall thin bodies, curly hair, large broad noses, brown eyes, and dark skin, in this case all physical adaptations to hot temperatures, high humidity, low elevations, and increased sunlight—that is, equatorial environments. All humans descend from recent and distant ancestors that were from one or both of these geographical regions (or from regions that lie between them), which explains the immensely diverse physical traits of the human species.

Confounding both popular belief and science, there are exceptions, even reversals, to this rule, such as instances in which white children have been born to black parents with no known Caucasian ancestry, and black children who have been born to white parents with no known African ancestry.[13] And since some whites become quite dark from sun exposure while some do not, and since blacks have dark skin in all environments, we know that it is not just heredity that determines traits like skin color. It is the way an individual reacts to his environment—and it is *this* particular trait that is inherited.[14]

British anthropologist Ashley Montagu has called the idea of race "man's most dangerous myth," for it catalogs people not merely by physically distinguishable populations, but by the common belief that these differences are inherently connected to higher or lower mental capacities, capacities that can allegedly be measured by both cultural achievements and IQ tests.[15] Yet no such measurement can be taken because no such link exists. "Race" then is one of those ideas that lies beyond infallible systemization; it is a nonsensical and thus worthless concept that "deifies all attempts at classification."[16]

In a word, human beings are simply not capable of being arranged into clear-cut categories, for there are far too many variables, from natural selection and environmental adaptation, to genetic mutations and the random modification of hereditary characters. The massive genetic diversity resulting from these sporadic, spontaneous, and often unknowable and untraceable influences makes the very concept of a "pure race" impossible.[17]

Indeed, the "diversity" of the human species is much smaller than popular culture imagines: the female eggs that created the world's present human population would all fit inside a one gallon jar, while the sperm cells that produced us would easily fit into an aspirin tablet. In fact, the hereditary material that formed all living human beings would only take up the space of one large multivitamin.[18]

The word "race" then turns out to be an invented construct, an arbitrary and convenient term that has no relationship to biology (skin color, hair and facial characteristics, body type, etc.), culture, religion, linguistics, or nationality. This, in turn, renders the concept of "racism" pointless, which is why the word race has been slowly disappearing from science books for many decades. Anthropologists, for instance, no longer classify humans by skin color, but rather by biological and genetic variability and the influence of these factors on different populations that are far more accurately called "ethnic groups" or "genogroups," rather than "races."[19] Anything else must be labeled false science and illogical theorizing based on faulty misconceptions about human biology.[20]

In truth what "racist" blacks do not like about non-Africans, what "racist" browns do not like about non-Hispanics, what "racist" yellows do not like about non-Asians, what "racist" reds do not like about non-Indians, and what "racist" whites do not like about non-Europeans, is, in almost all cases, social and cultural, not "racial."

Furthermore, if one is biased toward another due to their appearance, this is lookism, not racism. If one is biased toward another because of their age, this is ageism, not racism. If one is biased toward another due to their gender, this is sexism, not racism. All of these "isms" have, at one time or another, been misinterpreted and mischaracterized as "racism." Hence, I have put forth a replacement word for racism, *socioculturalism*: prejudice toward an individual or group based on their social or cultural background and conditions.

While it is doubtless time to rid our language of the ambiguous, artificial, obsolete, generalized, loaded, stereotyping, imprecise, limited, mystical, and meaningless word "race" and its "built-in confusion,"[21] I continue to use it, in this book because—as there is yet no public consensus agreement on an alternate—my word "socioculturalism" would only confuse my readers.

BOOK LAYOUT

☛ Although there is a natural beginning-to-end progression to the chapter layout, this book was designed so that it can also be read from back to front or even at random. As such, there is a small amount of repetition of some of the material in various sections.

MY VIEWS ON SLAVERY

☛ Today, even the most objective discussion of slavery brings automatic charges of "racism" from the unenlightened. In this atmosphere of political correctness gone mad it is therefore necessary to offer the following statements.

I do not like slavery. I do not approve of slavery. I would not want to enslave another person, and I certainly would not want to be a slave. Thus nothing in this book should be construed in any way as a defense of slavery. While as a historian I maintain that slavery was a harsh but necessary development in the early evolution of human civilization, the need for the institution, particularly on a large scale, has long since passed, and I believe that its illegality should be strongly enforced around the world today.

As for the imputation of racism, as a Christian I maintain—along with fanatical 19th-Century abolitionist William Lloyd Garrison—that "prejudice against color is rebellion against God."[22]

What the reader will find in the following pages then is not a justification of the institution, but rather a description of how American slavery came to be, and what it was actually like in early America. In particular I examine the facts behind so-called "slavery" in the Victorian South (as opposed to what Yankee myth has taught us it was like), and how both white and black Southerners viewed and experienced it (as opposed to how the anti-South movement has taught us it was viewed and experienced).

FOR PARENTS

☛ This is an academic work on the institution of slavery written for adults. As authentic slavery was and remains an unsightly and brutal business, some of this material, including the illustrations, may not be suitable for those under 18. Parental discretion is advised.

BOOK COVER IMAGE

☛ Why did I use a *British* ship on the cover of a book about *American* slavery? The answer to this question is addressed in Chapter 5, where the reader will learn that the South played no part in the instigation of either the American slave trade or American slavery. Even her subsequent role in helping to maintain slavery was minor in comparison to the contributions made by both her Yankee compatriots to the North and her English cousins across the Atlantic.

With Lincoln's election all of this changed. Since that day, November 6, 1860, the truth about American slavery and the South began to be buried in earnest. Not only that, but actual history was rewritten, revised, and redacted in an attempt to deflect blame for the institution from the North onto the South.

As I will discuss in this very book, the arrogance not to mention the ignorance behind this single act not only helped fuel the launching of the War for Southern Independence, but it provided pro-North, anti-South historians, writers, and politicians with the ideal material to create one of the greatest coverups in American history: the suppression of the truth about American slavery.

This work will bring these hidden facts back to light, and by doing so, give the South and her people their rightful and honorable place on the stage of world history once again.

FOREWORD

I AM AN AFRICAN-AMERICAN WOMAN, storyteller, author, and retired educator, with a background in publishing and sales. About mid-career I started thinking about retirement and decided that since I had taught school and managed a bookstore, it might be rewarding to become a storyteller. At the time I lived near one of the major storytelling centers of the country, Jonesborough, Tennessee. I started attending storytelling conferences, enlisted in East Tennessee State University, and received a Master of Education with a concentration in Reading and Storytelling.

I also have a passion for history. When I was a child in elementary school this grieved me. I worried that by the time I graduated from college, all the history that interested me would be told. There would be nothing I could add that would have scholastic value. I had no way of knowing that later in life I would encounter a group of people that would introduce me to an entire new approach to History and Storytelling. The organization was the Sons of Confederate Veterans (SCV). I met them through a colleague, Bill Harris. A few years later Bill and I would have a Confederate wedding ceremony during an SCV camp meeting.

My future husband and the SCV introduced me to a new concept, that being, living history, American Civil War Reenactment. I had lived in the southeastern part of the United States all my life, and knew nothing about reenactments. When I attended my first reenactment, I was absolutely dumbfounded. How could all of this be going on around me, and I know nothing about it? Needless to say, a new world of storytelling opened up before me.

I jumped in with both feet and started a strong kicking swim. Only one problem. I was an African-American woman who had leapt into the deep end of the Confederate side of the pool. Who would I portray during the reenactments? A runaway slave? That wouldn't do. How can you portray a runaway and be there at the same time? How is it that here I was a college graduate with a Masters degree, yet I was totally unprepared to find a place for myself in this aspect of Southern History? Good question. Let's examine that for a moment.

According to the official Yankee definition of a "soldier," some 1 million Southern blacks served in the Confederate armies, five times the number that served in the Union armies. These African-American Rebel soldiers were just two of the 3,000 who fought under the command of Confederate General Stonewall Jackson.

The only history that I had of the Civil War was that the South was wrong because they owned and wanted to keep slaves; the North was right because they were led by Abraham Lincoln, who wanted to and did free the slaves just before he led the nation to a glorious defeat of those amoral white Southerners. Later, forward thinking Northerners both black and white would descend upon the South to educate the poor freedman and set them on the road to upright civilized living. I asked myself, is that all there is to telling the story of my Southern ancestors during the Civil War and the antebellum years of this country?

The answer is easy. My professors had let me down. You see, one of the basic principles of good scholarship is discourse. Without discourse, there is no scholarship and to have discourse, one needs at least one other point of view. That is why when it comes to Southern history, you must *ask a Southerner*. How can you possibly understand a people's story if you do not ask the people to tell their story?

True scholars seek information that goes beyond simply verifying their own hypothesis. They seek information that will test and challenge the status quo. Without discourse information becomes stagnant and lacks the catalysts for generating new ideas and hypothesizes. Faced with this dilemma, I began to see that it was time to do my own research and return to the libraries and archives of southern communities and states. I have spent and still spend hours doing research that goes beyond the feeble history that I received from our educational institutions.

My research revealed that slaves had varied lives, had dreams and ambitions, loved their families, and worked to carve out a nation that we can and should be proud of today. Most of them did not run away, many of them purchased their freedom or lived as quasi free individuals. Here is a partial list of occupations that my research reveals were held by slaves: farmer, agronomist, shoemaker, overseer, household manager, weaver, mechanic, hunter, fisherman, pilot, boatman, bricklayer, brick maker, carpenter, blacksmith, harness maker, doctor, nurse, midwife, nanny, butler, teamster, coachman, wheelwright, basket maker, domestic, barber, merchant, seamstress, preacher, farm laborer, hotel staff, tavern and inn keeper, musician, composer, poet, storyteller, cooper, iron worker, charcoal maker, leather worker and all those untold. Remember that childhood fear that I had? It was just that, a childish thought. The truth is, there is so much history yet to be told about our Southern ancestors, there are not enough historians to tell it all.

If you are reading this foreword, read on, your good fortune awaits. I have spent years of research to discover just a portion of the enormous amount of information that Lochlainn Seabrook shares in this important historical work, *Everything You Were Taught About American Slavery Was Wrong, Ask a Southerner!* It is an in-depth book, but every hour spent reading it will be hours well spent.

Barbara G. Marthal, BA, M.Ed.
Mt. Juliet, Tennessee
December 2014

INTRODUCTION

"WE CANNOT ESCAPE HISTORY"

The Truth About American Slavery

THE MAINSTREAM VIEW OF AMERICAN SLAVERY

WE ARE ALL FAMILIAR WITH the traditional school textbook view of American slavery. Nearly every American, Canadian, Australian, and European child was raised on it. As adults we continue to be bombarded with it by every existing form of media, from newspapers and magazines to TV and the Internet. So profoundly have we all been inculcated with the mainstream view of slavery, that we have practically memorized it. For those who need a reminder of this leftist, one-sided, Northern perspective, it goes something like this:

> American slavery began in the South, at Jamestown, Virginia, with the arrival of 20 black slaves aboard a Dutch ship in the year 1619. These free men had been captured by the Dutch in the wilds of Africa, then dragged in chains and at gunpoint to the vessel, bound for the American South.
>
> In 1661 Virginia became the first colony to legally recognize slavery. Though few Southern whites actually prospered from slavery, every family owned one or more, and it quickly became the very foundation of the Southern colonies' commercial system—until the trade was permanently banned and halted by Congress in 1808. Up until then, both the transatlantic slave trade and slavery were engaged in only by the South. The American North never played a role in either: it never owned a single slave ship or a slave, for it was purely an antislavery, abolitionary region.
>
> Between 1619 and 1808, Southern slave traders forcibly brought between 10 and 50 million African slaves to the Americas. At least half died on board ship before their arrival, mainly due to whipping and other cruelties inflicted on them by their white overlords. En route countless thousands of African slaves committed suicide by jumping overboard, rather than face the life of endless pain and hardship that they knew surely awaited them in America's Southern states.
>
> After being purchased at auction and purposefully separated from his family members and friends, an African slave

was first stripped naked and beaten, an initial show of white dominance. A ball and chain was then attached to his ankle, and a metal collar—that was chained to dozens of other naked slaves—was placed around his neck. After being once again viciously whipped, he was set to work in Dixie's fields under the lash of a brutal white Southern overseer. There he labored beneath the hot blazing sun from sunrise to sunset, or even longer. He had no days off, no rewards, no recompense of any kind for his labors. Just endless sweat, blood, and tears from cradle to grave. As a result the typical Southern slave died young, covered with whip scars and often riddled with disease and other signs of malnourishment and maltreatment.

Slavery is not and never was an "inherently racist institution," as the liberal pro-North movement teaches. It began long ago as a non-racial, non-racist form of bondage, and it has retained this aspect into the present day. One of the first to racialize slavery was the 16th-Century American Yankee, who used white racism to justify the enslavement of not just blacks, but whites and reds as well. The chariot of this Mesopotamian king is being by led white slaves, while he is being sheltered from the sun by a white slave, all members of a neighboring Middle Eastern tribe who were captured in battle.

His always white master was typically an arrogant, upper class, aristocratic planter, who did little all day except lounge on the front gallery of his mansion sipping iced mint juleps and flirting with pretty Southern belles. Underneath his civilized veneer, however, he was nothing but an uneducated hayseed, a lazy, hedonistic, non-religious, racist redneck who detested books and big cities and lived only for his own personal gratification.

For fun, in his spare time he would whip his male slaves and ravish his female ones. To increase both his profit and opportunities for his sadistic pleasures, the Southern slaveholder regularly forced his army of human chattel into large-scale breeding programs, happily dividing slave families by mercilessly selling the "undesirables" while keeping the fit ones for himself. To help enforce white Southern racism, an extreme terrorist group was formed, the Ku Klux Klan, whose sole mission was to intimidate and kill slaves and free blacks.

All of this is to be expected from the American South, a region literally founded on human inequality and white superiority, one inhabited by a degraded and inbred people: moonshine-addicted Southern hillbillies, whose backward, alien land was then awash in poverty, illiteracy, immorality, atheism, debauchery, violence, bigotry, and misguided political ideals such as self-government and states' rights. It was this very so-called "civilization," the downcast "white trash" of the South, who ignorantly built their entire society on plantation slavery, after which every Southerner became a slave owner. In the Old South slavery was wholly accepted and embraced, for it was simply the natural order of things. Thank God the North won the War, and put a stop to all of this!

One of the constant dangers faced by "freed" blacks in the North was reenslavement. This freedman and freedwoman are being accosted, tied, and bound by Massachusetts slave dealers, who will "double their money" by reselling them a second time on the open New England market. Though illegal, the practice thrived across the North, and was largely ignored by Yankee law enforcement and the Yankee judicial system.

The average black Southern slave lived off stale bread and water, wore rags of coarse material (if he was lucky), and dwelt in a tiny, crowded, filthy, rat-infested hovel with dozens of other sickly suffering slaves. The white owners of Southern slaves refused them medical care when ill, worked them to near death, then abandoned them to their fate on the side of the road if and when they got too sick or too old to be of use.

The slave auction was once an everyday sight in New England, as well as the rest of the Northeastern states—the birthplace of both American slavery and the American slave trade. This slave auction is taking place at the great slave seaport in New London, Connecticut.

America's Southern slaves had no rights whatsoever. Their white owners could do whatever they wanted to them, including beatings, torture, rape, and murder. There were no laws against such things, and even if there were, the white racist, anti-abolitionist South would not have lifted a finger in protest.

Because Southern slaves were regarded as little more than human cattle—completely owned and controlled by their white masters—they were not allowed to marry, earn an income, own any personal possessions, partake in religion, leave the plantation, hire themselves out, celebrate holidays, grow their own food, or take days off either for health reasons or for recreation.

Not only were the slaves of the Old South whipped on a daily basis, many were actually mercilessly beaten with chains, roasted over fires, and hung by the ribs on meat hooks by their racist and savage white owners. Southern slaves were also barred from learning to read and write, so all were completely illiterate. These highly prejudicial policies insured that slaves remained dependent, powerless pawns in the white man's patriarchal, exploitative slave system.

Lacking any special skills, money, home, gardens, transportation, personal belongings, and above all any type of freedom, the typical Southern slave was reliant solely on his white owners for his survival. Yet, he was not allowed to mingle with whites, attend their churches, political meetings, parties, or funerals, or even sit next to them on trains.

The mainstream liberal media wants you to believe that Victorian white Southerners routinely mistreated and abused their black "slaves." Not only was the typical Southerner a gentle, religious, and tolerant humanitarian, but *all* of the South's African-American servants, like these loading cotton bales at New Orleans, Louisiana, were protected by hundreds of laws and statutes designed to keep them safe, healthy, and happy from birth to death.

Southern black slaves hated their Southern white owners, and Southern white slaveholders hated their black slaves in return. Thus when the Civil War opened in April 1861, not a single black man or woman chose to fight for let alone support the Confederacy. They could not have even if they had wanted to, for the ultra racist white South would have never allowed, and did not ever allow, blacks to serve in its armed forces. The Confederacy's racist President Jefferson Davis made sure of that!

In 1863, abolitionist and true friend of the black man, the "Great Emancipator" Abraham Lincoln, freed *all* of America's slaves with the issuance of the Emancipation Proclamation. Every one of the South's freed slaves immediately moved North, where they were welcomed with open arms into white Yankee society. Hundreds of thousands willingly joined the U.S. army, to fight the "treasonous, racist South" as well as for black civil rights and Lincoln's noble attempt to bring an end to slavery.

Despite "Lincoln's Dream" to live in a racially integrated nation, we must remind ourselves that American slavery was a creation of white Southern-Americans, and that it was an innately bigoted institution built on racism, exploitation, cruelty, psychological intimidation, and physical violence. As such, white Southern Americans will bear the burden of guilt, shame and the horrors of slavery and the Atlantic slave trade for all time. Not only does the South owe an apology to all American blacks, past, present, and future, but reparations as well.[23]

Relationships between white Southern slave owners and their black servants were the opposite of how anti-South historians have long portrayed them. White children, for example, respectfully referred to adult black house servants by name, as "Uncle" and "Aunty." In return, black servants often treated the master's children as their own, with the two groups ultimately forming one large interracial extended family.

The real problem with the above "history" of American slavery is that not one word of it is true, correct, or historical! This is merely what our politically correct gatekeepers want you to think and believe. In fact, as this very book will aptly illustrate, in every instance the opposite is true.

What happened to the truth about American slavery then?

Contrary to Northern myth the American South had nothing to do with the transatlantic slave trade, which was run solely by Yankees, Europeans, and Africans. Here, a previously enslaved African woman is being branded on Africa's Gold Coast before being loaded onto a Rhode Island slave ship anchored in the harbor. The man branding her is part of a group of African slave catchers, hired by New England slave merchants.

HOW THE LEFT PRESERVES ITS CIVIL WAR IDEOLOGY

The answer is that it has been aggressively and intentionally suppressed by the Left (as well as by some misinformed Conservatives). Why? Because the facts reveal that Lincoln was not the Great Emancipator, but rather the Great Racist, and his War was not only illegal and unnecessary, it was not fought over slavery, or even black civil rights.

The Barbary Wars pitted white Europeans and Americans against black and brown Africans. The cause? The enslavement in Africa of some 1.5 million whites by North African slavers. Here the squadron of U.S. Commodore Edward Preble attacks the white slavery port at Tripoli, Libya, August 3, 1803. Few pro-North slavery scholars write about or discuss this sordid chapter in African history.

To prevent the Truth from ever seeing the light of day, those who lord over our so-called "institutions of higher learning," that is, our liberal universities and their parochial university presses, have gone to extraordinary lengths, from simple deception to some of the most outrageous and malicious ploys ever concocted. For example, in an effort to enforce only their view of American slavery, that is, the pro-North perspective, the manuscripts of pro-South authors are summarily rejected. Not because they are not factual, but because they are!

Facts are one of the pro-North advocate's worst enemies, and anything, no matter how true, that opposes the liberal Civil War ideology of the school's publishing department must, at all costs, be kept out of the hands of the reading public. When books *are* published by such universities, they are thoroughly scoured and edited to prevent even a hint of the Truth from coming out. Everything must conform to the liberal bias of the mainstream gatekeepers.

Besides only publishing illiterature by carefully vetted fellow liberals, some of the tricks anti-truth, anti-South writers, publishers, editors, documentarians, filmmakers, and bloggers use include:

- Omitting anything and everything related to *Northern* slavery from both their books and the indexes of their books.

- Adding anything and everything related to *Southern* slavery to both their books and the indexes of their books.
- Using the word "slavery" when speaking of *Southern* slavery, while using the word "unfreedom" when speaking of either *Northern* or *African* slavery.
- Taking great care to publish only the works of anti-South authors, preferably those with a socialist, Marxist, communist, anti-European, anti-West, or even an anti-American perspective.
- Creating titles and book covers that both overtly and subliminally promote the *Northern* view of American slavery while denigrating the *Southern* view. (For example, always using Abraham Lincoln's image but never Jefferson Davis' image.)
- Eliminating from their writings, TV programs, blogs, articles, films, and books all references to the positive aspects of Southerners, Southern culture, Southern history, Southern heritage, and of course, Southern slavery.
- Neglecting to include Abraham Lincoln's name in books, blogs, and articles on the racist Yankee-founded American Colonization Society. (Lincoln was a lifelong supporter of the organization.)
- Mollifying domestic *African* slavery and ignoring American *Northern* slavery, while strongly and loudly condemning American *Southern* slavery.
- Flooding the public domain with photographs, documentaries, videos, short films, and full length feature films that paint Davis and the Old South in a negative light and Lincoln and the Old North in a positive one.[24]

OTHER TRICKS USED BY THE PRO-NORTH MOVEMENT

One of the anti-South movement's favorite stratagems is to pretend that the exception to the rule is the rule itself. In this way the rare and deranged Southern slave owner, who occasionally whipped his servants, is made out to be "typical"; the nonexistent Southern slave breeder becomes the "norm"; and the rarely occurring splitting up of Southern slave families becomes "standard practice" in the Old South.

The North's most nefarious deception, however, is her practice of overlaying the mild servitude of the South with the real atrocities and barbarities of authentic slavery, the kind that were once found in such ancient civilizations as Mesopotamia, Greece, and Rome. In other words, when you read about American slavery in a Northern-slanted history book, you are actually reading about slavery as it was practiced 2,000 to 3,000 years ago halfway around the world, not as it was practiced in the American South 200 to 300 years ago!

Be assured that the South-loathing authors of our school's history books will go to any length to convince America's young readers that slavery in Dixie was the most vile, heartless, and un-Christian institution that ever graced God's green earth; a pact with Satan himself, one that placed the always "racist" white Southerner up against the always "righteous" white Northerner.

This white Englishman is being torn from his family, to be enslaved and sent to work in the mines. The long history of the worldwide institution of white slavery has been suppressed by the pro-North movement—which only wants you to focus on Southern black slavery. Yet at least two-thirds of the original English colonists in America came over as white slaves and servants. White slavery continues to flourish into the present day, even in the United States.

Though such books are filled from beginning to end with fabrications based on presentism, the mindless copying of outdated antislavery works, spurious information from other radical anti-South titles, and disproven Victorian abolitionary tracts, few ever challenge them. But in *Everything You Were Taught About American Slavery is Wrong, Ask a Southerner!*, we will do just that. For facts cannot be destroyed. They merely go underground temporarily, only to later reappear stronger and brighter than ever—as they have in the following pages.

And so we know why the Truth about American slavery is not more generally known: the politically correct gatekeepers of our society do not want you to learn it, or even become aware of it. Just who are these lauded all-powerful "protectors," these highly biased PC thought police, who tell us what we can and cannot read?

The splitting up of slave families was rare and frowned upon—and in many places illegal—across the Old South, but common and accepted in the Old North. This angry slave in Boston, Massachusetts, has just been informed that he is to be sold and separated from his family.

IDENTIFYING THE LIBERAL PRO-NORTH GATEKEEPERS

They are comprised primarily of liberals, left-wingers, socialists, Marxists, communists, and other types of anti-Americans selected chiefly from our ultra progressive educational system. These are the same people who are running nearly all of America's media, including the TV industry, the radio industry, the newspaper industry, the magazine industry, the film industry, the public library system, the various branches of science, the publishing industry, the National Park Service, and social media on the Internet.

These are the same individuals who founded or who are now running most of our schools, colleges, and universities; the same ones who pack their faculties with hand-picked liberal, socialist, and communist professors, who brainwash their students with anti-American doctrines, and then create university presses so that they can publish these same doctrines in regurgitated book form by their well propagandized teachers and students. Only one viewpoint can be disseminated—and it is theirs. All others must be discounted, dismissed, rejected, suppressed, silenced, or discredited.

EXCISING HISTORY, SUPPRESSING FACTS

So thoroughly has the anti-South movement expunged the facts that most books on American slavery are literally useless to anyone interested in authentic history.

For example, there are books on the origins and development of slavery in my personal library that do not contain a single mention of the words "Africa" (the birthplace of African slavery) or "Massachusetts" (the birthplace of American slavery). I own hundreds of books on American history which either completely disregard slavery (out of ignorance or to hide the North's role), or which portray the savage forms of slavery practiced by ancient civilizations as if they were those of the Old American South. I even have books on world history that never once refer to slavery. Yet, it was slavery that made all of the world's great civilizations possible, from India, China, and Arabia, to ancient Greece, Rome, and Judea.

LINCOLN REWRITES AMERICAN HISTORY

The Underground Railroad did exist, but not in the way pro-North writers depict it. It was not a "railroad," it was not literally "underground," and at best only some 2,000 American slaves, North and South, took advantage of it during the entire Civil War. This old illustration commemorates one of the few black families who fled America for Canada using this method.

The redaction and rewriting of American history pertaining to American slavery is not new. Though extremist antebellum abolitionists like William Lloyd Garrison and Harriet Beecher Stowe were among the first to radically revise the facts in order to profit the North and impair the South, it was Lincoln who later had the biggest impact in the arena of revisionist history. In fact, the intolerant Big Brother progressive—who, like so many Liberals today, could not abide the right of free speech or opposing opinions—was successful beyond anything he could have imagined.

Big government Liberal President Abraham Lincoln, a former newspaperman who unconstitutionally closed down over 300 (mostly Conservative) *Northern* newspapers because they were printing articles he did not approve of, was a master of media manipulation. It is he who must be held accountable for instigating what I call "The Great Yankee Coverup": the revision, perversion, and suppression of authentic Civil War history in order to conceal his true motivations for making war on the Constitution and the American people. Since Lincoln's death, literally millions of Liberals, socialists, scallywags, and American progressives in general have taken up where he left off, making innumerable anti-South documentaries and movies, and publishing thousands of anti-South articles, blogs, and books a year to maintain the secret that no leftist wants you to know: Lincoln was not the "Great Emancipator" and his war was not over slavery.

To discourage and crush views contrary to his own, as well as to cleverly hide his true motivation for waging war (to install big government at Washington), crime boss Lincoln showed an almost unlimited capacity for committing outrages against the American people and the Constitution.

For instance, the criminal-minded president, who William H. Herndon (Lincoln's law partner and biographer) once described as a man who "cared little for simple facts, rules and methods,"[25] violated hundreds of laws,[26] then went on to invade sitting courts, disrupt their proceedings, and threaten, intimidate, and even arrest judges,[27] all to silence those who disagreed with him. He also deported Northern politicians, such as Ohio Congressman Clement L. Vallandigham, for advocating peace;[28] and, as Jefferson Davis mentioned, he also curbed the press, closing down over 300 Northern newspapers for printing antiwar articles.[29] Under Lincoln's direct orders, his thugocracy (administrative officials) had printing presses confiscated or destroyed and the papers' editors jailed.[30]

The following is a partial list of the hundreds of papers Lincoln suppressed and shut down:

The *Chicago Daily Times* (Illinois)
The *Christian Observer* (Pennsylvania)
The Day-Book (New York)
The *Democrat* (New Hampshire)
The *Farmer* (Maine)
The *Freeman's Journal* (New York)
The *Herald* (Missouri)
The *Journal* (Missouri)
The *Journal of Commerce* (New York)
The *Missourian* (Missouri)
The *Morning News* (New York)
The New York World (New York)
The *Philadelphia Evening Journal* (Pennsylvania)
The *Republican Watchman* (Pennsylvania)
The *Sentinel* (Connecticut)[31]

As always, the owners of these newspapers were imprisoned without legal representation or trial, a gross violation of both constitutional law and American civil rights. Unsurprisingly, objective constitutional and legal scholars now refer to the Lincoln administration as the lowest period for civil liberties up to that time. Some rank it as one of the worst in all of American history.[32]

Although you would never know it from reading mainstream history books, at one time the American North possessed hundreds of thousands of slaves, far more than the South. Here a wealthy white Pennsylvania slave owner and his black overseer are driving a group of newly purchased slaves to his plantation outside of Philadelphia.

Lincoln's Emancipation Proclamation contained no plans for freed black slaves, no provisions for housing, food, clothing, employment, or healthcare. They were merely "turned loose" to fend for themselves or end up on so-called "government plantations" like this one, malodorous squatter camps where poverty, sickness, hunger, thievery, and prostitution reigned. In February 1865, when Confederate diplomats asked Lincoln what he planned to do with America's 4.5 million freed slaves (North and South), he likened them to hogs, and jokingly replied: "Let 'em root, pig, or perish!" The president may have thought this was humorous, but he was the only one who laughed.

LINCOLN'S CONTROL OF THE PRESS

Here is another example of how Liberal Lincoln influenced and shaped the press to his own advantage.

On July 24, 1863, he referred to his soldiers as bearing the "burden of saving our country."[33] "Saving" it from what? The Union and its central government were still intact and functioning on and at all levels before, throughout, and after the conflict. In a December 27, 1864, letter to Dr. John MacLean, Lincoln foolishly asserts that "the fate of civilization upon this continent is involved in the issue of our contest."[34]

This type of anti-South propaganda came naturally to him, for as a former newspaper agent and journalist (for the Springfield, Illinois, *Sangamon Journal*) and a newspaper owner (of the *Illinois Staats-Anzeiger*), he was highly aware of the power of the press in shaping public opinion. Little wonder then that in true liberal fashion, newspaperman Lincoln often used and manipulated both the public and the media. Not only to assist with his own political aspirations, but in aiding and abetting the creation of what is now a large corpus of pretentious anti-South myths,[35] like those associated with American slavery. Well aware of his power over public opinion, and sounding very much like Hitler—one of the many dictators who has idolized him over the years[36]—here is how Lincoln expressed it on August 21, 1858:

> . . . *public sentiment is everything*. With public sentiment, nothing can fail; without it, nothing can succeed. *Consequently he who molds public sentiment goes deeper than he who enacts statutes or pronounces decisions*. He makes statutes and decisions possible or impossible to be executed.[37]

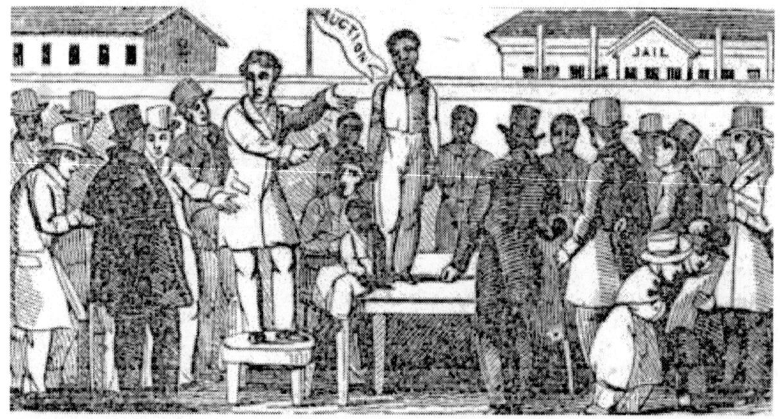

Slave auctions like this one at Washington, D.C., not far from the White House and the Capitol Building, were such a familiar sight to our nation's politicians that few took any notice of them. Coffles of shackled slaves were regularly marched right past the doors of Congress without so much as an objection. When a small movement finally arose to try and abolish the institution in the District, there were howls of protest. One of these voices was that of Abraham Lincoln, who on December 15, 1860, one month after being elected president, said: "I have no thought of recommending the abolition of slavery in the District of Columbia, nor the slave-trade among the slave States." Abolition in Washington finally came on April 16, 1862, with the passage of Lincoln's District of Columbia Emancipation Act. It had taken abolitionists several years to force the president's hand on the issue.

How much Lincoln's media blitz of disinformation contributed to the North's victory over the South is impossible to know, but contribute it certainly did. Though nearly every word of it is false, the world still considers Lincoln's wartime propaganda to be "Gospel." Indeed, it is Lincoln's view of the "Civil War" that is still taught in every school, not only in America, but around the globe.[38]

The North prides itself in being "the center of abolitionism" during the antebellum period. But this is just another Yankee myth. Abolitionists were widely detested across Yankeedom throughout the early 1800s, and even up and into the Civil War. Anti-abolitionist Abraham Lincoln himself once said that he did not mind having abolitionists in his party, "as long as I'm not tarred with the abolitionist brush." Attempts were regularly made on the lives of antislavery advocates, such as William Lloyd Garrison, who was dragged through the streets of Boston, Massachusetts, with a noose around his neck. Abolitionist Elijah P. Lovejoy had his printing presses destroyed and was later murdered by an angry anti-abolition mob in Illinois. In this illustration from 1839, abolitionist Reverend George Storrs is on his knees praying before an Anti-Slavery Society meeting at Northfield, New Hampshire, on December 14, 1835. In the middle of his benediction Storrs is grabbed by the collar by deputy sheriff David Tilton, who drags him from the pulpit and arrests him. A few months later, at Pittsfield, New Hampshire, on March 31, 1836, Storrs is arrested again for "preaching against the sin of slavery," this time by the authority of a writ issued by Moses Norris, Jr., Esquire. The Yankee attorney had the full support of the state behind him: New Hampshire Governor Isaac Hill later reappointed Norris, who went on to become one of the state's most popular senators. There was no such thing as "the abolitionist North."

FELLOW LIBERALS PICK UP WHERE LINCOLN LEFT OFF

Shortly after Lincoln's death in April 1865—at which time his friends, family members, and business associates began burning thousands of his personal papers, notes, and letters to prevent knowledge of his true feelings about his war and blacks from getting out to the public[39]—pro-North (that is, liberal) politicians, historians, and scholars picked up where Dishonest Abe left off, launching a massive effort to conceal the truth about slavery and his violent and bloody attack on the Constitution and the American people.

Why was such an effort needed?

THE REASON THE NORTH HAD TO SUPPRESS THE TRUTH

Because the Civil War was both illegal and unnecessary. Thus an explanation had to be established that would justify the death of millions of American men, women, and children,[40] and the destruction of billions of dollars of property. And that justification was *Southern slavery*! And so the effort to reshape and recast the War in the North's image, according to the North's political agenda, in conformity with the North's liberal ideology, began almost immediately.[41]

Since Lincoln's time, tens of thousands of books have been written by pro-North authors supporting our sixteenth president's intentionally fabricated view of his war, all in an effort to veil the facts. Naturally, one of the first casualties of this tidal wave of invented propaganda was the truth about American slavery. In the process, the North was painted as the innocent victim of the "racist, slavery-loving, traitorous South," which would stop at nothing to preserve its "peculiar institution," even if it meant fomenting war on the "unbigoted, slavery-hating, loyal North." Factual books by Southern authors, as well as books by Northern authors that told the truth, were and still are being ignored and banned, replaced by titles featuring the tall tales of Lincoln's modern day propagandists, which include all of the anti-South movement's standard lies about American slavery.

Pro-North historians would like you to believe that scenes such as this, of a slave family working in chains, shackles, and metal neck collars, was a common sight in the American South. Actually, this type of treatment of African-American servants was both illegal and unknown in Dixie. This illustration, in fact, is of slaves working on a Caribbean indigo plantation owned by a Yankee from Boston, Massachusetts.

PRO-NORTH WRITERS COPY EACH OTHER'S ERRORS

After the suppression of thousands of volumes of factual information, one might wonder where our liberal gatekeepers could find enough material to fill up the seemingly infinite pages of their invented literary works. Because such books are merely repetitions of fabrications, copied by one anti-South author from another, *ad infinitum*, there is an endless supply of Northern mythology regarding American slavery. When you have read one pro-North book on this topic, you have read them all, because they are mere error-filled facsimiles of all those that came before them. Nothing new, just the same old hackneyed untruths.

FINALLY, A BOOK OF FACTS ON AMERICAN SLAVERY!

Southerners have long wondered why Yankees call President Lincoln "the great friend of the black man" and the "Great Emancipator," when it was "Honest Abe" who not only stalled emancipation for as long as possible and refused to grant blacks equal rights, but also used slave labor to complete the dome on the U.S. Capitol Building, as well as the construction of numerous other edifices and roads around Washington, D.C.

If you have an open enquiring mind and hunger for the Truth, *Everything You Were Taught About American Slavery is Wrong, Ask a Southerner!* will be a truly enlightening intellectual journey. As long as it is in length, it could have been much longer, even spanning numerous volumes. Indeed, an entire book could be written around almost every entry.

Instead, to keep my book at a manageable size I chose to merely touch on what I consider to be the most relevant items pertaining to American slavery. I recommend that the interested reader carry on his or her own studies in this important arena of American history, then share them with others. This will help preserve authentic history for future generations. South-loathers have no love for facts and will never hesitate to censor and suppress the Truth. Do your part, won't you?

HOLLAND ON THE DISTORTION OF SOUTHERN HISTORY

I am not the first Southerner, of course, to express discontent over the manner in which my region has been portrayed concerning American slavery. It was 192 years ago, in 1822—39 years before the start of Lincoln's War—that South Carolinian Edwin Clifford Holland wrote these words:

> *The people of the North and East, are, or they affect to be, totally ignorant of our situation, and yet they insist upon legislating for us upon subjects, with a knowledge of which they appear to be wholly unacquainted. This is neither fair, nor honorable, nor wise, nor prudent.* It must be recollected, that *every State is sovereign and independent within the circle of her own territory, and that her citizens have an indisputable right to frame whatever laws their intelligence may deem necessary to its prosperity and happiness, provided they do not conflict with any of the great fundamental principles of the Federal Constitution.* This proposition, so apparently self evident and just, is, nevertheless, in a manner, controverted, and that too in an age when the principles of State Sovereignty have been as fully admitted as they have been freely discussed. *The people of the North and East, will, nevertheless, take the liberty of interfering in the designing of some of our most important local [Southern] regulations and of directing the steps of our constituted authorities. We are not only dictated to, but we are slandered in their [Northern] public prints, denounced in their pulpits, and calumniated in pamphlets and orations.*

Aggressive African chiefs, like this one, were responsible for enslaving untold millions of fellow Africans long before the opening of the transatlantic slave trade in the 15th and 16th Centuries.

For her enormous role in the development and maintenance of the institution of slavery, which continues to this day, Africa must certainly be named "the Slavery Capitol of the World." Traces of Africa's peak slavery period in the 1800s are still in evidence. This photo shows the termination of the Great Slavery Route that ended at Katumbella (modern Catumbela), Angola, on which countless thousands of black African slaves were marched along by their African enslavers before being sold a second time to Yankee slave ship owners. British author Henry Woodd Nevinson visited the area in 1906, and penned the following: The route "is touched by the tragedy of human suffering. . . . This is the path down which the caravans of slaves from the basin of the Upper Congo have been brought for generations, and down this path within the last three or four years the slaves were openly driven to the coast, shackled, tied together, and beaten along with whips. . . . The traffic still goes on, almost unchecked."

> . . . *We [in the South] are sneeringly upbraided with a want of common justice in the framing, or a lamentable want of mercy in the execution of our laws.* In many of the Northern and Eastern prints, there has been a great deal of that whining, canting, sickly kind of humanity, which is as disgraceful to the character of those journals, as it is contemptible in the eyes of all intelligent and reflecting men. Instead of meeting as we expected, and had a right to expect, the cordial and unaffected sympathy of those [fellow Americans] who wear the livery of our own color, who are connected to us by all the endearing affections of political brotherhood, whose hearts ought to beat with our own and whose hands ought to be the first to assist us in the hour of peril and of danger, *we have too frequently encountered a heartless indifference or selfish apathy* with respect to the horrors we have escaped, and what is still worse, the gibes and jeers of the idle and unfeeling, or the foul rebuke of the "humane" and the "religious." This then is the plain unvarnished statement of facts, that, at a period of the deepest and most awful anxiety, when

our whole [Southern] community was thrown into the most anxious and painful suspense; when the mother, petrified with fear, "strained her infant closer to her breast," and the listening father held his breath to catch the first notes of that tocsin that was to summon him to the defence of all that was dear to him in life, *against a merciless and vindictive foe [at the North]; we have had our motives misrepresented, our character defamed, and our laws ridiculed and reviled.* If this be religion or humanity we must confess that we have learned the meaning of these two important terms from a nomenclature widely different from those who have assigned to them a signification so directly the reverse of our own.

You are not supposed to know that during Lincoln's War nearly all Southern blacks supported the Confederacy. Most simply stayed on their farms, growing food crops and protecting their white and black families from the violent depredations of Northern troops. Others held bake sales and auctions in order to raise money for Rebel regiments. Some blacks supported the Confederacy by purchasing Confederate bonds. Many more willingly enlisted in the Confederate military, marching off to war wearing placards on their hats that read: "We will die by the South!" Some 300,000 black Confederates were known to have fought on the battlefield against the ruthless Northern invader. By some estimates as many as 1 million Southern blacks served in one capacity or another under Commander-in-Chief, President Jefferson Davis, in the Confederate army and navy. Among them were tens of thousands who served as teamsters, cooks, nurses, bridge and road builders, smithies, carpenters, couriers, and lookouts. Thousands more served as actual soldiers, providing some of the finest snipers, best musicians, and fiercest warriors in the South. These enthusiastic Southern black conscripts are being mustered out in March 1865, at Richmond, Virginia.

We repeat, *the people of the North and East are, or affect to be, totally ignorant of the actual state and character of our Negro Population; they represent the condition of their bondage as a perpetual revolution of labor and severity, rendered still more deplorable by an utter destitution of all the comforts of life.* Our Negroes, according to these candid and accurate observers, are in every respect illy provided, badly fed and badly clothed; worked beyond their physical capacity while in health; neglected while in sickness; going always to their labor with the most dogged reluctance, confined to it by the severity of the cart-whip, and denied, in fine, all the ordinary enjoyments of existence. *Now, the very reverse of this is the truth*; and it is within the province of those who are continually defaming us, to ascertain it; yet, notwithstanding that *the most abundant testimony is at hand to satisfy the most curious inquirer upon the subject, and every candid and enlightened observer finds himself at every step furnished with the most ample refutation of these charges, the calumny has nevertheless been industriously propagated and upheld with a malignity of design, and an utter contempt of truth, at war with every thing like fair argument, or the most ordinary regard for our feelings.*

According to Yankee mythology Southern slave owners never reunited slave families, they only separated them. The opposite was true. White Southern slaveholders, like Nathan Bedford Forrest, were responsible for thousands of slave family reunions. In this touching illustration a Southern slave couple has been brought back together after the woman's white master agreed to sell her to her husband's white master across town. Such inter-plantation arrangements were common, widely sanctioned, and socially encouraged throughout Dixie.

> We are told by these enlightened and exclusive patriots and philanthropists [at the North] that the odious state of bondage among us is a libel on the character of our country, the very Constitution of which, declares all men to be born equal; that it lessens the reputation of the Republic in the eyes of the civilized world, renders us as a people less acceptable in those of Heaven, and that its abolition is necessary to the greater security and more perfect happiness of the Union; *as if We were the original introducers of this system, or even, now, had it in our power, to sweep away, at one effort, the accumulated evils that have been the growth of centuries, and which will take more than centuries to remove.*[42]

CORRECTING INJUSTICE, PRESERVING THE TRUTH

The "total ignorance" regarding so-called "Southern slavery" that Holland speaks of is indeed a reality that we in Dixie have been living with for centuries. And despite the fact that this view is a fiction, it has unfairly poisoned the world's opinion of the South, the birthplace of the American abolition movement, while forcefully slanting the scales of history in favor of the North, the founder of both the American slave trade and American slavery!

Long before the Civil War, Southern hero President Jefferson Davis was well aware that slavery was doomed. His fight with Lincoln and the North was over the constitutional prerogatives of self-government and states' rights, not the "peculiar institution."

This book will address this injustice head on, and in so doing help rebalance the disequilibrium brought on by years of anti-South propaganda masquerading as "history." May this work stand as a testament to the truth about American slavery for generations to come. As Lincoln himself said: "We cannot escape history."

Lochlainn Seabrook
A slave of Christ (Galatians 1:10)
Nashville, Tennessee, USA
December 2014

WORLD SLAVERY TIME LINE

(Early dates are, of necessity, general estimations)

PREHISTORY: Slavery practiced by every known civilization, people, race, society, culture, and religion around the globe.
3000-1000 BC: Egyptians, Assyrians, Babylonians, Sumerians, Akkadians, Mesopotamians, Phoenicians, Mycenaeans, Arameans, East Indians, Chaldeans, Hittites, Scythians, Persians, Arabians, and Hebrews are enslaving both themselves and their neighbors.
1500 BC: Indigenous slavery is now endemic in Africa as well as across the Americas among Native-Americans like the Mayans.
500 BC: Africans begin exporting their own people as slaves.
200 BC: Rome and Greece are engaged in massive slavery programs and slave trading, both mainly involving whites.
150 BC: Britain's Druids are enslaving fellow whites on the island of Anglesey.
AD 30: Jesus speaks of slavery without condemning it.
AD 60: Paul speaks of slavery without condemning it.
AD 500-1500: The Christian Church sanctions slavery and even engages in various forms of bondage, from mild serfdom to brutal enslavement.
AD 500: The Celts and the Germans, like most other European peoples, are heavily engaged in slavery, primarily white slavery.
AD 700-1000: Islamic slavery is now widespread, bringing the first white

slavers to Africa.

AD 800: The Vikings begin enslaving fellow Europeans.

AD 990: Moorish merchants from the Barbary Coast (Northwest Africa) arrive in what is now Sudan, where they begin trading European goods for slaves from Central Africa.

1100s: The Inca and Aztec peoples are involved in indigenous slavery, which includes some of the most barbaric and terrifying forms of slavery ever known.

1434: Portuguese ship captain Antonio Gonzales lands on the Guinea coast and purchases a group of native African boys, whom he later sells to several Moorish families in the south of Spain.

1441: With the arrival of the Portuguese on Africa's shores, the transatlantic slave trade begins in earnest: Africa initiates slave trading with Europe, selling fellow Africans that have already been enslaved by African chiefs.

1492: Columbus lands in the Americas, carrying African slaves he purchased in Spain. He begins the mass enslavement of Native-Americans, instigating European slavery in the New World.

1501: Spain sends the first African slaves to the Americas when a group of black slaves are transported to Hispaniola and other Spanish colonies.

1526: Spaniard Lucas Vásquez de Ayllón sails 500 of his countrymen and 100 African-Haitian slaves to the area that would one day become the state of Virginia, in an attempt to found a Spanish colony. Within the year most of the settlers perish from disease, including de Ayllón, the slaves revolt, and the survivors return to Haiti. Had the endeavor succeeded, Spain would have been responsible for being the first to introduce black slaves into North America's Southern states.

1527: Native-Americans begin enslaving white Europeans when the Spanish-supported Narváez expedition (named after Spanish conquistador Pánfilo de Narváez) comes ashore on what is now Florida.

1562: For the first time, under Queen Elizabeth I, England recognizes the African slave trade by passing an act legalizing the purchase and sale of blacks. English merchant Sir John Hawkins begins slave trading voyages to Africa, opening up the infamous Cotton Triangle to the Americas.

1612: It is reported this year that Native-Americans have been busy enslaving white colonists who survived the rigors of the doomed English settlement at Roanoke, Virginia (which had been established 27 years earlier in 1585).

1619: On August 31 the Dutch become the first to *successfully* bring Africans to North America when one of their ships, bound for the Spanish colonies, accidently lands at Jamestown, Virginia. On board is a group of 20 blacks, along with 90 white European girls, all who are sold to the colonists, not as slaves (for authentic slavery was unknown in early Jamestown), but as indentured servants. Though this first North American purchase of African servants was considered an experimental trial, the "bargain" was so successful that demand for them quickly grew, eventually involving not just the Dutch, but the English, the French, and other European countries as well.

1621: The Dutch West India Company, the great slave trading corporation, is founded by the Dutch government.

1624: The Dutch West India Company founds and begins governing New Netherland—later to become known as the state of New York.

1625: The Dutch West India Company founds and settles New Amsterdam—later to become known as New York City.

1626: The Dutch bring the first African servant-laborers to New York when the West India Company takes eleven Congolese men from a passing Portuguese slave ship (bound for Brazil), and delivers them to the island of Manhattan.

1630: English Puritans found the Massachusetts Bay Colony at Boston, Massachusetts, and promptly order 180 white indentured servants to be shipped to the colony from England.

1636: America's first slave ship, the *Desire*, is constructed and outfitted at Marblehead, Massachusetts.

1637: Just seven years after the city's birth in 1630, Boston, Massachusetts, purchases and imports African slaves (whom New Englanders then referred to as "Moores") from Providence Island, a fellow Puritan colony off the coast of Nicaragua. American institutional slavery is born. This same year white Bay Staters fight a war against the Pequot Indians, capturing and enslaving the tribe's women and girls and "distributing" them to towns in Massachusetts and Connecticut. The captured Pequot boys are put to work on the *Desire*.

1638: The American North launches the North American slave trade when Yankee slavers in Boston, Massachusetts, sail the ship *Desire* to the West Indies, bringing back to Boston Harbor the first shipload of true African slaves, purchased earlier on the coast of Africa.

1641: The American North legally establishes North American slavery when Massachusetts becomes the first American colony (state) to permit, legitimize, and monetize the institution.

1643: The Yankee colonies of Massachusetts, Plymouth, Connecticut, and

New Haven form the "New England Confederation" (an early American forerunner of the 1861 Southern Confederacy), in part to govern the procurement, trade, maintenance, importation, and exportation of slaves.
1645: New Hampshire and Delaware now have slaves, while on the African coast of Guinea the crew of a Boston slave ship (in conjunction with those from several slave ships from London, England) attack a native village, killing a number of the inhabitants, and capturing two, who are promptly enslaved and taken back to New England.
1646: In June another early slave ship, the *Tamandere*, arrives in New Netherland (New York) with a cargo of African slaves. They are sold to colonial slave holders "for pork and peas."
1647: The Dutch West India Company begins encouraging the white inhabitants of New York to purchase African slaves.
1600s-1700s: England imposes slavery on the American colonies as a legally required institution.
1650: Connecticut passes a code of laws legalizing African slavery within its borders. The Dutch West India Company is bringing black slaves in ever greater numbers into New Netherland (New York). Virginia now has a large population of free landowning blacks, some who are also owners of black servants.
1653: Anthony Johnson, a black Angolan living as a free man in Northampton County, Virginia, is the wealthy owner of a large plantation estate and numerous black and white slaves. When one of his black servants tries to flee, Johnson sues in court to prove that the man is his personal "lifelong property"—a first in American history. Johnson wins, becoming what many believe is the first true, official, and legal slave owner in the U.S.
1655: By permission of the Dutch West India Company, the colonists of New Netherland (New York) begin importing black slaves directly from Angola (Africa) and Brazil.
1656: Due to pressure from England, Virginia's earliest law regarding slavery is passed, noting that if Indians send hostages (whatever their race) into their colony they will not be used as "slaves."
1660: Virginia removes obstacles to trading with the Dutch and other foreign nations, including the importation of "negroes."
1661: Virginia legalizes slavery. Thus prior to this year Virginia court records refer to bonded blacks as "negro servants" or just "negroes," genuine slavery being unknown.
1662: As England continues to force slavery on the American colonies, Virginia has no choice but to officially recognize black slavery within its

borders. Nonetheless, the type of "slavery" practiced in Virginia, and subsequently the rest of the Southern states, is *not* true slavery, but rather a benign form of servitude, in many ways similar to serfdom, vassalage, and even apprenticeship, wherein bondsmen have numerous rights and can even purchase their freedom.

1663: Maryland passes a law making all slaves and children of slaves, slaves for life. Under the same regulation white women who marry black slaves also become lifelong slaves, as do their children.

1664: The English take over the colony of New Netherland and rename it New York (after the Duke of York, later King James II). Slavery is officially legalized and greatly increases here under the new British authorities. The Dutch West Indian Company is replaced by England's far more ruthless slave trading business, the Royal African Company. New Jersey also legalizes slavery this year.

1665: New York borrows from the "Massachusetts Fundamentals," enacting a code of statutes known as "Duke's Laws," which allow unbaptized blacks and Indians to be enslaved.

1667: New England imports a "considerable number" of Native-American slaves from the Caribbean Islands and the Spanish Main.

1671: Maryland passes an act encouraging the importation of African slaves. Out of a total population of 40,000 people, Virginia now has 6,000 white servants but only 2,000 black servants.

1682: South Carolina legalizes slavery.

1686: African slaves in New York find their conditions so terrible they begin fleeing to Canada, then known as New France, for the first time.

1699: The English in New York legally justify the enslavement of Africans due to their "being Pagans." Additionally, New York military officials begin considering using African slaves as soldiers, to cut down on the expense of transporting white soldiers from England.

1700: Rhode Island and Pennsylvania legalize slavery, and New York slave ships are now traveling all the way to Madagascar for black slaves.

1705: In an attempt to prevent African slaves from escaping to Canada, New York officials pass an act prohibiting blacks from traveling more than 40 miles north of Albany without being accompanied by their master or mistress. The punishment for violation is death.

EARLY 1700S: The American South begins the North American abolition movement, with Virginia becoming the first colony to seek the abolition of slavery.

1712: On December 10 New York passes a law called "An Act for

Preventing, Suppressing and Punishing the Conspiracy and Insurrection of Negroes and other Slaves," which allows whipping, torture, and various cruel and unusual forms of execution for all convicted offenders.
1715: North Carolina legalizes slavery.
1723: Britain opens up slavery in Belize.
1732: On June 9, under English army officer James Edward Oglethorpe, the colony of Georgia is founded. The state's newly created charter bans negro slavery as "unjust and cruel," making it the first American colony to add this prohibition to its constitution.
1733: Black New York slaves are caught escaping to neighboring Indian tribes, seeking refuge from their horrid captivity under white colonists.
1749: Georgia legalizes slavery, the last of the original 13 colonies to do so.
1753: Virginia begins enacting laws to prohibit the importation of black slaves.
1775: New York passes its last slave law as a British colony when on April 3 it issues a statute for Orange County assessing the value of African slaves: "Males, 15 years old and under 40 years, £30; and females of the same age, £20. Males 40 years old and under old and under 15 years, £18; and females of the same age, £12. Males 7 years old and under 10 years, £10; and females of the same age, £8."
1776: Thomas Jefferson uses the Declaration of Independence to lambast England's King George III for forcing slavery on the 13 original American colonies, which are now in possession of some 500,000 slaves: 300,000 (or 60 percent) are located in the Northern colonies, only 200,000 (or 40 percent) are in the Southern colonies.
1778: Under Jefferson, Virginia becomes the first state to prohibit the importation of slaves—30 years before the U.S. Congress enacts a nationwide prohibition in 1808.
1802: Denmark abolishes the slave trade.
1807-1808: Both the U.S. (under Jefferson) and Great Britain (under William Bentinck) call for an end to the transatlantic slave trade. The ban is ignored and the trade continues.
1814: The Dutch abolish the slave trade in the Netherlands.
1823: Mexico abolishes slavery.
1827: New York "officially" ends slavery, as have most other Northern states by now. Yet both the trade and slavery carry on illicitly and sometimes even openly, not only in New York, but across the entire Northeast.
1831: Southerners are busy gradually freeing their slaves when New England meddler, fussbudget and troublemaker, abolitionist William Lloyd Garrison,

publishes his newspaper *The Liberator*, calling for the immediate, complete, and unconditional abolition of slavery in the South, with no financial compensation to slave owners. In it, *for the first time*, Southern slavery is referred to as a "sin" and slaveholders as "criminals." This "Garrisonian agitation," not slavery itself, forces the conservative, pro-Constitution South into greater conflict with the liberal, anti-Constitution North over the issue of states' rights, which opens the door for the upcoming "Civil War."
1834: Canada abolishes slavery.
1838: Belize abolishes slavery.
1842: Mexico abolishes the slave trade.
1845: Sweden abolishes slavery.
1848: France abolishes slavery at home and among it colonies. St. Croix abolishes slavery as well.
1860: On November 6 white supremacist and big government Liberal Abraham Lincoln (a Republican, the Liberal Party at the time) is elected sixteenth president of the U.S., on a platform promising *not* to interfere with slavery (as he clearly states in his Inaugural Address on March 4, 1861, and as was asserted obliquely in the 1860 Republican Party Platform). Had the Conservatives (at that time the Democrats) stood together and not divided their vote, Lincoln would have gone down in defeat. Instead, he won, in great part, because ten of the Southern states did not even bother putting him on their ballots, and also because the majority of Northerners at the time were anti-abolition, and his was the only party that pledged to allow slavery to continue unimpeded (though it was against the expansion of slavery outside the South). He thus became the first sectionally elected president in U.S. history, and that with only 39 percent of the popular American vote (due to our faulty, and by then already outdated, Electoral College).
1861: On March 11 the Southern Confederacy issues its new constitution, the Constitution of the Confederate States of America (named after the original name of the United States of America), with a clause prohibiting all foreign slave trading within its borders. On April 12 Lincoln tricks the Confederacy into firing the first shot at the Battle of Fort Sumter. Though no one is killed (the South only wanted all U.S. troops removed from the island—which now belongs to the C.S.), Lincoln accuses the South of aggressing on the U.S. flag, and on April 15 calls for 75,000 Federal troops to invade Dixie. Though some Northern blacks want to join the U.S. army, Lincoln refuses to allow "negroes" or "savages" (his name for Indians) to serve for the first two years of his war due to the "natural disgust" he and

other Yankees feel at the idea of the mixing of the races.
1862: On September 22 Lincoln issues his Preliminary Emancipation Proclamation, calling for an end to American slavery so that freed blacks can be deported from the U.S. and settled ("colonized") in foreign lands such as Africa, the Caribbean, Europe, and Latin America.
1863: On January 1, after two years of tremendous pressure from abolitionists in his party, a reluctant Lincoln issues his Final Emancipation Proclamation, calling for an end to slavery, though only in the Southern states—and then only in those areas not under Union control. As he notes in the document itself (which he revealingly refers to as a "*military* emancipation"), its real purpose is to enlist freed Southern blacks in the U.S. army, not grant them citizenship or any other civil rights. (The black deportation clause included in the preliminary proclamation has been removed by Lincoln's cabinet to prevent offending abolitionists in his party, whose votes he needs in the upcoming 1864 election.)
1865: On December 6 the Thirteenth Amendment, not Lincoln (now deceased), finally officially abolishes slavery across the U.S. (though not for criminals, who can still legally be enslaved).
1886: Cuba bans slavery.
1888: Brazil becomes the last country in the New World to outlaw slavery.
1895: Korea abolishes slavery.
1906: Iran's Constitution forbids slavery.
1910: China abolishes slavery.
1962: Saudi Arabia ends slavery.
PRESENT: Both slavery and the slave trade continue worldwide, mainly in Africa, the Middle East, South America, and parts of Asia. Yet various forms of slavery are still found even in the U.S. International antislavery organizations estimate that there are now more slave traders, slave owners, and slaves in the world than at any other time in human history.

EVERYTHING

You Were Taught About American Slavery Is Wrong

Ask a Southerner!

1

WE ALL DESCEND FROM SLAVE OWNERS AND SLAVES

WHAT YOU WERE TAUGHT: Slavery was an invention of America's Southern whites, in particular, African slavery.
THE TRUTH: This statement would certainly have amazed the thousands of Africans who were practicing slavery on each other millennia before the first European slave ships visited West Africa,[43] for Africans are a people "among whom slavery [has] existed from immemorial time."[44]

No one knows who actually invented slavery of course, for it was a worldwide phenomenon that arose simultaneously around the globe. But we do know that it dates from prehistory,[45] was once universally accepted on every part of the planet,[46] and that at one time it was found on every continent, in every single nation, and among every people, race, religion, and ethnic group.[47] Actually, "so far as we can trace back the history of the human race, we discover the existence of slavery."[48]

Slavery was, in fine, the economic system upon which *all* ancient civilizations were built,[49] for "slavery is the precursor to civilization."[50] As such it must certainly be counted as one of humanity's oldest social institutions and an essential feature of both society and economics.[51] It is, as the *Encyclopedia Britannica* puts it, a universal, useful, indispensable, and inevitable accompaniment of human culture,[52] one that eventually became so taken for granted that it was seen as a "divinely ordained institution" in every country.[53]

In 1837 America's seventh vice president, South Carolinian John C. Calhoun, rightly noted that

> there has never yet existed a wealthy and civilized society in which one portion of the community did not, in fact, live on the labor of the other.[54]

Slavery was once practiced in every known early civilization, and among all ancient peoples, societies, cultures, and religions.

In 1886 Yankee historian George Bancroft of Massachusetts wrote:

> Slavery and the slave-trade are older than the records of human society; they are found to have existed wherever the savage hunter began to assume the habits of pastoral or agricultural life; and . . . they have extended to every portion of the globe. The oldest monuments of human labor on the Egyptian soil are the results of slave labor. The founder of the Jewish people was a slave-holder and a purchaser of slaves. The Hebrews, when they broke from their own thraldom, planted slavery in the promised land. Tyre, the oldest commercial city of Phoenicia, was, like Babylon, a market "for the persons of men."[55]

In 1899 North Carolina planter and slave owner William Tasse Alexander penned:

> There is no injustice more revolting than slavery, and yet there is no fact so widespread in history. In antiquity the system of labor was everywhere slavery. It was found in Rome, in Greece, in Egypt, in Austria, in Gaul, among the Germans, and it is said even among the Scythians. It was recruited by war, by voluntary sale, by captivity for debt, and then by inheritance. It was not everywhere cruel, and in patriarchical life it was scarcely distinguishable from domestic service; in some countries, however, it approached the service of beasts of burden. The brutal insensibility with which Aristotle and [Marcus Terentius] Varro spoke of slaves is revolting; and the manner in which they were treated by the laws is even more so. These men who were of the same race, who had the same intellect and the same color as their owners, were declared incapable of holding property, of appealing to the law, of defending themselves; in a word, of conducting themselves like men in any of the circumstances of life. Only the law of the Hebrew people tempered servitude by humanity. Doubtless we might quote certain words of Euripides or Terence, of Epictetus or of Seneca, colored with a more tender pity and evincing some heart. We find also both in Greek and Roman laws, on the monuments, and in the inscriptions and epitaphs which our contemporaries have so carefully studied, the proof that the granting of freedom to slaves, in individual cases, was frequent, and that it was inspired, especially at the moment of death, by religious motives.
>
> *But the brutal fact of slavery is incontestable. The evil outweighed the good in an enormous measure; servitude remained from century to century, from country to country, during all antiquity, the universal fact, and the legitimateness of servitude, the universal doctrine.*[56]

In short, slavery is a natural byproduct of human society,[57] placing it alongside our other oldest human social institutions: hunting and gathering, religion, marriage, warfare, puberty rites, funerary rites, and prostitution.[58] Indeed, anthropologists consider slavery not an indication of barbarity, but an early sign of civilization: its emergence meant that humans had begun to enslave rather than kill one another.[59]

From its appearance in the prehistoric mists of time, slavery went on to be employed by the Mesopotamians (ancient Iraqis), Indians, Chinese, ancient Egyptians, Hebrews, Greeks, and Romans. In the pre-Columbian Americas slavery became an integral part of such Native-American peoples as the Maya and Inca,[60] who depended on large scale slave labor in warfare and farming.[61]

Among the Inca, villages were required by law to supply the

king's royal mansions with slaves. One of these leaders, Atahualpa, the last of the Incan kings, was well-known for his cruelty: though it was necessary for certain types of slaves to approach him (such as chefs, cupbearers, and porters), the megalomaniacal potentate ordered that such individuals must afterward be killed for coming into close proximity to his sacred person. Not only were these slaves "pitilessly slaughtered," but Atahualpa had their entire families executed, their houses burned down, and their villages destroyed. All of the peoples in the Cuzco region were oppressed in this manner, with some villages losing 25 percent of their total population.[62]

Northerner George Bancroft was a rare Yankee historian: he acknowledged that slavery was as old as mankind.

For the Aztecs slavery was not only vital to their economic, agricultural, and military systems, it also concerned diet: always in need of offerings to propitiate their voracious gods and goddesses, the cannibalistic Aztec people were highly proficient at human sacrifice, the first choice of victim usually being a slave. Spanish Conquistadors reported that Aztec slaves were purposefully fattened up in cages so that the most "succulent cuts" of their bodies (hands and thighs) could later be devoured at mealtime.[63]

Other Indian peoples who once practiced slavery include the Cherokee, Iroquois, Navaho, Seminole, Choctaw, Creek, Chickasaw, Cheyenne, Natchez, Arapaho, Kiowas, Paiute, Chinook, Yuchie, Pima, Papago, Halchidhoma, Guarani, Shasta, and Klamath. Again, some of the forms of slavery employed were particularly brutal, involving torture and cannibalistic rituals. It is said that slavery was as economically important to many Native-American tribes as it was to European-American slavers prior to the Civil War.[64]

The list of Indian and native peoples who practiced various forms of slavery and servitude also includes such Eskimo tribes as the Aleuts, the Koniagas, the Tlinkits, the Tsimshians, the Nootkas, the Bilballas, the Ahts, and the Puget Sound tribes. There were also the Fish Indians of British Columbia, the Kutchins, the Tacullies, the Atnas, the Koltschanes, the Similkameen people of British Columbia, the Delawares, the Ojibways, the Menomini, the Tuscaroras, the Okanagans, the Atnaks, the Nez Percé, the Shastika, the Shoshones, the Utahs, the Kioways, the Apaches, the Comanches, the Navajos, the Mojaves, the Cibola Pueblo, Panamanian Indians, Costa Rican Indians, the Caribs of the Antilles, the Continental Caribs, the Arawaks, the Saliva of Columbia, the Goajiro, the Brazilian natives, the Apiacas, the Mundrucus, the Mauhés, the Miranhas, the Guaycurû, the Mbayás, the Chiriguanos, the Záparos, the Conibas, the Yuracarés, the Mocéténès, the Chiquitos, the Moxos, the Enimagas, the Charruas, the Patagons, the Puelches, the Araucanians, and probably the Hurons, the Karayas, the Nishinan, the Flatheads, the Karoks, and the Hupas, among countless others.[65]

The native peoples of nearly every continent, in fact, are known to have engaged in some form of bondage and slave trading. Here is a brief sampling: the Solomon Island natives, the Fijians, the natives of New Guinea (such as the Papua), the Maori, the Tongas, the natives of Tahiti, the natives of Hawaii, the natives of the Marquesas Islands, the natives of Tukopia, the natives of Anaa, the natives of the Marshall islands, the natives of the Caroline Islands, the natives of Yap, the natives of the Gilbert Islands, the natives of Polynesia, the natives of Micronesia, the Battahs of Sumatra, the natives of Borneo, the natives of the Celebes Islands (modern Sulawesi) of Indonesia, the natives of the Little Sumda Islands, and the Moluccas, the natives of the Philippines, the natives of Bali, the natives of Java, and the natives of the Himalayas, India, Central Asia, Siberia, and the Caucasus.[66]

After the fall of Rome and the establishment of Christianity as the dominant religion in Europe, the Christian Church also accepted slavery,[67] never once trying to suppress it,[68] never publically denouncing it,[69] never even privately condemning it.[70] During the 1700s, for example, the Church of England owned a large slave plantation in the Caribbean.[71] Christianity also embraced serfdom,[72] a less harsh form of slavery that was nearly ubiquitous throughout Europe during the Middle Ages. Islam recognized slavery, as did all of Arabia[73] and Europe, with the Portuguese initiating the European-African slave trade in the year 1444,[74] after which they monopolized human trafficking for over a century.[75] By 1550 at least 10 percent of Lisbon's population were slaves.[76]

Since the master-slave relationship predates human history, American Southern whites were obviously not the inventors of American black slavery. In fact, Southern whites inherited the institution of African servitude very late in the game, many thousands of years after it had been practiced in Europe, the Middle East, Asia, and its ultimate source, of course, Africa.[77]

The Native-American Aztecs depended on slaves for every facet of their society, including human sacrifice.

Indeed, as both the American slave trade[78] *and* American slavery began in New England,[79] the South was actually the *last* region in America to adopt slavery, and it is this fact that has helped contribute to the Yankee myth that she is the one responsible for inventing it. Memories are short and propaganda is long, particularly *Yankee* propaganda.[80]

The reality is that slavery is a worldwide, omnipresent phenomenon, one that stubbornly persists into modern times, and which dates far back into the fog of prehistory on all continents, and among all races, ethnic groups, religions, societies, and peoples.[81] All of us then, no matter what our race, color, or nationality, have ancestors who enslaved others and who were themselves enslaved. *We are all descendants of slave owners and slaves.*

Early peoples traditionally enslaved those they captured during war, a usually degraded group that formed the majority of most ancient societies. It is from among these enormous enslaved populations and their masters that you will find many of your own ancestors.

2

INDIGENOUS AFRICAN SLAVERY

WHAT YOU WERE TAUGHT: American enslavement was especially painful for African-born blacks, who in their entire history had been free and had never known slavery or any other kind of bondage or captivity. For early Africa knew nothing of slavery: it never practiced it and had no interest in the slave trade, particularly in enslaving, trading, or purchasing its own inhabitants.

THE TRUTH: No region on earth has been more dependent on slavery over a longer period of time, practiced slavery more aggressively and widely on its own populace, or allowed slavery to become more entrenched, than Africa. Indeed, Africa has been so intimately involved with slavery over such an immense duration—with slave majorities thought to be as high as 90 percent of the population in some regions[82]—that its name is today synonymous with the institution. "The great womb of slavery," Yankee abolitionist Charles Sumner called it.[83]

Slavery was so intrinsic to the early African way of life that at one time slaves, known by their own people as "black ivory,"[84] could be found in nearly every African society, where—as in every other country where slavery is found—the minority population dominated and enslaved the majority population.[85] These were not merely "insignificant traces of slavery," as African apologists maintain, but rather true African slave societies, built on and around the bondage of their own people.[86]

So plentiful and in such demand were African slaves in Africa that they came to be used as money. In East Africa, for example, the government accepted slaves as payment, and sometimes soldiers were given slaves instead of wages.[87] And because slavery was a "central institution" in Africa,[88] slaves became "Africa's most important export."[89]

In 1861 Blake wrote that the responsibility for what later became the transatlantic slave trade must be laid at the feet of Africa, which introduced "a slavery confined entirely to negroes":

> *The nations and tribes of negroes in Africa, who thus ultimately became the universal prey of Europeans, were themselves equally guilty in subjecting men to perpetual bondage. In the most remote times, every Ethiopian man of consequence had his slaves, just as a Greek or Roman master had.* Savage as he was, he at least resembled the citizen of a civilized state in this. *He possessed his domestic slaves, or bondmen, hereditary on his property; and besides these, he was always acquiring slaves by whatever means he could, whether by purchase from slave-dealers, or by war with neighboring tribes. The slaves of a negro master in this case would be his own countrymen, or at least men of his own race and color; some of them born on the same spot with himself, some of them captives who had been brought from a distance of a thousand miles.* Of course, the farther a captive was taken from his home, the more valuable he would be, as having less chance of escape; and therefore it would be a more *common practice to sell a slave taken in war with a neighboring tribe, than to retain him as a laborer so near his home.* And *just as in the cities of the civilized countries, we find the slave population often outnumbering the free, so in the villages of the interior of Africa the negro slaves were often more numerous than the negro masters.* [Scottish explorer Mungo] Park, in his travels among the negroes, found that *in many villages the slaves were three times as numerous as the free persons; and it is likely that the proportion was not very different in more ancient times.* In ancient times, the Garamantes used to sell negroes to the Libyans; and so a great proportion of the slaves of the Carthaginians and the Egyptians must have been blacks brought northwards across the desert.[90]

Slavery's pivotal role in African society certainly explains why not a single organized slave revolt, or even an abolition movement for that matter, ever arose among the African populace during the entire pre-colonial period, and it is why slavery was finally only outlawed by the efforts of non-Africans (mainly Europeans).[91] It also explains why there has long been a belief among the native population that due to domestic African slavery, "the whole land has been laid under a curse which will never be removed."[92]

Let us now examine the historical facts concerning indigenous African slavery in more detail.

Africans were practicing slavery on themselves for thousands of years before the arrival of Europeans.[93] For

> negro slavery is not an invention of the white man. As Greeks enslaved Greeks, as Anglo-Saxons dealt in Anglo-Saxons, so *the earliest accounts of the land of the black men bear witness that negro masters held men of their own race as slaves, and sold them to others*. This the oldest Greek historian [Herodotus] commemorates.[94]

Africa's own slavery system dates back to prehistory, long before written records, and includes some of the most unusual, savage, and shocking forms of human bondage ever chronicled.

In what is known as the "Oriental Slave Trade" (as opposed to the "Occidental Slave Trade" of Europeans),[95] Africans have been enslaving one another dating back to at least 2,200 years ago. It is at this time, during the continent's Iron Age, that we begin to see historical evidence of African slavery, an institution already in progress over 1,600 years before the arrival of the first Arabic,[96] and later European and Yankee, slave ships.[97]

Yet, as with all slavery cultures, we can be sure that the institution was being practiced in Africa long before written records—such as in prehistoric Egypt, for instance.[98] In point of fact, "African slavery was coeval with the existence of the African race . . . . [and thus] has existed in Africa since its first [negro] settlement."[99]

It cannot be stressed enough that, it being a "characteristic part of African tradition" and a truly "universal" aspect of African society, *African slavery was of African origin*. Thus indigenous African slavery is nearly as old as Africa itself. Indeed, not only were slaves an integral part of the commerce of prehistoric and ancient Africa, but just as in early Sudan, as only one example, slave ownership was an accepted sign of wealth, and so was considered no different than owning precious metals or gems. Even the practice of exporting African slaves out of the country can be definitively dated back to at least the 5th Century BC. It can be truly said then that *early Africa literally revolved around the enslavement of its own people by its own rulers upon its own soil.*[100]

The native victims of the pre-conquest African slave trade were captured inland or in East Africa by their African brethren, then exported to Persia, Arabia, India, and China.[101] This means that the first European slavers to venture to Africa (Portuguese ship captain Antonio Gonzales arrived in 1434 and purchased several native African boys who he sold in Spain,[102] while Portugal's trade in slaves with the continent began in 1441)[103] only interrupted the booming, "well-developed" slave trade inaugurated by West Africans and various coastal tribes[104]—one that had already been going on there for untold centuries[105] with peoples like the Arabs.[106] It was only much later that Europeans helped stimulate the existing business.[107]

In 1846, while internal African slavery was still expanding, Estes noted how the transatlantic slave trade was helping to improve the condition of the African slave in his native homeland:

> . . . *the larger proportion of the population of Africa are in a state of perpetual, and most abject slavery. And it is a well known fact, that the larger number of them which have been sold into foreign slavery, were in a state of slavery in their own country: consequently . . . he is equally, if not more free, here [in the American South], than he was in Africa. They were sold by their African owners to the slave traders; and by these latter, brought to this country and sold to the planters.* Kidnapping, has, no doubt, been occasionally practised in Africa; but the number of slaves obtained in this manner, have been very few in comparison with *the great number which were obtained by purchase from their African*

> *Masters*.
>
> It has been often objected to the slave trade, that it has been the source of wars among the natives—gotten up, and urged on, by foreigners—with the view of getting a supply of slaves. . . . I have before remarked that *the several African tribes are in a state of perpetual hostility, and that one of the maxims of war among them is, "extermination or slavery." The old, the infirm, the helpless infant, and, in many instances, the female, are put to death; and that, too, very often, in the most brutal manner. The able-bodied men and women are retained alive, and reduced to slavery*. They may, or may not sell them into foreign slavery: that will depend greatly upon the supply at home. *Most intelligent travellers agree that these wars would occur with nearly the same frequency, if the slave trade had never existed*. But even admitting the fact that these wars have been rendered somewhat more frequent by the slave trade, there is an advantage resulting from this trade which will much more than counterbalance this evil. Where slaves are very numerous in Africa, they are in a measure worthless to their owners; consequently, no regard is paid to their lives, or to their interest, in any way. *On the death of a distinguished man, thousands of these worthless slaves are put to death*, in order that he may have suitable attendance in the future world. Now *the foreign slave trade, by raising the value of the slaves, has greatly tended to prevent the destruction of life in the cases referred to—and has, in fact, greatly tended to ameliorate the condition of the slave generally*. The number of slaves put to death in such cases, as might be inferred, will be in proportion to their value if they are valuable, and can, in consequence, be sold at a high price to foreigners, but few, comparatively, will be sacrificed; but if, on the contrary, the slaves have but little value on account of their great numbers, the sacrifices are numerous. *On some occasions, thousands of slaves are put to death, in order to satisfy the appetite of a merciless superstition*.[108]

Along with slavery, servitude, vassalage, and serfdom were also practiced among pre-European Africans, whose kingdoms, as Estes pointed out, routinely engaged in the mass subjugation of neighboring tribes.[109] The kingdom of Dahomey instigated an annual war every year for the sole purpose of acquiring slaves.[110] By controlling the slave ports of Allada and Ouidah, Abomey (the capital city of Dahomey) grew into one of the richest towns in Africa.[111] When rebellions broke out in Dahomey in the 1600s, Fon leaders quickly subdued the rebel leaders and enslaved them, along with their followers. All were sold to slavers then shipped to the West Indies and Brazil.[112] Slavery, once a "common feature" of Dahomey society, greatly enriched the coffers of this African people: at least one fifth of all the slaves shipped to the Americas came from the Bight of Benin, a region that includes Dahomey.[113]

The coffle of shackled African men on the left have been captured by African slavers at Kilgou in southeastern Sudan. They will be marched to one of Africa's many internal slave markets and sold at auction to fellow Africans. Such scenes were taking place thousands of years before the arrival of Europeans on Africa's northwest coast.

Many pre-conquest Africans were put into bondage for nothing more than breaking African laws,[114] such as not paying off a financial obligation. If the individual was not able to discharge the debt, he or she became a "lifetime slave."[115] Native African rulers—all who insisted on having slave trading stations set up near their palaces[116]—even went as far as enslaving the subjects of their own personal kingdoms and states, often setting fire to villages at night in order to seize the terror stricken inhabitants as they fled.[117] After capture they were locked in wretched "slave prisons" (known as barracoons),[118] sometimes for months at a time, after which they were summarily sold off to the highest bidder.[119] As enslaving POWs was also an innate part of the African slaving system, this was considered "normal proceeding."[120]

The early African word for war did not have the same meaning as ours. Its literal definition was "a piratical expedition for making slaves."[121] Estes writes that:

> The consequence is, *every imaginable evil which springs from the bosom of society* when not under the influence of moral, religious, and political restraints, *exists in Africa. Wars—bloody, destructive, and unrelenting wars—are constantly waged by the several tribes against each*

> *other. These wars are often undertaken with the open and avowed purpose of plunder, and in order to get prisoners for the purpose of supplying the slave market. Kings, and the most celebrated warriors engage readily in these wars for plunder, and even regard such expeditions as highly honorable.*[122]

Africans were so hungry for slaves that during the 15th and 16th Centuries the Portugese found a ready market on the continent's Gold Coast for selling African slaves back to their original captors and owners in exchange for gold[123]—a precious metal that was itself a product of African slave labor.[124] Phillips comments that:

> *The [African] chiefs were eager to foster trade and cultivate good will, for it brought them pompous trappings as well as useful goods.* "Grandy King George" of Old Calabar, for example, asked of his friend [English slave ship] Captain [Ambrose] Lace a mirror six feet square, an arm chair "for my salf to sat in," a gold mounted cane, a red and a blue coat with gold lace, a case of razors, pewter plates, brass flagons, knives and forks, bullet and cannon-ball molds, and sailcloth for his canoes, along with many other things for use in trade.[125]

African slaves recently being traded on Angola's Cuanza River.

At one time large regions of Africa were completely depopulated by "barbarous" African kings in order to furnish slaves to Arabic countries,[126] where, it was once said, "every family possessed at least one black slave."[127] In many cases victims were hunted down by African slave-catchers, then specifically bred for sale and export across the Atlantic to satiate the appetite of sugar, tobacco, coffee, indigo, and cotton plantations for cheap African labor.[128] More nefarious, in order to undermine respect for tradition and customs, the most powerful rulers often encouraged strife and violence among the general populace in order to fill the prisons with lawbreakers.[129] They then wrote up new laws that were punishable by enslavement in order to increase the number of slaves.[130] In the Songhai Empire, a large Islamic domain in 16th-Century West Africa, entire towns were turned into "slave villages," whose inhabitants had but one purpose in life: to serve the African king and his court.[131] When the slave supply ran low, the Songhai government simply raided Mossi territory, after which all the captives were turned into chattel and sold to the highest Muslim bidder in North Africa.[132]

In 1790 and 1791, a number of individuals who had either lived in Africa or had been involved in the African slave trade, gave testimony before the English House of Commons as to the pervasiveness of indigenous African slavery:

> The trade for slaves, (says Mr. Kiernan), in the river Senegal, was chiefly with the Moors, on the northern banks, who got them very often by war, and not seldom by kidnapping; that is, lying in wait near a village, where there was no open war, and seizing whom they could. *He has often heard of villages, and seen the remains of such, broken up by making the people slaves.* That the Moors used to cross the Senegal to catch the negroes was spoken of at Fort Louis as notorious; and he has seen instances of it where the persons so taken were ransomed.
>
> General Ruoke says, that kidnapping took place in the neighborhood of Goree. It was spoken of as *a common practice*. . . . He remembers two or three instances of negroes being brought to Goree, who had been kidnapped, but could not discover by whom. At their own request he immediately sent them back.
>
> Mr. Dalrymple found that the great droves (caffellas or caravans) of slaves brought from inland, by way of Galam, to Senegal and Gambia, were prisoners of war. Those sold to vessels at Goree, and near it, were procured either by the grand pillage, the lesser pillage, or by robbery of individuals, or in consequence of crimes. *The grand pillage is executed by the [African] king's soldiers, from three hundred to three thousand at a time, who attack and set fire to a village, and seize the inhabitants as they can. The smaller parties generally lie in wait about the villages, and take off all they can surprise; which is also done by individuals, who do not belong to the king, but are private robbers. These sell their prey on the coast*, where it is well known no questions as to the means of obtaining it are asked.
>
> As to kidnapping, it is so notorious about Goree, that he never heard any person deny it there. Two men while he was there offered a person, a messenger from Senegal to Rufisco, for sale, to

the garrison, who even boasted how they had obtained him. Many also were brought to Goree while he was there, procured in the same manner. These depredations are also practiced by the Moors: he saw many slaves in Africa who told him they were taken by them; particularly three, one of whom was a woman, who cried very much, and seemed to be in great distress; the two others were more reconciled to their fate.

Captain Wilson says, that slaves are either procured by intestine [internal] wars, or by kings breaking up villages, or crimes real or imputed, or kidnapping. *Villages are broken up by the king's troops surrounding them in the night, and seizing such of the inhabitants as suit their purpose. This practice is most common when there is no war with another state. It is universally acknowledged that free persons are sold for real or imputed crimes, for the benefit of their judges.* Soon after his arrival at Goree, king Damel sent a free man to him for sale, and was to have the price himself. One of the king's guards being asked whether the man was guilty of the crime imputed to him, answered, that was of no consequence, or ever inquired into. . . .

Kidnapping was acknowledged by all he [Wilson] conversed with, to be generally prevalent. It is the first principle of the natives, the principle of self-preservation, never to go unarmed, while a slave-vessel is on the [African] coast, for fear of being stolen. When he has met them thus armed, and inquired of them, through his interpreter, the reason of it, they have pointed to a French slave-vessel then lying at Portudal [in Senegal], and said their fears arose from that quarter.

. . . Mr. Wadstrom knows slaves to be procured between Senegal and Gambia, either by the general pillage or by robbery by individuals, or by stratagem and deceit. *The general pillage is executed by the king's troops on horseback, armed, who seize the unprepared.* Mr. Wadstrom, during the week he was at Joal, accompanying one of those embassies which the French governor sends yearly with presents to *the black kings*, to keep up the slave trade, saw parties sent out for this purpose, by king Barbesin, almost every day. *These parties went out generally in the evening, and were armed with bows and arrows, guns, pistols, sabres, and long lances. The king of Sallum practices the pillage also.* Mr. Wadstrom saw twenty-seven slaves from Sallum, twenty-three of whom were women and children, thus taken. He was told also by merchants at Goree, that *king Damel practices the pillage in like manner.*

Robbery was a general way of taking single slaves [in Africa]. He once saw a woman and a boy in the slave-hold at Goree; the latter had been taken by stealth from his parents in the interior parts above Cape Rouge, and he declared that *such robberies were very frequent in his country*; the former, at Rufisco, from her husband and children. He could state several instances of such robberies, he very often saw negroes thus taken brought to Goree. Ganna of Dacard was a noted man-stealer, and employed as such by the slave-merchants there. As instances of stratagem employed to obtain slaves, he relates that a French merchant taking a fancy to a negro, who was on a visit to Dacard, persuaded the village, for a certain price, to seize him. *He was accordingly taken from his wife, who wished to accompany him*, but the Frenchman had not merchandise enough to buy both. *Mr. Wadstrom saw this negro at Goree, the day he arrived from Dacard, chained, and lying on the ground, exceedingly distressed in his mind.* The king of Sallum also prevailed on a woman to come into his kingdom, and sell him some millet. On her arrival, he seized and sold her to a French officer, with whom Mr. Wadstrom saw this woman every day while at Goree. Mr. Wadstrom was on the island of St. Louis, up the Senegal also, and on the continent near the river, and says that *all the slaves sold at Senegal, are brought down the river, except those taken by the robbery of the Moors in the neighborhood, which is sometimes conducted by large parties, in what are called petty wars.*

Captain Hills saw, while lying between Goree and the continent, *the natives, in an evening, often go out in war dresses, as he found, to obtain slaves for king Damel, to be sold.* The reason was, that the king was then poor, not having received his usual dues from us. He never saw the parties that went out return with slaves, but has *often seen slaves in their huts tied back to back.* He remembers also that some robbers once brought him a man, bound, on board the [ship] *Zephyr*, to sell, but he, Captain Hills, would not buy him, but suffered him to escape. *The natives on the continent opposite to Goree all go armed, he imagines for fear of being taken.*

When in the river Gambia, wanting servants on board his ship, he expressed a wish for some volunteers. A black pilot in the boat called two boys who were on shore, carrying baskets of shallots, and asked Captain Hills if they would do, in which case he would take them off, and bring them to him. This he declined. From the ease with which the pilot did it, he concludes *this was customary.*

. . . Sometimes [Mr. Bowman] accompanied [African slave catchers working on behalf of their king] . . . a mile or so, and once joined the party, anxious to know by what means they obtained the slaves. Having traveled all day, they came to a small river, when he was told they had but a little way farther to go. Having crossed the river, they stopped till dark. Here Mr. Bowman (it was about the middle of the night) was afraid to go farther, and prevailed on the king's son to leave him a guard of four men. In half an hour he heard the war cry, by which he understood they had reached a town. In about half an hour more they returned, bringing from twenty-five to thirty men, women and children, some of the latter at the breast. At this time he saw the town in flames. When they had recrossed the river, it was just daylight, and they reached Scaffus about mid-day. The prisoners were carried to different parts of the town. *They are usually brought in with strings around their necks, and some have their hands tied across. He never saw any slaves there who had been convicted of crimes. He has been called up in the night to see fires, and told by the town's people that it was war carrying on.*

Whatever rivers he traded in, such as Sierra Leone, Junk, and little Cape Mount, *he has usually passed burnt and deserted villages, and learned from the natives in the boat with him, that war had been there, and the natives had been taken in the manner as before described, and carried to the ships [as slaves].*

He has also seen such upon the [African] Coast: while trading at Grand Bassa, he went on shore with four black traders to the town a mile off. On the way, there was a town deserted, (with only two or three houses standing), which seemed to have been a large one, as there were two fine plantations of rice ready for cutting down. A little further on they came to another village in much the same state. He was told that the first town had been taken by war, there being many ships then lying at Bassa. . . . In passing along to the trader's town, *he saw several villages deserted; these, the natives said, had been destroyed by war, and the people taken out and sold [into slavery].*

. . . Slaves, says Mr. Town, are brought from the country very distant from the coast. The king of Barra informed Mr. Town, that on the arrival of a ship, he has gone three hundred miles up the country with his guards, and driven down captives to the sea-side. *From Marraba, king of the Mandingoes, he has heard that they had marched slaves out of the country some hundred miles; that they had gone wood-ranging, to pick up every one they met with, whom they stripped naked, and, if men, bound; but if women, brought down loose; this he had [heard] from themselves, and also, that they often went to war with the Bullam nation, on purpose to get slaves.* They boasted that they should soon have a fine parcel for the shallops [shallow water sailing vessels], and the success often answered. Mr. Town has seen the prisoners (the men bound, the women and children loose) driven for sale to the water-side. *He has also known the natives to go in gangs, marauding and catching all they could.*

. . . Lieutenant Simpson says, from what he saw, he believes *the [internal African] slave trade is the occasion of wars among the natives.* From the natives of the Windward Coast he understood that *the villages were always at war*; and the black traders and others

> gave as a reason for it, that *the [African] kings wanted slaves*. If a trading canoe . . . saw a larger canoe coming from a village they were at war with, they instantly fled; and sometimes without receiving the value of their goods. On inquiry, he learned their reasons to be, that if taken, they would have been made slaves.[133]

It was not uncommon for African slave catchers themselves to be captured, enslaved, and sold by other Africans:

> In the Galenas river [Mr. Town] knew four blacks seize a man who had been to the sea-side to sell one or more slaves. This man was returning home with the goods received in exchange for these, and they plundered him, stripped him naked, and brought him to the trading shallop, which Mr. Town commanded, and sold him there.[134]

These practices were so accepted in Africa that it gave rise to a popular children's game called "slave-taking," in which young African boys would imitate their elders' slave-catching maneuvers, such as leaping, attacking, grabbing, and retreating.[135]

This Fulani woman and Susu man both belong to native African peoples who once vigorously and violently practiced slavery on other Africans.

The list of early African communities who practiced indigenous slavery includes almost every known people, among them: the Swahili,[136] the Fur of Darfur,[137] the Mandingos, the Ibos, the Efiks, the Krus, the Fantins, the Binis, the Sengalese,[138] the Mang'anja, the Nsenga, the Maravis, the Gaza Nguni,[139] the Malians,[140] the Gambians,[141] the Wolof, the Serer, the Fulbe,[142] the Hausas, the Mane, the Oyo, the Yao, the Chikunda,[143] the Susu,[144] the Fulani,[145] the Futa Jallon,[146] Kenyans,[147] Mozambicans,[148] the Akan,[149] inhabitants of the Loango kingdom[150] and the Benin kingdom,[151] the Yoruba of western Nigeria, the Fon of Dahomey (as mentioned),[152] and the Ashanti[153] (or Asante) of Ghana,[154] the latter where Osei Tutu, the founder and ruler of the Ashanti states, turned the African kingdom into one of the wealthiest regions on the continent through the capture and selling of African slaves.[155] There were also the peoples of the Dande and the Chidima,[156] as well as the Madagascarians,[157] one of whose specific slaving people were the Tanala.[158] All of these, as well as many others, were once considered primary slaving kingdoms, states, regions, or tribes.[159]

According to slavery scholar Herman J. Nieboer, the purchasing, keeping, and selling of slaves, or in some cases the practice of a form of bondage often more akin to servitude, is or was known among the Ama-Xosa, the Zulus, the Matabele, the Betchuanas, the Angoni, the Vawenda, the Batoka, the Ovaherero, the Hottentots, the Barotse, the Kimbunda, the Lovalé people, the Lunda, the Kioko, the Selles, the Manganja, the Banyai, the Wanyamwesi, the Azimba, the Wajiji, the Babisa, the Wazaramo, the Maravis, the Wasinja, the Wakerewe, the Wakikuyu, the Bondei, the Bihés, the Minugo, the Mpongwe, the Orungu, the Mbengas, the Apinchi, the Duallas, the Fiotes, the Bayanzi, the Bangala, the Baluba, the Manyuema, the Kabinda, the Ininga, the Galloa, the Wangata, the Bondo, the Camas, the Songo, the Bakele, the Okota, the Bakuba, the Tuchilangue, the Tupende, the Aduma, the Oschebo, the Hollo, the Milembue, the Waganda, the Calabarese, the inhabitants of Bonny, the Brass people, the Ewe, the Croos, the Gallinas, the Wolofs, the Saracolays, the Bambaras, the Toucouleurs, the Sereres, the Haussa, the Borgu, the Chillooks, the Diour, the Dinka, the Makaraka, the Niam-Niam, the Mombuttus, the Wangungo, the Boobies, the Sakalavas, the Namaqua, the Mucassequere, the Beduan, the Takue, the Marea, the Beni Amer, the Barea, the Kunama, the Bogos, the Gallas, the Somal, the Danakil, the Fulbe, the Moors of Senegambia, the Tuareg, and probably the Abukaja, the Warua, the Bateke, and the Wanyoro.[160] Hundreds more could be named, but these lists are sufficient to give an of idea of the widespread practice of various forms of enslavement across Africa.

Naturally, the main commodity in countless early African empires, states, and city-states was slaves. One from the latter category, the Hausa city-states, imported slaves from other African communities for use in construction and agriculture. When they ran low on human chattel, the Hausa illegally caught and enslaved Muslim peasants, sometimes selling them to fellow Africans in the North for guns and livestock.[161]

These Ashanti slaves are en route to the great African city of Kumasi in southern Ghana, where the males will be sold to African slaveholders as common laborers and the females as concubines or as involuntary participants in one of West Africa's vast slave breeding programs.

Regions such as Kanem, Ife, Zanzibar, Geti, Pate, Mombasa, Sofala, Kilwa, and Oyo were not only deeply involved in slaveholding, but they also often served as important marketplaces for trade in slaves. The primary route over which slaves from the African interior were marched ran from Kigoma and Tabora to Dodoma and finally Bagamoyo. Those who survived this perilous journey were sent to Zanzibar, and from there to the Arabian peninsula where they were sold at auction.[162] At one point 75 percent of Zanzibar's population was made up of African slaves.[163] (Little wonder that the archipelago refused to close its huge slave market until 1873, when it was forced to due to pressure from Britain.)[164] The main slave route from the area south of the Sudan traversed the desert from Timbuktu, Kano, and Bornu to Morocco and Benghazi on the Mediterranean, where African slaves were then exported to Turkey.[165]

Entire African civilizations were built on and maintained by slavery, using some of the world's most extreme, dehumanizing, exploitive, cruel, and savage forms of bondage ever known.[166] One of these was the aforementioned African state of Songhai, which enslaved people from the region of Bornu, then drove them across the Sahara Desert,[167] where they were sold in North Africa as well as in Turkey and the Middle East.[168] One early writer states that on the

> northern and eastern flanks of Guinea, where the Mohammedans operated and where the most vigorous of the African peoples dwelt, *the natives lent ready assistance in catching and buying slaves in the interior and driving them in coffles* [a line of slaves chained together and driven along] *to within reach of the Moorish and Arab traders. Their activities, reaching at length the very center of the continent, constituted without doubt the most cruel of all branches of the slave-trade. The routes across the burning Sahara sands in particular came to be strewn with negro skeletons.*[169]

The wanton brutality of the typical African slave dealer can be seen in the following extract, again taken from testimony of British slave dealers before the House of Commons in 1790 and 1791:

> Mr. Ellison says, that while one of the ships he belonged to [the *Briton*] was lying in Benin river, Capt. Lemma Lemma, a [black African] Benin trader, came on board to receive his customs. This man being on the deck, and happening to see a canoe with three people in it crossing the river, dispatched one of his own canoes to seize and take it. Upon overtaking it, they brought it to the ship. It contained three persons, an old man and a young man and woman. The chief mate bought the two latter, but the former being too old, was refused. Upon this, Lemma ordered the old man into the canoe, where his head was chopped off, and he was thrown overboard. Lemma had many war canoes, some of which had six or eight swivels; he seemed to be feared by the rest of the natives. Mr. Ellison did not see a canoe out on the river while Lemma was there, except this, and if they had known he had been out, they would not have come. He discovered by signs, that the old man killed was the father of the two other negroes, and that they were brought there by force.[170]

Slavery was so imbedded in African culture that native peoples often gave their towns names that were associated with the institution.

An example is the village of Atorkor, located today in what is the Volta region of Ghana. As controllers of the local slave supply, the main source of income among early Atorkorians was slave trading, hence the rough meaning of their village name: "purchase and leave."[171]

Like the slavery-practicing Bornu people of Nigeria, the Ashanti divided their slaves into castes:

1) *Akyere*: someone who was to be executed for a crime.
2) *Odonko*: a foreign-born slave.
3) *Awowa*: a creditor's pawn.
4) *Akoa pa*: a pawn who was to become a slave.[172]
5) *Domum*: someone captured during warfare.[173]

A typical 18th-Century slave trading caravan, bringing a group of freshly purchased slaves to Timbuktu, a city in the West African Republic of Mali. The slave catchers, the slave dealers, the slave drivers, the slave owners, and the slave purchasers in this process are all black Africans.

Into the early 1830s and beyond, at the town of Bonny (on Bonny Island in what is now Nigeria), an annual slave fair was held, at which 20,000 African slaves were auctioned off by African slavers. Many went to native African slaveholders, the rest were sold to foreign traders and shipped to Cuba and Brazil,[174] human trafficking that continued well into the late 1800s.[175] At what was once the kingdom of Bulozi, now modern day Zambia, as late as the end of the 19th Century, African slaves made up 33 percent of the total population.[176] In the late 1700s intrepid

Scottish explorer Mungo Park estimated that throughout the Niger River Valley region "slaves outnumbered the free three to one."[177] On this topic Estes wrote that:

> *The larger portion of the African population are in a state of the most abject slavery.* There is a difference of opinion among writers as to the proportion of slaves in that country; but *no one estimates the number at less than two-thirds of the whole population. Some even estimate the number as high as nine-tenths.* Slavery, in Africa, may originate from:
>
> 1st. A voluntary act on the part of the people. It occasionally happens that the blind veneration on the part of the people, for a distinguished chief or warrior, leads them to sink voluntarily into a state of slavery. But the number that become slaves from this cause are few, compared to the great number that are made slaves by—
>
> 2nd. War. Wars are undertaken with the express view of getting slaves. It frequently happens that a tribe, without the least provocation, will stealthily surround the village of a neighboring tribe at night whilst they are asleep, and all at once rush upon them, set fire to their houses—and whilst they are struggling to escape, they are seized, sent off, and sold to the Europeans as slaves, *or kept as slaves among themselves.*[178]

Though many Africa-sympathetic writers have tried to portray domestic African slavery as a trivial and "harmless institution" that routinely absorbed slaves into families as "quasi-kin," the facts strongly refute this. Indeed, in most cases authentic indigenous African slavery was actually "the antithesis of kinship."[179] For one thing, numerous African Kingdoms such as Uganda, Benin, and Dahomey,[180] and slaving peoples such as the Yoruba and the Ashanti, were well-known to ritually sacrifice their personal slaves in great Pagan ceremonials,[181] ranging from funerals and religious rites to political services.[182] The barbaric treatment of slaves is hardly compatible with the idea of kinship.[183] Let us consider the following:

> On the death of a king, or a distinguished [African] chief, hundreds of their courtiers, wives, and slaves are put to death, in order that they may have the benefit of their attendance in the future world. It often happens, that where the sword of the rude warrior is once drawn in such cases, it is not again readily sheathed; whole towns may be depopulated before the thirst for blood is satiated.[184]

Thus in 1800 the funeral of Ashanti King Quamina was accompanied by the ritual murder of 200 African slaves.[185] On another occasion the Ashanti people slaughtered some 2,600 African slaves at a single public sacrifice. In 1873, when the British seized Kumasi, a city in southern central Ghana, they discovered a huge brass bowl five feet in diameter. In it the Ashanti had collected the blood of countless thousands of sacrificed African slaves and used it to wash the footstools of deceased African kings.[186] Once, when the mother of a certain Ashanti king died, 3,000 African slaves were sacrificed at her tomb, and for two months afterward 200 additional slaves were put to death every week "in her honor."[187] Did anything in the American South ever compare to such horrific savagery?

African authorities, like this Susu chief and his staff, were responsible for the enslavement of thousands of fellow Africans, a fact now all but ignored by most historians.

On some occasions and among some African tribes, as Phillips notes, a rare type of kinship did develop between slave and master; but only when slaves were taken from *local* villages:

> Slavery . . . was generally prevalent except among the few tribes who gained their chief sustenance from hunting. Along with polygamy, it perhaps originated, if it ever had a distinct beginning, from the desire to lighten and improve the domestic service. Persons became slaves through capture, debt or malfeasance, or through the inheritance of the status. *While the ownership was absolute in the eyes of the law and captives were often treated with great cruelty, slaves born in the locality were generally regarded as members of their owner's family and were shown much consideration.* In the millet

> zone where there was much work to be done the slaveholdings were in many cases very large and the control relatively stringent; but in the banana districts an easy-going schedule prevailed for all. . . . *The Africans were in general eager traders in slaves as well as other goods, even before the time when the transatlantic trade, by giving excessive stimulus to raiding and trading, transformed the native economy and deranged the social order.*[188]

Domestic slavery was so commonplace on the continent that literally "*all peoples*" of Central Africa later played a role in supporting the European slave trade.[189] Indeed, of the four classes of slavery identified by slavery scholars—1) captives of war; 2) debtors and criminals; 3) individuals who have sold themselves or were sold as children into slavery; and 4) children of slaves—"Negro Africa" is one of the few regions on earth that possesses all four.[190] In the mid 1800s famed Scottish missionary David Livingstone spent 30 years on the continent[191] trying to drain what he called the "open sore of Africa," the African slave trade, in this case with Arabia.[192] He did not succeed.[193]

Blake gives this example of one British attempt at closing down African slavery, illustrating the virtual impossibility of ever turning the continent into a completely slave-free zone:

> When Dr. [Richard Robert] Madden, of England,[194] went to Egypt in 1840, as the bearer of a letter from the Anti-Slavery Convention to Mohammed Ali, the ruler of Egypt, congratulating him upon his having issued an order abolishing the slave hunts, to his great surprise, he found that the order, though issued, had never been enforced, and probably never would be. The truth is, that *Mohammed himself had brought the system of hunting slaves to a high degree of perfection. Nubia was his principal hunting ground, into which he permitted no intruder. His own expeditions were conducted on a grand scale*; and generally took place after the rainy season.[195]

Although countless African regions exported African slaves, the chief six were Senegambia, Sierra Leone, Gold Coast, Bight of Benin, Bight of Biafra, and West Central Africa, the last being responsible for some 45 percent of the total trade. Historians describe these areas as existing in a constant state of warfare for the main purpose of slave raiding:[196] neighbors that were captured during battle were immediately enslaved then appropriated for sale and export.[197] Often those incapable of hard labor, such as infants, children, and older women, were mercilessly slaughtered.[198] The rest were shackled and marched to the coast, where bonfires were lit along the beaches as signs to passing slave ships that the natives had slaves for sale.[199]

These Timbo women filling their gourds at the local water hole had to be on constant guard against stealthy and vicious native African slave hunters, who, at any moment, could rush in and take them captive, then rape, torture, and sell them into slavery. The Timbo, of course, were slavers themselves.

In the mid 1800s famous French-Italian slaver Theophile Conneau, better known as Theodore Canot, experienced one of these African slave wars and lived to tell about it. He was visiting a small African town in the area then known as Digby, himself hoping to purchase native slaves from his hosts. Overjoyed to see him in anticipation of profitable sales, he was the focus of a long night of feasting and song. Exhausted from the celebration, all had fallen asleep, when:

> About three in the morning, the sudden screams of women and children aroused me from profound torpor! Shrieks were followed by volleys of musketry. Then came a loud tattoo of knocks at my door, and appeals from the negro chief to rise and fly. "The town was besieged:—the head-men were on the point of escaping:—resistance was vain:—they had been betrayed:—there were no fighters to defend the stockade!"
>
> I was opening the door to comply with this advice, when

my Kroomen [members of the Kroo tribe, often hired as African guides by visiting white slavers], who know the country's ways even better than I, dissuaded me from departing, with the confident assurance that our assailants were unquestionably composed of the rival townsfolk, who had only temporarily discharged the bushmen to deceive my entertainer. The Kroos insisted that I had nothing to fear. We might, they said, be seized and even imprisoned; but after a brief detention, the captors would be glad enough to accept our ransom. If we fled, we might be slaughtered by mistake.

I had so much confidence in the sense and fidelity of the band that always accompanied me,—partly as boatmen and partly as body guard,—that I experienced very little personal alarm when I heard the shouts as the savages rushed through the town murdering every one they encountered. In a few moments our own door was battered down by the barbarians, and Jen-ken [the rival chief and head African slaver], torch in hand, made his appearance, claiming us as prisoners.

Of course, we submitted without resistance, for although fully armed, the odds were so great in those ante-revolver days, that we would have been overwhelmed by a single wave of the infuriated crowd. The barbarian chief instantly selected our house for his headquarters, and despatched his followers to complete their task. Prisoner after prisoner was thrust in. At times the heavy mash of a war club and the cry of strangling women, gave notice that the work of death was not yet ended. But the night of horror wore away. The gray dawn crept through our hovel's bars, and all was still save the groans of wounded captives, and the wailing of women and children.

By degrees, the warriors dropped in around their chieftain. A palaver-house, immediately in front of my quarters, was the general rendezvous; and scarcely a bushman appeared without the body of some maimed and bleeding victim. The mangled but living captives were tumbled on a heap in the centre, and soon, every avenue to the square was crowded with exulting savages. Rum was brought forth in abundance for the chiefs. Presently, slowly approaching from a distance, I heard the drums, horns, and war-bells; and, in less than fifteen minutes, a procession of women, whose naked limbs were smeared with chalk and ochre, poured into the palaver-house to join the beastly rites. Each of these devils was armed with a knife, and bore in her hand some cannibal trophy. Jen-ken's wife,—a corpulent wench of forty-five,—dragged along the ground, by a single limb, the slimy corpse of an infant ripped alive from its mother's womb. As her eyes met those of her husband the two fiends yelled forth a shout of mutual joy, while the lifeless babe was tossed in the air and caught as it descended on the point of a spear. Then came the refreshment, in the shape of rum, powder, and blood, which was quaffed by the brutes till they reeled off, with linked hands, in a wild dance around the pile of victims. As the women leaped and sang, the men applauded and encouraged. Soon, the ring was broken, and, with a yell, each female leaped on the body of a wounded prisoner and commenced the final sacrifice with the mockery of lascivious embraces!

In my wanderings in African forests I have often seen the tiger pounce upon its prey, and, with instinctive thirst, satiate its appetite for blood and abandon the drained corpse; but these African negresses were neither as decent nor as merciful as the beast of the wilderness. Their malignant pleasure seemed to consist in the invention of tortures, that would agonize but not slay. There was a devilish spell in the tragic scene that fascinated my eyes to the spot. A slow, lingering, tormenting mutilation was practised on the living, as well as on the dead; and, in every instance, the brutality of the women exceeded that of the men. I cannot picture the hellish joy with which they passed from body to body, digging out eyes, wrenching off lips, tearing the ears, and slicing the flesh from the quivering bones; while the queen of the harpies crept amid the butchery gathering the brains from each severed skull as a *bonne bouche* ["tasty mouthful"] for the approaching feast!

After the last victim yielded his life, it did not require long to kindle a fire, produce the requisite utensils, and fill the air with the odor of human flesh. Yet, before the various messes were half broiled, every mouth was tearing the dainty morsels with shouts of joy, denoting the combined satisfaction of revenge and appetite! In the midst of this appalling scene, I heard a fresh cry of exultation, as a pole was borne into the apartment, on which was impaled the living body of the conquered chieftain's wife. A hole was quickly dug, the stave planted and fagots supplied; but before a fire could be kindled the wretched woman was dead, so that the barbarians were defeated in their hellish scheme of burning her alive.

I do not know how long these brutalities lasted, for I remember very little after this last attempt, except that the bushmen packed in plantain leaves whatever flesh was left from the orgie, to be conveyed to their friends in the forest. This was the first time it had been my lot to behold the most savage development of African nature under the stimulus of war. The butchery made me sick, dizzy, paralyzed. I sank on the earth benumbed with stupor; nor was I aroused till nightfall, when my Kroomen bore me to the conqueror's town, and negotiated our redemption for the value of twenty slaves.[200]

The massacre at Digby (Africa) described in lurid detail by eyewitness Theodore Canot, occurred when a local African tribe attacked another in the middle of the night for the sole purpose of procuring slaves. In the ensuing melee hundreds were tortured and killed in the most brutal manner, such as this baby, who was flung into the air then impaled on a spear as it descended. It could be argued that the dead were the more fortunate of the victims in these types of raids, where the survivors could only look forward to a lifetime of misery, suffering, abuse, and eventually an ignoble death at the hands of their cold-blooded African masters and mistresses. Note the severed heads and limbs being carried by the participants, as well as the assailant inhumanely cutting body parts from a fallen but still living victim.

Africans continued to engage in the internal slave trade (the main pillar of the Afro-Arabic, Afro-European, and Afro-American slave trades) for centuries, despite the fact that it was extremely harmful to Africa's own people in a myriad of ways. The loss of adult males, for example, had a negative impact on African gender ratios, the gender division of labor, and dependency rates, as well as having the effect of intensifying warfare and increasing overall social inequality.[201] Indeed:

> *In Africa [slavery] . . . largely transformed the primitive scheme of life, and for the worse. It created new and often unwholesome wants; it destroyed old industries and it corrupted tribal institutions.* The rum, the guns, the utensils and the gewgaws were irresistible temptations. *Every chief and every tribesman acquired a potential interest in slave getting and slave selling. Charges of witchcraft, adultery, theft and other crimes were trumped up that the number of convicts for sale might be swelled; debtors were pressed that they might be adjudged insolvent and their persons delivered to the creditors; the sufferings of famine were left unrelieved that*

> *parents might be forced to sell their children or themselves; kidnapping increased until no man or woman and especially no child was safe outside a village; and wars and raids were multiplied until towns by hundreds were swept from the earth and great zones lay void of their former teeming population.*
>
> The [transatlantic] slave trade has well been called the systematic plunder of a continent. But in the irony of fate those Africans who lent their hands to the looting got nothing but deceptive rewards, while *the victims of the rapine were quite possibly better off on the American plantations than the captors who remained in the African jungle. The only participants who got unquestionable profit were the English, European and Yankee traders and manufacturers.*[202]

These domestic African problems do not mean, however, as some have suggested, that the continent was "forced against her will" to participate in the slave trade with Arabia, Europe, and later America. For since Africa was engaged in indigenous slavery for millennia prior to the Afro-European trade, *the transatlantic slave trade was merely a natural outgrowth of domestic African slavery.*[203]

African countries like Sierra Leone finally freed their *African* slaves in 1927.[204] But many tribes in various parts of the continent continue to engage in both the institution and the trade right into the present,[205] primarily in North,[206] Central, and West Africa, the latter where it has been reported that some 200,000 children alone are still sold into slavery each year.[207] There is evidence of a thriving slavery industry in both Southern Sudan and Mauritania (which, in 1980, banned slavery for the *third* time), while other forms of servitude, such as chattel slavery, forced prostitution, penal slavery, child labor, debt bondage (also known as pawnship), and forced military enlistment, continue unabated across Africa.[208] In 1993 a Mauritanian slave could be purchased for a mere $15. That same year the American Anti-Slavery Group (AASG) was formed for the sole purpose of trying to stop indigenous African slavery.[209] In essence, *intercontinental, large-scale, domestic African slavery is both pervasive and persistent, showing no signs of eradication any time soon.* As you are reading this, thousands of Africans are being enslaved by other Africans somewhere on the continent.

While 19th-Century Americans paid an average of $1,500 for an African servant (the current equivalent of $50,000),[210] as noted, today's Africans sell one another for as little as $15 a person; and they are treated, not as servants, as in America's Old South, but as true slaves: shackled and held at bayonet point, many slaves in modern Africa exist without an income, without civil rights, without proper diet or medical care, and without means or authority to buy their freedom.[211] This is *true* slavery, quite unlike what was practiced in Victorian Dixie.

This reality led many 19th-Century Southerners *and* Northerners to view American slavery as benign in comparison. In 1854 Southern abolitionist and slaveholder George Fitzhugh[212] spoke for many white Americans when he wrote that Africans were far better off being servants in the U.S. than being slaves in their native land, where there existed types of bondage that were infinitely worse.[213] However much we may condemn slavery today, Fitzhugh was correct. *Indigenous African slavery, a continent in which slavery was both universal and integral to the growth and maintenance of countless kingdoms, was of African origin and often unimaginably brutal in nature.*

WHAT YOU WERE TAUGHT: Even if one accepts the fact that pre-conquest Africans enslaved their own people, it could not have been more than a small minority who were enslaved, perhaps 1 percent or less.

THE TRUTH: Those who lived during or actually worked in the transatlantic slave trade are the only trustworthy sources for this statistic. One from the former category was Brantz Mayer, the 19th-Century editor and transcriptionist of the writings of the French-Italian slaver Theodore Canot. According to Mayer's readings of Canot's journals, "one sixth of Africa subjects the remaining five sixths to servitude."[214]

The total population of Africa around the time Canot worked as a slaver (mid 1800s) was about 100 million.[215] This means that as of 1850, 17 million Africans were free, the other 83 million were slaves—the former being the enslavers.

WHAT YOU WERE TAUGHT: All of America's black slaves were shipped directly from Africa.

THE TRUTH: The slaves brought back to the Northern colonies "were more generally drawn from the West Indies than directly from Africa."[216] In other words, most of North America's black slaves were purchased in the Caribbean (also known as the "Sugar Islands") having already been enslaved *twice*: first by their own African brothers, and second by the Dutch, English, French, Spanish, and Portuguese slave traders who bought them on Africa's West Coast.

Why the West Indies?

Profitability. It was simply better business to transport African slaves over the shortest distances possible to cut down on traveling time, illness, and death. Since the West Indies route shaved days off the journey, slave ship owners from places like Massachusetts, Rhode Island, Connecticut, Maryland, Pennsylvania, and New York preferred it over the much longer distance from Africa.[217]

These Africans were captured near their village by neighboring tribesmen, and are now being transported aboard a dhow (a three-masted Arabic sailing vessel) to the local slave market.

WHAT YOU WERE TAUGHT: Free native Africans were hunted down in the wilds of Africa by white American slavers before being shackled and loaded aboard slave ships.

THE TRUTH: What Yankee historians, New South professors, and the Liberal media will not tell you is that Africans were never actually hunted down and captured directly by the crews of slave ships. Rather, as is clear from the preceding entries, they were captives who had already been taken during yearly intertribal raids and then enslaved by enterprising African kings, kinglets, chiefs, and subchiefs,[218] who quite eagerly traded them to non-African slavers for rum, guns, gunpowder, textiles,[219] beads, iron, and cloth.[220]

This African chief (seated near center) is having his newly kidnaped slaves inspected to determine their value. After their sale the slaves are fettered, whipped, and loaded onto boats (right) that will carry them to their final home: the village of a distant African king, where they will live out their lives in hard service under their new black master.

Not all African slaves were obtained through domestic warfare, of course. Blake gives a list of the various other methods:

> In one case, it would be a negro master selling a number of his spare slaves; . . . In another case, it would be a father selling his son, or a son selling his old father, or a creditor selling his insolvent debtor. In a third, it would be a starving family voluntarily surrendering itself to slavery. When a scarcity occurred, instances used to be frequent of famishing negroes coming to the British stations in Africa and begging "to be put upon the slave-chain." In a fourth case it would be a savage selling the boy or girl he had kidnapped a week ago on purpose. In a fifth, it would be a petty negro chief disposing of twenty or thirty negroes taken alive in a recent attack upon a village at a little distance from his own.[221]

Still, for the most part, the majority of African slaves were the products of massive and intentional wars:

> *Sometimes these forays in quest of negroes to sell are on a very large scale,*

> *and then they are called slave-hunts. The king of one negro country collects a large army, and makes an expedition into the territories of another negro king, ravaging and making prisoners as he goes.* If the inhabitants make a stand against him, a battle ensues, in which the invading army is generally victorious. As many are killed as may be necessary to decide that such is the case; and *the captives are driven away in thousands, to be kept on the property of the victor till he finds opportunities of selling them. In 1794, the king of the southern Foulahs, a powerful tribe in Nigritia, was known to have an army of 16,000 men constantly employed in these slave-hunting expeditions into his neighbors' territories. The slaves they procured made the largest item in his revenue.*[222]

The aforementioned Dr. Madden, who lived in Africa while working for the British government, gave the following detailed description of a typical domestic African slave hunt in which Egyptian Arabs hunted down and enslaved fellow black Muslims in Nubia:

> The [slave] capturing expedition consists of 1000 to 2000 regular foot soldiers; 400 to 800 Mograbini [that is, mounted Bedouins] armed with guns and pistols; 300 to 500 of the militia on dromedaries with shields and spears; and 1000 or more on foot with bucklers and small lances. . . . The riders on the dromedaries present a peculiarly imposing spectacle; they are naked with the exception of a small piece of cotton, which is wrapt round their loins, and manifest an agility, which appears almost incredible. . . . The cries which they utter when attacking (which they always do in bodies, and at the full speed of the dromedaries;) the whizzing of the lances in the air; their long floating hair which reaches to their necks, this, together with the large shields which cover nearly the whole of their bodies, gives the riders a frightful appearance, and is enough to intimidate the most stout hearted person.
>
> . . . As soon as they arrive at the first mountains in Nubia the inhabitants are asked to give the appointed number of slaves as their customary tribute. . . . If the Sheik [head of the Arab tribe] does not yield to the demand, an attack is made upon the village. The cavalry and bearers of lances, surround the whole mountain, and the infantry endeavour to climb the heights.
>
> . . . Animated with avarice and revenge, they mind no impediment, not even death itself. One after another treads upon the corpse of his comrade, and thinks only of robbery and murder, and the village is at last taken in spite of the most desperate resistance. And then *the revenge is horrible. Neither the aged nor sick people are spared, women, and even children in their mother's womb, fall*

a sacrifice to their fury; the huts are plundered, the little possession of the unfortunate inhabitants carried away or destroyed, and all that fall alive into the hands of the robbers, are led as slaves into the camp. When the negroes see that their resistance is no longer of any avail, *they frequently prefer death to slavery*; and if they are not prevented, you may see the father rip up first the stomach of his wife, then of his children, and then of his own, that they may not fall alive into the hands of the enemy.

. . . After the Turks [that is, the Egyptian Arabs] have done all in their power to capture the living, they lead these unfortunate people into the camp; they then plunder the huts and the cattle, and several hundred soldiers are engaged in searching the mountain in every direction, in order to steal the hidden harvest, that the rest of the negroes, who were fortunate enough to escape, and have hid themselves in inaccessible caves, should not find anything on their return to nourish and continue their life.

. . . *No situation can be more dreadful, than that of those unfortunate people. On the one hand, the fear of falling into the power of the Turks, and the prospect of death on the other, drive these poor creatures to despair.* Their distress is immediately perceived in the camp, the cries of the children, and the bleating of the cattle, announce the sad condition of the village. The cattle run restlessly to and fro; and on the second or third day, they become unmanageable, and must be killed. The people in despair wrestle with death, and seek a way of deliverance, but in vain; *the cruel hunters surround their game with too great a vigilance to allow any to escape alive.* While *many of these unfortunate beings prefer death by their own hands to slavery, and while many hide themselves in caves, in order to escape this great misery*, others hold assemblies and consult about the surrender of themselves and families; but this does not soften the hard hearts of their murderers, indifferent about such sufferings, they wait with impatience for the moment when they will be able to seize their victims. . . . *[In all] cases they endeavour with satanic craftiness to bring destruction upon the unfortunate inhabitants.*

[As the enslaved negroes are marched along, they] have to suffer all kinds of cruelty from their tormentors, knocks with the butt ends of the guns, thrusts with bayonets, and stripes with whips, is the usual treatment of those miserable creatures, who by reason of physical, mental, or moral sufferings are not able to stand erect. The soldiers feel no compassion in such transportations, for as no personal interest induces them to preserve the unfortunate negroes, the only consideration with them is, to prevent every possible escape. . . . The [captors]. . . treat their prisoners worse than animals.

As soon as they have obtained about 500 or 600 slaves, they are sent to Lobeid with an escort of country people, and about fifty soldiers under the command of an officer. In order to prevent escape *a sheba is hung round the necks of the adults*. Such a sheba is a young tree, about eight feet long, and two inches thick, and which has a fork at the top, it is so tied to the neck of the poor creature, that the trunk of the tree hangs down in the front, and the fork closed behind the neck with a cross piece of timber, or tied together with stripes cut out of a fresh skin; and in this situation the slave, in order to be able to walk at all, is obliged to take the tree into his hands, and to carry it before him; but none can endure this very long, and to render it easier, the one in advance takes the tree of the man behind him on his shoulder. It is impossible for them to get their head free, and *it frequently occurs, that they have their necks wounded, which is followed by an inflammation, and sometimes, even by death*.

Boys, between ten and fifteen years of age, who cannot bear such a sheba, are tied together, two and two, with wooden clasps on their hands; this is done by placing the wood on the right arm of one, and on the left of another, above the wrist, and then lacing it tightly; the pieces of wood are scooped out at one end that the hand may fit in, but the openings are generally too narrow, by which *the hands are wounded, and dangerous ulcers created; but even if the hand should decay and fall off, no notice is taken of it, and the clasps are not removed before their arrival at Lobeid*.

Other boys are tied together by two and two with leather strings. It is therefore easy for the reader to imagine with what difficulty these poor creatures walk, and what sufferings they have to endure on their march; besides which, they have very miserable food. If their strength should fail them, and become too feeble to continue walking, they experience still greater cruelty. Boys under the above mentioned ages, as well as girls, women, and aged persons are allowed to walk at liberty. Many a mother carries her sucking babe, of a few days old, in her arms; others have to carry on their backs, or in their arms, two or three of their children, as they are too young and feeble to walk by themselves. Old people, tottering with their staves, the sick and wounded walk, surrounded by their daughters, wives or relations, and are assisted and even carried occasionally by them: if one of these unfortunate persons remains behind the line but one step, he is immediately forced to proceed by blows from the butt ends of the guns, or by stripes of the whip, and if they even then should not be able to move on, *from ten to twelve of them are tied with their hands to a cord, one end of which is fastened to the pommel of a camel, and the dying thus dragged along; no pity is shewn to those who sink down, they are not released, but dragged along with the rest, even if one should die before they arrive at the appointed halting place. Before the caravan halts, no refreshment, either*

> *of food or drink, is given to the debilitated negroes; the unfeeling Turks have no compassion, even if a drop of water should be sufficient to refresh the feeble, it is not given to him, but he is left to perish.*
>
> When the caravan reaches the place, which had been fixed for rest or an encampment, those who had been dragged are now loosened, *the dead and the dying thrown aside into the sand*, and the latter left to their fate. *No entreaties or sighs move the hearts of their tormentors; the wives and children are not even allowed to take leave of their dying husbands or fathers, or to press a farewell kiss on their dying lips; no one is allowed to approach these unfortunate persons, they are abandoned, and it is known, that frequently, when the caravan proceeds, these forsaken creatures are torn by wild beasts. No pieces of bread or drops of water are left behind; those who are left must starve with hunger, and languish in misery, being conscious of their state, and looking forward to such a horrible death.*
>
> After from six to fourteen days, the mournful cavalcade reaches Lobeid, and it is no wonder that *by such inhuman treatment, more than the eighth part of their prisoners perish on the way, no notice however is taken of it, as they are the property of government, and the interests of private individuals are not regarded.*
>
> As soon as all the slaves have arrived at Lobeid, the distribution takes place. The most suitable of them are made soldiers, and those who are considered to be under the value of 200 to 250 piastres, given to the soldiers at Cordofan and Sennaar, instead of the arrear pay. The soldiers then sell them again to slave-traders, in order to get ready money or goods. *The wearied slave frequently dies before he is sold, or has not the value of the taxed sum on account of his great age or other frailties; and thus the soldiers frequently lose the whole of their pay.*[223]

In this way, writes Blake,

> the men carrying the sheba, the boys tied together by the wrists, the women and children walking at their liberty, and the old and feeble tottering along leaning on their relations, the whole of the captives are driven into Egypt, there to be exposed for sale in the slave-market. Thus negroes and Nubians are distributed over the East, through Persia, Arabia, India, etc.[224]

Such tragic scenes of inhumanity and depravity have long been attributed to European slave dealers. But eyewitnesses like Madden prove, as is patently clear here, that *all* of the slave hunting, slave capturing, slave abusing, slave torturing, slave marching, slave marketing, slave dealing, and slave selling went on *inside* Africa, perpetuated by Africans upon other Africans upon African land.[225]

These African slaves were not captured by Europeans or Americans, and they are not destined for either Europe or North America. They were taken near Benguela, a city in western Angola, by fellow Africans and sold by fellow Africans to a European slave ship owner, who is now transporting them by boat to St. Thomas in the Caribbean. Here, they will be sold a second time and put to work on one of the island's many sugar, indigo, coffee, or cotton plantations.

Sometimes these intra-African militaristic style raids and battles were carried on by slave armies led by slave officers.[226] Though the attrition rate was extremely high (over the millennia millions upon millions of Africans died during these marauding attacks),[227] greedy African kings would often purposefully start such wars, known as "slave hunts,"[228] in order to obtain slaves, a practice that eventually became "endemic" across many parts of the continent.[229]

Again, this means that during the transatlantic slave trade, every one of the Africans brought to America on Yankee slave ships had already been enslaved in their home country by fellow Africans,[230] after which they were marched to the "Slave Coast" (a 240-mile maritime strip roughly extending between the Volta River and the Akinga River),[231] temporarily held in stockades (prisons), then sold to white slavers by local African governments.[232] In short, whites "bought slaves after they had been captured,"[233] and thus played no role in the actual enslaving process that took place in the interior, and had no idea what went on beyond the coastal areas.[234] As one Yankee slave ship owner himself admitted in the late 1700s:

> It is true, I have brought these slaves from Africa; but I have only transported them from one master to another.[235]

Before a Congressional committee on abolition another Northerner, Theodore Dwight of Connecticut, repeated the often acknowledged Yankee conviction that

> in importing Africans, we do them no harm; we only transfer them from a state of slavery at home to a state of slavery attended by fewer calamities here [in America].[236]

Yes, *African slavery was purely an African-on-African business.*

And here is proof: *until the first part of the 19th Century, no white man had ever set foot in the interior of tropical Africa.*[237] Even the Europeans who first came to Africa's shores in the 1400s had no knowledge of anything "south of the desert."[238] These were the African hinterlands, after all: utterly unnavigable and therefore unexplorable, due in great part to the ferocity of the native animals, and to the fact that it swarmed with cannibalistic tribes who practiced human sacrifice and other barbaric customs.[239]

Here the African slaves from the preceding photo have deboarded at St. Thomas. Sitting on the pier, they pensively await their fate.

At one time even radical abolitionists

admitted this much. In 1835 Reverend George Bourne—the Briton who inspired fanatical New England abolitionist William Lloyd Garrison[240]—noted that "no ancient and accessible part of the inhabited globe is so completely unknown as the interior of Africa."[241] Thus whites could not have had any knowledge of what went on in the central regions of the continent during most of the Atlantic slave trade.[242]

During the first half of the transatlantic slave trade, the so-called heart of Africa, the interior of the Dark Continent, was still completely unexplored by the West, and was thus unknown to white slave traders. More evidence that they did not participate in the capture and enslavement of native Africans, as anti-South writers preach. It was the ancient domestic African slave system itself that was fully responsible for this phase of the process; a process in which already enslaved Africans were carried to the coast by other Africans, then auctioned off to white ship owners. As one European slave trader understandably replied to a critic: "I have only transported them from one master to another."

Indeed, it was not until November 17, 1855, nearly four centuries after the African-European slave trade began, that Scottish missionary Dr. David Livingstone became the first white man to lay eyes on Victoria Falls on the Zambezi River.[243] Blake writes:

> [Africans] were drained away to meet the increasing demand [for slaves]; either *led captive by warlike visitants from the west [coast of Africa]*, or *handed from tribe to tribe till they reached the sea*. In this way, eventually, Central Africa, with its teeming myriads of negroes, came to be the great mother of slaves for exportation, and *the negro villages on the coast the warehouses, as it were, where the slaves*

> *were stowed* away till the ships of the white men arrived to carry them off.[244]

Even our nation's most racist chief executive and most notorious anti-abolitionist, President Abraham Lincoln, admitted that

> the African slave trader . . . does not catch free negroes and bring them here. He finds them already slaves in the hands of their black captors, and he honestly buys them at the rate of about a red cotton handkerchief a head. This is very cheap, and it is a great abridgement of the sacred right of self-government to hang men for engaging in this profitable trade![245]

In 1908 J. Clarence Stonebraker wrote:

> *Slave dealers only obtained their slaves by one tribe conquering another and delivering same into the hands of the slave dealers, or by the consent of parents, getting up their children and selling them. The very false stories that a vessel's crew could go into the jungles and drive out as many negroes as they wished is grossly vile, and was hatched along with many others by the unconscionable and incorrigible prejudice of [Northern] partisans, and for an equally vile purpose. Such things are still being taught and believed to an extent in the frigid [Yankee] section of our country . . .*[246]

In essence, it was African chiefs who first enslaved other Africans,[247] and it was African slave merchants, slave drivers known as *Slattees*,[248] who then forcibly marched them to the coast in chains and sold them to Arabs, Europeans, and eventually Yankees.[249] In plain English, up until at least 1820, "no *free* blacks ever came [to America] from Africa."[250]

It is obvious that Africa herself must be held accountable for taking part in the enslavement and forced deportation of some 10 to 50 million of her own people during the four centuries between the 15th and the 19th Centuries.[251]

WHAT YOU WERE TAUGHT: The majority of African slaves died during the terrible Middle Passage at sea, en route to the Americas.
THE TRUTH: There can be no doubt of the horrors of the Middle Passage—the ocean-crossing second leg of the slaves' three-part journey.

The typical small Yankee slave ship probably measured about 18 tons, sported a crew of five, and had an African cargo of about 100 men and women (and sometimes children), all who were arranged side-by-side and end-to-end like logs in the cramped, dark, steamy hold of the heaving ship.[252] Weather permitting, the slaves were daily brought to the upper deck—where the unruly only were chained to ring-bolts fastened to the floorboards from about 9:00 AM to 4:00 PM[253]—for fresh air, exercise (that is, being forced to jump up and down in their leg irons),[254] and sunshine, at which time their quarters were cleaned, ventilated, and disinfected with lime.[255] The journey, depending on the destination, could last from two to six weeks.[256]

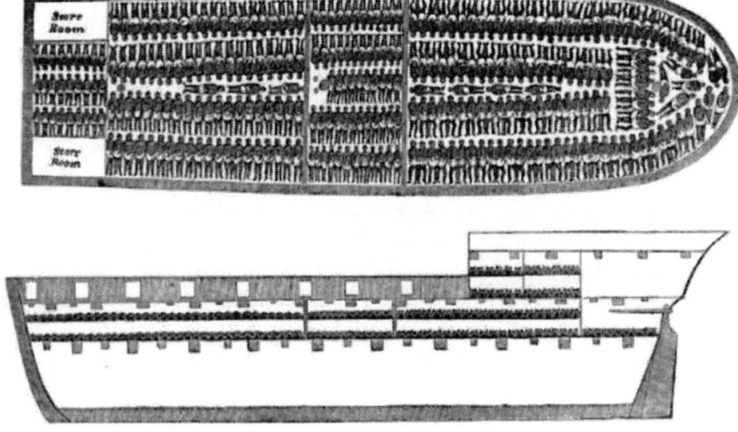

The decks of a slave ship during the infamous Middle Passage, as seen from above and the side. In the captain's effort to increase his profit margin, every square inch of the hold was used to accommodate as many men, women, and children as possible. Despite the obvious horrors that resulted from this barbarous custom, and contrary to Yankee myth, this, the second leg of the Slave Triangle, was not the most dangerous for the African individuals packed inside.

With only between 14 and 36 inches (and an average of 22 inches) of head clearance, bodily waste, dehydration, heat and humidity, poor diet, malodorous suffocating air, unhygienic conditions, seasickness, melancholy, pestilence, and disease (mainly dysentery, smallpox, scurvy, ophthalmia, and measles), caused unimaginable suffering, mental illness, and in some cases a slow agonizing death. The most despondent among them tried to take their own lives by refusing food and medicines. The truly deranged hurled themselves into the sea (thinking they could swim back to their homeland). Those whose ailments were deemed hopeless or who were contagious were tossed overboard, food for sharks. The heat in the hold below, which caused "steam to come up through gratings as if from a furnace,"[257] alone caused uncomprehensible suffering.[258] (The hold of a small slave ship was 36 feet in length, 7 feet wide, and only 3.5 feet in height; this is 252 square feet, about the size of an average modern living room. Into this small space were packed several hundred people.)[259]

It is estimated that some 9 million African-enslaved African slaves died on the Middle Passage,[260] traveling on vessels so abominably foul that one could smell them before they were sighted on the distant horizon.[261] Phillips writes:

> The discomfort in the densely packed quarters of the slave ships may be imagined by any who have sailed on tropic seas. With seasickness added it was wretched; when dysentery prevailed it became frightful; if water or food ran short the suffering was almost or quite beyond endurance; and in epidemics of scurvy, small-pox or ophthalmia the misery reached the limit of human experience. The average voyage however was rapid and smooth by virtue of the steadily blowing trade winds, the food if coarse was generally plenteous and wholesome, and the sanitation fairly adequate. *In a word, under stern and often brutal discipline, and with the poorest accommodations, the slaves encountered the then customary dangers and hardships of the sea.*[262]

Yet, despite these abysmal conditions, this was *not* the worst part of their three-leg journey. It was on their forced march inside *Africa* to the *African* coast, the Beginning Passage, chained together and forced violently along by their *African* owners,[263] that the majority of African slaves died—not on the infamous Middle Passage, as Yankee mythology has long insisted.[264] Phillips describes the Beginning Passage like this:

> *The coffles [single lines of shackled slaves] came from distances ranging to a thousand miles or more*, on rivers and paths whose shore ends the European traders could see but did not find inviting. *These paths, always of single-file narrowness, tortuously winding to avoid fallen trees and bad ground, never straightened even when obstructions had rotted and gone, branching and crossing in endless network, penetrating jungles and high-grass prairies, passing villages that were and villages that had been, skirting the lairs of savage beasts and the haunts of cannibal men, beset with drought and famine, storm and flood, were threaded only by negroes, bearing arms or bearing burdens. Many of the slaves fell exhausted on the*

paths and were cut out of the coffles to die. The survivors were sorted by the purchasers on the coast into the fit and the unfit, the latter to live in local slavery or to meet either violent or lingering deaths, the former to be taken shackled on board the strange vessels of the strange white men and carried to an unknown fate.[265]

Slave ships operating in the transatlantic trade came in many sizes and configurations, such as this schooner anchored off the coast of Guinea in West Africa. In the lower right a group of African slave dealers, paddling out to sell their human wares, has capsized in the surf.

English writer Henry Woodd Nevinson traversed West Central Africa (Angola) in 1904 and 1905, and saw and described firsthand the horrors of the Beginning Passage, though long after it had peaked in the mid 1800s. His journey took him through what is called the "Hungry Country," a heavily used slave-transporting route that had been active up until only recently. As Nevinson noted at the time, the native African slave traders "seem to have discovered that the palmy days when they used to parade their chained gangs through the country, and burn, flog, torture, and cut throats as they pleased, are over for the present." Nonetheless, even in the early 1900s there were still signs of recent human trafficking, though by now illicit and "underground":

That path [the 250 mile route from the Portuguese fort at Mashiko to the Cuanza River] is strewn with dead men's bones. You see the white thigh-bones lying in front of your feet, and at one side, among the undergrowth, you find the skull. *These are the skeletons of slaves who have been unable to keep up with the march, and so were murdered or left to die.* Of course the ordinary carriers and travellers die too. *It is very horrible to see a man beginning to break down in the middle of the Hungry Country. He must go on or die.* The caravan cannot wait for him, for it has food for only the limited number of days. I knew a distressful Irishman who entered the route with hardly any provision, broke down in the middle, and was driven along by his two carriers, who threatened his neck with their axes whenever he stopped, and only by that means succeeded in getting him through alive. Still worse was a case among my own carriers—a little [African] boy who had been brought to carry his father's food, as is the custom. He became crumpled up with rheumatism, and I found he had bad heart-disease as well. He kept on lying down in the path and refusing to go farther. Then he would creep away into the bush and hide himself to die. We had to track him out, and *his father beat him along the march till the blood ran down his back.*

But with slaves less trouble is taken. After a certain amount of beating and prodding, they are killed or left to die. Carriers [that is, free laborers] are always buried by their comrades. You pass many of their graves, hung with strips of rag or decorated with a broken gourd. But *slaves are never buried, and that is an evidence that the bones on the path are the bones of slaves.* The Biheans have a sentiment against burying slaves. They call it burying money. It is something like their strong objections to burying debtors. The man who buries a debtor becomes responsible for the debts; so *the body is hung up on a bush outside the village, and the jackals consume it, being responsible for nothing.*

Before the great change made by the "Bailundu war" of 1902, the horrors of the Hungry Country were undoubtedly worse than they are now. I have known Englishmen who passed through it four years ago and found slaves tied to the trees, with their veins cut so that they might die slowly, or laid beside the path with their hands and feet hewn off, or strung up on scaffolds with fires lighted beneath them. My carriers tell me that this last method of encouraging the others is still practised away from the pathway, but I never saw it done myself. I never saw distinct evidence of torture. The horrors of the road have certainly become less in the last three years, since the rebellion of 1902. Rebellion is always good. It always implies an unendurable wrong. It is the only shock that ever stirs the self-complacency of officials.

I have not seen torture in the Hungry Country. I have only seen murder. *Every bone scattered along that terrible foot-path from Mashiko to the Cuanza is the bone of a murdered man. The man may not have been killed by violence, though in most cases the sharp-cut hole in the skull shows where the fatal stroke was given. But if he was not killed by violence, he was taken from his home and sold, either for the buyer's use, or to sell again to a Bihean, to a Portuguese trader, or to the agents who superintend the "contract labor" for San Thomé* [the Caribbean island of St. Thomas].[266]

British journalist Henry Woodd Nevinson explored Angola in the early 1900s, where he discovered the atrocities of the still thriving indigenous African slave industry firsthand.

Nevinson only hints at the unthinkable barbarities that occurred on this particular "path" of the Beginning Passage, for other slaving routes wound some 800 miles into the interior of West Central Africa. Could the Middle Passage, even with all of its outrages, begin to compare?

What is not generally discussed is that slaving captains were well aware of the dangers of mortality during the oceangoing Middle Passage and, for both economic and humanitarian reasons, took great pains to reduce them. Naturally, the longer a slave ship was at sea, the greater the death rate of its human cargo, the ships' crews included—which, we will note, had a mortality rate nearly as high as the slaves that were being transported.[267]

Between 1784 and 1790, for instance, the 350 slave ships that sailed from Bristol and Liverpool, England, lost over half of their white crews due to the deplorable conditions at sea. Most died from ulcerations about the body. The white seamen who survived these slave voyages continually complained "of their ill treatment, bad feeding, and cruel usage," and usually came ashore in a sickly, emaciated, neglected, destitute, and debilitated state. One eyewitness described them as "the most miserable objects he ever met with in any country in his life." In some cases the crews were so brutally handled by their captains that they themselves jumped overboard, and if near enough to the shore, were rescued by canoes paddled out by native Africans.[268]

Slave ship captains thus sought not only the shortest routes possible, they also anchored at various stopping points along the way to replenish supplies and allow both their enslaved human cargo and their crews to rest. Thus the journey from the West African coast to the Caribbean Islands and Brazilian colonies, two of the shortest voyages, resulted in the lowest rates of Middle Passage mortality, between 5 and 10 percent. The longer routes, such as the month and a half journey from Saint Thomas to Lisbon, Portugal, could push slave mortality rates to as high as 30 percent.[269]

During his trek along one of Angola's slave trading paths to the coast, Nevinson came across this slave's grave, just one of thousands that dotted the 250-mile trail through the region's notorious Hungry Country. African slaves who were marched through this area never died of natural causes. Their end always came by way of the cruel hand of one of their African captors.

But not even this compared to the death rates that occurred during an African's initial capture, at which time untold millions of men, women, and children perished.[270] Later, during the subsequent Beginning Passage (the march from Africa's interior to the coast), at least two or three times as many individuals died as were shipped out on the Middle Passage.[271] This was due not just to the shock of capture, but also to exhaustion, hyperthermia, malnourishment, sleep deprivation, dehydration, illness, animal attacks, and the inevitable physical abuse suffered at the hands of their tyrannical African captors. All of this made the misery and the mortality rates of the Middle Passage—which were after all, as Phillips noted, merely part of "the then customary dangers and hardships of the sea"[272]—pale in comparison.

This coffle of African slaves is being driven to the coast by native African slave catchers, who work for native African slave dealers. The adult prisoners and their children were already serving as lifelong slaves of a local African chief when they were purchased from him for sale to Arab and European slave ship owners. It was this phase of the triangular trade, the overland Beginning Passage, not the subsequent seagoing Middle Passage, which proved to be the most hazardous for native African slaves.

Despite the outrages of the *African* Middle Passage, white men who actually worked in it insisted that it was not as terrible as the *European* Middle Passage that carried, for example, Irish slaves to early North America. One of these men was Henry Laurens, a wealthy South Carolinian rice planter and merchant, and president of the U.S. Confederate Congress (from 1777-1778). Laurens, who eventually got out of the African slave trade business due to its "barbarities," was once suddenly put in charge of several shiploads of Irish Protestants who were imported to his state in 1768. Of this experience he wrote to a friend:

> If you knew the whole affair it would make your humanity shudder. *I have been largely concerned in the African trade.* I quitted the profits arising from that gainful branch principally because of many acts from the masters and others concerned toward the wretched negroes from the time of purchasing to that of selling them again, some of which, although within my knowledge, were uncontrollable—yet *I never saw an instance of cruelty in ten or twelve years experience in that branch equal to the cruelty exercised upon those poor Irish. . . . Self interest prompted the baptized heathen [Yankee slave*

> *ship captains] to take some care of their wretched [African] slaves for a market, but no other care was taken of those poor Protestant Christians from Ireland but to deliver as many as possible alive on shore upon the cheapest terms, no matter how they fared upon the voyage nor in what condition they were landed.*[273]

In 1790 South Carolina Senator William Smith had this to say about the African Middle Passage:

> The cruelty of the method of transportation [during the Middle Passage] was alleged as a motive for abolishing the traffic; but surely the merchants would so far attend to their own interests as to preserve the lives and health of the slaves on the passage. *All voyages must be attended with inconveniences, and those from Africa to America not less than others. The confinement on board was no more than was necessary. The space allowed was more than to soldiers in a camp; for the cubical measurement of air breathed by encamped soldiers fell below that allowed in the slave-ships, in the ratio of seventeen to thirty.*[274]

WHAT YOU WERE TAUGHT: During the Middle Passage slaves were ruthlessly chained to the wooden hold from the beginning to the end of the voyage.

THE TRUTH: Experienced and knowledgeable captains *never* chained their human cargo during the Middle Passage, for a number of reasons, the most important which was humanitarian. Secondly, however, iron fetters created ulcerous wounds that could lead to death. The French-Italian slaver Theodore Canot noted that as the captain's "sole object is to land a healthy cargo, pecuniary interest, as well as natural feeling, urges the sparing of metal."[275]

Furthermore, females and children were *never* shackled after they boarded ship; only the adult males—and even this was typically temporary. For slaves, male or female, who earned the captain's trust during the first stage of the journey were allowed complete freedom on the upper decks (which usually meant relaxing in the sun), and were sometimes even given arms with which to help the schooner's crew fight off pirates. There was also the moment when land was first spotted, traditionally "a signal for merriment,"[276]

> for a well-behaved [slave] cargo is [then] invariably released from shackles, and allowed free [social] intercourse between the sexes

during the daytime on deck. Water tanks are thrown open for unrestricted use. "The cat" [a small whip known as the Cat o' Nine Tails] is cast into the sea. Strict discipline is relaxed. The day of danger or revolt is considered over, and the captain enjoys a new and refreshing life till the hour of landing. Sailors [the crew], with proverbial generosity, share their biscuits and clothing with the blacks. The women, who are generally without garments, appear in costume from the wardrobes of tars [sailors], petty officers, mates, and even captains. Sheets, table-cloths, and spare sails are torn to pieces for raiment, while shoes, boots, caps, oil-cloths, and monkey-jackets contribute to the gay masquerade of the "emigrants."[277]

WHAT YOU WERE TAUGHT: White Europeans were the first people to enslave Africans.

THE TRUTH: As previous entries have irrevocably proven, Africans were the first to enslave themselves. Indeed, indigenous African slavery existed long before whites and blacks even knew the other existed. Much later, thousands of years later, in the 8th Century Arabs became the first Caucasian people to enslave Africans. White Europeans were the *last* foreign people to enslave Africans, while white Southerners were the *last* in both the New World and North America to enslave them.

An African chief selecting a prospective slave from a neighboring village, a practice common across the continent for at least 5,000 years before the arrival of the white man.

We will note here that 21st-Century Africa is still deeply involved in the "peculiar institution": some 200,000 African children alone are enslaved each year by Africans, then sold through the African slavery system to other Africans.[278]

WHAT YOU WERE TAUGHT: All of the American South's 3.5 million slaves were cruelly purchased in Africa and dragged in manacles to America aboard slave ships.

THE TRUTH: Contrary to this popular Northern myth, of the South's 3.5 million black servants, only 14 percent—or about 500,000 individuals—were imported from Africa *by Yankee slavers* between the settling of Jamestown, Virginia (in 1607), and 1861. The other 3 million (86 percent) were all American-born, and were thus the result of natural reproduction.[279] Most of the South's 500,000 free blacks probably also derived from the latter group.[280]

WHAT YOU WERE TAUGHT: The first Africans brought to America's shores came as slaves.
THE TRUTH: This is another one of the pro-North movement's most treasured myths. It has made the rounds of so many history books over such a long period of time that it is now regarded as "gospel." Yet it is a false gospel.

The first blacks to step foot in North America (at Jamestown, Virginia) were not slaves: true slavery was unknown in the earliest North American colonies.[281] They were voluntary or indentured servants,[282] a type of legal status in which one contracts himself to work under another in exchange for travel expenses, room, board, and general maintenance, or for an apprenticeship.[283] Nor were they intentionally brought to our shores, for the Dutch ship that landed at Jamestown on August 31, 1619,[284] did so "by chance," having for its original destination the Spanish colonies further south. Thus the opening of the North American slave trade began accidently, and the first blacks to step ashore were servants purchased by the colonists as an "experiment."[285]

Though the first blacks brought to North America were purchased as slaves in their native Africa, they were sold as servants to the colonists at Jamestown, a significant distinction that you will never read in Yankee history books.

In 1913 John Henderson Russell made the following remarks about the status of these first North American Africans:

> From the quaint narrative of Master John Rolfe, who possibly wrote as an eyewitness of the introduction of negroes into Virginia, it is learned that "About the last of August [1619] came in a Dutch man of Warre [ship] that sold, us twenty negars." *In the very year of the arrival of this group of African immigrants a system of labor known as indented servitude received recognition in the laws of the colony. It was not an uncommon practice in this early period for ship masters to sell white servants to the planters; hence, an inference that these twenty negroes were slaves, drawn from the fact that they were sold to the colony or to the planters, would not be justified. Prior to 1619 every inhabitant of the colony was practically "a servant manipulated in the interest of the company, held in servitude beyond a stipulated term." The word "freeman" was just beginning to be used to distinguish persons set free from service to the London Company from persons still in a condition of servitude either to the company or to individual freemen.* Beyond all question the first twenty negroes brought in were not introduced as freemen. The only question is whether, upon entering the colony, they became servants or slaves. The possibility of their becoming slaves must be recognized because it is conceivable that a status different from that of any person in Virginia at that time was given to persons so different from white settlers as were the Africans.
>
> Since *it is the fact that the white population in the colony in 1619 had not been familiar in England with a system of slavery or with a model slave code*, and since they had developed in Virginia a system of servitude and were fortifying it by law, it is plausible that the Africans became servants in a condition similar to the status of white servants, who, after a term of service varying from two to eight years, were entitled to freedom. According to the "Lists of living and dead in Virginia" in 1623 and the "Muster Rolls of the Settlements in Virginia," *a census made in 1624-1625, there were in the colony twenty-three Africans. They are all listed as "servants," thus receiving the same class name as many white persons enumerated in the lists.* Some had names, as, for instance, "Angelo, a negro woman," and "John Pedro, a neger aged 30." Others apparently had no names, and were designated simply by the word "negro" under the caption "servants." *In the opinion of Thomas Jefferson, "the right to these negroes was common, or, perhaps, they lived on a footing with the whites, who, as well as themselves, were under the absolute direction of the president."*
>
> Were any or all of these negroes permitted to realize the freedom to which servants were entitled under the laws and

customs of servitude? *In the records of the county courts dating from 1632 to 1661 negroes are designated as "servants," "negro servants," or simply as "negroes," but never in the records which we have examined were they termed "slaves." By an order of the general court a negro brought from the West Indies to Virginia in 1625 was declared to "belong to Sir Francis Wyatt (then governor) as his servant." There is nothing in the record which indicates that "servant" meant the same as "slave."*[286]

As Russell hinted, and as our next entry reveals, blacks were not the only ones to emigrate as bonded laborers to what was to become the United States of America.

WHAT YOU WERE TAUGHT: Africans were the only enslaved people in early North America.

THE TRUTH: Our earlier discussion of Native-American slavery immediately disproves this statement. But there was another type of bondage that also preceded black servitude in North America, and which actually laid the groundwork for African slavery in the U.S.

The vast majority of white immigrants who came to America's original 13 English colonies—at least two-thirds[287]—came as white servants.[288] Made up primarily of English, Germans, Irish, and Scots, some 400,000 whites formed the first non-American servant population in the region's history, working as unskilled laborers on the budding nation's large new plantations.[289]

In fact, *white indentured servitude*, being much preferred over African slavery (Africans were considered "alien" by early white colonialists),[290] *was the institution that paved the way for black slavery in America*;[291] or as Brackett put it, white slavery made "a smoother pathway for the growth of [black] slavery."[292] In 1698, as just one example, not only were there more white servants in Virginia than there were Africans, but white indentured servants were being imported in far greater numbers than blacks at the time.[293]

Two of the signers of the Declaration of Independence arrived in the U.S. as indentured servants,[294] and at least two future U.S. presidents began their adult life as white servants.[295] One of these, our thirteenth president, Millard Fillmore, was indentured to a cloth maker. After "slaving away" for a number of years, Fillmore managed to purchase his freedom for $30, a fortune in the early 1800s (the equivalent of about $500 today).[296]

One of the reasons American President Andrew Johnson was conciliatory toward the South after Lincoln's War was that he himself had been enslaved in his youth.[297] Unlike Fillmore, however, Johnson did not wait to earn his way out of the institution. He simply ran away. His master, a tailor, posted a $10 reward in the Raleigh (North Carolina) *Gazette* for the young servant's capture and return, but never collected. Johnson escaped permanently, later to become America's seventeenth chief executive.[298]

White indentured servants working a colonial plantation in Virginia.

President Martin Van Buren's third great-grandfather, Cornelius Maesen Van Buren, emigrated from the Netherlands to New York as an indentured servant.[299] Henry Wilson, President Ulysses S. Grant's second vice president and a cofounder of the Free-Soil Party, worked as an indentured slave for eleven years, from age ten to 21.[300] Even one of Lincoln's ancestors, an early relation who was part of the Massachusetts Bay Colony, came to America as an indentured servant.[301]

Thirteen of the 30 members of Virginia's House of Burgesses came across the Atlantic as indentured servants, as did Adam Thoroughgood, the founder of the city of Norfolk, Virginia.[302] It was Virginia that passed the nation's first white servitude bill on July 30, 1619, legalizing the institution of white slavery within its borders.[303] Bancroft writes:

> Conditional servitude, under indentures or covenants, had from the first existed in Virginia. Once at least [King] James [I] sent over convicts, and once at least the city of London a hundred homeless children from its streets. The servant stood to his master in the relation of a debtor, bound to discharge by his labor the costs of emigration. *White servants came to be a usual article of merchandise. They were sold in England to be transported, and in Virginia were to be purchased on shipboard. Not the Scots only, who were taken in the field of Dunbar, were sold into servitude in New England, but the royalist prisoners of the battle of Worcester.* The leaders in the insurrection of

> Penruddoc, in spite of the remonstrance of [Sir Arthur] Haselrig and Henry Vane, were shipped to America. At the corresponding period, in Ireland, the exportation of Irish Catholics was frequent. *In 1672, the average price in the colonies, where five years of service were due, was about ten pounds, while a negro was worth twenty or twenty-five pounds.*[304]

White servitude was so popular in early Virginia that when Governor William Berkeley took a rough census in 1671, out of a statewide population of 40,000 people, he counted some 6,000 white servants (15 percent of the total) against only 2,000 black servants (5 percent of the total). Let us note here that at this time, because "the laws did not discriminate in any way between the races," Virginia's early black bondsmen and women worked right alongside the state's white bondsmen and women, and were considered legal members of their master's household.[305]

U.S. Vice President Henry Wilson spent eleven years of his youth working as an indentured servant, or white slave.

Victorian Roger Brooke Taney, fifth chief justice of the U.S. Supreme Court, descended from ancestors who, in the mid-1600s, emigrated from England to the British colony in Maryland as indentured servants.[306] So many whites arrived in America from Europe as retainers that as writer Hulbert Footner commented in the early 1900s, most of America's earliest European families proudly traced their beginnings to an indentured servant.[307]

Life was not easy for America's early white slaves, many who were sold by slave merchants side-by-side with African slaves.[308] In the colonies, for instance, white indentured servants, of both genders, were obliged to perform any labor asked of them. Their term lasted for up to five years, after which they were dismissed with nothing but the clothes on their backs—unless they were found guilty of misconduct, for which the length of their indenture could be extended. Maryland's white slaves were given a bonus: fifty acres of land on which to set up their own farms.[309]

Up until the end of the 17th Century, much of the American South's economy was based around, not African slavery, but European slavery; that is, indentured whites.[310] And free whites were not safe either. Across the Northern colonies whites were often sold into slavery as punishment for committing crimes.[311] In addition, many Southern whites lived under another form of servitude, one known as peonage, well into the 1880s.[312]

Chief Powhatan, shown here performing a ceremony with his entourage, was a member of the Virginia Algonquians, a group of Native-Americans that regularly enslaved white colonists beginning in the late 1500s. This form of white slavery lasted well into the 1800s.

White slavery was also practiced in the U.S. under the headright system.[313] To accrue property in the American British colonies, wealthy Europeans would pay for the oceanic passage of indentured white servants from England in exchange for land.[314] John Maddison, an ancestor of America's fourth president, James Madison, did just this, acquiring some 2,000 acres of property by 1664.[315] In 1896, of this chapter in American history, Herbert Baxter Adams wrote:

> *The first slaves that we hear of in North Carolina were white people, and their masters were Indians.* [English writer William] Strachey, in his *Travayle into Virginia* [1612], speaks of a story that he had from the Indians of an Indian chief, Eyanoco, who lived at Ritanoe,

somewhere in the region to the south of Virginia, and who had seven whites who escaped out of the massacre at Roanoke, and these he used to beat copper. It is not improbable that there is a shadow of truth in the statement, although the details must be fictitious. *That the Indians of the colony later on did enslave the whites whom they could take in their waters, or who were shipwrecked off the coast, we know from the preamble of an act of the Assembly about 1707. This form of white servitude left no trace in the life of the colony.*

The first laborers that the English took to the New World colonies were whites, who during the first years of their residence were obliged to serve the settlers in the capacity of bonded servants. These people were commonly called "servants" or "Christian servants," and as such are to be distinguished from slaves. In regard to them, as well as to the slaves, their history as it related to North Carolina begins in Virginia. There were three sources of the supply of these [white] servants: 1. There were indented [white] servants, people of no means who, being unable to pay for passage to America, agreed to assign themselves for a certain period to some ship-captain on condition that when he reached Virginia he might transfer his right for money to some one who would maintain and work the servant for the given period. 2. Transported [white] felons, who were such criminals, vagabonds, or other obnoxious persons as were sent to the colonies by order of the English courts. 3. Kidnapped [white] persons, usually children, who were stolen by traders or ship-captains in the London or Liverpool streets and taken to America, where they were assigned till of age to such planters as would pay the prices demanded for their passages. *From these three sources many [white] people came to Virginia during the first sixty years of its settlement.* At the time, however, at which North Carolina was being settled, the importation of these people was being checked. This was due to at least three causes: 1. The British government was actually exerting itself to replace the white servants with negro slaves. In this the King was interested. In 1661 the Royal African Company was organized. The Duke of York [later known as King James II] was at the head of the enterprise and the King was a large stockholder. 2. The conscience of the English public was awakening to the violations of right which the traders perpetrated on those whom they allured by false promises, or forced by fraud, to go with them. These two causes acted together in 1664 when a commission of inquiry, with the Duke of York at its head, was appointed to report on the condition of such exportation of [white] servants. At the same time arrangements were provided by which indented servants going to the colonies of their own free will might register their indentures at an office created for that purpose. Public sentiment thus aroused continued to grow until in 1686 an Order of Council was issued, which directed: a) that all contracts between emigrant servants and their masters should be executed before two magistrates and duly registered; b) that no adult should be taken away but by his or her own consent, and no child without the consent of the parent or master; c) that in cases of children under fourteen the consent of the parent as well as the master must be obtained, unless the parents were unknown. The process was supplemented by an order issued in 1671 to stop the transportation of felons to the continental colonies. 3. The incoming of negro slaves, who, when the experimental stage of slavery was past, were seen to be cheaper than white servants, was probably the most powerful of all the causes. The rivalry was between the whites and the blacks. The blacks won. It is impossible not to see in this an analogous process to that by which negro slavery supplanted Indian slavery in the West Indies. The abuses connected with Indian slavery touched the conscience of the people, and negroes who could better stand slavery were introduced to replace it. The abuses connected with white servitude touched the hearts of the British people, and again the negro was called in to bear the burden of the necessary labor. In each case it was a survival of the fittest. Both Indian slavery and white servitude were to go down before the black man's superior endurance, docility, and labor capacity.

The checking of the introduction of white servitude just at that time saved the colony of North Carolina for slavery. Whatever [white] servants were now taken thither would be carried into the place in ever decreasing numbers. Another cause operated to deprive the colony of even that number of [white] servants which would under these conditions have been its normal share. This was the poor harbors and the consequent lack of direct trade with Europe. The few ships that came through the inlets of the Currituck, Albemarle, and Pamlico Sounds brought few servants to be indented to the colonists. Furthermore, the poor economic conditions of those early days, when the farms were small and the exports inconsiderable, would have made it an unsafe venture for a trader to have tried to dispose of a shipload of [white] servants.

A few [white] servants very probably came to the colony from the first. In the Concessions of 1665 the Proprietors offered all masters or mistresses already in the colony eighty acres of land for each able-bodied manservant whom they had brought in, armed and victualled for six months, and forty acres for each weaker servant, "as women, children, and slaves." Those who should come in during the next three years were to have sixty and thirty acres respectively instead of eighty and forty acres as just stated. Those

> who should come later than that should get varying other amounts. This system was continued in its existing form for some time, but toward the end of the century it settled down to the habit of giving each [white] man who came into the colony fifty acres for every person, bond or free, whom he brought in with him. A further inducement was offered to the [white] servants themselves. The Concessions of 1665 offered to every Christian servant already in the colony forty acres at the expiration of his or her period of servitude. Those coming later were to have smaller amounts. This inducement could not have brought many servants into the government, for two years later they were offered fifty acres on the expiration of their terms of service. Although this offer was not mentioned in the instructions after 1681, it seems to have been allowed as late as 1737, and perhaps later.
>
> The Fundamental Constitutions, whose spirit was entirely feudal, provided for white servitude in that they tried to re-establish the mediaeval leet men and leet women [servants on the manors of lords]. They assumed the existence of such persons and directed that on every manor they should be subject to the lord of the manor without appeal. Such servants should not leave the lord's land without his written permission. Whenever a leet man or leet woman should marry, the lord of each should give the pair ten acres of land, for which he must not take as rent more than one-eighth of the yearly produce. It was also stipulated that "whoever shall voluntarily enter himself a leet man in the registry of the county court shall be a leet man," and " all children of leet men shall be leet men, and so to all generations."[316]

In summary, American white servitude lasted for over two centuries, involved the majority of the nation's first white immigrants,[317] and laid the foundation for American black servitude.[318]

WHAT YOU WERE TAUGHT: All or most of the African slaves exported from Africa during the transatlantic trade were taken to the American South, where they were sold directly to Southern plantation owners.

THE TRUTH: At least 90 percent of all African slaves slated for the Americas were taken to the Caribbean Islands and the Spanish and Portuguese colonies in Central and South America.[319]

WHAT YOU WERE TAUGHT: Europe forced the slave trade on an unwilling Africa, and dominated and controlled the industry until its demise in the 1800s.

THE TRUTH: As this chapter repeatedly and clearly shows, Africa is a continent that has been practicing both slave trading and slavery from time immemorial,[320] for many thousands of years before the arrival of white slavers, and in particular white European slavers.

Additionally, Europe had no method of inducement, either economically or militarily, to compel Africa to trade her slaves to outsiders. As such, Africa's involvement in the slave trade was both completely voluntary and entirely under her control.[321]

An African slave owner at his house in Angola, surrounded by some of his African slaves—originally captured by Africans and sold to other Africans by Africans. It is clear to objective students of history that Africa must accept responsibility for enslaving her own people and for her enormous role in launching and facilitating the 400 year old transatlantic slave trade.

Indeed, throughout the entire Atlantic slave trade, it was Africa which commanded the entire industry, including the number and the types of slaves that were sold. This it did by cleverly determining demand and supply, levying stiff taxes on European slavers, adjusting to market conditions, and preventing Europeans from forming monopolies.[322]

WHAT YOU WERE TAUGHT: American slavery was the worst for African women, for being a free people they had never known anything like slavery in their entire lives.

THE TRUTH: As we have illustrated, throughout the millennia countless millions of African women were enslaved by other Africans, including other African women. Slavery was, after all, once endemic to African society, with female slaves being considered nearly as valuable as male slaves. Those who were not used as manual agricultural laborers became concubines at the royal court, or were simply used to breed new generations of slaves. Indigenous African slavery is at least as old as Egypt, whose earliest known kingdoms and dynasties began some 5,000 years ago.[323] Thus bondage, often of the most savage and exploitive type, was nothing new to the first African female slaves who were brought to the New World.

Furthermore, the African-enslaved African-born woman would have been all too familiar with her own unique brand of slavery: just like true slaves, African women were *purchased* for marriage by their husbands, then legally required to perform *all* of the family's domestic menial labor. This enforced marital servitude lasted for the duration of an African woman's life, or until she could no longer perform her duties, at which time her husband would purchase additional wives to lighten her load or take over her chores.[324]

Prince Abdul Rahman Ibrahim Ibn Sori, commonly known by his nickname the "Prince of Slaves," began life as the son of a Timbo king in his native Africa, a people well-known for their custom of enslaving fellow Africans. One day while "Prince" was out on a slave catching mission, he himself was captured by African slavers, sold into slavery, and eventually transported to Mississippi, where he spent nearly half a century as a plantation overseer before he was freed and able to return to Africa.

WHAT YOU WERE TAUGHT: Slavery finally ended in Africa due to the efforts of Africans themselves. Whites, either American or European, showed no interest in abolition in Africa, and played no role in its destruction there.

THE TRUTH: First, as we have seen, indigenous African slavery has never ended, and is today nearly as pervasive in many parts of the continent as it was 300 years ago.[325]

Second, both white Americans and white Europeans played a very important role in the attempt to abolish African slavery. Indeed, since Africans themselves never created an organized abolition movement, or even once protested domestic slavery, during the entire pre-colonial period,[326] it was left to non-Africans to do the job, and this fell mainly to Europeans and Americans—a nearly futile task that went on for centuries, and is in fact still going on to this day.[327] This gave rise, in the mid 1800s, to the not uncommon phenomenon of Africans, who had been enslaved by other Africans, being rescued and set free by whites.[328]

In the early 19th Century, under the auspices of the newly formed "African Institution," the British not only put pressure on other European countries to help bring domestic African slavery to an end,[329] but they ordered naval patrols, such as the "African Squadron,"[330] to cruise the waters along the African coast to help enforce the new ban on slave exporting.[331] As a result, numerous battles were waged against, for example, the Dey (in 1816)[332] and the Ashanti (in 1823), who were conquered and forced to abolish slavery.[333]

Despite the efforts of this large "Anti-Slavery Squadron," so entrenched was the institution in Africa that for a time the transatlantic slave trade actually increased under Britain's watch.[334] Indeed, more slaves were "carried away" in ships from Africa in 1844 when it was illegal than 100 years earlier in 1744 when it was legal.[335]

Christian missionaries, like Scotsman Dr. David Livingstone, explored eastern Africa in order to uncover the primary slaving depots and bring worldwide attention to the problem of ongoing enslavement. German scholar Dr. Heinrich Barth spent several years traveling throughout western Africa, while British writer and military officer Sir Samuel Baker explored the northern regions.[336] Noted Welsh-American journalist, Sir Henry Morton Stanley, led numerous excursions into the central interior, also helping to open up the Dark Continent to the scrutiny of the Western world. For better or for worse, portions of Africa were soon colonized by European nations.

The main benefit of these early European explorations—which grouped together are tellingly called the "opening up of Africa"—to both the continent and its citizens, was the eventual legal abolition of indigenous slavery, as non-African countries began to impose Western social, religious, and commercial ideas on the native populace. Though slavery continues in Africa, it is now illegal in most areas and where it is not, it is now largely considered an illicit institution—thanks, in large part, to *white Europeans and Americans*.[337]

It is time that we give credit where credit is due: whites helped end, or at least curb, the millennia old indigenous African practice of enslaving other Africans.

Welsh explorer Sir Henry Morton Stanley was only one of thousands of white Britons who bravely assisted in the suppression of domestic African slavery. Africa has never been able to completely rid herself of the institution on her own, even to this day.

This early African city, filled with thousands of potential slaves, was a prime target for African slave dealers and slave catchers, who waged war on neighboring peoples for the express purpose of obtaining human chattel. The usual method was to launch a sudden and violent attack in the dead of night, then butcher the resistors, the weak, the elderly, the ill, and the very young, then capture and enslave the rest, particularly the fit and the healthy. Those who believe that slavery has been abolished in Africa are mistaken. In the time it has taken you to read this caption, dozens of Africans have been kidnaped and enslaved by other Africans. Most will suffer unspeakable horrors, as well as experience extreme forms of bondage unknown in Western history. Few will ever be seen by their families again.

3

AMERICAN SLAVERY AND RACE

WHAT YOU WERE TAUGHT: Slavery is and always has been a racist business predominated by whites. This was particularly true of American slavery.

THE TRUTH: Slavery is a business, period, one that has nothing to do with race, for slavery came into being long prior to the invention of either the word race or the false concept of race.[338] This is why, before the 1600s, there is no mention in the records of any known people using race as a basis for enslavement.

As we have seen, Africans, Native-Americans, Europeans, Asians, and Middle-Easterners, all peoples and races, in fact, were enslaving their own kind long before they discovered that there were colors and varieties of humans different than themselves. Even Chinese Buddhists once kept fellow Chinese slaves.[339] This is why, among the ancient Greeks and Romans, skin color and nationality bore no relationship to slavery whatsoever. All the races were enslaved indiscriminately,[340] from Syria, Judea, and Egypt, to Gaul, the Rhineland, and Greece.[341] In short, *anyone could become a slave owner and anyone could become a slave*—regardless of their ethnic background.[342] This has been true in all societies and in all nations throughout all of human history, *including early America*.

Let us take an example, Western slavery, which has its roots among Caucasians. Besides the overwhelming evidence of white-on-white slavery across ancient and Medieval Europe, any doubts about its Caucasoid origins vanish when we examine the etymology of the word slave itself: *originally a name of nationality*,[343] slave derives from the word "Slav,"[344] from the name of a European people, the Slavs,[345] today the largest European ethnic and language group inhabiting central and eastern Europe, as well as Siberia. (This group's 225 million people all speak one of the Slavonic languages.)[346] Authorities consider Russians, Bulgarians, Serbians, Poles, and Bohemians to be Slavs.[347]

Slavery in early Africa, as everywhere, was non-racial. Africans have hunted and enslaved their own kind from time immemorial, and they continue to do so to this day.

The word Slav became synonymous with slavery due to the enslavement, by other Europeans (mainly Celts[348] and Germans)[349] of thousands of Slavic individuals during Europe's early history.[350] Germans, for example captured Slavic men, women, and children during internecine conflicts, then traded them to Roman merchants for jewelry, farming equipment, wine, and household wares. The Slavic men seized in this manner were sold into slavery as gladiators, the women as domestic servants, and the children as field hands.[351]

In his monumental work, *The History of the Decline and Fall of the Roman Empire*, 18th-Century English historian Edward Gibbon commented on the manner in which the name Slavs or Slaves was converted from a national name to an appellative one:

> From the Euxine to the Adriatic, in the state of captives or subjects, or allies, or enemies, of the Greek empire they [the Slavonians] overspread the land; and the national appellation of the Slaves has been degraded by chance or malice from the signification of glory to that of servitude.[352]

As their names indicate, the Slovenes (of *Slove*nia), the Slovaks (of *Slova*kia), and the Yugoslavians (of Yugo*slavia*), are the modern (white) descendants of the ancient Slavs. The French word for slave is *esclave*, from the Greek *sklave*,[353] all pointing to European origins.

WHAT YOU WERE TAUGHT: Daniel Webster was correct when he said in his March 7, 1850, speech that the American South justified slavery on the same grounds as the ancient Greeks: on the racial inferiority of the black man.

THE TRUTH: As we have just discussed, slavery has *never* been based on racism, not black, red, yellow, brown, or white racism. And thus so-called "Southern slavery" could not have been founded on this idea either. This makes Webster's pronouncement on the South erroneous.[354] But we must take into account that he was a Yankee, and an uninformed one at that.

As for Webster's comment about the ancient Greeks, we will let Southern statistician James D. B. De Bow respond:

> *The Greeks never had Ethiopian [black] slaves*, nor was it until late in their history that they had Asiatic slaves. Slavery existed in Greece before the siege of Troy, and it was three or four centuries after this [that] authentic history commences, before they extended their conquests into Asia. The Grecian states that attained great power commenced their career of greatness . . . by conquering the nearest cities; and, as they gained strength, extending their conquests. *Greek slaves were mostly themselves Greeks, of the same language and color, and equal to, or but little inferior to their conquerors*.
>
> It is true, the Greeks held other nations to be barbarians who might be reduced to servitude, but *they knew nothing about Ethiopians, made no distinction as to the Asiatic nations; and without hesitation, made slaves of Greeks who were conquered*. Aristotle expresses the general principle of the Greeks thus: "with barbarians, the family consists of male and female slaves, but to the

> Greeks belong dominion over the barbarians, because the former have the understanding requisite to rule, the latter body only to obey." *In this there is nothing about Ethiopians* or the different tribes of Asia, and a few instances will show that *the principle of conquest was extended over the Greeks*.[355]

WHAT YOU WERE TAUGHT: As our schools teach only about black slavery, it is obvious that the idea of "white slavery" is a myth, or is at best overemphasized.

THE TRUTH: Actually, the reality of white slavery is completely *under* emphasized in our leftist schools, and for good reason: America's liberalistic teachers do not want the truth to be known, for it would expose and demolish their false teachings about racism and capitalism. So let us now correct this imbalance.

Ancient Romans enslaved fellow Romans both for labor and for sport. Most gladiators, such as those pictured here, were white slaves who were forced to battle each other and wild beasts as a form of public entertainment. Entire Roman families came to watch white slaves fight and die in the gruesome gladiatorial games at the Colosseum.

As discussed, in the beginning, not only did slavery exist among Native-Americans—for example, the Aztecs,[356] Incas,[357] and Mayans[358]—long before the arrival of Christopher Columbus[359] (the man responsible for starting the European-American slave trade),[360] but Western slavery itself was purely a white man's occupation and had nothing to do with Indians, Africans, or any other people of color, or even racism.

This bas-relief from an ancient Assyrian temple shows Assyrian soldiers brutally flaying then beheading imprisoned slaves. Both the soldiers and the slaves are white Middle Easterners.

Indeed, historically speaking, *both the earliest known slave traders and the earliest known slaves were Caucasians*: the Babylonians, Assyrians, Sumerians, Akkadians, Mesopotamians, Phoenicians, Egyptians, Mycenaeans, Arameans, East Indians, Chaldeans, Hittites, Scythians, Persians, Arabians, and Hebrews—at some point in their history—all either enslaved other whites or were themselves enslaved by other whites.[361] In India, for example, historic records show that Caucasian slavery was being practiced by 1750 BC, nearly 4,000 years ago,[362] though doubtlessly it arose there thousands of years earlier. Some maintain that white thralldom may have even once been an integral part of Hinduism, one of the world's oldest religions.[363]

During slavery's peak in Mesopotamia (ancient Iraq), nearly every household possessed several white slaves, a country where parents thought little of selling their children into slavery—to other whites.[364] White female slaves in ancient Iraq suffered doubly: as their bodies belonged to their masters, they could also be forced into prostitution.[365] In Assyria (which once stretched from Iraq to Egypt) white slaves were procured through warfare, then forced to work for life under the lash. Assyrian slaves were identified by their shaven heads and pierced ears, which set them apart from free citizens.[366]

In ancient Egypt slaves could be any color, race, or nationality. The slave in the foreground is a white Egyptian, paying homage to a white pharaoh.

If a Babylonian father got into debt, he would sell his entire family into slavery. Fortunately, the Law of Hammurabi stipulated that their bondage could last no more than three years.[367] Babylonia's enormous slave class was comprised primarily of whites taken in battle and from slave raids into neighboring states. A Caucasian woman was worth $20, a Caucasian man about $50. The former was bred to produce new slaves, the latter was either conscripted in the Babylonian army or put on forced labor gangs to build roads and dig canals. When a white master determined that his white slave was costing him more money than he was producing, he was promptly put to death.[368]

By 1300 BC, white slavery had become "widespread" in ancient Egypt, with white warrior-pharaohs bringing home thousands of Caucasian slaves as prisoners-of-war[369] from Palestine, Syria,[370] and Anatolia, or what is now part of Turkey and Lebanon.[371] The Egyptian King Rameses III (reigned 1187-1156 BC) enslaved some 113,000 people during his rule.[372] By the time of the ancient philosopher Thales, around 600 BC, it was said that most of the Greek cities of Asia Minor possessed large white slave populations.[373] Though a few of Egypt's slaves were of "negro blood," most were white, of North African Mediterranean descent.[374]

Like other early Caucasian peoples, the ancient Jews obtained their white slaves through warfare or purchase at the slave markets that dotted the Near and Middle East.[375] Hundreds of thousands of white slaves labored in Judea, working at such public work projects as the building of Solomon's Temple, where they hewed and transported heavy timber.[376] Known from the time of Moses (1391-1271 BC), white slavery was an ordinary aspect of Hebrew society,[377] one that required the writers of the Torah (Old Testament) to record dozens of complex laws in order to govern it.[378]

The three white Romans on the right have been captured by the Roman military. They are being led to a waiting ship, which will take them to a nearby slave port where they will be sold into slavery.

For example, both adults and children could be enslaved,[379] a man could sell himself into slavery,[380] a man's creditors could enslave him for unpaid bills,[381] thieves could be enslaved,[382] the children of indebted parents could be put into bondage,[383] the children of white slaves were themselves considered slaves,[384] and Hebrew daughters could be sold into slavery by their fathers.[385] All of these practices continued into the time of Jesus.[386]

The Phoenicians or Canaanites, from what is now roughly the area of Lebanon, were notorious slavers, obtaining white slaves indiscriminately from every nation they visited, one being early Spain. Slaves were gotten through any means necessary, including treachery, robbery, and cheating. Sometimes the piratical Phoenicians would anchor their vessels off the coast and, as a friendly gesture, invite the unsuspecting natives on board. When the boat was filled they would simply sail away, selling their human cargo at the next slave port.[387]

Many other peoples from the same period, such as Thracians,[388] Greeks,[389] and Romans, were slaves of white, Caucasian, or European extraction, enslaved by other Europeans.[390] The noted early Greek storyteller Aesop was a slave,[391] as was the famed Stoic philosopher and Greek sage Epictetus.[392]

The modern world vastly underestimates the popularity of white slavery in the ancient world. In 5th-Century Greece, for instance, fully one-third of the total population of Athens was made up of white slaves.[393] The same was true of the city of Attica, while half of the Greek city of Pergamum (Pergamon) were bonded Caucasians.[394]

Ancient Greek society, where nearly every slave owner and slave was white, was a classic example of a nonracist slave civilization. In this early artwork a group of Greek slaves (left) tend the horses and chariot of their wealthy Greek master (right).

As for ancient Greece herself—whose citizens considered slavery a prerequisite for the building and maintenance of civilization[395]—there was literally no known time at which she did not practice slavery. The result was that there were no Greek states in which slaves did not outnumber the free inhabitants.[396] One estimate puts the free population at 5 million (29 percent) and the slave population at 12 million (71 percent).[397] Translated into modern terms, if these numbers were applied to 21st-Century America, we would today have nearly 700 million white slaves catering to the needs of our free population of just over 300 million.

Greece put many of her white slaves to work in places of worship, males as well as females:

> Most of the temples of Greece possessed a great number of slaves, or serfs, who cultivated the sacred domains, exercised various humbler offices of religion, and were ready on all occasions to execute the orders of the priests. At Corinth, where the worship of [the goddess] Aphrodite chiefly prevailed, these slaves consisted almost exclusively of women, who, having on certain occasions burnt frankincense, and offered up public prayers to the goddess, were sumptuously feasted within the precincts of her fane.[398]

Although the Spartans and Thessalians were practicing slavery on other whites from earliest times, it was the Chians who were the first Grecian people to engage in a regular white slave trade. Unlike nearly all other early peoples, they purchased their slaves rather than capturing them during warfare. Later, the Chians paid dearly for introducing the trade into Greece: in retaliation "they were subjugated by the Mithridates, and delivered up to their own slaves, to be carried away captive to Colchis."[399]

Ancient Greek families who fell behind on their rent were split up by the authorities and sold into slavery, even the children.[400] Greek field slaves lived wretched lives in large "cellar barracks," under constant watch by armed guards.[401] At the Greek settlement of Ionia, white male and female slaves were acquired during warfare from the surrounding population, the former were sent to the mines, the latter into the textile industry.[402] These unfortunate souls were forced to wear fetters as they worked, and were frequently flogged.[403]

In ancient times slaves were frequently obtained through warfare. Those who survived the attack were made slaves of the victor, often while still on the battlefield amid the dying. This Caucasian archer is drawing his bow on a Caucasian enemy who has chosen death over subjugation.

At one time the city of Rome may have had as many as 330,000 white slaves.[404] Some estimates put the figure at 500,000, nearly half the population during the 1st Century AD.[405] Around the same period, during the era of my ancestor Emperor Tiberius Claudius, the entire Roman Empire contained some 120 million people, half of which were slaves, and nearly all of whom were white. But the proportion of white slaves to freemen in Italy was even higher than in the outer provinces: here, between 146 BC and AD 235, bondsmen and women outnumbered the free population three to one.[406]

Although no nation or people were off limits, most of Rome's white slaves came from Gaul, the Rhineland, Greece, Judea, Syria, or Egypt.[407] Even Roman leaders could be surprised at the Empire's enormous white slave population. When the famed Roman politician Tiberius Gracchus visited Etruria in the early 2nd Century BC, he was stunned at the number of Caucasian slaves he saw in the fields.[408] Some private Roman estates were served by as many as 20,000 white slaves each.[409] In short, an enormous proportion of the Empire was made up of bonded whites,[410] who functioned as the "vital supply of manpower" needed to build and maintain the old Roman commonwealth.[411]

In 1855 English educator and author Dr. Henry George Liddell wrote of the prodigious number of Roman slaves who were thrown into the market after the Second Punic War (218-201 BC):

> To punish the Bruttians for the fidelity with which they adhered to the cause of the great Carthaginian, the whole nation were made slaves; no less than 150,000 Epirotes were sold by [Lucius] Aemilius Paullus; 50,000 were sent home by Scipio from Carthage. These numbers are accidentally preserved; and if, according to this scale, we calculate the hosts of unhappy men sold in slavery during the Syrian, Macedonian, Illyrian, Grecian, and Spanish Wars, we shall be prepared to hear that [white] *slaves fit only for unskilled labour were plentiful and cheap*.
>
> There was also a [white] slave-trade regularly carried on in the East. The barbarous tribes on the coasts of the Black Sea—a practice not yet extinct—were *always ready to sell their own flesh and blood; Thrace and Sarmatia were the Guinea Coast of the Romans*. The entrepôt of this trade was Delos, which had been made a free port by Rome after the conquest of Macedonia. Strabo tells us that *in one day 10,000 slaves were sold there in open market*.[412]

Bancroft notes that white slavery across ancient Europe was so commonplace, and often so severe, that it inspired some of the earliest known antislavery statements. But the white institution carried on, eventually opening the door to the European trade in blacks:

> *Old as are the traditions of Greece, slavery is older*. The wrath of Achilles grew out of a quarrel for a slave; Grecian dames had servile attendants; the heroes before Troy made excursions into the neighboring villages and towns to enslave the inhabitants. Greek pirates, roving, like the corsairs of Barbary, in quest of men, laid the foundations of Greek commerce; each commercial town was a slave-mart; and every cottage near the sea-side was in danger from the kidnapper. *Greeks enslaved each other*. The language of Homer was the mother tongue of the Helots; *the Grecian city that warred on*

its neighbor city made of its captives a source of profit; the hero of Macedon sold men of his own kindred and language into hopeless slavery. More than four centuries before the Christian era, Alcidamas, a pupil of Gorgias, taught that "God has bent forth all men free; nature has made no man slave." While one class of Greek authors of that period confounded the authority of master and head of a family, others asserted that the relation of master and slave is conventional; that freedom is the law of nature, which knows no difference between master and slave; that slavery is the child of violence, and inherently unjust. "A man, O my master," so speaks the slave in a comedy of Philemon, "because he is a slave, does not cease to be a man. He is of the same flesh with you. Nature makes no slaves." Aristotle, though he recognises "living chattels" as a part of the complete family, has left on record his most deliberate judgment, that the prize of freedom should be placed within the reach of every slave. Yet the idea of universal free labor was only a dormant bud, not to be quickened for many centuries.

Slavery hastened the fall of the commonwealth of Rome. *The power of the father to sell his children, of the creditor to sell his insolvent debtor, of the warrior to sell his captive, carried it into the bosom of every family, into the conditions of every contract, into the heart of every unhappy land that was invaded by the Roman eagle.* The slave-markets of Rome were filled with men of various nations and colors. "Slaves are they!" writes Seneca; "say that they are men." The golden-mouthed orator Dion inveighs against hereditary shivery as at war with right. "By the law of nature, all men are born free," are the words of Ulpian. The Roman digests pronounce slavery "contrary to nature."

In the middle age the pirate and the kidnapper and the conqueror still continued the slave-trade. *The Saxon race carried the most repulsive forms of slavery to England, where not half the population could assert a right to freedom, and where the price of a man was but four times the price of an ox. In defiance of severe penalties, the Saxons long continued to sell their own kindred into slavery on the continent. Even after the conquest, slaves were exported from England to Ireland, till, in 1102, a national synod of the Irish, to remove the pretext for an invasion, decreed the emancipation of all their English slaves.*

The German nations made the shores of the Baltic the scenes of the same traffic; and the Dnieper formed the highway on which Russian merchants conveyed slaves from the markets of Russia to Constantinople. The wretched often submitted to bondage as the only refuge from want. But *it was the long wars between German and Slavonic tribes which imparted to the slave-trade so great activity that in every country of Western Europe the whole class of bondmen took and still retain the name of Slaves.*

> In Sicily, natives of Asia and Africa were exposed for sale. *From extreme poverty the Arab father would pawn even his children to the Italian merchant. Rome itself long remained a mart where Christian slaves were exposed for sale, to supply the market of Mahometans. The Venetians purchased alike infidels and Christians, and sold them again to the Arabs in Sicily and Spain. Christian and Jewish avarice supplied the slave-market of the Saracens.* The trade, though censured by the church and prohibited by the laws of Venice, was not effectually checked till the mere presence in a Venetian ship was made the sufficient evidence of freedom.
>
> In the twelfth century, Pope Alexander III had written that, "nature having made no slaves, all men have an equal right to liberty." Yet, as among Mahometans the captive Christian had no alternative but apostasy or servitude, the captive infidel was treated in Christendom with corresponding intolerance. In the camp of the leader whose pious arms redeemed the sepulchre of Christ from the mixed nations of Asia and Libya, the price of a war-horse was three slaves. *The Turks, whose law forbade the enslaving of Mussulmans, continued to sell Christian and other captives; and [Captain John] Smith, the third president of Virginia [1609-1610], relates that he was himself a runaway from Turkish bondage.*
>
> All this might have had no influence on the destinies of America but for the long and doubtful struggles between Christians and Moors in the west of Europe, where, for more than seven centuries, the two religions were arrayed against each other, and *bondage was the reciprocal doom of the captive. France and Italy were filled with Saracen slaves; the number of them sold into Christian bondage exceeded the number of all the Christians ever sold by the pirates of Barbary.* The clergy felt no sympathy for the unbeliever. The final victory of the Spaniards over the Moors of Granada, an event contemporary with the discovery of America, was signalized by a great emigration of the Moors to the coasts of Northern Africa, where each mercantile city became a nest of pirates, and every Christian the wonted booty of the corsair: an indiscriminate and retaliating bigotry gave to all Africans the denomination of Moors, and without scruple reduced them to bondage.[413]

Though the *Odyssey* and the *Iliad* portray kindly relationships between master and slaves,[414] often such servants were treated with extreme cruelty, for they had no rights[415]—which marks them as true slaves. Ancient Roman and Greek owners, for instance, could do anything they wanted to their white slaves,[416] except murder them.[417] (In Rome the latter law, known as the *Lex Petronia*, was not passed until about AD 61.)[418] Even then a disgruntled Roman slaveholder could hire the municipal executioner to legally torture and kill an unruly white slave, usually by burning him or her alive.[419] While the ruthless treatment of white slaves was the norm during the earlier republican period, protective laws began to appear in the 1st Century BC at the start of the imperial period.[420] Throughout all Roman periods, however:

> The condition of slaves and their personal treatment were sufficiently humiliating and grievous, and may well excite our pity and abhorrence. They were beaten, starved, tortured, and murdered at discretion; they were dead in a civil sense; they had neither name nor tribe; they were incapable of judicial process; and they were, in short, without appeal.[421]

The ancient Egyptians enslaved fellow white Egyptians and foreigners alike, whatever their race, making them one of the most powerful slavery societies the world has ever known.

Some early Italian slaveholders were exceptionally brutal, even by ancient Roman standards. One of these was Vedius Pollio, who took white slaves accused of "trivial mistakes or even accidents," and threw them into his fishpond filled with lamprey eels.[422] Similarly, after his capture, Syrian slave leader Eunus was cast into a cell to be eaten by rats.[423] Sick, injured, and aged white slaves were dropped off on the island of Aesculapius in the Tiber River, where they were left to die of starvation and exposure to the elements.[424] Those who managed to survive and recover were mercifully given their freedom.[425] Some slave owners merely went in for humiliation: in ancient Syria in order that their female owners could more easily step onto their coaches, female slaves had to get down on all fours to serve as a human footstool,[426] something never required of black servants in the American South!

The Colosseum at Rome, where white slaves were condemned by fellow whites to fight and die in bloody gladiatorial games, a sadistic form of public "amusement" that still perplexes the 21st-Century Western mind. The life of a slave-gladiator was devalued, and often short and brutish. But for the ancient Romans violent death brought honor and nobility, whatever one's skin color.

White slaves who were trained to become Roman gladiators[427] were treated with unthinkable ferocity in order to turn them into beasts.[428] Emperor Marcus Aurelius commanded that gladiators' swords be blunted in order to decrease pain and bloodshed, but the edict was soon suspended in order to appease the bloodlust of the crowds.[429] Ordinary white slaves did not have it easy either. Beatings, chaining, branding, and all manner of torture were not uncommon,[430] with the ill simply left to die—doctoring costing more than a new slave.[431] One of the milder slave penalties in Rome was forcing an individual to work in fetters, while "everyday punishments" included being beaten with sticks and scourging by whip. When a rich and powerful Roman slave owner died, his slaves could expect to be killed and buried with him, so that he might be waited on in the Afterlife.[432]

Countless industrial dungeons constellated the landscape of Italy and Sicily, purposefully built underground so that the slaves who worked in them could less easily escape.[433] When Eunus and the Cilician (Turkish) slave Athenio each led 10,000-man armies to fight to have these prisons shut down, some 60,000 slaves were released.[434] When the Roman General Fabius conquered Hannibal and subdued Tarentum, he sold 30,000 of the town's white inhabitants into perpetual slavery.[435]

By Roman law if a slave killed his master, he, along with all of the other slaves belonging to the household, were put to death. Untold numbers of white slaves lost their lives in just this way. In one case, when a slave murdered his owner, Pedanius Secundus, in the 1st Century AD, the rest of his slaves were condemned to death as well. Though there was a public outcry against the sentence, Emperor Nero sent his troops in to quell the mobs and carry out the executions.[436]

Cato the Elder wrote a book, *On Agriculture*, in which he outlines, in a harsh and inhumane manner, "how to get the best results from [white] slaves on the least money."[437] According to the Roman statesman:

> Slave laborers should get thirty-two quarts of wheat each during the winter, thirty-six in the summer. The overseer, housekeeper, foreman, and chief shepherd are to receive twenty-four quarts each. Let the supply for the fettered slaves [chain-gangs] be four pounds of bread through the winter, five pounds when they have begun to dig the vineyard . . . then afterwards switch them back to four pounds again. After the vintage for three months let them drink the thin wine of the skin of the grapes . . . Let the shackled slave receive additional wine proportioned to the work accomplished. . . . [For a relish for the slaves' food] store up as many fallen olives as you can; afterwards [use only] the ripe olives from which you can make very little oil, but be sparing with them that they may last as long as possible. When the olives are eaten, give the slaves fish-pickle and sour wine. Give each slave eighteen ounces of olive oil per month. In a year to give each slave eight quarts of salt is enough. . . . [For clothing] each slave receives one tunic, three and a half feet in length, plus a coarse cloak every other year. As often as you give each a tunic or a cloak, first take the old one to make out of it rag-garments. You must give the slaves good

> wooden shoes on alternate years.[438]

It was Plutarch who criticized Cato for insisting that his slaves should never be doing anything except laboring or sleeping,[439] and for working them to the point of near-death, then mercilessly selling them off.[440]

Despite these privations and cruelties, ancient white Italian slaves could annually look forward to Saturnalia, a pre-Christian holiday held in Rome from December 17 to December 23—timed to fall during the Winter Solstice as well as the Birthday of the great Pagan Sun-god Sol on December 25 (adopted centuries later as the birthday of the Christian "Sun of Righteousness," Jesus).[441] Of this Pagan revelry British folklorist Sir James George Frazier writes:

> . . . no feature of the festival is more remarkable . . . than the license granted to slaves at this time. The distinction between the free and the servile classes was temporarily abolished. The slave might rail at his master, intoxicate himself like his betters, sit down at table with them, and not even a word of reproof would be administered to him for conduct which at any other season might have been punished with stripes, imprisonment, or death. Nay, more, masters actually changed places with their slaves and waited on them at table; and not till the serf had done eating and drinking was the board cleared and dinner set for his master. So far was this inversion of ranks carried, that each household became for a time a mimic republic in which the high offices of state were discharged by the slaves, who gave their orders and laid down the law as if they were indeed invested with all the dignity of the consulship, the praetorship, and the bench. Like the pale reflection of power thus accorded to bondsmen at the Saturnalia was the mock kingship for which freemen cast lots at the same season. The person on whom the lot fell enjoyed the title of king, and issued commands of a playful and ludicrous nature to his temporary subjects. One of them he might order to mix the wine, another to drink, another to sing, another to dance, another to speak in his own dispraise, another to carry a flute-girl on his back round the house.[442]

Entire cities, even entire states of whites, were sold into slavery in ancient times. The citizens of Judea were enslaved in Babylon twice; the inhabitants of Miletos were taken to Persia and enslaved; and the whole population of Thebes was sold into bondage by Alexander the Great.[443]

Caucasian slavery was well-known and widespread across the Medieval Middle East,[444] peaking in the Islamic western Mediterranean region around 1700.[445] Turkey once enslaved its own citizens: between the years 1280 and 1566, the ten sultans who reigned over the empire possessed an enormous number of officials from among the ruling class, or Ottomans, as they were known. All of these Caucasian administrators worked as slaves under their respective rulers.[446] In an empire in which even ordinary citizens were virtual slaves, the sultan took 3,000 white male children a year from conquered Christians in the Balkans. The boys were then brought up in Turkey as Muslims, to be trained in the arts of warfare and administration.[447] The Ottomans also procured white slaves from Spain, Italy, Albania, Bosnia, Hungary, and Romania,[448] and it is recorded that in the 11th Century the Fatimid army of Egypt was comprised primarily of white warrior-slaves—mainly Turks who had been bought as children from nomadic families.[449]

Ancient slaves were used to perform undesirable mundane tasks. This white Middle Eastern slave is carrying water for her white master.

During the 9th Century, Arabs purchased Turkish boys to serve as slaves to the Abbasids, Islam's second dynasty, whose capital was centered at Baghdad. Arabs used adult Turks captured in war as slaves for the caliphs, Islamic spiritual leaders. Though plantation slaves were rare in the early Middle East, household slaves were common enough, most who were taken from the Arabs' large pool of war captives and those children sold into slavery by their parents. While early Islam recognized slavery and issued no prohibitions against it,[450] its prophet, Muhammad, ordered slave owners to treat their chattel humanely.[451]

Slavery was so vital to the financial stability of early Saudi Arabia that when the great Islamic leader began converting white slaves, he earned the wrath of the Quraysh (the ruling tribe of Mecca at the time), who believed that this was a threat to the country's economy.[452] After the Christian Crusades (1095-1291), Muslims

> began to obtain white slaves not only by war but also by purchase, even from parts of Western Europe. The Mohammedans of the Barbary States also obtained white slaves by piracy in the Mediterranean.[453]

During the Muslim hegemony in early Spain (which peaked around the year 1000), Arab invaders regularly captured, imprisoned, and enslaved native Christian Spaniards, particularly women, girls, and children, who were sold at auction for huge profits. Countless thousands of Spanish slaves procured by the armies of the Caliph served out their lives as manual laborers, building mosques and other structures.[454] The harem of one Islamic vizier contained some 500 white slave women.[455] In the 13th Century Baghdad's slave fortunes were reversed when Genghis Khan and his army of barbarian Mongols attacked the city. After slaughtering 800,000 of its white inhabitants, the city was ransacked and its surviving women were raped and sold into slavery.[456]

The white slaves taken by the Musulman overlords became their "most important source of revenue." Known as *Şaqāliba*,[457] when these slaves became too numerous, the Arabs simply massacred and beheaded them—men women, and children alike. At the palace of the now extinct Arab-Spanish town of Az Zahara, white Christian slave-girls numbered some 6,300. The entire native population of some Spanish cities were sold into Muslim slavery. Later, not to be outdone, African Moors entered Spain and routinely seized and enslaved untold thousands of Catholic Spaniards.[458] To this day slavery, in one form or another, is still found in parts of Saudi Arabia.[459]

The Koran itself recognizes slavery,[460] and mentions it numerous times, permitting Muslims to acquire slaves by conquest,[461] but enjoining slave owners to be merciful.[462] In ancient times entire Islamic armies were comprised of white slaves.[463] Some of these soldier-slaves rose up the ranks becoming officers themselves, or even governors. In some cases Muslim slaves attained their freedom, founded dynasties of their own, and became kings.[464]

In the early years of the Roman Empire three out of four residents of what we now call Italy were slaves, some 21 million in total. Though a tiny minority were black slaves from Nubia, in the main both the owners and their chattel were white,[465] culled from places like Carthage, Spain, Gaul, Macedonia, Greece, and Asia Minor.[466] (Contrast this number with the much smaller figure 3.5 million, the total number of black slaves in the American south in 1860,[467] an area many times the size of Italy.)[468] Rome acquired 150,000 white slaves from the Adriatic region alone.[469]

Unlike the humane, civilized, and reluctant slave owners of America's Old South, ancient Near and Middle Eastern slave owners long enjoyed the bizarre and fiendish custom of inflicting pain upon their slaves, even to the point of death. Here, white Mesopotamian officials callously torture a group of white slaves, the reasons for which today we can only attribute to psychopathy.

While some were the product of slave breeding,[470] most were acquired in war, as the "general maxim in their polity" was to immediately reduce all captives to a condition of slavery.[471] Slave dealers accompanied the Roman armies to expedite the process: when an enemy soldier was captured on the field, he was sold on the spot to the dealer for a "mere trifle," about 80 cents in modern currency. Often "many thousands" of captives were enslaved simultaneously in this fashion.[472]

Plutarch wrote that during the Gallic Wars (58-51 BC), Julius Caesar sacked at least 800 European towns and enslaved (or killed) some 3 million Caucasian men.[473] In one Belgian campaign Caesar captured and sold 53,000 whites into perpetual bondage,[474] all from a Germanic tribe known as the Aduatuci.[475] The 1st-Century Roman-Jewish historian Josephus too mentions the enslavement of Germans by Rome.[476]

Many of Rome's white thralls ended up in the huge slave gangs that sustained the *latifundia*, the great landed estates of the wealthy and powerful.[477] Such affluent Italian families kept white slaves "as a matter of course,"[478] for it was accepted custom that a wealthy Roman could enslave his neighbors anytime he pleased, and for any reason.[479] In 149 BC, when Rome attacked Carthage, it leveled the city, slaughtered most of its white inhabitants, then sold the survivors into slavery.[480]

Those who managed to evade capture during warfare were hunted down by Rome's infamous professional slave catchers—white men pursuing white men. Sometimes fellow whites were caught by Roman pirates,[481] who then sold them to rich landowners to be used as cheap labor.[482] These Roman buccaneers often engaged in the "wholesale kidnaping" of other whites, as they brazenly sailed throughout the Aegean and eastern Mediterranean Seas,[483] providing constant replenishment of the large Roman slave marts on the Greek island of Delos.[484]

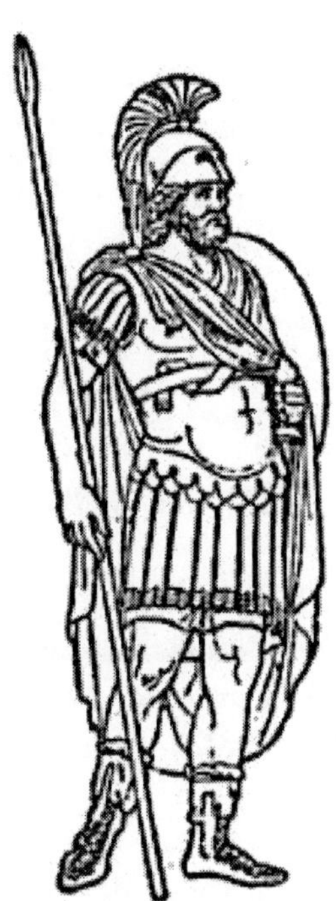

This Roman soldier, who was trained to secure slaves for the Empire, was most likely a slave himself.

After winning the Battle of Pydna (168 BC), Roman General Lucius Aemilius Paullus punished the people of Epirus (northwestern Greece) by selling 150,000 of their white inhabitants into slavery.[485] According to evidence found in early literature, the ancient Italians also captured and enslaved Gauls, or Celts.[486] After the 2nd-Century Roman General Gaius Marius' victories over the invading Germanic tribes, some 150,000 Teutons and Cimbri were sold into slavery.[487] In 146 BC, after sacking and burning Corinth, Roman General Lucius Mummius sold the entire white population of the Greek city into slavery.[488] It is said that Roman Emperor Trajan transformed all of eastern Asia into a "slave reservoir" in order to improve the Empire's infrastructure. It was these millions of white slaves who were used to build countless public projects, including hundreds of water-works as well as commercial and military highways, the latter which spanned tens of thousands of miles.[489]

Though we are speaking of white slavery here, race made no difference to the Romans. African black slaves, though rare in places like ancient Greece,[490] were considered just as good as Spanish ones, with blond Germans being favored above all others.[491] So popular was white slavery in Greece that the number one type of financial speculation among the Middle Class was to invest in slaves, often using one's savings or an inheritance.[492]

As in all parts of the ancient world, white slavery was found in Italy from "the earliest times of which we have any record."[493] After the First Punic War (264-241 BC), 75,000 whites from around the Mediterranean, including Sardinia, were put in bondage and sold at market.[494] The first slave rebellion ever recorded was by white slaves in Italy in the year 198 BC. Numerous other white slave uprisings took place in the following decades, "inflicting great damage upon Italy."[495]

Babylonians attacking a Mesopotamian city in a civil war that pitted Caucasians against Caucasians. The survivors were later enslaved: white slaves serving white masters, the norm in ancient Arabia.

One rebel servant army in Sicily contained some 200,000 white slaves, a power so great that they were able to hold off the Roman government for three years while defeating four Roman armies. When they were finally captured, the Romans crucified 20,000 of them as punishment.[496]

The most notable of the rebel Roman slaves was the gladiator Spartacus,[497] well-known to this day: a white man from Thrace, the slave revolt he led in 73 BC has become legendary.[498] After amassing an army of 120,000 white slaves, Spartacus was able to vanquish the Roman legions sent against him.[499] However, he was eventually killed in battle, and 6,000 of his followers were crucified on the Appian Way between Rome and Capua, their mangled rotting bodies a gruesome warning to other white slaves who might be considering a rebellion of their own.[500]

Since ancient Romans viewed slaves as "overgrown children," such revolts were seen as a form of parricide, punishable by death. Virgil said that any slave who participated in an insurrection would be abandoned in the lowest regions of Hell.[501] Hades must be overflowing with white slaves then.

In ancient Sicily, which was said to be "flooded with slaves," some 60,000 white bondsmen rebelled, murdering their owners and wreaking havoc in the area for years afterward.[502] At the Battle of Carrhae (53 BC), white Parthian soldiers conquered a Roman army four times the size of their own, then marched the 10,000 Italian survivors into Iran and sold them into slavery.[503] Since most industry and agriculture was run by white Roman slaves, it is not surprising that many from among the empire's more learned professions, such as doctors, tutors, clerks, managers, businessmen, and farm bailiffs, were actually slaves working under the ownership of kings and ministers.[504]

In a society like ancient Rome, where it was legal and common for slave owners to kill the unwanted infants of their white slaves,[505] we should not be shocked by any of this. Consider the following description of the life of a typical white slave living under the auspices of the Roman Empire, from Philip Smith's 1885 work, *A History of the World*:

> *When the slaves landed in Sicily, they were kept by the dealers in slave-pens, waiting for the purchasers. The wealthy capitalists would buy whole batches at once, brand or mark the slaves like cattle, and send them off to the country to work.* The young and robust were employed as shepherds, and the others in agricultural and other labour. *Some worked in fetters*, to prevent them running away. *All of them had hard service, and their masters supplied them scantily with food and clothing. They cared little about their slaves. They worked them while they were able to work, and the losses by death were replaced by fresh purchases.* This want of humanity and prudence in the masters soon produced intolerable mischief. The slaves who were employed in looking after sheep and cattle of necessity had more freedom than those who were kept to cultivating the ground. Their masters saw little of them, and left them unprovided with food, supposing that they would be able to look after themselves and cost nothing. Many of these greedy slave-owners were Italians, some of whom probably did not reside in Sicily, but entrusted the management of their estates to overseers, and consumed the produce of their wool and the profits of their cattle either at Rome or in some of the Italian towns. These slave shepherds, an active and vigorous set of men, soon found out ways of helping themselves. They began by robbing and murdering, even in frequented places, travellers who were alone or only in small companies. They next attacked the huts of the poorer people, plundered them of their property, and, if resistance was made, murdered them. It became unsafe for travellers to move about by night, nor could people any longer safely live on their lands in the country. The shepherds got possession of huts which the occupants abandoned, and of arms of

> various kinds also, and thus they became bolder and more confident. They went about with clubs and spears, and the staves which were used by herdsmen, dressed in wolfskins or hogskins, and already began to make a formidable appearance. They had a great number of fierce dogs with them, and abundance of food from the milk and flesh of their beasts. The island was filled with roaming bands of plunderers, just as if the masters had allowed their slaves to do what they liked.
>
> . . . Though all the slave-owners would suffer from the depredations of these robbers, every man would be unwilling that his own slaves should be put to death when they were caught, and would claim them as fugitive labourers; and thus disputes might easily arise between the governors and the owners. The true state of the case is probably this. *Slaves were bought cheap, and could be made profitable by working them hard*; and thus the greediness of gain, the total want of any humane feeling in the masters, the neglect of proper discipline among the slaves, and the careless feeling of security produced by many years of prosperity, brought things gradually to such a state, that repression of the disorder was beyond the power of the masters or the governors; for the masters could not reduce such sturdy fellows to obedience on estates far removed from towns, and a Roman governor of Sicily had no army at his command.[506]

Needless to say, the black slaves of the American South never experienced anything remotely like this, and were treated like royalty in comparison.[507]

Slavery, and in particular white slavery, was so ubiquitous in ancient Rome that the institution was known as the *ius gentium*: "the common law of all peoples."[508] Under Justinian I's edict that "making slaves is esteemed a right of nations,"[509] even the poorest families had at least one or more, and great white slave gangs (working the fields of massive estates) were a familiar sight throughout the region.[510]

Though, according to the Roman poet Horace, 200 slaves per household seems to have been the average,[511] the typical affluent Roman owned between 400 and 500 white slaves.[512] When Caius Caecilius Isadorus, who lived just prior to the birth of Jesus,[513] experienced a financial setback, he complained that he had been left with *only* 4,116 slaves—all white of course.[514] The Greek author Athenaeus claimed that a sizeable number of individual Romans personally owned as many as 10,000 to 20,000 white slaves.[515]

Slavery was so omnipresent in Rome that it was not uncommon for former slaves and even slaves themselves to own slaves.[516] By the 2nd Century AD there were so many white slaves across the Empire that they were outproducing free labor,[517] creating embitterment and widespread unemployment,[518] while ruining countless small farmers and small businessmen.[519] Flooded with slaves, both free enterprise[520] and free labor all but vanished[521] as Rome's white chattel took over and monopolized various crafts and occupations,[522] including accounting, literature, and medicine.[523]

The Parthenon at Athens. It was widely maintained among the ancient Greeks that Greece could not have developed without slavery, an opinion still held by many modern historians.

An idea of the number of white slaves in ancient Rome comes from the fact that for decades a minimum of 50,000 white slaves were kept at work in Italy's mines.[524] Then, as we saw, there was Spartacus, a single slave who was able to raise a slave army consisting of 120,000 men in just two weeks.[525]

Among Rome's large white slavery population were Jews, many who were impressed into the Roman legions in order to accompany their masters on the march.[526] Jewish leaders were so afraid that their entire population might disappear through enslavement that they created a new law requiring Jews to purchase the release of nearby Jewish slaves within seven years.[527]

When the supply of white slaves from military raids and outright war ran low, Roman slave dealers turned to "wholesale kidnaping."[528] White slavery remained "commonplace" throughout Italy and the entire eastern Mediterranean region well into the early Middle Ages.[529] White slaves were considered so invaluable to the running of society, that the wealthiest slave owners were willing to pay up to $20,000 for a single servant, the modern equivalent of many millions of dollars.[530] Naturally, other nations preyed upon what is now Italy for their own supply of slaves. Thus when the Normans stormed across southern Italy in the 11th Century they subjugated much of the local population.[531]

Just as early Romans obtained some of their white gladiators and slaves from Greece (as spoils of war), the early Greeks secured many of their white slaves in the same manner from Italy and Sicily.[532] In ancient Athens specifically—where the white slave population reached 400,000 individuals by the year 370 BC[533]—white slaves were purchased in great numbers from Thrace, as well as many countries in northern Europe.[534] There was also the Black Sea region, where white slaves were routinely exchanged for olive oil, silver, marble, lead, and works of art.[535]

In early Sparta, where white slaves existed in disproportionate numbers[536]—by some estimates, eight slaves to one freeman[537]—the Helots, or Greek serfs, worked the land as state slaves,[538] kept in thralldom by the "harsh measures" of their overlords, the ruling class known as the Spartiates.[539] They were "severely beaten every year," for example, "without having committed any fault, in order that they might never forget that they were slaves." In the words of the Greek historian Theopompos, "they were at all times cruelly and bitterly treated."[540]

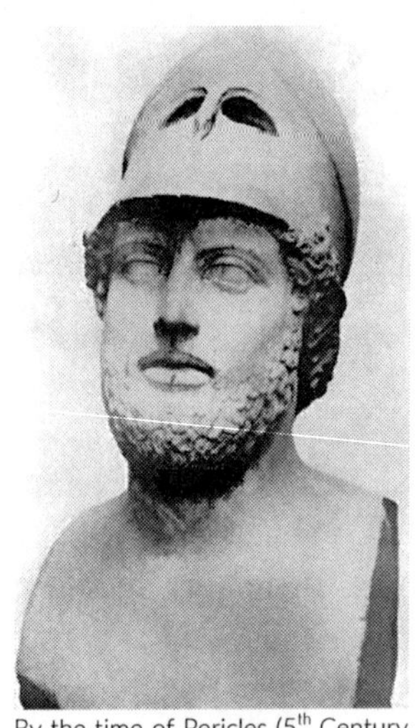

By the time of Pericles (5th Century BC), Greece was awash in white slaves. Though they greatly outnumbered the free population, white Greek slaves possessed no rights and were worked to death as a matter of course, many of them in the region's large silver mines.

It has been estimated that there were as many as 800,000 white Helot slaves.[541] There were so many that they posed a danger to the Spartan aristocracy, which was constantly trying to think up new ways to rid itself of their numbers. As property of the state, the "lowly" Helots could not be disposed of by their masters. So Sparta's officials simply declared annual war on them, an efficient way to exterminate their "overly abundant" white slave population with a clear conscience.[542]

Sometimes disguised, dagger-carrying assassins were sent out among them while their worked in the fields, in order to thin out their numbers. These hired killers usually performed their murderous work at night, "slaughtering all such of the Helots as they found abroad." On other occasions thousands of Helots at a time were lured into temples for the alleged purpose of being rewarded for their labors by emancipation. Instead, every last man was massacred, their corpses concealed, their fates never revealed to the public.[543]

For centuries, Athens, one of the great slave cities of ancient Europe, revolved on and around white slavery.

The first known use of slaves in Greece was as miners in the 5th Century BC.[544] At Laurium some 30,000 white slaves were employed in the town's silver mines.[545] As Greek slaves had no legal or political rights,[546] and since their masters held "life-and-death power" over them,[547] untold thousands died while working miserable ten-hour shifts in the dark damp mine shafts.[548] It is said that these manacled, overworked white laborers endured "almost every brutality."[549]

In 419 BC, when the Greek General Alcibiades subdued the island of Melos, he killed all of the men and sold the women and children into slavery.[550] The Helots of Greece were treated so inhumanely that it sparked a 30 year slave rebellion, from 650 to 620 BC. This white slave insurrection was only finally suppressed by the Spartans with great difficulty and viciousness.[551]

At Athens if a white slave was asked to give testimony in court, Greek law required that it be done under torture.[552] Indebted Attican[553] and Athenian families who were unable to pay their loans were split up and sold into slavery,[554] or they sold themselves.[555] White Greek sharecroppers could be turned into slaves for underproduction.[556] As in Rome, most of Greece's white slaves were procured through piracy, kidnaping, and war.[557]

White slaves in ancient Greece "greatly outnumbered the free population." Since it was considered "a real hardship to function with less than half a dozen slaves," nearly every freeman was a white slave owner.[558] In fact, all Athenian industry was built on white slavery. Thus the smallest farmer owned at least one or two bondsmen. Even Athens' policemen were slaves.[559]

By the year 338 BC there were some 150,000 white slaves working in Attica's mines alone. Nicias, an Athenian politician and military officer, is said to have owned over 1,000 white slaves. Ancient Greeks held slavery to be just as necessary as oxygen. As an essential aspect of both Greek society and Greek civilization itself,[560] it was a commonplace but important institution that was taken for granted,[561] like cooking utensils[562]—just as slavery was among all ancient peoples.[563] If slavery had been abolished at the height of Grecian civilization and free labor put in its place, the leisure upper classes would have disappeared, completely dissolving Greek society as a whole.[564]

Wealthy ancient Greeks, like the owner of this sumptuous country house, possessed an impressive array of white slaves who catered to their every whim and fancy.

This is why one cannot find a single antislavery statement in any of the literature of, for example, the ancient Middle East.[565] In fact, the only early Mediterranean people to discourage slavery were the Ptolemies, and this was purely for economic reasons: slavery would have competed with free labor.[566]

Without the economic foundation of white slavery, neither Athenian culture or the Roman imperial system could have developed. Actually, none of the world's ancient civilizations could have existed without the enslavement of whites,[567] for their bondage was the foundation of the economy and society of *all* early Western peoples dating back to prehistory.[568] In 1904 historian Philip Van Ness Myers wrote:

> *If ever slavery was justified by its fruits, it was in Greece. The brilliant civilization of the Greeks was its product, and could never have existed without it.* As one truthfully says, 'Without the slaves the Attic democracy would have been an impossibility, for they alone enabled the poor, as well as the rich, to take a part in public affairs.' Relieving the citizen of all drudgery, the system created a class characterized by elegant leisure, refinement, and culture.[569]

During the 10th Century, Verdun, France, was a major trading center of white slaves: imported from the Slavonic east, they were sold primarily to Spaniards to serve in the courts of the Caliphs.[570] As late as the 1700s the chamber of commerce at Nantes, France's main slave trading port, stated publicly that French colonial commerce would have been unachievable without slavery.[571] The institution reached its height in France in the 1700s when the country took over the oceangoing slave trade between Africa and Spain's colonies in South America.[572] Officially the French slave trade lasted 206 years, from 1642, when King Louis XIII authorized it,[573] to 1848, when it was finally legally abolished at home and throughout all of its colonies. During those two centuries millions of whites (and blacks) were bought, sold, and transported around the world by French slave dealers, traders, and shippers.

It is often said that slavery is as old as human history. Actually it is far older, dating back to prehistoric times, before the advent of recording keeping. With the dawn of the historic period some 5,000 years ago, we learn of the first known enslavers and the first slaves: both were Caucasians.

Britons were enslaving each other as early as the 5th Century, and among the English (as with the Germans) there had been a white slave class from their earliest days as a separate and distinct people. White English slaves had no rights whatever and were viewed as a part of the livestock of their owner's estate.[574] Bristol, England, was once a thriving slave port, where enslaved English men and women, known as "thralls," were sold to the Irish.[575]

In the late 6th Century the future Roman pope, Saint Gregory the Great, was startled to see fair-skinned slaves for sale at a slave market in Rome;[576] not because they were in bondage, but because of their "well formed features and beautiful blond hair." When he asked about them he was told that they were Angles (Anglo-Saxons), the people who gave their name to Angles' Land (England).[577] In the 9th Century, when Bishop Wilfrid I of York, England, was granted land by King Ethelwulf, the cleric found that he had also inherited 250 white male and female slaves attached to the property. He promptly baptized them and set them free.[578] Under Agilulf, the 7th-Century King of the Lombards, Jews were permitted to own white Christian slaves.[579]

Ancient Europe's casual and pragmatic view of white slavery was summed up by slavery approving Aristotle in the 4th Century BC.[580] According to the famed Greek philosopher, certain members of society are born to be slaves, "animated instruments,"[581] or "tools with voices," as he referred to them, natural-born servants who need to be enslaved for their own good.[582] Besides, he went on, as most Greek slaves were non-Greek, and therefore inferior, it was only right that they were ruled by a superior people.[583] Plato, who believed that slavery would continue indefinitely into the future,[584] held that slavery was simply the inherent fate of certain individuals.[585]

Roman diplomat Marcus Terentius Varro referred to slaves as "vocal agricultural instruments."[586] The Greek historian Xenophon held that civilization itself could not exist without a privileged class freed by white slave labor, so that its members could use their spare time to pursue the development of government, education, art, warfare, philosophy, and science.[587] Little wonder, as we have seen, that the word "slave" itself derives from the word "Slav," the name of a European people: the Slavs.[588]

In Europe, where avaricious white slave dealers routinely

enslaved white peasants for sale to Middle Eastern countries,[589] white slavery was such a dominant aspect of the region that it eventually spilled over into both Asia and the Arabic world. Throughout the 9th Century Swedish Vikings enslaved whites from the northern forests of Russia[590] (a country once literally known as the "nation of slaves"),[591] then traded them to Muslims for Oriental goods.[592] It was not until the latter half of the 19th Century that Russia abolished its own "widespread" system of slavery,[593] one dating back to the country's earliest chronicles,[594] emancipating some 10,000 white slaves in Uzbekistan alone.[595]

As the Vikings violently carved their way across 8th and 9th Century Europe, they fought, killed, and enslaved thousands of fellow white Europeans. The idea of "race" was unknown at the time.

The Vikings, who carried on a European-wide slave trade for many decades, captured and enslaved untold numbers of whites from Ireland all the way to what is now Slovakia. Males were sold as slave laborers while females were sold into harems.[596] As zealous practitioners of white slavery, the institution became a routine aspect of Viking culture for several centuries.[597]

During the Children's Crusade in 1212 thousands of French and German boys were kidnaped by white slave dealers and sold into captivity in Arabia.[598] German royal Henry the Lion turned captured Danish Christians into slaves, and Bavarian nobleman Diepold von Vohburg sold Italians into slavery.[599] Germans were so addicted to gaming that they would offer to sell themselves into bondage if they lost. As a result, many were bound, sold, and shipped away to pay their debt.[600]

In Western Europe specifically, white slavery existed long before the Roman Empire, with peoples like the Venetians specializing in the import of white slaves right up into the Medieval period.[601] Many of Venice's Caucasian bondsmen came from Egypt, Tunis, Morocco, and Muslim Spain.[602] Between the years 1414 and 1423 some 10,000 white slaves (among them Jews)[603] were sold just in Venice.[604] Considered its most important form of trade, Venice also exported white slave men, women, and children to places like Alexandria, the site of an enormous slave market.[605] The Genoese, Catalans, Flemings, and Florentines were also heavily engaged in slaving throughout the 1400s, using their profits to help in the colonization of the Cape Verde Islands and the Azores.[606] Phillips writes of this period:

> . . . so long as petty wars persisted, the enslavement of [white] captives continued to be at least sporadic, particularly in the south and east of Europe, and a considerable traffic in white slaves was maintained from east to west on the Mediterranean. The Venetians for instance, in spite of ecclesiastical prohibitions, imported frequent cargoes of young girls from the countries about the Black Sea, most of whom were doomed to concubinage and prostitution, and the rest to menial service.[607]

White slavery did not begin to disappear in Europe until the 12th Century,[608] though it continued to flourish in places like Florence, Italy, where in 1363 the government sanctioned the unlimited importation of white slaves. White slavery persisted in Southern Italy, Spain, Crete, and Sicily well into the 1500s. During the Renaissance, Genoese slavers established white slaving stations in the Crimea and in the Black Sea region in order to fully exploit the lucrative business.[609] In Mexico the Catholic Church's Spanish Inquisition also continued to enslave other whites from the 1400s onward.[610]

Despite increasing disapproval by the Church,[611] English slaves (mainly criminals and political prisoners) were sent to plantations in the New World throughout the 17th Century, and kidnaped English children were sold there as slaves as late as 1744.[612] As we have noted, many of the original 17th-Century American colonists were white slaves and white indentured servants from England, Ireland, and Scotland.[613]

Medieval European white slaves (serfs)—the "lowest grade of vassals"[614]—were legally the lord's chattel and had few rights, could not own property,[615] were viewed as human livestock, and were often sold for less than the cost of a horse.[616] If a serf died without children, all of his belongings reverted to his lord: legally a serf's possessions were only "on loan" to him for the duration of his life.[617] Under the Christian reign of Byzantine Emperor Justinian I, white slaves who accused their master of a crime were burned at the stake.[618] Parents from Thrace, what is now the southeastern Balkans, regularly sold their children into slavery to pay off their debts.[619]

Mediterranean Europe only stopped trading in white slaves when it was forced to: in 1453, when the Ottoman Empire conquered Constantinople—cutting off the flow of white slaves from the Balkans and the area around the Black Sea—it had no choice but to turn to Africa as a source for slaves. By the late 1400s black slaves were working in the vineyards and on the sugar plantations of Majorca and Sicily. Thus, Mediterranean Europeans had developed an "American" form of slavery even before Columbus sailed to the Americas.[620]

Europa, the ancient moon-goddess after which Europe was named, riding the sacred White Bull—Taurus of the modern Zodiac. Europeans were enthusiastically reducing one another to slavery long before the birth of Jesus. It was not until centuries later, in the 15th Century, that they began enslaving Africans. White people continue to enslave one another into the present.

White slavery was not just a phenomenon of the ancient world, the Middle Ages, or even the 1700s. In fact, whites have been continuously and enthusiastically enslaving one another right into the present day. Soviet dictator Joseph Stalin, for example, enslaved an estimated 12 million[621] to 18 million Caucasians during his reign of terror in the 1930s,[622] as many as 14.5 million more white slaves than the American South's 3.5 million black slaves. "Harshly treated," and forced to live in labor camps that were located in the northern wilderness of Siberia, Stalin's white slaves were assigned spirit-breaking work in mines and forests.[623]

Between 1941 and 1945, nearly 8 million Caucasians were enslaved across Europe under Nazi Germany, including children as young as six years of age. This means that the Nazis owned 4.5 million more white slaves than the American South owned black slaves. Under Nazi socialist leader Adolf Hitler and the Third Reich's infamous swastika,[624] white European families were routinely separated and forced to work in factories, fields, and mines, where they were dehumanized, beaten, whipped, and starved by their German overlords.[625]

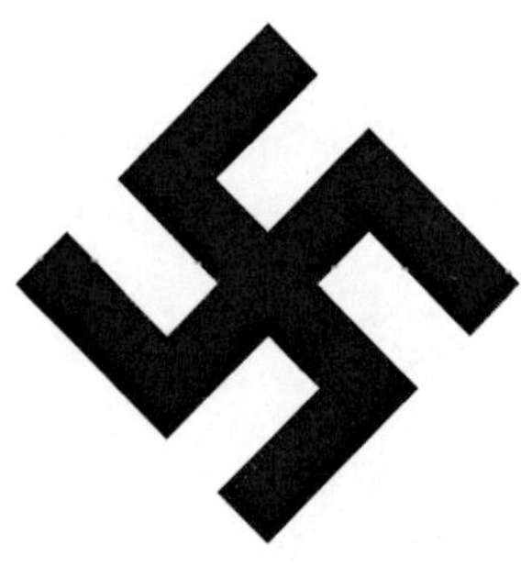

Though the Nazis' decision to adopt the swastika was based on an error (for it is not "Aryan"), today this archetypal, prehistoric solar symbol continues to be seen by many in the West as a frightening emblem of a dictatorial militaristic organization, one that thought nothing of enslaving, torturing, and murdering millions of fellow Caucasians.

By definition, *all* Nazi concentration camp prisoners were considered slaves, which is why Hitler's right-hand man, Heinrich Himmler, wanted the concentration camps themselves to be turned into modern factories—mainly for the production of German armaments. As sanitary conditions were poor, disease and mortality rates became "extraordinarily high."[626]

Among the millions of whites who were violently coerced into the Nazi Slave Labor Program were Poles, Russians, Slavs, Jews, and Italians. Many of Hitler's white slaves were housed five at a time in dog kennels only three feet tall. Imprisonment could last for as long as six months in camps that lacked water and even rudimentary sanitation. Overworked and underfed, millions of European slaves died at the hands of fellow whites during this period.[627]

White Nazi slavery was the largest revival of the institution in the 20th Century, and one of the fastest and most monumental expansions of slavery in world history.[628] If the Nazis had been victorious, Hitler was planning to operate a massive "slave empire" that ran from Europe's Eastern coast on the Atlantic Ocean to the Ural Mountains in Western Russia.[629] All of this occurred a mere 65 years ago, demolishing the Yankee-New South myth that "slavery is a white racist institution focused specifically on blacks."

Not all modern white slaves have been enslaved by other whites, however. It was common among some Caucasian peoples, such as the Russians, to voluntarily sell themselves into slavery during periods of economic duress.[630]

As the earliest recorded slave societies were built on the white ownership of white slaves (for example, ancient Mesopotamia, Babylon, Assyria, India, Phoenicia, Greece, Rome, and Judea),[631] and as Africans were practicing slavery on one another thousands of years before the arrival of Arab, Portuguese[632] (who were assisted by the Venetians, Genoese, Catalans, Flemings, and Florentines),[633] Spanish, French, Dutch, Danish, Swedish, English,[634] and finally, Yankee slave traders,[635] it is obvious that the institution of slavery itself is not by definition a white and black racial issue. Indeed, throughout the Western world every race, color, and nationality has been enslaved at one time or another, many to as late as 1450 and beyond, even into the present.[636]

And it is certainly not accurate to refer to slavery as the "South's peculiar institution," for slavery was neither Southern in origin or peculiar. Rather, as we have seen, it was a worldwide custom,[637] a "fact of life,"[638] literally a basic, most would say essential, building block in the foundation of all known human societies.[639] In short, slavery was once a universal "normal condition" around the globe.[640]

The institution is so inherent to human society that many anthropologists consider slavery a sign of civilization rather than a sign of primitiveness,[641] for during our species' hunting-gathering period enemies were simply killed rather than captured and put into bondage.[642] (Being nomadic, prehistoric peoples had no use for slaves. Instead, captive men were sacrificed to Pagan gods and goddesses or slaughtered outright, while captive women and children were absorbed into the group.)[643] Thus, for instance, 6th-Century prisoners taken by the English in warfare welcomed slavery, since it saved them from torture and ultimately death.[644]

Not surprisingly then, *throughout world history white slavery has been even more common than black slavery*. Ancient Germans,[645] ancient Celts (who enslaved cowardly soldiers),[646] and Druids on the Welsh island of Anglesey,[647] as just three more examples, were engaged in white slavery long before the start of the American-African slave trade.[648] Tacitus reports that early German slaveholders seldom struck their beleaguered white chattel. Instead, they "often" simply killed them; not as a result of discipline, but due to the "impulse of passion."[649] During the time of Constantine the Great, the East European Dacians enslaved Sarmatians (Iraqis living in what is now southern Russia) and the Sarmatians in turn enslaved the Limigantes (from what is now Hungary),[650] all Caucasians.

Queen Maeve, of Irish legend, oversaw an aggressive often warlike people whose entire society was built around white slavery. Black servants in the American South lived a life of ease, security, plenty, and comfort by comparison. A white slave under a Celtic master could expect few if any rights, and was savagely worked under harsh conditions. Treated the same as criminals, beggars, and prisoners, Celtic slaves could not own land, were forbidden personal possessions, and were often put to the fire as a form of punishment, or merely humiliation. The Celtic hero-god Crimthann was said to own two dogs that were worth 100 white female slaves. In Celtic myth even fairies have slaves. The very unit of value in early Celtic Ireland was the *cumal*, which meant "the price of a woman slave."

In early Ireland, where the white slave trade flourished for centuries, the aggressive, warring Iron Age Celtic people based their entire society on white slavery. When Saint Patrick—himself a former white slave of both the Irish and the Scots[651]—returned to the Emerald Isle in the 5th Century as a freeman, he referred to the institution as a "horrible and unspeakable crime," then wept with dismay when he discovered that his Irish female converts had been abducted and enslaved by the British chieftain King Coroticus.[652] Celtic white slaves, who were treated the same as beggars and were prohibited from owning anything,[653] where marked by mutilation, or sometimes less severely, by having their heads shaved.[654] According to Celtic mythology, even fairies enslave both their own kind and mortal humans.[655]

Russia engaged in white slavery up until quite recently,[656] and as late as the 1950s Caucasian slavery was still openly practiced in Turkey.[657]

WHAT YOU WERE TAUGHT: The captivity and subjugation of whites in Africa, particularly in the Barbary States, has been overemphasized. The phenomenon was rare and lasted only a few years, very few whites were ever enslaved, suspiciously no names of the enslaved were ever recorded, and as native Africans are a kind and meek people, their so-called "white slaves" would have been treated graciously and respectfully by their black masters. White slavery in the Barbary States certainly has no connection to American black slavery.
THE TRUTH: Wrong on all counts. In a 1908 travel guide, writer Burton Holmes noted:

> A hundred years ago a visit to the Barbary Coast was an experience not to be desired by voyagers from Christian lands, who then came not as tourists with cameras and guidebooks but as *prisoners or slaves in manacles and chains*.[658]

The primary period of the enslavement of whites by African peoples lasted some 300 years, roughly from the 16th Century to the 19th Century. Second, it has been conservatively estimated that between the years 1500 and 1800, 1 million to 1.5 million whites—from both Europe and America[659]—were enslaved by the Barbary States,[660] with an average of 5,000 white slaves entering the region each year. At about 14 new whites being imported a day, it was a commonplace occurrence. The city of Algiers, the capital of the African city of Algeria, alone possessed some 25,000 to 50,000 European bondsmen and women.[661] Over the centuries countless tens of thousands of additional whites were killed during the process of enslavement.[662]

White slavery in the Barbary States—now the area of North Africa comprising Morocco, Libya, Tunisia, and Algeria—arose long before black slavery in the United States, and aided in opening up the subsequent transatlantic slave trade between Africa, Europe, and America. These six newly kidnaped white British slaves are being driven along under the unyielding whip of a Berber slave merchant. Though this illustration portrays the African Arab slaver as a Caucasian, white Christian slaves from both Europe and America were abducted, sold, purchased, and owned by thousands of wealthy black Africans throughout the region as well. Unlike in the American South, white Barbary slave families were routinely split up and individual white slaves were daily subjected to the most horrific forms of abuse and even torture, including whipping, branding, starvation, exposure, and beheading.

There were so many white slaves serving on the Dark Continent that an abolition society called the "Knights Liberators of the White Slaves in Africa" was formed to rescue and emancipate them.[663] Indeed, several full scale U.S. military campaigns eventually broke out in an effort to put a stop to the merciless enslavement of white Christians in Africa: the Tripolitan War (or First Barbary War, 1801-1805) under President Thomas Jefferson,[664] and the Algerian War (or Second Barbary War, 1815) under President James Madison.[665] Shortly thereafter, in 1816, the British, led by Lord Exmouth (Edward Pellew), conducted their own assault on African white slavery in the conflict known as the "Battle of Algiers."[666]

A typical business day in Medieval Algiers began with the posting of the current white slave prices in the marketplace. This was accompanied by the usual cry of the white, brown, and black slave merchants: "Christian dogs are very cheap today!"[667] Then, upon the arrival of a Corsair slaving fleet at port,

> *Arab chiefs, with faces of dark bronze, or negroes, raised to wealth and influence by their courage or their villainy, would assemble to make bids for the human merchandise . . . Records tell of hundreds of [white] gentlemen,—doctors, lawyers, or scholars, of France or Spain or England who were knocked down to the highest bidder; their [white] wives, refined and delicate women, were torn from them and sold to brutal masters; [white] children were separated from their parents and educated in the religion of these robber lords.* One captive out of every eight was allotted to the dey, a ruler who invariably owed his position to the soldiery, and who almost invariably was doomed to perish by poison or the bowstring when some other leader should arise to win the support and favor of the fickle Janizaries, the veritable rulers of the land. . . . The pirates at one time grew so bold that they threatened to go to Great Britain and drag men out of their beds. Nor was this an idle threat. In 1631 they sacked the town of Baltimore in County Cork [Ireland] and carried off more than two hundred Irishmen. Ten years later, sixty men were taken from the shores of England near Penzance. The fishermen of Plymouth, Exeter, and Dartmouth for a long time after dared not put to sea. It is even stated that the Algerine fleet on one occasion ravaged the shores of Iceland in the Arctic Sea.[668]

At this African slave market in the souk (commercial quarter) of the Tunisian capital city of Tunis, untold thousands of white Europeans were separated from their families and sold into slavery, many who disappeared without a trace.

One of the many "Christian dogs" who was captured then later sold on the auction block at Algiers, was famed Spanish novelist and playwright Miguel de Cervantes, the author of *Don Quixote*. He served for five years in the house of a brutal Muslim master, only surviving to write his masterpiece by a daring escape. Of the African viceroy who ruled Algiers at the time, Cervantes wrote:

> Every day he hanged a [white] slave, impaled one, cut off the ears of another, and this upon so little animus or so entirely without cause that the Turks would own that he did it for the sake of doing it and because it was his nature.[669]

Barbary pirates in Northern Africa marching a captured white family (sitting forlornly on the right) to market. All three—the father, mother, and daughter—will most likely perish during their enslavement due to general maltreatment and excruciation, or they may simply be killed outright. The females will probably be forced into the sex slave trade, while the male will die a nameless common laborer.

Concerning the names of African white slaves, thousands were indeed recorded, those that follow being merely a small sample. In 1848 Englishman Edward Marsh collected notes from the meetings of the Religious Society of Friends, or Quakers, concerning the enslavement of fellow Quakers in Africa. Among the material was the following list of white men whose freedom the group had purchased in 1702. One of these individuals had been a white African slave for 26 years:

> An account of the captives which were lately redeemed at the cost of Friends:—*John King*, aged about 50 years, captive 18 years 5

months, convinced of the truth about 15 years, has a wife and four children living at Poole, in Dorsetshire, a seaman. *Thomas Walkenden*, born in London, aged about 50 years, captive 19 years 6 months, convinced 12 years back, no family, a seafaring man. *Richard Robinson*, born at Market-Harborough, Leicestershire, aged 33 years, captive 4 years, convinced 14 months, a single man, by trade a leather-dresser. *Robert Finley*, born at Erwin in Scotland, aged 43 years, captive 19 years, convinced 16 years, single man, a seafaring man. *James Burgin*, born in Kinton parish, near Exeter, Devonshire, aged 50 years, and captive 26 years 3 months, convinced 18 years 6 months, single, a seafaring man. *Joseph Bigland*, born at Lynn, Norfolk, aged about 50 years, captive 19 years 6 months, broke his leg on board the ship coming over, and at present in the Queen's Hospital at Plymouth for a cure.[670]

The start of the Barbary Wars in 1801, a full scale battle to free thousands of white Americans and Europeans held in the brutal African slave system.

Of the reality of the "phenomenon" of white slavery in Africa, Marsh wrote:

> The power of the Barbary states was at its height about 300 years ago [that is, in the 1500s]. Their corsairs became the scourge of Christendom, while *their much-dreaded system of slavery* assumed a front of new terrors. *Their ravages were not confined to the Mediterranean: they penetrated the ocean, and pressed even to the Straits of Dover and the Irish Channel*. From the chalky cliffs of England, and

> even from the distant western coasts of Ireland, the inhabitants were swept into cruel captivity. Several attempts were made, either to abate or remove this terrible nuisance by England, France, and Holland; but without complete success, until *the year 1816*. At that period, by negotiation in the first place, and subsequently by the terrible bombardment of Algiers by Lord Exmouth, upwards of *3000 Christian slaves were liberated from captivity*.[671]

One of many sea battles during the Barbary Wars. The fight to end white slavery in Africa lasted nearly two decades and cost the lives of scores of valiant American and European troops.

As for the treatment of Africa's white slaves, several items from Marsh's Quaker material are illuminating: letters from white Quaker slaves serving in Africa in the 1600s and 1700s. All were said to live "under the great severities of labour and undeserved stripes [whipping] that captives often endure . . . deep afflictions that they have suffered in that dark place of captivity in Algiers"[672]:

> 1685.—A letter from James Ellis, a young man, captive at Sallee, read, giving account that *they are in great misery: they work hard all the day, at night are chained, and beat most sadly*.
>
> 1685.—A letter from J. Ellis, read, that he is *put to hard labour and sore blows: they will not allow them clothes, scarce any bread*: they will deliver safe to them what is sent to the captives, nor take any thing from them; his redemption, he thinks, will be about 1000 dollars. *There are about 400 men, women, and children of English, and 1000 of other nations, all captives*.
>
> 1690.—There yet remain some English Friends captives at

Mequinez and three at Murbay, who have received the Truth there, it being three or four days journey distant, who correspond with each other by letters. One Friend (to wit Joseph Wasey) being lately redeemed [purchased and released] and newly come over, gave a large account to this meeting of *their miserable hard usage in captivity; having no lodging but under arches, in deep places on the cold ground, winter and summer, only water for their drink, and no bread allowed them by the king, but of old, rotten, stinking barley; and no clothes but a frock once in two years; and forced to hard labour (except three days in the year) and more especially on the Sixth-day of the week (which is their day of worship) they are compelled to carry heavy burdens on their heads, running from sun-rising to sun-setting, with brutish black boys following with whips and stripes at their pleasure. Many of the other captives perish and die, through their extreme hardships and want of food to sustain them, as in all likelihood, Friends there had, if Friends and their relations here had not sent them some relief: seven-pence a month, formerly allowed them by the king, being now taken from them. Their sufferings are lamentable*; yet, the Lord's power has wonderfully preserved them, and greatly restrained *the fury and cruelty of the [African] Emperor towards poor Friends there*; in whose behalf the said Joseph Wasey, did, by an interpreter, speak to the said Emperor; giving him an account of their innocent conversation and religion, which he heard with moderation, though *he often kills men in cold blood at his pleasure.* Joseph Wasey, also, signified that Friends' day time being taken up with *hard servitude*, they are necessitated to keep their meetings in the night season to wait upon God. And that the aforesaid captive Friends were very thankful for the relief [food and clothing] sent from hence, which was very refreshing to them.

1691.—An epistle to George Fox and George Whitehead from the Friends in slavery was read, stating *their having but three days in the year allowed them for rest*, and that they meet on nights to wait upon God. . . . Joseph Wasey, a late captive in Sallee, was here, and gave an account how the Lord's power was with Friends, notwithstanding *their great hardships and cruel usage . . . Their labour is, on every Sixth-day of the week, (which is the Moors' day of worship), to carry from sunrise to sunset baskets of earth on their heads, or other hard labour, and not suffered to sit down all the time, nor to ease themselves, without danger of stripes [whipping]; no clothes, but a frock once in about two years; no lodging but the ground, winter and summer; no drink but water; nor bread, but of perished barley; sometimes not suffered to sit down to eat that bread made of decayed corn which the cattle will not eat. The captives had [been] formerly allowed by the government seven s. [santimat?] per month each, but that allowance is now taken from them.*

1693.—A letter from James Ellis to his father, Josiah Ellis, dated Mequinez, in South Barbary, 2nd of Second Month, 1693, read, stating that *the condition of the captives was still very miserable . . . and that their taskmasters . . . have lately killed an Englishman . . . who had his head cut off by the tyrant's own hand with a sword.*

1693.—Joseph Bealing writes, that *there may be about two hundred and sixty captives of the English nation, and that all the [African slave] cruisers, except one, that belong to Sallee, are now at sea for the bringing in of more [white slaves], etc.* Accounts received of John Bealing's death, after seven days' illness, *having been a captive [slave] ten years.*[673]

On August 27, 1816, English naval commander Lord Exmouth (Edward Pellew) led Britain's effort to abolish white slavery in Africa, when his fleet attacked the Algerian capital at Algiers. After a thorough bombardment of the harbor, Exmouth subdued the Algerian fighters and some 3,000 white slaves were eventually freed.

In 1816 the following description of "the wretched condition" of some of the white slaves in Western Africa was given before Britain's House of Commons:

> *In one case, out of three hundred prisoners, fifty had died of ill-treatment on the first day of their arrival, and seventy during the first fortnight. The rest were kept in the most miserable condition, being allowed only a pound of bread a day, and subject to the lash from morning to night. No age, no sex was spared.* A Neapolitan lady of distinction, carried off with eight children, six of whom survived, had lately been seen by a British officer in *the thirteenth year of her captivity.*[674]

A bloody skirmish during the Barbary Wars known as "the fight of the gunboats."

Finally, let us address the pro-North teaching that white slavery in the Barbary States had no relationship to black slavery in the United States. This is false, and for this reason: white slavery on the Barbary Coast took root in the early 1500s, over 100 years before the rise of American black slavery, which began in Massachusetts in 1638.[675] As such, the former helped open the door to the latter, just as white slavery in early America herself paved the way for black slavery.[676]

WHAT YOU WERE TAUGHT: Just as racism is slowly disappearing from the world, slavery is also disappearing and will one day be completely extinct.

THE TRUTH: Since, as we have amply shown, race and slavery are not connected, this statement is nonsensical. More to the point, neither racism or slavery show any signs of declining, and never have. In fact, as both are inherited ancient survival mechanisms (the former an aspect of xenophobia, the latter an aspect of socioeconomics), we should not be surprised to learn that there is every indication that both are on the rise, concomitant with today's explosive growth in population worldwide.

In 1803 American ship Captain William Bainbridge fought bravely in the First Barbary War, but was captured and enslaved by his African adversaries for nearly two years.

In the case of slavery specifically, it continues to thrive and is universal in scope: according to Britain's Anti-Slavery Society, the institution is still found all over the world, even in the U.S., though it continues to flourish most consistently in Africa, the Middle East, the Far East, and parts of South America.[677]

Not only this, but studies reveal that the rate of slavery is actually increasing not decreasing, for *there are now more slaves in the world than at any other time in human history*:[678] in 1933, 5 million slaves were estimated to exist around the globe.[679] Yet, at the time of this writing, 2014, at least 30 million people are currently living under authentic slavery,[680] while an additional 200 million people worldwide are

In the 21st Century Africans continue to enslave one another in astonishing numbers. The black African master of these slaves is using them as porters to carry supplies from one village to another. As this photo shows, African slavers spare no one, not even children.

suffering under one type of bondage or another.[681] (Let us contrast these figures with the Old South, which never possessed more than 3.5 million servants,[682] 86 percent of these, in 1860, which were American born.)[683]

As for the U.S., according to a pre-2000 CIA study, 50,000 people (mostly women and children) were enslaved in the U.S.[684] At the time of this survey, this number was expected to rise—and indeed it has. As of 2013 there were 60,000 slaves in the U.S.[685] Both these slaves and their enslavers come in every race and color, more proof that slavery—whether modern, Victorian, Medieval, ancient, or prehistoric—is not, and never has been, based on skin color.

The celebrated European writer Miguel de Cervantes, author of *Don Quixote*, one of the better known of Africa's 1.5 million white slaves. Cervantes was sold at a slave auction in Algiers in 1575, then served for five years under a vile African master before he was able to escape to freedom.

While the American Southern slave owner purchased his slaves according to their age, health, and gender, the always persnickety, miserly, materialistic Yankee slave owner bought his by the pound. Here, at the slave port in Providence, Rhode Island, a Yankee slaver (far left) watches as dockside weighmasters apply various masses to the weighing pan of a large balance scale, in order to determine the exact weight of a newly arrived African female slave.

4

THE AMERICAN SLAVE TRADE

WHAT YOU WERE TAUGHT: The American slave trade got its start in the South. Thus, Southerners were "America's slave traders" and Dixie is the region responsible for bringing the first slaves to North American soil.

THE TRUTH: The only slave ships to ever sail from the U.S. left from Northern ports, all were commanded by Northern captains and funded by Northern businessmen, and all operated under the auspices of the U.S. flag.[686]

The South, on the other hand, did not own slave ships and never traded in foreign slaves.[687] Her slavery was strictly domestic. This is one of the reasons she banned the foreign slave trade in the Confederacy's new Constitution, penned by the Confederate Founding Fathers in 1861.[688] Thus, while no slave ship ever flew under the Confederate Flag, it is this very flag that is today universally viewed as a "symbol of slavery"!

Yankee slave ships "generally sailed from place to place peddling their slaves, with notice in advance when practicable."[689] In the mid 1790s, when French nobleman Duke de la Rochefoucauld Liancourt paid a visit to Georgia, he made these observations:

> The law of the land permits the importation of negroes, and this is the only state, the ports of which are not yet shut up against this

> odious trade. They are not, however, imported in great numbers in Savannah; in the course of last year arrived about six or seven hundred; during the first four months of this year four hundred and fifty have been landed, and two or three thousand more are expected. *Savannah employs no ship in the slave-trade; but it is carried on in ships belonging to New England, and especially to Rhode-Island. The cargo, however, is constantly carried to Savannah . . .*[690]

Yankee slave ships came in a vast assemblage of varieties and sizes. This Yankee clipper from Newport, Rhode Island—where 70 percent of all American slave voyages began—was refitted to serve as a slave ship in New England's lucrative 250 year old Cotton Triangle.

In the early 1830s Northerner Joseph Holt Ingraham visited New Orleans, where he made note of the arrival of *Yankee boats* stocked with goods from Pittsburgh and Cincinnati, "crowded, not infrequently, with slaves for the Southern market."[691] In her 1891 memoirs, Elizabeth Buffum Chace of Rhode Island recalled the following experience:

> My grandmother, Sarah Gould, was born near the year 1737, and her father, James Coggeshall, soon after her birth, purchased a little African girl, from a [Yankee] slave-ship just come into port [at Newport, Rhode Island], to serve as nurse-maid to the child. She remained a slave in the household, until the Friends [Quakers] abolished slavery among themselves in 1780. . . .[692]

With these facts in hand we must then ask ourselves: is it the flag of the U.S.A. or the flag of the C.S.A. that deserves to be called

"America's true slavery flag"? And is it the U.S. capital city (Washington, D.C.) or the C.S. capital city (Richmond, Virginia) that deserves the title of "America's true slavery capital"?[693]

American slave ships sailed under the United States flag, never the Confederate States flag. This 15-star U.S. flag would have been a familiar sight to Yankee slavers operating out of the Northeast in the year 1791.

The answers to these two questions were obvious and well-known until recently, when the pro-North movement took over our educational system and news media, then buried the Truth beneath a mountain of fabricated anti-South propaganda. In 1906, for example, Georgia State Representative William Henry Fleming gave an address before the Alumni of the University of Georgia that included this statement:

> If Charleston, South Carolina, was one of the chief ports of destination for slave-trading vessels, Salem, Massachusetts, was one of the chief ports from whence these vessels sailed.[694]

In his 1910 book *The White Man's Burden,* pastor, editor, and author Benjamin F. Riley writes:

> While the middle of the nineteenth century found the Negroes massed, for the most part, in the states of the South, from Maryland to Texas and Arkansas and Missouri, *they had traveled all the way across the continent from New England. If Southern planters bought the slaves, Northern traders, in the earlier years, sold and supplied them.*[695]

Charleston, South Carolina, the port of entry for thousands of African slaves—all brought from Africa and the West Indies by Yankee ships, commanded by Yankee captains, manned by Yankee crews, funded by Yankee bankers, and sold by Yankee merchants.

Northern politicians were well aware that they could not fool the public about the origins of slavery simply by deflecting the entire issue onto the South. One of these was U.S. Representative Jonathan Ogden Mosely of Connecticut. When, in the late 1700s, the idea of executing slave ship owners by hanging came up before a congressional committee on abolition, the Yankee politician remarked:

> We have been repeatedly told, and told with an air of triumph, by gentlemen from the South, that their citizens have no concern in this infamous traffic; that *people from the North are the importers of negroes, and thereby the seducers of Southern citizens to buy them*. We have a right to presume, then, that the citizens of the South will entertain no particular partiality for these wicked traffickers, but will be ready to subject them to the most exemplary punishment. So far as the people of Connecticut are concerned, I am sure that, should any citizen of the North be convicted under this law, so far from thinking it cruel in their Southern brethren to hang them, such a punishment of such culprits would be acknowledged with gratitude as a favor.[696]

Now we can better understand the words of U.S. Senator Jefferson Davis, soon to become the Southern Confederacy's first and—so far—only president, who, in 1848, rightly chastised his Northern brethren on the Senate floor for their abolitionist hypocrisy:

> You were the men who imported these negroes into this country; you enjoyed the benefits resulting from their carriage and sale; and you reaped the largest profit accruing from the introduction of slaves.[697]

Colonial Yankee slave ships flew one of these—or a variation of one of these—early U.S. naval flags from the late 1700s.

This is why, even after slavery had been pushed South by the Yankee,[698] it still mainly served financial interests in the North, as is obvious from 19th-Century records: during the 1850s alone, at least "25,000 slaves were annually sold South from the Northern slave states."[699] These figures do not include the most northern states, where the slave trade was still very active. In 1920 William E. Dodd wrote:

> While agricultural production was concentrated in the comparatively small [Southern] area where cotton could be grown and the returns all seemed to be going to the planters, *the evidence is conclusive that far the greater part of the proceeds was left in the hands of those who supplied the South with its necessaries and its luxuries*. The earnings of the slave plantations were thus consumed by [Northern sponsored] tariffs, freights, commissions, and profits which the Southerners had to pay. Southern towns were only marts of trade, not depositories of the crops of surrounding or distant areas. Thus while the [Southern] planters monopolized the cotton industry, drew to themselves the surplus of slaves, and apparently increased their wealth enormously, *they were really but custodians of these returns, administrators of the wealth of Northern men who really ultimately received the profits of Southern plantations and Southern slavery*.[700]

Hundreds of Yankee slave ships sailed out of New England harbors each year, bound for the Dark Continent. Hundreds more from New York, Pennsylvania, and Maryland annually plied the waters of the transatlantic slave trade. *All* of America's original African slaves arrived on one of these vessels, as Northern ship manifests from the period testify.

Clearly, as will become more evident in subsequent chapters, when it came to American slavery the North was the equivalent of a shrewd and aggressive drug dealer, the South a hapless and reluctant drug addict.

In 1860 alone it has been estimated that 85 vessels—all which had been fitted out in and which had sailed from New York City—brought as many as 60,000 African slaves into the U.S.[701] That same year the overwhelming extent of the nationwide power of the domineering Yankee industrialist and his numerous slaving seaports was described by Southerner Hinton R. Helper:

> It is a fact well known to every intelligent Southerner that we are compelled to go to the North for almost every article of utility and adornment, from matches, shoe-pegs and paintings up to cotton-mills, steamships and statuary; that *we have no foreign trade*, no princely merchants, nor respectable artists; that, in comparison with the free [Northern] states, we contribute nothing to the literature, polite arts and inventions of the age; that, for want of profitable employment at home, large numbers of our native population find themselves necessitated to emigrate to the West, whilst the free [Northern] states retain not only the larger proportion of those born within their own limits, but induce, annually, hundreds of thousands of foreigners to settle and remain amongst them; that almost everything produced at the North meets with ready sale, while, at the same time, there is no demand, even

among our own citizens, for the productions of Southern industry; that, owing to the absence of a proper system of business amongst us, *the North becomes, in one way or another, the proprietor and dispenser of all our floating wealth, and that we are dependent on Northern capitalists for the means necessary to build our railroads, canals and other public improvements*; that if we want to visit a foreign country, even though it may lie directly south of us, we find no convenient way of getting there except by taking passage through a Northern port; and that nearly all the profits arising from the exchange of commodities, from insurance and shipping offices, and from the thousand and one industrial pursuits of the country, accrue to the North, and are there invested in the erection of those magnificent cities and stupendous works of art which dazzle the eyes of the South, and attest the superiority of free [Northern] institutions!

The North is the Mecca of our merchants, and to it they must and do make two pilgrimages per annum—one in the spring and one in the fall. All our commercial, mechanical, manufactural, and literary supplies come from there. We want Bibles, brooms, buckets and books, and we go to the North; we want pens, ink, paper, wafers and envelopes, and we go to the North; we want shoes, hats, handkerchiefs, umbrellas and pocket knives, and we go to the North; we want furniture, crockery, glassware and pianos, and we go to the North; we want toys, primers, school-books, fashionable apparel, machinery, medicines, tomb-stones, and a thousand other things, and we go to the North for them all. Instead of keeping our money in circulation at home, by patronizing our own mechanics, manufacturers, and laborers, we send it all away to the North, and there it remains; it never falls into our hands again.

In one way or another we are more or less subservient to the North every day of our lives. In infancy we are swaddled in Northern muslin; in childhood we are humored with Northern gewgaws; in youth we are instructed out of Northern books; at the age of maturity we sow our "wild oats" on Northern soil; in middle-life we exhaust our wealth, energies and talents in the dishonorable vocation of entailing our dependence on our children and on our children's children, and, to the neglect of our own interests and the interests of those around us, in giving aid and succor to every department of Northern power; in the decline of life we remedy our eye-sight with Northern spectacles, and support our infirmities with Northern canes; in old age we are drugged with Northern physic; and, finally, when we die, our inanimate bodies, shrouded in Northern cambric, are stretched upon the bier, borne to the grave in a Northern carriage, entombed with a Northern spade, and memorized with a Northern slab![702]

As proof that the North was the only region of the country to engage in the African slave trade, consider the following: the only American ever tried, convicted, and executed for slaving was a Northerner: Captain Nathaniel Gordon of New York was put to death for the crime on February 21, 1862, by Lincoln's personal order,[703] as his February 4, 1862, letter reveals:

> Respite For Nathaniel Gordon.
> Abraham Lincoln, President Of The United States Of America, To all to whom these presents shall come, greeting:
>
> Whereas it appears that at a term of the Circuit Court of the United States of America for the southern district of New York, held in the month of November, A. D. 1861, Nathaniel Gordon was indicted and convicted for being engaged in the slave-trade, and was by the said court sentenced to be put to death by hanging by the neck on Friday the 7th day of February, A. D. 1862;
>
> And whereas a large number of respectable citizens have earnestly besought me to commute the said sentence of the said Nathaniel Gordon to a term of imprisonment for life, which application I have felt it to be my duty to refuse;
>
> And whereas it has seemed to me probable that the unsuccessful application made for the commutation of his sentence may have prevented the said Nathaniel Gordon from making the necessary preparation for the awful change which awaits him:
>
> Now, therefore, be it known that I, Abraham Lincoln, President of the United States of America, have granted and do hereby grant unto him, the said Nathaniel Gordon, a respite of the above-recited sentence until Friday, the 21st day of February, A. D. 1862, between the hours of twelve o'clock at noon and three o'clock in the afternoon of the said day, when the said sentence shall be executed.
>
> In granting this respite it becomes my painful duty to admonish the prisoner that, relinquishing all expectation of pardon by human authority, he refer himself alone to the mercy of the common God and Father of all men.
>
> In testimony whereof I have hereunto signed my name and caused the seal of the United States to be affixed.[704]

Furthermore, the last American slave ship to be captured by the U.S. government was a Northern one: the *Nightingale*, also from New York, confiscated on April 21, 1861. The ship, known fondly to Northerners as the "Prince of Slavers," was built in Maine, fitted out in

New Hampshire, sailed from Massachusetts, and had a New York captain. At the time of her seizure, this vessel, from the so-called "abolitionist North," had nearly 1,000 manacled Africans on board.[705] She was doing "business as usual" up until the first few weeks of the Civil War,[706] all the while proudly flying the U.S. flag from her mast.[707]

The notorious U.S. slave ship *Nightingale* had a purely Northern provenance. Constructed in Maine and outfitted in New Hampshire, she sailed from Massachusetts under the command of a New York captain. With some 1,000 African slaves in her hull, in 1861 she became famous for being the last slave ship to be seized by the U.S. government. Note the large U.S. flag flying from her stern.

Phillips gave this description of the average Yankee slave vessel:

> *The typical New England ship for the slave trade* was a sloop, schooner or barkentine of about fifty tons burthen, which when engaged in ordinary freighting would have but a single deck. *For a slaving voyage* a second flooring was laid some three feet below the regular deck, the space between forming the slave quarters. Such a vessel was handled by a captain, two mates, and from three to six men and boys. It is curious that a vessel of this type, with capacity in the hold for from 100 to 120 hogsheads of rum was reckoned by the *Rhode Islanders* to be "full bigg for dispatch," while among the Liverpool slave traders such a ship when offered for sale could not find a purchaser. The reason seems to have been that dry-goods and sundries required much more cargo space for the same value than did rum.[708]

Despite the fact that slave trading was far more inhumane than slaveholding,[709] vast fortunes were to be made from the barbaric business; which is precisely why Northern slave dealers, Northern bankers, Northern manufacturers, Northern shipbuilders, Northern shipowners, Northern seamen, and Northern merchants kept the slave trade going long after it had been banned in 1808 by then U.S. president and Southerner Thomas Jefferson.[710]

More evidence of the North's massive participation in the slave trade comes from the Quintuple Treaty, signed by England, France, Austria, Russia, and Prussia in 1841. Its purpose was to join some of the great world powers together in an effort to shut down the transatlantic slave trade. The treaty bestowed on these five nations the right to board any seagoing vessels that were "suspected of being engaged in the traffic of slaves," and confiscate both the ship and its cargo.

Thousands of wealthy and influential Yankees helped keep Northern slavery alive. One of these was Michigan politician Lewis Cass, who campaigned to keep the Northern slave trade open and unimpeded by countries like Britain.

One name is noticeably absent from the Quintuple Treaty list: the United States of America. If it too had signed, the document would have been called the Sextuple Treaty. The question is, why did the U.S. not append its signature to this all important edict? It was because of its deep and long-term involvement in slavery, the Cotton Triangle, and the African-European-American slave trade.

One of the United States' most vociferous opponents of the Quintuple Treaty was Northern politician and, at the time, American Minister in Paris, Lewis Cass of Michigan. Criticizing the ruling of conferring "the right to violate the American flag" as an outright "attack upon U.S. independence," Cass and his fellow Yankee constituents continued to support the North's slave-holding interests, protested any prohibitions against the American slave trade, and pushed to have the trade reopened where it had been closed.[711] (Seventeen years later Cass was still protesting the law that allowed British officers to search U.S. ships for evidence of slave trading.)[712]

Massachusetts statesman Daniel Webster used the anti-slave trade agreement known as the Webster-Ashburton Treaty to surreptitiously uphold Yankee slave interests.

The following year, on August 9, 1842, U.S. Secretary of State Daniel Webster and British diplomat Lord Ashburton signed the Webster-Ashburton Treaty, which, among other things, was meant to address the ongoing problem of the American slave trade. Once again the U.S. had the opportunity to shut it down. Instead, even though it had banned the slave trade 34 years earlier (in 1808), Webster refused to allow Britain to inspect Yankee slave ships—which were still audaciously plying their human wares across the Atlantic and up and down the east coast of the United States.[713]

Webster did agree to send American warships to the west coast of Africa to search for Yankee slave vessels sailing under the U.S. flag. But the promise was all a ruse. A Yankee slave ship from New York called the *Martha*, for example, was captured off the coast of Africa on June 6, 1850. The captain and crew were condemned to the penitentiary and the ship was seized. Though the boat was empty when boarded, as he was being led away the captain admitted that had he not been caught, he would "during the night, have shipped 1,800 slaves, and before daylight in the morning been clear of the coast." Three months later another Yankee slave ship, the *Chatsworth* of Baltimore, Maryland, was seized for the same reason. Condemned in court as a slaver, it was said that the capture of the *Chatsworth*, "as far as the American flag was concerned, would give a severe and unexpected blow to the slave-trade."[714] These represented the mere tip of the iceberg, however. Most U.S. slave ships continued in the dastardly traffic without fear, *and* without capture.

Obviously the U.S. had no intention of closing down the Yankee slave trade—which was by then so commonplace and accepted on the high seas that any slave shipowner could hoist a U.S. flag up their flagstaff and be completely protected by law.[715] Subsequently this part of the treaty was not fully implemented until the Yankees were forced to by the start of Lincoln's War, as well as by the trade's final death knell in America, the Thirteenth Amendment.[716]

African-American historian Dr. William E. B. Du Bois of Massachusetts reprimanded the North over its hypocrisy in criticizing so-called "Southern slavery." Said Du Bois, the American slave trade "is growing more profitable every year, and if you should hang all the Yankee merchants engaged in it, hundreds would fill their places."

In 1896 the vociferous pro-slavery policies of the American Northeast and her Yankee slavers led African-American scholar and Yankee intellectual William E. B. Du Bois to declare what has always been patently obvious to informed Southerners:

The American slave-trade finally came to be carried on principally by United States capital, in United States ships, officered by United States citizens, and under the United State flag. Executive reports repeatedly acknowledged this fact. In 1839 "a careful revision of these laws" is recommended by the President [Martin Van Buren], in order that "the integrity and honor of our flag may be carefully preserved." In June, 1841, the President declares: "There is reason to believe that the traffic is on the increase," and advocates "vigorous efforts." His message in December of the same year acknowledges: "That the American flag is grossly abused by the abandoned and profligate of other nations is but too probable." The special message of 1845 explains at length that "it would seem" that a regular policy of evading the laws is carried on: American vessels with the knowledge of the owners are chartered by notorious slave dealers in Brazil, aided by English capitalists, with this intent. The message of 1849 "earnestly" invites the attention of Congress "to an amendment of our existing laws relating to the African slave-trade, with a view to the effectual suppression of that barbarous traffic. It is not to be denied," continues the message, "that this trade is still, in part, carried on by means of vessels built in the United States, and owned or navigated by some of our citizens." Governor [Thomas] Buchanan of Liberia reported in 1839: *"The chief obstacle to the success of the very active measures pursued by the British government for the suppression of the slave-trade on the coast, is the American flag.* Never was the proud banner of freedom so extensively used by those pirates upon liberty and humanity, as at this season." One well-known American slaver [that is, a ship] was boarded fifteen times and twice taken into port, but always escaped by means of her papers. *Even American officers report that the English are doing all they can, but that the American flag protects the trade.* The evidence which literally poured in from our consuls and ministers at Brazil adds to the story of the guilt of the United States. *It was proven that the participation of United States citizens in the trade was large and systematic.* One of the most notorious slave merchants of Brazil said: "I am worried by the Americans, who insist upon my hiring their vessels for slave-trade." Minister [George H.] Proffit stated, in 1844, that the *"slave-trade is almost entirely carried on under our flag, in American-built vessels."* So, too, in Cuba: the British commissioners affirm that *American citizens were openly engaged in the traffic; vessels arrived undisguised at Havana from the United States, and cleared for Africa as slavers after an alleged sale. The American consul, [Nicholas P.] Trist, was proven to have consciously or unconsciously aided this trade by the issuance of blank clearance papers.*

The presence of American capital in these enterprises, and the connivance of the authorities, were proven in many cases and known in scores. In 1837 the English government informed the United States that from the papers of a captured slaver it appeared that the notorious slave-trading firm, Blanco and Carballo of Havana, who owned the vessel, had correspondents in the United States: "at Baltimore, Messrs. Peter Harmony and Co., in New York, Robert Barry, Esq." The slaver *Martha* of New York, captured by the *Perry*, contained among her papery curious revelations of the guilt of persons in America who were little suspected. The [Portuguese] slaver *Prova*, which was allowed to lie in the harbor of Charleston, South Carolina, and refit, was afterwards captured with two hundred and twenty-five slaves on board. *The real reason that prevented many belligerent Congressmen from pressing certain search claims against England lay in the fact that the unjustifiable detentions had unfortunately revealed so much American guilt that it was deemed wiser to let the matter end in talk. For instance, in 1850 Congress demanded information as to illegal searches, and President [Millard] Fillmore's report showed the uncomfortable fact that, of the ten American ships wrongly detained by English men-of-war, nine were proven red-handed slavers.*

The consul at Havana reported, in 1836, that whole cargoes of slaves fresh from Africa were being daily shipped to Texas in American [Yankee] vessels, that 1,000 had been sent within a few months, that the rate was increasing, and that many of these slaves "can scarcely fail to find their way into the United States." Moreover, the consul acknowledged that ships frequently cleared for the United States in ballast, taking on a cargo at some secret point. When with these facts we consider the law facilitating "recovery" of slaves from Texas, the repeated refusals to regulate the Texan trade, and the shelving of a proposed congressional investigation into these matters, conjecture becomes a practical certainty. It was estimated in 1838 that 15,000 Africans were annually taken to Texas, and "there are even grounds for suspicion that there are other places . . . where slaves are introduced." Between 1847 and 1853 the slave smuggler *Drake* had a slave depot in the Gulf, where sometimes as many as 1,600 Negroes were on hand, and the owners were continually importing and shipping. "The joint-stock company," writes this smuggler, "was a very extensive one, and connected with leading American and Spanish mercantile houses. Our island was visited almost weekly, by [slave purchasing] agents from Cuba, *New York, Baltimore, Philadelphia, Boston,* and New Orleans. . . . The seasoned and instructed slaves were taken to Texas, or Florida, overland, and to Cuba, in sailing-boats. As no squad contained more than half a dozen, no difficulty was found in posting them to the United States, without discovery, and generally without suspicion. . . . The Bay Island plantation sent ventures weekly to the Florida Keys.

> Slaves were taken into the great American swamps, and there kept till wanted for the market. Hundreds were sold as captured runaways from the Florida wilderness. We had agents in every slave State; and *our coasters were built in Maine*, and came out with lumber. *I could tell curious stories . . . of this business of smuggling Bozal [that is, fresh or newly acquired] negroes into the United States. It is growing more profitable every year, and if you should hang all the Yankee merchants engaged in it, hundreds would fill their places.*" Inherent probability and concurrent testimony confirm the substantial truth of such confessions. For instance, one traveller discovers on a Southern plantation Negroes who can speak no English. The careful reports of the Quakers "apprehend that many [slaves] are also introduced into the United States." Governor [George B.] Mathew of the Bahama Islands reports that "in more than one instance, Bahama vessels with coloured crews have been purposely wrecked on the coast of Florida, and the crews forcibly sold." This was brought to the notice of the United States authorities, but the district attorney of Florida could furnish no information. Such was the state of the slave-trade in 1850, on the threshold of the critical decade which by a herculean effort was destined finally to suppress it.[717]

And the Yankee slave trade only increased in intensity from then on.

In 1858, when British warships in the West Indies began a systematic search of U.S. vessels suspected of carrying slaves, resistance by Northern merchantmen was so fierce that British officers were forced to fire on several boats that refused to display their colors.[718]

The cotton bales on the wharf of this harbor at Savannah, Georgia, may have been picked, ginned, and packed by Southern slaves, but the slaves themselves were originally enslaved by fellow Africans and brought to America by Yankee slave ships—as the U.S. flags on the mastheads of these boats attest.

Why did American slave ships sail from the North and not the South? The answer is simple. It was the so-called "Cradle of Liberty," the Puritan North,[719] and more specifically intolerant and dogmatic Puritan Massachusetts,[720] that was, from the very beginning, America's first slave trading region:[721] though it had already long been enslaving Native-Americans, to test the waters so to speak, in 1637 Boston, Massachusetts (the city was then only seven years old) had a group of African slaves shipped in from Providence Island, a fellow Puritan colony located off the coast of Central America.[722]

In the early 1600s, prior to purchasing and importing African slaves, white New Englanders regularly attacked and murdered Indians. The survivors were sold as slaves in Massachusetts and Connecticut.

That same year New Englanders fought the Pequot Indians in Connecticut. At least 900 Native-Americans were killed. The surviving males were shipped to the West Indies to be sold off as slaves, while the Indian women and children were retained, enslaved, and sold to white plantation owners and families throughout Massachusetts and Connecticut. This was the usual New England penalty (particularly in Massachusetts) for any and all Indians known or suspected to have shed colonial English blood.[723]

Finding an enormous Yankee hunger for "sable servants," the next year, 1638, Massachusetts instigated the American slave trade when Boston began importing African slaves commercially for the first time.

This occurred when Captain William Pierce brought New England's first remunerative shipload of Africans from the West Indies aboard the 120-ton Salem vessel *Desire*[724] (built at Marblehead, Massachusetts, in 1636).[725]

A few short years later, in 1641, Massachusetts gave birth to American slavery when it became the first colony to legitimatize and monetize the institution.[726] By 1676 Boston slavers were routinely coming home with shiploads of human cargo from East Africa and Madagascar.[727] By 1680 the colony itself possessed 120 black slaves.[728]

After the termination of England's Royal African Company in 1697, New England as a whole took an even more aggressive approach to the African slave trade.[729] By 1708 Boston alone had 400 black slaves,[730] and by 1775 Massachusetts had over 5,000 black slaves and 30,000 bondservants.[731]

Both the American slave trade and American slavery got their start in the North, not in the South, as our liberal slanted history books teach. More specifically, the former was launched in Massachusetts in 1638, the latter in Massachusetts in 1641. To this day New England is still known not only for the fine craftsmanship of her 17th- and 18th-Century ships, but for her industrious worldwide maritime trade, which included galleons laden with black human cargo from Africa's Gold Coast.

But even this was not enough to satiate New England's enormous "retail" demand for African slaves,[732] who were sold on nearly every corner, from taverns and stores to warehouses and slave merchants' homes.[733] Thus the trade carried on, increasing in strength and scope every year for decades thereafter.

So intertwined did the institution become with Massachusetts' state economy that when abolitionists tried to introduce a bill in 1771 to "prevent the importation of negro slaves into this province," Governor Thomas Hutchinson refused to approve it.[734] Even manumission was discouraged, in the case of Massachusetts, by requiring that the owner post a £50 bond in the event that the slave he freed became dependent on the state.[735] All in all, the people of Massachusetts

> took their slave-trading and their slaveholding as part of their day's work and as part of God's goodness to His elect. In practical effect *the policy of colonial Massachusetts toward the backward races* merits neither praise nor censure; *it was merely commonplace.*[736]

By 1639 Connecticut had slaves,[737] and in 1650 the institution was formally legalized through the adoption of a code of laws.[738] Though negligible at this time, by 1775 the state owned some 6,500 African bondsmen and women.[739] By 1645 New Hampshire had slaves as well. The largest slave concentrations in New England were in Rockingham County, New Hampshire; Essex, Suffolk, Bristol, and Plymouth Counties, Massachusetts; New London, Hartford, and Fairfield Counties, Connecticut; and Newport and Washington Counties, Rhode Island. Let us bear in mind that most of the Southern states had not even been formed yet.[740]

Not long after it legalized slavery in 1652,[741] there were so many slaves in Rhode Island's Narragansett region that they made up half the population. The slavers of Rhode Island and those of Massachusetts combined to make New England the leading slave trading center in America and slavery "the hub of New England's economy,"[742] a region where eventually even "parish ministers all over New England owned slaves."[743]

At one time Rhode Island's slave traders owned and operated nearly 90 percent of America's slave trade.[744] Though the state's slave ship captains often wrote home from the African coast complaining of the difficulties of trading with the native African slave merchants there,[745] nonetheless by their standards they managed to achieve spectacular monetary success: by 1756 slaves made up at least 16 percent of Newport's population,[746] and as late as 1770 Rhode Island alone possessed some 150 slave ships,[747] which between 1804 and 1807 brought 20,000 of the 40,000 Africans transported to South Carolina during that period.[748] (The other 20,000 were brought to the Palmetto State by English slave ships.)[749]

By 1749 Rhode Island had 3,077 blacks, by 1756 at least 4,697, and in 1774, 3,668.[750] "Of this last number Newport contained 1,246, South Kingstown 440, Providence 303, Portsmouth 122, and Bristol 114."[751] By 1775 almost 2 out of every 25 people (6 percent) of Rhode Island's entire population were black slaves,[752] many of them belonging to the white aristocratic planters of the famed fertile Narragansett farming region.[753]

Providence, Rhode Island, was once one of early America's most active slave ports. Affluent Rhode Islanders, who controlled a large percentage of the transatlantic slave trade, greatly profited from New England's "peculiar institution." Providence merchant and slave trader Nicolas Brown, Sr. cofounded the college that would later be named Brown University in his family's honor.

A full two-thirds of Rhode Island's fleets and sailors were devoted to the slave trade. Even the region's state governors participated in it, Yankee politicians such as Jonathan Belcher of Massachusetts and Joseph Wanton of Rhode Island. It was well-known that slavery was so integral to New England's economy that without it she would have collapsed into financial ruin.[754] She was able to achieve this not just by purchasing millions of already enslaved blacks from Africa's shores,[755] but also by categorizing anyone a slave who had "slave blood" on the maternal side of their family. This would have included, of course, many Yankees who were considered white not black.[756]

Many notable New England families owe their present-day wealth and celebrity to slavery.[757] Among them: the Cabots (ancestors

Dane Hall in 1832, part of Harvard Law School, built with money made from the Yankee slave trade.

of Massachusetts Senators Henry Cabot Lodge, Sr. and Henry Cabot Lodge, Jr.), the Belchers, the Waldos (ancestors of Ralph Waldo Emerson), the Faneuils (after whom Boston's Faneuil Hall is named), the Royalls, the Pepperells (after whom the town of Pepperell, Massachusetts, is named), the DeWolfs (at least 500,000 descendants of their slaves are alive today),[758] the Champlains (after whom Lake Champlain is named), the Ellerys, the Gardners (after whom Boston's Isabella Stewart Gardner Museum is named), the Malbones, the Robinsons, the Crowninshields (after whom Crowninshield Island, Massachusetts, is named), and the Browns (after whom Rhode Island's Brown University is named).[759]

The slave trading Royall family, which made millions from their slave plantations in Antigua, donated money and land to what would become the Harvard Law School. The educational center still uses a seal from the Royall family crest.[760] Slavery was so integral to New England's culture, society, and economy that even South-hating Harriet Beecher Stowe, the infamous author of *Uncle Tom's Cabin*, had to acknowledge that:

> The Northern slaveholder traded in men and women whom he never saw, and of whose separations, tears, and miseries he determined never to hear.[761]

At least one half of the land in Brookline, Massachusetts, was once in the possession of slave owners, while in the town of Concord, Massachusetts, 50 percent of its government seats were occupied by slave owners.[762] In this quaint New England borough, where slavery continued well into the 1830s (decades after the official "abolition" of slavery there), those blacks fortunate enough to be freed were then, unfortunately, exiled to the woods surrounding Walden Pond, where they struggled for survival in fetid squatter camps.[763]

It was also in Massachusetts that the now wholly disgraced and defunct field of "race science"—or "niggerology," as many Yankees referred to it—got its start, at Harvard University in Cambridge, to be exact. It was this very pseudoscience, one which claimed that "blacks are inferior subhumans," that for hundreds of years allowed white Northerners to rationalize the exploitation of people of African descent.[764]

Famous Faneuil Hall, Boston, Massachusetts, named after noted New England slave merchant Peter Faneuil, who donated profits from the Yankee slave trade to help construct the building in 1742.

Walden Pond, Concord, Massachusetts, where the town's freed blacks were once cruelly banished by its white citizens. At least 50 percent of Concord's politicians were slave owners, just one reason why slavery continued there well into the 1830s, years after official state abolition in 1780.

About the same time, the 1830s, the Boston Female Anti-Slavery Society was complaining of the many "obstacles" it continued to encounter around the Bay State. The women pledged to "overcome" resistance to abolition, not just from countless "mobs" and the "judicial courts" of Massachusetts, but also from the state's "ecclesiastical councils."[765]

During the American Revolutionary War, Massachusetts political leader and Continental Army General William Heath (after whom the town of Heath, Massachusetts, is named), complained about the blacks in his regiments. Though thousands had bravely joined to help fellow white colonists fight the British, Heath was unhappy at the mixing of the two races. Fellow officer General Philip Schuyler of New York, who had similar misgivings, did not like the fact that whites were putting their "trust" in black slaves to defend American liberty.[766] In 1819, as other Northern states were passing statutes condemning slavery, it is well-known that "the New England legislatures remained silent."[767]

Little wonder that when William Lloyd Garrison went to Boston in 1830 to scrounge up support for the launch of his upcoming antislavery newspaper, *The Liberator*, he was turned down by some of the city's most notable men, including William Ellery Channing, Daniel Webster, Jeremiah Evarts, and Jeremiah Mason. His plea was even rejected by Lyman Beecher, the town's most influential Christian leader and the father of the aforementioned abolitionist author Harriet Beecher

Stowe. Garrison should not have been surprised: not only were many of Massachusetts' schools and churches segregated, nearly every one of Boston's clergymen—like the leaders of every major protestant denomination in the U.S.[768]—was a member of the American Colonization Society, a Yankee-founded organization devoted to deporting all blacks out of the country.[769] (One of its future members and leaders would be the notorious white supremacist Abraham Lincoln, who was to become America's sixteenth president.)[770] Boston itself was once a major center of such black colonization efforts,[771] whose main mission was "to return Negroes to Africa."[772]

Former Northern slave Frederick Douglass found white racism was so severe in Massachusetts that he could not secure a job there.

In 1788 the state of Massachusetts forbade the emigration of free blacks from outside its boundaries,[773] and well into the early 1800s restrictive Black Codes across New England prohibited African-Americans from voting, testifying in court, intermarrying with whites,[774] or gaining access to jobs, housing, and education. Banned from most restaurants and hotels, New England blacks were also subject to segregation in restaurants, in theaters,[775] on public transportation, and in churches and hospitals.[776]

Of course, since all of the Northern colonies (states) possessed slaves[777]—both African and Indian[778]—all of them also passed similar laws, statutes that not only held down the black man and curtailed his rights, but which also reenforced the Yankees' white supremacist ideology. In New York blacks could not own property, in New Jersey they could not own land, and in Pennsylvania any free black who refused to work was automatically enslaved.[779] In the early 1800s, under pressure from abolitionists, Massachusetts, Rhode Island, Maine, New

Hampshire, and Vermont began to allow black males to vote, though even this right was often undermined by the white racism that was so endemic to New England.[780]

Freed male blacks traveling to the North after Lincoln's War hoping to find employment were out of luck: though most had numerous skills in a variety of trades, the "fierce racial discrimination" of the Yankee prevented him from securing a job.[781] Long before, in the late 1830s, the famous former Northern slave and black civil rights leader Frederick Douglass, now a freedman, could not get a job as a caulker in New Bedford, Massachusetts, because of the color of his skin. White Yankee caulkers refused to work alongside him.[782]

Boston, Massachusetts. The founder of both the American slave trade and American slavery, as well as the primary site where hundreds of slave ships were manufactured and launched, Beantown was the epicenter of the Yankee slave system for a century and a half—until this title was taken over by New York City in the mid 1700s.

This particular form of racial discrimination continued on into the early 1900s and beyond, as Riley noted in 1910:

> *In the North the Negro is denied membership in the labor-unions, and then in order to seal hermetically the situation against him, an employer is forbidden to engage the services of non-union labor. In other words, the Negro is precluded altogether.* Should the employer engage the services of Negroes, the members of the labor unions, rather than work beside the colored men, decline to labor at all. Besides these, it is a fact well known, that *even in some of the menial functions of industry, the Negro is denied employment, purely on account of color. This*

pertains to certain hotels, restaurants, barber shops, and to domestic service as hostlers, butlers, maids, janitors, sextons, and other similar functions.[783]

When Ray S. Baker traveled through the North in the early 1900s, he was astounded to see widespread, lingering white racism:

> [Generally speaking] I was surprised at the general attitude [regarding blacks] which I encountered [in the North]. *It was one of hesitation and withdrawal. . . . the people one ordinarily meets [here] don't know anything about the Negro, don't discuss him, and don't care about him.* In Indianapolis, and indeed in other cities, the only white people I could find who were much interested in the Negroes were a few politicians, mostly of the lower sort, the charity workers and the police. . . . One of the first white men with whom I talked (at Indianapolis) said to me with some impatience: "*There are too many Negroes up here; they hurt the city.*"
>
> *[In Boston, Massachusetts] . . . several hotels, restaurants, and especially confectionery stores, will not serve Negroes, even the best of them. The discrimination is not made openly, but a Negro who goes to such places is informed that there are no accommodations, or he is overlooked and otherwise slighted, so that he does not come again. A strong prejudice exists against renting flats and houses in many white neighbourhoods to coloured people.*[784]

White Bostonians also showed great enthusiasm for keeping blacks out of their churches, as Baker writes:

> A quarter of the congregation of the Church of the Ascension is coloured and the vicar has had to refuse any further coloured attendance at the Sunday School. St. Peter's and St. Philip's Churches in Cambridge [Massachusetts] have also been confronted with the *colour problem*.
>
> *A proposition is now afoot to establish a Negro mission which shall gradually grow into a separate coloured Episcopal Church, a movement which causes much bitterness among the coloured people.* I shall not soon forget the expression of hopelessness in the face of a prominent white church leader as he exclaimed: "What shall we do with these Negroes! I for one would like to have them stay. I believe it is in accordance with the doctrine of Christ, but the proportion is growing so large that *white people are drifting away from us. Strangers avoid us.* Our organisation is expensive to keep up and the Negroes are able to contribute very little in proportion to their numbers. Think about it yourself: What shall we do? *If we allow the*

Negroes to attend freely it means that eventually all the white people will leave and we shall have a Negro church whether we want it or not."[785]

Harvard University, Cambridge, Massachusetts, birthplace of a "race science" called "niggerology," which held that blacks are a subhuman species that forms a bridge between man and apes. The less scientific of Boston's citizens believed Africans were a cross between a child, a madman, and an imbecile. Renowned Harvard scientist Dr. Louis Agassiz taught that the negro came from a regressive race that would never rise above a state of barbarity.

Baker encountered similar problems at Harvard University, long one of America's most liberal and progressive institutions:

> *Even at Harvard where the Negro has always enjoyed exceptional opportunities, conditions are undergoing a marked change.* A few years ago a large class of white students voluntarily chose a brilliant Negro student, R. C. Bruce, as valedictorian. But *last year a Negro baseball player was the cause of so much discussion and embarrassment to the athletic association that there will probably never be another coloured boy on the university teams. The line has already been drawn, indeed, in the medical department. Although a coloured doctor only a few years ago was house physician at the Boston Lying-in-Hospital, coloured students are no longer admitted to that institution.* One of them, Dr. Welker (an Iowa coloured man), cannot secure his degree because he hasn't had six obstetrical cases, and he can't get the six cases because he isn't admitted with his white classmates to the Lying-in-Hospital. It is a curious fact that *not only the white patients but some Negro patients object to the coloured doctors. In a recent address which has awakened much sharp comment among Boston Negroes, President [Charles William] Eliot of Harvard indicated his sympathy with the general policy of separate education in the South by remarking that if Negro students were in the majority at Harvard, or formed a large proportion of the total*

> *number, some separation of the races might follow.*
>
> And *this feeling is growing [in Boston]*, notwithstanding the fact that no Negro student has ever disgraced Harvard and that no students are more orderly or law-abiding than the Negroes. On the other hand, Negro students have frequently made distinguished records for scholarship . . .[786]

Along with hearing of countless examples of race riots at the North, Baker was also disturbed to learn that white Yankee mobs often roamed the streets actively seeking out blacks in order to do them harm:

> *In certain towns in Ohio, Indiana, and Illinois, on the borders of the old South, the feeling has reached a stage still more acute. At Springfield, Ohio, two race riots have occurred, in the first of which a Negro was lynched and in the second many Negroes were driven out of town and a row of coloured tenements was burned. There are counties and towns where no Negro is permitted to stop over night. At Syracuse, Ohio, Lawrenceburg, Ellwood, and Salem, Indiana, for example, Negroes have not been permitted to live for years. If a Negro appears he is warned of conditions, and if he does not leave immediately, he is visited by a crowd of boys and men and forced to leave.* A farmer who lives within a few miles of Indianapolis told me of a meeting, held only a short time ago by thirty-five farmers in his neighbourhood, in which *an agreement was passed to hire no Negroes, nor to permit Negroes to live anywhere in the region.*
>
> . . . In Indianapolis the Negro comes in contact with the "bungaloo gangs," crowds of rough and lawless white boys who set upon Negroes and beat them frightfully, often wholly without provocation. Although no law prevents Negroes from entering any park in Indianapolis, they are practically excluded from at least one of them by the danger of being assaulted by these gangs.
>
> *The street cars are free in all Northern cities, but the Negro nevertheless sometimes finds it dangerous to ride with white people.* Professor R. R. Wright, Jr., himself a Negro, and an acute observer of Negro conditions, tells this personal experience: "I came out on the car from the University of Pennsylvania one evening in May about eight o'clock. Just as the car turned off Twenty-seventh to Lombard Street, a crowd of about one hundred little white boys from six to about fourteen years of age attacked it. The car was crowded, but there were only about a dozen Negroes on it, about half of them women. The mob of boys got control of the car by pulling off the trolley. They threw stones into the car, and finally *some of them boarded the car and began to beat the Negroes with sticks, shouting as they did so, 'Kill the nigger!' 'Lynch 'em!' 'Hit*

> *that nigger!', etc. This all happened in Philadelphia. Doubtless these urchins had been reading in the daily papers the cry 'Kill the Negro!' and they were trying to carry out the injunction."*
>
> While I was in Indianapolis a clash of enough importance to be reported in the newspapers occurred between the races on a street car; and in New York, in the San Juan Hill district, one Sunday evening I saw an incident which illustrates *the almost instinctive race antagonism which exists in Northern cities*. The street was crowded. Several Negro boys were playing on the pavement. Stones were thrown. Instantly several white boys sided together and began to advance on the Negroes. In less time than it takes to tell it thirty or forty white boys and young men were chasing the Negroes down the street. At the next corner the Negroes were joined by dozens of their own race. Stones and sticks began to fly everywhere, and if it hadn't been for the prompt action of two policemen there would have been a riot similar to those which have occurred not once but many times in New York City during the past two years. Of course these instances are exceptional, but none the less significant.[787]

It is easy to understand why New Hampshire abolitionist Mary Baker Eddy invested most of her antislavery efforts not on the South but on the North, where due to entrenched attitudes among white Yankees, freed slaves were often reenslaved as soon as they were emancipated.[788] When Englishman Henry Latham visited Philadelphia in 1867, he found that Pennsylvanians were still segregating the two races, with white children and black children attending separate schools.[789] Thus when he traveled to Boston he was surprised to see white and black children sitting in class together. Why surprised? Latham answered the question this way:

Mary Baker Eddy, the Yankee founder of Christian Science, focused her abolitionist activities not on the South, but on the North, where white racism was far more firmly fixed.

> Here at Boston, far away from the South, is the only instance we have yet seen of the negro being received on an actual equality with the white.[790]

This type of Northern white racism worked to both justify and expedite Yankee slavery for centuries. Truly, as acclaimed British author H. G. Wells once said, "Negro slavery is as old as New England."[791]

Around the late 1660s New England was importing a "considerable number" of Native-Americans from the Spanish Main and the West Indies.[792] This is one reason Rhode Island boasted not only black slaves, but Indian slaves as well, forced to work alongside one another in the fields of the great Narragansett plantations. By 1770 New England possessed some 11,000 documented African slaves.[793]

One of Rhode Island's more notable slave traders was the wealthy Portuguese-born Jew, Aaron Lopez. Lopez, who possessed 27 African slaves and owned at least 30 slave ships, believed that blacks were subhuman animals who were best kept in leg irons and handcuffs. He routinely outfitted slave ships at Newport and was friends with a number of other famous New England slave traders, among them William English, Peleg Clarke, Nathaniel Waldron, and Nathaniel Briggs. Far from being criticized for his occupation, fellow Northerners lauded Lopez for his work, his very name becoming a synonym for scrupulousness, morality, and good character.[794]

So great were the profits made by slave traders like Lopez at Newport, Rhode Island,[795] that it has been said that the city was literally constructed over the graves of thousands of Africans,[796] for its prosperity was due solely to the slave trade.[797] The city itself once boasted the largest number of Yankee slavers in the U.S.[798] William Johnston writes:

> . . . for more than thirty years prior to 1764 Rhode Island sent to the coast [of Africa] annually eighteen vessels carrying 1,800 heads of rum. The commerce in rum and slaves afforded about ,£40,000 per annum for remittance from Rhode Island to Great Britain. *As the [slave] trade grew Newport became more and more the central market. . . . It is probable that the trade in Rhode Island was much more extensive than in the other New England colonies.* Dr. John Eliot says: "*The African trade was carried on in Massachusetts and commenced at an early period, but to a small extent compared with Rhode Island.*" Samuel Dexter says: "*Vessels from Rhode Island have brought slaves into Boston.* Whether any have been imported into that town by its own merchants I am unable to say." *In the latter half of the century Rhode Island still maintained this pre-eminence, and its chief mart, Newport.* During this period Bristol also became noted as a slave port, and Captain Simeon Potter, one of her famous slave traders, flourished

about 1764. . . .

The census of 1730 [shows a slight decline in slave numbers from the previous census,] but *it was popular to conceal numbers from the observation of the home government. [Rhode Island] families would average from five to forty slaves each. They owned slaves in proportion to their means of support.* The slaves and horses were about equal in number; the latter were raised for exportation. *Newport was the great slave market of New England.* There were some importers of slaves in Narragansett; among them were Rowland Robinson and Colonel Thomas Hazard. In Newport there were twenty-two still [rum] houses. *"The large exportation of New England rum to Africa, which in return brought slaves, increased the wealth of the place to an astonishing degree. There were but few of her merchants that were not directly or indirectly interested in the traffic. Some forty or fifty sail of vessels were in this employment, and it was thought a necessary appendage to have one or more slaves to act as domestics in their families." Newport was then the centre of the trade, while the Narragansett Plantations were the stronghold of the institution of slavery.*[799]

Rhode Island's official name, "Rhode Island and Providence Plantations," as well as the state's maritime flag, are both remnants of her days as one of the nation's leading slave powers.

By 1790—by which time Britain had transported some 2 million African slaves to North America and the Caribbean since 1690[800]—Liverpool had become England's primary slave port. Her only serious competition was from the Yankee slave ship owners of Bristol[801] and Newport, Rhode Island.[802] For England, and her offspring New England, were the primary participants in the transatlantic slave trade at the time.[803] Rhode Island's state flag still bears a ship's anchor, an apt reminder of her days as the nation's largest slave trader, one that imported 100,000 African slaves—20 percent of all those brought into the U.S.[804]—and whose main harbor, Newport, launched 70 percent of all American slave voyages prior to the American Revolution.[805]

It was not just slave trading that Rhode Island was involved in. The state also possessed thousands of crop and cattle plantations which depended almost exclusively on slave labor, many of them located in the town of Providence.[806] In fact, due to the number of plantations that once dotted the Renaissance City, to this day the official name of the state of Rhode Island is "Rhode Island and Providence Plantations,"[807] a carryover from the 1600s when the slavery-loving colony was first named.[808]

Vestiges of New England's "peculiar institution" are still obvious to this day, one of the more conspicuous being the pineapple. Though it is now seen as a "welcome" sign across the Northeast, this is a corruption of its original meaning: when New England slave traders returned from their ocean expeditions to the tropics to pick up slaves (mainly in the West Indies),[809] they would skewer a pineapple on their fencepost to let everyone in town know that they were "welcome" to come in and shop for slave products, as well as for slaves themselves.[810] The pineapple motif, that great symbol of Yankee slavery, is still commonly seen all over the U.S., not just in the North, but in the South as well.

Now a sign of hospitality, the pineapple motif began as a symbol of Yankee slavery, impaled on a slaver's gate to "welcome" customers in the market for slaves and slave products.

Even after slavery was abolished in the North, both Rhode Island and Massachusetts continued to amass huge profits from the slave trade,[811] the same profits that would later help Lincoln fund his "Civil War" on the South.[812] In 1861 Blake wrote the following about early Northern slavery in general:

> With the increase of wealth and luxury, the number of slaves increased also. There were in Massachusetts in 1754, as appears by an official census, twenty-four hundred and forty-eight negro slaves over sixteen years of age, about a thousand of them in Boston—a greater proportion to the free inhabitants than is to be found at present in the city of Baltimore. Connecticut exceeded Massachusetts in the ratio of its slave population, and Rhode Island exceeded Connecticut. Newport, grown to be the second commercial town in New England, had a proportion of slaves

> larger than Boston. . . . Manumissions . . . were not allowed except upon security that the freed slaves should not become a burden to the parish.[813]

In the 1860s, under Lincoln, Northern slavery continued unabated in America's Yankee capital city, Washington, D.C., until the middle of his administration. Up until that time he turned down numerous opportunities to abolish the institution here.

The District—where blacks were once fined $25, given 25 lashes with a bull whip, jailed for 30 days, then returned to slavery, just for receiving Garrison's abolitionist newspaper *The Liberator*;[814] where hospitals were strictly segregated so that blood plasma would not be used for both whites and blacks; and where even the White House press and photographers' pool was segregated until the 1950s[815]—had long been a major center for slave sales and boasted the nation's largest slave mart,[816] one located in full view of Northern members of Congress,[817] as Lincoln himself noted.[818]

Senator Joseph Stanton, Jr., of Rhode Island once spoke of his embarrassment after seeing "twenty or thirty negroes chained together and driven like mules to market" while on his way to the Capitol building.[819] In 1819, during a committee meeting on abolition in Washington, D.C., U.S. Representative James Tallmadge, Jr. of New York made the following comments:

> Since we have been engaged in this debate, we have witnessed an elucidation of this argument, of bettering the condition of slaves, by spreading them over the country. *A slave-driver, a trafficker in human flesh, as if sent by providence, has passed the door of your capitol, on his way to the west, driving before him about fifteen of these wretched victims of his power, collected in the course of his traffic, and by their removal, torn from every relation and from every tie which the human heart can hold dear. The males, who might raise the arm of vengeance, and retaliate for their wrongs, were hand-cuffed and chained to each other, while the females and children were marched in their rear, under the guidance of the driver's whip! Yes, sir, such has been the scene witnessed from the windows of congress hall, and viewed by members who compose the legislative councils of republican America!*[820]

In 1836 Yankee professor Dr. Ethan Allen Andrews referred to the "ten miles square" District as "the very seat and centre of the domestic slave-trade."[821] It was, as slavery scholar William O. Blake called it, the "great resort of [slave] traders."[822] Rightly so.

Numerous slave pens, located right across the street from the new Smithsonian building, overflowed with the human chattel of Yankee slave traders who lived and worked in the town. Most Northern politicians and statesmen alike, Lincoln included, passed by them on a daily basis without so much as a comment, criticism, or protest.[823] And for good reason: it was the auctioned brethren of these very slaves—that is, the *Northern* slaves sold at these *Northern* markets and pens, who had been brought to America on *Northern* slave ships, owned by *Northern* businessmen—who built the White House, the U.S. Capitol, and numerous other Federal buildings in the city, along with many of her city streets.[824]

African slaves being led to auction in front of the U.S. Capitol (top right) in Washington, D.C.

Yet many Southern politicians could not abide the idea of slavery in the nation's capitol, particularly after it began to increase in the early 1800s. One of these was John Randolph of Virginia, who

> in congress denounced this new traffic as heinous and abominable, inhuman and illegal, and moved a committee of inquiry, whose report justified some of the epithets. Governor [David Rogerson] Williams, of South Carolina, in a message to the legislature, denounced "this remorseless and merciless traffic, this ceaseless dragging along the streets and highways of a crowd of suffering victims to minister to insatiable avarice," as condemned alike by "enlightened humanity, wise policy and the prayers of the just." The legislature accordingly passed an act forbidding the

> introduction of slaves from abroad; which was repealed, however, in two years.[825]

Apparently the many advertisements of the city's slave dealers in the local papers,[826] the existence of slave pens, slave jails, auction blocks, thousands of chained African slaves laboring throughout the city,[827] and the sight of Yankee slave boats plying up and down the Potomac River,[828] bothered neither Lincoln or the U.S. Congress, for the town's citizens were allowed to own and trade in slaves right up through the first year of the Civil War. Antislavery pamphlets, such as *Slavery and the Slave Trade at the Nation's Capital*, highlighted the problem, while abolitionists, like Massachusetts Congressman Horace Mann, took every opportunity to speak out against both the ongoing slave trade and the practice of slavery in Washington, D.C. During a speech before the House of Representatives on February 23, 1849, Mann made the following comments:

> Sir, from the Western front of this Capitol, from the piazza that opens out from your Congressional Library, as you cast your eye along the horizon and over the conspicuous objects of the landscape,—the President's Mansion, the Smithsonian Institution, and the site of the Washington Monument, *you cannot fail to see the horrid and black receptacles where human beings are penned like cattle, and kept like cattle, that they may be sold like cattle*—as strictly and literally so as oxen and swine are kept and sold at the Smithfield shambles in London, or at the cattle fair in Brighton. In a communication made during the last session, by the Mayor of this city, to an honorable member of this House, *he acknowledges the existence of slave pens here. Up and down the beautiful river that sweeps along the western margin of the District, slavers come and go, bearing their freight of human souls to be vended in this market-place; and after they have changed hands, according to the forms of commerce, they are retransported—the father of a family to go, perhaps, to the rice fields of South Carolina, the mother to the cotton fields of Alabama, and the children to be scattered over the sugar plantations of Louisiana or Texas.*
>
> *Sir, it is notorious that the slave traders of this District advertise for slaves in the newspapers of the neighboring counties of Maryland, to be delivered in any numbers at their slave pens in this city; and that they have agents, in the city and out of it, who are engaged in supplying victims for their shambles.* [Just recently I believe,] one coffle of about sixty slaves came, chained and driven into this city; and at about the same time another coffle of a hundred. Here they were lodged for

a short period, were then sold, and went on their returnless way to the engulphing South.

Sir, *all this is done hereunder our own eyes, and within hearing of our own ears*. All this is done now, and it has been done for fifty years,—ever since the seat of the National Government was established in this place, and ever since Congress, in accordance with the Constitution, has exercised "exclusive legislation" over it. . . . [Thus by] authority of Congress, *the city of Washington is the Congo of America*.[829]

The U.S. Capitol Building, Washington, D.C. There were once so many African slaves, slave pens, slave markets, slave merchants, slave owners, and slave ships in and around the District that it was referred to as the "Congo of America . . . where man is bought and sold, as cattle are bought and sold." The wretched scenes of newly arriving Africans being led in coffles through the streets of Washington bothered few people, particularly Northern politicians. One of these was U.S. President-elect Abraham Lincoln who, a few months prior to his inauguration, said: "I have no thought of recommending the abolition of slavery in the District of Columbia, nor the slave-trade among the slave States."

Whites who lived in the "Congo of America"—the "heart of the Union . . . where man is bought and sold, as cattle are bought and sold"[830]—were greatly interested in keeping down the number of blacks in their city, which, in 1850, stood at 26 percent of the total population. In contrast, blacks in slave-owning St. Louis, Missouri, represented only 5.4 percent. Cincinnati, Ohio, was only 2.8 percent black. To maintain, or even decrease, the local black populace, Washington whites widely approved of the new Fugitive Slave Law. Why? Under it, runaway slaves had to be returned to their owners. Those who escaped, however, would blend back into the city's free black population, thereby swelling African-American numbers.[831]

To counter this trend, numerous anti-black laws were revisited in order to make them more stringent. New amendments required black emigrants to Washington, D.C. to "apply for residence" within five days of their arrival, or face a fine, a sentence in the workhouse, and banishment from town. "Secret meetings" by blacks were prohibited and anyone of African descent had to obtain the permission of the mayor to gather in public.[832] In one case a group of 24 "genteel colored men" met in the District to discuss charity works. They were arrested and fined. One was sentenced to hard labor, another was whipped.[833]

In a city where already severe black codes were rigidly enforced and where blacks merely suspected of petty crimes were often savagely beaten by Washington's police force, even law-abiding, hard-working blacks lived in constant fear, mainly of white gangs.[834] Without a "certificate of freedom," no free black in the city was safe from harassment and arrest by the police—who devoted the majority of their time to tracking down and capturing African-Americans. The "Negro business" was so profitable in the District that slave catchers were attracted to the town from far and wide.[835]

Blacks, enslaved and free, did not fare well in early Washington, D.C., where some of the nation's most stringent anti-black laws, known as Black Codes, were harshly regulated. This African slave is being whipped and beaten in a Washington jail cell for violating one of the town's many white racist statutes.

Throughout the 1850s, white Washingtonians continued to reinforce slavery by endorsing the kidnaping of free blacks (to be sold into slavery) and engaging in the slave trade, even though it had been outlawed, *again*, in 1850. And while blacks were three times more likely to be arrested than whites, black testimonies in court were regarded as both invalid and illegal, and overly punitive sentences were routinely handed out to black criminals.[836] Sometimes they were punished not so much for major crimes as for minor offenses, such as lighting off firecrackers, flying a kite in the wrong area, or swimming in the canal. The punishment? A "good whipping" with a Yankee lash.[837]

It was not just the 1,800 black slaves in the District that caused Northern whites so much distress. It was also the 9,000 free blacks who lived and worked in the city, all of whom were habitually treated with "fear and hatred." The depth of this loathing can be seen in the name of an area of the Third Ward, known by Northern whites at the time as "Nigger Hill."[838] In the mid 1850s a white Washingtonian was asked what he thought about the enormous numbers of slaves and free blacks in the District, to which he replied: "I am heartily sick of them; and should be glad to see the country rid of the whole concern. They are a regular nuisance!"[839]

It was into the white racist world of Washington, D.C., that white racist Lincoln walked in the spring of 1861.

If he was truly the "Great Emancipator," as Northern myth asserts, one would think that the first item on his agenda as president would have been to abolish slavery in the capital city. Instead, he stalled and deferred month after month, until over a year passed—infuriating the Radicals (abolitionists) in his party.[840] As he himself had said on December 15, 1860, one month after being elected president:

> I have no thought of recommending the abolition of slavery in the District of Columbia, nor the slave-trade among the slave States.[841]

Actually, the entire process of ridding the District of the North's "peculiar institution" was to take hundreds of years, in part because of Lincoln.[842]

Our sixteenth chief executive's delay tactics in cleansing Washington of slavery earned him yet another one of his many unflattering nicknames: "America's biggest slave owner." An angry Charles Sumner wrote:

> Do you know who, at this moment, is the largest slaveholder in this country? It is Abraham Lincoln; for he holds all of the three thousand slaves of the District, which is more than any other person in the country holds.[843]

After postponing abolition in Washington, D.C. for several years, President Abraham Lincoln finally bowed to pressure and signed his District of Columbia Emancipation Act into law in 1862. But it was not what abolitionists had hoped for: Lincoln's edict asked for continued financial support from Congress for his racist plan to deport all people of African heritage—preferably back "to their own native land," as he phrased it earlier during a public speech in 1854.

On April 14, 1862, while Lincoln was still refusing to free Washington's slaves, noted black bishop, Daniel A. Payne, head of the African Methodist Episcopal Church, decided to pay him a visit. "Do you intend to sign a bill of emancipation or not?" he asked the president impatiently. Lincoln obfuscated, told stories and jokes. Forty-five minutes later he still had not answered Payne's question, and the frustrated clergyman politely got up and left.[844]

Political expediency and constant pressure over the previous year, including his meeting with Bishop Payne, finally forced Lincoln's hand, and two days later, on April 16, 1862, the country witnessed the passage of the District of Columbia Emancipation Act. Because of the president, it had come neither quickly or easily.[845] In fact, the entire process, from bondage to emancipation, had taken hundreds of years. Not even the Compromise of 1850 had been able to shut it down.[846] But finally, to the great relief of the North's handful of vociferous abolitionists, slavery had at last been banned in Washington, D.C.[847]

This "humanitarian" act was tainted, however, by several things. One was the fact that Lincoln's emancipation proclamation in Washington, D.C. turned out to be for the benefit of white colonizationists like himself, not for the benefit of the slaves.[848] For he had included a clause in the bill calling for what he hoped would be their deportation after liberation.[849] It reads:

> Section 11: And be it further enacted, That the sum of *one hundred thousand dollars*, out of any money in the Treasury not otherwise appropriated, *is hereby appropriated, to be expended under the direction of the President of the United States, to aid in the colonization and settlement of such free persons of African descent now residing in said*

> *District, including those to be liberated by this act, as may desire to emigrate to the Republics of Hayti or Liberia, or such other country beyond the limits of the United States as the President may determine*: Provided, The expenditure for this purpose shall not exceed one hundred dollars for each emigrant.[850]

The day the bill was signed into law, April 16, 1862, President Lincoln even wrote a letter to the House and Senate applauding them for recognizing his call for the deportation of the city's newly freed blacks and for setting aside funds for their colonization.[851]

There was also the anger of the city's whites, most who had no taste for abolition to begin with.[852] At the same time, antislavery advocates fumed over Lincoln's concomitant demand of Congress that it appropriate funding to deport, to Liberia and Haiti, the very blacks he had just freed. (Though the crafty president finally liberated the city's slaves, cleverly he had never promised that he would not attempt to colonize them outside the U.S.)[853]

Lincoln's half-hearted attempt at ending slavery in the nation's capital, of course, had little effect on the endemic Yankee trade there. In 1864, some two years after the District of Columbia Emancipation Act had been issued, former Northern slave Sojourner Truth discovered, to her horror, that whites near Washington, D.C. were kidnaping the black children of freed Southern servants and forcing them back into Northern slavery. The small community the freed blacks lived in, ironically called "Freedman's Village," had been set up by the U.S. army to help newly emancipated African-Americans adjust to living in free white society. Truth used the court system to have the children released and returned to their parents; but not before her own life was threatened by the violent and unrepentant Yankee slavers. Lincoln, whose offices were not far away, must have been aware of these crimes, yet he did nothing. Indeed, it was Lincoln's overt complicity in the institution of slavery that often prompted Truth to refer to the U.S. flag, not as the "Stars and Stripes," but as the "Scars and Stripes."[854]

Not surprisingly, during the Lincoln administration Truth herself was often denied admission to the White House because she was black. On several occasions there were eyewitnesses, such as on February 25, 1865, when British journalist Fred Tomkins saw Truth being barred from entering. Other times she was forced to wait until the president

This obvious piece of pro-North propaganda, depicting President Lincoln showing a Bible to Sojourner Truth, would have us believe that the two were on cordial terms, that she was always warmly welcomed at the White House, and that Lincoln himself was a Bible-believing Christian. All of these assumptions are demonstrably false. Like Frederick Douglass and most other blacks at the time, Truth saw Lincoln as a serious impediment to black civil, legal, and social progress, and she was rarely admitted to the White House due to the color of her skin. As for the president's alleged "religiosity," he had none! From his earliest days as a politician, he was a publicly avowed "infidel" who opposed organized religion (particularly Christianity), told impious stories, denounced his wife's spiritualism, never prayed, never attended church, never joined any religious faith or denomination, never opened a Bible, and never spoke of Jesus. He was also well-known for his lack of belief in the divinity of Christ, Christian salvation, the sanctity of the Bible, and even in God Himself. According to his associates, Lincoln once wrote a "little book" declaring that the Bible was "uninspired" and historically inaccurate, that its miracles went against the laws of Nature, and that Jesus was a "bastard." This devilish volume was later burned by one of Lincoln's friends to protect his future reputation. It worked.

deigned to see her. According to Truth, she never felt completely welcomed at the White House while Lincoln was occupying it. Even in the rare instances when she *was* allowed entrance, it was never with any respect, or "reverence," as she put it.[855]

The legal prohibition of black suffrage "was imposed by numerous Northern states between 1807 and 1838,"[856] an idea that quickly spread across Yankeedom at the time. This particular form of white Yankee racism in and around Washington, D.C. carried on well into the Grant administration, as English tourist Henry Latham noted in 1867:

> The two Houses having passed a bill that every coloured man who had resided for one year in the district of Columbia should possess the suffrage, sent it up to the President [Grant], who returned it to-day with his veto, assigning his reasons. The chief reasons assigned were: that although Congress does constitutionally make State laws for the district of Columbia, yet they are not representatives elected by that district; that *a vote had recently been taken of the white citizens of the district, and they had almost unanimously refused the suffrage to the negroes; that the effect of the bill would be to alter the constitution of the district against the expressed wish of its citizens, and would result in its being filled with negroes coming in from the surrounding States.*[857]

Indeed, legalized white racism continued all the way into the 1940s in Washington, and it was not until the early 1950s that legislation was passed barring the city's restaurants from refusing to serve black patrons. It was not until 1956 that the District finally became fully and legally racially integrated.[858]

America's capital city was so central to slavery in the 1800s that she probably would have become the nation's slave trading capital instead of New York City. The only reason Washington, D.C. did not was due to geography: at the time she was only a mere sixty-eight square miles, with no room to expand.[859] Nonetheless, a vestige of Washington's original function as a leading slave market is its black population, which peaked at 71 percent in 1970, one of the highest of any city in the U.S.[860]

As the founder of both the American slave trade and American slavery, and with her long history of deep economic ties to the slave industry, it should come as no surprise to learn that the top five American cities with the largest black populations today are not in the South, but in the North and West (by rank they are New York City, New York; Chicago, Illinois; Detroit, Michigan; Philadelphia, Pennsylvania; and Los Angeles, California). Even the city with the highest percentage of blacks is in the North: Detroit.[861]

A slave port at Baltimore, Maryland. Unlike in the South, in the Old Line State—as with the other Northern states—a slave and his or her offspring were made "slaves for life."

Like our nation's capital city Washington, D.C.,[862] Baltimore, Maryland, and Philadelphia, Pennsylvania,[863] were also great slave ports,[864] the latter state having, by 1750, some 11,000 blacks, most of them slaves.[865] Maryland's Governor Leonard Calvert was purchasing black slaves as early as 1642.[866] Baltimore in particular was one of the nation's most important slave trading centers: her slave ships were said to be packed "like livestock" with black human cargo, with mortality rates reaching as high as 25 percent.[867] In 1663 the state passed a slavery law whose first section ordered that

> *"all negroes and other slaves within this province, and all negroes and other slaves to be hereafter imported into this province, shall serve during life; and all children born of any negro or other slave, shall be slaves, as their fathers were, for the term of their lives."* The second section recites that "divers free-born [white] English women, forgetful of their free condition, and to the disgrace of our nation, do intermarry with negro slaves"; and for deterring from such "shameful matches," it enacts that, *during their husbands' lives, white women so intermarrying shall be servants to the masters of their husbands, and that the issue of such marriages shall be slaves for life.*[868]

In 1671 Maryland issued a statute that promoted and encouraged the further importation of slaves from Africa. Around the same time it tried to ban interracial marriage.[869]

Another Maryland city, Annapolis, also became one of America's most prosperous towns due to its thriving slave trade. It was a Northern slave ship that brought Kunta Kinte, the lead character in Alex Haley's saga *Roots*, to Annapolis from West Africa in 1767. The city still goes by the nickname the "sailing capital of the world." By 1770 at least one-third, or 66,000, of Maryland's total population of 200,000 were slaves,[870] a number that continued to increase for the next several decades: in 1790 Maryland had 103,036 slaves; in 1810, 111,502. It was not until 1830 that the state began to see a decline, when the total number dropped to 102,994 slaves.[871]

Yankee slave owners did not like to report their slaves to the Census takers for fear of having to pay taxes on them. Sometimes it was just pure laziness or carelessness on the part of the enumerator. Either way, the result was the same: Northern slaves were always appallingly undercounted, leaving the false impression that slavery was insignificant in the North.

By 1775, on the eve of the American Revolution, one conservative estimate—based on the always woefully inaccurate and "willfully false" Census,[872] as well as the typical underreporting of *all* blacks by slave owners and Census takers[873]—counted some 46,102 slaves in the North as a whole.[874] At a Congressional committee meeting in 1805, Rhode Island was severely rebuked by abolitionist members for "furnishing ships for the business" of slave trading. But no one truly wanted to interrupt the flourishing Yankee commerce, so it was decided that the issue would be held over until the next session.[875]

It was New York City, however, that eventually came to be the main port of exit and entry for America's slave ships.[876]

Originally known as New Amsterdam, it grew to become the center of the Dutch colony of what was then called New Netherland (later renamed New York by the English), a territory founded in 1624 and governed by the great slave trading corporation, the Dutch West India Company, whose primary goal was to "extend the market for its human merchandise whithersoever its influence reached."[877] Today New York City's official flag still bears the colors of the original flag flown by Netherland's slave ships: blue, orange, and white.

Thus it was that slavery took root in New York at the very beginning, when it was established by the Dutch in 1624. This marked the start of the official recognition of slavery in the middle colonies, where the institution quickly became a "custom" in the region.[878]

A Dutch cottage in New York in 1679. The Empire State was steeped in slavery from its very inception: the colony of New Netherland, as it was then known, was founded in 1624 by the Dutch West India Company for the express purpose of expanding its slavery operations in the New World.

Though the Dutch West India Company brought the first African laborers to New Netherland in 1626[879] (at which time eleven men from Africa's Gold Coast were delivered to the island of Manhattan),[880] it was not until around 1650 that it officially introduced slavery to the colony.[881] Settlers from New England immediately began pouring south into what is now Long Island and Westchester, New York, becoming some of the corporation's "best customers for slaves." In 1651 the inhabitants of Gravesend (now part of Brooklyn) petitioned to have the slave supply increased. To stimulate slave sales the Dutch opened up the slave trade to private ships, hoping to make New Amsterdam (the future New York City) the central slave market for all of the surrounding English colonies.[882] Their desire would soon manifest.

By the time the slavery-obsessed English took over the colony of New Netherland in 1664 and renamed it New York, it "contained more slaves in proportion to its inhabitants than Virginia."[883] From then on the institution only increased. Between 1697 and 1790, for example,

Albany's slave population grew from 3 percent to 16 percent. Influential Albany plantation owners, like the Schuyler and Van Rensselaer families, made vast fortunes using black slaves to build up their estates. A number of their well-known homes stand in New York's capital city to this day,[884] including Ten Broeck Manor,[885] Cherry Hill Mansion,[886] and the Schuyler Mansion.[887] In 1665 New York passed Duke's Laws, named after the Duke of York (who later became King James II).[888] A codification of statutes borrowed from the Massachusetts Fundamentals, they allowed Indians and blacks who had not been baptized into the Christian religion to be enslaved.[889]

By the year 1700 New York Harbor was teeming with slave ships and slavery had become the foundation of the state's economy. New Yorkers believed that their "peculiar institution" was so vital to the North's economy that they blocked and delayed emancipation for over 100 years, with so-called "official abolition" not occurring until 1827.[890] New York's slave owners were a brutal lot, engaging in a myriad of cruel practices, from disenfranchisement and the separation of slave families to whipping and murder.[891]

By the year 1720 New York had become one of the largest slaveholding states in the North, with 4,000 slaves against a white population of only 31,000. The situation was unbearable to the North's few abolitionists, resulting in the nation's first antislavery essay: *The Selling of Joseph*, penned in Massachusetts by the famed Yankee judge who presided at the Salem witch trials, Samuel Sewall.[892] As in ancient Africa, Israel, and Thrace, slaves were such a valuable commodity in the North that they could be used as an insurance policy to cover their master's financial obligations,[893] or be sold to pay off the owner's creditors.[894] This led to the illegal Northern practice of falsely claiming free blacks as "personal property," then selling them to pay off debts.[895]

By the mid 1700s one-sixth of New York City's population was comprised of African slaves.[896] By 1756 New York state possessed some 13,000 adult black slaves, giving it the dubious distinction of having the largest slave force of any Northern colony at the time. That same year slaves accounted for 25 percent of the population in Kings, Queens, Richmond, New York City, and Westchester, making these areas the primary bastion of American slavery throughout the rest of the colonial period.[897] As mentioned, Yankees moving south to Westchester and

Long Island were among the most eager slave purchasers, and by 1750 at least one-tenth of the province of New York's householders were slave owners.[898] At New York City's peak, at least one-fifth of the town's population were slaves.[899] Little wonder that in 1785 New York's state legislators rejected a bill advocating gradual emancipation.[900]

On February 22, 1788, New York passed "An Act Concerning Slaves." The law, which severely tightened up the state's slavery statutes, enacted:

> *That every negro, mulatto, or mestee, within this state, who at the time of the passing of this act, is a slave, for his or her life, shall continue such, for and during his or her life*, unless he or she, shall be manumitted or set free, in the manner prescribed in and by this act, or in some future law of this state.
>
> That *the children of every negro, mulatto or mestee woman, being a slave, shall follow the state and condition of the mother, and be esteemed, reputed, taken and adjudged slaves to all intents and purposes whatsoever*.
>
> That *the baptizing of any negro, or other slave, shall not be deemed, adjudged, or taken, to be a manumission of such slave*.[901]

New York Harbor in the 1600s teemed with slaves, slave owners, slave dealers, and slave ships.

To further protect their human investment, New York insurance companies sold insurance policies to Yankee slave owners: in 1853, for instance, a New York slave was insured for $550.00 by a Northerner named John Yellmann[902]—the equivalent of nearly $20,000 in today's currency. Obviously, New Yorkers were loath to give up the lucrative institution,[903] which is why they continued it right through Lincoln's

War, though, as we saw earlier with New York slave ship Captain Nathaniel Gordon, as well as the New England slave ship *Nightingale*, it was by then a largely clandestine affair.[904]

What Northern and New South historians will not tell you is that there is only one reason that New York City is today America's largest and wealthiest municipality: for centuries it served as the literal heart of North America's slaving industry.[905] Many of the most famous New York names, in fact—names such as the Lehman Brothers, John Jacob Astor, Junius and Pierpont Morgan, Charles Tiffany, Archibald Gracie, and many others—are only known today because of the tremendous riches their families made from the town's "peculiar institution."[906] Many of today's wealthiest New York Jewish families descend from 18th-Century Jewish slave ship owners and slave traders, who eagerly participated with Northern colonial Christians in the Yankee's "peculiar institution."[907]

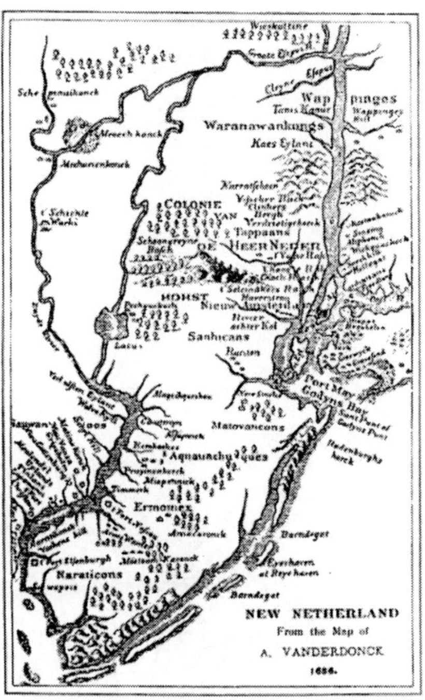

A 1656 Dutch map of New York, then called New Netherland. The selection of this specific area on North America's upper East Coast by the Dutch was no accident: the region—with its sea frontage and numerous natural harbors, bays, ports, and riverways—was strategically situated to expedite and maintain the maritime slave trade between Africa, the American Northeast, and the West Indies.

New York abolitionists were understandably infuriated. In 1854, 27 years after the state officially terminated slavery, an editorialist in the *New York Times* complained:

> *This City [New York City] and Baltimore [Maryland] are now, and have been for years, the great head-quarters of the African slave-trade. In the face of all our laws, in defiance of our treaty stipulations and in contempt of armed cruisers and men-of-war, that piratical traffic is largely carried on by ships fitted out in American ports, and under the protection of the American flag. If the authorities plead that they cannot stop this, they*

simply confess their own imbecility. If they will not do it, the moral guilt they incur is scarcely less than that of the slave-traders themselves.[908]

New York City, the center of America's cotton business as early as 1815, was so deeply connected to the Yankee slave trade and to Southern slavery that it opposed all early attempts at abolition within its borders,[909] and, along with New Jersey, was the last Northern state to resist the passage of emancipation laws.[910]

In 1664 the English took over the colony of New Netherland, renaming it New York after the Duke of York—who was later to become King James II. Instead of lessening, slavery only intensified under the new British government, which replaced the Dutch West Indian Company with an even more merciless and profit oriented slave trading organization: the Royal African Company. Note the British flag on the galleon to the right, which is bringing a new cargo of African slaves into New York Harbor.

Later, in December 1860, when the Southern states began seceding, New York City's mayor Fernando Wood advocated that his city secede as well, for it was primarily King Cotton that was keeping it economically stable.[911] When Lincoln's War finally erupted in April 1861, New York was one of the last states to recruit African-Americans: the state's governor, Horatio Seymour, refused to enlist them until he was forced to by the U.S. War Department.[912] This occurred on December 23, 1863, a year after the Emancipation Proclamation was issued and nearly three years after the War began.[913]

That same year, New York physician Dr. John H. Van Evrie came out with his book, *Negroes and Negro Slavery*, in which the Yankee white supremacist argued that blacks were naturally inferior to whites, were, in fact, a different species than whites, could not stand upright like whites, could not facially express emotions like whites, would never be able to speak English like whites, that slavery was the black man's natural occupation, and that the slave trade was "beneficial," among other white racist stereotypes.[914] Many fellow New Yorkers agreed with Van Evries, support that further fueled the massive and profitable slavery business, not only in the Empire State, but throughout the entire Northeast.

New York in 1746, now under control of the British, was quickly overtaking New England as America's slave trading capital.

In New York specifically slavery was so firmly fixed that it endured for at least 239 years:

1. Slavery in New York officially began (on the island of Manhattan) under the Dutch, and lasted for 38 years, from 1626 to 1664.
2. New York slavery then fell under the auspices of the English, lasting for 112 years, from 1664 to 1776.
3. After the formation of the U.S., New York slavery was turned over to the new state government, continuing on for another 51 years, from 1776 to 1827, when it was legally "abolished."[915]
4. Slavery in New York then persisted illegally for another 38 years, only being permanently shut down by the ratification of the Thirteenth Amendment in December 1865.[916]

New York's 239-year history of slavery is the longest of any state, and certainly far longer than any Southern state. It is greater even than Massachusetts, where both the American slave trade and American slavery got their start. This makes New York America's premier slave state, as close to a true slavocracy as any U.S. state has ever come.

As noted, the 1827 suspension of slavery in New York came and went, and still the human trafficking continued. Decades passed without so much as a murmur from the state's mayors, marshals, police, or state prosecutors. Not even New York judges felt inclined to impede the institution. Between 1837 and 1861, for instance, 125 New York slavers were tried for the crime of slave trading. Only 20 were convicted, receiving a mere two years in prison for a crime that was supposed to be punishable by execution under federal law.[917]

New York City's Federal Hall, Trinity Church, and Wall Street in 1789. Now part of the United States of America, New York's obsession with the slave trade continued to broaden and strengthen. One day she would earn the dubious honor of being the state having the deepest and longest involvement with slavery, far more even than Massachusetts, where both the institution and the trade got their start in the early 1600s. In effect, by this time New York was well on her way to becoming a true slave empire. Her progress was only checked by the passage of the Thirteenth Amendment on December 6, 1865.

That New York was addicted to the slave trade and refused to "break the habit" is shown by yet another well-known example, that of the ship *Wildfire*, which, on May 19, 1860, the *New York Times* referred to as the "American slave bark." A few weeks earlier, on April 30, the *Wildfire* had arrived at the port of Key West, Florida, packed to the stern with hundreds of male and female slaves fresh from the Congo River region. An artist made a famous woodcut from photos of the incident, which now appears in nearly every pro-North "history" book concerning American slavery. The image shows 507 slaves—the males in the front on the lower deck, the females in the back on the upper deck—in a state of utter misery and deprivation, dozens having already perished due to "inanition, exhaustion, and dysentery."

Anti-South writers continue to blame Dixie for the African slave trading voyage of the *Wildfire* and its subsequent enslavement of "free" Africans, just as they incriminate the Old South for all things concerning American slavery. However, the facts show that it is the North, not the

The ill-famed woodcut (based on actual photographs) of some 500 African slaves aboard the bark *Wildfire*, April 30, 1860, entering Florida waters. This image has long been used by pro-North writers to denounce and humiliate the South. As it turns out, however, it was the North and only the North that was responsible for the tragedy of the *Wildfire*.

South, who must take responsibility for this tragedy.

First, the *Wildfire* did not sail to Florida under its own volition that Spring day. On April 26 it had been seized by U.S. vessels off Cuba for illegally engaging in the slave trade, after which it was towed to Key West by the U.S.S. steamer *Mohawk*, under the command of one Lieutenant Craven. This, in fact, is what is actually being depicted in the infamous woodcut: the towing of the captured *Wildfire*.

Second, the bark was not a Southern vessel, as the South did not engage in the foreign slave trade—only the domestic trade. It was a Northern one, built in Amesbury, Massachusetts, by a Yankee named Simeon McKay of Boston, Massachusetts, and launched in April 1853. The original owner was also a Yankee from Beantown: A. L. Payson.[918]

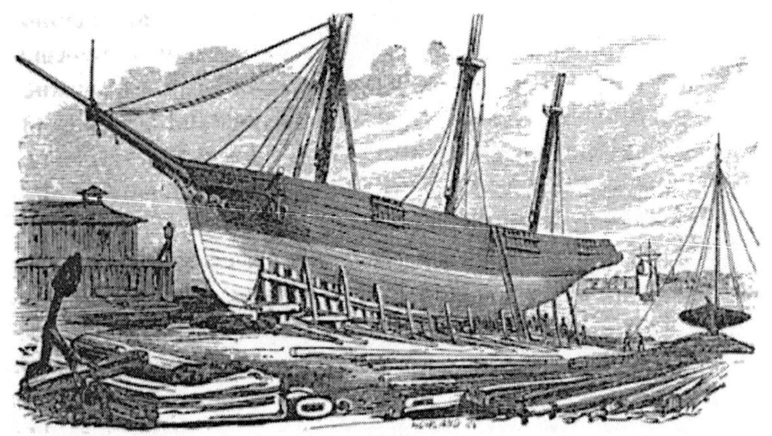

Yankee boat builders did not stop constructing slave ships until 1865, when they were forced to by the U.S. Congress and the court of public opinion.

Furthermore, at the time of its capture *Wildfire* was owned by a New Yorker, Pierre L. Pearce, and was operating out of New York City,[919] the port from which the clipper originally sailed to the Congo—then to Cuba, where it was finally impounded, then hauled to Key West.[920] The ship's master, Captain William Stanhope and his first mate George Hutchinson, as well as the 13-man crew, were all Northerners from New York and New Jersey,[921] making the entire venture strictly a Yankee one.

Third, the slaves aboard the *Wildfire* were not free blacks "caught in the wilds of Africa," as pro-North historians phrase it. Like all other

Africans brought to the Americas, they had already been slaves in their own country, after which they were purchased by white slave traders and transported back to the New World. As a journalist from *Harper's Weekly* was told when he asked a male slave named Francisco how he came to be on the *Wildfire*:

> I was a slave in Africa, and I do not wish to return there. I'd rather be a slave to the white man in this country than be a slave to the black man in my country.[922]

Fourth, far from evincing any bigotry, Southerners would have heartily welcomed the *Wildfire's* slaves, all who were freed upon their arrival in Florida.[923] For there blacks were considered, as soon-to-be Confederate General Nathan Bedford Forrest said, better laborers than whites; "the finest workers the South has ever known," in fact.[924]

Unfortunately for them, after disembarking at Key West, Yankee President James Buchanan of Pennsylvania, along with his Northern constituents, decided that the *Wildfire's* black chattel were not wanted, and that America would be better off without them. As such, on May 19, 1860, he sent a "special message" to Congress requesting funds to ship the slaves back to Africa "as soon as practicable." To that end, as Buchanan wrote:

> I would suggest that Congress might authorize the President to enter into a general agreement with the *[American] Colonization Society* binding them to receive on the coast of Africa, from an agent there, all the captured Africans which may be delivered to him, and to maintain them for a limited period, upon such terms and conditions as may combine humanity toward these unfortunates with a just economy.[925]

Congress approved the appropriation and the bark's longsuffering Africans were eventually sent to Liberia under the auspices of one of America's most racist Yankee organizations.[926]

Despite this temporary setback, the Northeast and her Wall Street Boys in New York City continued to fund and launch one famous slave trading ship after another, decades after legal abolition in the region. Among the more celebrated of these vessels were the *Haidee* (built in 1851 at Providence, Rhode Island), the *Lady Suffolk* (built in

1852 at Baltimore, Maryland), the *Sunny South* (built in 1854 at Williamsburg, New York), and of course the *Nightingale* (built in 1851 at Eliot, Maine, and Portsmouth, New Hampshire).[927]

The fact is that it was not Southern slavery, but rather the North's heavy dependence on the Yankee slave trade and on selling slaves to the South, that helped precipitate the Civil War: in March 1861 the newly constitutionally formed Confederate States of America adopted its Constitution, which included a clause banning slave trading with foreign nations.[928] "Foreign nations," of course, now included the United States of America. The North panicked, deciding it was better to beat the South into submission than allow her to cut off one of the Yankees' primary revenue streams.[929] Big government Liberal Abraham Lincoln, the only 1860 presidential candidate who promised *not* to interfere with slavery,[930] and who was put into office by Northern industrialists using profits from the Northern slave trade,[931] launched the War of Northern Aggression in April, just a few weeks later.[932]

An old illustration of the misnamed 703 ton clipper *Sunny South*, the only sailing ship ever built by Northerner George Steers (designer of the famous racing yacht *America*). Known as "one of the prettiest clippers ever launched at New York," in 1860 the *Sunny South* was seized by the British ship *Brisk*, with a cargo of 850 slaves on board. Though there was now one less Yankee slave ship on the prowl, her capture had no impact on the Yankee slave trade.

How can these things be true if they are not in our history books? Let us examine the facts.

Though Southerner George Mason tried, unsuccessfully, to prohibit the U.S. slave commerce as early as 1787[933]—referring to it as a "wicked, cruel, and unnatural trade"[934]—and though Southern President Thomas Jefferson finally permanently banned it in 1808,[935] the law (as even Lincoln observed)[936] was routinely ignored by Northerners[937] (mainly from New England and New York),[938] who vigorously continued to illegally traffic in human chattel,[939] even during and after the Civil War.[940] Not a single slaving captain or trader was punished by the U.S. until Gordon in 1862,[941] and for good reason: the federal government was completely controlled by slave interests right through to the Lincoln administration.[942] Indeed, as just mentioned, this is how "Honest Abe" funded his war: chiefly with profits from Northern slavery and the Yankee slave trade.[943]

These 17th-Century British galleons, sailing under the auspices of England's Royal African Company, were specifically outfitted for the transatlantic slave trade, and were responsible for bringing tens of thousands of African slaves into North America and the West Indies (the Caribbean). Ships sailing under Britain's sister organization, the East India Company, busied themselves transporting slaves from Madagascar to India and the East Indies (Asia). Britain's deep interest in the slave trade was later imposed on the American colonies against the wishes of Southerners like George Washington, Thomas Jefferson, and George Mason. This additional affliction on the already over-taxed colonies helped inspire both the American Revolutionary War in 1775 and the Declaration of Independence in 1776.

Yankee abolitionist, individualist, and natural rights advocate Lysander Spooner saw right through Lincoln's duplicitous treachery, correctly referring to the president's "Wall Street Boys"—that is, New York City's business establishment (bankers, merchants, manufacturers, and stockjobbers)[944]—as the "lenders of blood money." Wrote Spooner:

> *. . . these lenders of blood money had, for a long series of years previous to the war, been the willing accomplices of the slave-holders in perverting the government from the purposes of liberty and justice, to the greatest of crimes. They had been such accomplices for a purely pecuniary consideration, to wit, a control of the markets in the South; in other words,*

the privilege of holding the slave-holders themselves in industrial and commercial subjection to the manufacturers and merchants of the North (who afterwards furnished the money for the [Civil] war). And these Northern merchants and manufacturers, these lenders of blood money, were willing to continue to be the accomplices of the slaveholders in the future, for the same pecuniary considerations. But the slaveholders, either doubting the fidelity of their Northern allies, or feeling themselves strong enough to keep their slaves in subjection without Northern assistance, would no longer pay the price these Northern men demanded. And *it was to enforce this price in the future—that is, to monopolize the Southern markets, to maintain their industrial and commercial control over the South—that these Northern manufacturers and merchants lent some of the profits of their former monopolies for the [Civil] war, in order to secure themselves the same, or greater, monopolies in the future. These—and not any love of liberty or justice—were the motives on which the money for the [Civil] war was lent by the North.*[945]

Yankee abolitionist Lysander Spooner of Massachusetts was not fooled by Abraham Lincoln's political chicanery. Instead he accurately attributed the Civil War not to so-called "Southern slavery," but to the North's stubborn support of the Yankee slave trade.

Finally, the North was also responsible for creating the infamous "Cotton Triangle,"[946] or "Slave Triangle," as it is also known,[947] a three-way process easily understood by following the money.

1) Yankee slave ships sailed from the North to Africa where rum (made in Northern distilleries)[948] was traded for African slaves (already enslaved by other Africans).[949] The going rate was 115 gallons of rum for a healthy African male slave, 95 gallons for a healthy African female slave.[950] 2) These individuals were brought back to America and auctioned off at Southern ports, sold a second time as laborers in the cotton growing industry on Dixie's expansive plantations. The harvested cotton was then sold to New England's textile mills, whose products were peddled worldwide at huge profits. 3) These profits were then used to

fund more Northern slave expeditions to Africa, completing the Triangle,[951] each time accruing evermore vast fortunes for Yankee slavers.[952]

Phillips provides the following description of a typical New England triangular slave run, this particular one from the Ocean State, to Africa, to the West Indies, and back to New England. Yale University, the source of the original manuscript, calls it: "An estimate of a voyage from Rhode Island to the Coast of Guinea and from thence to Jamaica and so back to Rhode Island for a sloop of 60 Tons":

> Details of characteristic outfit, cargo, and expectations in *the New England branch of [the transatlantic slave] trade* may be had from an estimate made in 1752 for a projected voyage. A sloop of sixty tons, valued at £300 sterling, was to be overhauled and refitted, armed, furnished with handcuffs, medicines and miscellaneous chandlery [storerooms] at a cost of £65, and provisioned for £50 more. Its officers and crew, seven hands all told, were to draw aggregate wages of £10 per month for an estimated period of one year. Laden with eight thousand gallons of rum at l*s*. 8*d*. per gallon and with forty-five barrels, tierces and hogsheads of bread, flour, beef, pork, tar, tobacco, tallow and sugar—all at an estimated cost of £775—it was to sail for the Gold Coast [of Africa]. There, after paying the local charges from the cargo, some 35 slave men were to be bought at 100 gallons per head, 15 women at 85 gallons, and 15 boys and girls at 65 gallons; and the residue of the rum and miscellaneous cargo was expected to bring some seventy ounces of gold in exchange as well as to procure food supplies for the westward voyage. Recrossing the Atlantic, with an estimated death loss of a man, a woman and two children, the surviving slaves were to be sold in Jamaica at about £21, £18, and £14 for the respective classes. Of these proceeds about one-third was to be spent for a cargo of 105 hogsheads of molasses at 8*d*. per gallon, and the rest of the money remitted to London, whither the gold dust was also to be sent. The molasses upon reaching Newport [Rhode Island] was expected to bring twice as much as it had cost in the tropics. After deducting factor's commissions of from 2½ to 5 per cent. on all sales and purchases, and of "4 in 104" on the slave sales as the captain's allowance, after providing for insurance at four per cent. on ship and cargo for each leg of the voyage, and for leakage of ten per cent. of the rum and five per cent. of the molasses, and after charging off the whole cost of the ship's outfit and one-third of her original value, there remained the sum of £357, 8*s*. 2*d*. as the expected profits of the voyage.[953]

Thus it was that *every* American slave ship that ever sailed to Africa left and returned from, not a Southern C.S. port, but a Northern U.S. port. Again, this is why the only person ever arrested, tried, and executed for slaving was New Yorker Captain Gordon, who hailed from one of the many Northern states that openly and illegally continued to trade in slaves and practice slavery long after both had been officially abolished.[954]

WHAT YOU WERE TAUGHT: The Old South was deeply involved in the oceangoing slave trade, and possessed numerous slave ships, one of the more noteworthy being the *Clotilde*, which imported over 100 slaves into the South just before the Civil War.

THE TRUTH: It is true that the *Clotilde* sailed to Africa from Mobile, Alabama, in 1859, bringing back a cargo of already enslaved Africans. But it is not true that the South was "deeply involved" in the transatlantic slave trade, nor is it true that she "possessed numerous slave ships." And as far as the *Clotilde* is concerned, most of what we have been told about her is wrong.

The *Clotilde* ran under the U.S. flag—for the Southern Confederacy had not yet been formed—and her owner was not a Southerner, but a New England shipping magnate named Captain Timothy Meaher, of Maine.

More importantly, the *Clotilde* was not a *legitimate* Southern slave ship. There was no such thing: the practice of foreign slave trading had been banned by the U.S. Congress in 1808.[955] This is why the schooner had been constructed in secret, launched in secret, had returned to Mobile and unloaded her enslaved cargo in secret, and had been burned in an isolated Alabama bayou (near Mobile Bay) in secret. And it is also why Meaher went on the run in order to evade arrest for several years, and it is why, when he was finally captured, he was put on trial.

The point is that if the *Clotilde* had been an "authentic Southern slave ship" operating under "legal Southern slave trading laws," as pro-North writers continue to incorrectly insist, none of these things would have taken place. Indeed, the entire African slave voyage had been the result of a bet between Meaher and other transplanted Yankees in Mobile. The wager? That he could not successfully smuggle African slaves in under the nose of the U.S. government. But he could, and he did![956]

As for the comment that the South legally owned and operated a myriad of slave ships, this is patently false, for as just discussed, the foreign slave trade was made illegal in 1808, and when the Confederacy was formed in 1861 she immediately banned it as well. The illicit schooner *Clotilde* turns out to be the only *notable* example of an antebellum "Southern" slave ship. But she was not truly Southern, for her Yankee owner did not sail her with either the blessings of the Southern people or the sanction of Southern law.

How different this is from what occurred in the Old North, the region from which all of the nation's *legal* slave ships sailed—with the complete backing of the Yankee judicial system and the full support of a majority of the Northern populace!

Just as there was no such thing as a "Northern abolition ship," there was no such thing as a "Southern slave ship." All legal, and nearly all illegal, shipments of African slaves came to the U.S. aboard Yankee slave vessels, designed by Yankee engineers, constructed by Yankee shipbuilders, fitted out by Yankee riggers, piloted by Yankee ship captains, manned by Yankee crews, launched from Yankee marine ports, funded by Yankee businessmen, and supported by the Yankee population. Is it not now time to put the responsibility for American slavery where it belongs, instead of on a Southern scapegoat?

In a 1906 issue of *Harper's Weekly*, S. H. M. Byers wrote of the massive problem of Yankee slave trading, one that endured under the auspices of the United States government well into the Civil War years:

> The enormous extent of this traffic now appears almost beyond belief. For fifty years the human conscience of the American people was dead. The infamy was winked at, and *it flourished under the Stars and Stripes* when every other civilized nation of the earth was struggling for its suppression. *In the eight short years preceding 1848 the British government caught and destroyed 625 slave-ships and freed 40,000 of their victims. The American [U.S.] government was doing nothing at all.* Then, as later, controlled and directed by a section growing rich and arrogant out of the piracy of slaves, it folded its arms and stood unmoved. Its officials saw nothing. The cupidity of scoundrels on the Northern seaboard equalled the scoundrelism of the Southern slave-traders. Aside from the earnest, crying, but vain appeals of the Abolitionists there was no moral opposition to the trade. There was no anger, there was no pity. *New York city itself, in the short period of eighteen months, equipped and sent secretly from its harbor eighty-five slave-ships to prey upon helpless humanity beyond the sea. Seventeen million dollars a year was being made in the awful traffic.* Stephen A. Douglas declared that 15,000 chained and tortured human beings were brought into the United States in the single year 1859.[957]

In summarizing this chapter let us consider the words of Southern writer Edwin Clifford Holland, who, in 1822, wrote:

> The Northern and Eastern sections of our Union, then, in common with ourselves, Colonies of the British Empire, were at a very early period, actively and industriously engaged in the very traffic to which is to be attributed the introduction and existence of the sin of which they have since so loudly and clamorously complained. The "atrocious crime" of slavery among us as a [Southern] people, of which, *their [the North] own agency was, in a great degree, the proximate cause*, ought, in strict justice, therefore to be attributed to them, or, as will be shown, is less imputable to us. *Great Britain, and the then Northern and Eastern Colonies of her American possessions, were the first dealers in the odious and reproachful commerce that has entailed upon our country, the evil which we all lament, and if the latter made any early or obviously direct efforts, to abolish the trade, it was not so much from any "compunctious visitings" of conscience, or from any more enlightened feelings of philanthropy*, as from the operation of the acts

of the British Parliament, which, from time to time granted peculiar and exclusive privileges to British merchants, that amounted to a virtual prohibition, and debarred her Colonies from any participation in the trade. *When the latter [the Northern states] found that they were to be inundated by a [black slave] class of people, from the introduction of which, they no longer were to derive the commercial advantages they had hitherto possessed, exertions were then made to abolish the traffic*, or to lay it, under heavy imposts. *It was not until [the early 1800s] . . . that any very serious disposition was shown by them to interrupt the stream of wealth that poured its riches into their laps, or to divert it from the channels in which it had hitherto flowed.* The history of the times is emphatic upon this point. The first expression of the Legislation in the then North-American Colonies which took place upon this subject, was that of the "General Court of Massachusetts," in 1645, in which they prohibited the buying and selling of slaves, "except those who were condemned to servitude by the sentence of a court of justice, or those who were taken in time of war." In 1703, more than half a century after the qualified provisions of the act which we have just quoted, another effort was made to restrict the importation of slaves, by subjecting it to a heavy impost, which failed. From the complexion of these historical documents, it would appear that *it was from no very nice and scrupulous abhorrence of the "odious crime" of slavery, on the part of the Northern and Eastern Colonies, that they interdicted the trade in human flesh, but a necessary result of the commercial avarice of the mother country [England], which closed the door of the trade upon her Colonies, and shut up the gates of its African commerce to all but native born British merchants, and consequently destroyed all prospects of advantage on the part of the Colonies in this respect. It was not, then, so much the generous result of a more enlarged and enlightened philanthropy on the part of these [Northern] Colonies, as it was a calculating policy which dictated the steps that they took, in relation to the importation of slaves. If it were not, why delay the expression of their abhorrence of what they deemed a curse and a scourge upon the country, from the year 1645 to 1703, in the years intermediate between the two periods of which, the exclusive privileges to which we have referred were granted by the crown*; or why the distinction between the situation of the individual [African slave] who may have been fairly purchased on the Coast of Africa, and brought into the country, and that of him who was taken prisoner in awful war, fighting boldly against the enemies of his race, and manfully exerting all the energies which God and nature gave him, to repel the notorious and uninterrupted aggressions of the Colonists upon his liberty and life. The red man of the woods, who was the original proprietor of the soil on which they had settled, if taken captive while resisting the encroachments of his more civilized and unwelcome neighbors, was declared to be a slave, and could be bought and sold as such, at the discretion or caprice of those into whose hands the fortune of war may have thrown him; while the black man was no sooner landed on their shores, than he became invested with the privileges of a higher and more fortunate condition. *And yet these [Northern] Colonies now arrogate to themselves, the proud and peculiar distinction of having first interdicted the traffic in human flesh, and of having, from the purest and most disinterested humanity, first exhibited to the world the features of a system of legislation dignified by all that can ennoble humanity.*

We claim, on the part of the Colonists of the South, no particular exemption from the charge of having participated in this [slavery] commerce and in the reception in common with the Northern and Eastern Provinces, of the slaves that were imported in British ships; but they are certainly entitled to as much credit, on the score of humanity, as any portion of the Colonies, for *the early and active exertions which were made to suppress the growth of an evil, the frightful character of which appeared so evident.*[958]

The U.S.A. and only the U.S.A. is responsible for the American slave trade and American slavery, for it was her flag, not the Confederate flag, that flew from the masts of every legitimate slave ship between the early 1600s and the mid 1800s.

The whip! Where would Yankee mythology be without the whip? It is one of the mainstays of the entire artificial structure, and once it is removed the unstable edifice falls like the house of cards that it is. American society has been so indoctrinated by Northern anti-South propaganda that most people will assume that this early illustration depicts a white Southern slave owner whipping a Southern black slave. In fact, slave whipping was rare and strongly discouraged across the Old South, and was even illegal in many areas. Here we have the true "Lord of the Lash"; not a Southern slaveholder, but a Northern one. For the tormentor in this image is a white Bostonian and his naked victim—bound by cordage to a tree—is a black Yankee slave from Massachusetts. Such a scene should surprise no one. American slavery got its start in the Bay State, and it is the Northeastern U.S. where blacks had the least legal protection, and where they suffered under the nation's toughest and most inhumane Black Codes. Indeed, contrary to Yankee myth, America's Black Codes were invented, developed, and first implemented in the Northeast.

5

AMERICAN SLAVERY

WHAT YOU WERE TAUGHT: American slavery began in the South.
THE TRUTH: Like the American slave trade (which is connected with but distinct from American slavery), American slavery also got its start as a legal institution in the North. Its birthplace was, of course, none other than Massachusetts, the very *first* of the original 13 states (colonies) to legalize it in 1641.[959] In contrast, the *last* of the original 13 colonies to legalize slavery was a Southern one, Georgia, which officially sanctioned it 108 years later, in 1749.[960]

Boston, Massachusetts, the birthplace of American slavery. Though New York possessed African slaves as early as the 1620s, Massachusetts earns the title for having launched the institution in the American colonies by being the first to legitimize, monetize, and legalize it in 1641 by way of a series of Yankee laws and statutes.

Even the second, third, and fourth states to legalize slavery were all Northern ones: New Hampshire had slaves by 1645 and Delaware by the mid-1640s,[961] while Connecticut legalized slavery in 1650. It was not until 1661, 20 years after Massachusetts adopted slavery, that the first Southern state, Virginia, legalized the institution (becoming the fifth colony to do so).

A complete time table for the states is as follows:
The first colony to legalize slavery was Massachusetts, in 1641.
The second colony to legalize slavery was New Hampshire, in 1645.
The third colony to legalize slavery was Delaware, mid 1640s.
The fourth colony to legalize slavery was Connecticut, in 1650.
The fifth colony to legalize slavery was Virginia, in 1661.
The sixth colony to legalize slavery was Maryland, in 1663.
The seventh colony to legalize slavery was New York, in 1664.
The eighth colony to legalize slavery was New Jersey, in 1664.
The ninth colony to legalize slavery was South Carolina, in 1682.
The tenth colony to legalize slavery was Pennsylvania, in 1700.
The eleventh colony to legalize slavery was Rhode Island, in 1700.
The twelfth colony to legalize slavery was North Carolina, in 1715.
The thirteenth and last colony to legalize slavery was Georgia, in 1749.

In short, just as they initiated the American slave trade in 1638, this list clearly shows that the Northern states are also responsible for launching American slavery in 1641. Dixie played no role in either.[962]

WHAT YOU WERE TAUGHT: America is solely responsible for American slavery.

THE TRUTH: So-called "American" slavery was actually a "gift" of Europe, and more specifically of the English. But before we examine these facts, let us remind ourselves that slavery already existed in America long before the arrival of European explorers, for Native-Americans had been practicing it among themselves for thousands of years prior. In 1492 Christopher Columbus arrived in the West Indies, where he began enslaving millions of Native-Americans themselves (and, as a result, killing off most of the Indian population within a few years). Thus it is Columbus who must shoulder the responsibility for introducing European slavery in the Americas.

However, legal and widespread *black* slavery in the Americas got its start under the English flag,[963] when English merchant Sir John Hawkins instigated a series of slave voyages to Africa in 1562[964] (returning with a rich cargo of "ginger, sugar, and pearls"),[965] thereby "exciting the avarice of the British government."[966]

That same year, under Queen Elizabeth I, the English government legalized the purchase of negroes.[967] These momentous acts culminated in the notorious triangular trading system,[968] or Cotton Triangle, in which: 1) goods were exchanged for slaves in Africa, who were 2) used in the American colonies to produce sugar and cotton, goods that were 3) sold in New England to the region's numerous manufacturers.[969] The profits (60 percent of which went to the shareholders of Hawkins' operations) from these sales were used to fund additional trips to Africa, starting the Cotton Triangle all over again.[970]

In the latter half of the 16th Century English naval explorer and slave merchant Sir John Hawkins introduced black African slavery into the Americas for the first time. Some 75 years later the British government began forcing slavery on the original 13 American colonies, one of the triggers that inaugurated the American Revolutionary War.

Centuries later, the English were still the primary source of slaves in America. In one three year period, for example, between 1804 and 1807, English slave ships brought half of all slaves to South Carolina.[971] The other half were transported there by Rhode Island slave ships,[972] many of whose owners were of English heritage. Thus it was that Southern author Edwin Clifford Holland said of Hawkins: he was "guilty of having paved the way to the violence, barbarity, and bloodshed, that have stained the subsequent history of the slave trade."[973]

Behind this one man then lies the primary responsibility for American black slavery and all of its ills. Which in turn means, as New York politician James Tallmadge, Jr. correctly asserted in 1819, that England "committed the original sin of bringing slaves into our country."[974] In 1846 New York Presbyterian minister Albert Barnes spoke for all Southerners when he said that slavery was "a burden imposed on them by the joint wickedness and cupidity of our fatherland [England] and the [Yankees at the] North."[975] In 1850 Jefferson Davis concurred, reproaching "our British ancestors for the introduction of this institution upon the continent of America."[976]

Adding to the powerful impact of Hawkins' exploits on America was the organization of England's Royal African Company in 1661,[977] and its formation in 1672. Under the auspices of the company, which monopolized the trade until 1697 (the year it terminated),[978] all males of English nationality had the right to engage in the slave trade, which, in 1750, Parliament called "very advantageous to Great Britain." Indeed, the slave trade was "the cardinal point in the treaties of Great Britain with the European powers."[979]

By the 1700s Britain had become the world's major slave trading nation, a true slave power in every sense of the term:[980] between 1680 and 1786, she carried at least 2 million pre-enslaved Africans to North America and the Caribbean[981] (some 20,000 a year),[982] then forced the institution, as Thomas Jefferson complained, on the original 13 English-American colonies.[983] The 1824 edition of the *Encyclopedia Britannica* concurred: "The existence of slavery [in the U.S.] is a bequest from Britain; it is not the crime of the Americans, but their misfortune."[984]

After the Treaty of Utrecht in 1713 England was awarded the *Asiento*,[985] the shipping rights over the oceangoing slave trade between Africa and Latin America,[986] allowing the transport of 4,800 African slaves into the Spanish colonies every year.[987] From this point on she completely monopolized the lucrative African slave trade, outdoing even slave-trade obsessed Portugal and Spain.[988]

As a result, between 1713 and 1792 the yearly export of English goods to Africa for use in the slave trade increased tenfold, while in 1790 slave-produced merchandise brought to England from the West Indies constituted nearly 25 percent of all British imports. This means that the massive growth of British capitalism in the 1700s was due almost solely to African slavery. The nation's industrial revolution itself was born out of her "peculiar institution": Liverpool, as just one example, grew into a large manufacturing center thanks to slavery, which in turn stimulated industry in towns like Manchester.[989]

By 1770, from the British seaports of Liverpool, London, Bristol, and Lancaster alone, sailed 192 slave ships,[990] with cargo holds capable of transporting some 47,146 Africans.[991] It has been estimated that at least one third of the slaves carried away from Africa's west coast were paid for by cotton dealers whose goods were manufactured in Lancashire.[992] My cousin, the 17th-Century English statesman Prince Rupert, had long desired that England become the world's leading slave trading nation—and his wish came true.[993]

British man-of-war, 1738. Britain dominated the transatlantic slave trade, and in turn, early American slavery, for over a century. Even the *Encyclopedia Britannica* admits that American slavery was not "the crime of Americans," but an inheritance of Britain, and thus merely America's "misfortune."

By this time Britain was responsible for over half the world's slave trade. At her peak in 1790 she was exporting 38,000 Africans a year, more than French, Dutch, Danish, and Portuguese slave traders combined.[994] Britain held this position for years after, during which time she continued to fill North America with hundreds of thousands of enslaved Africans through her many colonial seaports in New England and throughout the American Northeast.[995] "The mother country" then "continued the traffic in utter disregard of the repeated remonstrances of the colonies."[996]

An example of the harsh slavery laws that were imposed on the British-American Colonies by their "mother country" comes from 1740, enacted under King George II. Made perpetual in 1783, the statute covered all of the Carolinas and even included free blacks:

> Whereas, in his Majesty's plantations, etc., slavery has been allowed, be it enacted, that all Negroes, Mulattoes, etc., who are

> or shall hereafter be in this province, and all their issue and offspring, born and to be born, shall be, and are hereby declared to be, and shall remain for ever hereafter, absolute slaves.[997]

This meant, in other words, that "it shall always be presumed that every negro is a slave, unless the contrary can be made to appear."[998]

In 1918 Ulrich B. Phillips described England's slave trade like this:

> The bursting of the South Sea bubble in 1720 shifted the bulk of the separate trading from London to the rival city of Bristol. But the removal of the duties in 1730 brought the previously unimportant port of Liverpool into the field with such vigor that ere long she had the larger half of all the English slave trade. Her merchants prospered by their necessary parsimony. The wages they paid were the lowest, and the commissions and extra allowances they gave in their early years were nil. By 1753 her ships in the slave traffic numbered eighty-seven, totaling about eight thousand tons burthen and rated to carry some twenty-five thousand slaves. Eight of these vessels were trading on the Gambia, thirty-eight on the Gold and Slave Coasts, five at Benin, three at New Calabar, twelve at Bonny, eleven at Old Calabar, and ten in Angola. For the year 1771 the number of slavers bound from Liverpool was reported at one hundred and seven with a capacity of 29,250 negroes, while fifty-eight went from London rated to carry 8,136, twenty-five from Bristol to carry 8,810, and five from Lancaster with room for 950. Of this total of 195 ships 43 traded in Senegambia, 29 on the Gold Coast, 56 on the Slave Coast, 63 in the bights of Benin and Biafra, and 4 in Angola. . . . By 1801 the Liverpool ships had increased to 150, with capacity for 52,557 slaves according to the reduced rating of five slaves to three tons of burthen as required by the parliamentary act of 1788. About half of these traded in the Gulf of Guinea, and half in the ports of Angola.[999]

To be fair, England was also the first Western power to advocate abolition, banning the slave trade in her own territory in 1807[1000] and slavery in 1831, and then in all of the British colonies in 1833,[1001] while in 1841 the Quintuple Treaty—which England signed with France, Russia, Austria, and Prussia—greatly aided in suppressing the oceangoing trade.[1002] Yet, there is a hypocritical irony here.

Though England introduced then forced the slave trade (and thus slavery) upon a reluctant young America,[1003] she later became the first to

The Georgian Era, 1714-1830, was presided over by the "four English Georges": King George I, King George II, King George III, and King George IV. All four monarchs had an influence, for good or ill, on American slavery. In particular was George III, the unlucky recipient of Thomas Jefferson's fiery document, the Declaration of Independence, which listed "a long train of abuses and usurpations" by Britain, including the imposition of slavery on the 13 colonies. Jefferson's famous antislavery passage was later edited out by his peers for fear of offending wealthy Yankee slave traders.

try and prevent America from practicing slavery and the slave trade,[1004] for *British abolition* (in the early 1830s) *coincided with the birth of the British working class.*[1005] In 1861 in the U.S., this was the exact same tactic used by the North: after bringing millions of shackled Africans to the Northeast between the 1600s and 1800s, *white Northern laborers finally began to protest against their presence.* As we will see in our next entry, it was then and only then that the Yankee began to find the institution unprofitable[1006] and the idea of permanently coexisting with people of African descent unbearable.[1007]

To this end, Northerners then, slowly, carefully, and methodically, began suppressing slavery in their own region over the next 100 years. Then (without actually abolishing it) they pushed the institution on a largely unwilling South.[1008] Yet, within a few short decades they commanded Dixie to *completely*, *immediately*, and *unconditionally* emancipate her black servants, nearly all recently acquired from Northern slave merchants.[1009]

WHAT YOU WERE TAUGHT: The Northern states hated the inhumanity of slavery and could not wait to abolish it. This is why the North emancipated its slaves before the South.

THE TRUTH: Slavery was officially extinguished in the Northern states first, not because the worldly Victorian Yankee began to feel shame or guilt, but because it became unprofitable,[1010] the same reason Europe finally abolished it.[1011] And slavery became unprofitable in the American North, in great part, due to the regions's largely rocky sandy soil and short cold summers, which made it unsuitable for large-scale farming.[1012]

There was also the North's enormous distance from both Africa (where slaves were picked up) and the tropics (where slaves were needed on sugar, coffee, cotton, pineapple, tobacco, and indigo plantations).[1013] This last factor made it much more profitable to sell slaves in the American South (which was a shorter distance from both Africa and the Caribbean).[1014] Another monetary consideration involved the difference in value between slave labor and the slaves themselves:

> An early realization that the price of negroes . . . was greater than the worth of their labor under ordinary circumstances in New England led *the Yankee participants in the African trade* to market their slave cargoes in the plantation colonies [in the American South] instead of bringing them home [to the Northern states].[1015]

New England's rocky sandy soil, long cold winters, short cool summers, and hilly terrain made large-scale farming unprofitable and field slavery impractical, just one of the many reasons Yankees pushed their "peculiar institution" southward—onto a largely unwilling populace, it should be added.

There was also the humanitarian doctrine of equality which was spreading to America after the French Revolution[1016] and the European Enlightenment.[1017] More importantly there was America's own Revolutionary War, which, due to the enormous numbers of blacks who willingly served on both the American side and the British side (usually for the promise of manumission), weakened the master-slave bond across the North.[1018]

Two black female slaves serving dinner to a New England family. The main reason Yankees finally got rid of slavery had nothing to do with humanitarianism, altruism, or even money. It was due to the entrenched white racism that was endemic to all of the Northern states. Like Lincoln, most Northerners simply could not abide the thought of living side by side with African-Americans as equals.

Another factor that aided in the gradual demise of Yankee slavery was the skyrocketing birth rate of whites in the North after 1750. This huge new supply of free workers greatly damaged the Yankee slave economy and wage rates fell, helping make slavery unnecessary, cumbersome, inefficient, uneconomical, and finally obsolete across the North.[1019]

Along with the North's growing blue-collar demographic came increasing racial intolerance toward non-whites. As early as the late 1700s Yankees "were frankly stating *an antipathy of their people toward negroes in any capacity whatever*."[1020] This, of course, now made abolition in the North absolutely essential, especially economically. Yankee John Adams of Massachusetts, who was to become America's second president two years later, wrote the following in a personal letter dated March 21, 1795:

Argument might have some weight in the abolition of slavery in the Massachusetts, but the real cause was the multiplication of labouring white people, who would no longer suffer the rich to employ these sable rivals so much to their injury. This principle has kept negro slavery out of France, England, and other parts of Europe. *The common people would not suffer the labour, by which alone they could obtain a subsistence, to be done by slaves. . . . The common white people, or rather the labouring people, were the cause of rendering negroes unprofitable servants. Their scoffs and insults, their continual insinuations, filled the negroes with discontent, made them lazy, idle, proud, vicious, and at length wholly useless to their masters, to such a degree that the abolition of slavery became a measure of economy.*[1021]

Here we have the most significant factor leading to the death of Northern slavery: *Northern white racism*. Most 18th- and 19th-Century Yanks simply preferred living in an all-white society,[1022] free from the "naturally disgusting" presence of the black man, as Lincoln and other white racist Northerners expressed it.[1023]

Each of these elements then contributed to the demise of Yankee slavery as well as its introduction into Dixie,[1024] a process, according to surviving chronicles, already well underway in the early 1700s. For example, we have record of

an advertisement in the Boston *Gazette* of August 17, 1761, *offering for sale young slaves just from Africa and proposing to take in exchange "any negro men, strong and hearty though not of the best moral character, which are proper subjects of transportation [to the South]"*; [there is also] . . . a letter of James Habersham of Georgia in 1764 telling of his purchase of a parcel of negroes at New York for work on his rice plantation. That *the disestablishment of slavery in the North during and after the American Revolution enhanced the exportation of negroes was recited in a Vermont statute of 1787, and is shown by occasional items in Southern archives.* One of these is the registry at Savannah of a bill of sale made at [the slave seaport of] New London [Connecticut] in 1787 for a mulatto boy "as a servant for the term of ten years only, at the expiration of which time he is to be free." Another is a report from an official at Norfolk to the Governor of Virginia [Robert Brooke], in 1795, relating that *the captain of a sloop from Boston with three negroes on board pleaded ignorance of the Virginia law against the bringing in of slaves.*[1025]

Phillips writes that while the North's abolitionary sentiments were sometimes based on a "humanitarian motive,"

> *it was supplemented, often in the same [Yankee] breasts, by the inhumane feeling of personal repugnance toward negroes.* The anti-slave-trade agitation in England also had a contributing influence. . . . *At the South racial repugnance was fainter, and humanitarianism though of positive weight was but one of several factors.*[1026]

And so, though the money-making aspects of the institution continued illegally (with the tacit approval of the U.S. government) until eight months after the "Civil War," up until that time the Northern states, one by one, had "officially" freed themselves from slavery.[1027] This they did *slowly*, *voluntarily*, and *gradually* over a long drawn out 239 year period (from 1626 to 1865), during which time—as the *Encyclopedia Britannica* flatly states—they "*simply transferred Northern slaves to Southern markets.*"[1028]

The North, the originator of both the American slave trade and American slavery, gave itself over 200 years to completely abolish slavery. Big government Liberal Abraham Lincoln, however, coerced the South into immediate abolition through the use of unconstitutional measures, war crimes, and violent force. Was this right or fair? To this day the traditional South says no.

Unfortunately, Lincoln and his liberal cohorts did not allow the same slow, deliberate, extended, natural "emancipation" process to unfold in the South as it had in their own region. Instead, in Dixie Dishonest Abe *forced* the abolition of slavery, abruptly, involuntarily, and at gunpoint, and within a period of *two short years*: 1863 to 1865. All of this from a region where abolitionists made up only a tiny but loud minority,[1029] as Lincoln himself was well aware.[1030]

Proof that the North was not truly an abolitionist area was that while it abolished slavery in its own backyard, the majority still did not want to end slavery in the South, for New England's textile mills, and the New York industrialists who owned them, were still making vast fortunes from Southern cotton, picked and ginned by millions of Southern slaves. Thus, a full scale Northern effort began to keep Southern slavery alive, and even strengthen and enlarge it. It was in this way that when the white North grew tired of dealing with blacks and slavery, she pushed the institution southward on a mostly unwilling populace,[1031] one that had been trying to abolish it since the early 1700s.[1032] For example, when New York slave owner John Bouiness freed one of his black servants in the North, at the same time he also had five other slaves sold in Virginia.[1033]

The Northern states never "abolished" slavery in the traditional legal sense. While Yankee slave ships continued their trips to Africa and the West Indies right up and into the Civil War, the Northern states from which they sailed had implemented a long, drawn out legislative process known as "gradual emancipation," which allowed for the casual unhurried extinction of the institution. This same right was later cruelly denied the Southern states.

It has been estimated that at least 99 percent of Yankee businessmen were anti-abolitionists who supported the continuation of Southern slavery, for, as mentioned, the cotton that Southern slaves picked was one the North's largest financial assets.[1034] Among the most vociferous of this group were New York's "Wall Street Boys,"[1035] which had bankrolled Lincoln's first (and later his second) presidential campaign using money they had made primarily from the Yankee slave trade.[1036] There was also the Boston elite, who made it known that they were quite willing to make huge concessions to the South in the interest of making money.[1037]

Around 1831 Rhode Islander Elizabeth Buffum Chace and her father Arnold Buffum, the first president of the New England Anti-

Slavery Society, decided to travel across their region in order to enlist Yankee support for their emancipation plan. In her 1891 memoirs Chace wrote:

> I remember well, how eager we were, in our revived Anti-Slavery zeal, to present the cause of the slave to everybody we met [in New England]; not doubting that, when their attention was called to it, they would be ready, as we were, to demand his immediate emancipation. But, alas! *their commercial relations, their political associations*, and with many, their religious fellowship with the people of the South, so blinded the eyes, hardened the hearts and stifled the consciences of *the North*, that *we found very few people who were ready to give any countenance or support to the new AntiSlavery movement.*[1038]

Is it any wonder then that the 1860 Republican Party Platform contained paragraphs promising to leave the "peculiar institution" alone,[1039] while declaring that Republicans were only against the extension of slavery, not slavery itself?[1040] That in his First Inaugural Address, March 4, 1861, Lincoln pledged not to disturb slavery?[1041] Or that American slavery did not come to a final end until December 6, 1865 (eight months after Lincoln's death), with the passage of the Thirteenth Amendment?[1042]

Here we have more proof, if more is needed, that the Civil War was not a contest over slavery. It was a Northern contest over slavery money, a Southern contest over constitutional rights (that is, self-determination).[1043]

WHAT YOU WERE TAUGHT: The Northern states legally abolished slavery quickly and completely.

THE TRUTH: We have already seen that the Northern states did not end slavery quickly, for it took them over 100 years, and in the case of New York, over 200 years, before they took steps to terminate it. We have also discussed the fact that they did not actually abolish Northern slavery completely, for the institution lingered, in a myriad of forms, until long after the end of Lincoln's War.

From these two facts, in turn, it is obvious that the Northern states never really "abolished" slavery in their region at all. This term, pertaining to Yankee slavery, is, in truth, a misnomer. What they actually did was merely suppress it until, over time, it naturally faded away due to neglect, unprofitability, and ultimately white racist hostility.[1044] As mentioned, the Northern states accomplished this through a slow, voluntarily, and gradual process—and, it should be emphasized, *without any interference from the South*.[1045]

This exposes the lie that the Northern states literally "abolished slavery" within their borders on a precise date in a specific year, as our Yankee-biased history books claim. For example: "Vermont in 1777," "Pennsylvania in 1780," "Massachusetts in 1780," "Connecticut in 1784," "Rhode Island in 1784," "New Jersey in 1804," and "New York in 1827."[1046]

The fact of the matter is that *none* of the Northern states ever actually abolished slavery; they only legislated it into "gradual extinction."[1047] This is why a few Yankee states, such as New Hampshire and Delaware, did not fully rid themselves of slavery until the passage of the Thirteenth Amendment, December 6, 1865 (though the U.S. government continued to allow the enslavement of criminals).[1048]

Just as there were—and still are—black slave owners in Africa, there were also black slave owners in early America. In fact, one out of four of all 17th-, 18th-, and 19th-Century free African-Americans, a largely wealthy class, owned black slaves.

In short, while Pennsylvania, Connecticut, Rhode Island, and New Hampshire all intentionally used a *gradual emancipation plan* (wherein freedom was guaranteed to all persons born in their states after the date of so-called "abolition"),[1049] the North as a whole gave herself over 200 leisurely years to eliminate slavery from within her borders. This is hardly what one would describe as "quick and complete abolition."[1050]

If only the Yankee had accorded this same privilege to his Southern compatriots! It would not have prevented Lincoln's War, of course, because the conflict was not about slavery.[1051] But it would have greatly eased the constitutional tensions that led Dixie into the War to begin with, and it is much more likely that the South today would be an independent, constitutional, confederate republic—just as our Southern ancestors intended before Lincoln repeatedly violated his oath of office.[1052]

WHAT YOU WERE TAUGHT: Only white Americans owned black slaves.

THE TRUTH: Liberal historians carefully hide the fact from the general public, but the reality is that there were tens of thousands of black slave owners in early America, most who were not counted in the U.S. Census (Census takers were prone to vastly underreporting blacks, free and enslaved).[1053] Additionally, some black slaveholders abused their African servants, another fact that you will seldom find in pro-North, anti-South history books.[1054]

One of the first slave owners in the American colonies was a black servant by the name of Anthony Johnson. After his arrival in 1621, he quickly worked off his term of indenture and began purchasing human chattel in Virginia.[1055] Later, in the chronicles of Northampton County, there is record of a suit brought by Johnson "for the purpose of recovering his negro servant."[1056] The African slaver from Angola, who owned both black *and* white servants, actually helped launch the American slave trade by forcing authorities to legally define the meaning of "slave ownership."[1057] In 1652 his son John Johnson imported and bought eleven white slaves, who worked under him at his Virginia plantation, located on the banks of the Pungoteague River.[1058]

In the mid 1790s, while he was traveling through South Carolina, French nobleman Duke de la Rochefoucauld Liancourt came across an enormous plantation with hundreds of black slaves, the owner who himself was black:

> In the township of St. Paul *a free negro*, who from his early youth carefully stored up the produce of his industry, *possesses a plantation of two hundred slaves. The severity excepted, with which this emancipated slave treats his negroes*, his conduct is said to be regular and good. His name is Pindaim, and he is eighty-five years old. He has married a white woman, and has given his daughter, a mulatto, to a white man.[1059]

In 1830 some 3,700 free Southern blacks owned nearly 12,000 black slaves,[1060] an average of almost four slaves a piece. That same year in the Deep South alone nearly 8,000 slaves were owned by some 1,500 black slave owners (about five slaves apiece). In Charleston, South Carolina, as another example, between the years 1820 and 1840, 75 percent of the city's free blacks owned slaves. Furthermore, *25 percent of all free American blacks owned slaves, South and North.*[1061]

A Mandingo chief and his enslaved swordbearer. The Mandingo people of Sierra Leone were one of the most aggressive and merciless slavers in the whole of Western Africa, often initiating wars on other villages for the sole purpose of obtaining slaves. The millennia old African custom of slave owning later came, quite naturally, across the Atlantic to America with the slaves aboard Yankee slave ships, where it flourished among tens of thousands of black slaveholders in both the South and the North.

As we are about to discuss in more detail, in 1861 the South's 300,000 white slave owners made up only 1 percent of the total U.S. white population of 30 million people.[1062] Thus, while only one Southern white out of every 300,000 owned slaves (1 percent), one Southern black out of every four owned slaves (25 percent). In other words, far more blacks owned black (and sometimes white) slaves than whites did: 25 percent compared to 1 percent.

Most black slave owners were not only proslavery, they were also pro-South, supporting the Confederate Cause during Lincoln's War as fervently as any white Southerner did. At church each Sunday, thousands of blacks would pray for those blacks, both their own slaves and their free friends, who wore the Rebel uniform. Their supplications were simple: they asked God to help all African-American Confederates kill as many Yankees as possible, then return home safely.[1063]

Wealthy blacks bought, sold, and exploited black slaves for profit, just as white slave owners did. The well-known Anna Kingsley, who began life—as was nearly always the case—as a slave in her native Africa, ended up in what is now Jacksonville, Florida, where she became one of early America's many black plantation owners and slaveholders.[1064]

These black servants, working a Southern cotton field, were not owned by a white family, but by one of the thousands of affluent black slave owning families that once thrived across the United States. On average black slaveholders owned far more slaves than white slaveholders did, a fact you will never read in any pro-North history book.

Some, like the African-American Metoyers, an anti-abolition family from Louisiana, owned huge numbers of black slaves; in their case, at least 400.[1065] At about $1,500 a piece,[1066] their servants were worth a total of $600,000, or $20 million in today's currency.[1067] This made the Metoyers among the wealthiest people in the U.S., black or white, then or now. Louisiana's all-black Confederate army unit, the Augustin Guards, was named after the family patriarch, Augustin Metoyer.[1068]

We have scores of written records chronicling the existence of black slave owners. Phillips writes:

> *The property of colored freemen oftentimes included slaves*. Such instances were quite numerous in pre-revolutionary San Domingo; and some in the British West Indies achieved notoriety through the exposure

of cruelties. On the continent *a negro planter in St. Paul's Parish, South Carolina, was reported before the close of the eighteenth century to have two hundred slaves as well as a white wife and son-in-law, and the returns of the first federal census appear to corroborate it. In Louisiana colored planters on a considerable scale became fairly numerous. Among them were Cyprien Ricard who bought at a sheriff's sale in 1851 an estate in Iberville Parish along with its ninety-one slaves for nearly a quarter of a million dollars; Marie Metoyer of Natchitoches Parish had fifty-eight slaves and more than two thousand acres of land when she died in 1840; Charles Roques of the same parish died in 1854 leaving forty-seven slaves and a thousand acres; and Martin Donato of St. Landry dying in 1848 bequeathed liberty to his slave wife and her seven children and left them eighty-nine slaves* and 4,500 arpents of land as well as notes and mortgages to a value of $46,000. *In rural Virginia and Maryland also there were free colored slaveholders in considerable numbers.*

Slaveholdings by colored townsmen were likewise fairly frequent. Among the 360 colored taxpayers in Charleston in 1860, for example, 130, including nine persons described as of Indian descent, were listed as possessing 390 slaves. The abundance of such holdings at New Orleans is evidenced by the multiplicity of applications from colored proprietors for authority to manumit slaves, with exemption from the legal requirement that the new freedmen must leave the state. A striking example of such petitions was that presented in 1832 by Marie Louise Bitaud, free woman of color, which recited that in the preceding year she had bought her daughter and grandchild at a cost of $700; that a lawyer had now told her that in view of her lack of free relatives to inherit her property, in case of death intestate her slaves would revert to the state; that she had become alarmed at this prospect; and she accordingly begged permission to manumit them without their having to leave Louisiana. The magistrates gave their consent on condition that the petitioner furnish a bond of $500 to insure the support and education of the grandson until his coming of age. This was duly done and the formalities completed.

Evidence of slaveholdings by colored freemen occurs also in the bills of sale filed in various public archives. One of these records that a citizen of Charleston sold in 1828 a man slave to the latter's free colored sister at a price of one dollar, "provided he is kindly treated and is never sold, he being an unfortunate individual and requiring much attention." In the same city a free colored man bought a slave sailmaker for $200. At Savannah in 1818 Richard Richardson sold a slave woman and child for $800 to Alex Hunter, guardian of the colored freeman Louis Mirault, in trust for him; and in 1833 Anthony Ordingsell, free colored, having obtained through his guardian an order of court, sold a slave woman to the highest bidder for $385.

It is clear that aside from the practice of holding slave relatives as a means of giving them virtual freedom, *an appreciable number of colored proprietors owned slaves purely as a productive investment*. It was doubtless a group of these who sent a joint communication to a New Orleans newspaper when secession and war were impending:

> *"The free colored population (native) of Louisiana . . . own slaves, and they are dearly attached to their native land, . . . and they are ready to shed their blood for her defence. They have no sympathy for abolitionism; no love for the North, but they have plenty for Louisiana. . . . They will fight for her in 1861 as they fought in 1814-1815. . . . If they have made no demonstration it is because they have no right to meddle with politics, but not because they are not well disposed. All they ask is to have a chance, and they will be worthy sons of Louisiana."*

Oral testimony gathered by the present writer from old residents in various quarters of the South supports the suggestion of this letter that *many of the well-to-do colored freemen tended to prize their distinctive position so strongly as to deplore any prospect of a general emancipation for fear it would submerge them in the great black mass.*[1069]

Black slavery was not just common among blacks. It was also found among America's 19th-Century Indians, who bought and sold African chattel right alongside black and white slave owners.[1070] In fact, one of the many reasons so many Native-Americans sided with the Southern Confederacy was that she promised to enforce the fugitive slave law in Indian Territory, making it a legal requirement to return runaway slaves to their original Indian owners.[1071]

While the average white slave owner owned five or less slaves (often only one or two),[1072] the average red slaveholder owned six. One Choctaw slaver owned 227.[1073] Again, it was *non-white* slave owners who individually owned the most slaves, not whites.[1074]

Slavery was practiced right up until the 1950s by some Native-American tribes, principally the Haida and the Tlingit peoples of the Pacific Northwest.[1075] Among the Haida, slaves performed all of the menial labor, ate only food scraps, were refused health care, and could not own property. And since there were no laws of protection, Haida slaves could be purchased, sold, beaten, molested, and even murdered at the whim of their owners.[1076] This is true slavery, the exact opposite of the much milder servitude experienced by Africans in the Old American South.

THE GENERAL

LAWS

And

LIBERTIES

of the

MASSACHUSETS

COLONY:

Revised & Re-printed.

By Order of the General Court Holden at *Boston,*
May 15th. 1672.

Edward Rawson Secr.

Whosoever therefore resisteth the Power, resisteth the Ordinance of God and they that resist receive to themselves Damnation. Rom. 13. 2.

CAMBRIDGE

Printed by Samuel Green, for John Usher of Boston.

1672.

The title page from a 1672 reprint of *The General Laws and Liberties of the Massachusetts Colony*, part of which laid out the statutes governing slavery during the founding and early development of Massachusetts. Note the Bible quote from Romans 13:2, no doubt directed, in part, to the state's white, black, and red slaves. The message? Those who resist Massachusetts' God-inspired laws will "receive damnation," a Yankee euphemism for arrest, imprisonment, torture, and possibly death. When it came to slavery such barbarous, rigid, merciless attitudes were all but unknown in the more civilized, easy-going, genteel South.

The Apache were just one of thousands of Native-American peoples who engaged in slavery. Most not only enslaved fellow Indians, but later also whites and blacks as well, utilizing crude, appalling, and horrific practices that defy the English language and baffle the modern mind.

6

SOUTHERN SLAVERY

WHAT YOU WERE TAUGHT: The type of black bondage practiced by the Old South was called "slavery."
THE TRUTH: This chestnut is perhaps Yankeedom's oldest and most enduring anti-South myth. The only problem is that it happens to be false.

Edward A. Pollard, Virginian, staunch Confederate, and editor of the pro-South Richmond *Examiner* during the War, said it best: there was never such a thing as "slavery" in the Old South. What North and New South writers conveniently and slanderously call Southern "slavery" was actually, Pollard rightly asserts, a "well-guarded and moderate system of negro servitude."[1077] As he wrote during Lincoln's War:

> In referring to the condition of the negro in this war, we use the term "*slavery*" . . . under strong protest. For *there is no such thing in the South; it is a term fastened upon us by the exaggeration and conceit of Northern literature, and most improperly acquiesced in by Southern writers. There is a system of African servitude in the South; in which the negro, so far from being under the absolute dominion of his master (which is the true meaning of the vile word "slavery"), has, by law of the land, his personal rights recognized and protected, and his comfort and "right" of "happiness" consulted, and by the practice of the system, has a sum of individual indulgences, which makes him altogether the most striking type in the world of cheerfulness and contentment.* And the system of servitude in the South has this peculiarity over other systems of servitude in the world: that it does not debase one of God's creatures from the condition of free-citizenship and membership in organized society and [which] thus rest on acts of debasement and

> disenfranchisement, but [instead it] elevates a savage, and rests on the solid basis of human improvement. *The European mind, adopting the nomenclature of our enemies, has designated as "slavery" what is really the most virtuous system of servitude in the world.*[1078]

As mentioned previously, the first blacks brought to British North America (on August 31, 1619)[1079] were not regarded as slaves, but as indentured servants, laborers with the same rights as white indentured servants.[1080] Indeed, 90 white girls, also indentured servants, were sold at Jamestown, Virginia, at the same time.[1081] Though in the case of the Africans this status would eventually change from voluntary servitude to involuntary servitude, most Southerners, unlike Northerners, correctly continued to refer to bonded blacks as "servants" (not "slaves") right up to and after Lincoln's War. As such, Southerners seldom used the phrase "African slavery." Like Jefferson Davis, they used the more correct term "African servitude."[1082] To this very day, unlike most Yankees, traditional Southerners still refer to the bonded blacks of 19th-Century America as "servants" rather than "slaves."[1083]

This iconic piece of Northern propaganda, showing a shackled slave pleading for his life and freedom, was often used as a weapon to try and shame Dixie into abolition. But there was no such thing as authentic slavery in the Old South, making both this fake image and the charge ludicrous.

What is the difference between slavery and servitude?

Slavery is the state of working under the complete control, ownership, subjugation, or absolute dominion of another, without pay, and usually for life.[1084] Additionally, true slaves have no rights of any kind,[1085] are generally debased and disenfranchised, and cannot purchase their freedom. In short, a genuine slave is seen by his or her owner as little different than a cow or a horse, just another piece of livestock to be owned and worked until "it" is no longer of value.[1086]

Servitude, on the other hand, is for a limited duration, the individual is not "owned" (his boss is not his "owner" or "master," but rather his employer), he is paid a wage, and he may hire himself out to work for others. Servants also possess a wide variety of personal and civil rights that are both recognized and protected by society and tempered by religious sentiment. In this way, under servitude a person's right to comfort and happiness are taken for granted and he or she is treated with common respect and decency.[1087] Finally, servants have the right and the power to buy their freedom.[1088]

Olaudah Equiano, born in Nigeria around 1745, was a member of the Igbo, one of the thousands of slave owning peoples of Africa. At a young age Equiano was himself enslaved by fellow Africans, then was later sold to a planter in Virginia and renamed Gustavus Vassa. After numerous adventures he ended up in the hands of a Northern slave owner, who allowed Vassa to purchase his freedom, something he would not have been able to do under the authentic slavery system of his own African homeland. Now a freeman, he eventually ended up in England, where he married, bore children, campaigned for abolition, wrote a celebrated memoir of his exploits, and died at the age of 52. Vassa was an example of a black man who lived in bondage on two continents, Africa and America, but who only experienced true slavery on one of them: Africa.

Among the more famous of those black American servants who purchased their liberty (or had it purchased for them) are Northern slave Frederick Douglass,[1089] black racist-militant Denmark Vesey,[1090] former African slave and later travel adventurer Gustavus Vassa (Olaudah Equiano),[1091] and Lincoln's own modiste, Elizabeth Keckley (who purchased her freedom with money she made hiring herself out as a dressmaker).[1092] Slightly lesser known are Lott Cary, Hiram Young, Free Frank McWorter, Venture Smith, Amos Fortune, John Parker, Samuel Berry, and Paul Jennings (one of President James Madison's servants).

Tens of thousands of others could be named. If any of these individuals had lived under authentic slavery (that is, without a single human right)[1093] they would have remained in bondage for life, as self-purchase is prohibited. The reality is that by the late antebellum period (1850-1860), most Southern manumissions (the emancipation of specific individuals) were the result of free blacks buying their own relatives then freeing them.[1094]

It is clear from these facts alone that the South practiced servitude, not slavery.

The use of the injurious and false word "slavery" instead of "servitude" for the type of bondage that was practiced in the Old South has been forced on us by Northern propagandists and by New South liberals. For this word, like the equally fallacious and deleterious Northern terms "copperhead," "rebel," "pro-slavery," and "slave state," all help to justify Lincoln's unjust war.

Sadly for Dixie, much of the outside world—misled by anti-South language like this—has never fully understood the true nature of so-called "Southern slavery." But those Southerners who lived through this period, and those today who have researched the institution objectively, understand that it was, in all actuality, a form of servitude not slavery, one not unlike serfdom. This fact is overtly preserved in the Latin words for both serf and servant, each a Western form of "slave": *servus* (male), *serva* (female).[1095] So-called Southern "slaves" then were actually serf-like servants, not slaves in the legal, technical, literal, or even in the stereotypical sense.

In fine, there was no such thing as "slavery" or a "slave state" in the Old South. This politicized nomenclature is an invention of enemies of Dixie, whose aim has been to defile the South in the eyes of the world and, as noted, to excuse Lincoln's unholy war on the Confederacy.

The truth is that Southerners who were labeled "proslavery" and Southern states that were labeled "slave states," were merely pro-states' rights. For as we are about to discuss, only a tiny minority of white Southerners actually owned servants (less than 4.8 percent in 1860).[1096] The South's ultimate goal was always the preservation of the right of self-determination (self-government), not the continuation of black servitude, no matter what the North chooses to believe or what name New South scallywags choose to call the institution.

In point of fact, if one were to take Northern history books and replace every instance of the word "slavery" with the word "servitude," the word "pro-slavery" with "pro-states' rights," the phrase "slave state" with "slavery optional state," and the term "free state" with "slavery prohibited state," one would have a much more accurate and honest portrait of the South-North conflict.

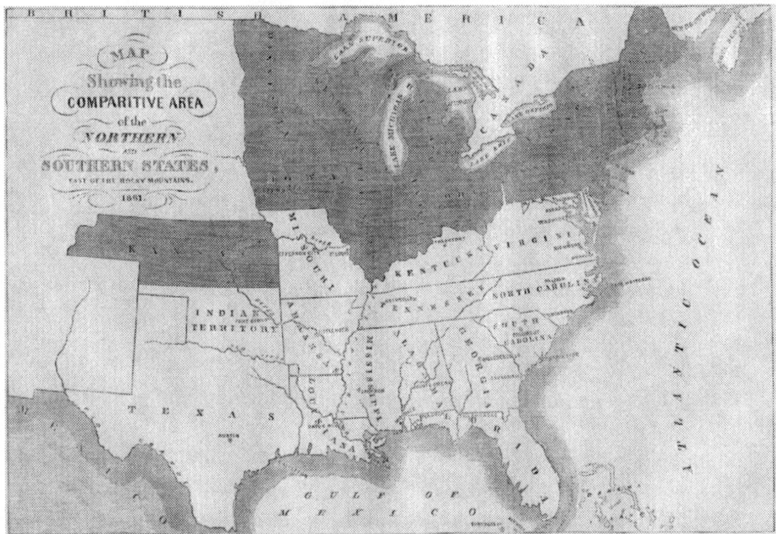

Early on, the Southern states of the U.S., delineated here in the lower half of this black and white map, were intentionally labeled the "slave states" by Northern propagandists. That this is nothing more than fallacious slander is clear from the facts that: 1) both the American slave trade and American slavery began in the North; 2) the North and only the North engaged in the transatlantic slave trade; and 3) the North was the slaving capital of North America for nearly 250 years. Conversely, not only did the South never participate in the transatlantic slave trade, she did not even practice authentic slavery. What *was* practiced in Dixie was technically a "mild form of servitude," one that shared many similarities with, and was, in many respects, nearly identical to serfdom and apprenticeship—a truism attested to by so-called Southern "slaves" themselves. In short, the so-called Southern "slave states," where the Constitution was respected, were actually "slavery optional states," where one could own or not own servants, while the so-called Northern "free states," where the Constitution was largely disregarded, were actually "slavery prohibited states," where one did not have a choice.

Pollard aptly described the situation from the South's perspective in 1866:

> *It is a remarkable circumstance that the South should have tamely allowed the Yankees to impose upon her political literature certain injurious terms, and should have adopted them to her own prejudice and shame. The world takes its impression from names; and the false party nomenclature which the North so easily fastened upon us, and which survives even in this war, has had a most important influence in obscuring our history, and especially in soliciting the prejudices of Europe.*
>
> *The proposition of Mr. [John C.] Calhoun to protect the Union by a certain constitutional and conservative barrier, the North designated*

> *Nullification, and the South adopted a name which was both a falsehood and a slander. The well-guarded and moderate system of negro servitude in the South, the North called Slavery; and this false and accursed name has been permitted to pass current in European literature, associating and carrying with it the horrors of barbarism, and defiling us in the eyes of the world. The Democratic party [the Conservative Party at the time] in the South, which claimed equality under the Constitution, as a principle, and not merely as a selfish interest, was branded by the North as a pro-slavery party, and the South submitted to the designation.*
>
> How little that great party deserved this title was well illustrated in the famous Kansas controversy; for the history of that controversy was simply this: *the South struggled for the principle of equality in the Territories, without reference to the selfish interests of so-called Slavery, and even with the admission of the hopelessness of those interests in Kansas; while the North contended for the narrow, selfish, practical consequence of making Kansas a part of her Free-soil possessions.*[1097]

In summary, Pollard notes:

> The peaceful and fortunate career on which Mr. [Thomas] Jefferson's administration launched the country was to meet with a singular interruption. That interruption was the sectional agitation which finally broke the bonds of the Union and plunged North and South into one of the fiercest wars of modern times. The occasion of that conflict was *what the Yankees called—by one of their convenient libels in political nomenclature—slavery; but what was in fact nothing more than a system of negro servitude in the South; well guarded by laws, which protected the negro laborer in the rights of humanity; moderated by Christian sentiments which provided for his welfare; and, altogether, one of the mildest and most beneficent systems of servitude in the world.*[1098]

WHAT YOU WERE TAUGHT: Southern slavery was rightly called the "Peculiar Institution."

THE TRUTH: Actually there was nothing "peculiar" whatsoever about slavery, and neither was it a specifically Southern institution, for it was once a worldwide phenomenon dating back to prehistoric times.[1099] Even some Victorian anti-South New Englanders recognized this fact. One of them was abolitionist Henry David Thoreau, who recorded the following in his journal on December 4, 1860:

> *Talk about slavery! It is not the peculiar institution of the South. It exists wherever men are bought and sold, wherever a man allows himself to be made a mere thing or a tool, and surrenders his inalienable rights of reason and conscience. Indeed, this slavery is more complete than that which enslaves the body alone. It exists in the Northern States, and I am reminded by what I find in the newspapers that it exists in Canada.* I never yet met with, or heard of, a judge who was not a slave of this kind, and so [became] the finest and most unfailing weapon of injustice. He fetches a slightly higher price than the black man only because he is a more valuable slave.[1100]

An institution that has been found on every continent and among nearly every civilization from earliest recorded history right into present-day America can hardly be considered "peculiar."[1101] In fact, as this very book shows, it would be more appropriately and accurately called the "ordinary institution."

WHAT YOU WERE TAUGHT: Southern slaves had no rights.
THE TRUTH: As touched on above, the South's servants had numerous rights, which is why they were not true slaves. As such, because having basic civil rights is one of the many things that separates servants from slaves, 19th-Century Southerners generally referred to their bondsmen and bondswomen as "servants," not "slaves."

Indeed in Virginia, the first American colony to receive Africans (in this case from the Dutch), "there was neither law nor custom then establishing the institution of slavery in the colony," which is why up until 1661 county records referred to bonded blacks as "negro servants," or in many cases simply as "negroes"—authentic slavery being unknown anywhere in the South at the time.[1102]

The South's slavery laws were founded on the Christian ideas, ethics, and principles of esteemed 18th-Century British politician and judicial scholar William Blackstone.

The complex wealth of material that formed the slavery laws of the Old South was founded on English common law, and in particular around the *Commentaries on the Laws of England*, a work by the noted English legal scholar Sir William Blackstone. Among the many civil and legal rights possessed by Southern servants was the right to own private property, the right to marry, the right to sue and to give evidence in court (in special cases), the right to have days off, the right to hire themselves out to others, the right to write up and sign their own work contracts, the right to practice religion and receive religious instruction, and the right to be supported by their temporary "owners" from birth to death, including in times of sickness and in old age. Female servants had the additional right to apply for domestic service (in the "Big House") and could not be forced into doing heavy labor.[1103]

In particular, all of Dixie's servants had the right to be treated justly and fairly. Violations of any and all of these laws and rights were prohibited by legal statute in *all* of the Southern states,[1104] particularly by the mid 1800s,[1105] just as Virginian James Madison noted far earlier in 1788 in *The Federalist Papers*:

> [The Southern slave is] protected . . . in his life and in his limbs against the violence of all others, even the master of his labor and his liberty . . .[1106]

Then as today, possessing such rights is what differentiates true servants from true slaves—the latter group which has no rights whatsoever.

In fact, some Southern servants were given so much freedom that they were believed to be freedmen (one recently emancipated) or even free blacks (one who has never known servitude). In one case in South Carolina this reality turned into a slaveholder's worst nightmare.

The year was 1836. George Broad of St. John's Parish, Berkeley County, having passed away "without blood relatives," bequeathed his entire slave force of 14 adults and their children to his neighbor John R. Dangerfield,

> in trust nevertheless and for this purpose only that the said John R. Dangerfield, his executors and assigns do permit and suffer the said slaves . . . to apply and appropriate their time and labor to their own proper use and behoof, without the intermeddling or interference of any person or persons whomsoever further than may be necessary for their protection under the laws of this state.[1107]

So-called "Southern slavery" was a largely casual affair. Black servants—like this nonchalant group lounging during one of their daily breaks—were given a wide range of freedoms and were often allowed to come and go as they pleased. On many Southern plantations the rules were so lax that the "slaves" were mistaken for freemen, a situation that sometimes led to social and legal issues. The black Southern bondsman often compared his time as a true slave back home in the barbaric wilds of Africa with his far safer, far healthier, and far more placid life as a true servant in the American South, always favoring the latter. This gave rise to the seldom discussed phenomenon of hundreds of thousands of Southern "slaves" refusing to be emancipated, before, during, and after Lincoln's War.

A year later Dangerfield was following Broad's will to the letter, when one particular day he had to leave his home on an errand. As always, his slaves were left to run the plantation on their own. That morning one of Broad's relatives, Rebecca Rhame, rode past in a buggy and saw what she perceived to be "freed slaves" roaming the property. Discovering no whites about, she attempted, "under the law," to seize all 14 servants. At this point Dangerfield rode up and a heated dispute ensued.

The matter quickly went to court, with Rhame suing Dangerfield in an attempt to procure possession of his servants, claiming this was her right under the South Carolina statute, which stated that "any slaves illegally set free might be seized by any persons as derelicts." Dangerfield's team countered, however, saying that they were still slaves, and that it was his custom (and right) to leave them on their own in "virtually complete freedom." The jury decided in favor of the defendant.[1108]

Let us give Southern hero Confederate President Jefferson Davis the final word on this subject:

> *Among the less-informed persons at the North there exists an opinion that the negro slave at the South was a mere chattel, having neither rights nor immunities protected by law or public opinion. Southern men knew such was not the case, and others desiring to know could readily learn the fact. On that error the lauded story of* Uncle Tom's Cabin *was founded, but it is strange that a utilitarian and shrewd people did not ask why a slave, especially valuable, was the object of privation and abuse? Had it been a horse they would have been better able to judge, and would most probably have rejected the story for its improbability.*[1109]

WHAT YOU WERE TAUGHT: Slavery was the "cornerstone" of the Confederacy, as its own vice president declared.
THE TRUTH: Few statements have ever been more garbled, more misunderstood, and as we will see momentarily, more purposefully misinterpreted, by enemies of the South than the one made by my close cousin, Confederate Vice President Alexander H. Stephens, on the eve of the Civil War. Here are the infamous words, uttered on March 21, 1861, during a speech at Savannah, Georgia, that stirred up the false "controversy":

> [The Confederacy's] cornerstone rests upon the great truth, that the negro is not equal to the white man; that slavery, subordination to the superior race, is his natural and normal condition.[1110]

First, let us compare these words with those of Yankee President Abraham Lincoln, delivered publicly a few years earlier on July 17, 1858, at Springfield, Illinois:

> *My declarations upon this subject of negro slavery may be misrepresented, but cannot be misunderstood.* I have said that I do not understand the Declaration [of Independence] to mean that all men were created equal in all respects. . . . Certainly *the negro is not our equal* in color—perhaps not in many other respects . . .[1111]

A few months later, on September 18, 1858, at Charleston, Illinois,

Lincoln made the following statement:

> I will say then that *I am not, nor ever have been, in favor of bringing about in any way the social and political equality of the white and black races—that I am not, nor ever have been, in favor of making voters or jurors of negroes, nor of qualifying them to hold office, nor to intermarry with white people*; and I will say in addition to this that *there is a physical difference between the white and black races which I believe will forever forbid the two races living together on terms of social and political equality*. And *inasmuch as they cannot so live, while they do remain together there must be the position of superior and inferior, and I as much as any other man am in favor of having the superior position assigned to the white race*.[1112]

Pro-North advocates often cite the "Cornerstone Speech" of Confederate Vice President Alexander Hamilton Stephens as "proof" that the Old South's socioeconomic structure rested on slavery. In fact, this is a perversion of Stephens' words; an intentional misinterpretation and misrepresentation by enemies of the South to further heap disgrace and ridicule on Dixie—as the vice president himself, as well as his defenders, often pointed out.

Our point here is that Vice President Stephens' racism was no different than President Lincoln's. Both men were products of a 19th-Century white society that saw blacks as an "inferior race," as Lincoln *always* referred to African-Americans.[1113] Thus, if critics of the South wish to avoid being called hypocrites, Northerner Lincoln must be denounced just as heartily as Southerner Stephens.[1114] As the "Great Emancipator" Lincoln himself said of "nearly all white people" living in America at the time:

> *There is a natural disgust in the minds of nearly all white people, to the idea of an indiscriminate amalgamation of the white and black races.*[1115]

While the deeply held lifelong white supremacy in Lincoln's speeches is obvious for all to see, the racism displayed in Stephens' speech turns out to be far less vicious and entrenched, as a closer examination reveals.

There were indeed a few Southerners who claimed that slavery was necessary for the operation of the Confederacy, and that this was the reason the Yankee government was determined to abolish it. However, there was never a period in Southern history when more than 5 percent of Southerners owned slaves (and it was usually far less).[1116] As such, it is clear that the South did not need slavery to survive, making Stephens' claim, if taken literally, both ludicrous and illogical.

The reality is that the Union was no threat to Southern slavery, for not only had Lincoln promised not to interfere with it,[1117] but slavery was still fully legal across the entire U.S. in 1861, the year Stephens gave his Cornerstone Speech. At the time Southern slavery was actually in more danger from the Southern abolitionist majority than the much smaller Northern abolitionist minority.

Why then did some Southerners, like the Rebel vice president, make such patently absurd comments?

Those few who declared that slavery was the "cornerstone" of the South were engaging in a clever but reckless political ploy, one used to try and agitate other Southerners in the tariff conflicts with the North.[1118] There were so few slave owners in the South in the early 1860s, that in an attempt to gain their support it is not surprising that the traditional political tactics of exaggeration, fear-mongering, and hyperbole were sometimes employed by Confederate leaders like

Stephens, just as they are still used by most politicians today, both Liberal and Conservative.

We must also consider the fact that if slavery had truly been the "cornerstone of the Confederacy," not to mention the cause of the Civil War, then the conflict would have ended with Lincoln's Final Emancipation Proclamation on January 1, 1863.[1119] Instead, it dragged on for over two more bloody years, not ending until Confederate abolitionist General Robert E. Lee reluctantly stacked arms at Appomattox on April 9, 1865.

Afterward, Southerner Lyon Gardiner Tyler, the son of America's tenth president, John Tyler,[1120] put the matter this way:

> The emancipation of slaves [on January 1, 1863] by the late war is the best evidence that the South never fought for slavery, but *against a foreign dictation and a sectional will.* Within the Union slavery was probably secure for many years to come. The war was nothing more than the outcome of a tyranny exerted for seventy-two years by the North over vital interests of the South.[1121]

It would be far more accurate then to say that *slavery was the cornerstone of the Union*, for as we have seen, not only would New England have gone bankrupt without it,[1122] it was the North's Wall Street Boys (Yankee financiers, merchants, stock traders, and industrialists) who made the most money from the institution and who were thus the most interested in keeping it alive.[1123]

Indeed, it was this very group, the Wall Street Boys, keen to put anyone into the Oval Office who would maintain the lucrative Northern slave trade and the equally profitable business of Southern slavery, that got Lincoln elected president. For he was the only candidate who promised to do just that.[1124] Later, these same backers rewarded "Honest Abe" by donating millions of dollars from their slave profits to fund his War against the South and get him reelected in 1864.[1125]

There is one other important point that must be made regarding Stephens' Cornerstone Speech. According to the newspaper reporter who transcribed the address, it

> *is not a perfect report*, but *only such a sketch* of the address of Mr. Stephens as embraces, *in his judgment*, the most important points presented by the orator.[1126]

What this means is that the speech we have today is not a literal word-for-word reproduction of what Stephens actually said. Nor is it even complete. It is merely, by the transcriber's own admission, a partial and imperfect interpretation of what was said—and that based on the reporter's own personal "judgment," viewpoint, and biases. This lends tremendous weight to Stephens' subsequent complaint that his words were misunderstood and thus grossly misrepresented.

When Stephens gave his "Cornerstone Speech" in March 1861, not only was slavery still fully protected and legal under the U.S. Constitution in all 34 states, but Northern states like New York were still funding the voyages of Yankee slave ships to Africa and the West Indies, and the Yankee slave trade was still one of the primary revenue streams in the North. In other words, at the outset of Lincoln's War, slavery was actually the cornerstone of the Union's economy, not the Confederacy's—the birthplace of the American abolition movement and a region where less than 5 percent of the population owned slaves that year.

In fact, it was widely known at the time that the vice president delivered his Cornerstone Speech "impromptu," and that the transcriptions later made of it were "imperfectly" reported.[1127]

Despite these facts, as well as the ignorant and vengeful manner in which anti-South proponents have tried to twist the import of Stephens' address, as Richard M. Johnston noted in 1884, its entire content can be summed up in this manner:

> On the subject of slavery there was no essential change in the new [1790 U.S.] Constitution from the old [that is, the Articles of Confederation, 1781-1789]. As Judge [Henry] Baldwin [of Connecticut], of the Supreme Court of the United States, had announced from the Bench several years before, that *[just as] slavery was the corner-stone of the old Constitution, so it is of the new.*[1128]

In other words, decades before the formation of the Southern Confederacy, Yankees widely regarded slavery as the cornerstone of the Union!

What follows is Southern Conservative Stephens' defense against the Northern Liberal charges that he (and the rest of the South) had intended to establish a "slave dynasty," and that he personally believed that the Southern Confederacy rested solely on the "cornerstone" of slavery. For the historical record, I will cite the pertinent paragraphs from this particular 1870 "colloquy" in full:

> In [only] one thing [have the Liberals] . . . done me full justice, and that was in [their] . . . assumption, that I had no sympathy with any conspirators or conspiracy aiming at the overthrow of the Constitution of the United States, with the view of establishing a "*Slavery Dynasty*" in its stead. If any such body of men existed in the country, they certainly had no sympathy from me. Nay, more, if any such body was organized in Washington or elsewhere, or had any existence anywhere, it was wholly unknown to me. *I think it had existence, if [my Liberal friends] . . . will allow me respectfully to say so, only in [their] . . . imagination[s], and that of others who have written fictions called histories. The only real conspiracy against the Constitution organized in Washington, as I understand it, was that of the seven Governors, from seven Northern States, who assembled there, and by their mischievous machinations caused Mr. [Abraham] Lincoln to change his purpose as to the evacuation of Fort Sumter. Caused him to fail to 'keep faith as to Fort Sumter.' This was the conspiracy which inaugurated the war. It was a conspiracy well typified by the Seven Headed monster Beast in the Apocalypse!* The analogy I will not stop to trace, striking as it is, but will follow the [Liberals]. . . .
>
> [They quote] . . . from my speech on the annexation of Texas. [They] . . . did not, however, quote fully. In that speech I said, and said truly, that I was "*no defender of slavery in the abstract*." I was speaking of it politically and not morally, and of slavery in the general sense of that term applied to men of the same race, and not as it existed in the States of this Union. This was true then, and now, and always with me. I said also on that occasion, in the next sentence, and now repeat, that
>
>> "Liberty always had charms for me, and I would rejoice to see all the sons of Adam's family, in every land and clime, in the enjoyment of those rights which are set forth in our Declaration of Independence as "natural and inalienable," if a stern necessity, bearing the marks and impress of the hand of the Creator himself, did not, in some cases, interpose and prevent. Such is the case with the States where slavery now exists."

Here is that speech. [The Liberals were] . . . as much at fault in [their] . . . memory in regard to it, as [they were] . . . in regard to the Union speech of 1860.

There is, moreover, nothing in the "Corner-Stone" speech, as [they call it] . . . , inconsistent with the sentiments delivered in the Texas speech. Here is the "Corner-Stone" speech, also. In it I said:

> "Many Governments have been founded upon the principle of the subordination and serfdom of certain classes of the same race; such were, and are in violation of the laws of nature. Our system commits no such violation of nature's laws. With us, all of the white race, however high or low, rich or poor, are equal in the eye of the law. Not so with the negro. Subordination is his place. He, by nature, or *by the curse against Canaan*, is fitted for that condition which he occupies in our system. The architect, in the construction of buildings, lays the foundation with the proper material—the granite; then comes the brick or the marble. The substratum of our society is made of the material fitted by nature for it, and by experience we know that it is lest, not only for the Superior, but for the Inferior race, that it should be so. *It is, indeed, in conformity with the ordinance of the Creator. It is not for us to inquire into the wisdom of his ordinances, or to question them. For his own purposes, he has made one race to differ from another, as he has made 'one star to differ from another star in glory.'*
>
> "The great objects of humanity are best attained when there is conformity to his laws and decrees, in the formation of Governments as well as in all things else. Our Confederacy is founded upon principles in strict conformity with these laws. This stone which was rejected by the first builders 'is become the chief of the corner'—the real 'corner-stone'—in our new edifice."

In the corner-stone metaphor, I did but repeat what Judge [Henry] Baldwin of the Supreme Court of the United States, had said of the Federal Government itself, in the case of *Johnson* vs.

Tompkins. In that case he declared that "the foundations of this Government are laid, and rest on the rights of property in slaves, and the whole fabric must fall by disturbing the corner-stone."

It was disturbed, as we have seen, and the only intended difference between the old "edifice" and the "new," in this respect, was to fix this corner-stone more firmly in its proper place in the latter, than it had been in the former. This is the substance of that speech; and there is no conflict between the sentiments expressed in both upon the same subject matter.

Stephens' "Cornerstone Speech" was misunderstood by Northerners at the time he gave it, and it is still being misunderstood by them today. If they care to educate themselves on the matter, they have the vice president's own explanation and rebuttal to help correct their confusion.

So much for all these points, irrelevant as all of them, and *ad hominem* as some of them are, which have been presented by the [Liberals]. . . . I assure [them], . . . none of them announced any truth which hurts in the least. . . . But what bearing have they upon the matter under immediate consideration?

How stands the issue between us as to the character of the conflict about slavery? My position was that in the Federal Councils and before Federal Authorities it was not a conflict between the advocates of the system of slavery, as it existed, and its opponents, as Mr. [Horace] Greeley has treated it throughout; but that it was in all its stages and phases so far as Federal Politics were concerned, a conflict between those who claimed [that is, the Liberals], and those who denied [that is, the Conservatives], that the Federal Authorities had any rightful power, under the Constitution, to take any action whatever upon it, with a view to its immediate or ultimate extinction, or its regulation in any way in contravention of the Rights of the States.

By [the Liberals'] . . . reference to the Congress of the Colonies and what occurred upon drawing up the Declaration of their Independence, or subsequently, [have they] . . . stated a single fact to unsettle or even jostle that position? *Why was the Declaration finally made without any allusion to the subject [of slavery]? Was it not because it was a matter over which each Sovereign State was to exercise its own discretion as it ought to? Was not Mr. [Thomas] Jefferson, the draftsman of that instrument, as much opposed to slavery as Mr. [John] Adams, or Dr. [Benjamin] Franklin, or Roger Sherman, or Robert R. Livingston, his colleagues on the committee, and all of whom, except himself, were Northern men?* Did he who penned that soul-stirring defiance to British power "truckle" [that is, bow down] to the "insolent" demands of any miserable "Slavery Oligarchy" or did John Adams, Dr. Franklin, Roger Sherman, or Robert R. Livingston, to say nothing of John Hancock, and others who voted for it, as it stands, so "truckle"? Did the Supreme Court so truckle in declaring the Constitution to be as they did, in the case I have read? Especially did Justice [John] McLean, well known to have been an opponent of slavery, as I have said, so truckle in delivering the opinion cited from him?

In a word, . . . [have my Liberal friends] . . . ventured to deny a single fact, stated by me . . . in relation to the nature of this conflict, and the position of the great names mentioned upon it, from the time of its first introduction in Congress down to the election of Mr. Lincoln? [They have] . . . not, and I am sure [they] . . . will not. *We are bound*, therefore, *to take it as a fact, admitted by silence, at least, that the conflict on this subject in the Federal Councils and before Federal Authorities, was not one between the "principles of human rights and human bondage" at all; but that it was a conflict between the advocates and supporters of a Federal [Confederate] Government, with limited and specific powers, on the one side [that is, the Conservatives], and those who favored Centralism and Consolidation on the other [that is, the Liberals].*

The States South were all on the side of the Constitution. They never invoked any stretch of Federal power to aid or protect that peculiar Institution, either in the States or Territories. Their position from the beginning to the end, upon the Territorial question, was "non-intervention," by Congress, either for or against the Institution. All they asked of Congress, in this particular, was simply not to be denied equal rights in settling and colonizing the common public domain, and that the people in these inchoate [that is, Southern] States might be permitted to act as they pleased upon the subject of the status of the Negro race amongst them, as upon all other subjects of internal policy, when they came to form their

Constitutions for admission into the Union, as perfect States upon an equal footing with the original Parties, without dictation or control from the Federal Authorities, one way or the other. They claimed the same Sovereign Right of local Self-government on the part of these new States which was the moving cause of the Declaration of Independence, and was the basis upon which our whole system of Government rested. This was their position on the admission of Missouri, and their position throughout. They never asked the Federal Government to extend, or strengthen their particular interest in any such way, as stated. No case of the kind can be named.[1129]

WHAT YOU WERE TAUGHT: Southerners waited and stalled for as long as possible before emancipating their slaves.

Lincoln stalled abolition for as long as possible after his election, earning the nickname the "tortoise president," awarded to him by his own party members.

THE TRUTH: It was the Union's white supremacist, black colonizationist, big government Liberal president, Abraham Lincoln, who procrastinated and delayed abolition for as long as possible. In contrast, the South had been, whenever and wherever possible, gradually emancipating its black servants for centuries prior to the issuance of Lincoln's fake and illegal Emancipation Proclamation in 1863.

In 1855, for example, British tourist to the Southern states, Sir Charles Lyell, said this about Southern black servants and their owners:

> Already their task-masters have taught them to speak, with more or less accuracy, one of the noblest of languages, to shake off many old superstitions, to acquire higher ideas of morality, and habits of neatness and cleanliness, and have converted thousands of them to Christianity. *Many they have emancipated, and the rest are gradually approaching to the condition of the ancient serfs of Europe half a century or more before their bondage died out.*
>
> *All this has been done at an enormous sacrifice of time and money, an expense, indeed, which all the governments of Europe and all the Christian missionaries, whether Romanist or Protestant, could never have effected in five centuries.*[1130]

Though it would not be practical to name the hundreds of thousands of Southern servant owners who liberated all or part of their slaves (or their relatives' slaves) prior to Lincoln's War, some of the more notable were George Washington, Thomas Jefferson, Robert E. Lee, Andrew Johnson, and Nathan Bedford Forrest.

Considering the facts that both the African-American slave trade and African-American slavery started in the North,[1131] that the American abolition movement began in the South,[1132] and that 95 percent of the South never owned or traded in slaves,[1133] this particular Yankee myth has no justification whatsoever.

WHAT YOU WERE TAUGHT: Southern slavery was an un-Christian, cruel, cold, impersonal, and despicable labor system that wasted and destroyed the lives of slaves and alienated the races.

THE TRUTH: Southern servants were legally registered as literal members of the families of their white, black, red, or brown owners, and, in nearly all cases, delicately cared for throughout their entire lives, very much as if they were the adopted children of their owners.[1134] Little wonder that many blacks did not welcome emancipation, preferring servitude instead![1135] As Dr. Henry A. White, history professor at Washington and Lee University, wrote in 1900:

> *The [Southern slavery] system produced no paupers and no orphans; food and clothing the negro did not lack; careful attention he received in sickness, and, without a burden [care] the aged servants spent their closing days. The plantation was an industrial school where the negro gradually acquired skill in the use of tools. A bond of affection was woven between Southern masters and servants which proved strong enough in 1861-'65 to keep the negroes at voluntary labour to furnish food for the armies that contended against [Lincoln's] military emancipation.*[1136] In the planter's home the African learned to set a higher value upon the domestic virtues which he saw illustrated in the lives of Christian men and women; for, be it remembered, the great body of the slave-holders of the South were devotees of the religious faith handed down through pious ancestors from [John] Knox, [Thomas] Cranmer, [John] Wesley, and [John] Bunyan. *With truth, perhaps, it may be said than no other economic system before or since that time has engendered a bond of personal affection between capital and labour so strong as that established by the institution of slavery.*[1137]

WHAT YOU WERE TAUGHT: While few in the North ever owned slaves, nearly every Southerner was once a slave owner. The

Confederacy was a nation of slaveholders, with most records showing that at least 25 percent of the South owned slaves.

THE TRUTH: We have already seen that American slavery got its start in the North,[1138] that many thousands of Yankee farmers owned slaves,[1139] that thousands of Yankee businessmen funded and operated the slave trade,[1140] and that conservative estimates infer that between 500,000[1141] and 1 million slaves were once held in the North[1142] (there were already 300,000 slaves in Yankeedom by 1776).[1143] As for slave ownership in the South, far from being "a nation of slaveholders," a "slavocracy," or a "slave regime," as the North ridiculously calls Old Dixie, the reality is that this group made up only a tiny fraction of Southern whites.

Like this Tennessee yeoman, over 95 percent of white Southerners were non-slave owners, men who farmed their own land without outside assistance—other than their own family members.

Land and slaves were costly in the 1800s, so invariably slavery was a rich man's business. Nearly all 19th-Century Southerners were poor farmers, however. Thus very few Southerners could afford to own slaves, even if they had wanted them (most, like General Robert E. Lee and Stonewall Jackson, did not want them). After honestly researching the statistics, even the most anti-South authors have had to admit that most of the slaves in the South were owned by a "relatively small proportion" of families.[1144] It was not possible then for there to be a "slave owning majority," a phrase that anti-South writers enjoy using. Quite the opposite. The large slaveholding families of the South, those with over 20 slaves, numbered only about 10,000.[1145] This was only 0.6 percent of the 1.5 million families who lived across the South in 1860.[1146]

The "25 percent" figure, in fact, is a common ruse used by anti-South proponents who, in a manifest attempt to tarnish the South, artificially inflate the numbers of white Southern slave owners (they completely ignore black and red slave owners) by calculating using the number of *households* ("families") instead of the *total number of white Southerners*. Using the lower number of households as opposed to the higher number of total whites, of course, gives a higher number of slave owners, which is why they use this method: it magnifies the "guilt" of the South while giving further justification for Lincoln's unjustifiable war.[1147]

The two districts of Camden and Ninety-Six, South Carolina, are excellent examples of this kind of anti-South trickery, for they were typical of Dixie's slave owning population percentage at the time. Out of a total of 91,704 white *individuals*, only 3,787 were slaveholders, just 4.1 percent. If we use the duplicitous Yankee method, however, and take 15,562—which is the number of white *families* in these two towns—and then calculate the number of slaveholders, we get 24.1 percent.[1148]

Obviously, the truth about Southern slave ownership is far different than what pro-North advocates would like you to believe!

According to the U.S. Censuses during the mid 1800s, slightly less than 5 percent of all Southerners owned slaves, and most of these owned less than five.[1149] In 1850 specifically, for instance, the Census shows that of the total population of 8,039,000 white Southerners, only 384,884 owned slaves: just 4.7 percent. Of these same whites that year only 46,274 owned 20 or more servants (0.5 percent of the total white population), only 2,500 owned 30 or more (0.03 percent),[1150] and a mere handful, 2,300, owned 100 or more (0.02 percent).[1151]

This last group, the extremely wealthy "Aristocratic Planters," the only group that anti-South writers like to focus on, actually made up only one-half of 1 percent of the total population of the South.[1152] Yet it is the "Aristocratic Planters" who pro-Northers claim were the norm! Furthermore, many of these wealthiest of slave owners lived in only one region of the South: the famous "Black Belt," a 5,000 square mile swath of rich fertile land (hence its name) that stretched across central Alabama to northeastern Mississippi.[1153] Thus massive slave ownership was not "universal," and the "Aristocratic Planters" who owned these large numbers of slaves were neither "typical" or "characteristic" of the South.

The Southern "Aristocratic Planter"—one of whom is shown here with his wife and daughter visiting the servants' quarters on his plantation in the 1700s—was the rarest of all slave owners in Dixie, comprising a mere 0.03 percent of the total white Southern population in 1860. In order to besmirch the South, however, pro-North historians paint him as the "typical" Southern slave owner.

The cold hard statistics of the U.S. government themselves back up these facts.

Continuing with our survey, ten years later, in 1860, now with a white population of 7,215,525, little had changed in the way of white slave ownership. According to the U.S. Census, that year only 4.8 percent (or 385,000) of all Southerners owned slaves, the other 95.2 percent did not.[1154] Of those that did, most owned less than five.[1155] Correcting for the mistakes of Census takers—which would include counting slave-hirers as slave owners and counting more than once those thousands of slave owners who annually moved the same slaves back and forth across multiple states—this figure, 4.8 percent, is no doubt too large. Either way, Southerners themselves believed that only about 5 percent of their number owned slaves, which is slightly high, but roughly accurate.[1156]

In 1860 there were still only 2,300 Aristocratic Planters (those who owned 100 or more slaves), now just 0.03 percent of the total white population, while only 8,000 owned as many as 50 slaves (0.11 percent). Of the total white Southern population in 1860, just 46,000 individuals met the criteria for actual "planter" status (that is, owning large acreage and 20 or more slaves), a mere 0.06 percent of Dixie's populace.[1157]

With slightly less than 5 percent of Southern whites as slave owners, what about the other 95 percent? They were non-servant owning, yeoman farmers, small landholders who operated without labor assistance,[1158] and who thus had no need for outside workers and no interest in the institution of slavery.[1159] In fact, there had been enormous tension between slaveholders and non-slaveholders from the very beginning, for the latter group resented the very existence of black servant labor in the South.[1160] Northern slave owner, and later U.S. president, General Ulysses S. Grant, admitted that:

> *The great bulk of the legal voters of the South were men who owned no slaves*; . . . [thus] their interest in the contest [to allegedly "abolish slavery"] was very meagre . . .[1161]

Even Lincoln himself acknowledged that "in all our slave States except South Carolina, a majority of the whole people of all colors are neither slaves nor masters."[1162] Southern scholar Shelby Foote correctly called this group "the slaveless majority," a phrase never heard, discussed, or even acknowledged in Yankee and scallywag "history" books.[1163] Yet it was the *slaveless majority* that made up the foundational mass of people in the Old South, slightly over 95 percent; the *slave owning minority* made up only 4.7 percent of the population.

Now let us compare these figures with Africa where, until only recently, slavery has been the primary form of labor since prehistoric times,[1164] and where the *slave owning majority* averaged 75 percent,[1165] and in some regions 90 percent.[1166] This means that until the late 19th Century, Africa never had a slaveless majority, or anything close to it. Rather it had a *slave owning majority* of up to 90 percent and a *slaveless minority* of as little as only 10 percent, nearly the complete reverse of what existed in the Old South.

In summary, agriculturalists maintain that an American farmer would need at least 20 laborers to achieve a decent level of "economies of scale" on a large farm. By this standard there were actually very few planters and plantations in the Old South.[1167] In other words, slave owning Southern whites were in the vast minority, non-slave owning Southerners were in the vast majority.

Yankee General and slave owner Ulysses S. Grant was well aware that the majority of Southerners were non-slave owners, and he said so. This exposes the pro-North lie that the South was a great "slavocracy." Today's anti-South historians, however, continue to disregard and suppress this fact.

WHAT YOU WERE TAUGHT: Contrary to the claim made by Southerners, Confederate General Robert E. Lee was indeed a slave owner, for he makes numerous references to them in his writings.

Despite the assertions of Yankee mythologists, Confederate General Robert E. Lee—like 95 percent of all Southerners—was not a slave owner, detested the institution, and campaigned vigorously for abolition.

THE TRUTH: It is true that there were black servants in the Lee household, and the South has never denied this. The question is, did they belong to General Lee?

The answer is that they did not.[1168] They belonged to the family of his wife, Mary Anne Randolph Custis. More specifically, they were the property of Mary's father, George Washington Parke Custis. General Lee had no choice but to "adopt" Mr. Custis' servants when he married his daughter in 1831, who, in the tradition of wealthy Southerners, had been given some of the family servants as a wedding gift.

As for General Lee himself, I can find no records of him ever personally, purchasing, possessing, or selling slaves for the express purpose of *slave ownership*. In fact, as has been widely known across the South for generations, the General's so-called "slaves" were merely an assortment of black servants he had involuntarily inherited from other family members, such as his father-in-law, Mr. Custis. All were treated respectfully, humanely, and, as was the popular custom in Dixie, like members of the Lee family, particularly the house servants.

In the Fall of 1862, five years after Mr. Custis' death on October 10, 1857, General Lee, who had been made the executor of Mr. Custis' will, immediately set about emancipating the Custis family servants, as was requested of him in that document. Thus it is clear that not only did the General *not* personally own slaves, but that the entire Lee clan was discussing personal abolition in their household at least five years before the start of Lincoln's War. We will note here that this was the same period in which Lincoln was most aggressively promoting the idea of deporting all blacks out of the U.S.—his lifelong obsession.[1169]

In short, abolitionist General Lee emancipated the Custis servants four months *before* black colonizationist Lincoln issued his fraudulent and unlawful Final Emancipation Proclamation on January 1, 1863. Slave-hating Lee was no slave owner.[1170]

WHAT YOU WERE TAUGHT: The horrible racist Black Codes were an invention of Southerners.
THE TRUTH: This is one of the most deeply cherished of the North's so-called "Civil War facts." But it turns out to be just another mendacious Yankee fairy tale.

Naturally, the Black Codes, laws meant to restrict the movements, freedoms, and rights of African-Americans, began in that part of the United States where not only both the American slave trade and American slavery got their start, but more importantly where racism was most severe.[1171] And that region, in the 1800s, was the North, as foreign visitors, Southerners, and even Northerners themselves repeatedly observed.[1172]

WHAT YOU WERE TAUGHT: Southern slavery was less efficient, and thus less profitable, than Northern free labor.
THE TRUTH: Southern slavery was actually more efficient *and* more profitable than Northern free labor. Even when all of slavery's attendant problems are taken into account, such as high start-up costs, the care of slaves too young or too old to perform labor, and runaways, illness, and death, slavery paid and paid well in the Old South.[1173]

Plantations that used slave labor, for example, were 50 percent more efficient than those that used free labor, giving the South an enormous advantage: her farms were 35 percent more productive than slave-free farms in the North,[1174] and 28 percent more efficient than slave-free farms in the South in 1860.[1175] Indeed, Southern slavery became more productive, and thus more lucrative, right up to the time of Lincoln's War.[1176]

This is why, between the 1600s and the 1700s, American slaves were responsible for producing at least 75 percent of the total value of all American products bought and sold in the Atlantic region alone. At the same time, owners were getting a 10 percent average return on their investment in servants, basically identical to what they could have expected to receive had they invested in manufacturing or railroads.[1177]

Northern and New South propagandists would have us believe that Southern slavery was inefficient, unremunerative, and nonproductive compared to Northern non-slave plantations. But the opposite is true. As just one example, Southern farms with servants were 35 percent more productive than Yankee farms with free laborers—translating into huge crop yields and profits for Dixie planters.

WHAT YOU WERE TAUGHT: The Old American South should have known better than to embrace slavery at a time when the entire world had already banned it.

THE TRUTH: This is patently false: in the 1700s and 1800s slavery was still legal in every country around the world, including the U.S. Indeed, both slavery and the slave trade were still protected by the U.S. Constitution. More to the point, slavery was perfectly lawful across America for a full 246 years:

- It was legal in the American colonies from 1619 (when the first African indentured servants[1178] were brought by the Dutch to the English settlers at Jamestown, Virginia)[1179] and 1641 (when Massachusetts became the first state to legalize it),[1180] to 1776 (the year the U.S.A. was formed).
- It was legal from 1776 to 1789 (the period of the American Confederacy lasted from 1781 to 1789).
- It was legal in the U.S.A. from 1789 to 1865, and in the C.S.A. from 1861 to 1865, the year the Thirteenth Amendment was ratified on December 6, finally ending the institution in every state. This is one reason why Northern slave owners, such as General Ulysses S. Grant, kept their slaves until after the War ended,[1181] and why other Yankees, like Lincoln, editor Horace Greeley, Union officer Nathaniel Prentiss Banks, and Union officer Benjamin F. "the Beast" Butler, approved of the idea of black colonization outside the U.S.[1182]

This bas-relief shows ancient white Mesopotamian slaves working on a construction project. Slavery was and is not only universal, it has been legal worldwide for thousands of years, and was not completely abolished in the U.S. until nearly a year after the Civil War.

Again, it should be remembered that slavery was also legal in Europe, Asia, Latin America, and Africa, and indeed in every other region and nation on earth at the time the Old South owned black servants. As we have seen, pre-European Africa had been practicing slavery, servitude, vassalage, and serfdom on its own people for thousands of years[1183] (in forms far more brutal than anything found in the American South),[1184] dating back to before the continent's Iron Age,[1185] to the very dawn of African history itself. In fact, Africa is the *only* region that engaged *continually* in the West African-European-American slave trade for its full 424 years.[1186]

It was just such facts that made the institution so understandable to many American black civil rights leaders. One of these was African-American educator, intellectual, and author William E. B. Du Bois, who wrote that he could forgive slavery for it "is a world-old habit."[1187]

WHAT YOU WERE TAUGHT: Slavery lasted far longer in the American South than it did in the American North.

THE TRUTH: The reverse is true. Southern slavery lasted from 1749, when Georgia became the first Southern state to legalize slavery,[1188] to 1865, the year the Thirteenth Amendment was ratified and American slavery was officially abolished, a mere 116 years.[1189]

In contrast, Northern slavery lasted from 1641, when Massachusetts became the first Northern state to legalize slavery,[1190] to 1865, a span of 224 years. This period increases if we count from 1626, the year New York imported the first black slaves into North America, a span of 239 years—ending in 1865.[1191]

Either way, the North practiced slavery for over a century longer than the South did, between 108 and 123 years longer.

These Southern servants, "slaves" to Yankees, and their descendants lived under the institution for only 116 years, while in the North black slaves endured it for some 239 years. And yet it is the Confederate flag that is associated with slavery and it is the South that has been labeled the "slave states," while in contrast, the U.S. flag is considered the flag of emancipation and the North has been labeled the "free states." Let us call this duplicitous Northern myth what it is: the overt hypocrisy of anti-South Yankee propaganda, another feeble attempt to hide the Truth about Lincoln's War from the American people.

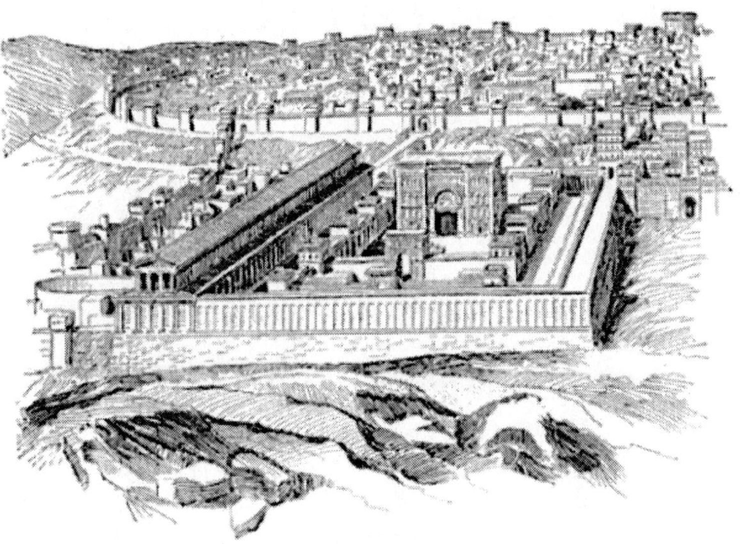

The Jewish Temple at Jerusalem. As the Bible records, the Hebrews were one of the most ardent slaving societies in the ancient world. The Old Testament brims with rules and regulations on the treatment of slaves, most of whom were fellow Semites from the same region. The Jewish approval and practice of slavery passed on into the early Christian Church through Jesus, Paul, and the Twelve Apostles, who accepted the institution as a natural aspect of society at the time. Later, most of the early Church Fathers, from Saint Augustine to Thomas Aquinas, also recognized and sanctioned slavery.

7

THE LIFESTYLE AND TREATMENT OF SOUTHERN SLAVES

WHAT YOU WERE TAUGHT: Southern slavery was so terrible in every way that Dixie's slaves were the most wretched people on earth. Downcast and dejected by his enslavement, feeling powerless, exploited, angry, and afraid, starving from lack of food, freezing from lack of proper clothing and shelter, the typical Southern slave lived a life of pure misery, filled with anguish, hopelessness, and despair due to a lifestyle that was far below the standards of even domestic livestock let alone impoverished humans, one unknown in the annals of world history.

THE TRUTH: The Northern mind deserves credit for creativity and imagination, but it ranks dead last when it comes to historical accuracy! In the late 1700s U.S. Representative Aedanus Burke of South Carolina gave the following reply to these types of silly anti-South charges:

> *"The negroes [in the South live] . . . better and in more comfortable houses than the poor of Europe."* He [then] referred to an advertisement which he had lately seen in a New York paper of a [black] woman and child to be sold. *"That," he declared, "was a species of cruelty unknown in the southern states. There the negroes have property, horses, cattle, hogs, and furniture. With respect to their ceremony of marriage, they took each other from love and friendship."*[1192]

Southern "slaves" were not the bedraggled, illiterate, oppressed race that our Yankee biased history books like to portray. This dapper slave couple, for example, George and Susan Page, worked for the Dabney family of Raymond, Mississippi, made famous by Susan Dabney Smedes' 1888 book, *Memorials of a Southern Planter*. When Susan's father, plantation owner Thomas Dabney, passed away in the late 1800s, former body servant George wrote to her, saying: "He was a good master to us all. You are all my children, and I love you all alike."

"As a general rule," wrote antislavery advocate Hinton Rowan Helper, in the South "poor white persons are regarded with less esteem and attention than negroes," with the condition of "vast numbers" of whites being "infinitely worse off."[1193] In 1819 a Virginian declared before Congress that Southern slaves "are treated with confidence and esteem, and their rights [are] respected."[1194]

Such truths were so obvious that many 19th-Century Northerners came to admit that Southern slavery was far from the miserable institution that radical Yankee abolitionists tried to portray. One of these was Reverend Nehemiah Adams, a stalwart New England abolitionist who visited the South in the 1850s *for the express purpose of validating his already negative view of Southern slavery*.

After leaving Boston, Massachusetts, Adams' ship arrived at the port of Savannah, Georgia. Filled with dread at what he expected to see, he tentatively stepped ashore, not realizing that his views on "Southern slavery" were about to change dramatically. Now let us allow the Yankee clergyman to speak for himself:

> The steam tug reached the landing, and the slaves were all about us. *One thing immediately surprised me; they were all in good humor, and some of them in a broad laugh. The delivery of every trunk from the tug to the wharf was the occasion of some hit, or repartee, and every burden was*

borne with a jolly word, grimace, or motion. The lifting of one leg in laughing seemed as natural as a Frenchman's shrug. I asked one of them to place a trunk with a lot of baggage; it was done; up went the hand to the hat — "Any thing more, please sir ?" What a contrast, I involuntarily said to myself, to that [black] troop at the Albany landing on our Western Railroad! and on those piles of boards, and on the roofs of the sheds, and at the piers, in New York! *I began to like these slaves. I began to laugh with them. It was irresistible. Who could have convinced me, an hour before, that slaves could have any other effect upon me than to make me feel sad?*

. . . One thing seemed clear; they were not so much cowed down as I expected. Perhaps, however, they were a fortunate set. I rode away, expecting soon to have some of my disagreeable anticipations verified.

. . . I shall now relate the impressions which were involuntarily made upon me while residing in some of the [Southern] slave States.

. . . All things being arranged at your resting-place, the first impulse is to see how the land lies, settle certain landmarks, and, above all things, find the post-office.

The city of Savannah abounds in parks, as they are called—squares, fenced in, with trees. Young [white] children and infants were there, with *very respectable colored nurses—young women, with bandanna and plaid cambric turbans, and superior in genteel appearance to any similar class, as a whole, in any of our cities. They could not be slaves. Are they slaves? "Certainly," says the friend at your side; "they each belong to some master or mistress."*

In behalf of a score of mothers of my acquaintance, and of some fathers, *I looked with covetous feelings upon the relation which I saw existed between these nurses and children. These women seemed not to have the air and manner of hirelings in the care and treatment of the children; their conversation with them, the degree of seemingly maternal feeling which was infused into their whole deportment, could not fail to strike a casual observer.*

Then these are slaves. Their care of the children, even if it be slave labor, is certainly equal to that which is free.

"But that was a freeman who just passed us?"

"No; he is Mr. W.'s servant, near us."

"He a slave?" Such a rhetorical lifting of the arm, such a line of grace as the hand described in descending easily from the hat to the side, such a glow of good feeling on recognizing neighbor B., with a supplementary act of respect to the stranger with him, were wholly foreign from my notions of a slave. "Where are your real slaves, such as we read of?"

"These are about a fair sample."

. . . Our [Yankee] fancies with regard to the condition of the slaves proceed from our northern repugnance to slavery, stimulated by many things that we read. The every-day life, the whole picture of society at the South, is not presented to us so frequently—indeed it cannot be, nor can it strike the mind as strongly—as slave auctions and separations of families, fugitives hiding in dismal swamps, and other things which appeal to our [Northern] sensibilities. Whatever else may be true of slavery, these things, we say, are indisputable; and they furnish materials for the fancy to build into a world of woe.

Without supposing that I had yet seen slavery, it was nevertheless true that *a load was lifted from my mind by the first superficial look at the slaves in the city.*

It was as though I had been let down by necessity into a cavern which I had peopled with disagreeable sights, and, on reaching bottom, found daylight streaming in, and the place cheerful.

A better-looking, happier, more courteous set of people I had never seen, than those colored men, women, and children whom I met the first few days of my stay in Savannah. It had a singular effect on my spirits. They all seemed glad to see me. I was tempted with some vain feelings, as though they meant to pay me some special respect. It was all the more grateful, because for months sickness and death had covered almost every thing, even the faces of friends at home [in New England], with sadness to my eye, and my spirits had drooped. But to be met and accosted with such extremely civil, benevolent looks, to see so many faces break into pleasant smiles in going by, made one feel that he was not alone in the world, even in a land of strangers.

How such unaffected politeness could have been learned under the lash I did not understand. It conflicted with my notions of slavery. I could not have dreamed that these people had been "down trodden," "their very manhood crushed out of them," "the galling yoke of slavery breaking every human feeling, and reducing them to the level of brutes." It was one of the pleasures of taking a walk to be greeted by all my colored friends. I felt that I had taken a whole new race of my fellow-men by the hand. I took care to notice each of them, and get his full smile and salutation; many a time I would gladly have stopped and paid a good price for a certain "good morning," courtesy, and bow; it was worth more than gold; its charm consisted in its being unbought, unconstrained, for I was an entire stranger. Timidity, a feeling of necessity, the leer of obliged deference, I nowhere saw; but the artless, free, and easy manner which burdened spirits never wear. It was difficult to pass the colored people in the streets without a smile awakened by the magnetism of their smiles. Let any one at the North, afflicted with depression of spirits, drop down among these negroes, walk these streets, form a passing acquaintance with some of them, and unless he is a hopeless case, he will find himself in moods of cheerfulness

> *never awakened surely by the countenances of the whites in any strange place.*[1195]

Thus far in my trip, wrote Reverend Adams,

> *with regard to slavery, the relations and feelings between the white and colored people at the south were not wholly as I had imagined them to be. [Already my first experiences] . . . gave me feelings of affection for the blacks and respect for their masters. Not a word had been said to me about slavery; my eyes taught me that some practical things in the system are wholly different from my anticipations.*[1196]

During Lincoln's War, Charles Francis Adams, Jr. (far left) of Boston, Massachusetts, a brevet brigadier general in the Union Army, was able to witness the truth about Southern slavery firsthand. Like thousands of other Yankees, he came away from the experience with a completely altered attitude about the "slave states," the "peculiar institution," and the "African race."

Union officer Charles Francis Adams, Jr. (the great-grandson of famed U.S. Founder President John Adams), grew to have similar sentiments about Southern slavery. In November 1864 he wrote the following to his father Charles, Sr.,[1197] Lincoln's ambassador to Great Britain:

> *I'm gradually getting to have very decided opinions on the negro question*; they're growing up in me as inborn convictions and are not the result of reflection. I note what you say of the African race and "the absence of all appearance of self reliance in their own power"

during this struggle. From this, greatly as it has disappointed me, I very unwillingly draw different conclusions from your own. *The conviction is forcing itself upon me that African slavery, as it existed in our slave states [the South], was indeed a patriarchal institution, under which the slaves were not, as a whole, unhappy, cruelly treated or overworked. I am forced to this conclusion.*[1198]

On November 9, 1862, the young Confederate diarist Sarah Morgan wrote sarcastically of Lincoln and the North's erroneous views of "Southern slavery." Sarah mingled, laughed, played, and worked with her family's black servants and knew the truth that the Yankee president dared not admit:

> If Lincoln could spend the grinding season on a [Southern] plantation, he would recall his [emancipation] proclamation.[1199] As it is, he has only proved himself a fool, without injuring us. Why last evening I took old [slave] Wilson's place at the baggasse chute, and kept the rollers free from cane until I had thrown down enough to fill several carts, and had my hands as black as his. What cruelty to slaves! And [our servant] black Frank thinks me cruel, too, when he meets me with a patronising grin, and shows me the nicest vats of candy, and peels cane for me. Oh! very cruel![1200]

Fashionably and expensively dressed black servants "promenading" through town on Sundays—wearing, among other things, top hats and bonnets, and carrying canes and parasols—almost always appalled Northern visitors to the South, for this image was the opposite of what they had been told to expect.[1201] After fighting for some time in Virginia, one of Lincoln's soldiers, a private from New Hampshire, wrote:

> *After now having seen Southern slavery for myself, I firmly believe that we Yanks have been fooled. It is nothing like we were taught. Why just the other day I saw slaves going to church who were as happy and cheerful as can be.*[1202]

During a visit to a Virginia plantation in 1842, Boston clergyman and slaveholder James W. Alexander included the following observations in a personal letter:

> *I am more and more convinced of the injustice we do the [Southern]*

> *slaveholders.* Of their feelings towards their negroes I can form a better notion than formerly, by examining my own towards the slaves who wait on my wife and mind my children. *It is a feeling most like that we have to near relations. [One of the slaves on this plantation] Nanette is a mild but active brown woman, with whom I would trust any interest we have. She is an invalid, however, and in the North would long since have died in an alms-house. As it is, she will be well housed, well fed, protected, and happy, if she lives to be 100. There are two blind [slave] women (80-90 [years of age]) on this estate, who have done nothing for years. It is touching to see them walking out, arm in arm, to bask in the sun.*[1203]

When New England landscape architect Frederick Law Olmsted traveled through Virginia in the early 1800s, he was stunned by the incongruity of what he had believed about Southern "slavery" and the reality of Southern servitude: the slaves he saw working in the fields were either whistling or singing.[1204] On one plantation he witnessed a group of 30 black field servants "grinning," leaning on their hoes, scarcely working. All were neatly dressed and overweight, hardly the portrait of the "brutal existence of the starving slave" presented by the North.[1205]

Victorian Yankee landscape architect, journalist, and author Frederick Law Olmsted visited Dixie in the early 1800s, and was shocked to learn that Southern slavery was nothing like he had been taught.

While riding through Georgia in January 1846, British tourist Charles Lyell came across a "long line" of "well dressed" slaves made up of men, women, and boys. The "merry" band was "talking and laughing" as they stopped to take a look at Lyell's coach.[1206] In 1846 Southern historian Matthew Estes wrote:

> *It has been remarked by almost every one who, has visited the South, and made himself acquainted with the condition of our slaves, that there is more light-hearted joyousness among them, than among any similar number of people in the world.* Having been born at the South, and reared on a plantation, I have enjoyed a fair opportunity of knowing the character and state of mind of our slaves. *I have ever found the slaves contented, happy, light-hearted, and full of amusement. The oldest negroes never get old in their feelings; but they continue light-hearted, and full of sport to the last.* Even when worn down by age and infirmity so as to be unable to get about, they still continue contented and happy in their feelings—as ready as ever to tell stories, and make merry.[1207]

During Englishman Robert Russell's tour of the U.S. in 1854, he stopped in Richmond, Virginia, where he was amazed to observe large numbers of carefree black slaves loafing about the town. "There was nothing repulsive in the appearance of the [negro] crowds about the corners of the streets," writes Russell, "as all were well-dressed and as light-hearted as one could possibly imagine."[1208] While strolling through Montgomery, Alabama, in the mid 1800s, Irish journalist William Howard Russell had the following experience:

> As I was walking . . . *I perceived a crowd of very well-dressed negroes, men and women*, in front of a plain brick building which I was informed was their Baptist meeting-house, into which white people rarely or never intrude. *These were domestic servants, or persons employed in stores, and their general appearance indicated much comfort and even luxury. I doubted if they all were slaves.* One of my companions went up to a woman in a straw hat, with bright red and green ribbon trimmings and artificial flowers, a gaudy Paisley shawl, and a rainbow-like gown blown out over her yellow boots by a prodigious crinoline, and asked her "Whom do you belong to?" She replied, "I b'long to Massa Smith, sar."[1209]

The Southern slave's state of felicity was indeed obvious, and as is plain from these eyewitness accounts, could be noted in part by the manner in which he clothed himself. Englishman Adam Hodgson visited the U.S. in 1819 and 1820, and had this say about the black servants he witnessed at Charleston, South Carolina:

> *I was pleased to see the slaves apparently enjoying themselves on this day in their best attire, and was amused with their manners towards each other.*

> *They generally use Sir and Madam in addressing each other, and make the most formal and particular inquiries after each other's families.*[1210]

The sight of sociable, cheerful, carefree, polite, well dressed slaves walking freely about town was a common one in the Old South, much to the consternation and shock of Yankee visitors and Northern transplants.

When Englishman James Silk Buckingham traveled to Richmond, Virginia, in the 1840s, he noted that:

> *On Sundays, when the slaves and servants are all at liberty after dinner, they move about in every thoroughfare, and are generally more gaily dressed than the whites. The females wear white muslin and light silk gowns, with caps, bonnets, ribbons and feathers; some carry reticules on the arm and many are seen with parasols, while nearly all of them carry a white pocket-handkerchief before them in the most fashionable style. The young men among the slaves wear white trousers, black stocks, broad-brimmed hats, and carry walking-sticks; and from the bowings, curtseying and greetings in the highway one might almost imagine one's self to be at Hayti [Haiti] and think that the coloured people had got possession of the town and held sway, while the whites were living among them by sufferance.*[1211]

New Yorker Joseph Holt Ingraham recorded the following

anecdote while visiting New Orleans, Louisiana, in the early 1830s:

> [Eventually] . . . we overtook a cart loaded with negroes, proceeding to the country. To our inquiry, one of them answered,—while the others exhibited ivory [teeth] enough to sheathe a ship's bottom [that is, smiled broadly], "We Wirginny niggurs, Massas: new massa, he juss buy us, and we be gwine to he plantation. Plenty sugar dere, massa!" *They all appeared contented and happy, and highly elated at their sweet anticipations. Say not that the slavery of the Louisiana negroes is a bitter draught.*[1212]

After visiting Charleston, South Carolina, in 1854, abolitionist Professor Charles Eliot Norton of Cambridge, Massachusetts, wrote:

> The change to a Northerner in coming South is always a great one when he steps over the boundary of the free states . . . Dr. [Nehemiah] Adams made no new discovery when he found that *the outside first aspect of slavery has nothing horrible and repulsive in it. The slaves do not go about looking unhappy, and are with difficulty, I fancy, persuaded to feel so. Whips and chains, oaths and brutality, are as common, for all that one sees, in the free as the slave states. We have come thus far, and might have gone ten times as far, I dare say, without seeing the first sign of Negro misery, or white tyranny.*[1213]

During a trip to South Carolina in 1854, Yankee Liberal Dr. Charles Eliot Norton noted—much to his surprise—that there were absolutely no indications of either "negro misery" or "white tyranny."

During his travels to America's old Southland, English novelist William M. Thackeray had a similar experience, as he discusses in his work, *Roundabout Papers*:

> *How they sang; how they laughed and grinned; how they scraped, bowed, and complimented you and each other, those negroes of the cities of the Southern parts of the then United States!* My business kept me in the towns; I was but in one negro-plantation village, and there were only women and little children, the men being out a-field. But *there was plenty of cheerfulness in the huts, under the great trees—I speak of what I saw—and amidst the dusky bondsmen of the [Southern] cities. I witnessed a curious gaiety; heard amongst the black folk endless singing, shouting, and laughter; and saw on holidays black gentlemen and ladies arrayed in such splendor and comfort as freeborn workmen in our [English] towns seldom exhibit.*[1214]

WHAT YOU WERE TAUGHT: Southern slavery was a lawless barbaric institution that gave slaves no legal rights, protection, or privileges. Thus slaves were not allowed to marry and have families.
THE TRUTH: This could not be more false, as Scotsman William Thomson noted in the 1840s after visiting the South: "The negroes are allowed to do as they please with regard to marriage."[1215] In point of fact, nearly all Southern servants were allowed, even exhorted, to marry and have children, for as modern studies show, in nearly all cases the married are more vigorous, more content, more productive, and more stable than the unmarried. As Southern servant owner James Hammond wrote in his plantation manual: "Marriage [among servants] is to be encouraged, as it adds to the comfort, happiness and health of those who enter upon it . . ."[1216] Thus in 1846 Southern historian Matthew Estes could write of the South that:

> *Most of our slaves live in the country on the plantations of their masters, where they early marry, and live as happily together as any people in the world. Having no apprehensions about supporting themselves and families, they marry much earlier than the great mass of poor whites . . .*[1217]

In 1858 we have record of a combined six-couple slave wedding on the Georgia plantation of Daniel R. Tucker, "with dinner and dancing to follow."[1218] Around the same time New Yorker Anson De Puy Van Buren was an eyewitness to a typical servant marriage, this one in

Mississippi:

> The wedding . . . took place at the plantation-house, on New Year's eve. Two of Major W.'s slaves were there united in marriage. Many of the young [white] folk, and very many of the blacks, were present on this occasion. Everything being ready, the two stepped forward to be married. The blooming bride, showily dressed, came forward in all her sable beauty, with eyes of sparkling blackness, and—"mouth with pearl and ruby glowing" . . . gave herself, as a New Year's gift, to a robust negro. The twain were pronounced—a sable unit, by a [white] minister residing in the neighborhood.[1219]

Countless others examples of legal slave marriages exist in the historical record, one of the most famous, of course, being the marriage between Northern slave, abolitionist, and feminist, Sojourner Truth, and a fellow Northern black slave named Thomas.[1220]

In 1914 Harrison Anthony Trexler made these remarks on antebellum slave marriages in Missouri:

> . . . *the Catholic church regularly married slaves and held the tie to be as sacred as any other marriage.* The following entry appears in the Cathedral records:
>
> > "On the twenty-fourth of December, Eighteen Hundred and twenty-eight the undersigned Parish priest at St. Louis received the mutual consent at Marriage between Silvester, slave of Mr. Bosseron, born in St. Louis, and Nora Helen, slave of Mr. Hough, born in the city of Washington, and gave them the nuptial benediction in the presence of the undersigned witnesses. Wm. Sautnier."
>
> Then follow the crosses which represent the signatures of Silvester, Nora Helen, and four other slaves and one free negro.
>
> Several old slaves were questioned regarding the subject of marriage, and their statements show differences in practice. One said that he and his wife liked one another, and as they both belonged to the same master they "took up" or "simply lived together," and that this arrangement was the custom and nothing was said. *A negro of Saline County who was a child in slavery days stated that his parents belonged to different persons, and, by the consent of both,*

> *were married by the squire. . . . After the War they were again married in conformity with the new state constitution. Doubtless the experience of many slave families was similar to this last.*[1221]

A typical Southern slave wedding in the 1700s featured high spirits, food, music, singing, and dancing, with everyone dressed in their finest attire. Both blacks and whites were invited to the gala affair from neighboring farms and plantations, which was usually planned out months in advance by the slaves' white mistress. Often the couple's master officiated, while a local black minister performed the service.

English tourist Henry Latham visited Jefferson Davis in 1867, and asked the Confederate president if what Yankee abolitionists had said about Southern slaves being prohibited from marrying and having religion were true, to which he replied:

> It is a *gross misrepresentation* on the part of the abolitionists, that the marriage-tie and religion were not observed upon the plantations. *It was simply a matter of interest with every planter that they should be regarded.*[1222]

Victorian blacks, like Victorian whites, needed little encouragement to "walk down the aisle," for marriage was practically a religion among them. Of this phenomenon, Mary Chesnut, who makes note of numerous legal Southern slave marriages in her diaries,[1223] writes that it was routine for black servants to marry, and that afterward they behaved just like any other married couple, for "tying the knot" was one of their great pleasures and the primary focus of their lives.[1224]

The reality is that black Southern servants courted and married in the same way that free blacks and whites did, their white and black owners allowing them to wed whomever they chose in their own manner and time.[1225] White owners often officiated at servant weddings, marrying the couples in their own homes or at nearby churches. On other occasions black pastors, who formed a major segment of the antebellum South's black leadership,[1226] performed the wedding services.[1227] In either case, the custom was almost universally approved of across the white South, as the words of early 19th-Century Christian authority Charles C. Jones show. Southern pastors, he wrote in 1842, should always solemnize the marriages of black servants,

> and *at their own homes and at such times as may best suit their convenience, for like the rest of mankind, they like to see their friends in their own houses, and give them on such joyous occasions, the best entertainment they can afford.* Some ministers are in the habit of requiring for their own convenience, the people to appear and be married at the church. The consequence is, they are called upon very seldom; the people contrive to have their marriages solemnized at home. Church marriages are not more popular with the lower than with the higher classes in society.
>
> The formal solemnization of their marriages is of great importance if their improvement in morals and religion is the object sought after. The effect is to elevate and throw around the marriage state peculiar sacredness. It is rendered "honorable in all." *Polygamy and licentiousness are rebuked and overthrown. Masters protect families more, and make greater efforts to preserve them from separation.*
>
> *That very great reforms can be made among the Negroes, in the sacredness and perpetuity of their marriage relations, admits of no question. The experiment has been tried and proven.*[1228]

The "slave weddin'" was often done up on a grand scale, with the white mistress of the house proudly sending out invitations to both her friends and the whites and servants of neighboring plantations. Planning and decorating could go on for weeks ahead of time, ending in the kind of fun-laden gala event—overflowing with food, drink, music, dancing, and wedding presents—that one only finds in the South.[1229]

To this day Yankee authors continue to pretend that the Old South prohibited marriage between slaves. Southern hero, Confederate President Jefferson Davis, called this particular Yankee myth "a gross misrepresentation" of the facts.

In 1858 a Swedish visitor to the United States, Fredrika Bremer, told of her experience attending the wedding of two black servant couples on a plantation in Columbia, South Carolina:

> I was one day invited by Professor F. to the weddings of two couples of his house slaves. The bridal pairs were young people, and *looked very well*, especially one of the bridegrooms, a negro black as night, and whom his master commended for the excellence of his character and his general intelligence, and one of the brides—but not of the bridegroom par excellence—were regularly handsome. *Both the brides were dressed very prettily in white, and wore garlands.* The clergyman entered the negro-company, stepped up to the bridal couples and very soon dismissed the marriage ceremony, after which *they began dancing in the same room. Negroes*

> *and negresses swung round in a lively waltz; ladies dressed and decked out in gauze and flowers, altogether like our [white European] ladies, the only difference being that these had more finery about them*, and considerably less grace; and, after all, they looked very much better in this borrowed and imitated finery than I should have believed possible. *While the black company danced zealously, the white people went to see the wedding dinner-table, which was splendidly covered with flowers and fine cakes, and seemed really almost to bend under the abundance of meats.*[1230]

A Southern black servant girl described her own marriage this way:

> We girls were all unmarried when we moved to Missouri, and excepting Millar, we all lived together till old master's family began to set up for themselves. I was the first that got married. It was the next year after we went to Missouri that I was married to Nathaniel Noll. *There was about three hundred people at my wedding. When a respectable colored girl gets married, it is the custom there, and in Kentucky, for all the neighbors, white and black, to come and see the ceremony. Colored people and whites associate more in the South than in the North. They go to parties together, and dance together. Colored people enjoy themselves more in the South than in any other part of the world . . . . We were married by Mr. Chandler, at my master's house.*[1231]

Intense devotion, commitment, and affection among married servants was well-known, and interplantation marriages were not uncommon. When the distance between the two farms was too great for convenient travel, it was the customary practice across the South for one of the owners to unite the pair through purchase.[1232] An 1854 letter from one white Georgia slave owner to another regarding this topic is elucidating:

> I have a girl Amanda that has your servant Phil for a husband. I should be very glad indeed if you would purchase her. She is a very good seamstress, an excellent cook—makes cake and preserves beautifully—and washes and irons very nicely, and cannot be excelled in cleaning up a house. Her disposition is very amiable. I have had her for years and I assure you that I have not exaggerated as regards her worth. . . . I will send her down to see you at any time.[1233]

The myth of forced or arranged marriages among Southern

slaves is just that, for it was discouraged and thus atypical. But even when, in those rare cases, it did occur, it would have been similar in many respects to the arranged marriages that one found, and still finds, in Africa.[1234] Thus, such a matrimonial bond was not altogether foreign to African-Americans in the antebellum South, most who have carried many of the old African customs right into the present day.

Of black servant weddings in the Old South generally, Ulrich B. Phillips writes:

> . . . *[white] marriage merriment in the great house would have its echo in the [servants'] quarters; and sometimes marriages among the slaves were grouped so as to give occasion for a general frolic.* Thus Daniel R. Tucker in 1858 sent a general invitation over the countryside in central Georgia to [as mentioned earlier] a sextuple wedding among his slaves, with dinner and dancing to follow. On the whole, the fiddle, the banjo and the bones were not seldom in requisition.[1235]

WHAT YOU WERE TAUGHT: Southern slaves were not allowed to live in their own homes or possess or farm their own land.
THE TRUTH: Marriage was just the beginning of a litany of civil, social, and human rights that were accorded to black servants in the South. They were also free to build their own homes, plant their own gardens, own their own livestock, buy their own clothes and furniture, and farm their own parcels of land. Indeed, a number of freedmen reported that as former servants nearly all of them had owned property, and that they loved nothing better than to amass wealth, property, and belongings.[1236]

After visiting the American South in the late 1820s, Scottish tourist Basil Hall wrote that on the typical plantation slaves

> are *allowed to have as much land as they choose to plant*, and the master's family is supplied entirely with poultry and eggs from this free work of *the slaves, who are regularly paid* at the following rates:—Eggs, 12½ cents (6d.) a-dozen; chickens, 12½ cents (6d.); fowls, 20 to 25 cents, or about a shilling a pair; ducks twice as much. But *they are left at liberty to carry their poultry to a better market if they can find one. The proceeds are mostly laid out in dress and trinkets.*[1237]

As was the norm throughout the South, these Virginia slaves owned their own home, land, outbuildings, livestock, farming equipment, carts, buggies, gardens, products, and supplies. Many Southern slaves owned more land and had a greater net worth than free blacks and whites in the same neighborhood.

We have numerous records of black servants who owned not just great swaths of real estate, but also hogs, horses, cows, jewelry, buggies, and wagons, and whose personal products included corn, rice, fowl, beehives, peanuts, fodder, syrup, hay, mules, butter, sugar, tea, and sheep, among hundreds of other items. Industrious black servants became wealthy selling their goods, had excellent credit, and owned more land than whites living in the same area.[1238]

WHAT YOU WERE TAUGHT: American slavery, particularly in the South, could have only come into existence and could have only been maintained by forceful laws and regulation. Otherwise it would have fallen to pieces.

THE TRUTH: In ancient times slavery began as a natural outgrowth of the social customs of a particular time and place. Thus in the beginning there were no laws regarding the institution whatsoever. This exact same phenomenon occurred in early America. It was only later on that laws regarding slavery were created.

Yet these first statutes did not arise for the express purpose of regulation, but rather as recognition of the institution and to give legal sanction to the native slave customs that were already in operation. It was only when the American slave population grew to an unmanageable size that laws began to be used to regulate and govern the slave system. In other words, slave laws only arose when they were required by circumstances.[1239]

Slavery was a natural outgrowth of the rise of human civilization thousands of years ago. As such, it is not the "peculiar Southern institution," but rather the "standard universal institution," one in which the American South played no role, either in its invention or its development. To the contrary, Dixie was the last Western region to practice slavery and the first to try to abolish it.

In 1819 Robert Walsh wrote factually *and* sympathetically of Dixie's slave laws:

> The laws of the [Southern] slaveholding states do not furnish a criterion for the character of their present white population or the condition of the slaves. *Those laws were enacted for the most part in seasons of particular alarm produced by attempts at insurrection, or when the black inhabitants were doubly formidable by reason of the greater proportion which they bore to the whites in number and the savage state and unhappy mood in which they arrived from Africa*. The real measure of danger was not understood but after long experience, and in the interval the precautions taken were naturally of the most jealous and rigorous aspect. That these have not all been repealed, or that some of them should be still enforced, is not inconsistent with *an improved spirit of legislation*, since *the evils against which they were intended to guard* are yet the subject of just apprehension.[1240]

In short, Southern slave laws did not create Southern slavery, Southern slavery created Southern slave laws. The institution was a natural byproduct of human society, which is why it was once found on every continent and among *all* races, creeds, nationalities, and religions.

WHAT YOU WERE TAUGHT: Since there were no laws against the it, Southern slave owners routinely split up slave families, and perversely even enjoyed doing so.

THE TRUTH: Though laws were lenient regarding the breaking up of slave families, the majority of Southern slaveholders always did everything possible to prevent this from occurring.[1241] Louisiana, as just one example, went one step further by legally banning the practice.[1242] But most Southern states did not require this law, as Southern white families considered it dishonorable to allow family units, whatever their race, to disintegrate. Their Christian upbringing and naturally humanitarian dispositions could simply not abide it.[1243]

Dixie icon Confederate General Nathan Bedford Forrest typified the Southern slaveholder: not only did he refuse to split up slave families, he helped reunite numerous family members who had been separated.

This is why, in fact, nearly all Southern slave owners went to such extraordinary lengths to maintain the unity of slave families. Confederate General Nathan Bedford Forrest, for instance, one of the wealthiest slave traders in the Old South, was known far and wide for his beneficent approach to servant families, often traveling great distances to purchase and reunite separated individuals. To avoid this problem to begin with, it was his routine practice to purchase all the members of a slave household if need be—even if he had to take a financial hit—in order to keep husbands, wives, and children together. Little wonder that at slave markets blacks lined up by the dozens begging Forrest to buy them.[1244]

Furthermore, Southern slave owners were compelled by law to legally register their servants, whether black or white, as literal members of their own families, making it even more emotionally difficult to separate husbands from wives, children from parents.[1245]

Foreign visitors to the antebellum South, as well as slaves themselves, reported that most Southern slaveholders refused to split up families, even accepting huge financial losses in order to do so. When this was absolutely impossible, separated family members were sold within traveling distance of one another.[1246] While visiting the South in 1835, professor Ethan Allen Andrews of Connecticut asked a slave dealer about this topic:

> In answer to my inquiries respecting the separation of families, he assured me that *they were at great pains to prevent such separation in all cases, in which it was practicable, and to obtain, if possible, whole families. . . . In one instance, he remarked, they had purchased, from one estate, more than fifty, in order to prevent the separation of family connections; and in selling them, they had been equally scrupulous to have them continue together. In this case, however, they had sacrificed not less than one or two thousand dollars* [about $55,000 in today's currency], *which they might have obtained by separating them, as they would have sold much better in smaller lots. The [slave men and] women, in general, looked [cheerful,] contented and happy . . .*[1247]

William Thomson of Scotland, who observed the workings of a number of Southern plantations firsthand, wrote the following in 1842:

> The [Southern] *slave owners are not apt to separate families*, although they are always liable to be sold; but, *in reality, they are not so much scattered as the families of working men in Scotland*, whose necessities compel them to separate at an age when the American slave is running about, gathering health and strength, and playing mischief. . . . *When a [slave] man and his wife, or a [slave] mother and her daughter, who love each other, are separated, they complain of it to their owners, who make an arrangement either to "buy or sell." This is frequently done.*[1248]

Southern belle Kate Stone voiced the sentiments of millions of white Southerners when she recorded the following in her journal on January 24, 1862. Kate's uncle, Ashburn Ragan, had just passed away, obliging the rest of her family to sell their servants:

> My grandpa John Ragan came by, but only to pick up Uncle Ashburn's Negroes, all of whom are to be separated and sent out to our various heirs. *Anytime one has to break apart a servant family, people who have spent decades together, it is a great sorrow and a terrible pain, both to them and to us. How I wished that Mamma could have bought them all herself, and kept them here with us.*[1249]

The separation of slave families was uncommon in the American South, and was only done under the most extenuating circumstances. This scene, for example, in which a terrified slave boy is being purchased and removed from his distraught mother and father, took place in New York—the state in which slavery was the most entrenched and long lasting.

Another example of this type of owner was Virginia planter William Massie who, in 1858, under financial duress, sold his family's beloved farm rather than split up and auction off the individual members of his servants' families. Massie, referring to "my little family, white and black," stated that his greatest happiness came from the knowledge that they would all continue together "permanently."[1250] Contrary to anti-South Northern myth, this was the typical rather than the atypical attitude among Southern slaveholders.

Yes, Southern slave dealers and slaveholders did sometimes split apart slave families. As we have seen, this was never purposeful, however. It was usually attributable to bureaucratic red tape, and nearly always accompanied by heartfelt agony. Where it was unavoidable the seller could always console himself with the fact that slave separations "were no more frequent than those suffered by free laborers at the North under the stress of economic necessity"[1251]—something that 21st-Century readers of this book may have very well experienced in their own families.

While American Southerners disliked separating slave families, this was an accepted custom across Africa. These African slaves in Suriname were long ago taken from their families of origin by ruthless African slavers, who placed profit above humanitarian concerns—quite unlike in Dixie.

However much we may decry the occasional breaking up of slave families in the Old South, it never approached the fearful conditions of 18th- and 19th-Century Africa herself, whose native slave catchers and slave dealers showed absolutely no concern about the separation of the African families they captured and sold as slaves to other Africans, and later to non-African slave traders.[1252]

WHAT YOU WERE TAUGHT: Southern slaves toiled for their masters for free, never earning a dime for their hard labor. Thus they drew no income and, obviously, could not own their own businesses.

THE TRUTH: This is yet another one of the great Northern slavery myths. Actually, not only were Southern servants financially compensated, they were also encouraged to own their own businesses. And not only this, the extra money they earned from plying their personal trades—added to their basic daily income—could be quite substantial,[1253] and greatly contributed to the thriving "black commerce" that existed across the South.[1254]

Let us look at one example. At Carnton Plantation in Franklin, Tennessee, one can still see evidence of the Southern practice of paying black servants: outside, on the east wall of the mansion, the doorstep (on the left) that leads into the master's office, is worn down from thousands of scuffling shoes that passed over it between 1826 and 1909. Most of the shoes that ground away this stone between 1826 and 1865 specifically belonged to the owners' (the McGavocks) black servants, who lined up here for both their daily work orders and their weekly pay packets.[1255]

While the average Southern servant's income seems to have been around $48 a year (or about $1,300 in today's currency, a substantial wage at the time), many ambitious blacks earned from $60 to over $300 a year ($1,600 to $8,000 in today's currency, respectively), many drawing "considerably higher wages" than whites doing the same type of labor.[1256] The products of home gardens (sold at market each Sunday)[1257] and work at outside odd jobs also brought in significant extra earnings,[1258] some of which were used to buy fancy cloth from which they created "fine clothing" for themselves. More often Southern servants saved their money and bought brand new clothing; or just as frequently were given nearly new, much appreciated hand-me-downs from their owners, as Smedes describes:

> Some of the [servant] women bought silk dresses; many had their Sunday dresses made by white mantua-makers. Of course they had the clothes of the master and mistress in addition; and in later years, as the house grew full of young masters and young mistresses, theirs were added. *As the family knew that the servants liked nothing so well as the well-made clothes that they laid aside, they wore their clothes but little. They justly considered that those who had labored for them had rights to them while still fresh. Under these circumstances it did not seem wasteful for a daughter of the house to distribute, at the end of a season, as many as a dozen or more dresses that had been made up but a few months before. It was quite funny to see among the [male slave] gallants three or four swallow-tail coats of the master's come in at the gate for the grand promenade on Sunday evenings, escorting the colored belles in all their bravery of hoop-skirts, and ruffles, and ribbons, and flowers.*[1259]

Far from being the "bedraggled, stupid, degraded, indolent slaves" of Northern lore, such commercialism made these Southern servants much more akin to proud peasants and enterprising small town traders.[1260] It was not uncommon for a servant to earn enough surplus money that he or she could make a contribution to the collection plate every Sunday at church.[1261] Thomson noted that

> *many of those [slaves] who are hired out make more money than the stipulated wages their owners require. With this [extra income] they are allowed to do as they please.*[1262]

Under the South's mild African servitude, there were no laws barring black slaves from earning money, owning possessions, or accruing wealth. Thus untold thousands of African-American servants amassed great fortunes, not only through their own hard work and thriving businesses, but by way of shrewd financial deals. This resulted in a booming internal "black commerce" that helped improve and stabilize the entire Southern economy for centuries.

When German scientist Dr. Johann David Schoepf traveled through South Carolina in the late 1700s, he found that:

> The gentlemen in the country have among their negroes, as the Russian nobility among their serfs, the most necessary handicraftsmen, cobblers, tailors, carpenters, smiths, and the like, whose work they command at the smallest possible price, or for nothing almost. There is hardly any trade or craft which has not

> been learned and is not carried on by negroes, partly free, partly slave; *the latter are hired out by their owners for day's wages.*[1263]

This was indeed a "frequent" practice. Phillips gives a few examples of Southern black slaves who were hired *and paid* for their labor:

> The following are typical of a multitude of newspaper advertisements: Michael Grantland at Richmond offered "good wages" for the year 1799 by piece or month for six or eight negro [slave] coopers. At the same time Edward Rumsey was calling for strong negro men of good character at $100 per year at his iron works in Botetourt County, Virginia, and *inviting free laboring men also to take employment with him.* In 1808 Daniel Weisinger and Company wanted three or four negro [slave] men to work in their factory at Frankfort, Kentucky, saying "they will be taught weaving, and *liberal wages will be paid for their services.*" George W. Evans at Augusta in 1818 "Wanted to hire, eight or ten white or black men for the purpose of cutting wood." A citizen of Charleston in 1821 called for eight good black [slave] carpenters *on weekly or monthly wages*, and in 1825 a blacksmith and wheelwright of the same city offered to take black apprentices. In many cases [free] whites and [enslaved] blacks worked together in the same employ, as in a boat-building yard on the Flint River in 1836, and in a cotton mill at Athens, Georgia, in 1839.[1264]

Tobacco factories, as Phillips continues, were among the largest employers of hired slaves, even offering financial bonuses for overtime. The primary supply of

> *slaves for hire* was probably comprised of the husbands and sons, and sometimes the daughters, of the cooks and housemaids of the merchants, lawyers and the like whose need of servants was limited but who *in many cases made a point of owning their slaves in families.* On the other hand, many townsmen whose capital was scant or whose need was temporary *used hired slaves even for their kitchen work*; and sometimes the filling of the demand involved the transfer of a slave from one town to another. Thus an innkeeper of Clarkesville, a summer resort in the Georgia mountains, published in the distant newspapers of Athens and Augusta in 1838 *his offer of liberal wages for a first rate [slave] cook.*[1265]

North Carolina slave Harriet Ann Jacobs (writing under the

pseudonym Linda Brent), described the working life of her father, Elijah Knox, this way:

> [He] was a carpenter, and considered so intelligent and skilful in his trade, that, when buildings out of the common line were to be erected, *he was sent for from long distances, to be head workman.* On condition of *paying his mistress two hundred dollars a year*, and *supporting himself, he was allowed to work at his trade, and manage his own affairs. [My parents] lived together in a comfortable home . . .*[1266]

Carnton Plantation, Franklin, Tennessee, photographed by the author, was once the home of his famous Confederate cousins, the McGavocks. Carnton Mansion still retains physical evidence of the Southern practice of paying slaves a weekly wage.

Servants who hunted and fished in their free time could earn, along with the raising of their own livestock and the production of personal foodstuffs, an appreciable income, which they funneled into their internal economy. This allowed them, in turn, to engage in daily commercial traffic with other servants on their plantation and those of neighboring farms.[1267] Adding to their economic stability was the fact that a black servant could bequeath or inherit property from other servants.[1268] Wrote Smedes:

> *The thrifty negroes made so much* on their chickens, peanuts, popcorn, molasses-cakes, baskets, mats, brooms, taking in sewing, and in other little ways, *that they were able to buy luxuries.*[1269]

A huge percentage of Southern blacks were foremen and managers on their owners' farms and plantations, and many more were skilled and much-needed artisans and craftsmen.[1270] These included: woodworkers, metalworkers, instrument makers, clothes makers, cooks, and basketmakers, occupations by which a stable financial independence could easily be achieved.[1271] Those among the latter two categories did their own advertising, hired themselves out, wrote up and settled their own contracts, collected their own money, paid their own bills, and rented or purchased their own homes and shops. The employers (misleadingly called "owners" or "masters" by Northerners) of this class of servants took a small fixed percentage from their employees' income (to offset the cost of their upkeep). Other than that, there was little, if any, distinction between slave artisans and free artisans.[1272] Indeed, they operated under the same system of occupational mobility that free laborers do. Thus those servants who showed promise at their jobs were promoted while those who did not were demoted.[1273]

Phillips noted that if slaves wanted to be hired out,

> and if other slaves were to utilize their talents in keeping cobbler and blacksmith shops and the like for public patronage, *they must be vested with fairly full control of their own activities.* To enable them to compete with whites and free negroes in the trades requiring isolated and occasional work their *masters early and increasingly fell into the habit of hiring many slaves to the slaves themselves, granting to each a large degree of industrial freedom in return for a stipulated weekly wage.* The rates of hire varied, of course, with the slave's capabilities and the conditions of business in their trades.[1274]

As is clear from this report, such was the freedom of the Southern "slave" that some of the more ambitious among them were able to hire other slaves, becoming foremen of their own all-slave work crews.[1275]

Hired hands or not, many of the South's servants were well respected, possessing business experience and acumen for which they were handsomely paid. During his visit to Hopeton Plantation in

Georgia in January 1846, Briton Sir Charles Lyell was astonished to witness the expertise of some of the estate's black "slaves":

> *I was agreeably surprised to see the rank held here by the black mechanics.* One day I observed a set of carpenters putting up sluices, and a lock in a canal of a kind unknown in this part of the world. The black foreman was carrying into execution a plan laid down for him on paper by [Hopeton's owner] Mr. [Hamilton] Couper, who had observed it himself many years ago in Holland. I also saw a steam-engine, of fifteen horse-power, made in England by [Matthew] Boulton and [James] Watt, and used in a mill for threshing rice, which had been managed by a negro for more than twelve years without an accident. *When these mechanics come to consult Mr. Couper on business, their manner of speaking to him is quite as independent as that of English artisans to their employers. Their aptitude for the practice of such mechanical arts may encourage every philanthropist who has had misgivings in regard to the progressive powers of the race* . . .[1276]

Such occupations brought in excellent wages, not only basic plantation income, but in extra income, money that was often saved up and used to purchase one's freedom, or the freedom of relatives and friends. Indeed, as the logical next step after self-hire was self-purchase, hired-out slaves often offered their new employers a payment program by which to pay off the cost of their original purchase price.[1277]

Famed British geologist Sir Charles Lyell, whose ideas influenced Charles Darwin, was impressed by the high level of expertise of the slaves he met on a Georgia plantation in 1846.

As a reminder: one cannot buy one's self out of slavery; only out of servitude. And as history has recorded, thousands of "slaves" bought their freedom both before and during Lincoln's War. No true slave has ever possessed this right.

Selling products from his

own land, a field servant could easily earn $300 a year above his base income, the equivalent of about $8,000 today, while a skilled black artisan, making his own products, could earn an extra $500 a year, the modern equivalent of about $13,500. Employers (that is, "owners" or "masters") also often invited their servants to become participants in a variety of profit sharing schemes, and along with financial bonuses and gifts of land for good service and performance, a servant's money earning potential was quite spectacular.[1278] Sometimes these cooperative business ventures were operated on a smaller scale, such as when plantation owners, like James and Mary Chesnut, shared the profits from their gardens with their servants.[1279] At other times the arrangement was more basic, as Olmsted explained concerning a Louisiana plantation he visited in the mid 1800s:

> *At Christmas, a sum of money, equal to one dollar for each hogshead of sugar made on the plantation, was divided among the negroes.* The last year this had amounted to over two dollars [about $50 in today's currency] a head. It was usually given to the heads of families. If any had been particularly careless or lazy, it was remembered at this Christmas dole. Of course, *the effect of this arrangement, small as was the amount received by each person, was to give the laborers a direct interest in the economical direction of their labor: the advantage of it was said to be very evident.*[1280]

The need for hired slaves was great enough to spawn an entirely new business in the South: brokerage firms that specialized in nothing but the coordination of the demand and supply of hireable servants. "Servants to hire by the day or month," was the typical ad that ran in local papers.[1281] Some of these types of temporary jobs could last as long as a year.[1282]

> *Slave wages, generally quoted for the year and most frequently for unskilled able-bodied hands, ranged materially higher, of course, in the cotton belt than in the upper South.* Women usually brought about half the wages of men, though they were sometimes let merely for the keep of themselves and their children. In middle Georgia the wages of prime men ranged about $100 in the first decade of the nineteenth century, dropped to $60 or $75 during the war of 1812, and then rose to near $150 by 1818. The panic of the next year sent them down again; and in the 'twenties they commonly ranged between $100 and $125. Flush times then raised them in such wise that the

contractors digging a canal on the Georgia coast found themselves obliged in 1838 to offer $18 per month together with the customary weekly rations of three and a half pounds of bacon and ten quarts of corn and also the services of a staff physician as a sort of substitute for life and health insurance. The beginning of the distressful 'forties eased the market so that the town of Milledgeville could get its street gang on a scale of $125; at the middle of the decade slaveowners were willing to take almost any wages offered; and in its final year the Georgia Railroad paid only $70 to $75 for section hands. In 1850, however, this rate leaped to $100 and $110, and caused a partial substitution of white laborers for the hired slaves. . . . *In 1860 there was a culmination of this rise of slave wages throughout the South*, contemporaneous with that of their purchase prices. First-rate hands were engaged by the Petersburg tobacco factories at $225; and in northwestern Louisiana the prime field hands in a parcel of slaves hired for the year brought from $300 to $360 each, and a blacksmith $430. *The general average then prevalent for prime unskilled slaves, however, was probably not much above two hundred dollars.*[1283]

Enterprising Southern slaves could earn enough money to indulge in leisurely pursuits, such as reading, hunting, fishing, shopping and selling in town, household chores, and visiting friends on nearby farms.

Englishman Robert Russell visited Virginia in 1854 and made these remarks about the Southern custom of hiring and paying slaves:

> Richmond was at this time literally swarming with negroes, who were standing in crowds at the corners of the streets in different parts of the town. *The most of the slaves who are hired out and who change masters, usually do so at Christmas.* Many had not got places for themselves. The general system seems to be that *the owners allow the slaves, male and female, to seek out masters for themselves.* I went up and spoke to one man who was offering himself for hire as a coachman. He showed me a slip of paper on which was written, "Isaac, for hire, apply to Mr. ___, 140 dollars per annum." According to his own account, he was not quite healthy, and would not be worth more than 700 dollars. I was rather amused at the efforts of a market gardener to hire a young [black] woman [slave] as a domestic servant. The price that her owner put upon her services was not objected to by him, but they could not agree about other terms. The grand obstacle was, that she would not consent to work in the garden, even when she had nothing else to do. [Later I] . . . learned that she was pleading for other privileges—her friends and favourites must also be allowed to visit her. At length she agreed to go and visit her proposed home and see how things looked. It would thus seem that *the feelings and wishes of the slaves are often humoured.*
>
> . . . I walked into a tobacco manufactory at Richmond, and one of the partners, an intelligent gentleman, showed me over the premises. About eighty [black slave] hands were constantly employed, but none had yet returned to work since Christmas. A considerable time is always lost about this season, as the slaves cannot be readily collected to resume work. No women are employed, as the labour is heavy, and *the slaves are all hired in*, and their owners receive from 120 to 125 dollars a year; . . . but they have to supply clothing. Everything is done by piece-work, and the slaves usually work ten hours a day. *Each earns for himself from two to five dollars a month, which enables him to obtain something more than the mere necessaries of life. . . . In such establishments the negroes are all hired in . . .*[1284]

Clearly, hired out slave hands could net considerable sums for themselves and their employers. In Virginia in 1863, as one example, it cost $30 a month to hire a slave (about $800 today), while a Confederate soldier was paid only $11 a month (about $250 today).[1285]

All told, a skilled hard working Southern black servant could easily earn today's equivalent of $25,000 annually. This was considered "great wealth" in 1840: the average American income for whites that year was $100, or only about $2,400 in today's currency. And as the employers ("owners") of servants only expropriated an average of about 12 percent of a servant's yearly income, a considerable sum could be saved up. Shrewd and enterprising servants used this money wisely, either for self-purchase, additional business investments, or for improving their quality of life.[1286] Some of the more ambitious Southern "slaves" managed to reach a level of independence comparable to free blacks: allowed to work entirely for themselves, such individuals were essentially liberated from the control of their "master" in exchange for a fixed yearly wage.[1287]

In early South Carolina, French author and traveler Duke de la Rochefoucauld Liancourt, encountered a former black slave who had earned and saved enough money under Southern African servitude to buy his freedom and purchase a large plantation and some 200 black slaves.

During the 1850s the South's 200,000 industrial slaves (about 5 percent of Dixie's servant population) performed a wide assortment of jobs, from construction work, iron work, mining, and wood-chopping to tanning leather, milling, sugar refining, and shipbuilding, as well as positions in the region's textile, hemp, tobacco, salt, and chemical factories. Most of the South's transportation laborers were slaves, such as turnpike, rafting, canal boat, railroad, and steamboat workers. All were handsomely compensated for working overtime, and additional cash could be procured by working on holidays and Sundays. Slaves who worked as supervisors were paid what would now be considered a weekly wage, and many were able to amass small fortunes and bulging bank accounts.[1288]

One of the thousands of non-Southern eyewitnesses of Dixie's flourishing black commerce was French author Duke de la Rochefoucauld Liancourt. While visiting South Carolina in the late 1700s he came across a former black slave, "who from his early youth [had] carefully stored up the produce of his industry," which allowed him to purchase his own large plantation and 200 black slaves.[1289]

Blacks themselves testified to the economic and social freedom they experienced under the mild institution of "Southern slavery." In 1860, after observing blacks and whites working closely together on an Alabama plantation, British author Laurence Oliphant interviewed the farm's black bondsmen, who candidly told him that they could earn more as slaves than as freemen, and that slaves who were poor had only themselves to blame.[1290]

James Chesnut, Jr., and his equally celebrated wife, diarist Mary Chesnut, were just two of the thousands of reluctant Southern slaveholders who disliked slavery, supported abolition, referred to their black chattel as "servants," and viewed Southern slavery as "peasantry."

The South's internal black servant economy flourished for decades under the sagacious control of hard working African-Americans who acquired, exchanged, hawked, peddled, and bartered their wares, including real estate, at market for such commodities as blankets, whiskey, and sugar. We know of a number of these individuals from archival state records, for some servants accumulated substantial debts between themselves and ended up in court.[1291]

One of the most common paths black servants took toward financial stability and even wealth was cotton production. Both males and females grew and sold their own cotton, individually and collectively, often selling larger bales and bigger crops, and at higher prices, than many white cotton farmers.[1292]

South Carolina servants noted that during this period many fellow blacks walked around with large rolls of money, money that was later depleted by Lincoln's War. "If we had not been set free in 1865," they opined, "you would have discovered many wealthy black slaves laden with the money we had made from our extra crop production." So great was the wealth produced by Dixie's black slaves that many amassed a significant amount of property, ranging from homes, land, and cattle ranches, to boats, carriages, and entire stables of horses.[1293]

Working on their own land in cooperative units and collective family groups, producing and selling their own goods, practicing bequeathment and inheritance, all gave Southern black servants, particularly those of the low-country of South Carolina and Georgia, a great degree of autonomy, power, and prestige, both within and without the slave community. And in fact in many ways they were much more similar to what we would now term "proto-peasants"[1294] than they were even to servants.[1295]

Hence Chesnut noted that what Northerners and scallywags called Southern "slaves" were actually known by most Southerners as "operatives," "tenants," and "peasants." This is why Chesnut, like countless other Southerners, often referred to the institution of Southern black servitude as "peasantry,"[1296] for as this very book reveals, it has almost nothing in common with authentic slavery.

WHAT YOU WERE TAUGHT: Southern slaves were not allowed to maintain family relationships with off-plantation relatives or cultivate new relationships without their owner's permission.

THE TRUTH: African-Americans in the Old South, whether bonded or free, took great interest in relationships, and as there were no civil laws regarding a slave's social life, they had complete liberty to stay in touch with distant relations, strike up new acquaintances, and, as we are about to see, visit friends, romantic interests, and family members on other homesteads, farms, and estates.[1297]

As such, Southern servants routinely developed powerful, secure, long-lasting kinship bonds with others, both black and white, and on- and off-plantation. Naturally, affection for relations among slaves was identical to that of Southern whites, and there was keen interest throughout the black community in genealogy, with many slaves keeping careful record of aunts, uncles, nieces, nephews, and cousins.[1298]

WHAT YOU WERE TAUGHT: Southern slaves were illiterate and unskilled, and thus were only used for the most menial jobs around the plantation.
THE TRUTH: The North has comforted itself with this notion for a century and a half. But it happens to be incorrect.

As plantation workers, Southern black servants were generally divided into two broad categories: house servants and field servants. House servants were occupied with cleaning, cooking, sewing, washing, weaving, and tending children.

Dixie's black slaves could be friends with whomever they liked, and just as often as not they chose to socialize with whites. There were no laws against interracial friendships and, unlike in the North, in the South the two races greatly enjoyed one another's companionship.

Field servants, a more diverse group, were organized by skill, experience, aptitude, and intelligence, and were assigned various occupations that included: managers, foremen, drivers, plowmen, hoe hands, harrowers, seed sowers, coverers, sorters, ginners, packers, milkmaids, gardeners, stock minders, carpenters, coopers, rakers, drillers, droppers, still operators, masons, rail-splitters, and blacksmiths.[1299]

But servants did not just clean house, muck out stalls, milk cows, construct barrels, make horseshoes, and till the soil. Far from being merely "meek, illiterate cotton pickers," as the North prefers to label them, early 19th-Century records reveal that the occupations of Southern black servants covered a spectacularly wide spectrum of professionalism, including: highly skilled craftsmen and craftswomen, weavers, seamstresses, musicians, nurses, stewards, teamsters, coachmen, furniture makers, and even technically advanced architects and engineers. Even "lowly" field hands were required to have a vast number of skills ranging from a detailed knowledge of farming (planting, cultivating, and harvesting), land management, and dairying, to the use and maintenance of farm machinery and building construction.[1300]

WHAT YOU WERE TAUGHT: Southern slave owners worked their slaves seven days a week, 365 days a year, with long hours stretching into the nighttime and no time off.

THE TRUTH: Southern black servants worked from sunrise to early afternoon (eight hours) five days a week,[1301] with one to three hours off for lunch.[1302] This made their average work week from 25 to 40 hours long,[1303] far below the norm at the time for both free-laboring whites and blacks, who put in between 70 and 75 hours a week.[1304] Phillips writes of the typical slave worker's schedule in the Carolinas and Georgia:

> As to schedules of work, the Carolina and Georgia lowlanders dealt in tasks; all the rest in hours. [Plantation owner Alexander] Telfair wrote briefly:
>
> > "The negroes [are] to be tasked when the work allows it. I require a reasonable day's work, well done—the task to be regulated by the state of the ground and the strength of the negro."
>
> [Planter P. C.] Weston wrote with more elaboration:
>
> > "A task is as much work as the meanest [i.e., best] full hand can do in nine hours, working industriously. . . . *This task is never to be*

> *increased, and no work is to be done over task except under the most urgent necessity; which over-work is to be reported to the proprietor, who will pay for it. No negro is to be put into a task which [he] cannot finish with tolerable ease. It is a bad plan to punish for not finishing tasks; it is subversive of discipline to leave tasks unfinished, and contrary to justice to punish for what cannot be done. In nothing does a good manager so much excel a bad as in being able to discern what a hand is capable of doing, and in never attempting to make him do more.*"

In [planter James] Hammond's schedule the first horn was blown an hour before daylight as a summons for work-hands to rise and do their cooking and other preparations for the day. Then at the summons of the plow driver, at first break of day, the plowmen went to the stables whose doors the overseer opened. At the second horn, "just at good daylight," the hoe gang set out for the field. At half past eleven the plowmen carried their mules to a shelter house in the fields, and at noon the hoe hands laid off for dinner, to resume work at one o'clock, except that in hot weather *the intermission was extended to a maximum of three and a half hours.* The plowmen led the way home by a quarter of an hour in the evening, and the hoe hands followed at sunset. *"No work," said Hammond, "must ever be required after dark."* [Planter Joseph A. S.] Acklen contented himself with specifying that

> "the negroes must all rise at the ringing of the first bell in the morning, and retire when the last bell rings at night . . ."

[Plantation owner J. W.] Fowler's rule was of the same tenor:

> "All hands should be required to retire to rest and sleep at a suitable hour and permitted to remain there until such time as it will be necessary to get out in time to reach their work by the time they can see well how to work."[1305]

Three and a half hours off for lunch is far more than any modern office or factory worker could expect from his or her boss today!

All Southern servants were given Sundays off, time which most used to attend church[1306] (for them a blend of African customs and

European-American customs)—since the first day of the week was as important to most servants as it was to their masters.[1307] As Susan Dabney Smedes noted, the typical slave approached Sabbath mornings with great enthusiasm:

> In the afternoon the [white girls of the community] . . . held a service and Sunday-school for the negroes, and the large library was well filled by them. They delighted in the chants and hymns, and knew much of the service and the catechism by heart.
>
> Many years after they were free, a brawny blacksmith sent a message to his teachers of these days, "Tell de ladies I ain't forgit what dey teach me in de Sunday-school."[1308]

On those few Southern farms and plantations where there were black servants, Saturday nights were set aside for great "slave parties," complete with whiskey, barbeques, music, and dancing. As with modern Christian Americans, Christmas was the favorite time of year among Dixie's black servant population, a few days to a few weeks of relaxation, celebration, gift-giving, and the usual over indulgence of turkey, eggnog, and sugary desserts, as well as singing carols around the Christmas tree.

When servants absolutely had to work on a Sunday (such as during the important sugar harvest season), they were well remunerated with generous financial bonuses and extra days off.[1309]

On Saturdays, the day traditionally set aside for servants to work their own land, they labored either a half day,[1310] or had the entire day free. Each year they also had about a week's worth of work free holidays (such as Christmas, Good Friday, Independence Day, and the post harvest period), with odd days off as rewards.[1311] On many plantations there was a servant-only party held every Saturday night, complete with whiskey, a barbeque, music (items often contributed by the white owners), and dancing.[1312] At slave parties, commonly held in barns or out in the fields, the fiddle and banjo were always present, while bones, stomping feet, and hand-clapping kept the beat as individuals danced various jigs and shuffles.[1313] Lyell writes:

> The [black] labourers *begin work at six o'clock in the morning*, have an hour's rest at nine for breakfast, and many have *finished their assigned task by two o'clock*, all of them by three o'clock. In summer they divide their work differently, going to bed in the middle of the day, then rising to finish their task, and *afterwards spending a great part of the night in chatting, merry-making, preaching, and psalm-singing. At Christmas they claim a week's holidays, when they hold a kind of Saturnalia, and the owners can get no work done.*[1314]

In 1863 Irishman and war correspondent William Howard Russell gave this account of a plantation he visited in Louisiana:

> Each [Southern servant] . . . gets five pounds of pork a week, and as much Indian corn bread as he can eat, with a portion of molasses, and occasionally they have fish for breakfast. All the carpenters' and smiths' work, the erection of sheds, repairing of carts and ploughs, and the baking of bricks for the farm buildings, are done on the estate by the slaves. The machinery comes from the manufacturing cities of the North; but great efforts are made to procure it from New Orleans, where factories have been already established. *On the borders of the forest the negroes are allowed to plant corn for their own use, and sometimes they have an overplus, which they sell to their masters. Except when there is any harvest pressure on their hands, they have from noon on Saturday till dawn on Monday morning to do as they please . . .*[1315]

We will note here that some of these slave-to-master sales were "paid" on credit. By the time Lincoln's War ended, many owners were so in debt to their former servants that there was no possibility of ever repaying them.[1316]

Christmas was the favored time of year since Southern servants would get at least three days or more of liberty from their tasks. Slaves who had been hired out to off-plantation employers were given up to two weeks or more for their holiday vacation.[1317] Alcohol and eggnog flowed freely around candle-decorated Christmas trees, as the races intermingled in joyful celebration and the owners handed out presents to their black charges. Servants were allowed to invite friends and family from neighboring farms, and they in turn were permitted to attend Christmas parties on other homesteads.[1318] While visiting a Mississippi plantation in the 1850s, New Yorker Anson De Puy Van Buren was present for the residents' Christmas celebration, which he described like this:

> *Throughout the country [of the South], on every plantation, there is a merry time—a joyous leisure from all work; merry Christmas is with them all. The negroes, whole troops of them mounted on mules, male and female, laughing and singing, go from one plantation to another; thus gathering in jolly groups they feast and frolic and dance the time away.*
>
> *They are all dressed in their best*, many of them in broadcloth. They have their nice white dickies on, their boots are blacked, and a white or silk handkerchief is sure to display itself from some one of their pockets, or from their hand. A negro is your true frolicker. His sable periphery will hold more merriment, fun and pent up animal spirit, than any other human being's.
>
> To see a group of them on the floor, or on the lawn, beneath the shade of the China-trees, when "hornpipes, jigs, strathspeys and reels, put life and mettle in their heels," whirling in the giddy mazes of the dance with their buxom dulcenas, each seeming to vie with the other in dancing the most; it is *one of the finest specimens of animated nature I ever gazed upon*.
>
> No restraint of the ettiquettish ball-room, to fetter their actions and motions, but, *charged like galvanic batteries, full of music, they dance with a vigorous vim*.
>
> Restraint! whew! they'd burst like steamers. No. They must dance untrammeled; the action must be suited to the spirit, the spirit to the action—perfect *lusus naturaes*! What luxury of motion, what looks—breathing and sighs! what oglings, exclamations and enjoyment!
>
> This is dancing. It knocks the spangles off your light fantastic tripping, and sends it whirling out of the ballroom.[1319]

Unlike Caribbean and South American slaves, who were worked through all types of weather,[1320] Southern servants had rainy days off.[1321] But "lazin' 'round" was not usually an option on such days. The men used the time to do menial outside labor around their homes, such as house repairs and mending fences,[1322] while the women performed indoor activities, such as sewing, weaving, light house cleaning, and caring for poultry.[1323] Robert Q. Mallard, the white son of a wealthy Georgia slaveholder, gave this description of the typical Southern field slave's labors:

> As for their work [Southern field hands], *they were never called out in the rain, and open sheds were always provided in distant fields against thunder showers*. In some parts of the South they were, *with an interval of a noon day rest of several hours*, in the field from "sun up" to "sun down," but *in all such instances their food was cooked for them, and they were generously fed upon full rations of bacon*. With us the work was, in the main, extremely light. It was the duty of the men to split the pine rails with which the plantation was enclosed, to clear the forest from the "new ground" prepared for tillage. The women and the "thrash gang"—i.e., the half grown boys and girls—made up the fences, the men commonly drove the plow, *the women never handled anything heavier than the hoe*; in the harvest both used the sickle, the men threshed the rice and trod the cotton foot-gin, while to the women was assigned the easier task of sorting the lint of its specks and loaves. Our lands were light and friable and easily worked, and for a large part of spring and summer the hands were allotted task work; and *many is the time I have in the spring season seen the industrious [black] laborer shouldering his hoe, with the sun high in the sky, ready to work his own allotted patch in the rice field, or to go "churning" or lounging and gossiping in the village street!*[1324]

Female servants were allowed a month to recover after childbirth, far more time than was accorded the peasant women of Europe during the same period.[1325] Southern slave children were not obliged to begin working until age twelve, though many servant owners postponed this day until the age of 14 or 15.[1326] Compare this to the children of poor white families in the North, who were put to work as soon as possible,[1327] or to Victorian European children: Germany allowed adolescents as young as nine to be employed in various industries until the mid 1800s, while in France and England in particular, children as young as eight were set to work in factories.[1328] Of the latter country

David Henry Montgomery writes:

> *. . . negro slaves were not the only slaves in [England in] those days. There were white slaves as well,—women and children born in England, but condemned by their necessities to work under ground in the coal mines, or exhaust their strength in the cotton mills, driven by brutal masters who cared . . . little for the welfare of those under them . . .* Parliament at length turned its attention to these abuses and greatly alleviated them by the passage of acts, forbidding the employment of women in the collieries, and of young children in the factories.[1329]

Our Yankee biased history books tell us that Southern slaves were "worked to death" from morning till night, seven days a week, 365 days a year, from the age of five until death. Actually they labored less hours a week than a modern office or factory worker, and had Saturdays, Sundays, sick days, rainy days, and holidays off. And unlike what was found in Europe at the time—where child labor was the norm—Southern slaves were not usually put to work until the age of 15, then were retired in their 60s.

We repeat: black slave children were not allowed to work in the Old South; not due just to Southern humanitarianism, but also by law.

On Sundays Southern servants could attend their own black-only "Negro churches" and at night they could participate in all-black promenades and other types of social gatherings.[1330] With about twelve days a year lost due to sickness, the average slave ended up working about 265 days a year, slightly less than today's 21st-Century office worker.[1331] After careful observation during his visit to the American South in the 1840s, Scotsman William Thomson noted that "those of them employed as house servants have not one-fourth so much work as a Scotch servant lass."[1332] In fact, contrary to Yankee mythology, Southern servants did not do *all* of the work on a plantation. The children of the owners usually did most of the chores, for example.[1333]

On their days off servants had near complete freedom. They could hunt, fish,[1334] nap, rest, play games, garden, spend time with their families, take weekend jaunts into town, almost anything they desired. Visits to family members, friends, and lovers on nearby farms and plantations was a favorite pastime. Servants could also continue working for the plantation and receive extra pay and bonuses, or hire themselves out (or have their owners hire them out) to do odd jobs for additional revenue[1335]—a right, by the way, that was denied slaves in many Northern states, such as Pennsylvania.[1336]

But many chose to use their free days to work at their own businesses, earning additional extra money and raising their status, not only on the plantation, but in the community around them. A host of highly respected black servants rose up the economic ladder in just this fashion, earning their way to increased social freedom and financial prosperity and independence.[1337] Lyell tells us that at a certain Southern plantation he visited, the black servants

> are allowed Indian meal, rice, and milk; and occasionally pork and soup. *As their rations are more than they can eat, they either return part of it to the overseer, who makes them an allowance of money for it at the end of the week, or they keep it to feed their fowls, which they usually sell, as well as their eggs, for cash, to buy molasses, tobacco, and other luxuries. When disposed to exert themselves, they get through the day's task in five hours, and then amuse themselves in fishing, and sell the fish they take; or some of them employ their spare time in making canoes out of large cypress trees, leave being readily granted them to remove such timber, as it aids the landowner to clear the swamps. They sell the canoes for about four dollars, for their own profit.*
>
> *If the [white] mistress pays a visit to Savannah, the nearest town, she is overwhelmed with commissions [purchase orders], so many of the slaves wishing to lay out their small gains in various indulgences, especially articles of dress, of which they are passionately fond.* The stuff

must be of the finest quality, and many instructions are given as to the precise colour or fashionable shade. White muslin, with figured patterns, is the rage just now.[1338]

The Southern "slave" was not a slave. He was a servant, with all the rights and freedoms of a servant.

WHAT YOU WERE TAUGHT: Southern slavery was a pathological economic system, and was exploitive and harmful to blacks in every way and on every level.

THE TRUTH: Today in the 21st Century we have nothing good to say about 19th-Century Southern servitude ("slavery" to Yanks), for there was truly almost nothing wholly good about it. For one thing, in the long run it hurt both employer ("owner") and employee ("slave"), community and city, state and nation. Did it not go against the very foundation of both American religion and the Constitution? Moreover, the loss of personal freedom is arguably one of the worst fates that can befall a person, as any prisoner or former convict will aver.

And it is certainly true that the time and energy of black servants was exploited, and it is just as true that they did not have the same rights or freedoms that their employers ("masters") or free blacks had.

By the same token it is an implacable reality that in comparison to the life of free laborers, slave life on the plantation, in fact, benefitted Southern servants in a number of ways. How?

According to modern day cliometricians (economic historians), due to the well-known superior quality of black labor, large slave plantations were 34 percent more efficient than free labor Southern farms, and 40 percent more efficient than Northern free labor farms.[1339] The extra wealth derived from this increased productivity was passed onto the servants in the form of higher wages, greater independence, and better quality housing, food, clothing, and health care.[1340]

In addition, though slave owners were clearly "rational capitalists" (*slaves began profiting their owners within three to five years,*[1341] *roughly the same as a modern day business*) and the plantation was unquestionably a for-profit business, as we have seen, on some levels it also functioned as a communal enterprise. For instance, servile blacks paid less for their clothes than did free blacks, and servants could also save on interest charges: a free black could expect to pay exorbitant rates, while a servant could take advantage of the far lower rates offered by his owner.[1342]

Just as ancient Rome's white slaves often had far better social, political, and financial opportunities than Europe's free laborers,[1343] and just as ancient peoples who were defeated in battle often benefitted from enslavement (since it put an end to their economic strife while giving them social stability),[1344] so too did black Southern servants compared with many of their free neighbors. In fact, servitude benefitted Southern blacks in many ways.

For example, in comparison to free blacks, and even in comparison to many free whites, black Southern servants lived longer, had lower suicide rates, earned more money, had better diets, suffered less illness, were better skilled, lived in bigger and better houses, had superior health care, and had lower death rates and lower maternal death rates in childbearing.[1345] Other studies have shown that adult Southern servants could expect to live at least as long as free adults, and that they were, on the whole, "remarkably well off" in the areas of diet, housing, clothing, and medical care.[1346] Additional surveys have revealed that *the health care of Southern slaves was identical to that of their white owners*, and that infant mortality among black servants was the same as for Southern whites.[1347] Estes writes that:

> According to the census of the United States for 1840, *mortality, and all diseases among the colored population, increases as you advance*

north. This result may, in part, be owing to the wretched condition of the free Negroes at the North . . .[1348]

Using data from this same U.S. Census (1840), South Carolina politician John C. Calhoun made note of this discrepancy in a letter to British diplomat Sir Richard Parkenham, dated April 18, 1844:

> *Taking the two extremes of North and South—in the state of Maine, the number of negroes returned as deaf and dumb, blind, insane, and idiots, by the census of 1840, is one out of every twelve; and in Florida, by the same returns, is one out of every eleven hundred and five; or seventy-two to one in favor of the slaves of Florida, as compared with the free blacks of Maine.*
>
> In addition, *it deserves to be remarked, that in Massachusetts,* where . . . [abolition took place] . . . now more than sixty years ago, where the greatest zeal has been exhibited in their behalf, and where their number is comparatively few (but little more than eight thousand, in a population of seven hundred and thirty thousand), *the condition of the African is among the most wretched. By the latest authentic accounts, there was one out of every twenty-one of the black population, in jails or houses of correction; and one out of every thirteen was either deaf and dumb, blind, idiots, insane, or in prison.*[1349]

What pro-North historians will not tell you is this: not only did Southern servitude benefit blacks in numerous ways, but slave plantations were far more efficient than free labor plantations. Additionally, the incredible wealth that slave plantations produced ultimately trickled down to the servants, providing them with a quality of life—in wages, health care, housing, clothing, food, and so on—that was far superior to that of many free lower and middle class blacks and whites at the time.

We can get an idea of the excellent health care provided to Southern slaves from the plantation manual of owner James Hammond. In his set of precise and humanitarian instructions to his overseers he writes:

> *No negro will be allowed to remain at his own house when sick, but must be confined to the hospital. Every reasonable complaint must be promptly attended to; and with any marked or general symptom of sickness, however trivial, a negro may lie up a day or so at least. . . . Each case has to be examined carefully by the master or overseer to ascertain the disease. The remedies next are to be chosen with the utmost discrimination; . . . the directions for treatment, diet, etc., most implicitly followed; the effects and changes cautiously observed. . . . In cases where there is the slightest uncertainty, the books must be taken to the bedside and a careful and thorough examination of the case and comparison of remedies made before administering them. The overseer must record in the prescription book every dose of medicine administered.*[1350]

There was also the fact that it was impossible for a servant to ever experience homelessness or joblessness, or suffer from starvation or neglected health problems. Why? Because their *Southern owners were legally obligated to care for them at all times and through any type of hardship, from the cradle to the grave.*

When a black servant became too old or too ill to work, or if a black child became orphaned, for instance, their masters and mistresses bore the legal responsibility of looking after their welfare until the day of their deaths—or freedom, whichever came first.[1351] This means that *at any one time a full one-third of Southern slaves were not working,*[1352] and were therefore nonproductive members of their owners' plantations. Yet, they remained under the medical protection and physical guardianship of their masters, who essentially "paid them to do nothing," making this an early form of socialized health care that was unknown in the U.S. until the creation of Medicare in 1965.

In the 1830s Yankee author Joseph Holt Ingraham commented on this unique aspect of Southern "slavery":

> *Nor are [Southern] planters indifferent to the comfort of their gray-headed slaves. I have been much affected at beholding many exhibitions of their kindly feeling towards them. They always address them in a mild and pleasant manner—as "Uncle," or "Aunty"—titles as peculiar to the old*

> *negro and negress, as "boy" and "girl," to all under forty years of age. Some old Africans are allowed to spend their last years in their houses, without doing any kind of labour; these, if not too infirm, cultivate little patches of ground, on which they raise a few vegetables—for vegetables grow nearly all the year round in this climate—and make a little money to purchase a few extra comforts. They are also always receiving presents from their masters and mistresses, [as well as] . . . the negroes on the estate, the latter of whom are extremely desirous of seeing the old people comfortable. A relation of the extra comforts which some planters allow their slaves, would hardly obtain credit at the North. But you must recollect that Southern planters are men—and men of feeling—generous and high-minded, and possessing as much of the "milk of human kindness" as the sons of colder climes . . .*[1353]

Here is another example of how Southern slaveholders actually treated their servants, as opposed to the tall tales told in Northern slanted history books. In 1860 there were an estimated 3,427 Southern slaves who were listed in the Census as either "blind," "deaf and dumb," "insane," or "idiotic."[1354] All of the needs of these individuals were tended to by their owners; not simply due to legal requirement, but, as mentioned, also from the great Southern philanthropic impulse. This is what Southerners to this day regard as true humanitarianism. Of this legally required but altruistic custom, Lyell offered the following example of a Georgia plantation owner:

> *There are 500 negroes on the Hopeton estate, a great many of whom are children, and some old and superannuated [retired]. The latter class, who would be supported in a poor-house in England, enjoy here, to the end of their days, the society of their neighbours and kinsfolk, and live at large in separate houses assigned to them.*[1355]

In 1840 Thomson observed the same thing as he toured the American South:

> *I took particular notice how masters treated the old slaves after they were unable to work in the fields. Their laws provide that they shall be fed and clothed; but I found that a better feeling than necessity prompted the planters to minister to the wants of their aged servants. They have their houses, blankets, shoes, clothing, and their allowance of corn, the same as prime hands. I knew some of them that had been toddling about for twenty years after they were unable to work.* Many of these old hands keep themselves in tobacco, molasses, etc., by feeding a pig, or raising

> a few chickens. To feed them, they will cultivate a little patch of ground, but as frequently steal corn from "Massa" for this purpose; and, after all, if the planter's family want to buy any of their eggs or chickens, they will not sell them to them one cent cheaper than the regular market price. *These old hands are a sort of privileged persons, and are never abused or neglected.*[1356]

Chesnut noted that Southern servants employed their own time, meaning that they worked as employees under their owners, who in turn paid their medical bills and provided their food and clothing[1357]—the latter which typically consisted of two cotton outfits for Spring and Summer and two woolen outfits for Fall and Winter, along with four pairs of shoes and a surplus of socks and undergarments.[1358] The diarist herself hired and paid several servants during Lincoln's War.[1359] Servants in this category, most who could read and write, lived basically as free blacks did.[1360]

Southern servants, like this one suffering from an illness (center), received immediate on-site medical care from birth to death, paid for by their owner (far right). This is a right that no true slave could ever expect. Typically, the doctor (kneeling) was the same one used by the owner and his family. In other words, Southern black servants had access to the same high quality health care as wealthy whites—the only difference being that for the former it was free.

The weight of the responsibility for caring for servants was such that a universal joke arose in the South: it was not the servants that one need fear would run away. It was their employers. English novelist William M. Thackeray characterized slave ownership this way: it is similar to owning an elephant when all that is needed is a horse.[1361]

Chesnut writes that nearly all Southerners considered slaves an annoyance rather than a benefit, one that never came close to paying off. "It is far simpler and cheaper," she noted with some exasperation, "to hire a free laborer than to own a man whose father, mother, wife, and numerous children have to be fed, clothed, houses, nursed, and have their taxes and doctor's bills paid throughout their entire lives."[1362]

Indeed, a slave did not even begin to pay for himself until sometime between the ages of 20 and 25. Up until that time his every need was provided for and paid for, *without remuneration*, by his owner. Sometime after age 40 the slave's value began to drop, and from that point until his death the owner once again lost money. Until that day, by both civil and humanitarian law the owner was responsible for his slave's food, health, clothing, room, and board.[1363] In 1886 Susan Dabney Smedes referred to owning slaves as "the incubus":

> There were . . . [many] who felt that slavery was a yoke upon the white man's neck almost as galling as on the slaves; and *it was a saying that the mistress of a plantation was the most complete slave on it. I can testify to the truth of this in my mother's life and experience. There was no hour of the day that she was not called upon to minister to their real or imaginary wants*. Who can wonder that we longed for a lifting of the incubus, and that in the family of [my father] Thomas Dabney the first feeling, when the [Civil] war ended, was of joy that one dreadful responsibility, at least, was removed?[1364]

Phillips writes that nearly all Southern servant owners, particularly those who owned more than a dozen, experienced numerous

> stresses in plantation management. An owner of ninety-six slaves told [Yankee Frederick Law] Olmsted that *such was the trouble and annoyance his negroes caused him*, in spite of his having an overseer, and such the loneliness of his isolated life, that he was torn between a desire to sell out at once and a temptation to hold on for a while in the expectation of higher prices. At the home of another Virginian, Olmsted wrote:
>
> > "During three hours or more in which I was in company with the proprietor I do not think there were ten consecutive minutes uninterrupted by some of the slaves requiring

> his personal direction or assistance. He was even obliged three times to leave the dinner table. 'You see,' said he smiling, as he came in the last time, 'a farmer's life in this country is no sinecure' [that is, easy occupation]."

A third Virginian, endorsing Olmsted's observations, wrote that *a planter's cares and troubles were endless; the slaves, men, women and children, infirm and aged, had wants innumerable; some were indolent, some obstinate, some fractious, and each class required different treatment.* With the daily wants of food, clothing and the like, "the poor man's time and thoughts, indeed every faculty of mind, must be exercised on behalf of those who have no minds of their own."

Harriet Martineau wrote on her tour of the South:

> *"Nothing struck me more than the patience of slave-owners . . . with their slaves. . . . When I considered how they love to be called 'fiery Southerners,' I could not but marvel at their mild forbearance under the hourly provocations to which they are liable in their homes. Persons from New England, France or England, becoming slave-holders, are found to be the most severe masters and mistresses, however good their tempers may always have appeared previously. They cannot, like the native [Southern] proprietor, sit waiting half an hour for the second course [of a meal], or see everything done in the worst possible manner, their rooms dirty, their property wasted, their plans frustrated, their infants slighted,—themselves deluded by artifices—they cannot, like the native proprietor, endure all this unruffled."*

It is clear from every sort of evidence, if evidence were needed, that life among negro slaves and the successful management of them promoted, and wellnigh necessitated, a blending of foresight and firmness with kindliness and patience. The lack of the former qualities was likely to bring financial ruin; the lack of the latter would make life not worth living; the possession of all meant a toleration of slackness in every concern not vital to routine. A plantation was a bed of roses only if the thorns were turned aside.[1365]

Thousands of Southern servant owners, such as fire-eating die-hard Confederate Rebel Edmund Ruffin,[1366] agreed. Ruffin, like thousands of others, eventually auctioned off his black servants; not because they were poor producers, but because they were excellent consumers, making the expense of maintaining them nearly impossible.[1367]

As so many other Southern slaveholders did, Virginian Edmund Ruffin, "the man who fired the first shot at Fort Sumter," complained that servants were more trouble and expense than they were worth—wholly contradicting the standard Northern view of Victorian Southerners as "zealous" slave owners.

Let us contrast all of this with Victorian free laborers who, just like employees today, had no one to care for them during times of want and difficulty, no protection against joblessness, ill-health, homelessness, or starvation. Joseph T. Derry noted that:

> *The fidelity of the slaves was due to the fact that most masters treated them kindly. Their toil was not unrequited, for they were supplied with whatever they needed and were cared for in sickness and in old age. Many of them*

> *were allowed opportunities for making money for themselves.* Much attention had always been given to their religious instruction. Southern ladies labored for the conversion of their slaves. Missionaries sent by the Southern churches preached to them on the plantations. *In malarial districts, where negroes only could live with safety, some of these devoted missionaries laid down their lives. The negroes had churches of their own in the towns and on many of the plantations.* In the churches of the whites there were always galleries set apart for them, and *in the city churches it was often difficult to say which were the better dressed, the masters or the slaves.*[1368]

Southern servitude then functioned much like a social welfare program with built-in health and life insurance, operating in some ways like an early form of socialism. Yes, servants helped defray these costs through their work and through monthly percentage payments to their employers. But they earned wages at the same time as well, both via their regular work and also from their personal extracurricular labors. In all, most Southern slaves were so highly indulged and protected by their owners that *being a "slave" came to be an enviable status symbol among many blacks*. Such bold facts have forced even the most South-loathing, biased historians to admit an obvious truth: *Southern servants were treated far better than servants in any other part of the New World.*[1369]

Would servile blacks have given all these benefits up for freedom? Some would have, and some certainly did. A few (as we will see, very few) fled north on the Underground Railroad,[1370] while others purchased their freedom with their hard earned savings.

But, after contemplating the quasi-freedom of living in the North, where the anti-African Black Codes were strictly enforced and where white racism was far more deeply entrenched, many Southern blacks reconsidered. When Lincoln's War came, this group, most of whom were third, fourth, and fifth generation Southern Americans, quite consciously chose to remain in the South, in their own homes, on the plantations with their "white families."[1371]

Then, when "Honest Abe" freed them, and he and the North tried to deport them back to Africa, with one voice this group cried "no!" For they quite rightly considered themselves true Americans and true Southerners. After all, by 1860, 99 percent of all blacks were native-born Americans, a larger percentage than for whites.[1372] As black educator and former Southern servant Booker T. Washington wrote:

> I was born in the South. I have lived and labored in the South. I wish to be buried in the South.[1373]

Thus it was that a majority of Southern blacks would not be removed from their homes, or their home nation, the place of their birth and that of all their known ancestors.

WHAT YOU WERE TAUGHT: The original Southern KKK was an all-white, racist, anti-black terrorist organization, used to intimidate and murder slaves and free blacks. Its founder and first leader was Confederate General Nathan Bedford Forrest, the South's most violent and racist slaveholder.

Contrary to Yankee myth, Confederate General Nathan Bedford Forrest of Tennessee did not launch or lead the Southern KKK. Actually, he was responsible for shutting down the organization when it began to reflect white racist sentiment. But enemies of the South do not like to give him credit for this.

THE TRUTH: This statement contains a number of Yankee myths, all of them absurd fallacies created by the pro-North, pro-Lincoln propaganda machine. Let us take them apart one at a time.

The names of the six men who founded the KKK on Christmas Eve 1865 in a haunted house in Pulaski, Tennessee, are well-known.[1374] They are: J. Calvin Jones, Captain John C. Lester, Richard R. Reed, Captain James R. Crowe, Frank O. McCord, and Captain John B. Kennedy.[1375] Forrest did not begin to associate with the organization until two years later, in 1867.[1376] Obviously then he could not have been either the founder or the first leader, known as the Grand Wizard.[1377]

The members of this, the original Reconstruction KKK, never wrote anything down, so there is no hard physical evidence stating who the first Grand Wizard was. Where then did South-haters come up with the name Forrest? They fabricated it. The mysterious man's true identity was eventually revealed by Ora Susan Paine, the widow of my cousin George W. Gordon.[1378] According to Ora's sworn testimony,

Gordon served as the organization's first Grand Wizard from 1865 to 1869.[1379]

As for Forrest being a cruel and racist slaver, here are the facts: Prior to Lincoln's War, Forrest's reputation as a kind and beneficent slaveholder was so widespread that at auction slaves would line up, begging him to purchase them.[1380] Forrest did not sell to known brutal slavers, never split up black families,[1381] and was, in fact, instrumental in bringing several broken slave families back together, himself sometimes traveling great distances to purchase and reunite lost loved ones. Eyewitnesses often commented on the cleanliness, erudition, new starched clothing, and impeccable manners of his servants.[1382]

General Forrest emancipated nearly all of his slaves in 1859, five years before Lincoln signed the Emancipation Proclamation.[1383] Afterward, most of his freedmen and women voluntarily remained on his plantations, now working as full-time paid employees (many returned from distant states to work for him).[1384] The rest, about 45 black men, Forrest invited into his Confederate cavalry unit.[1385] Of these, he selected seven to serve as his personal armed guards.[1386] All fought with bravery and honor throughout Lincoln's War, and afterward received military pensions and attended Forrest's cavalry reunions.[1387]

In the latter years of his life Forrest labored vigorously for social equality for blacks and enthusiastically campaigned to repopulate the devastated South with new African immigrants. At his funeral on Halloween Day in Memphis in 1877, fully one-third of the grieving attendees were black.[1388] It beggars credulity to find any trace of racism or malevolence in the life or character of such a man!

While the founding of the original KKK in 1865 did indeed occur in the South (as mentioned, at Pulaski, Tennessee),[1389] it was not a purely Southern entity. This is because it borrowed heavily from numerous similar secret *Northern* organizations that long preceded it.

One of these was the anti-Catholic, anti-immigrant group known as The Order of the Star Spangled Banner, founded in Boston, Massachusetts, in 1849. The original Southern KKK adopted many of the Order's traditions, such as its esoteric signals, handclasps, rituals, and codes, and later, it seems, even some of it strong arm tactics, including nighttime terrorist attacks, and general deception, fraud, and hocus-pocus antics (known as "dark lantern tactics").[1390]

In 1854 The Order of the Star Spangled Banner evolved into the Know-Nothing or American Party, a rabid anti-immigration, anti-Catholic, anti-foreigner movement that got its start in New York.[1391] When this too dissolved in 1856, the organization's racially intolerant members cast about for a political group to join. By 1860 there was only one logical choice: the party of white supremacy, white racism, and white separatism. The Liberal Party of Abraham Lincoln.[1392]

As the KKK was founded nearly three years after the Emancipation Proclamation was issued (January 1, 1863), and a month after the Thirteenth Amendment ended slavery across the U.S. (on December 6, 1865), it is obvious that the organization was not and could not have been used to "intimidate and murder slaves." By the latter date they had completely disappeared from the South.

This 1868 illustration shows the true focus of the original Southern KKK: not blacks, but carpetbaggers; treacherous Northern whites who came South after Lincoln's War in order to prey on the ravaged region.

Neither was its original purpose to frighten blacks, for it was not an anti-black organization. The Reconstruction KKK was an *anti-Yankee* group, one that quite correctly described itself as an institution of "chivalry, humanity, mercy, and patriotism."[1393] Far from being a "terrorist" organization, during the first two years of its existence this social aid organization[1394] was comprised of thousands of white *and* black members,[1395] for its sole mission was to protect and care for the weak, the disenfranchised, and the innocent, whatever their race. This explains why there was an all-black Ku Klux Klan that operated for several years in the Nashville area.[1396]

The KKK's other primary goal was to help maintain law and order across the South. Though Lincoln's Reconstruction program had called for military rule, its implementation had the opposite effect. Lawlessness and vicious criminal behavior became commonplace, problems exacerbated by the appearance of thick-skinned, greedy carpetbaggers (Northerners) and treasonous, unscrupulous scallywags (Northernized Southerners), both groups which sought to prey on and exploit the long-suffering Southern survivors of Lincoln's War.[1397]

The ignorant continue to foolishly believe that the Confederate flag is a white racist symbol representing the campaign to "bring back American black slavery." This photo of a KKK parade in 1925 in Washington, D.C. (the Capitol is just visible center rear), destroys this absurd Northern falsehood. Taken before the Confederate flag began to be used by equally uninformed 21st-Century white supremacist groups, we see that the original flag symbol used by today's KKK was—and still is—the U.S. flag, the same one under which Yankee slave ships sailed to and from Africa for nearly 250 years.

In 1869 the social atmosphere in the South changed dramatically. By this time the government-sponsored black Loyal Leagues and the Freedmen's Bureau had been formed, organizations meant to aid Southern blacks dispossessed by Lincoln's cruel, illegal, and unplanned emancipation (note that no U.S. government leagues were ever formed to aid dispossessed Southern whites specifically). Instead, carpetbaggers and scallywags used the Leagues to inculcate freed slaves in pro-North, anti-South propaganda,[1398] training them to use weapons and military tactics to taunt, punish, and even murder their former owners.[1399]

As part of their counter-Reconstruction efforts, KKK members responded by carrying coffins through the streets with the names of prominent Bureau leaders on them. Underneath their names were the words: "Dead, Damned, and Delivered!"[1400] The Bureau, as it turned out, was not only unnecessary, as Southerners had long maintained, but it was an absolute hindrance to any kind of racial harmony in the South—one of the reasons Yankees created it to begin with. This is why former Confederates saw it as nothing less than the imposition of an alien government, reinforced by an occupying army.[1401]

These ten Ku Klux Klan members from around 1870—posing in front of a real skull and crossbones with hat bands that read "KKK"—were not from the Old South, as pro-North historians would have you believe. They were from the New North—Watertown, New York, to be exact—and were known as "Watertown Division 289," just one of hundreds of KKK chapters that sprung up across the North after Lincoln's War. While anti-Southers want you to think they are one and the same, the truth is that the new modern Northern KKK has no connection with the old deceased Southern KKK: the former is an anti-black organization, the latter was an anti-Yankee organization.

The Bureau's overt political efforts to create racial warfare in Dixie (by attempting to make former black servants hate their former white owners) were intended to further divide the Southern people by breaking down their morale. Ultimately, to the great remorse of Northern Radicals (Yankee abolitionists), it did not work. But various white elements in the KKK began to understandably turn their attention, some of it violent, toward African-Americans, particularly those who were committing hate crimes against white families under the directives of the U.S. government's Black Leagues. Again, these particular white groups were acting out of self-preservation, not racism.[1402]

Proof of this is that when carpetbag rule ended that year, in 1869, this, the original KKK, immediately came to an end as well all across the "Invisible Empire" (that is, the Southern states). For when Southerners were allowed to begin taking back political control of their own states, there was no longer any need for a self-protective social welfare organization like the KKK. This is why former Confederate officer and Southern hero General Forrest, the Klan's most famous and influential supporter, called in its members and shut the entire fraternity down in March of that year.[1403]

After Lincoln's War, General Forrest, seen here leading another victory against the Yanks, was thoroughly interrogated by a U.S. government committee investigating the KKK. He was found entirely innocent of any wrongdoing and cleared of all charges, facts that are conveniently left out of our Yankee biased history books.

On June 27, 1871, Forrest was put on the witness stand before a highly prejudicial, South-loathing, U.S. governmental investigative committee on Klan activities. The General not only truthfully denied being the leader of the KKK, but he also honestly disclaimed even being a member (though he did state that he was "in sympathy" with the Klan and that he had been a member of the Pale Faces, a Mason-like organization). The KKK was nothing more than a defensive body, he rightly asserted, organized to counter the nefarious work of the North's Freedmen's Bureau, Union League, and various Loyal Leagues, all anti-South organizations.[1404]

After a severe grilling the committee sided with Forrest, finding him innocent of all charges in association with the organization,[1405] and concluding that he was not and had never been either the founder of or the first leader of the KKK,[1406] facts that are never mentioned by Forrest's critics. Also never acknowledged by the anti-South movement is the fact that by the end of 1871 the KKK had all but vanished from most areas of the South,[1407] due almost solely to Forrest's efforts.

Still, now inaccurately associated with bigotry, the damage had been done, and to this day the original Reconstruction KKK has been branded, unfairly and unhistorically, with the racist label.

We will note here for the record that the KKK of today, which emerged in the 1920s, is in no way similar or even connected to the original KKK of the Southern postbellum period, which lasted a mere three years and four months: December 1865 to March 1869. Indeed, there are indications that the modern KKK is far more popular in the North and West than in the South, with flourishing clans in Indiana, New York, California, Oregon, and Connecticut, just to name a few.[1408] Illinois, Lincoln's adopted home state, has also seen a recent resurgence of Klan activity.[1409]

WHAT YOU WERE TAUGHT: For blacks the plantation system of the Old South was akin to Nazi concentration camps, for they endured the worst suffering man has ever afflicted on his fellow human beings. Consequently, most were never able to raise themselves out of poverty, nor overcome the enormous psychological damage that resulted.

THE TRUTH: It was controversial American historian Stanley Elkins who first promoted this hair-brained notion in 1959, and unfortunately it has been making the rounds in pro-North, anti-South books ever since.[1410] Not only is this correlation an insult to the memories of those who actually experienced the real Nazi prison system of Germany, but it is an entirely unjustifiable postulate; one with absolutely no evidence for it, and mountains of evidence against it.

Elkins believed that slavery, particularly Southern slavery, "infantilized" blacks under a brutal, racist, totalitarian-like regime, turning them into depersonalized automatons; permanently broken human beings stripped of all legal rights, dignity, and personal will, who clung to life under the endless daily cruelty of their white oppressors.

To Elkins and his devotees, Southern servants were "helpless dependents" who were transformed by slavery into the lethargic, illiterate, docile, cartoonish black character that Northerners derogatorily call "Sambo."[1411]

Obviously, as this very book shows, Elkins' judgement could not have been more in error, and today few but the most uneducated and ill informed embrace this theory. Radical abolitionists, like William Lloyd Garrison and Harriet Beecher Stowe, were using a similar line of reasoning in the 1800s, and, because it is a complete fabrication, it received little support then as now.

Frederick Douglass was just one of thousands of former slaves who achieved the American Dream after his emancipation, debunking the Yankee myth that slavery permanently "destroyed" the hearts, minds, souls, and ambition of blacks.

Not even educated Victorian blacks accepted it. One of these was former Northern slave Frederick Douglass, who strenuously disapproved of the idea that black servants were nothing but feeble victims, powerless to sculpt their own destinies.[1412] He was, after all, living proof. After accruing the money to purchase his freedom, he traveled, educated himself, married twice, bore five children, founded a newspaper, became a successful author, editor, journalist, and lecturer, and was appointed to a series of important political positions: in 1871 President Ulysses S. Grant made him assistant secretary of the Santo Domingo commission; from 1877 to 1881 he was marshal of the District of Columbia; from 1881 to 1886 her served as recorder of deeds for the District; and from 1889 to 1891 he was the American minister resident and consul-general in the Republic of Haiti.[1413] And he achieved all of this despite the stiff Yankee resistance he met at nearly every step across the racist North.

Thousands of other examples could be given of strong, courageous, intelligent, enterprising black men and women who rose Phoenix-like from the ashes of servitude to create successful and fulfilling lives. For our purposes, however, only one example is needed: in one fell swoop Douglass' life decimated Elkins' absurd theory, and the book you now hold in your hand, the final nail in that theory's coffin, stands as an eternal testament to the Truth for all those who have "ears to hear."[1414]

The liberality with which the majority of Southern slaveholders governed their servants and plantations can be gleaned from the following comments from an 1820s pamphlet written by Zephaniah Kingsley, a Florida planter:

> About twenty-five years ago I settled a plantation on St. John's River in Florida with about fifty new negroes, many of whom I brought from the [U.S.] Coast myself. *They were mostly fine young men and women*, and nearly in equal numbers. *I never interfered in their connubial concerns nor domestic affairs, but let them regulate these after their own manner. I taught them nothing but what was useful, and what I thought would add to their physical and moral happiness. I encouraged as much as possible dancing, merriment and dress, for which Saturday afternoon and night and Sunday morning were dedicated. [Part of their leisure] was usually employed in hoeing their corn and getting a supply of fish for the week. Both men and women were very industrious. Many of them made twenty bushels of corn to sell, and they vied with each other in dress and dancing. . . . They were perfectly honest and obedient, and appeared perfectly happy, having no fear but that of offending me; and I hardly ever had to apply [any] other correction than shaming them. If I exceeded this, the punishment was quite light, for they hardly ever failed in doing their work well. My object was to excite their ambition and attachment by kindness, not to depress their spirits by fear and punishment. . . . Perfect confidence, friendship and good understanding reigned between us.*[1415]

Two of the kindest and most broad-minded Southern slave owners were Confederate President Jefferson Davis and his brother Joseph, who ran Hurricane Plantation and Brierfield Plantation in

Warren County, Mississippi:

> *There the slaves were not only encouraged to earn money for themselves in every way they might, but the discipline of the plantations was vested in courts composed wholly of slaves, proceeding formally and imposing penalties to be inflicted by slave constables except when the master intervened with his power of pardon. [This arrangement] . . . was maintained for a number of years in full effect until in 1862 when the district was invaded by Federal troops.*[1416]

WHAT YOU WERE TAUGHT: Southern slave owners largely disregarded the personal welfare of their slaves, forcing them to live in filth, poverty, squalor, and rags.
THE TRUTH: By direct order of the South's plantation owners, the average Southern black "slave" was clean, well-groomed, well-mannered, well-fed, and wore fresh clothing each day. In 1809 Virginia planter John Taylor, for example, recommended that all servants be supplied with "fireproof brick houses, warm clothing, and abundant, varied food," among many other provisions.[1417] This approach was not only good business (for a sick or unhappy servant is of little or no use), but it was the accepted humanitarian practice across the South—the region where the American abolition movement began, and where slavery was only reluctantly accepted by the great majority of the population.

Phillips made the following comments about the typical planter's attitude toward cleanliness, hygiene, and Southern servants:

> *In the matter of sanitation, [servant owner Joseph A. S.] Acklen directed the overseer to see that the negroes kept clean in person, to inspect their houses at least once a week and especially during the summer, to examine their bedding and see to its being well aired, to require that their clothes be mended, "and everything attended to which conduces to their comfort and happiness."* In these regards, as in various others, [planter J. W.] Fowler incorporated Acklen's rules in his own, almost verbatim. *[Planter James] Hammond scheduled an elaborate cleaning of the houses every spring and fall. The houses were to be completely emptied and their contents sunned, the walls and floors were to be scrubbed, the mattresses to be emptied and stuffed with fresh hay or shucks, the yards swept and the ground under the houses sprinkled with lime. Furthermore, every house was to be whitewashed inside and out once a year; and the negroes must appear once a week in clean clothes, "and every negro habitually uncleanly in*

person must be washed and scrubbed by order of the overseer—the driver and two other negroes officiating."[1418]

In 1863 two black servants and one white servant from New Orleans, Louisiana, posed for this photograph, showing not only the high quality clothing of the average Southern "slave," but pride of personal hygiene, cleanliness, appearance, and dignity as well.

Concerning the typical clothing worn by Southern servants:

> [James] Hammond's clothing allowance was for each man in the fall two cotton shirts, a pair of woolen pants and a woolen jacket, and in the spring two cotton shirts and two pairs of cotton pants, with privilege of substitution when desired; for each woman six yards of woolen cloth and six yards of cotton cloth in the fall, six yards of light and six of heavy cotton cloth in the spring, with needles, thread and buttons on each occasion. Each worker was to have a pair of stout shoes in the fall, and a heavy blanket every third year. Children's cloth allowances were proportionate and their mothers were required to dress them in clean clothes twice a week.[1419]

WHAT YOU WERE TAUGHT: All Southern states had antiliteracy laws, and all or nearly all Southern slave owners prohibited their slaves from learning to read and write.

THE TRUTH: Antiliteracy laws were not enacted in "all" of the Southern states. Actually, only four Southern states ever bothered to ratify such laws: Virginia, Georgia, North Carolina, and South Carolina, and even here the statutes were only loosely obeyed and routinely ignored. Kentucky and Tennessee never issued them,[1420] and the rest of the Southern states simply ignored the entire issue since it was both inhumane and illogical.

The fact is that, just as Mary Chesnut did, millions of Southern slave owners intentionally taught their servants to read and write; or just as often the servants taught themselves.[1421] Thus the Northern myth that slave owners prevented their servants from becoming literate for fear of them becoming "too smart," "impudent," and "uppity" is just that, a Northern myth—certainly true of ancient Rome, but completely false when it came to the Victorian American South.[1422]

While there were some Southern slave owners who tolerated or even endorsed this counterproductive concept, again, these were the exception rather than the rule. Writing in 1850, Lyell was one of those who discovered this reality first-hand:

> *I am told that the old colonial statutes against teaching the slaves to read were almost in abeyance, and had become a dead letter, until revived by the reaction against the Abolition agitation [which began in the early 1830s], since which they have been rigorously enforced and made more stringent. Nevertheless, the negroes are often taught to read, and they learn much in Sunday schools, and for the most part are desirous of instruction.*[1423]

This attitude on the part of the owners is not surprising: the more abilities and talents a servant had, the more valuable he was (in financial worth and productivity), not only to his employer, but also to himself, to his family, and to both white and black society. With this, his personal power and station in life increased, allowing him potential for greater advancement in life. This truly benefitted everyone on the Southern plantation, from the lowliest field hand to the wealthiest and largest land owner.[1424] As Jefferson Davis said in 1867:

> *Negroes were never prevented from learning to read*; and some of them could write. . . . *Our negroes were not living as the abolitionists say; but were steady and happy* and tolerably moral. Do you suppose that could have been a very bad mode of life for them, which has raised them to a position to which they have never anywhere been able to attain in Africa, by their own unaided efforts?[1425]

The observations of eyewitnesses bear out these facts. Joseph T. Derry, for instance, noted that many Southern servants

> *were taught [to read and write] by their young masters and mistresses, and in the churches on the Sabbath could be seen many slaves who had hymn books and knew how to use them.* Your author has seen in the Sunday school room of Trinity Methodist Church in Charleston, South Carolina, and of St. Paul's Episcopal Church in Augusta, Georgia, negro Sabbath Schools taught by the best ladies and gentlemen of those cities. *At Lexington, in Virginia, Major Thomas J. Jackson, afterwards the noted "Stonewall" Jackson, was the superintendent of a negro Sunday School.* One of the largest churches of Charleston was a negro Presbyterian Church, whose pastor, Dr. [John L.] Girardeau, a celebrated preacher, and learned gentleman, could never be induced to leave it for any other charge.[1426]

Author Joseph T. Derry saw the widespread schooling of Southern slaves firsthand, overturning the old Yankee myth that they were banned from being educated.

It was well-known across the South that every plantation had at least one or more literate servants. Urban areas in particular were filled with them. Owners routinely ridiculed the antiliteracy laws of their state (if there were any) and gave instruction in "readin' and writin'" to any slave who requested it. Favorite house servants came in for special attention in this regard, but it was white children teaching black children that accounted for a great deal of this type of education. Sometimes literate servants held "late night schools" in order to give instruction to their fellows—nearly always with the full approval of their owners. Black Yankee sociologist William E. B. Du Bois estimated that by 1860 at least 5 percent of the South's servant population was literate, though this figure is certainly far too low.[1427]

Many Southern black slaves were able to read and write, and those who could not displayed an eagerness to learn. While some taught one another and some were taught by their owners' children, many others were instructed in the "three r's" by the owners themselves. Laws that forbade the education of slaves were considered silly, and thus were scoffed at, routinely ignored, and almost never enforced.

Of the Southern black man's yearning for education and general betterment, another eyewitness, Sidney Andrews, wrote:

> However poor or ignorant or unclean or improvident he may be, I never yet found a negro who had not at least a vague desire for a better condition, an undefined longing for something called freedom, a shrewd instinct of self-preservation. These three ideas—or, let me say, shadows of ideas—do not make the creature a man, but they lift him out of the bounds of brutedom. . . . The negroes . . . are much interested in the matter [of education]. They all seem anxious to learn to read.[1428]

As is clear from both statistics and eyewitness accounts, being Christians and innately altruistic, white Southern slave owners in their thousands readily responded in kind to this yearning among their servants.

WHAT YOU WERE TAUGHT: Southern slaves were not allowed to learn a craft or trade, and were prevented from either occupational or scholastic advancement.

THE TRUTH: In essence, in the Victorian South the average American black servant worked for his room and board, which was provided to him by his owner-employer. Intelligent servants, and those with special skills, could easily advance, and were often placed in occupations of status, which in turn allowed them to earn an income that quite often led to prosperity, and even freedom, if they chose it.

Thus in thousands of villages and cities across the Old South, we have records of servants who were highly sought after, and highly paid, for their work as artisans and furniture makers. One method of attaining this level was through actual apprenticeship programs, which were offered by numerous Southern slave owners.[1429]

More to the point, as we have seen, so-called "Southern slavery" was often itself a form of apprenticeship, a type of servitude in which one is legally bound to work for an employer for a predetermined amount of time in return for training in a specific trade.[1430] This was why, after all, anti-abolitionist and black colonizationist Abraham Lincoln—who opposed the spread of slavery, not slavery itself—suggested that servants be "subject to apprenticeship" after emancipation.[1431]

Thus the Chesnuts, like many other Southern slaveholders, apprenticed their black servants, even issuing them "degrees" for attaining various levels of achievement, just as in a regular school.[1432] During his travels through Dixie, Lyell commented on what he considered the surprisingly large population of skilled black workers, whose expertise was in such demand that white employment was being adversely affected. There are, he wrote, vast

> *numbers of coloured mechanics in all these Southern States very expert at trades requiring much more skill and knowledge than the functions of ordinary work-people in factories.* Several New Englanders, indeed, who have come from the North to South Carolina and Georgia, complain to me that they cannot push on their children here, as

> carpenters, cabinet-makers, blacksmiths, and in other such crafts, *because the planters bring up the most intelligent of their slaves to these occupations*. The landlord of an inn confessed to me, that, being a carrier, he felt himself obliged to have various kinds of work done by coloured artisans, because they were the slaves of planters who employed him in his own line. "They interfere," said he, "with the fair competition of white mechanics . . ."[1433]

WHAT YOU WERE TAUGHT: White Southern slaveholders did not allow their chattel to practice religion, denying them the right to be baptized, be ordained in any capacity, worship in white churches, take the Sacrament, sing hymns, associate with white Christians, or any of the other religious rights and customs that were available to whites.
THE TRUTH: It was in the Old North that black slaves and free blacks were so often barred from the rights of white Christians,[1434] while it was in the Old South that they were warmly welcomed into the religious folds of their white sisters and brothers.

As this book brims with references of the nearly wholesale, open-hearted Christianization of Southern black servants, I need not go into great detail here, other than to cite a few eyewitness examples, both from non-Southerners. Yankee author Joseph Holt Ingraham described the typical Sunday morning on a Southern plantation in the 1830s:

> *No scene can be livelier or more interesting to a Northerner, than that which the negro quarters of a well-regulated [Southern] plantation present on a Sabbath morning, just before church hours. In every cabin the men are shaving and dressing; the women, arrayed in their gay muslins, are arranging their frizzly hair, in which they take no little pride, or investigating the condition of their children; the old people, neatly clothed, are quietly conversing or smoking about the doors; and those of the younger portion who are not undergoing the infliction of the wash-tub, are enjoying themselves in the shade of the trees, or around some little pond, with as much zest as though slavery and freedom were synonymous terms.* When all are dressed, and the hour arrives for worship, they lock up their cabins, and the whole population of the little village proceeds to the chapel, where divine service is performed, sometimes by an officiating clergyman, and often by the planter himself, if a church-member. *The whole plantation is also frequently formed into a Sabbath class, which is instructed by the planter or some member of his family; and often, such is the anxiety of the master that they should perfectly understand what they are taught, a hard matter in the present state of their intellect, that no means calculated to advance their progress*

are left untried. I was not long since shown a manuscript catechism, drawn up with great care and judgment by a distinguished planter, on a plan admirably adapted to the comprehension of the negroes.[1435]

Southern servants were among the most religious of an already ultra religious region. Church attendance, baptism, and sermonizing were taken seriously, and black preachers were a common sight on Dixie's backroads. As in this scene, enslaved blacks and free whites often met together to worship.

Our second even more detailed account comes from the keen observations of William Thomson of Scotland, who witnessed the following during his travels in South Carolina in the first half of the 19th Century, noting that "the negroes are allowed to do as they please with regard to . . . becoming members of churches."[1436] In 1842, addressing his fellow countrymen in Britain, he remarked:

> On my arrival in South Carolina, the first thing that particularly attracted my attention was negro slavery. Two days after my arrival in Beaufort, the quarterly meeting of the Baptist Church occurred, being Sunday the 11th October 1840; and, as I understood that some sixteen or eighteen negro slaves were to be baptized, *I went to the river in the morning at seven o'clock, and found the banks crowded with some hundreds of black faces, and a few white people.*
>
> It was a beautiful morning, with a clearer sky than is often seen in Scotland. I almost expected to see something ridiculous, but, in reality, *the whole affair had rather an imposing and solemn effect. The black people behaved themselves decently, and with great propriety, much more so than a parcel of young [white] gentlemen*

who were looking on, enjoying the scene in their own way, but not much to their credit, as men of sense or good feeling. The parson, who was dressed in a white gown, went into the river, till the water came up to his waist. A very large fat negro man, named Jacob, one of the deacons of the church, led the people into the river, and stood by, while the parson immersed them, I suppose, to see that none of them were carried off by the stream. . . . They went into the river one by one, the men first, and then the women. The effect was really solemn, as the clear voice of the pastor resounded through the crowd, and along the banks of the river, with the words—"I baptize thee in the name of the Father, and of the Son, and of the Holy Ghost—Amen;" and when all was done, they came up from the river, in a body, singing the beautiful hymn—

"I'm not ashamed to own my Lord,
Or to defend his cause:
Maintain the glory of his cross,
And honour all his laws."

At eleven o'clock we went to church, which was very crowded. I believe there are about twelve or fourteen hundred negro members belonging to it, partly house servants, but mostly slaves from the cotton plantations in the neighbourhood. In the church, the negroes (with the exception of those who were baptized in the morning), were seated in the gallery, the men on the one side, and the women on the other. They had a very strange appearance to me. It was a novel sight to see so many blacks. . . . *In their outward appearance, they were the most serious and attentive congregation I have seen.* After prayer and praise, the negroes who were baptized in the morning, were requested by the pastor to stand up, when he addressed himself to them; telling them particularly their duty to God and to their masters, and to hold fast by the profession of Christianity they had that day made. Then the pastor, the Rev. Mr. Fullen, who was standing, surrounded by his elders, immediately before the pulpit, told them to come forward, and receive the right hand of fellowship. *As they came forward, he took them by the hand, and bade them welcome as brethren in Christ. I took particular notice of the shaking of hands. It was a real transaction; and in the act, the women made a curtsey, and the men a bow, with a better grace than many of the servant lads and lasses in this country would have done.* All, except one, were new members; and on this one they had been exercising church discipline; I believe, for incontinence; but, after a reprimand before the congregation, he was bid "Go in peace, and sin no more." *All [white Southern] churches admit them as members, after instructing them in the great features of Christianity and some of the most practical and useful dogmas*. I frequently conversed with them on this subject, and they generally had a tolerable scriptural idea of Hell and the Devil, of God and Heaven, and of Jesus Christ, who died for their sins; or, with the ideas of a little schoolboy, they would tell me that Heaven is good, and that Hell is bad,—that the wicked will be punished in the one, and the good enjoy the other. Yet *some of them are learned in the Scriptures*. I have heard them praying and exhorting in their own homely way; but, as with their white brethren, this does not appear to have any practical effect on their conduct.

In the afternoon the Sacrament of the Supper was administered. There were black deacons, who handed round the bread and wine to the negroes. They all used the same wine and bread. . . . The negroes have generally fine voices, and they joined in the psalmody of the church. . . . *They appeared to pay great attention to the service*; but I was sorry to observe that the minister never turned his eye to the galleries, nor addressed himself to the limited capacities of the slaves. Judging from the discourse, and the manner of the minister, one would not have known there was an ignorant negro in the house, although *there were five or six times as many black skins as white*.

It would be a hard task to describe the dress of the slaves. The men could not have presented a greater variety of dress if a cart-load of clothes, beggars' duds, gentlemen's dresscoats, with silk-velvet collars, good hats, shocking bad hats, the miserable remnants of black and white "castors" that had served a severe apprenticeship to their masters, and all sorts of inexpressibles, had been all mixed together, and each one sent blindfolded to put on what first came to hand; and this would, indeed, convey some idea of their dress. About one-half of them had shoes on. I have often heard it said, it is the life of an old hat to cock it well, but never saw the thing so well illustrated as I did here. Their plantation dress, although coarse, is far more becoming; but they are so vain, and their taste is so little cultivated, that they prefer, when going to meeting, the very rags and tatters of an old dress coat to their own Osnaburg jacket.[1437] *A few were as well dressed as many white men*.

The dresses of the females were about as varied as those of the men. One uniform custom prevails of wearing gaudy-coloured handkerchiefs on the head, *a la turban*, many of them tartan, the bright and heart-warming colours of which seemed strangely out of place on the head of a slave.

I was told a ludicrous circumstance that had occurred lately. It is customary, when the church is thronged, for the slaves to sit on the stairs; sometimes they bring stools with them, on which they sit about the doors. One Sunday, an old slave, whose black head was turned grey, sat down at the door on the remainder of an old chair. From the heat of the day, and perhaps partly from the soporific quality of the discourse, the old man fell asleep, and was nodding very comfortably. This attracted little attention from the congregation, but it did not escape the observation of a ram that was feeding close by. Every nod the negro gave, the ram approached a little closer. He stood at bay, in the attitude of boxing, just for a sufficient length of time to attract the attention of the minister and a great part of the congregation, who saw what was coming, but had not time to interfere before the unconscious old man gave a larger nod than usual. The ram considering this a fair challenge, came bang up against his head with a crack that would have fractured the skull of any white man, and sent him in at the church door on his back, with the broken chair on the top of him, shouting murder, amidst the ill suppressed laughter of the congregation.

After the services of the day were over, I was amused with their appearance and manners, when they congregated in crowds and groups around the church, after the manner of the people in country parishes in Scotland, but with much more of light-hearted happiness in their black and glistening faces. Their politeness, too, was pleasing, though it amounted to the ridiculous—*a shaking of hands, such bowing and scraping; the young [black] wenches kissing each other for very joy. "How you do, Miss Diana?" "Pretty well, Massa Talleyrand; how you do?" Curtseying, chattering, and laughing, and showing rows of pearly teeth that a duchess might envy. What a contrast appears between these and their task-masters, as they lead their ladies to their carriages, through the crowd,—thin and delicate, with care and disease written upon their wrinkled but haughty brows. Surely, I said to myself, these men suffer more of the evils and the curses that always follow slavery than the slaves themselves.*[1438]

For the ultimate authority on the facts pertaining to the Southern servant and religion, we need go no further than Southern historian Matthew Estes, who was born and raised in the South. In 1846 he recorded the following, in one fell swoop destroying this particular anti-South myth, cruelly fabricated by the North and the New South:

Our [Southern] slave population cannot, at this time, be less than three millions of souls; and of this number, at the lowest possible estimate, we have six hundred thousand Church communicants. Four times this number regularly attend Divine service: thus *we have at least two millions of slaves, who regularly attend preaching. Nearly one half of some of our most popular religious denominations, are colored persons.*

In proportion to numbers, our negroes are not in the

least behind the whites in religious zeal and activity. *Our blacks, in fact, have very strong religious sentiments—possess great earnestness and zeal in their religious devotions, and in the discharge of the practical duties growing out of their religious profession.* Infidelity [that is, atheism] among them is almost entirely unknown, even where they are well-informed in Christianity. *I need hardly repeat that this sin is exceedingly common among the whites, especially at the North, and more especially still, in the good abolition city of Boston [Massachusetts].*

. . . In most cases where the negroes, from any cause, are deprived of regular preaching, they have meetings of their own, and regular services by persons of their own color.

Missionaries are now regularly sent among the blacks in all cases where they live remote from places of regular worship. In many cases, masters owning a large number of slaves, will build meeting-houses, and employ preachers themselves to preach to their negroes. In some parts of the country, Sabbath schools are opened on every Sabbath day for the benefit of the negroes, and this would have been almost universal but for the interference of abolitionists: so these friends may thank themselves for this restriction of the privileges of the negro. Many of our negroes can read the New Testament as well as the great mass of uneducated whites; and even where they cannot read, they acquire an extent of Scripture knowledge which is truly surprising. Having nothing but memory to depend upon, they retain with more tenacity than even the [most] educated among the whites.

We have, in this town, six different Churches belonging to as many different denominations of Christians. In all of these Churches we have Divine Service from two to four times every week, and *in all of them provision is made for the accommodation of the colored people: and what is; more, they are not only permitted, but urged to attend, by their masters*; for all at the South are aware of the difference between religious and irreligious negroes. The most devout of our slaves are the most faithful and honest in the discharge of their duties to their masters. *The negroes generally avail themselves of the opportunity of attending preaching, especially on Lords-day afternoon, when in this and most other towns, special preaching is held for their benefit.* In two of the largest denominations of this place, *special preaching to the negroes, on Sunday, is never neglected; and the result is, that the number of black communicants is very numerous*: in one Church they number several hundred, and in another nearly an equal number. From this statement of facts, the conclusion follows that *our slave population possess very high religious advantages, and that their actual religious condition is equal to that of the great body of the laboring population of most European countries, and not much inferior to the laboring population of the Northern States of this Union.*[1439]

WHAT YOU WERE TAUGHT: Southern slavery was harsh, brutal, and horrific in every way.

THE TRUTH: The true nature of Southern "slavery" was summed up by Virginian Thomas Jefferson in 1781, when he made reference to "the mild treatment our slaves experience,"[1440] while in 1866, another Virginian, Edward A. Pollard, described Southern "slavery" as "altogether, one of the mildest and most beneficent systems of servitude in the world."[1441] As comparative slavery studies show, when contrasted with indigenous African slavery, this is absolutely true. Southern historian Matthew Estes writes that

> *the government to which our Southern negroes are subject, are milder than that to which the hired servant in England, and elsewhere, is subject.*[1442]

U.S. President Thomas Jefferson recognized Southern "slavery" for what it was: a "mild" form of servitude, one virtually unknown outside Dixie.

America's twenty-eighth president, Woodrow Wilson, agreed. In his book *Division and Reunion: 1829-1889*, he writes that in the South, black servants were almost always overindulged, and with great tenderness, by their masters:

> *There was a slave mart even in the District of Columbia itself, where Congress sat and northern members observed. But in the heart of the South conditions were different, were more normal. Domestic slaves were almost uniformly dealt with indulgently and even affectionately by their masters. Among those masters who had the sensibility and breeding of gentlemen, the dignity and responsibility of ownership were apt to produce a noble and gracious type of manhood, and relationships really patriarchal. "On principle, in habit, and even on grounds of self-interest, the greater part of the slave-owners were humane in the treatment of their slaves,—kind, indulgent, not over-exacting, and sincerely interested in the physical well-being of their dependents,"—is the judgment of an eminently competent northern observer who visited the South in 1844. "Field hands" on the ordinary plantation came constantly under their master's eye, were comfortably quartered, and were kept from overwork both by their own laziness and by the slack discipline to which they were subjected. They were often commanded in brutal language, but they were not often compelled to obey by brutal treatment.*[1443]

In 1833 Timothy Flint noted that slaveholders in Alabama were "generally and honorably, with some few exceptions, kind and indulgent masters to their slaves."[1444] During the post-Civil War era English tourist Henry Latham made the following comments after a conversation with a Georgia farmer:

> *He described the former easy life of the slaves; their copious diet, their short hours of work, and provision in sickness, infancy, and age, as compared with their present [emancipated] condition; and asserted that cases of cruelty were as rare as cases of cruelty to his cows and horses inflicted by an English farmer. Cases, he admitted, there were, but very rare; and the love which a man always has for his own property was sufficient to ensure the slave being still cared for in his old age, after the motive from self-interest had ceased.*[1445]

As we have seen, Southern slaves were even allowed to choose their own work schedule and workload, which they did by carefully limiting their output so as not to overstress themselves.[1446]

Slaveholder Chesnut noted that across the South black servants were almost universally considered to be the most comfortable, most indolent, the fattest, and the happiest "peasantry" that ever graced the earth. "Indeed," she wrote, "they are so well situated and so coddled by us that it is sometimes easy to forget that slavery is an evil."[1447]

My kinsman William Giles Harding of Belle Meade Plantation, in Nashville, Tennessee, was like nearly every other Southern slave owner: an abolitionist, a humanitarian, and a kindly and generous master whose freed slaves stayed with him after Lincoln's War.

The South Carolina diarist added that she and her fellow Southern slaveholders were never afraid of their servants fleeing to the other side during Lincoln's War. Why? Because they were simply too contented where they were. Writes Chesnut:

> General [Robert E.] Lee and Mr. [Jefferson] Davis want the negroes put into the army. Mr. [James] Chesnut and [Confederate] Major [Charles Scott] Venable discussed the subject one night, but would they fight on our side or desert to the enemy? *They don't go to the*

> *enemy, because they are comfortable as they are, and expect to be free anyway.*[1448]

Southern black servants were so well taken care of that they not only had better appetites than free blacks,[1449] but, according to Census records, they were the same height as whites (and an inch taller than the average British Royal Marine of the day). Height, of course, is one of the standard measures of one's nutritional history,[1450] and indeed studies show that Southern slaves consumed more calories than free Northern laborers.[1451]

In 1888, 23 years after Lincoln's War, William S. Speer wrote the following about my cousin General William Giles Harding of Belle Meade Plantation in Nashville, Tennessee. Before the War, Speer noted, General Harding

> *was opposed, as his father before him had been, to purchasing slaves, and also opposed to trusting his slaves to the charge of an overseer. Consequently he would never invest in a cotton or sugar plantation, but kept his slaves under his immediate supervision, a course generally thought to be a less profitable method of working slave labor, but by him considered the more humane. During the civil war his slaves remained faithful to him, and a goodly number remain with him at this writing. He cares for them in sickness and in health as formerly. They are contented, happy set; well fed; well clothed; fat, sleek and merry.*[1452]

Victorian Virginian and social theorist George Fitzhugh, just one of the South's many slave owning abolitionists,[1453] contrasted America's moderate slavery with that found in Africa, where extremely barbaric forms of bondage were found.[1454] Even though he was one of the more vociferous antislavery men in Dixie, Southern defender and Alabama attorney Daniel Robinson Hundley was still impressed by the institution's gentility, leniency, moderateness, and informality, particularly when compared with other types of slavery around the world:

> . . . we might compare the present condition of the Southern slaves with the condition of other laborers elsewhere. . . . Certainly we believe the comparison, if made, would show that *the negroes of the South are happier as a class than the peasants of other countries.* We know from actual observation that *they fare better than the poor of any*

of our cities—are more warmly clad, work less, and are a thousand-fold more cheerful and contented. We know, too, that they are infinitely better off than the peons of Mexico, who are bought by the year for any nominal sum which they are presumed to owe the purchaser, and are liable in their old age to be turned adrift without a home, and with not a living soul to take an interest in their welfare. We also believe, and so must every thoughtful honest man, that *their lot is even enviable compared to that of the poor [Chinese] Coolies and other free apprentices*, those new-fangled slaves whom Cant and Hypocrisy are engaged in selling for a term of years to our tropical neighbors.[1455]

Southern slavery was a relaxed institution, and thus the typical Southern slave was relaxed as well. It was so informal that many owners, like Mary Chesnut, found themselves being bossed around by their black servants.

The stark contrast between the Northern view of Southern "slavery" and the reality of Southern servitude was also noted by Northerners. One Yank who visited the South in 1844 was genuinely surprised to find that:

> On principle, in habit, and even on grounds of self-interest, *the greater part of the slave-owners were humane in the treatment of their slaves,—kind, indulgent, not over-exacting, and sincerely interested in the physical well-being of their dependents.*[1456]

Even many anti-South writers have had to grudgingly concede that just prior to Lincoln's War, slavery in the South had attained its most gentle and civilized level for such an institution.[1457] So casual were Southern "slave owners" toward their "sable charges" that, as Chesnut writes, she and other white masters and mistresses often took orders from their servants.[1458]

Little wonder that so few Southern black servants ever tried to escape. Which of them would want to trade the relatively easy life of a "contented peasant" in Dixie for the grueling and dangerous existence of a runaway, chased from town to town both day and night by lawmen, bounty hunters, and hound dogs? As we have seen, Chesnut and other Southern servant owners often jokingly complained that it was so costly and labor intensive, so complicated and difficult owning and maintaining black servants, that it was usually the owner, not the servants, who most often considered running away.

In the mid 1800s, while riding a train over the Georgia-Alabama line during his travels through the American South, first-time British visitor Charles Lyell had the following experience:

> At one of the stations we saw a runaway slave, who had been caught and handcuffed; the first I had fallen in with in irons in the course of the present journey. On seeing him, a *New Englander* [on the train], who had been with us in the stage before we reached Chehaw [Georgia], began to hold forth on the miserable condition of the negroes in Alabama, Louisiana, Mississippi, and some other States which I had not yet visited. For a time I took for granted all he said of the sufferings of the coloured race in those regions, the cruelty of the overseers, their opposition to the improvement and education of the blacks, and especially to their conversion to Christianity. I began to shudder at what I was doomed to witness in the course of my further journeyings in the South and West. He was very intelligent, and so well informed on politics and political economy, that at first I thought myself fortunate in meeting with a man so competent to give me an unprejudiced opinion on matters of which he had been an eye-witness. At length, however, suspecting a disposition to exaggerate, and a [liberal, left-wing]

party-feeling on the subject, I gradually led him to speak of districts with which I was already familiar, especially South Carolina and Georgia. I immediately discovered that there also he had everywhere seen the same horrors and misery. He went so far as to declare that the piny woods all around us were full of hundreds of runaways, who subsisted on venison and wild hogs; assured me that I had been deceived if I imagined that the coloured men in the upper [Southern] country, where they have mingled more with the whites, were more progressive; nor was it true that the Baptists and Methodists had been successful in making proselytes. Few planters, he affirmed, had any liking for their negroes; and, lastly, that a war with England about Oregon, unprincipled as would be the measure on the part of the democratic faction, would have at least its bright side, for it might put an end to slavery. "How in the world," asked I, "could it effect this object?" "England," he replied, "would declare all the slaves in the South free, and thus cripple her enemy by promoting a servile war. The negroes would rise, and although, no doubt, there would be a great loss of life and property, the South would nevertheless be a gainer by ridding herself of this most vicious and impoverishing institution." This man had talked to me so rationally on a variety of topics so long as he was restrained by the company of Southern fellow-passengers from entering on the exciting question of slavery, that I now became extremely curious to know what business had brought him to the South, and made him a traveller there for several years. I was told by the conductor that he was "a wrecker;" and I learnt, in explanation of the term, that he was a commercial agent, and partner of a northern house which had great connexions in the South. To him had been assigned the unenviable task, in those times of bankruptcy and repudiation which followed the financial crisis of 1839-40, of seeking out and recovering bad debts, or of seeing what could be saved out of the wreck of insolvent firms or the estates of bankrupt planters. He had come, therefore, into contact with many adventurers who had been overtrading, and speculators who had grown unscrupulous, when tried by pecuniary difficulties. Every year, on revisiting the Free States [in the North], he had contrasted their progress with the condition of the South, which by comparison seemed absolutely stationary. His thoughts had been perpetually directed to the economical and moral evils of slavery, especially its injuriousness to the fortunes and characters of that class of the white aristocracy with which he had most to do. *In short, he had seen what was bad in the system through the magnifying and distorting medium of his own pecuniary losses, and had imbibed a strong anti-negro feeling, which he endeavoured to conceal from himself, under the cloak of a love of freedom and progress. While he was inveighing against*

> *the cruelty of slavery, he had evidently discovered no remedy for the mischief but one, the hope of which he confessedly cherished, for he was ready to precipitate measures which would cause the Africans to suffer that fate which the aboriginal Indians have experienced throughout the Union* [that is, the colonization or deportation of all blacks, Lincoln's own plan for dealing with America's "racial problem"].
>
> *When I inquired if, in reality, there were hundreds of runaway slaves in the woods, every one [of the Southerners on the train] laughed at the idea. As a general rule, they said, the negroes are well fed, and, when they are so, will very rarely attempt to escape unless they have committed some crime: even when some punishment is hanging over them, they are more afraid of hunger than of a whipping.*[1459]

This is not a defense of either slavery or servitude. It is simply an explanation of why slave owning Southerners called the blacks who worked for them "servants," "domestics," "maids," "butlers," "menservants," "womenservants," "hands," "operatives," "tenants," and "peasants," but almost never "slaves." Indeed, most bonded blacks referred to themselves as "servants."[1460]

Whites also often referred to their black chattel either by their Christian names (Maggie, Bill, etc.), or by their occupational titles: "washerwoman,"[1461] "body servant,"[1462] "housekeeper,"[1463] "chambermaid,"[1464] and "dairy maid."[1465] As a race, most Southern whites simply called them "Negroes,"[1466] while they usually referred to their form of servitude as the "domestic institution."[1467]

In short, the word "slave" and the concept of authentic slavery (that is, one having no human rights)[1468] were completely unknown in the South. Only in the North—where anti-South mythology and propaganda were (and still are) accepted as fact—were these erroneous terms used on a daily basis for servitude in Dixie.

WHAT YOU WERE TAUGHT: Slavery had a destructive impact on the psychology of the slave owner, turning him into a savage beast without a shred of tolerance, mercy, or humanity.

THE TRUTH: There can be little question that early American slavery had an effect on the psyche of the average slaveholder. Because slavery requires a degree of exploitation of fellow human beings, this influence could sometimes be harmful, particularly to the sensitive. However, to say that it was always damaging, and that this damage literally turned the slave owner into a bestial and imperious individual, is wholly without merit. Prior to Lincoln's War slavery was seen by nearly all Southerners as a serious business; not a business they necessarily wanted to be involved in, but one to be taken seriously nonetheless. Southerners would know: they had been censured by Yankees for this very thing in the halls of the U.S. Congress since the late 1700s.[1469] We also have the existence of hundreds of dry, statistic-laden plantation manuals from the antebellum period, another confirmation of this fact. Almost without exception, the slave owning writers of these handbooks were gentle, kindly, and respectful toward their human chattel, more verification of the falsity of the above accusation.

Though, as I have made clear throughout this book, I cannot and will not ever defend slavery, let us consider the words of pro-slavery

Anti-South writers have long regaled us with horrid images of filthy wretched black slaves being lorded over by evil conniving white masters, a whip in one hand and shackles in the other. This is so far from the facts of the matter that educated Southerners still laugh at this preposterous characterization. The true relationship between slave and master is much more accurately depicted in this old illustration, showing a happy, confident, well fed black house servant and a gentle, undemanding owner. Were all master-slave relationships in the Old South like this? Of course not. However, most were, and we have the accounts of thousands of eyewitnesses to prove it.

South Carolina Senator William Smith, who, in the late 1700s, cast a different perspective on the question. It is said, he noted,

> "that slavery vitiates and debases the mind of the slave-holder; but where is the proof? Do the citizens of the south exhibit more ferocity in their manners, more barbarity in their dispositions, than those of the other states? Slavery was first introduced into the West Indies by [Bartolomé de] Las Casas from motives of humanity. The French promote the slave-trade by premiums; and are not the French a polished people, sensible of the rights of mankind, and actuated by just sentiments? The Spaniards encourage slavery, and they are people of the nicest honor, proverbially so. The Greeks and Romans held slaves, and are not their glorious achievements still held up as incitements to great and magnanimous actions? Sparta teemed with slaves at the time of her greatest fame as a valiant republic. Much had been said of the cruel treatment of slaves in the southern states and the West Indies." As to the southern states, from experience and information, [Senator Smith] denied the fact; he believed in his conscience that *the slaves in South Carolina were a happier people than the lower order of whites in many countries he had visited*. As to the West Indies, Lord [George Brydges] Rodney and Admiral [Samuel] Barrington, both of whom had spent some time there, had lately declared in the house of commons that *they had never heard of a negro being cruelly treated, and that they should rejoice exceedingly if the English day-laborers were half as happy*.[1470]

WHAT YOU WERE TAUGHT: All Southern slaves were forced to live either outside in the elements or in crude hovels, usually in tents or dilapidated or abandoned cabins.

THE TRUTH: This is one of the great stereotypes of Northern myth, that the abodes of Dixie's black servants were filthy, poorly-made shanties, filled with lice and rats. It just happens to be untrue.

If you have ever visited a historic Southern antebellum home, chances are that there was a sturdy brick building located somewhere on the property, not far from the main house. The perceptive will immediately notice the high quality of the design and materials that were used. This was no accident. This is the house servants' home, or what Yankees wrongly refer to as the "slave quarters," and it was built by the tenants themselves—African-American experts in the crafts of masonry, carpentry, and general construction. Indeed, this highly skilled craftsmanship is the reason so many of these houses are still standing hundreds of years later.

Typically about 1,000 square feet, some may consider such a home small. But, cozy, well made, and constructed for *one* family only, it was the pride of the inhabitants, which ensured that it was kept clean and tidy. President Wilson noted that, contrary to Northern generalities about Old Dixie, Southern servants were quite "comfortably quartered."[1471] Of the typical slave accommodations, Lyell writes:

> *The negro houses are as neat as the greater part of the cottages in Scotland* (no flattering compliment it must be confessed), are provided always with a back door, and a hall, as they call it, in which is a chest, a table, two or three chairs, and a few shelves for crockery. On the door of the sleeping apartment they keep a large wooden padlock, to guard their valuables from their neighbours when they are at work in the field . . . *A little yard is often attached*, in which are seen their chickens, and usually a yelping cur, kept for their amusement.[1472]

These well constructed "slave" cabins on a plantation in Columbia, South Carolina, in 1862 were built by the servants themselves, many of whom were well paid professional carpenters. Some of the fashionably dressed inhabitants can be seen sitting and standing proudly outside their homes.

While many will look back from today's perspective and wish that the black occupants of such houses had been free citizens with the same rights as whites, the truth is that, at the time, these dwellings were highly prized by those who lived in them. You can be sure that there were free blacks, *and free whites*, living nearby with far less. In fact, there are free Americans of all races today living in smaller, less well built homes, as even the most causal observer must acknowledge.

This photo, taken by the author, of the "slaves' quarters" at Carnton Plantation in Franklin, Tennessee, shows the high level of design, masonry, and carpentry that went into its construction. Built by some of Tennessee's early black servants to house two families, one on each side, the sturdy brick building is roughly 200 years old, and has withstood both time and the elements—and outlasted Lincoln's War as well. All of the plantation's other outbuildings have long since disappeared. In fact, this is one of the oldest structures in Williamson County, a testament to the expertise of its African-American builders. Not only was it of a higher standard than the homes of many of Franklin's free blacks and whites at the time, to this day it is superior in quality and craftsmanship to many houses across the U.S., South, North, East, and West.

This is why both Northern and foreign visitors to the South in the 1800s reported that most slave houses were of a much higher standard than the homes of poor and even many middle class whites. Southern servants' quarters actually compared very favorably with those of the average working class family around the world,[1473] as Hinton R. Helper, Fanny Kemble, Sir Charles Lyell, Frederick Law Olmsted, Harriet Martineau, Basil Hall, James Stirling, and a myriad of other early American tourists noted in their writings.[1474]

Right into the early 1900s, for instance, entire families from among London's laboring poor existed in tiny, single-room flats that were not even fit for livestock. Indeed, the rural and urban poor in most countries have always lived in what we today would consider sordidness, most in filthy ruined shacks that are far below the level of the Victorian South's clean, fairly spacious, well constructed slave housing.[1475]

Southern slaves themselves were well aware of the difference between their standard of living and that of many of the free whites around them—the poorest who, as blacks often remarked, lived in rude windowless huts made of mud and sticks.[1476] Phillips pointed out that these differences were still obvious several generations after the War ended and the homes had begun to deteriorate:

> *As for housing, the vestiges of the old slave quarters, some of which have stood abandoned for half a century, denote in many cases a sounder construction and greater comfort than most of the negroes in freedom have since been able to command.*[1477]

Comparing their homes with those of free African-Americans, and even indigent European-Americans, resulted in enormous pride and appreciation among black servants. After the War former slaves reminisced sympathetically about how poor whites would often come to their door begging for handouts and assistance, recalling that the suffering of many whites rivaled, or even far exceeded, their own.[1478]

Eyewitness accounts of the similarities between Southern servant housing and the housing of Europe's poor are particularly instructive. In 1837 Martineau described the homes of England's lower class this way:

> *In the dwellings of the English poor, parents and children are crowded into one room, for want of space and of furniture.* All wise parents above the rank of poor, make it a primary consideration so to arrange their families as that each member may, at some hour, have some place where he may enter in, and shut his door, and feel himself alone. If possible, the sleeping places are so ordered.[1479]

Scotsman James Stirling, who viewed Dixie's servants' quarters only at a distance, had this to say on the subject:

> The dwellings of the [Southern] slaves which we have seen from the railway seem in fit keeping with their clothing. As far as such a passing glance can inform one, they consist of a log hut of one apartment, with a brick chimney outside, a door, and an aperture with a wooden shutter for a window. *They resemble considerably the poor chalets on the Swiss table-lands, where they drive their cattle to in summer. Altogether, taking into consideration the difference of climate, they seem to me much on a par, as to comfort, with the hovels of our [white Scottish] Highland cottiers.*[1480]

Neat rows of well made comfortable "slave" homes, like these on a Mississippi plantation, belie the Yankee myth that Southern black servants lived in crude squalid shacks. Actually such homes were the envy of lower class free whites and blacks for miles around.

In 1861 Yankee tourist Frederick Law Olmsted gave this description of a Louisiana plantation house and its servants' quarters:

> Fronting upon the river, and but six or eight rods from the public road, which everywhere runs close along the shore inside the levee, was the mansion of the proprietor: an old Creole house, the lower story of brick and the second of wood, with a broad gallery, shaded by the extended roof, running all around it; the roof steep, and shedding water on four sides, with ornaments of turned wood where lines met, and broken by several small dormer windows. The gallery was supported by round brick columns, and arches. The parlors, library and sleeping rooms of the white family were all on the second floor. Between the house and the street was a yard,

planted formally with orange-trees and other evergreens. A little on one side of the house stood a large two-story, square dove-cot, which is a universal appendage of a sugar-planter's house. *In the rear of the house was another large yard, in which, irregularly placed, were houses for the family servants*, a kitchen, stable, carriage-house, smoke-house, etc. Behind this rear-yard there was a vegetable garden, of an acre or more, in the charge of a negro gardener; a line of fig-trees were planted along the fence, but all the ground inclosed was intended to be cropped with vegetables for the family, and for the supply of "the people." I was pleased to notice, however, that the negro-gardener had, of his own accord, planted some violets and other flowering plants. From a corner of the court a road ran to the sugar-works and the negro settlement, which were five or six hundred yards from the house.

The negro houses were exactly like those I described on the Georgia Rice Plantation, except that they *were provided with broad galleries in front. They were as neat and well-made externally as the cottages usually provided by large manufacturing companies in New-England, to be rented to their workmen.*[1481]

In 1892 Southerner Robert Q. Mallard offered these perceptive remarks:

Compare the average house of the [Southern] slave with the one-roomed mud hovel of the Irish tiller in Roman Catholic Ireland, with no privacy by day or night; the suitable and substantial clothing and bed covering supplied the slave with the scanty and sometimes ragged raiment of the poor in our great cities, and even laborers in our factories; their big fires, wood ad libitum, with the miserable, smouldering embers over which the poor sewing women crouch shivering in Northern cities; the excellent nursing and good medical attention given the [Southern] slave, with the condition of many of the poor work-people, who dare not, or will not in their pride, call in a physician, for whose services they are unable to pay; compare the hours of labor in the open air, not pushed to exhaustion and comparatively short, with the long and drastic work of many artisans, against which there is a constant demand for restrictive legislation; and add to this the consideration, that if the white master lived in comparative luxury upon the fruit of the labor of his slaves, he had all the care and forethought and responsibility of directing and organizing the labor for united efficiency; in a word, that he supplemented the African brawn with Anglo-Saxon brain; and it will be perceived that no laboring population in the world were ever better off than the Southern slaves; and that there never was a [more] false accusation made against the Southern planter than this, harped upon by abolitionists of old, and repeated sometimes by Northern preachers now, that "he kept back the hire of the laborer." The plain truth is just this, that no tillers of the soil, in ancient or modern times, received such ample compensation for their labors. He was not [always] paid down, it is true, in cash, but he was amply compensated for his toil in free quarters, free medical attention, free food, free firewood, free support of sick, infirm, aged and young, and the free supply of that organizing faculty which utilized labor and made it more productive and capable of supporting, without the remotest fear of starvation, or even of scarcity, and without appeal to public charity, of entire slave communities, often as large as that of a good-sized village of whites![1482]

This slave nursery on an Alabama farm was located near the center of the servants' homes, which were part of the larger "slave village," an all black community that could be found on nearly all big plantations in Dixie. Children remained in the nursery until they were between 12 and 15 years old, living a carefree existence at the expense of their owners. The nursery, like most of the South's houses and buildings, was designed and constructed by fine Southern black craftsmen, both free and bonded.

WHAT YOU WERE TAUGHT: Every black man and woman living in the Old South was a slave. There was no such thing as a "free black" person in Dixie.

THE TRUTH: There were at least 250,000 known free blacks living across Dixie in the early to mid 1800s.[1483] By 1860 there were some 500,000,[1484] more than double the number of free blacks living in the North. Let us look at a few specific examples.

Though there had been free, slave owning, landowning blacks living and working in Virginia nearly from its inception in the early 1600s,[1485] the state's free black population greatly increased in the late 1700s,[1486] more than doubling between 1790 and 1810, a span of only 20 years.[1487] By 1860 nearly 11 percent of Virginia's black population was free, numbering 58,042 individuals. Officially Tennessee, as another example, had 7,300 free blacks in 1860, though there were no doubt thousands more, not only in the Volunteer State, but across the rest of the South as well, who went unrecorded.[1488] In 1790 the city of Charleston, South Carolina, alone had 586 free blacks, 7 percent of the total white population of 8,089 individuals.[1489]

When he passed through Fredericksburg, Virginia, in 1835, Yankee Professor Ethan Allen Andrews commented on the many free blacks living in the town, saying:

> Some of the best mechanics of the city are colored men, and among them are several master-workmen, who employ considerable numbers of colored laborers.[1490]

Phillips referred to the South's innumerable free blacks as "industrious, well-mannered, and respected members of society."[1491]

For more specific proof, let us turn to the 1860 U.S. Census. Though obviously hopelessly imprecise and "willfully false"[1492] when it comes to providing accurate numbers, the Census gives the following figures of free blacks living in the Southern states that year:

Alabama: 2,265 free black men and women
Arkansas: 608 free black men and women
Georgia: 2,932 free black men and women
Florida: 932 free black men and women
Kentucky: 10,011 free black men and women
Louisiana: 17,462 free black men and women
Mississippi: 930 free black men and women

Missouri: 2,618 free black men and women
North Carolina: 27,463 free black men and women
South Carolina: 8,960 free black men and women
Tennessee: 6,422 free black men and women
Texas: 397 free black men and women
Virginia: 54,333 free black men and women[1493]
TOTAL: 134,733 free black men and women

Some might describe the following two states and the District as "Southern," so for the moment let us consider them as well:

Delaware: 18,733 free black men and women
Washington, D.C.: 10,059 free black men and women
Maryland: 74,723 free black men and women[1494]
COMBINED TOTAL: 238,248 free black men and women

In contrast we will note here that the total number of free black men and women living in the 16 Northern and Western states in 1860 was 196,016.[1495] Thus, there were nearly 45,000 *more* free blacks living in the South that year than in the North. If we take what is almost certainly the more accurate number of 500,000 free Southern blacks in 1860,[1496] there were over 300,000 more in Dixie than in Yankeedom.

WHAT YOU WERE TAUGHT: Due to the damaging effects of Southern slavery, Northern urban black families were stronger and healthier than Southern rural black families.
THE TRUTH: As countless studies have shown, the opposite is true. In fact, it was because of what is called the South's healthier and culturally richer "antebellum experience" that Dixie's rural black families had better, closer relations with one another than the members of Yankee urban black families.[1497]

WHAT YOU WERE TAUGHT: All Southern slave owners were white.
THE TRUTH: There were thousands of free Southern blacks who were extremely wealthy slave owners themselves,[1498] black masters and mistresses who bought and sold others of their race with the same

alacrity and commercial mindedness that white slave owners did.[1499] Many, like early African-American servant owner Anthony Johnson, owned white slaves as well.[1500] This particular practice became common enough by the late 1600s that several states tried to ban free blacks and Indians from purchasing or owning Caucasian slaves and servants.[1501]

In the deep South, just one specific region of Dixie, nearly 25 percent of free blacks owned black slaves.[1502] This is in stark contrast to white Southern slave owners, who made up only 1 percent of the entire total U.S. population in 1860! The Census for that year alone shows that 10,000 black slaves were owned by other blacks.[1503]

One of these was the Metoyer family of Louisiana, an African-American slaveholding clan that owned 400 black servants. At about $2,000 a piece in 1860, their slaves were worth a total of $22,000,000 in today's currency, making the Metoyer's one of the most affluent families in all of American history, black or white.[1504]

A free black slave owner. Countless thousands of such men and women lived across the South prior to Lincoln's War. The African-American Metoyer family of Louisiana, as just one example, owned a sprawling plantation and some 400 black slaves.

The third largest slaveholder in South Carolina was William Ellison, a former black slave who owned 97 African servants, worth a total of about $5,250,000 today.[1505] One of the richest men in the state, he was wealthier than 90 percent of his white neighbors.[1506] The Ellison family became the social core of Charleston's many black slave owners and was a staunch supporter of the

Southern Cause.[1507] Of his black clan it was written: "They were the epitome of loyal Rebels."[1508]

One of Ellison's fellow South Carolinians, John Stanley, was a black man who owned 163 black slaves, worth about $9,000,000 today. In 1860 the African-American women of Charleston, who owned 70 percent of the town's black-owned slaves, used the wealth they accumulated from the so-called "peculiar institution" to start up their own prosperous businesses.[1509]

Black slave owning families could be quite large and were always wealthy. Had they lived today they would have been considered part of the 1 percent of the upper class or ultra rich of American society.

Born into slavery, Horace King of Russell County, Alabama, was later freed, after which he founded a highly lucrative bridge building company using slave labor. King, a generous Confederate benefactor, donated money and purchased uniforms for Rebel soldiers throughout Lincoln's War.[1510] In 1905 it was noted that he had been

> a constant and liberal contributor to the support of the Confederacy. He also furnished clothes and money to the sons of his former master who were in the army, and erected a monument over the grave of their father.[1511]

Andrew Durnford of Louisiana was a free black millionaire who owned 75 black slaves. Durnford complained about both the price of his slaves and their poor work ethic, calling them "rascally negroes." Unlike George Washington, Thomas Jefferson, Nathan Bedford Forrest, and thousands of other white Southern slave owners, Durnford never freed any of his slaves (except one body servant who he favored). Indeed, he never expressed any misgivings about the institution at all.[1512]

Countless other examples of black slavers abound, such as the Virginia black who owned 71 slaves; the Louisiana black who owned 75; and two in South Carolina who each owned 84 slaves.[1513] All were black planters of great wealth and influence in their communities.

Then there was William Johnson of Natchez, Mississippi. A free African-American, Johnson saved up his money, purchased a plantation, and bought 15 black slaves. His famous farm, called "Hardscrabble," is today part of the Natchez National Historical Park.[1514]

When Lincoln's invaders began their illicit raid on the South, they were appalled to often come across entire plantations without a single white person. Both the owners and the servants were black. This was something new and radical to the Northern mind. But it was well-known and accepted in the South, where race relations were normalized by constant and close association.[1515]

It was not just blacks who traded in and owned other blacks. There were thousands of Native-American slave owners as well,[1516] particularly in the lower South.[1517] Despite Lincoln's early racist military ban on Indian and black enlistment,[1518] some of these tribes, along with their black slaves, eventually fought in the Western Territories for the Union throughout the entire war.[1519]

There were many other Native-American slave owners who supported and fought for Davis and the Confederacy, however, among them the Five Civilized Tribes, as they were known.[1520] Some of the more famous examples from among this group were followers of Cherokee chief Stand Watie,[1521] the last Confederate officer to surrender to Lincoln (on June 23, 1865). Watie's strongest Confederate allies were the southeastern Indian slave owners who had been relocated to the West by a callous Union army.[1522]

The 1860 Census lists how many slaves were owned by the various Indians tribes, numbers that must be considered vastly undercounted due to the many inherent errors of the enumeration process and constant underreporting by owners:[1523]

Choctaw: 385 red slave owners, 2,297 black slaves.
Cherokee: 384 red slave owners, 2,504 black slaves.
Creek: 267 red slave owners, 1,651 black slaves.

Chickasaw: 118 red slave owners, 917 black slaves.[1524]

The average white slave owner owned five or less slaves,[1525] but the average Native-American slaveholder owned six. It is known that one Choctaw slaver owned 227 black slaves.[1526] Again, *it was non-white slave owners who individually owned the most slaves, not whites.*

Native-Americans with a freshly captured European-American female. Like the fellow Indians they regularly seized in battle, this white woman too will be turned into an Indian slave, as was the custom among most native peoples for thousands of years previous to the arrival of Europeans.

In 1900 Nieboer made these comments on black slave owning tribes:

> According to the census of 1860 several Indian tribes had Negro-slaves. Our informant enumerates the *Choctaws, Cherokees, Creeks and Chickasaws. Slavery was carried on to a great extent; some owners had from 50 to 200 slaves.*
>
> . . . The *Creeks* already in Bartram's time (1789) had slaves. He tells us of a chief who kept 15 Negroes; they were slaves until they married Indian women, and then acquired the privileges of the tribe. Schoolcraft informs us that "if an Indian should murder a Negro, the law is satisfied with the value of the Negro being paid to the owner."
>
> The *Seminoles* also had Negro-slaves . . . The Shahnees [Shawnees] . . . also kept a few Negro slaves. Amongst the French *Creoles* the rich possessed slaves, Negroes imported from Africa and Indians overcome and taken in battle.[1527]

The full extent of Native-American slave ownership will never be known, but we do have proof that—besides the Choctaw, Chickasaw, Cherokee, and Creek—the Seminoles[1528] also possessed African-American slaves.[1529] The Apaches, among others, not only kept fellow red slaves but white slaves as well,[1530] a custom among Native-Americans that began as early as 1527. By the 19th Century, Indians had enslaved tens of thousands of European-Americans,[1531] a fact seldom discussed in our liberal-oriented, Northern-slanted history books.

As was the norm among the Great Plains Indians, the Cheyenne were enthusiastic slave owners without racial bias of any kind. Any man, woman, or child—whatever their skin color—who fell into their hands could become a lifelong slave under Cheyenne leaders, like Chief Wolf Robe, seen here in 1904.

Evidence for red slaveholders comes from the reports, journals, and diaries of the many whites who came in contact with them,[1532] often in order to purchase Indian slaves directly from its ultimate source: Native-Americans themselves.[1533] This inevitably led to the common practice, mainly in Northern states like New York, of the purchase of already enslaved Indians by white colonists.[1534]

In Chapter 1 we discussed dozens of other Native-American peoples who practiced slavery on fellow reds—as well as on whites and blacks—from every region of North, Central, and South America. Among the more famous of these were the Mayans, the Aztecs, and the Incas, notorious for their primitive, rapacious, and heartless slave systems, many which entailed ritual torture and murder.[1535]

Of course, neither red, black, or white American slave owners would have ever even had the opportunity to become involved in this occupation had it not been for their brown brethren, the Hispanics and Latinos.[1536]

Both the European and the American slave industries got their start with a 15th-Century Portuguese explorer, Henry the Navigator, who, while searching for gold along the West African coast in the early 1400s, happened upon a vast indigenous slave industry run by local African slave owners and slave traders.[1537] Henry wasted no time in involving Portugal in the sordid business. This resulted in the first African slaves to be brought to the New World, the black human cargo which was dropped off in St. Domingo in 1503.[1538] The owners, captains, and crews on these ships were all Hispanic-Europeans.[1539]

Portuguese explorer Henry the Navigator helped open up the African slave trade to the Americas in 1503.

Over the next few centuries African and Hispanic slavers were responsible for the capture, sale, and shipment of literally millions of blacks from Africa to Latin-American colonies and nations, such as Hispaniola and Cuba,[1540] the latter being one of the last Western nations to ban slavery, in 1886, 21 years after the Thirteenth Amendment (not Lincoln) outlawed it across the U.S. Between 1580 and 1680 Portugal was responsible for taking 1 million Africans to its Brazilian colony alone.[1541]

The very word *negro* is a legacy of those dark days: because Portuguese and Spaniards were the first Europeans to involve themselves in the native African slave business, the word *negro*, Spanish for "black," was later adopted by the English as the logical word for Africans.[1542] As a result of the Medieval Portuguese slave trade, today at least one-sixth of the total population of Latin America is negro or mulatto.[1543]

Christopher Columbus launched European-American slavery in 1492 when he transported African slaves to the Caribbean, then immediately began enslaving the native Indian population.

Under the auspices of the Spanish government, the Hispanic slave industry persisted with the arrival of Italian explorer Christopher Columbus in the Caribbean islands in 1492, who many historians credit with the founding of European-American slavery itself.[1544] Already carrying African slaves on his ships that he had probably purchased from Spain,[1545] at Hispaniola Columbus enslaved thousands of the native Indian inhabitants (whom he referred to as "cannibal pagans"),[1546] reducing their free population from 1 million to a mere 60,000, in just 15 years.[1547] Contrast this with the black slave population of America's South, which was so well treated, well fed, well housed, and well clothed that far from diminishing in numbers, it rapidly increased by millions from the beginning of the institution in Georgia in 1749 (the Peach State was the first Southern state to start using slaves),[1548] to its end in 1865.[1549]

It was actually Hispanics who were the first to bring both Africans and African slavery to what is now the United States. This occurred in 1526 when a Spanish Colonial judge named Lucas Vásquez de Ayllón (a man also known to have enslaved Indians),[1550] sailed 500 Spaniards and 100 African-Haitian slaves to what may have been present day Virginia, in an attempt to establish a colony. The experiment ended when most of the group perished from local diseases.[1551] Had these settlers lived, Hispanics would also have been directly responsible for being the first to introduce black slaves into the Southern states.

Here is more evidence that American black slavery was not a creation of the South. It was a creation of Europe, and more specifically of Hispanic Europe, which introduced the institution to Latin America long before it was introduced to the American South by Yankees. Neither were these early African slaves first used on cotton plantations in the South, as Northern folklore asserts. They were first sent to work on plantations in such places as Barbados, Curacao, Antigua, and Brazil.

Early Spanish explorers brought a particularly gruesome and heartless form of Christian slavery to the Americas, one that had no regard for either the indigenous people or even life itself. Those who resisted enslavement were tortured, gutted, and burned alive, as shown here.

Brown slave trading and brown slave ownership were further augmented with the Spanish Conquest of the Americas by men like Hernán Cortés and their conquistadors. They regarded the Native-Americans they encountered as an "inferior race," a vice-ridden caste whose sole function was to serve as beasts of burden, and who could only be saved from their wretched Paganistic lives by conversion to Christianity. The most efficient way to accomplish this, so they believed, was to enslave them and put them to work in the mines. As such, sometime in the early 1500s the Spanish crown required "the baptism of all pagan slaves upon their disembarkation in the colonial ports."[1552]

But this Christianization went only one way. It is said that the Spaniards treated their horses far better than they did their Indian servants.[1553] The result? By 1618 Mexico's native population dropped from 20 million to 1.6 million.[1554]

It was in 1517 that a Spanish priest, Bartolomé de Las Casas, recommended to Spain's Queen Isabella that the native Indian slaves of Hispaniola be replaced with African slaves.[1555] The Spanish monarch agreed, for it was found that Indians did not do as well under slavery as Africans. Why? Because slavery in the Americas primarily surrounded agriculture, and Native-Americans were mainly nomadic hunter-gatherers, while Africans were mainly farmers, with an agricultural tradition that dated back thousands of years. Spain embarked on the African slave trade, hiring the Portugese to bring back some 4,000 African slaves a year from their "slave factories," that is, European settlements, on the continent's coast.[1556] Each slave factory contained a fort, the most remarkable which

According to de Las Casas' 1656 book *The Tears of the Indians*, during its conquest and enslavement of the Americas, Spain tortured and killed some 20 million natives. At least 4 million of these, including "men, women, youths, and children," he wrote "were by the Spaniards consumed by fire." Note the living Indian baby being tossed into the fire in this 400 year old illustration. The number of those who died "under the intolerable yoke and burdens of their captivity" also numbered in the millions. The Spanish Catholic enslavers referred to their butchery and wholesale massacres as "chastisements."

> were St. George del Mina, erected by the Portuguese, though it subsequently fell into the hands of the Dutch; Cape Coast Castle, the principal establishment of the English; Fort Louis, at the mouth of the Senegal, generally occupied by the French; and Goree, situated upon an island of the same name, near Cape Verde. Most of these forts mounted from fifty to sixty pieces of cannon, and contained large reservoirs for water, and were not only impregnable to the negroes, but capable of standing a regular siege

by a European force.[1557]

By 1560 some 100,000 African slaves had been transported to the Americas through this trade system.[1558] Thus, though he was only partially correct, U.S. President John Quincy Adams said on April 29, 1819:

> The negro slave trade was the child of humanity [that is, compassion]—the contrivance of Las Casa to mitigate the condition of the American Indians.[1559]

As the Indian labor supply proved evermore insufficient,[1560] there followed an Hispanic-induced flood of thousands of enslaved Africans to the New World as well, one that both nearly destroyed the Native-American population (due to the "unparalleled cruelty of the Spaniards")[1561] and which opened the door to the slave industry across what would one day become the United States of America.[1562]

A Southern black overseer on horseback (far right) directs a group of black slaves to keep their bovine charges under control during a cattle drive. The smaller the Southern plantation the more likely that the owner, white or black, would employ a black overseer, a practice almost completely unknown on antebellum Yankee slave plantations. In fact, between 70 and 100 percent of *all* Southern slave plantations engaged black overseers.

WHAT YOU WERE TAUGHT: Contrary to Southern myth, there was no such thing as a black overseer on any Southern plantation.
THE TRUTH: Black-owned plantations had black overseers, of course, but on white-owned Southern plantations the vast majority of overseers were black as well. In her journals, for example, Chesnut makes frequent reference to James Team, the married black overseer of her father-in-law's numerous plantations, a position Team held his entire life. Of him Chesnut writes that he had the support and esteem of the whole world. The highly regarded African-American supervisor was also a planter himself, one worth $13,500 in 1860,[1563] about $350,000 in today's currency. Many other black servants operated at even higher levels of supervision, such as general manager. This position was only one rung down from actual plantation ownership.[1564]

Let us break these numbers down more specifically. On small white-owned Southern plantations (with one to 15 servants), almost all overseers were black, nearly 100 percent. On moderate sized white-owned Southern plantations (16 to 50 servants), more than five out of six used black overseers, about 84 percent. On large white-owned Southern plantations (over 50 servants), 75 percent of the overseers were black. And on extra large white-owned Southern plantations (over 100 servants), 70 percent employed black overseers.[1565]

It was in this way that blacks played a vital role not only in plantation management, but also in the financial success of both individual farms and of the Southern economy as a whole. Such interracial business relationships were virtually unheard of in the North before or after Lincoln's War.

WHAT YOU WERE TAUGHT: In order to further dehumanize them, Southern slaves were prohibited from giving themselves either first or last names, a right retained by their owners. In rare cases where they were allowed, slaves were forced to the take last names of their owners, the well-known despicable "slave names"—many which are used to this day.
THE TRUTH: First, there were no laws in the South against black servants naming themselves. Second, they usually chose their own names, and always without the consent or knowledge of their owners.[1566] Third, black servants did not refer to these as "slave names," but rather

as "entitles," since, as individuals with their own separate identities, they felt they had a right to own a proper first and last name. These were ideas and customs with which nearly all white Southerners agreed.[1567]

Fourth, entitles were seldom taken from their owners' names. Typically black servants chose both their first and last names based on their own parents' names, or just as often on unrelated whites (famous or unknown) whom they trusted or admired, or simply because they liked a particular moniker. Northern slave Frederick Douglass, for example, took his surname from the Douglas family, the powerful, noble Scottish clan featured in Sir Walter Scott's famous 1810 poem, *The Lady of the Lake*.[1568]

In many cases Southern blacks simply chose standard occupational names (Miller, Butler, Carpenter, Mason, Baker, Wheelwright), while others preferred native African names and words, such as Phiba, Cudjo, and Juba. Over time such names would usually become anglicized—in these three particular examples as Phoebe, Joe, and Jack respectively.[1569]

Many Southern plantation owners had little or no contact with their field servants. This job was left to the farm's "field marshal" or overseer, who was usually "a faithful, trusty negro" handpicked from the farm's servant population. It was the black overseer's reputation for brutality and even violence that earned him, not the plantation owner, the nickname "slave driver."

WHAT YOU WERE TAUGHT: Southern slaveholders were rightly given the nickname "slave drivers" for the unrelenting and often violent force they used to push their laboring slaves.
THE TRUTH: The plantation owner rarely if ever had anything to do with his servants, particularly his field servants. The latter group was put under the charge of the farm's field marshal, or as he was better known, the overseer. As we have just discussed, the majority of South's overseers were black servants,[1570] and it was these who, due to their special brand of ferocity (as compared to the more docile white overseer), were called "slave drivers."

The black slave driver carried a whip and never hesitated to use it on his African-American charges,[1571] as New Yorker Anson De Puy Van Buren noted during his stay at a Mississippi plantation in the late 1850s:

> The [black] overseer [always "a faithful, trusty negro"] has his horse and saddle, and rides over the field, or changes and walks, as he sees fit. He is always distinguished by his "insignia" of office— his "baton"—*the whip, which is ever in his hand. He has entire command of the slaves;—the correcting and punishing is all left to him. He decides on the most trivial, or weighty matters. The planter has nothing to do with them. The overseer is often the cause, especially if he is a hot-spur in temper, of much trouble among the slaves.* His residence at the "quarters," though it may be like the rest, is a sort of a governor's-house among the negro cabins.[1572]

WHAT YOU WERE TAUGHT: Southern slave laws were intentionally designed to be overly stringent, exceptionally restrictive, and even unnecessarily harsh and sadistic. For their purpose was not to protect black slaves, but to protect their white owners.
THE TRUTH: Though Louisiana, like all of the other states North and South, developed her own slave laws based on earlier European statutes, we can get the general tone of Southern slave laws as a whole by examining those of the Pelican State:

> Louisiana alone in all the Union, because of her origin and formative experience as a Latin colony, had a scheme of law largely peculiar to herself. The foundation of this lay in the *Code Noir* ["Black Codes"] decreed by Louis XIV for that colony in 1724. In it slaves were declared to be chattels, but *those of working age were*

> *not to be sold in execution of debt apart from the lands on which they worked, and neither husbands and wives nor mothers and young children were to be sold into separate ownership under any circumstances.* All slaves, furthermore, were to be baptized into the Catholic church, and were to be *exempt from field work on Sundays and holidays; and their marriages were to be legally recognized.* Children, of course, were to follow the status and ownership of their mothers. *All slaves were to be adequately clothed and fed, under penalty of confiscation*, and the superannuated were to be maintained on the same basis as the able-bodied. *Slaves might make business contracts under their masters' approval*, but could not sue or be sued or give evidence against whites, except in cases of necessity and where the white testimony was in default. *They might acquire property legally recognized as their own when their masters expressly permitted them to work or trade on their personal accounts*, though not otherwise. *Manumission was restricted only by the requirement of court approval; and slaves employed by their masters in tutorial capacity were declared* ipso facto *free.* In police regards, the travel and assemblage of slaves were restrained, and no one was allowed to trade with them without their masters' leave; slaves were forbidden to have weapons except when commissioned by their masters to hunt; fugitives were made liable to severe punishments, and free negroes likewise for harboring them. *Negroes whether slave or free, however, were to be tried by the same courts and by the same procedure as white persons*; and though masters were authorized to apply shackles and lashes for disciplinary purpose, *the killing of slaves by them was declared criminal even to the degree of murder.*
>
> *Nearly all the provisions of this relatively liberal code were adopted afresh when Louisiana became a territory and then a state of the Union.*[1573]

It bears repeating here that the more restrictive the Black Code, the more often it was ignored by white slave owners, not only in Louisiana, but across the entire South. This made the truly "mild form of African servitude" that existed in Dixie even more relaxed and informal than it was originally intended to be.

WHAT YOU WERE TAUGHT: The white Old South was so racist and repressive toward blacks, both free and bonded, that it would not even allow them to participate in the development of their region; nor did it recognize the few contributions blacks made to the South.
THE TRUTH: In the beginning it was the North not the South that prevented blacks from merging with or even contributing to white

society, as former Northern slave Frederick Douglass and many others complained.[1574]

White Southerners, on the other hand, have long paid homage to the scores of contributions blacks have made to Dixie. This is quite unlike Yankee leaders, such as the so-called "Great Emancipator," who never acknowledged or even mentioned any of these African-influenced gifts to American culture and society. (Indeed, Lincoln never once thanked American blacks for anything, including their courageous service in the Union army and navy. He never even sent condolences to the thousands of black families whose sons died in his unnecessary and illegal War.)[1575]

For example, many if not most of the large antebellum homes in the South were built by blacks: they constructed (or sometimes helped construct) the plantation mansions and all of the outbuildings, including barns, greenhouses, carriage houses, sheds, fences, and corrals. They planted the gardens (both decorative and vegetable), orchards, shrubbery, and trees, took care of the livestock, tilled the soil, and planted, maintained, and harvested the food crops. The wood used to build all of these structures was cut by black servants in sawmills, while the house bricks were often handmade, fired in kilns by these same highly skilled artisans. The sawmill and kiln themselves were usually made by talented black servants, a privileged group known as the "slave mechanic class": master carpenters, engineers, and millwrights.[1576]

Tour any one of the South's beautifully preserved prewar homes and you will see numerous examples of superb African craftsmanship, from superb ornamental "gingerbread" and carefully designed floor patterns, to elaborate wooden staircases, mantelpieces, and window frames.

None of this was unusual, though pro-North historians would have you believe otherwise. The truth is that early black architects, craftsmen, iron workers, and woodcarvers were responsible for at least 90 percent of the South's "big houses," as well as even many of her smaller homes, not to mention countless generic buildings, churches, mills, machinery, pieces of artwork, and home furnishings. Even much of the South's so-called "traditional" craftsmanship was done by blacks, including her boats, bridges, and graveyard decorations. Early blacks also gave America the banjo (a true African instrument in both name and design), countless new foods, dances, manners, folkways, folklore, and words, such as "boogie," "gumbo," "tote," "goober," "okra," "jazz," "mumbo-jumbo," and "un-huh" and "unh-uh." They also bequeathed to the world a voluminous body of superlative African-American literature.[1577]

The author's photo of "Rattle and Snap," an antebellum mansion at Mount Pleasant, Tennessee. Most of the South's large prewar homes were built by the region's "slave mechanic class," which included black architects, engineers, carpenters, craftsmen, millwrights, iron workers, artisans, painters, and wood carvers. This group also constructed, and often designed, the South's smaller homes, her churches, stores, and barns, as well as her craftwork, home furnishings, and funerary art. These important contributions to Southern culture and heritage are seldom acknowledged, particularly in the North.

Such architectural features as steep hip roofs, central fireplaces, broad porches with wide overhanging roofs, and the use of dirt (and sometimes moss) to build walls, were all elements of African origin, introduced to America by both free and bonded blacks. According to old building records most of the plantations of Louisiana, as just one example, were built almost exclusively by African architects. In the 1800s Yankee architect Olmsted visited the Pelican State during his travels through the South, and wrote that the best houses and most beautiful grounds he found there actually belonged to black, not white, owners.[1578]

The following, written in 1912 by a Northern engineer, Mr. J. D. Smith, from Chicago, Illinois, is illustrative, for Smith had learned his trade from a slave:

> *During the days of slavery the Negro mechanic was a man of importance. He was a most valuable slave to his master. He would always sell for from two to three times as much in the market as the unskilled slaveman. When a fine Negro mechanic was to be sold at public auction, or private sale, the wealthy slave owners would vie with each other for the prize and run the bidding often up into high figures.*
>
> The slave owners early saw the aptitude of the Negro to learn handicraft, and fully appreciating what vast importance and value this would be to them (the masters) *selected their brightest young slavemen and had them taught in the different kinds of trades. Hence on every large plantation you could find the Negro carpenter, blacksmith, brick and stone mason. These trades comprehended and included much more in their scope in those days than they do now. Carpentry was in its glory then. What is done now by varied and complicated machinery was wrot then by hand.* The invention of the planing machine is an event within the knowledge of many persons living today. Most of our wood-working machinery has come into use long since the days of slavery. *The same work done now with the machine, was done then by hand. The carpenter's chest of tools in slavery times was a very elaborate and expensive outfit. His "kit" not only included all the tools that the average carpenter carries now, but also the tools for performing all the work done by the various kinds of "wood-working" machines. There is little opportunity for the carpenter of today to acquire, or display, genius and skill in his trade as could the [slave] artisan of old.*
>
> *One only needs to go down South and examine hundreds of old southern mansions, and splendid old church edifices, still intact, to be convinced of the fact of the cleverness of the Negro artisan, who constructed nine-tenths of them, and many of them still provoke the admiration of all who see them, and are not to be despised by the men of our day.*
>
> There are few, if any, of the carpenters of today who, if they had the hand tools, could get out the "stuff" and make one of those old style massive panel doors,—who could work out by hand the mouldings, the stiles, the mullions, etc., and build one of those windows, which are to be found today in many of the churches and public buildings of the South; *all of which testify to the cleverness of the Negro's skill as artisan in the broadest sense of the term. For the carpenter in those days was also the "cabinet maker," the wood turner, coffin maker, generally the pattern maker, and the maker of most things made of wood.*

The Negro blacksmith held almost absolute sway in his line, which included the many branches of forgery, and other trades which are now classified under different heads from that of the regular blacksmith. *The blacksmith in the days of slavery was expected to make any and everything wrot of iron. He was to all intents and purposes the "machine blacksmith," "horseshoer," "carriage and wagon ironer and trimmer,""gunsmith,""wheelwright;" and often whittled out and ironed the hames [a type of horse collar], the plowstocks, and the "single-tree" for the farmers, and did a hundred other things too numerous to mention. They were experts at tempering edge tools, by what is generally known as the water process. But many of them had secret processes of their own for tempering tools which they guarded with zealous care.*

It was the good fortune of your humble servant to have served his time as an apprentice in a general blacksmithing shop, or shop of all work, presided over by an ex-slave genius known thruout the state as a "master mechanic." *In slavery times this man hired his own time,—paying his master a certain stipulated amount of money each year, and all he made over and above that amount was his own.*

The Negro machinists were also becoming numerous before the downfall of slavery. The slave owners were generally the owners of all the factories, machine shops, flour-mills, saw-mills, gin-houses and threshing machines. They owned all the railroads and the shops connected with them. *In all of these the white laborer and mechanic had been supplanted almost entirely by the slave mechanics at the time of the breaking out of the Civil War. Many of the railroads in the South had their entire train crews, except the conductors, made up of the slaves—including engineers and firemen. The "Georgia Central" had inaugurated just such a movement, and had many Negro engineers on its locomotives and Negro machinists in its shops.* So it will be seen at once that the liberation of the slaves was also the salvation of the poor white man of the South. It saved him from being completely ousted, as a laborer and a mechanic, by the masters, to make place for the slaves whom they were having trained for those positions. . . . While the poor whites and masters were [off] fighting [Yankees], these same black men were at home working to support those fighting . . . . *The Negro mechanic could be found, during the conflict, in the machine shops, building engines and railroad cars, in the gun factories making arms of all kinds for the soldiers, in the various shops building wagons, and making harness, bridles and saddles, for the armies of the South. Negro engineers handled the throttle in many cases to haul the soldiers to the front . . . . All of the flour mills, and most of every other kind of mill of the South, was largely in charge of black men.*

The author's photo of Ferguson Hall, Spring Hill, Tennessee, once the antebellum home of the author's cousin Martin Cheairs. Many African-American artistic motifs have been incorporated into this famous house, which is also the site of the May 7, 1863, murder of Confederate Major General Earl Van Dorn—shot down by a jealous local husband, Dr. James B. Peters, over alleged rumors of an affair between his wife Jessie McKissack Peters and Van Dorn.

Much has been said of the new Negro for the new century, but with all his training he will have to take a long stride in mechanical skill before he reaches the point of practical efficiency where the old Negro of the old century left off. It was the good fortune of the writer once to fall into the hands of an uncle who was master of what would now be half a dozen distinct trades. He was generally known as a millwright, or mill builder. A millwright now, is only a man who merely sets up the machinery, and his work is now confined mostly to the hanging of shafting, pulleys and belting. *In the days of slavery the millwright had to know how to construct everything about the mill, from foundation to roofs. This uncle could take his men with their "cross-cut saws" and "broad axes" and go into the forests, hew the timbers with which to build the dams across the rivers and streams of water, to erect the "mill house" frames, get out all the necessary timber and lumber at the saw-mill. Then he would, without a sign of a drawing on paper, lay out and cut every piece, every mortise and tenon, every brace and rafter with their proper angles, etc., with perfect precision before they put the whole together. I have seen my uncle go into the forest, fell a great tree, hew out of it an immense stick or shaft from four feet to five feet in diameter, and from twenty to thirty feet long, having as many as sixteen to twenty faces on its surface, or as they termed it, "sixteen" and "twenty square." He would then take it to the mill seat and mortise it, make the arms, and all the intricate parts for a great*

> *"overshot" water wheel to drive the huge mill machinery. This is a feat most difficult even for modern mechanics who have a thoro knowledge of mathematics and the laws of mechanics.*
>
> It is difficult for us to understand how those men [black artisans and mechanics] with little or no knowledge of mathematics, or mechanical rules, could take a crude stick of timber, shape it, and then go to work and cut out a huge screw and the "Tap-blocks" for those old style cotton presses.[1579]

As one example of the scope of Southern black artisans, let us look at my home state, Tennessee. Of the 480,243 blacks living in the Volunteer State in 1900, there were:

MALE
5 engineers (civil and mechanical)
100 millers
993 barbers
340 painters
5,542 steam railway employees
235 plasterers
532 brick and tile makers
137 plumbers and gas fitters
980 blacksmiths and wheelwrights
45 printers
315 boot and shoe makers
94 steam boiler makers
160 butchers
709 engineers and firemen (stationary)
1,308 carpenters and joiners
30 cabinet makers
31 cotton and other textile mill operatives
1,242 iron and steel workers
87 machinists
1,387 marble and stone cutters and masons

FEMALE
1,377 dressmakers and seamstresses
7 milliners
6 tailoresses[1580]

Many of these skilled African-Americans worked for the Confederacy during Lincoln's War, while others were their proud descendants.

If you are a Southerner living in an antebellum house, chances are nearly 100 percent that many of the aspects of your home were either built by African-Americans or influenced by African-American culture. As Dixie has been a melting pot of hundreds of ethnic groups, religions, and skin colors from its inception at Jamestown in 1607, this fact is something that nearly all Southerners, whatever their race, have always been proud of—and continue to be to this day.

From its inception during Lincoln's War, the beautiful but beleaguered, slandered, and greatly misunderstood Confederate Battle Flag, has represented Southerners of all races, not just white Southerners.

WHAT YOU WERE TAUGHT: The Old South was a region built on white racism and the servile exploitation of the black race, making the Confederate Flag a symbol of white supremacy.

THE TRUTH: As we will see in subsequent chapters, this description would be more properly applicable to the Old North, not the Old South.

In fact, Dixie has always been a multiracial, multiethnic, multicultural society, as is obvious from the region's military rolls, created during Lincoln's War. Under the beautiful Confederate Battle Flag (designed by my cousin Confederate General P. G. T. Beauregard),[1581] every known race donned Rebel gray or butternut and fought against the Yankee invaders. This included not just 1 million European-Americans[1582] and 300,000 to as many as 1 million African-Americans,[1583] but also 70,000 Native-Americans, 60,000 Latin-

Americans,[1584] 50,000 foreigners,[1585] 12,000 Jewish-Americans,[1586] and 10,000 Asian-Americans.[1587]

These statistics prove to the world like nothing else can, that from the beginning the Confederacy fought, not to exploit and oppress the black race or any other race, but for the constitutional rights and personal freedom of all her people. Those who say anything different are either lying or are ignorant of genuine Southern history, plain and simple.[1588]

Some from the anti-Confederate Flag movement, like the racially intolerant Northern-based NAACP, know full well the true meaning of what we in Dixie call the "Southern Cross." Unfortunately, such groups (which even other blacks, like Reverend Jesse Lee Peterson, have labeled "hate groups")[1589] have a vested interest in fanning the flames of racism, for without racial divisiveness the world's race-baiters would go out of business.[1590]

Our most racist liberal president, Abraham Lincoln, thought along similar lines. He, along with the Radicals (that is, abolitionists) in his party, believed that by pitting whites and blacks against each other, the resulting tension, emotion, and fear would divide and weaken the South, allowing him to manipulate and overcome her people easier. Happily, Lincoln's attempt to poison Southern race relations failed, for the majority of whites and blacks saw through the ruse and remained loyal to one another both during and after his War.[1591]

The South did not immediately become a multiracial, multiethnic, multicultural society in 1861 with the start of Lincoln's War, of course. As noted, the South has always been a racially inclusive region. Native-Americans were inhabiting the South for tens of thousands of years prior to European settlement,[1592] and for a short time blacks were in the area now known as Virginia as early as 1526,[1593] long before the European ancestors of most of today's white Southerners arrived. It is for this very reason that by 1860, 99 percent of all blacks were native born Americans, a larger percentage than for whites.[1594]

Hispanics too had a hand in the development of the Southern states. Spanish explorer Juan Ponce de León was in Florida in 1513, and in 1565 Spaniards founded St. Augustine, the oldest continually occupied city in the U.S. It is true, as has been said, that the American South once spoke Spanish.[1595]

British General James E. Oglethorpe, founder of the colony of Georgia, meeting with Native-Americans in 1733. The American South has been a multiracial society from the beginning.

Contrary to popular thought, the South is not a "white region," and never was. Indeed, Dixie is the unique and special place it is today because of the culinary, architectural, sartorial, political, social, artistic, musical, and literary contributions made by all the races, in particular, those of European descent and those of African descent.[1596] If one section of the U.S. had to be called a "melting pot" of multiracial influences, it would be the South, not the North.

The Confederate Battle Flag then turns out to be anything but a symbol of white racism or white supremacy. Those who created it never intended it to have this meaning, and those who fought under it never thought of it as having this meaning. The descendants of those soldiers today have also never perceived it in this way, as I myself can testify.

If anything it would be more accurate to call our flag a symbol of racial inclusiveness and multiculturalism, one founded on the Christian principles extolled by Jesus, whose main tenants were love and universal brotherhood.[1597] The Confederate Battle Flag itself was designed around the Christian crosses of Great Britain's flag (Saint George's Cross), Scotland's flag (Saint Andrew's Cross), and Ireland's flag (Saint Patrick's Cross).[1598]

Our beloved Battle Flag then, the winsome Southern Cross, is an emblem of not only small government, capitalism, personal liberty, and self-government, but also of American patriotism, strict constitutionalism, Christian love, and Southern heritage. Indeed, these are the very reasons that Conservative Confederate President Jefferson Davis described the Southern Confederacy as "the last best hope of liberty."[1599] As such, the Confederate Battle Flag is one that all Southerners, and all lovers of freedom, can revere unreservedly, as well as display with pride and honor whenever and wherever possible. Conservative Founder and Southern abolitionist Thomas Jefferson, the "Father of the Declaration of Independence," would heartily approve.

As for the charge of exploiting Southern blacks, let us end this chapter with Matthew Estes' brief comparison of the treatment of the Southern slave by his Southern master with that of the African slave by his African master in his native African homeland:

> *It is almost needless to attempt a comparison between the government of the negro here [in the American South], and in Africa. The whole continent of Africa cannot furnish a government that permits so wide a range of human liberty, and that so thoroughly secures human rights, as the governments under which the slaves live in this country. Political and domestic slavery are almost universal in Africa. Three-fourths—some say, nine-tenths—of the whole population, are in a state of the most abject domestic slavery: a slavery, the grinding oppression of which is unknown in this country. With a few inconsiderable exceptions, all the African tribes are subject to the most absolute [tyrannical] forms of government.* The sovereign has a power over the lives and fortunes of his subjects, greater than any European monarch. A few of the smaller tribes, have what are called free governments, but *in all such cases, the population is licentious, turbulent, and unhappy. They are the most illy regulated of all the governments in Africa. All the larger and more important kingdoms, are absolute despotisms.*[1600]

Far from being an emblem of exclusive white racism, as the North and the New South fraudulently teach, the Confederate Battle Flag (top) is a Christian symbol of racial inclusiveness, one patterned on the designs of (bottom left to right) Ireland's Saint Patrick's Cross, Scotland's Saint Andrew's Cross, and England's Saint George's Cross. The Christian Cross itself is the emblem of Jesus, who preached the gospel of universal love (John 13:34).

Anti-South writers have fabricated the myth of the "runaway slave" to confuse students of history and denigrate the South. According to this particular fiction, Southern black servitude was so horrendous that slaves took every opportunity to flee for their lives. The truth is that while there were indeed occasional runaways, mainly from the rare cruel Southern master, fugitive slaves were an infrequent peculiarity that never occurred on the typical Southern farm or plantation. The reason for this was simple enough: Southern servitude actually benefitted servants in a myriad of ways by providing safety, stability, and security in the legally sanctioned forms of lifelong free housing, clothing, food, employment, and healthcare. In many Southern communities black servants were actually the envy of free blacks and whites, many who struggled with financial issues that inevitably led to serious housing and health problems, among other things. In truth, runaway slaves were a far more serious problem in the Old North, where the region's rigorous Black Codes often made life unbearable for black servants. Southern blacks who allowed Yankees to talk them into moving North had it especially hard, and usually deeply regretted the decision. While hard at work on the cold stony soil of New England's bleak plantations, it was not uncommon to hear them yearningly singing their favorite Southern tunes. One of those most often heard wafting across the fields of Massachusetts, for example, was the 1859 song, *I Wish I Was in Dixie's Land*: "Oh, I wish I was in the land of cotton, old times there are not forgotten. Look away! Look away! Look away! Dixie Land. Oh, I wish I was in Dixie, hooray! hooray! In Dixie land I'll take my stand, to live and die in Dixie. Away, away, away down south in Dixie. Away, away, away down south in Dixie."

8

SOUTHERN SLAVERY AND THE BIBLE

WHAT YOU WERE TAUGHT: Southerners once used the Bible to justify slavery.

THE TRUTH: This is true. But there were scores of logical reasons for this practice, all of which your teachers have withheld from you. In fact, as with so many other aspects of Southern history, this particular piece of anti-South folklore turns out to be one-sided and disingenuous; just one more arrow in the South-hater's quiver, one meant to further hurt, anger, and humiliate Dixie and her people.

To begin with, using the Bible to justify slavery was not specifically a Southern tradition, or even an American one. Both the North and the South engaged in the practice before, during, and even after the War.[1601] New England Puritans, such as Cotton Mather,[1602] were particularly enthusiastic about the biblical approval of slavery,[1603] which is why Connecticut's original bondage law cited a proslavery passage from the book of Exodus.[1604] When Massachusetts became the first American colony to legalize slavery in 1641,[1605] its pro-slavery statute ordered that black slaves were to be guaranteed

> all the liberties and Christian usages which the law of God established in Israel concerning such persons doeth morally require. This exempts none from servitude who shall be judged thereto by authority.[1606]

Of this law Hildreth wrote:

> This article gives express sanction to the slave trade, and the practice of holding negroes and Indians in perpetual bondage, anticipating by twenty years any thing of the sort to be found in the statutes of Virginia or Maryland.[1607]

It was not just Americans who used the Good Book to support slavery, however. This was a worldwide custom dating back to the earliest days of Christianity.[1608]

In early Medieval times, for instance, the European Church itself upheld the laws of feudalism, which was little more than a slave state in which serfs were bought and sold with the land. Though serfs had no civil rights and lived or died at the mercy of their owners,[1609] their plight was completely ignored by the Church. Why? Because the Bible makes no mention of serfdom or feudalism.[1610] Since both were legal, and because Jesus commanded his followers to obey the laws of the land,[1611] the Church backed away from the entire issue.[1612] The result? Slavery continued on for another 1,000 years throughout Europe's Christian nations.[1613] As every single one of these countries was a Christian nation (many of their national flags, such as Denmark's, still possess the Christian cross), this was a business that could only be called one thing: the Christian slave trade.[1614]

Most early American Christian Yankees, like Puritan Cotton Mather of Boston, Massachusetts, agreed with the Bible's implicit support of slavery.

While modern Christians understandably condemn authentic slavery, many of the early Church Fathers perceived it quite differently, seeing it merely as a result of the Fall of Man in the Garden of Eden.[1615] Both Saint Gregory of Nazianzus and Saint Augustine viewed the institution similarly, as a consequence of Original Sin. Saint Thomas

Aquinas taught that slavery was a punishment from God,[1616] while Saint Ambrose, the Bishop of Milan, argued that slaves should be happy because their condition gave them an opportunity to perfect the Christian ideals of patience, humility, and forgiveness.[1617]

The European-American trade in African slaves itself was a Christian undertaking,[1618] supported by the widely accepted Catholic idea that "heathen" peoples, wherever they were to be found, needed to be converted to the "true religion," the best means available being baptism then enslavement.[1619] This was believed to be particularly true in the case of "Pagan Africans," for they had already been slaves in their own land.[1620]

Saint Augustine held that slavery was a punishment for "original sin," a common belief in the 5th Century.

With such facts at hand and with such Christian luminaries and the Bible supporting slavery, it is hardly surprising that centuries later Victorian Christians across America argued that slavery must be a divinely sanctioned institution.

WHAT YOU WERE TAUGHT: In early America the Bible was used to justify African slavery because of prevailing sentiments about white superiority.

THE TRUTH: This could not have been the reason, for the Holy Scriptures say nothing about race in connection with slavery. Rather the Bible was used to defend slavery in great part because both Jesus and Saint Paul,[1621] Christianity's two most important figures, mention servitude and slavery numerous times without ever speaking out against them.[1622]

In the Gospel of Matthew, for example, Jesus is approached by a slave owning Pagan, a wealthy Roman centurion who possessed numerous slaves, one of whom was deathly ill, requiring immediate attention if he was to survive. After seeing the soldier's incredible belief in the Indwelling Christ,[1623] Jesus addresses him:

> "Verily I say unto you, I have not found so great a faith, no, not in Israel. . . . Go thy way; and as thou hast believed, so be it done unto thee." And his servant was healed in the selfsame hour.[1624]

There is not a single word of condemnation here concerning the centurion's slaves. Based on the faith of the owner,[1625] Jesus simply commands the man's slave to be healed, then goes on his way.[1626]

Jesus spoke of slavery numerous times without imprecating it, to early Southern Christians a sign of his tacit approval of the institution.

In the case of Paul, in the Epistle of Philemon we find him returning a runaway slave, named Onesimus, to his master, Philemon, with no comment about the injustices or evils of slavery.[1627] This is hardly the action of an abolitionist. Rather it is the action of a law-abiding, proslavery advocate,[1628] as Paul's own words to the slaves at Colossae (located in what is now southeast Turkey) testify:

> Servants, obey in all things your masters according to the flesh; not with eyeservice, as menpleasers; but in singleness of heart, fearing God.[1629]

Saint Paul tolerated slavery in great part because of his mystical belief that merely being a Christian obliterated the social, ethnic, racial, and even gender lines that traditionally separate people from one another. Wrote Paul:

> There is neither Jew nor Greek, there is neither bond nor free, there is neither male nor female: for ye are all one in Christ Jesus.[1630]

Saint Paul once returned a slave to his owner, and admonished slaves themselves to be obedient to their masters.

Saint Peter agreed with Paul on the topic of slavery and even issued the same command for slaves to be obedient to their owners, again without condemnation of the institution:

> Servants, be subject to your masters with all fear; not only to the good and gentle, but also to the froward.[1631]

Indeed, there is no unequivocal admonition against slavery anywhere in the New Testament.[1632] Slaveholding appears nowhere in its many lists of "offences," while the Apostles are seen readily receiving slave owners into the Church without the slightest censure.[1633] Jesus himself demands that one who desires to be his chief disciple should be the slave of all,[1634] and later, after His resurrection, the apostles are called "slaves of the Lord."[1635] In today's totalitarian environment of political correctness, how many Christians would be willing to publically refer themselves as "slaves of the Lord"?

Why did neither Jesus or his apostles denounce slavery?

Slavery was so accepted, so integral to ancient Roman and Middle Eastern society, that even espousing the idea of abolition would have caused widespread violence,[1636] resulting in massive social disorder and financial upheaval.[1637] After Rome's destruction of the Jerusalem Temple in the year AD 70, for example, no one took any notice of the fact that most of the surviving Jews were sold into slavery.[1638] Why? Because it was both the custom and a common occurrence at the time throughout the Roman Empire.

In addition, Jesus as well as Paul commanded complete obedience to the constitutional laws of the land.[1639] Abolition then, in this particular situation, would not have agreed with the teachings of Jesus and the Christian Church.[1640] These exact sentiments would be echoed 2,000 years later by good Christians across the American South.

The Old Testament (or Torah) is also completely silent on the evils of slavery. Instead it offers many examples of both the backhanded approval of slavery and its full sanction by God.[1641] Indeed, the institution was openly practiced by the early Hebrews throughout their entire era,[1642] with one of the more famous of them, Joseph, shown being sold into slavery by his own brothers.[1643]

If this was not enough to rationalize slavery, Christian supporters of the institution could always turn to the book of Genesis and read of the idea that Africans bore the "mark of Cain," a people cursed by Noah to be the "servants of servants"—meaning the "lowest of slaves."[1644]

Also known as the "Curse of Ham" (actually the curse of Ham's son Canaan, and his descendants), early Americans, like the Mormons, construed these passages to mean that Africans had inherited the "affliction" of black skin and a life of servitude under white rule.[1645] As the Old Testament authors state it:

> And Ham, the father of Canaan, saw the nakedness of his father, and told his two brethren without. And Shem and Japheth took a garment, and laid it upon both their shoulders, and went backward, and covered the nakedness of their father; and their faces were backward, and they saw not their father's nakedness. And Noah awoke from his wine, and knew what his younger son had done unto him. And he said, Cursed be Canaan; a servant of servants shall he be unto his brethren. And he said, Blessed be the Lord God of Shem; and Canaan shall be his servant. God shall enlarge Japheth, and he shall dwell in the tents of Shem; and Canaan shall be his servant.[1646]

Nowhere in the Old Testament or the New Testament is there a single word of disapproval regarding slavery. On the contrary, slavery is openly practiced by both Jews and Christians, not only with God's blessing, but sometimes under God's actual command.

As one of the many 19th-Century, Northern Christian denominations that believed in the Curse of Ham, it is worth noting here that early on the Mormons showed an intense interest in purchasing and owning slaves. Mormon leader Brigham Young, for example, not only welcomed white slave owners into his church, he settled Utah's Salt Lake Valley area using Mormon slave owners and their slaves. And in 1852, as the first territorial governor of Utah, Young asked the legislature to legalize slavery, making it the only territory west of the Missouri River and north of the Missouri Compromise line to allow the institution.[1647] Said Young in 1855: "The blacks should be used like servants, and not like brutes, but they must serve."[1648]

Early Latter Day Saints leader Brigham Young happily received slave owners into the Mormon Church, and even settled Utah's Salt Lake area with African slaves. "Blacks should be used like servants," he once commented.

All Mormons once held that blacks would continue to be an "inferior race" in the "Next World." Not surprisingly, blacks, being of the "lineage of Cain," were not allowed to join the Mormon priesthood or participate in Temple ordinances until 1978, 148 years after the church's founding in 1830 by Yankee polygamist and former Mason, Joseph Smith. The change only came after decades of severe criticism, denunciation, and charges of racism from around the world. Little wonder that in the early 1900s, the Utah branch of the new racially exclusive KKK (as distinct from the South's original racially inclusive KKK) flourished with the membership of Mormon ministers.[1649] Despite the church's modern 1978 concession, belief in the Mark of Cain and the Curse of Ham still survives among many individual Mormons and Mormon groups.[1650]

This 1843 illustration of a post-flood scene of Noah and his three sons (from the book of Genesis) captures the traditional belief of the period, one once widely held in both the American North and the American South. On the far left is Ham and his wife, "the parents of the negro race." Left center is Japheth and his wife, "the parents of the white race." Behind the altar is Shem and his wife, "the parents of the red race." On the far right is Noah and his wife, the progenitors of all the races. The view that the three main "races" spring from Noah's three sons is still popular among Bible literalists.

Of course, the Mormon Church was far from being the only early Northern Christian faith that supported slavery. In fact, there were so many pro-slavery Christian Yankees in the 19th Century that Southern abolitionist James G. Birney wrote an entire book about the issue, called, *The American Churches: The Bulwarks of American Slavery*.[1651] Naturally, the proliferation of pro-slavery sentiment in the North's Christian communities is exactly what one would expect in the region where both the American slave trade and American slavery got their start.[1652]

WHAT YOU WERE TAUGHT: The Quakers were a strictly antislavery Christian denomination that pushed for abolition from the time of their founding by Englishman George Fox in the 17th Century. Yankee Quaker groups in the early American North were particularly and strongly abolitionist.

THE TRUTH: It is true that for thousands of years, from ancient times to the dawn of the formation of the U.S., few, except a small number of Quakers, spoke out against the institution of slavery. Yet, even among this normally highly conscientious religious community, overt racism toward blacks was often witnessed,[1653] with some, like atheist Lincoln (whose ancestors were Quakers),[1654] supporting the American Colonization Society—which sought to make America "white from coast to coast."[1655]

Like Jesus, Quaker founder George Fox never spoke out against slavery, providing thousands of his followers in both England and America with full justification for owning African chattel.

Quaker founder George Fox himself accepted the existence of slavery, never publicly denounced it, and referred to black servants as "neigors" (niggers),[1656] which is why so many Quakers later justified owning slaves.[1657] One of the more famous of these was Yankee Quaker William Penn, after whom the state of Pennsylvania is named, a man known to have bought, owned, and sold slaves.[1658]

By and large Quaker slaveholders believed that blacks were inherently flawed creatures,[1659] "natural servants" who needed to be worked for at least several years before being were freed.[1660] New England Quakers in particular were busily engaged in the Yankee slave trade throughout the 1700s.[1661]

By 1768 the situation had become so disruptive and controversial that Quaker authorities tried to force fellow Friends in Pennsylvania to manumit their slaves. But the scheme failed for lack of interest and support.[1662] Eight years on, however, in 1776, Quakers, like abolitionist Anthony Benezet, sought to have all slaveholding members expelled from the Church.[1663] His view held sway, and those who refused to relinquish their black bondsmen and bondswomen were disowned and excommunicated.[1664]

Let us not judge the Quakers too harshly. Nearly every known major theologian, philosopher, politician, and writer of every race and creed who lived during this time period supported the idea of slavery.[1665]

WHAT YOU WERE TAUGHT: Defending slavery based on the Bible and the practices of the early Christian Church is silly, misguided, and illogical.

THE TRUTH: Only to those living in the 21st Century. To Westerners living in 16th-, 17th-, 18th-, and 19th-Century America, the Bible was the standard to which everything in life was held. Thus slavery, the Bible, and Christianity were seen as inseparable, and Yankee John H. Hopkins, the Bishop of Vermont, described the reason in 1863:

> . . . slaves and slaveholders were in the Church from the beginning; . . . slavery was held to be consistent with Christian principles by the Fathers and Councils, and by all Protestant divines and commentators up to the very close of the last century; . . . this fact was universal among all churches and sects throughout the Christian world. . . . [Thus I believe] that *our Southern brethren committed no sin in having slaves, and that they were men as of much piety as any ministers in our [Northern] Communion.* [For I also believe] that the plain precepts and practice of the Apostles sanctioned the institution . . .[1666]

Now let us look at the issue from our early American ancestors' point of view, beginning with the Old Testament.

The Old Testament's 39 books are completely silent on the evils of slavery. Instead they offer scores of examples of both the backhanded approval of slavery and its full sanction by God.[1667] As mentioned, slavery was institutionalized by the Hebrews and practiced throughout their whole existence.[1668] Many of the Old Testament Patriarchs were slave owners, such as Jacob, Joseph, and Job. Abraham, the man to whom God gave the covenant that is "the cornerstone of the whole Christian system," was both a slave owner and a slave dealer.[1669]

From these facts alone it is apparent that in the Old South slavery was not a racial white-black issue, but rather a religious one. And it was for just this reason that books, like Albert Taylor Bledsoe's *An Essay on Liberty and Slavery* (published in 1856), were owned, read, and embraced by many families across Dixie.

Bledsoe, a brilliant unreconstructed Southerner, observed in his book, for example, that Abraham, the father of Judaism, owned over 1,000 (white) slaves, but was not condemned by God. Rather he received God's greatest blessing: a divine promise sealed for all eternity.

How, then, Bledsoe asked "could these professing [Northern] Christians proceed to condemn and excommunicate a poor brother [that is, a Christian, Southern slave owner] for having merely approved what Abraham had practiced?"[1670]

Indeed, the Fourth and Tenth Commandments recognize slavery as "moral law,"[1671] and the book of Leviticus actually requires early Jews to buy and own slaves.[1672] Although details are lacking on ancient Jewish slavery, it was probably similar, if not identical, to the institution as it was practiced by surrounding early peoples.[1673] For under Hebrew law a slave was defined as a "possession," one that could be bought and sold like livestock.[1674]

Ancient Hebrew patriarch Abraham was a slave dealer who personally owned over 1,000 white slaves.

Men like Abraham were not the only ancient Semites who practiced slavery with the consent and even the encouragement of God. According to the Bible, the entire Hebrew people, spiritual precursors of the Christian faith, had the full sanction of the Almighty behind them in their acceptance of the institution. Here, in the Book of Leviticus, is what God Himself has to say on the matter:

> I am the Lord your God, which brought you forth out of the land of Egypt, to give you the land of Canaan, and to be your God.
>
> . . . Both thy bondmen [male slaves], and thy bondmaids [female slaves], which thou shalt have, shall be of the heathen that are round about you; *of them shall ye buy bondmen and bondmaids*.
>
> Moreover of the children of the strangers that do sojourn among you, *of them shall ye buy*, and of their families that are with you, which they begat in your land: and *they shall be your possession*.
>
> And ye shall *take them as an inheritance for your children after you, to inherit them for a possession; they shall be your bondmen [slaves] for ever* . . .[1675]

The Bible not only permits Hebrews to enslave foreigners permanently,[1676] it even allows a father to sell his children into slavery.[1677] Early Hebrew laws ordained that a slave had no human rights, and that slaves could not marry, but only "mate." The children of these unions were considered the property of the parents' owner.[1678]

According to Exodus 21:3, if a male slave was freed, his wife and children had to remain behind in slavery if the woman had been given to him by the owner.[1679] During the Dark Ages (AD 500-1000), while some early Christians were now beginning to discuss the incompatibility between slavery and Jesus' message of brotherly love, according to the Talmud, God sanctioned slavery among the Jews up until at least the year 400.[1680]

Jesus never condoned slavery, but neither did He condemn it. He simply accepted it as a legal aspect of the ancient Roman world, exhorting His followers to obey the laws of the land. "Render to Caesar the things that are Caesar's, and to God the things that are God's."

We find a similar situation in the New Testament. Antislavery proponents have long tried, but have never been able to find any disapproval of the institution in any of its 27 books—for none exists.[1681] As mentioned, both Jesus and Paul refer to servitude and slavery numerous times without a single protest.[1682] Paul goes even further by referring to himself as "the slave of Christ,"[1683] while the Disciples are often called the "slaves of the Lord."[1684]

Far from objecting to slavery, Jesus told his Disciples that whoever wanted to be chief among them should be the "slave of all."[1685] And in one of His many parables Jesus refers to a slave owner who whipped his slave. Again, never once does Christ say anything against either slavery, or even the brutal beating. The moral of the story is simply that much is asked of those to whom much is given.[1686]

Medieval Western slavery had Christian roots. As the Bible nowhere disapproves of slavery but instead actually condones and encourages it,[1687] the early Christian Church never came out completely against it,[1688] and countless Christians were themselves slave owners.[1689] In fact, having incorporated Aristotle's pro-slavery sentiment into its sacred canon,[1690] Catholicism tolerated and supported the institution[1691] for 1,000 years after the decline of Rome,[1692] and even operated as a large scale and lucrative slaveholder during the early Middle Ages—which helps explain its stolid resistance to abolition at the time.[1693]

Many Protestants were of the same mind. John Wesley, founder of the Methodist Church, did not consider it a sin for his parishioners to own slaves and believed that one could be a good Christian and a slaveholder. Thus countless slave owners filled not just the Church's pews, but also the various Methodist Societies that dotted the U.S. and the West Indies in the late 1700s.[1694]

Around the time of Constantine the Great (AD 400), the Church banned Jews from keeping slaves. Not because it was against the institution, but because, in accordance with Mosaic Law, Jews were setting their slaves free after only seven years of service—considered a transgression against the Church.[1695] Catholics in the Latin American colonies imported untold millions of African slaves in the 1500s, sales that were approved by Church leaders.[1696]

The Medieval Papacy certainly had little to say on the matter; and in fact beginning in the 14th Century, the popes routinely threatened their critics and foes with slavery.[1697] One Church leader, Pope Sixtus IV, who possessed 250 personal "servants,"[1698] issued a decree ordering all wayward Florentines to be sold into slavery.[1699] Pope Clement V placed the citizens of Venice under slavery in 1309, and in the early 16th Century Pope Paul III condemned all of the English who supported Henry VIII to slavery.[1700] Phillips writes:

> Venice . . . had treaties with certain Saracen rulers at the beginning of the fourteenth century authorizing her merchants not only to frequent the African ports, but to go in caravans to interior points and stay at will. The principal commodities procured were ivory, gold, honey and negro slaves.[1701]

Saint Peter's Square and Basilica at the Vatican, Rome, Italy. The pre-Reformation Christian Church (Catholicism) never officially came out against slavery, stubbornly resisting abolition for over 1,000 years. In fact, the early Catholic Church itself engaged in both the mass purchase and the mass sale of slaves, with one pope owning some 250 enthralled servants. Over the centuries thousands were sold into slavery by various popes. One of them, Clement V, enslaved all of Venice in 1309.

During the 15th Century, while Christian Rome was serving as a major slave market, Ferdinand the Catholic of Aragon gave Pope Innocent VIII 100 Moorish slaves as a gift. The pontiff promptly divided them up and gave them to his cardinals as presents.[1702] In early Jamaica, where African slaves lived squalid lives without legal protection, or even marriage and family, Christian priests were considered the "most finished debauchees" of all those who embraced the institution.[1703] In mid 16th-Century Brazil, Jesuit priests not only approved of slavery, but each had several of their own.[1704] During this same period, after their brutal torture and enslavement by Christian Spain and Portugal, Native-Americans were forced to convert to Catholicism as part of the Church's "official policy."[1705]

It was due to just such Church practices that canon law

recognized slaves as one of the three basic social classes (along with the clergy and freemen), and it is why numerous clerics were themselves slave owners.[1706] It is also why the Spanish Inquisition thought nothing of enslaving other Christian Europeans over a period of several centuries, beginning in the 1400s.[1707]

We have seen that many of the early Church Fathers, such as Saint Gregory of Nazianzus, Bishop Ambrose, Saint Augustine, and Thomas Aquinas sanctioned the institution,[1708] viewing it as a social system that helped maintain an orderly society,[1709] while Martin Luther believed that slavery was ordained by God.[1710] Later, among the early American colonists of the 17th and 18th Centuries, Christians and Jews helped one another run the African slave trade[1711] out of the Northeast,[1712] eventually turning New York City into the country's largest and most thriving slave port—for decades the veritable capital of the American slave trade.[1713]

Like the majority of ancient intellectuals, 4th-Century Greek philosopher Aristotle believed that slaves were fated to serve others, just as the free were predestined to rule over them.

Thus when it came to the Bible and the "peculiar institution," our Southern predecessors and ancestors were in good company.

As we have noted, Aristotle believed that "from the hour of their birth some are marked out for subjection, others for rule,"[1714] and nearly all early Christians agreed. Thus when a group of European slaves asked for their freedom in 1525, like Saint Paul, Martin Luther unsympathetically replied that "those in bondage need to accept their lot in life, for in order for the world to function, both free men and enslaved men are needed."[1715]

Long before Luther's time the Catholic Church, indeed all of Christendom, was actively involved in slavery,[1716] which is why Catholic philosophers, such as 15th-Century Christian Thomas More, thought it befitting for menial laborers, the poor, and criminals to be made into slaves.[1717]

Early Christians also defended slavery as a form of evangelism, one that introduced the saving grace of the Gospel of Christ to "ignorant African savages," none who, they believed, would see Heaven without a proper baptism. As one writer put it, the

> barbarians of Africa . . . are much better off when slaves among us than when free at home, to cut throats and eat one another.[1718]

This particular defense was especially aggravating to 19th-Century black civil rights leaders, like former Northern slave Frederick Douglass. Concerning America's centuries old defense and maintenance of slavery, he wrote:

> . . . I can see no reason, but the most deceitful one, for calling the religion of this land Christianity. I look upon it as the climax of all misnomers, the boldest of all frauds, and the grossest of all libels.[1719]

Whether one agrees with Douglass or not, it must always be borne in mind that in early America the general populace read the Bible quite literally; that is, its words were taken at face value.

And so it was in the extremely religious world of the Old Victorian South. Who are we to judge the region by 21st-Century standards? As Victorian Southerner Mary Chesnut herself knowingly said in vindication of the existence of servitude in Dixie: "We are all but creatures of our own time and place, of the 19th Century."[1720]

The point is that we should not evaluate our predecessors by the standards, values, and morals of our day—an outlook known as presentism. It is not fair, scientific, or historically accurate. After all, how will our hopefully more enlightened descendants evaluate us 150 years from now? If they judge us the way many people today judge our Victorian ancestors, especially our *Southern* Victorian ancestors, we will not stand up very well.

Old South Southerners were, after all, a product of their times, just as we are. And like nearly all 19th-Century Americans they were taught by their society, parents, church, school, and the science of the day, that servitude was inherent to human society, that it was, as we have just seen, an institution decreed by God himself.

How could it have been any different? At the time there was not a single egalitarian, nonracist, co-racial society on earth that early Americans could have used as a model. In every nation on the planet, one race, whether it was white, black, red, yellow, or brown, dominated all others, usually in what we would now think of as an inhumane and racist manner.

Human history records not a single example of a completely racist-free society. One race has always racially dominated another. In 1790, for example, while these African slaves were gathering cane under a white slave owner on a Caribbean sugar plantation, their black relatives back in Northwest Africa were viciously torturing, killing, and enslaving thousands of white Europeans and Americans. Since globally racism is even more severe now than it was 200 years ago, it remains to be seen whether our species can ever truly divest itself of this seemingly biologically hard-wired trait. Either way, we should take care not to judge our ancestors based on current social mores and political ideologies.

More to the point, *forced labor* has been the rule since the dawn of time.[1721] On the other hand, *unforced labor*, if there truly is such a thing, has always been the exception.[1722] And, as noted, as of the mid 1800s there had never been a single known instance of a purely nonracist society in all of recorded history.[1723]

Knowing these facts gives us a much better understanding of those blacks, whites, browns, and reds who practiced slavery during America's past—and often used the Bible to justify it.

While we can certainly agree or disagree with the ancient belief that slavery is an inherent element of human society, we are in no position to condemn early Americans for embracing it. What deeds are we committing today that we will be severely castigated for in the year 2161?

Let us hope that our future critics are fair in their assessment of us, and that they take into account our current social, political, and religious beliefs, as well as our level of scientific knowledge. For in all of these fields we will look extremely primitive to 22nd-Century Americans living 150 years from now.

Two white male slaves (left) and one white female slave (right) hard at work in an English mine in the 1800s. Contrary to pro-North, abolitionist mythology, there is no such thing as "unforced labor." Since we must earn a living, by nature all labor is forced. Many early Americans argued this very point when it came to what they considered the minor differences between a *slave laborer* working in a field and a *wage laborer* working in a factory. For example, if the three individuals pictured here were not forced to do this work as slaves, they would be forced to do it, or something else, as "free" laborers.

You would never know it from reading our Yankee-authored, mainstream American history books, but hundreds of thousands of Southern blacks fought for the Confederacy. In this illustration black and white Confederate scouts surveil a Union camp in Virginia in preparation for an attack. Note the Rebel uniform, rifle, belted cartridge box, and hat (taken off to help avoid detection by the enemy) of the black Confederate soldier in the foreground.

9

NORTHERN SLAVERY

WHAT YOU WERE TAUGHT: There was no such thing as slavery in the American North. Thus there were no Northern slaves and no Northern slave owners.

THE TRUTH: This statement is obviously false because both the North American slave trade and North American slavery got their start in the northeastern United States (the former in 1638,[1724] the latter in 1641).[1725] Additionally, it is a historic fact that *all* of the original Northern colonies and subsequent Northern states possessed slaves,[1726] both Indian and African.[1727] In fact, in 1776, of the 500,000 slaves in the 13 colonies, 300,000 (or 60 percent) were possessed by the Northern ones, only 200,000 (or 40 percent) by the Southern ones.[1728]

Yankee slave dealers trading an African slave for a horse on Africa's Gold Coast.

In 1776, 1790, 1800, 1810, 1820, 1830, 1840, 1850, and 1860 (the latter eight years from the Census), the approximate number of slaves in each of the *Northern* states are listed below. Note that some of these states were not yet officially formed, or were mere territories, at the time these figures were enumerated. Also, "not recorded" does not mean that the state possessed no slaves that particular year. Only that its slaves, if it had any, were not counted in the Census. Lastly, these numbers do not include either Native-American slaves or the hundreds of thousands of African slaves who were brought by Yankee slave ships through the various Northern seaports.

Connecticut: year 1776: 5,000 slaves; year 1790: 2,759 slaves; year 1800: 951 slaves; year 1810: 310 slaves; year 1820: 97 slaves; year 1830: not recorded; year 1840: not recorded; year 1850: not recorded; year 1860: not recorded.

Delaware: year 1776: 9,000 slaves; year 1790: 8,887 slaves; year 1800: 6,153 slaves; year 1810: 4,177 slaves; year 1820: 4,509 slaves; year 1830: 3,292 slaves; year 1840: 2,605 slaves; year 1850: 2,290 slaves; year 1860: 2,290 slaves.

District of Columbia: year 1776: not recorded; year 1790: not recorded; year 1800: 3,244 slaves; year 1810: 5,395 slaves; year 1820: 6,377 slaves; year 1830: 6,119 slaves; year 1840: 4,694 slaves; year 1850: 3,687 slaves; year 1860: 3,687 slaves.

Illinois: year 1810: 168 slaves; year 1820: 917 slaves; year 1830: 747 slaves; year 1840: 331 slaves; year 1850: not recorded; year 1860: not recorded.

Indiana: year 1776: not recorded; year 1790: not recorded; year 1800: 135 slaves; year 1810: 235 slaves; year 1820: 190 slaves; year 1830: not recorded; year 1840: not recorded; year 1850: not recorded; year 1860: not recorded.

Maryland: year 1776: 80,000 slaves; year 1790: 103,036 slaves; year 1800: 105,635 slaves; year 1810: 111,502 slaves; year 1820: 107,397 slaves; year 1830: 102,994 slaves; year 1840: 89,737 slaves; year 1850: 90,368 slaves; year 1860: 90,368 slaves.

Massachusetts: year 1776: 3,500 slaves; year 1790: not recorded; year 1800: not recorded; year 1810: not recorded; year 1820: not recorded; year 1830: not recorded; year 1840: not recorded; year 1850: not recorded; year 1860: not recorded.

Michigan: year 1810: 24 slaves; year 1820: not recorded; year 1830: not recorded; year 1840: not recorded; year 1850: not recorded; year 1860: not recorded.

New Hampshire: year 1776: 629 slaves; year 1790: 158 slaves; year 1800: eight slaves; year 1810: not recorded; year 1820: not recorded; year 1830: not recorded; year 1840: not recorded; year 1850: not recorded; year 1860: not recorded.

New Jersey: year 1776: 7,600 slaves; year 1790: 11,423 slaves; year 1800: 12,422 slaves; year 1810: 10,851 slaves; year 1820: 7,557 slaves; year 1830: 2,254 slaves; year 1840: 674 slaves;

year 1850: 236 slaves; year 1860: not recorded.

New York: year 1776: 15,000 slaves; year 1790: 21,324 slaves; year 1800: 20,343 slaves; year 1810: 15,017 slaves; year 1820: 10,088 slaves; year 1830: not recorded; year 1840: four slaves; year 1850: not recorded; year 1860: not recorded.

Pennsylvania: year 1776: 10,000 slaves; year 1790: 3,737 slaves; year 1800: 1,706 slaves; year 1810: 795 slaves; year 1820: 211 slaves; year 1830: not recorded; year 1840: 64 slaves; year 1850: not recorded; year 1860: not recorded.

Rhode Island: year 1776: 4,373 slaves; year 1790: 952 slaves; year 1800: 381 slaves; year 1810: 108 slaves; year 1820: 48 slaves; year 1830: not recorded; year 1840: not recorded; year 1850: not recorded; year 1860: not recorded.

Vermont: year 1776: not recorded; year 1790: 17 slaves; year 1800: not recorded; year 1810: not recorded; year 1820: not recorded; year 1830: not recorded; year 1840: not recorded; year 1850: not recorded; year 1860: not recorded.[1729]

Since the largest and most enduring slave state in the Union was, of course, New York, let us focus on her slave population specifically, as well as some of her counties:

1698: New York state, 2,170 slaves.
1703: New York state, 2,283 slaves.
1703: Five New York counties (not specified), 1,301 slaves.
1712: New York state, 2,425 slaves.
1712: Five New York counties (not specified), 1,775 slaves.
1714: Dutchess County, 29 slaves.
1723: New York state, 6,171 "negroes and other slaves."
1731: New York state, 7,231 slaves.
1737: New York state, 8,941 slaves.
1746: All New York counties except Albany, 9,107 slaves.
1749: New York state, 10,692 slaves.
1756: New York state, 13,542 slaves.
1771: New York state, 19,883 slaves.
1774: New York state, 21,149 slaves.
1776: New York state, 21,993 slaves (about 11.5 percent of the total

population).[1730]
1786: New York state, 18,889 slaves.[1731]
1787-1865: New York state, number of slaves not recorded.

Between the years 1701 and 1726, 1,573 slaves were imported into New York from the West Indies, and another 822 from the coast of Africa, totaling 2,395. The greatest number of African slaves were transported to New York in 1718, when 447 were brought from the West Indies and 70 from Africa, for a total of 517 that year. All of these were imported by "private traders" from New York; that is, Yankee slave ship owners from the American Northeast.[1732]

The crew of a Yankee slave ship, branding newly purchased female slaves and their children on Africa's Slave Coast before returning with them to New England. Since both the American slave trade and American slavery got their start in the American North, it is obvious that, contrary to what our anti-South history books teach, the entire Northeast not only traded in slaves and owned slaves, but engaged in these practices far earlier, far more vigorously, and far longer than the American South.

Due to the ever present errors in the Census, as well as the widespread Yankee custom of underreporting slaves by Northern slaveholders (to avoid taxes) and Census takers (simple carelessness),[1733] we can be sure that *all* of the preceding numbers are on the low side. Respected Yankee historian and African-American atheist William E. B. Du Bois, for example, stated that many of these figures are certainly incorrect "as not including the complete census."[1734]

All of the combined facts and figures from above automatically make early Northerners not only slave traders and slave owners, but the *first* officially recognized and the *first* legally authorized white North American slave traders and slave owners.

Massachusetts, whose legalization of slavery in 1641 occurred 147 years before it became a state in 1788, wrote this law into its "Body of Liberties," which was later consolidated into the "Articles of the New England Confederation" (the Yankees' pre-Civil War Confederacy).[1735] This legislative act automatically legalized slavery in what is now Connecticut, as well as in the southeastern portion of Massachusetts, then known as "New Plymouth" (which included all of Cape Cod).[1736] The pro-slavery paragraph of the Body of Liberties reads:

> There shall never be any bond slaverie, villinage or captivitie amongst us unles it be lawfull captives taken in just warres [wars], and such strangers as willingly selle themselves or are sold to us. And these shall have all the liberties and Christian usages which the law of God established in Israell concerning such persons doeth morally require. This exempts none from servitude who shall be judged thereto by authoritie.[1737]

The Yankee's enthusiastic attitude toward slavery can be easily gleaned from a letter written a few years later by Bay Stater Emanuel Downing to his brother-in-law Governor John Winthrop, one of the founders of the Massachusetts Bay Colony. In it Downing explains why he hopes to have a war with the local Narragansett Indians, referring to African slaves as "Moores":

> If upon a just warre the Lord should deliver them into our hands, we might easily have [Indian] men, women and children enough to exchange for Moores, which wil be more gaynful pilladge for us than wee conceive, for *I doe not see how wee can thrive untill wee get into a stock of [black] slaves sufficient to doe all our buisines*, for our children's children will hardly see this great continent filled with people, soe that our [white] servants will still desire freedome to plant for themselves, and not stay but for verie great wages. And I suppose you know verie well how we shall mayntayne 20 Moores cheaper than one [white] Englishe servant.[1738]

In 1643 the four Yankee colonies of Massachusetts, Plymouth, Connecticut, and New Haven formed the "New England Confederation" (this was 218 years before the South formed its own Confederation in 1861), joining forces for the "common concern," which included the purchase, maintenance, and sale of slaves, whatever their race. These Yankee Confederates were particularly interested in black slaves, stipulating that any Indian found guilty of a crime would be seized in satisfaction, "either to serve or to be shipped out and exchanged for negroes as the cause will justly beare."[1739]

In 1645 a Boston slave ship, working with several other slave ships from London, England, attacked a native African village on the coast of Guinea on Sunday. Many of the inhabitants were killed and a number were taken prisoner. Two of the captives were brought aboard the Boston schooner and promptly enslaved. After being transported to New England, however, a Massachusetts judge found the captain and crew guilty of "murder, man-stealing, and Sabbath-breaking," and ordered the slaves back to Africa. If they had been purchased instead of kidnaped, however, no law would have been broken under Massachusetts statutes.[1740] For by then the African slave trade had become a legal and "regular business" in New England.[1741]

New England was sending slave ships to the West Coast of Africa some 140 years before the United States of America was formed.

While the Massachusetts general court evaluated both red and black slaves as "private property" suitable for exportation as "merchandise,"[1742] Rhode Island and New Hampshire more specifically taxed them as "livestock." New Jersey and Pennsylvania—the latter state where blacks were present even before William Penn's colony was founded[1743]—preferred to see their slaves as assessable possessions, while New York evaluated its slaves using a poll tax. Everywhere across the North black slaves were registered by Yankee families on the same lists as their horses, cattle, tools, kitchen goods, and other common farm and household items.[1744] How different from the South, where slaves were civilly registered as literal members of their owner's family.[1745]

The official records show that as of the year 1800 there were 36,505 black slaves in the North, working on farms and plantations in a myriad of occupations, from agricultural to mechanical.[1746] As most slaves were not counted in the Census (Northern Census takers did not like to include blacks, and Yankee slave owners preferred not to report their slaves due to taxation[1747]—making the Census "willfully false"),[1748] we know that this number was actually much higher.

In fact, statistics from the time period reveal that in the early 1700s, 42 percent of all New York households owned slaves, and that the share of slaves in both New York and New Jersey was larger than that of North Carolina.[1749] By 1690, in Perth Amboy, New Jersey, as just one example, nearly every white inhabitant owned one or more black slaves.[1750] This means that nearly 100 percent of the whites in some Northern cities were slaveholders. By 1775, 12 percent of the population of eastern New Jersey was comprised of slaves.[1751] By 1776 there were at least 300,000 slaves in the North.[1752] An advertisement in New York's Oswego *Herald* dated 1799, gives an idea of the casual widespread acceptance of African slavery across Yankeedom at the time:

> A YOUNG WENCH—FOR SALE. She is a good cook and ready at all kinds of house-work. None can exceed her if she is kept from liquor. She is 24 years of age—no husband nor children. Price $200 [about $4,000 in today's currency]; inquire of the printer.[1753]

Based on mathematics alone it is clear that many Yankees were far more rapacious slavers than Southerners: not only did most Southern towns have no slaves or slave owners at all, but the percentage of overall Southern slave owners never went above 5 percent (it usually hovered between 3 and 4 percent).[1754]

Beyond the hopelessly inaccurate and paltry 1776 and 1790 statistics cited above, it is difficult to know precisely how many slaves and slave owners there were in the antebellum North. We know that blacks were in North America, at least briefly, as early as 1526.[1755] As the U.S. Census did not officially begin until 1790, we have no hard data for the number of Northern slaves in the intervening 264 years. During that period we can be sure, however, that many millions lived, worked, and died in the North, the majority unrecorded, their names unchronicled, their births, lives, descendants, and deaths forever unknown.

Slave auctions, like this one in 17th-Century Boston, Massachusetts, were once an everyday affair in New England: accepted, legal, and well attended.

This unfortunate dearth of information regarding Northern slavery has long helped the North avoid acknowledging that it once imported, exported, owned, and maintained hundreds of thousands of African slaves, and that it alone is responsible for launching the U.S. slave trade and instigating American slavery. But authentic history cannot be ignored, suppressed, or rewritten. The record stands clear, defiant, and intractable: the American North and African slavery were once inextricably bound together, a deeply symbiotic relationship that was finally only torn asunder by the passage of the Thirteenth Amendment on December 6, 1865, nearly a year *after* Lincoln died.[1756]

It was only in the late 1700s, when Northerners finally began to find slavery unprofitable[1757] (due to the Industrial Revolution and their generally poor soil and cold climate)[1758] and uncomfortable (due to rampant white Northern racism),[1759] that they began to slowly dissolve the institution,[1760] eventually liberating over 300,000 slaves.[1761] Nonetheless, nearly 100 years later, in 1860, near the start of the Civil War, historian Dr. Clement Eaton believes there were at least 500,000 black slaves still left in the North,[1762] while Southern historian Don Hinkle maintains that their number was closer to 1 million.[1763]

Taking the higher number, 1 million slaves, and an average ownership of two slaves apiece, we get 500,000 Northern white slave owners, 2.5 percent of the 20 million white Northerners in 1860.[1764] Numbered among these were many famous Yanks, such as General Ulysses S. Grant,[1765] as well as General Winfield Scott, Admiral David G. Farragut, General George H. Thomas, and the family of Lincoln's wife, Mary Todd.[1766]

Millions of slaves must have lived and died in the Northern states between the 1600s and 1865. If all their names had been recorded, no single volume could contain them all.[1767] An abbreviated list of some of the better known Northern slaves whose names *were* recorded includes:

Crispus Attucks (Massachusetts)
Frederick Douglass (Maryland)
Sojourner Truth (New York)
Harriet Tubman (Maryland)
Amos Fortune (Massachusetts)
James Derham (Pennsylvania)
Prince Whipple (New Hampshire)
Daniel Coker (Maryland)
Theophilus Thompson (Maryland)
Richard Pierpoint (New York)
Quock Walker (Massachusetts)
Lisette Denison Forth (Michigan)
Amanda Smith (Maryland)
Briton Hammon (Massachusetts)
Samuel Green (Maryland)
Jane Johnson (Washington, D.C.)
Phillis Wheatley (Massachusetts)
Josiah Henson (Maryland)
Seymour Burr (Connecticut)
James Roberts (Maryland)
Prince Estabrook (Massachusetts)
Cynthia Hesdra (New York)
Venture Smith (Connecticut)
Francis Burns (New York)
Anthony Bowen (Maryland)
Ayuba Suleiman Diallo (Maryland)
Henry Highland Garnet (Maryland)
Pyrrhus Concer (New York)
Felix Holbrook (Massachusetts)
Leonard Black (Maryland)
John Jea (New York)
Charles Ball (Maryland)
William S. Crowdy (Maryland)
Peter Salem (Massachusetts)
Mary Edmonson (Maryland)
Emily Edmonson (Maryland)
Elizabeth Freeman (New York)
Lewis Charlton (Maryland)
Elijah Abel (Maryland)
Richard Allen (Pennsylvania)
Decatur Dorsey (Maryland)
Benjamin Bradley (Maryland)
Molly Williams (New York)
Solomon Bayley (Delaware)
John Edward Bruce (Maryland)
James H. Bronson (Pennsylvania)[1768]

WHAT YOU WERE TAUGHT: Slavery could not have begun in the North because Northerners had no use for slavery.

THE TRUTH: Both the North American slave trade *and* North American slavery got their start in what is now the Northeastern part of the U.S., and for very specific reasons.

Black slavery took root in the North due to two insurmountable problems: the high cost of white labor due to a shortage of white labor.[1769] The main issue, however, was that during the colonial period land was so cheap, often free, that there was no need for whites to work for a wage under an employer. Instead they could simply claim a piece of land and become independent farmers and tradesmen themselves, owning and running their own businesses and farms.[1770]

Unlike the later emerging Southern slave owner, the early Northern slave owner put every one of his able-bodied slaves to work, from the youngest to the oldest. African slavery in the American North grew out of the need for cheap, plentiful labor, white servants being scarce and expensive at the time.

Still, as Thomas Jefferson pointed out in 1811, assistance was needed to clear forests, cultivate the soil, and harvest crops on these new huge tracts of land, acreage that was out of proportion to the small amount of white labor available.[1771]

For help early American colonists turned to Native-Americans, but found, like Spain's Queen Isabella, that they did not do well under servitude. Additionally, indentured white slaves (mainly Englishmen and women) were not only scarce in numbers, but those who could be found were prone to buying their freedom as soon as they reached America's Western frontier.[1772]

Along with white slaves, white European convicts had once been a source of American labor as well, but the British government eventually began to cut back on their importation to the New World. For these reasons, a large inexpensive work force was needed. And so in the early 1600s, America's North, as Europe had already done, turned to Africa.[1773]

WHAT YOU WERE TAUGHT: There is no evidence, especially physical evidence, for Northern slavery. Therefore it did not exist.
THE TRUTH: If evidence for Northern slavery is scarce it is because, in great part, enemies of the South have suppressed it for fear that the Truth about Lincoln and his War will be revealed—as it is in this very book. However, there is another more practical reason: time.

In the late 1700s and early 1800s the white North pushed slavery South,[1774] accomplishing two goals simultaneously: it rid itself of the "naturally disgusting" and "dangerous presence" of blacks (as Lincoln variously referred to it),[1775] while maintaining the institution in order to continue reaping its huge financial profits. As *unofficial* abolition began in the North nearly 100 years before the South (as we have seen, however, the American abolition movement was born in the South),[1776] it was largely forgotten as attention was transferred to the South,

Thanks to the industrious efforts of unbiased archaeologists, massive evidence of Northern slavery is now being unearthed—much to the chagrin of Yankee and New South liberals, who would rather the truth not be known.

the most recent region in the U.S. to practice slavery.

Not only this, but scientifically speaking this means that archaeological evidence of Southern slavery is more recent, closer to the earth's surface, and thus easier to discover, while physical evidence of Northern slavery, being older, lies deeper in the ground, and its artifacts are less well preserved and more difficult to find.

Hundreds of African slave skeletons discovered on early American *Northern* farms and plantations reveal a cold fact that anti-South historians have long tried to suppress: Northern slavery was once a thriving region wide industry, with far higher rates of slave ownership than in the Old South.

Despite this problem, archaeological proof of Northern slavery is being brought to light like never before. Near Salem, Massachusetts, for instance, scientists have uncovered traces of a 13,000 acre plantation once owned by a Yankee named Samuel Browne. Near Browne's farm, one that traded its products for Caribbean rum and molasses, a massive slave cemetery was discovered, the final resting place of some 100 African-American slaves who worked there between the years 1718 and 1780.[1777]

An 8,000 acre plantation was also recently found at Shelter Island, Long Island, New York. The enormous homestead which supplied products for slave plantations in Barbados itself used slave labor: some 20 black servants lived in bondage here in the late 1600s.[1778]

With a conservative estimate of about 40,000 slaves living in New York, New Jersey, Delaware, and Pennsylvania alone in 1780, it is not surprising that an African burial ground with 420 skeletons was recently uncovered in what is now Lower Manhattan, New York. It has been estimated that between the 1690s and 1794, as many as 20,000 African slaves (including some free blacks), were buried at the site, which has since been added to the National Register of Historic Places. Today the history and recollection of those buried in this particular New York black cemetery has been preserved with a large public memorial: the "African Burial Ground National Monument."[1779]

More and more Northern slave cemeteries and slave plantations like those discussed here are being discovered and excavated each year, making it more and more difficult for the anti-South movement to hide the truth about Lincoln's War.[1780]

The ubiquitous pineapple "welcome" motif is not what it appears to be. Pro-North advocates have cleverly disguised its true origins in order to conceal what it actually represents: the North's 250 year preoccupation with African slavery.

WHAT YOU WERE TAUGHT: If Northern slavery had existed there would still be cultural traces of it.

THE TRUTH: For those who care to look, cultural vestiges of the North's "peculiar institution" are still obvious to this day, particularly in New England. One of the more conspicuous of these, as discussed earlier, is the pineapple symbol, commonly seen decorating front doors, gates, store fronts, street signs, and driveways.

Though the emblem of the pineapple is now seen as a "welcome" sign across the Northeast, this is an intentional corruption to mask its original meaning: when New England slave traders returned from their ocean expeditions to the tropics to pick up slaves, they would impale a pineapple on their fencepost to let the townspeople know that they were "welcome" to come in and shop for both slave products and for slaves themselves.[1781]

We will note that the pineapple motif, that great symbol of Yankee slavery, is still commonly seen all over the U.S., not just in the North, but in the South as well. Here, scallywags and transplanted Yankees have convinced many of the unsuspecting inhabitants of Dixie that the pineapple is an innocent emblem of friendship and hospitality. All who read this now know the truth: it is a cultural remnant of the Old North's 250 year old obsession with slavery and the slave trade.

WHAT YOU WERE TAUGHT: Northern slavery, if it truly existed, would have made more of an impact on early writers, authors, and historians, and hundreds of books would have been written on the subject. As it is, there are none.

THE TRUTH: It only seems like there "are none" because America's liberal run schools and universities refuse to teach or even acknowledge them, our politically correct bookstores refuse to sell them, our socialistic government owned public libraries refuse to stock them, and our left-leaning publishers refuse to reprint them.

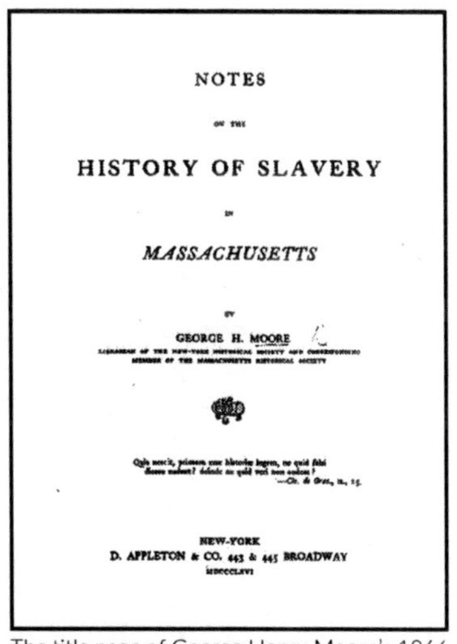

NOTES

HISTORY OF SLAVERY

MASSACHUSETTS

GEORGE H. MOORE

NEW-YORK
D. APPLETON & CO. 443 & 445 BROADWAY

The title page of George Henry Moore's 1866 work, *Notes on the History of Slavery in Massachusetts*. Anti-South proponents tell us that such books do not exist, our U.S. government-controlled public libraries refuse to stock them, and our liberal educators and professors will not teach what is in them.

Actually hundreds of pre-20th-Century and early 20th Century books *have* been written on this topic, titles such as Horace Mann's *Slavery and the Slave-Trade in the District of Columbia* (1849), Camilla Ware's *Slavery In Vermont, and in Other Parts of the United States* (1858), George H. Moore's *Notes on the History of Slavery in Massachusetts* (1866), Jeffrey R. Brackett's *The Negro in Maryland* (1889), Bernard C. Steiner's *History of Slavery in Connecticut* (1893), William D. Johnston's *Slavery in Rhode Island, 1755-1776* (1894), Henry Scofield Cooley's *A Study of Slavery in New Jersey* (1896), Ansel J. Northrup's *Slavery in New York* (1900), Edward Raymond Turner's *Slavery in Pennsylvania* (1911), and Frank U. Quillin's *The Color Line in Ohio: A History of Race Prejudice in a Typical Northern State* (1913).

The modern age has seen no let up on books that focus on Northern slavery and the Northern slave trade. These include such titles as Lorenzo Johnston Greene's *The Negro in Colonial New England, 1620-1776* (1942), Edgar J. McManus' *Black Bondage in the North* (1973), Jay Coughtry's *The Notorious Triangle: Rhode Island and the African Slave Trade, 1700-1807* (1981), Joanne Pope Melish's *Disowning Slavery: Gradual Emancipation and "Race" in New England 1780-1860* (1998), Anne Farrow, Joel Lang, and Jennifer Frank's *Complicity: How the North Promoted, Prolonged, and Profited From Slavery* (2005), and Elise Lemire's *Black Walden: Slavery and Its Aftermath in Concord, Massachusetts* (2009). The book you now hold in your hand, *Everything You Were Taught About American Slavery Is Wrong, Ask a Southerner!* (2014), is just the latest in a long line of such titles.

Taken together, the information these and scores of other similar works cover would span countless volumes and series.

One of New York's more famous slave owners, Catherine Schuyler.

We may add to this enlightening and invaluable material those bits and pieces of the historical record that have not yet been lost or suppressed. One of these is the remnants of a 1755 census taken of slaves older than 14 years of age, who lived throughout some 40 towns across the state of New York. Though hopelessly incomplete, and thus far from revealing the true scope of Northern slavery, these particular New York reports

> enumerate 2456 slaves, about one-third of the total negro population of the specified age; and they yield unusually definite data as to the scale of slaveholdings. Lewis Morris of Morrisania [New York] had twenty-nine slaves above fourteen years old; Peter DeLancy of Westchester Borough had twelve; and the following had ten each: Thomas Dongan of Staten Island, Martinus Hoffman of Dutchess County, David Jones of Oyster Bay, Rutgert Van Brunt of New Utrecht, and Isaac Willett of Westchester Borough. Seventy-two others had from five to nine each, and 1048 had still smaller holdings. *The average quota was two slaves of working age, and presumably the same number of slave children. That is to say, the typical [New York] slaveholding family had a single small family of slaves in its service.* From available data it may be confidently surmised, furthermore, that *at least one household in every ten among the eighty-three thousand white inhabitants of the colony held one or more slaves.* These two features—*the multiplicity of slaveholdings* and the virtually uniform pettiness of their scale—*constituted a [slave] regime never paralleled in equal volume elsewhere.*[1782]

Now let us take a few examples concerning the discussion of the existence of Northern slavery, the first from Mary Gay Humphreys' 1897 portrait of Albany, New York, slave owner Catherine Van Rensselaer, better known by her married name, Catherine Schuyler:

> *There was a retinue of servants attached to each of the prominent [New York] houses.* Slavery preserved in Albany in great measure its patriarchal form. *In the Schuyler household the slaves all descended from two old women brought from Africa when they were young.* Mrs. Grant gives an amusing account of the "rivalries in excellence" between these two tribes.
>
> > "Diana was determined that in no respect of excellence Maria's children should surpass hers; and Maria was equally determined that

> Diana's brood should not surpass hers. If Maria's son Prince cut down wood with more dexterity and despatch than any one in the province, the mighty Caesar, son of Diana, cut down wheat and threshed it better than he. His sister Betty, who to her misfortune was a beauty of her kind, and possessed wit equal to her beauty, was the best seamstress and laundress I have known, and plain unpretending Rachel, sister to Prince, wife to Tytus alias Tyte, and head cook, dressed dinners that might have pleased Apicius."

For every department of the household there was a slave allotted. They hoed, drilled, shod horses, made cider, raised hemp and tobacco, looked after the horses and the garden, made and mended the shoes, spun, wove, made nets, canoes, attended to the fishing, carpentering, each household sufficient unto itself. Slavery probably never took a more unobjectionable form. The negroes were treated with even familiarity; each was allowed his own garden, and was encouraged to raise pets. *As in the South, each boy had his boy, and each girl her maid who was given to her on her marriage.* Here they lived, and multiplied to old age, no slave being sold unless he proved unmanageable or to be a corrupt influence; and in this case, the threat to send the refractory one to Jamaica or the Barbadoes was usually sufficient. Later, in the more demoralizing days following the Revolution, there were negro troubles at Albany similar to those in earlier times in New York. Such a period was in 1793, when the "Bet of Philip Van Schaick, a handsome wench," and Dinah, prompted by Pomp, a favorite Albany negro, carried coals in a shoe and occasioned one of the famous fires of Albany. The two girls were tried, sentenced, and speedily executed, in accordance with the summary judgment of the times. Pomp, from his great popularity, had a stay, but subsequently suffered the same fate. [The celebration of] Pinxter, one of the three Dutch fetes of the year, belonged to the negroes. It was observed the Monday following Whitsunday, and generally continued through the week. There was a colored harlequin. For many years this was personated by a well-known Guinea negro known as King Charley. Dressed in a cast-off coat of the military, decked out with colored ribbons, his legs bare and a little black hat with a pompon on one side, he was seated on a hollow log, which had each end covered with skins and served as a drum for dancing. Other negroes had eel pots covered with skin which they beat with their hands while they sang a song that had a refrain "Hi-a bomba bomba," which it was supposed was brought over from Africa. To this music the negroes danced. There were also gingerbread booths and side shows, and under the charge of the elderly women all the young gentry were taken out to see the sights.[1783]

New Yorkers loved their slaves, and when they could not procure them fast enough they simply enslaved any free black who happened to be passing by. Such was the fate that befell this unfortunate free black man in New York City in 1836, nine years after the institution was allegedly "abolished" in the state in 1827. Though illegal, police seldom arrested those who practiced this heinous injustice. The exact number of free blacks who were enslaved, or just as often reenslaved, in New York and the rest of the North is not known, but it was easily in the tens of thousands.

Our second sample on the reality of Northern slavery also comes from a 19th-Century work pertaining to the Empire State: Joseph Shannon's *Manual of the Corporation of the City of New York*, written in 1869:

> *The institution of slavery, as it existed in early times in New York, was a source of constant anxiety to the inhabitants of this city*, arising from the turbulent character of that class of the population. This arose partly from the fact that *the slave trade was then in active operation, and New York city was the mart from whence the other parts of the colony were supplied*. A slave market was established where the imported negroes were exposed for sale, and where other slaves stood for hire. The negroes, when newly arrived, were ill at ease, and differed greatly from the same class who had been born on the soil. Ignorant of the language of the country, and unused to labor in the fields, and to the restraint under which they were held, the imported negroes were disposed to deeds of desperate outrage, reckless of the fact that no good result to them could arise from their wild endeavors to rid themselves of thraldom. Their known dispositions, however, excited fear, which was kept alive by the

occasional murders in different parts of the country, and especially by various plots of still more serious nature.

Among these was one in the spring of 1712. At this time a combination of from thirty to fifty newly-imported negroes was formed, with the intention to make a general assault upon the town. Their plans were laid with secresy, and do not appear to have been suspected before they were ripe for execution. The design appears to have been simply to murder the people and burn the town, and the time selected for beginning their bloody work was midnight of the 6th of April, 1712. The method adopted was to set fire to a house and await the coming forth of the inmates, when they, as well as others who came to quench the flames, were to be killed. The negroes were well armed, while it might reasonably be expected that citizens aroused from their slumbers by the cry of fire would be defenseless. The alarm took place at about two o'clock, and the whole town was at once in uproar. Upon reaching the burning house one citizen after another was dispatched until those numbered among the killed and mortally wounded amounted to about twenty persons. The cry of murder, added to the general din, soon changed the character of the affray. The citizens speedily armed and charged upon the blacks, who, after a brief resistance, fled to the woods, pursued by the excited crowd of whites. Meantime, as morning broke, the whole town was placed under arms under apprehension that the conspiracy was more generally diffused, and that there was danger of a general uprising of the slave population.

This state of things continued several days, in the course of which a large number of suspected negroes were arrested in the town, while the hunt was being continued throughout the forest, with which nearly all the upper part of Manhattan Island was then covered. These wild fastnesses offered peculiar facilities for concealment, as their rocks and caves were almost unapproachable. The negroes, however, had no friends to whom they could fly for ultimate safety, and starvation brought them forth from their hiding-places.

Some of these misguided persons committed suicide in the woods, using for that purpose the arms which they had brought with them. *Others were taken, and were brought to summary punishment in the most tormenting manner; some by burning at the stake; others by being broken on the wheel; and others by being hung up alive.* No leniency was shown to any who were known to have been in any way cognizant of the plot. Self-preservation was felt to exist in putting the abject race in fear, and thus extreme measures were resorted to without stint.

The horrors of that event long dwelt as a cause of disquiet

> to the townspeople, and occasioned a morbid subject of household gossip, until the minds of the inhabitants became infected with one ever-existing apprehension—that of a negro plot. The influence of this state of feeling affected even the best classes of the population [of New York], so that in the course of a generation afterward, upon the happening of some suspicious circumstances, as to which the proof in the light of history appears entirely inadequate to sustain the grave accusations, *hundreds of the negro race were visited with terrible punishment.*[1784]

Let us compare all of this with the treatment of slaves in the early 19th-Century South, as noted by Yankee author Joseph Holt Ingraham:

> [White] Northerners are entirely unaccustomed to their [slaves'] habits, which are perfectly understood and appreciated by [white] Southerners, who have been familiar with Africans from childhood; whom they have had for their nurses, playmates, and "bearers"; and between whom and themselves a reciprocal and *very natural attachment exists, which, on the gentleman's part, involuntarily extends to the whole coloured race, exhibited in a kindly feeling and condescending familiarity, for which he receives gratitude in return. On the part of the slave, this attachment is manifested by an affection and faithfulness which only cease with life.* Of this state of feeling, which a Southern life and education can only give, *the Northerner knows nothing. . . . The slave always prefers a Southern master, because he knows he will be understood by him.* His kindly feelings towards, and his sympathies with slaves, as such, are as honourable to his heart as gratifying to the subjects of them. He treats with suitable allowance those peculiarities of the race, which the unpractised Northerner will construe into idleness, obstinacy, revenge, or hatred.[1785]

WHAT YOU WERE TAUGHT: The North should be given full credit, as well as the nation's eternal approval, honor, and acknowledgment, for its great humanitarian act of abolishing slavery.
THE TRUTH: Writing in 1846, Southern historian Matthew Estes addressed this falsehood head on:

> Our Northern friends take great credit to themselves for abolishing slavery as though they had accomplished some wonderful work. But is it true that they practically abolished slavery? It is true, that most of the old States at the North passed laws abolishing slavery, but *when the time arrived for those laws to take effect there was no slavery*

> *to abolish. Persons owning slaves, with but few exceptions, just as soon as the agitation of the subject commenced, sent them off to the South and sold them*—hence as [Alexis] de Tocqueville has very justly said [in 1832], *"though the Northern States have passed laws abolishing slavery, no actual abolition has taken place."*
>
> *Another fact in connection with negro slavery at the North is, that it could never be made profitable there. It was very early ascertained that the region was not adapted to the constitution of the negro—hence one of the causes of the great mortality among the blacks at the North.* Nor is the North adapted to the growth of those products in the cultivation of which slave labor is most profitable [e.g., cotton]. *From this it appears that our Northern friends are entitled to no particular credit for abolishing slavery; they almost invariably sold their negroes before the law could take effect which they had passed abolishing slavery.*[1786]

In other words, Yankees rid themselves of slavery for almost every reason *except* a humanitarian one.

The American North prides itself in being the nation's "birthplace of abolition," as well as the region which elected the man they call the "Great Emancipator," our sixteenth president, Abraham Lincoln. Not only was the North not the birthplace of abolition and Lincoln not the Great Emancipator, but, as eyewitnesses living at the time rightly observed, Northerners finally only destroyed slavery in their region because of its hilly, rocky, sandy soil, long cold winters, and entrenched Yankee racism. After pushing the institution southward, the North continued its heavy involvement with the slave trade and slavery, though now more surreptitiously, still greatly profiting from both.

WHAT YOU WERE TAUGHT: Millions of Southern slaves were saved by the Underground Railroad, which allowed them to flee North and escape the horrors of the South's "peculiar institution." Canada was the preferred final destination, since it was an abolitionist nation from the beginning and had never known slavery.

THE TRUTH: Though the Underground Railroad functioned throughout most of the War, only about 2,000 slaves (just 500 servants a year) out of 4.5 million (North and South) availed themselves of it—a mere 0.04 percent of the total.[1787] Some reckon there were as many as 4,000 total (1,000 Southern slaves a year)[1788]—only 0.08 percent of the total.[1789]

There was no actual "Underground Railroad," of course, for it was not underground, it was not a railroad, and it was not secret. There were no "hidden tunnels." It was not even organized. There were no set roads, routes, or stopping stations, nor were there "thousands of agents," as Yankee mythologists maintain. The entire so-called "underground system" turns out to be nothing but a few sporadic groups of whites and blacks scattered throughout the North who wanted to help escaped slaves in their bid for freedom—none who came from the Deep South, by the way, but more typically from Maryland and Delaware, as well as the Border States. Here, at a port in Camden, New Jersey, a family of runaway slaves is being secretly deboarded from a steamboat at night, while an assistant blocks the attempts of a passenger trying to interfere. The family will be transported to the next "station" (that is, whoever will take them in temporarily), and from there sent northward to a concealed location in Canada.

Either way, according to scholarly studies, antebellum Southern slaves did not use the Railroad: the fugitive slaves that passed through New York, for instance, all came from Maryland and Delaware. Black

Southern escapees preferred staying in Dixie, simply disappearing into the anonymity of the big Southern cities where they easily merged with the large free black population.[1790] (This is not surprising: even after Lincoln's Final Emancipation Proclamation was issued, 95 percent of all Southern slaves voluntarily stayed at home in Dixie, defending both their owners' farms, and the owners themselves, from marauding Yanks.)[1791]

It is telling that the definitive early source on the railroad, William Still's 1872 book, *The Underground Railroad: A Record of Facts, Authentic Narratives, Letters, Etc.*, features not millions, not thousands, not even hundreds, but a mere handful of black slaves who were, as the author phrases it, "plucked from the jaws of slavery" via this particular method. And nearly all of these testimonials are of single individuals, with the exception of a few rare slave groups usually comprising no more than four to six people.[1792]

Out of 4.5 million Northern and Southern slaves in 1861, only some 2,000—like this one, who escaped detection in a shipping box—ever used the Underground Railroad. Ineffective, disorganized, and inefficient, it served mainly as a psychological crutch for a few Yankee liberals and abolitionists who wanted to believe that they were helping to end slavery.

Another 19th-Century authority on the subject, Wilbur H. Siebert, believed that tens of thousands of fugitive slaves had escaped to Canada, but admitted that he had no proof, and that the Census only records 4,669 of such individuals: 2,502 black males and 2,167 black females.[1793] But not even these statistics have turned out to be accurate.

As to the comment about Canada, that country did not exist during Lincoln's War: it was founded on July 1, 1867, two years after the conflict's cessation. Up until that year the region had been owned by various countries, including France, Spain, and Britain.

It is true that what is now Canada was free of slavery during our "Civil War," or as we in the American South like to call it, our "Second War for Southern Independence" (1861-1865). However, if those American slaves who traveled north on the Underground Railroad had tried to enter the area just 27 years earlier, they might have found themselves enslaved a second time. This is because slavery was practiced throughout all of Canada for hundreds of years prior to its founding.

In particular was the area known as New France (1534-1763), where Native-Americans were used as slaves, and where Africans had long been imported in order to invigorate the economy. African slavery came to Nova Scotia in 1749, and it was found in Quebec, New Brunswick, and Prince Edward Island before 1780. What should be called "Canadian slavery" did not end legally until August 1, 1834, the day the British Emancipation Act was implemented.[1794]

Most American black slaves seeking freedom in Canada made the attempt on their own, not via the Underground Railroad. This runaway slave was in the process of fleeing his owner's plantation in Rhode Island when a New England slave catcher and his dogs caught up with him.

In any discussion of the Underground Railroad and Canada, we must also consider that many Northern American states possessed laws that sought to prevent slaves from escaping to Canada. One of these was New York, which in 1705 issued a statute providing the death penalty for any slave caught traveling more than 40 miles north of Albany.[1795]

In the end, as nearly all enslaved American blacks seeking freedom did so on their own and without any assistance, the so-called "Underground Railroad" was little more than a morale booster for abolitionists as opposed to an actual effective escape system for slaves.[1796]

Anti-South historians tell us that "all Southern blacks were slaves." The truth is that in 1860, of Dixie's 4 million blacks, at least 500,000 of them, or 12.5 percent, were free, many of them owners of black slaves themselves. These three well dressed, well fed, obviously well contented Southern blacks were among the hundreds of thousands of free African-Americans who thrived for centuries across the Old South, decimating Northern myth to the contrary.

10

THE MASTER-SLAVE RELATIONSHIP IN THE SOUTH

WHAT YOU WERE TAUGHT: The relationship between Southern slaves and their masters was unhappy, unhealthy, abusive, and exploitive. **THE TRUTH:** Slave-master relationships were much the same as today's employee-employer relationships: most were productive, some were not. The facts are that the majority of Southern owners and their slaves had what can only be called warm relations, in many cases bordering on deep familial love, wherein whites and blacks considered each other "family." So close were they that on the typical Southern plantation both races hunted and fished together, celebrated holidays together, and attended sports events and church together.[1797]

In 1908, Luther W. Hopkins, a former Confederate soldier in Jeb Stuart's cavalry, wrote the following, revealing the true nature of the slave-master relationship across the South in the mid 1800s:

> *There was a peculiar relationship existing between the slave owner's family and the slaves that the North never did and never will understand. On the part of the white children it was love, pure and simple, for the slave, while on the part of the adult it was more than friendship, and, I might add, the feeling was reciprocated by the slaves.* The children addressed the adult blacks as Uncle and Aunt, and treated them with as much respect

as they did their blood relatives. It was Uncle Reuben and Aunt Dinah. The adult white also addressed the older colored people in the same way. *With but few exceptions, the two races lived together in perfect harmony. If a slave-owner was cruel to his slaves, it was because he was a cruel man, and all who came in contact with him, both man and beast, suffered at his hands.* Even his children did not escape. Such men are found everywhere. *The old black mammy, with her head tied up in a white cloth, was loved, respected and honored by every inmate of the home, regardless of color.*

An integral part of all large Southern plantations, the authoritarian mammy was both respected and adored. She sometimes wielded more power than the white mistress of the house, and was considered a true member of the family. Her commission covered a wide range of household duties, from rearing the owner's children to managing the other servants. This former mammy, known as Mammy Prater, was 115 years old at the time this photograph was taken, many years after Lincoln's War.

The following incident will be of interest: Hon. John Randolph Tucker, one of Virginia's most gifted and learned sons, who represented his State in the U.S. Congress, always celebrated

> his birthday. I remember to have attended one of these celebrations. It was shortly after the close of the war. Mr. Tucker was then between forty-five and fifty years of age. He had grown children. Fun making was one of his characteristics. On these annual occasions, it was his custom to dress himself in a long white gown and bring into the parlor his old black nurse, whom he called "mammy." She sat in her rocking-chair with her head tied up in the conventional snow-white cloth. Mr. Tucker, dressed up as a child in his nightgown, would toddle in and climb up into her lap, and she would lull him to sleep with an old time nursery song, no doubt one of her own compositions. This could not possibly have occurred had the skin of his nurse been white.
>
> When a daughter married and set up her own home, fortunate was she if she took with her the mammy. In many homes the slaves were present at family prayers. The kitchen and the cabin furnished the white children places of resort that were full of pleasure.
>
> This was the relation between white and colored as I remember it from a child in my part of Virginia. And tonight, as I write these lines, while the clock tolls off the hour of eleven, I cannot keep out of my mind the words of that little poem by Elizabeth Akers:
>
> > "Backward, turn backward, oh time in thy flight, and make me a child again, just for tonight."
>
> *How anyone could have desired to break up this happy relationship was beyond the conception of the child, and more or less incomprehensible to the adult.*[1798]

We know from family journals, travel logs, letters, and legal documents that most white Southern slave owners referred to their black charges as "servants," not "slaves," and that they considered them "a part of the family." Contrary to what our Northern influenced text books teach, this was the norm across the South. Mary Chesnut said that their black housekeeper and children's nurse, Mammy Baldwin, was always loved, cared for, and looked upon as one of the family.[1799]

This sentiment was always mutual and returned in kind. Indeed, most Southerners, both European and African, came to feel that they had two families: a white one and a black one, a relationship often marked by the most heartfelt tenderness and authentic love.[1800] When white plantation owner and onetime slaveholder Thomas Dabney died in the late 1800s, his former body servant George Page wrote back to one of Dabney's daughters:

> He was a good master to us all [i.e., both blacks and whites]. You are all my children, and I love you all alike.[1801]

This happy Southern servant girl, shown here caring for one of her master's children, was typical on slave plantations, not atypical, as anti-South historians preach. The relationship between black female servants and their white female owners was so close that, if necessary, both would breast-feed each other's infants. Such relationships created extremely personal kinship bonds between Southern whites and blacks, particularly among the women, something virtually unknown among the white slave owning families in the Old North.

This type of relationship existed in the South from the earliest days of colonial America right up until Lincoln's War. On June 8, 1845, for instance, as President Andrew Jackson lay near death at his Tennessee home, the Hermitage, anguished family members and weeping black servants surrounded his bed, listening intently as the dying Southerner uttered his last wish: "I hope to meet you all again one day in Heaven: both white and black."[1802]

Many of the letters that white Southern slave owners sent home from the battlefield were addressed to both their white biological family and their black servant family. Indeed, it was perfectly normal for a white Reb to tenderly inquire as to the general well-being of the African-Americans back at his farm, "my black family," as he would commonly refer to them.[1803] Similarly, Southern white civilians used the phrase, "my family—black and white," on a routine basis.[1804]

Even pro-North, anti-South writers have been forced to

acknowledge that intimate bonds of affection did in fact develop between the two races;[1805] that typically servants were made to feel like members of the owners' family, essentially becoming part of their white kinship group[1806]—that is, as part of the owner's extended family;[1807] and that there were innumerable cases of lifelong relationships built around love and mutual respect between Southern slave owners and their chattel.[1808]

So beloved were Southern servants that often white communities banded together to raise the money to purchase and free them. Such was the case of Mobile, Alabama, slave Pierre Chastang who, "in recognition of public services in the war of 1812 and the yellow fever epidemic of 1819 was bought and freed by popular subscription." A Georgia slave named Sam was freed in 1834 by the state legislature for stopping a fire that threatened to burn down the state capitol building. The cost for Sam's emancipation was $1,800 (about $50,000 in today's currency), which was happily paid for by Georgia's white taxpayers.[1809]

One of the more renowned emancipations of this type was that which concerned a Mississippi slave nicknamed the "Prince of Slaves," or "Prince" for short. In his previous life Prince had been a high-ranking member of the Timbo people in Africa, where his name had been Abdul Rahman Ibrahim Ibn Sori. Though he was the son of a Timbo king, he had been captured by fellow Africans during a local war, then bartered to Yankee slave traders, after which he was transported to America and sold South. In the early 1800s he pleaded his case for freedom. Kentucky slaveholder Henry Clay and many others came to Prince's defense, and eventually his kindly owner freed him at great financial loss. When it was discovered that Prince's wife was still enslaved, the citizens of Natchez, Mississippi, generously raised the funds for her purchase as well, with additional money for a "flowing Moorish costume in which Prince was promptly arrayed." In 1828 the couple sailed off to Morocco, all expenses paid.[1810]

Such situations were not exceptional in the Old South, nor were they confined to enslaved blacks. As Phillips writes:

> *Each [Southern] locality was likely to have some outstanding [black] figure. . . .* In Georgia the most notable was [a free black man named] Austin Dabney, who as a mulatto youth served in the Revolutionary army and attached himself ever afterward to the white family who saved his life when he had been wounded in

> battle. The Georgia legislature by special act gave him a farm; he was welcomed in the tavern circle of chatting lawyers whenever his favorite Judge Dooly held court at his home village; and once when the formality of drawing his pension carried him to Savannah the governor of the state, seeing him pass, dragged him from his horse and quartered him as a guest in his house.[1811]

Pro-North historians never mention these wonderful interracial acts of Southern kindness, for they do not want you to know that most Southern European-Americans respected and even loved the African-Americans who lived and worked among them. Such was certainly the case with New Orleans slaveholder John McDonogh, who emancipated his entire slave force in 1842. His parting words to them were: "I can say with truth and heartfelt satisfaction that a more virtuous people does not exist in any country."[1812]

Mammy Harriet, a loyal and beloved servant, worked in the household of slave owner Thomas Dabney for many years.

It was indeed often said of the Old South that there were "many ties of affection between the races."[1813] Yankee antislavery advocate Dr. Ethan Allen Andrews admitted that many people fail

> to estimate properly the amount of happiness occasioned by the mutual affection between the [Southern] white and the colored members of the same family.[1814]

During his travels in the South in the late 1850s, New Yorker Anson De Puy Van Buren observed the following incident on a Mississippi plantation:

> The next day, I was witness to a really affecting scene; one that remained very vividly impressed upon my mind. Major W. and his brother-in-law, Mr. H., had held, for many years, their slaves in conjunction; working them on the same plantation. To-day, Mr. H. was to take his slaves to a plantation he had recently purchased, in another part of the State. Major W., his lady and family, went out, as the negroes stopped at the gate, to bid them good-bye. *They shook hands with them one by one, as they passed on, and cried as if their*

> *own children, brothers and sisters, were leaving home. The family, negroes and all, were in tears.* But poor old Eastern—uncle Eastern, as the children always call him—he too was to go. He had been the faithful servant in the W. family for many, very many years. But he had built their fires for the last time. And all the kind acts and offices he had performed for the family, which had bound him to them during a service going back to the earliest childhood of the oldest of the household, were now to cease.
>
> This faithful old Eumaeus [in Greek mythology the loyal servant of Odysseus], shook hands and bade his master and mistress, and all the children, good-bye, with eyes suffused with tears, and voice too full for utterance. They all wept. He was truly the fitting one to close so affecting a scene.[1815]

Such warm sentiments between the races were almost always lifelong. When a famous Georgia planter was writing out his will in 1817, he included the following clause regarding his black servants:

> It is my most ardent desire that in whatsoever hands fortune may place said negroes, that all the justice and indulgence may be shown them that is consistent with a state of slavery. I flatter myself with the hope that none of my relations or connections will be so ungrateful to my memory as to treat or use them otherwise.[1816]

These types of relationships help explain why in so many instances when Union armies invaded a Southern town, black servants fled with their white families rather than into the arms of the enemy. Even in those rare situations where blacks did seek refuge with the advancing Union armies, loyalty and devotion to their white "brothers and sisters" often continued. In one such incident, at the Battle of Sharpsburg (Antietam to Yanks) on September 17, 1862, eyewitnesses reported a Southern black slave who pulled his injured white owner to safety before sprinting across a field through gunfire and into the Federal line.[1817]

We have other indications concerning the true relationship between whites and blacks in the Old South. There is the example of a black female servant named Maria Otey,[1818] who worked at Carnton Plantation in Franklin, Tennessee. The personal maid of the plantation's mistress, Carrie (Winder) McGavock, Maria raised three generations of McGavock children, then voluntarily returned to Carnton from Alabama after the War to continue working for the family, this time as a paid employee. The freedwoman would hardly have come back to the McGavocks' plantation had she been abused or seen other servants abused there.[1819]

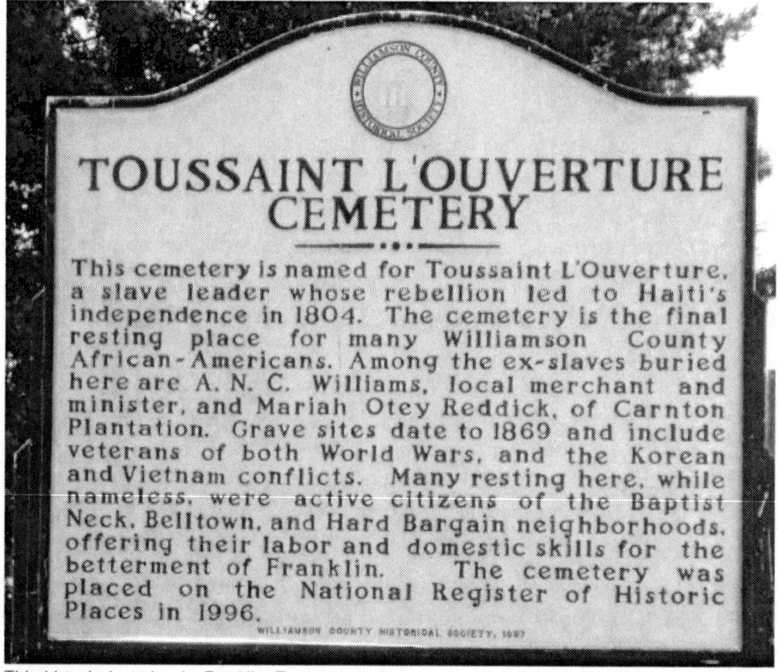

This historical marker in Franklin, Tennessee, photographed by the author, mentions Maria Otey Reddick, the famous servant of the McGavock family of Carnton Plantation. Like literally millions of other Southern slaves, Maria faithfully served her white family before, during, and after Lincoln's War.

Maria, who married another black servant, Bolling Reddick (of Virginia),[1820] and who was thereafter known as "Maria Reddick," bore eight children at the plantation.[1821] As a result she had her own long and interesting history at Carnton. As late as 1971 there were still living individuals who could recall the image of Maria quietly sewing, sitting and talking with other Franklin women, or reminiscing about the good old days before the "late unpleasantness," as many Southerners still refer to Lincoln's War.[1822]

Maria had begun as a servant of Carrie's father Colonel Van Perkins Winder, Sr. in Louisiana.[1823] On Carrie's marriage to John W.

McGavock in 1848, Mr. Winder gave the 16 year old African-American from Mississippi to Carrie as a wedding gift.[1824]

The author's photo of Carnton Mansion's back porticos.

Maria was so devoted to the McGavock family that she gave the eulogy at Carrie's funeral in 1905, then stayed on to work for the family until 1919, eight years after the last McGavock sold Carnton and moved out. Maria, who is buried in Franklin's Toussaint L'Ouverture (African-American) Cemetery,[1825] dedicated 71 years of her life to serving the McGavocks, longer than most of the McGavocks themselves lived.[1826]

WHAT YOU WERE TAUGHT: The "beloved" mammy, who supposedly adored her "white family" as much as her black one, is just another fabrication of Southern myth. There was no such thing. All black female slaves detested their white owners, who in return were loathed, degraded, abused, and exploited by them.

THE TRUTH: The mammy was no fictional anti-black stereotype, as the North falsely asserts. An actual foster mother rather than just a type of "nurse," many a white Southern youngster grew from childhood into adulthood under the mammy's eagle-eyed daily supervision. Fans of Margaret Mitchell's book and film *Gone With the Wind* will be very familiar with the indispensable African-American mammy, one integral to 19th-Century Southern culture and much beloved by Victorian white Southerners.

The mammy, who typically lived in a cabin near the "big house," was chosen for her loving, maternal, even-tempered personality, and was always considered by her white owners to be a virtual member of their own family.[1827] Given a wide range of powers over the mansion and its occupants, she had an authentic fondness for her white "chillun," and was sometimes perceived as being more devoted to them than to her own offspring.[1828]

So close was the mammy to the master's and mistress' offspring that it was usually she who they would turn to for love and security, not their real mother. For the mammy not only socialized the children, but she also often ran the household, interceded with parents on the children's behalf, punished the children for misbehaving, washed and dressed them, told them bedtime stories, sang them songs, rocked them to sleep, and even breast-fed them when necessary.[1829] Little wonder that white children often voluntarily spent more time with their mammy than with their biological mothers.[1830]

Just as they would with biological family members, Southern slave owners shared in all the joys and despairs, successes and failures, of their black servants. The two groups were not considered separate, but rather one great extended family, made up of white and black "kinfolk." Here a white master and mistress console their mammy after she is told that one of her relatives has been in a serious accident.

So common was the need for lactating mammies (known as "black wet nurses") that white families routinely ran ads in local newspapers for them. And the lack of prejudice ran both ways: white Southern mistresses, many from the middle- and upper-classes, were also known to breast-feed the infant children of their black servants. Like the white children who were nursed by black mammies, blacks who were breast-fed by whites also referred to them as "Ma." This sharing in the role of infant nurturer enabled Southern white and black women to form female bonds wholly unknown among whites and blacks in the North. Much of the world Mitchell depicted was indeed real, not a wishful dream world as anti-South proponents proclaim.[1831]

Though today the uninformed North and New South consider her an "invented racist stereotype" from a "dark chapter in America's past," at least up until the year 1923 the black mammy was still held in high esteem by Southern whites.

It was in that year that several Southern senators proposed the erection of a monument called "The Black Mammy of the South," in Washington, D.C. The reasoning behind the statue was wholly honorific: recognition of the mammy's many contributions to the South, as well as her image as the embodiment of love, devotion, and faithfulness. But Washington, D.C.'s Black Mammy statue never materialized. Soon after the monument's proposal the idea was permanently shelved out of respect for the sensitivities of African-Americans, most who apparently saw her as a disgraceful reminder that they descend from slaves owned by whites.[1832]

This is unfortunate. For while it is perhaps understandable—given the universal dissemination of the North's skewed anti-South version of the "Civil War"—that some blacks today harbor a deep resentment toward whites over slavery, it is not justifiable. For one thing, such individuals completely ignore the reality of America's tens of thousands of black, brown, and red slave owners. They also disregard their own native African, slave owning ancestors, without whose contributions American slavery could have never been created in the first place.

Additionally, as this very book shows, the earliest recorded slavers and slaves were both white. And let us not forget that the entire world once operated on and around slavery, an institution that has been endemic to nearly every known people, race, and society since the beginning of time. This is why, in 1927, pro-North historian Hendrik Willem Van Loon urged his fellow Yankees to stop condemning Southerners for keeping slaves. "For slavery has existed," he observed, "across the entire globe since humans first became bipedal."[1833]

After emancipation, the Dabney family's black matriarch Mammy Maria did what millions of other black servants did: she remained on the plantation with her white family. Mississippi girl Susan Dabney Smedes, the daughter of the estate's owner Thomas Dabney, recorded the transformation for posterity:

> In this time of change and discouragement Mammy Maria's strong, true love for the house showed itself, and was indeed a help and support. *She had never in her life received what could be called an order from any younger member of the family. To her everything was put in the form of a request.* She was too much beloved for any one of her "white children" to wish to alter this relationship now. But mammy decided herself on changing her manner to us. Instead of her independent way of letting us know her views, and *expecting us to follow her advice*, she addressed her young mistresses in a manner marked by the most studied deference. The slightest expressed wish, though couched as ever in the form of a request, was a command to mammy, and was obeyed with more punctilious exactness than if it had come from the father or mother. She and they had been *bons camarades* ["good friends"] many a year together, and understood each other,—*there was no need to obey strictly, or to obey at all, if she saw a better way.* But here was a different state of things,—here was upheaval and rebellion. The servants hardly meant it so; most of it was thoughtlessness on their part, but the result was discomfort and perplexity to mammy's "white children." Her loyal heart showed her this way of giving comfort to us.[1834]

Modern African-Americans themselves would do well to consider the manner in which their own 19th-Century American ancestors saw the situation between whites and blacks. Thanks to the insidious lies propounded by pro-North writers, 21st-Century blacks are filled with countless misconceptions about what actually went on in the Old South. The following sample from the period is reality, not fantasy.

On September 29, 1865, just five months after Lincoln's War came to an end at Appomattox, a group of North Carolina blacks held a "Negro Convention" that issued the following declaration:

> Born upon the same soil and brought up in an intimacy of relationship unknown in any other state of Society, we have formed attachments for the white race which must be as enduring as life.[1835]

As authentic history attests, this was a view that millions of fellow Southern blacks could relate to.

The Southern mammy has long been vilified by the unenlightened. But the truth about her place in Southern history cannot be erased, and her vital role in Southern culture cannot be obliterated. While the blinkered, the biased, and the uneducated will continue to slander her, those who know the facts will always hold the mammy and her honorific role in the highest esteem.

According to copious eyewitness accounts, Union soldiers were prone to the brutal treatment of Southerners, particularly white and black women. Among the many outrages they committed against Dixie's "fairer sex" were harassment, molestation, beatings, whippings, rape, and murder. Freed black females were sometimes reenslaved by particularly cruel Yankee officers, while Southern black servant women were often torn from their homes and physically coerced into slave labor in Federal military camps. Here the home of a Southern white woman, whose husband and sons are off fighting in the Confederate army, has been illegally entered by a group of belligerent and menacing Union soldiers. Her house furnishings will be destroyed, her black servants kidnaped, and she herself violated. More than likely her house will be burned to the ground. Though they clearly violated the Geneva Conventions, the U.S. government virtually ignored these types of war crimes, and compensation was never given to Southern families for the destruction of their homes, farms, property, and lives, making a mockery of the Yankees' so-called "Reconstruction" program.

11

THE NORTHERN MYTH OF SOUTHERN SLAVE ABUSE

WHAT YOU WERE TAUGHT: Because there were no laws protecting slaves in the South, Southern slave owners were often extremely cruel, and daily whipped, beat, mutilated, raped, tortured, and even murdered their human chattel without fear of reprisal. Southern slaves were beaten with chains, hanged, burned to death, locked in cages, and hung on meat hooks on a regular basis.

THE TRUTH: None of this is true, at least it was not true of the Old South. The region where such outrages were most likely to be committed was in the Old North. In New York, for example, where a 1702 law authorized masters to chastise their human chattel at their own discretion,[1836] slaves convicted of heinous crimes, such as murder, were subject to all manner of hideous fates. These included being "burned at the stake," "gibbeted alive," and "broken on the wheel." This is precisely what occurred in 1712, when New York authorities hanged 13 slaves, burned four of them alive (one over a "slow fire"), "broke" one on the wheel,[1837] and left another to starve to death chained to the floor.[1838]

In 1741 the Empire State executed 31 blacks:[1839] 13 were burned at the stake, 18 were hanged, while another 71 were transported out of state.[1840] On another occasion a New York slave named Tom, found guilty of killing two people, was ordered to be "roasted over a slow fire so that he will suffer in torment for at least eight to ten hours."[1841] Such executions were often performed in public, in full view of ordinary New Yorkers. While this was going on, Southern states like South Carolina were banning the public punishment of blacks. The naturally humanitarian Southerner found such scenes "distressing," quite unlike his more thick-skinned Yankee compatriot to the North.[1842]

As is clear from this old illustration, there was nothing many 18th-Century white New Yorkers enjoyed more than a public slave burning. This African victim was found guilty of theft. After being branded and then tortured for several hours, he was tied to a stake in the town square and set alight. Even young children were taken to view public slave executions, a not uncommon spectacle in the Old North. In 1741 alone New York burned 13 black slaves at the stake.

Pennsylvania—a state whose founder William Penn was a well-known slave owner[1843]—liked to brand, castrate, and hang its black criminals,[1844] while New Jersey preferred cutting off the ears of its African outlaws or burning them at the stake (even for "ordinary crimes").[1845] But it was New York that took the prize for the most sadistic punishments by adding psychological torment to their penalties.[1846]

In one famous case in 1708, a black New York female was tied down and burned alive with a bucket of cool water suspended in front of her face. In another case two New York slaves were convicted of murdering a white family. One was roasted over a "slow fire," the other was impaled on a spear then hung, while still alive, in chains to extend his misery for as long as possible.[1847] It could take as long as ten hours for death to come. The fire was left to burn until the body was "consumed to ashes," an attempt to further frighten potential black criminals in the crowd.[1848] When there were too many African outlaws to contend with at one time, New York simply shipped them south, which is precisely what it did in 1816 when it sent 40 of its slave convicts to New Orleans—"much to the disquiet of the Louisiana authorities."[1849]

Not to be outdone by her Northern neighbors, Massachusetts was writing up and enforcing particularly severe laws against blacks as early as the 1600s. In 1681, for instance, Maria, a female slave from Roxbury who confessed to arson, was sentenced by Governor Thomas Hinckley to be immediately taken from the court and burned alive. Around the same time Jack, a black male slave from Weathersfield, was also convicted of arson. Though his "crime" was accidental not intentional, he was sent to the gallows, after which his body was thrown onto Maria's fire and "burned to ashes."[1850]

Thousands of such examples could be given.

As for the horrific, bestial, and sickening form of *Southern* slavery depicted in fictitious books like *Uncle Tom's Cabin*, this never occurred anywhere in everyday life in Dixie. The very idea of this kind of depraved slavery came from the overly agitated imaginations of sentimental novelists and South-loathing, antislavery activists who cared more about abolishing slavery and deporting blacks out of the country than the facts. Andrews wrote that those Northerners who thought of Southern "slavery only as a system of whips and fetters—of unfeeling tyranny, on the one part, and of fear mingled with hatred, on the other," were wholly misled. This being

> the usual picture of slavery which is presented to the people of North . . . it is no wonder that Southern masters, who know how wide from the truth this representation is, are not particularly ready to listen to the counsel of those, whom they perceive to be so ill-informed on the subject.[1851]

This Massachusetts slave is being punished for accidently breaking a farm tool. Yankees, descendants of intolerant English Puritans, believed that a severe penalty for minor offences, even unintentional ones, was the best method of controlling their slaves. In the more easy going South, where the slave laws were lax and master and slave were more likely to be friends, such punishments were almost unheard of.

Were there inhumane Southern slave owners and slave traders? Of course. There are unthinking vicious people in every type of business. Were there slave owners who were racists? No question.

Racists of every color exist in every occupation. Were there atrocities committed on Southern farms? Absolutely. Some blacks were mistreated and some did indeed suffer torture, rape, and death at the hands of their deranged owners. These incidents are well-known and have been repeated in thousands of anti-South books for generations. And they are still being peddled today by rabid South-haters.

What the readers of these works are not told is that not only did such incidents also occur in the North, but in the South they were the rare exception rather than the common rule, just as they are in today's business world. For as Chesnut wisely intimated, a man who was cruel to his servants was a man who was capable of being cruel to anyone, black or white, enslaved or free.[1852] Estes observed that a

> passionate, ill-tempered man, not being able to govern himself, cannot of course be expected to govern others. Such persons are unfit to govern any one; they always govern their families badly, and their negroes are always turbulent, disobedient, and unruly.[1853]

Let us be clear. The type of person who commits such crimes is suffering from an illness known as antisocial personality disorder (APD), or what is popularly known as sociopathy or psychopathy, a mental disease that is rare in every time period and in every society. In 1908 British physician Joseph Shaw Bolton, M.D., reckoned that only about 2 percent of the general population can be classified as psychopathic.[1854]

APD is a disease in which the afflicted individual (a sociopath or psychopath) operates without a conscience, without empathy, and subsequently without remorse, viewing others as mere objects to be exploited and manipulated for personal gain and pleasure.[1855] Such people may be adjudged legally insane, for they are both a liability and a menace to society.[1856] To re-emphasize, this serious form of psychosis is uncommon today, just as it was uncommon in the mid-1800s.

Those few psychopaths who were involved in inhumane slaving practices in the South were strongly condemned by all thinking Southerners and, whenever possible, were arrested, tried, convicted, and imprisoned. The most serious offenders were executed.

We should also bear in mind that white-on-white violence (like black-on-black violence) was far more common than white-on-black violence. In other words, antisocial whites were far more likely to physically abuse other whites than blacks.[1857] To believe otherwise, as Northern myth has asserted for decades, is not only illogical and ridiculous, it is also not supported by the historical record.

When a Southern slave owner was put in the extraordinarily rare position where force was needed (such as with a violent and aggressive servant), he was not motivated by innate cruelty, by sadistic tendencies, or by APD. He was motivated by the same thing that motivates modern free labor bosses: the desire for maximum profits.[1858] After all, the slave owner was, as every unbiased study has shown, a "rational capitalist" whose primary interest was the profit and loss sheet.[1859]

This illustration of a white Southern slave owner viciously whipping his servant (from the author's book, *Honest Jeff and Dishonest Abe: A Southern Children's Guide to the Civil War*), is a fantasy created by the anti-South movement. In fact, whipping was extremely rare in the Old South. Not only was it considered unmanly, inhumane, and un-Christian to hurt one's servants, but it was also both bad business and against the law. Those few ignorant owners who violated this statute were reported to the sheriff by concerned neighbors. The outlaw was then arrested, tried, and imprisoned. In some cases exceptionally cruel Southern slave owners were hanged and their slaves were confiscated.

While today's supervisors use the threat of demotion and termination for inferior work or bad behavior, Victorian slavers used the threat of force, for this was then the accepted approach to discipline. One of the instruments of force sometimes resorted to, of course, was the infamous whip.

But whipping was not a corrective tool created specifically for the American Southern slave trade. Throughout the 16th, 17th, 18th, and 19th Centuries, black African slave owners regularly used the whip on their white American and European slaves, particularly in the region of West Africa.[1860] It was said that "none were spared" by these bestial African slavers, not women, the aged, or even children.[1861]

Moreover, whipping was the standard form of punishment in the U.S. from the 1600s to the 1800s for law-breakers of every kind, whether black, white, brown, or red. This particular penal custom was a gift of the English, who left us records of "rogues" being "graciously whipped" from as early as the late 1500s. The practice was then brought to America with the first wave of Anglo immigrants.[1862]

As early as 1659 the Puritan government at Boston, Massachusetts, regularly whipped Quakers, Baptists, and Catholics, a custom carried to the colony from England under the intolerant Puritan moralist Oliver Cromwell.[1863] Naturally Bay Staters also whipped their black citizens, even for crimes as seemingly insignificant as "striking a Christian."[1864] In 1698, Pennsylvanian Gabriel Thomas wrote that:

> Thieves of all sorts, are oblig'd to restore four fold after they have been Whipt and Imprison'd, according to the nature of their Crime; and if they be not of Ability to restore four fold, they must be in Servitude till 'tis satisfied.[1865]

Here we see that at the time Northern criminals were not only whipped and imprisoned for their misdeeds, but they could also be enslaved under Northern law if they were unable to repay their victims "four fold."

Whipping in Europe was already an age old custom by this time, of course. On February 28, 1574, for instance, as part of the Spanish Inquisition, Catholic inquisitors in Mexico ordered 61 English "heretics" to receive 300 lashes by whip, after which they were turned into galley slaves for ten years. (These were the lucky ones: two other Englishmen and an Irishman from the group became the first individuals to be burnt at the stake for heresy in the New World.)[1866] In 1685, despite the passage of humane laws for the treatment of African slaves under the new Negro Code, France continued to dole out the whip for recalcitrant servants.[1867]

In the U.S. the Pennsylvania custom of flogging black slaves continued well into the 1800s, as it was the punishment for the crime of stealing one's master's belongings. Blacks who carried weapons such as guns or clubs in the Keystone State could expect to receive "21 lashes," while those caught on the streets on Sunday were given 39. The same law applied in New Jersey, and in fact in nearly all Northern cities and counties. In New York's slave-heavy Westchester County, slaves who took weapons off their masters' plantations were flogged according to the mood of the presiding judge. New England slaves who violated the region's strict curfew laws (to be off the streets by 9:00 PM), were picked up and arrested by the Yankees' infamous "slave police," and given a solid whipping. Though Connecticut, Massachusetts, and New Hampshire all had particularly harsh punishments for breaking the slave curfew, Rhode Island went one step further by allowing "unlimited flogging" of its black transgressors.[1868]

Along with the North's ever present "slave police," the "Negro Whipper" was a civil authority figure required by law in every Northern town prior to the Civil War. Handy with the cat-'o-nine-tails and other forms of torture, this one is preparing to lay 39 lashes on the bare back of a white indentured female slave convicted of committing an offence on a Yankee plantation. Pro-North writers never mention the Yankee Negro Whipper, and for obvious reasons. However, he was a central figure in the Old North and therefore must be recorded for posterity.

In Connecticut, which issued an anti-manumission law in 1702 and set up harsh black codes as early as 1730, the slave police were always on active duty.[1869] Here, slaves convicted of uttering "defamatory words" were arrested, whipped, and sold on the auction block in order to recoup court costs. Connecticut and Pennsylvania—the latter state which upheld its stringent Black Codes until the late 1700s[1870]—whipped blacks who entered a bar or a pub, and both branding (on the forehead with the letter "T") and whipping were the customary penalty for black thieves across the North. Yankee slaves who met in groups without permission were in for serious reprisals as well, as were those who gambled or traveled off their owner's farm or plantation without a pass. All could expect a brutal lashing (usually ten to 30) by the town's "Negro Whipper," a civil authority figure who was required by law in every Northern city.[1871] New Yorkers passed a law in 1708 allowing "40 lashes" to be given to any slave caught swearing.[1872]

Along with branding, "hard labor," and "spare diet," early Massachusetts routinely parceled out "severe whippings" to all races as punishment for crimes ranging from theft, debt, and cursing to drunkenness, prostitution, and piracy.[1873] By law white men in the Bay State who had intimate relations with black women were whipped. White women who "mixed" with black men, free or bonded, were whipped, then both were sold into slavery, the males out of state.[1874] In the early 1700s Rhode Island "made a by-law to the effect that if any negro slave be found at any negro house or cottage, both slave and free negro should be whipped."[1875]

Delaware doled out "sixty lashes upon the bare back" to anyone of any race found guilty of kidnaping or assisting in the kidnaping of free blacks.[1876] In Maryland anyone caught allowing a white servant they did not own to stay overnight, was given a fine of £100, or a whipping if they could not pay the penalty. Owners who abused their white servants in any way could get ten lashes, while white servants who misbehaved could receive 39 lashes.[1877]

The truth, contrary to Northern folklore, is that from New England to the Deep South, the whipping post was the centerpiece of the village green in hundreds of towns and cities across early America. The standard punishment for horse thieves, for example, nearly all who were white, was "three good whippings," each one consisting of 39 lashes.[1878]

To give an accurate idea of the widespread acceptance of whipping at the time, here is how Edward Raymond Turner described the practice in Pennsylvania:

> . . . an act forbidding the use of fireworks without the governor's permission, states that the slave instead of being imprisoned shall be publicly whipped. Another provides that if a slave set fire to any woodlands or marshes he shall be whipped not exceeding twenty-one lashes. As far back as 1700 whipping had been made the punishment of a slave who carried weapons without his master's permission. In 1750-1751 participation in a horse-race or shooting-match entailed first fifteen lashes, and then twenty-one, together with six days' imprisonment for the first offense, and ten days' imprisonment thereafter. In 1760 hunting on Indians' lands or on other people's lands, shooting in the city, or hunting on Sunday, were forbidden under penalty of whipping up to thirty-one lashes. In 1750-1751 the penalty for offending against the night watch in Philadelphia was made twenty-one lashes and imprisonment in the work-house for three days at hard labor; for the second offence, thirty-one lashes and six days. Sometimes it was provided that a slave might be punished as a free man, if his master would stand [testify] for him. Thus a slave offending against the regulations for wagoners was to be whipped, or fined, if his master would pay the fine.[1879]

Whipping was a standard military punishment at the time as well. During the Revolutionary War, while the "father of the nation," George Washington, served as general of the Continental Army, he regularly whipped his white soldiers for a host of offences ranging from drunkenness to desertion. His floggings were so violent that Congress had to create a rule regulating the number of times a whip could be applied to a soldier's bare back.[1880]

In 1812 an enlightened and more humane Congress made courts-martial whippings unlawful (in one of the more outrageous cases a white U.S. soldier had been branded, had his head shaved, and was given 50 lashes). Military officers, however, believed it was the only sure means of enforcing discipline. Congress had no choice but to later lift its ban, and whipping was reinstated in 1833.[1881]

During Lincoln's War white farmers in the South risked being whipped for violating the governmental ban on growing cotton instead of food.[1882] And it is well-known that both white and black Yankee soldiers used the whip on "stubborn" captured Southern blacks between 1861 and 1865.[1883] Even black Union soldiers were known to whip white civilians during the War.[1884]

Our liberal anti-South historians like to pretend that whipping was used only by Southern slave owners. The truth is that it was an ordinary form of punishment for lawbreakers—whatever their skin color or gender—throughout all of early America. It was also the standard penalty used by the U.S. military. For instance, while George Washington (seen here entertaining family and friends at home) was serving as general of the Continental Army, he routinely had his soldiers flogged. Though legal and accepted, the severity of his whippings was not, and Congress had to step in to regulate them.

The whip then was the normal American penalty for bad behavior. Thus it was only natural that on occasion it was also used to enforce authority on Southern plantations. In fact, black slaves themselves, such as those who worked in positions of power (for example, mammies, overseers, and drivers), regularly used the whip on other black slaves when the situation warranted it.[1885] And we will note that there were extremely cruel *black* slave owners who occasionally used it on their black chattel as well.[1886] While visiting Hopeton Plantation in Georgia, Lyell had the following experience:

> One day, when walking alone, I came upon a "gang" of negroes, who were digging a trench. *They were superintended by a black "driver," who held a whip in his hand.* Some of the labourers were using spades, others cutting away the roots and stumps of trees which they had encountered in the line of the ditch. Their mode of

> proceeding in their task was somewhat leisurely, and eight hours a day of this work are exacted, though they can accomplish the same in five hours, if they undertake it by the task. The digging of a given number of feet in length, breadth, and depth is, in this case, assigned to each ditcher, and a deduction made when they fall in with the stump or root. The names of gangs and drivers are odious, and *the sight of the whip was painful to me as a mark of degradation, reminding me that the lower orders of slaves are kept to their work by mere bodily fear, and that their treatment must depend on the individual character of the owner or overseer. That the whip is rarely used, and often held for weeks over them, merely* in terrorem, *is, I have no doubt, true on all well-governed estates; and it is not that formidable weapon which I have seen exhibited as formerly in use in the West Indies.* It is a thong of leather, half an inch wide and a quarter of an inch thick. No ordinary driver is allowed to give more than six lashes for any offence, the head driver twelve, and the overseer twenty-four. When an estate is under superior management, the system is remarkably effective in preventing crime. *The most severe punishment required in the last forty years for a body of 500 negroes at Hopeton was for the theft of one negro from another. In that period there has been no criminal act of the highest grade, for which a delinquent could be committed to the Penitentiary in Georgia*, and there have been only six cases of assault and battery. As a race, the negroes are mild and forgiving, and by no means so prone to indulge in drinking as the white man or the Indian. There were more serious quarrels, and more broken heads, among the Irish in a few years, when they came to dig the Brunswick Canal, than had been known among the negroes in all the surrounding plantations for half a century. The murder of a husband by a black woman, whom he had beaten very violently, is the greatest crime remembered in this part of Georgia for a great length of time.[1887]

Such intimidation was not imposed to create submissive and docile slaves, as Northern mythologists have long claimed. Rather it was used to create the largest and best product at the lowest cost in the most efficient manner. In such a social climate we should not be surprised to learn that black slave parents often brutally whipped their disobedient offspring (with switches), while black male slaves were known to whip their wives when they felt it was "necessary."[1888]

These were mere echoes of what was transpiring in Victorian England at the time. Here, factory-working children as young as seven—who were required to work 16 hour shifts—were routinely whipped to keep them awake at their posts.[1889]

Mary Todd Lincoln, wife of Abraham Lincoln, "whipped" their children on occasion, as the president himself noted in a personal letter dated October 22, 1846; yet another fact glossed over by pro-North writers, who continue to decry the rare application of the whip on slaves in the Old South, while neglecting to mention that it was used in every state in the Union at the time.

In most Western nations this approach to discipline lasted well into the 20th Century, and there are, no doubt, people reading this book who will recall being strapped with a belt, whipped with a switch, or spanked with a paddle as a youngster. It is well-known, for example, that President Jimmy Carter (whose great-grandfather Littleberry Walker Carter fought for the Confederacy in Lincoln's War) was whipped as a child.[1890] Even Lincoln's wife Mary Todd Lincoln often whipped their children, as the Yankee president acknowledged in a letter dated October 22, 1846.[1891] Writing that same year, Southern historian Matthew Estes noted that:

> Fathers, mothers and teachers, are bound to use the rod occasionally in order that due subordination may be kept up among the children. But this is not all: *flogging is practised in the armies and navies of all countries.* In Great Britain, flogging is carried to great extremes in her armies and navies. *The soldiers and sailors are taken up and flogged in a manner unknown among Southern masters. They make use of instruments of torture that are never used by the Southern slave-holder. Flogging, then, is not confined to Southern slaveholders, but is [also] . . . practised by others.*
>
> But after all, I am satisfied from much observation, experience and inquiry, that much exaggeration has prevailed on this subject [of whipping on Southern plantations]. *All well-managed plantations dispense with flogging almost entirely. I am well acquainted with large plantations, where the whip is never used from one end of the year to the other; and this I learn, from inquiry, is generally the case.*[1892]

In 18th-Century America then the whipping of a slave, while rare, was considered no more exceptional or barbaric than the whipping of an unruly child by its parents.[1893] Southern hero General Nathan Bedford Forrest, like most Victorian Southern children, was routinely whipped for bad behavior as a schoolboy,[1894] so it was only natural that later in life, as a slave trader and slave owner, he may have occasionally used the whip on the rare felonious black servant. This will appall some. But the offense is greatly lessened when we learn that as a military officer in the Confederate army he also whipped his white soldiers for insubordination.[1895]

It is important to note that the 19th-Century U.S. judicial system expected slave owners (Northern and Southern) to attend to disciplinary matters themselves, and not clog up the courts with petty grievances concerning disobedient slaves.[1896] As such, use of the whip was an accepted and recognized form of penalizing black servants.[1897]

In the end physical discipline on Southern plantations was about pure economics. Too much force would have increased rather than decreased the cost of labor, which is just one of the many reasons why African-American, Native-American, and European-American slave owners did not use physical coercion on their human chattel unless absolutely necessary.[1898] Phillips writes:

The theory of rigid coercion and complete exploitation was as strange to the bulk of the [Southern] planters as the doctrine and practice of moderation was to those [Yankees] who viewed the regime from afar and with the mind's eye. A planter in explaining his mildness might well have said it was due to his being neither a knave nor a fool. *He refrained from the use of fetters not so much because they would have hampered the slaves in their work as because the general use of them never crossed his mind. And since chains and bolts were out of the question, the whole system of control must be moderate; slaves must be impelled as little as possible by fear, and as much as might be by loyalty, pride and the prospect of reward.*[1899]

Discipline is typically generational: as adults we tend to discipline others the way our parents disciplined us. Confederate General Nathan Bedford Forrest, seen here with his famous "critter company," was whipped as a child. Later in life he also occasionally whipped both his slaves and his soldiers. From far being aberrant behavior, as Northern-biased writers would have you believe, whipping was absolutely typical, legal, and accepted among all races across both the Old North and the Old South for nearly 300 years.

Yes, threat of punishment was also important in sustaining the power hierarchy on the early plantation. But it is for this very same reason that it is also vital today in the modern office. Obviously the balance between a superior and his or her subordinates cannot be achieved, however, if the former resorts to brute violence.

Slave owners, most who were experienced, professional, and highly intelligent businessmen, understood this, as did the authors of a variety of Victorian plantation manuals, all which strongly discouraged farm managers from using any kind of corporal punishment on their servants.

Here is what one such work, the popular 19th-Century *Instructions to Managers*, had to say on the subject:

> The most vital ingredient in managing servants is how their superiors act toward them and treat them. It is true that there needs to be a certain amount of discipline on a farm. However, remember that when a servant's work is finished it is only right to *treat him with humanity, sympathy, and even permissiveness.* Kindness and rewards are much more effective than punishment.[1900]

These were words that nearly all Southern slave owners, black, white, brown, or red, understood and agreed with. This made whipping and other severe forms of physical discipline on Southern plantations extremely rare—and for good reason. Not only was it bad for morale, it also increased the cost of labor while reducing the value of those slaves it was used on (whip marks, for instance, indicated an unmanageable individual), which is why *all* early plantation manuals strongly advised against the practice.[1901]

Plantation owners themselves encouraged servants to bring them complaints concerning cruel drivers and overseers, or anyone else who hurt or even interfered with them,[1902] for everywhere in the South "a bad master was universally execrated."[1903] To further discourage cruelty to slaves, in most parts of the South slave owners could not punish their servants without first holding a "plantation trial," the jury of which was made up solely of slave friends of the accused.[1904]

Naturally, the majority of Southerners considered those who used the whip to be inhumane,[1905] and those who wielded it against their servants were routinely reported by neighbors to the authorities for cruelty.[1906] Southern historian Matthew Estes noted in 1846 that

> *this public sentiment is growing stronger and stronger every year: a man now who treats his slaves with any considerable degree of cruelty, is shunned by the community as though he were the veriest monster in*

existence.[1907]

In the mid 1830s Yankee author Reverend Joseph Holt Ingraham of Maine wrote of the alleged "severity" of the Southern slaveholder:

> It is now popular to treat slaves with kindness; and *those planters who are known to be inhumanly rigorous to their slaves, are scarcely countenanced by the more intelligent and humane portion of the community. Such instances, however, are very rare*; but there are unprincipled men everywhere, who will give vent to their ill feelings and bad passions, not with less good-will upon the back of an *indented apprentice*, than upon that of a purchased slave.[1908]

All Southerners condemned "the barbarous use of slaves" as "bringing on the community, the State and the city the contumely and opprobrium of the civilized world."[1909] As President Woodrow Wilson explains,

> *public opinion in the South*, while it recognized the necessity for maintaining the discipline of subordination among the hosts of slaves, *was as intolerant of the graver forms of cruelty as was the opinion of the best people in the North*. . . . It sometimes happened that husbands were sold away from their wives, children away from their parents; *but even this evil was in most instances checked by the wisdom and moral feeling of the slave-owners. Even in the ruder [Southern] communities public opinion demanded that when negroes were sold, families should be kept together, particularly mothers and their children. Slave-dealers were universally detested, and even ostracised; and the domestic slave-trade was tolerated only because it was deemed necessary for the economic distribution of the slave population.*[1910]

In 1845 a public debate on slavery took place in Cincinnati, Ohio, between Southerner Nathan Lewis Rice and Northerner Jonathan Blanchard. During the disputation Rice made the following statements regarding the alleged "cruelties" of the Southern slave owner, highlighting the hypocrisy of abolitionists in the "slave-free states":

> I remember, that very recently a black man was murdered in the streets of Indianapolis, for no crime whatever. Had such a thing happened in a slave-holding State [in the South], we should not soon have heard the last of it. It would have stood prominent in abolition books, tracts and papers. But it happened in a free State

> [in the North]; and therefore, we hear little concerning it. . . . Why are such things so lightly passed over, when they occur in a free State, and so bitterly denounced when they occur in the slave-holding States? Let impartial justice be done.
>
> . . . Some years since, as I am credibly informed, a citizen of Danville, Ky., sold a negro woman from her husband to a slave-trader. It was soon known in the town; and *such was the excitement [that is, the negative response of the white citizens] that he was constrained to follow the slave-holder, and re-purchase the woman at considerable loss. He could scarcely have lived there, if he had not done so. Not a great many years ago, a prominent citizen of Lexington came near being mobbed, because he had cruelly chastised a negro woman*. And Dr. Drake, of Louisville, whilst travelling through Alabama, not long since, met a sheriff and his posse returning from the penitentiary where they had safely lodged a man who owned a plantation and a number of slaves. He had been *convicted of the murder of one of his slaves*, chiefly on circumstantial evidence derived through his slaves, and was *sentenced for ten years*, if my memory serves me. *Such facts show the real state of feeling in the slave-holding States.*[1911]

Agriculturalist Samuel Martin gave these recommendations in his plantation manual in the late 1700s. Though he owned a sugar plantation in Antigua, this same advice is found in all of the early American farm handbooks:

> . . . as it is the interest of every planter to preserve his negroes in health and strength; so *every act of cruelty is not less repugnant to the master's real profit, than it is contrary to the laws of humanity*: and if a manager considers his own ease, and his employer's interest, he will *treat all negroes under his care with due benevolence*. . . . [He who] treats them with kindness and good-nature, will reap a much larger product, and with infinitely more ease and self-satisfaction, than the most cruel taskmaster . . .[1912]

Southern planter Joseph A. S. Acklen made these remarks in his plantation manual:

> . . . *if ever any of my negroes are cruelly or inhumanly treated, bruised, maimed or otherwise injured, the overseer will be promptly discharged and his salary withheld.*[1913]

Since whipping was usually considered more an indication of a bad-tempered overseer or an inattentive manager than an unruly servant,[1914] far from being a common item on Southern plantations, most slave owners simply permanently banned the whip from their property.[1915] This is why Confederate President Jefferson Davis could honestly say that when it came to the alleged "sadistic" treatment of Southern slaves, it "probably exists to a smaller extent [here] than in any other relation of labor to capital" in the world.[1916]

This white overseer is whipping a shackled black slave on a coffee plantation on the island of Montserrat. Though this occurred with some frequency in the Caribbean and in the Old North, such scenes were almost unheard of in the Old South, where there existed an easy going acceptance, tolerance, friendship, and even love between the races.

Southerners hated unmerciful slave owners and the use of the whip was widely regarded as unneeded and indefensible.[1917] This is why, of course, there is abundant historical evidence "of the care taken by humane [Southern] planters to protect their slaves from abuse by overseers."[1918] According to one white plantation owner's "Rules in the Management of a Southern Estate":

> I will most certainly discharge any overseer for striking any of my negroes with a club or the butt of his whip, or in any way injuring one of my negroes. *My negroes are not to be abused or injured in any way*; and, at the same time, they must be kept under strict discipline, which can be accomplished *by talking to them . . .*[1919]

Another Southern planter, P. C. Weston of South Carolina, gave these instructions to his overseer in 1856:

> The proprietor, in the first place, wishes the overseer most distinctly to understand that *his first object is to be, under all circumstances, the care and well being of the negroes*. The proprietor is always ready to excuse such errors as may proceed from want of judgment; but *he never can or will excuse any cruelty, severity or want of care towards the negroes*. For the well being, however, of the negroes it is absolutely necessary to maintain obedience, order and discipline, to see that the tasks are punctually and carefully performed, and to conduct the business steadily and firmly, without weakness on the one hand or harshness on the other.[1920]

Plantation owner Charles Manigault of Georgia required his overseers to take a pledge, promising that they would treat his servants "all with kindness and consideration in sickness and health."[1921] In 1857 J. W. Fowler of Coahoma County, Mississippi, provided his overseer with these detailed rules for governing the black servants on his plantation:

> The health, happiness, good discipline and obedience; good, sufficient and comfortable clothing, a sufficiency of good wholesome and nutritious food for both man and beast being indispensably necessary to successful planting, as well as for reasonable dividends for the amount of capital invested, without saying anything about the Master's duty to his dependants, to himself and his God—I do hereby establish the following rules and regulations for the management of my Prairie Plantation, and require an observance of the same by any and all Overseers I may at any time have in charge thereof to wit:
>
> *Punishment must never be cruel or abusive, for it is absolutely mean and unmanly to whip a negro from mere passion or malice, and any man who can do this is entirely unworthy and unfit to have control of either man or beast.*
>
> *My negroes are permitted to come to me with their complaints and grievances and in no instance shall they be punished for doing so. On*

examination, should I find they have been cruelly treated, it shall be considered a good and sufficient cause for the immediate discharge of the Overseer.

Prove and show by your conduct toward the negroes that you feel a kind and considerate regard for them. Never cruelly punish or overwork them, never require them to do what they cannot reasonably accomplish or otherwise abuse them, but seek to render their situation as comfortable and contented as possible.

See that their necessities are supplied, that their food and clothing be good and sufficient, their houses comfortable; and *be kind and attentive to them in sickness and old age.*

See that the negroes are regularly fed and that their food be wholesome, nutritious and well cooked.

See that they keep themselves well cleaned: at least once a week (especially during summer) inspect their houses and see that they have been swept clean, examine their bedding and see that they are occasionally well aired; their clothes mended and *everything attended to that conduces to their health, comfort and happiness.*

If any of the negroes have been reported sick, be prompt to see what ails them and that proper medicine and attention be given them. Use good judgment and discretion in turning out those who are getting well.

I greatly desire that the Gospel be preached to the Negroes when the services of a suitable person can be procured. This should be done on the Sabbath; day time is preferable, if convenient to the Minister.

Christianity, humanity and order elevate all—injure none—whilst infidelity, selfishness and disorder curse some—delude others and degrade all. I therefore want all of my people encouraged to cultivate religious feeling and morality, and punished for inhumanity to their children or stock—for profanity, lying and stealing.

All hands should be required to retire to rest and sleep at a suitable hour and permitted to remain there until such time as it will be necessary to get out in time to reach their work by the time they can see well how to work—particularly so when the nights are short and the mornings very cold and inclement.

Allow such as may desire it a suitable piece of ground to raise potatoes, tobacco. They may raise chickens also *with privileges of marketing the same at suitable leisure times.*[1922]

What is more, the violence, unethical treatment, and immorality portrayed between black slaves and their masters and mistresses in fantasy fiction books like *Uncle Tom's Cabin*, was not only uncommon but was a punishable crime in the South.[1923] Phillips writes:

> *The killing or injury of a slave except under circumstances justified by law rendered the offender liable both to the master's claim for damages and to criminal prosecution. . . .* [An example occurred in Virginia in 1775. When] William Pitman was found guilty and sentenced by the Virginia General Court to be hanged for the beating of his slave to death, the *Virginia Gazette* said: "This man has justly incurred the penalties of the law and we hear will certainly suffer, which ought to be a warning to others to treat their slaves with more moderation." *In the nineteenth century the laws generally held the maiming or murder of slaves to be felonies in the same degree and with the same penalties as in cases where the victims were whites; and when the statutes were silent in the premises the courts felt themselves free to remedy the defect.*[1924]

In fact, by the early 1800s *all* Southern states had passed anti-cruelty laws that provided fines, imprisonment, and even execution for those who mistreated their servants, and more than one sadistic slaver died at the business end of a lawman's gun.[1925] Furthermore, killing a slave was also punishable by death in *all* of the Southern states, and was considered on par with killing a white person. This is quite unlike the laws of the Old Testament, which "allowed the master to take the life of his slave without any particular penalty."[1926]

Let me repeat once more that whipping was not a corrective tool created especially for the institution of Southern slavery, as the North and New South teaches. From the 1600s to the 1800s it was the standard form of punishment in the U.S. for misdemeanors; and it was applied to lawbreakers of every kind, whether male or female, whether black, white, brown, or red.[1927] As such, *far more American whites were whipped by the local sheriff than American blacks.*[1928]

During Lincoln's War Yankee troops whipped Southern noncombatants as readily as they whipped Rebel soldiers. In Screven County, Georgia, for instance, a white citizen who was found armed was given 200 lashes by a Union officer.[1929] It is well-known that both white and black Yankee soldiers used the whip on "stubborn" captured Southern blacks between 1861 and 1865.[1930] "Insubordinate" black Yankee soldiers were sometimes whipped by their white superiors as well.[1931] Black Union soldiers were known to whip white civilians during the War.[1932]

We do not read of such incidents in our history books because the pro-North movement does not want you to know about them. Such facts would utterly expose their great Yankee Coverup by revealing the truth, not only about slavery, but about Lincoln and his war on the American people and the Constitution.

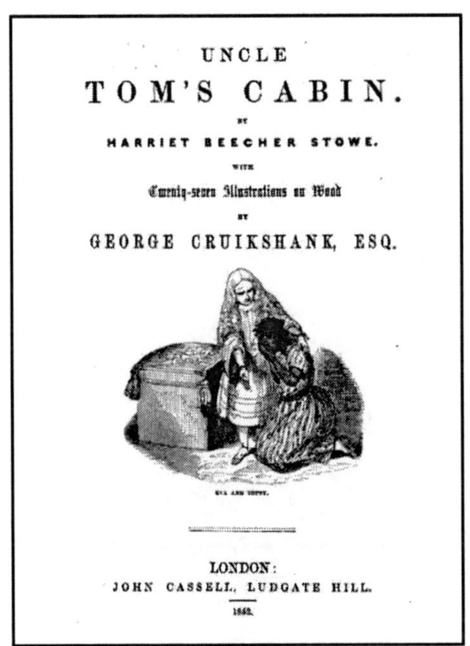

UNCLE
TOM'S CABIN.
BY
HARRIET BEECHER STOWE.
WITH
Twenty-seven Illustrations on Wood
BY
GEORGE CRUIKSHANK, ESQ.

LONDON:
JOHN CASSELL, LUDGATE HILL.

The title page from Stowe's bestselling fantasy novel, *Uncle Tom's Cabin*, without a doubt one of the most fallacious and damaging pieces of anti-South propaganda ever penned.

It is true that aboard Yankee slave ships unruly black slaves on their way from Africa to the Americas were sometimes whipped during the infamous Middle Passage. But what Northern mythology leaves out is the fact that on these same slave runs not only were the whippers usually fellow slaves (who were assigned the task of "constable"),[1933] but that disorderly white crewmen were also whipped. Often they were flogged (as well as beaten and chained) for minor infractions (such as complaining) or even simple accidents.[1934] In fact, eyewitnesses described the maritime practice as "constant flogging," with men dying from their wounds on a daily basis, both black *and* white.[1935]

During Lincoln's War, Southern cotton plantations were "taken over" (that is, stolen) from their owners, and white Yankee officers and Northern businessmen were put in charge. Freed blacks were then transferred to these farms to labor at the same menial jobs they had performed while slaves (Lincoln's idea of "emancipation"). Naturally, their white Yankee overseers were permitted to use the whip. At times the use of the lash became so frequent that it had to be disallowed, but the practice continued behind closed doors.[1936]

Even after Lincoln's War was over Yankees continued to use the whip as a method of punishment across the South during "Reconstruction."[1937] Native-Americans too relied on the lash during this period: when freed blacks were caught coming into Indian territory they were soundly flogged.[1938] And in the North, postwar whites in Massachusetts routinely whipped blacks who overstayed their welcome, for the limit a nonresident black could remain in the so-called "abolitionist" Bay State was just two months.[1939]

In post Civil War Massachusetts, out-of-state blacks who stayed past the two-month deadline were hunted down, whipped, and extradited. No one protested because the lash was legal and accepted across the U.S. at the time.

In early America then the whip was the normal penalty for unwanted behavior. Thus it was only natural that it was also occasionally used to enforce authority on Southern plantations. In fact, *black slaves themselves, such as those who worked in positions of power (for example, mammies, overseers, drivers, and managers), regularly used the whip on other black servants when the situation warranted it.*[1940] (As mentioned earlier, contrary to Yankee myth, some 70 percent of white Southern plantations were managed by blacks.)[1941]

And we will note that *black slave owners*—of which there were tens of thousands across the South[1942]—*used it on their black servants as well.*[1943] Black overseers on white plantations could be quite generous with the lash, as former Virginia slave Henry Clay Bruce noted in 1895:

> Mrs. Prudence Perkinson and her son Lemuel, lived about one mile from our place, and they owned about fifty field hands, as they were called. They also had an overseer or negro-driver whose pay consisted of a certain percentage of the crop.
>
> The larger the crop the larger his share would be, and having no money interest in the slaves he drove them night and day without mercy. *This [black] overseer was a mean and cruel man and would, if not checked by her, whip some one every day.* Lemuel Perkinson, was a man who spent his time in pleasure seeking, such as fox-hunting, fishing, horse racing and other sports, and was away from home a great deal, so much so that he paid little attention to the management of the farm. It was left to the care of his mother and the overseer. Mrs Sarah Perkinson, wife of Lemuel Perkinson, was a dear good woman and was beloved by all her slaves as long as I knew her, and I am informed that *she is living now and is still beloved by her ex-slaves.* Mrs. Prudence Perkinson would not allow her overseer to whip a grown slave without her consent, because I have known of cases where the overseer was about to whip a slave when he would break loose and run to his old mistress. If it was a bad case she would punish the slave by taking off her slipper and slapping his jaws with it. They were quite willing to take that *rather than be punished by the overseer who would often have them take off the shirt to be whipped on their bare backs.*[1944]

After living among Southern planters for several years, Scotsman William Thomson offered this observation:

> *The driver [on Dixie's plantations] is always a black man, who has the immediate oversight of the hands in the field. Sometimes he carries a bundle of small wands, perhaps five or six; some have a horsewhip, which they apply to the shoulders of the women, and the bare buttocks of the men, when they make bad work or misbehave in any way; but this sort of punishment is not very severe.* It is when the "cow-skin," a piece of hide twisted into the appearance of a riding-switch, sometimes painted red, is applied to their bare back for some heinous offence, that *they make the woods ring with their cries*, which I have heard; but I never saw the punishment inflicted, and I hope never shall.[1945]

As there were far worse penalties (such as being branded with a hot iron or being shot before a firing squad), use of the whip was an accepted and recognized form of penalizing not only black servants, but criminals of all colors and social statuses.

Southern mammies sometimes whipped fellow black kitchen aids who fell behind on their duties.[1946] Not even black slave children could escape the lash: black slave parents used it on their offspring whenever it was deemed necessary.[1947] At times the whipping was so severe that their white owners grew concerned, or even had to intervene.[1948] One observer of the disciplinary actions of slave parents remarked that it

> owes its chief efficiency to excited passion, and consequently exists in the extreme of laxity or severity. *They ofttimes when under no restraint, beat their children unmercifully.*[1949]

The early American custom of flogging was not just found among whites. It was known nationwide and practiced by all races. Blacks caught trespassing on Indian land, for example, were whipped by their Native-American captors.

Still, the innate savagery of the whip offended all thinking Southerners, just one of the many reasons why African-American, Native-American, Latin-American, and European-American slave owners did not use physical coercion on their human chattel unless absolutely necessary.[1950] Even in the most severe cases owners were much more likely to rely on traditional methods of punishment, such as withdrawal of privileges, being assigned unpleasant tasks, or temporary confinement.[1951]

All in all, actual use of the whip was indeed often unnecessary, for it was mainly seen across early America as a symbol of law and order.

Knowing it existed, and that it *could* be used, was usually enough to keep even the most incorrigible citizens, free or enslaved, white or black, in line.[1952]

After Lincoln's War, Susan Dabney Smedes, the daughter of Thomas Dabney, a Mississippi plantation and slave owner, summed up the Southern view of black servants and discipline:

> *It may be thought that Southerners could punish their servants, and so have everything go on just as they pleased. But he who says this knows little of human nature.* "I cannot punish people with whom I associate every day," [my father] Thomas Dabney said, and *he expressed the sentiment of thousands of other slave-owners. It was true that discipline had sometimes to be used, but not often, in very many instances only once in a lifetime, and in many more, never.* [Our servant] George Page, who in his youth, and in his middle age, was about his master's person and knew him well, said, "Marster is a heap more strict with his [own] children than he is with [us] his servants. He does not overlook things in his children like he does in his [servant] people."
>
> *Apart from the humane point of view, common sense, joined with that great instructor, responsibility, taught slave-owners that very little can be effected by fear of punishment.*
>
> Fear and punishment only tend to harden the rebellious heart. What, then, was to be done with a grown servant who was too lazy or too ill-tempered to do half work, *with abundant and comfortable support insured whether the work was done or not?* It is clear that unless the moral nature could be appealed to, that servant had to be endured. It would not have answered to set that one free; that would have made dissatisfaction among the others. *Very many [Southern] slave-owners looked on slavery as an incubus, and longed to be rid of it*, but they were not able to give up their young and valuable negroes, *nor were they willing to set adrift the aged and helpless.* To have provided for this class, without any compensation for the loss of the other, would have reduced them to penury.[1953]

In 1900 Dr. Henry A. White also debunked the Yankee myth of the so-called "routine abuse" of Southern servants:

> Self-interest restrained harsh masters from cruelty, and *a wholesome public sentiment enforced the practice of kindness toward the quiet wards of the plantation. Cruelty was the exception. Not often was the lash used*; not often were negro families separated by sale, except as penalty for misdemeanor, or in the distribution of estates to heirs or to creditors.[1954]

In 1833 Yankee Timothy Flint made the following revealing comments after visiting the Southern states:

> As [Louisiana] contains a greater number of slaves, in proportion to its population, than any other in the western country, we shall bring into one compass all the general remarks which we shall make upon the aspect and character of slavery in the Mississippi valley. [Statistics show] . . . that considerably more than one half of the whole population of this state are slaves. Formerly, they did not increase in this state, and required importations from abroad to keep up the number. But, since experience and humanity have dictated more rational and humane modes of managing the sick and the children, *by carrying them during the sickly months to the same places of healthy retirement, to which their masters retire*, they are found to increase as rapidly here as they do elsewhere. It is well known, that under favorable circumstances they are more prolific than the whites.
>
> . . . It is not among the objects of this work to discuss the moral character of slavery, or to contemplate the subject in any of its abstract bearings. *We can pronounce, from what we consider a thorough knowledge of the subject, that the condition of the slaves here [in the South], the treatment which they receive, and the character of their masters, have been much misrepresented in the non-slave-holding states.* We pretend to none but historical knowledge of the state of things which has existed here in past time. *At present, we are persuaded there are but few of those brutal and cruel masters, which the greatest portion of the planters were formerly supposed to be.* The masters now study popularity with their slaves. If there must be the odium of severity, it is thrown upon the overseer, who becomes a kind of scape goat to bear away the offences of the master. *There is now no part of the slave holding-country in the south-west, where it would not be a deep stain upon the moral character to be generally reputed a cruel master. In many plantations no punishment is inflicted except after a trial by jury, composed of the fellow-servants of the party accused. Festival prizes and rewards are instituted, as stimulants to exertion, and compensations for superior accomplishments of labor. They are generally well fed and clothed*, and that not by an arbitrary award, which might vary with the feelings of the master, but by periodical apportionment, like the distributed rations of soldiers, of what has been experimented to be sufficient to render them comfortable. *Considerable attention is paid to their quarters, and most of them are comfortably lodged and housed.*
>
> *Nor are they destitute, as has been supposed, of any legal protection coming between them and the cupidity and cruelty of their masters.* The '*code noir*' [black code] of Louisiana is a curious

collection of statutes, drawn partly from French and Spanish law and usage, and partly from the customs of the islands, and usages which have grown out of the peculiar circumstances of Louisiana while a colony. It has the aspect, it must be admitted, of being formed rather for the advantage of the master than the servant, for it prescribes an unlimited homage and obedience to the former. It makes a misdemeanor on his part towards his master a very different offence from a wanton abuse of power towards the servant. But, at the same time, *it defines crimes that the master can commit in relation to the slave, and prescribes the mode of trial, and the kind and degree of punishment. It constitutes unnecessary correction, maiming, and murder, punishable offences in a master. It is very minute in prescribing the number of hours which the master may lawfully exact to be employed in labor, and the number of hours which he must allow his slave for meal times and for rest. It prescribes the time and extent of his holidays. In short, it settles with minuteness and detail the whole circle of relations between master and slave, defining and prescribing what the former may and may not exact of the latter. Yet, after all these minute provisions, the slave finds the chief alleviation of his hard condition, and his best security against cruel treatment, and his most valid bond for kind and proper deportment towards him, in the increasing light, humanity, and force of public opinion.*

This political illustration is from Robert Seth McCallen's 1907 left-wing book, *Master and Slave*, in which socialism and labor unions are glowingly compared with the ugly "greediness" of capitalism. McCallen refers to America's common white factory workers as "slaves" and their bosses as "masters." Though they were Conservatives, and thus the opposite of Socialists, this was the same idea put forth by traditional antebellum Southerners decades earlier, on the eve of Lincoln's War.

> *That the slave is, also, in the general circumstances of his condition, as happy as this relation will admit of his being, is an unquestionable fact.* That *he seldom performs as much labor, or performs it as well as a free man*, proves all that can be desired, in regard to the value of those motives, which freedom only can supply. In all the better managed plantations, the mode of building the quarters is fixed. The arrangement of the little village has a fashion by which it is settled. Interest, if not humanity, has defined the amount of food and rest necessary for their health; and there is, in a large and respectable plantation, as much precision in the rules, as much exactness in the times of going to sleep, awakening, going to labor, and resting before and after meals, as in a garrison under military discipline, or in a ship of war. A bell gives all the signals. Every slave, at the assigned hour in the morning, is forthcoming to his labor, or his case is reported either as one of idleness, obstinacy, or sickness, in which case *he is sent to the hospital, and there he is attended by a physician, who, for the most part, has a yearly salary for attending to all the sick of the plantation*. The union of physical force, directed by one will, is now well understood to have a much greater effect upon the amount of labor which a number of hands, so managed, can bring about, than the same force directed by as many wills as there are hands. Hence, it happens that while one free man, circumstances being the same, will perform more labor than one slave, *one hundred slaves will accomplish more on one plantation, than so many hired free men, acting at their own discretion*. Hence, too, it is, that such a prodigious quantity of cotton and sugar is made here, in proportion to the number of laboring hands. The whole process of agriculture is managed by system. Every thing goes straight forward. There is no pulling down to-day the scheme of yesterday, and *the whole amount of force is directed by the teaching of experience to the best result.*
>
> *If we could lay out of the question the intrinsic evils of the case, that would be a cheering sight which is presented by a large Louisiana plantation.* The fields are as level and as regular in their figures as gardens. They sometimes contain three or four hundred acres in one enclosure; and we have seen from a dozen to twenty ploughs all making their straight furrows through a field a mile in depth, with a regularity, which it would be supposed, could only be obtained by a line. *The plough is generally worked by a single mule, and guided by a single hand, who cheers the long course of his furrow with a song.*[1955]

Despite the obvious truth about the alleged "horrors of Southern slavery," pro-North and New South educators and writers have always relished perverting that truth in order to conceal the North's role in giving birth to American slavery, while unfairly casting Dixie in the worst light possible. This reprehensible distortion of the facts began even before Lincoln's War, as Englishman Sir Charles Lyell recorded in his 1855 book, *A Second Visit to the United States of North America*. The following was recorded during his travels through New Orleans, Louisiana:

> A rich merchant of Pennsylvania, who was boarding at the St. Louis Hotel, showed me a letter he had just received from Philadelphia, in which his correspondent expressed a hope that his feelings had not often been shocked by the sufferings of the slaves [in the South]. "Doubtless," said the writer, "you must often witness great horrors." The Philadelphian then told me, that after residing here [in Louisiana] several years, and having a strong feeling of the evils as well as impolicy of slavery, *he had never been forced to see nor hear of any castigation of a slave in any establishment with which he had intercourse.* "Once," he added, "in New Jersey (a free State) he remembered having seen a free negro child whipped by its master." The tale of suffering to which his Pennsylvanian correspondent particularly alluded, was not authentic, or, at least, grossly exaggerated. It had been copied from the Abolitionist papers of the North into the Southern papers, sometimes with and sometimes without comment.
>
> . . . We ascertained that Miss [Harriet] Martineau's story of [Louisiana native and psychopath] Madame [Marie Delphine] LaLaurie's cruelty to her slaves was perfectly correct.[1956] Instances of such savage conduct are rare, as was indeed sufficiently proved by the indignation which it excited in the whole city [of New Orleans]. A New England lady settled here told me, she had promised to set free her two female coloured servants at her death. I asked if she had no fear of their poisoning her. "On the contrary," she replied, "they would be in despair were I to die."
>
> *One of the families which we visited at New Orleans was plunged in grief by the death of a little negro girl, suddenly carried off by a brain fever, in the house. She was the daughter of a domestic servant, and the sorrow for her loss was such as might have been felt for a [blood] relation.*[1957]

During a visit to Maryland in the mid 1800s, Englishman Sir Adlard Welby made these remarks:

> This is a Slave State; an institution hateful to English ears; yet I will observe again that after travelling through three slave States, I am obliged to go back to theory to raise any abhorrence of it: *not once during the journey did I witness an instance of cruel treatment, nor could I discover anything to excite commiseration in the faces or gait of the people of colour—they walk, talk, and appear at least as independent as their masters*; in animal spirits they have greatly the advantage . . .[1958]

Kentucky politician and slave owner Henry Clay openly discussed what his Yankee compatriots would not: the self-evident similarities between the South's black agricultural slaves and the North's white industrial slaves.

After Scottish ship captain Basil Hall visited America's Southern states in the years 1827 and 1828, he made these statements:

> I have no wish, God knows! to defend slavery in the abstract; neither do I say that it is the best state of things which might be supposed to exist in those countries; but I do think it is highly important that we should look this great and established evil fairly in the face, and consider its bearings with as little prejudice as possible. There is no other chance for its gradual improvement, I am well convinced, but this calm course, which has for its object the discovery of what is possible—not what is desirable.
>
> One of the results which actual observation has left on my mind is, that there are few situations in life, where a man of sense and feeling can exert himself to better purpose, than in the management of slaves. *So far, therefore, from thinking unkindly of slave-holders, an acquaintance with their proceedings has taught me to respect many of them in the highest degree; and nothing, during my recent journey, gave me more satisfaction than the conclusion to which I was gradually brought, that the planters of the Southern States of America, generally speaking, have a sincere desire to manage their estates with the least possible severity.* I do not say that undue severity is nowhere exercised; but *the discipline, taken upon the average, as far as I could learn, is not more strict than is necessary for the maintenance of a proper degree of authority*, without which, the whole framework of society in that quarter would be blown to atoms.[1959]

In 1819 Englishman William Faux visited a plantation in South Carolina, and left with these impressions of the owner and the management of his servants:

> This gentleman (Mr. Mickle, senior) appears to me to be a rare example of pure and undefiled religion; kind and gentle in manners. . . . Seeing such a swarm, or rather herd, of young negroes, creeping and dancing about the door and yard of his mansion, *all appearing healthy, happy, and frolicsome, and withal fat and decently clothed, both young and old*, I felt induced to praise the economy under which they lived. "Aye," said he, "I have many black people, but I never bought nor sold any in my life. All that you see came to me with my estate by virtue of my father's will. They are all, old and young, true and faithful to my interests; *they need no task-master, no overseer; they will do all, and more than I expect them to do; and I can trust them with untold gold.* All the adults are well instructed, and all are members of Christian churches in the

> neighbourhood; and their conduct is becoming their professions. *I respect them as my children, and they look on me as their friend and father.* Were they to be taken from me, it would be the most unhappy event of their lives." *This conversation induced me to view more attentively the faces of the adult slaves; and I was astonished at the free, easy, sober, intelligent, and thoughtful impression, which such an economy as Mr. Mickle's had indelibly made on their countenances.* Blush, ye black whites of America, when ye behold these white blacks![1960]

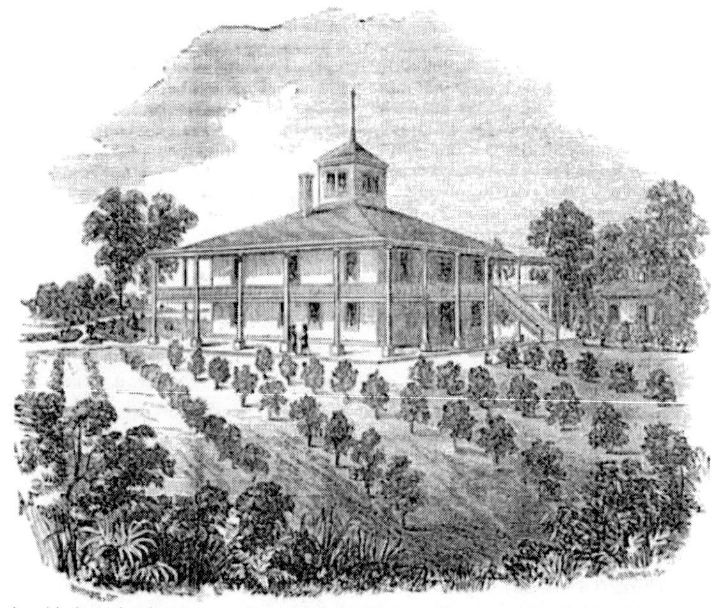

An old plantation house near Augusta, Georgia. According to pro-North historians, every manner of abuse took place on Southern farms between master and slave, from regular whippings and chainings to intentional starvation and slave breeding. The historical record proves that such accusations are actually the opposite of reality. They must therefore all be relegated to the fairy realm of Yankee mythology, where they belong.

From these and thousands of other eyewitness accounts, the deceptions and falsehoods that have been fabricated about the "horrors" of Southern slavery are completely decimated. As Phillips writes: "There was clearly no general prevalence of severity or strain" in the management of Southern servants.[1961] Even the most virulent antislavery campaigners, such as Massachusetts abolitionist and Harvard professor Theophilus Parsons, had to acknowledge that among Southern slave owners:

> Slavery is compatible with much excellence of heart and character and conduct. I have no doubt whatever, that there are many slaveholders who are kind and just men. That they heartily acknowledge their duty to their slaves, and endeavor conscientiously to discharge their duty.[1962]

Were their instances of abuse? Yes, just as there were in the Old North. But in the Old South these occurrences were few and far between, and less severe than anti-South writers have ever admitted. Was slavery an abominable but necessary blight on the history of mankind? Absolutely. But so have been a thousand other evils around the world, none of which generate any notice because they are not connected to the American South—the favorite whipping boy for uneducated South-loathers and progressive ideologues.

Famous Kentucky slave owner Senator Henry Clay, Lincoln's favorite politician,[1963] was fond of contrasting the bonded black slaves of the South—who worked under an employer called a "master," with the "free" white slaves of the North—who labored under an employer called a "boss."[1964] The subject was important enough to elicit a number of books on the topic, one of the better known being John T. McEnnis' 1888 work, *The White Slaves of Free America*.

To put it another way, both regions exploited labor: the South bonded servitude, the North wage servitude.[1965] After living in the American South for several years, Scotsman William Thomson described his views on this very topic to his British countrymen, by favorably comparing agricultural slavery to the industrial slavery experienced by the millions of free white "wage slaves" working in the world's factories and mines:

> . . . it will appear to those who knew my opinions on [American] slavery before I visited that country, that, like most others, who can judge dispassionately, *I have changed my opinions considerably*. Although there are [indeed] . . . cases of great cruelty, *domestic slavery, in the southern and slave states of America, is not that horrid system of cruelty and oppression that is represented in this country [Britain]*. [While it is true that they are denied certain things] . . . I believe, *they laugh and sing more than any class of men on earth. I have seen them laughing at the jokes of the auctioneer who was selling them at public auction*, like the beasts that perish. This, by some, will be called strong evidence of the great evils of the system. Well, be it

so. *I only wish, without being in their stead, I could laugh as hearty and as often as they do.*

I must bring this chapter on slavery to a conclusion, although I have not expressed one hair of the observations I made in my travels through the southern states. Yet, one remark more. *I have seen children in factories, both in England and Scotland, under ten years of age, working twelve hours a-day, till their little hands were bleeding. I have seen these children whipped, when their emaciated limbs could no longer support them to their work; and I believe there is not a planter in America whose blood would not rise, and whose arm would not be lifted up to defend even the negroes from such cruelty; especially the native [Southern] planter, who is much better to his negroes than the planters that have been brought up in free [Northern] states. This is an acknowledged fact, and therefore I need not illustrate it.* If I were to look for the cause of the comparative kindly feeling of the native [Southern] planter, it would partly be found in his *having been nursed and tended in infancy by some careful negro, and having made playmates of the little black fellows of his father's house.* I acknowledge that the miserably degraded state of the [white] factory slave, or the equally unnatural condition of the [white] miners, is no apology for the continuance of negro slavery; and I only make the comparison to show how difficult it is, under the present irrational state of society, to render pleasant the condition of the "hewers of wood and drawers of water." *I consider myself in some degree qualified to make this comparison, for I have witnessed negro slavery in mostly all the slave-holding states in America; having lived for weeks on cotton plantations, observing closely the actual condition of the negroes; and can assert, without fear of contradiction from any man who has any knowledge of the subject, that I have never witnessed one-fifth of the real suffering that I have seen in manufacturing establishments in Great Britain.* In regard to their moral condition, let those who have had the temerity, who have dared to lay their hands on fellow-men, to claim them as property, let them answer for themselves in this matter to the Almighty, who still permitteth this extraordinary condition of society to exist.

Let none suppose that my object is to defend slavery: but, dearly as I love personal liberty, I love justice and truth as well, which compel me to say that *the condition of the [American Southern] negroes is not so anomalous as that of the labouring men of this country [Britain]. [Dixie's black servants] . . . have no responsibility, no fear that their children may be left to want, no provision to make for age, no fear of being neglected in sickness, or of being compelled, in their old age to beg their bread from door to door. Whereas the labouring men of this boasted country have all the care and responsibility of freemen, and none of their [the slaves'] valued privileges. They are used as animals of burden, and have not even the right of shifting the load from one shoulder to the other, without the consent of their task-masters.* I do not make these comparisons between the negro and the worst-off class of manufacturing people for any invidious purpose, but only to enable me to convey a correct idea of their condition, by comparing them with a class that live amongst ourselves, and whose condition we know.[1966]

White wage slaves working in a Yankee woolen mill. Southerners argued that there was little difference between the lower-class, white peasant workers who were forced to labor in Northern factories and the bonded blacks who were forced to work on Southern cotton plantations. Actually, as they noted, there *was* one important difference: Southern slaves could not be fired, and had guaranteed lifelong pensions, housing, food, clothing, and healthcare—unlike their "free" white counterparts to the North.

Let us now highlight the mild nature of Southern black servitude as engaged in by the white man by comparing it with the authentic slavery practiced by another early eager American slave owner, the red man.

Though bondage among Native-Americans ran the gamut, from moderate serfdom to true slavery, a number of tribes practiced primitive and bestial forms that nearly defy description, and which incorporated treatment that confounds the modern mind. Of the "wild tribes of North Mexico," for example, H. H. Bancroft writes that in raiding and war:

> Seldom is sex or age spared, and when prisoners [slaves] are taken, they are handed over to the women for torture, who treat them most inhumanly, heaping upon them every insult devisable, besides searing their flesh with burning brands, and finally burning them at the stake, or sacrificing them in some equally cruel manner. Many cook and eat the flesh of their captives, reserving the bones as trophies.[1967]

Nieboer writes that:

> Among the wild tribes of Central Mexico, the heads of the slain [slaves] were placed on poles and paraded through their villages in token of victory, the inhabitants meanwhile dancing round them. Young [slave] children were sometimes spared, and reared to fight in the ranks of their conquerors, and in order to brutalize their youthful minds and eradicate all feelings of affection toward their own kindred, the youthful captives were given to drink the brains and blood of their murdered parents.[1968]

Honduran Indians enslaved their conquered enemies as well, cutting off their noses to mark them as chattel. Costa Rican natives enslaved the children of their military conquests. If and when their parents were subjugated rather than murdered, they were branded on the face and had one of their front teeth knocked out. Those who escaped slavery were killed and eaten, after which their heads were cut off and proudly displayed as trophies. When a Costa Rican Indian master died, *all* of his slaves were killed and buried with him.[1969]

The Apiaca people of Brazil likewise killed all of the adults captured in war, retaining their children as slaves. When these youngsters reached twelve years of age, they were butchered and eaten. Among the Pimas tribe, males were crucified or tortured to death and their women and children were immediately sold into slavery. The ancient Fijians "barbarously tortured" then enslaved their captives. The head-hunting Bontoc people of the Philippines used to capture their neighbors and tie them to trees. After subjecting them to extreme torture, they cut off their heads, then kidnaped their children, presumably for slavery.[1970]

After beating and whipping their white captives, Native-American tribes often burned them at the stake. Those victims who survived the brutal round of tortures that were inflicted on them were later enslaved. Here a white U.S. officer is trying to rescue a soldier who has been set afire by a band of Plains Indians. Such barbaric practices were unknown on the slave plantations of the American South.

When the Klamath Indians of Oregon made war on nearby tribes, all of the men were slaughtered and the women and children abducted. The latter were sold into slavery, the former, along with some of their own females, were sold into the sex slave trade (forced prostitution). Klamath children who interfered with the sale of their mothers were "killed without compunction." Among the early Charrúa people of Uruguay, during warfare all the men were murdered; the women and children were preserved and forced into concubinage and slavery.[1971]

We find similar shocking traditions among the Pacific Islanders. Slaves on the Marquesas Islands, for instance, were considered enemies, had no rights, and could be treated in any fashion or even killed at any time. Those who survived were either sacrificed and eaten or, in rarer instances, adopted into the tribe. In Tahiti slaves could be murdered without notice, and in New Zealand countless numbers of slaves "were killed at the feasts held in commemoration of dead chiefs."[1972]

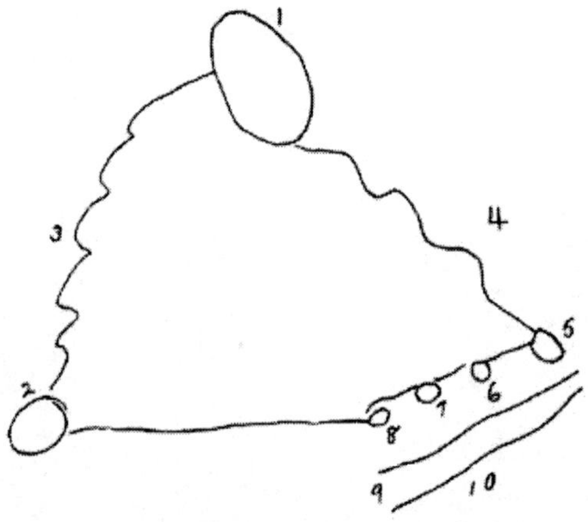

Map Drawn by Kazoola.

(1) Tarkar Village. (2) Dahomey's Land. (3) Wavering line showing stealthy march of Dahomeyans through forest. (4) Route by which captive Tarkars were taken to the sea. (5), (6), (7), (8), Eko, Budigree, Adaché, Whydah, towns through which Tarkars passed. (9) River. (10) Beach and sea.

This map was drawn by Kazoola (later Cudjo Lewis), an African of the Tarkar people, showing his capture, enslavement, and march to the African coast by fellow Africans, the Dahomeys. He ended up being illegally smuggled aboard the schooner *Clotilde* onto a plantation in Mobile, Alabama, in 1859. Pro-North writers focus only this last item, completely ignoring Kazoola's time as a slave in Africa, and the fact that his purchaser in Mobile was not a Southerner, but a New England ship captain by the name of Timothy Meaher of Maine.

The Indians of Southern California never took male prisoners. Instead they "tormented them in a most cruel manner" until dead, then sold or kept their wives as slaves.[1973] Of the early natives of Hawaii it was said that:

> The wives and children of those whom they had defeated were frequently made slaves, and attached to the soil for its cultivation, and, together with the captives, treated with great cruelty. Captives were sometimes spared, though perhaps spared only to be slaves, or to be sacrificed when the priests should require human victims.[1974]

In Neiboer's 1900 work entitled *Slavery as an Industrial System*, we find the following observations concerning the head-hunting natives of New Georgia (Solomon Islands):

> I was informed that slaves are kept chiefly for their heads, which are demanded whenever any occasion necessitates them, such as the death of the owner.[1975] On their expeditions it is not heads alone that they bring back, but slaves as well. These are either bought or captured alive, and it is from among these slaves that the victims are selected in case a head is required. They appear to be well treated in other ways, and to have as much liberty as they please; in fact, [they] seem to be on a perfect footing of equality and familiarity with their captors. But any day a head may be wanted to celebrate the completion of a new canoe or other work, and one of the luckless slaves is unexpectedly called upon to furnish it. Mercifully for the victim, the blow falls from behind and unexpectedly. These slaves are often employed as guides to lead a party of head-hunters unexpectedly upon the mountain villages on Ysabel, whence they originally came.[1976]

In 1887 H. P. Guppy also wrote of the treatment of slaves in the Solomon Islands:

> The servitude to which the victims of this [slave] traffic are doomed is not usually an arduous one. But there is one grave contingency attached to his thraldom which must be always before the mind of the captive, however lightly his chains of service may lie upon him. When a head is required to satisfy the offended honour of a neighbouring chief, or when a life has to be sacrificed on the completion of a tambu house or at the launching of a new war-canoe, the victim chosen is usually the man who is not a free-born native of the village. He may have been bought as a child and have lived amongst them from his boyhood up, a slave only in name, and enjoying all the rights of his fellow natives. But no feelings of compassion can save him from his doom; and the only consideration which he receives at the hands of those with whom

> he may have lived on terms of equality for many years is to be found in the circumstance that he gets no warning of his fate.[1977]

The Acropolis in ancient Athens overlooked a nation of slave owners and slaves, a time period in which there were few if any laws regarding the treatment of servants. In Sparta, where free boys where whipped as a form of military discipline, adult slaves were beaten everyday merely to remind them that they were chattel. In early Sicily slaves were branded and forced to work round the clock.

Let us not leave out Africa, where some of the world's most brutish and disturbing forms of slavery have existed since Pharaonic times. Phillips described one of the many disadvantages of being an African enslaved by fellow Africans:

> One of the chief hardships of the slaves was the liability of being put to death at their master's funeral in order that their spirits might continue in his service. In such case it was customary on the Gold Coast to give the victim notice of his approaching death by suddenly thrusting a knife through each cheek with the blades crossing in his mouth so that he might not curse his master before he died. With his hands tied behind him he would then be led to the ceremonial slaughter.[1978]

In the early 1900s S. H. M. Byers relayed the following story of a black Alabama woman named Abacky, who had survived enslavement at Ataka in her native Africa:

> In slow, soft tones of awful earnestness she spoke of their peaceful

> farm and village life in Africa; how they tilled the ground, planting yams and rice; how some of the women traded in products with other tribes—and all was peaceful; and then one summer morning, just at the daybreak, they heard sudden shouts and firing of guns. Men, women, and children sprang from their beds, only to be killed or captured.
>
> It was the "raiders" of the terrible King Dahomey, come to enslave the village! The surprise was so complete that in half an hour all was over. The young and strong were chained together by the necks, the feeble and the old left dead or dying in their burning village.[1979]

Note that many of these descriptions are of indigenous peoples living in the late 1800s, just a little over 100 years ago.

In comparing the treatment of Southern black servants with the treatment of other types of slaves around the globe, we should also not neglect the ancient world, a lawless period when slaveholders were free to use the most inconceivably harsh methods of coercion and correction on their slaves.

Male Spartan slaves, for example, were regularly beaten for no other reason than to remind them that they were slaves. In early Sicily masters "treated their slaves with extraordinary rigor, branding them like cattle, and compelling them to toil incessantly." In Rome, where masters could work their chattel as many hours a day as they pleased, female slaves were "barbarously punished" by their mistresses for the slightest mistake in "arrangement of the hair or a part of the dress." As punishment for disobedience a male Roman slave was branded on the forehead, hung up by the hands with weights attached to the feet, then sent to the dreaded *ergastulum*, a private prison where he was forced to labor for years in chains.[1980]

Physical torture in the ancient world was not confined to slaves. In early Sparta the boys of free families were annually whipped to toughen up their constitution and inure them to pain. Despite the fact that this trial was so severe that it was not uncommon for some of the boys to die, their fathers encouraged them, standing on the sidelines "exhorting their sons to fortitude." If the lads showed any weakness during their brutal scourging, the number of lashings was doubled. If any one of them cried out, even once, in pain, he was permanently disgraced. The one who remained silent throughout his entire flogging was crowned "and received the praises of the whole city."[1981]

There is not a single record of anything approaching these barbaric customs in the annals of America's Old South. In contrast, Southern slavery was, as this very book testifies, a mild and highly tolerant form of involuntary servitude in which servants were accorded numerous rights, protections, and freedoms, and could even purchase their own independence. Dixie's black servants were fortunate indeed not to have lived under the "peculiar institution" of the pre-Colonial Native-American, the Pacific Islander, or his fellow African neighbors.

WHAT YOU WERE TAUGHT: Most Southern white male slave owners purchased female slaves for illicit sexual purposes, such as concubinage. This is proved by the high prices that were paid for many young female slaves.

THE TRUTH: Anyone who studies the records of these particular types of sales will quickly see the fallacy of this statement. "In virtually every case" the black women who brought unusually high prices were described as "fine seamstresses, parlor maids, laundresses, hotel cooks, and the like." In other words, these were highly intelligent, trained, and experienced individuals who rightfully commanded exceptional prices.

Additionally, most of these particularly talented females were purchased as part of family groups, or were themselves already married. Although there were doubtless occasions of purchase for the purpose of concubinage (such purchases were known, for example, in Louisiana), the truth is that the practice was not only infrequent and uncommon, it was frowned upon by Southern white society.[1982]

WHAT YOU WERE TAUGHT: Almost all Southern slave owners engaged in money-making slave breeding schemes, treating their African chattel as little more than domestic livestock in order to create new generations of slaves.

THE TRUTH: This is one of the more common anti-South myths, one still being perpetuated by the biased and the uninformed. One of these was esteemed Yankee anthropologist Margaret Mead, who made the fantastic claim that black slaves in the U.S. were ruthlessly bred like cattle, after which the resulting children were ripped away from the parents and sold on the auction block.[1983]

Such nonsense does not hold up to scrutiny. Like so much of Northern anti-South propaganda, this myth too comes from unreliable sources, mainly highly prejudicial Yankees writing for Northern and European audiences, whom they intended to infect with their South-loathing disinformation.

Ancient civilizations engaged in *authentic* slavery, which involved extremely inhumane forms of bondage and treatment. This was in stark contrast to the Old American South, where the practice of servitude was temperate and benign by comparison.

As it turns out, the few truly "exceptional cases" of Southern slave breeding were nefariously and purposefully "made to appear as the general rule," an age old pro-North deception. The fact is that slaves naturally reproduced, and thus increased "without any consideration for their master's wishes in the matter."[1984] Any time the owner sold these surplus servants (for in most cases they could not afford to own more than a set number), abolitionists cried "foul!," claiming they were selling slaves who had been intentionally bred for that purpose. In response Winfield Hazlitt Collins wrote the following in 1904:

> A planter could stop raising hogs whenever he might choose, but *it seemed to be hardly within the province of the master to limit the increase of his negroes*. And the better they were treated evidently the faster

> the increase. A man who had one or two hundred negroes, and had scruples about selling them, unless he should be able to add to his landed estate as they increased was in a bad predicament. It seems some *such men had the welfare of their negroes at heart and used every means to keep them*. . . . [Out of purely humanitarian motives] sometimes men who were in prosperous circumstances would buy land as fast as their slaves increased and settle them on it.[1985]

Andrews made these comments:

> A gentleman in one of the poorer counties of Virginia has nearly 200 slaves whom he employs upon a second rate plantation of 8,000 or 10,000 acres, and who constantly brought him into debt, at length *he found it necessary to purchase a smaller plantation of good land in another county which he continues to cultivate for no other purpose than to support his negroes*.[1986]

Besides, as slavery scholar Phillips writes, regulating childbearing in any way, especially by artificially increasing it, is extremely damaging to the health of the offspring who are born as a result of this coercive method:

> With physical comforts provided, the [slave] birth-rate [took] . . care of itself. The pickaninnies [black children] were winsome, and their *parents, free of expense and anxiety for their sustenance, could hardly have more of them than they wanted*. A Virginian told [Yankee tourist Frederick Law] Olmsted, "he never heard of babies coming so fast as they did on his plantation; it was perfectly surprising"; and in Georgia, Howell Cobb's negroes increased "like rabbits." In Mississippi M. W. Philips' [black servant] woman Amy had borne eleven children when at the age of thirty she was married by her master to a new husband, and had eight more thereafter, including a set of triplets. But the culminating instance is the following as reported by a newspaper at Lynchburg, Virginia: "*Very Remarkable.* There is now living in the vicinity of Campbell a negro woman belonging to a gentleman by the name of Todd; this woman is in her forty-second year and has had forty-one children and at this time is pregnant with her forty-second child, and possibly with her forty-third, as she has frequently had doublets." *Had childbearing been regulated in the interest of the masters, Todd's woman would have had less than forty-one and Amy less than her nineteen, for such excesses impaired the vitality of the children. Most of Amy's, for example, died a few hours or days after birth*.[1987]

Slavery scholar Ulrich B. Phillips searched for years for evidence of so-called "slave breeding in the Old South," but came up empty-handed. Where he *did* find it, however, was in New England. This white Rhode Island slave owner, standing on his porch, has just informed one of his black female slaves that she must become a "breeder" in his slave breeding program, or he will barter her off to a neighbor in exchange for several sheep.

Phillips took great interest in this topic, and after years of thorough investigation he could find only one genuine case of slave breeding, and that came not from the South, but from New England! Wrote Phillips:

> It has been said by various anti-slavery spokesmen that many slaveowners systematically bred slaves for the market. *They have adduced no shred of supporting evidence however; and although the present writer has long been alert for such data he has found but a single concrete item in the premises.* This one came, curiously enough, *from colonial Massachusetts*, where John Josslyn recorded in 1636:
>
> > "Mr. Maverick's negro woman came to my chamber window and in her own country

> language and tune sang very loud and shril. Going out to her, she used a great deal of respect towards me, and willingly would have expressed her grief in English. But I apprehended it by her countenance and deportment, whereupon I repaired to my host to learn of him the cause, for that I understood before that she had been a queen in her own countrey, and observed a very humble and dutiful garb used towards her by another negro who was her maid. Mr. Maverick was desirous to have a breed of negroes, and therefore seeing she would not yield to perswasions to company with a negro young man he had in his house, he commanded him . . . to go to bed to her—which was no sooner done than she kickt him out again. This she took in high disdain beyond her slavery, and this was the cause of her grief."

> As for the ante-bellum South, the available plantation instructions, journals and correspondence contain no hint of such a practice [as slave breeding]. . . . [In fact,] it is extremely doubtful that any appreciable number of masters attempted any direct hastening of slave increase [through slave breeding]. The whole tone of the [Southern] community was hostile to such a practice.[1988]

The final nail in the coffin of this particular myth comes from statistics: slaves were not sold until they were ten years of age or older. Thus, if the so-called "slave breeding states" (that is, the Border States) had actually been engaging in this practice, one would expect to find more slave children under ten in them than in the so-called "slave buying states" in the deep South. According to the Census records of 1830, 1840, 1850, and 1860, however, the opposite is true.[1989] Collins adds that

> Southerners generally have denied the accusation [of slave breeding]. When Andrew Stevenson, of Virginia, was minister to England, he was, upon one occasion, taunted by Daniel O'Connell with belonging to a State that was noted for breeding slaves for the South. *He indignantly denied the charge.* And in 1839 the editor of the Cincinnati *Gazette* was much abused for asserting that Virginia

bred slaves as a matter of pecuniary gain.

. . . *It would seem that these States are not only practically freed from the charge of multiplying slaves and raising them for market as a business, but that, as a rule, they did not sell their slaves unless compelled to do so by pecuniary or other embarrassments.*

Probably many planters were as conscientious about their slaves as [Thomas] Jefferson appears to have been. In a letter he says:

> "I cannot decide to sell my lands. I have sold too much of them already, and they are the only sure provision for my children, nor would I willingly sell the slaves as long as there remains any prospect of paying my debts with their labor."[1990]

Jefferson's attitude was the norm, just one of the many reasons why Southern slave families were rarely split up,[1991] with some states like Louisiana banning the practice altogether.[1992]

In the 1850s Yankee clergyman and abolitionist Nehemiah Adams traveled through Dixie to see for himself what Southern slavery was really like. Afterward, concerning slave breeding specifically, he proffered this observation:

> *The charge of vilely multiplying negroes in Virginia, is one of those exaggerations of which this subject is full*, and is reduced to this—that Virginia, being an old State, fully stocked, *the surplus black population naturally flows off where their numbers are less.*[1993]

In the early 1800s Dr. Gamaliel Bailey of New Jersey was the editor of an antislavery paper called the *National Era*. As an abolitionist he was constantly on the lookout for abuses in the South, such as slave breeding. After years of close scrutiny into the matter he came to these conclusions:

> The sale of slaves to the South is carried on to a great extent. *The slave holders do not, so far as I can learn [however,] raise them for that special purpose.* But here [for example] is a man with a score of slaves, located on an exhausted plantation. It must furnish support for all; but while they increase, its capacity of supply decreases. The result is he must emancipate or sell. But he has fallen into debt, and he sells to relieve himself of debt and also from the excess

> of mouths. Or he requires money to educate his children; or his negroes are sold under execution [of his estate after death]. From these and other causes, large numbers of slaves are continually disappearing from the State.
>
> . . . *There are many planters who cannot be persuaded to sell their slaves. They have far more than they can find work for, and could at any time obtain a high price for them. The temptation is strong for they want more money and fewer dependents. But they resist it, and nothing can induce them to part with a single slave, though they know that they would be greatly the gainers in a pecuniary sense, were they to sell one-half of them.*[1994]

In summation, the evidence is definitive: there was no such thing as "slave breeding" in the Old South, period,[1995] for this was a deeply Christian and humanitarian region, the birthplace, in fact, of the American abolition movement.[1996] To the contrary, as has been amply demonstrated, not only did Southern slave owners encourage traditional marriage and family life among their servants,[1997] but the servants themselves desired and enthusiastically pursued these institutions themselves.[1998] In fact, since both Dixie's slave dealers and her slave owners preferred married slaves,[1999] and as purchasing was cheaper than forced reproduction,[2000] these two facts alone completely rule out the possibility of so-called "Southern slave breeding." It was simply not humane, efficient, or profitable.

As so many others did, Yankee journalist and abolitionist Gamaliel Bailey searched for but could not find instances of slave breeding in the South.

WHAT YOU WERE TAUGHT: After purchasing their slaves from slave ship owners, Southern slave dealers maintained their slaves in horrible conditions before selling them at auction. These "slave pens" were similar to Nazi concentration camps, foul, unsanitary, damp, dark, and disease-ridden. The slaves who were kept in these loathsome stalls suffered untold miseries, such as dehydration, starvation, and exposure to the elements. After being stripped naked, they were whipped, beaten, and chained. As a result most died before they could be sold.

The Southern slave dealers themselves were filthy barbarians, much despised by both the slaves and their communities.

THE TRUTH: More ridiculous anti-South falderal, not one word of which has any basis in fact. But you need not take my word for it. What follows is an eyewitness description of a typical slave stockade in 1835, this one belonging to slave dealers Isaac Franklin and John Armfield of Alexandria, Virginia:

> In addition to a brick residence and office, it comprised two courts, for the [slave] men and women respectively, each with whitewashed walls, padlocked gates, cleanly barracks and eating sheds, and a hospital which at this time had no occupants. In the men's yards "the slaves, fifty or sixty in number, were standing or moving about in groups, some amusing themselves with rude sports, and others engaged in conversation which was often interrupted by *loud laughter* in all the varied tones peculiar to negroes." They were mostly young men, but comprised a few boys of from ten to fifteen years old [all who looked *"cheerful and contented"*]. In the women's yard the ages ranged similarly, and but one woman had a young child. *The slaves were neatly dressed* in ["comfortable"] clothes from a tailor shop within the walls, and additional clothing was already stored ready to be sent with the coffle and issued to its members at the end of the southward journey. In a yard behind the stockade there were wagons and tents made ready for the departure. Shipments were commonly made by the firm once every two months in a vessel for New Orleans, but the present lot was to march overland. Whether by land or sea, the destination was Natchez, where the senior partner managed the selling end of the business. Armfield himself was "a man of fine personal appearance, and of engaging and graceful manners"; and *his firm was said to have gained the confidence of all the countryside by its honorable dealings and by its resolute efforts to discourage kidnapping. It was said to be highly esteemed even among the negroes.*[2001]

Ethan Allen Andrews, the eyewitness in the above account, writes that:

> I was assured, in Alexandria [Virginia], that *it was not uncommon for servants in that town, when about to be sold, to request that they might be sold to Mr. Armfield*; and his clerk told me that *they had numerous applications from servants, requesting that they would purchase them.*[2002]

The slave enclosure of Isaac Franklin and John Armfield in Alexandria, Virginia, around 1835. Actually a typical slave dealership where white and black customers could purchase African servants, uneducated pro-North writers continue to incorrectly refer to such facilities as "slave prisons," as if the blacks held inside were criminals being punished. Eyewitnesses tell us that the offices and grounds at Franklin and Armfield were spotless, and that the servants themselves were clean, well dressed, and "cheerful." Since many of them had been true slaves in their native Africa, life in Virginia must have seemed paradisiacal by comparison. It was well-known that local black servants who faced being sold requested that they be purchased by Franklin and Armfield. One man who visited the facility saw blacks laughing and playing sports in the yard, hardly what could be termed a "slave prison."

WHAT YOU WERE TAUGHT: The lynching of slaves and free blacks was a familiar and accepted tradition in the racist Old South. Of course, only blacks were killed in this manner, and always for nothing more than being of African origin.

THE TRUTH: To begin with, lynching—that is, murder without the sanction of law—in the South was "far from habitual," which is what one would expect in the region where the American abolition movement got its start and where the majority of early abolition societies existed.

Second, when lynching did occur, the victim could be any color and any race, and the execution of whites by this method was certainly not uncommon.

Third, as late as the mid 1850s, as Olmsted noted, "the whole South is maintained in a frontier condition . . . that is everywhere permanent."[2003] Lynching then was an understandable and natural development in Dixie, particularly in her more rural regions, at a time when courts, police, and the general population were sparse, where law enforcement was often located a great distance away, and where the wheels of law turned slowly, if at all.[2004]

Fourth, only the most heinous criminals were executed in this fashion. For example, lynching was considered especially appropriate for rapists, pederasts, murderers, and especially abusive slave owners.

One from this last category was an upper class Creole and Louisiana psychopath named Madame Marie Delphine LaLaurie, who became notorious for the cruelties, torture, and murder of her black servants in the 1830s. When eventually her horrid crimes were discovered, a large angry mob of white citizens gathered outside her house in New Orleans, prepared to do their worst. Martineau picks up the story from here:

> *The rage of the crowd, especially of the French creoles, was excessive.* The lady [LaLaurie] shut herself up in the house with her [two] trembling daughters, while the street was filled from end to end with a yelling crowd of gentlemen. She consulted her coachman as to what she had best do. He advised that she should have her coach to the door after dinner, and appear to go forth for her afternoon drive, as usual; escaping or returning, according to the aspect of affairs. It is not told whether she ate her dinner that day, or prevailed on her remaining slaves to wait upon her. The carriage appeared at the door; she was ready, and stepped into it. Her assurance seems to have paralyzed the crowd. The moment the door was shut they appeared to repent having allowed her to enter, and *they tried to upset the carriage, to hold the horses, to make a snatch at the lady*. But the coachman laid about him with his whip, made the horses plunge, and drove off. He took the road to the lake, where he could not be intercepted, as it winds through the swamp. He outstripped the crowd, galloped to the lake, bribed the master of a schooner which was lying there to put off instantly with the lady to Mobile [Alabama]. She escaped to France, and took up her abode in Paris under a feigned name, but not for long. Late one evening a party of gentlemen called on her, and told her she was Madame Lalaurie, and that she had better be off. She fled that night, and is supposed to be now skulking about in some French province under a false name.
>
> The New-Orleans mob met the carriage returning from the lake. What became of the coachman I do not know. *The carriage was broken to pieces and thrown into the swamp, and the horses stabbed and left dead upon the road. The house was gutted, the two poor girls [LaLaurie's daughters] having just time to escape from a window.*

Royal Street, New Orleans, Louisiana. In this 1920s photo, the majestic (now considered haunted) house of Madame Marie Delphine LaLaurie can be seen on the left. The Southern outrage over LaLaurie's crimes reveals not only the deep humanitarianism that has always existed in Dixie, but the facts that cruel slave owners were not tolerated and that lynchings in the Old South were not focused specifically on blacks, but on lawbreakers of all races.

They are now living, in great poverty, in one of the faubourgs. *The piano, tables, and chairs were burned before the house. The feather-beds were ripped up, and the feathers emptied into the street, where they afforded a delicate footing for some days. The house stands, and is meant to stand, in its ruined state.* It was the strange sight of its gaping windows and empty walls, in the midst of a busy street, which excited my wonder, and was the cause of my being told the story the first time. I gathered other particulars afterward from eyewitnesses.

The crowd at first intended to proceed to the examination of other premises, whose proprietors were under suspicion of cruelty to their slaves; but the shouts of triumph which went up from the whole negro population of the city showed that this would not be safe. Fearing a general rising, the gentlemen organized themselves into a patrol, to watch the city night and day till the commotion should have subsided. *They sent circulars to all proprietors suspected of cruelty, warning them that the eyes of the city were upon them. . . . It may be doubted whether any more such people exist [as Madame LaLaurie]. . .*[2005]

While the mob never caught LaLaurie, it is certain she would have been killed on the spot if they had, making clear that the South's "lynch law" was not only saved for the worst outlaws, but was applied equally to all races and both genders. Phillips notes that:

> While the records have no parallel for Madame LaLaurie in her systematic and wholesale torture of slaves, *there were thousands of [Southern] masters and mistresses as tolerant and kindly as she was fiendish; and these were virtually without restraint of public authority in their benevolent rule.* Lawmakers and magistrates by personal status in their own plantation provinces, *they ruled with a large degree of consent and cooperation by the governed*, for indeed no other course was feasible in the long run by men and women of normal type. *Concessions and friendly services beyond the countenance and contemplation of the statutes were habitual with those whose name was legion.*[2006]

It is plain from such facts that the vast majority of Southerners, from the northern Border States to the most southern edge of the Deep South, were wholly racially unbiased when it came to lynching. Just as self evident, they were also vigorously hostile to cruel and unjust slave owners, and would absolutely not tolerate them in their midst—even if it meant risking their own safety and freedom to illegally murder a barbaric slaveholder without due process of law.

With the final ratification of the Thirteenth Amendment on December 6, 1865, eight months after Lincoln's death, the United States became one of the last civilized countries in the world to abolish slavery, thanks in great part to the anti-abolitionist shenanigans of Lincoln himself. Throughout his entire presidential tenure he used various clever stall tactics to delay abolition and derail black civil rights. Such racist-based procrastination did not go unnoticed by fellow Northern politicians, who began referring to him sneeringly as "the slow coach at Washington." Even Lincoln's Emancipation Proclamation had only been issued under ongoing pressure from radical abolitionists, dire military needs, and political expediency—and that three years *after* he became chief executive. In contrast to the U.S., as this illustration commemorates, slavery in the West Indies was officially abolished on August 1, 1838, and, as was the case everywhere in the world—except the United States—*without war or bloodshed.* Indeed, few countries eradicated slavery after the U.S. One of them was Brazil, which did not end the institution within its borders until 1888.

12

SLAVERY AND LINCOLN'S WAR

WHAT YOU WERE TAUGHT: In the American Civil War the North fought to abolish slavery.

THE TRUTH: Not according to the man who inaugurated that war. "We did not fight the South in order to abolish slavery . . ." Lincoln repeated endlessly to abolitionist politicians and his antislavery friends. But they refused to listen. Even when they did, they would not accept his reasoning. Still Lincoln continued to hammer the point home: "We didn't go into the war to put down slavery . . ."[2007]

Eventually he became so frustrated that on August 15, 1864, he issued the following statement, angrily calling those who claimed the war was over slavery "my enemies":

> My enemies pretend I am now carrying on this war for the sole purpose of abolition. So long as I am President, it shall be carried on for the sole purpose of restoring the Union.[2008]

Indeed, from the very beginning of his first presidential term Lincoln made it clear that he had no interest in slavery whatsoever; not in abolishing it; not even in tampering with it. On March 4, 1861, for example, a little over a month before the start of the War, he gave his First Inaugural Address, a speech that included these now famous words:

Apprehension seems to exist among the people of the Southern States, that by the accession of a Republican [then Liberal] administration, their property, and their peace, and personal security, are to be endangered. There has never been any reasonable cause for such apprehension. Indeed, the most ample evidence to the contrary has all the while existed, and been open to their inspection. It is found in nearly all the published speeches of him who now addresses you. I do but quote from one of those speeches when I declare that "*I have no purpose, directly or indirectly, to interfere with the institution of slavery in the States where it exists. I believe I have no lawful right to do so, and I have no inclination to do so*." Those who nominated and elected me did so with full knowledge that I had made this, and many similar declarations, and had never recanted them. . . . I now reiterate these sentiments, and in doing so I only press upon the public attention the most conclusive evidence of which the case is susceptible that *the property, peace, and security of no section are to be in any wise endangered by the now incoming Administration.*[2009]

America's sixteenth chief executive, Abraham Lincoln, was quite clear: the Civil War was not over slavery. Only "my enemies" would claim that it was, he noted angrily on August 15, 1864, to his abolitionist detractors. This makes all those who continue to contradict the president, not the "friends of Abe," but his literal adversaries.

If Lincoln believed, as was true, that he had no legal right to meddle with the institution, *and* he actually promised not to meddle with it, both just five weeks prior to the War, it is obvious that for the man who started the conflict, it was not about slavery.[2010]

In this same March 4 speech, over a month before the Battle of Fort Sumter (the first engagement of the War), he stated absolutely clearly that his one and only issue with the Southern states was money. My main purpose, he declared in his First Inaugural Address, is

> to collect the duties and imposts; but beyond what may be necessary for these objects, there will be no invasion—no using of force against or among the people anywhere.[2011]

Strangely, just as many today refuse to accept Lincoln's actual statements, many in his own time also did not seem to be able to take the man at his word. One of these was abolitionist Reverend Charles Edward Lester, who was immovable on the subject: the focus of the War must be on abolition, he preached unwaveringly. In the summer of 1861, after impatiently revoking an attempt by one of his officials to emancipate slaves (just one of at least five known times the president would do this),[2012] Lincoln took Lester aside and scolded him and other Northern abolitionists who were pushing for emancipation. Said "Honest Abe" sternly:

> I think [Massachusetts Senator Charles] Sumner, and the rest of you, would upset our apple-cart altogether, if you had your way. . . . We didn't go into the war to put down Slavery, but to put the flag back, and to act differently at this moment, would, I have no doubt, not only weaken our cause, but smack of bad faith; for I never should have had votes enough to send me here, if the people had supposed I should try to use my power to upset Slavery. Why, the first thing you'd see, would be a mutiny in the army. No! We must wait until every other means has been exhausted. This thunderbolt will keep.[2013]

We will note here Lincoln's unambiguous assertion that the Northern people would have never elected him, and that Northern soldiers would have mutinied, if he had tried to "use his power to upset slavery."

On August 22, 1862, in his now famous public reply to

abolitionist Horace Greeley (who had vigorously attacked the president in the press for delaying emancipation), Lincoln restated his purpose for making war on the South, this time even more succinctly:

> As to the policy I "seem to be pursuing," as you say, I have not meant to leave any one in doubt. I would save the Union. I would save it the shortest way under the Constitution. The sooner the national authority can be restored, the nearer the Union will be "the Union as it was." If there be those who would not save the Union unless they could at the same time save slavery, I do not agree with them. If there be those who would not save the Union unless they could at the same time destroy slavery, I do not agree with them. *My paramount object in this struggle is to save the Union, and it is not either to save or destroy slavery. If I could save the Union without freeing any slave, I would do it*; and if I could save it by freeing all the slaves, I would do it; and if I could save it by freeing some and leaving others alone I would also do that. *What I do about slavery, and the colored race, I do because I believe it helps to save the Union; and what I forbear, I forbear because I do not believe it would help to save the Union.*[2014]

Lincoln could not have been any more plain speaking than this.

If he did not initiate an illegal war against the South to end slavery, why then did he do it?

As the above reply to Greeley shows, his public claim was that it was to "save the Union." But this was just a smokescreen for Lincoln's true covert agenda: the inauguration of his American System plan, in which the government was to be changed from Thomas Jefferson's conservative confederation (a weak decentralized government supported by small, but strong, self-sufficient nations called "states"), into Henry Clay's liberal federation (a strong central government ruling over weak subservient states). Like nearly all Liberals, Lincoln wanted desperately to enlarge both the Federal government and the powers of the president, neither which he could fully do if the South seceded. And here is the reason that to this day Liberals like Dishonest Abe detest the concept of states' rights.

There were other reasons he went to war as well.

Lincoln did not want to lose the South's prosperous seaports, riverways, and farmland, nor her 8 million white citizens and their numerous electoral votes. Above all, there was the South's cotton and her 3.5 million black servants, the bread and butter of wealthy Yankee industrialists, who had financially supported his presidential campaign using earnings derived from the profits of both the Northern slave trade and Southern slavery.[2015]

Yankee abolitionist and New York *Tribune* owner Horace Greeley frequently attacked Lincoln for delaying emancipation. The president's reply to this charge was always the same, just as it was to Greeley on August 22, 1862: "My paramount object in this struggle is to save the Union, and it is not either to save or destroy slavery."

But Lincoln had no hope of keeping the South within the Union unless he could destroy the idea of state's rights in Dixie. To do this, he reasoned, he had to eradicate the South's political will and psychologically exhaust its people through militarily conquering the region.

Why did the South fight? To maintain the original confederate government of the Founding Fathers and, of course, to protect its new republic from the invasion of Northern forces. It had little choice in the matter. At Fort Sumter Lincoln had cruelly ordained the course the South would have to take over the next four years: kill or be killed.

The Battle of Malvern Hill, July 1, 1862, matched Confederate General Robert E. Lee against Union General George B. McClellan. Neither the Rebel soldiers or the Yankee soldiers on this battlefield believed that the War was over slavery. The former held that they were fighting for states' rights, the latter for the preservation of the Union.

Confederate diplomats who, during the early stages of the War, went to Europe seeking formal recognition, made sure that Europeans understood the true causes of the conflict. It was obvious, they told the English and French courts, that the Yankees had no interest in abolishing slavery. They had entered into war against the South because, having formed a despotism under Lincoln, and having lost the wealth of the Southern states, they needed to force Dixie back into the U.S. in order to re-subjugate her. This Lincoln called "preserving the Union"![2016]

But the Confederate diplomats had, at that particular time (1861 and 1862), little trouble convincing Europe that the War was not about slavery, for Europeans themselves saw no connection between abolition and the conflict. Why? Because Lincoln had not sided with the abolitionists, had not proposed emancipation, had promised not to interfere with the slavery, and had in fact definitively stated that his only goal was to "restore the proper practical relations between the seceded states and the Union."[2017]

In short, we are dealing with two Yankee myths in one here. First, that the South went into battle against Lincoln to preserve slavery, and second, that the North fought to preserve the Union. Both are equally false. In his monument to the Confederacy, *The Rise and Fall of the Confederate States*, Jefferson Davis delineated the matter accurately:

> . . . the war was, on the part of the United States Government, one of aggression and usurpation, and, on the part of the South, was for the defense of an inherent, unalienable right.[2018]

What was that right? The right of self-determination as laid out in the Declaration of Independence, the Articles of Confederation, the Bill of Rights, and the Constitution itself (see the Ninth and Tenth Amendments in particular).

The Confederacy's chief executive President Jefferson Davis publicly declared that the North fought for national dominance while the South fought for the right of self-government. No mention of slavery.

The "Civil War" then did not concern slavery. Rather it was a battle between liberal, progressive, Northern industrialists who cared little for the Constitution, and conservative, traditional, Southern agriculturalists who were strict constitutionalists. This Liberal vs. Conservative conflict still rages today, of course, just as potently as it did in the 1860s.[2019]

Where then does slavery fit into the picture?

We know slavery was not the cause of or even a contributing factor of the War, not only because of what Lincoln himself said and did, but also because:

1. The U.S. Congress too asserted that the War had no connection to slavery. On July 22, 1861, it issued the following resolution:

> . . . this war is not waged upon our part in any spirit of oppression, nor for any purpose of conquest or subjugation, *nor purpose of overthrowing or interfering with the rights or established institutions [that is, slavery] of those States*; but to defend and maintain the supremacy of the Constitution and to preserve the Union with all the dignity, equality, and rights of the several States unimpaired; that as soon as these objects are accomplished the war ought to cease.[2020]

2. The South knew the institution was doomed long prior to the War, and had made many attempts, under Southerners like Thomas Jefferson, to abolish it since the earliest history of the U.S.[2021] Indeed, as we will see, the American abolition movement began in the South.[2022] Abolitionist Jefferson himself, a Founding Father from Virginia, had included a clause in the original draft of the Declaration of Independence that would have permanently banned the slave trade. Unfortunately, as he observed, it was later removed because, in part, it offended wealthy Northern merchants whose livelihoods depended on both the Yankee slave trade and Southern slavery.[2023]

3. The vast majority of Northerners and Southerners simply did not care enough about the issue of slavery to die over it. In the North, where according to European visitors like Alexis de Tocqueville, white racism was far worse than in the South[2024] (one of the main reasons the North abolished slavery before the South did),[2025] most Yankees were

positively hostile toward the idea of fighting for abolition, preferring to keep their distance from blacks altogether (just one of the reasons many Northerners both *wanted* the South to secede and were against abolition).[2026]

The U.S. Capitol at Washington, D.C. The Yankee Congressmen who met here between 1861 and 1865 repeatedly announced to the public that the North was not fighting for the purpose of "overthrowing or interfering with the rights or established institutions" of the Southern states; but to "preserve the Union with all the dignity, equality, and rights of the several States unimpaired." "As soon as these objects are accomplished," Congress pledged, "the war ought to cease." Again no reference to slavery—except a promise not to overthrow it or interfere with it.

4. In the South only a tiny fraction, less than five percent, of the populace owned slaves.[2027] The other 95.2 percent had no stake in the institution and therefore cared little about its outcome. Even the 4.8 percent of the Southern population that did own servants were fully aware that the institution was going extinct, and most, like South Carolinian slave owner Mary Chesnut,[2028] were quite happy about it.[2029]

The South's hesitation to abolish slavery was never about whether it should be done or not. *It was about how and when it should be done.*[2030] Unfortunately, Lincoln took this choice away from Southerners by force, even though just a few decades earlier the North had granted itself unlimited time to abolish slavery in its own region. All this being true, what then would be the average Southerner's motivation for fighting over slavery?

As for the Northern soldiery, Lincoln's own men made it clear during and after the War that they would have never even joined the military, let alone fought, if they had thought the battle was an abolitionary one. Most of Lincoln's military officers were of the same mind. Cigar-chomping Yankee General Ulysses S. Grant, for example, an Ohio slave owner who kept his slaves until eight months *after* the War was over[2031] (only setting them free because he was forced to by the ratification of the Thirteenth Amendment on December 6, 1865),[2032] spoke for nearly all Federal soldiers when he said:

> The sole object of this war is to restore the union. Should I be convinced it has any other object, or that the government designs using its soldiers to execute the wishes of the Abolitionists, I pledge to you my honor as a man and a soldier, I would resign my commission and carry my sword to the other side.[2033]

Most Northern newspapers too understood the true foundations of the conflict. On October 8, 1861, Washington, D.C.'s *National Intelligencer* wrote:

> The existing war has no direct relation to slavery. It is a war for the restoration of the Union under the existing Constitution.[2034]

The same sentiment was expressed by nearly all Confederate officers and soldiers, as well. After the War, Moses Jacob Ezekiel, one of 12,000 Jews who fought for the Confederacy[2035] against anti-Semites Lincoln and Grant,[2036] spoke on behalf of every Southern military man, saying: "We did not fight to maintain slavery. We took up arms for states' rights, free trade, and in defense of our families, homes, and land."[2037] Confederate Colonel Joseph F. Burke declared similarly:

> It has often been said that we were fighting for the perpetuation of slavery. This was not so. We were simply fighting for our right to keep slaves if we wanted to. We were fighting for State rights—rights to be allowed to make our laws for our particular States.[2038]

As further proof, consider the early American debates over continuing or ending the foreign slave trade: the South showed scarcely any interest in the slavery issue itself, but was always mainly concerned with guarding "against precedents tending to infringe states rights."[2039]

The idea that the American Civil War was about slavery is an outrageous fraud and a demonstrable perjury, created by the anti-South movement to conceal the truth about Lincoln and his War. In fact, the conflict was merely a continuation of the age old fight between Yankee liberalism and Dixie conservatism—the same one that began the moment the original 13 colonies decided to form a Union, and the same one that endures to this day. In the late 1800s Confederate Vice President Alexander H. Stephens rightly referred to the Civil War as a struggle between Northern consolidationists (who wanted to consolidate all power in the Federal government) and Southern constitutionalists (who wanted to preserve the sovereign powers of the individual states as promised in the Constitution).

In a June 22, 1861, letter, my cousin, the celebrated "Fightin' Bishop," Confederate General Leonidas Polk, penned the following:

> The North seems bent on overrunning the country and sponging us out at all hazards. . . . I believe most solemnly that it is for *constitutional liberty*, which seems to have fled to us for refuge, for our hearth-stones, and our altars that we strike. I hope I shall be supported in the work and have grace to do my duty.[2040]

In 1863, in her excellent pro-South work, *My Imprisonment and the First*

Year of Abolition Rule at Washington, famed Confederate female spy Rose O'Neal Greenhow wrote:

> It is not my purpose to elucidate the causes which have brought about the downfall of the American Republic. I do not pretend to the character of a publicist, or that of a philosophical historian. But as an attentive, and, I trust, impartial observer, I think I can correct some grave misconceptions of the events which have gained credence.
>
> *In the first place, slavery, although the occasion, was not the producing cause of the dissolution.* The cord which bound the sections together was strained beyond its strength, and, of course, snapped at the point where the fretting of the strands was greatest.
>
> *The contest on the part of the North was for supreme control, especially in relation to the fiscal action of the Government. This object could not be fully attained by a mere numerical majority. A majority of States was also necessary. To secure this majority, and thus complete the political ascendency of the North, the policy of 'no more Slave States' was formally set forth.*

Confederate patriot Rose O'Neal Greenhow articulated what all Southerners knew and understood at the time: the North fought for domination, the South fought for freedom.

> A political party was formed [the Republican Party, then the Liberal Party], whose sole principle was the exclusion of slavery from the territories. There was no moral sentiment involved in this. It did not alter the status of slavery. It made not a human being free; nor did it propose to do so. 'Sir,' said Mr. [Daniel] Webster in the Senate, 'this is not a moral question: it is a question of political power.' Lord [John] Russell has more recently corroborated this bold assertion, by saying, that *'this was a struggle on one side for supremacy, and on the other for independence.'*
>
> On the other hand, *the Southern States, struggling for equality, and seeking to maintain the equilibrium of the Government,* insisted upon the rights of their citizens to enter and live in the new territories upon terms of equality with the men north of Mason and Dixon's line. *They contended for the right of extending their social institutions, not to propagate slavery—not to make a single human being a slave that would otherwise be free—but simply to preserve the equilibrium of power between the two sections.*
>
> It is true that the anti-slavery fanaticism was brought to bear; and it is also true that there followed a rancorous agitation which divided churches, rent asunder political parties, diminished and embittered the intercourse of society, and unfitted Congress for the performance of its constitutional duties, and resulted in the estrangement of the Southern people from their Northern connection. But this estrangement was not an active or stimulating motive, and manifested itself rather in the want of any general anxiety to restrain the movement for disunion.[2041]

Foreigners too were acutely aware that slavery had nothing to do with Lincoln's War. In their opinion it was about money. German progressive and socialist Karl Marx, no friend of the Conservative, anti-socialist South (but a true friend of Liberal Lincoln),[2042] elucidated the sentiments of much of Europe, and certainly of London, England, where he wrote the following on October 20, 1861:

> *The war between the North and the South is a tariff war. The war is further, not for any principle, does not touch the question of slavery, and in fact turns on the Northern lust for sovereignty.*[2043]

As early as 1833, Virginian John Tyler, soon to become America's tenth president, gave the Southern people's viewpoint of the Yankee tariff:

> In plain terms . . . [it is] an unwarranted extension of the powers of the government and an appeal to the numerical majority of the North to grow rich at the expense of their section.[2044]

During the War Yankee General Ulysses S. Grant swore that if he ever became convinced that the U.S. government was fighting to overthrow slavery, "I would resign my commission and carry my sword to the other side."

Far earlier, in the 1820s, John C. Calhoun wrote that when it came to South-North tensions, the Northern tariff was always "the great central interest, around which all the others revolved."[2045] No less than Woodrow Wilson, America's twenty-eighth president, would later concur with these comments. For it was very evident, he wrote in 1892, that because of the North's increasing tariff pressures on the South,

> that she was to suffer almost in direct proportion as other sections of the country gained advantage from such legislation.[2046]

Lincoln himself admitted that, at its foundation, his War was about the almighty dollar. Just prior to the conflict, several Southern peace commissioners had an interview with the newly sworn in president, an attempt to avoid the coming bloodbath. At the meeting, one of the commissioners, Alexander H. Stuart, pleaded for time and further discussions, to which Lincoln replied anxiously:

> If I do that [that is, recognize the Southern Confederacy], what will become of my revenue? I might as well shut up housekeeping at once.[2047]

Southerner and U.S. President Woodrow Wilson asserted that the North did not go to war over slavery, but over money and power.

Southerners well understood Lincoln's primary goal, which is the main reason they wanted to separate from the North: Dixie was tired of having her destiny and money controlled by unfriendly materialistic Yankees, who saw the Cotton States only as profit-making machines for Northern textile mills. This machinery was sustained, of course, by the toil of former black Northern slaves who had been sent South when their Yankee owners decided that they could no longer tolerate them. Here is how Confederate Major Robert Stiles, who served under General Robert E. Lee, put it in 1910:

> What now of the essential spirit of these young [Confederate] volunteers? Why did they volunteer? For what did they give their lives? We can never appreciate the story of their deeds as soldiers until we answer this question correctly.
>
> *Surely it was not for slavery they fought. The great majority of them had never owned a slave and had little or no interest in the institution.* My own father, for example, had freed his slaves long years before; that is, all save one, who would not be "emancipated,"—our dear "Mammy" who clung to us when we moved to the North and never recognized any change in her condition or her relations to us. *The great conflict will never be properly comprehended by the man who looks upon it as a war for the preservation of slavery.*[2048]

German socialist Karl Marx said that the American Civil War was purely a tariff war, one that "does not touch the question of slavery."

As Stiles notes, white Southerners were apathetic toward slavery in great part because so few possessed slaves: as mentioned, less than 5 percent owned black servants, even at the peak of the institution in 1860. No rational Southerner was about to risk his life, his family, his business, or his homeland, for a handful of slave owners. Slave owners themselves would have far preferred giving up their servants rather than die to keep them. Consider the following words from Confederate General Randolph H. McKim, penned in 1918:

> Stonewall Jackson never owned but two slaves—a man and a woman—whom he bought at their earnest solicitation. And he kept account of the wages he would have paid for white labor, and when he considered himself reimbursed for the purchase money gave them their freedom. [Confederate] Gen. Joseph E. Johnston never owned a slave, nor did Gen. A. P. Hill, nor Gen. Fitzhugh Lee. Gen. J. E. B. Stuart, the famous cavalry leader, never owned but two, and he rid himself of these long before the war.
>
> To these facts as to the attitude of the leaders and commanders of the Confederacy, should be added the testimony of the rank and file of the Southern armies. *With one voice they avowed then, with one voice they avow now, that they were not marching and fighting and suffering and dying for slavery but for the right of self-government. Old soldiers, known to the writer, declare they never met a Southern soldier who had drawn his sword to perpetuate slavery. What they had at heart was the preservation of the supreme and sacred right of self-government.* They had the same pride in their cause as [General Robert E.] Lee had when he expressed his absolute belief in its nobility and justice, and his resolute determination to fight for it so long as there was any possibility of success. To use his own words, "Let each man resolve that the right of self-government, liberty and peace, shall find in him a defender."
>
> And *what was true of the soldiers of the South was true also . . . of the soldiers of the North. Slavery was not the issue in their minds. As a general rule, at least, they were not fighting to free the slaves but to preserve the Union.*[2049]

Put simply, slavery was never more than an ancillary matter in the South and in the North. What Yankee myth misleadingly calls the "slavery issue" was actually the *states' rights issue*: in accordance with the Constitution the Southern people merely wanted to be able to choose the manner and time in which to dismantle slavery and emancipate their slaves.[2050] No one likes to be told what to do, particularly by an aggressive, meddlesome, despotic foreigner, which is exactly how Southerners viewed Lincoln at the time, the man they rightly called "the Military Dictator at Washington."[2051] Lyell, visiting the South from England, recorded the following conversation in the 1850s:

> An intelligent Louisianian said to me, "Were we to emancipate our negroes as suddenly as your [British] Government did the West Indians, they would be a doomed race; but there can be no doubt that white labour is more profitable even in this climate." "Then, why do you not encourage it?" I asked. *"It must be the work of time,"* he replied; "the prejudices of owners have to be overcome, and the sugar and cotton crop is easily lost, if not taken in at once when ripe; the canes being damaged by a slight frost, and the cotton requiring to be picked dry as soon as mature, and being ruined by rain. Very lately a planter, five miles below New Orleans, having resolved to dispense with slave labour, hired one hundred Irish and German emigrants at very high wages. In the middle of the harvest they all struck for double pay. No others were to be had, and it was impossible to purchase slaves in a few days. In that short time he lost produce to the value of ten thousand dollars [about $300,000 today]."[2052]

This is the type of math a first-grader could understand. Yet it was beyond the greatest minds of the North at the time!

Prior to the beginning of his War in April 1861, Lincoln was asked: "Why not simply allow the new Southern Confederacy to separate in peace?" The president revealingly countered: "If I do that what will become of my revenue?"

So what was really behind Lincoln's total war against Dixie? It was fought, like all wars, over money, power, ego, greed, and politics—though today's Yankee-scallywag PC thought police do not want you to know this.

Decades before Lincoln's War, South Carolinian John C. Calhoun, U.S. vice president under Andrew Jackson, was expressing his displeasure over the massive tariffs that the North was unfairly imposing on the South. It was this very cultural condescension, political oppression, and fiscal dominance that later led to the War for Southern Independence, not slavery.

From the Northern point of view then at least, Lincoln was correct: the Civil War was very much about his "revenue." But if that is all it had been about, the proud and honorable people of Dixie would never have gone to war with him.

For them the conflict between the two regions involved a number of other long-simmering issues, as history has attested. In essence it was a battle between Southern agrarianism and Northern industrialism;[2053] between the farming and commerce capitalism of the South and the finance and industry capitalism of the North;[2054] between Southern free trade and Northern protective tariffs;[2055] between Southern traditionalism and Northern progressivism; between Southern ruralism (the countryman) and Northern urbanism (the townsman); between Southern conservatism and Northern liberalism; between the South's desire to maintain Thomas Jefferson's "Confederate Republic" and the North's desire to change it into Alexander Hamilton's federate democracy.[2056]

Since these issues long preceded sectional debates over slavery, and in fact were at their bitterest level in 1860, and since they continued "long after slavery was abolished"—as Britain's representative in Washington, D.C., Minister Augustus J. Foster, pointed out—it is obvious that slavery was not the cause of the Civil War. Indeed, in the

1820s, decades before Southern slavery was even considered a "problem,"[2057] anti-South Yankee Daniel Webster noted that plans for a Southern Confederacy were already well under way.[2058]

A Northerner, Gunning Bedford, Jr. of Delaware, predicted the American Civil War as early as 1787. On June 30 he stood before the Constitutional Convention and said:

> . . . the larger states proceed as if our eyes were already perfectly blinded. Impartiality, with them, is already out of the question; the reported plan is their political creed and they support it, right or wrong. Even the diminutive state of Georgia has an eye to her future wealth and greatness. South Carolina, puffed up with the possession of her wealth and negroes, and North Carolina, are all, from different views, united with the great states. And these latter, although it is said *they can never, from interested views, form a coalition,* we find closely united in one scheme of interest and ambition, (notwithstanding they endeavor to amuse us with the purity of their principle and the rectitude of their intentions,) in asserting that the general government must be drawn from an equal representation of the people. Pretences to support ambition are never wanting. Their cry is, Where is the danger? and they insist that although the powers of the general government will be increased, yet it will be for the good of the whole; and although the three great states form nearly a majority of the people of America, they never will hurt or injure the lesser states. *I do not gentlemen trust you.* If you possess the power, the abuse of it could not be checked; and what then would prevent you from exercising it to our destruction? . . . . The small states never can agree to the Virginia plan; and why then is it still urged? . . . *Is it come to this, then, that the sword must decide this controversy, and that the horrors of war must be added to the rest of our misfortunes?* . . . The states will never again be entrapped into a measure like this. The people will say, The *small* states would confederate, and grant further powers to Congress; but you, the *large* states, would not. Then the fault would be yours, and all the nations of the earth will justify us. But what is to become of our public debts, if we dissolve the Union? Where is your plighted faith? Will you crush the smaller states, or must they be left unmolested? Sooner than be ruined, there are *foreign powers who will take us by the hand.*[2059]

Though South Carolina's "negroes" are mentioned, Bedford was not discussing slavery here. This was a debate between himself and Southerner James Madison over proportional representation in the

Senate.[2060]

Even when Southern secession came, the word slavery was scarcely mentioned in the secession documents of the eleven states who broke away from the Union.[2061] What *was* mentioned were the topics of self-determination, personal liberty, states' rights, and the Union's "frequent violations" of the Constitution.[2062] As Confederate General John B. Gordon declared to the women of York, Pennsylvania, during the War:

> Our Southern homes have been pillaged, sacked and burned; our mothers, wives and little ones driven forth amid the brutal insults of your soldiers. Is it any wonder that we fight with desperation? A natural revenge would prompt us to retaliate in kind, but we scorn to war on women and children. *We are fighting for the God-given rights of liberty and independence as handed down to us in the Constitution by our fathers.* So fear not: if a torch is applied to a single dwelling, or an insult to a female of your town by a soldier of this command, point me out the man and you shall have his life.[2063]

Delaware Congressman Gunning Bedford, Jr. predicted Lincoln's War 74 years before it occurred. It would not be over slavery. It would be due to the sharp differences between the heavily populated Northern states and the more sparsely populated Southern states. "They can never form a coalition," said Bedford prophetically.

Despite Lincoln's undisguised obfuscation concerning the *true* purpose of his War, he, along with his cabinet and military officers, were, as we have just seen, publicly clear on at least one thing: the conflict was not over slavery, it was over the preservation of the Union. Lincoln maintained this falsehood until literally the last day of his life. On April 11, 1865, at the White House, four days before his death, and just as so-called "Reconstruction" was beginning, the president gave his last public speech. The Emancipation Proclamation was already over two years old. Still Lincoln once again reiterated the same old lie:

> We all agree that the seceded States, so called, are out of their proper practical relation with the Union, and that *the sole object of the government, civil and military, in regard to those States, is to again get them into that proper practical relation.*[2064]

No talk here of slavery, of abolition, of civil rights for African-Americans, of incorporating blacks into American society. Just preserving the Union. This was Lincoln's mantra at the start of the War, during the War, and after the War. As he literally says in the above quote, it was his "sole object."

Why then do Yankees and New South Southerners continue to maintain that it was about slavery? The answer is that secession was legal,[2065] making abolition the only possible defense (to Yankees and scallywags anyway) for the North's illegal invasion of the South and the needless deaths of nearly three million Americans.[2066]

Prior to becoming America's tenth president in 1841, Virginian John Tyler denounced the North's economic preeminence over the South in the war of the tariffs, calling it "an unwarranted extension of the powers of the government." The accumulation of such complaints finally boiled over in 1860 with the election of big government Liberal and anti-states' rights partisan Abraham Lincoln, leading to the secession of the Southern states and the North's subsequent invasion of Dixie.

Yet, no matter how well this particular Yankee myth is gussied up, no matter how long and forcefully it is presented as "fact" to a largely uninformed public, it can never and will never justify what the North did between 1861 and 1865. In 1870, Northern abolitionist Lysander Spooner put Lincoln, his "Wall Street Boys," and their War in proper perspective:

> *The pretence that the "abolition of slavery" was either a motive or justification for the war, is a fraud of the same character with that of "maintaining the national honor." Who, but such usurpers, robbers, and murderers as they, ever established slavery? Or what government, except one resting upon the sword, like the one we now have [war criminal and former slave owner Ulysses S. Grant was then president of the U.S.], was ever capable of maintaining slavery? And why did these men abolish slavery? Not from any love of liberty in general—not as an act of justice to the black man himself, but only "as a war measure," and because they wanted his assistance, and that of his friends, in carrying on the [Civil] war they had undertaken for maintaining and intensifying that political, commercial, and industrial slavery, to which they have subjected the great body of the people, both white and black.* And yet these imposters now cry out that they have abolished the chattel slavery of the black man—although that was not the motive of the war—as if they thought they could thereby conceal, atone for, or justify that other slavery which they were fighting to perpetuate, and to render more rigorous and inexorable than it ever was before. *There was no difference of principle—but only of degree—between the slavery they boast they have abolished, and the [political] slavery they were fighting to preserve; for all restraints upon men's natural liberty, not necessary for the simple maintenance of justice, are of the nature of slavery, and differ from each other only in degree.*[2067]

WHAT YOU WERE TAUGHT: We know the Civil War was fought over slavery because on several occasions Lincoln asserted, or at least implied, that it was.

THE TRUTH: It is true that Lincoln made a number of such comments, like the following from his December 1, 1862, Message to Congress: "Without slavery the rebellion never could have existed; without slavery it could not continue." On January 31, 1865, he referred to slavery as "the original disturbing cause." And there is his famous remark, on March 4, 1865, that "all knew that the slavery interest was, somehow, the cause of the war."[2068] Such comments, however, completely contradict those we examined in the previous entry, in which Lincoln repeatedly and clearly states that he went to war with the South to "preserve the Union." Why the two opposing views?

Vermonter Stephen A. Douglas, the "Little Giant" who beat Lincoln in the Illinois senatorial debates in 1858, often commented on his opponent's rank duplicity. "Lincoln carefully crafts his words," said an appalled Douglas, "to fit his audience and the occasion." This handily explains, of course, why Dishonest Abe sometimes asserted that "slavery was the cause of the war." The guileful demagogue never acknowledged the fact that such statements wholly contradicted dozens of others he made before and after.

The ultimate demagogue, Lincoln always carefully crafted his words to fit the moment and his audience. This suited the devilish bureaucrat, whose ambiguous speech, obfuscationary tricks, passivity, prevarication, stall tactics, secrecy, shady back-room dealings, deception, pseudo-religiosity, opportunism, do-nothing policies, and political double-talk kept him out of prison and got him elected twice with under 50 percent of the American vote.[2069]

Illinois Senator Stephen A. Douglas put Lincoln's stupendous talent for duping the American people this way: "He has a fertile genius in devising language to conceal his thoughts."[2070] This is, of course, why, as Douglas also once said:

> Lincoln is to be voted in the south as a proslavery man, and he is to be voted for in the north as an Abolitionist . . . [for] he can trim his principles any way in any section, so as to secure votes.[2071]

The truth of the matter is that *privately*, as opposed to *publicly*, Lincoln never once wavered about what lay behind the conflict. His *public* statements concerning slavery as the "cause" of the War were meant strictly for Northern abolitionists, whose votes and financial backing he always desperately wanted and needed.

WHAT YOU WERE TAUGHT: The South fought to preserve slavery.
THE TRUTH: According to the president of the Confederate States of America, Jefferson Davis, this was not at all the reason the South went to War against the North. And who would know this better than the South's chief executive, its highest leader? According to Davis:

> The truth remains intact and incontrovertible, that *the existence of African servitude was in no wise the cause of the conflict, but only an incident*. In the later controversies that arose, however, its effect in operating as a lever upon the passions, prejudices, or sympathies of mankind, was so potent that it has been spread like a thick cloud over the whole horizon of historic truth.[2072]

To summarize, Liberal Lincoln and the progressive North fought for money and power; Conservative Davis and the traditional South fought for the constitutional right of self-government. To say otherwise is both a lie and an insult to the intelligence of the American people.

This black teamster was only one of an estimated 1 million Southern African-Americans who served in the Confederate military in one capacity or another.

13

APOLOGIES AND REPARATIONS

WHAT YOU WERE TAUGHT: The South should be ashamed of itself for practicing slavery.
THE TRUTH: The white South does feel shame for its involvement in slavery, and it has apologized for it repeatedly over the years—and continues to do so, at every opportunity.[2073]

The Northern states were responsible for both the American slave trade and American slavery, yet they have never issued a formal apology, or even acknowledged their culpability in the matter. The blame has all gone South.

What the South wants to know is why the North has not also apologized for its role in the "peculiar institution"? After all, it was Northerners (in Massachusetts) who first introduced the slave trade to the American colonies in 1638;[2074] it was Northern ship builders who constructed America's first slave ships; it was Northern businessmen who financed these ships; it was these Northern slave ships which first sailed to Africa; it was Northern ports that harbored the first American slave ships;[2075] it was a Northern state (the colony of Massachusetts) that first legalized slavery in 1641;[2076] it was Yankee businessmen who owned and operated the entire American slave trading business; it was New England slavers who transported African slaves to every port in the Americas;[2077] it was the North that first prospered from slavery; and finally, it was the North that sold its slaves to the South when it finally found them to be both disagreeable and unprofitable.[2078]

New Englander Henry Ward Beecher publicly criticized his region for its "responsibility for the existence of slavery," something few Yankees did then or now.

Thus when New England abolitionist William Lloyd Garrison campaigned for the secession of the Northern states from the Union, so that they could break their association with the "horrid slave states" to the South, another Yankee "antislavery reformer,"[2079] Henry Ward Beecher, disagreed, saying:

> . . . Union with slaveholders was not a sound principle of political action [on which to secede]. Secession from the Union was neither right nor expedient. It was not right, because the North as well as the South was responsible for the existence of slavery; the North as

well as the South had entertained and maintained it; *the importation of slaves was carried on by New England shipping merchants and defended by New England representatives; and when the proposition came before the Constitutional Convention [in 1787] for the prohibition of the slave-trade, New England voted for the clause that it should not be abolished until 1808. Thus the North shared with the South in the responsibility for the sin and shame of slavery*, and it had no right, Pilate-like, to wash its hands and say, "We are guiltless of this matter." It was under sacred obligation to remain in the partnership and work for the renovation of the nation. As it was not right, so neither was it expedient.[2080]

An Ibo family from southern Nigeria. The Ibo were once one of the great slave owning peoples of Africa. Neither the Ibo or any of the other thousands of African tribes, people, and ethnic groups who once practiced slavery on fellow Africans, and who aided in the development and maintenance of the transatlantic slave trade, have ever given an official apology for their participation in American slavery.

An apology for African slavery in America is also due not only from England (which imposed slavery on the American colonies), but also from the thousands of descendants of early slave owning African-Americans, Native-Americans, and Latin-Americans, as well as from Africa herself: as we saw in Chapter 2, Africa not only practiced slavery long prior to the arrival of Europeans, but greatly expedited and even encouraged Europeans in developing the Atlantic slave trade.[2081]

WHAT YOU WERE TAUGHT: The American South owes modern day blacks reparations for slavery, which should be paid out by the living descendants of early slave masters.

THE TRUTH: While today's New South Southerner may be receptive to this proposal, traditional Southerners understand that it would be difficult if not impossible to fulfill it for the following reasons.

The Dutch were the first to successfully transport blacks to North America in 1619 (an earlier attempt by Spain failed in 1526). In 1624 they founded the colony of New Netherland (later to become the state of New York) for the express purpose of opening up the slave trade to America's British colonies, dominating the sordid business for decades afterward. If reparations are to be paid American blacks for slavery, should not the Netherlands be the first in line?

A white female being sold on the auction block at a slave market in downtown Boston, Massachusetts. At one time hundreds of thousands of European-Americans also served as slaves and indentured servants across the U.S. Are not the descendants of these individuals owed reparations as well?

First, slavery was legal across the entire U.S. from 1776 to 1865,[2082] and was practiced by both by Southerners *and* Northerners. The North was itself the instigator of North American slavery[2083] and the epicenter of the American slave trade for decades.[2084] Because of this the North would also have to contribute. But why would it after spreading the falsehood, for the last 150 years, that "the South is totally responsible for American slavery"? By doing so it would be admitting its role in inaugurating and maintaining slavery for several hundred years, something it clearly does not want to do.

Second, European-Americans, as we have seen, were not the only ones who bought, sold, and owned blacks slaves. Tens of thousands of African-Americans, as well as untold scores of Native-Americans, Asian-Americans, and Latin-Americans, were also slave traders and slaveholders.[2085] Additionally, most Southern whites did not own slaves.[2086]

Scores of Native-American peoples, such as this member of the Nez Percé tribe, enslaved hundreds of thousands of other Indians, as well as whites, blacks, and browns. Such facts underscore the complications involved in paying reparations to American blacks for the "sin" of slavery.

Third, reparations for American blacks would, allegedly, be paid by Americans. But it was not Americans who were responsible for the founding of the American slave trade in the Western hemisphere. It was an Italian, one by the name of Cristoforo Colombo, or Christopher Columbus, as we know him in English.[2087] If recompense is to be awarded American blacks, should it not then be paid by Italy, his birthplace, and by Spain, the nation that financed his expeditions to the Americas?

Fourth, in 1619 the Dutch were the first to successfully bring blacks (as indentured servants)[2088] to North America.[2089] Thus the Netherlands would also need to help pay reparations. Great Britain and Portugal too, like Spain, were deeply involved in opening up slave trade routes between Africa and the New World.[2090]

Queen Isabella of Spain bids farewell to Columbus as he prepares for his first voyage to the New World on August 3, 1492. Columbus, who brought Africans to the Caribbean, eventually enslaved millions of Native-Americans, making him the founder of European-American slavery. Spain in turn funded the expedition, making her partly responsible for helping launch African slavery in the Americas.

Lastly, other racial and ethnic groups in early America besides blacks were also held in various types of bondage, from slavery to servitude, from indenture to involuntary apprenticeship. Among these were European-Americans themselves, the great majority who, like one of Lincoln's ancestors (an early relation who was part of the Massachusetts Bay Colony), came to America as indentured servants.[2091]

With these facts in mind, who would decide—and *how* would they decide—which European nations, and which European-Americans, African-Americans, Native-Americans, Asian-Americans, and Latin-Americans are obligated to pay reparations for slavery and who are not?

Explorer Hernán Cortés was one of the many early Spaniards who aided in bringing the European slave trade to the Americas. In 1519, arriving in Mexico, he came across the Aztec Indians, whom he viewed as an inferior, devil-worshiping race. To rid them of this "evil," he believed that he would have to destroy their cities, convert them to Christianity, and turn them into slaves. Amid the inevitable mass destruction and slaughter that followed, Cortés crushed the Aztec Empire and ruthlessly enslaved thousands of the region's Native-Americans. While we certainly feel pity for his Indian victims, this must be balanced with the fact that the Aztecs had been wantonly and savagely enslaving one another for centuries prior to Cortés' arrival—yet another important item left out of our anti-West, liberally biased history books.

14

THE AMERICAN ABOLITION MOVEMENT

WHAT YOU WERE TAUGHT: The American abolition movement started in the North, that thriving center of abolitionist sentiment.
THE TRUTH: The American abolition movement began in the South. While Northern colonies like Massachusetts were busy legalizing slavery and expanding the slave trade, Southern colonies—who considered anything connected to human bondage an "evil"[2092]—were busy trying to put a stop to both.

Indeed, the very first American colony to attempt to abolish the entire ugly institution, in particular the slave trade, was a Southern one: Virginia,[2093] which began issuing official statutes as early as 1753 in an attempt to block the importation of slaves.[2094] In 1732, when English military officer James Edward Oglethorpe founded the Southern colony of Georgia, it becomes the first to place a prohibition against commercial trafficking in slaves into her state constitution,[2095] calling the institution "unjust and cruel."[2096] North Carolina and South Carolina both passed restrictions on the trade in 1787, as did Tennessee in 1805.[2097]

In point of fact, at one time or another *all* of the antebellum Southern states tried to stop both the importation of slaves[2098] and the kidnaping and selling of slaves within their borders.[2099] In other words, the reality is that *up until the year 1800, nearly all Southerners were abolitionists.*[2100]

While all of this was going on, the Northern states were busy bringing in as many African slaves as possible through their seaports. In 1776 alone, for example, the year the Declaration of Independence was issued, New Hampshire imported 627 slaves; Massachusetts imported 3,500; Rhode Island, 4,376; Connecticut, 6,000; New Jersey, 7,600; Delaware, 9,000; New York, 15,000; and Maryland, 80,000.[2101]

The American abolition movement began in the South, not in the North. This is just one reason why, long prior to the Civil War, Southern slave owners were emancipating their servants by the thousands, whenever and wherever possible. At a financial loss of several million dollars, this white slaveholder in Georgia is setting all of his slaves free in 1829, a full 34 years before Lincoln issued his fake and illegal Emancipation Proclamation in 1863. While some servants will refuse his offer of freedom (preferring the securities of Southern servitude to the uncertainties of liberation), as was the custom in Dixie, nearly all will stay on with their former master to continue working on his estate, now as independent laborers known as "plantation hands."

In 1835, when Yankee tourist Professor Ethan Allen Andrews told a Virginia slave owner that "the whole public sentiment of the North is decidedly opposed to slavery," the man replied sharply: "So also is that of the South, with but a few exceptions."[2102] After visiting the South in the early 1800s, British-American scientist George William Featherstonhaugh wrote:

> All Christian men must unite in the wish that slavery was extinguished in every part of the world, and *from my personal knowledge of the sentiments of many of the leading gentlemen in the Southern States, I am persuaded that they look to the ultimate abolition of slavery with satisfaction.*[2103]

There were a number of good reasons for the near universal

abolitionism across Dixie:

> At the South . . . *humanitarianism* though of positive weight was but one of several factors. The distinctively *Southern considerations against the trade* were that its continuance would lower the prices of slaves already on hand, or at least prevent those prices from rising; that it would so increase the staple exports as to spoil the world's market for them; that it would drain out money and keep the community in debt; that *it would retard the civilization of the negroes already on hand*; and that by raising the proportion of blacks in the population it would intensify the danger of slave insurrections.[2104]

Featherstonhaugh also spoke of the reasons why the South was hesitant to provide "immediate, complete, and uncompensated emancipation," as pushy Yankee abolitionists demanded, to her millions of black servants:

> [Southerner] Mr. [James] Madison, the Ex-President, with whom I have often conversed freely on this subject, has told me more than once that he could not die in peace if he believed that so great a disgrace to his country [i.e., slavery] was not to be blotted out some day or other. *He once informed me that he had assembled all his slaves—and they were numerous—and offered to manumit them immediately; but they instantly declined it*, alleging that they had been born on his estate, had always been provided for by him with raiment and food, in sickness and in health, and if they were made free they would have no home to go to, and no friend to protect and care for them. *They preferred, therefore, to live and die as his slaves*, who had always been a kind master to them. *This, no doubt, is the situation of many humane right-thinking proprietors in the Southern States; they have inherited valuable plantations with the negroes born upon them, and these look up to their master as the only friend they have on earth. The most zealous, therefore, of the Abolitionists of the Free States [in the North], when they denounce slavery and call for its immediate abolition, overlook the conditions upon which alone it could be effected. They neither propose to provide a home for the slaves when they are manumitted, nor a compensation to their proprietors*. Without slaves the plantations would be worthless; there are no white men to cultivate them; the newly-freed and improvident negroes could not be made available, and there would be no purchasers to buy the land, and no tenants to rent it. *The Abolitionists, therefore, call upon the [Southern] planters to bring ruin upon their families without helping the negro*. In the mean time the Abolitionists, not uniting in some great practical

measure to effect the emancipation of all slaves at the national expense, suffer the evil to go on increasing; the negro population amounts now to about two millions, and the question—as to the Southern States—will, with the tide of time, be a most appalling one, viz. whether the white or the black race is to predominate.

The uncompromising obloquy which has been cast at the Southern planters, by their not too scrupulous adversaries [at the North], is therefore not deserved by them; and it is but fair to consider them as only indirectly responsible for such scenes as arise out of the revolting traffic which is carried on by these sordid, illiterate, and vulgar [Yankee] slave-drivers—men who can have nothing whatever in common with the gentlemen of the Southern States. This land traffic, in fact, has grown out of the wide-spreading population of the United States, the annexation of Louisiana, and the increased cultivation of cotton and sugar. The fertile lowlands of that territory can only be worked by blacks, and are almost of illimitable extent. Hence negroes have risen greatly in price, from 500 to 1000 dollars, according to their capacity. Slaves being thus in demand, a detestable branch of business—where sometimes a great deal of money is made—has very naturally arisen in a country filled with speculators.[2105]

These historical facts have forced even the most diehard anti-South historians to acknowledge the bold reality that *Southerners, particularly between 1808 and 1831, played a much greater role in the antislavery movement than Northerners did.*[2106]

Among the Virginians who were ardent abolitionists, even advocating "entire emancipation,"[2107] was America's first president, George Washington. In 1794, when he began to sell off some of his property, he said that his main motive, "one more powerful than all the rest," was to

> liberate a certain species of property I possess [that is, slaves], very repugnantly to my own feelings, but which imperious necessity compels, until I can substitute some other expedient by which expenses not in my power to avoid, however well disposed I may be to do it, can be defrayed.[2108]

Washington was so against the institution that he beseeched God to help bring about emancipation in both the South and the North as soon as possible. Said the Southerner:

> Not only do I pray for it on the score of human dignity, but I can

clearly foresee that nothing but the rooting out of slavery can perpetuate the existence of our union by consolidating it in a common bond of principle.[2109]

As with the vast majority of Southerners, U.S. President George Washington detested slavery and could not wait to cleanse the country of it. A Virginian, Washington was, in fact, one of America's first abolitionists.

As such, he spent much of his adult life trying to come up with a plan "by which slavery may be abolished by slow, sure and imperceptible degrees."[2110] It was, Washington asserted to everyone he knew, among his "first wishes to see some plan adopted by which slavery may be abolished by law."[2111]

Our fifth president, James Monroe of Virginia, denounced slavery in the strongest terms, saying:

> We have found that this evil has preyed upon the very vitals of the Union; and has been prejudicial to all the States in which it has existed.[2112]

On January 19, 1832, General William H. Brodnax of Dinwiddie, Virginia, uttered the following before the Virginia legislature:

> That slavery in Virginia is an evil, and a transcendent evil, it would be more than idle for any human being to doubt or deny. It is a mildew, which has blighted every region it has touched, from the creation of the world. Illustrations from the history of other countries and other times might be instructive; but we have evidence nearer at hand, in the short histories of the different States of this great confederacy, which are impressive in their admonitions, and conclusive in their character.[2113]

U.S. President James Monroe, another early Southerner who campaigned for the destruction of slavery.

In 1827, before the legislature of Virginia, Governor William Branch Giles spoke out against the custom of enslaving free blacks accused of crimes:

> Slavery must be admitted to be a punishment of the highest order; and according to every just rule for the apportionment of punishment to crimes, it would seem that it ought to be applied only to crimes of the highest order. It seems but an act of justice to this unfortunate, degraded class of persons, to state that the number of convicts among free colored persons, compared with

> the white population, is extremely small; and would serve to show, that even this description of our population is less demoralized than is generally supposed.[2114]

In 1832 Virginia politician Charles James Faulkner, who later served under Confederate General Stonewall Jackson during Lincoln's War, gave a speech to the Virginia legislature that included these strong antislavery words:

> Slavery, it is admitted, is an evil. It is an institution which presses heavily against the best interests of the State. It banishes free white labor—it exterminates the mechanic—the artisan—the manufacturer. It converts the energy of a community into indolence—its power into imbecility—its efficiency into weakness. Being thus injurious, have we not a right to demand its extermination?[2115]

Southern Congressman Charles J. Faulkner, later a Confederate officer in Lincoln's War, held that slavery was "an evil," one that needed to be "exterminated" as soon as a proper plan was formed.

Since the American abolition movement got its start in the South, and more specifically in Virginia,[2116] we should not be surprised to learn that it was in the Old Dominion State that voluntary emancipation found its greatest success. We have seen that there was already a large, free black, landowning, black slave owning population in Virginia dating from the early 1600s.[2117] But in 1782, at the urging of Thomas Jefferson, this number greatly increased when Virginia legislators passed a law legally permitting the state's slaveholders to emancipate their slaves.[2118]

The response was immediate and overwhelming. Between that year and 1790 some 10,000 black servants were voluntarily freed by their white owners. In contrast, slave owners in the Northern states showed much greater reluctance to give up their black chattel. New Jersey, for example, did not pass its emancipation act until 1804, which is why it still had over 3,500 slaves as late as 1830.[2119] There were a number of Northern states, such as Connecticut, that banned manumissions altogether.[2120]

As stipulated in his father-in-law's will, Confederate General Robert E. Lee, gladly freed his wife's family's slaves in 1862. Lee hated the institution and was one of the first to push for emancipation and black enlistment in the Confederate military.

After the American Revolutionary War ended in 1783, though the U.S. government had not yet even given citizenship to blacks, numerous Southern states began passing laws allowing African-Americans to own property, testify in court, vote, and travel without restrictions.[2121] In addition, many white Southerners were manumitting their slaves as fast as possible. Thus by 1810 the free black population of the Upper South had risen from 1 percent to 10 percent in less than 30 years.[2122] Across the entire South there were 100,000 free blacks by that year, nearly 5 percent of the free population.[2123]

By 1860 there were 500,000 free blacks in the South,[2124] more than two times as many as were then living in the North. Some 60,000 of these were from Virginia alone, about the same as the number of free blacks living in all of New England and New York.[2125] Phillips writes that:

> Manumissions were in fact so common in the deeds and wills of the [Southern] men of 1776 that the number of colored freemen in the South exceeded thirty-five thousand in 1790 and was nearly doubled in each of the next two decades.[2126]

Southern emancipations on a large scale were practically an everyday occurrence. Monroe Edwards of Louisiana, for example, set 160 slaves free by deed in 1840; in his will George W. P. Custis of Virginia (Robert E. Lee's father-in-law) liberated some 300 slaves at his death in 1857; and in 1833 Virginian John Randolph manumitted nearly 400 slaves via his will.[2127] It was Randolph who said:

> Virginia is so impoverished by the system of slavery, that the tables will sooner or later be turned, and the slaves will advertise for runaway masters.[2128]

Another noteworthy slaveholder who participated in this early Southern manumission program was Virginian Robert Carter (III) of Nomini Hall, known as America's "First Emancipator" for freeing his 500 slaves in 1791.[2129] This was a financial sacrifice of monumental proportions: at approximately $1,000 a piece, these 500 individuals had a value of $15 million in today's currency. By this time, the late 1700s, Virginia herself had "effectively annulled" slavery: blacks could no longer be imported into the state, schools had been established for their education, and numerous Southern societies had sprung up whose sole mission was to legally protect the slaves that still existed.[2130] From this same period comes a revealing declaration by a Virginia slaveholder named Paxton. Reflecting the feelings of millions of other Southerners, Paxton went on record as saying that "the best blood in Virginia flows in the veins of slaves!"[2131]

In 1807, under another Virginian, President Thomas Jefferson, the Southern states enthusiastically voted to end the slave trade by 1808, the year the Constitution had set as the earliest date Congress could decide on the issue.[2132] In fact:

> Jefferson denounced the whole system of slavery, in the most emphatic terms, as fatal to manners and industry, and endangering the very principles on which the liberties of the state were founded—"a perpetual exercise of the most unremitting despotism on the one part, and degrading submission on the other."[2133]

Southerner and U.S. President Thomas Jefferson was one of the first and most vociferous enemies of slavery the world has ever known. His fight to destroy the unwanted institution went on for decades, but complete American abolition would not come until 1865—39 years after his death in 1826.

As Beecher noted, the American slave trade could have been brought to a halt in 1787, except for the efforts of Yankees: this was the year a vote was taken at the Constitutional Convention in Philadelphia to close the trade as soon as practicable, or keep it open until 1808. The New England states voted for the latter option.[2134]

Unfortunately for African-Americans, little changed on January 1, 1808. As even Lincoln later remarked,[2135] Yankees completely ignored the 1808 ban, and continued the trade illegally right through to the end of the Civil War.[2136] Indeed, between 1808 and 1860, Northern slave ships imported at least 270,000 additional African slaves into the U.S.—all unlawfully.[2137]

Actually, Jefferson's attack on slavery had begun even long before the formation of the U.S., while the states were still colonial possessions of England. As a member of the House of Burgesses in 1769, for instance, he asked the British crown for permission to emancipate all slaves in the American colonies[2138] (his request was rejected due to pressure put on the British government by English slave traders).[2139] This was nearly a century (96 years) before the Thirteenth Amendment abolished slavery in the U.S. in December 1865.[2140]

In 1776, now a member of the Confederate (or Continental) Congress, Jefferson referred to slavery as a "wickedness" and again tried to get rid of the trade, this time by adding a condemnation of England for forcing it on the original 13 colonies (that is, for not allowing them to close it down) to his rough draft of the Declaration of Independence. This issue was recognized 43 years later when, in 1819, New York politician James Tallmadge, Jr. told a congressional abolition committee that slavery is "an evil brought upon us without our own fault, before the formation of our government."[2141]

We will note here that Jefferson must have known that England would never allow abolition in the American colonies as long as she had not yet destroyed slavery on her own soil.[2142] And at the time she had no intention whatsoever of jeopardizing the lucrative trade, which had been, until recently, wholly monopolized by the great British slaving corporation known as the Royal African Company. Historian Israel Smith Clare writes:

> The Royal African Company's grip upon the English colonies [in America] was . . . [immense]. *Virginia and South Carolina vainly*

> *imposed a prohibitory duty upon the importation of slaves, as their acts were annulled by the royal command.* The Mother Country upheld the slave trade because the profits of the Royal African Company and of the private [English and Yankee] slave traders were enormous, and because the dependence of the colonists in agriculture, manufactures and commerce, as well as in government, was assured so long as they were confined to slave labor. *This was openly avowed in England.* Thus the colonies were at the mercy of the Royal African Company so long as that company was in existence, no matter how much they resisted its action and policy.[2143]

Despite this, as Clare continues:

> *The repugnance of the colonies to the slave trade brought out renewed expressions of opposition and abhorrence. In 1770 the Virginia assembly attempted to restrict the traffic, but her royal governor received instructions from the authorities in England to veto all colonial acts affecting the interests of the slave dealers.* The efforts of other colonies in this direction encountered similar obstacles. Bill of colonial assemblies and petitions to the king, caused by startling development of the infamous traffic, were alike ineffectual, and over six thousand slaves were imported into South Carolina alone from Africa and the West Indies in less than nine months [by English slave ships]. A public meeting in Fairfax county, Virginia, in 1774—of which young George Washington was chairman—passed the following resolution:
>
> > "It is the opinion of this meeting that during our present difficulties and distress no slaves ought to be imported into any of the British colonies on this continent; and *we take this opportunity of declaring our most earnest wishes to see an entire stop forever put to such a wicked, cruel and unnatural trade.*"[2144]

Though by 1776 the Royal African Company was no longer in operation, British slaving interests still dominated the transatlantic trade, with much of their human African cargo ending up in North America, and worse still, in heavily abolitionist Virginia. Thus Jefferson had good reason to include his censure of the British Crown in the Declaration of Independence. The pertinent portion of the document, written between June 12 and 27 of that year, reads:

> [King George III] . . . has waged cruel war against human nature itself, violating it's most sacred rights of life & liberty in the persons of a distant [African] people who never offended him, captivating & carrying them to slavery in another hemisphere, or to incur miserable death in their transportations thither. This piratical warfare, the opprobrium of infidel powers, is the warfare of the Christian king of Great Britain. Determined to keep open a market where men should be bought & sold, he has prostituted his negative for suppressing every legislative attempt to prohibit or to restrain this execrable commerce, and that this assemblage of horrors might want no fact of distinguished die, he is now exciting those very people to rise in arms against us, and to purchase that liberty of which he has deprived them, by murdering the people upon whom he also obtruded them; thus paying off former crimes which he urges them to commit against the lives of another.[2145]

Though Jefferson managed to push through a bill outlawing the slave trade in 1808, the statute was disregarded by Yankee slave ship owners, who continued to sail to Africa and back with untold thousands of already enslaved Africans, right into the 1860s.

The real question is, why are these powerful antislavery words (Clause 20 in Jefferson's draft)—*written by a Southerner*—not in the Declaration of Independence as we know it today? According to an irritated Jefferson, his denunciation of slavery was removed by committee from the final draft because, in great part, it would have angered not only Northern slave traders,[2146] but also Northern businessmen,[2147] nearly all who were deeply involved in the slave industry,[2148] the same Yankee industry, as we have seen, whose profits were later used by Lincoln to fund his "Civil War."[2149] Wrote Jefferson:

> The clause reprobating the enslaving [of] the inhabitants of Africa was struck out in compliance to . . . *our Northern brethren* [who] I also believe felt a little tender under these censures; for though their people have very few slaves themselves, yet *they had been pretty considerable carriers of them to others*.[2150]

Britain's King George III. Jefferson's indictment of the monarch for imposing slavery on the early American colonies was left out of the final draft of the Declaration of Independence, for fear of offending Northern businessmen involved in the Yankee slave trade—much to Jefferson's displeasure.

While his antislavery clause was withdrawn from the first draft of the Declaration of Independence, the final version, adopted on July 4, 1776, did retain Jefferson's belief that "all men are created equal, that they are endowed by their Creator with certain unalienable Rights, that among these are Life, Liberty and the pursuit of Happiness."[2151]

We will note here that Northern Liberal Lincoln did not agree with Southern Conservative Jefferson on this point. As Lincoln stated on June 26, 1857, during a speech in Springfield, Illinois:

> *There is a natural disgust in the minds of nearly all [Northern] white people at the idea of an indiscriminate amalgamation of the white and black races*; . . . [Yet my opponent Judge Stephen A. Douglas] . . . finds . . . [my political party] insisting that the Declaration of Independence includes all men, black as well as white, and forthwith he boldly denies that it includes Negroes at all, and proceeds to argue gravely that all who contend it does do so only because they want to vote, and eat, and sleep, and marry with Negroes! He will have it that they cannot be consistent else.
>
> Now I protest against the counterfeit logic which concludes that, because I do not want a *black woman* for a slave, I must necessarily want her for a wife. I need not have her for either. I can just leave her alone. *In some respects she certainly is not my equal*; but in her natural right to eat the bread she earns with her own hands without asking leave of anyone else, she is my equal and the equal of all others. . . .
>
> I think the authors of that notable instrument [the Declaration of Independence] intended to include all men, *but they did not intend to declare all men equal in all respects. They did not mean to say all were equal in color, size, intellect, moral developments, or social capacity*. . . .
>
> I have now briefly expressed my view of the meaning and object of that part of the Declaration of Independence which declares that 'all men are created equal.'[2152]

Again in 1776, now a member of the Virginia House of Delegates, Jefferson's draft of the Virginia Constitution contained a clause calling for the total emancipation of all slaves in his state. This was 89 years prior to Lincoln's bogus and felonious Emancipation Proclamation.

In 1777 Jefferson assisted in creating America's first Constitution, known as the Articles of Confederation.[2153] In doing so he said: "It is our duty to lay every discouragement on the importation of slaves."[2154] But the final document, ratified on March 1, 1781, was not allowed to say anything about the trade.

In 1778 he introduced a bill to Congress to prevent the further "evil" of the importation of slaves[2155] "either by land or sea,"[2156] which temporarily halted the trade, though not the institution itself.[2157] The bill must have soon been overturned, or ignored, because it was not long before he was once again trying to push through new antislavery proposals.

Big government Liberal Abraham Lincoln did not agree with Jefferson that "all men are created equal." In 1857 he told an Illinois audience that he, like "nearly all" other Northern whites, felt a "natural disgust" at the idea of the white and black races mixing together.

In 1781, his last year as governor of Virginia, Jefferson began penning his famous booklet, *Notes on the State of Virginia*, in which he called slavery a "tyranny," a "blot in our country," and "a great political and moral evil," further adding that "the minds of our citizens may be ripening for a complete emancipation."[2158] Nearly every Southerner agreed. "I tremble for my country," Jefferson wrote in his *Notes*, "when I reflect that God is just; that his justice cannot sleep forever."[2159]

In 1782, as we have seen, Jefferson pushed through legislation allowing the emancipation of black servants in Virginia.[2160] In 1784, having by this time been elected to Congress under the Articles of Confederation,[2161] he wrote a report on the temporary government of the Western Territory which included a clause that read: "After the year 1800 of the Christian era, there shall be neither slavery nor involuntary servitude in any of the said states."[2162] Congress again ultimately deleted this sentence from the document.

In 1785 Jefferson and fellow Virginian George Wythe, as commissioners in charge of revising the state's statutes, agreed on a bill for gradual emancipation. Unfortunately, when the act came before the House of Delegates that year, Jefferson was absent (at Paris, serving as U.S. minister to France). With no strong voice to advocate in favor of the bill, it was "not brought forward."[2163]

In 1787, while the U.S. was still a Confederacy (and was in fact called "the Confederacy" by Americans[2164] and the "Confederate States of America" by foreigners),[2165] Jefferson authored the Northwest Ordinance, which established rules regarding how states were to be created from the Western Territories and admitted to the Union. In it he included a clause completely prohibiting slavery in the new Western states that were to be created. It read: "There shall be neither slavery nor involuntary servitude in the said territory."[2166] At the time, of course, slavery was still legally practiced in all of the Northern states.

In 1796 Jefferson created a bill on the subject of slavery, saying: "Nothing is more certainly written in the book of fate than that these people are to be free."[2167] The bill, however, was "kept back."[2168]

In 1800, in a memorandum outlining his "services to my country," Jefferson, now vice president of the U.S. under President John Adams, proudly and rightfully noted that he was responsible for formulating the "act prohibiting the importation of slaves." But his plan to end slavery by that year failed.[2169]

Thus it was on December 2, 1806, now as America's third president, that he addressed the Senate and the House of Representatives in his Sixth Annual Message, to bring a special reminder to the American people: on January 1, 1808, the American slave trade would come to an end, Jefferson stated authoritatively. To strengthen his edict, he timed it to coincide with the passage of England's famous Abolition Act,[2170] which was set to permanently halt the British slave trade on the same day.[2171] In the meantime, he encouraged citizens everywhere to try to prevent new Northern slave expeditions from leaving for Africa and to "interpose your authority constitutionally" by withdrawing "from all further participation in those violations of human rights which have been so long continued on the unoffending inhabitants of Africa."[2172]

Due to resistance from wealthy Northern industrialists, who would eventually become known as the "Wall Street Boys," most who were heavily involved in the slave trade and had absolutely no interest in black civil rights, President Jefferson's promise never materialized.[2173] Nonetheless, it should be emphasized that this particular Southern attempt to end American slavery occurred 55 years before Lincoln's Emancipation and 57 years before the passage of the Thirteenth Amendment, which finally and officially ended all aspects of American slavery (except for criminals).[2174]

Southerner Patrick Henry possessed what he called an "abhorrence of slavery," and referred to the institution as an "lamentable evil."

Jefferson was far from being the only ardent emancipator from either Virginia or the South. Indeed, thanks largely to his efforts as well as those of even earlier Southern abolitionists, "from 1732 until the Revolution there were only six months in which slaves could be brought into Virginia free of duty."[2175] One of these individuals was Patrick Henry, who helped inspire the American Revolution, another one of the great slavery reformers from Dixie.[2176] Like the vast majority of Southern slave owners, Henry did not buy his African chattel. He had inherited them, and quite unwillingly. How can anyone seriously believe, he wrote, that I am a master of slaves of my own purchase? I am drawn along by the general inconvenience of living here without them. I will not—I can not justify it! I believe a time will come when an opportunity will be offered to abolish *this lamentable evil.* Every thing we can do is to improve it, if it happens in our day; if not, let us transmit to our descendants, together with our slaves, a pity for their unhappy lot, and *an abhorrence of slavery.*[2177]

In 1790 Virginian Fernando Fairfax drafted his "Plan for Liberating the Negroes within the United States," while six years later, in 1796, St. George Tucker, one of the earliest abolitionists in the U.S., drew up another even more elaborate emancipation program.[2178]

About the same time another Southerner, James Madison, joined Thomas Jefferson in formulating ideas for permanently ending slavery in Virginia.[2179] In 1788, in *The Federalist Papers*, Madison wrote passionately on the subject of abolition *from the South's point of view*:

> *It were doubtless to be wished that the power of prohibiting the importation of slaves had not been postponed until the year 1808, or rather, that it had been suffered to have immediate operation.* But it is not difficult to account either for this restriction on the general government or for the manner in which the whole clause is expressed. *It ought to be considered as a great point gained in favor of humanity that a period of twenty years may terminate forever within these States a traffic which has so long and so loudly upbraided the barbarism of modern policy; that within that period it will receive a considerable discouragement from the Federal Government and may be totally abolished* by the concurrence of the few States which continue the *unnatural traffic* in the prohibitory example which is given by so large a majority of the Union. *Happy would it be for the unfortunate Africans if an equal prospect lay before them of being redeemed from the oppression of their European brethren. . . .*
>
> We [in the Southern states] subscribe to the doctrine . . . that representation relates more immediately to persons, and taxation more immediately to property; and we join in the application of this distinction to the case of our slaves. But *we deny the fact that slaves are considered merely as property, and in no respect whatever as persons.* The true state of the case is that they partake of both these qualities, being considered by our laws in some respects as persons, and in other respects as property. In being compelled to labor, not merely for himself, but for a master—in being vendible by one master to another master, and being subject, at all times, to being restrained in his liberty and chastised in his body by the capricious will of his owner, the slave may appear to be

degraded from the human rank and classed with that of the irrational animals which fall under the legal denomination of property. In being protected, on the other hand, in his life and in his limbs against the violence of all others, even the master of his labor and his liberty, and in being punished himself for all violence committed against others, *the slave is no less regarded by the law as a member of society, not as a part of the irrational creation—as a moral person, not a mere object of property.* The Federal Constitution, therefore, decides with great propriety on the case of our slaves when it views them in the mixed character of persons and property. This is, in fact, their true character. It is the character bestowed on them by the laws under which they live, and it will not be disputed that these are the proper criterion, because *it is only under the pretext that the laws have transformed negroes into subjects of property that a place is denied to them in the computation of numbers, and it is admitted that if the laws were to restore the rights which have been taken away the negroes would no longer be refused an equal share of representation with the other inhabitants.*[2180]

In 1788 Southerner and U.S. President James Madison condemned the laws that viewed slaves as "property" and which would allow the slave trade to continue until 1808.

Southerner and U.S. Founding Father George Mason felt that slavery always "brings the judgment of heaven upon a country," and lamented the fact that Yankee businessmen had gotten involved in the trade.

Twenty years before that, the Virginia Declaration of Rights—first drafted in 1776 by native son and antislavery advocate George Mason—included the phrase that all men are "born equally free and independent," and are possessed of certain "natural, essential, and unalienable rights."[2181] Mason himself noted:

> "Slavery discourages arts and manufactures. The poor despise labor when performed by slaves. They prevent the immigration of whites, who really enrich and strengthen a country. They produce a pernicious effect on manners. Every master of slaves is born a petty tyrant. They bring the judgment of heaven on a country." He lamented that some of our [north] eastern brethren [that is, Yankees], from a lust of gain, had embarked in this nefarious traffic [the slave trade]. As to the states being in possession of the right to import, that was the case of many other rights now to be given up. He held it essential, in every point of view, that the general government should have power to prevent the increase of slavery.[2182]

In 1790 the Virginia Abolition Society was formed, and Southern slave owner Robert Pleasants was made its first president. In 1791 the organization, which now numbered nearly 100 members, sent a petition against slavery to the Virginia Assembly, as well as one to Congress, in the hopes of bringing an end to the transatlantic slave trade. Pleasants often corresponded with other Southern abolitionists, among them Patrick Henry, Thomas Jefferson, James Madison, George Washington, and George St. Tucker, garnering their support for his efforts. Of Pleasants, Stephen Beauregard Weeks writes that he

> died on April 4, 1801, aged 79. He is spoken of in the monthly [abolition] meeting memorial as "an indulgent and prudent master." He was a philanthropist as well. He emancipated eighty slaves. In a memorial to the Governor and Council of Virginia he says that he "did, about the year 1777, place divers [that is, a number] of his Negroes on lands of his own, at a small distance from his habitation, and for their encouragement to industry, and to remove every inducement to theft and dishonesty, supported them for the term of one year, and allowed them the full benefit of their labor."[2183]

In 1816 a myriad of manumission societies began to burst forth in North Carolina. The strongest and most aggressive branch, headed by Moses Swaim, was in Guilford County. There were 147 members at the first meeting that year in July. Around the same time the Manumission Society of Tennessee was founded. The formation of both organizations was inspired by the work of Southern abolitionist Charles Osborn, a North Carolinian by birth, who had moved to Tennessee as a child, where he began preaching against slavery in 1806. His followers held that Osborn—who refused to eat or use any slave-grown produce—was the first American to preach the idea of "immediate and unconditional emancipation," and that his journal, *The Philanthropist*, was the first in the nation to print it.[2184]

A myriad of other early Southerners stepped forward to push the abolitionist cause. Among them was another North Carolinian, Calvin A. Wiley, as well as Reverend James Lyons of Mississippi. Both men campaigned for legal reforms that would lift the ban on educating slaves, help protect slave marriages, ban the splitting up of slave families, and allow slaves to testify in court.[2185] Their efforts were heartily welcomed throughout the abolitionist South. Louisiana, as just one example, eventually prohibited both the breaking up of servant families[2186] and the prevention of blacks exiled to their state from other states from becoming American citizens,[2187] facts you will read in few American history books.

A friend of Mary Chesnut's, Confederate General James Johnston Pettigrew, wrote an antislavery essay in 1862—the same year Lincoln was trying to figure out how to prevent abolitionists from pressuring him into issuing an emancipation proclamation. A South Carolina slave owner and abolitionist, Chesnut not only read it but highly approved of Pettigrew's words and ideas, and told him so, much to the officer's pleasure.[2188] Sadly the North Carolinian died shortly after the Battle of Gettysburg and never saw the fruition of his dream of ending slavery in the South.[2189]

Of the 130 abolition societies established before 1827 by Northern abolitionist Benjamin Lundy, over 100, comprising four-fifths of the total membership, were in the South.[2190] Southern Quakers were among the first to come out against the spread of the institution.[2191] Early North Carolina, as another example, had a number of well-known "forceful" antislavery leaders, such as Benjamin Sherwood Hedrick and Daniel Reaves Goodlow.[2192] And in South Carolina the famed Quaker sisters Sarah and Angelina Grimké were just two among millions of Southerners fighting for the cause of abolition.[2193] The Southern abolition movement involved so many Southerners, so many Southern states, and covered such a large span of time, that the latter wrote an entire book on the subject.[2194]

Other Southerners of note who came out against the "peculiar institution" were Bishop William Meade,[2195] Christopher Gadsden, Nathaniel Macon,[2196] Samuel Doak, Gideon Blackburn, John Rankin, David Nelson, James H. Dickey, James Gilliland, Samuel Crothers, Dyer Burgess, James Lemen, Edward Coles, William T. Allan, James A. Thome, William Ladd, James G. Birney, and George Bourne, cofounder of the "American Anti-Slavery Society" in 1833.[2197] On August 14, 1776, South Carolina rice planter and slave owner Henry Laurens wrote the following to his son John, who was also antislavery:

> You know, my dear son, *I abhor slavery*. I was born in a country in which slavery had been established by British Parliaments and the

laws of the country for ages before my existence. I found the Christian religion and slavery growing under the same authority and cultivation. *I nevertheless dislike it.* In former days there was no combating the prejudices of men, supported by interest. *The day I hope is approaching when from principles of gratitude and justice every man will strive to be foremost in complying with the golden rule.* £20,000 sterling [about £2.5 million, or $4 million in today's currency] would my negroes produce if sold at auction tomorrow. I am not the man who enslaved them; they are indebted to Englishmen for that favour. Nevertheless *I am devising means for manumitting many of them and for cutting off the entail of slavery.*[2198]

Prior to 1827 Northern abolitionist Benjamin Lundy founded some 130 abolition societies across America. At least 100, or four-fifths of them, were located in the South.

In 1778 Jefferson managed to push through a bill that temporarily blocked the importation of African slaves,[2199] and in the early 1800s he and Madison were still discussing, and fully expecting, their home state of Virginia to move toward abolishing slavery. In 1794 North Carolina also prohibited the foreign slave trade,[2200] and in 1798 South Carolina Senator William Harper put forth an amendment "prohibiting the introduction into the new Mississippi territory of slaves from without the limits of the United States." (It passed without opposition.) That same year Georgia revised its constitution, adding a clause expressly banning the importation of slaves "from Africa or any foreign place."[2201]

Around the same time South Carolina Congressman William Lowndes came forward, saying that "personally, he was opposed to the slave-trade, and that he wished the time were already arrived when it might be constitutionally prohibited by Congress." In 1807 U.S. Representative Peter Early of Georgia stood before a congressional committee and said: "We of the South consider slavery a dreadful evil . . ."[2202] John Randolph of Virginia denounced the ever increasing slave traffic in Washington, D.C. as "heinous and abominable, inhuman and illegal." South Carolina's Governor David Rogerson Williams condemned it as well, as opposed to "enlightened humanity, wise policy and the prayers of the just."[2203]

Southern Congressman John Randolph deplored the Yankee slave trafficking in and around Washington, D.C., calling it "abominable, inhuman, and illegal."

Following the intense abolitionist activities of the late 1700s, by the early 1800s the Southern abolition movement was in full swing. Weeks writes:

> It is to be noted . . . that *during the whole of this period the anti-slavery sentiment was strong in Virginia*. This sentiment is shown clearly by the great debates in the Virginia Assembly in January, 1832, on the question of gradual emancipation. This debate was precipitated by the Nat Turner insurrection in August, 1831. Emancipation was advocated by most of the leading men of the day, including Mr. Moore, of Rockbridge; Mr. Rives, of Campbell; Mr. [William B.] Preston, who was afterwards in [U.S. President Zachary] Taylor's

> cabinet; George W. Summers, afterwards member of Congress; Thomas J. Randolph, the grandson of [Thomas] Jefferson; Thomas Marshall; James McDowell, Jr., afterwards governor of Virginia and member of Congress; and Charles J. Faulkner, M. C. and minister to France. While there were members who denied the advisability of action, *there were none who defended the principles of slavery*. The *Whig* and the *Enquirer* were both equally vehement in their denunciations of the institution.[2204]

Thus it was that in 1863, when Lincoln illegally forced Virginia to cede her northwest territory (in order to form West Virginia), she stipulated that it be a slave-free region.[2205]

Southerner Robert E. Lee believed that slavery had such an overwhelmingly and obvious negative impact on both whites and blacks that "it is idle to expatiate on its disadvantages."

In the 1850s Yankee minister Nehemiah Adams traveled through the South and found, contrary to all that he had heard about "racist Southerners," a vast and thriving abolition movement, complete with fiery abolitionist speakers and widely disseminated antislavery tracts. A stunned Adams noted that white Southerners everywhere could not wait to abolish the institution, "till no wrong, no pain, should be the fruit of it which is not incidental to every human lot."[2206]

On December 27, 1856, five years before Lincoln's War, here is what one famous antislavery Virginian, Robert E. Lee, had to say about the institution:

> There are few, I believe, in this enlightened age, but what will acknowledge that *slavery as an institution is a moral and political evil in any country. It is idle to expatiate on its disadvantages. I think it is a greater evil to the white than to the colored race.*[2207]

In January 1865, almost a year before the U.S. abolished slavery, Confederate official Judah P. Benjamin announced the C.S. government's pledge to enact total abolition across all of the Southern states.

Most of the General's Southern compatriots agreed with him, which is why the Confederate States of America sought to end slavery before the United States of America did: in January 1865, nearly a year before the U.S. issued the Thirteenth Amendment (on December 6) banning slavery across the nation, Confederate Secretary of State Judah P. Benjamin ordered Confederate commissioner Duncan F. Kenner to England to announce the C.S.'s commitment to full emancipation.[2208]

Even before Lee spoke the words recorded above, white Southerners everywhere were adopting ever more liberal reforms that, along with the forces of industrialization, urbanization, and the Enlightenment, would have inevitably led to eventual abolition and emancipation all across the South. That is, if Lincoln had not interfered by illegally invading what was by then a constitutionally-formed foreign country.[2209] After the War started, Southerners in their thousands continued to come out against slavery. Among them of course was Lee, who said:

> If I owned the four millions of slaves [in the South], I would cheerfully sacrifice them to the preservation of the Union . . .[2210]

The true irony of all this of course is that, as Lee intimated, the North ended up using slavery as justification for its illegal invasion of Dixie, and yet it was the North who sold these same slaves to the South to begin with.[2211]

WHAT YOU WERE TAUGHT: The North never fully embraced slavery. Only the South.
THE TRUTH: Since American slavery got its start in the North, and since the American abolition movement got its start in the South, this statement is obviously untrue for these two reasons alone. In fact, contrary to Northern mythology, not only did the Old South never fully embrace slavery, it never invited it to begin with.

What our current Northern-slanted history books do not teach is that up until the year 1831—the year meddlesome busybody and Yankee abolitionist William Lloyd Garrison began publishing his arrogant, slanderous anti-South newspaper, *The Liberator*—not only was slavery not considered an "issue,"[2212] but hundreds of thousands of Southerners had been busy quietly, earnestly, and gradually manumitting their slaves.[2213] Surprising? Hardly. Nearly every Southern man and woman was both an antislavery advocate[2214] *and* an abolitionist,[2215] two categories of individuals that were in the vast minority in the North at the time.[2216]

In late 1861 slave owner Mary Chesnut, for example, writes that both she and her husband James Chesnut, Jr. (President Jefferson Davis' aide-de-camp) literally hated slavery.[2217] And I will never get used to the word "nigger," she wrote emphatically.[2218] "All Southerners detest the institution more than Harriet Beecher Stowe ever could; we abhor slavery, know that it is doomed, and are happy about it,"[2219] she emphasized. In an earlier diary entry dated June 29, 1861, the Southern belle included the following words: "slavery has got to go, of course!"[2220]

Such statements are all but ignored, or even suppressed, by Northern and New South writers. But we traditional Southerners are well aware of them, and I record them here for future generations.

The masthead of William Lloyd Garrison's anti-South abolition newspaper *The Liberator*. Though it displays the biblical quote "thou shalt love they neighbor," Garrison had no love for his white neighbors to the South, the very people who had launched the American abolition movement decades before he was born. Garrison also uses an image of Jesus, whom he has saying: "I come to break the bonds of the oppressors." But Jesus fully accepted the institution of slavery and never spoke out against it. Indeed, our Lord commanded obedience to the laws of the land. But Garrison, like all radical abolitionists, ignored the fact that slavery was legal both in ancient Israel and in the Victorian South.

The diarist once described a letter she had written to her husband while he was on their plantation in Mississippi in 1842. "It is the most ardent abolitionist document," she noted, one she kept so that the South's allegedly highly educated foes to the North might one day learn the truth about so-called Southern slavery.[2221]

So far, 170 years later, few anti-South partisans have shown any interest in becoming "educated" when it comes to the facts about American slavery!

Speaking for the entire white slave owning class, after the War Mississippian Susan Dabney Smedes wrote:

> Now that the institution [of slavery] is swept away, I venture to express the conviction that *there is not an intelligent white man or woman in the South who would have it recalled, if a wish could do it.* Those [whites] who suffered and lost most—those who were *reduced from a life of affluence to one of grinding poverty* [due to the emancipation of their servants]—are content to pay the price.
>
> . . . It may not be out of place to give an illustration of how [Alcey] one of the Burleigh [a related Dabney family plantation in Virginia] servants carried her point over the heads of the white family.

> After the mistress had passed away, Alcey resolved that she would not cook any more, and she took her own way of getting assigned to field work. She systematically disobeyed orders and stole or destroyed the greater part of the provisions given to her for the table. No special notice was taken, so she resolved to show more plainly that she was tired of the kitchen. Instead of getting the chickens for dinner from the coop, as usual, she unearthed from some corner an old hen that had been sitting for six weeks, and served her up as a fricassee! We had company to dinner that day; that would have deterred most of the servants, but not Alcey. She achieved her object, for she was sent to the field the next day, without so much as a reprimand, if I remember rightly. We were very sorry, for she was the most accomplished cook whom we had had in Mississippi. But what was to be done? No master could have made her cook unless by making a brute of himself, and using such measures as would lower him in his own eyes. Her master merely said, "Choose any one whom you like as your cook, and let Alcey go out to the field."[2222]

Old South Southerners like the Dabneys and the Chesnuts, being innately humanitarian, deplored the institution of African slavery and felt that they had, quite rightly, unwillingly inherited the "incubus" from their Northern neighbors, who in turn had inherited it, by force, from Great Britain,[2223] which had inherited it from its ultimate source: Africa herself.[2224] Writing in 1817, radical Yankee abolitionist Jesse Torrey was forced to make the following comments:

> . . . the possessors of slaves, with whom I have conversed, while travelling through several slave districts [in the South], frequently acknowledged that they "have inherited a curse from their ancestors, and that it would be better for the country if the slaves were all out of it."[2225]

Hence, in the early 1800s Virginia's eccentric antislavery advocate, Senator John Randolph, could truthfully say that "slavery was foisted on the South, and was never an institution she sought out,"[2226] while Virginia Senator John Taylor could declare that "slavery was an inherited disaster that Southerners would have to endure but never accept."[2227] In 1900 Dr. Henry A. White wrote of this monstrous process:

> *Unto the ships of New England the slave-carrying-trade was transferred after the [American] Revolution. Even before that war, her [Yankee]*

skippers had taken cargoes of rum from Cape Cod and Narragansett to exchange for flesh and blood on the coast of Africa. Fresh impetus was now given to this kind of barter. Wealth was rapidly heaped up in Rhode Island through the traffic of her fleet of slave vessels. *Gradually the negroes of Northern masters were sent to the Southern markets, and thus were the Southern States filled up with the alien race.*[2228]

An enlightened and educated Southerner, U.S. President Woodrow Wilson was well aware of the realities of American slavery, particularly so-called "Southern slavery." "There was no region on earth," he argued, "where one could find more vigorous disapproval of slavery than in Dixie."

Clearly, 17th-Century Southerners, now "saddled" with slavery, would have preferred that it had never come to America's shores to begin with. This is why both the civil rights movement and the abolition movement began in, and were so strong in, the South from the earliest days of the nation. And this is why the region tried to ban slavery long before the North did. As Southerner and U.S. President Woodrow Wilson writes, nowhere in early America were there more sincere, more openly declared denunciations of the "evil influence" of slavery on both whites and blacks than in the South:[2229]

> A mild antislavery sentiment, born of the philanthropic spirit, had existed in all parts of the country from the first. *Nowhere were there to be found clearer or more plainly spoken condemnations of its evil influence at once upon masters and slaves and upon the whole structure and spirit of society than representative southern men had uttered.*[2230]

WHAT YOU WERE TAUGHT: In contrast to the Old South, the Old North was 100 percent antislavery, pro-abolition, and pro-African-American.

THE TRUTH: This myth would be laughable if it had not been accepted as factual by hundreds of millions of Americans, even the educated, over the past 150 years, which has caused irreparable damage to the South's reputation as a result.

If one chooses to judge early Southerners by today's mores and ideas, then he must judge early Northerners by the same ones. To make our point, let us begin with an example of a well-known Yankee racist and slave owner, one who would now be considered an overt white supremacist, Benjamin Franklin.[2231]

The famous Boston inventor and statesman detested slavery; not because it hurt blacks, but because it hurt whites. How? By forcing an "unnatural intermingling" of the two races, whereby the white race was thought to be diluted and degenerated by the black one.[2232]

In Franklin's view whites were a civilized, light, happy, righteous, forgiving, Christian people, while the majority of blacks, he declared, "are of a plotting Disposition, dark, sullen, malicious, revengeful, and cruel in the highest Degree."[2233] Because of these perceived differences, Franklin came to believe in maintaining the "racial purity" of the European-American race, a goal that was threatened by the introduction of black slavery into the U.S., which he feared would make whites darker.

Franklin, who as a newspaper publisher had printed advertisements for slave sales,[2234] noted with revulsion how "the introduction of slaves" always "greatly diminished the whites," and how slaves always "pejorate the families that use them; the white children become proud, disgusted with labor, and, being educated in idleness, are rendered unfit to get a living by industry."[2235]

Yankee statesman and inventor Benjamin Franklin held the typical white Northern view of slavery at the time: he was not against the institution because it hurt blacks, but because the "unnatural intermingling" of the two races "degraded" whites.

While advocating the banning of slavery, Franklin felt that it was also proper to be biased toward one's own race, making him what we would call today an abolitionist-racist. Franklin was no isolated character in this regard.[2236]

Studies of 19th-Century society show that nearly all white Northerners were of the same mind as the famed printer and writer. Indeed, Franklin could have been speaking for most Yankees and Northerners when he voted to prohibit the institution while at the same time complaining about the problem of disappearing whites in the face of an ever increasing population of blacks.[2237] It is a fact, Franklin wrote, that

> the number of purely white people in the world is proportionably very small. All Africa is black or tawny; Asia chiefly tawny; America (exclusive of the new comers) wholly so. And in Europe, the Spaniards, Italians, French, Russians, and Swedes, are generally of what we call a swarthy complexion; as are the Germans also, *the Saxons only excepted, who, with the English, make the principal body of white people on the face of the earth. I could wish their numbers were increased*. And while we are, as I may call it, scouring our planet, by clearing America of woods, and so making this side of our globe reflect a brighter light to the eyes of inhabitants in Mars or Venus, why should we, in the sight of superior beings, darken its people? *Why increase the sons of Africa, by planting them in America, where we have so fair an opportunity, by excluding all blacks and tawnys, of increasing the lovely white and red?* But perhaps *I am partial to the complexion of my country*, for such kind of partiality is natural to mankind.[2238]

The vast majority of Southerners, even if they were slaveholders, never looked at other races the way Yankees did. In fact, there are few records, written or verbal, of this type of racism, or any other kind, in the typical Southern family. Most would be more accurately described as the true friends of American blacks—quite unlike Northerners such as Franklin, and later the notorious white supremacist Abraham Lincoln.

The case of Benjamin Franklin highlights an uncomfortable truth for those who embrace Northern mythology: *authentic* abolitionism—that is, the belief that slave owning is wrong, that slavery should be abolished, *and* that blacks should be accepted into American life as equals—was actually quite rare in the Old North, with true abolitionists never representing more than the tiniest percentage of the Northern population.[2239] Even then, what little abolitionist sentiment there was in Yankeedom was not based on sympathy for the black man so much as it was on the self interest of the white man,[2240] as Lincoln would later go on to prove so overtly as America's sixteenth chief executive.[2241]

In 1858 Lincoln himself admitted as much when he discussed abolition with an Illinois audience. After emancipating America's black servants, what then?, he asked rhetorically:

> *Free them, and make them politically and socially, our equals? My own feelings will not admit of this*; and if mine would, we well know that those of the great mass of white people will not.[2242]

As the future U.S. president intimates here, abolitionists were detested by nearly all Northern whites, who saw them as troublemakers, malcontents, agitators, and revolutionaries who threatened white Yankee hegemony. This is why a furious New England mob attacked abolitionist William Lloyd Garrison in Boston, Massachusetts, threatened to tar and feather him[2243] and then tried to lynch him,[2244] dragging him through the streets with a noose around his neck;[2245] it is why he was arrested in 1829, tried and convicted by a Northern jury and sent to prison for several months[2246] for libeling a slave trader;[2247] and it is why subscriptions for his weekly abolitionist periodical, *The Liberator*, never exceeded 3,000, were bought mainly by blacks not whites,[2248] and, like every other Yankee antislavery paper, was both continuously in debt and short-lived.[2249]

South-loathing, Yankee busybody William Lloyd Garrison was so disliked in the North for his abolitionism that he was not only arrested and imprisoned, but numerous attempts were made on his life by fellow Northerners.

As hard evidence for the widespread existence of anti-abolitionist sentiment in the North prior to Lincoln's War, we need look no further than the doleful story of Prudence Crandall.

Crandall was a white New England teacher who founded the "High School for Young Colored Ladies and Misses" in Canterbury, Connecticut, in 1834. One would think that fellow Yanks, had they been true non-racist egalitarians, would have applauded her efforts. Instead, for trying to offer blacks a free education in New England, Crandall, a Quaker and abolitionist, was harassed, persecuted, arrested (three times), imprisoned, and had her home burned down, while Northern white mobs attacked and stoned her school, tore it from its foundations using a team of 100 oxen, then physically drove her out of the state.[2250]

Here is an account of Crandall's brief time in Connecticut, penned by fellow Quaker Jessie Gidley Carter:

> People who tried to establish schools for the negroes [in the North] at first found this a very hard thing to do. Many [Yankee] slaveholders said that the negroes were not bright enough to learn, or else that if they were taught they would become dangerous to the country. . . . the Friends [that is, the Quakers] and others were steadily and faithfully working for better things. The story of Prudence Crandall shows how earnest the friends of the slaves were and how much they were willing to suffer for their ideas.
>
> Prudence Crandall was a young Quaker schoolteacher in Connecticut. In the summer of 1832, she bought a house in the town of Canterbury, where she opened a boarding and day school for girls. The school had the support of the leading townspeople, until a colored girl, Sarah Harris, became one of its pupils. Sarah was a bright student, who wanted to fit herself to be a teacher of her own race. She was a good girl, she had pleasant manners, she had been through the district school, and both teacher and pupils of the little boarding school were willing to have her stay and study with them. The [white New England] parents of the other girls, however, were deeply offended.
>
> "If Sarah Harris stays," they declared, "we will take our daughters out."
>
> This put Prudence Crandall into a very hard place. She could not afford to lose the money from her richer pupils. She was already in debt. And yet, as she thought of the great need of Sarah Harris and of many other colored girls, ready and eager to learn, although there was no one to teach them, her duty seemed clear. She took courage and said that if the white girls were taken out, she would open her school for girls of the negro race. This made the people of the town very indignant. A town-meeting was called, where more than *a thousand excited people met to protest against the bold action of this one little Quaker woman.*
>
> *"That nigger school shall never be allowed in Canterbury nor in any other town in this State!"* cried out one of the angry men.
>
> The friends of Prudence Crandall were not allowed to say anything, and the meeting broke up with much noise and confusion.
>
> Prudence Crandall did not show any fear. She received

fifteen or twenty colored pupils from New York, Philadelphia, Providence, and Boston. This was in Fourth Month, 1833. In a little less than a year and a half, the school had to be given up; and during that time the teacher and the students patiently bore many hardships. *The stores of the town would sell them nothing; and people insulted the colored girls on the street and tried to make their life miserable at the school itself. Not satisfied with such things as this, the leading men of the town influenced the State Legislature to pass a law called the "Black Law," which said that no one should set up any school in Connecticut for teaching any colored person not a native of the State. When the people of Canterbury heard that the law was passed, they were wild with excitement, ringing bells and firing cannon to show their joy.*

Prudence Crandall's "School for Colored Girls" being attacked and torched by local townspeople in Canterbury, Connecticut. "Your nigger school shall never be allowed in Canterbury nor in any other town in this State!" the furious Yankee mob shouted. The building was later ripped from its foundation by a team of 100 oxen and destroyed. Crandall was only one of hundreds of Yankee abolitionists who were criticized, harassed, assaulted, and driven from the region for promoting racial equality. Her story highlights the utter disdain the majority of Northerners had for both blacks and abolition at the time.

For breaking this law, Prudence Crandall was then taken to jail and shut up in a murderer's cell, as this happened to be the only one empty. The courageous young teacher was very willing to bear the disgrace for the sake of the cause. The next day, her friends gave bonds for her and the jailer let her go; but the story of her unfair imprisonment quickly spread over the country and roused much interest and sympathy. Twice her case was tried in court, but the juries could not agree, and the decision was never given. All this time the little school had been going on; but soon after the trials in court, some of Prudence Crandall's enemies tried to set fire to her house, and, a few nights afterward, a number of persons attacked the place with iron bars and clubs and broke the windows. It is hard to believe that people who pretended to be Christians could

> be so cruel to a houseful of frightened girls. In the face of such danger, Prudence Crandall saw that she must at last give up her school. This was in Ninth Month, 1834. Four years later, the "Black Law" was repealed. It seems a strange law to have been made at this time in the North, for the Northern States had been "free States" for years . . .[2251]

Miss Carter would not have thought this Northern law "strange" had she spent time in the far more racially tolerant South.

None of Connecticut's white population shed a tear for Crandall. Instead, the state, and in particular her politicians, were quite happy to see her, and her school, disappear. Their smug parting comment sums up the North's feelings perfectly during this period: "Once open this door, and New-England will become the Liberia of America," they shrieked as Crandall left Connecticut for the last time.[2252] New Hampshire whites followed suit by destroying their state's own black schools.[2253]

More proof that abolitionists were widely detested in the North comes from the grim story of white abolitionist publisher Elijah Parish Lovejoy, who was shot to death in Alton, Illinois, by a white gang. Prior to Lovejoy's murder at the hands of his fellow Illinoisans, his printing office had been destroyed three times by Northern anti-abolitionists. He died trying to protect it during their fourth attempt.[2254]

Being a Yankee abolitionist, Elijah P. Lovejoy of Maine was never cordially received by fellow Northerners. As is pictured here, Northern anti-abolition mobs repeatedly broke into his publishing office and destroyed his printing equipment. On November 7, 1837, he was cornered in a warehouse in Alton, Illinois, which mobs attempted to set ablaze. When Lovejoy came out to try and prevent torches from being applied to the wooden roof, he was shot to death. He was 34 years old.

We should not be surprised at the Prairie State's attitude toward blacks. Illinois, Lincoln's adopted home state, became one of the most anti-black states in the nation, in great part, as we will see, because of Lincoln himself.

Illustrations of the Old North's hatred of both abolition and black Americans could fill volumes, but we only have room for a few more examples.

In 1827 a citizen of Chillicothe, Ohio, spoke for "all" of the whites in his city when he wrote:

> In most of the towns of Ohio, there are a number of free blacks, who with few exceptions, are little less than a nuisance and their numbers are every year increasing by immigration, as well as other causes. *All* of the whites would willingly do something to free themselves from this evil.[2255]

Nine years later, on July 12, 1836, a white mob in New Richmond, Ohio, broke into the printing office of antislavery advocate James G. Birney, the founder and publisher of the abolitionist publication, *The Philanthropist*—a mouthpiece for the Ohio chapter of the Anti-Slavery Society. Fortunately, Birney, a former Southern slave owner who had traveled North hoping to convert racist Yankees to abolitionism, was not onsite at the time, and the gang merely destroyed some of his printing equipment. But the matter did not end there.

The town called a large meeting, where an appointed committee (that included former speaker of the Ohio House of Representatives David T. Disney) passed several anti-abolitionary resolutions. Birney was warned of more potential mob violence and ordered to cease publication of his paper. He refused, then fled for his life.

Soon "wanted" handbills began appearing on the town's bulletin boards and walls, seeking the public's assistance in capturing Birney. One read:

> A FUGITIVE FROM JUSTICE. 100 DOLLARS REWARD. The above sum will be paid for the delivery of one James G. Birney, a fugitive from justice, now abiding in the city of Cincinnati. [The] said Birney, in all his associations and feelings, is black, although his external appearance is white. The above reward will be paid, and no questions asked. . . .[2256]

As countless "anti-abolition meetings" began to spring up across Ohio, the Cincinnati *Whig* published this editorial:

> We are informed on indisputable authority that a large number of boarders have left the Franklin House [hotel] in this city; have left it on account of the reception of Mr. Birney, editor of *The Philanthropist* as a boarder. *There is no doubt an overwhelming majority in the city are opposed to the wild schemes of the abolitionists.*[2257]

In the 1830s Southern abolitionist James G. Birney moved North in the hopes of spreading abolitionism in what was, and still is, the most racist region in the U.S. He was met with extreme opposition and became a fugitive of the law, chased from county to county by violent, Northern anti-abolitionist gangs who sought his life.

Not to be discouraged, violent anti-abolitionist gangs soon resumed their search for Birney. On July 30, after tossing his printing press into the Ohio River, they set about ransacking the homes of the city's blacks, whom they tormented and ill-treated. Unable to find Birney himself (who was still "out of town"), the dangerous mob dispersed, leaving a taint of menace in the air for weeks after.[2258]

On March 2, 1835, Northern abolitionist and antislavery speaker Theodore D. Weld, himself a former Yankee slave owner,[2259] wrote to his friend Elizur Wright about his experiences in the town of Circleville, Ohio:

> Went next to Circleville, the capitol of Pickaway Co. *I had long heard of Circleville as violent in the extreme against abolition.* Found two decided and open abolitionists and a few others in a state of transition. *The Presbyterian minister, Mr. Benton, said among his people, that I was a rebel, had made all the mischief at Lane Seminary, and surely a man should not be countenanced who was such a disturber of the peace. Further, he said, as I was told, that the distinguished faculty of Lane Seminary had felt themselves impelled from solemn sense of duty to warn the public against me, declaring in their official capacity that I was a remarkable instance of monomania* [one who is mentally ill due to a single object, in Weld's case, abolition]. *Through his influence the Presbyterian church was shut against me.* Finally, the vestry room of the Episcopal church was procured.
>
> *At the second lecture, the mob gathered and threw eggs and stones through the window. One of the stones was so well aimed that it struck me on the head and for a moment stunned me.* Paused a few minutes till the dizziness had ceased, and then went on and completed my lecture. Meanwhile, some of the gentlemen had hung their cloaks up at the window, so that my head could not be so easily used as a target. The injury was not serious, though for a few days I had frequent turns of dizziness.
>
> *The next day the mob were so loud in threats that the trustees of the church did not feel at liberty to grant the use of the vestry*, but some of them very cheerfully united with other friends, and procured a large room in the centre of the village, recently fitted up for a store and counting room. This would hold comfortably one hundred persons. The next night I lectured there. Room full. *Stones and clubs flew merrily against the shutters. At the close as I came out, curses were showered in profusion. A large crowd had gathered round the door. Lamp black, nails, divers pockets full of stones and eggs had been provided for the occasion, and many had disguised their persons, smeared their faces to avoid recognition.* But the Lord restrained them and not a hair of my head was injured.
>
> *Next evening same state of things, with increase of violent demonstrations. The next, such was the uproar that a number of gentlemen insisted upon forming an escort and seeing me safe to my lodgings, which they did. This state of things lasted till I had lectured six or seven times*, then hushed down and for the latter part of the course had a smooth sea.[2260]

When abolitionists John W. Alvord and James A. Thome tried

to lecture at the Methodist Church in Willoughby, Ohio, they were met by the angry pastor, who promised to stand in the doorway with a club, if necessary, to prevent them from entering. They decided to try their luck at Middlebury, Ohio, but a mob gathered and threw eggs and glass bottles at them, forcing them to retreat.[2261]

Weld was not allowed to lecture at Zanesville, Ohio, and in the county of Putnam not only was he attacked by a mob, but because he had invited blacks to attend his speeches, white Northern gangs attacked them as well. Soon Ohio passed a series of laws prohibiting the hiring of blacks. Whites who ignored these statutes were arrested and jailed.[2262]

Yankee abolitionist Theodore Dwight Weld was constantly hunted by white Northern mobs, stoned, egged, and harassed, driven from lecture hall to lecture hall. It became so routine that he eventually accepted this violent persecution as part of his job.

In 1836 Northern abolitionists sought to hold the Ohio Anti-Slavery Convention at Granville, but the schoolhouse at which James A. Thome was to lecture was torn down by angry white mobs before he could appear. The townspeople purposefully brought in hooligans and bullies to scare off the abolitionists. When they refused to budge, a violent riot broke out, resulting in a number of injuries. Eventually the antislavery group was driven out of the area, riding for their lives on horseback amid a hail of eggs and expletives.[2263]

Scores of other examples could be given. For instance, in New York anti-black mobs stormed the home of abolitionist Lewis Tappan. After robbing the house of its valuables, what was left was thrown out into the street and burned. In the ensuing melee the church, home, and store of Reverend A. L. Cox were nearly destroyed, along with the church of Reverend H. G. Ludlow, the homes of 20 black families, a black school, and three black churches.[2264]

A black parade honoring emancipation in the West Indies was dispersed by a raging white mob in 1839 in Pittsburgh, Pennsylvania. Dozens of blacks were hurt and the Presbyterian Church and the African Hall were torched. In August 1834 an anti-abolition riot erupted in Philadelphia, Pennsylvania. Known as "the Passover Riot," the three-day rampage left 45 black homes and a black Presbyterian church in ruins. On May 16, 1838, just two days after it opened, Philadelphia's Pennsylvania Hall was broken into by a furious anti-abolition gang, which ransacked the interior then set fire to the building, leaving nothing but a smoldering pile of ashes. Why? They objected to the presence of the Female Anti-Slavery Convention that was in session at the hall.[2265]

A few decades earlier, around 1800, the Pennsylvania Abolition Society had introduced a proposition calling for "the immediate and total abolition of slavery." It failed to pass for lack of support. Pennsylvania abolitionists got the same result in 1804 when they tried to push through an act that would have freed all slaves over the age of 28. In 1805, when Congressman James Sloan of New Jersey proposed a bill that would free the children of slaves in Washington, D.C., the bill was rejected by a vote of 77 to 31.[2266]

In the early 1800s Yankee abolitionist Lewis Tappan was pursued by white, Northern, anti-black mobs, who burgled his house, plundered its valuables, and burned the remaining items in the street.

Prior to 1840, New England abolitionist Henry B. Stanton (husband of New York's famed women's rights activist, Elizabeth Cady Stanton) was attacked 150 times, while Weld grew so accustomed to hecklers and mob violence that he came to regard it as a routine part of his job.[2267] In Ohio all of this led up to the Cincinnati Riots of 1842, in which roving gangs of white anti-abolitionists set out to destroy the town in protest.

So aggressive, brutal, and massive was their force that neither city officials or the military could stop them. The purpose behind the riots? Northern whites wanted to discourage blacks from moving to or even visiting the state.[2268] Thus they passed a law requiring all blacks "who could not give guaranties of their good behavior" to be evicted from the city.[2269] As this was an impossibility, Cincinnati was able to appreciably whittle down its black population.

Yet, there was a more significant and even simpler reason for the North's open animosity toward abolitionists: not only was racism toward blacks at its deepest and darkest in the North, but, as we have discussed, the slavery business itself began and was headquartered in the North.

New York City, the capital of the North's economy, was also the capital of American slavery right up to the end of Lincoln's War, and for good reason: the two were inextricably linked. And it was for this very reason, that is, pure economic interest, that the North was far more interested in maintaining the institution than the South. As one wealthy New York businessman said to Boston abolitionist Reverend Samuel J. May in 1835:

> Mr. May, we [New Yorkers] are not such fools as not to know that slavery is a great evil, a great wrong. But it was consented to by the founders of our Republic. It was provided for in the Constitution of our Union. A great portion of the property of the Southerners is invested under its sanction; *and the business of the North* as well as the South *has become adjusted to it. There are millions upon millions of dollars due from Southerners to the merchants and mechanics of New York alone, the payment of which would be jeopardized by any rupture between the North and the South. We cannot afford, sir, to let you and your associates succeed in your endeavor to overthrow slavery. It is not a matter of principle with us; it is a matter of business necessity. We cannot afford to let you succeed; and I have called you out to let you know, and to let your fellow laborers know, that we do not mean to allow you to succeed. "We mean, sir," said he with increased emphasis,—"we mean, sir, to put you Abolitionists down— by fair means if we can, by foul means if we must."*[2270]

WHAT YOU WERE TAUGHT: The Confederacy never tried to, or even wanted to, abolish slavery.

THE TRUTH: On November 7, 1864, President Jefferson Davis took his first step toward becoming America's true and only "Great

Emancipator" when he asked the Confederate Congress to allow the government to purchase 40,000 slaves with the intention of emancipating them after the War.[2271] The non-racist Davis, who—while racist Lincoln was busy trying to convert new members to the American Colonization Society—adopted an orphaned black boy (named Jim Limber) during the War,[2272] said to the Confederate Congress:

> The policy of engaging to liberate the negro on his discharge after [military] service faithfully rendered seems to me preferable to that of granting immediate manumission, or that of retaining him in servitude.[2273]

(Shortly we will discuss why, unlike the North, the South was, correctly, against *immediate* emancipation.)

Confederate President Jefferson Davis proposed complete abolition in the South a year before the U.S. issued the Thirteenth Amendment in December 1865, a fact you will never read in any mainstream American history book.

Then, as noted earlier, in January 1865, under Davis' ruling, Confederate Secretary of State Judah P. Benjamin sent Confederate commissioner Duncan F. Kenner to England to declare the South's commitment to abolition.[2274]

In essence what Davis' plan amounted to was complete emancipation, only 24 months after Lincoln reluctantly issued his

Emancipation Proclamation (which purposefully did not free a single slave in the North or South), and a year before the Thirteenth Amendment finally freed all bonded blacks in the U.S. Thus the South was realistically discussing authentic abolition for both its black soldiers and its black servants long before the U.S. actually ended slavery on December 6, 1865. Had not Lincoln interfered, official, legal, full, and complete Southern emancipation would have soon followed.

WHAT YOU WERE TAUGHT: The North abolished the slave trade before the South did.
THE TRUTH: The Rebels put an end to the slave trade long before the Yanks. Article One, Section Nine, Clauses One and Two of the Constitution of the Confederate States of America, written up in early 1861, clearly forbids the foreign slave trade. They read:

> 1) The importation of negroes of the African race from any foreign country other than the slaveholding States or territories of the United States of America, is hereby forbidden; and Congress is required to pass such laws as shall effectually prevent the same.
>
> 2) Congress shall also have power to prohibit the introduction of slaves from any State not a member of, or territory not belonging to, this Confederacy.[2275]

These words were written five years before the U.S. banned the foreign slave trade. Indeed the original U.S. Constitution, also Article 1, Section 9, Clause 1, allowed the

> . . . importation of such Persons as any of the States now existing shall think proper to admit . . .[2276]

Those referred to here as "such Persons" were, of course, slaves.

Wisely, the abolitionist Confederacy did not include this clause in her constitution when she used the U.S. Constitution as a template, yet pro-North historians never give her credit for this.

From Thomas Jefferson to Jefferson Davis, it is clear that the South, not the North, initiated the American abolition movement. It is any wonder that the South was well-known to have treated its black servants better than the North treated its free blacks?[2277]

WHAT YOU WERE TAUGHT: There is no good reason why the South continued to postpone emancipation before and during the War, particularly after Lincoln's Emancipation Proclamation. For this the South deserves the eternal condemnation of the world.

THE TRUTH: This is strong language coming from the region, namely the North, that not only founded American slavery *and* became the center of the American slave trade, but which outlawed slavery in its own time and way (that is, when the institution became unprofitable and unbearable), postponed emancipation for as long as possible (finally only relenting under enormous political pressure), then unfairly turned around and tried to force the South to abolish slavery before she was ready[2278]—this despite the fact that many early enlightened New Englanders campaigned to leave abolition up to each individual state.[2279]

After Lincoln's War, here is how former Confederate soldier Luther W. Hopkins explained the situation in the South during the 1850s:

> Somewhere between childhood and youth we [Southern] children all learned that there was a race of people up North called Abolitionists, who were so mean that they sent secret agents through the country to persuade the colored people to leave their homes and go North, where they could be free. That these agents were disguised as peddlers or otherwise, and that they visited the cabins of the slaves during the late hours of the night, and went so far as to urge them to rise up in a body and declare their freedom, and if necessary to murder those who held them as slaves [was obvious to everyone]. This delusion, if it were a delusion, might have been dispelled had not [anti-South Yankee abolitionist] John Brown and his men appeared upon the scene to give an ocular demonstration of their real intent [popularly known as John Brown's Raid on Harper's Ferry, it occurred October 16, 1859]. The few men with him may have been the only following that he had, but the damage had been done. Virginia was fighting mad. What had been whispered about the abolitionists in secret was now proclaimed from the housetops. John Brown was an abolitionist, and all abolitionists were John Browns, so the youths, at least, reasoned. The words abolitionist and Yankee were for the most part synonymous terms; the former being hard to pronounce, the child usually employed the latter. Some of the young children did not know that a Yankee was a human being . . .[2280]

It was just this kind of Northern abolitionist pressure on the South, and the inevitable accompanying charge of racism, that delayed emancipation in Dixie.[2281] How?

Human nature being what it is, Newton's Third Law of Motion is applicable here: "For every action, there is an equal and opposite reaction." The harder the North pushed the South toward emancipation, the harder the South resisted. Not because she was against abolition—as we have thoroughly documented, the American abolition movement got its start in the South—but because 19th-Century Southerners, just like Southerners today, did not like being told what to do, how to do it, why they should do it, and when to do it.

Two months before the start of Lincoln's War, in a February 1861 letter to his wife Varina, Jefferson Davis acknowledged the well-known fact that the secession of the Southern states would mean the end of slavery in Dixie.

What our Yankee biased history books do not teach is that from the 1700s on, nearly all Southerners desired, and expected, slavery to come to an end naturally—either by soil depletion[2282] or by the weight of its own weaknesses, or by both. This is why, being a leisurely people, they felt no great urgency to hurry the process along. And this is why thousands of slave owners, like Nathan Bedford Forrest, emancipated their slaves even before Lincoln's War,[2283] while others, like Robert E. Lee, liberated their family's servants before the Emancipation Proclamation was issued.[2284] Why hold on, such Southerners reasoned, to something that was soon to disappear of its own accord across the U.S. as completely as the American Mastodon?

Jefferson Davis too knew that slavery's days were numbered. The Confederate chief executive understood that the secession of the Southern states would mean the demise of slavery, but he supported the creation of the Confederacy anyway, writing to his wife Varina in

February 1861: "In any case [whether we are successful in establishing the Confederacy or not,] our slave property will eventually be lost."[2285]

In the late 1700s Continental Congress member and Connecticut Senator Roger Sherman was absolutely sure that

> the abolition of slavery seemed to be going on in the United States, and that the good sense of the people of the several states would by degrees complete it.[2286]

His Yankee colleague Connecticut Senator Oliver Ellsworth said:

> The morality or wisdom of slavery are considerations belonging to the states themselves. . . . Let us not intermeddle. As population increases poor laborers will be so plenty as to render slaves useless. Slavery in time will not be a speck in our country.[2287]

American Founding Father and Yankee statesman Oliver Ellsworth was against interfering with the states on the issue of slavery. Like many other Northerners and *all* Southerners, he understood that slavery would eventually come to a natural end on its own, without any need for outside coercion.

The very fact that neither the word "slave" or the word "slavery" appear anywhere in the U.S. Constitution (though slavery was still legal under the original document), is an indication that its creators assumed that the institution would one day disappear. James Madison admitted that this silence was purposeful, for as Blake writes,

> it was the belief of at least a large portion of the [constitutional] delegates that slavery could not long survive the final stoppage of the slave-trade, which was expected to (and did) occur in 1808.[2288]

More proof that the Civil War was *not* about slavery comes from Lincoln himself. Knowing that its demise was a forgone conclusion, in his writings and speeches he repeatedly refers to the natural, inevitable, "ultimate extinction of slavery," a widely held and understood view in the antebellum period.

Even Lincoln was fully aware that slavery was soon to end, which is one of the many reasons we know that his War was not over slavery. In fact, according to a speech the Big Brother Liberal gave at Columbus, Ohio, on September 16, 1859: "The *whole* country looked forward to the ultimate extinction of the institution."[2289] The "whole country" at that time, of course, included the American South. In short, from the very beginning the entire country, South and North, understood perfectly well that "the institution of slavery was doomed to die."[2290]

According to an 1863 work by Yankee legal scholar Theophilus Parsons, "our national [American] life has been, from its beginning, working against slavery."[2291] Of that same period historian Israel Smith Clare wrote:

> *The wisest and best men of the time, both in the North and in the South, looked forward with confidence and hope to the speedy extinction of an institution so repugnant to the principles of Christian civilization and so fraught with danger to society, religion and the state.*[2292]

Why then did Dixie seem to "resist" abolition so intensely after the 1830s? Understanding the answer to this question is vital to an understanding of Southern culture, the Confederacy, and Lincoln's War.

At first the North acknowledged that it had instigated both slavery and the slave trade. In 1835, for example, famed abolitionist and Unitarian theologian William Ellery Channing of Boston, Massachusetts, stated that:

> Our ancestors at the North were concerned in the slave-trade. Some of us can recollect individuals of the colored race, who were born in Africa, and grew old under our parental roofs. Our ancestors committed a deed now branded as piracy.[2293]

All other Northerners fully accepted this fact as well—at least up until 1831, the year the mouthy, Radical Yankee abolitionist and gossip-monger William Lloyd Garrison launched his antislavery gazette, *The Liberator*.

Though, like Harriet Beecher Stowe, Garrison knew absolutely nothing about either the South or black servitude, he published articles in his paper condemning Southern slavery as a "crime" and Southern slave owners as "criminals." Though he was totally ignorant of the overwhelming cost, complexities, and challenges of true abolition, he called for *complete*, *unconditional*, and *immediate* emancipation across the South,[2294] with *no* financial compensation for slave owners.[2295] "This is," Garrison bellowed, "the right of the slave and the duty of the master!"[2296]

As part of his offensive campaign, later called the "Garrisonian agitation,"[2297] the fanatical crusader—from the Puritanical state of Massachusetts, well-known for its dogmatic intolerance and uncompromising attitudes[2298]—labeled the U.S. Constitution (under which slavery was still legal) "a covenant with death and an agreement with hell,"[2299] then filled his columns with misinformation, disinformation, and outright lies regarding the institution, all carefully calculated to whip the North into an anti-South frenzy.[2300] Fearing the consequences of unfairly attacking Southerners, U.S. Representative Henry Randolph Storrs of New York tried to impart some common sense to other Yankee politicians, preaching that "for the sake of union and harmony, Northern men must learn to sacrifice their prejudices [against the South]."[2301]

But such sagaciousness fell on deaf ears. Instead, many Yankees promptly fell in line behind Garrison. One result, in 1833, was the formation of the National Anti-Slavery Society and the ensuing creation of various subchapters throughout all of the Northern states. To Southerners their one and only purpose was to denounce the South with absurd and false rhetoric "calculated to inflame the public mind" against the citizens of Dixie.[2302]

It worked—on the naive and uneducated. Shortly thereafter, in 1835, when Yankee Professor Ethan Allen Andrews asked a fellow New Englander what he thought about Southern slavery, the man answered:

> It is quite time that something be done about the slaves at the South. According to all accounts they are very badly used, and *if their masters will not set them at liberty they ought to be made to do it*.[2303]

Yankees continue their 200 year long worship of radical Yankee abolitionist William Lloyd Garrison, of Newburyport, Massachusetts, as is clear from this statue of the South-hating meddler located in Boston. This blind idolization would not be so enthusiastic if New Englanders knew that, like Lincoln, he once supported the American Colonization Society, which sought the deportation of all African-Americans. Garrison was the first to begin calling Southern slavery a "crime" and Southern slave owners "criminals," this from a Bostonian, the veritable birthplace of American slavery!

The Liberator did indeed cause a furor. But not the kind that would weaken Southern slavery. Instead, Garrison and his paper helped strengthen it,[2304] becoming one of the many embers that "kindled a fire which all the waters of the ocean cannot put out, which seas of blood can only extinguish."[2305] Forty-two years later this conflict would come to be known as the "American Civil War," or as we call it here in Dixie, the War for Southern Independence.

One of Garrison's "embers" ignited a particularly horrific slave insurrection in Virginia: the notorious Nat Turner Rebellion of 1831,[2306] in which some 60 whites (most of them abolitionists and non-slave owners) were butchered in their sleep. Not even newborn babies were spared Turner's axes.[2307]

An unremorseful Turner and his racist madmen were all caught within a few weeks. Many of the mob, including their psychopathic leader, swung from the hangman's rope. But the bloody mayhem was all for naught. In fact, if Turner was trying to end slavery, he had done the worst thing possible: his "rebellion" not only did not advance the cause of African-Americans, it actually reversed it. For in its aftermath at least 100 blacks were killed,[2308] terrified whites passed new exceptionally harsh slave codes,[2309] and abolitionist sentiment, once strong across the entire South, was considerably dampened for decades thereafter.[2310]

This was a revolutionary change in attitude for white Southerners, who had for so long viewed their black servants as "family" and free blacks as fellow citizens of Dixie. Thus, while nearly every Southerner had once been an abolitionist,[2311] after 1831 the idea of emancipation was considered "too dangerous," and blacks everywhere, bonded and free, now began to be viewed with suspicion.[2312]

Between Garrison's increasingly vociferous attacks on Dixie and Turner's bloody killing spree, white Southerners had had enough. The spreading of the "infernal doctrines" of a handful of prying Yankee abolitionists had thrown the whole South "into a state of insecurity."[2313] Now, instead of discussing abolition, they dug in their heels and built up a defensive wall of resentment and fear. No one, especially Yankees, would tell them what to do—particularly when they and their family's lives were at stake.[2314]

One other important development that must be mentioned was Eli Whitney's 1793 invention of the cotton gin, which greatly increased the need for manual laborers,[2315] and which in turn greatly increased the value of slaves.[2316] For Southern planters this made both "King Cotton" and slavery more profitable, the expansion of the Cotton Kingdom more attractive,[2317] and *immediate, complete, and uncompensated emancipation* absolutely impossible.

Was slavery truly an ethical transgression against God, as Garrison and his ilk maintained? Since from beginning to end the Bible sanctions the institution, and since Northerners had been the ones responsible for bringing African slaves to America, *Southerners saw slavery more as a political issue rather than a moral one;* or more specifically, *as a temporary but necessary evil rather than a premeditated crime*. After all, "the negroes brought from Africa were unquestionably brought from a state of slavery." And *all* African slaves themselves admitted that "as slaves, they were infinitely better off in America than in Africa." What then was so "immoral" about slavery?, Southerners often asked their critics from the North.[2318]

The needless and malevolent abolition agitation stirred up by Garrison must be counted as one of the main sparks that later ignited the Civil War. This was not due to the slavery issue, as pro-North writers claim, but because of his insinuation that physical force would be needed to end slavery in Dixie—which brought the long simmering states' rights issue to the foreground. This ended 29 years later in the secession of the Southern states with the election of another violent and intolerant, constitutionally ignorant aggressor, Abraham Lincoln.

Thus the Southern approach to the situation was legal, political, and constitutional, instead of religious, emotional, and ethical, the approach taken by Northerners.

How would the South end slavery? Legally, this was her decision. *Why* would the South destroy slavery? That was her political choice. *When* would the South end slavery? It was her right to decide this for herself, as the U.S. Constitution clearly affirmed.[2319] Any Northern attempt to weaken or block the South's power to make these decisions was clearly "against the true spirit and meaning of the Constitution, and an infringement of the rights of the states affected, and a breach of the public faith on which they entered into the [U.S.] confederacy . . ."[2320] In 1867 a Southerner complained to English tourist Henry Latham:

> Mr. Lincoln at his [1864] election had not the vote of a single Southern State. He was chosen to carry out the views of the North. The South said, "If you do not mean to abide by the Constitution, let us go out and live by ourselves. We mean to abide by it." But the North knew that they could not stand without us. How have they observed the Constitution? "No State shall be coerced," says the Constitution: have they not coerced us? "No State shall be divided:" have they not divided Virginia [illegally creating West Virginia]? Slavery is recognised by the Constitution: have they not set the slaves against their masters? I wish we were all colonies of England again.[2321]

This illustration of the "Nat Turner Rebellion" from the 1830s was headlined "Horrid Massacre in Virginia." It shows Turner's black racist gang—spurred on by the wild-eyed rantings of William Lloyd Garrison—murdering innocent, white, non-slave owning families with axes, swords, and knives. 1) A white mother futilely trying to protect her children. 2) Turner's owner Joseph Travis (known as a kindly, inoffensive man who never mistreated Turner), about to be butchered by his assailants. 3) John T. Barrow fending off hatchet blows from Turner's madmen while his wife escapes.

Unlike Lincoln, who believed that the Federal government should have the power to force states to adopt doctrines against their wishes, other Northerners were more constitutionally aware, recognizing the South's right of self-determination in this regard. One of them, Illinois Senator Stephen A. Douglas, wisely observed:

> The whole South is rallying to the support of the doctrine that if the people of a Territory want slavery they have a right to have it, and if they do not want it that no power on earth can force it upon them.[2322]

State independence from the Federal government. This important states' right was what the traditional conservative South wanted in the 19th Century, and it is what she still wants in the 21st Century.

In 1895 Southern historian Joseph Tyrone Derry described the situation like this:

> [Following both the interference of William Lloyd Garrison and the terrors caused by the Nat Turner Rebellion in 1831, the] South was thoroughly aroused. Conservative men in the North [then the Democrats] denounced the Abolitionists and broke up their meetings. *Those in the Southern States who had favored a gradual emancipation of the slaves changed their views.* Up to 1835 free negroes with property were allowed to vote in North Carolina; but in that year North Carolina changed her State constitution and took from these free negroes the right to vote. Virginia passed laws forbidding free negroes to enter her borders. Even Ohio, a State which did not allow slavery, passed similar laws.
>
> There were many men in the North opposed to slavery who did not sympathize with extreme men of the Garrison sort. But *the conduct of the fanatics caused the people of the South to regard all antislavery men as belonging to the same class.* In 1837 many efforts were made by Northern men to procure the abolition of slavery in the District of Columbia. Mr. [John C.] Calhoun of South Carolina introduced into the Senate a series of resolutions to the effect that the Federal Government was created by the States with a view to their increased security against all dangers, domestic as well as foreign; that the citizens of one State had no right to interfere with the domestic institutions of another State; and that the Federal Government had no right to interfere with slavery in either the States or the Territories of the Union. *The Senate by a large majority adopted these resolutions.*
>
> In 1838 an attempt was made in the [U.S.] House of Representatives to renew the slavery agitation. But Mr. [Charles Gordon] Atherton of New Hampshire introduced a series of resolutions, whose purport was that, *under the Constitution of the United States, Congress had no right to interfere with slavery in the several States of the Confederacy*; that Congress had no right to do indirectly what it could not do directly, and therefore should not interfere with slavery either in the District of Columbia or in the Territories. *These resolutions were adopted by an overwhelming majority of the House of Representatives.* Henry Clay, who had warmly favored the resolutions, and most of the other public men of the country, hoped that this exciting agitation would now be abandoned.
>
> *But the Abolitionists cared nothing for the restraints of the*

> *Constitution*. Neither of the great parties of the country [the Democrats and the Whigs] was at this time connected with the anti-slavery agitators. *The mass of the American people regarded the Abolitionists as men disloyal to the Constitution and as the foes of the Federal Union*.
>
> A Slaveholders' Convention met at Annapolis in Maryland in 1842 to consider what measures must be taken to secure the safety of the Southern people. Considering the fact that the terrible massacres that had occurred in Hayti [Haiti] (one of the West Indies) were the work of free negroes, and that free negroes had been the fomenters of discord in many places, *they concluded that the only security for the South lay in restricting the privileges of free negroes and in throwing greater restrictions around the slaves*.
>
> *Thus the utter disregard of the restraints of the Constitution shown by the ultra Abolitionists of the Garrison type in their attack upon slaveholders, and their determination to effect their purpose regardless of consequences, alarmed the Southern people and put a complete stop to the idea of gradual emancipation, which, previous to their work, had begun to make considerable progress in the border Southern States. The violent abuse of all slaveholders indulged in by the Abolitionists made it impossible for those Southern men, who really disliked the institution of slavery, to speak a word for even gradual emancipation, for fear that they should be regarded as the enemies of the South and the allies of the Abolitionists. Without the work of the agitators the abolition of slavery would have been gradual and in some places long delayed, but it would have been free from that bitterness which estranged two great sections of our country and brought about the most dreadful war of the nineteenth century*.[2323]

The South's reaction to the North's constant meddling was particularly strong after Lincoln's dire 1861 predictions of coming "negro insurrections," anarchy, and widespread white deaths across Dixie. There could be only one reaction, and it was universal in the South: "resentment at [the Yankees'] impertinent interference," for this interference had been, up until then, "wholly mischievous in its direct operation upon the condition of the slaves."[2324] In other words, it had been underhanded, malicious, and intentional. Not meant for the good of black Southern servants, but for the purpose of irritating, harassing, provoking, and disrupting the white South.

Thus, it was at this point that Southern antislavery sentiment once again began to rapidly disintegrate, and the South, out of legitimate fear—as well as Southern pride and honor—understandably began to resist the idea of abolition.[2325] For in the end it was not the destruction of slavery that the South was against—just as Confederate President Jefferson Davis emphasized in 1867, only two years after Lincoln's War:

> *All the thinking men in the South recognised the fact, that as an economical question, it would be much better for all parties that the negroes should be free, and work for wages.*[2326]

Yankee clergyman Henry Ward Beecher was one of the many Northerners who opposed the irrational ideas and tactics of Garrison and other radical abolitionists. Beecher knew that the "immediate" emancipation of Southern slaves, as Garrison demanded, would create insurmountable turmoil in Dixie. For this Beecher's liberal enemies resorted, as usual, to *ad hominem* attacks, calling him, among other things, "Benedict Arnold" and "Lucifer."

What the Southern Confederacy (the C.S.A.) *was* against was the premature, forced destruction of slavery, and that by a foreign power (the U.S.A.), whose Northern states had been unmercifully dominating, ridiculing, and undermining her for decades.[2327]

In 1780, when an abolitionist act was passed in Pennsylvania giving freedom "to all persons thereafter born in that state," several members of the state assembly entered a protest against it, denouncing the statute as "impudent" and "premature," and as likely to have a "dangerous effect" on the economics of the region.[2328] Thus, a half a century later, despite the Garrisonian agitation, even some Yankees understood the South's stance on the issue on the eve of Lincoln's War.

One of these was New England antislavery reformer Henry Ward Beecher, whose ideas are here paraphrased by Beecher's biographer Lyman Abbott. Beecher, from Connecticut, is responding to inflammatory, inaccurate, and unhistorical remarks made by Garrison in *The Liberator*, January 1, 1847:

> *The [Southern] slaveholder was not a man-stealer. The original slave-dealer in Africa was; but the [Southern] man who found himself in a slave state, the owner of slaves bequeathed to him by his ancestors, was as truly under the domination of the slave system as the slave himself.* What could he do? Emancipate his slaves? In one state, if he did so, a tax was laid upon the emancipated slave for the very purpose of sending him back into slavery again; in another state, if he did so, he must give bonds that the slave would never become a pauper, or the act of manumission was illegal; in another state, he could not emancipate him legally unless he carried him out of the state. What should this man do, who had a hundred slaves in his possession, and no money with which to provide for them? Should he set his slaves free, run away from responsibility, and leave them to be sold again at the auction block to the highest bidder? This in many cases would have been the result of [William Lloyd Garrison's] "immediate, unconditional emancipation," and *this would not have been liberation*. It was therefore not true [as Garrison held] that immediate, unconditional emancipation was the duty of the hour. *It certainly was not the duty of the Northern readers of [Garrison's abolition newspaper]* The Liberator*: they had no more political power to emancipate the slaves in the Southern States than they had to emancipate the slaves in Turkey. It was not necessarily the duty of the individual slaveholder: if he undertook immediate, unconditional emancipation, he would in many cases only pass his slave from one state of servitude to another and a worse state.* Whether it was the duty of the individual state must at least be gravely questioned. *When a great wrong has been done by a community, and has been wrought into the social fabric of the community, it cannot be abolished by a single act of legislation. When an individual is engaged in wrong-doing, it is his duty immediately to cease wrong-doing; the doctrine of immediatism, [which I apply] . . . to the individual, is sound. When a community has become pervaded by a social injustice which has been wrought into its very structure, it is not always its duty, by an immediate act of legislation, to destroy the structure, in order that it may destroy the evil; the duty of*

> *immediatism, applied to the community by Mr. Garrison, was unsound.* The single-taxer traces land ownership back to robbery: the Romans stole the land from the Europeans, the Normans from the Anglo-Saxons, the Anglo-Saxons from the Indians; therefore the single-taxer proposes to abolish all ownership in land. Even if it be true that all land ownership is a kind of robbery, it does not follow that it ought to be instantly abolished, with the result of overturning in a day the whole fabric of civilization built upon the private ownership of land.[2329]

Henry Clay, a slave owner from Kentucky, understood the serious ramifications and problems that would result from "immediate, unconditional, complete, and uncompensated emancipation" in the South if it were to be pushed through by the North. "Does any considerate man believe it to be possible to effect such an object without convulsion, revolution, and bloodshed?" Clay rightly asked. Yet, this is precisely what Lincoln wanted!

Despite such wisdom coming from a fellow Yankee, most of Beecher's Northern compatriots, being both ill-informed and dictatorial, would not be moved—which is why they resorted to name-calling, labeling Beecher everything from a "Benedict Arnold" and "Lucifer," to a "recreant son of Massachusetts" whose words are "a blow struck at freedom and the constitutional rights of the free states."[2330] Instead of offering understanding and compromise, radical Yankee abolitionists gave the South increasingly impossible stipulations, including expecting her to instantly release 3.5 million slaves without a workable plan for either them or their owners. Think of it: demands were imposed on the South that would only worsen an already existing problem—without offering any solution.[2331]

Naturally, Dixie dug in her heels, for if the abolition of slavery was to become a reality, it would have to come peaceably and gradually. Garrison's "unconditional and immediate emancipation" could only bring with it a "national upheaval," destructively impacting every level of Southern society.[2332] In 1839, during a debate in the Senate, Kentucky slave owner Henry Clay took aim at those Northerners who were then called the "ultra-Abolitionists," a group of radical anti-South extremists who were hell bent on ending slavery "without regard to consequences, however calamitous":

> With them, the rights of property are nothing; the deficiency of the powers of the General Government is nothing; the acknowledged and incontestible powers of the States are nothing; civil war, a dissolution of the Union, and the overthrow of a government in which are concentrated the fondest hopes of the civilized world, are nothing. A single idea has taken possession of their minds, and onward they pursue it, overlooking all barriers, reckless and regardless of all consequences. . . . Utterly destitute of constitutional or other rightful power, living in totally distinct communities as alien to the communities in which the subject on which they would operate resides, so far as concerns political power over that subject, as if they lived in Africa or Asia, they nevertheless promulgate to the world their purpose to be to manumit forthwith, . . . and without moral preparation, three millions of negro slaves, under jurisdictions altogether separated from those under which they live. . . . *Does any considerate man believe it to be possible to effect such an object without convulsion, revolution, and bloodshed?*[2333]

The entire South agreed! A tiny minority of boisterous and bigoted Northerners were attacking an aspect of Dixie's way of life,[2334] labeling it "immoral," and the South would not stand for it.[2335]

The North no doubt expected the negative response it got from the South, which was part of its original intention to begin with: by constantly pressuring Dixie to abolish slavery prematurely, the North knew it would be met with stubborn resistance. This allowed Lincoln to paint the South as the "bad guy," which in turn gave him the excuse to later force the issue at the tip of a bayonet. This only occurred, of course, when on January 1, 1863—the day he grudgingly issued the Final Emancipation Proclamation—it suddenly served his agenda to underhandedly alter the character of the war from a *political* one meant to "preserve the Union" to a *moral* one meant to "abolish slavery."[2336]

The reasoning behind this could have only come from his

Northern constituents, and more particularly from New England, "the center of the rationalizing process." For it was here, in this region steeped in self-righteous Puritanism, that complicated matters were always simplified into a single issue, then justified through the lense of morality.[2337]

Neither Southerners or Britons were fooled by Lincoln's bait-and-switch tactic, however. The perspicacious *London Spectator* noted:

> *The [Lincoln] government liberates the enemy's slaves as it would the enemy's cattle, simply to weaken them in the coming conflict. . . . The principle is not that a human being cannot justly own another, but that he cannot own him unless he is loyal to the United States.*[2338]

In a word, the ill will created by Northern abolitionists' indiscriminate accusations against Dixie made it impossible for Southerners to make any immediate movement toward abolition.[2339] While visiting the South in 1835, Yankee Professor Ethan Allen Andrews asked countless Southerners about their meddlesome neighbors to the North. Here are his observations:

> Since I entered the slave-holding country, I have seen but one man who did not deprecate, wholly and absolutely, the direct interference of northern abolitionists with the institutions of the south. "I was an abolitionist," has been the language of numbers of those with whom I have conversed, *"I was an abolitionist, and was laboring industriously to bring about a prospective system of emancipation. I even saw, as I believed, the certain and complete success of the friends of the colored race, at no distant period, when these northern abolitionists interfered, and by their extravagant and impracticable schemes, frustrated all our hopes.* We have no expectation that, in our day, the prospects of the slaves will ever again be as favorable, as they were at the moment when this ill-omened interference commenced. *Our people have become exasperated, the friends of the slaves alarmed, and nothing remains, but that we should all unite in repelling the officious intermeddling of persons who do not understand the subject with which they are interfering. We will not be driven by northern clamors, or northern associations, to do that which we would gladly accomplish, in a prudent manner, if left to ourselves."*
>
> *These views and feelings may be unintelligible to men who know nothing of southern society; but they are sentiments in which almost every man, woman and child, south of Pennsylvania, fully unites. Equally united are they in the opinion that the servitude of the slaves is far more*

rigorous now, than it would have been, had there been no interference with them. In proportion to the danger of revolt and insurrection, have been the severity of the enactments for controlling them, and the diligence with which the laws have been executed.[2340]

Due to political expediency, halfway through his war Lincoln decided to shift the character of the conflict from "preserving the Union" to "abolishing slavery." Both were rank falsehoods, however, carefully calculated to procure Northern and abolitionist votes in the upcoming 1864 presidential election. Part of this ruse was the issuance of the Final Emancipation Proclamation on January 1, 1863, which, revealingly, could not and did not legally free a single slave South or North.

Was the South being stubborn? Hardly. It merely expected to be treated with the same respect and dignity that the U.S. government normally accorded any foreign nation. Yet this was something the North seemed incapable of doing where slavery and her neighbor to the South were concerned. Along with the fact that less than 5 percent of Southerners were slave owners,[2341] it is obvious then that the South's resistance to abolition was primarily psychological and constitutional. This is precisely what Hugh Williamson, North Carolina's representative at the Constitutional Convention in Philadelphia in 1787, said before his

Yankee opponents:

> . . . we are expressly prohibited by the Constitution from giving liberty to a single slave. *That business remains with the individual states; it is not committed to Congress, who have no right to intermeddle with it.*[2342]

There was a set of additional reasons, however, for proceeding cautiously with Southern abolition; reasons of a much more practical nature.

Southerners understood that the abolition of slavery was not something that could be accomplished overnight. It was a complex procedure that had taken other countries years, decades, centuries, to complete, and it would take Dixie just as long, or longer. Time was needed to prepare, from designing laws and rules to regulate the process of readying 3.5 million former slaves for a life of freedom, to finding the capital ($3 billion, or $57 billion in today's currency)[2343] to compensate former slave owners and establish housing and jobs for freedmen and women. U.S. President Woodrow Wilson wrote sympathetically of this situation:

> While the [Industrial] Revolution was in progress, a series of inventions brought the whole modern machinery of cotton manufacture into existence. Following immediately upon the heels of this great industrial change, came Eli Whitney's invention of the cotton-gin (1793), which enabled even the unskilful slave to cleanse a thousand pounds of cotton of its seeds in a single day, instead of five or six pounds, as formerly. At once, almost at a single bound, the South became the chief cotton field of the world. In 1792, the year before Whitney's invention, the export of cotton from the United States amounted to only 138,328 pounds; by 1804 it had swelled to 38,118,041; and at the time of the first struggle touching the extension of slavery (the Missouri compromise), it had risen to 127,860,152, and its value from seven and a half to more than twenty-two millions of dollars. Before this tremendous development of cotton culture had taken place, slavery had hardly had more than habit and the perils of emancipation to support it in the South: southern life and industry had shaped themselves to it, and *the slaves were too numerous and too ignorant to be safely set free.* But when the cotton-gin supplied the means of indefinitely expanding the production of marketable cotton by the use of slave labor, another and even more powerful argument for its retention

was furnished. After that, slavery seemed nothing less than the indispensable economic instrument of southern society.[2344]

African enslaved African women on the coast of Nigeria, awaiting their second sale to arriving Portuguese slave ships. In campaigning for "immediate emancipation" in the South, Lincoln—as well as his liberal Northern critics, the radical abolitionists—did not seem troubled by the fact that such women would be mercilessly slaughtered if their plan was ever implemented. For it was the custom along the slave coast of Africa for African slave dealers to simply murder unsellable slaves. But the more humanitarian Southerner was very concerned about this potential problem, just one of the many reasons he wanted to take a deliberate, slow, and methodical course toward full abolition.

There was also the potential issue of large-scale massacres in West Africa following a sudden emancipation in the American South, for it was a well-known custom that African chiefs and African slave dealers killed any slaves that were transported to their coast and could not be sold.[2345] How could such a slaughter be stopped? Who would be in charge of policing the African coast in an attempt to prevent the carnage, and where would the money come from to outfit dozens of U.S. ships and their crews?

Georgia Senator James Jackson made the following pertinent observations in 1790 before the U.S. Congress:

> . . . *I should be for total abolition. [But let] charity and humanity begin at home; let the gentlemen in the Northern States who own slaves and advocate their cause, set the example of emancipation. Let them prove their own humanity; let them pull the beam out of their own eye previous to discovering the mote in their neighbor's. That is an argument that would speak for itself.* Gentlemen have talked of our [the South] raising alarms; but it is at a reality, not at a bug-bear [a frightening phantom]. *The whole tenor of the resolutions has been contrary to southern interests*; and [immediate] manumission, emancipation, and abolition have been their intention. [I admire those Northern men who have spoken candidly about these subjects.] . . . I wish the same might be done by other members, who appear to me to *conceal their real designs under the specious pretext of concern for the interests of the Southern States.*[2346]

In 1857, anticipating the many very real problems that would be associated with a hurried and unplanned mass liberation of slaves, South Carolina secessionist Representative Lawrence M. Keitt stood in front of Congress and said:

> History tells us . . . that when the working classes stepped out of the condition of bondage, by the process of emancipation, they branched into four recurring subdivisions—the hireling, the beggar, the thief, and the prostitute . . .[2347]

Some Yankees understood the situation quite well. Said New Jersey politician Elias Boudinot:

> It would be a piece of inhumanity to turn these unhappy people loose, to murder each other or to perish for want of the necessities of life.[2348]

The conservative South wanted to do everything in its power to try and prevent these types of social disasters; the liberal North showed no concern about them whatsoever. Phillips put it this way. The Southern

> people were not to be stampeded in the cause of inherent rights or any other abstract philosophy. It was a condition and not a theory which confronted them.[2349]

South Carolina Representative Lawrence M. Keitt spoke out against the idea of rushing Southern abolition. History teaches, he correctly observed, that this usually leads to "four recurring subdivisions—the hireling, the beggar, the thief, and the prostitute."

The dilemma facing the South affected everyone, of every race, of every economic class, of every educational background. This was not something to be taken lightly.

The topic was front and center across the South from the 1700s onward, and was discussed by commentators from every part of the globe, not just the U.S. Tocqueville, for example,

> *demonstrated beyond a doubt, that the abolition of slavery in the South was a far different problem from, and a far graver problem than, its abolition in the North.* This was true (1) because the climate of the South was far more favorable to slave labor than the climate of the North; (2) because of the nature of the Northern and of the Southern crops, the former requiring attention only at intervals, the latter requiring almost constant attention; (3) because of the tendency of slavery to move toward the South.
>
> He pointed out the fact that in 1830 there was in Maine only one negro for every three hundred of the whites; in Massachusetts one negro for every one hundred; in Virginia

> forty-two for every one hundred; in South Carolina fifty-five for every one hundred. And *his conclusion was that "the most Southern States of the Union cannot abolish slavery without incurring very great danger, which the North had no reason to apprehend when it emancipated its black population. . . . The Northern States had nothing to fear from the contrast, because in them the blacks were few in number, and the white population was very considerable.* But if this faint dawn of freedom were to show two millions of men their true position, the oppressors would have reason to tremble." He disclaimed any sympathy with the principle of negro slavery, but said . . . *"The question of slavery was a question of commerce and manufacture for the slave-owners in the North; for those of the South, it is a question of life and death."*[2350]

Eminent Virginia professor Dr. Early Lee Fox made the following comments, noting that *Southern* slavery, as opposed to *Northern* slavery, was far more complicated, and included the fact that many black servants South of the Mason-Dixon Line simply refused to be emancipated, yet another impediment to Southern abolition that you will never read about in any pro-North "history" book:

> Dr. William Thornton had pointed out clearly in 1804 the seriousness of the problem of the abolition of slavery in the South as compared with its abolition in the North. *At that time he said that, in the North, the comparatively few slaves were so distributed among the population that a general emancipation fell but lightly upon each owner; whereas, in the South, "it would perhaps be requiring too much from humanity, to expect those who hold slaves to emancipate them, and thus reduce their own families from affluence to absolute misery. And there is frequently no alternative."* He deprecates the evils of slavery, but "it has been not only a query with others, but with myself, whether this partial good does not increase the general evil. . . . Evil therefore rests on evil till a mountain rises whose summit is shadowed by a cloud of sin."
>
> And many years later Henry Clay, in a speech on the subject of Abolition petitions, made in the United States Senate, February 7, 1839, estimated the value of property in slaves, in the South, at $1,200,000,000 [$31 billion in today's currency]—owned by persons of all classes, those who could afford to emancipate their slaves and very many who could not. *Slave property, he said, "is the subject of mortgages, deeds of trust, and family settlements. It has been made the basis of numerous debts contracted upon its faith, and is the sole reliance, in many instances, of creditors within and*

without the slave States, for the payments of debt due to them."

It is also to be observed that those proprietors who were most anxious to emancipate their slaves were the very ones from whom the slaves received the most consideration. Scores of instances could be noted of the proffer of their freedom, by such masters, to their slaves, and of the slave's refusal to go free. . . . There are significant statements in a note, appended by himself, to the will of Reverend Thomas S. Witherspoon [a relative of both the author and actress Reese Witherspoon], of Alabama:

> *"It will be plainly seen that my intention is to liberate them [six slaves] by colonizing them in some of the colonies of free blacks. This I would do now, but they utterly refuse to leave me, protesting that they will not leave me until my death. . . .* I cannot meet death in peace while the consciousness of the fact is left that these faithful and pious servants are to be left in bondage. I feel that I am responsible to God for them. . . . I am a Presbyterian minister. . . . *My slaves I inherited from my father and through my deceased wife, all but one, whom I purchased to keep him with his wife."*[2351]

The famous slave owning Dabney family of Mississippi also experienced this situation firsthand, as daughter Susan Dabney Smedes writes in her 1888 book, *Memorials of a Southern Planter*:

> [My father Thomas Dabney] was at [our family plantation] Burleigh when he heard of General [Robert E.] Lee's surrender. On the day that the news reached him, he called his son Thomas [Jr.] to him, and they rode together to the field where the negroes were at work. *He informed them of the news that had reached him, and that they were now free.* His advice was that they should continue to work the crop as they had been doing. At the end of the year they should receive such compensation for their labor as he thought just.
>
> From this time till January 1, 1866, no apparent change took place among the Burleigh negroes. Those who worked in the fields went out as usual, and cultivated and gathered in the crops. In the house, they went about their customary duties. We expected them to go away, or to demand wages, or at least to give some sign that they knew they were free. But, except that they were very quiet and serious, and more obedient and kind than they had ever been known to be for more than a few weeks, at a time of

sickness or other affliction, *we saw no change in them.*

At Christmas such compensation was made them for their services as seemed just. Afterwards fixed wages were offered and accepted. Thomas called them up now and told them that as they no longer belonged to him they must discontinue calling him "master."

The archetypal image of the "Slave Unshackled." Though pro-North writers would have you believe otherwise, few in the predominately abolitionist Old South ever cared about preserving slavery. The main topic of discussion was always about how and when to abolish it.

"Yes, marster," "yes, marster," was the answer to this. "They seem to bring in 'master' and say it oftener than they ever did," was his comment, as he related the occurrence to his children. This was true. The name seemed to grow into a term of endearment. *As time went on, and under the changed order of things, negroes whom he had never known became tenants on his plantation; these new people called him master also. . . . They were proud of living on his place, on account of the good name that he had won for himself as a master. Not infrequently they were heard to express a regret that they had not belonged to him when they saw the feeling that existed between himself and his former slaves. Sometimes he came to us with a puzzled look to ask who those negroes were who had just called him old master and shaken hands with him.*

"I cannot recall their faces," he would say; "surely, I

never owned them?"

Finally the negroes on the neighboring plantations, and wherever he went, came to call him old master. They seemed to take pride in thus claiming a relationship with him, as it were; and he grew accustomed to the voluntary homage.[2352]

This phenomenon, of slaves refusing emancipation, was repeated tens of thousands of times across the South before, during, and even after Lincoln's War.

And so Dixie had a number of perfectly good reasons for postponing abolition, not one of them having to do with either so-called "Southern racism" or the absurd "slavery was the cornerstone of the Confederacy" theory.

Tragically, the Northern agenda called for the *complete*, *immediate*, and *unconditional* destruction of Southern slavery,[2353] without compensation to slaveholders,[2354] a contemptuous attitude that only bred further bad blood, stalled Southern abolition, and ultimately helped send the two nations into battle. Is it any wonder that after Lincoln's War a former Union soldier offered the following description of antebellum America to a British visitor?

> You had no idea of the intensity of the hatred between North and South when the war broke out. They would not pray together. In the same cities there were churches for Northerners and churches for Southerners. At the beginning of the war, the Union men in the South had to fly for their lives. Some took to the woods; they were hunted with dogs, shot, and hung.[2355]

Of the aggressive and violent Northern approach to foreign diplomacy regarding the Constitution, states' rights, and slavery, Mary Chesnut opined:

> We separated North from South because of incompatibility of temper. We are divorced because we have hated each other so.[2356]

But this "marital" acrimony was completely unnecessary. Southerners, based on their thorough knowledge of ancient Roman and Greek history, had understood from the earliest days of the American colonies that *slavery is arguably worse for the slaveholder than it is for the slave*, and that both classes would benefit from its cessation.[2357]

Again, their only desire was that they be allowed the constitutional right to terminate the institution in their own time and way. This meant that any contrary Northern opinion on the matter was, as Georgia Governor George M. Troup called it, nothing but "officious and impertinent intermeddlings with our domestic concerns."[2358] Anticipating the formation of the Southern Confederacy 37 years later, in 1824 a congressional committee representing the sentiments of Troup, relayed his thoughts regarding the North's unwanted intrusion into Southern society to the U.S. House of Representatives:

> The hour is come or is rapidly approaching, when *the states, from Virginia to Georgia, from Missouri to Louisiana, must confederate*, and, as one man, say to the Union: We will no longer submit our retained rights to the sniveling insinuations of bad men on the floor of congress—our constitutional rights to the dark and strained construction of designing men upon judicial benches; that *we detest the doctrine, and disclaim the principle, of unlimited submission to the general government*.
>
> Let our Northern brethern, then, if there is no peace in union, if the compact has become too heavy to be longer borne, in the name of all the mercies, find peace among themselves. Let them continue to rejoice in their self-righteousness; let them bask in their own elysium, while they depict all south of the Potomac as a hideous reverse. As Athens, as Sparta, as Rome was, we will be: they held slaves; we hold them. Let the North, then, form national roads for themselves; let them guard with tariffs their own interest; let them deepen their public debt until a high-minded aristocracy shall arise out of it. We want none of all those blessings. But in the simplicity of the patriarchal government, *we would still remain master and servant under our own vine and our own fig tree, and confide for safety upon Him who, of old time, looked down upon this state of things without wrath*.[2359]

Virginian St. George Tucker agreed, pronouncing the Northern aggression over Southern slavery nothing but "a mischievous attempt, an improper interference, and, at best, an act of imprudence." Southerners rightly saw this uninvited Yankee tampering as an attack on their constitutional rights, and were understandably fed up with being lectured by bossy, "misguided and misinformed" Northerners on "lessons in religion and morality." "Suppose Congress were to forbid the [North] eastern fishery, or to put restrictions on it; would the [North] eastern states submit?" asked one Southerner of his Yankee compatriots. The answer is obvious, as were the true but hidden motivations behind the interference: "to create disunion among the [Southern] states, and to excite the most horrible [slave] insurrections."[2360]

The South, cradle of the American abolition movement, had been trying to figure out how to rid itself of slavery even before the formation of the U.S. The North's constant interference not only did not help the situation, it delayed and almost completely stalled it. Georgia Governor George M. Troup referred to the Yankees' incessant tampering as "officious and impertinent intermeddlings with our domestic concerns."

Southerners were appalled that the North forced its "free" laborers to toil for up to 14 hours a day in unventilated mills for mere pennies, and even refused its workers health care, paid leave, or pensions. Despite this, Southerners respected the Yankee's constitutional right to treat his employees as he wished, and asked only the same courtesy in return.[2361] Derry phrased the situation like this:

> *There were ills connected with slavery which the good people of the South tried faithfully to remedy.* The best and kindest of masters firmly believed that the freedom of the large number of negroes who lived in the South would bring ruin to master and slave alike, and *many*

> *of the slaves themselves shared in this feeling.* It was the kindly sentiment that prevailed between the ruling and the servile class that prevented the latter from being a menace to the South, when the vast armies of the North were thundering at the gates of her cities, or ravaging her fields.
>
> . . . A great deal has been said by the enemies of the South about the aggressions of the slave power. *The Southern people always felt that the aggression was entirely on the other side.* The most extreme Southerner had never asked for more than protection to himself in the right to carry with him into the common territories of the Union any property that he might possess including slaves, with the understanding, however, that when the territory adopted a constitution and applied for admission into the Union as a State, it could exclude slavery if it chose. *All that he asked was that his Northern brethren should not interfere either directly or indirectly with the institutions of the South.*[2362]

If Lincoln had only followed this sage advice, Southern slavery would have come to a natural end by itself, untold thousands of lives and billions of dollars in property would have been spared, and the South today would be living in its own free, separate, sovereign, prosperous, and happy land: the Confederate States of America (C.S.A.).

Let us point out here that contrary to what you have been taught, this name was no mere whim of fancy on the part of Dixie. The Southern Founding Fathers intentionally borrowed it from the name the U.S. Founding Fathers originally gave to the United States of America: "the Confederacy," which for all practical purposes means the "Confederate States of America." And this is exactly what Alexis de Tocqueville called the U.S. in 1832[2363]—29 years *before* Jefferson Davis and his cabinet formed the *Southern* Confederates States of America.

This is why, after all, George Washington, Andrew Jackson, and St. George Tucker referred to the U.S. as a "Confederate Republic";[2364] it is why, when Thomas Jefferson referred to it, he used the hopeful phrase a "lasting Confederacy";[2365] it is why Samuel Adams called the U.S. a "Confederation";[2366] it is why Alexander Hamilton called it the "American Confederacy";[2367] and it is why James Madison referred to the U.S. as "the present Confederation of the American States."[2368]

In 1861 Southerners had given their own new republic this same name, and for the same reason: the desire to live in a country made up of powerful, self-governing, independent states operating under a small, weak central government. Tragically, Davis, his advisors, and his military officers all woefully underestimated the arrogance, aggressiveness, guile, inhumanity, greed, self-delusion, and violence of their chief foe, big government Liberal, megalomanic Abraham Lincoln, who, just as progressives do today, despised the idea of states' rights, and who put socialistic idealism not only above the political intentions of the Constitution and the Founding Generation, but above commonsense and practicality as well.[2369]

In the 1830s, decades before the secession of the Southern states and the formation of the Southern Confederacy in 1861, French traveler and historian Alexis de Tocqueville journeyed through what he called the "Confederate States of America" (that is, the United States) and noted that racism was far more serious in the North than in the South. He was only one of many who made this observation during the antebellum era.

WHAT YOU WERE TAUGHT: Harriet Beecher Stowe's book *Uncle Tom's Cabin* portrays Southern slavery exactly as it was: cruel and inhumane. For this she has rightfully earned the respect and thanks of the world.

THE TRUTH: All Western societies today recognize the immorality of slavery and condemn it as an affront to civilized humanity. At the same time it must be acknowledged that the idea that every aspect of Southern "slavery" as it was practiced in the 17th, 18th, and 19th Centuries was hideously vicious and barbaric, is an invention of anti-South propagandists.

Indeed, this particular stereotype derives almost wholly from one of the North's most infamous anti-South propagandists, novice Yankee author Harriet Beecher Stowe. An abolitionist from Connecticut who moved to Ohio, Stowe worked tirelessly to rid the nation of slavery by writing such provocative books as *Uncle Tom's Cabin*, published on

March 20, 1852.[2370] We can certainly applaud her for her efforts.

There was just one problem with Stowe's antislavery works, however: they were all based on information she had gained secondhand, and that from unreliable biased sources.[2371] For Stowe never stepped foot on a Southern plantation, had no firsthand knowledge of slavery, and never even visited the South.[2372] In fact, like most Northerners then as now, she had no idea what a plantation was or how slavery was practiced, and even less knowledge of what life was like outside Cincinnati, where her notorious novel was written.[2373]

So she made up stories based on how she wanted to think Southern "slavery" was practiced, chronicling what she believed the institution to be rather than what it actually was. Her characters were drawn from her vivid imagination and from slanted and vitriolic South-loathing abolitionist tracts; South-hating leaflets put out by Northern antislavery societies that were filled with little more than two-dimensional cartoon-like stereotypes that never existed in Dixie.[2374] Even William Lloyd Garrison, the renowned Yankee abolitionist, admitted that *Uncle Tom's Cabin* could only be read as fiction, not as a true story.[2375] Southerners en masse simply referred to the book as "that damn Yankee lie."[2376] It was, in fact, nothing but an anti-Fugitive Law pamphlet disguised as a novel.[2377]

President Woodrow Wilson rightly asserted that the abuses portrayed in Stowe's book "were in every sense exceptional" in the South,[2378] calling her book the "product of the sympathetic imagination, which the historian must reject as quite misleading."[2379]

In her diaries Chesnut describes *Uncle Tom's Cabin* as "sickening,"[2380] and Stowe herself as "nasty" and "coarse."[2381] As for the woman's highly inventive mind, Chesnut calls it detestable and repugnant. "Stowe writes her books by making things up out of thin air,"[2382] the diarist penned, a common and accurate complaint across the South.

Stowe's portrait of "Southern plantation life" was indeed full of inaccuracies[2383] and gross generalizations and contradictions.[2384] Highly distorted and irrational, her black characters were atypical,[2385] for the entire book presented nothing but a highly distorted and even perverted picture of the institution as it was practiced in Dixie.[2386] All this without a word of "how the North [too] is implicated in the guilt of slavery," as

Southern abolitionist Angelina Grimké phrased it in 1837.[2387] *Uncle Tom's Cabin* was considered so pernicious by Tennesseans that petitions were sent to local theater managers to ban theatrical performances of the book. Southern parents denounced the play as highly "exaggerated," correctly complaining that it would have "a very bad effect on the children who might see the drama."[2388]

Understandably besieged by overwhelming criticism from both Southerners and Northerners for her wildly embellished tales—even many blacks, both then and today, have complained that she made her black hero Tom "too good to be true."[2389] Stowe, later finally bowing to criticism and pressure, conceded that her book was not meant to be taken literally, and that it was more a work of art than fact (this despite her strange claim that God had commanded her to write it).[2390]

Yankee scandalmonger Harriet Beecher Stowe, the author of *Uncle Tom's Cabin*, a purely fictitious novel based on ignorance, slanderous falsehoods, misrepresentations, blatant disinformation, and the fabrications of South-hating abolitionist tracts. Stowe, in fact, had never visited the South and knew absolutely nothing about Southern culture, society, or servitude. U.S. President Woodrow Wilson said that her book was nothing but a product of her imagination, one that would be rejected by true historians as "misleading." Southern belle Mary Chesnut called her book "sickening" and Stowe herself "nasty."

Unbeknownst to most of those who are familiar with her highly fictitious tale, the extremely cruel slave owner in her book, Simon Legree (whose surname she misspells),[2391] along with all of the other evil folks brought forth from her overwrought imagination, are *Northerners*, whose poor, exploited, and mistreated slaves live and work on imaginary farms in states Stowe never visited.[2392] Furthermore, while Legree himself was a transplanted Yankee from Connecticut, most of the

Southern characters in Stowe's book are portrayed as outstanding and empathetic individuals.[2393]

The reality is that *Uncle Tom's Cabin* was a work of Yankee propaganda, a political fabrication full of both misinformation and disinformation, meant to rouse Northern passions against the institution of slavery, a common ploy of Northern abolitionists. Stowe, in fact, knew literally nothing about blacks, slavery, the South, plantation life, or African-American culture. And, as discussed in Chapter 7, the violence, unethical treatment, and immorality she portrayed between black slaves and their masters and mistresses was not only rare, but was illegal in the South, punishable by law, and condemned by all good Southern people.[2394] Her portrait of plantation life was, in the end, highly contorted and irrational, while her black characters were aberrant.[2395]

It is important to note that Stowe's novel was actually inspired by the book *Truth Is Stranger Than Fiction*, the autobiography of Josiah Henson, a *Northern* slave.[2396] In her appeal to end slavery Stowe tried to incite Northern hatred toward the South by denigrating the people of Dixie. But in fact she revealingly based most of her story on the behavior of *Northern* slave owners from Maryland, Henson's birthplace. So much for this disreputable piece of anti-South fiction.

We have other evidence that Southern slavery was not what we have been taught by Northern and New South historians and textbooks.

In the 1850s a Boston minister named Nehemiah Adams traveled to the South to examine the phenomenon of "cruel slave owners" for himself. Dr. Adams was shocked to discover that there was no truth in the Northern anti-South myths he had heard for so long. In the fascinating account of his journey, entitled, *A Southside View of Slavery*, Adams writes of the whip:

> The white overseers have it in their power, of course, to perpetuate many tyrannical and cruel acts . . . [But] [t]here is a public sentiment to which they are amenable; *a cruel, neglectful master is marked and despised; and if cruel or neglectful by proxy, he does not escape reprobation*. . . . This is a brand upon a man which he and his family are made to feel deeply.[2397]

In 1835 James Madison was paid a visit by English author Harriet

Martineau, at which time he

> *mentioned the astonishment of some strangers, who had an idea that slaves were always whipped all day long, at seeing his negroes go to church one Sunday. They were gayly dressed, the women in brightly-coloured calicoes; and, when a sprinkling of rain came, up went a dozen umbrellas. The astonished strangers veered round to the conclusion that [Southern] slaves were very happy . . .*[2398]

It was an oft observed fact that Southern servants were frequently better dressed on Sundays than their free white farming neighbors.[2399] These and a thousand other facts destroy the dark, heartless, anti-South fantasy world Stowe created.

Nonetheless, she accomplished her goal, for the best-selling 1852-book, which was translated into 23 languages and sold millions of copies, was instrumental in ending slavery by shaping public opinion.[2400] And happy she must have been, for Stowe, like her liberal Yankee heroes Abraham Lincoln[2401] and Horace Greeley[2402] (and, at one time famed Northern abolitionists William Lloyd Garrison,[2403] Gerrit Smith,[2404] Lewis Tappan, Elizur Wright,[2405] and Theodore D. Weld—a former Yankee slave owner),[2406] was an ardent black colonizationist who looked forward to the day when all people of African descent would be shipped out of America. And this could not be accomplished until all slaves (then considered personal property) were freed.[2407]

Like Yankee abolitionists Gerrit Smith (pictured here), Horace Greeley, William Lloyd Garrison, Lewis Tappan, Elizur Wright, and Theodore D. Weld—and of course anti-abolitionist Lincoln—Stowe too once supported the American Colonization Society, whose primary goal was to make America "white from coast to coast." No pro-North advocate or Southern scallywag wants you to know these facts, of course, which is why they have suppressed them for 150 years.

Yet even pro-North writers have had to admit that it was *Uncle Tom's Cabin* that allowed abolitionists to finally win the propaganda war.[2408] According to

Yankee legend, after meeting her in 1862, midway through the South-North conflict, Lincoln himself referred to Stowe as "the little lady who started this great war,"[2409] a statement as fictitious as her book.

While this is an outright lie (war criminal Lincoln never once took responsibility for any of his own felonious actions), Stowe's real contribution was nearly as evil: *Uncle Tom's Cabin* helped prolong the conflict that Lincoln started by at least two years. During that period, after the Emancipation Proclamation was issued (January 1, 1863 to April 9, 1865), hundreds of thousands of Southerners *and* Northerners died, while slavery dragged on, all unnecessarily. And for this Stowe has been apotheosized and extolled by the North and the New South!

Stowe's book created other problems as well. Her fallacious perception of the South was taken as genuine fact by many Victorian Yankees, which has unfairly damaged the South's image and reputation right into the present day. *Uncle Tom's Cabin* also helped whip up Northern support for the abolition movement, which anti-abolitionist Lincoln later cunningly used to his advantage against the Confederacy.

The truths that Stowe ignored were legion. The facts are that black servant families in the South were rarely separated; slaves were almost never sold after purchase; whites did not buy slaves to elevate their social status; "slave breeding" was nonexistent;[2410] and, as we have seen, slaves were not poorly fed, poorly housed, poorly clothed, or poorly cared for: enslaved blacks actually had larger houses, as well as better clothes, diets, and medical care than free blacks, and even many free whites. Lastly, the death and suicide rates among Southern slaves were lower than those for whites, while slaves' life spans were longer; and we have the statistical studies of slavery scholars to prove it.[2411] (Compare these statistics with those of Brazil—in 1888,[2412] the last country in the New World to abolish slavery[2413]—where the treatment of slaves was so dismal and conditions were so barbaric that the average life expectancy of the typical Brazilian slave was only 18 to 22 years of age.)[2414]

Despite these plain facts, a majority of Victorian Yankees, just as many do today, refused to accept the truth. Englishman Sir Charles Lyell relates this story:

> To inquire into the condition of the negroes, and the evils arising out of the relation of master and slave, was not the object of my

> visit [to the American South in the 1850s]; but when I afterwards related to an Abolitionist in Massachusetts, how little actual suffering had obtruded itself on my notice, he told me that great pains must have been taken by the [Southern] planters to conceal from me the true state of things, while they had taken care to propitiate me by hospitable attentions.[2415]

WHAT YOU WERE TAUGHT: Southern slave owners were so tyrannical, cruel, and violent that Southern slaves were in constant rebellion, regularly forming gangs and even entire armies and justifiably murdering their masters. This is why there were hundreds if not thousands of slave revolts across the American South before and during the Civil War.

THE TRUTH: This Northern myth completely disregards the many both planned and real slave insurrections in its own region, two examples of the latter which occurred in New York, one in 1712, the other in 1741.[2416] More importantly, it ignores the fact that in the South there was not a single known slave revolt during Lincoln's War,[2417] and in fact as we are about to see, over a period of several hundred years only three so-called Southern "slave revolts" were significant enough to have been given the names of their instigators.[2418]

Southern black servitude was not at all what pro-North writers claim. In fact, it was the opposite of authentic slavery, which is what was practiced in the ancient world in places like Greece and Rome.

To begin with, if black servants were treated cruelly there was literally nothing to prevent them from rising up on their farms and plantations, overthrowing their owners, and leaving.[2419] Southern plantations were not armed concentration camps with barbed wire, security guards, and white racist militias specially trained to maintain law and order over blacks, as these large farms have been painted by the North.

On the contrary, by and large Southern plantations were, in

typical Southern fashion, relaxed, flexible, and informal, with few set rules and with both masters and servants coming and going, sometimes for days and even weeks at a time. This is the complete reverse of what one finds under authentic slavery (that is, a slavery system without any human rights),[2420] such as on the ancient Roman *latifundium*, those great Italian estates where the overseers and conditions were strict, unsparing, and brutal, and "where humanity and profits were incompatible." In comparison to the Roman slave system, writes Phillips, the Southern servant system "was essentially mild."[2421]

Mary Chesnut, as just one example, writes of how she often left her servants "on their own to do as they pleased, something they were well used to."[2422] Such historical facts reveal that a great deal of mutual trust and respect existed between servants and their owners, hardly the type of atmosphere that would foster rebellion, rioting, mayhem, and murder.

One must also consider that there was a wide disparity in population. On the average large Southern plantation, for instance, there were commonly 100 blacks to six whites, a European-American family that typically consisted of a father, mother, and four children. That is a ratio of about 17 to one. The ratio on such plantations between *adult* slaves and *adult* white males was even greater: about 30 to one.[2423] A force contemplating revolt with these types of odds on their side could be completely confident of victory. Why not rise up and mutiny then if life under Southern servitude was in every way unbearable?

Even on smaller plantations where there were typically five to ten times as many blacks as whites, black servants could have effortlessly overpowered their owners at any time, particularly at night.

The fact is they seldom if ever did.

In many antebellum Southern towns, blacks equaled whites in population; in others they actually outnumbered whites. While they were never the majority in the South, blacks once made up a huge percentage of the overall population: according to the 1860 U.S. Census, of the South's 12 million inhabitants in 1860, exactly one third of them, or 4 million, were black.[2424] Of these, 3.5 million were servants, 500,000 were free.[2425]

Just as revealing is the fact that in 1860 a majority of the Southern states had black populations that were nearly equal to the white population, and two Southern states, Mississippi and South Carolina, actually possessed more blacks than whites that year. The former had 436,696 blacks to only 354,700 whites, the latter with 402,541 blacks to only 301,271 whites. Some states like Florida, with 61,753 blacks to 78,686 whites, and Louisiana, with 333,010 blacks and 376,280 whites, were nearly dead even.[2426] Furthermore, in all of the rice-growing regions of the South blacks outnumbered whites two to one.[2427]

The point is that had Southern blacks wished to arm themselves and fight, they could have easily overthrown and killed their owners, wrecked Southern plantations, burned Southern cities to the ground, and emancipated themselves. And yet, there were virtually no major, and scarcely any minor, slave insurrections in any city in Dixie at any time between 1619 and 1865, despite the North's numerous cruel and un-Christian attempts to incite such revolts in the South.[2428]

In particular, as mentioned, not a single slave rebellion took place during Lincoln's War.[2429]

The racist North attributed the dearth of Southern slave rebellions to "the natural docility, laziness, and imbecility of the Negro." But Southerners who lived in daily close contact with African-Americans well knew that blacks possessed none of these attributes, and that their "low state" was not their natural condition. It was caused by the "degrading environment" of servitude.[2430]

Slave rebellions were extremely rare in the Old South, more proof that the life of a black servant in Dixie was not the punishing, brutal, depraved existence portrayed by anti-South historians. The slave uprising pictured here took place in New York, and resulted in the deaths of a number of blacks.

Thus, contrary to the Northern white view of blacks, the average Southern white regarded the average Southern black as ambitious, hard working, skilled, and highly intelligent, which is why, after Lincoln's War, former Confederates, such as General Nathan Bedford Forrest, wanted to help repopulate the South with African immigrants.[2431] Of his Southern black brothers and sisters, Forrest said:

> They are the best laborers we have ever had in the South. . . . there is no need for a war of the races. I want to see the whole country prosper.[2432]

One would have to search long and hard to find an example of a Yankee officer, or any Northerner for that matter, expressing similar sentiments.

So the question remains: in the 116 years that slavery existed in Dixie,[2433] why, when it would have been so simple to do so, did slaves not rise up, overtake the South, and free themselves? This question is particularly interestingly in light of the fact that during Lincoln's War, white women, children, and seniors were left alone on their farms for four years, sometimes outnumbered ten to one by their black servants. Why did the slaves on these estates not rise up en masse and either revolt or simply walk away? It would have been ridiculously easy to do.

There were indeed a few black insurrections in the South, but scarcely enough to be counted on one hand. And of these some were actually instigated by anti-South whites, not Southern blacks.

Moreover, most were so insignificant that they were never even reported. Of the four most important antebellum slave revolts, the first two do not even deserve the name "rebellion," for no rebellion ever actually took place. Let us look at all four of these.

1. "The Gabriel Prosser Rebellion": In 1800 Virginia slave and Methodist Gabriel Prosser set out to form a posse and "kill all the whites" in the name of God. But inclement weather delayed his massacre and he was never able to reassemble his mob.

2. "The Denmark Vesey Rebellion": In 1822 South Carolina slave and black racist Denmark Vesey, also a Methodist, planned to assail the city of Charleston and murder as many whites as possible. Before he could begin his attack, however, his scheme was discovered and he and 34 of his fellow black accomplices were hanged.[2434]

3. "The Nat Turner Rebellion": This, the third important slave

"revolt," only received publicity because of the exceptionally heinous crimes that the psychotic Turner, again a Methodist, and his henchmen committed in 1831. For it was not a rebellion in the true sense of the word. It lasted only twelve hours, covered only a few square miles, and in no way advanced the cause of blacks.

Indeed, it reversed it. In its aftermath whites passed new exceptionally harsh slave codes, and abolitionist sentiment, once strong across the entire South, was considerably dampened for several years. Despite these facts, pro-North historians have had little choice but to admit that Turner's was "the most serious uprising in the history of American slavery."[2435]

Additionally, this incident cannot be attributed specifically to *Southern* slavery. Why? Because it occurred 30 years before the Civil War, when both slavery and the slave trade were still being openly practiced by tens of thousands of people in the North. In fact, much if not all of the responsibility for the Nat Turner Rebellion must lie with William Lloyd Garrison's Northern newspaper, *The Liberator*, which was read primarily by blacks, not whites.[2436]

The Yankee paper's articles were filled with antislavery and anti-South propaganda of the most inaccurate, overly embellished, vituperative, melodramatic, and absurd kind. Here is a sample from *The Liberator*, dated January 1, 1847:

> Three millions of the American people are in chains and slavery—held as chattels personal, and bought and sold as marketable commodities. Seventy thousand infants, the offspring of slave parents, kidnapped as soon as born, and permanently added to the slave population of Christian (!), Republican (!!), Democratic (!!!) America every year. Immediate, unconditional emancipation. *Slave-holders, slave-traders, and slave-drivers are to be placed on the same level of infamy, and in the same fiendish category, as kidnappers and men-stealers—a race of monsters unparalleled in their assumption of power, and their despotic cruelty.* The existing Constitution of the United States is a covenant with death, and an agreement with hell. No Union with Slave-holders![2437]

Sadly, Turner and his followers, inflamed by this truly comical nonsense, sought their revenge on a white society that was almost wholly innocent of Garrison's accusations and lies.[2438] Since we are striving to preserve the truth about both American slavery and Southern slavery, a brief overview of this "slave revolt" will be beneficial.

At 2:00 A.M., on August 21, 1831, Turner, an escaped servant operating under a series of obscure and dubious "signs from Heaven," led a 50-member gang of vicious blacks on a murderous rampage through Jerusalem, Southampton County, Virginia. Using axes, hatchets, and knives rather than firearms (to avoid detection), they tortured, butchered, and killed entire European-American families, mostly women and children, almost none who owned slaves or who even had slave owning relatives.

THE
CONFESSIONS
OF
NAT TURNER,
THE LEADER
OF
THE LATE INSURRECTION
IN SOUTHAMPTON, VA.
AS FULLY AND VOLUNTARILY MADE TO
THOMAS R. GRAY,
In the prison where he was confined, and acknowledged by him to be such, when read before the Court of Southampton: with the certificate, under seal of the Court convened at Jerusalem, Nov. 5, 1831, for his trial.
ALSO,
AN AUTHENTIC ACCOUNT
OF THE
WHOLE INSURRECTION,
WITH
Lists of the Whites who were Murdered,
AND OF THE
Negroes brought before the Court of Southampton, and there sentenced, &c.

RICHMOND:
PUBLISHED BY THOMAS R. GRAY.
T. W. WHITE, PRINTER.
1832.

The title page of Thomas R. Gray's 1832 book, in which Nat Turner confessed to his crimes prior to his execution on November 11, 1831.

Under Turner's racist orders to "kill all whites," Caucasian men, women, children, and even newborn infants, were all slain with equal and unmerciful ferocity, usually while asleep in their beds. As their victims slumbered peacefully, Turner and his butchers sank freshly sharpened axes deep into their skulls. Most never woke up. Those who did were greeted with scenes of horror beyond all description. Of this diabolical massacre one historian notes that all that was left afterward were pillaged homes and headless bodies strewn across the town.[2439]

Turner later gleefully bragged of his foul deeds. At a plantation owned by the Whitehead family, for example, he boasted that he grabbed a struggling Margaret Whitehead, "and after repeated blows with a sword, I killed her by a blow on the head, with a fence rail."[2440]

During Turner's psychopathic killing spree nearly 60 innocent defenseless whites died, many who were, like a majority of Southerners, ardent abolitionists.

Four weeks later Turner and most of his fellow murderers were captured. The violent outlaw never showed any remorse for his crimes, and on November 11, he and some 20 of his followers were hanged for their senseless outrages. "Senseless" because Virginia was the most zealous antislavery state in the South, perhaps even in the entire nation at the time, with a strong abolition movement that dated back to before the formation of the U.S. Indeed, as we have shown, the entire American abolition movement got its start in Virginia.[2441]

4. "The John Brown Slave Rebellion": The final antebellum "slave rebellion" of any consequence has also been misnamed, for it was not instigated by slaves, or even by free blacks, but by a white Northerner.

This particular "revolt" occurred in 1859, 28 years after Turner's debacle, and was headed by New Englander John Brown, an antislavery-obsessed madman from Torrington, Connecticut.

To Brown, Southern blacks, for reasons he and many other Northerners could not comprehend, were unwilling to mutiny, overrun their plantations, and kill their white owners and their families. Brown decided that a white man needed to goad them into action, by organizing and arming them in an effort to start a slave war against Southern whites.[2442]

The fanatic began his insane escapade when pro-states' rights forces (known wrongly by Northerners as "pro-slavery" forces) burned down the town of Lawrence, Kansas, on May 21, 1856, in anger over increasing anti-states' rights sentiment (known wrongly by Northerners as "antislavery" sentiment) in the area. The "Sacking of Lawrence," as it is called, outraged abolitionist Brown, who immediately called for revenge.[2443]

On the evening of May 24, during a surprise night attack, he hacked five unarmed, pro-states' rights men to death with swords at Pottawatomie Creek, Kansas. Brown's innocent victims were: William Sherman, Allen Wilkinson, William Doyle, James Doyle, and Drury Doyle. Instead of helping his cause, however, Brown's purposeless and bloody binge only further incited Southern whites against him, heightening tensions in the Kansas Territory guerrilla war that would one day become known as "Bleeding Kansas."[2444]

Not surprisingly, Southern blacks did not support Brown either. Indeed, while he did his best to galvanize African-Americans to turn against their owners and join him, after several years he managed to interest only five former black servants in enlisting in his mob. The other 16 men in his 22-man team were white, many of them his own family members.

Brown next intended to capture the Federal armory at Harpers Ferry, Virginia (in what is now part of Jefferson County, West Virginia), then emancipate all the servants in the area. He assumed that learning of his "noble crusade," thousands of freed blacks would unite with him, after which he would lead the resulting army across the South, liberating the region's remaining bondsmen and bondswomen as he went.

The murderous escapades of Yankee abolitionist, South-hating, demented serial killer John Brown were supported by numerous high profile Yankees, among them Abraham Lincoln, poet Henry Wadsworth Longfellow, author Henry David Thoreau, clergyman Theodore Parker, and famed detective Allan Pinkerton. Why anyone would champion an individual whose main goal was to slaughter innocent Southerners and overthrow the South's economy is still a mystery here in Dixie 155 years later.

The plan was so absurd, so unworkable, so impossible, that even black abolition leaders, like Frederick Douglass, tried to dissuade him from going through with it, calling the scheme suicidal.[2445]

Brown was not one to be reasoned with, however. Like Turner, he claimed to have had numerous visions in which God appointed him to "free the slaves." The Bible-thumping Connecticuter could not have been very familiar with the Good Book, however, because, as we saw in Chapter 8, throughout the Old and New Testaments, far from condemning slavery, God overtly encourages it, Jesus ignores it, and Saint Paul condones it.

With delusional un-biblical reveries filling his head, and with thousands of dollars in support money from other wrong-headed Northerners, on October 16, 1859, the serial-killer led his tiny band of mercenaries on an attack against the arsenal buildings at Harpers Ferry.[2446] A two-day skirmish ensued, which ended on the 18th with Brown's capture by future Confederate hero Robert E. Lee and his U.S. forces.

The ill-informed Brown was tried and convicted, and on December 2 he was executed by hanging for treason against the state of Virginia.[2447] In the crowd was a cousin of mine, a man soon to become known as "Stonewall Jackson," who no doubt retained the memory of this bizarre episode in American history until the day he himself died a few years later, on May 10, 1863. Ironically, General Jackson passed away in the middle of Lincoln's own failed attempt to start a black insurrection in the South.

South-hating Northerners, such as Henry David Thoreau, Ralph Waldo Emerson, Horace Greeley, Louisa May Alcott, William Cullen Bryant, William Henry Seward, Henry Wadsworth Longfellow, Franklin Benjamin Sanborn, and James Russell Lowell—some of these individuals who had actually bankrolled Brown—hailed him as a martyred saint, one who had died, like Jesus, to save mankind from sin.[2448]

But what was the South's sin? Slavery? As we have proven over and over in this very book, this "sin" started in the North which then pushed it southward,[2449] a fact Thoreau, Emerson, Greeley, and the others never discussed let alone acknowledged.

Despite Brown's deification in the North, even Lincoln, whose favorite song was now *John Brown's Body*,[2450] pronounced the radical's "slave revolt" a failure, as he noted on February 27, 1860, during his Cooper Union Speech:

> John Brown's effort was peculiar. *It was not a slave insurrection. It was an attempt by white men to get up a revolt among slaves, in which the slaves refused to participate. In fact, it was so absurd that the slaves, with all their ignorance, saw plainly enough it could not succeed.*[2451]

Our sixteenth president was rarely so honest and accurate.

WHAT YOU WERE TAUGHT: New Englander John Brown was a great Christian abolitionist who wished only to free the black man from his shackles. He should not have been executed, but instead revered, as many Northerners did, for his work to inaugurate emancipation and black civil rights. The John Brown Rebellion was righteous and godly.
THE TRUTH: Calling Brown's uprising at Harper's Ferry, Virginia, a "rebellion" stretches credulity to the breaking point, for the crazed New Englander can hardly be placed in the same category with Prosser, Vesey, and Turner. For one thing, Brown was a white man; for another, not a single Southern slave left his or her home to follow him,[2452] as even Lincoln himself noted.[2453]

Brown's "rebellion" was also a dismal failure, one that ended not only in the deaths of hundreds of people across the U.S.,[2454] but with his own as well: the misguided psychopath eventually hung on the gallows for his murder of dozens of innocent Southerners, most who did not even own slaves and, like a majority of white Virginians, were abolitionists.[2455]

Nor is the Brown Rebellion what our history books claim it was: a righteous campaign against the South's so-called "peculiar institution."

John Brown (center) lying wounded next to his son in the aftermath of the so-called "John Brown Slave Rebellion" at Harper's Ferry, Virginia, October 18, 1859. Despite the backing of rich and powerful Northerners, Brown's attempt to launch a slave rebellion in the South was a dismal failure, doomed from the start by lack of interest among Southern blacks. After his capture by then U.S. military officer Robert E. Lee, Brown was convicted and hanged. The future "Stonewall" Jackson was in the audience.

It was not, in fact, his opposition to slavery that fueled his plans (the overwhelming majority of Southerners, 95.2 percent, did not own slaves, had no connection to it, and cared nothing about it).[2456] It was his desire to start up a massive slave insurrection across Dixie, an act that he hoped would both disrupt the South's economy and put all white Southerners in peril.[2457]

Concordian Henry David Thoreau, Yankee author of *Walden*, literally worshiped John Brown, likening him to the martyred Jesus and referring to him as an "angel of light."

A tragic irony that is seldom mentioned in our history books is the fact that one of the five people Brown and his men killed during their "uprising" to "save blacks from the sin of slavery," was a free Southern black man named Heyward Shepherd, who had refused to join his band of hair-brained assassins. Seventy-five years later, on October 10, 1931, the United Daughters of the Confederacy erected a monument at Harper's Ferry dedicated to Shepherd and the millions of other blacks who remained loyal to the South during Lincoln's War.[2458] If the other Southern states followed suit, Dixie would be filled with thousands of memorials to these courageous black men and women.

In the final analysis we must agree with another black man who also turned down Brown's offer to join him: abolitionist leader Frederick Douglass, who held that Brown's plan was a suicide mission from which there would be no escape and only hell to pay.[2459]

It is true that Brown was idolized and even worshiped by many. Indeed, he received almost unanimous support from New England whites, who gleefully engaged in his blasphemous apotheosization—and still do. But was this vulgar deification right?

We in the South do not think so. In order to better understand Dixie's position, let us examine a few of those who did.

Foremost among Brown's admirers was Henry David Thoreau (author of the classic American work, *Walden*), who evinced a deep sympathy for the New England robber, kidnapper, and murderer. After Brown's death, though he had been widely known as a true enemy of the South, one whose stated mission was the indiscriminate slaughter of Southern women and children,[2460] Thoreau proclaimed him an unfairly executed saint.[2461] This was the same man Southerners considered a demented zealot.[2462]

On December 2, 1859, the day of Brown's execution, New Englander Thoreau wrote his famous *Plea for Captain John Brown*, which contained the following incredible statements:

> Some eighteen hundred years ago Christ was crucified; this morning, perchance, Captain Brown was hung. These are the two ends of a chain which is not without its links. He is not Old Brown any longer; he is an angel of light.[2463]

Thoreau's literal worship of the South-loathing Brown did not end there. That same day the famed nonconformist asked that he be allowed to ring the bells of the First Parish Church in Concord, Massachusetts, in honor of "Old Ossawatomie," as Brown was popularly known.[2464] Wisely, the town's selectmen turned down his request,[2465] no doubt because Negrophobia and white racism were the ruling sentiments (abolitionists were a tiny and much hated minority)[2466] in New England at the time, and they did not want to stir up trouble.[2467] Despite Thoreau's experience in Concord, however, in a number of Northern towns guns were fired in salute and church bells rang in honor of the deceased criminal-turned-divinity.[2468]

In countless other Northern places of worship Brown was reverently called "the first martyr for slavery," "God's servant," "one comparable to Saint Stephen," and "a man who had certainly gone straight to Heaven."[2469] Referring to the fanatic from the Constitution State as a true hero whose execution had been "cowardly," other Northerners cried that he should have been allowed to live, and that America was in desperate need of "the religion of John Brown." After all, they claimed, his goals were truly noble: to abolish slavery and humiliate the South, for her people were arrogant, dictatorial, and low-born, and thus needed to be humbled.[2470] Here was a sentiment that, at the time, the majority of Northerners agree with.

Brown's demise had indeed deified him in the North, where he was celebrated in countless songs, poems, and speeches.[2471] Clearly, to Yankee antislavery advocates, psychopath Brown had died with the halo of martyrdom and was nothing less than a crucified god, one who deserved to be worshiped in the "Church of Liberty."[2472]

Besides Thoreau, John Brown had many other supporters from Concord, Massachusetts, where slave owners once dominated the town and freed slaves were cruelly exiled to the shores of Walden Pond. Among them were Louisa May Alcott, author of *Little Women*, and celebrated Transcendentalist Ralph Waldo Emerson. One Concordian who did not back Brown was Nathaniel Hawthorne, author of *The Scarlet Letter*. Of the Connecticut maniac, Hawthorne wrote: "Nobody was ever more justly hanged."

We also have the example of one of Thoreau's Yankee friends, Louisa May Alcott (the celebrated author of *Little Women*), who asserted that the late John Brown was now to be known as "St. John the Just."[2473] And let us not forget Ralph Waldo Emerson, who called John Brown "a saint . . . whose martyrdom . . . will make the gallows as glorious as the cross."[2474]

Emerson must have heartily applauded when one of his own

protégés, American journalist Franklin Benjamin Sanborn, became a member of the Secret Six,[2475] a group that financially supported Brown's Lincolnesque plan to start a slave revolt in the South,[2476] beginning with the seizure of Harper's Ferry.[2477]

Another New Englander who belonged to the Secret Six was fanatical abolitionist Samuel Gridley Howe,[2478] whose wife, Julia Ward, later composed the words to *The Battle Hymn of the Republic*.[2479] The original song, however, had been called *John Brown's Body Lies A-mouldering in the Grave*, a tune very popular with Lincoln's troops during his illegal War on the Constitution and the South.[2480]

Emerson, no doubt, loved both versions of this song, in particular the former, which euphemistically called for the North to "trample out the vintage [i.e., the Old South] where the grapes of wrath [the fruits of secession] are stored." Though Brown had butchered innocent non-slave owning families and had been a fugitive on the run from the law, the Transcendentalist and Boston Brahmin described his fellow Yankee as

> a fair specimen of the best stock of New England . . . a romantic character absolutely without any vulgar trait . . . All women are drawn to him by their predominance of sentiment. All gentlemen, of course, are on his side.[2481]

Another member of the Secret Six, New England liberal Theodore Parker,[2482] held that Brown was "not only a martyr . . . but also a saint,"[2483] while New England poet Henry Wadsworth Longfellow vowed that the day of Brown's execution "will be a great day in our history; the date of a new Revolution, quite as much needed as the old one."[2484]

Of Brown, New England poet William Cullen Bryant said: "History . . . will record his name among those of its martyrs and heroes,"[2485] while New England journalist and founder of the New York *Tribune* newspaper, Horace Greeley, eulogized Brown's "grandeur and nobility."[2486]

Some New Englanders not only supported Brown's insane plot to destroy the South through inciting a slave insurrection, but were also involved in equally preposterous plans to break him out of prison after he was captured. One of these was Reverend Thomas Wentworth

Higginson,[2487] who was active in devising several schemes to rescue and free Brown. Among the plots was a raid by sea; the kidnaping of Virginia Governor Henry A. Wise (who was to be held hostage in exchange for Brown); and, strangely, an overland charge of German refugees who would release Brown from prison and escape on the cavalry horses used by his guards.[2488]

After Brown's death, Higginson publically stated that he loved, admired, and defended Brown.[2489] Later, as a Union colonel in Lincoln's War, Higginson would go on to command the first all black force in Lincoln's highly segregated U.S. Army,[2490] a "slave regiment" known as the First Regiment of the South Carolina Volunteers.[2491] (Despite Higginson's seemingly non-racist views, his command of a black-only troop actually turned out to be a product of the North's deeply held racism.)

A complete list of the names of New Englanders who adored Brown and despised the South would require dozens of pages, but among them must also be mentioned the noted poet, essayist, and diplomat, James Russell Lowell, and also Massachusetts Governor John Albion Andrew, who said of Brown, his murder spree, and his attempt to wreck the South with a slave revolt: "John Brown was right, and I know it."[2492]

One of Brown's greatest admirers was Boston Brahmin Ralph Waldo Emerson, who, like Thoreau and many other South-haters, compared the Yankee psychopath to Christ. Brown's martyrdom, wrote Emerson, "will make the gallows as glorious as the cross."

Support from such luminaries did nothing to discourage Brown from viewing himself, as he did, as an "instrument of God,"[2493] even one comparable to

Christ, believing that his own death would bring salvation to millions.[2494]

All of this, of course, was calculated to hurt and infuriate the South. And it did.

In this characteristic piece of Yankee disinformation, an apotheosized John Brown is portrayed Christ-like, leaving jail en route to his death on the scaffold. On the way he is stopped by hundreds of blacks who wish to shower him with gratitude for fighting for their freedom. Of course, as with nearly all Yankee myths, the reality was the opposite: not a single Southern black slave enlisted in his violent gang of thugs, or even supported him. Indeed, one of the five Virginians Brown killed during his uprising was a free black man who had spurned his offer to become an anti-South terrorist. Leading black abolitionists declared Brown's plan to invade the South, start up a massive slave army, destroy Dixie, and completely abolish slavery, a pointless and futile suicide mission. And it was, for Southern slavery was nothing like the Connecticut madman had been taught and believed it to be.

In her diary on November 27, 1861, confused and angry Southern belle Mary Chesnut wrote of the odd animosity Yankees feel toward the South, in particular those self-righteous New Englanders, like Thoreau and Emerson,[2495] who "helped encourage John Brown to travel down to Dixie to kill Southerners in the name of Christianity."[2496]

While it is clear that New Englanders felt they were superior to the "inferior" South, what Chesnut may not have fully realized was that much of this invective originated in the region's profound racism toward blacks, as this very book reveals.[2497]

New Englanders were not the only Northerners who loved the South-hating Brown.[2498] While a fugitive on the run for numerous heinous crimes, Brown was given money, food, and supplies, and treated like a hero in countless Northern states, including Iowa and Illinois. In Cleveland, Ohio, where Brown was virtually deified by his admirers,[2499] Allan Pinkerton, famed founder of the U.S. detective agency (and soon to become Lincoln's chief of intelligence),[2500] gave the gangster $500 he had raised, the equivalent of nearly $12,000 today.[2501] Lincoln himself contributed financially to Brown, money that eventually went to fund his attack on Harper's Ferry.[2502]

It was New York, however, that rivaled New England in its support of the lunatic. In the city of Rochester, for example, Brown was allowed to give public lectures,[2503] while New Yorkers, such as William H. Seward (Lincoln's future secretary of state), said of him that his "utter sense of morality" allowed him to rise above his critics to the point where "his crimes would be all but forgotten."[2504]

Orchard House, Concord, Massachusetts, the childhood home of Louisa May Alcott, famous for her Victorian novel, *Little Women*. Like many uninformed Yankees at the time, Alcott held that John Brown was a divine being, come to earth to teach "the terrible Southerners" about the evils of slavery and "save" the black race from its "inevitable destruction" in Dixie. "St. John the Just," Alcott called Brown, insulting 12 million Southerners, white and black, with one little phrase.

Sometimes Northern hatred of the South was even more subtle, such as with Emerson's and Thoreau's friend, Long Islander Walt Whitman, author of the infamous *Leaves of Grass*, and whose brother, George Whitman, was a Yankee officer.

Walt—who during his walks often saw the mysterious, sad-faced president riding with his cavalry escort to and from the Soldiers' Home in Washington, D.C.—was particularly drawn to Lincoln,[2505] even stating publically that he "loved" him.[2506] After the president's assassination, the bard, a long-standing member of the antislavery Free-Soil Party, over-glorified Lincoln in flowery prose in his famous poems, "O Captain! My Captain!" and "When Lilacs Last in the Dooryard Bloom'd."[2507]

It was Lincoln, of course, who shared Brown's vision,[2508] and who later adopted the maniac's deranged plan to destroy the South.

Victorian South-loathing came in a myriad of forms, some subtle, some overt. New Jersey poet Walt Whitman, for example, once proclaimed that he "loved" Abraham Lincoln, then filled his notebooks with turgid verses about the liberal anti-South president after his assassination. In turn it was "Honest Abe" who shared John Brown's Yankee worldview of a subordinate, humbled South, later borrowing his insane plan to obliterate Dixie through violence and slave insurrections.

15

RACE RELATIONS IN 19th-CENTURY AMERICA

WHAT YOU WERE TAUGHT: White racism was always far worse in the South than it was in the North, which is why American slavery got its start in the Southern states.

THE TRUTH: In Chapters 4 and 5 we examined abundant evidence showing that both the American slave trade and American slavery were born in the North, in Massachusetts in 1638[2509] and 1641,[2510] respectively.

As for the other half of this particular Northern teaching, it is self-evident that the opposite is true; that, as Phillips put it, the "antipathy [toward blacks] was palpably more severe at the North in general than in the South."[2511] And here is why.

Wherever the various races have the least amount of contact, racism tends to increase—no matter what the skin color of the dominant or majority race. And this is precisely the situation we find in the Old South and the Old North, for in the latter region most whites had little if any interaction with blacks, making racism far more ingrained. Thus we find that Jim Crow laws, along with both legal and customary segregation, for instance, were "universal" in all of the Northern states, but were "unusual" in the South.[2512] Indeed, during the antebellum period there was no segregation anywhere in Dixie, yet it was endemic to America's northeastern states right up to, and far beyond, the 1860s.[2513]

The North's onerous Black Codes forbade, among many other things, black immigration and black civil rights, and even banned blacks from attending public schools. Little wonder that those blacks who managed to survive in the North were generally less educated and less skilled than Southern blacks. Up to 1855 it was this very type of oppression that prevented blacks from serving as jurors in all but one Northern state: Massachusetts.[2514]

Edward Everett, governor of Massachusetts, was fully aware of the blatant white racism in his region, observing that the lives of so-called "free" Northern blacks were weighted down by "disability, discouragement, and hardship" on all sides.

Even after Lincoln's admittedly fake and illegal Emancipation Proclamation was issued (on January 1, 1863),[2515] literally nothing changed for African-Americans living north of the Mason-Dixon Line. When former slaves managed to make economic progress there, they found themselves blocked at every turn by a hostile racist Northern government, the very body that had "emancipated" them. This blockage was accomplished not only by Black Codes, by also through the implementation of severe Jim Crow laws and public segregation laws.[2516]

Trade unions and a highly discriminatory legal system further undermined black efforts to merge into Northern society.[2517] All of this was done under the auspices of President Lincoln, and later, after his death, with the authorization of his cabinet, all of whom he had carefully hand-picked.[2518]

While on the topic of our sixteenth president and Northern racism, we should point out that "The Land of Lincoln," Illinois, Lincoln's adopted home state, was one of the most anti-black Jim Crow states in America at the time,[2519] in large part because of his work to restrict black civil rights there—all which he dismissed as nothing more than "false issues."[2520] White Illinoisans, for instance, arguably among the most racist Northerners in the 1850s and 60s, threatened to start "a war of extermination" if blacks were given equal rights in their state.[2521] It was said that Illinois' Black Codes were so stringent that the civil rights of African-Americans were "virtually nonexistent" there.[2522] Thus it was that Massachusetts Governor Edward Everett once described the condition of "free" blacks in the North as one of "disability, discouragement, and hardship."[2523] And here is proof.

In the early 1800s a group of 19 free blacks were so despondent over the treatment they received from whites in Illinois that they penned a letter to the state's chapter of the American Colonization Society, begging to be transported to the African colony of Liberia. Their desperation was so severe that they even offered themselves as lifelong slaves to the ACS in exchange for ship fare. Their leader, named Smith, only hints at the conditions blacks had to deal with in the Old North:

> We are ready to start from Shawneetown [Illinois] at any moment, and wish the time to come as soon as possible [to go to Liberia]; for *though we are free in name we are not free in fact. We are in as bad, or worse condition than slaves* . . . being compelled to leave the State, or give security, and those of the whites who would befriend us are debarred by the fear of public opinion. If only those who deserve such treatment, if any do, were the only ones to suffer we should be content; but on the contrary, *if one misbehaves, all the colored people in the neighborhood are the sufferers, and that frequently by unlawful means; dragged from our beds at the hour of midnight, stripped naked, in presence of our children and wives, by a set of men alike lost to mercy, decency and Christianity, and flogged till they are satisfied, before we know for what; and when we are informed, it is probably the first time we heard of the offence.* Such is our situation and such the condition from which your Society can extricate us. *We deem it [that is, so-called "freedom" in the North] worse than slavery.* We say again we wish to go to Liberia, and if no way else is provided, we had as lief soon indent ourselves to the Society for life for our passage, *so we can live among our own color.* Let me know as soon as possible, whether you can help us, and how soon, and how much.[2524]

English abolitionist Marshall Hall visited the U.S. in the mid 1800s, and discovered, to his horror, a thriving racial bigotry among Northern whites—especially Illinois whites—one he aptly termed "the second slavery." Writes Hall:

> In some of the States, termed free, in Ohio, in Indiana, but *especially in Illinois*, [the black man] . . . is absolutely prohibited and excluded by State-law, and by recent State-law too, from taking up his abode and pursuing some humble calling of industry. *If he attempt to do so, he is actually driven, or sold, from the state, re-sold into slavery!* What words can adequately characterize such legislation? . . . What a contrast does this Illinois present with Old England! In England, the moment the slave's foot touches the soil, he is free. *In Illinois, the moment the free-man of colour touches the soil, of his own country too, even the country of his birth, he becomes—an alien, or—a slave!*[2525]

The average Yankee had no interest in the mixing of the races, and created numerous laws to keep them separated. Here a white New England headmaster blocks a black parent from bringing her two children to an all-white school in New Hampshire.

Reverend John Orcutt of Connecticut, an agent of the American Colonization Society, wrote the following in his report after traveling across the U.S.:

> *Not only are free negroes forbidden to come into Indiana by express statute, but it is made a penal offense for a white person to induce such immigration*. . . . When a State constitution was adopted in Oregon, four-fifths of the electors said by their vote we will not have slavery! and they *also said by about the same majority, "we will have no*

> *free negroes!" Illinois too, has a similar prohibitory law against free negroes. . . .* Already in the Eastern States, the black man finds himself on equal footing with the whites nowhere, except in the State prisons, where he is on the same level, and fully represented! No wonder that some of the free colored people at the North should begin to inquire with solicitude what they shall do. *I saw several at the West who said, "We must go somewhere!"*[2526]

In 1862, Lincoln, who as an attorney had once defended a slave owner in court (and lost), helped the citizens of Illinois amend their state constitution to include a passage that read, "no negro or mulatto shall immigrate or settle in this state."[2527] He even urged the Illinois legislature to set aside funding to deport all free blacks from the state in order to prevent *miscegenation* (that is, racial interbreeding),[2528] a racist word invented, not by Southerners, but by Northerners.[2529]

With men like Lincoln serving in its government it is certainly no surprise that Illinois was so anti-black. After all, it was Old Abe himself who, on July 17, 1858, made a public speech at Springfield, Illinois, that included the following words: "What I would most desire would be the separation of the white and black races."[2530]

A year earlier, on June 26, 1857, during another address at Springfield, here is what the die-hard colonizationist said to his Northern audience about the horrors of race-mixing and the benefits of "separating" the races. In this statement he reveals one of the main reasons he was against slavery and in favor of black deportation: his absolute dread of miscegenation, amalgamation, or mongrelization, as it was also known. Stated Lincoln to his Northern audience:

> *Judge [Stephen] Douglas is especially horrified at the thought of the mixing of blood by the white and black races: agreed for once—a thousand times agreed.* There are white men enough to marry all the white women, and black men enough to marry all the black women; and so let them be married. . . . *A separation of the races is the only perfect preventive of amalgamation; but as an immediate separation is impossible the next best thing is to keep them apart where they are not already together. If white and black people never get together in Kansas, they will never mix blood in Kansas.* That is at least one self-evident truth. A few free colored persons may get into the free States, in any event; but their number is too insignificant to amount to much in the way of *mixing blood*. . . . In 1850 there were in the United States 405,751 mulattoes. Very few of these are the offspring of whites

> and free blacks; nearly all have sprung from the black slaves and white masters. *These statistics show that slavery is the greatest source of amalgamation.*[2531]

Though his conclusions were in error,[2532] Lincoln's opinion was clear enough: by nature, slavery forces the races to intermingle, which in turn brings about the undesirable birth of "mullatoes." Only a "separation of the races" could fully prevent this, he maintained. Thus one of Lincoln's party members, Illinois Senator Lyman Trumbull, noted that:

> *There is a great aversion in the West—I know it to be so in my state—against having free Negroes come among us. Our people want nothing to do with the Negro.*[2533]

For Northern white supremacists like Lincoln, one of the more negative aspects of slavery was that it brought the two races into close proximity. For it led to what was then fearfully regarded in the white North as "amalgamation," "miscegenation," or "mongrelization," and the inevitable "dilution of the white race" through the creation of the dreaded "mulatto." This old illustration gives the Northern white racist view of "amalgamation," a dire warning of the potential consequences of both slavery and emancipation. Lincoln admitted publicly that he was "horrified at the thought of the mixing of blood by the white and black races," revealing his true motivation for being antislavery. "Statistics show," he repeatedly preached, "that slavery is the greatest source of amalgamation." Lincoln's ultimate solution to the "race problem" was emancipation then black colonization: the deportation of freed African-Americans to all-black colonies in Liberia, or any other foreign country that would take them.

Even after the War white Illinoisans continued to discriminate against blacks. One postbellum Illinois law, for example, required that free blacks possess a "certificate of freedom" and post a bond of $1,000 to reside in the state. Those who violated these conditions were subject to arrest, after which they were hired out as a laborer (what Yankees would call a slave) for one year.[2534]

Illinois was far from being the only Northern state that feared "race-mixing," or which issued these types of Black Codes. Massachusetts had some of the most stringent anti-miscegenation rules on the books. Blacks convicted of violating New England's racist puritanical laws were sold and deported, usually to the West Indies, where they faced a life of bitter toil on England's sprawling sugar plantations.[2535] Massachusetts, New Jersey, Pennsylvania, and Connecticut all heartily approved of castration as another means of "curing" black males of intermingling with white females, and also as a punishment for rape or even attempted rape of white females.[2536]

Like Massachusetts,[2537] Pennsylvania passed severe laws against interracial "mixing." A 1726 statute upheld the longtime custom of punishing free blacks who had relations with white women by forcing them into slavery for seven years. Any African-American, free or enslaved, who married a white female was to be forced into slavery for life.[2538]

Writing in the 1840s, Scottish-born Anne M. Grant made the following observations of New York slave owners:

> . . . *these colonists had not the smallest scruple of conscience with regard to the right by which they held them [their black slaves] in subjection.* Had that been the case, their singular humanity would have been incompatible with continued injustice. But the truth is, that of law the generality of those people knew little; and of philosophy, nothing at all. *They sought their code of morality in the Bible, and imagined that they there found this hapless race condemned to perpetual slavery*; and thought nothing remained for them but to lighten the chains of their fellow Christians, after having made them such. I neither "extenuate," nor "set down in malice," but merely record the fact. At the same time it is but justice to record, also, a singular instance of moral delicacy distinguishing this settlement from every other in the like circumstances; though, from their simple and kindly modes of life, they were from infancy in habits of familiarity with their negroes, yet being early taught that nature had placed

> between them a barrier, which it was in a high degree criminal and disgraceful to pass, *they considered a mixture of such distinct races with abhorrence, as a violation of her laws.* This greatly conduced to the preservation of family happiness and concord. An ambiguous race, which the law does not acknowledge, and who (if they have any moral sense, must be as much ashamed of their parents as these last are of them) are certainly a dangerous, because degraded part of the community. How much more so must be those unfortunate beings who stand in the predicament of the bat in the fable, whom both birds and beasts disowned? I am sorry to say that the progress of the British army, when it arrived, might be traced by a spurious and ambiguous race of this kind. *But of a mulatto born before their arrival, I only remember a single instance; and from the regret and wonder it occasioned, considered it as singular.*[2539]

As for the Yankee Black Codes, in fact, at one time all of the Northern states had rigorous laws on the books that restricted the movements of blacks and limited black civil rights. Michigan, whose Black Laws strongly suggested that blacks traveling through the state not stop, but continue onto Canada, banned blacks from voting because, as they saw it, blacks belong to a disgraced race of humans.[2540] Another example was Iowa, where, in 1857, the white populace rejected black suffrage by a vote of 49,000 to 8,000.[2541]

Illinois Senator Lyman Trumbull spoke for Lincoln, as well as most other white Northerners at the time, when he made this public pronouncement: "There is a great aversion in the West—I know it to be so in my state—against having free Negroes come among us. Our people want nothing to do with the Negro."

Naturally, New York City, America's slavery capital for decades, had its own set of strict Black Codes, all which were considered particularly savage. Offences by black servants could garner punishments ranging from beatings and whippings to deportation and even execution. In 1741 the mere hint of a slave revolt resulted in the public killing of 27 slaves, each one who was hanged or burned at the stake.[2542]

New York as a whole was arguably the most racially intolerant state, perhaps second only to Illinois and Massachusetts. This is certainly why, for instance, New York City had far less black artisans than Southern towns such as the far more racially tolerant New Orleans.[2543] Between 1702 and 1741 alone the Empire State passed a massive series of statutes that, among other things, allowed blacks convicted of heinous acts to be executed "in such a manner as the enormity of their crimes might be deemed to merit." Along with this law manumissions were restricted, free New York blacks were prohibited from holding real estate, and the state's entire set of Black Codes was strengthened in an effort to gain greater control over both slaves and blacks in general.[2544] Well into the 1830s, as just one example, not even free blacks were allowed to drive their own hacks or carts.[2545] This same law was also active in Baltimore, Maryland, while in Philadelphia, Pennsylvania, free blacks were not allowed to drive an omnibus.[2546]

Hundreds of such illustrations from the racist Old North could be given. No wonder so many blacks wanted to get as far away from Yankeedom as possible, requesting that they be sent as far South as possible (to places like New Orleans),[2547] or even out of the country.[2548]

On November 14, 1864, Lincoln himself admitted that Louisiana was less racist than his own state, saying:

> A very fair proportion of the people of Louisiana, have inaugurated a new state government, making an excellent new constitution—*better for the poor black man than we have in Illinois*.[2549]

What Lincoln deceptively does not mention here is that Illinois' blacks were largely "poor" (that is, devoid of basic civil rights) because of he himself!

In 1857, for example, Lincoln aided in the white supremacist movement in his state by asking the Illinois legislature to appropriate funds for the deportation of all blacks out of the state. Why? As we have seen, to help prevent one of his greatest fears: the dilution of the white race through interracial reproduction.[2550]

Whites from central Illinois in particular had little use for blacks, considering them, not human beings, but lowly creatures, little more than livestock "with wool on their heads."[2551] Wrote one newspaper editor from the area, who could not abide the idea of free blacks moving to Illinois: "We don't want any Negroes around here. Send them all to the Northeast!"[2552]

An Illinois senator, Joseph Kitchell, was of the same mind as the rest of the whites in his state, including Lincoln. The residence of Negroes among us, he announced,

> *even as servants . . . is productive of moral and political evil. . . . The natural difference between them and ourselves forbids the idea that they should ever be permitted to participate with us in the political affairs of our government.*[2553]

Illinoisans passed countless anti-integration and anti-immigration laws to prevent blacks from settling in or even traveling through their state, with punishments ranging from whipping to being sold back into slavery at public auction.[2554] In 1862 Illinois voters adopted a constitutional provision that barred the further admission of blacks into their state,[2555] a Black Code that Lincoln allowed to remain on the books until 1865, the year his War finally came to an end.[2556] In 1863, for instance, eight blacks were arrested and convicted for entering Illinois unlawfully. Of these, seven were sold back into slavery (temporarily) to pay off their fines[2557]—all under Lincoln's watch.

As we have seen, black Illinois residents complained bitterly of their treatment. Another example in this class was John Jones, a wealthy African-American living in Chicago, who sent the following to Governor Richard Yates. It began like this:

> *We, the colored people of Illinois are highly displeased with the degradation we are suffering under in our State. Though we were born here, we are viewed as strangers. A black man cannot even buy a burial plot in Chicago for himself. The hatred toward us all comes from the anti-Negro laws passed by the whites of Illinois.*[2558]

Prior to the Revolutionary War, New Jersey barred all free blacks from coming into the state. Only black slaves, accompanied by their owners, were allowed.[2559] To gain maximum control over its slaves the Garden State adopted New York's Black Codes, considered some of the harshest in the nation.[2560] If more than three slaves gathered without the permission of their owners, the penalty was to be "whipt upon the naked back, at [the] discretion of any justice of the peace, not to exceed forty lashes." New York law not only permitted slave owners to "punish their slaves for their crimes and offenses at [their own] discretion," it also allowed and even encouraged every city and town in the state

> to have and appoint a Common Whipper for their slaves . . . to agree upon such sum [fee] to be paid him by the master or mistress of slaves per head, as they shall think fit, not exceeding three shillings per head, for all such slaves as shall be whipt.[2561]

Unlike in the Old South, where black servants were protected by a veritable bible of laws, the Old North's racist and unsparing Black Codes often allowed white Yankee slave owners the freedom to punish their slaves "at their discretion." This, of course, allowed for a wide array of abuses. Here, aboard a boat in New York Harbor, a white slave owner (right) has cut the throat of one of his slaves, who falls to the deck, blood spilling from his neck. While the whites in the background appear unfazed by this wanton act of brutality, in the South such a scene would have incited mass social outrage, and ended with the slave owner's immediate arrest and trial, and ultimately, his execution.

According to eyewitnesses, by 1835, due to white racism, conditions for free blacks in Maryland were far worse than they were for the state's slaves.[2562] Massachusetts, which restricted interracial marriage[2563] (and which was the first state to do so),[2564] also forbade trading with slaves, restricted manumission, and imposed whipping of "any negro or mulatto who should strike a Christian."[2565] The Bay State also segregated its railroads, theaters, and lecture halls, and would only permit blacks with state citizenship to enter its borders. Due to white racism, Philadelphia's prisons were segregated around the same time. In 1804 Ohio would not let blacks enter the state unless they paid "good behavior" bonds costing between $500 and $1,000. To discourage blacks from coming across its borders, Illinois followed suit in 1814.[2566]

All of the Northern states had similar Black Codes on their books at the time, a social phenomenon that did not go unnoticed by foreign visitors. As we are about to see, as early as 1831 individuals like French aristocrat Alexis de Tocqueville, who toured the South and the North that year, noticed that Southerners were "much more tolerant and compassionate" toward blacks than Northerners. This is why, while visiting America in the 1850s, Englishman Sir Charles Lyell observed that the Southern states justifiably "make louder professions than the Northerners of democratic principles and love of equality."[2567]

The racial discrepancy between the South and the North was also remarked on by British journalists, even in the middle of Lincoln's War. In 1862 the *North British Review* noted that in the North, "where slavers are fitted out by scores . . . free Negroes are treated like lepers."[2568] This was the same year Lincoln issued his Preliminary Emancipation Proclamation, which, of course, called for continued efforts to deport all freed blacks out of the U.S.[2569]

After his tour of the states in 1831, Tocqueville summed up his observations this way:

> Whosoever has inhabited the United States must have perceived that in those parts of the Union in which the negroes are no longer slaves, they have in no wise drawn nearer to the whites. On the contrary, *the prejudice of the race appears to be stronger in the States which have abolished slavery than in those where it still exists; and nowhere is it so intolerant as in those States where servitude never has been known.*
>
> It is true that in the North of the Union marriages may be legally contracted between negroes and whites; but *public opinion would stigmatize a man who should connect himself with a negress as infamous, and it would be difficult to meet with a single instance of such a union.* The electoral franchise has been conferred upon the negroes in almost all the States in which slavery has been abolished; but if they come forward to vote, *their lives are in danger.* If oppressed, they may bring an action at law, but they will find none but whites among their judges; and although they may legally serve as jurors, *prejudice repulses them from that office. The same schools do not receive the child of the black and of the European. In the theatres, gold can not procure a seat for the servile race beside their former masters; in the hospitals they lie apart; and although they are allowed to invoke the same Divinity as the whites, it must be at a different altar, and in their own churches with their own clergy.* The gates of Heaven are not closed against these unhappy beings; but their inferiority is continued to the very confines of the other world; *when the negro is defunct, his bones are cast aside, and the distinction of condition prevails even in the equality of death. The [Northern] negro is free, but he can share neither*

the rights, nor the pleasures, nor the labour, nor the afflictions, nor the tomb of him whose equal he has been declared to be; and he can not meet him upon fair terms in life or in death.

In the South, where slavery still exists, the negroes are less carefully kept apart; they sometimes share the labour and the recreations of the whites; the whites consent to intermix with them to a certain extent, and although the legislation treats them more harshly, *the habits of the [Southern] people are more tolerant and compassionate. In the South the master is not afraid to raise his slave to his own standing,* because he knows that he can in a moment reduce him to the dust at pleasure. *In the North the white no longer distinctly perceives the barrier which separates him from the degraded race, and he shuns the negro with the more pertinacity, since he fears lest they should some day be confounded together.*

Among the Americans of the South, Nature sometimes reasserts her rights, and restores a transient equality between the blacks and the whites; but in the North pride restrains the most imperious of human passions. The American of the Northern States would perhaps allow the negress to share his licentious pleasures if the laws of his country did not declare that she may aspire to be the legitimate partner of his bed; but he recoils with horror from her who might become his wife.

Thus it is, *in the United States, that the prejudice which repels the negroes seems to increase in proportion as they are emancipated, and inequality is sanctioned by the manners while it is effaced from the laws of the country.* But if the relative position of the two races which inhabit the United States is such as I have described, it may be asked why the Americans have abolished slavery in the North of the Union, why they maintain it in the South, and why they aggravate its hardships there? The answer is easily given. It is not for the good of the negroes, but for that of the whites, that measures are taken to abolish slavery in the United States.[2570]

What Tocqueville refers to as "those States where servitude never has been known" is a reference to what were then called the Western Territories (today the Western states), at the time an area with the least number of blacks and where slavery had never been practiced. It was here that he found white racism toward blacks the strongest.

To emphasize these facts, the Frenchman goes on to point out that while slaves had been freed in the North and now had so-called "full equal rights," Northern white society continued to strongly discourage blacks, often with the threat of death, from voting, sitting on juries, or attending white schools or white churches. According to Tocqueville blacks in the "abolitionist North" were not even permitted to sit next to whites in theaters, take a sick bed next to them in Northern hospitals, or be buried next to them in death.

Early foreign visitors to the American colonies, and later the U.S., frequently commented on the severity of white racism in the North as compared to the more racially tolerant South. Pro-North writers conveniently leave this fact out of their articles, books, teleplays, screenplays, and blogs.

Englishman Lyell noted that in Louisiana free blacks were allowed to be witnesses in court, while this privilege was denied them in many of the Northern states at the time, such as Indiana[2571]—where "there was little hostility to slavery, and bitter hostility to abolitionism."[2572] He then goes on to tell this story, which seems to have taken place in the 1830s or early 1840s:

> Mr. Richard Henry Wilde, formerly senator [representative] for Georgia, told me that he once knew a coloured freeman who had been brought up as a saddler, and was a good workman. To his surprise he found him one day at Saratoga, in the State of New York, acting as servant at a hotel. "Could you not get higher wages," he inquired, "as a saddler?" "Yes," answered he; "but no sooner was I engaged by a 'boss,' than all the other workmen quitted." They did so, not because he was a slave, for he had long been emancipated, but because he was a negro.[2573]

In the 1840s English writer James Silk Buckingham wrote that "the prejudice of colour is not nearly so strong in the South as in the

North."[2574] Here is how Robert Young Hayne, a South Carolina senator, described the treatment of those few Southern blacks who fled to the North:

> *. . . there does not exist on the face of the whole earth, a population so poor, so wretched, so vile, so loathsome, so utterly destitute of all the comforts, conveniences, and decencies of life, as the unfortunate blacks of Philadelphia, and New York and Boston. Liberty has been to them the greatest of calamities, the heaviest of curses. Sir, I have had some opportunities of making comparison between the condition of the free negroes of the North, and the slaves of the South, and the comparison has left not only an indelible impression of the superior advantages of the latter, but has gone far to reconcile me to slavery itself.* Never have I felt so forcibly that touching description, 'the foxes have holes, and the birds of the air have nests, but the Son of Man hath not where to lay his head,' as when I have seen *this unhappy race, naked and houseless, almost starving in the streets, and abandoned by all the world.* Sir, *I have seen, in the neighborhood of one of the most moral, religious and refined cities of the North, a family of free blacks driven to the caves of the rocks, and there obtaining a precarious subsistence from charity and plunder.*[2575]

Only a few years later, in 1835, Virginian James Madison met with English author Harriet Martineau at his home, Montpellier, and regaled her with stories of how the Northern states erected numerous barriers in an attempt to thwart Negro emigration. With regard to slavery, Martineau wrote of their celebrated conversation, he was despairing:

> *He talked more on the subject of slavery than on any other, acknowledging, without limitation or hesitation, all the evils with which it has ever been charged. . . . [He then] pointed out how the free [Northern] states discourage the settlement of blacks*; how Canada disagrees with them; how Hayti shuts them out; so that Africa is their only refuge.[2576]

In contrast to this explicit Yankee racism, there was Madison himself, who:

> As long as he was able . . . always superintended his own slaves, and had no overseer, and they were always well cared for. Another [white] visitor at Montpellier had been greatly surprised to see . . . [a group of Madison's female slaves] neatly dressed in bright calicoes, going to church; and when a shower came, to see the

dozen umbrellas that were raised. . . . [So kindly disposed was Madison toward his slaves that he had recently] parted with some of his best land [in order] to feed the increasing numbers.[2577]

In 1841, after traveling through Philadelphia, an English Quaker, Joseph Sturge, met with former Illinois Governor Edward Coles. Writes Sturge:

> *In the course of conversation, the Governor spoke of the prejudice against colour prevailing here as much stronger than in the slave States [the South]. I may add, from my own observation, and much concurring testimony, that Philadelphia appears to be the metropolis of this odious prejudice, and that there is probably no city in the known world, where dislike, amounting to hatred of the coloured population, prevails more than in the city of brotherly love!*[2578]

In 1835 English intellectual and writer Harriet Martineau met with former U.S. President James Madison of Virginia, at which time he discussed the problems of white Northern racism with her.

After a visit to New York City, English writer Edward Dicey recorded his observations concerning Yankee racism and Northern blacks. In the North, Dicey noted:

> *Everywhere and at all seasons the coloured people form a separate community.* In the public streets you hardly ever see a coloured person in company with a white, except in the capacity of servant. . . . On board the river steamboats, the commonest and homeliest of working [white] men has a right to dine, and does dine, at the public meals; but, *for coloured passengers, there is always a separate table.* At the great [Northern] hotels there is, as with us [in England], a servants' table, but *the coloured servants are not allowed to dine in common with the white.* At the inns, in the barbers' shops, on board the steamers, and in most hotels, the servants are more often than not coloured people. . . . *White [Northern] servants will not associate with black on terms of equality. . . . I hardly ever remember seeing a black employed as shopman, or placed in any post of responsibility. As a rule, the blacks you meet in the Free [that is, Northern] States are shabbily, if not squalidly dressed; and, as far as I could learn, the instances of black men having made money by trade in the North, are very few in number.*[2579]

While blacks were "degraded" in the North, they were "upgraded" in the South, as Englishman Lyell penned in 1855:

> I have heard apologists in the North endeavouring to account for the degraded position which the negroes hold, socially and politically, in the Free States, by saying they belong to a race which is kept in a state of slavery in the South. But, if they really desired to accelerate emancipation, they would begin by setting an example to the Southern States, and treating the black race with more respect and more on a footing of equality. I once heard some Irish workmen complain in New York, "that the niggers shut them out from all the easiest ways of getting a livelihood;" and *many white mechanics, who had emigrated from the North to the Slave States, declared to me that every opening in their trades was closed to them, because black artisans were employed by their owners in preference.*[2580]

Among the many racist-abolitionist Yankees Lyell came across while visiting the North, there was one whom he felt deserved special mention:

> One of the most reasonable advocates of immediate emancipation whom I met with in the North, said to me, "You are like many of our politicians, who can look on one side only of a great question. Grant the possibility of these three millions of coloured people or even twelve millions of them fifty years hence, being capable of

amalgamating with the whites, such a result might be to you perhaps, as a philanthropist or physiologist, a very interesting experiment; but *would not the progress of the whites be retarded, and our race deteriorated, nearly in the same proportion as the negroes would gain? Why not consider the interests of the white race by hastening the abolition of slavery*. The whites constitute nearly six-sevenths of our whole population. As a philanthropist, you are bound to look to the greatest good of the two races collectively, or the advantage of the whole population of the Union."[2581]

Compare all of this to the South, where whites and blacks worked in close association with one another on a daily basis, creating race relations that, on the whole, were friendlier and warmer than in any other region in America, as the following example illustrates. In his book *The Cotton Kingdom*, Connecticut landscape architect Frederick Law Olmsted, betraying typical Yankee bigotry, wrote of a "scandalous" experience he had during a train ride through the Old Dominion State:[2582]

> *I am struck with the close cohabitation and association of black and white—negro women are carrying black and white babies together in their arms; black and white children are playing together . . .; black and white faces are constantly thrust together out of the doors, to see the train go by. . . . A fine-looking, well-dressed, and well-behaved coloured young man sat, together with a white man, on a seat in the cars. I suppose the man was his master; but he was much the less like a gentleman of the two. The railroad company advertise to take coloured people only in second-class trains; but servants seem to go with their masters everywhere.* Once, to-day, seeing a [white] lady entering the car at a way-station, with a family behind her, and that she was looking about to find a place where they could be seated together, I rose, and offered her my seat, which had several vacancies round it. She accepted it, without thanking me, and immediately installed in it a stout negro woman; took the adjoining seat herself, and seated the rest of her party before her. It consisted of a white girl, probably her daughter, and a bright and very pretty mulatto girl. *They all talked and laughed together; and the girls munched confectionary out of the same paper, with a familiarity and closeness of intimacy that would have been noticed with astonishment, if not with manifest displeasure, in almost any chance company at the North.*[2583]

This scene, however, would have "astonished" or "displeased" very few white Southerners, nearly all who were accustomed to, and enjoyed, the company of blacks, as this incident clearly shows.

Mary Chesnut too writes of an incident that reveals the true state of race relations in the Old South. One hot August day during the War she found herself traveling on a river boat in Alabama, one overseen, not by a white deck hand, but by a black one, as was the norm in the South. Writes Mary in her diary:

> Montgomery, July 30th.—Coming on here from Portland there was no stateroom for me. My mother alone had one. My aunt and I sat nodding in armchairs, for the floors and sofas were covered with sleepers, too. *On the floor that night, so hot that even a little covering of clothes could not be borne, lay a motley crew. Black, white, and yellow disported themselves in promiscuous array. Children and their nurses, bared to the view, were wrapped in the profoundest slumber. No caste prejudices were here. Neither [abolitionists] Garrison, John Brown, nor Gerrit Smith ever dreamed of equality more untrammeled.*[2584]

This early illustration portrays a typical romantic relationship between a white Southern woman and a black Southern man—one that would have horrified Lincoln and his fellow Yankee cohorts. Such relationships were much more common and accepted in less racially prejudicial Dixie than in the far more biased puritanical North. Liberal educators do not want you to know this, however, so they did not teach it to you, and they are not teaching it to your children. This book will help preserve such historical facts.

Naturally such scenes contradict Yankee myth, so they are ignored by pro-North historians.

And let us not forget that it was a Southern state, Virginia, that would later vote the first American black into its highest office: in 1989, Lawrence Douglas Wilder, the grandson of Southern black servants, became the first elected black governor in the U.S. Even the first *non-elected* African-American governor was from a Southern state: as lieutenant governor of Louisiana, Pinckney B. S. Pinchback succeeded to the position in 1872 when Governor Henry Clay Warmoth was impeached and forced to step down.

The first two blacks to

serve in the U.S. Congress were also from the South: Hiram Rhodes Revels of Mississippi entered the Senate February 23, 1870; Joseph Hayne Rainey of South Carolina entered the House of Representatives December 12, 1870. Despite these bold facts, it is the South, not the North, that continues to be unfairly associated with racism.

European-American revulsion toward blacks was so deeply rooted in the North that many white Yanks, even those who considered themselves "friends of the Negro," promoted the idea of using whites as slaves rather than their "sable-skinned" fellow Americans. One of these was Puritan abolitionist Samuel Sewall, who was a judge at the infamous Salem Witch Trials in 1692.[2585] Though he hated slavery, he could not abide the thought of free blacks living among New England whites. Wrote Sewall:

> And all things considered, *it would conduce more to the Welfare of the Province, to have White Servants for a Term of Years, than to have [Black] Slaves for Life. Few can endure to hear of a Negro's being made free*; and indeed they can seldom use their freedom well; yet their continual aspiring after their forbidden Liberty, renders them Unwilling Servants. And *there is such a disparity in their Conditions, Colour & Hair, that they can never embody with us, and grow up into orderly Families*, to the Peopling of the Land: but still remain in our Body Politick as a kind of extravasat Blood.[2586]

Northern white racism was severe enough that it actually helped spawn the phenomenon of all-black churches, still with us today. As early Northern whites could not bear sitting next to African-Americans in church, blacks had little choice. Thus in 1787, in Philadelphia, Pennsylvania, two former Northern slaves, Richard Allen and Absalom Jones, started what was probably the first African-American-only church, the Mother Zion African Methodist Episcopal Church, when white members at nearby Saint George's Church denied them the right to worship there.[2587] In an effort to further segregate themselves from white Yankee racists, in 1816 additional branches of the Church sprouted up in places like Baltimore, Maryland.[2588]

Over a century later Northern racism was, if anything, even more unyielding and firmly established, which is why it has been truly said that on the eve of Lincoln's War "the negro was safer in South Carolina than New York, in Richmond than in Boston."[2589]

Here is an illustration. When Lincoln illegally instituted the first military draft in U.S. history, 50,000 Northerners took to the streets in New York in protest. They did not vent their anger in peaceful demonstrations against the government, however. These so-called Northern "humanitarians and abolitionists" turned on the blacks of their state, chasing, beating, and even lynching them. Many were hanged from trees and lampposts, while the bodies of dead blacks were burned in the streets. At least 100 people were killed and damage was estimated to be at least $1.5 million ($33.5 million in today's currency).[2590]

Samuel Sewall, Yankee judge at the infamous Salem witch trials, was typical of many New Englanders at the time. As one who detested African-Americans more than slavery itself, he recommended the use of white slaves instead of black ones, maintaining that individuals of African heritage would never be able to merge with European-American society.

So deep was the racism of white New Yorkers that these same mobs attacked and flogged white abolitionists, even destroying their homes and businesses. The "New York Draft Riots," as they are still deceptively called by Northern and New South historians, lasted five days (July 12-16, 1863) and were finally only quelled when Lincoln sent in Union troops returning from the Battle of Gettysburg (fought July 1-3, 1863).[2591]

In the early 1840s Scottish tourist William Thomson witnessed a racist white mob in Cincinnati, Ohio, that rioted for two full days. After destroying the building of an abolition organization and throwing its printing press into the Ohio River, they managed to kill or drive out every one of the "numerous" blacks who lived in the town:

> Many of them fled to the authorities of the town for protection; and the jail-yard was crowded with the poor creatures who had fled for their lives.
>
> An arrangement was immediately come to, between the authorities and the citizens; to the effect that no negro should be

allowed to live in the city who could not find a white man to become his security, and be answerable for his conduct.[2592]

In 1863 famed white British actress Frances "Fanny" Kemble wrote the following to a Northerner about Northern blacks:

> *They are not slaves indeed, but they are pariahs; debarred from all fellowship save with their own despised race—scorned by the lowest white ruffian in your streets, not tolerated as companions even by the foreign menials in your kitchen. They are free certainly, but they are also degraded, rejected, the offscum and the offscouring of the very dregs of your society; they are free from the chain, the whip, the enforced task and unpaid toil of slavery; but they are not the less under a ban. Their kinship with slaves forever bars them from a full share of the freeman's inheritance of equal rights, and equal consideration and respect. All hands are extended to thrust them out, all fingers point at their dusky skin, all tongues—the most vulgar, as well as the self-styled most refined—have learned to turn the very name of their race into an insult and a reproach.*[2593]

English abolitionist Marshall Hall said of Northern racism:

> I am utterly at a loss to imagine the source of that prejudice which subsists against him [the Negro] in the Northern states, *a prejudice unknown in the South, where the domestic relations between the African and the European are so much more intimate.*[2594]

While traveling on a Red River steamboat in Louisiana, Olmsted talked to a free black barber who had briefly attended school in West Troy, New York. Concerning white racism in the two regions:

> *He said that colored people could associate with whites much more easily and comfortably at the South than at the North; this was one reason he preferred to live at the South. He was kept at a greater distance from white people, and more insulted on account of his color, at the North than in Louisiana.*[2595]

During his visit to Richmond, Virginia, Olmsted heard about a black slave who had bought his freedom so he could go and live with his brother in Philadelphia, Pennsylvania. However, he returned abruptly a short time later. When his former owner asked him why, he replied:

Oh, I don't like dat Philadelphy, massa; ain't no chance for colored folks dere. Spec' if I'd been a runaway de wite folks dere take care o' me; but I couldn't git anythin' to do, so I jis borrow ten dollar of my broder an' cum back to old Virginny.[2596]

In his 1913 book *The Color Line in Ohio: A History of Race Prejudice in a Typical Northern State*, Frank U. Quillin writes:

John Randolph, of Roanoke, [Virginia] before his death in 1833 set free 518 slaves and bought for them a large estate in Mercer County, Ohio. It was arranged that each one was to have 40 acres and a cabin. *The white inhabitants of the county rose en masse against the influx of the negroes, and Judge Leigh distributed them around Troy, Piqua, Sidney and Xenia.*[2597]

Phillips made these comments concerning white racism in the North:

. . . *in Connecticut the citizens of New Haven resolved in a public meeting in 1831 that a projected college for negroes in that place would not be tolerated, and shortly afterward the townsmen of Canterbury broke up the school which [Quaker] Prudence Crandall attempted to establish there for colored girls.*[2598] The legislatures of various Northern states, furthermore, excluded free immigrants as well as discriminating sharply against those who were already inhabitants. *Wherever the negroes clustered numerously, from Boston to Philadelphia and Cincinnati, they were not only browbeaten and excluded from the trades but were occasionally the victims of brutal outrage whether from mobs or individual persecutors.*[2599]

On August 15, 1862, a black Massachusetts justice of the peace, John S. Rock, made the following remarks about white racism there. According to Rock, the Bay State did not compare favorably with Southern states, such as South Carolina:

The masses seem to think that we [blacks] are oppressed only in the South. This is a mistake; *we are oppressed everywhere in this slavery-cursed land. Massachusetts has a great name, and deserves much credit for what she has done, but the position of the colored people in Massachusetts is far from being an enviable one. While colored men have many rights, they have few privileges here. . . . The educated colored man meets, on the one hand, the embittered prejudices of the whites.* And on the other the jealousies of his own race. . . . *You can hardly imagine the humiliation and contempt a colored lad must feel by graduating the first in his class, and then being rejected everywhere else because of his color.*

No where in the United States is the colored man of talent appreciated. *Even in Boston, which has a great reputation for being anti-slavery, he has no field for his talent.* Some persons think that, because we have the right of suffrage [in Massachusetts] . . . there is less prejudice here than there is farther South. In some respects this is true, and in others it is not true. *We are colonized in Boston. It is five times as difficult to get a house in a good location in Boston as it is in Philadelphia, and it is ten times more difficult for a colored mechanic to get employment than in Charleston [South Carolina]. . . . if we don't like that state of things, there is an appropriation to colonize us.*[2600]

In the 1850s noted Yankee landscape architect, journalist, and social commentator, Frederick Law Olmsted, visited the American South, where he found himself appalled by the informality, familiarity, mutual respect, and even tenderness that existed between the white and black races—something altogether unheard of in his native Connecticut. While in Louisiana, Olmsted met a black man who had once lived and worked in New York, and who articulated the sentiment of thousands of other Southern African-Americans. "I much prefer living in the South sir," he told the stunned white Yankee tourist, "for I'm much more warmly accepted here than I ever would be in the North."

Sadly for Northern blacks, white Northern abolitionists were often among the most racist of an already overwhelmingly racist population.

Yankee antislavery advocates, for example, often told former Northern slave, black civil rights leader, and lecturer, Frederick Douglass, that he should try not to appear overly intellectual before his white audiences. "People won't believe that you ever were a slave, Frederick, if you keep on this way," said one. "Better have a little of the plantation speech than not; it is not best that you seem too learned," said another abolitionist.[2601] (All this despite the fact that Douglass was half-white,[2602] and that he was then a well respected educator whose second wife was a European-American.)[2603]

According to Douglass, due to the color of his skin, as late as the late 1830s he could still not get a job as a caulker in New Bedford, Massachusetts.[2604] White workers promised to strike if he was hired, so he was forced to go back to performing menial work as a common laborer.[2605] Just one example of the lack of love for the black man in the so-called "free" North. Had Douglass moved to Louisiana instead of Massachusetts, he would have had no problem securing employment.[2606]

Many Northern white abolitionists liked to refer to blacks, as Lincoln often did, using the "n" word,[2607] and comments about their "niggerly odour"[2608] and "woolly heads" were not uncommon at New England antislavery meetings.[2609] These were terms one never heard at Southern abolition meetings, which were attended by whites *and* blacks. Shortly after Lincoln's War, Yankee General Philip H. Sheridan, then serving in Louisiana, spoke for millions of Northerners when he made this comment concerning the beauty, speed, and stride of Southern horses:

> The horses of New Orleans have rather a good time of it. They are to the mules what the white man was to the negro—they do the trotting matches, draw the carriages, and carry the gentlemen, while their servants, the mules, do all the hard work, draw the carts, and do the ploughing and field work.[2610]

Even Northern Quakers, allegedly the most ardent of the abolitionists, often displayed overt prejudice: blacks were regularly denied membership, Quaker meeting halls were segregated, and many

Quakers belonged to Lincoln's favorite organization, the Northern-founded American Colonization Society, whose main objective was to "free the U.S. of the presence of the black race."[2611] Such attitudes underscore the fact that the constitution of the American Anti-Slavery Society, an organization established in Philadelphia, Pennsylvania, in 1833, did not even mention social equality as one of its goals.[2612]

It was because of this nearly ubiquitous white Yankee racism that Southern Congressmen enjoyed comparing

> the happy, well-fed, healthy, and moral condition of the southern slaves, with the condition of the miserable, vicious, and degraded free blacks of the North.[2613]

Northern President Abraham Lincoln, white racist, white supremacist, white separatist, and proponent of American apartheid, was well-known for his use of the word "nigger," a personal prejudice that carried beyond the grave: blacks were prohibited from attending his funeral on April 19, 1865.

Such are the facts of what Northern mythologists and South-haters still deceptively refer to as the "abolitionist North."

This is the same region that barred blacks from voting, jury duty, holding political office, interracial marriage, hotels, restaurants, theaters, stagecoaches, trains, schools, steamboats, churches, lecture halls, hospitals, and even cemeteries, right up to and beyond the Civil War.[2614] Even African-Americans who risked their lives for the Union, such as black Yankee officers, were repeatedly denied first-class railroad accommodations across the North.[2615] Is it any wonder that blacks were barred from Lincoln's funeral, but were welcomed at the funeral of Confederate General Nathan Bedford Forrest?[2616]

Why was the white North so much more racist than the white

South? It was due, in great part, to a lack of familiarity with blacks.

In the South whites intermingled with both free and servile blacks on a daily basis, developing strong, lasting, and affectionate bonds,[2617] especially with their own personal African servants.[2618] In a very real sense, the servant family and their household thus became part of the owner's extended family.[2619] This intimate association helped banish both white and black racism, while nurturing warm even loving relationships that often endured for life.[2620]

As Booker T. Washington and hundreds of others have noted, warm relationships between white Southern slave owners and their black servants was the norm, the entire group considering itself one large extended family. Thus, just as one would expect from such an intimate, interracial familial unit, black servants were profoundly affected by the emotional ups and downs of their white owners, *and* vice versa. The Southern black servants pictured here share in the grief of their white family, which has just learned that one of their sons, a Confederate soldier serving under Stonewall Jackson, has been shot down and killed at the Battle of Cedar Mountain, August 9, 1862. The entire family, both white and black, will go into mourning for several months.

There was indeed a human dimension to Southern servitude ("slavery") that was completely lacking in Northern free labor: Northern black employees, for example, could be fired and made penniless and homeless at a moment's notice, and often were.[2621] Southern black servants, however, were assured permanent employment, *and* their every need was provided for by their "owners" (employers)[2622]—including food, clothing, housing, and health care—from cradle to grave.[2623]

In reality, at the time it was much harder for most blacks to live free, which is why, when given a choice, many actually preferred bondage in the South over so-called "liberty" in the North.[2624] When a group of Louisiana slaves were freed by their owner's will in 1852 and sent to New York, they

> found themselves in such misery there that they begged the executor [of their master's will] to carry them back, saying he might keep them as slaves or sell them—that they had been happy before but were wretched now.[2625]

Racism was so firmly fixed in Northern culture that many abolitionist-minded Northerners and politicians were forced to promote emancipation using racist arguments, otherwise no one would listen to them. Knowing that Northern blacks would have preferred to live in the more tolerant South, some radical Republicans (the Liberal Party of the day) called for abolition because it would offer the benefit of starting a mass migration of blacks out of the North and into the South! And indeed, after Lincoln issued the Emancipation Proclamation, a fearful U.S. government (no doubt with Lincoln's blessing) inaugurated the policy of "containment,"[2626] in which freed blacks were to be prevented from coming North by keeping them "hemmed in," as Stephen A. Douglas put it, across the South.[2627]

On September 16, 1859, in a speech at Columbus, Ohio, Lincoln voiced his specific concerns on this subject. For, if slavery is allowed to re-spread back up North, he said fearfully:

> They will be ready for Jeff Davis and [Alexander H.] Stephens and other leaders of that company, to sound the bugle for the revival of the slave-trade, for the second Dred Scott decision, *for the flood of slavery to be poured over the Free States, while we shall be here tied down and helpless, and run over like sheep.*[2628]

The fear was of the "africanization" of America. Here was the real reason Lincoln and other Northern racists made such statements.[2629]

Of course, the idea of preventing a "black tidal wave" from pouring forth into the Northern states was already being considered long prior to the Proclamation, or even to Lincoln's presidency. In 1818, for example, Congressman Jonathan Mason of Massachusetts supported the strengthening of the old fugitive slave act, for he had a personal interest in the question, from his fear lest, if the bill failed to pass, *his own town of Boston might be inconveniently infested by southern runaways.*[2630]

Other Northern states quickly followed suit:

> *The States of Illinois and Indiana, alarmed at the numbers of blacks that were threatening to pour in on them by reason of the [abolitionist efforts of] North Carolina Quakers*, hastened to pass acts, Illinois in 1831, and Indiana a little later, forbidding masters to carry negroes there for the purpose of giving them freedom, and also forbidding negroes already free to migrate thither.[2631]

Lincoln's associate justice of the Supreme Court, David Davis. In 1862, after Davis complained to his boss that an "excess" of freed Southern blacks coming into Illinois could potentially jeopardize the 1864 election, Lincoln issued a human "blockade" to prevent any more African-Americans from entering the Prairie State. If this did not work, Lincoln believed, they could be deported and colonized in Africa—an idea he had referred to in a speech at Peoria, Illinois, on October 16, 1854. Or, he could simply corral them in an all-black state (to be created by his administration)—a typically Northern idea he had announced publicly at the Lincoln-Douglas Debate on September 15, 1858.

Southern Quakers cited an 1826 assessment which reported

> "that *the prejudice against a coloured population, was [very] . . . great in Indiana* . . . and that there was as much of it in the minds of members of our Society there as in other people, that they say as others do that they [Southern slaves] ought to be free, but they do not want them there [in the North], and he says *notwithstanding, that it's called a free state, a free black person is not allowed as much priveledge there by law, as in North Carolina." When a company [of freed Southern slaves] reached there [Indiana] about 1837 they found they could not stay; they turned to Pennsylvania, but they were not allowed to remain there either, and it was not until they reached Africa that they found a resting place.*[2632]

In 1832 Northern Quakers noted that there were no longer any "openings for negroes in the North," the result of a hostile white racism that is well demonstrated in the following excerpts from a letter penned by Edward Bettle of Philadelphia, Pennsylvania, to Nathan Mendenhall of North Carolina. It is dated May 21, 1832:

> Thy favour of the 15th, just came to hand this morning and in the absense of father from the city, I opened it, and am communicating the contents relative to the black people, to some of the Friends [Northern Quakers] who are mentioned in thy letter—*they all united in the earnest desire that no more of the blacks may at present be sent to these parts, as the effect of such a measure would probably be disastrous to the peace and comfort of the whole coloured population of Pennsylvania.* A law was before our Legislature at its last session, which the friends of the negroes had great difficulty in postponing, making similar provisions to the law of Indiana, to which thou has referred, and containing the further most obnoxious provision that all free people of colour now resident in Pennsylvania should be obliged to carry passes in traveling from one county of the state to another, and that should give security against becoming chargeable to the public, whenever they might change their residence from one part of the state to another. This act was brought before our Legislature in consequence of the arrival at Chester [Pennsylvania] I believe of some fugitives from Southampton, Virginia . . . *the public mind here is more roused even among respectable persons against these poor people, than it has been for several years*, and on the 27th, of this month, an adjourned session of the Legislature will take place; when the bill I have just alluded to is again to be taken up and I have no doubt if your blacks arrive here (as they will if now shipped) while the

> subject is under discussion that very circumstance will be the means of causing *the passage of a bill which will bring the utmost trouble upon the coloured population in our state and at the same time prevent any such persons from other states ever emigrating to Pennsylvania.*
>
> *This same law is also very severe in its provisions against fugitive slaves*, repealing some very good acts passed a few years ago upon that subject, and thus leaving the kidnappers, fair scope for their nefarious labours. *Under all these circumstances, we do sincerely hope you may not have shipped the blacks when this reaches you. An expedition is to sail to Liberia [Africa] from Norfolk [Virginia] in a short time as I am informed, perhaps you might get your company into that ship.* Very respectfully thy friend, Edward Bettle.[2633]

Such anti-black sentiments only increased in intensity in the North over the following decades. As late as 1905 the Charity Organization Society of New York could still comment that:

> In the cities of the North the Negro has a more severe struggle for mere existence than on southern plantations or in southern towns. His difficulties are accurately reflected in the high death-rates—especially in the frightful mortality of the Negro child.[2634]

In 1862 it was this same Yankee bigotry that prompted David Davis, associate justice of the Supreme Court under Lincoln, to go to the president and complain that an "excess" of Southern blacks venturing into Illinois would jeopardize the upcoming election. Lincoln agreed, issuing what John Y. Simon referred to as a human "blockade," one meant to halt even the possibility of a "negro influx" northward. From then on Southern blacks made refugees by Lincoln's War were restricted to camps set up in the South by Union officers, where they were forced to work cotton under armed guard.[2635] No white Northerner, especially Lincoln, wanted to be "tied down and helpless, and run over like sheep" by an advancing horde of Southern blacks.[2636]

Here we have yet another apt example of the North's idea of "emancipation," one buttressed by the racist Yankee organization, the American Colonization Society. This group in turn fueled fears across the North of an "African threat" stemming from Dixie,[2637] necessitating the need of a system of racial proscription "for all persons of color" throughout Yankeedom.[2638] Northern Governor Joseph A. Wright of

Indiana once said:

> *The subject of the colonization of the free blacks is now beginning to receive that attention which it demands. . . . We of the north are adopting extraordinary means for removing them, by prohibiting them from holding property, excluding them from the protection of the law, and denying them any rights whatever.*[2639]

This overt racism, which was rooted in antebellum Yankee bigotry, helps explain why Nat Turner, John Brown, and Lincoln could not manage to instigate even a tiny slave insurrection in the South, for even if blacks chose to leave Dixie where would they go? Certainly not North! And it is also why the infamous "Southern" Black Codes (which restricted the advancement of black civil rights) actually originated in the North, where they existed long prior to those adopted later by Southerners,[2640] and where interest in black civil rights was virtually nonexistent.[2641]

Indiana Governor Joseph Albert Wright was just one of thousands of Yankee authorities who believed that the only way to solve the North's "racial issue" was to expel blacks from the country. "We of the north," bragged Wright, "are adopting extraordinary means for removing them, by prohibiting them from holding property, excluding them from the protection of the law, and denying them any rights whatever."

We will note that rampant Northern racism endured well into the 20th Century. When 750,000 Southern blacks headed North to join in the prosperity of the labor boom in the early 1900s, for instance, Northern whites, far from welcoming them, instead regarded them as "dangerous and loathsome competition." As a result, between June and December 1919 alone 26 race riots exploded across America, the worst one occurring in the nation's capital city, Washington, D.C. Terribly violent racially based riots, such as those witnessed in recent years in Detroit, Harlem, Jersey City, and Philadelphia, continue in the North into the present day,[2642] along with an ever increasing rate of hate crimes.

Some of the most recent of these have included the appearance of nooses (an anti-black symbol) and swastikas (an anti-Jewish symbol) in police stations, U.S. Coast Guard stations, post offices, and college campuses in New York and Connecticut.[2643]

Why are such facts left out of our history books? It is because they do not fit in with the great anti-South agenda: in order to justify Lincoln's illegal war on Dixie, his subversion of the Constitution, his illicit slaughter of millions, and the permanent emotional scar he left across the Mason-Dixon Line, the South and her people must always be made to look as terrible as possible, in every way possible.

It is a testament to humanity's innate love of Truth that so many people, both North and South, and even foreigners, are now standing up to this outrageous cultural attack, one meant to erase all traces of authentic Southern history, and replace them with anti-South propaganda, liberal disinformation, Yankee myth, and New South fairy tales.

WHAT YOU WERE TAUGHT: Early American free and enslaved blacks were devoid of racism toward whites, and were, of course, completely incapable of being prejudiced toward other blacks. In other words, there was no racism within the black community. Racism was and still is strictly a white problem. This makes the horrid treatment white Southerners imposed on black slaves in the 1800s even more tragic.

THE TRUTH: Black racism among early American blacks, both toward whites and toward their own kind, was well-known in the 1700s and 1800s. Why is this fact not more generally known? Because the gatekeepers who govern our media, libraries, and book publishing companies have carefully withheld it from the public. Such individuals and organizations only profit if they can convince fellow Americans that there is an ongoing "race war" being waged by whites (not true), and that only whites are capable of racial bigotry (an absurd claim by any standard). Thus, they are deeply invested in hiding the reality of black racism.

America's history of black racism and black racial separatism (the black movement to live apart from whites) is nearly as long as that of whites. Black racism toward Caucasians was particularly strong during the 1800s: many African-Americans at this time were revolted by the sight of white skin, a vestige of the native African belief that "only black skin is beautiful."[2644]

Early American black nationalism (loyalty only to Africa), some of which grew out of a revulsion toward white racism, was expedited by a black Massachusetts Quaker named Paul Cuffee, who—infuriated by having to live in the presence of whites—financed the emigration of nearly 40 other blacks to Sierra Leone in 1815.[2645] As occurred in the early 1800s,[2646] in 1877 a number of blacks again sought out the American Colonization Society (a Northern white supremacist organization of which Lincoln had been a lifelong supporter), asking for help in resettling them in Liberia[2647]—a colony that had been created by the ACS to begin with in 1822.[2648]

In the 1920s, with the ongoing growth of black racism, a full-fledged, black-sponsored "Back-to-Africa" movement emerged. Its founder, Jamaican-born black nationalist Marcus Garvey, promoted the ideas of black pride, economic independence from whites, and the establishment of a black-only state in Africa. (Unfortunately for supporters of the Back-to-Africa movement, Garvey was later convicted of fraud, imprisoned, and eventually deported.)[2649] Even earlier, in the 19th Century, African-American abolitionist and black racist Martin R. Delany had advocated a separation of the races, with an emphasis on black separatism specifically.[2650]

African-American Paul Cuffee is often honored as a Revolutionary War patriot. What is not usually mentioned is that he was a black racist who learned to detest whites in the ultra white racist state of Massachusetts, where he was born in 1759. Also seldom discussed is the fact that Cuffee's father was a native African of the slave owning Ashanti people, who himself had been enslaved by fellow Africans and brought to New England aboard a Yankee slave ship.

Delany and Garvey were not the first nor the last American blacks to push for black separatism. The idea continues today among numerous African-American groups, many with extreme racist ideologies (that whites are an "inferior race," for example).[2651] Some of these groups are quite well-known, with former members today even inhabiting the halls of the U.S. Congress—all, we should add, without the slightest protest (quite unlike what occurred when European-American rights advocate David Duke became a Louisiana state representative). Like Lincoln and most other 19th-Century white Northerners, the majority of today's black racists continue to campaign against interracial marriage while promoting racial separation.[2652]

These cases may appear extreme and uncommon, but not when compared with the story of Virginia slave Nat Turner, who presents one of the more notable examples of black racism, in this case toward whites.

In August 1831 Turner led a group of fellow black supremacists and black racists on a whites-only killing spree across the Dominion State. Though he admitted that his own master, Joseph Travis, had always been gentle, respectful, and kind toward him, he murdered Travis and his entire family in their sleep.[2653] Why? Because they were white.

After committing this heinous crime Turner's gang left the Travis home to go looking for more white families to slaughter, when they realized that despite having killed both parents and all of the family's children (with axes to the head), they had left a tiny baby sleeping in its cradle. Turner sent two of his henchmen back into the house to finish the job. As he later coldly testified, "Henry and Will returned and killed it."[2654]

Over the next 48 hours some 55 whites were viciously murdered[2655] before Turner was captured (cowering in a cave), arrested, tried, and finally hanged on November 11, 1831.[2656]

What was it all for?

We have seen that it could not have been because Turner hated his master, for Turner was overweight (from being overindulged) and had near complete freedom on the Travis family farm.[2657] And it could not have been because he hated slave owners in general, because most of the families he dispatched did not own a single slave, and never had. They were Virginians, after all, the birthplace of the American abolition movement.[2658]

It was psychopathy combined with black racism, pure and simple, one that may have been subconsciously inspired by the old African belief that Europeans are an "inferior race" due to their pale skin color.[2659]

As for early evidence of black racism toward other blacks, we have an abundance of that as well.

To begin with, there was a rigid, and often not very well hidden, caste system among slaves on Southern plantations. The mammy, for instance, looked down her nose on the house servants, the house servants believed they were superior to the field servants, and so on.[2660] This hierarchal prejudice quite naturally extended itself to skin color among blacks as well.

Worldwide, blacks have long differentiated their own race based on gradations of skin color, and it was no different in the Old South. Those of African descent have nearly always accorded higher status to light skinned blacks (known as "coloreds") than dark skinned ones: the lighter the skin the more elevated their stature in the eyes of other blacks, and vice versa.

In the European-American community this would be considered a form of racism, and it is. But liberal historians, professors, and authors would rather you not be aware of this phenomenon, so they neglect to mention it—despite the fact that to this day, even if it is not always spoken of openly, skin color is held to be of "considerable importance" in the African-American community. Phillips writes:

> *The variety in complexion, status and attainment among [Southern] . . . slaves led to a somewhat elaborate gradation of colored society.* One stratum comprised the fairly numerous quadroons and mulattoes along with certain exceptional blacks. *The men among these had a pride of place as butlers and coachmen, painters and carpenters; the women fitted themselves trimly with the cast-off silks and muslins of their mistresses, walked with mincing tread, and spoke in quiet tones with impressive nicety of grammar.* This element was a conscious aristocracy of its kind, but its members were more or less irked by the knowledge that no matter how great their merits they could not cross the boundary into white society. The bulk of the real negroes on the other hand, with an occasional mulatto among them, went their own way, the women frankly indulging a native predilection for gaudy colors, carrying their burdens on their heads, arms akimbo, and laying as great store in their kerchief turbans as their paler cousins did in their beflowered bonnets. The men of this class wore their shreds and patches with an easy swing, doffed their wool hats to white men as they passed, called themselves niggers or darkies as a matter of course, took the joys and sorrows of the day as they came, improvised words to the music of their work, and customarily murdered the Queen's English, all with a true if

humble nonchalance and a freedom from carking care.[2661]

In the Victorian South, as another example, free *colored* slave owners were almost always higher on the social status ladder than free *black* slave owners. Thus in 1790, around the time of the Haitian Revolution (1791-1804), when free colored refugees began pouring into the American South, at Charleston, South Carolina, they founded the male-only "Brown Fellowship Society,"[2662] which, as the name reveals, was for brown skinned men only. Considering themselves superior to darker skinned blacks, anyone with skin blacker than their own was banned from membership. Only mulattos (an individual with one-half black ancestry), quadroons (an individual with one-quarter black ancestry), and octoroons (an individual with one-eighth black ancestry), were allowed entrance.[2663]

The arrest of black racist Nat Turner in the Fall of 1831. By murdering some 60 innocent non-slave owning whites, Turner did far more damage to the cause of abolition than good. In the ensuing mayhem that followed, 100 blacks died, the South enacted new laws restricting African-Americans, and the negative feelings between South and North greatly intensified.

As many of the colored members were slaveholders themselves, the Society showed no trace of abolitionism, and never lifted a finger to help their bonded African brethren. Early black racism toward other blacks was so entrenched that dark skinned blacks had no hope of ever joining the ranks of the Brown Fellowship Society. So they established their own: in 1843, under the leadership of Thomas Smalls, "The Society for Free Blacks of Dark Complexion" was formed.

Meanwhile, the Brown Fellowship Society found it increasingly difficult to sustain its racist and sexist membership policies. After Lincoln's War, they changed their name to the "Century Fellowship Society," and opened their doors to all black men and black women.[2664] Black racism within the group continued in other forms, however: *white* men and women were still prohibited from membership.

Race relations in the Old South were nothing like what our liberally biased historians and teachers claim. Indeed, they were the opposite of what we have been taught. Southern European-Americans and Southern African-Americans, both free and enslaved, enjoyed one another's company and regularly sought out personal friendships and relationships with each other. Here a white girl and one of her family's black servants share a few agreeable moments together on the back gallery overlooking Virginia's beautiful Shenandoah River.

White slavery is the Great Secret that no pro-North writer, liberal college professor, or anti-South scallywag wants you to know about. But as the majority of whites came to early North America under some form of bondage, as ancient Europeans enslaved millions of their own people, and as Africa at one time enslaved up to 1.5 million whites, this is a worldwide phenomenon that can no longer be concealed. In this old illustration a white Massachusetts slave owner (on horseback, far left) and his white slave driver march a coffle of indentured white slaves off to a nearby plantation under the sting of the whip.

16

THE EMANCIPATION PROCLAMATION

WHAT YOU WERE TAUGHT: Lincoln issued the Emancipation Proclamation to free all of America's slaves, which it did in 1863.
THE TRUTH: While the North has long comforted itself with this picturesque notion, the facts reveal something quite different.

It is well-known to most Southerners today that the Final Emancipation Proclamation, issued January 1, 1863, only "freed" slaves in the South, and even then, only in specific areas of the South. Lincoln's edict purposefully excluded Tennessee, for example (the entire state had been under Yankee control since the fall of Nashville, February 25, 1862),[2665] all of the Border States,[2666] and numerous Northern-occupied parishes in Louisiana and several counties in Virginia.[2667]

The Final Emancipation Proclamation, in fact, was issued only in areas of the South *not* under Union control; that is, it only freed *Southern* slaves who had sided with the Confederacy.[2668] It did not ban slavery anywhere in the North, where thousands of Yankees still practiced it, including Union officers like General Ulysses S. Grant and his family.[2669] As Lincoln states in the proclamation itself, the North and those places exempted "are for the present left precisely as if this proclamation were not issued."[2670] Lincoln could not have made the meaning of this sentence more clear: *slavery was to be allowed to continue in the U.S. (that is, the North) and in any areas of the C.S. (that is, the South) controlled by the U.S. (that is, by the Union armies).*

The question Southerners have been asking Northerners for the past century and a half is why, if Lincoln was so interested in black equality, did he only abolish slavery in the South where he had no jurisdiction but not in the North where he had full control?

The answer is obvious to most Southerners today, just as it was to a majority of them in 1863: the Emancipation Proclamation was nothing more than a clever political illusion, for he did not free slaves where he legally could (in the North and in the Border States), yet he sought to free them (in the South) where he had no legal right to do so.[2671] If Northerners had asked themselves this same question at the time, they would have never created the myth of Lincoln the "Great Emancipator" to begin with!

One of the North's countless overly sentimentalized images of Lincoln's Emancipation Proclamation. The document—which was not only illegal (and therefore powerless) but which freed no slaves either in the South or the North—was just one part of the president's overall plot to bring down the Confederacy through the use of force, economic disruption, and the instigation of slave insurrections across the South. In all these aspects the Emancipation Proclamation was a failure, and Lincoln later grudgingly admitted that it was "the greatest folly of my life." However, after Lincoln's death it did give the North and pro-North Southerners (scallywags) a convenient myth to embellish in an effort to help hide the truth about the president and his War. This vile myth is with us to this day, and is still being taught in nearly every elementary school, junior high school, high school, college, and university in the United States.

In truth our sixteenth president did not issue the Emancipation Proclamation for the specific purpose of trying to establish black civil rights across the U.S. If that had indeed been his intention he would have also banned slavery in the North and in non-Union occupied areas of the South.

Actually, being the penultimate politician, Lincoln had five primary goals in mind when he wrote out the edict, not a single one of them having anything to do with black equality or even true abolition.

Lincoln revealed the first of these in the proclamation itself by calling it a "war measure" instead of a "civil rights measure,"[2672] a connivance he had been developing for many months, perhaps for several years. And what a brilliant idea it was. After all, no one could argue against emancipation—not even the most pro-South Northerners or pro-North Southerners—if Lincoln could prove that freeing the slaves was vital to winning the War.[2673] And it would indeed prove to be vital. But not for the reasons Yankee myth has long claimed.

Since the beginning of the conflict Lincoln had been trying to court and maintain support from Europe, mainly Britain and France. For he knew if Europe sided with the South, giving her weaponry, ammunition, ships, clothing, and other types of supplies, the Union would have no hope of winning. Only by keeping Europe on his side could Lincoln achieve his true goal: *total conquest of the wealth-producing South and the eradication of states' rights.*

In part, the Emancipation Proclamation was calculated to do just that, for as Europe had much earlier abolished slavery herself, Lincoln assumed that she would automatically support the side most dedicated to humanitarian ideals. His edict not only made it appear that the North was the region most interested in abolition, but midway through the War it also transformed the North's purpose for fighting Dixie from "preserving the Union" to that of "ending slavery."[2674] The proclamation thus reenforced Lincoln's lie to Europe that "slavery is the basis of the war." I sincerely hope that this fact will "obtain the favor of Europe," he implored deceptively.[2675]

But Lincoln's wish utterly failed in this regard. Europe repeatedly stated, quite emphatically and clearly, that slavery had nothing whatsoever to do with which side she would support, if either.[2676]

The second reason Lincoln had for issuing the Emancipation Proclamation was to incite a massive "slave rebellion" in the South, which he hoped would bring about chaos, destabilize Southern society, and destroy her economy.[2677] Thus he states in the proclamation that the U.S. government will do nothing to stop any acts that Southern slaves wish to engage in against the Confederacy to attain their freedom.[2678]

To every thinking Southerner, Lincoln here was not only breaking the laws of civilized warfare, he was clearly inviting their black servants to insurrection, mayhem, violence, rape, and murder.[2679] This was understood as far away as Europe. In England, for instance, the aristocracy widely regarded both Lincoln's Preliminary Emancipation Proclamation (issued September 22, 1862) and his Final Emancipation Proclamation (issued January 1, 1863) as nothing less than naked attempts to incite African-American riots across the South.[2680] They were right, of course.

Unfortunately for Lincoln, like psychopath John Brown's futile attempt at Harper's Ferry to trigger black riots in the South, his own nefarious plan came to naught. There was not a single slave rebellion anywhere in the South after he issued the proclamation,[2681] as he himself later grudgingly admitted.[2682]

The truth is that of the South's 3.5 million black servants,[2683] the "vast majority,"[2684] 95 percent (19 out of 20), remained in the South, all the while maintaining their loyalty to Dixie.[2685] Ignoring Lincoln's fake proclamation of freedom, they instead pledged their allegiance to their home states, to the South, and to their white families.[2686] Remaining at home they ran their owner's farms, grew food, produced provisions for the Confederate military, and protected their master's family and property while he was away on the battlefield.[2687] In 1910 Pastor Benjamin F. Riley noted that the Southern black servant

> sustained the armies of the Confederacy during the great Civil War; he was the guardian of the helpless women and children of the South while the husbands and sons were at the distant front doing battle . . .; against him was not a whisper of unfaithfulness or of disloyalty during all this trying and bloody period; when the land was invaded by the [Northern] armies . . . he remained faithful still, and often at great personal risk of life, secreted from the invader [his owner's] . . . horses and mules, and buried the treasures of the family that they might not fall into the hands of the enemies of the whites . . .; *in many thousands of instances he declined to accept freedom when it was offered by the invading army, preferring to remain loyal and steadfast to the charge committed to him by the absent master, all this and more the Negro slave did. There was not a day during the trying period of the Civil War when he might not have disbanded the Southern armies. An outbreak on his part against the defenseless homes of the South would have*

> *occasioned the utter dissolution of the Southern armies, and turned the anxious faces of the veterans in gray toward their homes. But no Southern soldier ever dreamed of the possibility of a condition like this. So far as his home was concerned, it was not any apprehension of the unfaithfulness of the slaves which occasioned the slightest alarm.*[2688]

This romanticized illustration shows grateful blacks thanking John Brown (center) one last time before he ascends the steps to his death on the gallows. Actually, African-Americans did not thank Brown for anything, none joined his cause, and most, like former Northern slave Frederick Douglass pronounced him insane. Lincoln, however, using the Emancipation Proclamation, later adopted parts of Brown's monstrous plan to destroy the South through invasion, violence, destabilization, and attempts to foment slave rebellions. Both plots failed. There was not a single slave insurrection across Dixie between 1859 (when Brown attacked Harpers Ferry) and 1865 (the end of the Civil War), and Brown's life ended in the hangman's noose, while Lincoln's came to a close with an assassin's bullet.

In an effort to raise money for the Southern war effort many Southern slaves and freemen bought Confederate bonds.[2689] Others held bake sales and auctions, while still others donated clothing and other goods in an effort to help support Confederate soldiers.[2690] Those untold thousands of African-Americans who marched off to resist Lincoln and his illegal invaders, proudly stood up for "ole Jeff Davis," wearing placards on their hats that read: "We will die by the South."[2691] Among them were tens of thousands who served the Confederacy as teamsters, bridge and road builders, musicians, nurses, carpenters, smithies, couriers, lookouts, and cooks[2692]—many from among the last occupation who had been trained by the best culinary schools in Paris.[2693]

By most objective estimates at least 300,000 Southern blacks donned Rebel uniforms, marched unhesitatingly onto the battlefield, and fought fearlessly for the Southern Cause.[2694] Those who were crack shots served as sharpshooters, helping to bring down thousands of Yankee interlopers.[2695] But if we use Yankee General August Valentine Kautz's definition of a "private soldier,"[2696] then as many as 1 million Southern blacks served in one capacity or another in the Confederate military. This means that 50 percent of the South's soldiers were black,[2697] and that five times, or 500 percent, more blacks fought for the Confederacy than for the Union.[2698]

Slave rebellions, like this one in early 19th-Century Rhode Island, were extremely rare in the South. Northerners ignorantly assumed that the South's 3.5 million black servants were miserable, starving, abused, fettered wretches, pining away for freedom on military prison-like plantations, run by rich, cruel, racist white planters. Nothing could have been further from the truth, of course, which is why all Yankee attempts at provoking slave revolts in Dixie ended unsuccessfully. The most celebrated of these was Lincoln's Emancipation Proclamation, which stirred not a single Southern servant to rebel against his master. The edict, in fact, was widely criticized in both the South and the North, and even around the world, as nothing more than a desperate, disreputable, last ditch attempt by a weakening army and an ineffectual commander-in-chief, to wreck the South by freeing her slaves.

Here too Lincoln once again failed in his goal, for far from initiating a full scale slave rebellion in the South, his overt racism and selfish political scheming only turned most Southern blacks further against him, while renewing their love for Dixie. Of this situation, Derry writes:

> *The conduct of the slaves during the war gives strong proof of the kind feeling that existed between them and their masters.* The great majority of them remained on the plantations and by their labor supplied the armies in the field. Many negro men went with their young masters to war, faithfully waited on them, nursed them when sick, and, if they died in camp or in battle, returned with the lifeless bodies to lay them beside their kindred dead in the family burying-ground.[2699]

The third motivation behind white supremacist Lincoln's Emancipation Proclamation was to provide much needed manpower for his all-white army and navy, both which, after two years of fighting, were quickly diminishing in numbers due to what I call "the four D's": desertion, defection, disease, and death.

His "military emancipation," as Lincoln openly called it,[2700] would offset these losses by freeing up the South's 3.5 million black slaves, all of whom he assumed would speedily come North and gratefully enlist in the Union military effort. Lincoln himself said as much in a letter to Tennessee's Military Governor Andrew Johnson on March 26, 1863, just three months after issuing the Emancipation Proclamation:

> *The colored population is the great available and yet unavailed of force for restoring the Union. The bare sight of fifty thousand armed and drilled black soldiers upon the banks of the Mississippi would end the rebellion at once . . .*[2701]

With racist Lincoln there was always racial reasoning behind his schemes, as he noted on August 26, 1863, in a letter to James C. Conkling:

> *I thought that whatever negroes can be got to do as soldiers, leaves just so much less for white soldiers to do in saving the Union.*[2702]

As we have just seen, however, Lincoln's assumption that Southern blacks would leave their lives of comfort and security to join his dying armies was an absurd fantasy. This was, in part, because the president, who consistently and vehemently proclaimed that he was not an abolitionist,[2703] did not promise citizenship to blacks—newly freed or already free (and indeed blacks would not become U.S. citizens until

1868, three years after Lincoln's death).[2704]

Whatever the many reasons for the apathetic response by Southern blacks to his proclamation, between 1863 and 1865 only a small fraction, less than 90,000, of the South's 3.5 million servants ended up in Lincoln's military.[2705] (Even then, as we will see, many of these so-called black "enrollments" were not voluntary; they were forced under threat of physical violence.)[2706] As stated, this indicates that five times more blacks fought for the Confederacy than for the Union, a fact one will never find in any pro-North history book on the Civil War.

In March 1863 Lincoln told Tennessee's military governor Andrew Johnson (soon to become Lincoln's second vice president) that the purpose of the Emancipation Proclamation was to use the "colored population" to "end the rebellion at once."

The fourth principal reason Lincoln had for issuing the Emancipation Proclamation again had nothing to do with African-American civil rights. The 1864 election was just around the corner and he was desperate to be reelected. But he faced a major problem: he had lost the eleven Confederate states and their 88 electoral votes (obviously the Confederacy, now a separate nation, did not vote in the Union's 1860 election),[2707] along with the support of both anti-war activists and abolitionists.[2708] How to accrue additional votes? he asked himself.

Again the answer was the Emancipation Proclamation. He would free millions of Southern blacks in the expectation that most would enlist and, as U.S. soldiers, would gratefully cast their votes to reelect him for a second term (he never offered *non-military* blacks the franchise). As noted, however, the incumbent president's scheme in this regard was completely unsuccessful.

The fifth and final reason for signing the Emancipation Proclamation into law concerned Lincoln's lifelong goal, known today by educated blacks as "Abraham Lincoln's white dream": the colonization of all African-Americans in foreign lands. Lincoln could not even begin this deportation process as long as the South's 3.5 million black servants were considered the "property" of their owners. Emancipation, however, would instantly transform them into "freemen," allowing their legal expatriation; or so "Honest Abe" believed.

Lincoln never referred to his Emancipation Proclamation as an "abolitionary measure," or even as a "black civil rights emancipation," because it was neither—and was never meant to be. He disclosed its true purpose by calling it a "war measure," and even more revealingly, a "military emancipation."

But this aspect of the Final Emancipation Proclamation also failed, for not only would it have been financially impossible for the U.S. government to pay for the emigration of millions of people, the idiotic bigoted plan had absolutely no support, except for a handful of Lincoln's fellow white supremacists and white separatists.[2709]

All in all then, from Lincoln's perspective at least, the Emancipation Proclamation was a pathetic blunder. Little more than a transparent and cynical political move, his "war measure" and "military emancipation" did not help gain European support; it did not incite a single slave rebellion in the South and in turn disrupt the Confederacy's economy; it did not motivate Southern blacks to enlist in his army; it did not inspire Southern blacks to vote for him; and finally, it did not allow him to launch his nationwide black deportation program.

The fact that it actually freed no slaves did not trouble Lincoln in the least, as this was never the intention of his proclamation to begin with.

WHAT YOU WERE TAUGHT: Lincoln issued the Emancipation Proclamation voluntarily.

THE TRUTH: From the first day of his presidency Lincoln had to be cajoled, pushed, and pressured, even threatened, to do something about abolishing slavery. Every step of the way he resisted.[2710] It took him over two years—from November 6, 1860, the day he was elected president, to January 1, 1863, the day he issued the Final Emancipation Proclamation—to even begin taking abolition seriously. Even then he never became a full-blooded authentic abolitionist. He was always an emancipationist-colonizationist at heart (that is, a "free 'em up and ship 'em out" advocate), and nothing ever changed his mind on the subject.

In a private conversation Lincoln told former Northern slave Sojourner Truth that he had never wanted to issue the Emancipation Proclamation, and only did so because Southerners had not "behaved themselves" (that is, seceded). Otherwise he had been prepared to allow the South to keep slavery indefinitely, as he himself intimated in his Inaugural Address on March 4, 1861.

It was just such bullheadedness and illogical stall tactics that prompted severe criticism from abolitionists in his party. Wendell Phillips, for instance, began calling him "a first-rate second-rate man,"[2711] while famed antislavery advocate William Lloyd Garrison angrily referred to Lincoln's policies as "stumbling, halting, prevaricating, irresolute, weak, besotted."[2712]

On September 13, 1862, just prior to issuing the Preliminary Emancipation Proclamation (on the 22nd) Lincoln wavered, procrastinated, and resisted, seriously questioning whether it was the right thing to do—even when pressed by a group of angry clergymen.[2713] At the same time he continued to refuse to enlist freedmen as combatants, or give blacks either citizenship or voting rights.[2714]

In short, there was nothing voluntary about Lincoln's issuance of the proclamation. It would be more accurate to say that it was done with great reluctance, doubt, and misgiving.

Indeed, the president himself once intimated that he felt forced to free the slaves, and that he would not have done so had the South not "rebelled." In a rare conversation in the Oval Office with former Northern slave Sojourner Truth (for most of his administration Lincoln barred Truth and other free blacks from entering the White House),[2715] he noted that it was only because Southerners had not "behaved themselves" that he had been "compelled" to issue his abolitionary edict.[2716] Otherwise, according to Lincoln himself, there would have been no Emancipation Proclamation, the institution of slavery would have remained untouched, and the South's 3.5 million slaves, along with the 500,000 to 1 million black slaves in the North, would have continued in bondage indefinitely.[2717]

WHAT YOU WERE TAUGHT: Lincoln issued the Emancipation Proclamation in a timely manner.

THE TRUTH: If Lincoln's goal was truly to "free the slaves" we must ask ourselves why he waited so long to issue his proclamation. From the first day of his inauguration, both white and black civil rights leaders—men like Horace Greeley, Benjamin F. Wade, Thaddeus Stevens, John C. Frémont, David Hunter, John W. Phelps, Theodore Tilton, Wendell Phillips, Frederick Douglass, Henry Ward Beecher, and George B. Cheever[2718]—put constant pressure on the president to abolish slavery. Yet time and time again he refused.

First the year 1861 passed. Then 1862. Nearly two years into the War, Lincoln still would not be moved to emancipate America's slaves, earning him the well deserved nicknames the "tortoise President"[2719] and the "slow coach at Washington."[2720]

As discussed above, it was only the need to maintain European support, the manpower shortage crisis, his desire to start a slave insurrection in the South, his desperation to be reelected, and his black colonization goals that finally prompted Lincoln to issue the Final Emancipation Proclamation on January 1, 1863. This is why the topics of black suffrage and black citizenship—the ultimate dream of Victorian blacks and abolitionists—are never once mentioned in that document.

For Lincoln it was merely a "war measure" and a "military emancipation" (that is, something utilized for the sole purpose of winning the conflict), which is exactly how he termed it.[2721]

Abolitionist Wendell Phillips of Massachusetts was one of the few who truly understood what was behind Lincoln's phony liberation edict. In 1863, during a speech at Music Hall in New Haven, Connecticut, he made this pronouncement:

> *Lincoln was badgered into emancipation. After he issued it he said it was the greatest folly of his life. It was like the Pope's bull against the comet.*[2722]

It was indeed a futile and ridiculous act.

When it came to issuing the Emancipation Proclamation, like other Yankee abolitionists, Wendell Phillips had little patience with Lincoln's ongoing delay tactics. "He had to be badgered into it," complained the frustrated Boston civil rights attorney.

If most of Lincoln's other Northern constituents did not notice the diabolical hypocrisy of the Emancipation Proclamation, Southerners and Europeans certainly did. Agreeing with President Jefferson Davis, the Richmond *Examiner* called it "the most shocking crime perpetuated by a politician in U.S. history."[2723] English newspapers, like the London *Times*, called it "a tragic document," while the London *Spectator* termed it "a deceitful fabrication."[2724]

And what rank hypocrisy it was, for at the time not only was slavery still alive and well in the North,[2725] but free Northern blacks were still not allowed to vote, sit on juries, attend white churches, be buried in white cemeteries, marry whites, or even become U.S. citizens.[2726]

Let us also consider the fact that, like the true anti-abolitionist that he was, Lincoln routinely prevented U.S. officials and military officers possessed of abolitionist leanings, such as John Charles Frémont,[2727] Simon Cameron,[2728] John W. Phelps,[2729] Jim Lane,[2730] and David Hunter,[2731] from freeing Southern slaves,[2732] actions for which he was, of course, angrily denounced by antislavery advocates.[2733] Certainly, countermanding the emancipations of fellow U.S. officials proves once and for all, if nothing else does, that Lincoln did not wage war against the South over slavery.[2734]

Union General John Charles Frémont was only one of many U.S. officials who tried to free slaves during the War, but was prevented from doing so by Lincoln. In fact, Lincoln relieved Frémont of his command over the incident. When the general's wife, Jessie Frémont, went to the president to try and plead her husband's case, he scolded her: "He should have never bothered with the Negro in the first place. This is a war for a momentous national purpose, and the black man has nothing whatsoever to do with it." Pro-North writers do not want you to know about such scandals because they expose the real Lincoln, an emancipationist-colonizationist who disguised himself as an abolitionist in order to curry votes in the North.

Indeed, the primary reason Lincoln delayed issuing the Emancipation Proclamation was that the War was never about slavery. As he said repeatedly to the Radicals (abolitionists) in his party: "We didn't go into the war to put down slavery . . ."[2735] When he finally did issue it, it was against his own wishes, and then only for the reasons discussed in this chapter.[2736] For this lassitude he was severely criticized by abolitionists such as Phillips—soon to become the president of the Anti-Slavery Society—who angrily denounced him as "the slavehound of Illinois."[2737]

So unmistakably clear was Lincoln's procrastination toward emancipation that some of the more vociferous antislavery groups saw it as a sign of traitorousness. "Lincoln," they complained, "is not only a Southerner by birth, he has a brother-in-law [Confederate Captain Nathaniel Dawson] who fights for the Confederacy."[2738] "Obviously," they cried, "his sympathies lie with the South and with slavery, for he could end the War tomorrow if he would only go after the slave owners."[2739]

Lincoln's hesitation to emancipate America's slaves was more than evident in a letter he penned on September 13, 1862, in reply "To A Committee From The Religious Denominations Of Chicago, Asking The President To Issue A Proclamation Of Emancipation." The letter really should have been called "The Emancipation Proclamation: My Many Excuses for Blocking It and Delaying Its Issuance." It is worth citing in full. Wrote Lincoln:

> The subject presented in the memorial is one upon which I have thought much for weeks past, and I may even say for months. I am approached with the most opposite opinions and advice, and that by religious men who are equally certain that they represent the divine will. I am sure that either the one or the other class is mistaken in that belief, and perhaps in some respects both. I hope it will not be irreverent for me to say that if it is probable that God would reveal his will to others on a point so connected with my duty, it might be supposed he would reveal it directly to me; for, unless I am more deceived in myself than I often am, it is my earnest desire to know the will of Providence in this matter. And if I can learn what it is, I will do it. These are not, however, the days of miracles, and I suppose it will be granted that I am not to expect a direct revelation. I must study the plain physical facts of the case, ascertain what is possible, and learn what appears to be wise and right.
>
> The subject is difficult, and good men do not agree. For instance, *the other day four gentlemen of standing and intelligence from New York called as a delegation on business connected with the war; but, before leaving, two of them earnestly beset me to proclaim general emancipation, upon which the other two at once attacked them*. You know also that the last session of Congress had a decided majority of antislavery men, yet they could not unite on this policy. And the same is true of the religious people. Why, the rebel soldiers are praying with a great deal more earnestness, I fear, than our own troops, and expecting God to favor their side; for one of our soldiers who had been taken prisoner told Senator Wilson a few days since that he met with nothing so discouraging as the evident sincerity of those he was among in their prayers. But we will talk over the merits of the case.
>
> *What good would a proclamation of emancipation from me do, especially as we are now situated? I do not want to issue a document that*

the whole world will see must necessarily be inoperative, like the Pope's bull against the comet. Would my word free the slaves, when I cannot even enforce the Constitution in the rebel States? Is there a single court, or magistrate, or individual that would be influenced by it there? And what reason is there to think it would have any greater effect upon the slaves than the late law of Congress, which I approved, and which offers protection and freedom to the slaves of rebel masters who come within our lines? Yet I cannot learn that that law has caused a single slave to come over to us. And suppose they could be induced by a proclamation of freedom from me to throw themselves upon us, what should we do with them? How can we feed and care for such a multitude? General [Benjamin F.] Butler wrote me a few days since that he was issuing more rations to the slaves who have rushed to him than to all the white troops under his command. They eat, and that is all; though it is true General Butler is feeding the whites also by the thousand, for it nearly amounts to a famine there. If, now, the pressure of the war should call off our forces from New Orleans to defend some other point, what is to prevent the masters from reducing the blacks to slavery again? For I am told that whenever the rebels take any black prisoners, free or slave, they immediately auction them off. They did so with those they took from a boat that was aground in the Tennessee River a few days ago. And then I am very ungenerously attacked for it! For instance, when, after the late battles at and near Bull Run, an expedition went out from Washington under a flag of truce to bury the dead and bring in the wounded, and the rebels seized the blacks who went along to help, and sent them into slavery,[2740] Horace Greeley said in his paper that the government would probably do nothing about it. What could I do?

Now, then, tell me, if you please, what possible result of good would follow the issuing of such a proclamation as you desire? Understand, I raise no objections against it on legal or constitutional grounds; for, as commander-in-chief of the army and navy, in time of war I suppose I have a right to take any measure which may best subdue the enemy; *nor do I urge objections of a moral nature, in view of possible consequences of insurrection and massacre at the South. I view this matter as a practical war measure, to be decided on according to the advantages or disadvantages it may offer to the suppression of the rebellion.*

I admit that slavery is the root of the rebellion, or at least its *sine qua non* [Lincoln is again revealing his demagoguery here]. The ambition of politicians may have instigated them to act, but they would have been impotent without slavery as their instrument. I will also concede that emancipation would help us in Europe, and convince them that we are incited by something more than ambition. *I grant, further, that it would help somewhat at the*

North, though not so much, I fear, as you and those you represent imagine. Still, some additional strength would be added in that way to the war, and then, unquestionably, it would weaken the rebels by drawing off their laborers, which is of great importance; but I am not so sure we could do much with the blacks. If we were to arm them, I fear that in a few weeks the arms would be in the hands of the rebels; and, indeed, thus far we have not had arms enough to equip our white troops. I will mention another thing, though it meet only your scorn and contempt. There are fifty thousand bayonets [that is, black soldiers] in the Union armies from the border slave States. It would be a serious matter if, in consequence of a proclamation such as you desire, they should go over to the rebels. *I do not think they all would*—not so many, indeed, as a year ago, or as six months ago—not so many to-day as yesterday. Every day increases their Union feeling. They are also getting their pride enlisted, and want to beat the rebels. Let me say one thing more: I think you should admit that we already have an important principle to rally and unite the people, in the fact that constitutional government is at stake. This is a fundamental idea going down about as deep as anything. [Note: it was Lincoln who was trying to destroy constitutional government; the South was trying to preserve it!]

Do not misunderstand me because I have mentioned these objections. *They indicate the difficulties that have thus far prevented my action in some such way as you desire. I have not decided against a proclamation of liberty to the slaves, but hold the matter under advisement*; and I can assure you that the subject is on my mind, by day and night, more than any other. Whatever shall appear to be God's will, I will do. I trust that in the freedom with which I have canvassed your views I have not in any respect injured your feelings.[2741]

Even earlier, on March 1, 1859, Lincoln said to a large Chicago audience:

I do not wish to be misunderstood upon this subject of slavery in this country. I suppose it may long exist; and perhaps the best way for it to come to an end peaceably is for it to exist for a length of time.[2742]

Thus spoke the North's "tortoise President," a self-proclaimed atheist and enemy of Christianity who pretended to be religious, an anti-abolitionist who pretended to hate slavery, and a white supremacist who pretended to like blacks; certainly one of the most faithless, conniving, tyrannical, morally bankrupt men ever to have inhabited the halls of the

U.S. government![2743]

Yankee Senator Willard Saulsbury spoke for millions of Southerners and not a few Northerners, when he called Lincoln "a weak and imbecile man." "If I wanted to paint a tyrant," said the Delawarian, "I would paint the hideous form of Abraham Lincoln."

Let us note here that it was this very type of duplicitous demagoguery that inspired such absolute loathing for Lincoln, not just in the South, but by fellow Northern politicians. In 1863, before the U.S. Congress, for example, Yankee Senator Willard Saulsbury of Delaware stood up and, intimating that Lincoln was an "enemy of the country," declared the following:

> Thus has it been with Mr. Lincoln—a weak and imbecile man; the weakest man that I ever knew in a high place; for I have seen him and conversed with him, and I say here, in my place in the Senate of the United States, that I never did see or converse with so weak and imbecile a man as Abraham Lincoln, President of the United States. . . . if I wanted to paint a tyrant, if I wanted to paint a despot, a man perfectly regardless of every constitutional right of the people, who's sworn servant, not ruler, he is, I would paint the hideous form of Abraham Lincoln.[2744]

Likewise, Garrison once said of Lincoln, "he may be a giant in height, but he is a midget in intellect,"[2745] while one of Lincoln's officers, Union General George B. McClellan, felt that:

> The president is nothing more than a well meaning baboon. He is the original gorilla. What a specimen to be at the head of our affairs now![2746]

These were sentiments that all Southerners could relate to!

Union General George B. McClellan and his wife Ellen Mary McClellan were a rare Yankee couple that traditional Southerners could truly understand. "Lincoln is a well meaning baboon," the General once said, "the original gorilla."

More proof of Lincoln's lack of sentiment towards African-Americans comes from the manner in which he issued the Emancipation Proclamation: in January 1863, and again in December 1865, the U.S., under both Lincoln's Emancipation Proclamation and his pet project the Thirteenth Amendment respectively, abolished slavery suddenly, illegally, and violently.[2747] And all of this occurred without restitution to owners, even though compensation (buying every Southern slave from their owners at market value and then freeing them) would have cost the nation ten times less than what it cost to go to war[2748]—a fact that even the money-obsessed president himself once alluded to.[2749]

There was nothing "timely" about Lincoln's so-called "emancipation" program.

WHAT YOU WERE TAUGHT: Lincoln wanted to end slavery as quickly as possible.
THE TRUTH: Lincoln had no such definitive goal in mind and was actually quite malleable on the topic. In his Annual Message to Congress December 1, 1862, for example, he proposed three new amendments to the Constitution. In the first, Article One, he said:

> Every state wherein slavery now exists which shall abolish the same therein at any time or times before the first day of January in the year of our Lord one thousand and nine hundred, shall receive compensation from the United States . . .[2750]

In other words, as a compromise with the South Lincoln was prepared to give any Southern state that wished to practice slavery another 38 years, until January 1, 1900, to abolish it.

In the same speech Lincoln explained Article One so that there would be no misunderstanding:

> The plan leaves to each State choosing to act under it to abolish slavery now, or at the end of the century, or at any intermediate time, or by degrees extending over the whole or any part of the period . . .[2751]

Clearly Lincoln was in no hurry to end slavery.

WHAT YOU WERE TAUGHT: Lincoln planned on making the abolition of slavery permanent.
THE TRUTH: Far from intending to destroy slavery forever, Lincoln acknowledged that his Emancipation Proclamation was neither permanent or unchangeable, and that he would consider allowing the Southern states to reinstate slavery and maintain it permanently if only they would rejoin the Union and pay their taxes.[2752]

The only permanence Lincoln demanded pertained to slaves themselves: once a servant was set free he could never be reenslaved, he declared,[2753] a law in perfect keeping with his lifelong black colonizationist goal to free the slaves and, along with free blacks, ship as many out of the country as possible.[2754]

As for the time of emancipation and the duration of emancipation laws in the South, however, he was entirely flexible. That Lincoln viewed his Emancipation Proclamation in this exact manner is supported by reams of evidence, though nearly all of it has been buried under a mountain of Yankee mythology. Let us examine some of it here.

Lincoln was once severely criticized by Northern Democrats, for instance, because he had absent-mindedly called for *complete* and *permanent* emancipation in all the Southern states. Realizing his error, on July 18, 1864, he immediately sent out a notice humbly rescinding the demand. It read:

> Any proposition which embraces the restoration of peace, the integrity of the whole Union, and the abandonment of slavery . . . will be received and considered . . . and will be met by liberal terms on other substantial and collateral points . . .[2755]

Yankee historians have long wondered what "substantial and collateral points" Lincoln was so willing to "receive and consider." But we Southern historians have been perfectly aware of them since the 1860s.

Lincoln himself spoke openly of at least one of these, one that included the possibility of ending the War without total and lasting abolition. On August 17, 1864, in a letter to the Honorable Charles R. Robinson, Lincoln responded to the many attacks on his emancipation plan with these startling words:

> To me it seems plain that saying reunion and abandonment of slavery would be considered, if offered, is not saying that nothing *else* or *less* would be considered, if offered. . . . If [Confederate President] Jefferson Davis wishes, for himself, or for the benefit of his friends at the North, to know what I would do if he were to offer peace and reunion, saying nothing about slavery, let him try me.[2756]

Six months later, on February 3, 1865, at the Hampton Roads Peace Conference (the one and only time imperious Lincoln agreed to meet with Confederate peace delegates), the U.S. president reiterated that his primary concern was "preserving the Union." And he would go to nearly any length to do so, he told the Rebel peace representatives, Vice President Alexander H. Stephens, Senator Robert M. T. Hunter, and Assistant Secretary of War John A. Campbell. These lengths included allowing the South to continue practicing slavery after it rejoined the U.S.[2757] According to those present, Lincoln's

> . . . own opinion was, that as the Proclamation was a *war measure*, and would have effect only from its being an exercise of the war power, as soon as the war ceased, it would be inoperative for the future. It would be held to apply only to such slaves as had come under its operation while it was in active exercise. This was his individual opinion . . .[2758]

Confederate Vice President Alexander H. Stephens attended the Hampton Roads Peace Conference on February 3, 1865. It was at this infamous meeting that Lincoln told the startled Rebel official and two other Southern diplomats that since the Emancipation Proclamation was a "war measure," its "effect" would end with the termination of the war. In other words, according to Lincoln himself, once the Confederacy surrendered and rejoined the Union, the Southern states would be allowed to resume practicing slavery if they so desired. This is a fact you will find in few if any pro-North American history books.

In true Lincolnian fashion, the Yankee president preached against slavery in public, but behind closed doors he was busy supporting loophole laws, like the proposed 1861 Corwin Amendment to the U.S. Constitution, which would have allowed slavery to continue in perpetuity without any interference from the national government.[2759] It was passed by the U.S. House of Representatives on February 28, 1861, and by the U.S. Senate on March 2, 1861, two days before his presidential inauguration[2760]—during which Lincoln publicly mentioned the "proposed amendment" in his address on March 4. "I have no objection to its being made express and irrevocable," he stated emphatically before the nation that day.[2761]

By this time three states had actually ratified the Corwin Amendment, and certainly the rest would have as well, if given the chance. However, the act was dropped with the start of the Battle of Fort Sumter, on April 12, 1861. Had hostilities not exploded between the South and the North that Spring day, what can only be called "Lincoln's proslavery amendment" would have been signed into law, and American slavery would have continued indefinitely.[2762]

Lincoln fully supported the antebellum 1861 Corwin Amendment, named after Yankee Representative Thomas Corwin of Ohio. The measure read: "No amendment shall be made to the Constitution which will authorize or give to Congress the power to abolish or interfere, within any State, with the domestic institutions thereof, including that of persons held to labor or service by the laws of said State." Its meaning is clear. The main reason the amendment was not ratified was because of the start of the Civil War. How different the U.S. would be today if Lincoln's Corwin Amendment had passed!

Further evidence that Lincoln did not set out to make abolition in the South permanent is his "Ten Percent Plan," issued in December 1863[2763] as part of his "Proclamation of Amnesty and Reconstruction."[2764] Here a Confederate state could be readmitted to the Union if just 10 percent of its citizens took an oath of allegiance to the U.S.[2765] Afterward, that state, under its own new state government, could reestablish slavery if it so desired.[2766] Though he later changed his mind, in August of 1864 Lincoln even momentarily considered offering Jefferson Davis a truce *without the condition of emancipation*, believing that slavery would eventually be dealt with "by peaceful means."[2767]

The final death blow to this particular Yankee myth came that same year (1864) when, according to Confederate Secretary of State Judah P. Benjamin (thanks to the South, America's first Jewish statesman),[2768] far from demanding unconditional, immediate, and complete abolition (as William Lloyd Garrison had),[2769] Lincoln let it be known that he was willing to let the issue be decided on by a general vote in both the South and the North.[2770]

Famed Victorian novelist and social campaigner Charles Dickens correctly observed that the primary motivation behind Lincoln's invasion of the South was money.

Despite overwhelming evidence to the contrary, much of it from Lincoln's own pen, pro-North writers continue to pretend that the Yankee president wanted to end slavery quickly and permanently, and that he issued the Emancipation Proclamation for the sole purpose of granting blacks full civil rights.

But all of the purposeful misrepresentation, obfuscation, and subterfuge in the world cannot hide the Truth, as even 19th-Century foreigners understood. Here is how one of them, English novelist Charles Dickens, put it in December 1861. In the "War Between the States":

> The Northern onslaught upon slavery is no more than a piece of specious humbug disguised to conceal its desire for economic control of the United States. Union means so many millions a year lost to the South; secession means loss of the same millions to the North. The love of money is the root of this as many, many other evils. The quarrel between the North and South is, as it stands, solely a fiscal quarrel.[2771]

This ridiculous and misleading piece of pro-North propaganda, from the author's book *Honest Jeff and Dishonest Abe: A Southern Children's Guide to the Civil War*, portrays Lincoln as "The Great Emancipator." He was anything but. Not only did he delay abolition for as long as possible and block black advancement at every turn, he also supported the Corwin Amendment, campaigned to have all blacks deported, and refused to issue the Emancipation Proclamation until he was forced to by political expediency: he was running out of white soldiers *and* he needed the abolitionist vote for his reelection in 1864. And still the unenlightened continue to call him "The Great Emancipator"! As Lincoln was the ultimate demagogue, a more appropriate title would be "The Great Impersonator," which is how the author refers to him in the title of his book of the same name.

The author's cousin, Confederate General Stonewall Jackson—who referred to Yankees as the "boastful host which is ravaging our beautiful country"—is seen here attacking the right wing at the Battle of Chancellorsville in the Spring of 1863. Not one of these Rebel soldiers was fighting to "preserve slavery," as our Yankee slanted history books teach. Only a tiny minority of the South's troops were slave owners, and most of her officers were abolitionists who supported the idea of black enlistment. One of these was Jackson himself, whose tender, respectful, generous, sympathetic, and even loving relationships with African-Americans was well-known in his day. Indeed, this is why, though he had slaves in his household, he was not a true slave owner in the technical sense. He had not desired them or purchased them for his family's personal use. Instead, due to his kindly tolerant nature, all had been bought at the request of their original owners or by the slaves themselves. In 1855 Jackson founded a Sunday school for 100 African-Americans at Lexington, Virginia. He funded the little church with his own money and taught there when he was not busy at the Virginia Military Institute. Later, during Lincoln's War, he enlisted and racially integrated 3,000 armed black soldiers into his army in the fight against Yankee oppression—much to the "shock and awe" of Federal soldiers and officers. Jackson, who was absolutely typical of Southern whites at the time, not atypical, as pro-North writers continue to falsely maintain, has rightly earned a permanent place in the Confederate pantheon of Southern heroes.

17

ABRAHAM LINCOLN, BLACKS, AND SLAVERY

WHAT YOU WERE TAUGHT: Lincoln was America's greatest abolitionist.

THE TRUTH: Far from being an abolitionist Lincoln actually detested the group as a whole,[2772] constantly tried to distance himself from it, and always spoke of abolitionists in the negative.[2773] Indeed, he considered the very concept of abolition itself a pernicious influence, which is why he often made public comments on how he loathed and distrusted abolitionists and considered its members a public nuisance.[2774] Real abolitionists like Massachusetts-born Lysander Spooner, of course, detested and suspected him in return.[2775]

Once when he was asked if he minded having abolitionists in his political party, Lincoln snapped back: "As long as I'm not tarred with the abolitionist brush."[2776] For the rest of his life, when speaking of abolitionists, he always referred to them with barely disguised revulsion, and as a group quite distinct and separate from himself.

As early as 1837, while Lincoln was still a young member of his state's legislature, he made it a practice to send anti-abolition statements to the U.S. House of Representatives, as he did on March 3 under the title "Protest in the Illinois Legislature on the Subject of Slavery." Here, the obviously irritated lawyer wrote that when it came to slavery, "the promulgation of abolition doctrines tends rather to increase than abate its evils."[2777] His views on this topic never changed.

Lincoln's home at Springfield, Illinois. The president's friend, William Henry Herndon, tried for decades to turn him into an abolitionist, but to no avail. "Abolition is a greater evil than slavery," Lincoln once said.

Antislavery advocate William H. Herndon, Lincoln's law partner and later his biographer, labored throughout his entire friendship with Lincoln trying to convert him to abolitionism. But he would not be moved. This is because the U.S. president equated abolitionism with slavery, seeing both as two dangerous sides of the same coin.[2778] Eradicating slavery, Lincoln warned once, will produce "a greater evil" than slavery, an evil that is a hazard "even to the cause of human liberty itself."[2779] No other American ever held more extreme anti-abolitionist views than these.

As further proof, during the War several abolitionist Yankee officers tried to emancipate blacks, but were actually forbidden by anti-abolitionist Lincoln. As we saw in the previous chapter, one of these was the famous "Pathfinder," Union General John Charles Frémont, who declared martial law, then freed slaves in Missouri.[2780] Lincoln rescinded both orders, had the slaves returned to their owners, and relieved Frémont of his command—despite a tearful face-to-face plea from Frémont's famous wife, Jessie (Ann Benton).[2781]

Frémont's successor, abolitionist General David Hunter, also bucked Lincoln's racism by trying his own hand at emancipation. Hunter's "General Order No. 11" declared all slaves in the Union-held territories of South Carolina, Georgia, and Florida "forever free." Lincoln was not amused and again revoked the proclamation.[2782] But the slavery-hating Hunter continued to disobey the chief executive. When Hunter formed the 1st South Carolina Regiment, made up of blacks he had (illegally) enlisted in that state, Lincoln promptly ordered him to disband the group,[2783] reaffirming that he would not free the slaves until "it shall have become a necessity indispensable to the maintenance of the Government . . ."[2784]

Others in Lincoln's cabinet and military who tried to abolish slavery were also blocked by the white supremacist president, among them Simon Cameron,[2785] John W. Phelps, and Jim Lane.[2786]

Naturally Lincoln was heartily despised for such actions by abolitionists, who, from the very first day of his presidency, were extremely cautious of him. Why? Because he had not yet called for the immediate end of slavery. Even in the final months of 1862, two years into his first term, antislavery forces continued to express their unhappiness with Lincoln over his reluctance, even his refusal, to emancipate the nation's slaves.[2787] It was just such efforts to hinder abolition that earned him the popular nickname the "tortoise President."[2788]

Yankee General David Hunter attempted to free slaves and form an all-black Union regiment. Lincoln countermanded both actions.

In the end, Lincoln hoped, abolitionists would be condemned, cursed, and hated; or as he put it, "receive their just execration . . ."[2789] His anti-abolitionist sentiments were so obvious that even some pro-North historians have been forced to acknowledge them.[2790] Our sixteenth president was no abolitionist.[2791]

WHAT YOU WERE TAUGHT: Lincoln was a proponent of giving U.S. citizenship to both American black slaves and free blacks.

THE TRUTH: Throughout his political career Illinoisan Lincoln was repeatedly challenged as to whether he was in favor of "negro citizenship," and he repeatedly gave the same answer, as he did at Charleston, Illinois, on September 18, 1858:

> . . . very frankly . . . *I am not in favor of Negro citizenship*. . . . Now, my opinion is that the different States have the power to make a negro a citizen, under the constitution of the United States, if they choose. . . . *If the State of Illinois had that power, I should be against the exercise of it*. That is all I have to say about it.[2792]

To his last days Lincoln continued to hesitate to give blacks full civil rights, including voting rights and citizenship. Even his postwar "Reconstruction" plans for the nation did not include complete black enfranchisement.[2793]

To put a period on this myth once and for all, we have the observable fact that he never once publicly thanked blacks, Northern or Southern, for the countless sacrifices they made during his War, or for the many contributions they had made to American society.[2794]

WHAT YOU WERE TAUGHT: Lincoln's Gettysburg Address is rightly considered one of the most honest, historically accurate, and beautiful speeches ever given by a U.S. president.
THE TRUTH: Lincoln's most celebrated address, delivered November 19, 1863, at the dedication of the cemetery at Gettysburg, Pennsylvania, was meant to promote his overriding message that the "slave-obsessed" South, by seceding, threatened to obliterate the U.S. government. Even though the South had no such intentions—and, of course, his prediction never came close to occurring—the mendacious allure of Lincoln's words at Gettysburg has brainwashed six generations of Americans against the South.[2795]

To the citizens of Dixie, and to all respecters of the truth, the Gettysburg Address must go down in history as one of the most dishonorable, cynical, erroneous, and cruelly ironic speeches ever uttered, for in it Lincoln promises to uphold the Constitution, when in fact he did the opposite. He blames the South for the War, when it was a conflict that he not only wanted but that he also wickedly instigated. Finally, he praises America's true political heritage. Yet two years later, on April 9, 1865, at Appomattox,[2796] he overturned it, then caused it to "perish from the earth." What was that political heritage? It was our original Jeffersonian Confederate Republic, a constitutional government "of the people, by the people, for the people."[2797]

Here is what Maryland journalist H. L. Mencken had to say

about Lincoln's most famous declamation:

> The Gettysburg speech was at once the shortest and the most famous oration in American history. . . the highest emotion reduced to a few poetical phrases. Lincoln himself never even remotely approached it. It is genuinely stupendous. But let us not forget that it is poetry, not logic; beauty, not sense. Think of the argument in it. Put it into the cold words of everyday. The doctrine is simply this: that the Union soldiers who died at Gettysburg sacrificed their lives to the cause of self-determination—that government of the people, by the people, for the people, should not perish from the earth. *It is difficult to imagine anything more untrue. The Union soldiers in the battle actually fought against self-determination; it was the Confederates who fought for the right of their people to govern themselves.*[2798]

In this November 19, 1863, photograph of the crowd gathering for Lincoln's Gettysburg Address, the hatless president can just be seen upper left of center. (Only his head and shoulders are visible. He is facing the audience, to the left of the tall gentleman wearing a top hat.) The Gettysburg Address must be counted as one of the most disingenuous, hypocritical, contrived speeches ever given. Not one word of it is true, and its main thrust, that the North was fighting to sustain "a government of the people, by the people, for the people," is manifestly false, as H. L. Mencken and many others have pointed out. It was the South that was fighting to maintain the constitutional right of self-government. Plainly, the North was fighting to destroy it: Lincoln referred to secession as an "ingenious sophism."

British journalist Alistair Cooke concurred, calling Lincoln's Gettysburg Address "a classic work of oratory of highly questionable reasoning."[2799] As a Southern historian, I agree as well, but I will be more direct. The Gettysburg Address is a malevolent fiction, written by an incorrigible criminal, created for the sole purpose of justifying an unjustifiable war.

Despite the obvious anti-South political propagandizing at the root of this speech, incredibly, it continues to be lauded by thousands of pro-North scholars, authors, and academicians, with hundreds of books being entirely and worshipfully devoted to it.[2800] Astounding. And here is the reason we in the traditional South do not trust pro-North books: at their best they are subjective and biased, at their worst they are vindictive and historically inaccurate. Yet it is from these very types of Yankee-slanted works that our children are being taught American history today.

WHAT YOU WERE TAUGHT: The public response to Lincoln's Gettysburg Address was overwhelmingly positive, particularly during the speech itself, at which time it was received with rapt attention, constant cheers, tear swollen eyes, and thunderous applause.
THE TRUTH: Contrary to this silly Northern myth, Lincoln's own words tell quite a different story. According to his friend Ward Hill Lamon, after the speech Lincoln said to him:

> I tell you, Hill, that speech fell on the audience like a wet blanket. I am distressed about it. . . . It is a flat failure and the people are disappointed.[2801]

It is little wonder the Northern public responded this way. Victorian Americans, of course, had not yet been blinded by the anti-South movement's postwar political deification of Lincoln. Instead, at the time most saw him simply as what he really was: a demagogic rhetorician reciting vacuous pro-North nonsense.[2802]

WHAT YOU WERE TAUGHT: After issuing the Emancipation Proclamation Lincoln kindly gave all freed blacks "forty acres and a mule" as a head start on their new lives of freedom.
THE TRUTH: Lincoln never gave freed blacks anything, not even the most basic of human rights. In regard to this particular myth, what he did do was *promise* freed Southern blacks "forty acres and a mule." But

as with most of the North's other pledges to blacks, this one too turned out to be a lie:[2803] there were no mules,[2804] only deprivation, starvation, and vagrancy.[2805] And Lincoln's so-called "black land giveaways" were only meant to be temporary[2806]—and most of those that were issued ultimately went to rich white Northerners,[2807] railroads, land speculators, and lumber companies.[2808] Throughout the Sea Islands of South Carolina and Georgia, as just two examples, 90 percent of the land was sold to affluent Yankees,[2809] even though all the while Union General William T. Sherman pretended that it had been set aside "for the exclusive use of the negroes in the vicinity."[2810]

In this highly romanticized pro-North illustration of Lincoln's Gettysburg Address, his rapt audience hangs on every word, half of them holding back tears of emotion, the other half cheering their support. Lincoln is shown in a melodramatic pose, arms raised, bellowing out his message on the evils of the Confederacy and the great sacrifices of the Northern people in the cause of "preserving the Union." The reality of the scene, of course, was nothing like this. Of his speech that day Lincoln later declared that it was a "flat failure," one that "fell on the audience like a wet blanket." "I am distressed about it," he admitted to his friend Ward Hill Lamon, "and the people are disappointed."

White Southerners too were appalled at Lincoln's inhumanity. An incredulous General Robert E. Lee posed a rhetorical query to the Yankee president:

> What will you do with the freed people? That is a serious question today. Unless some humane course, based on wisdom and Christian principles, is adopted, you do them a great injustice in

setting them free.[2811]

Lincoln did not listen to General Lee, nor to his Northern constituents, or even his own cabinet members. Instead, he blindly inaugurated the very "great injustice" Lee had warned him about; the unplanned liberation of some 4.5 million former servants (North and South), catapulting them into a social and civil nightmare that, 150 years later, many of their descendants have yet to fully recover from.

WHAT YOU WERE TAUGHT: Lincoln's Emancipation Proclamation included a generous plan to incorporate freedmen and freedwomen into American society.

THE TRUTH: The Emancipation Proclamation contains no plans whatsoever for freed blacks, other than a self-serving push to enlist as many black males into the Union army as possible, one of the main purposes for issuing the edict to begin with.[2812] Indeed, this is why Lincoln himself referred to it as a "military emancipation," not a "civil rights emancipation."[2813]

Lincoln signing the Emancipation Proclamation. Contrary to Yankee mythology, the document did not promise freed blacks "forty acres and a mule." Nor did it offer any kind of organized plan to assist the millions of people who were to be suddenly turned loose on the streets of America.

The tragic fact is that Lincoln had no organized plan to admit freed blacks into American society as equal citizens;[2814] nothing to help the elderly, the ill, or orphaned blacks who could not work and who had previously been under the lifelong care of their owners;[2815] no education, no loans or grants, no job training, no housing, to ease freedmen and freedwomen into the world of capitalism, competition, and a free, highly skilled, and often hostile labor force. All were merely "liberated" to roam the streets and make their way as best they could; or as Lincoln flippantly put it, to "root, pig, or perish."[2816] After the reality of Lincoln's double-dealing politics sank in, all hope of free land, or anything else, for blacks evaporated.[2817]

We will note here that Lincoln and the U.S. Congress did eventually create the Bureau of Refugees, Freedmen, and Abandoned Lands. But this was in March 1865,[2818] over two years after the Emancipation Proclamation and just one month before the War ended—far too late to mitigate the myriad of problems caused by the president's sudden, violent, and unplanned abolition in January 1863. Even then, it was none too successful, for it had a habit of crowding freed blacks "into filthy shanties, for which exorbitant rates were charged."[2819]

Subsequently, finding that the Bureau violated states' rights and that it was "demoralizing thousands of negroes," in early 1866 President Andrew Johnson wisely vetoed a bill that would have kept the corrupt governmental department in operation indefinitely. This was to be Andrew's "first and last victory over the radicals [that is, the liberal abolitionists] in Congress."[2820]

Even foreigners understood what Lincoln could not or would not. After visiting the American South, Englishman Sir Charles Lyell made the following remarks in 1855:

> I am aware that there is some danger, when one hears the philanthropist declaiming in terms of gross exaggeration on the horrors of slavery and the crimes of the [Southern] planters, of being tempted by a spirit of contradiction, or rather by a love of justice, to counteract misrepresentation, by taking too favourable a view of the condition and prospects of the negroes. But *there is another reason, also, which causes the traveller in the South to moderate his enthusiasm for emancipation. He is forced continually to think of the responsibility which would be incurred, if several millions of human beings were hastily set aside, like so many machines, by withdrawing from them suddenly the protection afforded by their present monopoly of labour. In the opening of the market freely to white competitors, before the race is more improved, consists their danger.*[2821]

In 1867, while on a steamboat chugging out of Mobile, Alabama, Englishman Henry Latham asked a former slave working on the boat whether he was better off now or before emancipation, to which he gave this intentionally humorous but revealing response:

> Well, when I tumbled overboard before, the captain he stopped the ship, and put back and picked me up; and they gave me a glass of hot whisky and water; and then they gave me twenty lashes for falling overboard. But now if I tumble overboard, the captain he'd say, "What's dat? Oh! Only dat dam nigger—go ahead."[2822]

In 1910 Pastor Benjamin F. Riley, though white, aptly described Lincoln's impulsive and chaotic emancipation through the eyes of thousands of still living blacks who had experienced slavery and liberation firsthand:

> *. . . the Negro was turned loose at the period of his emancipation without a penny in his pocket, without a loaf of bread, and without a shelter over his head.* He had not a barleycorn of land, nothing which he could call his own but his muscle and will. He had enriched the states of the South with the cotton bale for many generations, he had equally enriched New England and the Middle States by the same means, and even while the hubbub of abolitionism was rampant, he was the chief means of the enrichment of the land, and *what was the compensation afforded him? He was usually given a miserable hut in which to live; the scantiest clothing, of the coarsest sort; he was maintained on a peck of corn meal and three pounds of bacon a week; he was denied any rights save those of the scantiest nature; he was forbidden intellectual development, as that would have unfitted him for the profitable servitude to which he was subjected; . . . he knew nothing but to labor from day to day, and from year to year, till he found his last resting place in the humble grave, into which a stream of seven generations of slaves passed before the boon of freedom came.*[2823]

In 1886 Susan Dabney Smedes offered these comments on her deceased father Thomas Dabney, a former Mississippi slave owner:

> My father was so well assured of the contentment and well-being of his slaves, while he owned them, and *saw so much of their suffering, which he was not able to relieve after they were freed*, that he did not, for many years, believe that it was better for them to be free than held as slaves. But during the last winter of his life he expressed the opinion that it was well for them to have their freedom.[2824]

Black civil rights leader William E. B. Du Bois of Massachusetts summed up Lincoln's emancipation "plan" this way: "former slaves are now free to do whatever they want with the nothing they never had to begin with."[2825] Of the Yankee president's "root, pig, or perish" emancipation program, former slave Thomas Hall later spoke for millions of Southern blacks:

> Lincoln got the praise for freeing us, but did he do it? He give us freedom without giving us any chance to live to ourselves and we still had to depend on the Southern white man for work, food, and clothing, and he held us through our necessity and want in a state of servitude but little better than slavery. *Lincoln done but little for the negro race and from a living standpoint nothing.*[2826]

A sentimental pro-North drawing of Lincoln issuing the Emancipation Proclamation. Though the illegal document officially freed no slaves, it did accomplish one thing: the quality of life for blacks immediately plummeted, remaining far below even slavery levels for almost 100 years.

WHAT YOU WERE TAUGHT: Life greatly improved immediately following Lincoln's Emancipation Proclamation.
THE TRUTH: One of the primary consequences of Lincoln's victory over the Constitution and the rights of the American people, particularly in the South, was that the quality of life for blacks instantly plummeted, then remained below slavery levels for nearly the next 100 years.

After his War, for instance, black life span dropped 10 percent, diets and health deteriorated, disease and sickness rates went up 20 percent, the number of skilled blacks declined, and the gap between white and black wages widened, trends that did not even begin to reverse until the onset of World War II, 75 years later, in 1939.[2827] At least one out of four blacks died in a number of communities.[2828]

Of life after "liberation," Adeline Grey, a black South Carolina servant, wrote that when "liberation" came she could still vividly remember it, while slavery was but a dim memory. Why? Because "life was much more difficult and painful after emancipation than before."[2829]

The "pain" of emancipation was due, in great part, to the fact that Lincoln never pushed through any kind of organized, gradual, or compensated emancipation plan, as nearly every other Western nation had done when it abolished slavery.[2830] And Lincoln's promise to freedmen of "forty acres and a mule" was little more than a carrot on the end of a stick, used to lure blacks into a false sense of governmental protection after emancipation (as we will recall, Lincoln's so-called "black land giveaways" were never meant to be permanent,[2831] and what little of these were dispersed went primarily to wealthy white Northerners).[2832]

In truth, prior to emancipation Lincoln set up no effectual homestead act, no substantive support plans, and no land redistribution program. As such, freed blacks were literally cast out into the streets with no education, no jobs, no housing, no job training, no grants or loans, only to simply "root, pig, or perish," as Lincoln callously put it.[2833] The occasion for this brutish comment was related by one of the South's most honorable and intelligent gentlemen, Confederate Vice President Alexander H. Stephens.

On February 3, 1865, only two months before his death, Lincoln attended a peace conference on board the presidential steamer *River Queen*, anchored at Fort Monroe, at Hampton Roads, Hampton,

Virginia. A Southern committee, headed by Stephens, had come to the Yankee garrison to negotiate for peace. Besides Stephens and Lincoln, U.S. Secretary of State William H. Seward, Confederate Senator Robert M. T. Hunter, and Confederate Assistant Secretary of War John A. Campbell were also in attendance. According to Stephens:

> Other matters were then talked over relating to the evils of immediate emancipation, if that policy should be pressed, especially the sufferings which would necessarily attend the old and the infirm, as well as the women and children, who were unable to support themselves. These were fully admitted by Mr. Lincoln, but in reference to them, in that event, he illustrated all he could say by telling the anecdote, which has been published in the papers, about the Illinois farmer and his hogs. The conversation then took another turn.[2834]

The "anecdote" Stephens refers to is as follows:

> An Illinois farmer was congratulating himself with a neighbor upon a great discovery he had made, by which he would economize much time and labor in gathering and taking care of the food crop for his hogs, as well as trouble in looking after and feeding them during the winter. "What is it?" said the neighbor. "Why, it is," said the farmer, "to plant plenty of potatoes, and when they are mature, without either digging or housing them, turn the hogs in the field and let them get their own food as they want it." "But," said the neighbor, "how will they do when the winter corn and the ground is hard frozen ?" "Well," said the farmer, "let 'em root!"[2835]

This story, proudly related by Lincoln to the group at the Hampton Roads Peace Conference, was his way of explaining how he handled the fact that he had freed millions of slaves without job training, education, housing, loans, or grants. Lincoln's exact words? "Let them root, pig, or perish"!

Why was there no plan for a smooth transition from captivity to freedom? Lincoln took the answer to his grave. As a former female slave later recollected of those times: "We had no idea what to do. There was no place to go after we were freed. We were just turned loose with no direction and no assistance," she bemoaned.[2836]

Under Lincoln's "root, pig, or perish" emancipation plan, blacks who as servants had lived quality lives equal to and often superior to many whites and free blacks, now found themselves living out in the open or in makeshift tents, begging for food and work. There was now less labor available to them under freedom than there had been under servitude, and thus the black economy plunged.[2837]

On February 3, 1865, according to eyewitness testimony, when Confederate diplomats asked Lincoln what his plan was for the South's 3.5 million black servants after their emancipation, he compared them to hogs, saying: "Let 'em root, pig, or perish." And this is precisely what occurred!

Disease, homelessness, starvation, beggary, prostitution, poverty, and thievery now became the lot of untold thousands of former black servants. Even many of those who managed to become sharecroppers eventually found themselves in a state of peonage (a debt that tied them to the land), living in crude filthy shacks, suffering from illiteracy, ill health, and malnutrition. All of this was a far cry from the excellent quality of life experienced by Southern blacks when they had lived under servitude.[2838]

Black house servant Sarah Debro of North Carolina was "freed" then put to work by her Yankee "emancipators" as a field hand, a job she had never performed before. Here, in 1937, is what Sarah, who worked for the Cain family, had to say about Lincoln's "emancipation":

> After the War Yankees came round orderin' us Negroes about like slaves, even though we was "free." The Yanks gave us houses they had built. They told us to go live in 'em. But they were horrible little things, with no windows, and made of mud and sticks, like poor white folks live in. We was used to much better. As servants we had had warm dry houses made of wood, with nice brick chimneys and glass windows. I told my Mammy that I didn't want to live in the Yankees' house. She beat me and sent me to bed. I laid there and looked up at the ceilin'. I could see the stars through the cracks in the roof. I cried myself to sleep. I always had plenty to eat when we worked for Master. But under Yankee freedom we was always starvin'. It was a horrible time, so bad that I would have much rather been a slave than a freed girl. In between doin' slave work and tryin' to find something to eat, I had to fight off dem Yankee mens. Dey was always tryin' to have their way with me. Dem Yanks are cruel people. When I look back in time I still think fondly of my days as a slave.[2839]

She did not realize it, but Sarah Debro was among the fortunate.

Most freed black servants were given neither a home or a job, and many were not able to fight off the sexual advances and violent treatment of Yankee soldiers. As Chesnut said of Lincoln's emancipation debacle, "the Yanks have let loose Satan himself, and have no idea how to handle him."[2840] From the perspective of 1867, four years after the Emancipation Proclamation and two years after the Thirteenth Amendment, Englishman Henry Latham spoke these words:

> It is considered that *of the 4,000,000 negroes 1,000,000 have perished since their emancipation*. They were without habits of prudence and forethought, and labour had been the badge of their servility. They were ignorant and helpless. Their first impulse when set free was to wander away from the old homes and see the world. They could not realize that they were free upon the plantations where they had toiled as slaves. Then they soon gravitated to the larger cities, where vice and want made terrible havoc among them.
>
> They felt the instinct which is said to drive all loose

> population without anchor westward. It is computed that 37,000 negroes have moved from South Carolina to Mississippi and Texas. It requires the energy of the white man to strike out for the far West at once.
>
> Not only were they thinned by death, but they ceased to multiply as before. As long as there was a profit in rearing them, *the masters took care that the women were attended to in child-birth, and the babies properly nourished. . . . After the emancipation it was nobody's interest that the little children should be cared for. Babies were an incumbrance in wandering about; the maternal instincts were weak; life had no great charms for them, and infanticide became terribly common. The year after Mr. Lincoln proclaimed emancipation, there were more black babies floating down the Mississippi River than there were aged Hindoos in the Ganges. The little children died off more rapidly than the adults.*
>
> The mortality has been so great, that some have predicted a solution of the negro difficulty in the disappearance of the whole coloured race in the next fifty years. This would be a melancholy fiasco; but ungrateful captives when set free sometimes do refuse to live, although toils and dangers have been incurred by their deliverers. Even in New York and Philadelphia there are not now nearly as many negroes as there were before the war. In the parts where they have lived in the greatest security during the war, and where they may be supposed to have congregated, and where the largest subscriptions were raised to preserve them from famine, they have been fading away. In the colder climate of the Northern States, after a generation or two the coloured families die out.[2841]

Just prior to Lincoln's War, Southern plantation owner James Hammond wrote:

> I believe that our slaves are the happiest three millions of human beings on whom the sun shines. Into their Eden is coming Satan in the guise of an abolitionist.[2842]

While it is not true that the Old South's system of servitude was an "Eden" for all blacks, we can certainly say that the institution as practiced in Dixie was nothing like Harriet Beecher Stowe and other Northern propagandists have painted it. In fact, for many of both races, life in the Old South was exactly as Margaret Mitchell depicted it in her classic Southern novel, *Gone With the Wind*. What Northerners and New South scallywags disparagingly call her "make-believe world," did exist after all,[2843] and those who read her book will see a part of the Old South as it really was, without the distortions, lies, slanders, and South-hating propaganda of Yankee folklore.[2844]

With all its dangers and uncertainties, would "enslaved" blacks have traded servitude for freedom? Of course, and some did. But, weighing things in the balance, many more—95 percent of all Southern black servants—did not.[2845] Instead, this group chose to remain in their homeland after "emancipation," on their masters' plantations, where safety and certainty reigned.[2846] As we have seen, only about 2,000 slaves (a mere 500 Northern and Southern servants a year) out of 4.5 million availed themselves of the Underground Railroad during the War—just 0.04 percent of the total.[2847] The rest voluntarily stayed at home, defending both their owners' farms, and the owners themselves, from marauding Yanks.[2848]

Though Southern black servants yearned for freedom, most had no desire to leave the secure and comfortable lives they had long known on the plantation. Nothing, not the Emancipation Proclamation, not even the arrival of Union troops, their so-called "liberators," could convince them to desert their homes, their white extended families, their family cemeteries, or the South itself.

What occurred at the Confederate home of Sarah Morgan's parents was the norm, not the exception, as Northern myth insists. On the day of Jubilee (emancipation) in New Orleans, Louisiana, her family's slaves were (illegally) "set free" by arrogant Yankee officers, who ordered the servants to leave with them. All refused, however. One servant named Margret, snapped back at the Union soldiers: "I don't want to be any free-er than I is now—I'll stay with my mistress." Another of the Morgan's servants, a black man, was tossed a musket and commanded to join the Federal army, to which he replied: "I am only a slave, but I am a secesh nigger, and won't fight in such a damned crew!"[2849]

During his travels Yankee Nehemiah Adams met a number of black slaves in the Old South who were dreading being freed upon their masters' deaths. After being liberated, wrote Adams:

> Such servants sometimes select new masters, and prevail on them to buy them, preferring the feeling of protection, the gratification of loving and serving a white person, to abstract liberty.[2850]

It was this same loyal, stay-at-home group—representing 95 percent of all Southern blacks (a group even recognized by Lincoln)[2851]—that eventually inspired the concept of sharecropping: as nearly all slaves refused to leave their plantations after emancipation, owners simply subdivided their land into small plots and turned them over to their new freedmen and freedwomen. This saved blacks from having to seek employment elsewhere (or worse, try and raise money to buy their own land), while it saved plantation owners the trouble of trying to find new employees.[2852]

There was something far deeper going on here than just mere practicality, however.

Former slaves quite rightly considered themselves true Americans and true Southerners. After all, by 1860, 99 percent of all blacks were native-born Americans, a larger percentage than for whites.[2853] Educator and former Southern servant Booker T. Washington eloquently spoke for the 95 percent of Southern blacks who remained in Dixie after Lincoln's emancipation, when he wrote:

> I was born in the South, I have lived and labored in the South, and I expect to die and be buried in the South.[2854]

On September 29, 1865, just five months after Lincoln's War came to an end at Appomattox, North Carolina blacks held a "Negro Convention" which issued the following declaration:

> *Born upon the same soil and brought up in an intimacy of relationship unknown in any other state of society, we have formed attachments for the white race which must be as enduring as life, and we can conceive of no reason that our God-bestowed freedom should now sever the kindly ties which have so long united us. . .*

> We acknowledge with gratitude that there are those among former slave masters who have promptly conceded our freedom and have *manifested a just and humane disposition towards their former slaves*. . . .
>
> Though associated with many memories of suffering, as well as of enjoyment, *we have always loved our homes, and dreaded, as the worst of evils, a forcible separation from them. Now that freedom and a new career are before us, we love this land and people more than ever before. Here we have toiled and suffered; our parents, wives, and children are buried here; and in this land we will remain, unless forcibly driven away.*[2855]

Virginia born African-American educator and orator, Booker T. Washington, represented the voice of millions of other black Southerners when he said: "I was born in the South, I have lived and labored in the South, and I expect to die and be buried in the South." This is a sentiment that few white Yankees then or now comprehend. But it was, and still is, well understood by traditional white Southerners.

So strong was their attachment to Dixie that as late as the 1880s, a generation after the Civil War, 90 percent of all Southern blacks still lived in the plantation belts of the Deep South.[2856]

Yet the scars left by that illegal, bloody, and unnecessary conflict remained; and they remain to this day. The man behind all of this is the one many Americans, both black and white, tenderly call the "Great Emancipator"!

With such a legacy, what many in the South really want to know is why, year after year, Lincoln is continually voted America's "favorite," "best," and "greatest president"?[2857] And why do Northerners sometimes refer to him as "Father Abraham," equate him with men like Moses and even Jesus, and liken his mother Nancy Hanks (a relative of actor Tom Hanks)[2858] to the Virgin Mary?[2859] Lincoln did not even end slavery, as pro-North historians pretend. The Thirteenth Amendment ended it eight months after he died.[2860]

The man himself repeatedly said he was not qualified to be the nation's highest leader. In a letter to Thomas J. Pickett of Rock Island, Illinois, for example, dated April 16, 1859, Lincoln wrote:

> I do not think myself fit for the presidency. I certainly am flattered, and grateful that some partial friends think of me in that connection.[2861]

To this day, millions of traditional Southerners agree with this sentiment and only wish that Lincoln had followed his own judgement.

WHAT YOU WERE TAUGHT: Lincoln was a humanitarian and a non-racist, and in particular was an admirer and respecter of African-Americans.

THE TRUTH: This may be how he is seen by most people today, but this is not how he was perceived during his life, and for good reason. Though Lincoln's own words refute this Yankee myth,[2862] let us allow one of Lincoln's so-called "friends," former *Northern* slave Frederick Douglass, to reveal the facts.

When it came to people of color Lincoln's words often lacked "the genuine spark of humanity," Douglass once observed acidly.[2863] As for his supposed "love of the black man," Douglass set the record straight for all those willing to read his words: "Lincoln was a hypocrite who was only proud of his own race and nationality. Though voted into office as an antislavery Liberal, he was actually a prejudiced, black colonizationist, with nothing but contempt and even hatred for the Negro," the black orator stated.[2864]

Years later, on April 14, 1876, Douglass elaborated on his feelings about Lincoln in a speech he gave at Washington, D.C. Former Union general, now U.S. President Ulysses S. Grant (today still known in the South, like Lincoln, as a war criminal), was in attendance. The old Yankee warhorse must have cringed as he listened to Douglass utter the following words to his largely black audience:

> It must be admitted, truth compels me to admit, even here in the presence of the monument we have erected to his memory, *Abraham Lincoln was not, in the fullest sense of the word, either our man*

or our model. In his interests, in his associations, in his habits of thought, and in his prejudices, he was a white man.

He was preeminently the white man's President, entirely devoted to the welfare of white men. He was ready and willing at any time during the first years of his administration to deny, postpone, and sacrifice the rights of humanity in the coloured people to promote the welfare of the white people of this country. . . . He came into the Presidential chair upon one principle alone, namely, opposition to the extension of slavery. His arguments in furtherance of this policy had then motive and mainspring in his patriotic devotion to the interests of his own race. To protect, defend, and perpetuate slavery in the States where it existed, Abraham Lincoln was not less ready than any other President to draw the sword of the nation. He was ready to execute all the supposed constitutional guarantees of the United States Constitution in favour of the slave system anywhere inside the slave States. He was willing to pursue, recapture, and send back the fugitive slave to his master, and to suppress a slave rising for liberty, though his guilty master were already in arms against the Government. The race to which we belong were not the special objects of his consideration.[2865]

Contrary to so-called Northern "history," it is clear that "Honest Abe's" attitude toward African-Americans was nothing like we have been taught.

In this old pro-North illustration, in which Lincoln is incongruously compared with his political opposite, George Washington, we are treated to yet more absurd Yankee propaganda. The caption (not shown) reads: "Behold oh America, your sons. The greatest among men." The image text itself reads: "Under providence Washington made our country and Lincoln saved our country." Washington is holding a copy of the U.S. Constitution, Lincoln is holding a copy of the Emancipation Proclamation. The Constitution officialized the workings of the U.S. government, the Emancipation Proclamation officialized Lincoln's violation of the Constitution. No connection.

Lincoln used slave labor not only to finish work on the U.S. Capitol Building at Washington, D.C., but to construct numerous other federal structures and roads in the District as well. Progressive Northerners and New South scallywags may consider these the acts of an "abolitionist," but traditional Southerners do not and never will.

In the South we know and teach the Truth: Lincoln was no abolitionist;[2866] hated the entire movement;[2867] said abolition was worse than slavery;[2868] stalled the Emancipation Proclamation for as long as possible[2869]—and then only issued it for military, political, and colonization purposes;[2870] was a leader in the American Colonization Society;[2871] forced slaves to complete the construction of the Capitol dome in Washington, D.C.;[2872] implemented extreme racist military policies;[2873] used profits from Northern slavery to fund his War;[2874] often referred to blacks as "niggers";[2875] said he was willing to allow slavery to continue in perpetuity if the Southern states would come back into the Union;[2876] pushed nonstop right up to the last day of his life for the deportation of all American blacks;[2877] as a lawyer defended slave owners in court;[2878] backed the proslavery Corwin Amendment to the Constitution in 1861;[2879] and continually blocked black enlistment, black suffrage, and black citizenship.[2880]

The truth is that during Lincoln's two terms in office, he was extremely disliked in both the North and the South.[2881] Indeed, not only was Grant far more popular,[2882] but Americans considered Lincoln one of the worst if not the worst chief executive up to that time,[2883] some even referring to him as "America's most hated president."[2884]

To hide these facts is criminal, an insult to the South, and a disservice to both authentic American history and posterity.

In the late 1700s and early 1800s Toussaint L'Ouverture, "the Black Napoleon," led the Haitian Revolution against the French government, the only known successful mass slave revolt in world history. Despite this fact, pro-North educators continue to teach that there were dozens if not hundreds of victorious slave insurrections in America's Old South. In fact, there were none during Lincoln's War and only three antebellum slave rebellions consequential enough to be given names. All three of these insurrections ended in failure, their leaders arrested and executed.

18

LINCOLN'S BLACK COLONIZATION PLAN

WHAT YOU WERE TAUGHT: After issuing the Emancipation Proclamation, Lincoln planned to fully incorporate former black slaves into American society.

THE TRUTH: Lincoln planned on doing nothing of the kind. Actually, after abolition his number one goal for freed blacks was to ship as many of them out of the country as possible.[2885]

So adamant was he about expatriating American blacks that he was willing to settle them almost anyplace—as long as it was, as he said, "without the United States."[2886] This included Europe, Latin America, or the Caribbean, or anywhere else they would be accepted. As such, he funded experimental black colonies in what are now Panama and Belize, as well as in Haiti.[2887] But the president seemed to have a special interest in the African colony of Liberia. Indeed, Africa was always his first choice. He would even pay the resettlement costs of any and all African-Americans willing to volunteer to be shipped out of the U.S.: the more the better, the sooner the better.[2888]

If his deportation plan turned out to be unworkable, Old Abe had, in his opinion, another solution nearly as good: corral American blacks in their own all-black state, preferably one far from his own home state of Illinois. This idea, yet another one of his many harebrained racist notions, was presented by Lincoln to the public on September 15, 1858, at one of his infamous debates with Senator Stephen A. Douglas.[2889]

Lincoln's true feelings about blacks were never in doubt at the time. Just two months earlier, on July 17, 1858, for instance, our future sixteenth chief executive told an audience at Springfield, Illinois:

> What I would most desire would be the separation of the white and black races.[2890]

Lincoln spent his entire adult life publicly campaigning for racial segregation, or what the author calls American apartheid, pleading for "the separation of the white and black races." His racist ideas, such as black colonization, had long been supported by other fellow Yankees, including William Lloyd Garrison, Harriet Beecher Stowe, Horace Greeley, Rufus King, Edward Everett, John Maclean, Jr., William Alexander Duer, Jeremiah Day, Jared Sparks, Henry Rutgers, and John Dickinson, among thousands of others. Pro-North historians have been suppressing these facts for a century and a half.

Why was Lincoln so anti-black? Being a Victorian Northerner, it all came down to white racism and money.

Like other white racist politicians before him, Lincoln was at first confused about how to deal with slavery: free them and they would compete with whites for jobs and land; keep them enslaved and, as he himself glibly put it, "the inferior race bears the superior down."[2891]

In 1842 Scotsman William Thomson wisely wrote of Southern slavery that "it is a curse entailed on them: and how are they to get clear of it?"[2892] In 1820 Thomas Jefferson phrased the seemingly insurmountable problem more picturesquely:

> We have the wolf by the ears, and we can neither hold him, nor safely let him go.[2893]

If the brilliant, highly educated, Christian Southerner Thomas Jefferson was at a loss as to how to deal with slavery, the slow, self-taught, atheist Northerner Abraham Lincoln was not. Eventually he hit upon a simple solution, one that he described bluntly on October 16, 1854, in a speech at Peoria, Illinois:

> If all earthly power were given me, I should not know what to do as to the existing institution. My first impulse would be to free all the slaves, and send them to Liberia [Africa]—to their own native land.[2894]

Seven years later, now in the White House, the new president's support for what was called "black colonization" was, if anything, even stronger, as is evidenced in his political documents. The most famous of these, of course, is the Emancipation Proclamation.

What historians call the Emancipation Proclamation was actually the final version of a document that underwent several minor and major revisions in draft form.[2895] As such, it would be more accurate to call the last one, issued January 1, 1863, the Final Emancipation Proclamation.

The document that is of most interest to us in regards to this particular Yankee myth, however, is known as the Preliminary Emancipation Proclamation, and what an interesting article it is. If only it was studied as closely as the Final Emancipation Proclamation, our sixteenth president would never have been wrongly apotheosized as the "Great Emancipator"!

The Preliminary Emancipation Proclamation, which Lincoln said he "fixed up a little" over the previous weekend,[2896] then read to his cabinet on September 22, 1862—just four months before issuing the Final Emancipation Proclamation—contained the following remarkable statement:

> it is my purpose . . . to again recommend . . . that the effort to colonize [that is, deport] persons of African descent with their consent upon this continent or elsewhere . . . will be continued.[2897]

Why did this sensational clause, directed at the U.S. Congress, not make it into the Final Emancipation Proclamation? Against his wishes Lincoln's own cabinet members talked him out of including it because it might further alienate abolitionists, a group that was already bitterly disappointed with Lincoln's refusal to abolish slavery after being in the White House for over two years. Lincoln would need their votes in his upcoming bid for reelection in 1864. Promising to deport newly freed blacks out of the country was hardly the way to win the hearts, minds, and votes of the vociferous antislavery crowd. And so the item on black colonization, one of Lincoln's most ardent lifelong aspirations, was struck from the Final Emancipation Proclamation.[2898]

U.S. President Thomas Jefferson compared the dangers of abolishing slavery with holding a wolf by the ears. Unfortunately for the South, Lincoln did not understand this elemental concept—or he did and did not care.

Thus this version, the only one known by the public today, is *not* the Emancipation Proclamation Lincoln wanted. It was the one forced on him by his cabinet and by political expediency.[2899]

But this did nothing to slow down his campaign to expel all African-Americans from the country. Indeed, shortly thereafter, just one month before issuing the Final Emancipation Proclamation, he reemphasized his position on the issue, lest anyone should forget. In his Second Annual Message to Congress on December 1, 1862, Lincoln stated unambiguously:

> I cannot make it better known than it already is, that I strongly favor colonization.[2900]

Lincoln showing his cabinet the *Final* Emancipation Proclamation. At a previous meeting they had discussed the president's September 22, 1862, *Preliminary* Emancipation Proclamation, at which time they talked him into removing his infamous black colonization clause because it would offend abolitionists in his party. The redacted material included Lincoln's request of Congress that it apportion funds for his black colonization plan, which would deport freed slaves to foreign lands. The secretly deleted clause read: "It is my purpose . . . to again recommend . . . that the effort to colonize persons of African descent with their consent upon this continent or elsewhere . . . will be continued." Thus, the Final Emancipation Proclamation—*the only one known to the public*—is not the document Lincoln had originally wanted. It was the one that was forced on him by political expediency.

In this same speech he once again asks Congress to set aside funding for black deportation,[2901] even suggesting that it be added as an amendment to the Constitution in order to expedite it.[2902] According to Lincoln:

> Congress may appropriate money and otherwise provide for colonizing free colored persons, with their own consent, at any place or places without the United States.[2903]

While Congress continued to allocate money for Lincoln's bizarre deportation scheme, by this time few politicians besides the president actually believed it was feasible.[2904]

When it came to the Northern populace, however, Lincoln was far from being alone in his desire to rid America of blacks. At the time, all across the North, white racism was deeply entrenched, far more so than in the much more racially tolerant South.[2905] Even Thaddeus Stevens, one of the North's most infamous and fervent abolitionists, had founded a colonization society devoted to freeing and deporting blacks.[2906]

Speaking for his Yankee constituents, Indiana Senator Albert Smith White presented the following in an April 7, 1862, report to the U.S. Congress:

> Much of the objection to emancipation arises from *the opposition of a large portion of our [Northern] people to the intermixture of the races*, and from the association of white and black labor. The committee would do nothing to favor such a policy; apart from *the antipathy which nature has ordained, the presence of a race among us who cannot, and ought not to, be admitted to our social and political privileges, will be a perpetual source of injury and inquietude to both. This is a question of color, and is unaffected by the relation of master and slave. The introduction of the negro, whether bond or free, into the same field of labor with the white man, is the opprobrium of the latter*; and we cannot believe that the thousands of non-slaveholding citizens in the rebellious [Southern] States who live by industry are fighting to continue the negro within our limits even in a state of vassalage, but more probably from a vague apprehension that he is to become their competitor in his own right. We wish to disabuse our laboring countrymen, and the whole Caucasian race who may seek a home here [in the North], of this error. We are satisfied that the labor of our cotton fields, as well as of our corn fields, may be performed by the white man, and we would offer to these sons of labor the emoluments of both. There is no sounder maxim in political economy than that the cultivators of the soil should be the owners of the soil. *The committee conclude that the highest interests of the white race, whether Anglo-Saxon, Celt, or Scandinavian, require that the whole country should be held and occupied by those races alone.*
>
> . . . It is useless, now, to enter upon any philosophical inquiry whether nature has or has not made the negro inferior to the Caucasian. *The belief is indelibly fixed upon the public mind that such inequality does exist. There are irreconcilable differences between the two races which separate them, as with a wall of fire.* There is no instance afforded us in history where liberated slaves, even of the same race, have lived any considerable period in harmony with

their former masters when denied equality with them in social and political privileges. But *the [Northern] Anglo-American never will give his consent that the negro, no matter how free, shall be elevated to such equality*. It matters not how wealthy, how intelligent, or how morally meritorious the negro may become, so long as he remains among us the recollection of the former relation of master and slave will be perpetuated by the changeless color of the Ethiop's skin, and that color will alike be perpetuated by the degrading tradition of his former bondage.

When it came to America's multiracial society, liberal Indiana Senator Albert Smith White held the typical progressive Yankee view: blacks are inferior to whites, the two races should not intermix, the black race "degrades" the white one, the U.S. should be an all-white nation, and black colonization was the only feasible solution to the "racial problem." "There are irreconcilable differences between the two races which separate them, as with a wall of fire," White assured his left-wing constituents in an 1862 report to the U.S. Congress.

> . . . To appreciate and understand this difficulty, *it is only necessary for one to observe that, in proportion as the legal barriers established by slavery have been removed by emancipation [here in the North], the prejudice of caste becomes stronger, and public opinion more intolerant to the negro race.*
>
> To remove this obstacle is a work well worthy of the efforts of a great people anxious for their own future well-being, and moved by a spirit of humanity towards an enslaved and degraded class of their fellow beings. How, then, can the separation of the races after emancipation be accomplished? *Colonization appears to be the only mode in which this can be done. The home for the African must not be within the limits of the present territory of the Union. The [Northern] Anglo-American looks upon every acre of our present domain as intended for him, and not for the negro. A home, therefore, must be sought for the African beyond our own limits and in those warmer regions to which his constitution is better adapted than to our own climate, and which doubtless the Almighty intended the colored races should inhabit and cultivate. Hayti and others of the West India islands, Central America and the upper portions of South America, and Liberia, are all interesting fields of inquiry in relation to the future of the liberated negroes of the United States.* There they may be provided with homes in a climate suited to their highest physical, intellectual, and moral development, and there, under the beneficent protection and friendship of the freest and most powerful of all the governments of the world, they may enjoy true liberty with all its attendant blessings, and achieve the high destiny which the Almighty has intended man should everywhere accomplish.
>
> *If the good which would thus be effected for an oppressed people, by their removal from our midst and their settlement in other parts of the globe, were the only object to be attained by the system of colonization, that alone would be worthy the high and holy ambition of a great nation. . . .* [Let us acknowledge] the truth that *the retention of the negro among us with half privileges is but a bitter mockery to him, and that our duty is to find for him a congenial home and country [outside the U.S.].*[2907]

Smith, a member of the select committee on Emancipation and Colonization, was speaking for nearly every Northerner when he presented this bill to the U.S. House of Representatives on July 16, 1862, requesting $20 million from Congress to expatriate African-Americans. The committee was evidently quite determined to fully publicize its racist campaign. Attached to the document was this note:

> Resolved, that ten thousand copies of the bill entitled "An act giving

the aid of the United States to certain States upon the adoption by them of a system of emancipation, and to provide for the colonization of free negroes," together with the report of the select committee, be printed in pamphlet form for the use of the House.[2908]

New York University alumnus and celebrated Yankee historian, James Ford Rhodes of Ohio, expressed the common Victorian Northern view of black slaves, describing them as "filthy, stupid, and brutish." This is the opposite of how the typical Southerner would have depicted his African servants in the 1800s.

On this very day, while Lincoln and the Republican Party (then the Liberal Party) were trying to come up with the money to exile blacks to foreign lands, Jefferson Davis and the Democratic Party (then the Conservative Party) were busy seeking recognition of the Confederacy in France, while trying to oust Yankee forces out of West Tennessee, now under the command of General Ulysses S. Grant.[2909]

As is obvious from Smith's resolution, it was the common Yankee belief, even among most Northern abolitionists,[2910] that people of African descent were inferior to those of European descent, inferior in intellect, morality, psychology, emotionality, creativity, and physicality. They were a kind of "bridge," or even a separate species, between apes and man, many white Northerners staunchly maintained.[2911]

Respected Yankee historian James Ford Rhodes, for instance, described slaves as "indolent and filthy," "stupid" and "duplicitous," with "brute-like countenances."[2912] Esteemed New York physician and Union officer Robert Wilson Shufeldt, who wrote a book called, *The Negro: A Menace to American Society*, came to the anthropological conclusion that blacks were an inferior race whose presence could only degrade the

European-American community. As such, like Lincoln, Shufeldt spent much of his life developing ideas and methods by which to rid the United States of its African population. By way of deportation and colonization, wrote the Cornell University alumnus,

> *we have it in our power to render the negro race extinct in the United States in very short order.*[2913]

In Massachusetts blacks were widely regarded as a cross between a juvenile, a lunatic, and a "retard."[2914] Other Northerners were even less charitable. Famed Harvard scientist Louis Agassiz declared that "the negro race groped in barbarism and never originated a regular organization among themselves."[2915] Agassiz, like his English associate Charles Darwin (who originated the idea of natural selection, or "survival of the fittest"),[2916] believed that blacks were so evolutionarily feeble that once freed from slavery they would eventually "die out" in the U.S.[2917]

Respected Harvard University professor Dr. Louis Agassiz referred to African negroes as a "race groping in barbarism," one that "never originated a regular organization among themselves."

English naturalist Charles Darwin held that blacks were so evolutionarily weak that after their emancipation in America they would simply go extinct. Such views were adopted by millions of people across the northern U.S., and even influenced Yankee scientists.

Thus no Northerners blinked, except a few authentic abolitionists,[2918] when on September 16, 1858, Lincoln made the following remarks during a senatorial debate with rival Stephen A. Douglas at Columbus, Ohio:

> . . . this is the true complexion of all I have ever said in regard to the institution of slavery and the black race. This is the whole of it, and *anything that argues me into his idea of perfect social and political equality with the negro is but a specious and fantastic arrangement of words*, by which a man can prove a horse-chestnut to be a chestnut horse. I will say here, while upon this subject, that *I have no purpose either directly or indirectly to interfere with the institution of slavery in the States where it exists*. I believe *I have no lawful right to do so*, and I have no inclination to do so. *I have no purpose to introduce political and social equality between the white and the black races*. There is a physical difference between the two which, in my judgment, will probably forever forbid their living together upon the footing of perfect equality, and *inasmuch as it becomes a necessity that there must be a difference, I, as well as Judge Douglas, am in favor of the race to which I belong having the superior position. I have never said anything to the contrary* . . . I agree with Judge Douglas, *he [the black man] is not my*

> *equal in many respects—certainly not in color, perhaps not in moral or intellectual endowments.*[2919]

Lincoln preferred the idea of living in a black-free America, and his own words prove it.

What then was the solution to "America's racial problem," as white Northerners referred to the presence of blacks in the U.S.? For Lincoln and many other Yankees there was only one: black colonization, resettling African-Americans in colonies outside the U.S. To this end Lincoln spent years developing his own deportation scheme, one he openly and enthusiastically promoted to both his cabinet members and to the public throughout his entire political career.

As he did whenever the opportunity arose, President Lincoln used his First Annual Message to Congress on December 3, 1861, to promote the idea of deporting blacks, in this case, free blacks:

> It might be well to consider, too, whether the free colored people already in the United States could not, so far as individuals may desire, be included in such colonization.[2920]

As a result of this speech, in 1861 and 1862 the U.S. Congress had $600,000 (about $15 million in today's currency) set aside to aid in Lincoln's colonization plan to send as many free blacks as possible out of the country.[2921]

The first Congressional effort to fund Lincoln's black deportation plan came on April 16, 1862, with the passage of the District of Columbia Act, when $100,000 ($2.4 million in today's currency) was set aside for slaves who were to be freed in Washington, D.C. The second effort came on July 16, 1862, when Congress earmarked$500,000 ($12 million today) to deport slaves whose owners supported the Confederacy. It was on this same day, as we have just seen, that the select committee on Emancipation and Colonization suggested that $20 million ($500 million today) be appropriated to evict all captured slaves to a "home and country" more "congenial" to the "African temperament."[2922]

None of this is surprising when we learn that Lincoln was a rank and file member of the American Colonization Society (ACS),[2923] a popular Yankee organization founded in 1816 in Washington, D.C., by a Northerner, New Jerseyan Reverend Robert Finley.[2924] The stated purpose of the ACS was to make America white from coast to coast[2925] through the governmental purchase of slaves,[2926] the remuneration of slave owners,[2927] and the shipping of both *freed* and *free* blacks "back to their own native land (Africa)," as zealous colonizationist Lincoln so bluntly put it.[2928]

The motivating idea of the ACS was that the freed negro "should be sent where he would never provoke friction with the whites," with Africa being "considered the most desirable place for the realization of this object."[2929] In 1819 the Board of Managers of the ACS issued a statement declaring that their goal was "the happiness of the free people of colour and the reduction of the number of slaves in America."[2930] The actual charter of the ACS states that its object is

> to promote and execute a plan for colonizing, with their consent, the free people of color residing in our country, either in Africa, or such other places as Congress shall deem expedient.[2931]

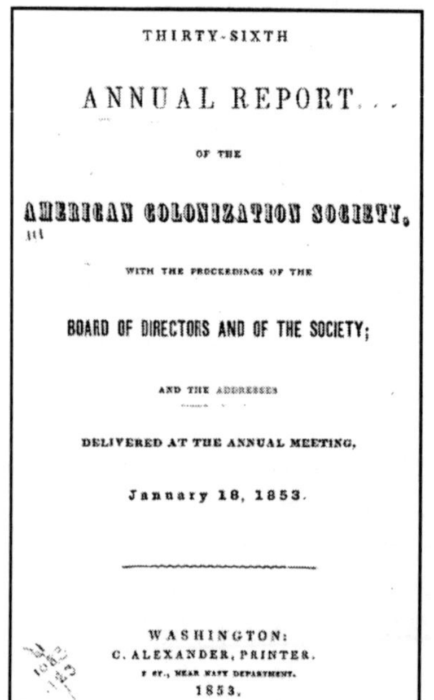

THIRTY-SIXTH

ANNUAL REPORT

OF THE

AMERICAN COLONIZATION SOCIETY,

WITH THE PROCEEDINGS OF THE

BOARD OF DIRECTORS AND OF THE SOCIETY;

AND THE ADDRESSES

DELIVERED AT THE ANNUAL MEETING,

January 18, 1853.

WASHINGTON:
C. ALEXANDER, PRINTER,
F ST., NEAR NAVY DEPARTMENT.
1853.

The cover of the American Colonization Society's 36th Annual Report, dated January 18, 1853, Washington, D.C. It includes proceedings from the Board of Directors of the ACS.

ACS supporter Samuel J. Mills of Connecticut put it this way: "We must save the negroes [through deportation], or the negroes will ruin us,"[2932] a sentiment then widely held across Yankeedom.

In 1837 a number of Yankee ACS state societies established black deportation settlements in Liberia, including Monrovia (founded by the ACS headquarters at Washington, D.C.), Bassa Cove (set up by the New York and Pennsylvania chapters), and Cape Palmas (created by the Maryland chapter).[2933]

Besides Lincoln, other early leaders, officers, and supporters of the ACS included such famed Yankees as New England statesman

Daniel Webster[2934] (after whom the town of Webster, Massachusetts, was named), New Yorker William H. Seward (Lincoln's secretary of state and the man who coordinated the purchase of what is now the state of Alaska), and Marylander Francis Scott Key (author of the U.S. National Anthem, *The Star-Spangled Banner*),[2935] a man considered by some to be a co-founder of the ACS.[2936] Two other men who played a role in the creation of the ACS were Northerner and British emigrant Dr. William Thornton (architectural designer of the U.S. Capitol at Washington, D.C.) and Yankee missionary Samuel John Mills of Connecticut (founder of the American Bible Society).[2937]

Lincoln's secretary of state, William Henry Seward of New York, supporter of the American Colonization Society.

Yankees who served as vice presidents of the ACS included William Phillips of Massachusetts, John E. Howard of Maryland, Robert Ralston of Pennsylvania, John Mason of Washington, D.C., and Reverend Robert Finley, as mentioned, of New Jersey.[2938] Massachusetts Governor Levi Lincoln, Jr. (a relative of Abraham Lincoln) was considered a "friend" of the ACS, as was fellow Bay Stater George Bancroft, U.S. secretary of the navy, and later U.S. minister to the United Kingdom.[2939]

Other famous Yankee supporters (at some point in their lives) of deporting blacks were abolitionists William Lloyd Garrison (founder of the defamatory abolitionist paper *The Liberator*),[2940] New Jersey Governor Joseph Bloomfield (after which Bloomfield County, New Jersey is named),[2941] Horace Greeley (owner of the liberal New York *Tribune*), and Harriet Beecher Stowe (author of the worldwide bestselling antislavery fantasy *Uncle Tom's Cabin*).[2942] New Yorker Gerrit Smith, noted Victorian social reformer, U.S. presidential nominee, and longtime member of the ACS, once said: "I remain an unwavering friend of the Colonization mode of abolishing slavery in the United States."[2943]

Among the many other early backers of black colonization was Senator Rufus King of Massachusetts, who, in 1824, proposed a resolution to have funds set aside to

> aid the emancipation of slaves, within any of the United States, and to aid the removal of such slaves, and the removal of such free persons of color, in any of the said United States . . . to any territory or country without the limits of the United States of America.[2944]

Author of the lyrics of the U.S. National Anthem, *The Star-Spangled Banner*, Francis Scott Key of Maryland, supporter of the American Colonization Society.

The number of well-known Yankees who belonged to the ACS, championed the ACS, or at least condoned the idea of black deportation and colonization, reached many thousands. For the historical record let us list a few additional individuals of note:

- Edward Everett of Massachusetts, president of Harvard University and governor of Massachusetts, after whom Everett, Massachusetts, is named.
- John Maclean, Jr. of New Jersey, president of Princeton University.
- William Alexander Duer of New York, president of Columbia

University.

- Jeremiah Day of Connecticut, president of Yale University.
- Jared Sparks of Connecticut, president of Harvard University.
- Henry Rutgers of New York, Revolutionary War hero after whom Rutgers University is named.
- John Dickinson of Maryland, U.S. congressman after whom Dickinson College is named.
- William Tudor of Massachusetts, state senator and founder of the Massachusetts Historical Society.
- Elisha Whittlesey of Ohio, U.S. representative.
- Theodore Frelinghuysen of New Jersey, U.S. senator.
- Elijah Paine of Vermont, U.S. senator.
- Roger Sherman of Connecticut, U.S. senator.
- Thomas March Clark of Rhode Island, Episcopal bishop.
- Richard Rush of Pennsylvania, U.S. attorney general.
- John Eager Howard of Maryland, governor of Maryland.
- Benjamin Franklin Butler of New York, controversial Union general during Lincoln's War.[2945]

President of Columbia College, later Columbia University, William Alexander Duer of New York, supporter of the American Colonization Society.

President of Harvard University, Jared Sparks of Connecticut, supporter of the American Colonization Society.

Author Early Lee Fox writes that from its inception in 1816 the ACS received nearly unanimous support from states across the North:

> Prior to 1826 the legislatures of . . . Maryland, . . . Ohio, New Jersey, Connecticut, Rhode Island and Indiana had officially approved the colonization project as carried on by the Society. In 1827 Vermont and Kentucky expressed themselves, through their legislatures, favorable to the Society, as did Ohio, and Kentucky again, in 1828; Pennsylvania and Indiana, in 1829; Massachusetts, in 1831; and New York and Maryland, in 1832. The Delaware Legislature likewise gave its approval. The resolution of the Massachusetts Legislature was in the following words:
>
> > "*That the Legislature of Massachusetts view with great interest the efforts made by the American Colonization Society in establishing an asylum on the Coast of Africa for the free people of color of the United States*; and that, in the opinion of this Legislature, it is a subject eminently deserving the attention and aid of Congress, so far as shall be consistent with the powers of Congress, the rights of the several States of the Union, and the rights of the individuals who are the objects of those efforts."

> *The Pennsylvania Legislature declared, "Their removal [that of the free people of color] from among us would not only be beneficial to them, but highly auspicious to the best interests of our country." The Indiana Legislature expressed "unqualified approbation."*[2946]

While the ACS was always popular and well supported in many Northern cities, such as New Haven, Connecticut, Baltimore, Maryland (even the town's Methodist Church endorsed it), and Philadelphia (home of "The Young Men's Colonization Society of Pennsylvania"),[2947] the nation's largest and most enthusiastic ACS chapter was in Boston, Massachusetts, the birthplace of American slavery[2948]—where both antislavery and anti-black sentiment (the two were not mutually exclusive in New England at the time) remained high well into the late 1800s.[2949] It was a U.S. Representative from this very town, Massachusetts pastor Joseph Barker, who at a congressional committee meeting in the late 1700s, argued that

> the United States ought not only to declare all illegally imported Africans free, but . . . convey them safely back to their native country.[2950]

Naturally the Massachusetts legislature took an interest in the idea of an organization dedicated to deporting blacks long before the ACS was formed. As Yankee Dr. William Thornton pointed out, by at least about the year 1788

> *the Americans in New England were desirous of sending all free blacks from that country, and offered ships and every [thing] necessary for their support.*[2951]

According to the "Annual Report of the Board of Managers of the Massachusetts Colonization Society," clergyman Daniel Waldo, its president, along with his sister Elizabeth Waldo, both of Massachusetts, left a total of $22,000 (about $300,000 today) to the ACS in their wills in the 1800s.[2952] The Waldos were relatives of famed New England Transcendentalist Ralph Waldo Emerson—a man who, as we have seen, hated the racially tolerant South,[2953] yet loved the racially intolerant John Brown.[2954] According to this particular New England branch of the ACS, it is:

> Resolved, that the cause of African Colonization is worthy of our earnest and liberal support, on account of its beneficial influence, both on the emigrants themselves, and on the natives of Africa.[2955]

The American Colonization Society issued this one cent token in 1833 for use in its African colony Liberia. The front of the coin (left) shows a freed American slave planting a palm tree in Liberia, with an incoming Yankee ship importing more freedmen and women. The back of the coin (right) displays the organization's name and founding year. The development of Liberia delighted President Lincoln, who was himself not only a devoted benefactor of the colony, but who was at one time an ACS official in Illinois. His ongoing efforts in the cause of black deportation prompted one of his party's liberal members, Massachusetts-born Samuel Clarke Pomeroy, to suggest naming a freedmen's colony in Latin American "Linconia."

In the year 1846 dozens of villages and towns across Massachusetts gave thousands of dollars in donations to the state's chapter of the American Colonization Society, in the hope of helping fund the deportation of freed American slaves to foreign lands. Among these Massachusetts cities were: Amherst, Andover, Attleboro, Auburn, Beverly, Blandford, Bradford, Bridgewater, Brimfield, Brookfield, Byfield, Cabotsville, Cambridge, Canton, Chester, Conway, Dudley, Dunstable, Enfield, Essex, Fairhaven, Foxboro, Framingham, Franklin, Gardner, Georgetown, Gloucester, Granby, Hadley, Harvard, Haverhill, Holden, Holliston, Hopkinton, Leicester, Leominster, Lowell, Lynn, Manchester (By-the-Sea), Mansfield, Marblehead, Medfield, Medway, Middlefield, Milton, New Bedford, Newbury, Newburyport, Northampton, Northbridge, Oxford, Palmer, Paxton, Plymouth, Reading, Rockport, Rowley, Salem, Sharon, Shrewsbury, Southampton, Southbridge, Spencer, Springfield, Stockbridge, Sturbridge, Sudbury,

Sutton, Taunton, Upton, Uxbridge, Walpole, Waltham, Ware, Westboro, Westford, Williamsburg, Woburn, Worcester, and Wrentham.[2956]

Though the Massachusetts chapter of the ACS boasted thousands of annual members during its existence, that same year, 1846, it listed 23 "Life Members" from such towns as Newburyport, Boston, Dedham, Bedford, Ipswich, Worcester, Harvard, Rockport, Manchester, Williamsburg, Medway, Northampton, Uxbridge, Taunton, Granby, and Framingham.[2957] Bay State ACS members wanted slave owners throughout the South

> to know that when they are ready to give up their slaves, we are ready to receive them, if of suitable character, and place them in a better situation than can be found for them in the United States.[2958]

Like the Massachusetts chapter and the rest of its members and supporters, the mother organization, the national ACS, believed that in order to preserve white American culture, all American blacks, both free and emancipated ("freed"), would have to be evicted then resettled outside the U.S., a daft racist notion that enlightened modern blacks have appropriately labeled "Abraham Lincoln's white dream."[2959] Though he would have loved to force the issue, President Lincoln finally agreed that only those who *volunteered* would be thrown out of the country, or "by the mutual consent of the people to be deported," as he put it.[2960] Revealingly, Lincoln, like every other ACS member, seemed unconcerned that the blacks he sent back to Africa would, in all likelihood, be recaptured, reenslaved, and resold back into the brutal indigenous African slave market by native slave catchers and slave dealers!

So enamored was Lincoln with the ACS—at one time headed by his beloved political idol, slave owner Henry Clay[2961]—that he eventually became a leader of the Illinois chapter,[2962] a state whose legislature he personally convinced to finance the deportation of free blacks.[2963]

During his famous February 27, 1860, Cooper Union speech in New York, the soon-to-be Republican presidential nominee brought up, as he so often did, the topic of colonization, hoping to make new converts. Quoting Thomas Jefferson's autobiography,[2964] Lincoln said hopefully:

> In the language of Mr. Jefferson, uttered many years ago, "*It is still in our power to direct the process of emancipation, and deportation, peaceably, and in such slow degrees, as that the evil will wear off insensibly; and their places be . . . filled up by free white laborers.*"[2965]

It was just such racist rhetoric that prompted other ACS supporters to glorify Lincoln. One of these was liberal Kansas senator Samuel C. Pomeroy, a Yankee from Massachusetts, who was so enamored with the president's enthusiastic efforts to deport blacks that he recommended naming an ACS colony in Latin America "Linconia."[2966]

For Lincoln it is clear that colonization served a dual purpose. Not only would it help protect whites from having to compete with freed blacks for jobs, it would also help prevent that most dreaded of all racists' nightmares: "amalgamation," that is, miscegenation, the mixing and interbreeding of the races.[2967] As discussed previously, it was thus that on June 26, 1857, at Springfield, Illinois, anti-miscegenationist Lincoln lectured his Northern audience on the many benefits of "a separation of the races," saying:

> Judge [Stephen] Douglas is especially horrified at the thought of the mixing of blood by the white and black races: agreed for once—a thousand times agreed. . . . . *A separation of the races is the only perfect preventive of amalgamation*; but as an immediate separation is impossible *the next best thing is to keep them apart where they are not already together. . . . statistics show that slavery is the greatest source of amalgamation.*[2968]

And here we find one of the real reasons Lincoln was both antislavery and pro-colonization. According to the Northern president, it was slavery that put whites and blacks in close proximity to one another, inevitably increasing the chances of interracial coupling, one of the greatest taboos to white separatists like Lincoln. Apparently he had spent some time researching the topic for, as he fearfully put it, "statistics show that slavery is the greatest source of amalgamation . . ."[2969]

Not content to let the issue go, during the same speech Lincoln made these stunning comments:

> *I have said that the separation of the races is the only perfect preventive of amalgamation.* I have no right to say all the members of the Republican party [then the Liberal Party] are in favor of this, nor to

say that as a party they are in favor of it. There is nothing in their platform directly on the subject. But I can say *a very large proportion of its members are for it, and that the chief plank in their platform—opposition to the spread of slavery—is most favorable to that separation.*

Such separation, if ever effected at all, must be effected by colonization; and no political party, as such, is now doing anything directly for colonization. Party operations at present only favor or retard colonization incidentally. The enterprise is a difficult one; but "where there is a will there is a way," and *what colonization needs most is a hearty will.* Will springs from the two elements of moral sense and *self-interest. Let us be brought to believe it is morally right, and at the same time favorable to, or at least not against, our interest to transfer the African to his native clime, and we shall find a way to do it, however great the task may be.* The children of Israel, to such numbers as to include four hundred thousand fighting men, went out of Egyptian bondage in a body.[2970]

Lincoln was so obsessed with black colonization that he even discussed the topic of deporting blacks in his eulogy at Henry Clay's funeral on July 6, 1852.

Even in his eulogy to Henry Clay at Clay's funeral on July 6, 1852, Lincoln managed to bring up the topic of colonization, no doubt something many in the audience found crass and improper. Besides preventing an increase in the population of mulattos, or "mongrels," as Lincoln called all mixed-racial, light brown-skinned people (such as Mexicans),[2971] sending blacks back to Africa would have an added benefit, he insensitively noted that day at Springfield, Illinois: that of disseminating Christianity and civilization, with God's blessing, among a primitive and barbaric people. Quoting slave-owner Clay, Lincoln went on to say:

> "*There is a moral fitness in the idea of returning Africa her children,* whose ancestors have been torn from her by the ruthless hand of fraud and violence. Transplanted in a foreign land, they will carry back to their native soil the rich fruits of religion, civilization, law, and liberty. May it not be one of the great designs of the Ruler of the universe . . . thus to transform an original crime, into a signal blessing to that most unfortunate portion of the globe?"[2972]

Lincoln, referring to himself not as one of the "friends of the black man," but as one of the "friends of colonization,"[2973] then called the possibility of successful black deportation a "glorious consummation,"[2974] adding that Clay's

> suggestion of the possible ultimate redemption of the African race and African continent, was made twenty-five years ago. *Every succeeding year has added strength to the hope of its realization.—May it indeed be realized!*[2975]

This type of white racism, which continued in both the North and in the Republican Party (again, the Liberals of Victorian America) until well into the 1870s,[2976] was in fact what delayed the legalization of interracial marriage in the U.S. until 1967, when the ban was finally eliminated by the Supreme Court.[2977] Naturally, such bigotry earned Lincoln the devotion of numerous modern white supremacists, among them: William P. Pickett (author of *The Negro Problem: Abraham Lincoln's Solution*), James K. Vardaman (the popular Mississippi politician known as the "the Great White Chief"), and Thomas Dixon, Jr. (the playwright who inspired D. W. Griffith's controversial film, *The Birth of a Nation*).[2978]

Lincoln left no question as to why he was so passionate about colonization. It would, he said, not only restore "a captive people to their long-lost father-land," but at the same time it would free "our land from the *dangerous presence* of slavery . . ."[2979] And colonization was not just for black servants or newly freed blacks, he asserted. It would also help relieve white society "from the *troublesome presence* of the free negroes . . ." If Clay's dream of colonization could become a reality, he concluded, it would certainly be the most "valuable labor" the U.S. statesman had ever provided his country.[2980]

Lincoln was talking here about a man who had not only been the U.S. secretary of state for four years under President John Quincy Adams, but who had also served as the speaker of the House of Representatives three times between 1811 and 1825. Still Lincoln felt that, if successful, the realization of black colonization would be Clay's greatest contribution to America!

President Jefferson Davis' well educated slaves were not about to be fooled by Lincoln's efforts to deport them to Liberia, which was, after all, nothing more than a convenient dumping ground for a race that Yankees no longer had any use for.

Even Lincoln's District of Columbia Emancipation Act turned out to be for the benefit of, not blacks, but emancipationist-colonizationists like himself:[2981] the bill, issued on April 16, 1862—and then only after a year of intense pressure from abolitionists—finally ended slavery in Washington, D.C. Yet in it the Northern president included a colonization clause pushing for continued efforts to fund the deportation of all Negroes out of the city upon their liberation.[2982] As discussed earlier, that same day Lincoln wrote a letter to the House and Senate applauding them for recognizing his call for the expatriation of the town's newly freed blacks, and for putting money aside for their eventual colonization outside the U.S.[2983]

Educated blacks were understandably furious. After one of Jefferson Davis' servants purchased his freedom, someone advised him to go to Liberia, to which he replied snappily:

> No, I am not so foolish as to trust my life and property in a country that is governed by black men.[2984]

Like black teacher and former Southern servant Booker T. Washington, this was an African-American who had been born in the South, had lived in the South, had labored in the South, and who wanted to be buried in the South.[2985] All perfectly understandable to white Southerners.

Unfortunately for black civil rights, this simple and obvious concept completely escaped most white Northerners who, like Lincoln, wished for nothing less than American apartheid: the geographical separation of the races across the U.S.[2986]

What Lincoln never understood, and what is completely unknown to the average American today, is that the racial segregation he so desperately craved is merely another form of slavery—in this case one known as "collective slavery," which is exactly how apartheid is defined by Anti-Slavery International, the world's oldest international human rights organization.[2987] Thus, it must go down as one of American history's greatest ironies that Lincoln is credited (wrongly) with ending chattel slavery, yet he actually spent his entire adult life promoting another form of the institution, collective slavery (that is, apartheid), one just as onerous, degrading, and exploitative.

While volumes could be written about our sixteenth president's efforts to deport African-Americans, let us look at just one more example of the enthusiasm with which he approached this subject.

On August 14, 1862, almost a year-and-a-half into his war, Lincoln requested that a group of five blacks meet with him at the White House. They were the first *free* African-Americans to ever enter those hallowed halls (out of necessity *enslaved* blacks had, of course, been allowed access). But the event was not something that pro-North writers, liberal educators, progressive Yankees, and New South scallywags would want recorded in the pages of American history[2988]—which is precisely why it is left out of our history books.

The fact that these five black men were hand-picked by Reverend James Mitchell, Lincoln's commissioner of *emigration*, hints at the enormous social fiasco Lincoln was about to create, surely the worst to ever occur inside the White House.

None of the black men who were hurriedly ushered into the president's office that day were well-known. In fact, four of them were lowly "contrabands" (captured Southern slaves), as Lincoln and other Northerners derogatorily referred to them.[2989] The awestruck, passive group had been selected purposefully to avoid a "scene." For as it turns out, Lincoln wanted a captive uneducated audience that would sit and listen to a racist monologue on the advantages of black deportation (colonization), not one that would engage him in an intellectual debate about slavery.[2990]

As the colored delegation sat in stunned silence, Lincoln removed a crumbled up piece of paper from inside his large stovepipe hat. On it was a speech, written in hastily scrawled words. In his thin high voice, Lincoln began to read aloud to the men gathered before him. What follows is an exact chronicle of the scene from Lincoln's personal friends and official biographers, John G. Nicolay and John Hay:

> August 14, 1862. — Address On Colonization To A Deputation Of Colored Men.
>
> Washington, Thursday, August 14, 1862.
>
> This afternoon the President of the United States gave an audience to a committee of colored men at the White House. They were introduced by Rev. J. [James] Mitchell, Commissioner of Emigration. E. M. Thomas, the chairman, remarked that they were there by invitation to hear what the Executive had to say to them.
>
> Having all been seated, *the President, after a few preliminary observations, informed them that a sum of money had been appropriated by Congress, and placed at his disposition, for the purpose of aiding the colonization in some country of the people, or a portion of them, of African descent, thereby making it his duty, as it had for a long time been his inclination, to favor that cause.* And why, he asked, should the people of your race be colonized, and where? Why should they leave this country? This is, perhaps, the first question for proper consideration. *You and we are different races. We have between us a broader difference than exists between almost any other two races. Whether*

it is right or wrong I need not discuss; but this physical difference is a great disadvantage to us both, as I think. Your race suffer very greatly, many of them, by living among us, while ours suffer from your presence. In a word, we suffer on each side. If this is admitted, it affords a reason, at least, why we should be separated. You here are freemen, I suppose?

A voice: Yes, sir.

The President: Perhaps you have long been free, or all your lives. Your race is suffering, in my judgment, the greatest wrong inflicted on any people. But even when you cease to be slaves, you are yet far removed from being placed on an equality with the white race. You are cut off from many of the advantages which the other race enjoys. The aspiration of men is to enjoy equality with the best when free, but *on this broad continent not a single man of your race is made the equal of a single man of ours. Go where you are treated the best, and the ban is still upon you.* I do not propose to discuss this, but to present it as a fact with which we have to deal. I cannot alter it if I would. It is a fact about which we all think and feel alike, I and you. We look to our condition. Owing to the existence of the two races on this continent, I need not recount to you the effects upon white men, growing out of the institution of slavery.

I believe in its general evil effects on the white race. See our present condition—the country engaged in war—our white men cutting one another's throats—none knowing how far it will extend—and then consider what we know to be the truth. But for your race among us there could not be war, although *many men engaged on either side do not care for you one way or the other.* Nevertheless, I repeat, without the institution of slavery, and the colored race as a basis, the war could not have an existence. *It is better for us both, therefore, to be separated.* I know that there are free men among you who, even if they could better their condition, are not as much inclined to go out of the country as those who, being slaves, could obtain their freedom on this condition. I suppose one of the principal difficulties in the way of colonization is that the free colored man cannot see that his comfort would be advanced by it. *You may believe that you can live in Washington, or elsewhere in the United States, the remainder of your life as easily, perhaps more so, than you can in any foreign country; and hence you may come to the conclusion that you have nothing to do with the idea of going to a foreign country.*

This is (I speak in no unkind sense) an extremely selfish view of the case. You ought to do something to help those who are not so fortunate as yourselves. There is an unwillingness on the part of our people, harsh as it may be, for you free colored people to remain with us. Now, if you could give a start to the white people, you would open a wide door for many to be made free. If we deal with those who are not free at the beginning, and whose intellects are clouded by slavery, we have very poor material to start with. *If intelligent colored men, such as are before me, would move in this matter, much might be accomplished. It is exceedingly important that we have [black] men at the beginning capable of thinking as white men, and not those who have been systematically oppressed.* There is much to encourage you. *For the sake of your race you should sacrifice something of your present comfort for the purpose of being as grand in that respect as the white people.* It is a cheering thought throughout life, that something can be done to ameliorate the condition of those who have been subject to the hard usages of the world. It is difficult to make a man miserable while he feels he is worthy of himself and claims kindred to the great God who made him. In the American Revolutionary war sacrifices were made by men engaged in it, but they were cheered by the future. General Washington himself endured greater physical hardships than if he had remained a British subject, yet he was a happy man because he was engaged in benefiting his race, in doing something for the children of his neighbors, having none of his own.

The colony of *Liberia* has been in existence a long time. In a certain sense it is a success. The old President of Liberia, [Joseph Jenkins] Roberts, has just been with me—the first time I ever saw him. He says they have within the bounds of that colony between three and four hundred thousand people, or more than in some of our old States, such as Rhode Island or Delaware, or in some of our newer States, and less than in some of our larger ones. They are not all American colonists or their descendants. Something less than 12,000 have been sent thither from this country. Many of the original settlers have died; yet, like people elsewhere, their offspring outnumber those deceased. *The question is, if the colored people are persuaded to go anywhere, why not there?*

One reason for unwillingness to do so is that some of you would rather remain within reach of the country of your nativity. I do not know how much attachment you may have toward our race. It does not strike me that you have the greatest reason to love them. But still you are attached to them, at all events.

The place I am thinking about for a colony is in Central America. It is nearer to us than Liberia—not much more than one fourth as far as Liberia, and within seven days' run by steamers. Unlike Liberia, it is a great line of travel—it is a highway. The country is a very excellent one for any people, and with great natural resources and advantages, and especially because of the similarity of climate with your native soil, thus being suited to your physical condition. The particular place I have in view is to be a great highway from the Atlantic or Caribbean Sea to the Pacific Ocean, and this particular place has all the advantages for a colony. On both sides there are harbors—among the finest in the world. Again, there is evidence of very rich coal-mines. A certain amount of coal is valuable in any country. Why I attach so much importance to coal is, it will afford an opportunity to the inhabitants for immediate employment till they get ready to settle permanently in their homes. If you take colonists where there is no good landing, there is a bad show; and so where there is nothing to cultivate and of which to make a farm. But if something is started so that you can get your daily bread as soon as you reach there, it is a great advantage. Coal land is the best thing I know of with which to commence an enterprise.

To return—you have been talked to upon this subject, and told that a speculation is intended by gentlemen who have an interest in the country, including the coal-mines. We have been mistaken all our lives if we do not know whites, as well as blacks, look to their self-interest. Unless among those deficient of intellect, everybody you trade with makes something. You meet with these things here and everywhere. If such persons have what will be an advantage to them, the question is, whether it cannot be made of advantage to you? You are intelligent, and know that success does not so much depend on external help as on self-reliance. Much, therefore, depends upon yourselves. As to the coal-mines, I think I see the means available for your self-reliance. *I shall, if I get a sufficient number of you engaged, have provision made that you shall not be wronged. If you will engage in the enterprise, I will spend some of the money intrusted to me. I am not sure you will succeed. The government may lose the money, but we cannot succeed unless we try; and we think, with care, we can succeed. The political affairs in Central America are not in quite as satisfactory a condition as I wish. There are contending factions in that quarter; but, it is true, all the factions are agreed alike on the subject of colonization, and want it, and are more generous than we are here.*

To your colored race they have no objection. I would endeavor to have you made the equals, and have the best assurance that you should be, the equals of the best.

The practical thing I want to ascertain is, whether I can get a number of able-bodied men, with their wives and children, who are willing to go when I present evidence of encouragement and protection. Could I get a hundred tolerably intelligent men, with their wives and children, and able to "cut their own fodder," so to speak? Can I have fifty? If I could find twenty-five able-bodied men, with a mixture of women and children,—good things in the family relation, I think,— I could make a successful commencement. I want you to let me know whether this can be done or not. This is the practical part of my wish to see you. These are subjects of very great importance—worthy of a month's study, instead of a speech delivered in an hour. *I ask you, then, to consider seriously, not pertaining to yourselves merely, nor for your race and ours for the present time, but as one of the things, if successfully managed, for the good of mankind*—not confined to the present generation, but as

From age to age descends the lay
To millions yet to be,
Till far its echoes roll away Into eternity.

The above is merely given as the substance of the President's remarks.

The chairman of the delegation briefly replied that they would hold a consultation, and in a short time give an answer.

The President said: Take your full time—no hurry at all.

The delegation then withdrew.[2991]

The black committee did take its "full time." Lincoln waited and waited, but did not receive an immediate answer to his question concerning how many African-Americans would allow themselves to be shipped to Central America, or "back to Africa." Unbeknownst to the "Great Emancipator," there was good reason for this: after being forcefully urged to leave their lifelong homes for strange foreign lands, after being called "extremely selfish" if they did not consider his colonization plan, and after being told to "think like white men" in order to come to the proper conclusion, the five black delegates were in a state of humiliation, confusion, anger, and shock, and needed time to formulate a response!

On August 14, 1862, big government Liberal Lincoln initiated the greatest social debacle that has ever taken place in the White House: he invited a group of free blacks into his office to ask them if he could deport them, along with their families and friends, to foreign colonies in order to make life easier for Northern whites. Naturally, the incident caused an uproar among abolitionists and educated blacks, who forcefully denounced the president for his stupidity and racial insensitivity—then asked him to mind his own business. Lincoln, of course, completely ignored the colossal backlash, continuing his pointless campaign to colonize American blacks. You will never read about this racist scandal in any conventional history book.

A few days later their reply finally arrived at the White

House. The missive was brief and to the point. Furious, the black committee members scolded Lincoln for campaigning for the deportation of America's colored people, and asked him to please mind his own business![2992]

Lincoln must have scratched his head in bewilderment. He never grasped what every black and nearly every white Southerner understood instinctively: if America was ever to rid herself of color prejudice, Lincoln's black colonization plans were certainly not the "solution." In fact, it was obvious to nearly everyone that the deportation of blacks would only aggravate the problem;[2993] obvious to everyone, that is, except Lincoln. But then again, he was never truly interested in working toward a racist-free, color-blind society.

When educated black leaders heard about the White House conference they were enraged. Easily seeing through the charade, Frederick Douglass, prominent abolitionist, former Northern slave, and Lincoln's confidant, publicly denounced the president for his white racial pride, disdain for blacks, and rank dishonesty.[2994] Furthermore, wrote a fuming Douglass in his newspaper:

> The tone of frankness and benevolence which he assumes in his speech to the colored committee is too thin a mask not to be seen through. *The genuine spark of humanity is missing* in it. It expresses merely the desire to get rid of them . . .[2995]

A New Jersey newspaper printed the response of an exasperated black citizen. In lambasting the "meddlesome, impudent" president, he asked Lincoln to remember that in God's eyes there is only one race on earth: the human race.[2996] But being a devout atheist or "infidel," as he termed it, Lincoln never understood, or believed, this simple but powerful truth.[2997]

Most American blacks had been against colonization from the beginning, for they knew that it was not for their benefit, but for the benefit of its white patrons. In 1835, for example, Yankee Dr. Ethan Allen Andrews was told by an ACS member in Maryland that "no man will be viewed by the colored people as their friend, who advocates the cause of colonization."[2998] After hearing what Lincoln had told the committee at the Executive Mansion, African-Americans across the country were indeed disgusted.

And they had every right to be, for by 1862 nearly all blacks in both the U.S. and the C.S. were native born Americans. Most were fourth and fifth generation Americans[2999]—some were as much as sixth and seventh generation Americans, or more (though only briefly, blacks, for example, were in the area now known as Virginia by 1526).[3000] A great many whites, however, were not more than first, second, or third generation Americans.

In light of this, which race was more American, the white or the black one? blacks rightly asked. After all by 1860, 99 percent of all blacks were native born Americans, a larger percentage than for whites.[3001]

We already know how Lincoln would have answered this question. The fact remained that the vast majority of African-Americans had no intention of taking the president up on his offer to be shipped to a foreign land, for it meant leaving behind their loved ones (both black and white), their homes and farms, and their family cemeteries, filled with ancestors dating back to the early 1600s, and in some cases, even beyond.

Black civil rights leader and former Northern slave Frederick Douglass blasted Lincoln for his apathy and callousness toward African-Americans, particularly for asking to deport the black committee that visited him at the White House on August 14, 1862. As for Lincoln's overall racial policy toward blacks, "the genuine spark of humanity is missing in it," a furious Douglass later remarked.

Angered by Lincoln's endless and insensitive promotion of colonization, blacks from Long Island, New York, put their foot down, stating publicly:

> This is our native country; we have as strong attachment naturally to our native hills, valleys, plains, luxuriant forests, flowing streams, mighty rivers and lofty mountains, as any other people.[3002]

Taking a spiritual approach, a group of black men from Pennsylvania wrote up "An Appeal From the Colored Men of Philadelphia to the President of the United States." It read:

> We can find nothing in the religion of our Lord and Master teaching us that color is the standard by which He judges His creatures, either in this life or in the life to come. . . . We ask, that by the standard of justice and humanity we may be weighed, and that men shall not longer be measured by their stature or color.[3003]

On August 28, 1862, just two weeks after Lincoln's racial debacle at the White House, African-American Robert Purvis spoke for nearly all American blacks in an open letter to the president:

> *The children of the black man have enriched the soil by their tears, and sweat, and blood. Sir, we were born here, and here we choose to remain. For twenty years we were goaded and harassed by systematic efforts to make us colonize. We were coaxed and mobbed, and mobbed and coaxed, but we refused to budge. We planted ourselves upon our inalienable rights, and were proof against all the efforts that were made to expatriate us.* For the last fifteen years we have enjoyed comparative quiet. Now again the malign project is broached, and again, as before, in the name of humanity are we invited to leave.
>
> *In God's name what good do you expect to accomplish by such a course? If you will not let our brethren in bonds go free, if you will not let us, as did our fathers, share in the privileges of the government, if you will not let us even help fight the battles of the country, in Heaven's name, at least, let us alone.* Is that too great a boon to ask of your magnanimity?
>
> *I elect to stay on the soil on which I was born, and on the plot of ground which I have fairly bought and honestly paid for. Don't advise me to leave, and don't add insult to injury by telling me it's for my own good; of that I am to be the judge. It is in vain that you talk to me about the 'two races,' and their 'mutual antagonism.' In the matter of rights there is but one race, and that is the human race.* 'God has made of one blood all nations to dwell on all the face of the earth' [Acts 17:26]. *And it is not true that there is a mutual antagonism between the white and colored people of this community. You may antagonize us, but we do not antagonize you. You may hate us, but we do not hate you.*[3004]

All such "appeals" were forwarded directly to the president. If he ever read any of them, no one would have known. For despite them he continued to pursue his plan to deport all blacks out of the U.S. as vigorously as ever.

In 1921 Charles Manly Melden, a former slave, gave a number of reasons why black colonization would never work, two of which follow:

> 1) *It is a physical impossibility. One who speaks of deporting the colored race scarcely can realize what a stupendous undertaking it would be to tear up twelve million people, transport them across continents and oceans, and settle them in a new land.* Russia was defeated by Japan because she could not send troops and supplies fast enough across the Siberian wastes. Great Britain found the task of conquering the Boers made more difficult by the long distances her armies had to travel. America found it no easy task to put two million soldiers in France. Where would the ships be found to carry these multitudes of colored people? If Secretary Daniels's estimate of five tons to a man is correct, it would require fifty million tons of shipping. Where would this be found? Who would pay the expense? It took $150,000,000 to get the Japanese army back to its island home after the Russian War. The Jews interested in resettling Palestine figure that it would cost $250,000,000 to move one million people—a low enough estimate. Multiply this by twelve and the miles to be covered by a larger number, and *the cost of moving the Negroes from America to Africa is seen to be unthinkable.*
>
> 2) *The Negro is not willing to go. Neither the most earnest advocate of deportation nor the most inveterate enemy of the Negro would suggest exiling him without his consent. This he will never give. Why should he? This is his home, his native land.* There has been no legal importation of slaves since 1808, one hundred and thirteen years ago. *Every Negro has an American history of three generations, nearly four. His roots run deeper into American soil than those of a majority of his fellow citizens who claim to be to the manner born. This is the only home that he has ever known, the only one he wishes to know. He has built himself into its civilization and is a part of its history. He has won his title as an American by his centuries of toil, by his patriotic devotion sealed with his blood shed on many a battlefield, by his tears and his prayers.*
>
> This nation has no more loyal sons than the Negroes. The *Times-Picayune*, New Orleans, recently said: "The South is loyal to the core, despite the utmost efforts of the Kaiser's emissaries. And whatever may be the Negro's faults, the dream of dual allegiance is not among them. Poor as he is, no amount of foreign gold tempts him to treason against the flag under which he was born; I. W. W. ["Industrial Workers of the World," an international socialistic labor union] vainly breathes its doctrines

into his ear. This fidelity will be more and more clearly recognized as the war proceeds and America is summoned to make sacrifices on a grander and grander scale." I have elsewhere spoken of the Negro as a patriot in times of storm and stress, and need not enlarge upon the subject here. *Suffice it to say that the home of the American Negro is America. Here he was born, here he has lived and worked, and here he will stay.*[3005]

In his memoirs Union General Benjamin Franklin Butler disclosed what no pro-North advocate wants you to know: right up to the last day of his life President Lincoln supported the goals of the American Colonization Society, and continued his personal crusade to have blacks deported to foreign lands. There will never be peace in America "unless we can get rid of the negroes," Lincoln told Butler at a private meeting just days before his assassination. The Yankee officer replied by offering up his own idea: send them all to a colony in Panama. Lincoln agreed, saying: "There is meat in that, General Butler; there is meat in that."

If Lincoln was aware of any of this type of thinking, he never let on. Instead, he continued to pound home his views on the deportation of African-Americans. His March 12, 1864, "Message to the Senate," for example, was devoted solely to the idea of ridding the U.S. of its black citizens:

> To the Senate of the United States: In obedience to the resolution of the Senate of the 28th of January last, I communicate herewith a report, with accompanying papers from the Secretary of the Interior, *showing what portion of the appropriations for the colonization of persons of African descent has been expended, and the several steps which have been taken for the execution of the acts of Congress on that subject.* Abraham Lincoln.[3006]

On December 6, 1864, during his Fourth Annual Message to Congress, Lincoln brought up Liberia again. This time it was to suggest stopping the slave trade there. Not to abolish the evils of slavery, but so that no more African slaves would be exported to the U.S. After all, Liberia was the very country that he wanted to deport American blacks to. He then asserts, as we will recall, that Liberia will "derive new vigor from American influence." Not from ending slavery there, but from the influx of thousands of deported African-Americans he planned on sending to the colony. Said Lincoln:

> Official correspondence has been freely opened with Liberia, and it gives us a pleasing view of social and political progress in that republic. *It may be expected to derive new vigor from American influence, improved by the rapid disappearance of slavery in the United States.*
>
> I solicit your authority to furnish to the republic a gunboat, at moderate cost, to be reimbursed to the United States by instalments. *Such a vessel is needed for the safety of that State against the native African races*, and in Liberian hands it would be more effective in arresting the African slave-trade than a squadron in our own hands. The possession of the least organized naval force would stimulate a generous ambition in the republic, and the confidence which we should manifest by furnishing *it would win forbearance and favor toward the colony from all civilized nations.*[3007]

Contrary to Yankee myth, Lincoln never abandoned his obsession with exiling all blacks from the U.S. In fact, he lobbied feverishly for colonization right up to the day he died, two years after issuing the Emancipation Proclamation, as Yankee General Benjamin "the Beast" Butler attests. According to Butler, in April 1865, just days before Lincoln was assassinated by Northerner John Wilkes Booth, the president called the general to the White House to discuss the practicalities of black expatriation.[3008] Of the meeting Butler writes:

A conversation was held between us after the negotiations had failed at Hampton Roads [February 3, 1865], and in the course of the conversation he [Lincoln] said to me: —

'But what shall we do with the negroes after they are free? I can hardly believe that the South and North can live in peace, unless we can get rid of the negroes. Certainly they cannot if we don't get rid of the negroes whom we have armed and disciplined and who have fought with us, to the amount, I believe of some one hundred and fifty thousand men. I believe that it would be better to export them all to some fertile country with a good climate, which they could have to themselves.

'You have been a staunch friend of the race from the time you first advised me to enlist them at New Orleans. You have had a good deal of experience in moving bodies of men by water,—your movement up the James was a magnificent one. Now we shall have no use for our very large navy; what, then, are our difficulties in sending all the blacks away?'[3009]

Butler responded by discussing his own idea of how to "send all the blacks away." The solution was simple: settle a colony for them in the Isthmus of Darien (modern Panama). To this Lincoln agreed, replying: "There is meat in that, General Butler; there is meat in that."[3010]

In 1922 historian J. G. de Roulhac Hamilton put it like this:

Lincoln's belief in colonization of the negro as a practical solution of the question never faltered. It was a major policy of his during the war in connection with emancipation.[3011]

Of this distasteful aspect of Lincoln's political career, in 1919 Charles H. Wesley wrote:

From the earliest period of his public life it is easily discernable that Abraham Lincoln was an ardent believer and supporter of the colonization idea. It was his plan not only to emancipate the Negro, but to colonize him in some foreign land. His views were presented not only to interested men of the white race, but to persons of color as well. As may have been expected, the plan for colonization failed, both because in principle such a plan would have been a great injustice to the newly emancipated race, and in practice it would have proved an impracticable and unsuccessful solution of the so-called race problem.[3012]

Emancipation first. Colonization second. This was Lincoln's plan for blacks from the beginning to the very end of his life. Had he survived Booth's attack, there is no question that he would have done everything in his power to fulfill the second half of his program. Thus it was, in great part, Booth who finally freed American blacks, not Abraham Lincoln. For the stark reality is that African-Americans, whether enslaved or free, would have never been completely liberated while Lincoln was alive—and indeed they were not.[3013] Booth's bullet was the true "Great Emancipator."[3014]

Lincoln's entire mad colonization scheme was eventually tossed out after his death, not only due to lack of support and interest (the average income of the ACS for the first six years of its existence was a mere $3,276 a year),[3015] but more importantly, as Melden pointed out in 1921, because of the enormous costs and logistical complications that would have been involved.[3016] Indeed, it was because of these very impediments that in the first decade after the formation of the American Colonization Society in 1816, only 200 slaves were able to be freed and deported, and not more than 4,000 by 1860.[3017]

Southern icon Confederate General Nathan Bedford Forrest is widely criticized by the uninformed for being a "racist." But it was Forrest who, after the War, repeatedly called for *importing* blacks into the country. It was Lincoln who repeatedly called for *deporting* blacks out of the country. Yet it is Lincoln and not Forrest who anti-South advocates consider a "friend of the black man." The pro-North version of the Civil War simply does not stand up to the facts. Revisionist history never does.

During one ten-year period, between 1820 and 1830, for example, a mere 356 emancipated slaves were evicted and exiled from Northern states under the auspices of the ACS: one from Massachusetts, 4 from Washington, D.C., 32 from Rhode Island, 57 from New York, and 63 from Pennsylvania.[3018]

Nearly everybody seemed to be aware of the numerous obstacles involved in ridding the U.S. of every last black citizen. Everyone except our sixteenth president.

Just as bizarre, while he was alive, the man who longed so desperately for American apartheid, seemed completely oblivious of the bold fact that whites and blacks could indeed live together, peacefully, harmoniously, even affectionately. One hundred largely quiet years of Southern slavery, whatever one thought of it at the time, had proven this for all who had eyes to see.[3019]

Blacks in the U.S. would never have been completely free while colonizationist Lincoln was alive. This is precisely why full and legal emancipation did not come until eight months after his death, with the passage of the Thirteenth Amendment in December 1865. This makes John Wilkes Booth the true "Great Emancipator," for it was his bullet that finally opened the door of liberty for all African-Americans, both "free" and bonded.

But Lincoln did not view blacks and whites as equals, therefore he could not perceive what was plain to everyone else, particularly Southerners, most of whom had no use for colonization and actually campaigned against it.[3020] After the War one famous Southerner, Confederate hero General Nathan Bedford Forrest, called for the repopulation of Dixie with both freedmen *and* new black immigrants from Africa.[3021]

Lincoln would not have been happy with such ideas. But he *would* have been happy to know that the Yankee-founded American Colonization Society flourished for an astounding 146 years, finally only disbanding due to lack of support in 1963.[3022]

WHAT YOU WERE TAUGHT: Lincoln's primary goal in life was to abolish slavery.

THE TRUTH: Lincoln always did what was most politically expedient at the moment,[3023] a trait for which he was roundly criticized,[3024] even by members of his own party and constituency. However, there was one topic on which he never wavered: slavery. But contrary to Yankee myth, Lincoln's number one goal when it came to slavery was never to totally eliminate it. It was merely to *limit* its growth, as he himself said on countless occasions.

On December 22, 1860, in a letter to Southerner and soon-to-be Confederate Vice President Alexander H. Stephens, Lincoln wrote: "You think slavery . . . ought to be extended; while we think it . . . ought to be restricted." "Honest Abe," for once being completely honest, ended his letter to Stephens with this sensational statement: This is the "only substantial difference between us."[3025]

Just a few months later, on March 4, 1861, he would repeat the same sentiment almost word for word in his First Inaugural Address:

> One section of our country believes slavery . . . ought to be extended, while the other believes it . . . ought not . . . be extended. This is the only substantial dispute.[3026]

Thus, just prior to the War, Lincoln held that the only real difference between the South's view of slavery and the North's was that the former wanted to allow it to spread (mainly into the new Western Territories, eventually to become America's Western states), while the latter wanted to contain it where it already existed (that is, mainly in the South). No mention of emancipation or abolition. Just limitation.

Six years earlier, in his debate with Stephen A. Douglas on October 16, 1854, at Peoria, Illinois, Lincoln outlined his reasons for wanting to restrict, not end, slavery:

> Whether slavery shall go into Nebraska, or other new Territories, is not a matter of exclusive concern to the people who may go there. The whole nation is interested that the best use shall be made of these Territories. *We want them for homes of free white people. This they cannot be, to any considerable extent, if slavery shall be planted within them. Slave States are places for poor white people to remove from, not to remove to. New free States are the places for poor people to go to, and better their condition. For this use the nation needs these Territories.*[3027]

Four years later, on October 15, 1858, at Alton, Illinois, in his seventh and final joint debate with Douglas, Lincoln reasserted his views on the matter, this time even more vigorously:

> Now, irrespective of the moral aspect of this question as to whether there is a right or wrong in enslaving a negro, *I am still in favor of our*

new Territories being in such a condition that white men may find a home—may find some spot where they can better their condition—where they can settle upon new soil, and better their condition in life. I am in favor of this not merely (I must say it here as I have elsewhere) for our own people [that is, whites] who are born amongst us, but as an outlet for free white people everywhere, the world over—in which Hans, and Baptiste, and Patrick, and all other men from all the world, may find new homes and better their condition in life.[3028]

As he declared in a speech on June 26, 1857, the deportation of blacks is the only way to prevent whites from having to live in close association with them. But,

as an *immediate* separation is impossible the next best thing is to *keep them apart where they are not already together.*[3029]

Liberal Illinois Senator Lyman Trumbull of Connecticut fully agreed with Lincoln that it was more important to contain slavery than abolish it. To this end the newly named Liberal Party, the "Republican Party," was convinced that the still largely undeveloped Western Territories should remain "as white as New England." Trumbull left no doubt as to where Lincoln and the Republicans stood on the matter: ours is "the white man's party," he declared. His boss concurred. "If there was a necessary conflict between the white man and the negro, I should be for the white man," Lincoln once proudly stated publicly.

Thus, even if his colonization plan did not work out, he knew of other ways of "keeping whites and blacks apart where they are not already together."

Limiting the spread of slavery into the North was important to Lincoln and other Yankee racists for a number of reasons, some of which we have already discussed. Here is another. By forcing slavery to stay in the South they believed that it would also serve as an ideal method of "race control": keeping blacks in bondage in Dixie meant that Northerners need not worry about a "flood of darkies" coming over the Mason-Dixon Line any time soon, with whites "tied down and helpless, and run over like sheep," as Lincoln bluntly put it.[3030] With slavery confined to the South, Yanks could continue to promote antislavery views without fear of having to actually deal with the "unthinkable horror" of how to handle 3.5 million newly freed, hungry, homeless, and jobless blacks, many of them illiterate, armed, and angry.

This is why for Lincoln the issue was never about permanent and total emancipation. Rather it was about containing the spread of slavery so that racist whites like himself would not have to intermingle with blacks.[3031] "If we do not let them [blacks] get together in the [Western] Territories," he said publicly on July 10, 1858, "they won't mix [with whites] there."[3032]

Congressman David Wilmot of Pennsylvania, the author of the 1846 Wilmot Proviso (which sought to keep slavery from spreading West) and later a member of Lincoln's Liberal Party, considered it his special mission to resist Yankee abolitionists. Like Lincoln, Wilmot believed that America was meant for whites only, and that slavery was a barrier to that goal. On the debate over whether the "peculiar institution" should be abolished or simply contained in the South, Wilmot said: "I have no squeamish sensitiveness upon the subject of slavery, no morbid sympathy for the slave. I plead the cause and the rights of white freemen. I would preserve to free white labor a fair country, a rich inheritance, where the sons of toil, of my own race and own color, can live without the disgrace which association with negro slavery brings upon free labor."

More specifically, as U.S. President Woodrow Wilson writes, in Lincoln's mind it was not a question of slavery continuing in the South or anywhere else. It was a question of keeping it out of the newly developing Western Territories.[3033] On this issue in particular Lincoln had the "almost unanimous" support of the North, nearly all of whose inhabitants agreed with the president that the territories should remain "as white as New England."[3034] One of Lincoln's own senators, Lyman Trumbull, summed up the president's feelings on the matter perfectly when he referred to their political party as "the white man's party."[3035]

Lincoln was not the first to want to prevent the spread of slavery because, as his group asserted, it would both harm and compete with white society. In fact, he was merely following in the footsteps of a long list of Northerners who had preceded him.

Years before, in 1846, Northern Representative David Wilmot of Pennsylvania, introduced his Wilmot Proviso to try and prevent the spread of slavery into Western lands acquired from Mexico in the Mexican-American War (1846-1848). His proposition, later known as the "free-soil" position, was not for the sake of blacks, however, as Northern historians insist. It was for the sake of whites.[3036]

We will note here that the Free-Soilers, a short-lived coalition party formed in New York in 1848, were not abolitionists demanding free land giveaways from the government, as Yankee propaganda has always portrayed them. To Free-Soilers the term "free-soil" actually meant "soil that is free of black people."[3037] For their objection to slavery was not due to a sympathy for blacks, but a sympathy for their own race: they did not want African-Americans settling in the Western Territories where they would compete with whites for jobs and land.[3038]

Free-Soilers never tried to hide what was at the heart of the matter: white racism. They simply wanted their part of the U.S. (principally the Western states and territories) to remain "free of negroes." Little wonder that they had almost unanimous support across the largely anti-abolitionist, anti-black, pro-colonizationist North.[3039] Wilmot himself affirmed:

> *I have no squeamish sensitiveness upon the subject of slavery, no morbid sympathy for the slave. I plead the cause and the rights of white freemen. I would preserve to free white labor a fair country, a rich inheritance, where the sons of toil, of my own race and own color, can live without the disgrace*

> *which association with negro slavery brings upon free labor.* I stand for the inviolability of free territory. It shall remain free, so far as my voice or vote can aid in the preservation of its free character. . . . *The white laborer of the North claims your service; he demands that you stand firm to his interests and his rights, that you preserve the future homes of his children, on the distant shores of the Pacific, from the degradation and dishonor of negro servitude. Where the negro slave labors, the free white man cannot labor by his side without sharing in his degradation and disgrace.*[3040]

Wilmot, who once proudly commented that he had spent much of his adult life (like Lincoln) fighting against Northern Abolitionists,[3041] later remarked to a colleague:

> By God, sir, men born and nursed of white women are not going to be ruled by men who were brought up on the milk of some damn Negro wench![3042]

Lincoln, a lifelong supporter and one-time member of the American Colonization Society, could not have agreed more.

If blacks would not go to Liberia voluntarily, Northerners often forced them to under the threat of physical violence, as this old illustration shows. In 1834 Southern minister Robert Jefferson Breckinridge watched as agents of the Yankee-founded American Colonization Society "sent out two shiploads of vagabonds [freed slaves] that were coerced away as truly as if it had been done with the cartwhip." That same year New York businessman Thomas C. Brown said: "I am acquainted with several [former slaves], who informed me that they received several hundred lashes to make them willing to go [to Liberia]" An eyewitness account from 1836 informs us that on one occasion, when a Northern ACS agent was attempting to force 65 freed Southern blacks to leave for Liberia, 22 of them escaped at Pittsburgh, Pennsylvania, and in New York City. The attitude of the majority of Northerners concerning African-Americans and black colonization was summed up on January 20, 1836, by New York Reverend T. Spicer of the Troy Methodist Conference: "When emancipated, the slaves should be colonized in Africa, or somewhere else, whether they be willing or not."

On September 15, 1858, at one of the Lincoln-Douglas Debates, Lincoln shared one of his many ideas for preventing a tidal wave of blacks from coming North and mixing with whites: corralling African-Americans in their own all-black state. After reading a quote by newspaper editor Z. B. Mayo of DeKalb County, Illinois, he appended his own comment (in italics):

> [Quoting Mayo] "Our opinion is that it would be best for all concerned to have the colored population in a State by themselves." *In this I agree with him* [Lincoln's comment].[3043]

In his 1921 book *From Slave to Citizen*, former slave Charles Manly Melden commented on this absurd racist plan; that is, the "Organization of a Negro State":

> It has been proposed to set apart a certain territory and assemble the Negroes there and leave them to their own devices. This plan is open to most of the objections to [black deportation] . . . besides having some of its own. Even its most eloquent and persistent advocate, [Atlanta journalist] John Temple Graves, has seen its futility and has abandoned it. All such suggested solutions of the Negro problem may be dismissed as impracticable. They are By-Ways. They lead only to the entanglements and bewilderments of a political and social wilderness. Not the House of the Interpreter, but the Prison of Giant Despair is the fate of those who pursue them.[3044]

The Abraham Lincoln who publicly supported the concept of an all-black state is the same one, the so-called "Great Emancipator," who made the following comments:

> *[I give] the most solemn pledge that I will to the very last stand by the law of this State, which forbids the marrying of white people with negroes.*[3045]

> I do not perceive how I can express myself, more plainly, than I have done . . . *I have expressly disclaimed all intention to bring about social and political equality between the white and black races . . . I say . . . that Congress, which lays the foundations of society, should . . . be strongly opposed to the incorporation of slavery among its elements. But it does not follow that social and political equality between whites and blacks, must be incorporated . . .*[3046]

> *[Southerners, we] mean to marry your girls when we have a chance—the white ones, I mean . . .*[3047]
>
> *If there was a necessary conflict between the white man and the negro, I should be for the white man . . .*[3048]
>
> In the course of his reply, Senator Douglas remarked, in substance, that he had always considered *this government was made for the white people and not for the negroes. Why, in point of mere fact, I think so too.*[3049]

Reading such statements, is it surprising that Lincoln was so interested in apartheid, black deportation, and limiting instead of abolishing slavery? Not at all. As he himself states in his own words, he had good reason for his beliefs: jobs, housing, and racism.

"I cannot make it better known than it already is, that I strongly favor colonization." U.S. President Abraham Lincoln, December 1, 1862, from his Second Annual Message to Congress.

The brutality of the early American Spanish explorers knew no bounds. After simply slaughtering much of the Native-American population, the survivors were made lifelong slaves. Those who fought back were typically beaten, skinned, disemboweled, or roasted. Here Spanish conquistadors torment then burn and dismember their Indian victims, hanging their severed limbs up in a ghastly public display. Many pro-North writers would like you to believe that these types of outrages also took place in America's Old South. But not a shred of proof of this ridiculous allegation has ever surfaced. Why? Because such atrocities did not occur! All forms of slave abuse in the South were illegal, and carried stiff penalties, fines, imprisonment, and in extreme cases, even the death sentence. This is just one reason why, according to eyewitnesses, including black servants themselves, Southern servitude was a bastion of tolerance, safety, comfort, and security for Dixie's "slaves," completely unlike the types of bondage found elsewhere in the world.

19

THE CONFEDERACY, BLACK SLAVES, AND FREEDMEN

WHAT YOU WERE TAUGHT: Southern blacks did not support the Confederacy. Why would they?

THE TRUTH: Almost all Victorian Southern blacks, in their millions, supported the Confederacy, and for a number of rational and practical reasons. And we will note here that enlightened modern day blacks continue to endorse and back the ideals of the Southern Confederacy, and proudly display the Confederate Flag, the many reasons for which will be described in this chapter.[3050]

WHAT YOU WERE TAUGHT: Blacks never served in any capacity in the Confederate military.

THE TRUTH: We have reliable records showing that not only did millions of Southern blacks serve in the Confederate army, their service began at least four months before the start of Lincoln's War. Though at this early date they worked mainly as laborers, as we will see shortly, they still must be counted as "Confederate soldiers." Of this first Confederate black enlistment, Joseph Thomas Wilson writes:

> . . . the negro at the South had taken an active part in the

preparations for war, building breastworks, mounting cannon, digging rifle-pits and entrenchments, to shield and protect his rebelling master.

January 1st, 1861, Hon. J. P. Walker, at Mobile, Ala. received from R. R. Riordan, Esq., of Charleston, S.C., a dispatch rejoicing that—

> "Large gangs of negroes from plantations are at work on the redoubts, which are substantially made of sand-bags and coated with sheet-iron."

These doubtless were slaves, and mere machines; but the Charleston *Mercury* of January 3rd, brought the intelligence that—

> "One hundred and fifty able-bodied free colored men yesterday offered their services gratuitously to the governor, to hasten forward the important work of throwing up redoubts, wherever needed, along our coast."

Only the fire-eaters [radical anti-North Southerners] based their hope of success against the North,—the National Government,—upon the stubborn energies of the white [Confederate] soldiery; the deliberate men rested their hopes,—based their expectations, more upon the docility of the negro, than upon the audacity of their white troops.

The legislature of Tennessee, which secretly placed that State in the Southern Confederacy, enacted in June, 1861, a law authorizing the governor—

> "To receive into the military service of the State all male free persons of color, between the age of 15 and 50, who should receive $8 per month, clothing and rations."

And then it further provided—

> "That in the event a sufficient number of free persons of color to meet the wants of the State shall not tender their service, the Governor is empowered, through the sheriffs of the different counties, to press such persons until the requisite number is obtained."

> A few months after, the Memphis *Avalanche*, of September 3rd, 1861, exultingly announced the appearance on the streets of Memphis, of two regiments of negroes, under command of confederate officers. On the 7th of September, again the *Avalanche* said:
>
> > "Upwards of 1000 negroes armed with spades and pickaxes have passed through the city within the past few days. Their destination is unknown, but it is supposed that they are on their way to the 'other side of Jordan.'"
>
> Nor were the negroes in Virginia behind those of the other Southern States. In April [1861], the Lynchburg *Republican* chronicled the enrollment of a company of free negroes in that city, also one at Petersburg.
>
> Thus instead of revolts among the negroes, slaves and free, as predicted by some Union men at the North, many became possessed of a fervor,—originating generally in fear,—stimulated by an enthusiasm of the whites, that swept the populace like a mighty sea current into the channel of war. The negro who boasted the loudest of his desire to fight the Yankees; who showed the greatest anxiety to aid the confederates, was granted the most freedom and received the approval of his master.[3051]

The support of Southern whites for this idea, not to mention the bold enthusiasm with which thousands of Southern blacks wished to don Confederate gray to defend their homeland—even if just to work in the trenches—can be seen in a statement made by Confederate Secretary of State Judah P. Benjamin in early 1865:

> We have 680,000 blacks capable of bearing arms, and who ought now to be in the field. Let us now say to every negro who wishes to go into the ranks on condition of being free, go and fight—you are free. *My own negroes have been to me and said, "Master, set us free and we'll fight for you."*[3052]

WHAT YOU WERE TAUGHT: No black man ever fought as a soldier for the Confederacy.

THE TRUTH: From the previous entry we see that Confederate Secretary of State Benjamin was planning on putting, at the very least, nearly 700,000 armed Southern black soldiers "in the field."[3053] But this was in early 1865.

Far earlier, from even before the start of the conflict, however, we have an unofficial estimate of 300,000 Southern black males who armed themselves, enlisted, and served heroically under the Rebels' Stars and Bars, 100,000 more blacks than served under the Yanks' Stars and Stripes.[3054] This number is even more impressive when we consider that Southern blacks were exempt from the Confederate draft: though many were impressed into service, the rest volunteered.[3055]

This photograph destroys two Yankee fictions at one time: 1) that Southern whites and blacks detested one another, and 2) that there was no such thing as a black Confederate soldier. Andrew Martin Chandler (left) and one of his family's servants, Silas Chandler (right), are shown here in official Confederate uniforms, full fledged soldiers in the 44th Mississippi Infantry. Armed to the teeth in preparation for the fight against the illicit Northern invaders, such brave young men, white and black, were prepared to face death side-by-side if need be. This type of interracial pairing was repeated hundreds of thousands of times across the South during Lincoln's War. While Dixie's black servants were sometimes ordered to go into battle to accompany white loved ones, just as often they went of their own accord, anxious to put on Confederate gray and show "Marse Linkum" who was boss.

Additionally, when raw percentages are taken into account, far more blacks fought for the Confederacy than for the Union. The Union possessed about 3 million soldiers. Of these about 200,000 were black, 6 percent of the total. The Confederacy had about 1 million soldiers.[3056]

Of these an estimated 300,000 were black,[3057] 30 percent of the total. Simply put: 30 percent of Davis' army was black, but only 6 percent of Lincoln's army was black.

And these numbers are conservative if we use the definition of a "private soldier" as determined by German-American Union General August Valentine Kautz in 1864:

> In the fullest sense, *any man in the military service who receives pay, whether sworn in or not, is a soldier*, because he is subject to military law. Under this general head, laborers, teamsters, sutlers, chaplains, etc., are soldiers.[3058]

By Kautz's definition of a "private soldier," some 2 million Southerners fought for the Confederacy: 1 million whites and perhaps as many as 1 million blacks. As most of the 4 million blacks (3.5 million servants, 500,000 free) living in the South at the time of Lincoln's War remained loyal to Confederacy, and as at least 1 million of these either worked in or fought in the Rebel army and navy in some capacity, Kautz' definition raises the percentage of Southern blacks who defended the Confederacy as real soldiers to as much as 50 percent of the total Confederate soldier population[3059]—five times or 500 percent more than fought for the Union!

Many blacks were willingly impressed into Confederate military service impromptu, as the following example illustrates:

> [Mississippi plantation and slave owner Thomas Dabney's] fourteen-year-old son, Benjamin, caught the war fever, and his father gave his consent for him to go into the ranks. He sent a trusted body-servant [William, to enlist] with his sons.
>
> "William," he said, "I wish you to stand by your young masters, and to look after them as well as you can. And if they are killed, I want you to bring them home to me."
>
> "Yes, marster."
>
> "And here is my sword, William. I give it to you to take to the war. You can fight with it, too, if you see a chance."
>
> *"Yes, marster, I will show them the English of it."*
>
> *And William, who was about six feet two inches in height, threw his head back and looked proud of that trust.*
>
> William was armed with the master's own sword, which he had had sharpened before handing it to him. It had been his when, at the age of fourteen years, he had gone to Old Point

> Comfort, where the British were expected to land. The edge had been ground off when peace was declared after the war of 1812, and it had not been sharpened till the Confederate war broke out.[3060]

There were so many black Rebels on the battlefield that Northern soldiers, most who were overtly racist,[3061] were dumbstruck at the sight. And their fear was justified: Confederate blacks were known to be ferocious fighters, fearless soldiers, and crack shots. Indeed, the first Northerner killed in the War, Major Theodore Winthrop of the 7th Regiment, New York State Militia, was brought down by a black Confederate sharpshooter at the Battle of Bethel Church, June 10, 1861.[3062]

Union General August V. Kautz defined a soldier as "any man in the military service who receives pay, whether sworn in or not." By this definition as many as 1 million blacks served in the Confederate military, roughly 50 percent of the total Confederate soldier population. Thus five times or 500 percent more blacks fought for Davis than for Lincoln.

General Stonewall Jackson's army alone contained some 3,000 black soldiers.[3063] Clad "in all kinds of uniforms," and armed with "rifles, muskets, sabres, bowie-knives, dirks, etc.," to the shocked Yankee soldiers they were "manifestly an integral portion of the Southern Confederacy."[3064] On March 1, 1865, Union Colonel John G. Parkhurst sent a battlefield dispatch to Union General William D. Whipple, reporting that: "The rebel authorities are enrolling negroes in Mississippi preparatory to putting them into service."[3065]

If more proof of Southern black support for the Confederacy is needed we need look no further than a letter written by former Northern slave Frederick Douglass to Lincoln in 1862. In it the black civil rights leader uses the example of the overwhelming number of blacks in the Confederate army to urge the president to allow blacks to officially enlist in the Union army (Lincoln had steadfastly refused up until that time).[3066] Wrote Douglass:

> *There are at the present moment, many colored men in the Confederate Army doing duty not only as cooks, servants and laborers, but as real soldiers, having muskets on their shoulders and bullets in their pockets, ready to shoot down loyal [Yankee] troops, and do all that soldiers may do to destroy the Federal government and build up that of the traitors and rebels.* There were such soldiers at Manassas, and they are probably there still. There is a negro in the [Confederate] army as well as in the fence, and our Government is likely to find it out before the war comes to an end. *That the negroes are numerous in the rebel army, and do for that army its heaviest work, is beyond question.*[3067]

Unfortunately, the reality of the black Confederate soldier does not conform to Northern and New South myths about Southern blacks and slavery, and so it has been disregarded and suppressed. But we are bringing it back into the light of day for all to see.

WHAT YOU WERE TAUGHT: The South never officially enlisted blacks in it military forces as soldiers.
THE TRUTH: While blacks fought *unofficially* for the South from day one, the Confederacy began *official* black enlistment on March 13, 1865, with congressional passage of the "Act to Increase the Military Force of the Confederate States."[3068] The initial bill, also known as the "Negro Soldier Law," only allowed for the enrollment of blacks, not their emancipation, an unfortunate oversight that President Jefferson Davis quickly resolved. A few days later, on March 23, through the War Department, Davis issued General Order No. 14, which stated in part:

> . . . No slave will be accepted as a recruit unless with his own consent and with the approbation of his master by a written instrument *conferring, as far as he may, the rights of a freedman . . .*[3069]

In other words, Southern slaves could now not only officially enlist, but they were immediately emancipated and fought under the Confederate flag as free men, on the same footing as Southern white soldiers. The hope was that the Confederacy could now sign up at least 200,000 Southern blacks for military duty—a proposal first put forth by Mississippi Senator Albert G. Brown on February 8, 1865.[3070]

The buildup, drama, and excitement accompanying this important chapter in Southern history was recorded in a diary written by the clerk of the Confederate War Department, J. B. Jones, a few extracts of which follow:

> February 14th, 1865.—Yesterday some progress was made with the measure of 200,000 negroes for the [Confederate] army. Something must be done and soon.
>
> February 16th.—Did nothing yesterday; it is supposed, however, that the bill recruiting negro troops will pass. I fear when it is too late.
>
> February 17th.—A letter from General [Robert E.] Lee to General [Henry A.] Wise is published, thanking the latter's brigade for resolutions recently adopted declaring that they would consent to gradual emancipation for the sake of independence and peace. From all signs slavery [in the South] is doomed. But if 200,000 negro recruits can be made to fight and can be enlisted, General Lee may maintain the war very easily and successfully, and the [Union] powers at Washington may soon become disposed to abate the hard terms of peace now exacted.
>
> February 21st.—The negro bill has passed one house and will pass the other to-day, but the measure may come too late. The enemy is enclosing us on all sides with great vigor and rapidity.
>
> February 22nd.—Yesterday the Senate postponed action on the negro bill. What this means I cannot conjecture, unless there are dispatches from abroad with assurance of recognition, based on stipulations of emancipation, which can not be carried into effect without the consent of the States, and a majority of these seem in a fair way of falling into the hands of the Federal generals.
>
> February 24th.—Yesterday the Senate voted down the bill to put 200,000 negroes into the army. The papers to-day contain a letter from General Lee, advocating the measure as a necessity. [Virginia Senator] Mr. [Andrew] Hunter's vote defeated it. He has many negroes, and will probably lose them; but the loss of popularity and fear of forfeiting all chance of the succession may have operated

upon him as a politician. What madness! "Under which king, Benzonian?"

February 25th.—Mr. Hunter's eyes seem blood-shot since he voted against Lee's plan of organizing negro troops.

February 26th.—*Mr. Hunter is now reproached by the slave-holders he thought to please for defeating the negro bill.* They say his vote will make Virginia a free State, inasmuch as General Lee must evacuate it for want of negro troops.

March 2nd.—Negro bill still hangs fire in Congress.

March 9th.—Yesterday *the Senate passed the negro troops bill*—Mr. Hunter voting for it under instruction.

March 10th.—The president [Jefferson Davis] has the reins now, and Congress will be more obedient; but can they leave the city? *Advertisements for recruiting negro troops are in the papers this morning.*

March 17th.—*We shall have a negro army. Letters are pouring into the department from men of military skill and character asking authority to raise companies, battalions, and regiments of negro troops.* It is a desperate remedy for the desperate case, and may be successful. If 200,000 efficient soldiers can be made of this material there is no conjecturing when the next campaign may end. Possibly "over the border," for a little success will elate our spirits extravagantly, and the blackened ruins of our towns, and the moans of women and children bereft of shelter, will appeal strongly to the army for vengeance.

March 19th.—Unless food and men can be had Virginia must be lost. The negro experiment will soon be tested. Curtis says that the *letters are pouring into the department from all quarters asking authority to raise and command negro troops.* 100,000 troops from this source might do wonders.[3071]

WHAT YOU WERE TAUGHT: All Southern blacks fled North as soon as Lincoln issued the Emancipation Proclamation.
THE TRUTH: Almost no Southern blacks went North when Lincoln issued his famous edict on January 1, 1863, much to the relief of Northern whites,[3072] most who, like Lincoln himself, feared that a massive "flood" of freed slaves would immediately head north and "run

over the helpless Yankees like sheep," as the president put it.[3073]

Indeed, this is one of the many reasons Lincoln hesitated for so long to issue the Emancipation Proclamation: he and his Northern constituents believed that abolishing Southern slavery would push millions of African-Americans northward to intermix with their children, dilute and corrupt the white race, endanger racial purity, threaten prosperity, lower moral standards, scare off visitors and tourists, discourage new business, spread diseases, frighten away new students of local colleges, encourage further Negro immigration, drive down property values and wages, instigate a massive crime wave, thwart black colonization, "abolitionize" and "Africanize" the local white populace, and worst of all, take away jobs from whites.[3074]

Black Confederate soldiers building fortifications on James Island, South Carolina, under Rebel General Pierre G. T. Beauregard.

But "Honest Abe" and his Yankee neighbors need not have worried. Southern historical studies reveal that only 5 percent or less left Dixie for the North. A full 95 percent of the South's black servants remained right where they were after "emancipation,"[3075] preferring to stay with their families and friends on the land of their birth, on the farms and plantations they loved, near the graves of their time-honored ancestors.[3076] Of the loyal post-emancipation servants in her own family,

Mississippian Susan Dabney Smedes wrote: "They were our greatest comfort during the war."[3077] Revealingly, her memoirs, entitled *Memorials of a Southern Planter*, contain only three illustrations. One is of her father Thomas Dabney. The other two are of a few of the family's beloved black servants.[3078]

WHAT YOU WERE TAUGHT: No black man or woman ever aided the Confederate Cause.

THE TRUTH: Postwar Southern whites credited Southern blacks with literally saving the Confederacy from complete and utter destruction. In fact, Southern blacks were more important to the Southern Cause (self-government) during Lincoln's War than they were before it. Their talents, intelligence, courage, experience, fortitude, and labor were absolutely vital to the South's survival, and Dixie would have lost the War much sooner without their assistance.

Confederate Private Louis Napoleon Nelson fought under Rebel General Nathan Bedford Forrest, and was the only known black Confederate chaplain. Nelson lived into the early 1900s, attended 39 Confederate reunions, and at his funeral ceremony his coffin was draped with a Confederate flag. His grandson, African-American educator and lifetime member of the SCV, Nelson W. Winbush, wrote the foreword to the author's bestselling book, *Everything You Were Taught About the Civil War is Wrong, Ask a Southerner!*

Distinguished African-American historian Benjamin Quarles maintains that the Southern black's contributions to the Confederate Cause were beyond counting,[3079] and with good reason. The support of countless Southern slaves (and also free Southern blacks) who served in the Confederate army as teamsters, construction workers, drivers, cooks, nurses, body servants, and orderlies,[3080] not to mention the hundreds of thousands who served as soldiers,[3081] helped prolong the South's military efforts against Lincoln and his Yankee invaders.[3082]

Just as importantly, with the bulk of young and middle-aged white males away on the battlefield, it was primarily the bravery, strength, strong work ethic, and ingeniousness of Southern African-American servants—who remained at home and kept the farms going, provided food and supplies for the Confederate armies, and protected white females and their children against the ravages of Lincoln's violent blue-coated meddlers—that spared Dixie from utter annihilation.[3083]

Black Confederate soldiers with the First Louisiana Native Guards, surveilling and protecting the New Orleans, Opelousas, and Great Western Railroad in 1861.

Yankee commanders on the battlefield frequently complained of this very reality, which is one of the reasons they suggested "emancipating" Southern black slaves. Not to give blacks freedom and equal rights with whites, but to eliminate the Confederacy's primary support system: millions of loyal Southern blacks who refused to leave their homes, farms, and plantations. For by remaining in the South they helped maintain Southern resolve, supported Confederate troops, and protected Southern families.

After the War, white Confederate soldier Luther W. Hopkins had this to say about Southern blacks and their relationship to white Southerners:

> *Now I want to say that I shall ever have a tender spot in my breast for the colored people, owing to what I know of the race, judged from my association with them from early childhood up to and including the years of the Civil War, and, indeed, some years after.*
>
> My home in Loudoun county [Virginia], on the border

> line between the North and South, gave me an unusual opportunity of judging how far the negro could be trusted in caring for and protecting the homes of the men who were in the Southern armies. Scattered all through the South, and especially in the border States, there were white men who were not in sympathy with the South, and some of them acted as spies and guides for the Northern troops as they marched and counter-marched through the land. But *I never knew of negroes being guilty of like conduct. They not only watched over and protected the women and children in their homes, but were equally as faithful and careful to protect the Southern soldier from capture when he returned home to see his loved ones.*
>
> *No soldier in Loudoun or Fauquier counties ever feared that his or his neighbor's servants would betray him to the enemy. The negro always said, in speaking of the Southern soldiers, "our soldiers,"* although he well knew that the success of the North meant his freedom, while the success of the South meant the [temporary] continuation of slavery.
>
> *Another remarkable thing. No one ever heard of a negro slave, or, so far as I know, a free negro of the South, offering an insult or an indignity to a white woman.* They were frequently commissioned to escort the daughters of the family to church or to school, or on any expedition taking them from home. Sometimes the distance was long and across fields and through lonely woods, but *the . . . colored man always delivered his charge safely, and would have died in his footsteps to do it if the occasion required.* Freedom, education, or both, or something else, has developed in the negro a trait that no one ever dreamed he possessed until after the close of the Civil War. Hence, *I have a great respect for the race.*[3084]

Many blacks, though they did not wear Confederate uniforms, served the Confederate armies in a myriad of clever and dangerous ways. This next account, of the Union's Kilpatrick-Dahlgren Raid (February 28–March 3, 1864), illustrates just such an example. Related by Confederate Brigadier Generals Armistead L. Long and Marcus J. Wright, it is the story of a Southern servant, Martin Robinson, who had been captured by Union soldiers. Known to Yankees by the derogatory term "contraband" (one probably coined by Yankee General Benjamin "the Beast" Butler for all captured Southern blacks),[3085] the courageous African-American paid the ultimate price for remaining loyal to the Southland that he loved:

> [Union General Hugh Judson] Kilpatrick, having failed to meet

> [Union Colonel Ulric] Dahlgren at the appointed time before Richmond, determined not to wait, but to attack [the Rebels] at once. He crossed the outer line of defences without resistance, but on reaching the second line he was so warmly [that is, violently] received that he was obliged to retire, and with difficulty made good his retreat through the Confederate lines. This lack of co-operation in the Federal forces was due to the fact that Dahlgren put in the responsible position of guide *a contraband [Robinson] who showed his fidelity to the Southern cause by misleading him from his proposed line of march, and thus created a delay which prevented his forming a junction with Kilpatrick*. We are told that the negro was executed on the alleged charge of treachery [Dahlgren hanged Robinson on the spot, using the reins of his horse]. When Dahlgren approached the neighborhood of Richmond he was met by a Confederate force and signally defeated; he himself was killed, and only a remnant of his command escaped destruction.[3086]

Truly, the citizens of Richmond, Virginia, should immortalize Robinson in marble for his devotion to the South!

During Lincoln's War Union General Ulric Dahlgren was tricked by a black Southern slave who had remained loyal to the Confederacy, just one of thousands of such instances. For his cunning and daring the brave African-American paid the ultimate price: after he was found out, Dahlgren murdered him on the spot. The Yankee officer himself died in battle only days later. Amid the papers found on Dahlgren's corpse were orders for the assassination of Confederate President Jefferson Davis—more evidence of the type of unlawful Yankee treachery that went on throughout the conflict. As the orders almost certainly came from war criminal Lincoln, the affair triggered outrage across the South. Union officials later destroyed the "Dahlgren Papers," as they are known, in order to conceal their crime. Fortunately, Davis had made the material public, and several copies survive.

Thousands of similar stories have come down to us from wartime eyewitnesses. Even Lincoln recognized the immense contribution of Southern black soldiers to the Confederacy, as he stated on March 17, 1865:

> There is one thing about *the negro's fighting for the rebels* which we can know as well as they can, and that is that they cannot at the same time *fight in their armies* and stay at home and make bread for them.[3087]

Yankee Quartermaster-General Montgomery C. Meigs had the same complaint, as he grumbled in an official report on November 18, 1862:

> *The labor of the colored man supports the rebel soldier, enables him to leave his plantation to meet our armies, builds his fortifications, cooks his food, and sometimes aids him on picket by rare skill with the rifle.*[3088]

Meigs then recommended liberating Southern blacks; again, not for the purpose of civil rights. He, like Lincoln, merely wanted to employ them in the Northern army, and then only if segregated and "put under strict military control." As the Union officer wrote:

> In all these modes it [that is, the labor of Southern blacks] is available to assist our Army, and it is probable that there will be less outrage, less loss of life, by freeing these people, if put under strict military control, than if left to learn slowly that war has removed the white men who have heretofore held them in check, and to yield at last to the temptation to insurrection and massacre.[3089]

Like Lincoln's, Meigs' wish for a Southern black "insurrection and massacre" also failed to materialize, and millions of Dixie's African-Americans remained at home where they continued to support the Confederate Cause in whatever way they could. It was from this very phenomenon that the Southern tradition of sharecropping began: after the War planters subdivided their land into small plots known as "fragmented plantations," that were then tilled by millions of former black servants. Pro-North historians, of course, never mention where these men and women came from, but we will: they never left the South to begin with! When Lincoln illegally invaded the Confederacy in 1861 they refused to forsake their homeland, families, friends, farms, and businesses.[3090]

Southerner turned Union general, Montgomery C. Meigs, was upset that so many Southern blacks were fighting for the Confederacy. His solution to the problem? Free Southern slaves in an attempt to start slave rebellions across Dixie, then force them to enlist in the Union military and fight in racially segregated units.

Is any of this surprising? Not when we study the history of the black Southern servant in wartime:

> Seventy years ago [at the start of the American Revolution in 1776], Lord Dunmore [John Murray], Governor of Virginia, offered liberty to the slaves of Virginia, if they would join the British force against their masters. This they refused to do, notwithstanding the many tempting offers that were made them: *they preferred adversity with their masters, to freedom and gold without them. During the late war [of 1812], several attempts were made to induce the negroes to abandon their masters; but this they always refused, though circumstances were highly favorable to the success of any attempt of the kind.*[3091]

Hopkins gives us the following wartime story, yet another example showing the undying fidelity that Southern blacks had for both whites and for their Dixie homeland:

> . . . there was not a day that we [Confederate soldiers] were not in danger of being surrounded and captured. The bluecoats were scouting through the country almost continuously in search of Mosby's "gang," as they called it. We had to keep on guard and watch the roads and hilltops every hour of the day. We had the advantage of knowing the country and the hiding places and the short cuts, and then *we had our loyal servants, always willing to aid us to escape "them Yankees."*
>
> For instance, I made a visit to Sunny Bank, the home of my brother-in-law, E. C. Broun. My horse was hitched to the rack, and I was inside enjoying the hospitalities of an old Virginia home, when one of the little darkies rushed in and said, "Yankees." They were soon all around the house, but, before they got there, one of the servants took the saddle and bridle off my steed, hid them, and turned him loose in the garden, where he posed as the old family driving nag, while I went to the back porch, climbed a ladder, and lifting a trap-door, got in between the ceiling and the roof. The trapdoor was so adjusted that it did not show an opening. The ladder was taken away, and there I stayed until the enemy departed. I got back home safely, eight miles off, and had other close calls, but *owing to the fidelity of the colored people, who were always on the watch, and whose loyalty to the Confederate soldiers, whether they belonged to the family in which they lived or not, was touching and beautiful beyond comprehension. They always called the Confederates "Our Soldiers," and the other side "Them Yankees."*[3092]

In May 1865, one month after War's end,[3093] South Carolina diarist Mary Chesnut remarked that in her region there was not a single case of a servant betraying their master or mistress, and that on most plantations "things looked unchanged." Former black slaves, now free laborers known as "plantation hands," were still working in the fields of their original white families, as if not one of them had ever seen a Yankee or even knew they existed.[3094]

Thus it could truly be said that while white Southern soldiers lost on the battlefield, Southern black servants won the War on the home front by helping to preserve both white and black families and their agricultural holdings across Dixie. Except for the many Southern lives themselves that were expended in the fight against the North, no single greater contribution to the South's War effort can be named.

WHAT YOU WERE TAUGHT: During the Civil War the Southern armies were all white.

THE TRUTH: Actually, like Southern society itself at the time, as now, the Rebel military was a highly multiracial, multiethnic, multicultural group comprised of every race and dozens of different nationalities.

Though—thanks to the vicious Yankee custom of burning down Southern courthouses[3095]—exact statistics are impossible to come by, Southern historians have determined that the following numbers are roughly accurate. In descending numerical order the Confederate army and navy was composed of about 1 million European-Americans,[3096] 300,000 to 1 million African-Americans,[3097] 70,000 Native-Americans, 60,000 Latin-Americans,[3098] 50,000 foreigners,[3099] 12,000 Jewish-Americans,[3100] and 10,000 Asian-Americans.[3101]

A group of Cherokee Confederate veterans, gathered for a Confederate reunion in New Orleans, Louisiana, in 1903. An estimated 70,000 Indians fought for the Confederacy, primarily members from the Cherokee, Choctaw, Chickasaw, Seminole, Osage, and Creek tribes. Despite being outnumbered three to one, thousands of European-Americans, African-Americans, Native-Americans, Latin-Americans, Asian-Americans, Jewish-Americans, and foreigners combined to create a Confederate force so powerful that it was able to hold off the Union army and navy for four years. The Confederate military was, in fact, a mirror image of Dixie's multiracial, multiethnic, multicultural society. Pro-North advocates do not want you to know any of this, of course, which is why they have withheld these facts from you, and it is why they will withhold them from your children and your grandchildren.

True Southerners, of all races, continue to be proud of our region's multiracial history, and of the many contributions made to Dixie by individuals of all colors, creeds, and nationalities.[3102] For it is my theory that what I call "racism-phobes"—that is, those who fear that they see racism in everything and who label everyone they dislike a "racist"—are actually themselves latent racists.[3103] It is to the South's credit that to this day one still sees little racism of any kind in our region, from any one race toward any other.

WHAT YOU WERE TAUGHT: No Confederate officer or politician ever called for the enlistment and emancipation of blacks.
THE TRUTH: Numerous Southern militiamen and politicians had long sought enlistment and emancipation of blacks. One of these was General Robert E. Lee, across the South still one of the most beloved and highly regarded Confederate officers.

On December 27, 1856, five years before Lincoln's War, Lee—who unlike General Grant and many other Northern officers,[3104] never owned slaves in the literal or technical sense,[3105] and who had always been opposed to slavery—wrote a letter to his wife Mary Anna in which he stated that slavery is a "moral and political evil," worse even for the white race than for the black race.[3106]

Lee's sentiment is just what one would expect from a Virginian, the state where the American abolition movement began,[3107] and whose native sons, most notably U.S. Presidents George Washington[3108] and Thomas Jefferson,[3109] struggled for so long to rid America of the institution; and this while the North was sending hundreds of slave ships to Africa, and whose main port cities, like New York, Providence, Philadelphia, Baltimore, and Boston, were functioning as the literal epicenters of slave trading in the Western hemisphere.[3110]

Regarding the enlistment of Southern blacks, Lee made his views clear in a letter to Southern Congressman Ethelbert Barksdale on February 18, 1865:

> . . . *in my opinion, the negroes, under proper circumstances, will make efficient soldiers.* I think we could at least do as well with them as the enemy . . . Under good officers, and good instructions, *I do not see why they should not become soldiers. . . . They furnish a more promising material than many armies of which we read in history . . . I think those who are employed should be freed. It would be neither just nor wise, in my opinion, to require them to serve as slaves. . . .* I have no doubt that if Congress would authorize their reception into service, and empower the President [Jefferson Davis] to call upon individuals or States for such as they are willing to contribute, with the condition of emancipation to all enrolled, *a sufficient number would be forthcoming to enable us to try the experiment.* If it proved successful,

> most of the objections to the measure would disappear, and if individuals still remained unwilling to send their negroes to the army, *the force of public opinion in the [Southern] States would soon bring about such legislation as would remove all obstacles.*[3111]

General Lee mentions that "the force of public opinion" in the abolitionist South would push black enlistment through eventually, no matter what the military thought. However, as Representative Barksdale stated before the House in early 1865, *all* Confederate soldiers, whatever their rank, wanted black enlistment. This sentiment was backed up by such establishments as the renowned Virginia Military Institute, which agreed, if called upon, to train Southern blacks in the art of soldiering.[3112]

Long before Lincoln's War, Robert E. Lee referred to slavery as a "moral and political evil," and during the conflict he called for abolition and black enlistment.

But Lee was far from being the first prominent Confederate to advocate emancipation and enlistment of Southern blacks. Another example was my cousin Confederate General Pierre G. T. Beauregard, the "Hero of Fort Sumter" and co-designer of the Confederate Battle Flag.[3113]

Yet another important Southerner was Louisiana governor and commander-in-chief Thomas O. Moore, who, on March 24, 1862, commissioned the first black militia in the Confederacy (the Native Guards of Louisiana). Moore called on the all-black unit, one that had already been protecting New Orleans for several months, to "maintain their organization, and . . . hold themselves prepared for such orders as may be transmitted to them." Their purpose? To guard homes, property, and Southern rights against "the pollution of a ruthless

[Northern] invader."[3114] In 1890 Joseph Thomas Wilson made note of this landmark decision in his book, *The Black Phalanx*:

> The leaders at the South in preparing for hostilities showed the people of the North, and the authorities at Washington, that they intended to carry on the war with no want of spirit; that every energy, every nerve, was to be taxed to its utmost tension, *and that not only every white man, but, if necessary, every black man should be made to contribute to the success of the cause for which the war was inaugurated. Consequently, with the enrollment of the whites began the employment of the blacks.*
>
> *Prejudice against the negro at the North was so strong that it required the arm of public authority to protect him from assault, though he declared in favor of the Union. Not so at the South, for as early as April, 1861, the free negroes of New Orleans, La., held a public meeting and began the organization of a battalion, with officers of their own race, with the approval of the State government, which commissioned their negro officers.* When the Louisiana militia was reviewed, the Native Guards (negro) made up, in part, the first division of the State troops. Elated at the success of *being first to place [Confederate] negroes in the field together with [Confederate] white troops*, the commanding general sent the news over the wires to the jubilant confederacy:
>
>> "New Orleans, Nov. 23rd, 1861. Over 28,000 troops were reviewed to-day by Governor Moore, Major-General [Mansfield] Lovell and Brigadier-General [Daniel] Ruggles. *The line was over seven miles long; one regiment comprised 1,400 free colored men.*"[3115]

In the summer of 1863 both a number of Southerners and the Alabama legislature asked the Confederate government to enlist blacks,[3116] and on November 11, 1863, in a letter to Confederate Secretary of War James A. Seddon, Confederate Major Samuel W. Melton suggested that conscription be extended to include "free negroes."[3117] These men had the solid backing of civilian Confederate leaders as well. In October 1864, for example, the governors of North Carolina, South Carolina, Georgia, Alabama, and Mississippi enacted a bill proposing black enlistment, while on March 6, 1865, the Virginia legislature passed a resolution allowing the recruitment of African-Americans within its borders.[3118]

Another noteworthy pro-black white Confederate officer was General Patrick R. Cleburne, known as the "Stonewall Jackson of the West" for his bold tactics on the battlefield.[3119] A native of Ireland and a division commander in the Army of Tennessee, at an officers' meeting on January 2, 1864, the Irishman disclosed a written proposal that would soon become known as the "Cleburne Memorial." Calling for the immediate enlistment and training of black soldiers, it promised complete emancipation for *all* Southern slaves at the end of the War.[3120]

Cleburne, who died eleven months later fighting Yankee interlopers at the Battle of Franklin II,[3121] wrote:

> Adequately to meet the causes which are now threatening ruin to our country, we propose . . . that we retain in service for the war all troops now in service, and that we *immediately commence training a large reserve of the most courageous of our slaves, and further that we guarantee freedom within a reasonable time to every slave in the South who shall remain true to the Confederacy in this war. As between the loss of independence and the loss of slavery, we assume that every patriot will freely give up the latter—give up the negro slave rather than be a slave himself.* If we are correct in this assumption it only remains to show how this great national sacrifice is, in all human probabilities, to change the current of success and sweep the [Yankee] invader from our country. . . . The immediate effect of *the emancipation and enrollment of negroes* on the military strength of the South would be: To enable us to have armies numerically superior to those of the North, and a reserve of any size we might think necessary; to enable us to take the offensive, move forward, and forage on the enemy. It would open to us in prospective another and almost untouched source of supply, and furnish us with the means of preventing temporary disaster, and carrying on a protracted struggle. *It would instantly remove all the vulnerability, embarrassment, and inherent weakness which result from slavery.* . . . We can only get a sufficiency by making the negro share the danger and hardships of the war. If we arm and train him and make him fight for the country in her hour of dire distress, *every consideration of principle and policy demand that we should set him and his whole race who side with us free. It is a first principle with mankind that he who offers his life in defense of the State should receive from her in return his freedom and his happiness, and we believe in acknowledgment of this principle. The Constitution of the Southern States has reserved to their respective governments the power to free slaves for meritorious services to the State.* It is politic besides. For many years, ever since the agitation of the subject of slavery commenced, the negro has been dreaming of

freedom, and his vivid imagination has surrounded that condition with so many gratifications that it has become the paradise of his hopes. To attain it he will tempt dangers and difficulties not exceeded by the bravest soldier in the field. The hope of freedom is perhaps the only moral incentive that can be applied to him in his present condition. It would be preposterous then to expect him to fight against it with any degree of enthusiasm, therefore we must bind him to our cause by no doubtful bonds; we must leave no possible loop-hole for treachery to creep in. The slaves are dangerous now, but armed, trained, and collected in an army they would be a thousand fold more dangerous: therefore *when we make soldiers of them we must make free men of them beyond all question*, and thus enlist their sympathies also. *We can do this more effectually than the North can now do, for we can give the negro not only his own freedom, but that of his wife and child, and can secure it to him in his old home.* . . . .

In January 1864 Confederate General Patrick Ronayne Cleburne issued the "Cleburne Memorial," which called for the immediate "emancipation and enrollment of negroes" in the Rebel army and navy. The beloved Irishman never saw the fruition of his dream: he was killed later that year by a Yankee bullet at the Battle of Franklin II. Anti-South proponents would have you believe that Cleburne's position on abolition and black enlistment was rare in the Confederacy. Actually, according to Southern Congressman Ethelbert Barksdale, "all Confederate soldiers," whatever their rank, held the same view—as did nearly the entire Southern civilian population.

> *If, then, we touch the institution at all, we would do best to make the most of it, and by emancipating the whole race upon reasonable terms, and within such reasonable time as will prepare both races for the change, secure to ourselves all the advantages, and to our enemies all the disadvantages that can arise, both at home and abroad, from such a sacrifice. Satisfy the negro that if he faithfully adheres to our standard during the war he shall receive his freedom and that of his race. Give him as an earnest of our intentions such immediate immunities as will impress him with our sincerity and be in keeping with his new condition, enroll a portion of his class as soldiers of the Confederacy, and we change the race from a dreaded weakness to a position of strength. . . . It is said slavery is all we are fighting for, and if we give it up we give up all. Even if this were true, which we deny, slavery is not all our enemies are fighting for. It is merely the pretense to establish sectional superiority and a more centralized form of government, and to deprive us of our rights and liberties. We have now briefly proposed a plan which we believe will save our country. It may be imperfect, but in all human probability it would give us our independence.*[3122]

Cleburne's proposal was signed by over a dozen other Confederate officers. When it came to African-Americans, anti-abolitionist Lincoln never came close to espousing such humanitarian ideas.

WHAT YOU WERE TAUGHT: Southern slaves detested their white owners before, during, and after the War, particularly former Confederate soldiers.

THE TRUTH: The opposite is true. Throughout the antebellum, bellum, and postbellum periods we have thousands of stories of warm relations between Southern whites and Southern blacks,[3123] and of free blacks and slaves providing various forms of support for both the war effort[3124] and for former white slave owners who had been made indigent by Lincoln's War. In 1901, esteemed former Virginia slave and black educator Booker T. Washington wrote:

> *As a rule, not only did the members of my race entertain no feelings of bitterness against . . . [Southern] whites before and during the war, but there are many instances of Negroes tenderly caring for their former masters and mistresses who for some reason have become poor and dependent since the war.* I know of instances where the former masters of slaves have for years been supplied with money by their former slaves to keep them from suffering. I have known of still other cases in

which the former slaves have assisted in the education of the descendants of their former owners. I know of a case on a large plantation in the South in which a young white man, the son of the former owner of the estate, has become so reduced in purse and self control by reason of drink that he is a pitiable creature; and yet, notwithstanding the poverty of the coloured people themselves on this plantation, *they have for years supplied this young white man with the necessities of life*. One sends him a little coffee or sugar, another a little meat, and so on. Nothing that the coloured people possess is too good for the son of "old Mars Tom," who will perhaps never be permitted to suffer while any remain on the place who knew directly or indirectly of "old Mars Tom."[3125]

The warm Civil War relations between Confederate whites and blacks has carried down into the present day. These two buddies, photographed by the author, recently attended an event honoring Confederate General Nathan Bedford Forrest at Chapel Hill, Tennessee. Dressed in period style Rebel uniforms, they are posing in front of an original outbuilding that still stands on the grounds of the Nathan Bedford Forrest Boyhood Home. Can we have any doubt that, had they lived at the time, these two young men would have wanted to join the Confederate army and fight alongside their fathers, brothers, and friends?

There were no official slave seaports in Dixie. All of America's legal slave ships entered and departed via seaports located north of the Mason-Dixon Line, throughout the northeastern states and New England. This slaving port is in New York City.

20

THE UNION, BLACK SLAVES, AND FREEDMEN

WHAT YOU WERE TAUGHT: The North, under President Lincoln, enlisted blacks long before the South did under President Davis.
THE TRUTH: The opposite is true. The South, which recognized the importance of blacks and the War long prior to the North,[3126] began black enlistment even before the conflict's first major fight: the Battle of First Manassas (First Bull Run to Yanks) on July 18, 1861.[3127] In June 1861, one year and three months before the Union officially sanctioned the recruitment of blacks in August 1862,[3128] and almost two years before Lincoln began arming blacks in March 1863, the Tennessee legislature passed a statute allowing Governor Isham G. Harris to receive into military service "all male free persons of color, between the ages of 15 and 50 . . ."[3129]

On February 4, 1862, the Virginia legislature passed a bill to enroll all of the state's free Negroes for service in the Confederate army. Earlier, on November 23, 1861, a seven-mile long line of Confederate soldiers was marched through the streets of New Orleans. Among them was a regiment of 1,400 free black volunteers.[3130] Hundreds of other such examples could be given. We have already seen that perhaps as many as five times more—or 500 percent more—blacks fought for the

Confederacy than for the Union.[3131]

Anti-South proponents have carefully suppressed such facts, making our already Northern-slanted history books even more incomplete, inaccurate, and misleading than they already are.

In June 1861 the Tennessee legislature gave Governor Isham G. Harris legal permission to begin enlisting all free black and colored males between the ages of 15 and 50 into the Confederate military. This was over a year before Lincoln began recruiting blacks, and nearly two years before he began arming blacks.

WHAT YOU WERE TAUGHT: The Union formed all-black troops before the Confederacy did.

THE TRUTH: The South's first all-black militia was officially formed on April 23, 1861, only nine days after the first battle of the War at Fort Sumter, South Carolina. The unit, known as the "Native Guards (colored)," was "duly and legally enrolled as a part of the militia of the State, its officers being commissioned by Thomas O. Moore, Governor and Commander-in-Chief of the State of Louisiana . . ."[3132]

In contrast, the North's first all-black militia, the First South Carolina Volunteers, was not commissioned until over a year and a half later (on November 7, 1862), under Yankee Colonel Thomas Wentworth Higginson.[3133]

WHAT YOU WERE TAUGHT: The Confederacy was racist towards her black soldiers, and treated them unfairly and abused them. The Union was not racist toward hers, and treated them equally with white soldiers.

THE TRUTH: We have discussed the facts that Lincoln postponed both the emancipation of slaves and the enlistment of blacks into the Union army for as long as possible, and that Northern racism was at the root of these delay tactics. There was certainly white racism in Old Dixie, and her people have never tried to hide this fact as the North has tried to conceal its own wartime white racism. But because, as Tocqueville and others have pointed out, white racism was far less severe in the South,[3134] the Confederacy treated its black soldiers far more equitably than the Union did its black soldiers. In fact, the Rebel military was ordered to do so by the Confederate government.

Early in the War, under Lincoln's orders, Yankee Secretary of War Simon Cameron declared that the U.S. had "no intention" of enlisting either "coloreds" (African-Americans) or "savages" (Native-Americans).

Like their commander-in-chief at Washington, D.C.,[3135] white Yankee soldiers were well-known for their racial bigotry and utter intolerance of blacks.[3136] Here then were the two primary reasons Lincoln would not permit blacks to serve as active combatants in the U.S. military during the first half of his War.[3137] The following communications between Jacob Dodson, a black volunteer from Washington, D.C., and Lincoln's secretary of war, Simon Cameron, are instructive. On April 23, 1861, Dodson wrote the following to Cameron:

> Sir: I desire to inform you that I know of some 300 reliable colored free citizens of this city who desire to enter the service for the defense of the city. I have been three times across the Rocky Mountains in the service of the country with [John C.] Frémont and others. I can be found about the Senate Chamber, as I have been employed about the premises for some years. Yours respectfully, Jacob Dodson (colored).[3138]

Just as Yankee General William T. Sherman "fought negro recruiting to the end,"[3139] Cameron too was against black enlistment,[3140] which is why, taking orders from his superior, President Lincoln, he sent the following terse response to the patriotic African-American on April 29, 1861:

> Jacob Dodson (colored). Sir: In reply to your letter of the 23rd instant, I have to say that *this Department has no intention at present to call in the service of the Government any colored soldiers*. With respect, etc. Simon Cameron, Secretary of War.[3141]

On September 13, 1862, Lincoln himself—also of the same mind—was approached by a group of abolitionist clergyman, asking about the possibility of arming blacks. The diehard black colonizationist's reply evinced absolutely no confidence in the idea of the African-American soldier:

> . . . I am not so sure we could do much with the blacks. If we were to arm them, I fear that in a few weeks the arms would be in the hands of the rebels; and, indeed, thus far we have not had arms enough to equip our white troops.[3142]

This was just a few days prior to his issuing his Preliminary Emancipation Proclamation!

Lincoln's hesitation was warranted, but not for the reason he states: when he finally allowed full-fledged black recruitment, white soldiers hissed and booed, desertions increased, and officers reported a widespread general "demoralization" across the entire Federal military.[3143]

The mere mention of the idea of "black enlistment" brought many white regiments close to insurrection.[3144] A Yankee soldier with the Ninetieth Illinois reported on the general feeling among his fellow

Union compatriots at the time: "Not one of our boys wants to give guns to the Negroes. This is a white man's war and that's the way we want to keep it. Besides we have no desire to fight next to blacks on the battlefield," he asserted.[3145] Yankee Corporal Felix Brannigan, of the Seventy-fourth New York Regiment, was even less convivial, saying:

> We don't want to fight side and side with the nigger. We think we are a too superior race for that.[3146]

During the first two years of the War, when Northern blacks tried to join the Union army, they were quickly turned away at Federal recruiting stations by Lincoln's orders. Those who managed to sneak into service were soon discovered, honorably discharged, and sent home. Neither Lincoln, his officers, or his soldiers wanted blacks in Union trenches. "We don't want to fight side and side with the nigger," said Yankee Corporal Felix Brannigan of the Seventy-fourth New York Regiment, a sentiment echoed by most white U.S. soldiers.

Union soldiers like Brannigan were supported by a majority of the Northern populace. At the mere mention of black enlistment, white mobs in Ohio, for example, roamed the streets yelling, "kill the nigger!" (This was not an isolated occurrence. As late as 1865 many Northern states were still rejecting black suffrage, among them Connecticut, Wisconsin, and Minnesota.)[3147] Not surprisingly, when blacks secretly managed to enlist in the U.S. army without being noticed, Lincoln had them quietly removed and honorably discharged.[3148] Wilson writes that:

> *The [Northern] opposition to [U.S.] negro soldiers did not cease with many of the Union generals even after the [Lincoln] Government at Washington issued its mandate for their [black] enlistment and impressment,* and notwithstanding that the many thousands in the service, with their display of gallantry, dash and courage, as exhibited at Port Hudson, Milliken's Bend, Wagner, and in a hundred other battles, had astonished and aroused the civilized world. In view of all this . . . *General [William T.] Sherman wrote to the Washington authorities, in September, 1864, protesting against negro troops being organized in his department.* If Whitelaw Reid's [book] *Ohio in the War*, is to be relied upon, Sherman's [racist] treatment of the negroes in his march to the sea was [similar to a massacre.[3149] Yet still it was] . . . *in keeping with that of the [Union] authorities of his state* . . .[3150]

Lincoln's racist prohibition against black enlistment was in stark contrast to America's history of negro soldiery. African-Americans, like the man above on the far left, fought, for example, at many of the Revolutionary War's most important engagements, including the Battles of Lexington, Concord, Ticonderoga, Brandywine, Saratoga, and Yorktown, to name but a few.

How un-American all of this Northern racism was. For blacks had served in official capacities in *all* of America's wars prior to 1861, all the way back to the first Revolutionary War against the British Empire in 1775, when 4,000 African-Americans served in the Continental Army, along with thousands more in the state militia.[3151] In fact, the first person killed by British troops during the Boston Massacre in 1770 was an American black named Crispus Attucks, while black soldiers were present thereafter at nearly all of the Revolutionary battles including those at Lexington, Concord, Bunker Hill, Breed's Hill, Stony Points, Ticonderoga, White Plains, Stillwater, Bennington, Trenton, Brandywine, Princeton, Bemis Heights, Eutaw, Saratoga, Savannah, Fort Griswold, Red Bank, Long Island, Monmouth, and Yorktown.[3152] Two heroic blacks even made the famous crossing with George Washington over the Delaware River on December 25, 1776.[3153] Blacks also served in the War of 1812 and under Andrew Jackson at the Battle of New Orleans in 1814.[3154]

The first soldier to die in the American Revolutionary War was a black Yankee slave from Framingham, Massachusetts, named Crispus Attucks, shown here falling before British fire at the conflict known as the Boston Massacre, March 5, 1770. Either Lincoln was ignorant of U.S. history or he was aware of it and did not care: he continued to bar blacks from enlisting in his army until he was forced to change his mind due to the appalling loss of his white soldiers. The result was the Emancipation Proclamation, which the president grudgingly issued on January 1, 1863, allowing blacks to serve as legitimate uniformed soldiers in the U.S. military for the first time.

In 1820, before the U.S. House of Representatives, South Carolinian Charles Pinckney revealed what everyone seemed to know except Lincoln and his Yankee cronies; namely that the "colored population" of the United States was of inestimable value in both peacetime and war:

> At the commencement of our Revolutionary struggle with Great Britain, all the States had this class of people [African-Americans].

> The New England States had numbers of them; the Northern and Middle States had still more, although less than the Southern. They all entered into the great contest with similar views. *Like brethren, they contended for the benefit of the whole, leaving to each the right to pursue its happiness in its own way. They thus nobly toiled and bled together, really like brethren.* And it is a remarkable fact, that, notwithstanding, *in the course of the Revolution, the Southern States were continually overrun by the British, and every negro in them had an opportunity of running away, yet few did. They then were, as they still are, as valuable a part of our population to the Union as any other equal number of inhabitants. They were in numerous instances the pioneers, and in all, the laborers of your armies. To their hands were owing the erection of the greatest part of the fortifications raised for the protection of our country. Fort Moultrie gave, at an early period of the inexperience and untried valor of our citizens, immortality to American arms. And in the Northern States, numerous bodies of them were enrolled, and fought, side-by-side with the whites, the battles of the [American] Revolution.*[3155]

Massachusetts slave Peter Salem at the June 17, 1775, Battle of Bunker Hill, one of the many American blacks who fought in our nation's Revolutionary War. Two black men even made the famous Delaware River crossing with George Washington on December 25, 1776. A mere 47 years later, under the leftist Lincoln administration, the U.S. government banned black enlistment.

It was only under Lincoln, 47 years later, that the United States of America completely barred blacks (as well as Native-Americans, whom the Lincoln administration referred to as "savages")[3156] from enlisting in the armed services, questioning their intelligence, stamina, and courage. Thus, it was Lincoln who injected white racism and racial integration in the U.S. military for the first time, a situation that lasted well into the 1940s.

Like Lincoln, Union General William Tecumseh Sherman held that blacks, or "niggers," as the two often referred to them, were inferior to whites and that the two races should be kept apart. Naturally he was also against black enlistment. "I would prefer to have this a white man's war," Sherman declared during the conflict.

Little wonder that for nearly two years into Lincoln's presidency he and his administration viewed African-Americans as a "bother,"[3157] and continued to refuse to even consider the idea of black U.S. soldiers. Instead they maintained that the war did not in any way involve either free or enslaved blacks, only whites.[3158]

As discussed in previous chapters, the real reason was, of course, that Lincoln and most of his white officers and soldiers were racists and did not want to intermingle with blacks—on or off the battlefield. As Yankee war hero General William T. Sherman said:

> *I would prefer to have this a white man's war* . . . With my opinions of negroes and my experience, *yea prejudice*, I cannot trust them yet. Time may change this but I cannot bring myself to trust negroes with arms in positions of danger and trust.[3159]

Echoing his commander-in-chief at Washington,[3160] this was the real thrust of the issue in Yankeedom. Indeed, Sherman was the man responsible for the following "stain" upon the record of his "March to the Sea":

> Thousands of [free and freed Southern] negroes accompanied the [Union] column, by the express permission of General Sherman. Once or twice great crowds of these unfortunate creatures were driven back from the bridges, when the [U.S.] army was crossing rivers, and, the bridges being taken up as soon as the army had crossed, were left to the cruelty of the Rebel cavalry and of the enraged masters whom they had been encouraged to desert. [Union] General Jeff C. Davis seems to have been prominent in this barbarism, but it called forth no rebuke from General Sherman himself.[3161]

As the War progressed and the U.S. army's white soldiery continued to decrease at alarming rates, Yankee opinion, once bitterly opposed, began to soften toward the idea of black enlistment. Iowa's Civil War Governor Samuel Jordan Kirkwood, a member of Lincoln's Republican Party, expressed the typical liberal Northern view at the time: It would be better, he argued, to sacrifice the lives of "niggers" than the lives of the nation's white sons.

After Lincoln finally relented and began allowing black enlistment, he put his African-American recruits into segregated regiments, for his white soldiers would not fight next to them on the battlefield. This did not help matters, however. Widespread disgust and desertion set in among white U.S. troops after the Emancipation Proclamation was issued in January 1863. Here, several blacks are being mustered into Union service amidst an angry white crowd in Illinois.

Northern white outrage at the idea of enlisting blacks was somewhat mitigated when Lincoln ordered the army and navy to be racially segregated, but newly recruited blacks were not happy with the president's command that all colored troops were to be officered by whites.[3162] Even pro-North historians have had to concede that white Northern soldiers were "bitterly hostile . . . to Negro troops."[3163]

Others in Lincoln's party put the matter more bluntly. Samuel J. Kirkwood, Iowa's governor, said that he would rather sacrifice the lives of "niggers" than the lives of the nation's white sons.[3164] Another man from Lincoln's party, Illinois Senator John A. "Black Jack" Logan, a Union general in the War, stated publicly that he would rather that "six niggers" be killed than a single white man.[3165] In the winter of 1864, the London *Telegraph* printed what the North has still yet to find the courage and honesty to acknowledge: "Not once did Lincoln ever consider arming blacks on his own. It was only when he could not afford to lose anymore white soldiers that the decision came."[3166]

Lincoln later admitted that he relied much more heavily on his nearly 200,000 black soldiers than his 2,700,000 white soldiers. Why? Because, as he himself flatly asserted, "without our black soldiers the War would have stripped the North of much of its white population."[3167] Since his first priority was the preservation of the white race, white culture, and white jobs, he could simply not allow this to occur; thus the need for the Emancipation Proclamation and black enlistment.

In mid 1864 Lincoln initiated his involuntary black enlistment plan, which involved physically forcing Southern blacks to join the U.S. military.

Preferring to stand by the Confederacy and its cause (self-determination), the vast majority (95 percent) of Southern slaves had no use for a racist army like Lincoln's. Yet, he had decided he needed soldiers, warm bodies on the battlefield—whatever their color.

To this end, beginning in the summer of 1864, Lincoln sent 1,045 agents into occupied areas of Dixie to "round up" black recruits. Using barbaric methods nearly identical to those of bounty hunters and slave catchers,[3168] only 5,052 Southern blacks were enrolled in this manner,[3169] a failure of such magnitude that the original act that had authorized the procedure was repealed after only eight months. An embarrassed Yankee provost marshal general later drily remarked in his report:

> No material advantage to the service resulted from this undertaking [Lincoln's involuntary black enlistment program]. All, or nearly all, of the [Negro] recruits to be had in the rebel States were being obtained through the proper military officers and agents of the War Department. Without increasing the number of men enlisted, the law enabled States in the North to lay claim to credits for the men enlisted in the South, and thus reduce their quota for draft. To obtain these credits local bounties were lavishly provided. They were unnecessary, and did not have the effect of increasing the number of [Negro] recruits obtained, but in many instances [they] enriched bounty brokers and corrupted military officers.[3170]

But black Southern resistance was no impediment to Lincoln. In fact, it only seemed to rouse the dictator in him. Those blacks who refused to enroll voluntarily were taken, at gunpoint, from the peace and safety of their farms and plantations, to the filth, hardships, and dangers of life on the battlefield.[3171] As a result, at least 50 percent of these reluctant soldiers died alone in muddy ditches fighting for the Yanks against their own native homeland, the South.[3172]

Those blacks who resisted the North's "involuntary enlistment" program were usually shot or bayoneted on the spot, without trial. When blacks rebelled against the abuse of white Yankee soldiers, they were whipped.[3173] Those who deserted were mercilessly tracked through the wilderness by Northern bounty hunters and their hound dogs.[3174] Both white and black Union soldiers mistreated Southern slaves who remained loyal to Dixie, entering their homes, shooting bullets through their walls, overturning furniture, and stealing various personal items.[3175] A Northerner visiting South Carolina told how Southern blacks were "hunted like wild beasts and ruthlessly dragged from their families" by Yankee military recruiters.[3176]

These freshly captured Southern black slaves, some of them shackled by their Yankee abductors, are being marched off under the whip to "enlist" in the Union army. Pro-North writers pretend that African-Americans by the tens of thousands willingly joined Lincoln's militias, but this is far from the truth. For many the process was involuntary, brutal, and diabolical, to say the least. Blacks who resisted Lincoln's racist "recruiting tactics" were beaten, whipped, and sometimes murdered where they stood. According to eyewitnesses, a bullet or bayonet thrust usually did the job.

African-Americans who made it through Lincoln's barbaric military enlistment program were treated very differently than his European-American soldiers. These black recruits, who are being subjected to medical examinations, will be consigned to slave-like labor and paid half that of white U.S. soldiers.

The Yankees' own *Official Records* reveal what most Northerners and scallywags will still not admit. In December 1864, a disgusted Yankee General Rufus Saxton reported on Lincoln's racist and often violent "recruiting tactics." Southern blacks, Saxton said,

> were hunted to their hiding places by armed parties of their own people [that is, Unionized blacks], and, if found, compelled to enlist. This [Union] conscription order is still in force. [Black] men have been seized and forced to enlist who had large families of young children dependent upon them for support and fine crops of cotton and corn nearly ready for harvest, without an opportunity of making provision for the one or securing the other.
>
> Three [black] boys, one only fourteen years of age, were seized in a field where they were at work and sent to a [Union] regiment serving in a distant part of the department without the knowledge or consent of their parents.
>
> A [black] man on his way to enlist as a volunteer was stopped by a [Union] recruiting party. He told them where he was going and was passing on when he was again ordered to halt. He did not stop and was shot dead, and was left where he fell. It is supposed the [Union] soldiers desired to bring him in and get the bounty offered for bringing in recruits.

> Another [black] man who had a wife and family was shot as he was entering a boat to fish, on the pretense that he was a deserter. He fell in the water and was left. His wound, though very severe, was not mortal. An employee [black] in the [U.S.] Quartermasters Department was taken, and without being allowed to communicate with the quartermaster or settle his accounts or provide for his family, was taken to Hilton Head and enrolled, although he had a certificate of exemption from the military service from a medical officer.
>
> I protested against the order of the [Union] major-general commanding (General Foster) and sent him reports of these proceedings, but had no power to prevent them. The order has never to my knowledge been revoked.[3177]

As this old illustration shows, both Southern and Northern blacks who tried to avoid Union enlistment were summarily tracked down by slave catchers and their hound dogs, then physically forced, often through extreme intimidation and ferocity, to join Lincoln's army. Blacks who were unlucky enough to find themselves in the U.S. military were often the recipients of racist banter, pranks, humiliation, general degradation, and even violence. Exactly how many blacks secretly fled U.S. military service for the warmth of the more tolerant South is unknown, but the figure must be in the many thousands. The slave in this image was ultimately torn to pieces by the pursuing dogs and left to die in the river, a not uncommon occurrence that was recorded by numerous observers.

Of Lincoln's "shot-gun policy" of coercive black enlistment, it was said that "it always succeeded in getting his conscript."[3178] What the president did not seem to grasp, however, was that the very definition of recruitment insinuates *voluntary* enlistment. Thus, many of Lincoln's black "recruits" were actually more akin to prisoners of war than enlisted soldiers. Yet, he still counted them as legitimate servicemen, which, of course, greatly over exaggerated the number of "black Union soldiers."

Speaking before the Confederate Congress on December 7,

1863, President Jefferson Davis commented on the Yankees' conduct toward Southern blacks; or as he put it, the "unrelenting warfare [that has] been waged by these pretended friends of human rights and liberties against the unfortunate negroes":

> *Wherever the enemy have been able to gain access, they have forced into the ranks of their army every able-bodied [black] man that they could seize, and have either left the aged, the women, and the children to perish by starvation, or have gathered them into camps, where they have been wasted by a frightful mortality. Without clothing or shelter, often without food, incapable, without supervision, of taking the most ordinary precaution against disease, these helpless dependents, accustomed to have their wants supplied by the foresight of their masters, are being rapidly exterminated wherever brought in contact with the [Yankee] invaders. By the Northern man, on whose deep rooted prejudices no kindly restraining influence is exercised, they are treated with aversion and neglect. There is little hazard in predicting that, in all localities where the enemy have gained a temporary foothold, the negroes, who under our care increased six fold in number since their importation into the [Yankee] colonies of Great Britain, will have been reduced by mortality during the war to not more than one half their previous number.*
>
> Information on this subject is derived not only from our own observation and from the *reports of the negroes who succeeded in escaping from the enemy*, but full confirmation is afforded by statements published in the Northern journals, humane persons engaged in making appeals to the charitable for aid in preventing the ravages of disease, exposure, and starvation among the negro women and children who are crowded into [Union] encampments.[3179]

Those few Southern blacks who enlisted in the U.S. army voluntarily were treated little better by their white Union brothers. What follows is a description of an experience by a black Southern soldier who was then serving in the Fifty-fourth Massachusetts Volunteers. On this unfortunate occasion he crossed paths with a group of Federal soldiers from Connecticut, who happened to be in occupied New Orleans at the time:

> I attempted to pass Jackson Square in New Orleans one day in my uniform, when I was met by two white soldiers of the 24th Conn. They halted me and then ordered me to undress. I refused, when they seized me and began to tear my coat off, I resisted, but to no

> good purpose: a half a dozen others came up and began to assist. I recognized a sergeant in the crowd, an old shipmate on board of a New Bedford, Mass., Whaler; he came to my rescue, my clothing was restored and I was let go.[3180]

This black boy was coerced into U.S. military service, then "employed" as a personal slave, or what Southerners called a "body servant," under a Yankee officer.

As for those who underwent Lincoln's violent forced enlistment, most Southern blacks fled from his armies at their first opportunity,[3181] back to the comfort, warmth, security, and domesticity of their homes in the South.[3182] The Yankee top brass was not amused. While stationed at Camden, South Carolina, one of Sherman's officers, Lieutenant Thomas J. Myers, wrote to his wife on February 26, 1865:

> The damned [Southern] niggers, as a general rule, preferred to stay at home, particularly when they found out that we [Yanks] only wanted the able bodied men (and to tell you the truth the youngest and best looking women).[3183]

Northern newspapers too were confused by the homesick Southern black's propensity for fleeing back to Dixie whenever the chance arose. In the summer of 1862 Rhode Island's *Providence Post* wrote that

> most Southern blacks evince no friendliness toward the Yankees whatsoever. And neither have they attempted to flee north out of Dixie, or attack and overwhelm their white owners, as was expected. In fact, the few who have crossed over into Union lines show no urge to work or fight; only a desire to live off Northern whites, for their hearts are still with the Southern Confederacy.[3184]

Elizabeth Keckley, a *Northern* slave who worked for the Lincolns at the White House after she purchased her freedom, explained the Southern black attachment to Dixie:

> Well, the emancipated [Southern] slaves, in coming North, left old associations behind them, and the love for the past was so strong that they could not find much beauty in the new life so suddenly opened to them. *Thousands of the disappointed, huddled together in camps, fretted and pined like children for the 'good old times.'* In visiting them in the interests of the Relief Society of which I was president, they would crowd around me with pitiful stories of distress. *Often I heard them declare that they would rather go back to slavery in the South, and be with their old masters, than to enjoy the freedom of the North. I believe they were sincere in these declarations . . .*[3185]

Angering abolitionists and black civil right leaders alike, after Lincoln permitted black enlistment he consigned many African-Americans to simple picket duty. Yet this is exactly what he had pledged to do in his Final Emancipation Proclamation, issued on January 1, 1863.

Blacks who survived the Yankees' brutal "enlistment" process and could not escape back South, did not have it easy. Even after they were allowed to become combatants and carry weapons, they were still prohibited from serving as officers. Instead, Lincoln put most of them on "fatigue duty"[3186] or impressed them into "heavy labor."[3187] The rest were sent off to serve as garrison troops, tedious guard duty watching over Union forts, stations, and prisons, just as he had promised to do in his

Final Proclamation Emancipation.[3188]

The reason? Neither he nor his officers felt that blacks were intelligent or trustworthy enough to hold important positions, nor did they have any confidence that blacks could lead assaults.[3189] (Compare this with the Confederacy where, at the very beginning of the War, in April 1861, blacks were appointed commissioned officers in Louisiana.)[3190]

Untold numbers of blacks deserted Lincoln's armies. But why would they if, as pro-North writers claim, Union soldiers were egalitarian abolitionists coming to rescue them from the horrors of so-called "Southern slavery"? The truth is that blacks serving in the U.S. military suffered extreme persecution, from racist slander and insufficient pay to slave labor conditions and even physical beatings. The black man suspended from this particular Union army noose, Private William Johnson, was one of the unlucky ones: a member of the First New York Cavalry, Twenty-Third U.S. Colored Troops, after he was caught trying to desert, in June 1864 he was marched up the scaffold, had his wrists and ankles tied, and was hanged—taking the record of his personal sufferings at Union hands to the grave. The realities of black U.S. military abuse and desertion have been wholly ignored by anti-South partisans, another futile attempt to prevent the facts from coming out.

Black soldiers, Lincoln believed, would not be much of a bother after emancipation and enlistment,[3191] except that they might lose their weapons, by then a rare and valuable item.[3192] It was due to just such sentiments that on August 11, 1862, U.S. General Ulysses S. Grant issued the following order to his officers:

> Fugitive slaves may be employed as *laborers* in the quartermaster's, subsistence, and engineer departments, and whenever by such employment a [white] soldier may be saved to the ranks. They may be employed as *teamsters*, as company *cooks* (not exceeding four to a company), or as *hospital attendants* and *nurses*. *Officers may employ them as private servants [that is, slaves], in which latter case the fugitive will not be paid or, rationed by the Government. Negroes not thus employed will be deemed "unauthorized persons," and must be excluded from the camps.*[3193]

During the first half of the Civil War, blacks in the Union army were not uniformed, armed, drilled, and sent into battle, as pro-North historians claim. Instead, being an "inferior race," as Lincoln referred to them, they were given menial tasks and drudge work, from laundry and filling sandbags, to digging ditches and cooking. In this scene black U.S. "soldiers" are serving food to an all-white Yankee regiment—segregated by Lincoln's order.

Many of the thousands of blacks Lincoln refused to arm after emancipation were herded like cattle onto "government plantations," Southern farms whose peaceful and harmless white owners had been driven off or killed.[3194] Here so-called "freed" black men, women, and children, were put to work doing ordinary labor, the same drudgery they had performed previously as slaves (mainly laundry, cooking, and cleaning), and from which Lincoln was allegedly trying to free them. A ten-hour work day, 26 days a month, was mandatory. The pay was $10 a month ($0.26 a day, or 2.6 cents an hour). "Insubordination" was punishable by "imprisonment in darkness on bread and water."[3195] This was Lincoln's idea of "emancipation."

Many "freed" blacks were simply returned to the status of domestics and body servants,[3196] the latter being slave-like personal attendants whose only job was to wait on Yankee officers.[3197] Grant, who, like Lincoln, was not fond of African-Americans (once, after having excluded them from his picket lines, Grant was harshly reprimanded by Union General Henry W. Halleck),[3198] was known for intentionally keeping his black soldiers "in the rear, guarding his wagon trains."[3199]

Most other blacks in this particular group drove supply wagons, cooked for white soldiers, or worked on fortifications.[3200] This is not what they had signed up for.

This slave-like treatment of newly freed Southern blacks was no accident. As mentioned, Lincoln had carefully worded his Emancipation Proclamation so that black soldiers would remain subservient to white soldiers. Rather than warmly welcoming blacks into the Union military as legitimate armed combatants, Lincoln's edict states that

> . . . such [black] persons of suitable condition, will be received into the armed service of the United States to garrison forts, positions, stations, and other places, and to man vessels of all sorts in said service.[3201]

Compared to their black counterparts in the Union armies, black Confederate soldiers had it good. Not only did they fight in racially integrated troops, they were treated as equals, paid the same as whites, given pensions, assigned important military positions, and honored at postwar reunions. Here a group of white and black Confederate infantrymen enjoy a campfire story told by a black sharpshooter.

This, in essence, confined most black U.S. soldiers to "post and garrison duty"—if they were lucky.[3202]

The rest could expect to work as common laborers, digging ditches, constructing bridges, filling sandbags, unloading ships, and draining swamps.[3203] Others would end up working as laundresses, longshoremen, commissary workers, medical assistants, masons, carpenters, blacksmiths, orderlies, pioneers, or spies, almost anything except armed soldiers. This was, after all, as both Lincoln and the U.S. Congress maintained, a "white man's war."[3204] A newly "freed" black servant once complained to Mary Chesnut about the treatment he and other freedmen were receiving from Lincoln and his Yankee officers: "They have removed the chains from our feet, but left them on our wrists," he told her bitterly.[3205]

Despite black resistance to Lincoln's idea of "colored enlistment," he had the support of most of his party members. One Northern senator later put the matter this way:

> The shovel and the spade and the ax have ruined thousands of the young [white] men of the country, and sent hundreds of them to their graves . . . we could have employed thousands of colored men at low rates of wages to do that ditching, and thus saved the health, the strength, and the lives of our brave [white] soldiers.[3206]

Lincoln could not have agreed more. But his prejudice did not stop there.

After exploiting "freed" African-Americans as little more than enslaved automatons, he ordered all black troops to be segregated[3207] and led by white officers[3208]—an order followed closely at conflicts like the Battle of Nashville.[3209] These were certainly the fortunate ones.

Confederate President Jefferson Davis was one of thousands who witnessed Lincoln's savage Southern black recruitment process firsthand. Wrote Davis: "Wherever the enemy have been able to gain access, they have forced into the ranks of their army every able-bodied [black] man that they could seize, and have either left the aged, the women, and the children to perish by starvation, or have gathered them into camps, where they have been wasted by a frightful mortality."

Lincoln indeed used most of the blacks in his military, not for soldiering, but as road and bridge builders, chefs, and as "officers' servants"—in the North a euphemism for "slaves."[3210] Some U.S. officers, such as General Benjamin F. Butler—who, like Lincoln, was at first against Negro enlistment in the Union military—openly used the Southern blacks they came across as slave work forces for their own army projects.[3211] These projects, of course, required heavy labor and other monotonous mundane duties, the exact type of work from which Lincoln wanted his white soldiers spared.[3212]

Union General Grant was thinking along the same lines, which is why he immediately put the "contrabands" he encountered to work picking, ginning, and baling cotton. For though they were now under so-called Union "protection," they "slaved away" under constant guard to prevent their "escape," making them little more than bonded laborers—now in the North rather than in the South.[3213] This begs the question: if they were now truly free men, as Yankees then as today claim, why would they want to flee from their Northern "emancipators"?

This early American postal stamp memorializes something that today's pro-North movement would rather you not know about: Union General Benjamin F. Butler's use of freed Southern blacks—or "contraband of war," as he derogatorily called them—as slave laborers for his many army projects.

As black soldiers who were segregated from whites, Lincoln had them named the "United States Colored Troops" (USCT),[3214] a title never officially used by the Confederacy, whose military was fully integrated from day one. Thus, the 300,000 Southern blacks who eventually fought for the South[3215] joined seamlessly with the Confederate military's 1,000,000 European-Americans,[3216] 70,000 Native-Americans, 60,000 Latin-Americans,[3217] 50,000 foreigners,[3218]

12,000 Jewish-Americans,[3219] and 10,000 Asian-Americans.[3220] As in Southern society itself, there was no segregation among the South's military forces.[3221] For unlike in the North, Southern troops neither wanted it or needed it.

Appallingly—but perhaps not surprisingly with white supremacist Lincoln acting as commander-in-chief—white Yankee troops sometimes used the fog of war to kill their own fellow black soldiers.[3222] Apparently some saw this as an efficient and safe method of disposing of those whom Lincoln liked to refer to as an "inferior race."[3223]

At the Battle of the Crater blundering Yankee General Ambrose E. Burnside presided over the "Petersburg fiasco," which included the mass slaughter of black Union soldiers by racist white Union soldiers. Relieved of his command over the "embarrassing incident," he later resigned his commission. The tragic affair reveals the true depth of racism that existed not only among Lincoln's white troops throughout the conflict, but among Northerners in general: after the War Burnside was lauded by white New Englanders, who eagerly elected him governor of Rhode Island three times.

One such incident occurred at the Battle of the Crater on July 30, 1864, at Petersburg, Virginia, a conflict that pitted Yankee General Ambrose E. Burnside[3224] against Rebel General Robert E. Lee.[3225]

Even before the fight began many of Burnside's white soldiers had expressed the sentiment that they would not be "caught in the company of niggers." Thus, when in the heat of battle their black comrades were driven back into a 30-foot deep bomb crater by the Confederates, they were met with a "fate worse than death": under the looming powder smoke, waiting white Yankee soldiers bayoneted them, then later bragged lustfully of the cold-blooded murders.[3226]

Of this outrage Yankee General Benjamin F. Butler later lamented that "in the [Union] Army of the Potomac negro troops were thought of no value . . ."[3227] Indeed, some 1,327 black Yankee soldiers were killed at the Battle of the Crater, the largest single loss of African-Americans during the entire War—due, in great part, to the racism of Lincoln's white soldiers. Yet despite their valor and the great sacrifice of life, white Northerners blamed Burnside's black soldiers for the Yankee defeat.[3228] Grant referred to the battle as the "saddest affair" of the entire War. Not because his white soldiers mercilessly slaughtered their black comrades, but because the Union lost a total of 4,000 men against the South's 1,500.[3229]

A war correspondent for the New York *Evening Post* described what he witnessed in the typical Yankee army camp:

> White Yankee soldiers and their officers routinely approached negro soldiers in the harshest, most vulgar, and most inhumane manner I have ever seen, only speaking to them with depraved curse words, vicious criticisms, and violent threats.[3230]

The Battle of the Crater, July 30, 1864, one of the most shameful episodes in Yankee history. The truth about the racist disaster has been kept out of our history books and is not taught in our schools, all for fear of tarnishing the liberal North's Civil War reputation. But facts are facts.

Lincoln's navy was no less difficult for African-Americans. Aboard the USS *Constellation*, for instance, a white eyewitness reported that white Yankee sailors routinely referred to their fellow African soldiers as "God damn nigger," "bitch," and "black dog," and that they constantly shoved and "kicked them around." While this is not unexpected considering what we know of white Northern racism at the time, what is unexpected is the fact that only three of the crew of 36 were white.[3231]

Yes, life was not easy for blacks in Lincoln's military forces, as another case, that of Alexander

Thomas Augusta, illustrates.

A highly trained black physician from Virginia, Dr. Augusta was one of only eight black doctors commissioned by the U.S. government during the entire War.[3232] After receiving his commission in April 1863, Augusta was on his way to Baltimore, Maryland, to begin his service, when a group of Northern whites assaulted him on a train. After having his uniform defaced, he was able to escape to a nearby military post, where he reported the incident. He was then escorted back to the train under a heavily armed U.S. military squad and a detachment of detectives, who protected Augusta for the rest of his journey with drawn pistols. This was only the beginning of the doctor's troubles, however.[3233]

Dr. Alexander T. Augusta, a free born African-American from Virginia, was a distinguished physician who made the mistake of joining the Union army during the Civil War. The breveted lieutenant colonel and chief surgeon of the Seventh U.S. Colored Troops withstood years of harassment and even physical abuse from white U.S. soldiers due to his skin color. At one Yankee military camp, after the white medical staff complained of Augusta's presence, Lincoln had him removed and put on "detached service" at half the pay of a white U.S. private.

In February 1864, now head surgeon at the Union's Camp Stanton in southern Maryland, Augusta was shocked to learn that his white assistants had written a private letter to Lincoln requesting that his position be terminated. Why? Because of the "unexpected, unusual, and most unpleasant relationship in which we have been placed." In other words, they did not want to serve under a black man. Lincoln, of course, obliged the whites, and Augusta was quickly expelled from Camp Stanton and put on "detached service."

The black physician was appalled once again when he discovered that he was to be paid the same amount as a lowly black Union private ($7 a month). Under Lincoln's racist unequal pay system, this was $6 less than what even white privates were paid ($13 a month). After numerous letters of complaint, the U.S. government eventually agreed to pay Augusta according to his rank—one year later.[3234] If this is how Lincoln treated the highest ranking black officer in the Union military, it is not surprising that he treated all his other black soldiers so poorly.[3235] Thus it was that Union General Grant ordered that his troops be segregated in areas where there were high numbers of freed slaves, or as he put it:

> *The soldiers should all be white troops. The reasons for this are obvious. Without mentioning many of them, the presence of black troops, lately slaves, demoralizes labor, both by their advice and furnishing in their camps a resort for the freedmen for long distances around. White troops generally excite no opposition, and, therefore, a smaller number of them can maintain order in a given district.*[3236]

Union General Ulysses S. Grant was no friend of African-Americans. Not only did he assert that he would rather fight for the Confederacy than fight for abolition, he also kept his slaves until he was forced to free them by the Thirteenth Amendment. Not surprisingly he spent much of the War writing up orders that restricted the activities and rights of black Union soldiers. One of his "solutions" to the ever escalating racial tension in Yankee camps was to segregate troops wherever and whenever possible, a bigoted program in perfect keeping with Lincoln's own discriminatory policies. Wrote Grant coldly: "The soldiers should all be white troops. The reasons for this are obvious."

In plain English, most white Union soldiers did not want blacks in U.S. military camps. Not only because of their skin color, but, as Yankee General Henry W. Halleck inferred in his infamous "General Order Number Three," because they were sure to carry military information back to the Confederacy—a curious admission indeed, considering Southern blacks were supposedly fleeing *North* from the Rebel armies. To this end, Halleck directed the "expulsion and absolute exclusion from Union lines" of any and all blacks.[3237]

After earlier promising equal pay,[3238] Lincoln's order (via the Militia Act of July 17, 1862)[3239] that black soldiers receive half the pay of white soldiers,[3240] infuriated both blacks and abolitionists.[3241] This was a "necessary concession" to white Northern racism,[3242] Lincoln explained to a stunned Frederick Douglass in the summer of 1863.[3243] Many of Lincoln's black soldiers were *never* paid. Former slave Susie King Taylor wrote:

> I was the wife of one of those [black] men who did not get a penny for eighteen months for their services, only their rations and clothing.[3244]

There was also the issue of white Union recruitment: Lincoln and his cabinet feared that granting equal pay to black soldiers would discourage Northern whites from enlisting,[3245] most who did not want to fight next to blacks anyway, however noble the Union cause.[3246]

Adding fuel to the fire, black Yankee officers, those rare few that existed,[3247] were paid the same as white Yankee privates.[3248] Yet when the Confederacy also finally officially enlisted blacks, March 23, 1863, they were immediately integrated and given equal pay and equal treatment with white soldiers.[3249]

Resistance by white Union soldiers to black officers was so severe that even Lincoln's 100 black commissioned officers,[3250] representing just 0.003 percent of the entire Union military force of 3,000,000 men, *were ultimately replaced by whites*.[3251] U.S. General Nathaniel P. Banks discussed this topic in an official field report dated February 12, 1863. Speaking of the Union's all-black First, Second, and Third Louisiana Native Guards (infantry), Banks wrote:

> The three regiments first named have ten companies each; their

> field and staff officers are white men, but *they have negro company officers, whom I am replacing, as vacancies occur, by white ones, being entirely satisfied that the appointment of colored officers is detrimental to the service.*
>
> It [that is, black officership] converts what, with judicious management and good officers, is capable of much usefulness into *a source of constant embarrassment and annoyance. It demoralizes both the white troops and the negroes. The officers of the Fourth Regiment will be white men.*[3252]

Though blacks seem to have been more readily accepted into Lincoln's navy than his army,[3253] as noted, they were still confronted by rank bigotry from all sides. At the start of Yankee black enlistment, for instance, African-American sailors were not allowed to rise above the lowest rank, known as "Boy."[3254]

Union Major General Henry Wager Halleck, who had as little faith in the idea of arming blacks as Lincoln did, was the man responsible for issuing the infamous General Order Number Three, which called for the "expulsion and absolute exclusion [of blacks] from Union lines."

When Governor John Albion Andrew of Massachusetts went to Lincoln to ask that he be allowed to grant qualified blacks military commissions, the president said absolutely not. As usual, the reason he gave for this decision was that the racist Northern public would not accept them.[3255] However, this was only partially true, for Lincoln himself would also not accept black officers.

Let us note here that unlike Lincoln's black soldiers—most who were violently forced into service, Southern blacks were recruited voluntarily, "with their own consent."[3256] And while Lincoln's black soldiers served as *freed*men, Confederate black soldiers served as *free*men, an enormous difference to all concerned.[3257] All except for Lincoln, that is.

Though he made many promises to his black soldiers regarding the inequality of their pay, Lincoln did little or nothing to fulfill them, and full and equal pay was not granted to black Yankee soldiers until *after* the War. The money involved was so small that there is only one way to explain the procrastination: Northern white racism.[3258] Just as a fish rots from the head down, that racism, of course, started at the top—with the president.

Union General Nathaniel Prentice Banks found that appointing negro officers to lead all-black U.S. troops was "detrimental to the service." This practice is, he wrote, "a source of constant embarrassment and annoyance. It demoralizes both the white troops and the negroes. The officers of the [all-black] Fourth Regiment will be white men."

Lincoln was certainly his own worst enemy in this regard, for though he desperately needed blacks to join, most refused the "offer." Even Frederick Douglass, who constantly encouraged other blacks to become Union soldiers, had little success at this game. After he gave a recruitment speech before a black audience in New York City, only one man came forward. Insulted, Douglass told the crowd that he felt sorry for them, insinuating that they were cowards.

But it was not cowardice. It was Lincoln's racist military policies that made many blacks think twice about enlisting. A man named Robert Johnson stood up, faced Douglass squarely, and said of "the Negroes of New York":

> If the [U.S.] government wanted their services, let it guarantee to them all the rights of citizens and soldiers, and, instead of one man,

> he would insure them 5,000 men in twenty days.[3259]

Johnson was entirely correct. But guaranteeing black soldiers full civil rights was something that neither Lincoln, his cabinet, nor most of his officers were prepared to do, which is precisely why the majority of African-Americans had to be physically forced into Yankee military service.

Douglass himself eventually conceded that the trouble lay not with blacks or cowardice, but with Lincoln and his racial bigotry. "Why should Negroes enlist when the U.S. military is so prejudiced against them?" he asked the president rhetorically.[3260]

In October 1862 a *Northern* reporter for the New York *Tribune* visited Union troops in North Carolina and wrote the following report on the condition of black Yankee soldiers. The situation of the miserable lowly Negroes, he said,

> is such as should excite the sympathy of every Christian man. *I am sorry to say that they are treated with great sternness and severity amounting to positive cruelty, by our own soldiers who seem to regard them as hardly better than beasts. Not a few of our [Union] officers conduct themselves in the most unfeeling manner toward these unfortunate creatures* . . .[3261]

This type of white Yankee racism continued well into the War. During inclement weather, for example, white Union soldiers were known to beat black Union soldiers, then push them out into the freezing night air in order to have the tents all to themselves.[3262]

Most white Union officers never completely accepted the idea of commanding all-black troops, as there was "no prestige" in it. In fact so few white officers could be found who were willing to "lower" themselves to leading blacks that white privates, induced with the promise of promotion,[3263] finally had to be virtually coerced into taking the positions.[3264]

The situation got so out of hand that Federal officers had to be ordered to "treat black soldiers as soldiers," and the word "nigger," along with degrading disciplinary action and routine offensive language aimed at blacks, had to be banned with harsh punishments.[3265] Meanwhile white Union soldiers continued to put on minstrel shows that satirized and humiliated African-Americans, a not uncommon form of entertainment, particularly on Yankee warships.[3266]

But Northern white racism in the U.S. army often manifested in far more serious and diabolical ways. Southern diaries, letters, and journals are replete with reports of incredible Yankee brutality against not only white Southern women they came across, but black Southern women as well, even against those that had at first cheered them on as liberators. Yankee soldiers' crimes against black females included robbery, pillage, beatings, torture, rape, and even murder.[3267]

Southern black males were often treated even worse by their Northern "emancipators." As mentioned, those who survived such crimes were taken, against their will and at gunpoint, from their homes directly to the battlefield, where at least 50 percent of them perished.[3268]

One of the few times "Honest Abe" was actually honest was when he was confronted about his unequal and unfair pay scale for white and black Union soldiers. It is, he would reply, a "necessary concession" to white Northern racism.

Should we be shocked by any of this? Not when we realize that this was all merely a continuation of Lincoln's policy of coercion, the same one he had used to invade the South in an attempt to destroy states' rights to begin with.[3269]

Newly "freed" black males were often used as Yankee shock troops, sent first into battle in conflicts usually known beforehand to be hopeless, where they would draw fire and take the brunt of the violence.[3270] The purpose of this Union practice, of course, was to spare the lives of Northern whites—as Lincoln's Secretary of War Edwin B. Stanton later admitted to English visitor Henry Latham.[3271] This is almost certainly what Lincoln was intimating in his letter to James C. Conkling on August 26, 1863, when he wrote:

> . . . whatever negroes can be got to do as soldiers, leaves just so much less for white soldiers to do in saving the Union.[3272]

Naturally, this included receiving cold Confederate steel.[3273]

Lincoln's friend, Yankee savage and Union General William T. Sherman, had similar ideas about how to use black men, as he impatiently noted in a personal letter to Halleck on September 4, 1864:

> *I am honest in my belief that it is not fair to our men to count negroes as equals.* Cannot we at this day drop theories, and be reasonable men? *Let us capture negroes, of course, and use them to the best of advantage.*[3274]

Blacks who fought and died for the Union did not get much in return for their suffering and sacrifices. Lincoln refused to give black U.S. soldiers bounties, bonuses, pensions, or support for dependents, all which were routinely accorded to white soldiers. Even medical aid was to go to whites first.

As we have seen, blacks who were finally allowed to enlist in the Union army by their reluctant president, however, were in for a rude awakening if they expected to don a fancy new blue uniform and fight next to whites on the battlefield. For at the beginning of black enlistment, Lincoln turned nearly all freed black males into common workers who performed what can only be described as "forced labor";[3275] in other words, slavery. Their work, in fact, was identical to the drudgery they had experienced as slaves. Black military duties under Lincoln included construction, serving officers (known in the South as "body servants"), cooking, washing clothes and dishes, tending livestock, and cleaning stables.[3276]

This so-called "Freedmen's labor system," authorized by Lincoln and overseen by Yankee General Nathaniel Prentiss Banks, was so blatantly racist that Banks was roundly criticized by other Northerners, who accused him of "forcing blacks back into slavery." The brutal U.S. government program was also rife with corruption and fraud: freed blacks were regularly whipped, while their already paltry wages were often "withheld" by unscrupulous and inhumane white Northerners, who pocketed the money then disappeared.[3277]

The fact that one of Lincoln's top officers, the cross-eyed General Benjamin "the Beast" Butler, insisted on referring to freed Southern blacks as "contraband" (that is, illegal goods) certainly did not help the cause of black civil rights.[3278] Instead, it revealed that the North still regarded blacks as inferior to whites[3279] and as the legitimate property of whites—even after so-called "emancipation."[3280]

But Lincoln never objected to the dehumanizing title. In fact he approved it. The name stuck and continued to be widely used in the North, even after the War.[3281] This was to be expected, as the North's commander-in-chief, Abraham Lincoln, who led the North by example, always referred to whites as the "superior race"[3282] and blacks (and all non-whites, in fact) as the "inferior race."[3283]

Southern blacks were far from being truly free after Lincoln's Emancipation Proclamation. This is why Lincoln and the rest of the North referred to them as "freedmen" rather than "freemen": they had been freed from the "shackles of slavery," but they were not yet free from the shackles of Northern racism, or what English abolitionist Marshall Hall astutely called "the second slavery."[3284] This is precisely what tourists like Yankee antislavery advocate Dr. Ethan Allen Andrews discovered when he traveled through New York in 1835.[3285] And it is the same bigotry that Southern historian Matthew Estes wrote about in 1846:

At the North, bitter and deep-rooted prejudices exist against the colored race: whilst there is a legal equality, there is the most striking practical inequality in all departments of life. The two races are kept apart in every relation of life.[3286]

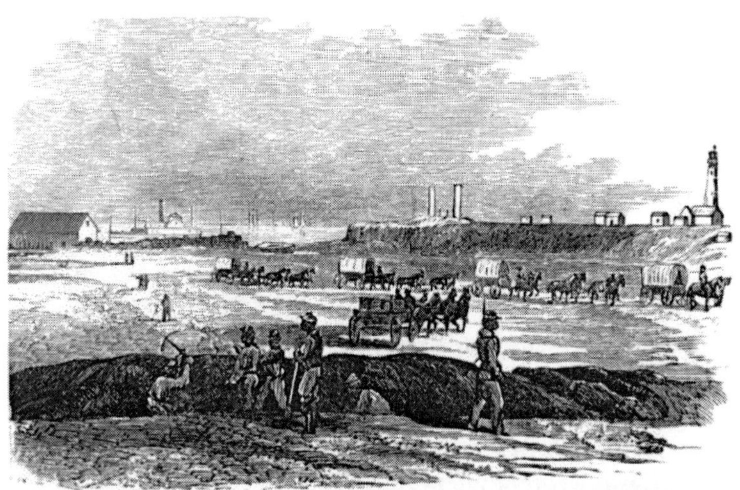

Halfway through his war Lincoln made it clear that he wanted to begin enlisting blacks because, as he put it, "whatever negroes can be got to do as soldiers, leaves just so much less for white soldiers to do in saving the Union." The black U.S. soldiers here are throwing up earthworks, a job considered unfit for white U.S. soldiers. While the South has acknowledged that the Confederacy sometimes also utilized blacks in this capacity, the North will never admit what is so obvious to Southerners: Lincoln and his Union officers often used their black troops as mere slave labor. Not out of necessity, as in the Confederacy, which had far less soldiers, but out of pure unadulterated white racism.

Lincoln's own personal racism seemed boundless. Along with the above bigoted policies, he literally refused to grant Northern black soldiers equal treatment in any way.[3287] As we have discussed, he gave his black soldiers half the pay of white soldiers:[3288] white U.S. privates were paid $13 per month, while black U.S. privates were paid just seven $7 per month.[3289] Contrast this with the Confederacy: in some Southern states blacks were actually paid up to three times the rate of whites for military service.[3290]

Three of the seven dollars of the black Union soldiers' monthly pay was a deduction for clothing, a deduction not imposed on white Union soldiers. Often even this small amount was withheld from black recruits by Yank officers, who simply "skimmed" the money for themselves, only one of dozens of ways the U.S. defrauded African-Americans during the War.[3291] Naturally, Northern black soldiers began to fight back. While some all-black Yankee regiments threatened to mutiny, others, like the Massachusetts Fifty-fourth and Fifty-fifth, declined to accept their pay vouchers until they were paid the same as all-white regiments.[3292]

But this rebellion was a mainly symbolic gesture, for Lincoln also refused to give black soldiers bounties,[3293] bonuses, pensions, or support for dependents, all which were routinely accorded to white soldiers.[3294] They were also purposefully given inferior or obsolete weapons, some completely unworkable.[3295] "Honest Abe" would not even allow black soldiers equal medical treatment. Medicines and emergency care were to go to whites first, blacks second.[3296]

As if this type of Northern prejudice was not enough, Lincoln made sure that most black units were stationed in out-of-the-way sectors, and that their white officers were those judged unfit for service in more vital departments.[3297] One wonders how many black Yankee soldiers finally realized that it was Lincoln and the Union who were their enemies, not Davis and the Confederacy!

To add to the insult, blacks in Lincoln's army could not officially be promoted beyond the level of noncommissioned officer.[3298] And in those rare cases when they were, black officers, as noted, were paid the same as white privates. At least 18 blacks who protested Lincoln's inequitable wages were charged with "mutiny" and executed by hanging or firing squad.[3299] These executions went on even after Lincoln's death and the War had ended. As late as December 1, 1865, six black U.S. privates accused of "mutiny" (that is, for protesting Lincoln's racist pay scale) were rounded up and killed by musketry at Fernandina, Florida. This was a full year-and-a-half after the U.S. Congress authorized retroactive equal pay for black soldiers in June 1864.[3300]

During his life, Lincoln, an avowed atheist and anti-Christian,[3301] had not been the forgiving type, and neither were many of those who followed in his footsteps.

An eyewitness living on Hilton Head Island, South Carolina, in 1862, reported that the occupying white Yankee soldiers there repeatedly talked down to blacks using the foulest and most disrespectful language imaginable, while in Norfolk, Virginia, a freed black woman wrote of seeing other blacks being continually abused psychologically, verbally, and physically by Union troops.[3302] These Yankee crimes included the destruction of property, pillage, assault and battery, and even rape, against innocent blacks who had fled to them, believing them to be emancipators. This same African-American woman forlornly penned: I'm nothing more than one of master Lincoln's slaves now.[3303]

Eyewitnesses of the interaction between white Union officers and black Union soldiers often described a variety of abuses, such as disrespectful language and assault. Though this white racism was endemic to Yankee culture, it was further fueled by the U.S. military's own commander-in-chief. It was Lincoln, after all, who once said: "What I would most desire is the separation of the white and black races." Should we surprised then that he segregated his troops and assigned blacks to do slave-like tasks that whites refused to do? The black U.S. soldiers in this illustration are unloading government stores from a Yankee river boat near Richmond, Virginia, as their white superiors stand nearby conversing.

It is obvious that even after reluctantly allowing blacks into the U.S. army and navy, Lincoln and his military men continued to see them as little more than servile laborers and cannon-fodder.[3304] The result? With 38,000 killed,[3305] the mortality rate among Lincoln's black soldiers was 40 percent higher than for white soldiers.[3306] But as we have so readily seen, this was just how Lincoln planned it.[3307]

In comparison to the Yankees' grossly unjust treatment of her black soldiers, the Southern Confederacy's approach was the epitome of equality. Not only were blacks paid equal with whites and integrated into all military units under President Davis' General Order No. 14, issued March 23, 1865, but:

> *All [white Confederate] officers . . . are enjoined to a provident, considerate, and humane attention to whatever concerns the health, comfort, instruction, and discipline of those [black] troops, and to the uniform observance of kindness, forbearance, and indulgence in their treatment of them, and especially that they will protect them from injustice and oppression.*[3308]

In sharp contrast to the equal rights accorded to African-American combatants in the Confederacy, Lincoln's prejudices against his own "sable soldiery" continued throughout the War. Black civil rights leaders, like Sojourner Truth, complained to the U.S. president about his pitiful treatment of black soldiers, but to no avail.[3309] Another, celebrated African-American orator, Frederick Douglass, expressed his displeasure with Lincoln's long-time reluctance to allow blacks to enroll in the Union military. "Mr. President," he asked, "if blacks were good enough to serve under U.S. General George Washington, why are they not now good enough to serve under U.S. General George B. McClellan?"[3310]

Most black men who eventually joined Lincoln's army probably did not want to serve under McClellan anyway. Like so many other U.S. officers, he spent much of his time enforcing the Fugitive Slave Law of 1850, which required runaway servants to be returned to their owners. This was the same law that Lincoln promised to strengthen in his First Inaugural Address,[3311] despite the fact that overturning it, or even ignoring it, would have helped bring slavery to an end much sooner.[3312]

Southern female servants and their children, meanwhile, could expect little better in the way of treatment from their "Northern liberators." After being driven from their homes in livestock-like droves, they were set to work on "U.S. government plantations," so-called "abandoned" Southern farms.[3313] In reality these were Confederate plantations whose original owners had been ousted or murdered,[3314] replaced by Yankee bosses who often withheld food, clothing, bedding, and medicine from their new black charges, resulting in an appalling death toll.[3315] Though their numbers were never recorded, eyewitnesses testify that the vast majority of blacks rounded up and put in Yankee "contraband camps" did indeed die, the U.S. government apparently placing little importance on their survival.[3316]

Southern blacks were so frightened of Lincoln's soldiers that they went to almost any length to avoid being taken away by them, for they knew that they would very likely be tortured, forced into labor camps, or even killed. Some simply wanted to avoid hearing the Yanks' horrible un-Christian language or having to gaze upon what they had heard were their "hideous looking" faces. One of the most ingenious methods Southern blacks came up with to escape being "freed" by Yankees was to feign illness. Many a Southern black, for instance, was spared "a fate worse than death" by faking a limp, wearing a perfectly good arm in a sling, or taking to bed with a host of alarming moaning sounds.[3317]

Unlike Union President Abraham Lincoln, Confederate President Jefferson Davis would not tolerate racial prejudice in his armies. His General Order Number Fourteen, for example, commanded all white Confederate officers to provide "a provident, considerate, and humane attention to whatever concerns the health, comfort, instruction, and discipline of those [black] troops, and to the uniform observance of kindness, forbearance, and indulgence in their treatment of them, and especially that they will protect them from injustice and oppression."

The dread of Northern racism was great enough in Dixie that during the War whites "refugeed" their servants by sending them further South for protection.[3318] But almost none had to be coerced, for no Southern black wanted to be "freed," then reenslaved by the invading Union army, only to end up fighting against their own homeland and people. Thus most went further South voluntarily, requested to be moved, or simply moved "down yonder" on their own.[3319]

The reality of this fact was brought to life by Southern belle Mary Chesnut. In 1862 she noted in her journal that after Confederate General Richard Taylor's home had been attacked and (typically) looted by foraying Yanks, his black servants then deliberately moved themselves southward to the city of Algiers, not far from New Orleans. Apparently the white Yankee penchant for intimidating and abusing Southern blacks was contagious. According to Chesnut, black Union soldiers treated Southern blacks even worse than white Union soldiers did.[3320]

Here black U.S. "soldiers" are hard at work repairing a railroad—like all army projects, one that was overseen by white Union officers. As the Emancipation Proclamation itself clearly states, white supremacist Lincoln never pretended that his black troops were to be anything but common laborers, slaves, in fact, who were to be assigned the lowest, dirtiest, and most undesirable jobs. It is the pro-North historians who came after him who have tried to conceal this fact from the public.

Throughout the War, despite the "elevated" standing that Lincoln's all-black Yankee troops eventually acquired over their former status as "subhumans," they continued to suffer racial discrimination, humiliation, abuse, and harassment at the hands of fellow whites,[3321] for few Northerners liked the idea of working alongside the common former slave.[3322] As we have seen, racial tension in Lincoln's armies would only deteriorate from this point on.

After the War, Yanks viewed Southern blacks no better than they had during the conflict. We have record of an incident in South Carolina, for instance, of a black man running up to thank a white Federal officer for Lincoln's emancipation. The grateful former servant threw his arms around the Union general, embracing him affectionately. But the Yank violently pulled himself away, quickly pulled a gun, and shot the innocent man dead. "I want nothing to do with such ridiculous falderal," he yelled sternly, and walked calmly away.[3323]

It was not just Southern blacks who feared white Yankees, of course. Tens of thousands of Northern blacks, as well, experienced the horrors of "Yankee rule" between 1641—the year slavery was first legalized in an American colony (Massachusetts),[3324] and 1862—the year the North officially, and finally, ceased trading in slaves.[3325]

When it came to blacks, Union General William T. Sherman and Lincoln shared identical views. Both wanted to limit slavery, not abolish it; bar blacks from the franchise; prevent the races from intermingling; and maintain the subordinate position of blacks in American society. Paralleling the sentiments of his commander in the White House, Sherman once remarked: "A nigger as such is a most excellent fellow, but he is not fit to marry, associate, or vote with me or mine."

As the innocent victims of the instigators of the American slave trade, Northern blacks certainly had much to fear from their Yankee masters. This is why former Northern slave Sojourner Truth often referred to the U.S. flag, not as the "Stars and Stripes," but as the "Scars and Stripes."[3326] Her attitude is not surprising considering the facts that: Lincoln used slave labor to build or complete many of Washington D.C.'s most important Federal structures (including the White House and the U.S. Capitol);[3327] the District once possessed America's largest slave mart;[3328] and slavery continued to be practiced within sight of these same buildings well after Lincoln issued his Final Emancipation Proclamation.[3329]

The fears of Northern blacks were particularly understandable when we consider that it was Lincoln (the man leading the Northern government) who repeatedly referred to blacks using the word "nigger"[3330] and described them as a base and primitive type of human,[3331] while it was Grant (the man leading the Northern military) who disliked Jews[3332] and blacks,[3333] and refused to fight for abolition.[3334] And let us not forget that it was William T. Sherman, to this day still one of the North's most idolized war heroes, who said:

> *A nigger as such is a most excellent fellow, but he is not fit to marry, associate, or vote with me or mine.*[3335]

Neither should we forget the manner in which Sherman was described by a fellow Ohioan in 1868:

> [Sherman] was at first very doubtful about emancipation; and *he never gave up his hostility to negro troops.* In 1864 *he objected to changing the status of the free negroes*, and declared that *he much preferred to keep them for some time to come in a subordinate state.* At the close of the war he insisted "that the United States can not make negroes vote in the South, any more than they can in the North, without revolution." And to Chief-Justice [Salmon] Chase he wrote about the same time: "The assertion openly of your ideas of universal negro suffrage, as a fixed policy of our General Government, will produce new war, sooner or later, more bloody and destructive than the last." He believes in a strong Government and a strong standing army; and *would rather limit than extend the suffrage [of blacks].*[3336]

With such information at hand, can there be any doubt that white Southerners saved thousands of black lives during Lincoln's War by refugeeing them further South, particularly after the Yankee chief executive issued his Final Emancipation Proclamation?[3337]

The "demoralization" caused by Lincoln's emancipation was indeed widespread, particularly among U.S. officers. One of the most demoralized of these was Yankee General Joseph "Fighting Joe"

Hooker,[3338] who sent the president a scathing letter about his proclamation, reporting that much of the Union army was solidly against the idea of freeing enslaved blacks. Wrote Hooker:

> At that time . . . *a majority of the officers, especially those high in rank, were hostile to the policy of the Government in the conduct of the war. The emancipation proclamation had been published a short time before, and a large element of the army had taken sides antagonistic to it, declaring that they would never have embarked in the war had they anticipated the action of the Government.*[3339]

Union General Fitz John Porter was just one of scores of Yankee officers who noted the widespread negative reaction among Federal troops to Lincoln's Emancipation Proclamation.

Even in those troops where abolition sentiment was deepest, the average Yankee soldier was hesitant to interfere with slavery, an institution that he was used to and which he, like Lincoln himself, knew to be legal under the Constitution.[3340] So accepted was slavery among most Union officers that they nearly always allowed Southern slaveholders into their lines to search for runaway servants.[3341]

Another disgruntled Yankee general, the infamous Fitz John Porter,[3342] wrote that Lincoln's Emancipation Proclamation was widely jeered throughout the Union army, inducing disgust, dissatisfaction, and words of infidelity toward the U.S. president that were very close to treasonous.[3343]

Shortly after the Battle of Sharpsburg, one Yankee soldier wrote that the Emancipation Proclamation was solidly denounced by most of the men in Lincoln's armies for one simple reason: none wanted to fight for the black man, but only to preserve the Union. "Subdue the Rebs first, talk about the civil rights of the nigger afterward," they fumed.[3344]

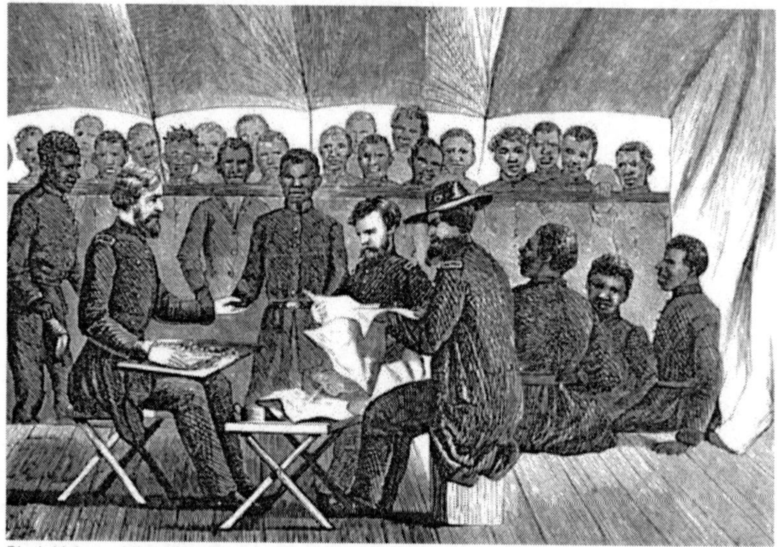

Black Union soldiers lining up to collect their monthly military salary, which was half that of white Union soldiers. The disgruntled expression on this black Union soldier's face, as he is being handed his pay packet, speaks volumes. African-Americans in Lincoln's armies received little sympathy for this and other gross injustices. Indeed, those who protested were viewed as agitators and troublemakers, and were swiftly arrested and punished. As late as December 1, 1865, six black U.S. privates found guilty of protesting Lincoln's racist pay scale, were charged with "mutiny," rounded up, and killed by musketry at Fernandina, Florida. Earlier, at least 18 blacks who had also protested Lincoln's inequitable wages, were executed by hanging and firing squad on the same charge.

In July 1862 a Yankee soldier from New York remarked that just about everyone in the U.S. army was infuriated with Lincoln and the Negro issue, and that most wanted nothing more than to put a noose around the neck of Northern abolitionist Horace Greeley.[3345] Another Union soldier said "I really don't care what happens to the 'Nigger,' and I'm certainly not going to risk my life for him. I'd rather fight him than Johnny Reb." Yet another U.S. serviceman wrote: "No doubt the ideal way to solve the dilemma of the black man would be to shoot all of them."[3346] One of the many thousands of Yankees who defected over to the Confederate side announced: "I'd just as soon live with Satan in Hell than lift a finger to free the slaves."[3347]

In early 1863, not long after Lincoln issued his Emancipation Proclamation, a Yankee soldier from his home state, Illinois, expressed the following sentiment: "I have suffered long and hard through this war, all for the 'poor nigger.' Yet I see no evidence that my suffering has helped him in anyway."[3348] Not atypical was the comment of a New

England soldier. In 1863, while stationed in New Orleans, he wrote to his brother: "I was out walking today and came upon a small black baby crawling along. My first instinct was to crush the horrid thing to death, there and then."[3349]

In the summer of 1862, some of McClellan's staff "seriously discussed" marching to Washington to "intimidate the president," in the hopes that he would refrain from interfering with slavery and simply bring the War to a quick and peaceful close. Union General John Pope noted that troops in the U.S. Army of the Potomac made frequent comments about Lincoln's flaws and the possibility of replacing him with someone more able.[3350]

Born a free man in the South, when war came Martin R. Delany switched allegiances, becoming one of the few black officers in the Union military, and the only one to achieve the rank of major. The sight of an African-American commander was so upsetting to Lincoln's white troops that eventually most of them had to be replaced with European-American officers.

The president's military men were not the only ones disappointed with his new focus on abolishing slavery for the sole purpose of enlisting blacks. Northern Catholics—who had once declared that abolitionist Garrison was a "hoary hypocrite" who should be immediately sent to Africa where he could live in "love and harmony with the wild negroes"[3351]—were highly displeased as well. New York's Archbishop John Hughes asserted that he and his flock, along with the overwhelming majority of Union troops, had no intention of fighting a bloody and costly war just to satisfy a group of rabid Yankee abolitionists.[3352]

The racial abuse of black U.S. soldiers became so severe throughout Lincoln's armies that Union General Lorenzo Thomas was forced to issue a warning of dismissal for violators. The admonition was roundly ignored and Thomas ended up ejecting a number of his more racist white Federal officers.

White racism among Lincoln's soldiers got so out of hand that eventually he had to legally ban the use of the "n" word in the military, the "demeaning punishment" of blacks, and any and all "insulting language" directed toward black soldiers.[3353] Yankee General Lorenzo Thomas, for example, promised white soldiers a quick dismissal from the army if they persisted in abusing and tormenting black soldiers. The threat had little impact and Thomas ended up removing a number of white Union officers who refused to treat blacks equitably.[3354]

Yankee slave owner General Grant, no friend of the black man, faced a similar problem in his ranks. It became so serious that on April 22, 1863, just four months after the Emancipation Proclamation was issued, he had to send out a general order demanding

> that all commanders will especially exert themselves in carrying out the policy of the Administration, not only in organizing colored regiments and rendering them efficient, but also in *removing prejudice against them*.[3355]

Lincoln still had a long way to go to get white Northerners used to the idea of fighting alongside black soldiers.

None understood this more perfectly than Southern blacks themselves, particularly those who Lincoln had violently dragooned into his military.

If pro-North historians are correct, Lincoln gave all "emancipated" Southern slaves "forty acres and a mule" to start their "wonderful new lives of liberty." In reality, he had most removed onto "government plantations," like this one. These were Southern farms whose inoffensive and nonaggressive white owners had been driven off or murdered. Here so-called "freed" black men, women, and children, were put to work doing ordinary labor, like laundry (above), the same drudgery they had often performed previously as slaves, and from which Lincoln was allegedly trying to free them. A ten-hour work day, 26 days a month, was mandatory. The pay was $10 a month ($0.26 a day, or 2.6 cents an hour). "Insubordination" was punishable by "imprisonment in darkness on bread and water." This was a harsh aspect of the real emancipation behind Lincoln's Emancipation Proclamation, one that you will never hear about from any unenlightened liberal, anti-South proponent, New South scallywag, or pro-Lincolnite.

James Ward, a former black servant from Virginia, risked his life fleeing back home through Yankee lines in order to warn other Southern slaves about the racist horrors of life as a black Union soldier in Lincoln's armies. Among these he related how he and other blacks were continually forced to the front lines in the heat of battle, while whites who had been ahead of them were allowed to fall back. "I'd rather be owned by the cruelest slaver in the South," Ward attested, "than live free in the North. They call this freedom, but if it is, I'd prefer slavery any day, thank you."[3356]

Liberal Lincoln was never progressive enough for ultra left-wing leaning Yankees like Horace Greeley. The Northern abolitionist often scolded the president for his racism, and for allowing the U.S. military to be governed by bigoted policies. One of Greeley's biggest complaints was the "invincible antipathy to niggers" displayed by Union officers, most who refused to lead all-black troops—even if the position came with a promotion.

While Lincoln was quickly instituting new martial laws to protect his black soldiers from racial abuse, Northern white soldiers, appalled and nauseated by his emancipation, began deserting in great numbers. At the same time, white Yankee officers began resigning their commands, complaining that leading black troops was less prestigious than leading white ones (white officers of white troops in particular looked down their noses at white officers of black troops).[3357]

One of the inevitable results of Lincoln's racist military policies was that many black Union regiments eventually came to be led by white privates, for few white officers could be found who were willing to command them.[3358] Those privates who signed up usually did so, not out of sympathy for the black man, but because an automatic promotion came with the position.[3359] As Greeley noted:

> There were few, if any, instances of a White sergeant or corporal whose dignity or whose nose revolted at the proximity of Blacks as private soldiers, if he might secure a lieutenancy by deeming them not unsavory, or not quite intolerably so; while there is no case on record where a soldier deemed fit for a captaincy in a colored regiment rejected it and clung to the ranks, in deference to his invincible antipathy to "niggers."[3360]

A typical example was the case of white New Yorker Daniel Ullmann. In January 1863, the non-racist Ullmann was appointed brigadier general and ordered to raise an all-black Louisiana volunteer infantry for the Union. After acquiring the proper number of black soldiers, he set out to find officers for the unit, who, by Lincoln's order, had to be white. Ullmann found it to be an impossible task and his quest nearly failed for lack of interest. Outraged, he later wrote that many Yankee officers and volunteers absolutely refused to have anything to do with the "Negro service," even if it meant a promotion.[3361]

On December 4, 1863, from Port Hudson, Louisiana, General Ullmann wrote to Senator Henry Wilson concerning the difficulties he was having due to the overt Yankee racism coming from Washington, D.C.:

> I have long had it in view to write to you, as the head of the Military Committee of the Senate, on a subject of grave importance, namely, the organization of colored troops.
>
> You are well acquainted with my status in the premises. I have had every opportunity during the last seven months to examine this policy in all its bearings.
>
> The first point to settle is whether it be intended to make these men soldiers or mere laborers; if the latter, the mode pursued is the right one, and I have nothing more to say. If the former, then there are some vital changes to be made. I fear that *many high officials outside of Washington have no other intention than that these men shall be used as diggers and drudges*. Now, I am well satisfied from my seven months intercourse with them that with just treatment they can be made soldiers of as high an average as any in the world. Their qualifications in most respects are equal to any and in one superior, to wit, their habit of subordination. All that is necessary is to give them a fair chance, which has not been done. *Since I have been in command such has been the amount of fatigue work thrust upon the organization that it has been with the utmost difficulty that any time could be set aside for drill. Months have passed at times without the possibility of any drill at all. The amount of actual labor performed by these men has been enormous. Much of it was done by them in the trenches during the siege of this place, whilst more exposed to the severe fire of the enemy than any other of our troops. They discharged their duties with cheerfulness, alacrity, and marked courage.*
>
> Then, again, *I have been forced to put in their hands arms almost entirely unserviceable, and in other respects their equipments have been of the poorest kind*. But there is another injustice done to these

men, which they appreciate as well and feel as keenly as anybody. It is a mistake to think that these poor fellows do not understand these matters just as well as we do. They are all the constant subject of conversation among them. *The point is this: While other soldiers are fed, clothed, have superior arms, and are paid $13 per month, and the non-commissioned officers receive, respectively, $17 and $20, they are fed, have unserviceable arms, and receive $10 per month, from which is deducted $3 for clothing, and no addition whatever for non-commissioned officers, and have no clothing allowance.*

Now, *general, I assure you that these poor fellows*, with all their warm, enthusiastic patriotism—and it is even greater than that of most other troops—*are deeply sensible to this gross injustice. It breaks down their 'morale,' and to an extent which I, who command and come into constant contact with them, daily deplore. . . .*

In late Summer of 1863 Lincoln's old friend James Cook Conkling invited the president to Springfield, Illinois, to speak on the subject of negro enlistment in the U.S. military. Lincoln refused, of course, for it was not something he truly approved of, but which, by this time, he had been forced into by political and military necessity. In lieu of appearing in person, he sent Conkling a letter to be read aloud at the meeting, one brimming with justificative comments about the realities of white racism across the North.

There is one other notion that must be eradicated, i.e., that anybody can command negro troops. So far from this, they require a superior grade of officers, though *I well know that those [Northern] prophets who declare that negroes never will make soldiers* are striving to force their prophecies to work out their own fulfillment by *appointing ignoramuses and boors to be officers over men who are as keensighted as any to notice the shortcomings of those placed over them*. Men have been made field officers in this section who are not fit to be non-commissioned officers—men so ignorant that they cannot write three consecutive sentences without violating orthography and syntax.

This unhappy group of captured Southern slaves, "contraband" to Yankees, have been Unionized (that is, inculcated with fictitious anti-South propaganda), and are now ready to be put into service. Most will end up doing slave labor for the U.S. military. The rest will be used as shock troops, forced onto the front lines to take the brunt of the initial attack, sparing the lives of white Federal soldiers.

My own judgment is, that in the great future before us we shall have to draw largely from this element for soldiers, and the sooner we set about it in earnest the better. This will be best accomplished by establishing the better regiments on the same footing and permanence as the Regular Army, if not actually a part of it. . . .

Notwithstanding *the persistent hostility, open and covert, which strove to defeat my mission here as a pioneer*, the progress made in the right direction is eminently encouraging, and I feel strong to carry it out to a successful issue if the right help shall come from Washington. I shall be glad if you will submit this letter to the Honorable the Secretary of War [Edwin M. Stanton]. I am, my dear general, your very faithful friend and obedient servant, Daniel Ullmann, Brigadier-General, Commanding.[3362]

With a bigoted president in the White House and little interest from other white officers (despite the offer of a promotion), Ullmann faced a long and uphill battle, as his own letter intimates.

U.S. black soldiers hard at work on river obstructions. This is not what they had signed up for.

But those few Yankees, like Ullmann, who strove for equal rights in Lincoln's armies, had another problem as well: most white Northern soldiers, as well as civilians, were against both the Emancipation Proclamation and black enlistment. Nowhere was this more true than in Lincoln's hometown, Springfield, Illinois. In August 1863, in an attempt to get an explanation from him, his Springfield constituents, including old friend James C. Conkling, invited Lincoln to speak on the topic of black enlistment. The president could not make it, and instead sent a letter to Conkling to be read aloud before the audience.

Bristling with defensiveness, in the letter we find Lincoln commenting on a variety of issues, including the Northern public's "dissatisfaction about the negro," its "dislike of both the emancipation proclamation" and its "unconstitutionality," and the fact that Northern whites, by and large, "will not fight to free negroes. . . ."[3363] Lincoln's missive is enlightening, for it demonstrates not only the depth of Northern racism at the time, but also the near total lack of support he had from other Yankees pertaining to emancipation and black soldiers.

As repeatedly noted, the very fact that Lincoln and his officers accepted and used the racist term "contraband,"[3364] reveals that the North still regarded blacks as inferior to whites[3365] (the "superior race," as Lincoln referred to them),[3366] and as the legitimate property of whites, even after emancipation.[3367] Likewise, Lincoln and his cohorts never referred to liberated blacks as "freemen." Instead they called them "freedmen": one who had been emancipated but who was still tainted with the odium of being both black and a former slave.

A man from Massachusetts wrote of the effect of Lincoln's emancipation decree on the Northern civilian population and their soldiers: "It has divided both. Lincoln's soldiers in particular hate to think that the War has anything to do with liberating the Negro," he noted.[3368]

Those Northerners who believed that Lincoln had abolished slavery to aid "the poor Negro" by enrolling him in the armed services, had it all wrong, however.

Contrary to Yankee myth, just 90,000, or only half, of Lincoln's roughly 180,000 black troops were from the South. The other 50 percent were from the North, culled from the *purposefully uncounted* and *undocumented* 500,000 to 1 million black slaves still living in the Union in the 1860s.

Our sixteenth president never claimed the Emancipation Proclamation was for the benefit of blacks, that it was a civil rights measure meant to forward their position in American society.[3369] In fact, he publicly referred to black civil rights as "false issues,"[3370] while quite clearly pronouncing his proclamation "a fit and necessary *war measure*"[3371]—a "military emancipation," as he more honestly put it[3372]—one whose sole aim was to deprive the South of her black military personnel (which numbered in the hundreds of thousands), then enlist them in the Union armies to fight against their own homeland, the Confederacy. It was unconstitutional under any other circumstances, as Lincoln himself well knew, conceding that it had "no constitutional or legal justification, except as a military measure."[3373] He even emphasized that his proclamation was meant to be temporary; that slavery could be reestablished once the War had ended.[3374]

So much for the Yankee myths about the Union's equitable treatment of freed slaves and their "freedom" under Lincoln's Emancipation Proclamation.

WHAT YOU WERE TAUGHT: All of the 180,000 blacks who fought for Lincoln and the Union were freed slaves from the South.

THE TRUTH: Just half, or 90,000, of the 180,000 blacks who eventually fought for Lincoln were "emancipated" Southern blacks. As discussed earlier, it is important to note, however, that a large percentage of these men did not enroll voluntarily. They were forced to join up at gunpoint—or risk physical assault, a whipping, or even being murdered.[3375]

The other 50 percent of Lincoln's African-American soldiers were made up of both free and freed Northern blacks,[3376] the latter who were "emancipated" from the intentionally uncounted and undocumented pool of 500,000 to 1 million black slaves who were still in bondage in the "abolitionist" North in 1860.[3377]

WHAT YOU WERE TAUGHT: Neither Union soldiers or Union officers, like Ulysses S. Grant, owned slaves. Why would they? They fought to have slavery abolished.

THE TRUTH: We have already well proven that the "Civil War" was not fought over slavery, as Presidents Jefferson Davis[3378] and Abraham Lincoln[3379] both attested on numerous occasions. And we have discussed Grant's promise that he would not fight for abolition.[3380] As for the reality of Yankee slaveholders, let us look at the record.

Since both the U.S. slave trade and U.S. slavery got their start in the North, no one should be appalled to learn that in 1860, one year before Lincoln's War, thousands of slaves still remained in the North. Estimates range from 500,000[3381] to 1 million.[3382] Using the higher number, 1 million slaves, and (as in the South) an average ownership of four slaves per owner, this means there were some 250,000 Northern white slaveholders (that is, 1.25 percent of the North's 20 million whites) in 1860.[3383]

Few if any of these Yankee slaves were counted in the always inaccurate Census due to underreporting by slave owners (who wished to avoid paying taxes on their slaves) and careless and inept Census takers.[3384] These black men and women had to be owned by someone, however—and they were not Southerners! They could have only been owned by Northerners, many who were in the U.S. military at the time.

Indeed, thousands of Yankees are known to have owned slaves right up to and through Lincoln's War. Among them were the families of Union General George H. Thomas, Union Admiral David G. Farragut, Union General Winfield Scott, and the family of Lincoln's wife, Mary Todd.[3385]

Unlike Confederate icons Robert E. Lee and Stonewall Jackson, who had slaves in their households but were not personal slave owners themselves, Yankee icon Ulysses S. Grant was an authentic slaveholder who bought, sold, and sometimes temporarily leased, Northern black slaves. Pro-North historians do not want you to know the facts about Grant, but they can no longer hide the truth about the man who became our eighteenth president, and who once uttered these words: "I never was an abolitionist, not even what could be called anti-slavery."

Arguably the most famous Yankee slaveholder was Union General Ulysses S. Grant, an Ohioan who evinced no sympathy for the situation of American blacks, never discussed the Underground Railroad, and as an officer in the Mexican War, was waited on by servants—one, a Mexican man named Gregorio, whom he took home with him after the War to entertain his family. Grant never showed any personal interest in his colored servants—except perhaps those who attended him while he was slowly dying in New York in 1885.[3386]

Upon his marriage to Julia Boggs Dent in 1848, Grant inherited a small army of 30 black Maryland slaves that belonged to her family.[3387] Later, in 1858, he was known to still own "three or four slaves, given to his wife by her father," Colonel Frederick Dent.[3388] Grant leased several additional slaves and personally purchased at least one, a 35 year old black man named William Jones. Never once did he reveal a desire to sell either his own slaves or Julia's.[3389] Instead, like his wife, and most other Northerners at the time, Grant assumed that the white race was superior to non-white races. On the eve of Lincoln's War in early 1861, for instance, Grant grew increasingly excited over the possibility that a conflict with the South would greatly depreciate black labor, then, he happily exclaimed, "the nigger will never disturb this country again."[3390] In an 1862 letter to his father, Jesse Root Grant, General Grant wrote:

> I have no hobby of my own with regard to the negro, either to effect his freedom or to continue his bondage.[3391]

This apathy for the black man continued throughout Lincoln's War. In 1863 Grant penned: "I never was an abolitionist, not even what could be called anti-slavery."[3392] Even after the issuance of Lincoln's Emancipation Proclamation Grant maintained the same sentiment, noting sourly that white Americans were still "just as free to avoid the social intimacy with the blacks as ever they were . . ."[3393]

Upon his marriage to Julia Boggs Dent, Grant inherited some 30 black slaves from her family. It is said that the couple continued to view blacks as slaves even after the end of the Civil War and the ratification of the Thirteenth Amendment.

As Lincoln's fake and illegal Emancipation Proclamation on January 1, 1863, did not liberate slaves in the North (or anywhere else, for that matter),[3394] Grant was permitted to keep his black chattel, which is precisely what he did. In fact, he did not free them until he was forced to by the passage of the Thirteenth Amendment on December 6, 1865,[3395] which occurred eight months *after* the War was over.[3396]

And what or who was behind the Thirteenth Amendment? It was not Grant, Lincoln, Garrison, or any other Northerner. It was proposed by a *Southern* man, John Henderson of Missouri.[3397]

But the amendment seemed to have little meaning to Grant or his wife Julia, the latter, who as late as 1876, still looked upon all blacks as slaves.[3398]

WHAT YOU WERE TAUGHT: Southern blacks could not wait for the arrival of the Northern armies and greeted them with open arms.
THE TRUTH: Those few Southern blacks who welcomed the sight of the invading Yankee troops only did so because their heads had been filled with anti-South, pro-North propaganda by the Freedmen's Bureau, by Union sympathizers, and by misinformed fellow African-Americans.

The reality is that most Southern blacks wanted nothing to do with Lincoln, the North, the U.S. government, or Federal soldiers. The more typical response to the arrival of the Union armies is illustrated in the following account. It was recorded shortly after the War by a former white Confederate soldier who witnessed the scene firsthand:

> In a raid by the Federals, on the Mississippi river, they took off [with] the son of [Jenkins,] a negro man belonging to Senator Henry. The boy was about ten years old; and when Jenkins ascertained that his son was on board the Yankee boat, he immediately repaired to the boat, foaming at the mouth, like an enraged tiger. He went on board, knife in hand, and demanded his boy. "Give me back my boy!" exclaimed he, in those terrible, fierce tones that electrify with fear all who hear them, "or I will make the deck of this boat slippery with your blood. You are nothing but a set of vile robbers and plunderers, and I will spill the last drop of my blood but I will have my child. Give him to me, or I will plunge my knife into the heart of the first man I reach." The captain of the boat seeing the desperate determination of Jenkins, told the [Union] soldiers they had better give him up, or some of them would be killed, and he was given up. Hurrah for Jenkins! He had previously resisted all appeals to him [by Yankees] to desert his master, and he took his boy back to his contented home in triumph. He is one amongst a thousand [Southern blacks who would have done the same].[3399]

Confederate General Robert E. Lee's son, Robert, Jr., wrote of the following incident concerning a Yankee raid on their property in the Summer of 1863. One of the family's servants, captured by U.S. soldiers, hazarded life and limb to not only return to the home and people he loved, but to protect the Lees' horses:

> The next day I found out that all the horses but one had been saved by the faithfulness of our servants. The one lost, my brother's favourite and best horse, was [accidently] ridden straight into the [Union] column [of troops] by Scott, a negro servant, who had him out for exercise. Before he knew our enemies [were there], he and the horse were prisoners. Scott watched his opportunity, and, not being guarded, soon got away. By crawling through a culvert, under the road, while the cavalry was passing along, he made his way into a deep ditch in the adjoining field, thence succeeded in reaching the farm where the rest of the horses were, and hurried them off to a safe place in the woods, just as the Federal cavalry rode up to get them.[3400]

Countless such examples could be given.

If Southern slaves were treated so terribly, and if they detested their white owners and the South so vehemently—as anti-South writers enjoy repeatedly telling us—why did nearly all of Dixie's black servants resist Yankee capture? And why did those who were taken prisoner or "freed" always try to return home, at great risk, at the first opportunity? Why do we never read about any of these brave, intelligent, and faithful African-Americans in pro-North histories?

In this early illustration the U.S. provost guard (Federal military police) is implementing Lincoln's dishonorable and illegal plan to physically coerce blacks into Union military service. Awakened in the middle of the night when they are least likely to resist, these African-Americans will be marched to the nearest Union camp and prepared to serve as menial laborers on various army projects. Those who resist "enlistment" will be threatened. That failing they will be beaten, whipped, or killed.

It is because their stories would expose the truth, revealing Lincoln's War for what it really was: not a battle to "preserve the Union" or "abolish slavery," but an illegal, unjust, and unnecessary assault on the Constitution and the American people.

The Southern Confederacy took its name from the original name of the United States of America: the "Confederate States of America." This proves that by seceding the South was not trying to destroy the Union, as Lincoln absurdly complained. Rather it was trying to recapture and preserve the original one, which they knew was about to be torn asunder by Lincoln's Constitution-loathing, dictatorial, left-wing politics. This old illustration shows some of the Confederacy's most important military officers. Clockwise from upper right: Stonewall Jackson, John Bell Hood, James Longstreet, Braxton Bragg, and Joseph E. Johnston. Center: Robert E. Lee.

21

FINAL WORDS

WHAT YOU WERE TAUGHT: All in all, American slavery manifested at its worst in the South, where white racism was rampant and man's inhumanity to man was most obvious.

THE TRUTH: Let us allow two men, Englishman Henry Latham and Southern historian Ulrich B. Phillips, to reply to this charge, and in doing so summarize the main messages of this book. We will begin with Latham:

> At the time the [civil] war broke out, it is estimated that there were, roughly speaking, 4,000,000 slaves in the Southern States. Their former masters state, and I believe with truth, that the *slaves as a rule were neither over-worked nor treated with cruelty. It is absurd to suppose the contrary.* That which is valuable and cannot be easily replaced is always taken care of. It is where there are no restrictions upon the importation, and the supply is abundant, as in the Chinese coolie trade, that you find the temptation to cruelty not over-ridden by self-interest. It is difficult also, I believe, to gainsay the position, that *nowhere where the negro is left to himself in Africa has he reached any higher stage of civilization than he possessed as a Southern slave. His hours of labour were shorter and his diet more plentiful, than those of the English agricultural labourer. He had such clothing and shelter as the climate required. The slaves of the [Southern planter] planter were in the same position as the cattle of the English farmer; and the interest that the farmer has in seeing his beasts well cared for operated in favour of the negro slave as strongly as it does in favour of all other chattels. It was the interest of the planter that, as long as his slaves were fit for work, they should be kept in working order; that as children they should be so reared as to make them strong and healthy; and*

when they were past work, that kindly feeling which a man always has towards everything which he calls his own, was sufficiently strong to ensure them a sustenance in old age. No doubt there were sometimes wicked cases of wanton cruelty, which were not common, and were exceptional as the cases are in this country [England] which are brought into court by the Society for the Prevention of Cruelty to Animals. I am willing to accept the Southerners' statement that as regards health, happiness, education, and morality, the negro-slaves were as well off as any other 4,000,000 of their race. That the slaves were not greatly discontented with their lot seems clear from the fact that the traveller can with difficulty find in the South an able-bodied white man who did not bear arms in the Confederate army. When the masters went to the war, they in fact left their wives, their children, and their goods in the keeping of their slaves. The plantations were left in charge of the old men, the women and children; yet, during the war, the crops were sown and harvested as when the masters were at home; and there were no outrages or insurrections on the plantations, except when the Northern armies passed by.

Fact: The transatlantic slave trade and American slavery were merely extensions of domestic African slavery, which has been continuous since ancient Egyptian times and beyond into the mists of prehistory. Indeed, Africa has the distinction of being the continent with the most enduring, most varied, and most barbaric forms of slavery ever known anywhere in the world. It is because of this, Africa's own ancient and entrenched history of indigenous bondage, that the words "Africa" and "African" have long been synonymous with slavery, not because of the Old American South.

The position taken by the ablest apologists for the slave-owner would affirm that *the treatment of the slaves was nearly as good as the fact of their slavery admitted; that the institution was not created by the present generation, but by their forefathers. They had not originated, but inherited it, and had to make the best of it. It was in no way peculiar to the Southern States of America; it had existed over the whole world. It was a condition of society recognised by the Old Testament as the natural state of things, and when mentioned in the New Testament, not reprobated.* It had been abolished by some nations, it was still retained by others. *It was retained by the Southern States, because they had no other labour to substitute for it*, and if the negro was emancipated it would not be possible to rely upon his labour. The civilization of the white race is the result of more than a thousand years of trial and training. The negro race was in the first stage of this probation; they had not yet completed their first century of slavery. *Those among them who possessed industry and steadiness of character could earn enough to purchase their emancipation.*

This ancient Assyrian palace at Nineveh on the Tigris River was occupied by a small group of leaders who ruled over tens of thousands of slaves—the usual ratio of free men to bondsmen in early societies. Slavery was so integral to human civilization that it could not have originated and evolved without it. The same holds true for the United States, which was built and developed on the backs of European, African, Indian, Latino, and Asian slaves and servants.

. . . It is hardly worth while to consider how far it is true that *slavery is a probation for the first steps in civilization, an education for future self-government.* It may, I think, be taken as a fact that, before the war, such speculations as to the future of the negro race did not occupy the minds of Southern planters more than the British stockbreeder is at present influenced by Dr. [Charles] Darwin's theories.

Nor is it worth while to consider how far it was probable, if the North had never interfered with the strong hand, that a gradual emancipation would have taken place in time. The only existing safety-valve through which the slave could escape into freedom was by purchase, and on that safety-valve was this weight—the more industrious the man the more valuable the slave. The living surrounded by slave-labour had so affected the Southern character that it was not easy for them to appreciate the benefits which a gradual emancipation would have brought about. They laughed at the doctrine of the dignity of labour. Hard hands and the sweat of the brow were the portion of the slave, servile. With the lower class of white men who owned no slaves, emancipation was disliked because it would raise the servile race to an equality with themselves. The slave-owners saw clearly that, however gradually brought about, emancipation would result in loss to them; for free labour, however competitive, can never be as profitable to the master as slave-labour has been—capital would have to give up a larger share of profits to the workman. The hearts of the white race were hardened . . . *They saw only that the slaves were not discontented with their lot, and that all things were prosperous.*

The institution of slavery broke down in the Southern States of America, not by reason of any injustice to the negroes, but in consequence of the effect produced by slavery upon the character and temper of the white race.[3401]

It is nothing but a fabrication of the uninformed to suggest that slavery was and is built on racism. Ancient peoples like the European Vikings were enslaving their own kind from their earliest appearance in the historical record. The same can be said for every other early ethnic group, race, people, culture, society, religion, and civilization, from India and Australia, to Native America and China. This non-racist practice continues into the present day, most notably in Africa.

The Stock Exchange, Wall Street, New York City, 1800s. Both American slavery and the American slave trade got their start in the North—at the maritime city of Boston, Massachusetts, to be exact—with other important slave ports later opening up in Rhode Island, Pennsylvania, Connecticut, New York, and Washington, D.C., among others. The South played no role whatsoever in the American slave trade. Slavery itself was inflicted on Dixie by Yankee slaving interests, such as the notorious "Wall Street Boys": affluent Northern businessmen and politicians who were heavily financially invested in keeping the Yankee slaving industry alive, but who did not want to have to live with blacks in their midst.

Phillips summarized his findings on American slavery this way, no doubt with an emphasis on Southern servitude:

> The government of slaves was for the ninety and nine by men, and only for the hundredth by laws. There were injustice, oppression, brutality and heartburning in the [slave] regime,—*but where in the struggling world are these absent? There were also gentleness, kind-hearted friendship and mutual loyalty* to a degree hard for him to believe who regards the system with a theorist's eye and a partisan squint. *For him on the other hand who has known the considerate and cordial, courteous and charming men and women, white and black, which that picturesque life in its best phases produced, it is impossible to agree that its basis and its operation were wholly evil*, the law and the prophets to the contrary notwithstanding.[3402]

The truest truth is that enemies of the American South have borrowed descriptions of the slave trade, slave revolts, and slavery as they were described and practiced in places like ancient Rome and Greece. Legally viewed and treated as human livestock, these were authentic slaves who toiled in chains, were ruthlessly beaten and whipped, torn from their families, forced to live in squalor, and killed when they became useless to their masters.[3403] As I have proven throughout this work, nothing could have been further from the mild involuntary servitude that existed in the Old American South, a region where slavery was forcefully imposed by Yankees, who had had it imposed on them by England. This makes England, the American Northeast, and Africa the culprits, and the *only* culprits, in the launching and maintenance of both the slave trade and slavery in the United States.

New York City, first known as New Amsterdam, was America's largest, most lucrative, and most important slave port for over a century, earning it the well deserved title, the "slave capital of the U.S." New York state herself holds the American record for practicing slavery longer than any other state: from 1626 to 1865, an astounding 239 years. Indeed, both the massive wealth and the dense population of today's modern metropolis ultimately derive from New York City's early and long involvement in the slave trade. New York's "Wall Street Boys," who financed the city's slave ship builders, slave ship captains, slave ship crews, and slave ship voyages, used profits from the slave trade to fund the two elections of Abraham Lincoln, as well as his armies during the Civil War.

This was a reality that even some early Yankees, like U.S. Representative John W. Taylor of New York, understood, believed, and accepted. In 1819 Taylor spoke before Congress:

> *How often and how eloquently have I heard Southern gentlemen deplore the existence of slavery! What willingness, nay, what solicitude have they not manifested to be relieved from this burden! How have they wept over the unfortunate policy that first introduced slaves into this country! How have they disclaimed the guilt and shame of that original sin, and thrown it back on their ancestors! I have heard with pleasure this avowal of regret, [and] I have confided in its sincerity. . . .*[3404]

The average Southern white family did not own slaves, and had little or no interest in the institution. According to the Census, only 4.8 percent of Dixie's white male population were slave owners in the late 1850s. In fact on average, Southern African-American slaveholders and Southern Native-American slaveholders owned more black slaves than Southern European-Americans, a statistic that has been strategically left out of our Yankee biased history books.

In 1846 another Northerner, Presbyterian minister and antislavery agitator Albert Barnes of New York, also evinced sympathy for the South, and in doing so exposed the hypocrisy of his fellow Yankee brethren:

> There is a hesitancy at the North in speaking of it [slavery] as an evil; a desire to apologize for it, and even to defend it as a scripture institution, which by no means meets the convictions of the great

body of *men at the South*, and for which they *do not thank us. They regard slavery as an unmixed evil—as the direst calamity of their portion of the republic. They consider it to be contrary to the spirit of the Bible. They look upon it as a curse in the midst of which they were born; as an evil entailed upon them without their consent, and which they desire above all things to get rid of. They remember with little gratitude the laws and cupidity of the mother country [England] by which it was imposed on them, and the Northern [Yankee] ships by which the inhabitants of Africa were conveyed to their shores*; and they little thank the professors in Theological Seminaries, and the pastors of the churches, and the editors of papers, and the ecclesiastical bodies at the North, who labour to convince the world that it is not an evil, and that it is one of the designs and tendencies of Christianity to rivet the curse on them for ever. *Such men ask for no defence of slavery from the North.* They look for a more manly voice—for more decided tones in behalf of freedom, from those whom God has favoured with the entire blessings of liberty, and they ask of us that we will aid them to free themselves from *a burden imposed on them by the joint wickedness and cupidity of our fatherland and the North*; not that we will engage in the miserable business of attempting to convince the world that the South must always groan under this malediction, and that even the influence of Christianity will be only to make the evil there eternal. *There have been more published defences of slavery from the Bible at the North, than there have been at the South. A Christian man can look with some respect on a defence of slavery at the South—for they who are there live in the midst of it, and it is natural for us to love and defend the institutions in the midst of which we were born; but what respect can we have for such a defence emanating from the North?*[3405]

The abuse of slaves was almost unheard of in America's humanitarian South, the cradle of the American abolition movement—which spawned a plethora of laws and regulations protecting black servants from the rare cruel master. Where slave abuse was both legal and widespread was in the American North. In this early illustration a living slave is being gleefully burned at the stake in Philadelphia, Pennsylvania. His crime? Being on the street after curfew.

The separation of slave families was not only frowned on in the American South, it was illegal in some cities and states, such as Louisiana. In the less racially tolerant North, however, the splitting up of slave families was both accepted and routine. This slave mother in Illinois is being torn from her son.

For those who find it difficult to let go of the lies, misinformation, disinformation, distortions, tall tales, and biased exaggeration of Yankee slanted books on slavery, here is a final reminder of *true* slavery as it existed in Africa up until recently. Bear in mind that this 1847 description by Matthew Estes comes from even earlier eyewitnesses, such as scientists, historians, and clergymen, who traveled through the Dark Continent in the late 18th and early 19th Centuries, at which time these customs were still very actively, openly, and legally being practiced. Thus the entire account is written in the present tense:

> . . . the Wag of Dahomey is engaged in perpetual wars, not only with a view to acquire Slaves, but in order to get his enemies, to water the graves of his ancestors with their blood. The tombs, palaces, and temples of his capitol, are ornamented with the skulls and jaw-bones of his enemies captured in war. The floors of his private chambers, and halls of audience, are paved with these bones; and it is considered a sufficient cause for war, that the graves of his ancestors want "more watering," or that his palace wants a new covering. *It very often happens that a tribe, without the least previous warning, or without the least provocation, will surround by night the village of a neighboring tribe, set fire to the houses, and either put the whole village to the slaughter, or spare such as they think will make useful Slaves—slaughtering the old men, children, and many of the women.*
>
> *The African Master has the most unlimited control over his Slaves, especially those whom he has purchased with his money, or taken in war. He can, if he sees proper, put them to death, or otherwise treat them*

in the most inhuman manner. Travellers in Africa mention numerous instances of inhumanity to servants. Sometimes they are confined to the earth until they are nearly stung to death by a large poisonous ant of that country: at other times they are almost burned to death; and where they become useless from age, infirmity, or from any other cause, they are put to death, as any planter would put to death a worthless dog. Our Negroes here [in the American South] are in Paradise, in comparison with the Negro Slaves in Africa.[3406]

White slavery existed in Europe and North America long prior to black slavery. This white mother and daughter were kidnaped from their home in France and taken to Cuba, where they are being sold together at auction. They will be put on a slave ship bound for New York City, and sold a second time to a Northern slave merchant, who will in turn sell them, a third time, to a wealthy Yankee family. The reality of white slavery, an institution dating back to ancient Greece and beyond, highlights an inescapable fact: whatever our race, nationality, or skin color, our family trees are full of ancestors who were slave owners and slaves.

The facts have been laid bare, so that now any further imputation of Dixie as the "founder and champion of American slavery" and the "enemy and delayer of abolition," can only derive from those whom Southern advocate Edwin C. Holland referred to as the "totally ignorant."[3407] For the Truth regarding American slavery will be available in this book forevermore, for all to see, read, absorb, and share.

The End

Both C.S. President Jefferson Davis and U.S. President Abraham Lincoln declared that the Civil War had nothing to do with American slavery. At the heart of it the South fought to preserve the Constitution, the North fought to destroy it. Anyone who says different is either lying or is ignorant of authentic American history, and is certainly in no position to critique Southern history or those who seek to save and maintain it. As the ancient saying goes: "It is unwise to comment on things you do not understand," and few understand Southern history less than those who idolize Lincoln and loathe the South. To conceal the facts about Lincoln and his war on the Constitution, pro-North advocates haughtily dismiss any material that reveals the Truth as "Lost Cause mythology," pro-South authors are minimized as "Lost Cause scribblers," and pro-South defenders are discounted as "Lost Cause partisans." Our Southern-written history books are discredited as "slanted" and "biased," and our historians are disparaged as "parochial zealots." But this type of arrogance does not make the Truth go away. The cause for which the South fought was not "lost" on April 9, 1865, and it is far from "lost" today. The Founding Fathers' self-governing precepts concerning states' rights—as tacitly embodied in the both the C.S. Constitution (Article 6, Clauses 5 and 6) and the U.S. Constitution (Ninth and Tenth Amendments)—form the very bedrock upon which the Declaration of Independence was earlier constructed, and from this grew the world's greatest republic: the "Confederate States of America," as Tocqueville and others originally referred to the United States of America. When the South seceded it was only following in the footsteps of our Revolutionary sires, who preferred death to living under a dictatorship. Hence, in 1861 the newly seceded states took the name the "Confederate States of America." Attempting to trivialize and obliterate these facts shows the utter desperation of the pro-North movement in its ongoing efforts to suppress the Truth. In the end the Southern Cause was not the preservation of American slavery, as you have been taught by anti-South mythologists, propagandists, and Lincoln devotees. Our ancestors' Cause was the preservation of what Thomas Jefferson called our great "Confederate Republic": a small weak federal government operating under the auspices of a group of all powerful sovereign states. Or as Robert E. Lee put it on January 6, 1866: "All the South has ever desired was that the Union as established by our forefathers should be preserved; and that the government as originally organized should be administered in purity and truth." Lincoln's War, the "Civil War," continues into the present, now pitting 21st-Century Conservatives against 21st-Century Liberals. For lovers of freedom this is a fight for the ultimate noble cause, one whose goal is priceless to all true Americans. This is why traditional Southerners, like Stonewall Jackson, referred to the Confederate Cause, not as "the Lost Cause," but as "the Precious Cause." Using American slavery to try and hide these facts, as the anti-South crowd does, is not only hypocritical and shameful, it is an insult to the memories of all those white, black, red, brown, and yellow Confederates who gave their lives to preserve the ideals of the original Constitution, one known as "the Articles of Confederation." We in the South hold these Truths to be self-evident.

NOTES

1. On Lincoln's socialistic and Marxist tendencies, see e.g., McCarty, passim; Kennedy and Benson, passim.
2. For a full discussion on the legality of the Southern Confederacy of 1861, see Seabrook, TAOCE, passim; Seabrook, TCOTCSOAE, passim; Seabrook, EYWTATCWIW, passim; Seabrook, AL, passim.
3. See e.g., Seabrook, TQNBF, pp. 91, 116, 118.
4. See e.g., R. Taylor, pp. vii, 1, 2, 15, 46, 125, 296, 308, 362.
5. See e.g., Seabrook, TQNBF, p. 6.
6. See e.g., A. H. Stephens, RAHS, p. 56.
7. See e.g., Seabrook, TQJD, pp. 30, 38, 76.
8. See e.g., J. Davis, RFCG, Vol. 2, pp. 4, 161, 454, 610.
9. Dunn and Dobzhansky, p. 105. For a late 19th-Century view on this topic, see W. T. Alexander, pp. 21-24.
10. Montague, TCOR, p. 11.
11. Acts 17:24, 26.
12. See Dunn and Dobzhansky, pp. 6-7.
13. W. T. Alexander, pp. 21-23.
14. See Dunn and Dobzhansky, pp. 16-17. It is interesting to note here that motor ability and emotional balance tests reveal that 50 percent of the differences between twins are due to environmental factors; less than half are due to heredity. Dunn and Dobzhansky, p. 22.
15. Montague, MMDM, p. 44.
16. Montague, TCOR, p. xiii.
17. Montague, SOR, pp. 150-151.
18. Dunn and Dobzhansky, p. 14.
19. Montague, TCOR, pp. 17, 23.
20. See Mead, SATCOR, passim. Seel also Dahlberg, passim. For an early 20th-Century discussion on the falsity of "race," see Beard, pp. 229-263.
21. Alland, p. 128.
22. Garrison and Garrison, Vol.2, p. 292. This is the only time I have ever agreed with Garrison on anything.
23. This text is my paraphrasal of what one finds in countless modern textbooks and early abolitionist works concerning the subject of American slavery. This avalanche of erroneous, cherry-picked, one-sided, largely anti-South material is at first fabricated, then copied later by hundreds even thousands of subsequent authors as "fact," and finally introduced into our schools by American "educators" as authentic "history." See e.g., Elkins, passim; Knowles and Prewitt, pp. 135-137, passim; Blake, passim; Brinton, Christopher, and Wolff, pp. 271-273; Weld, passim; J. Torrey, passim; Bennett, BTM, passim; Cash, passim; J. M. Burns, passim; Nevins and Commager, passim; H. U. Faulkner, passim; Garraty, TAN, pp. 73-76; Melden, passim; B. F. Riley, passim; Bonhoeffer, pp. 185-186; Macionis, pp. 244-225; Dormon and Jones, passim. Let the reader be the judge as to whether these writings are factual or not.
24. The list of anti-South films alone that have been made, and that continue to be made, are beyond counting. Since the making of the first motion pictures in the late 1800s, a conservative estimate would put the number at several tens of thousands, with dozens still being produced each year.
25. Rubenzer and Faschingbauer, p. 224.
26. For a large but still partial list, as well as a discussion, of Lincoln's war crimes, see Seabrook, L, pp. 758-859.
27. L. Johnson, p. 125.
28. Napolitano, p. 69.
29. L. Johnson, p. 125.
30. D. H. Donald, WNWCW, p. 87.
31. C. Adams, p. 43.
32. Neely, p. 53.
33. Nicolay and Hay, ALCW, Vol. 2, p. 375.

34. Nicolay and Hay, ALCW, Vol. 2, p. 622.
35. Mitgang, pp. 8-12, 205. The *Sangamon Journal* (later the *Illinois Journal*) is sometimes written *Sangamo Journal*. See Mitgang, p. 11. The two words are white American translations of the Algonquian word *saginawa*, meaning "river's mouth." The *Sangamo*, or the *Sangamon*, later came to refer to Illinois' once vast prairie lands. Faragher, pp. 74-75.
36. For more on Hitler and Lincoln, see Seabrook, AL, pp. 124, 293, 299, 304, 400, 401.
37. Nicolay and Hay, ALCW, Vol. 1, p. 298. Emphasis added.
38. How different the outcome of his War would have been if, for instance, "Honest Abe" had not used the press to spread lies throughout Europe about the South's "rebellion," declaring that she had split from the Union to preserve slavery, that the Confederacy was not a legitimate sovereign nation, and that secession was illegal. Such fallacies delayed, and finally killed off, any hope of official European support for Dixie, in turn destroying one of the South's last great chances for victory. Such was the mind of the man Americans annually vote our "greatest president."
39. Seabrook, L, pp. 13-14.
40. As we will discuss, pro-North historians intentionally vastly undercount the number of Civil War casualties among both soldiers and civilians—of all races.
41. Northernization of the South was one of Lincoln's chief goals. As he told Interior Department official T. J. Barnett during the War: "The entire South needs to be obliterated and replaced with new businessmen and new ideas." Seabrook, AL, p. 530. My paraphrasal.
42. E. C. Holland, pp. 10-11, 13-15. Emphasis added.
43. B. Davidson, TAST, pp. 30, 32.
44. G. Bancroft, Vol. 1, p. 123.
45. Rodriguez, THEOWS, Vol. 1, p. xiii.
46. Stimpson, p. 29.
47. C. Morris, s.v. "Slavery."
48. Blake, p. 17.
49. Braddy, s.v. "Slave."
50. Estes, p. 121.
51. See Meltzer, passim.
52. Encyc. Brit., "slavery."
53. Durant, p. 20.
54. McKitrick, p. 13.
55. G. Bancroft, Vol. 1, p. 119.
56. W. T. Alexander, pp. 119-120. Emphasis added.
57. R. S. Phillips, s.v. "Slavery."
58. For a discussion of the authentic history of prostitution, see Seabrook, *Aphrodite's Trade*, passim.
59. Encyc. Brit., "slavery"; Meltzer, Vol. 1, p. 2.
60. J. Campbell, pp. 212-213.
61. R. S. Phillips, s.v. "Slavery."
62. de la Vega, pp. 192, 355.
63. Mendelssohn, p. 173. For more on the Aztec religion, see Gardner, pp. 284-305.
64. Meltzer, Vol. 2, pp. 61-73.
65. Nieboer, pp. 47-86.
66. Nieboer, pp. 88-138.
67. R. S. Phillips, s.v. "Slavery."
68. McDannald, s.v. "Slavery."
69. Encyc. Brit., s.v. "slavery."
70. Bunson, s.v. "Slavery."
71. Website: www.nytimes.com/2013/11/07/opinion/slavery-isnt-a-thing-of-the-past.html?_r=0.
72. U. B. Phillips, ANS, p. 10.
73. Coughlan, p. 80.
74. Crane, Feinberg, Berman, and Hall, p. 152.
75. R. S. Phillips, s.v. "Slavery."
76. Coughlan, p. 80.

77. B. Mayer, p. vi.
78. Cartmell, p. 26; Norwood, p. 31; Meltzer, Vol. 2, p. 139.
79. G. H. Moore, p. 5; R. S. Phillips, s.v. "Slavery."
80. See Cottrol, passim.
81. Meltzer, Vol. 1, pp. 1-6. The one early people who seem to have completely eschewed slavery were the Minoans of ancient Crete. For more on the fascinating world of the Minoans, see Gimbutas, passim. Some believe that the Australian aborigines did not engage in slavery (see e.g., Nieboer, pp. 85-87), but this is debatable.
82. Estes, pp. 133-134.
83. Sumner, WSITBS, p. 12.
84. T. A. Bailey, p. 215.
85. B. Mayer, p. v.
86. Rodriguez, THEOWS, Vol. 1, s.v. "Africa."
87. Drescher and Engerman, pp. 32, 44, 45, 372.
88. Rodriguez, THEOWS, Vol. 1, s.v. "Africa."
89. Garraty, TAN, p. 42.
90. Blake, p. 94. Emphasis added.
91. Drescher and Engerman, p. 1.
92. Nevinson, p. 110.
93. B. Davidson, TAST, p. 30.
94. G. Bancroft, Vol. 1, p. 122. Emphasis added.
95. Craig, Graham, Kagan, Ozment, and Turner, p. 571.
96. See Moore and Dunbar, pp. 112-116.
97. B. Davidson, TAST, p. 30.
98. Bridgwater, s.v. "slavery." See also Eban, p. 20.
99. Estes, p. 81. My paraphrasal.
100. Coughlan, pp. 80, 83-84, 85.
101. Craig, Graham, Kagan, Ozment, and Turner, p. 252.
102. Blake, p. 95.
103. Penrose, p. 49; F. R. Willis, pp. 687-688; J. H. Parry, p. 27; Herring, p. 104; Burne, p. 424.
104. Coughlan, p. 86; Rodriguez, THEOWS, Vol. 1, s.v. "Africa."
105. Crane, Feinberg, Berman, and Hall, p. 152.
106. U. B. Phillips, ANS, p. 9.
107. Moore and Dunbar, pp. 103, 106; Durant and Durant, pp. 31-32.
108. Estes, pp. 92-94. Emphasis added.
109. Dormon and Jones, pp. 62-63.
110. Herskovits, p. 35.
111. Burne, pp. 677, 696.
112. Garraty, TAN, p. 50.
113. Rodriguez, THEOWS, Vol. 1, s.v. "Dahomey"; Barraclough, pp. 166-167.
114. Bennett, BTM, p. 47.
115. Dormon and Jones, p. 63.
116. U. B. Phillips, ANS, p. 27.
117. Encyc. Brit., "slavery."
118. In 1854 slaver Theodore Canot described a typical barracoon, this one in Spain: "Independent of all these [islets] were other islands, devoted to the barracoons or slave-prisons, ten or twelve of which contained from one hundred to five hundred slaves in each. These barracoons were made of rough staves or poles of the hardest trees, four or six inches in diameter, driven five feet in the ground, and clamped together by double rows of iron bars. Their roofs were constructed of similar wood, strongly secured, and overlaid with a thick thatch of long and wiry grass, rendering the interior both dry and cool. At the ends, watch-houses—built near the entrance—were tenanted by sentinels, with loaded muskets. Each barracoon was tended by two or four Spaniards or Portuguese; but I have rarely met a more wretched class of human beings, upon whom fever and dropsy seemed to have emptied their vials." B. Mayer, p. 327.
119. B. Davidson, TBMB, p. 21.

120. J. H. Parry, p. 150.
121. Blake, p. 116.
122. Estes, p. 54. Emphasis added.
123. Rodriguez, THEOWS, Vol. 1, s.v. "Gold Coast"; Drescher and Engerman, p. 33.
124. Kishlansky, Geary, and O'Brien, p. 530; Shillington, p. 196.
125. U. B. Phillips, ANS, p. 34. Emphasis added.
126. Encyc. Brit., "slavery"; J. H. Parry, pp. 64-65, 150.
127. Petherick, p. 216. My paraphrasal.
128. M. Harris, p. 119.
129. Coughlan, p. 84.
130. Crane, Feinberg, Berman, and Hall, p. 71.
131. Drescher and Engerman, p. 33.
132. Shillington, p. 104.
133. Blake, pp. 108-112, 114. Emphasis added.
134. Blake, pp. 112-113.
135. Blake, p. 115.
136. Dowley, p. 563.
137. Rodriguez, THEOWS, Vol. 1, s.v. "Darfur-Egypt Slave Trade."
138. Bennett, BTM, pp. 46-47.
139. Drescher and Engerman, pp. 38-39, 49.
140. Cappelluti and Grossman, p. 161.
141. Carruth, p. 1518.
142. Rodriguez, THEOWS, Vol. 1, s.v. "Ceddo."
143. Shillington, pp. 175, 188, 251, 252.
144. Isichei, pp. 225, 301, 380; Miers and Klein, pp. 226-227.
145. Rodriguez, THEOWS, Vol. 1, s.v. "The Hausa."
146. Drescher and Engerman, p. 34.
147. Carruth, p. 1531.
148. Carruth, p. 1544.
149. Rodriguez, THEOWS, Vol. 1, s.v. "Historiography, African."
150. Carruth, p. 1517.
151. V. M. Dean, p. 163.
152. Coughlan, p. 84.
153. Barraclough, pp. 166-167.
154. Moore and Dunbar, pp. 86-87; Carruth, pp. 1519, 1585; Cappelluti and Grossman, p. 159; Craig, Graham, Kagan, Ozment, and Turner, pp. 556-557; Crane, Feinberg, Berman, and Hall, pp. 60-64.
155. Burne, p. 678.
156. Drescher and Engerman, p. 38.
157. Barraclough, pp. 166-167; Shillington, p. 216.
158. Linton, pp. 352-353.
159. Coughlan, p. 84.
160. Nieboer, pp. 139-163.
161. Shillington, p. 188.
162. Crane, Feinberg, Berman, and Hall, pp. 62-64, 201.
163. Drescher and Engerman, p. 44.
164. Easton, TWH, p. 679.
165. Encyc. Brit., s.v. "slavery."
166. See B. Davidson, TAST, pp. 120-121, 123-124, 229, 242, 251; Stavrianos, p. 570; Drescher and Engerman, p. 48.
167. Barraclough, pp. 166-167.
168. Crane, Feinberg, Berman, and Hall, p. 62.
169. U. B. Phillips, ANS, p. 9. Emphasis added.
170. Blake, p. 116.

171. A. C. Bailey, p. 82.
172. Dormon and Jones, p. 93.
173. Rodriguez, THEOWS, Vol. 1, s.v. "The Ashanti."
174. McCulloch, Vol. 1, p. 359.
175. Blake, pp. 356-357.
176. Drescher and Engerman, p. 38.
177. U. B. Phillips, ANS, p. 27.
178. Estes, pp. 54-55. Emphasis added.
179. Barnard and Spencer, s.v. "Slavery"; Rodriguez, THEOWS, Vol. 1, s.v. "Historiography, African."
180. Encyc. Brit., s.v. "slavery."
181. Dormon and Jones, p. 64.
182. Lovejoy, TIS, p. 15.
183. Mbiti, p. 60.
184. Estes, p. 53.
185. U. B. Phillips, ANS, pp. 7-8.
186. Moore and Dunbar, p. 129.
187. Estes, p. 105.
188. U. B. Phillips, ANS, p. 6. Emphasis added.
189. Herskovits, p. 42.
190. Doubleday's Encyc., s.v. "slavery."
191. Haines and Walsh, p. 875.
192. Dowley, pp. 564-565.
193. Easton, TWH, pp. 683-684.
194. Madden was born in Ireland, but later worked on behalf of the British government, particularly on the problem of African abolition.
195. Blake, p. 103. Emphasis added.
196. Crane, Feinberg, Berman, and Hall, p. 120.
197. Garraty, TAN, p. 42.
198. Nieboer, p. 142.
199. U. B. Phillips, ANS, p. 29.
200. B. Mayer, pp. 383-386.
201. J. Thornton, pp. 304, 306.
202. U. B. Phillips, ANS, p. 45. Emphasis added.
203. See J. Thornton, pp. 72-74.
204. Doubleday's Encyc., s.v. "slavery."
205. Coughlan, p. 80.
206. Chadwick, p. 243.
207. Website: www.infoplease.com/spot/slavery1.html. For more information on modern day slavery, see Website: www.antislavery.org/english/slavery_today/default.aspx.
208. Braddy, s.v. "Slave"; Drescher and Engerman, pp. 5, 163-168.
209. Rodriguez, THEOWS, Vol. 1, s.v. "American Anti-Slavery Group."
210. Seabrook, L, p. 349.
211. Website: www.infoplease.com/spot/slavery1.html.
212. See Fox, p. 48.
213. McKissack and McKissack, p. 119.
214. B. Mayer, p. v.
215. Cameron, p. 189.
216. U. B. Phillips, ANS, p. 113.
217. U. B. Phillips, ANS, p. 113.
218. Palmer and Colton, p. 231.
219. Furnas, p. 115.
220. Drescher and Engerman, p. 44.
221. Blake, p. 102.

222. Blake, p. 102. Emphasis added.
223. Madden, EAMA, pp. 180-181, 184, 186-187, 188, 189, 192-196. Emphasis added.
224. Blake, pp. 103-106.
225. Kishlansky, Geary, and O'Brien, p. 530.
226. Drescher and Engerman, p. 30.
227. Coughlan, pp. 82-83.
228. Blake, p. 102.
229. Blassingame, p.14.
230. Crane, Feinberg, Berman, and Hall, p. 120.
231. C. Morris, s.v. "Slave Coast."
232. Garraty, HV, p. 77; Crane, Feinberg, Berman, and Hall, p. 70.
233. Blake, p. 103.
234. J. Thornton, p. 307.
235. Blake, p. 441.
236. Blake, p. 442.
237. Coughlan, p. 84.
238. Blake, p. 95.
239. Easton, TWH, p. 679.
240. T. Bourne, pp. 68-71.
241. G. Bourne, p. 69.
242. B. Davidson, TBMB, p. 26.
243. Wallechinsky and Wallace, p. 422.
244. Blake, p. 99. Emphasis added.
245. Nicolay and Hay, ALCW, Vol. 1, p. 197.
246. Stonebraker, pp. 50-51. Emphasis added.
247. Hacker, p. 18.
248. Blake, p. 101.
249. Shillington, pp. 174, 175.
250. Blake, p. 455. Emphasis added.
251. Blassingame, p. 3; Crane, Feinberg, Berman, and Hall, pp. 70-71.
252. Burne, p. 737.
253. Blake, p. 127.
254. Blake, pp. 127-128.
255. B. Mayer, p. 253; U. B. Phillips, ANS, p. 35.
256. B. Davidson, TBMB, p. 22.
257. On a proper slave ship gratings are placed over all of the hatches and bulkheads, which, when exposed by lifting the covers, allow ventilation into the hold below. See B. Mayer, pp. 105, 335.
258. For a fuller if not always completely trustworthy and unbiased discussion on the Middle Passage, see Blake, Chapter 10.
259. Blake, p. 284.
260. Clark, p. 323.
261. T. A. Bailey, p. 215.
262. U. B. Phillips, ANS, p. 37. Emphasis added.
263. Crane, Feinberg, Berman, and Hall, p. 70.
264. Drescher and Engerman, p. 34.
265. U. B. Phillips, ANS, p. 31. Emphasis added.
266. Nevinson, pp. 113-116. Emphasis added.
267. See Drescher and Engerman, p. 375.
268. Blake, pp. 136, 138, 142. One experienced crewman noted that "it was no uncommon thing for the captains [of slave ships] to send on shore, a few hours before they sail, their lame, emaciated, and sick seamen, leaving them to perish." Blake, p. 137.
269. J. Thornton, pp. 158-160.
270. Coughlan, pp. 82-83.

271. Drescher and Engerman, p. 34.
272. U. B. Phillips, ANS, p. 37. Emphasis added.
273. D. D. Wallace, pp. 67-68. Emphasis added.
274. Blake, p. 412. Emphasis added.
275. B. Mayer, p. 106.
276. B. Mayer, pp. 313, 330-332.
277. B. Mayer, p. 330.
278. Website: www.infoplease.com/spot/slavery1.html. For more information on modern day slavery, see Website: www.antislavery.org/english/slavery_today/default.aspx.
279. Garraty and McCaughey, p. 214.
280. Bennett, BTM, p. 87.
281. U. B. Phillips, ANS, p. 75.
282. M. Lerner, Vol. 2, p. 503.
283. Ransom, p. 41.
284. See U. B. Phillips, ANS, p. 74.
285. Blake, p. 98.
286. J. H. Russell, pp. 22-24. Emphasis added.
287. Drescher and Engerman, p. 239.
288. Stampp, p. 16.
289. Drescher and Engerman, p. 239.
290. Garraty and McCaughey, p. 26.
291. Wilson and Ferris, s.v. "Plantations." Many Northern whites, like Yankee judge Samuel Sewall, disliked blacks so much that they advocated using white slaves instead. See Sewall, Vol. 2, pp. 17-18.
292. Brackett, p. 25.
293. J. T. Adams, p. 53.
294. Smelser, ACRH, p. 58.
295. Shenkman and Reiger, p. 96; DeGregorio, s.v. "Millard Fillmore" (pp. 188-189); DeGregorio, s.v. "Andrew Johnson" (pp. 248-249).
296. Furnas, p. 108.
297. DeGregorio, s.v. "Andrew Johnson."
298. Shenkman and Reiger, p. 96.
299. DeGregorio, s.v. "Martin Van Buren."
300. DeGregorio, s.v. "Ulysses S. Grant."
301. Furnas, p. 108.
302. See Website: www.virginiabeachhistory.org/thoroughgoodhouse.html.
303. Bennett, BTM, p. 443.
304. G. Bancroft, Vol. 1, p. 125. Emphasis added.
305. U. B. Phillips, ANS, pp. 75, 76.
306. Roger's wife, Anne Phoebe Charlton Key, was a sister of Francis Scott Key, who wrote the U.S. National Anthem, *The Star Spangled Banner*. Like Abraham Lincoln, lawyer-poet Francis Scott Key detested abolitionists and the abolition movement. Indeed, he was a co-founder of the American Colonization Society (ACS), a Yankee organization dedicated to the idea of deporting all freed American blacks out of the country, preferably to Liberia, Africa—a colony set up in 1822 by the ACS for this express purpose. Lincoln mentioned Liberia many times in his speeches and writings as the best solution to the "race problem." See Seabrook, L, pp. 584-633.
307. Furnas, p. 108.
308. Bennett, BTM, p. 50.
309. Morison and Commager, Vol. 1, p. 51.
310. Carman and Syrett, p. 39.
311. E. J. McManus, BBITN, p. 57.
312. Goodwyn, p. 72.
313. Hacker, pp. 17-18.
314. Bedford and Colbourn, p. 13.
315. DeGregorio, s.v. "James Madison" (pp. 55-56).

316. H. B. Adams, Vol. 14, pp. 243-247.
317. Bennett, BTM, p. 443.
318. Brackett, p. 25; Wilson and Ferris, s.v. "Plantations."
319. Bedford and Colbourn, p. 30.
320. Blake, p. 98.
321. See J. Thorton, p. 125.
322. Drescher and Engerman, p. 275.
323. Grun, pp. 2-3; Burne, p. 39; Barraclough, pp. 44-45, 166-167.
324. U. B. Phillips, ANS, pp. 5-6. We will note here that the lot of the early African woman was not uncommon among world cultures. For instance, the wives of early Native-American men were, in many ways, far worse. See e.g., Nieboer, pp. 240-243.
325. Braddy, s.v. "Slave"; Drescher and Engerman, pp. 5, 163-168.
326. Drescher and Engerman, p. 1.
327. See e.g., Miers, passim; Miers and Roberts, passim; Miers and Kopytoff, passim; F. Morton, FSAFS, passim; Scully, passim; Lovejoy, TIS, passim; Lovejoy and Hogendorn, passim; Klein, passim. Also see Drescher and Engerman, pp. 31-32.
328. B. Davidson, TBMB, p. 25.
329. Rodriguez, THEOWS, Vol. 1, s.v. "Abolition, Africa."
330. Rodriguez, THEOWS, Vol. 1, s.v. "African Squadron."
331. See Blake, p. 305.
332. Dey is an old title given to ruling officials in North Africa's Ottoman Empire.
333. Ruoff, p. 88.
334. Shillington, p. 236.
335. Blake, p. 281.
336. Encyc. Brit., s.v. "slavery."
337. See Cloughlan, pp. 126-127; Montgomery, TLFOEH, p. 332.
338. See "Notes to the Reader."
339. Rodriguez, THEOWS, Vol. 1, s.v. "Asian/Buddhist Monastic Slavery."
340. Palmer and Colton, p. 230.
341. Bunson, s.v. "Slavery."
342. Drescher and Engerman, pp. 193, 246, 322.
343. Encyc. Brit., "slavery."
344. Garraty, TAN, p. 15.
345. Mish, s.v. "slave."
346. Rosenbaum, s.v. "Slavs"; "Slavonic Languages."
347. Meine, s.v. "Slav."
348. Gwatkin and Whitney, Vol. 2, pp. 421, 430.
349. Encyc. Brit., "slavery."
350. Meltzer, Vol. 1, p. 3.
351. Simons, p. 18.
352. Gibbon, Vol. 5, p. 406.
353. Meine, s.v. "Slave."
354. Webster's exact words in the speech were: "There was slavery among the Greeks; and the ingenious philosophy of the Greeks found, or sought to find, a justification for it exactly upon the grounds which have been assumed for such a justification in this country; that is, a natural and original difference among the races of mankind, and the inferiority of the black or colored race to the white. The Greeks justified their system of slavery upon that idea precisely. They held the African and some of the Asiatic tribes to be inferior to the white race . . ." Webster, p. 108.
355. De Bow, p. 515. Emphasis added.
356. See e.g., Meltzer, Vol. 2, pp. 60, 61, 62, 63, 64; Drescher and Engerman, p. 371; Vaillant, pp. 124, 126, 133, 200, 220, 221, 225-226, 255, 258; Johnson and Earle, p. 267.
357. See e.g., Drescher and Engerman, p. 389; MacQuarrie, pp. 21-23, 31, 58, 201, 209-210, 229-230, 311, 353-356; Howells, p. 298.

358. See e.g., Meltzer, Vol. 2, pp. 61, 62, 64; Drescher and Engerman, pp. 147-148; R. S. Phillips, s.v. "Slavery"; Hendelson, s.v. "slavery."
359. Garraty and McCaughey, p. 7; Leonard, p. 102.
360. Meltzer, Vol. 2, p. 4.
361. Durant, pp. 125, 159, 229, 275, 293, 337-338; Meltzer, Vol. 1, pp. 9-201; Nye, p. 46; McKenzie, s.v. "Slave, slavery"; Hartman and Saunders, pp. 54, 62, 70, 383, 446; Kramer, pp. 81-83; Eban, p. 20; Westermann, p. 90; Breasted, AT, pp. 83, 153, 218, 220; Magoffin and Duncalf, pp. 76, 100, 112, 113; Becker and Duncalf, pp. 41-42, 50; McKay, Hill, and Buckler, Vol. 1, pp. 30, 44, 67; Swain, p. 47; Jones and Pennick, p. 184; Warnock and Anderson, p. 94; Wells, Vol. 1, p. 186; Childe, p. 163; Andrewes, p. 26; Hayes, Baldwin, and Cole, p. 15; Johnson and Earle, p. 248; Breasted, TCOC, p. 75; Cappelluti and Grossman, pp. 94-96; Craig, Graham, Kagan, Ozment, and Turner, pp. 11-12; Estes, pp. 13-30.
362. Drescher and Engerman, p. 77.
363. British and Foreign Anti-Slavery Society, p. iv.
364. Kramer, p. 83.
365. F. R. Willis, pp. 21, 115.
366. Durant, p. 275.
367. Westermann, p. 36.
368. Durant, p. 229.
369. Mendelssohn, p. 147.
370. McKay, Hill, and Buckler, Vol. 1, pp. 25-26.
371. Murnane, p. 37.
372. Durant, p. 159.
373. B. Russell, p. 24.
374. Cobb, AHSOS, p. 44.
375. Riedel, Tracy, and Moskowitz, p. 298.
376. Durant, p. 337.
377. Estes, pp. 13-30.
378. Blake, pp. 17-18.
379. 2 Samuel 8:2.
380. Exodus 21:2.
381. Leviticus 25:39.
382. Exodus 22:1-7.
383. 2 Kings 4:1; Isaiah 50:1.
384. Exodus 21:4.
385. Exodus 21:7.
386. Durant, p. 337.
387. Durant, p. 293.
388. Langer, p. 68.
389. Breasted, TCOC, p. 312.
390. David, pp. 62-90; Craig, Graham, Kagan, Ozment, and Turner, pp. 92, 104.
391. Blake, p. 32.
392. Easton, TWH, p. 84.
393. Burne, p. 137.
394. Becker and Duncalf, pp. 92, 174.
395. Marvin Perry, p. 49.
396. Blake, pp. 23-24.
397. Beard, p. 50.
398. Aphrodite, or Aphrogeneia, whose name means "born of sea foam," was honored every year across Greece at her festival, called Aphrodisia. Blake, p. 31. Aphrodite was known as Venus in Rome, the name of the great Pagan "Morning Star" mentioned in the New Testament. See Revelation 2:28; 22:16.
399. Blake, pp. 25-26, 27.
400. Becker and Duncalf, p. 83.
401. F. R. Willis, p. 185.
402. B. Russell, p. 9.

403. Blake, p. 28.
404. Becker and Duncalf, pp. 92, 174.
405. Warnock and Anderson, p. 314.
406. Blake, p. 53.
407. Bunson, s.v. "Slavery."
408. Burne, p. 160.
409. Myers, p. 408.
410. Easton, THOTP, p. 356.
411. Starr, p. 236.
412. Liddell, Vol. 2, p. 143. Emphasis added.
413. G. Bancroft, Vol. 1, pp. 119-122. Emphasis added.
414. Westermann, p. 90.
415. Westermann, p. 149; Becker and Duncalf, p. 175.
416. Starr, pp. 270-271.
417. McKay, Hill, and Buckler, Vol. 1, p. 91.
418. Bunson, s.v. "Lex Petronia"; "Slavery."
419. Ariès and Duby, pp. 59, 65-67, 69.
420. Blake, pp. 49-53, 55-56.
421. Blake, p. 20.
422. Encyc. Brit., s.v. "slavery." Note: The original Latin seems to be referring to *moray* eels not *lamprey* eels.
423. Blake, p. 47.
424. Myers, p. 524.
425. Blake, p. 19.
426. Blake, p. 33.
427. C. Morris, s.v. "Slavery."
428. Westermann, pp. 354-355.
429. B. Russell, p. 262.
430. McKay, Hill, and Buckler, Vol. 1, p. 13; Breasted, TCOC, p. 562.
431. Myers, pp. 408, 409.
432. Blake, pp. 52, 53.
433. Blake, p. 20.
434. Liddell, Vol. 2, pp. 145-147, 250-252.
435. Estes, p. 31.
436. Bunson, s.v. "Secundus, Pedanius."
437. Westermann, p. 333.
438. Paraphrased from Oliver, pp. 91-92.
439. B. Russell, p. 237.
440. Starr, p. 271.
441. Seabrook, CBC, passim. See also Malachi 4:2.
442. Frazier, Vol. 9, pp. 307-308.
443. Blake, p. 25.
444. B. Russell, p. 422.
445. Eltis and Engerman, p. 152.
446. Winks, Brinton, Christopher, and Wolff, Vol. 1, p. 242.
447. McKay, Hill, and Buckler, Vol. 1, p. 546.
448. McKay, Hill, and Buckler, Vol. 2, p. 726.
449. J. McManus, pp. 59, 97.
450. Hayes, Baldwin, and Cole, p. 130.
451. Goldschmidt, pp. 79, 106; Hendelson, s.v. "slavery."
452. Dimont, p. 189.
453. C. Morris, s.v. "Slavery." For more on the Crusades, see Runciman, passim.
454. Bertrand, pp. 31, 50, 63, 70.

455. Jayyusi, p. 693.
456. Dimont, p. 193.
457. Jayyusi, p. 691.
458. Bertrand, pp. 59, 63, 66-67, 91-92, 149-150.
459. Coughlan, p. 80.
460. Hayes, Baldwin, and Cole, p. 130.
461. C. Morris, s.v. "Slavery."
462. See e.g., Dawood, pp. 60, 63, 70, 89, 192, 241, 248-249, 297, 398, 406, 426.
463. Jayyusi, pp. 691-693.
464. Zaehner, pp. 181-182. For the U.S. perspective on Arabic and Islamic history, see Diller, pp. 125-128.
465. Fogel, p. 17.
466. Breasted, TCOC, p. 561.
467. W. J. Cooper, JDA, p. 378.
468. To put these numbers into perspective: Italy is 116,345 square miles. The Confederacy was 850,000 square miles. Thus, while the American South was 87 percent larger than Italy, ancient Italians owned 84 percent more slaves than Southerners.
469. Breasted, AT, p. 642.
470. Thompson and Johnson, p. 13.
471. Blake, p. 18.
472. Blake, p. 49.
473. Herm, p. 189.
474. Easton, THOTP, p. 356; Becker and Duncalf, p. 174; Estes, p. 31.
475. T. R. Holmes, p. 59.
476. Josephus, p. 584.
477. Bark, pp. 118-120; S. B. Clough, p. 130.
478. Heer, p. 80.
479. Beard, p. 51.
480. Marvin Perry, p. 87.
481. Breasted, TCOC, p. 562.
482. Swain, pp. 172, 211.
483. Smith, Muzzey, and Lloyd, p. 103.
484. Van Nostrand and Schaeffer, p. 137.
485. Hadas, p. 41; Westermann, pp. 332-333.
486. Boardman, Griffin, and Murray, p. 47.
487. Becker and Duncalf, p. 174.
488. Hadas, p. 45.
489. Beard, p. 50.
490. Frost, p. 83.
491. McKay, Hill, and Buckler, Vol. 1, p. 147.
492. Frost, p. 76.
493. Blake, p. 46.
494. F. R. Willis, p. 185.
495. Swain, pp. 178-179.
496. Myers, p. 409.
497. M. Grant, TWOR, p. 27; Peters, p. 342.
498. Neilson, s.v. "Spartacus"; Westermann, p. 355; Boardman, Griffin, and Murray, p. 436; Wells, Vol. 1, p. 371.
499. Boren, p. 69.
500. F. R. Willis, p. 189.
501. Ariès and Duby, p. 61.
502. Smith, Muzzey, and Lloyd, p. 103.
503. Wells, Vol. 1, p. 372.

504. Childe, pp. 266-267, 282; Van Nostrand and Schaeffer, p. 131.
505. Ariès and Duby, p. 9.
506. Philip Smith, Vol. 2, pp. 546-547. Emphasis added.
507. For an in-depth evaluation of so-called "slavery" in the Old South, see Seabrook, TMOCP, pp. 65-231.
508. Drescher and Engerman, p. 283.
509. Blake, p. 19.
510. Swain, pp. 189-190, 211.
511. Blake, p. 48.
512. F. R. Willis, p. 185.
513. Estes, p. 31.
514. Celeste, pp. 141-142.
515. Blake, p. 47.
516. Drescher and Engerman, p. 193.
517. Bone, p. 161.
518. Boren, p. 49.
519. Winks, Brinton, Christopher, and Wolff, Vol. 1, p. 138; Myers, pp. 408, 409.
520. Dimont, p. 92.
521. Dimont, p. 92.
522. McDannald, s.v. "Slavery."
523. C. Morris, s.v. "Slavery."
524. Estes, p. 32.
525. Beard, p. 50.
526. Baigent, Leigh, and Lincoln, p. 278.
527. Dimont, pp. 120-121.
528. Van Nostrand and Schaeffer, p. 137.
529. Winks, Brinton, Christopher, and Wolff, Vol. 1, p. 138.
530. Myers, p. 524.
531. Drescher and Engerman, p. 272.
532. Van Nostrand and Schaeffer, pp. 131, 137.
533. Dunner, p. 880.
534. Blake, p. 49.
535. Wells, Vol. 1, p. 233.
536. Clough, Garsoian, and Hicks, p. 64.
537. De Bow, p. 515.
538. Rodriguez, THEOWS, Vol. 1, s.v. "Helots."
539. Ferguson and Bruun, Vol. 1, pp. 37, 44.
540. Blake, p. 43. My paraphrasal.
541. Blake, p. 39.
542. Andrewes, pp. 93, 139-140.
543. Blake, pp. 43-44.
544. Drescher and Engerman, p. 279.
545. Andrewes, pp. 136-137.
546. McNeill, pp. 224-225; Cappelluti and Grossman, p. 178.
547. Warnock and Anderson, p. 94.
548. McKay, Hill, and Buckler, Vol. 1, p. 91.
549. Brinton, Christopher, and Wolff, Vol. 1, p. 62.
550. Bone, p. 100.
551. F. R. Willis, p. 111.
552. A. R. Burn, p. 245.
553. Kagan, p. 256.
554. McKay, Hill, and Buckler, Vol. 1, p. 78.
555. Breasted, AT, p. 345.

556. F. R. Willis, p. 115.
557. McKay, Hill, and Buckler, Vol. 1, p. 114; Warnock and Anderson, p. 94.
558. Myers, p. 335.
559. Childe, p. 216.
560. J. M. White, p. 61.
561. Breasted, AT, p. 349.
562. Myers, p. 335.
563. Winks, Brinton, Christopher, and Wolff, Vol. 1, pp. 38-39, 48, 64; McKay, Hill, and Buckler, Vol. 1, p. 91.
564. Andrewes, p. 133.
565. McKenzie, s.v. "Slave, slavery."
566. McKay, Hill, and Buckler, Vol. 1, p. 114.
567. Doubleday's Encyc., s.v. "slavery."
568. Hendelson, s.v. "slavery."
569. Myers, p. 336. Emphasis added.
570. Heer, p. 74.
571. Chambers, Grew, Herlihy, Rabb, and Woloch, p. 662.
572. Blitzer, p. 171.
573. Burne, p. 656.
574. J. R. Green, Vol. 1. pp. 17, 27-28.
575. Hall, Albion, and Pope, p. 25.
576. Hall, Albion, and Pope, p. 11.
577. Bede, pp. 99-100.
578. Bede, p. 229.
579. B. Russell, p. 384.
580. Hale, p. 359; Wells, Vol. 1, p. 266.
581. Muller, p. 121.
582. Drescher and Engerman, pp. 195, 230.
583. Greer, p. 17.
584. Cornford, p. 54.
585. Warnock and Anderson, p. 94.
586. Myers, p. 524.
587. Dunner, p. 880.
588. Mish, s.v. "slave."
589. Van Nostrand and Schaeffer, p. 281.
590. Simons, p. 128.
591. Radzinsky, p. 33.
592. Boorstin, pp. 208-209.
593. See Bruford, p. 108.
594. Drescher and Engerman, p. 344.
595. Stavrianos, p. 528.
596. Seabrook, TMOCP, p. 209.
597. G. Jones, pp. 3, 23, 109, 119, 127, 131, 146-150, 164, 215-218, 256.
598. Van Nostrand and Schaeffer, p. 307.
599. Heer, p. 49.
600. Blake, p. 18.
601. Hayes, Baldwin, and Cole, p. 182.
602. Van Nostrand and Schaeffer, p. 307.
603. Gamoran, pp. 20-21.
604. McKay, Hill, and Buckler, Vol. 1, pp. 408-409, 494.
605. Plumb, p. 5.
606. Van Nostrand and Schaeffer, p. 446.
607. U. B. Phillips, ANS, p. 10.

608. Doubleday's Encyc., s.v. "slavery."
609. McKay, Hill, and Buckler, Vol. 1, p. 494.
610. See e.g., Burne, p. 528.
611. Myers, p. 524; E. A. Livingstone, s.v. "Slavery."
612. Doubleday's Encyc., s.v. "slavery."
613. A. O'Brien, p. 524.
614. Blake, p. 370.
615. Mills, pp. 171-178.
616. Thompson and Johnson, p. 329.
617. Tuchman, p. 172. For more on the role of the serf and the vassal in early feudalism, see Ganshof, passim.
618. Encyc. Brit., s.v. "slavery."
619. Andrewes, p. 135.
620. McKay, Hill, and Buckler, Vol. 1, p. 494.
621. Rayfield, p. 180.
622. Montefiore, p. 643.
623. I. L. Gordon, p. 362.
624. Note: Contrary to popular thought, the swastika (from the Sanskrit "amen") was not invented by the Nazis. It is an ancient religious symbol that originated in prehistoric times. One was found, for example, on a cave wall containing Stone Age art that dates back 10,000 years. This truly universal emblem appeared not only in ancient India, Persia, Japan, Libya, Greece, Rome, Britain, and Scandinavia, but it was also used in Medieval Christian church design, art, and heraldry, where it was known as the gamma cross. Swastikas with clockwise pointing arms represent the Sun and the Masculine Principle. Counterclockwise pointing arms signify the Moon and the Feminine Principle. B. G. Walker, TWDOSASO, pp. 61-62.
625. Meltzer, Vol. 2, pp. 270-277.
626. Speer, pp. 472-474.
627. Shirer, pp. 946-951. For more on the Nazi enslavement of Jews specifically, see Parkes, pp. 189-235.
628. Drescher and Engerman, p. 289.
629. Shirer, pp. 946-951.
630. Fogel, p. 454.
631. Meltzer, Vol. 1, pp. 9-201; Craig, Graham, Kagan, Ozment, and Turner, pp. 11-12; Magoffin and Duncalf, p. 76; Dunner, pp. 878-881; McKenzie, s.v. "Slave, slavery"; Hendelson, s.v. "slavery."
632. Boorstin, pp. 166-167, 209; Encyc. Brit., s.v. "slavery"; Greer, p. 210; Carruth, p. 1502; V. M. Dean, p. 177.
633. Van Nostrand and Schaeffer, p. 446.
634. Trevelyan, Vol. 2, pp. 113-114; Moore and Dunbar, p. 109; Goubert, pp. 237-238; Hendelson, s.v. "slavery."
635. Shillington, pp. 174-176; A. C. Bailey, pp. 11-12; Meltzer, Vol. 2, p. 10.
636. Winks, Brinton, Christopher, and Wolff, Vol. 1, p. 338; Dormon and Jones, p. 62.
637. Van Loon, p. 350.
638. McKay, Hill, and Buckler, Vol. 1, p. 12.
639. For more on the important topic of white slavery, see A. E. Smith, passim; Jordan and Walsh, passim; Hoffman, passim; Hildreth, TWS, passim; Ballagh, passim; Baepler, passim; Sumner, WSITBS, passim.
640. Dormon and Jones, p. 62.
641. The World Book Encyc., "slavery."
642. Encyc. Brit., s.v. "slavery." As human society became more organized and agriculture was discovered, a system of division of labor was needed to increase food production and profitability. In this early period before the domestication of animals, people naturally turned to other humans for the needed labor, which they procured through war, kidnaping, exchange, barter, and outright purchase. In this way enslavement was eventually substituted for butchery. Dunner, pp. 877-878.
643. Wells, Vol. 1, p. 185. Even after the Agricultural Revolution some 10,000 years ago, forms of this practice continued in Greece well into the 8th Century BC, the time of Homer. Andrewes, p. 46.

644. J. R. Green, Vol. 1, p. 27.
645. Van Nostrand and Schaeffer, p. 278; Hayes, Baldwin, and Cole, pp. 79-80.
646. Rodriguez, THEOWS, Vol. 1, s.v. "Celts."
647. Druidic slave chains were found in Llyn Cerrig Bach in 1943, a small lake located on the west side of the island. These, along with numerous other Iron Age items that were discovered, date from the period 150 BC to AD 50. Celtic Druids seem to have thrown them into the lake as votive offerings. Costello, p. 266.
648. K. C. Davis, p. 5.
649. McGarry and Hohl, Vol. 1, p. 105.
650. M. Grant, CTG, pp. 61, 63-64.
651. Bryant, pp. 41, 48-49, 107.
652. Cahill, pp. 81, 110, 112, 134.
653. Pinkerton, Vol. 2, p. 252.
654. Rhys, CB, p. 73.
655. Briggs, pp. 103, 123, 133, 145, 152.
656. Encyc. Brit., "slavery."
657. Compton's Encyc., s.v. "slavery and serfdom."
658. B. Holmes, p. 5. Emphasis added.
659. E. T. Clough, p. 89.
660. Mostert, p. 285; Jamieson, p. 17.
661. Milton, p. 271.
662. Löwenheim, p. 11.
663. Sumner, WSITBS, p. 45.
664. Muehlbauer and Ulbrich, pp. 124-125.
665. Jamieson, p. 229. See also Fremont-Barnes, passim; Boyde, passim.
666. Osler, pp. 294-325.
667. E. T. Clough, p. 85.
668. B. Holmes, pp. 33-35.
669. B. Holmes, pp. 30-31.
670. Marsh, pp. 21-22. Emphasis added.
671. Marsh, pp. 5-6. Emphasis added.
672. Marsh, pp. 10, 18.
673. Marsh, pp. 11-17. Emphasis added.
674. Osler, pp. 291-292. Emphasis added.
675. Meltzer, Vol. 2, p. 139.
676. Brackett, p. 25; Wilson and Ferris, s.v. "Plantations."
677. Chadwick, p. 243; The World Book Encyc., s.v. "slavery."
678. Website: www.foreignpolicy.com/articles/2008/02/19/a_world_enslaved.
679. McDannald, s.v. "Slavery."
680. Website: www.csmonitor.com/2004/0901/p16s01-wogi.html.
681. Website: www.pbs.org/newshour/bb/law/jan-june01/slavery_3-8.html.
682. W. J. Cooper, JDA, p. 378; Quarles, TNITCW, p. xiii.
683. Garraty and McCaughey, p. 214. See also Fogel and Engerman, pp. 23-24.
684. Website: www.pbs.org/newshour/bb/law/jan-june01/slavery_3-8.html.
685. Website: www.nytimes.com/2013/11/07/opinion/slavery-isnt-a-thing-of-the-past.html?_r=0.
686. Lott, pp. 35-60.
687. Ashe, p. 10.
688. Seabrook, TCOTCSOAE, passim; Stonebraker, p. 46.
689. U. B. Phillips, ANS, p. 41.
690. de la Rochefoucauld Liancourt, Vol. 2, pp. 461-462. Emphasis added.
691. Flint, Vol.1 , p. 106.
692. Chace, p. 7.
693. Lott, pp. 65-68.

694. B. F. Riley, p. 30.
695. B. F. Riley, p. 30. Emphasis added.
696. Blake, pp. 440-441. Emphasis added.
697. Dunbar, Vol. 1, p. 218.
698. See Estes, p. 229.
699. W. H. Collins, p. 60.
700. Dodd, TCK, pp. 29-30. Emphasis added.
701. W. H. Collins, pp. 19-20.
702. Helper, COTICOTS, pp. 12-13. Emphasis added.
703. S. Foote, Vol. 1, p. 537. Lincoln also refers to Captain Gordon, along with several other seized Yankee slave ships, in his First Annual Message to Congress. See Nicolay and Hay, ALCW, Vol. 2, p. 101.
704. Nicolay and Hay, ALCW, Vol. 2, pp. 121-122.
705. Farrow, Lang, and Frank, pp. 131-132.
706. Kennedy, pp. 104-105.
707. For more on the *Nightingale*, see A. H. Clark, pp. 164-165, 343.
708. U. B. Phillips, ANS, pp. 34-35. Emphasis added.
709. Ahlstrom, p. 649.
710. Rosenbaum and Brinkley, s.v. "Slavery"; Crane, Feinberg, Berman, and Hall, p. 73; Coughlan, p. 84.
711. Ward and Gooch, Vol. 1, pp. 244-247.
712. T. A. Bailey, p. 283.
713. R. S. Phillips, s.v. "Northeast Boundary Dispute"; Garraty, TAN, p. 365.
714. Blake, pp. 346-354.
715. T. A. Bailey, p. 215.
716. Bedford and Colbourn, p. 196; Boller and Story, pp. 180-181. However, under the Thirteenth Amendment enslavement was still allowed in the U.S. for criminals. Wallechinsky and Wallace, p. 427.
717. Du Bois, TSOTAST, pp. 162-167. Emphasis added.
718. T. A. Bailey, p. 283.
719. Ahlstrom, p. 649.
720. J. T. Adams, p. 253.
721. R. S. Phillips, s.v. "Slavery."
722. G. Bancroft, Vol. 1, p. 293.
723. Hildreth, THOTUSOA, Vol. 1, pp. 251, 492.
724. Meltzer, Vol. 2, p. 139. Also see Cartmell, p. 26.
725. Norwood, p. 31.
726. G. H. Moore, p. 5; Blake, p. 370; R. S. Phillips, s.v. "Slavery"; Bennett, BTM, p. 443.
727. E. J. McManus, BBITN, pp. 9, 10, 11.
728. U. B. Phillips, ASN, p. 103.
729. H. U. Faulkner, p. 58.
730. U. B. Phillips, ASN, p. 103.
731. Bowen, p. 217.
732. Wertenbaker, TPO, p. 198.
733. Bennett, BTM, p. 50.
734. G. H. Moore, pp. 130-132.
735. E. J. McManus, BBITN, p. 146.
736. U. B. Phillips, ANS, p. 104. Emphasis added.
737. See B. C. Steiner, passim.
738. Hildreth, THOTUSOA, Vol. 1, pp. 371-372; Blake, p. 371.
739. U. B. Phillips, ANS, p. 105.
740. Seabrook, TMOCP, p. 173.
741. E. J. McManus, BBITN, p. 59.
742. For more on the history of the New England slavery system, see Greene, passim.
743. Goodell, p. 106.

744. For more on the topic of slavery in Rhode Island, as well as in other New England states, see Website: www.boston.com/bostonglobe/ideas/articles/2010/09/26/new_englands_hidden_history/?page=1.
745. The Massachusetts Historical Society maintains numerous examples of these letters in their "Collections." U. B. Phillips, ANS, p. 28.
746. David, p. 135.
747. Pendleton, p. 56; Coughlan, p. 84.
748. U. B. Phillips, ANS, p. 138.
749. Blake, p. 445.
750. Johnston, p. 18.
751. U. B. Phillips, ASN, p. 106.
752. Ahlstrom, p. 649; Zilversmit, pp. 4-7.
753. E. Channing, pp. 6, 12.
754. E. J. McManus, BBITN, pp. 6-7.
755. Kishlansky, Geary, and O'Brien, p. 530.
756. E. J. McManus, BBITN, p. 60.
757. K. C. Davis, pp. 20, 23.
758. Website: www.tracesofthetrade.org/guides-and-materials/historical/the-dewolf-family/.
759. Meltzer, Vol. 2, pp. 145, 148; C. Johnson, TPIGTTS, pp. 125-126.
760. The Royall's original home and slave quarters have been turned into a museum located in Medford, MA. See Website: www.royallhouse.org.
761. A. T. Rice, TNAR, p. 607.
762. Francie Latour, "New England's Hidden History," *The Boston Globe*, September 26, 2010.
763. See Lemire, passim.
764. Farrow, Lang, and Frank, pp. 179-191.
765. Boston Female Anti-Slavery Society, p. 5, passim.
766. E. J. McManus, BBITN, p. 156.
767. Blake, p. 481.
768. Dowley, p. 547.
769. Nye, pp. 30, 49.
770. W. B. Garrison, LNOK, p. 186.
771. J. M. McPherson, NCW, pp. 78-79.
772. H. U. Faulkner, p. 318.
773. Smelser, DR, p. 44.
774. E. J. McManus, BBITN, p. 183.
775. J. M. Burns, p. 393.
776. Garraty and McCaughey, p. 146.
777. Garraty, TAN, p. 83.
778. J. T. Adams, p. 53.
779. McManus BBITN, pp. 67-68.
780. J. M. Burns, p. 392.
781. Genovese, p. 451.
782. F. Douglass, NLFD, p. 116.
783. B. F. Riley, pp. 43-44. Emphasis added.
784. R. S. Baker, pp. 117-118, 120. Emphasis added.
785. R. S. Baker, pp. 121-122. Emphasis added.
786. R. S. Baker, p. 123. Emphasis added.
787. R. S. Baker, pp. 124-125, 126. Emphasis added.
788. S. Wilbur, pp. 37-38, 40, 43, 48-49, 51.
789. Latham, p. 249.
790. Latham, p. 238.
791. Wells, Vol. 2, p. 705.
792. Hildreth, THOTUSOA, Vol. 1, p. 524; Blake, p. 372.
793. Furnas, pp. 117, 119.

794. Friedman, pp. 123-127.
795. K. C. Davis, p. 7.
796. M. M. Smith, p. 25.
797. Kishlansky, Geary, and O'Brien, p. 531.
798. Coughlan, p. 83.
799. Johnston, pp. 16-17, 19-20. Emphasis added.
800. Crane, Feinberg, Berman, and Hall, p. 71.
801. For more on Bristol, Rhode Island, and the African slave trade, see M. A. D. Howe, BRI, passim.
802. Garraty, HV, p. 77.
803. Palmer and Colton, p. 230.
804. C. Johnson, TPIGTTS, p. 125.
805. Farrow, Lang, and Frank, p. 99.
806. Hacker, pp. 19, 25.
807. For more on Rhode Island and the African slave trade, see Coughtry, passim.
808. October 25, 2010, *America Live*, FOX News. For early evidence of Rhode Island's official full name, "Rhode Island and Providence Plantations," see Article 1 of *The Treaty With Great Britain*, the famous secession contract between England's King George III and America's original 13 colonies, signed at Paris, France, November 30, 1782. J. Williams, p. 365; Rouse, pp. 78-79. Rhode Island's true official name was also mentioned in the first draft of the Preamble to the U.S. Constitution, written about August 1787. J. B. Scott, pp. 84-85. See also pp. 86-87.
809. U. B. Phillips, ANS, p. 113.
810. Manegold, pp. 132-134.
811. Rosenbaum and Brinkley, s.v. "Slavery."
812. Spooner, NT, No. 6, p. 54. See also Graham, BM, passim; Melish, passim.
813. Blake, pp. 380-381.
814. Adams and Sanders, p. 144; Nye, p. 54; Buckley, p. 61.
815. Adams and Sanders, pp. 272, 281.
816. De Angelis, p. 49.
817. W. Wilson, DR, p. 125.
818. Nicolay and Hay, ALCW, Vol. 1, p. 185.
819. Blake, p. 433.
820. Blake, p. 463. Emphasis added.
821. E. A. Andrews, p. 122.
822. Blake, p. 449.
823. C. M. Green, W, p. 180.
824. De Angelis, pp. 12-18; Lott, p. 65; J. J. Holland, passim.
825. Blake, pp. 449-450.
826. E. A. Andrews, p. 122.
827. De Angelis, p. 49.
828. Lott, pp. 61, 64.
829. Mann, pp. 2-3, 6. Emphasis added.
830. M. Hall, p. 135.
831. C. M. Green, W, pp. 180-181.
832. C. M. Green, W, p. 181.
833. J. M. Burns, p. 564.
834. C. M. Green, W, p. 182.
835. Leech, p. 291.
836. C. M. Green, W, p. 186.
837. Leech, p. 292.
838. Leech, p. 292. Many other Northern cities have had areas called "Nigger Hill" as well, such as Boston, Massachusetts. See e.g., Bartlett, WP, p. 8; Furnas, p. 515.
839. W. Chambers, p. 257.
840. Hendelson, s.v. "Lincoln, Abraham."

841. Nicolay and Hay, ALCW, Vol. 1, p. 659. Lincoln made this statement in a "strictly confidential" letter to North Carolinian John A. Gilmer. The president-elect was interested in appointing Gilmer secretary of the treasury. Desperate to have a Southerner in his cabinet, in his letter Lincoln laid out his position on slavery, hoping to allay any fears Gilmer might have about the future of the institution. Gilmer saw through it and the ploy failed. New Englander Salmon P. Chase became Lincoln's first secretary of the treasury.
842. J. C. Perry, p. 191.
843. Shotwell, p. 436.
844. Cromwell, pp. 121-122.
845. Though earlier in his presidency Lincoln had promised that he would never interfere with slavery in Washington, D.C., as usual, when it benefitted him he changed his mind. In this case, he needed the abolitionist vote for his upcoming bid for reelection. Additionally, freeing Washington's slaves allowed him to press Congress harder for black deportation and colonization.
846. Bedford and Colbourn, pp. 207-209.
847. This did not end segregation, of course. If anything it exasperated the problem of Northern white racism. Indeed, total integration was not achieved in Washington, D.C. until 1956. See Weintraub, p. 147.
848. It is a well-known fact of American history that Northern whites never once changed their laws or institutions primarily for the welfare of blacks, and Lincoln was no exception to this rule. See E. J. McManus, BBITN, p. 197.
849. *The National Almanac* (1863), p. 250; Quarles, TNITCW, p. 144.
850. Sanger, p. 378. Emphasis added.
851. Nicolay and Hay, ALCW, Vol. 2, p. 144.
852. Lincoln and the abolitionists, Caucasian Washingtonians declared, were determined to make the city "a hell on earth for the white man." Leech, pp. 295, 298.
853. Buckley, p. 86; Leech, p. 298.
854. Truth, p. 254. See also McKissack and McKissack, pp. 142, 143, 144.
855. Greenberg and Waugh, pp. 352-353.
856. U. B. Phillips, ANS, p. 448.
857. Latham, p. 73. Emphasis added.
858. Weintraub, p. 147.
859. Lott, p. 64.
860. Website: www.usatoday.com/news/washington/2007-09-01-dcdemographics_N.htm.
861. Website: http://afgen.com/popula.html. Some of these blacks, of course, went north to look for jobs during World War II. Nonetheless, a large number of them descend from Northern, not Southern, slaves. For more on America's black population centers, see S. Roberts, pp. 123, 127, 129, 137.
862. See Adams and Sanders, pp. 144, 272, 281; Nye, p. 54; Buckley, p. 61; De Angelis, pp. 12-18, 49; W. Wilson, DR, p. 125; C. M. Green, W, pp. 180-181; Lott, pp. 61, 64, 65; Leech, pp. 291-292.
863. For more on the history of slavery in Pennsylvania, see Turner, passim.
864. Lott, pp. 6-7.
865. U. B. Phillips, ANS, p. 112.
866. Brackett, p. 26.
867. Nye, p. 27.
868. Blake, p. 372. Emphasis added.
869. Blake, pp. 372, 373.
870. Nevins and Commager, p. 36.
871. E. A. Andrews, p. 41.
872. Siebert, p. xiii.
873. E. J. McManus, BBITN, pp. 196, 199; Johnston, p. 19.
874. W. Wilson, DR, p. 124; Ahlstrom, p. 649.
875. Blake, p. 434.
876. Farrow, Lang, and Frank, pp. xxvii, 4-5, 82-90; Hacker, p. 525; Ellis, FB, p. 103.
877. U. B. Phillips, ANS, p. 107.
878. Hurd, Vol. 1, pp. 277-278.

879. Heston, p. 40.
880. T. W. Foote, pp. 36-37.
881. Blake, p. 371.
882. U. B. Phillips, ANS, pp. 108-109.
883. Ripley and Dana, Vol. 12, p. 371.
884. Williams-Meyers, pp. 22, 54. See also pp. 87-93.
885. Website: www.sites.google.com/site/tenbroeckmansion/Home.
886. Website: www.historiccherryhill.org.
887. Website: www.nysparks.state.ny.us/historic-sites/33/details.aspx.
888. Blake, p. 373.
889. Commissioners of Statutory Revision, p. 18.
890. Seabrook, TMOCP, pp. 174-175.
891. Stewart, p. xxvi.
892. McKissack and McKissack, p. 3. Strangely, while Sewall had understandable sympathy for enslaved blacks, he had absolutely none for the free whites who were hanged (or crushed under rock) for witchcraft, due, in great part, to his judicial support of the accusations. To his credit Sewall later expressed remorse over his actions, even asking his church congregation for forgiveness. This is small solace, however, to the living descendants and relations of his victims.
893. E. J. McManus, BBITN, p. 62.
894. Greene, pp. 172-173.
895. Such ploys were not always successful. See E. J. McManus, BBITN, p. 149.
896. Blake, p. 381.
897. E. J. McManus, BBITN, pp. 16, 17.
898. David, p. 135.
899. Countryman, p. 11.
900. Blake, p. 406.
901. A. J. Northrup, p. 289. Emphasis added.
902. McKissack and McKissack, pp. 3, 4, 23.
903. See Stewart, passim.
904. Seabrook, EYWTACWW, pp. 79-80.
905. Farrow, Lang, and Frank, pp. 82-90.
906. Farrow, Lang, and Frank, pp. 4-5.
907. Dimont, p. 359.
908. *New York Times*, November 24, 1854. Emphasis added.
909. Hacker, p. 525.
910. Ellis, FB, p. 103.
911. Farrow, Lang, and Frank, p. xxvii.
912. Buckley, p. 103.
913. February 4, 2011, *Who Do You Think You Are?*, NBC.
914. See Van Evries, passim.
915. A. J. Northrup, pp. 246-247.
916. Wallechinsky and Wallace, p. 427.
917. C. Johnson, AVAFP, pp. 43-44.
918. Crothers, p. 16.
919. Howard, pp. 220, 233.
920. Knoblock, p. 238.
921. Blair (no page numbers).
922. *Harper's Weekly*, June 2, 1860. My paraphrasal.
923. The *Wildfire* was then condemned and sold for $6,500, after which it disappears from the records. Zimmerman, pp. 21-22.
924. Seabrook, ARB, p. 457.
925. J. D. Richardson, ACOTMAPOTP, Vol. 5, p. 594. Emphasis added.
926. American Colonization Society, pp. 9-22.

927. Knoblock, pp. 236-240; Providence Institution for Savings, pp. 37-39; J. L. M. Willis, pp. 24, 25.
928. Seabrook, TCOTCSOAE, p. 65.
929. Stonebraker, p. 81.
930. Nicolay and Hay, ALCW, Vol. 2, p. 1. See also Boller and Story, pp. 166 (the Republican Party Platform of 1860, paragraph 4), 180; J. T. Adams, p. 255.
931. Spooner, NT, No. 6, p. 54. See also Graham, BM, passim; Melish, passim.
932. See Spooner, NT, No. 6, p. 54; Pollard, LC, p. 154; Graham, BM, passim.
933. C. Johnson, TPIGTTS, p. 107.
934. Rutland, p. 35.
935. DeGregorio, s.v. "Thomas Jefferson" (p. 50).
936. Nicolay and Hay, ALCW, Vol. 2, p. 6.
937. Coughlan, p. 84.
938. Morison and Commager, Vol. 1, p. 245.
939. Faust, s.v. "slavery."
940. See Stampp, p. 271; Meltzer, Vol. 2, pp. 247-248; C. Johnson, TPIGTTS, pp. 126-128; Rosenbaum and Brinkley, s.v. "Slave Trade"; Durden, p. 288; Crane, Feinberg, Berman, and Hall, p. 73.
941. In 1862, an old law, the 1842 Treaty of Washington, was revived and strengthened, requiring U.S. and British ships to search and detain any vessel suspected of trading in slaves. This and only this finally put an effective end to Yankee slave trading. J. C. Miller, pp. 146-147.
942. Meltzer, Vol. 2, p. 247.
943. See Spooner, NT, No. 6, p. 54; Pollard, LC, p. 154.
944. Burns, Peltason, Cronin, Magleby, and O'Brien, p. 151.
945. Seabrook, L, pp. 84-85. Emphasis added.
946. Shillington, p. 178.
947. Weintraub, p. 54.
948. Wertenbaker, TPO, p. 198.
949. Crane, Feinberg, Berman, and Hall, p. 120.
950. Garraty, TAN, p. 65.
951. For more on the Cotton and Slave Triangles, see Farrow, Lang, and Frank, pp. 48-49, 50.
952. Garraty, TAN, p. 80.
953. U. B. Phillips, ANS, pp. 38-39.
954. O. Williams, p. 83.
955. DeGregorio, s.v. "Thomas Jefferson" (p. 50).
956. See S. H. M. Byers, "The Last Slave Ship," *Harper's Monthly Magazine*, Vol. 113, June to November 1906, pp. 742-746.
957. S. H. M. Byers, "The Last Slave Ship," *Harper's Monthly Magazine*, Vol. 113, June to November 1906, pp. 743-744. Emphasis added.
958. E. C. Holland, pp. 23-26. Emphasis added.
959. G. H. Moore, p. 5; Blake, p. 370; R. S. Phillips, s.v. "Slavery"; Bennett, BTM, p. 443. Massachusetts was also the first state to ban interracial marriage. See Wilson and Ferris, s.v. "Miscegenation"; K. C. Davis, p. 9.
960. McKissack and McKissack, p. 3.
961. For the history of slavery in Delaware, see W. H. Williams, passim.
962. Simpson, p. 78; Blake, p. 370.
963. G. Bancroft, Vol. 1, p. 125.
964. D. L. Jensen, p. 322; Burne, p. 516.
965. Estes, p. 87.
966. W. H. Collins, p. 3.
967. Blake, p. 98.
968. Rodriguez, THEOWS, Vol. 1, s.v. "Hawkins, John."
969. Coughlan, p. 82.
970. L. B. Smith, p. 183.
971. U. B. Phillips, ANS, p. 138.
972. Blake, p. 445.

973. E. C. Holland, p. 20.
974. Blake, p. 464.
975. A. Barnes, p. 10.
976. Blake, p. 571.
977. H. B. Adams, Vol. 14, p. 244.
978. H. U. Faulkner, p. 58.
979. Clare, Vol. 5, p. 3199.
980. Drescher and Engerman, p. 10.
981. Crane, Feinberg, Berman, and Hall, pp. 71, 73.
982. Encyc. Brit., s.v. "slavery."
983. Foley, p. 970.
984. Supplement to the Ency. Brit., p. 694.
985. W. H. Collins, p. 7.
986. Blitzer, p. 172.
987. Burne, p. 678.
988. Ferguson and Bruun, Vol. 2, p. 541.
989. Palmer and Colton, p. 230.
990. C. Morris, s.v. "Slavery."
991. Encyc. Brit., s.v. "slavery."
992. Madden, TIOC, pp. xxiii-xxiv.
993. Burne, p. 631.
994. Encyc. Brit., s.v. "slavery."
995. Albrecht-Carrié, p. 134. (Also see the map on p. 177.)
996. Estes, p. 90.
997. Macaulay, p. 3.
998. F. Hall, p. 422.
999. U. B. Phillips, ANS, pp. 32-33.
1000. Rickard, p. 177.
1001. Braddy, s.v. "Slave"; C. Morris, s.v. "Slavery." In 1833 some 800,000 Africans were set free in the British colonies, and £20 million was dispersed among their former owners as compensation. Montgomery, TLFOEH, p. 354.
1002. McDannald, s.v. "Slavery."
1003. Foley, p. 970.
1004. See Ward and Gooch, Vol. 1, pp. 244-247.
1005. Bonhoeffer, p. 356.
1006. Bedford and Colbourn, p. 85; W. T. Alexander, p. 240.
1007. See e.g., Lincoln's comments in Nicolay and Hay, ALCW, Vol. 1, p. 231.
1008. Estes, pp. 229-230.
1009. Burne, p. 862.
1010. W. T. Alexander, p. 240; Bedford and Colbourn, p. 85; P. M. Roberts, p. 198; Garraty and McCaughey, p. 81; Rosenbaum and Brinkley, s.v. "Slavery"; "Slave States."
1011. Crane, Feinberg, Berman, and Hall, p. 120.
1012. Meltzer, Vol. 2, pp. 141-142; Roche, pp. 14-15.
1013. Behrens, p. 147.
1014. Furnas, pp. 119, 121.
1015. U. B. Phillips, ANS, p. 102. Emphasis added.
1016. Bridgwater, s.v. "slavery."
1017. S. P. Elliott, s.v. "Slavery."
1018. See Quarles, TNITAR, passim; E. J. McManus, BBITN, p. 159.
1019. E. J. McManus, BBITN, pp. 175-179.
1020. U. B. Phillips, ANS, p. 131. Emphasis added.
1021. *Collections of the Massachusetts Historical Society*, Vol. 3, 5th Series, p. 402. Emphasis added.
1022. Litwack, NS, pp. 4, 6.

1023. Nicolay and Hay, ALCW, Vol. 1, pp. 231-232.
1024. Seabrook, TMOCP, p. 182.
1025. U. B. Phillips, ANS, pp. 187-188. Emphasis added.
1026. U. B. Phillips, ANS, p. 133.
1027. Estes, pp. 229-230.
1028. Encyc. Brit., s.v. "slavery."
1029. See e.g., Chace, pp. 11-12.
1030. Boller and Story, p. 180.
1031. Estes, pp. 229-230.
1032. J. Williams, pp. 27-50; Encyc. Brit., s.v. "slavery."
1033. E. J. McManus, BBITN, p. 148.
1034. J. T. Adams, p. 199.
1035. C. Adams, pp. 4, 58.
1036. Curti, Thorpe, and Baker, p. 572; Rosenbaum and Brinkley, s.v. "Slavery."
1037. Zinn, p. 185.
1038. Chace, pp. 11-12. Emphasis added.
1039. Boller and Story, p. 166.
1040. J. T. Adams, p. 255.
1041. Nicolay and Hay, ALCW, Vol. 2, p. 1.
1042. Findlay and Findlay, p. 227; Fogel, p. 207.
1043. For more on New England's so-called "abolition" of slavery, see Melish, passim.
1044. Estes, pp. 229-230.
1045. There *were* Southerners who did not like the fact that Yankee abolitionists intended to destroy slavery in the North. However, these Southerners did not send 75,000 troops into the region with the order to annihilate everything in their path, they did not seek to overturn the Constitution, nor did they kill hundreds of thousands of innocent civilians and non-combatants. Lincoln did do all of this, however, and yet it is the South who is still blamed for the War.
1046. The Northwest Ordinance, issued in 1787 and inspired by Southerner Thomas Jefferson, banned slavery throughout the Northwest Territory, an area that included what would soon become the Midwestern states of Illinois, Wisconsin, Ohio, Michigan, and Indiana.
1047. U. B. Phillips, ANS, p. 120.
1048. Wallechinsky and Wallace, p. 427.
1049. Blake, pp. 405-406.
1050. For more on gradual emancipation in New England, see Melish, passim.
1051. See Seabrook, TUAL, p. 40; Seabrook, EYWTATCWIW, p. 46.
1052. For more on the Southern Confederacy, see Seabrook, C101, passim.
1053. See Johnston, p. 19; E. J. McManus, BBITN, pp. 196, 199.
1054. Drescher and Engerman, p. 215.
1055. Bennett, BTM, p. 37.
1056. Wise, p. 286; *The Outlook*, p. 109.
1057. C. Johnson, TPIGTTS, pp. 81-84.
1058. Bennett, BTM, pp. 37-38.
1059. de la Rochefoucauld Liancourt, Vol. 2, p. 457. Emphasis added.
1060. Rodriguez, THEOWS, Vol. 1, s.v. "Black Slaveowners."
1061. Greenberg and Waugh, p. 376.
1062. See Foner, FSFLFM, pp. 87-88. See also Hacker, p. 581; Quarles, TNITCW, p. xiii; Weintraub, p. 70; W. J. Cooper, JDA, p. 378; Rosenbaum and Brinkley, s.v. "Civil War"; C. Eaton, HSC, p. 93; Hinkle, p. 125.
1063. Wiley, SN, pp. 106, 148.
1064. See Website: www.nps.gov/timu/historyculture/kp.htm.
1065. Greenberg and Waugh, pp. 392-393.
1066. M. M. Smith, p. 205. In 1860 a male slave could bring as much as $1,800, or about $56,000 in today's currency. Coughlan, p. 84.

1067. In the 1850s prime field slaves could fetch up to $1,800, about $51,000 in today's money. Garraty and McCaughey, p. 214.
1068. Greenberg and Waugh, p. 393.
1069. U. B. Phillips, ANS, pp. 433-436. Emphasis added.
1070. Grissom, pp. 131, 182; Stonebraker, p. 46; J. C. Perry, pp. 96, 99, 101, 174; Rosenbaum and Brinkley, s.v. "Five Civilized Tribes"; M. Perry, p. 183; Simmons, s.v. "Stand Watie"; "Indians, in the War"; Jahoda, pp. 85, 148, 154, 225, 241, 246, 247, 249.
1071. C. Eaton, HSC, p. 49.
1072. Gragg, p. 84; DiLorenzo, LU, p. 174.
1073. J. C. Perry, p. 101.
1074. For more on black slave owners, see Johnson and Roark, passim; Koger, passim.
1075. L. Donald, passim, and Ruby, passim.
1076. Robinson, pp. 56-57.
1077. Pollard, SHW, Vol. 2, p. 296.
1078. Pollard, SHW, Vol. 2, p. 202. Emphasis added.
1079. See U. B. Phillips, ANS, p. 74.
1080. Ransom, p. 41.
1081. Burne, p. 581.
1082. W. J. Cooper, JDA, p. 666. For an example of Davis using the word servitude, see J. D. Richardson, ACOTMAPOTC, Vol. 1, p. 494.
1083. Grissom, p. 128.
1084. Meine, s.v. "Slavery."
1085. Bruford, p. 107.
1086. Stampp, p. 192.
1087. Fogel and Engerman, pp. 151-152, 241; M. M. Smith, pp. 184-185.
1088. Fogel, p. 194.
1089. Nye, pp. 146-147. Douglass' independence was purchased by British sympathizers.
1090. Garraty and McCaughey, p. 159; Rosenbaum, s.v. "Vesey, Denmark"; Bowman, CWDD, s.v. "May 1822." Vesey bought his freedom in 1800 using money he had won in a lottery.
1091. K. C. Davis, p. 23.
1092. C. Johnson, TPIGTTS, pp. 131, 188-189; Quarles, TNITCW, p. 128.
1093. Bruford, p. 107.
1094. Fogel, p. 194.
1095. Traupman, s.v. "slave."
1096. M. M. Smith, pp. 4-5.
1097. Pollard, SHW, Vol. 2, pp. 296-297. Emphasis added.
1098. Pollard, SHW, Vol. 2, p. 562. Emphasis added.
1099. Meltzer, Vol. 1, pp. 1-35.
1100. B. Torrey, Vol. 14, p. 292. Emphasis added.
1101. As in most other modern countries, slavery is still alive and well in 21st-Century America: according to a recent CIA study, 50,000 people (mostly women and children) of all colors and races are enslaved in the U.S. each year. Website: www.pbs.org/newshour/bb/law/jan-june01/slavery_3-8.html.
1102. U. B. Phillips, ANS, p. 75.
1103. R. S. Phillips, s.v "Slavery"; Fogel, pp. 187-193; M. M. Smith, pp. 175-182, 184-185, 188-197; Wiley, SN, pp. 137-138; Fogel and Engerman, pp. 56, 151-152, 241; Stampp, pp. 58-59, 72.
1104. H. A. White, p. 63.
1105. Dormon and Jones, p. 149.
1106. M. M. Miller, Vol. 1, p. 359.
1107. U. B. Phillips, ANS, p. 505.
1108. For the entire story, see U. B. Phillips, ANS, pp. 505-506.
1109. Seabrook, TQJD, p. 55. Emphasis added.
1110. F. Moore, Vol. 1, p. 45.
1111. Nicolay and Hay, ALCW, Vol. 1, p. 272. Emphasis added.
1112. Nicolay and Hay, ALCW, Vol. 1, p. 539. Emphasis added.

1113. See e.g., Nicolay and Hay, ALCW, Vol. 1, pp. 257, 259, 449, 469.
1114. Kennedy, pp. 191, 233.
1115. Nicolay and Hay, ALCW, Vol. 1, p. 231. Emphasis added.
1116. M. M. Smith, pp. 4-5.
1117. Nicolay and Hay, ALCW, Vol. 2, p. 1; Boller and Story, p. 180.
1118. C. Adams, p. 4.
1119. Parker, p. 343.
1120. To his great credit, Virginian John Tyler, America's tenth president, was the only man of that office, former or future, to either join the Confederacy or serve in the Confederate government. Though he did not fight in Lincoln's War (being too old at the time), he served as a member of the Provisional Congress of the Confederacy. He was later elected to the Confederate House of Representatives, but passed away before taking his seat. Tyler was an example of the overt anti-South bias that has long permeated the U.S. government: because of his devotion to the Confederate Cause, Northerners in his day regarded him as a traitor, his death in 1862 was ignored in Washington, and an official U.S. memorial was not placed over his grave until 1915—53 years after he died. DeGregorio, s.v. "John Tyler." In total, six men who would become U.S. presidents fought in the War for Southern Independence; unfortunately for history, all got it wrong by siding with big government Liberal Lincoln and the North: Benjamin Harrison, James A. Garfield, Ulysses S. Grant, Rutherford B. Hayes, Chester A. Arthur, and William McKinley.
1121. Tyler, LTT, Vol. 2, p. 567.
1122. E. J. McManus, BBITN, pp. 6-7.
1123. C. Adams, pp. 4, 58.
1124. Nicolay and Hay, ALCW, Vol. 2, p. 1.
1125. See Spooner, NT, No. 6, p. 54; Graham, BM, passim.
1126. Seabrook, TAHSR, p. 205. Emphasis added.
1127. Seabrook, TQAHS, pp. 328-329.
1128. Seabrook, TQAHS, p. 329. Emphasis added.
1129. Seabrook, TAHSR, pp. 654-657. Emphasis added.
1130. Lyell, Vol. 2, p. 96. Emphasis added.
1131. Meltzer, Vol. 2, p. 139; G. H. Moore, p. 5; R. S. Phillips, s.v. "Slavery"; Blake, p. 370.
1132. Derry, p. 67.
1133. M. M. Smith, pp. 4-5.
1134. H. A. White, p. 63.
1135. See e.g., Seabrook, TMOCP, pp. 145-146.
1136. Lincoln called his "Emancipation Proclamation" exactly what it was: not a civil rights emancipation, but a "military emancipation." In other words, its true purpose was to "liberate" black servants, not so they could be free, but so the liberal Yankee president could use them in his armies. See e.g., Seabrook, L, p. 647.
1137. H. A. White, pp. 63-64. Emphasis added.
1138. G. H. Moore, p. 5; Blake, p. 370; R. S. Phillips, s.v. "Slavery"; Bennett, BTM, p. 443.
1139. For example, see David, p. 135.
1140. See Spooner, NT, No. 6, p. 54; Graham, BM, passim.
1141. Eaton, HSC, p. 93.
1142. Hinkle, p. 125.
1143. Rutherford, FA, p. 61.
1144. See e.g., Dormon and Jones, p. 155.
1145. Long and Long, p. 702.
1146. E. M. Thomas, p. 6.
1147. Be aware of this cowardly and treacherous pro-North trick, one found in nearly every anti-South book.
1148. U. B. Phillips, ANS, p. 156.
1149. Gragg, p. 84; DiLorenzo, LU, p. 174; Wilkens, p. 153.
1150. Wilson and Ferris, s.v. "Plantations."
1151. E. M. Thomas, p. 6.

1152. S. A. Channing, p. 8. The largest Southern slave owner I have been able to find was South Carolina Governor William Aiken who, in the mid 1800s, possessed some 700 slaves "of all ages" on a single plantation on Jehossee Island. See U. B. Phillips, ANS, p. 89. This number paled in comparison to many African kings and chiefs, of course, whose chattel were not only true slaves—not servants, as in the American South—but who also suffered under extremely cruel and primitive forms of enslavement. See Chapter 2 of this book.
1153. Some maintain that the still regionally distinct Black Belt once stretched into Tennessee and all the way into Georgia and the Carolinas. See Rodriguez, THEOWS, Vol. 1, s.v. "Black Belt."
1154. M. M. Smith, pp. 4-5.
1155. Gragg, p. 84; DiLorenzo, LU, p. 174.
1156. Parker, p. 343.
1157. E. M. Thomas, p. 6.
1158. White, Foscue, and McKnight, p. 209.
1159. Kennedy and Kennedy, SWR, p. 83.
1160. Ransom, p. 174.
1161. U. S. Grant, Vol. 1, p. 223. Emphasis added.
1162. Nicolay and Hay, ALCW, Vol. 1, p. 581.
1163. S. Foote, Vol. 3, p. 755.
1164. W. E. Channing, p. 97.
1165. Drescher and Engerman, p. 32.
1166. Estes, pp. 133-134.
1167. Wilson and Ferris, s.v. "Plantations."
1168. Munford, p. 156.
1169. See Seabrook, AL, pp. 241-260.
1170. Seabrook, TQREL, pp. 110-111.
1171. DiLorenzo, RL, pp. 26-27. See also Kennedy, p. 219.
1172. See e.g., Tocqueville, Vol. 1, pp. 357-358; Buckingham, TSSOA, Vol. 2, p. 112; Hawthorne, Vol. 2, pp. 109-110; M. D. Peterson, JM, p. 377; Sturge, p. 40; Dicey, Vol. 1, pp. 70-72.
1173. Stampp, pp. 408-418; E. M. Thomas, pp. 14-15.
1174. Fogel, pp. 73-76. See also Fogel and Engerman, pp. 158-257. This explains other studies which show that after emancipation blacks produced 50 percent less than when they were slaves. Garraty and McCaughey, p. 268.
1175. Drescher and Engerman, p. 180.
1176. See Fogel and Engerman, pp. 38-106.
1177. Drescher and Engerman, pp. 109, 179.
1178. Bennett, BTM, p. 34; Burne, p. 581.
1179. Encyc. Brit., s.v. "slavery"; Macionis, p. 224.
1180. G. H. Moore, pp. 5, 11, 17-19; Blake, p. 370.
1181. Wallechinsky, Wallace, and Wallace, p. 11; Woods, p. 67. Grant did not free his slaves until he was forced to by the ratification of the Thirteenth Amendment on December 6, 1865, eight months after Lincoln's War ended.
1182. Adams and Sanders, pp. 215-216.
1183. Lott, pp. 17, 19.
1184. See B. Davidson, TAST, pp. 120-121, 123-124.
1185. B. Davidson, TAST, p. 30.
1186. Coughlan, p. 80. I am dating this period from the arrival of the Portugese in Africa in 1441, to the ratification of America's Thirteenth Amendment in 1865.
1187. Du Bois, D, p. 172.
1188. McKissack and McKissack, p. 3.
1189. Rutherford, FA, p. 38; Wallechinsky, Wallace, and Wallace, p. 11; Woods, p. 67.
1190. G. H. Moore, p. 5; Blake, p. 370; R. S. Phillips, s.v. "Slavery"; Bennett, BTM, p. 443.
1191. A. J. Northrup, pp. 246-247.
1192. Blake, p. 411. Emphasis added.
1193. Helper, ICS, p. 42.

1194. Blake, p. 480.
1195. N. Adams, pp. 15-19. Emphasis added.
1196. N. Adams, p. 23. Emphasis added.
1197. As a Yankee diplomat in England, Charles Francis Adams, Sr. created numerous problems for the Confederacy. One of his most monstrous actions was issuing Lincoln's order to threaten Great Britain with war should she aid the American South in any way. Such tactics were, of course, hypocritical since the U.S. herself had aided and supported "belligerent" nations in the past. For more on Adams and this topic, see Owsley, pp. 401-412.
1198. W. C. Ford, Vol. 2, p. 215. Emphasis added.
1199. Sarah is referring here to Lincoln's *Preliminary* Emancipation Proclamation (as opposed to the one best known to the public today, the *Final* Emancipation Proclamation). Calling for abolition then black deportation, the president issued the preliminary version on September 22, 1862.
1200. S. M. Dawson, pp. 277-278.
1201. Stampp, p. 289.
1202. Wiley, LBY, p. 43. My paraphrasal. Emphasis added.
1203. J. Hall, Vol. 1, p. 352. Emphasis added.
1204. Stampp, p. 164.
1205. Olmsted, AJITSSS, pp. 386-388.
1206. U. B. Phillips, ANS, p. 198.
1207. Estes, pp. 96-97. Emphasis added.
1208. R. Russell, p. 151.
1209. W. H. Russell, p. Vol. 1, p. 167. Emphasis added.
1210. Hodgson, Vol. 1, p. 97. Emphasis added.
1211. Buckingham, TSSOA, Vol. 2, p. 427. Emphasis added.
1212. Ingraham, Vol. 1, pp. 190-191. Emphasis added.
1213. C. E. Norton, Vol. 1, p. 121. Emphasis added.
1214. Thackeray, p. 127. Emphasis added.
1215. Thomson, p. 181.
1216. U. B. Phillips, ANS, p. 269.
1217. Estes, p. 115. Emphasis added.
1218. U. B. Phillips, ANS, p. 314.
1219. A. D. P. Van Buren, pp. 122-123.
1220. McKissack and McKissack, p. 32. Sojourner Truth, originally named Isabella Baumfree, was born in 1797 in Ulster Country, New York, on the estate of Northern slave owners, the Dutch-American Hardenberghs. Truth gave her biography orally to a European-American woman named Olive Gilbert, who recorded the story, resulting in the book, *Narrative of Sojourner Truth*. It was first published in 1850. Truth, pp. iii, v.
1221. Trexler, pp. 87-88. Emphasis added.
1222. Latham, p. 112. Emphasis added.
1223. See e.g., Chesnut, MCCW, p. 465.
1224. Chesnut, DD, p. 114.
1225. Genovese, p. 464.
1226. J. M. Burns, p. 387.
1227. Olmsted, AJITBC, p. 154; C. P. Patterson, p. 18.
1228. C. C. Jones, p. 233. Emphasis added.
1229. Smedes, ASP, p. 42; Power, Vol. 2, p. 50; Mooney, p. 93. See also Ross, p. 240.
1230. Bremer, Vol. 1, p. 376. Emphasis added.
1231. Redpath, p. 313. Emphasis added.
1232. Genovese, pp. 474-475.
1233. U. B. Phillips, ANS, p. 513.
1234. Botkin, p. 161; U. B. Phillips, LALITOS, pp. 203-204; Yetman, p. 39; Herskovits, p. 64; Parrinder, p. 97.
1235. U. B. Phillips, ANS, p. 314. Emphasis added.
1236. M. M. Smith, p. 182; U. B. Phillips, ANS, p. 268.

1237. B. Hall, pp. 224-225. Emphasis added.
1238. M. M. Smith, pp. 175-179.
1239. U. B. Phillips, ANS, pp. 489-490.
1240. R. Walsh, p. 405. Emphasis added.
1241. Genovese, p. 453.
1242. Stroud, p. 50; Goodell, p. 46; U. B. Phillips, ANS, p. 493.
1243. Heyward, p. 88; Eaton, HC, pp. 120-121; L. Morton, p. 111.
1244. Seabrook, ARB, p. 214.
1245. H. A. White, p. 63.
1246. Genovese, p. 453.
1247. E. A. Andrews, pp. 137-138, 139. Emphasis added.
1248. Thomson, p. 182. Emphasis added.
1249. K. Stone, p. 84. My paraphrasal. Emphasis added.
1250. U. B. Phillips, LALITOS, p. 243.
1251. U. B. Phillips, ANS, p. 202.
1252. See e.g., Blake, p. 118.
1253. Fogel and Engerman, pp. 127, 128.
1254. M. M. Smith, p. 189. Also see Berlin and Morgan, passim.
1255. For more on Franklin, Tennessee's most famous Confederate family, the McGavocks, see Seabrook, TMOCP, passim.
1256. Fogel and Engerman, pp. 151, 241.
1257. U. B. Phillips, ANS, p. 268.
1258. Sitterson, p. 97; J. G. Taylor, p. 33.
1259. Smedes, ASP, p. 71. Emphasis added.
1260. Genovese, pp. 531, 535-536, 557.
1261. Smedes, ASP, p. 106.
1262. Thomson, pp. 183-184. Emphasis added.
1263. Schoepf, Vol. 1, p. 221. Emphasis added.
1264. U. B. Phillips, ANS, p. 406. Emphasis added.
1265. U. B. Phillips, ANS, pp. 407, 408. Emphasis added.
1266. Jacobs, p. 11. Emphasis added.
1267. Drescher and Engerman, p. 202.
1268. M. M. Smith, pp. 180-181.
1269. Smedes, ASP, p. 71. Emphasis added.
1270. Lancaster and Plumb, p. 46.
1271. Wilson and Ferris, s.v. "Black Life."
1272. Fogel and Engerman, pp. 151, 241.
1273. Drescher and Engerman, p. 301.
1274. U. B. Phillips, ANS, p. 411. Emphasis added.
1275. See also U. B. Phillips, ANS, p. 414.
1276. Lyell, Vol. 1, p. 360. Emphasis added.
1277. U. B. Phillips, ANS, pp. 412-413.
1278. Fogel and Engerman, p. 56.
1279. Chesnut, MCCW, p. 285.
1280. Olmsted. AJITSSS, p. 660. Emphasis added.
1281. U. B. Phillips, ANS, pp. 408-409.
1282. Rodriguez, THEOWS, Vol. 1, s.v. "Hiring of Slaves."
1283. U. B. Phillips, ANS, pp. 409, 410. Emphasis added.
1284. R. Russell, pp. 151-152. Emphasis added.
1285. Eaton, HSC, p. 104.
1286. Fogel and Engerman, pp. 148, 153.
1287. Drescher and Engerman, p. 36.
1288. Starobin, passim; R. L. Lewis, passim; Drescher and Engerman, p. 243.

1289. de la Rochefoucauld Liancourt, Vol. 2, p. 457.
1290. M. M. Smith, p. 185.
1291. Seabrook, TMOCP, p. 135.
1292. Seabrook, TMOCP, p. 135.
1293. M. M. Smith, pp. 186, 188-191.
1294. A proto-peasant is an early or primitive type of (free) farmer, yeoman, or agricultural laborer.
1295. M. M. Smith, p. 182.
1296. Chesnut, MCCW, pp. 246, 428.
1297. Sitterson, p. 97; J. G. Taylor, p. 33.
1298. Bedford and Colbourn, p. 178.
1299. We will note here that off the plantation, the labor that black female servants performed was basically the same as free white women. This was because whether one was white, black, free, or bonded, women's work was nearly identical within the same social classes in early America. In this sense slavery was easier for women than men, the latter who lost one of their greatest freedoms upon enslavement: choice of employment. See G. Lerner, p. 241; Drescher and Engerman, p. 221.
1300. Fogel and Engerman, pp. 38-41.
1301. Drescher and Engerman, p. 36.
1302. U. B. Phillips, ANS, p. 268.
1303. Rosenbaum and Brinkley, s.v. "Slavery"; M. M. Smith, p. 189.
1304. See e.g., S. A. Hill, p. 21; Perlman, pp. 60-61.
1305. U. B. Phillips, ANS, pp. 267-268. Emphasis added.
1306. Rosenbaum and Brinkley, s.v. "Slavery"; M. M. Smith, p. 189.
1307. J. M. Burns, p. 387.
1308. Smedes, ASP, p. 198.
1309. Fisk University, pp. 55, 109; Yetman, pp. 16, 144, 155.
1310. Genovese, p. 566.
1311. Rosenbaum and Brinkley, s.v. "Slavery"; M. M. Smith, p. 189.
1312. W. H. Russell, Vol. 1, p. 140; Genovese, p. 569; J. G. Taylor, p. 128.
1313. Bennett, BTM, p. 104.
1314. Lyell, Vol. 1, pp. 354-355.
1315. W. H. Russell, Vol. 2, p. 275. Emphasis added.
1316. Chesnut, MCCW, p. 792.
1317. R. Russell, p. 152.
1318. See Yetman, p. 332; K. Stone, p. 76; J. G. Taylor, p. 200; Sydnor, p. 80; Redpath, p. 138; Saxon, Dreyer, and Tallant, p. 232; Olmsted, AJITSSS, pp. 75, 101-102; Olmsted, AJITBC, pp. 51-52; H. Hamilton, pp. 35-36.
1319. A. D. P. Van Buren, pp. 117-118. Emphasis added.
1320. Genovese, p. 567.
1321. C. S. Davis, p. 4; U. B. Phillips, LALITOS, p. 5.
1322. Drescher and Engerman, p. 36.
1323. Smedes, ASP, p. 71; Sellers, p. 72; Dick, p. 92.
1324. Mallard, pp. 34-35. Emphasis added.
1325. Lyell, Vol. 1, p. 356.
1326. H. C. Bruce, pp. 14-15, 24; C. S. Davis, p. 58; Yetman, pp. 40, 144, 202, 264; Heyward, pp. 178-179.
1327. Paulding, p. 223.
1328. Hobsbawm, pp. 50-51; Kuczynski, pp. 105-106.
1329. Montgomery, TLFOEH, p. 354. Emphasis added.
1330. Chesnut, MCCW, pp. 458, 607, 734.
1331. Fogel and Engerman, p. 208.
1332. Thomson, p. 190.
1333. For an example of this on a New England slave plantation, see McLoughlin, p. 4.
1334. For more on the hunting and fishing activities of Southern servants, see Genovese, pp. 486-488.
1335. Sitterson, p. 97; J. G. Taylor, p. 33; U. B. Phillips, ANS, p. 268.

1336. U. B. Phillips, ANS, p. 113.
1337. Fogel and Engerman, p. 149.
1338. Lyell, Vol. 1, pp. 356-357. Emphasis added.
1339. Fogel and Engerman, pp. 192-193, 209-210.
1340. Seabrook, TMOCP, p. 138.
1341. Drescher and Engerman, pp. 183, 333.
1342. Fogel and Engerman, pp. 156-157.
1343. Muller, p. 207.
1344. Aron, p. 207.
1345. Fogel and Engerman, pp. 84, 109-123, 124-125, 241, 261.
1346. Drescher and Engerman, p. 182.
1347. Bedford and Colbourn, p. 181.
1348. Estes, p. 89. Emphasis added.
1349. Estes, pp. 139-140. Emphasis added.
1350. U. B. Phillips, ANS, p. 263.
1351. Thornton and Ekelund, p. 96.
1352. Drescher and Engerman, p. 302.
1353. Paulding, pp. 225-226. Emphasis added.
1354. Blake, p. 829.
1355. Lyell, Vol. 1, p. 353. Emphasis added.
1356. Thomson, p. 184.
1357. Chesnut, MCCW, p. 243.
1358. Genovese, p. 551.
1359. Chesnut, MCCW, p. 589.
1360. Genovese, pp. 392, 393.
1361. Thackeray, p. 127. A modern analogy would be owning a four-wheel drive pickup truck when all that is needed is a regular car.
1362. Chesnut, MCCW, p. 803. My paraphrasal.
1363. U. B. Phillips, ANS, pp. 359-360.
1364. Smedes, MOASP, p. 191.
1365. U. B. Phillips, ANS, pp. 286-287. Emphasis added.
1366. Ruffin, a professional agriculturist who pioneered crop rotation and who is said to have been the person who fired the first shot at the Battle of Fort Sumter I, committed suicide after the War rather than live in ignoble humiliation under Yankee rule. To this day Ruffin is considered an archetypal Confederate hero among traditional Southerners, one typifying Dixie's age old love of personal liberty, states' rights, and political independence.
1367. S. A. Channing, p. 128.
1368. Derry, p. 114. Emphasis added.
1369. See e.g., Dormon and Jones, p. 160.
1370. Rosenbaum and Brinkley, s.v. "Underground Railroad."
1371. Seabrook, TMOCP, p. 141.
1372. Fogel and Engerman, pp. 23-24.
1373. Scott and Stowe, p. 321. Dr. Washington's expectation was fulfilled. He was buried in Tuskegee, Alabama, on November 17, 1915.
1374. Henry, FWMF, p. 443.
1375. Seabrook, ARB, pp. 446-447; Lester and Wilson, pp. 19-21.
1376. For more on the facts about Forrest and his life, see my books: 1) *Nathan Bedford Forrest: Southern Hero, American Patriot*; 2) *A Rebel Born: A Defense of Nathan Bedford Forrest*; 3) *Forrest! 99 Reasons to Love Nathan Bedford Forrest*; 4) *The Quotable Nathan Bedford Forrest*; 5) *Give 'Em Hell Boys: The Complete Military Correspondence of Nathan Bedford Forrest*; 6) *Saddle, Sword, and Gun: A Biography of Nathan Bedford Forrest For Teens*; and 7) my screenplay, *A Rebel Born*—based on the book of the same name, and which is to be made into a full length feature film (it is presently in pre-production).
1377. Seabrook, F, p. 86.
1378. Wills, p. 336.

1379. Seabrook, ARB, p. 448. Gordon was one of the unlucky 702 Rebels captured at the Battle of Franklin II, November 30, 1864.
1380. Seabrook, ARB, pp. 221, 222.
1381. Seabrook, ARB, p. 149.
1382. Seabrook, ARB, pp. 214, 221.
1383. Seabrook, ARB, pp. 206, 219-220.
1384. Seabrook, ARB, p. 26.
1385. Seabrook, ARB, p. 259.
1386. Seabrook, ARB, p. 144.
1387. Seabrook, ARB, p. 261.
1388. Seabrook, ARB, p. 26.
1389. C. Adams, p. 151.
1390. Wade, p. 39.
1391. Weintraub, p. 89.
1392. Wade, p. 39. As noted earlier, Lincoln's Republican Party was what we would now call the Democratic Party (i.e., Liberals), while the Democratic Party of the mid 1800s was what we would now refer to as the Republican Party (i.e., Conservatives). Thus, though Lincoln was a Republican, today he would be considered a Democrat.
1393. Fleming, p. 665.
1394. Seabrook, NBF, p. 56.
1395. Hurst, p. 305; Lester and Wilson, p. 26; Rogers, KKS, p. 34.
1396. Seabrook, ARB, p. 441; Horn, IE, pp. 362-363. We will note that at one time (1920s-1930s) even the modern KKK—though it has no connection with the original KKK of the Reconstruction period—possessed African-American members, and treated both whites and blacks the same. Terkel, p. 239. In Indiana, for example, white Klansmen decided to broaden their racial base by organizing a "colored division" whose uniform was comprised of white capes, blue masks, and red robes. Blee, p. 169.
1397. Few things were worse to traditional Southerners than the scallywag. Known widely across the South as "vile, vindictive, unprincipled," and "scaly, scabby runts in a herd of cattle" (J. H. Franklin, pp. 98, 101), Wade Hampton referred to them as "the mean, lousy and filthy kind that are not fit for butchers or dogs." Harrell, Gaustad, Boles, Griffith, Miller, and Woods, p. 525. Known by Southern conservatives as "the lepers of the community," scallywags were hated even more than carpetbaggers. A former governor of North Carolina said: "We have no problem with Northerners per se, even those who fought against us in Lincoln's War. What we can't and won't abide is one of our own here in the South turning against us. Such a man will never get respect and will never be trusted." (My paraphrasal.) Foner, R, p. 297. To this day, revulsion toward the scallywag is a sentiment still very much alive across the South.
1398. Horn, IE, pp. 124, 169, 264-265; Simpson, p. 62.
1399. C. Adams, p. 153; Weintraub, p. 75.
1400. *Index to Reports of the Committees of the House of Representatives for the Second Session of the Forty-Third Congress, 1874-1875*, p. 344.
1401. See J. H. Franklin, pp. 38-39.
1402. C. Adams, pp. 153-155.
1403. Seabrook, ARB, p. 443; Lytle, p. 385; Morton, p. 345; Hurst, p. 327.
1404. *Reports of the Committees of the Senate of the United States for the Second Session of the Forty-second Congress*, pp. 22, 33, 34.
1405. Henry, FWMF, p. 448.
1406. Kelly, Michael. "History Tells the Real Story of Forrest," *The Daily News Journal*, December 9, 2006.
1407. Butler and Watson, p. 293.
1408. See Wade, passim.
1409. December 17, 2000, *Sunday Morning News*, CNN.
1410. See e.g., Wyatt-Brown, passim; Cash, passim.
1411. See Elkins, passim.
1412. Drescher and Engerman, p. 235.
1413. Encyc. Brit., s.v. "Douglass, Frederick."

1414. Mark 4:23.
1415. U. B. Phillips, ANS, p. 294. Emphasis added.
1416. U. B. Phillips, ANS, p. 296. Emphasis added.
1417. U. B. Phillips, ANS, p. 275.
1418. U. B. Phillips, ANS, p. 267. Emphasis added.
1419. U. B. Phillips, ANS, pp. 266-267.
1420. Rodriguez, THEOWS, Vol. 1, s.v. "Antiliteracy Laws."
1421. Chesnut, MCCW, p. 263.
1422. See e.g., Starr, pp. 210-211.
1423. Lyell, Vol. 1, pp. 360-361. Emphasis added.
1424. Much has been made of a 19th-Century American law that prohibited teaching slaves to read and write. South-loathers maintain that the thinking behind this counterproductive regulation was to keep black servants in a permanent state of ignorance and docile subservience, a hopelessly irrational interpretation. The fact is that most Southern servant employers ("slave owners" to Northerners) wisely disregarded the law, for reasons given in the associated paragraph.
1425. Latham, p. 112. Emphasis added.
1426. Derry, pp. 114-115. For more on Dr. Girardeau, see G. A. Blackburn, passim.
1427. Genovese, pp. 563-564.
1428. S. Andrews, pp. 227, 336.
1429. For several examples, see Phillips, ANS, pp. 342, 406.
1430. Fogel and Engerman, pp. 36, 150.
1431. Nicolay and Hay, ALCW, Vol. 2, p. 91. As is patently clear, Lincoln was never interested in abolishing slavery. An advocate of American apartheid, his main goal was to limit the spread of slavery outside the South and deport willing blacks to Africa, South America, and the Carribean. This is why American slavery was not abolished until eight months after Lincoln died. For more on these topics see my books *Abraham Lincoln: The Southern View*; *Lincolnology: The Real Abraham Lincoln Revealed in His Own Words*; *The Great Impersonator: 99 Reasons to Dislike Abraham Lincoln*; and *The Unquotable Abraham Lincoln: The President's Quotes They Don't Want You to Know!*
1432. Chesnut, DD, p. 167.
1433. Lyell, Vol. 2, p. 34. Emphasis added.
1434. See Tocqueville, Vol. 1, pp. 357-358; J. M. McPherson, NCW, pp. 245-270; Litwack, pp. 104-112; Greenberg and Waugh, p. 152.
1435. Paulding, p. 224. Emphasis added.
1436. Thomson, p. 181.
1437. Osnaburg clothing, or "osnaburgs," as they were irreverently called, was rough textured cotton clothing made by the servants themselves. The durable material was provided by their owners, but not much appreciated due to its scratchiness.
1438. Thomson, pp. 173-181. Emphasis added.
1439. Estes, pp. 99-102. Emphasis added.
1440. Foley, p. 815.
1441. Pollard, SHW, Vol. 2, p. 562.
1442. Estes, p. 131. Emphasis added.
1443. W. Wilson, DR, pp. 125-126. Emphasis added.
1444. Flint, Vol. 1, p. 234.
1445. Latham, p. 131. Emphasis added.
1446. Blassingame, pp. 180, 182.
1447. Chesnut, MCCW, p. 428. My paraphrasal.
1448. Chesnut, DD, p. 224.
1449. See Fogel, pp. 137, 138-140.
1450. C. Johnson, TPIGTTS, p. 130. American females, for example, are much taller today than ever before in the nation's history, due almost solely to healthier diets in childhood.
1451. Bedford and Colbourn, p. 181.
1452. Speer, p. 2. Emphasis added.
1453. Fox, p. 48.

1454. McKissack and McKissack, p. 119.
1455. Hundley, pp. 289-290. Emphasis added.
1456. W. Wilson, DR, p. 126. Emphasis added.
1457. M. M. Smith, p. 32.
1458. Chesnut, MCCW, p. 721.
1459. Lyell, Vol. 2, pp. 37-40. Emphasis added.
1460. See e.g., Chesnut, MCCW, p. 491.
1461. Chesnut, DD, p. 397.
1462. Chesnut, DD, p. 84.
1463. Chesnut, DD, p. 169.
1464. Chesnut, DD, p. 169.
1465. Chesnut, MCCW, p. 350.
1466. Chesnut, DD, p. 181.
1467. M. M. Smith, p. 191.
1468. Bruford, p. 107.
1469. Blake, p. 414.
1470. Blake, p. 412. Emphasis added.
1471. W. Wilson, DR, p. 126.
1472. Lyell, Vol. 1, p. 355. Emphasis added.
1473. Bedford and Colbourn, p. 181.
1474. Genovese, p. 526.
1475. Genovese, pp. 526-527, 533-534.
1476. Gragg, pp. 87-88.
1477. U. B. Phillips, ANS, p. 298. Emphasis added.
1478. Genovese, p. 24.
1479. Martineau, SIA, Vol. 2, p. 357. Emphasis added.
1480. Stirling, p. 264. Emphasis added.
1481. Olmsted, AJITSSS, pp. 659-660.
1482. Mallard, pp. 35-37. Emphasis added.
1483. Rosenbaum and Brinkley, s.v. "Free Blacks."
1484. Seabrook, EYWTACWW, p. 158. Also see Ransom, pp. 214-215; W. J. Cooper, JDA, p. 378; Quarles, TNITCW, p. xiii; Stephenson, ALU, p. 168; Bennett, BTM, p. 87.
1485. U. B. Phillips, ANS, p. 75.
1486. Bedford and Colbourn, p. 85.
1487. Drescher and Engerman, p. 213.
1488. *The Civil War Book of Lists*, pp. 193, 195.
1489. U. B. Phillips, ANS, p. 97.
1490. E. A. Andrews, p. 162.
1491. U. B. Phillips, ANS, p. 430.
1492. Siebert, p. xiii.
1493. Blake, p. 827.
1494. Blake, p. 827.
1495. Blake, p. 827.
1496. Seabrook, EYWTACWW, p. 158. Also see Ransom, pp. 214-215; W. J. Cooper, JDA, p. 378; Quarles, TNITCW, p. xiii; Stephenson, ALU, p. 168; Bennett, BTM, p. 87.
1497. Powdermaker, p. 143; Bernard, p. 21.
1498. Long and Long, p. 702.
1499. Genovese, pp. 406-408.
1500. C. Johnson, TPIGTTS, pp. 81-85.
1501. Blake, p. 372.
1502. Greenberg and Waugh, pp. 376-377.
1503. Kennedy and Kennedy, SWR, pp. 64-65.
1504. Greenberg and Waugh, p. 376.

1505. Greenberg and Waugh, p. 376.
1506. C. Johnson, TPIGTTS, pp. 133-134.
1507. Greenberg and Waugh, pp. 386-387.
1508. Johnson and Roark, p. 208. My paraphrasal.
1509. Greenberg and Waugh, p. 376.
1510. Greenberg and Waugh, p. 377.
1511. Fleming, p. 208.
1512. J. C. Perry, p. 178.
1513. Stampp, p. 194.
1514. J. C. Perry, p. 173. For more on the Natchez National Historical Park, see Website: www.nps.gov/natc/index.htm. For more on black slave owners, see Koger, passim; Johnson and Roark, passim.
1515. J. C. Perry, pp. 175-176.
1516. Rosenbaum and Brinkley, s.v. "Five Civilized Tribes."
1517. M. Perry, p. 183.
1518. *ORA*, Ser. 3, Vol. 1, p. 184.
1519. Grissom, p. 182.
1520. The Five Civilized Tribes were the Cherokee, Seminole, Choctaw, Creek, and Chickasaw. Quite unlike Lincoln and the North, Davis and the South enlisted Native-Americans almost from the beginning of the War. Also unlike Lincoln, Confederate Indians were treated as equals, not as an "inferior race," as Lincoln called them. Davis even signed a treaty with the Five Civilized Tribes promising not to "trouble or molest" them from that day forward. E. M. Thomas, p. 188. After the War, however, the U.S. military drove the Indians off their lands, nearly to extinction. Many of the U.S. officers involved were the same ones who had illegally invaded the Confederacy and had engaged in the cultural genocide of the Southern people.
1521. Warner, GG, s.v. "Stand Watie."
1522. Simmons, s.v. "Stand Watie."
1523. See E. J. McManus, BBITN, pp. 196, 199.
1524. J. C. Perry, p. 99.
1525. Gragg, p. 84; DiLorenzo, LU, p. 174.
1526. J. C. Perry, p. 101.
1527. Nieboer, pp. 70-71. Emphasis added.
1528. Rosenbaum and Brinkley, s.v. "Five Civilized Tribes."
1529. Simmons, s.v. "Indians, in the War."
1530. Nieboer, pp. 67-68.
1531. Rodriguez, THEOWS, Vol. 1, s.v. "Amerindian Slavery, General."
1532. See Jahoda, pp. 85, 148, 154, 225, 241, 246, 247, 249; J. C. Perry, pp. 96, 99, 101; Grissom, p. 182. Native-Americans also made captives (slaves) out of some of the earliest whites to land on North America's shores, European-Americans such as Virginia Dare, the first child born of English parents in America. Furnas, p. 28.
1533. Drescher and Engerman, p. 296.
1534. A. J. Northrup, p. 309.
1535. See Chapter 1.
1536. "Hispanics" here is used to indicate those born in, or deriving ancestry, from Spain or Portugal. "Latinos" refers to those of Latin-American origin; that is, those of mixed European (that is, Caucasian) heritage and Native-American (that is, Asian) heritage. Hispanics were responsible for bringing *European* slavery to the New World (it already existed among Native-Americans), while Latinos were responsible for expanding it across the Americas. For more on the history of Hispanic slavery, see Rodriguez, THEOWS, Vol. 1, s.v. "Historiography, Latin American."
1537. Stimpson, p. 30.
1538. C. Morris, s.v. "Slavery."
1539. Lott, p. 18.
1540. See Burne, p. 453. For more on Cuban slavery, see Blake, pp. 356-357.
1541. Crane, Feinberg, Berman, and Hall, p. 71.

1542. Garraty and McCaughey, p. 25.
1543. Greer, p. 216.
1544. Meltzer, Vol. 2, p. 4.
1545. Drescher and Engerman, p. 371.
1546. Stimpson, p. 30.
1547. Burne, p. 449.
1548. McKissack and McKissack, p. 3.
1549. Rutherford, FA, p. 38; Wallechinsky, Wallace, and Wallace, p. 11; Woods, p. 67.
1550. E. B. Andrews, p. 73.
1551. Furnas, p. 27; Meltzer, Vol. 2, p. 127
1552. U. B. Phillips, ANS, p. 16.
1553. Bertrand, pp. 185-186, 188; Albrecht-Carrié, p. 44.
1554. Diamond, p. 210.
1555. Bennett, BTM, p. 34; Swain, p. 730.
1556. Coughlan, p. 82; Blake, p. 99.
1557. Blake, p. 100.
1558. Palmer and Colton, p. 92.
1559. C. F. Adams, Vol. 4, p. 355.
1560. Albrecht-Carrié, p. 44.
1561. It is said that Spain murdered, by burning and hanging, some 50 million Native-Americans between the 1500s and the 1600s alone. Lubasz, p. 52.
1562. Kennedy, pp. 21-23.
1563. Chesnut, MCCW, pp. 75, 255.
1564. Fogel and Engerman, pp. 210-212.
1565. Fogel and Engerman, pp. 200-201.
1566. Genovese, p. 445.
1567. Yetman, pp. 21, 35, 59, 112, 182.
1568. Rubin, p. 159.
1569. Genovese, pp. 448-449.
1570. Fogel and Engerman, pp. 200-201.
1571. Genovese, pp. 356, 368, 371, 374, 378-380.
1572. A. D. P. Van Buren, p. 151. Emphasis added.
1573. U. B. Phillips, ANS, pp. 493-494. Emphasis added.
1574. F. Douglass, NLFD, p. 116.
1575. Seabrook, AL, p. 467.
1576. Bennett, BTM, p. 91.
1577. Wilson and Ferris, s.v. "African Influences." See also W. E. B. Du Bois, TGOBF, passim.
1578. Wilson and Ferris, s.v. "Architecture, Black."
1579. Du Bois and Dill, pp. 34-37.
1580. Du Bois and Dill, p. 76.
1581. J. McPherson, BCF, p. 342.
1582. Eaton, HSC, p. 93.
1583. Barrow, Segars, and Rosenburg, BC, p. 97; Hinkle, p. 106; *The United Daughters of the Confederacy Magazine*, Vols. 54-55, 1991, p. 32.
1584. Hinkle, p. 108. See also Quintero, Gonzales, and Velazquez, passim.
1585. Lonn, p. 218.
1586. Rosen, p. 161.
1587. Hinkle, 108; Blackerby, passim.
1588. Seabrook, EYWTATCWIW, p. 200.
1589. See Peterson's Brotherhood Organization of a New Destiny (BOND) Website: www.bondinfo.org.
1590. Hinkle, pp. 132-133. Sadly, in today's ultra politically correct society, it pays, and pays well, to be a race-merchant.
1591. Seabrook, AL, pp. 236, 506. See also Bultman, p. 285; C. Johnson, TPIGTTS, pp. 37-38.

1592. Barraclough, pp. 46-47.
1593. Meltzer, Vol. 2, p. 127; Furnas, p. 27.
1594. Fogel and Engerman, pp. 23-24.
1595. C. Johnson, TPIGTTS, pp. 78-79.
1596. For examples of black contributions to American culture, see Wilson and Ferris, s.v. "Black life." See also M. M. Smith, p. 30.
1597. Matthew 22:36-40; John 13:34; 15:17; 1 John 4:8, 16. See also Seabrook, JLOA, passim.
1598. For more on the topic of the development of the Confederate Battle Flag, as well as the Confederacy's many other flags, see Cannon, passim.
1599. M. B. Davidson, Vol. 2, p. 385.
1600. Estes, pp. 133-134. Note: modern day American blacks who are enamored with Africa and sincerely believe that moving there would greatly improve and enhance their lives, would do well to read Ken Hamblin's book, *Pick a Better Country: An Unassuming Colored Guy Speaks His Mind About America*, and also Keith B. Richburg's book, *Out of America: A Black Man Confronts Africa*.
1601. For a Northern example, see A. M. Grant, pp. 37-38.
1602. Wertenbaker, TPO, p. 198.
1603. Greene, pp. 167-169.
1604. B. C. Steiner, pp. 11-12.
1605. Blake, p. 370.
1606. G. Bancroft, Vol. 1, p. 284; Norwood, p. 32.
1607. Hildreth, THOTUSOA, Vol. 1, p. 278.
1608. Muller, p. 154.
1609. See Mills, pp. 171-178.
1610. B. G. Walker, TWEOMAS, s.v. "Slavery."
1611. Mark 12:16-17.
1612. Seabrook, TMOCP, p. 202.
1613. C. Morris, s.v. "Slavery."
1614. Blake, pp. 102-103.
1615. Morrall, p. 20.
1616. Cross and Livingstone, s.v. "Slavery."
1617. Muller, p. 186.
1618. Ahlstrom, pp. 52, 635.
1619. Bertrand, pp. 185, 194.
1620. Stimpson, pp. 30-31.
1621. As is revealed in my book *The Secret Jesus*, the true founder of traditional mainstream Christianity was not Jesus but Paul, who in turn based his teachings on the Pagan ideas of Mark—ideas, it should be noted, that were completely at odds with the teachings of Jesus.
1622. See e.g., Matthew 8:5-13; Matthew 10:24-25; Luke 12:47; Ephesians 6:5; I Timothy 6:1; Titus 2:9-10.
1623. Colossians 3:11. For more on the Indwelling Christ that exists in each one of us, see Seabrook, CIAAIA, passim.
1624. Matthew 8:10.
1625. For more on using the power of faith to heal disease, alter one's life, and shape one's destiny, see Seabrook, JATLOA, passim; Seabrook, TBATLOA, passim.
1626. Priest, BDOS, p. 538.
1627. Philemon 1:1-25.
1628. See Bonhoeffer, p. 321.
1629. Colossians 3:22.
1630. Galatians 3:28.
1631. 1 Peter 2:18.
1632. Bonhoeffer, p. 321; Estes, p. 33.
1633. Armstrong, p. 102.
1634. Matthew 20:27; Mark 10:44.
1635. Acts 4:29; 16:17; Galatians 1:10.

1636. Bunson, s.v. "Slavery."
1637. Estes, pp. 37-38.
1638. Baigent, Leigh, and Lincoln, TML, p. 74.
1639. See e.g., Matthew 22:21; Romans 13:1.
1640. T. C. Butler, s.v. "Slave/servant."
1641. See e.g., Exodus 21:26-27; Proverbs 29:19.
1642. Estes, pp. 13-30.
1643. Genesis 37:26-28.
1644. Genesis 4:1-15; 9:25. See Metzger and Coogan, s.v. "Slavery and the Bible."
1645. The non-Bible based Mormons, or more officially, the members of the Church of Jesus Christ of Latter-Day Saints (LDS), have long embraced a belief in the "mark of Cain," though understandably this fact has been largely kept from the general public.
1646. Genesis 9:22-27.
1647. B. H. Johnson, p. 140; Olson, p. 148.
1648. Trexler, p. 124.
1649. W. C. Wade, p. 143.
1650. Belief in the "Curse of Ham" is not the Mormon Church's only politically incorrect, non-biblical dogma. It still embraces beliefs in both a Father-God and a Mother-Goddess (as well as a "plurality" of other deities), the secret ritual of baptism for the dead (condemned in 1 Cor. 15:29 by Saint Paul as a Pagan practice), the belief that Jesus and Satan are brothers, the posthumous attainment of self-godhood (in order to rule other planets after earthly death), and the continuance of male polygamy after death—a tenant particularly distressing to many female LDS members. For more on these topics from an LDS perspective, see the church's excellent publication: *Encyclopedia of Mormonism*, by Daniel H. Ludlow, s.v. "Cain," "Race, Racism," "Blacks," "Devils," "Priesthood," "Mother in Heaven," "Godhood," "Baptism for the Dead," passim. For a non-Mormon Christian view of the LDS church see: *Mormonism Unmasked*, by R. Philip Roberts. Revealingly, the scandalous non-Christian Joseph Smith, murdered in an Illinois jail by an angry Christian mob, was an admirer of the equally scandalous non-Christian Abraham Lincoln of Illinois. See e.g., Nicolay and Hay, ALAH, Vol. 1, p. 182. For more on Lincoln's anti-Christian atheism, see Seabrook, L, pp. 918-938.
1651. See Birney, passim.
1652. Meltzer, Vol. 2, p. 139; G. H. Moore, p. 5; R. S. Phillips, s.v. "Slavery"; Blake, p. 370.
1653. Litwack, NS, pp. 205-208, 221.
1654. Barton, pp. 236-237.
1655. M. Perry, p. 85.
1656. See e.g., Penney, Vol. 2, p. 195.
1657. Garraty, TAN, p. 75; A. J. Northrup, p. 292; U. B. Phillips, ANS, p. 98.
1658. Dunn and Dunn, Vol. 2, pp. 66-67, 256; G. Bancroft, Vol. 1, p. 418.
1659. Garraty and McCaughey, p. 29.
1660. E. J. McManus, BBITN, p. 147.
1661. Furnas, p. 120.
1662. Bedford and Colbourn, p. 30.
1663. Ahlstrom, p. 650.
1664. Encyc. Brit., s.v. "slavery." See also Soderlund, passim.
1665. Seabrook, TMOCP, p. 213.
1666. J. H. Hopkins, pp. 11, 14. Emphasis added.
1667. See e.g., Exodus 21:26-27; Proverbs 29:19.
1668. Dunner, p. 879.
1669. See Seabrook, TAHSR, pp. 158-162.
1670. Bledsoe, ELS, p. 142.
1671. Exodus 20: 10, 17.
1672. Leviticus 25:44-46. See also W. Smith, s.v. "slave."
1673. McKay, Hill, and Buckler, Vol. 1, p. 44.
1674. See Exodus 12:44; Leviticus 25:44-46; Ecclesiastes 2:7.
1675. Leviticus 25:38, 44-46. Emphasis added.

1676. T. C. Butler, s.v. "Slave/servant."
1677. Exodus 21:1-6; Deuteronomy 15:12.
1678. Seabrook, TMOCP, p. 212.
1679. McKenzie, s.v. "Slave, slavery."
1680. Metzger and Coogan, s.v. "Slavery."
1681. E. A. Livingstone, s.v. "Slavery."
1682. See e.g., Matthew 8:5-13; 10:24-25; Luke 12:47; Ephesians 6:5; I Timothy 6:1; Titus 2:9-10.
1683. Galatians 1:10.
1684. Acts 4:29; 16:17.
1685. Mark 10:44.
1686. Luke 12:42-48.
1687. Seabrook, TAHSR, pp. 158-162, 651-653.
1688. McKay, Hill, and Buckler, Vol. 1, p. 281.
1689. Marvin Perry, p. 125.
1690. Childe, p. 232.
1691. B. G. Walker, TWEOMAS, s.v. "Slavery"; Muller, p. 154.
1692. Warnock and Anderson, p. 94.
1693. Winks, Brinton, Christopher, and Wolff, Vol. 1, p. 138.
1694. Bascom, pp. 26-27.
1695. Dimont, pp. 154-155.
1696. Drescher and Engerman, p. 152.
1697. Heer, pp. 49-50.
1698. De Rosa, p. 170.
1699. Reyes, p. 120.
1700. Heer, p. 50.
1701. U. B. Phillips, ANS, p. 10.
1702. Thompson and Johnson, p. 873.
1703. E. O. Wilson, p. 549.
1704. Herring, p. 226.
1705. Hinnells, p. 188.
1706. Simons, p. 88.
1707. See e.g., Burne, p. 528.
1708. Dunner, p. 882; Muller, p. 186; Cross and Livingston, s.v. "Slavery."
1709. Boardman, Griffin, and Murray, p. 418.
1710. Dunner, pp. 883-884.
1711. Dimont, p. 359.
1712. Seabrook, EYWTACWW, pp. 69-98.
1713. Farrow, Lang, and Frank, pp. xxvii, 4-5, 82-90; Hacker, p. 525; Ellis, FB, p. 103.
1714. A. J. Grant, p. 221.
1715. Fogel and Engerman, p. 31. My paraphrasal.
1716. L. M. Graham, pp. 459-461.
1717. Fogel and Engerman, pp. 29-31.
1718. Brackett, p. 32.
1719. F. Douglass, NLFD, pp. xi, 118.
1720. Chesnut, MCCW, p. 246. My paraphrasal.
1721. Drescher and Engerman, p. 204.
1722. Since all humans, no matter what their race, nationality, or socioeconomic background, *have* to work to survive, some slavery scholars—myself included—consider all labor "forced."
1723. Ellis, FB, p. 107. To this day there is still no completely egalitarian society on earth, for most people around the globe, whatever their skin color, seem unable to accept the fact that "race" is an illusion—as discussed in my "Notes to the Reader," a sociological theory that has no real basis in biology. We are all one species and descend from a single common prehistoric ancestor, symbolized in the pre-biblical Babylonian creation myth as the "first man" Adapa, in the pre-biblical Sumerian creation myth as Adamu, and in the later biblical Jewish creation myth as Adam. In reality the apparent physical differences

among us stem primarily from one factor: where on the planet our distant ancestors originated. Dark skinned people tend to evolve in hot equatorial regions, light skinned people tend to evolve in cool boreal regions. Thus, as Ashley Montagu postulated decades ago, when speaking of modern *Homo sapiens* it would be more accurate to replace the word "race" with the word "variety."

1724. Meltzer, Vol. 2, p. 139.

1725. G. H. Moore, p. 5; R. S. Phillips, s.v. "Slavery"; Blake, p. 370.

1726. Blake, p. 380.

1727. J. T. Adams, p. 53.

1728. Rutherford, FA, p. 61.

1729. Blake, pp. 388, 421, 430, 447, 498, 502, 524, 563, 827.

1730. It has been estimated that there were 169,148 whites in the state of New York in 1776. A. J. Northrup, p. 284.

1731. A. J. Northrup, pp. 284-285.

1732. A. J. Northrup, p. 285.

1733. E. J. McManus, BBITN, pp. 196, 199; Johnston, p. 19.

1734. A. J. Northrup, p. 286.

1735. Blake, p. 370.

1736. Greene, p. 125.

1737. U. B. Phillips, ANS, p. 100.

1738. U. B. Phillips, ANS, pp. 100-101. Emphasis added.

1739. U. B. Phillips, ANS, p. 101.

1740. Blake, p. 370.

1741. Hildreth, THOTUSOA, Vol. 1, pp. 282-283.

1742. U. B. Phillips, ANS, p. 101.

1743. U. B. Phillips, ANS, p. 112.

1744. E. J. McManus, BBITN, p. 61.

1745. H. A. White, p. 63.

1746. Litwack, NS, pp. 3-4. Northern plantations date back to at least the Pilgrims, who were establishing them as early as the 1600s, long before they were found in the South. October 25, 2010, *America Live*, FOX News.

1747. Johnston, p. 19; E. J. McManus, BBITN, pp. 196, 199.

1748. Siebert, p. xiii.

1749. Fogel, pp. 203-204.

1750. E. J. McManus, BBITN, p. 5.

1751. Ahlstrom, p. 649.

1752. Rutherford, FA, p. 61.

1753. A. J. Northrup, p. 293.

1754. M. M. Smith, pp. 4-5.

1755. Meltzer, Vol. 2, p. 127; Furnas, p. 27.

1756. R. S. Phillips, s.v. "Emancipation Proclamation."

1757. W. T. Alexander, p. 240; Bedford and Colbourn, p. 85.

1758. Roche, pp. 16-17.

1759. U. B. Phillips, ANS, pp. 119-120.

1760. P. M. Roberts, p. 198; Garraty and McCaughey, p. 81.

1761. Rutherford, FA, p. 61.

1762. Eaton, HSC, p. 93.

1763. Hinkle, p. 125.

1764. For the Northern white population in 1860, see Katcher, CWSB, p. 46.

1765. Rutherford, FA, p. 38; Wallechinsky, Wallace, and Wallace, p. 11; Woods, p. 67.

1766. McElroy, p. 357.

1767. A few years ago I had occasion to travel to Massachusetts on business, where I found myself, as I often do, exploring a cemetery, this one named Woodlawn, in the town of Acton. It was here that I experienced the most interesting part of my journey: the discovery of a small gray headstone that read simply, "Peter, slave." Revealingly, Peter's grave was completely isolated, situated by a road many yards

from the surrounding graves of white Yankees. This is quite unlike what one finds in the South. Here, where relations between Victorian whites and blacks were far warmer and more intimate than in the North, the graves of both races are often located right next to one another. For more on the subject of white-black relationships in the Old South, see my books *A Rebel Born: A Defense of Nathan Bedford Forrest* (pp. 151-155), and *The McGavocks of Carnton Plantation: A Southern History*, passim.
1768. Many of these individuals were slaves in more than one Northern state.
1769. See e.g., O. Williams, p. 6.
1770. Smelser, ACRH, p. 59.
1771. Foley, p. 323.
1772. Seabrook, TMOCP, pp. 172-173.
1773. White, Foscue, and McKnight, p. 38.
1774. Estes, pp. 229-230.
1775. Nicolay and Hay, ALCW, Vol. 1, pp. 176, 231.
1776. Derry, p. 67.
1777. Website: www.factasy.com/civil_war/2008/03/02/slave_owners_slaves_and_life_plantation.
1778. Website: www.factasy.com/civil_war/2008/03/02/slave_owners_slaves_and_life_plantation.
1779. See Rodriguez, THEOWS, Vol. 1, s.v. "African Burial Ground."
1780. As just one example of a large and successful New Englander slaveholding family, see McLoughlin, passim. See also Chan, passim; Di Bonaventura, passim.
1781. Manegold, pp. 132-134.
1782. U. B. Phillips, ANS, pp. 109-110. Emphasis added.
1783. Humphreys, pp. 37-39. Emphasis added.
1784. Shannon, pp. 775-776. Emphasis added.
1785. Paulding, pp. 221-222. Emphasis added.
1786. Estes, pp. 229-230. Emphasis added.
1787. Shenkman, p. 124.
1788. J. M. Burns, p. 393.
1789. Rosenbaum and Brinkley, s.v. "Underground Railroad."
1790. See Foner, GTF, passim.
1791. Gragg, pp. 191-192.
1792. See Still, passim.
1793. Siebert, p. 220.
1794. Drescher and Engerman, pp. 106-107. See also Winks, passim.
1795. U. B. Phillips, ANS, p. 110.
1796. J. M. Burns, p. 393.
1797. U. B. Phillips, ANS, pp. 314-316.
1798. L. W. Hopkins, pp. 14-17. Emphasis added.
1799. Chesnut, MCCW, p. 250.
1800. Wiley, LJR, p. 328.
1801. Smedes, MOASP, p. 341.
1802. *Andrew Jackson*, History Channel, June 26, 2008.
1803. Garraty and McCaughey, p. 254.
1804. Fox-Genovese, p. 133.
1805. Rosenbaum and Brinkley, s.v. "Slavery."
1806. M. M. Smith, pp. 37, 194.
1807. Drescher and Engerman, p. 175.
1808. Garraty and McCaughey, p. 217.
1809. U. B. Phillips, ANS, p. 428.
1810. U. B. Phillips, ANS, pp. 428-429.
1811. U. B. Phillips, ANS, p. 430.
1812. U. B. Phillips, ANS, p. 428. Emphasis added.
1813. Derry, p. 115.
1814. E. A. Andrews, p. 34.

1815. A. D. P. Van Buren, p. 123. Emphasis added.
1816. U. B. Phillips, ANS, pp. 329-330.
1817. S. A. Channing, p. 129.
1818. Maria was born in Mississippi.
1819. Seabrook, TMOCP, pp. 221-222.
1820. Bolling's first name is also spelled Boling and Bowling in some records.
1821. Some sources refer to her as Mariah Reddick.
1822. V. M. Bowman, p. 62.
1823. The wife of Col. Van Perkins Winder, Sr., Carrie's mother, was Martha Ann Grundy, a daughter of Tennessee senator, Felix Grundy.
1824. V. M. Bowman, p. 62.
1825. This Franklin cemetery was named after François Dominique Toussaint, a self-educated slave who led the black Haitian Rebellion in 1791. Taking the name of a series of hard-hitting campaigns to free his fellow servants, L'Ouverture (meaning "the opening"), he conquered Santo Domingo in 1801 and took over governorship. In the ongoing conflict with France he was captured and sent to a prison at Fort-de-Joux in the French Jura. Toussaint L'Ouverture died in a dungeon there in 1803, becoming a martyr for the cause of universal black emancipation. The Negro Haitian Rebellion was still a daily topic of discussion by white Americans in the mid-1800s and was no doubt occasionally brought up at the McGavocks' dinner table.
1826. According to her gravestone, Maria passed away in 1922. For a detailed history of the McGavocks, see Seabrook, TMOCP, passim; Seabrook, CPGS, passim. Also see Seabrook, EOTBOF, passim.
1827. C. Johnson, TPIGTTS, p. 15.
1828. Drescher and Engerman, p. 176.
1829. Blassingame, p. 167.
1830. Cash, p. 51.
1831. M. M. Smith, pp. 33, 262-265. See also C. Johnson, TPIGTTS, pp. 14-15.
1832. Adams and Sanders, p. 249.
1833. Van Loon, p. 350. My paraphrasal.
1834. Smedes, ASP, p. 193. Emphasis added.
1835. Ashe, p. 40; S. Andrews, pp. 128-129.
1836. U. B. Phillips, ANS, p. 110.
1837. A. J. Northrup, pp. 267-268.
1838. Garraty, TAN, p. 84.
1839. Garraty, TAN, p. 84.
1840. Blake, p. 379.
1841. E. J. McManus, BBITN, pp. 129-130. My paraphrasal.
1842. U. B. Phillips, ANS, p. 418.
1843. G. Bancroft, Vol. 1, p. 418.
1844. E. J. McManus, BBITN, p. 85.
1845. U. B. Phillips, ANS, p. 112.
1846. E. J. McManus, BBITN, p. 85.
1847. E. J. McManus, BBITN, pp. 85-86.
1848. U. B. Phillips, ASN, p. 469.
1849. U. B. Phillips, ASN, p. 456.
1850. U. B. Phillips, ASN, p. 102.
1851. E. A. Andrews, pp. 34-35.
1852. Chesnut, MCCW, p. 642.
1853. Estes, p. 257.
1854. Joseph Shaw Bolton, "Amentia and Dementia: A Clinico-Pathological Study," *The Journal of Mental Science*, Vol. 54, No. 224, January 1908, p. 25.
1855. Hinsie and Campbell, s.v. "psychopathic personality."
1856. Drake, pp. 1, 90.
1857. Garraty and McCaughey, p. 25.
1858. See Estes, p. 126.

1859. Drescher and Engerman, p. 183.
1860. Marsh, pp. 11, 14.
1861. Osler, pp. 291-292.
1862. Hacker, p. 35.
1863. Burne, p. 631.
1864. U. B. Phillips, ASN, p. 103.
1865. G. Thomas, p. 47.
1866. In 1568 these 71 unfortunate "heretics" had been left behind in Mexico by English slave trader and explorer Sir John Hawkins. Burne, p. 528.
1867. Burne, p. 663.
1868. E. J. McManus, BBITN, pp. 57, 69, 73.
1869. U. B. Phillips, ASN, pp. 104-105.
1870. U. B. Phillips, ANS, p. 113.
1871. E. J. McManus, BBITN, pp. 75-78.
1872. A. J. Northrup, p. 265.
1873. See e.g., Whitmore, pp. xxvii, xxix, xxxii, xxxiv, xxxvii, 13, 52, 59, 61, 63, 78, 92, 145, 186, 210, 237.
1874. E. J. McManus, BBITN, pp. 64-65.
1875. E. Channing, p. 11.
1876. W. H. Collins, pp. 85-86.
1877. Brackett, p. 22.
1878. Coit, pp 37, 48.
1879. Turner, SIP, pp. 34-35.
1880. M. Jensen, NN, p. 33.
1881. Alotta, p. 3.
1882. S. A. Channing, p. 29.
1883. Wiley, SN, pp. 213, 244, 245.
1884. Henry, ATSF, p. 246.
1885. Genovese, pp. 356, 368, 371, 374, 378-380.
1886. Genovese, p. 408.
1887. Lyell, Vol. 1, pp. 357-358. Emphasis added.
1888. See Genovese, pp. 470, 482, 504, 508-511.
1889. E. P. Thompson, pp. 339-349.
1890. DeGregorio, s.v. "Jimmy Carter" (p. 619).
1891. Nicolay and Hay, ALCW, Vol. 1, p. 89.
1892. Estes, p. 136. Emphasis added.
1893. Horn, IE, p. 68.
1894. Lytle, p. 14; Parks, p. 82.
1895. Wyeth, TDF, p. 279.
1896. O. Williams, pp. 42-43.
1897. Horn, IE, p. 68.
1898. Fogel and Engerman, pp. 232, 238-239.
1899. U. B. Phillips, ANS, pp. 293-294. Emphasis added.
1900. Fogel and Engerman, p. 240. My paraphrasal. Emphasis added.
1901. Fogel and Engerman, pp. 232, 238-239, 240.
1902. U. B. Phillips, ANS, p. 270.
1903. Smedes, MOASP, p. 191.
1904. Flint, Vol. 1, p. 248.
1905. Stampp, pp. 178, 179.
1906. U. B. Phillips, ANS, p. 328.
1907. Estes, p. 131. Emphasis added.
1908. Paulding, p. 223. Emphasis added.
1909. Jervey, p. 68.

1910. W. Wilson, DR, p. 127. Emphasis added.
1911. Blanchard and Rice, pp. 132-133. Emphasis added.
1912. A. Young, pp. 238-239. Emphasis added.
1913. U. B. Phillips, ANS, p. 270. Emphasis added.
1914. U. B. Phillips, ANS, pp. 274, 276.
1915. Fogel and Engerman, p. 146.
1916. *Appendix to the Congressional Globe*, 31st Congress, 1st Session, 1850, Vol. 23, Part 1, p. 150.
1917. Stampp, pp. 178, 179.
1918. Jervey, p. 67.
1919. *De Bow's Review*, Vol. 22, Third Series, Vol. 2, New Orleans, LA, 1857, p. 379. Emphasis added.
1920. U. B. Phillips, ANS, p. 261. Emphasis added.
1921. U. B. Phillips, ANS, p. 261.
1922. U. B. Phillips, PAFD, Vol. 1, pp. 112-114. Emphasis added.
1923. Fox-Genovese, p. 360.
1924. U. B. Phillips, ANS, p. 509. Emphasis added.
1925. Stampp, pp. 219-222.
1926. Estes, pp. 125, 126.
1927. Fogel and Engerman, p. 146.
1928. Ashe, p. 64.
1929. Harwell, p. 339.
1930. Wiley, SN, pp. 213, 244, 245.
1931. See Quarles, TNITCW, pp. 208-209; Wiley, SN, pp. 316-317.
1932. Henry, ATSF, p. 246.
1933. B. Mayer, pp. 104-105.
1934. Blake, pp. 136-142.
1935. Blassingame, p. 15.
1936. See e.g., Wiley, SN, pp. 213, 214, 244, 245.
1937. See e.g., J. Davis, RFCG, Vol. 2, p. 626.
1938. Grissom, p. 183.
1939. E. J. McManus, BBITN, p. 183.
1940. See Fogel, p. 26; Genovese, pp. 356, 368, 371, 374, 378-380, 385, 386, 542.
1941. Fogel and Engerman, pp. 210-215.
1942. See e.g., J. C. Perry, p. 174; Grissom, p. 131; Stonebraker, p. 46; C. Johnson, TPIGTTS, pp. 81-84; Greenberg and Waugh, p. 376.
1943. Drescher and Engerman, pp. 214, 215.
1944. H. C. Bruce, p. 27. Emphasis added.
1945. Thomson, pp. 190-191. Emphasis added.
1946. Genovese, p. 542.
1947. See e.g., Genovese, pp. 470, 508.
1948. Ellison, p. 96; Rose, RFR, p. 135; Baldwin, pp. 40-41; Swint, p. 123. Black slave parents were often seen by whites as "only too much disposed to resort to blows and slap in family matters," as one Victorian author put it. See Mallard, p. 52.
1949. C. C. Jones, p. 113. Emphasis added.
1950. See Fogel and Engerman, pp. 232, 238-239.
1951. Drescher and Engerman, p. 207.
1952. See Seabrook, AL, pp. 137-160.
1953. Smedes, ASP, pp. 190-191. Emphasis added.
1954. H. A. White, p. 63. Emphasis added.
1955. Flint, Vol. 1, pp. 248-250. Emphasis added.
1956. Madame Marie Delphine LaLaurie, a wealthy New Orleans socialite, became notorious for the torture and murder of her black servants in the 1830s.
1957. Lyell, Vol. 2, pp. 163-164. Emphasis added.
1958. Thwaites, p. 289. Emphasis added.

1959. B. Hall, pp. 227-228. Emphasis added.
1960. Faux, pp. 67-68. Emphasis added.
1961. U. B. Phillips, ANS, p. 307.
1962. Parsons, p. 27.
1963. Seabrook, AL, p. 47.
1964. Blake, p. 480.
1965. J. T. Adams, p. 200.
1966. Thomson, pp. 192-195. Emphasis added.
1967. Nieboer, pp. 71-72.
1968. Nieboer, p. 72.
1969. Nieboer, pp. 72-73.
1970. Nieboer, pp. 68, 75-76, 93, 114.
1971. Neiboer, pp. 63-64, 82.
1972. Neiboer, pp. 101, 315-316.
1973. Neiboer, p. 64.
1974. Neiboer, p. 100.
1975. This sentence is a quote by ethnographer B. T. Somerville. Neiboer, p. 90.
1976. This section is a quote by naturalist C. M. Woodford. Nieboer, p. 90.
1977. Nieboer, p. 92.
1978. U. B. Phillips, ANS, p. 6.
1979. S. H. M. Byers, "The Last Slave Ship," *Harper's Monthly Magazine*, Vol. 113, June to November 1906, p. 743.
1980. Blake, pp. 43, 47, 52.
1981. Blake, p. 41.
1982. U. B. Phillips, ANS, pp. 193-194.
1983. Mead, MAF, p. 148.
1984. W. H. Collins, pp. 70-71.
1985. W. H. Collins, p. 73. Emphasis added.
1986. E. A. Andrews, p. 119. Emphasis added.
1987. U. B. Phillips, ANS, pp. 298-299. Emphasis added.
1988. U. B. Phillips, ANS, pp. 361, 362. Emphasis added.
1989. W. H. Collins, pp. 74-77.
1990. W. H. Collins, pp. 78-80.
1991. Genovese, p. 453.
1992. Stroud, p. 50; Goodell, p. 46; U. B. Phillips, ANS, p. 493.
1993. N. Adams, p. 78. Emphasis added.
1994. W. H. Collins, pp. 82-83. Emphasis added.
1995. Drescher and Engerman, p. 218.
1996. Derry, p. 67.
1997. See e.g., Seabrook, TAHSR, pp. 12-13; Genovese, pp. 463-465.
1998. See e.g., Chesnut, DD, p. 114.
1999. E. A. Andrews, p. 139.
2000. See Blake, pp. 50-51.
2001. U. B. Phillips, ANS, pp. 194-195. Emphasis added. The building that housed Franklin and Armfield's offices still stands at 1315 Duke Street, Alexandria, Virginia.
2002. E. A. Andrews, p. 150. Emphasis added.
2003. Olmsted, AJITBC, pp. 413-414.
2004. U. B. Phillips, ANS, pp. 511-512.
2005. Martineau, ROWT, Vol. 1, pp. 266-267. Emphasis added.
2006. U. B. Phillips, ANS, p. 512. Emphasis added.
2007. Lester, p. 359.
2008. Seabrook, TUAL, p. 40.
2009. Nicolay and Hay, ALCW, Vol. 2, p. 1. Emphasis added.

2010. Seabrook, AL, p. 62.
2011. Nicolay and Hay, ALCW, Vol. 2, pp. 3-4.
2012. Seabrook, AL, p. 302.
2013. Lester, pp. 359-360.
2014. Nicolay and Hay, ALCW, Vol. 2, pp. 227-228. Emphasis added.
2015. Spooner, NT, No. 6, p. 54. See also Graham, BM, passim; Melish, passim.
2016. F. Moore, Vol. 4, pp. 201.
2017. Nicolay and Hay, ALCW, Vol. 2, p. 674; See also Owsley, KCD, pp. 65-66.
2018. J. Davis, RFCG, Vol. 2, p. 764.
2019. For more on this particular subject see my books on Lincoln's War, in particular, *Everything You Were Taught About the Civil War is Wrong, Ask a Southerner!*
2020. E. McPherson, PHUSAGR, p. 286. Emphasis added.
2021. DeGregorio, s.v. "Thomas Jefferson."
2022. Kennedy, p. 91.
2023. Foley, p. 813.
2024. Tocqueville, Vol. 1, pp. 357-358.
2025. Litwack, NS, pp. 4, 6.
2026. For the typical Yankee soldier's feelings concerning abolition, seee.g., Henderson, Vol. 2, p. 411; Murphy, p. 86; Page Smith, Vol. 5, pp. 308-309; Barrow, Segars, and Rosenburg, BC, p. 45; E. L. Jordan, p. 141; Wiley, LBY, p. 281; D. H. Donald, L, p. 385; B. Thornton, p. 176; S. Foote, Vol. 1, p. 538.
2027. M. M. Smith, pp. 4-5.
2028. Chesnut, DD, p. 74.
2029. Stampp, pp. 425-426.
2030. Garraty, HV, p. 302; Simpson, pp. 80-81.
2031. T. N. Page, p. 57; R. H. McKim, p. 31.
2032. Rutherford, FA, p. 38; Wallechinsky, Wallace, and Wallace, p. 11; Woods, p. 67.
2033. Meriwether, p. 219.
2034. Rhodes, Vol. 3, p. 476.
2035. Rosen, p. 161; Gamoran, p. 203.
2036. Simmons, s.v. "General Order, Number Eleven"; Horwitz, p. 204.
2037. Ferris and Greenberg, p. 114. My paraphrasal.
2038. Parker, p. 343.
2039. U. B. Phillips, ANS, p. 147.
2040. Polk, Vol. 1, pp. 324, 325. Emphasis added.
2041. Greenhow, pp. 324-326. Emphasis added.
2042. In late November 1864, Marx wrote Lincoln a letter congratulating him on his "re-election by a large majority." The missive included Marx's sincere hope that Lincoln would "lead his country through the matchless struggle for the rescue of an enchained race and the reconstruction of a social world." The two socialistic men had much in common, far more than most modern day Lincoln apologists are prepared to admit. For Marx's letter, and the White House's reply, see Schlüter, pp. 188-193.
2043. Thornton and Ekelund, p. 103; C. Adams, p. 79; I. C. Martin, p. 72. Emphasis added.
2044. Tyler, LTT, Vol. 3, p. 28.
2045. Anonymous, p. 32.
2046. W. Wilson, DR, p. 50.
2047. Christian, p. 14.
2048. Stiles, pp. 49-50. Emphasis added.
2049. McKim, pp. 31-33. Emphasis added.
2050. See e.g., Munford, pp. 52-53.
2051. Mitgang, p. 264.
2052. Lyell, Vol. 2, p. 162-163.
2053. Simpson, pp. 69, 74.
2054. Coit, pp. 170, 175.
2055. Rozwenc, p. 50.

2056. Seabrook, EYWTATCWIW, passim.
2057. DeGregorio, s.v. "John Quincy Adams" (p. 97).
2058. Coit, pp. 170-171, 186.
2059. Elliot, Vol. 1, pp. 472-473. Emphasis added.
2060. Collier and Collier, pp. 167-168.
2061. C. Johnson, TPIGTTS, p. 140.
2062. See E. M. Thomas, pp. 307-322.
2063. Oglesby, p. 42. Emphasis added.
2064. Nicolay and Hay, ALCW, Vol. 2, p. 674. Emphasis added.
2065. For more on the constitutionality and legality of secession, see Bledsoe, DT, passim; Graham, CHS, passim; Howe, passim; Perkins, passim; Powell, passim; Samuel, passim.
2066. We estimate, contrary to heavily manipulated and undercounted Yankee statistics, that during Lincoln's War some 2 million Southerners of all races perished, and that at least 1 million Northerners died. Seabrook, ARB, pp. 130, 131.
2067. Spooner, NT, No. 6, pp. 56-57. Emphasis added.
2068. Seabrook, L, pp. 242-243.
2069. Seabrook, L, pp. 244-245.
2070. Nicolay and Hay, ALCW, Vol. 1, p. 468.
2071. Nicolay and Hay, ALCW, Vol. 1, pp. 433, 451.
2072. J. Davis, RFCG, Vol. 1, p. 80. Emphasis added.
2073. Strangely, most black Southerners today do not express shame for their ancestral involvement in black slavery, nor have they ever apologized for it. As far as I am aware, neither have Native-Americans or Latin-Americans.
2074. Meltzer, Vol. 2, p. 139. Also see Cartmell, p. 26; Norwood, p. 31.
2075. Lott, pp. 35-60.
2076. G. H. Moore, pp. 5, 11, 17-19; Blake, p. 370.
2077. Drescher and Engerman, p. 372.
2078. W. T. Alexander, p. 240; Bedford and Colbourn, p. 85; Rosenbaum and Brinkley, s.v. "Slavery"; Melish, passim.
2079. L. Abbott, p. 155.
2080. L. Abbott, p. 149. Emphasis added. Note: this text is a paraphrasal by Beecher's editor Lyman Abbott.
2081. Seabrook, AL, pp. 161-165.
2082. Fogel, p. 207.
2083. G. H. Moore, pp. 5, 11, 17-19.
2084. R. S. Phillips, s.v. "Slavery."
2085. Greenberg and Waugh, p. 376; Grissom, pp. 131, 182; Stonebraker, p. 46; J. C. Perry, pp. 96, 99, 101, 174.
2086. Kennedy and Kennedy, SWR, p. 83; M. M. Smith, pp. 4-5.
2087. Meltzer, Vol. 2, p. 4.
2088. Encyc. Brit., s.v. "slavery."
2089. M. Perry, p. 49.
2090. Lott, p. 18; Furnas, p. 27; Garraty and McCaughey, p. 25; Garraty, HV, p. 77.
2091. Furnas, p. 108.
2092. M. B. Davidson, Vol. 2, p. 340.
2093. Derry, p. 67.
2094. W. H. Collins, p. 84.
2095. Seabrook, TQJD, p. 68.
2096. Blake, p. 379.
2097. U. B. Phillips, ANS, pp. 132, 138-139.
2098. U. B. Phillips, ANS, p. 202.
2099. W. H. Collins, pp. 84-85.
2100. Seabrook, TMOCP, p. 185.
2101. W. H. Collins, p. 9.

2102. E. A. Andrews, p. 176.
2103. Featherstonhaugh, Vol. 1, pp. 126-127. Emphasis added.
2104. U. B. Phillips, ANS, pp. 133-134. Emphasis added.
2105. Featherstonhaugh, Vol. 1, pp. 127-129. Emphasis added.
2106. Ahlstrom, p. 650.
2107. U. B. Phillips, ANS, p. 286.
2108. Nell, p. 218.
2109. Beard and Beard, Vol. 1, pp. 652-653.
2110. U. B. Phillips, ANS, p. 123.
2111. Blake, p. 389.
2112. Child, p. 11.
2113. Brodnax, p. 10.
2114. Child, p. 6.
2115. Child, p, 8.
2116. Derry, p. 67.
2117. U. B. Phillips, ANS, p. 75.
2118. Burne, pp. 740, 741.
2119. Garraty and McCaughey, p. 81.
2120. See U. B. Phillips, ASN, pp. 104-105.
2121. Adams and Sanders, p. 118.
2122. See Kolchin, pp. 78, 81, 89-90, 94, 128.
2123. Drescher and Engerman, p. 213.
2124. Seabrook, EYWTACWW, p. 158. Also see Ransom, pp. 214-215; Bennett, BTM, p. 87; W. J. Cooper, JDA, p. 378; Quarles, TNITCW, p. xiii; Stephenson, ALU, p. 168.
2125. J. H. Russell, pp. 9, 12-13.
2126. U. B. Phillips, ANS, p. 426.
2127. U. B. Phillips, ANS, pp. 426-427.
2128. Child, p. 5.
2129. McLoughlin, p. 205. See also Levy, passim; L. Morton, passim.
2130. Schoepf, Vol. 1, p. 149.
2131. Grimké, p. 10.
2132. W. Wilson, DR, pp. 113-114.
2133. Blake, p. 389.
2134. L. Abbott, p. 149.
2135. Nicolay and Hay, ALCW, Vol. 2, p. 6.
2136. Faust, s.v. "slavery"; Stampp, p. 271; Meltzer, Vol. 2, pp. 247-248; C. Johnson, TPIGTTS, pp. 126-128; Rosenbaum and Brinkley, s.v. "Slave Trade"; Durden, p. 288; Crane, Feinberg, Berman, and Hall, p. 73.
2137. W. H. Collins, p. 20.
2138. Burne, p. 718.
2139. H. U. Faulkner, p. 58.
2140. Foley, pp. 816-817.
2141. Blake, p. 464.
2142. See Blake, p. 385.
2143. Clare, Vol. 5, p. 3199. Emphasis added.
2144. Clare, Vol. 5, p. 3218. Emphasis added.
2145. Foley, p. 970.
2146. Bowen, pp. 600-601.
2147. Foley, p. 246.
2148. K. C. Davis, pp. 10, 30. John Adams' favorite part of Jefferson's draft of the Declaration of Independence was his attack on King George for foisting slavery on the American colonies. J. C. Miller, p. 8. Primarily opposites on the political spectrum, Southerner Jefferson and Northerner Adams at least had abolition in common.
2149. See Spooner, NT, No. 6, p. 54.

2150. Friedenwald, p. 130. Emphasis added.
2151. Foley, p. 399.
2152. Nicolay and Hay, ALCW, Vol. 1, pp. 231-233. Emphasis added.
2153. See M. Jensen, AC, passim.
2154. Foley, p. 973.
2155. E. C. Holland, p. 23.
2156. W. H. Collins, p. 10.
2157. Foley, p. 812.
2158. Jefferson, NSV, pp. 145, 146.
2159. Bergh, Vol. 2, p. 227.
2160. Burne, pp. 740, 741.
2161. R. Sobel, s.v. "Jefferson, Thomas."
2162. Foley, p. 811.
2163. Blake, p. 406.
2164. The U.S.A. was first created as a confederacy (a weak central government in compact with powerful, fully independent nation-states), and existed in this form from 1781 to 1789. As such, it was called "the Confederacy" by all early Americans between these years. Thomas Jefferson's writings alone contain dozens of references to "the Confederacy" during this period. Likewise, our first Constitution was known as the "Articles of Confederation." Despite the renaming of our nation as the "United States of America" after 1789, many Americans, both South and North, continued to refer to her as the Confederacy, some right up until the time of Lincoln's War in 1861. Lincoln himself publicly referred to the U.S. as "the Confederacy" that very year. Here is more evidence that the South fought, not over slavery, as Yankee myth asserts, but to maintain the original Confederacy of the Founding Fathers, most who were Southerners and true believers in confederation. This is why the seceded states called themselves "the Confederacy." For more information on Jefferson, Lincoln, and the original American Confederacy, see my books, *Confederacy 101: Amazing Facts You Never Knew About America's Oldest Political Tradition*; *The Articles of Confederation Explained*; *Abraham Lincoln: The Southern View*; *Lincolnology: The Real Lincoln Revealed in His Own Words*; and *Everything You Were Taught About the Civil War is Wrong, Ask a Southerner!* For more on the period of the U.S. Confederacy, see M. Jensen, NN, passim.
2165. See e.g., Tocqueville, Vol. 1, p. 154.
2166. Cluskey, p. 186.
2167. Foley, p. 816.
2168. P. L. Ford, Vol. 1, p. 76.
2169. Foley, p. 442.
2170. Blake, p. 445.
2171. C. Morris, s.v. "Slavery."
2172. Foley, p. 811.
2173. Ransom, p. 253.
2174. Wallechinsky and Wallace, p. 427.
2175. W. H. Collins, p. 5.
2176. Encyc. Brit., s.v. "slavery."
2177. Blake, p. 389. Emphasis added.
2178. U. B. Phillips, ANS, p. 124.
2179. Ellis, FB, p. 105.
2180. M. M. Miller, Vol. 1, pp. 358-359. Madison is here discussing the concept of "slave representation." Emphasis added.
2181. McCullough, p. 221.
2182. Blake, p. 397.
2183. Weeks, p. 214.
2184. Weeks, pp. 234-236.
2185. Eaton, HSC, pp. 237-238.
2186. Stroud, p. 50; Goodell, p. 46; U. B. Phillips, ANS, p. 493.
2187. Lyell, Vol. 2, p. 162.
2188. Chesnut, MCCW, p. 357.

2189. Warner, GG, s.v. "James Johnston Pettigrew."
2190. Cash, p. 63.
2191. McDannald, s.v. "Slavery."
2192. H. C. Bailey, p. 197.
2193. Oates, AF, p. 29; M. Perry, passim.
2194. See Grimké, passim.
2195. Fox, pp. 48-49.
2196. U. B. Phillips, ANS, pp. 124-125, 126.
2197. Dumond, pp. 7-8.
2198. D. D. Wallace, p. 446. Emphasis added.
2199. U. B. Phillips, ANS, p. 121.
2200. M. D. Peterson, JM, p. 371; Ellis, AS, pp. 102, 173.
2201. Blake, p. 427.
2202. Blake, pp. 432, 438.
2203. Blake, p. 450.
2204. Weeks, p. 243. Emphasis added.
2205. Derry, p. 67.
2206. N. Adams, p. 77.
2207. Seabrook, TQREL, p. 106. Emphasis added.
2208. Quarles, TNITCW, p. 280.
2209. E. M. Thomas, p. 242.
2210. Seabrook, TQREL, p. 106.
2211. Kennedy and Kennedy, SWR, p. 73.
2212. DeGregorio, s.v. "John Quincy Adams" (p. 97).
2213. Derry, p. 70.
2214. "Antislavery" is defined here as the belief that slavery is unjust. Holding this view did not necessarily mean that one was also an abolitionist, that is, one who held that slave owning was also wrong.
2215. Weintraub, p. 54.
2216. Adams and Sanders, pp. 144, 148-149. See also Chace, pp. 11-12.
2217. Chesnut, DD, pp. 114, 163.
2218. Chesnut, MCCW, p. 729.
2219. My paraphrasal.
2220. Chesnut, DD, p. 74.
2221. Chesnut, MCCW, pp. 729, 245, 246. My paraphrasal.
2222. Smedes, ASP, pp. 191-192.
2223. Simpson, pp. 77-78, 85.
2224. B. Mayer, p. vi.
2225. J. Torrey, p. 12.
2226. Coit, p. 166. My paraphrasal. Randolph, my cousin, was known to attend senate meetings carrying a whip and wearing spurs and multiple overcoats, some that dragged along the ground as he strode imperiously up and down the aisles in his buckskin breeches and leather boots. Coit, p. 162.
2227. Woods, p. 33. My paraphrasal. John Taylor "of Caroline," a die-hard Jeffersonian and vehement anti-Federalist, would later inspire the supporters of states' rights (like John C. Calhoun), as well as members of the libertarian and Tea Party movements, with his strict constructionist views of the Constitution.
2228. H. A. White, p. 65. Emphasis added.
2229. W. Wilson, DR, pp. 110-111.
2230. W. Wilson, DR, pp. 119-120. Emphasis added.
2231. Hale and Merritt, Vol. 3, p. 838.
2232. Seabrook, TMOCP, p. 67.
2233. Website: www.historycarper.com/resources/twobf3/slavery.htm.
2234. K. C. Davis, p. 37.
2235. B. Franklin, LWBF, Vol. 2, p. 422.

2236. Franklin was so Anglocentric and xenophobic that he even complained about Germans immigrating to Pennsylvania. Adams and Sanders, p. 327.
2237. Goodman, pp. 332, 333, 334, 336.
2238. Sparks, Vol. 2, pp. 320-321. Emphasis added.
2239. Adams and Sanders, pp. 144, 148-149.
2240. Drescher and Engerman, p. 23.
2241. See Seabrook, AL, passim; Seabrook, TUAL, passim; Seabrook, L, passim; Seabrook, TGI, passim.
2242. Nicolay and Hay, ALCW, Vol. 1, p. 288. Emphasis added.
2243. Thornton and Daugherty, p. 337.
2244. Bedford and Colbourn, p. 187.
2245. H. U. Faulkner, p. 319.
2246. McKissack and McKissack, p. 170.
2247. Rodriguez, THEOWS, Vol. 1, s.v. "Garrison, William Lloyd."
2248. Furnas, p. 408; Rosenbaum and Brinkley, s.v. "Liberator, The."
2249. Drescher and Engerman, p. 52.
2250. Buckley, p. 62; Dumond, pp. 59-60; *Acts and Resolves Passed by the General Assembly of the State of Rhode Island and Providence Plantations*, January Session, 1911, p. 299.
2251. *Quaker Biographies*, Vol. 5, pp. 140-143. Emphasis added.
2252. Garrison and Garrison, Vol. 1, p. 323.
2253. Bedford and Colbourn, p. 187.
2254. Thornton and Daugherty, p. 356.
2255. Fox, p. 32. Emphasis added.
2256. Birney, p. 5.
2257. Birney, p. 5. Emphasis added.
2258. Dumond, pp. 55-56.
2259. Birney, pp. 3-4.
2260. *The Liberator*, April 4, 1835, p. 3. Emphasis added.
2261. W. B. Shaw, pp. 381-382.
2262. W. B. Shaw, p. 382.
2263. W. B. Shaw, p. 382.
2264. Dumond, p. 58.
2265. Dumond, pp. 58-59.
2266. Blake, pp. 428, 434.
2267. Dumond, p. 58.
2268. W. B. Shaw, pp. 382-383.
2269. Fox, p. 33.
2270. O. Johnson, pp. 184-185. Emphasis added.
2271. Long and Long, pp. 593-594.
2272. C. Johnson, TPIGTTS, pp. 187-188.
2273. J. D. Richardson, ACOTMAPOTC, Vol. 1, p. 494.
2274. Quarles, TNITCW, p. 280.
2275. Seabrook, TCOTCSOAE, pp. 65-66.
2276. E. McPherson, PHUSAGR, p. 93.
2277. Kennedy, p. 91.
2278. P. M. Roberts, p. 198; Garraty and McCaughey, p. 81; Bedford and Colbourn, p. 85; Rosenbaum and Brinkley, s.v. "Slavery"; "Slave States."
2279. See e.g., McLoughlin, p. 199.
2280. L. W. Hopkins, pp. 17-18.
2281. Melish, passim.
2282. See Robinson, pp. 540-541.
2283. Seabrook, ARB, pp. 220-221.
2284. Seabrook, TQREL, pp. 110-111.
2285. McKim, p. 31.

2286. U. B. Phillips, ANS, p. 129.
2287. Blake, p. 397; U. B. Phillips, ANS, p. 129.
2288. Blake, p. 402.
2289. Seabrook, L, p. 44. Emphasis added.
2290. Fox, p. 45.
2291. Parsons, p. 24.
2292. Clare, Vol. 5, p. 3291. Emphasis added.
2293. W. E. Channing, pp. 57-58.
2294. Burne, p. 862.
2295. Bedford and Colbourn, p. 187.
2296. Derry, pp. 70-71.
2297. U. B. Phillips, ANS, p. 497.
2298. J. T. Adams, p. 253.
2299. L. Abbott, pp. 145, 148.
2300. Simpson, pp. 79-80.
2301. Blake, p. 450.
2302. Blake, p. 502.
2303. E. A. Andrews, pp. 16-17. My paraphrasal. Emphasis added.
2304. Ironically, though he was partly responsible for inflaming already existing sectional animosities, Garrison himself believed that allowing the South to secede peacefully was preferable to war between the two regions. W. B. Garrison, LNOK, p. 144.
2305. Blake, p. 457.
2306. For the complete *true* story of the Nat Turner Rebellion, see T. R. Gray, passim.
2307. Stampp, pp. 132-134; Blassingame, pp. 129-131.
2308. Bowman, CWDD, s.v. "August 1831."
2309. J. M. Burns, p. 392.
2310. Rosenbaum and Brinkley, s.v. "Slave Revolts."
2311. Simpson, p. 85.
2312. Stonebraker, p. 250.
2313. Blake, p. 448.
2314. Garraty, HV, p. 302.
2315. U. B. Phillips, ANS, p. 160.
2316. A. J. Northrup, p. 292.
2317. Robinson, p. 541.
2318. Blake, p. 441.
2319. Simpson, pp. 80-81.
2320. Blake, p. 511.
2321. Latham, pp. 37-38.
2322. Nicolay and Hay, ALCW, Vol. 1, p. 495.
2323. Derry, pp. 71-74. Emphasis added.
2324. E. A. Andrews, pp. 176, 197.
2325. White, Foscue, and McKnight, p. 211; Coit, pp. 298-299.
2326. Latham, p. 112. Emphasis added.
2327. Coit, p. 306.
2328. Blake, p. 389.
2329. L. Abbott, pp. 151-153. Emphasis added.
2330. L. Abbott, p. 165.
2331. J. T. Adams, p. 253.
2332. Fox, p. 48.
2333. Fox, p. 147. Emphasis added.
2334. See e.g., Chace, pp. 11-12.
2335. J. T. Adams, p. 251.

2336. Mitgang, p. 413; Simpson, pp. 73-74; C. Adams, pp. 93-94; L. H. Johnson, p. 133; Crocker, p. 59.
2337. J. T. Adams, p. 255.
2338. F. Bancroft, TLOWHS, Vol. 2, p. 339. Emphasis added.
2339. Eaton, HSC, p. 28.
2340. E. A. Andrews, pp. 156-157. Emphasis added.
2341. M. M. Smith, pp. 4-5.
2342. Hildreth, THOTUSOA, Vol. 1, pp 201-202. Emphasis added.
2343. Wallechinsky and Wallace, p. 425.
2344. W. Wilson, DR, pp. 124-125. Emphasis added.
2345. Blake, p. 412.
2346. Hildreth, THOTUSOA, Vol. 1, pp. 200-201. Emphasis added.
2347. *Appendix to the Congressional Globe*, 34th Congress, 3rd Session, 1857, Part 2, p. 141.
2348. Hildreth, THOTUSOA, Vol. 1, p. 200.
2349. U. B. Phillips, ANS, p. 121.
2350. Fox, pp. 19-20. Emphasis added.
2351. Fox, pp. 21-22. Emphasis added.
2352. Smedes, MOASP, pp. 228-229. Emphasis added.
2353. Burne, p. 862.
2354. Bedford and Colbourn, p. 187.
2355. Latham, pp. 123-124.
2356. Chesnut, DD, p. 20.
2357. Beard, p. 51.
2358. Blake, p. 499.
2359. Blake, pp. 499-500. Emphasis added.
2360. Blake, pp. 408, 409, 411, 417, 423.
2361. J. T. Adams, p. 201.
2362. Derry, pp. 104, 115. Emphasis added.
2363. Tocqueville, Vol. 1, p. 154.
2364. Seabrook, TAHSR, pp. 404, 479, 536, 571-572, 578; Seabrook, AL, p. 507.
2365. Bergh, Vol. 1, p. 48.
2366. Banks, p. 186.
2367. Hamilton, Madison, and Jay, p. 106.
2368. Hamilton, Madison, and Jay, p. 89. See also M. D. Peterson, JM, pp. 102-103; Hacker, p. 213.
2369. For more on the original U.S. Confederacy, see Seabrook, AL, passim.
2370. Prior to its publication in book form, Stowe's novel appeared as a serial in the columns of the *National Era*. Thornton and Daugherty, p. 92.
2371. Rosenbaum and Brinkley, s.v. "Uncle Tom's Cabin."
2372. Garraty and McCaughey, p. 230.
2373. Northern propaganda has long defined a plantation as "a large, Southern cotton estate, ruled by racist, indolent whites, and worked by black slave labor." In reality, a plantation is nothing more than a term for a large farm, and has nothing to do with the South, cotton, white planters, or black slavery. Indeed, in the 1700s and early 1800s, plantations, with and without slaves, were common across the North as well. See Seabrook, EYWTACWW, pp. 91-94. The origins of the plantation predates even the voyages of Columbus, with a history that extends over five continents, enduring long after the American "Civil War" was over. Curtin, RFPC, p. xiii. Webster thus correctly defines a plantation as simply "a place that is planted or under cultivation; an agricultural estate usually worked by resident labor." Mish, s.v. "plantation." Rhodes Island's original name, for example, was "Rhode Island and Providence Plantations," a carryover from the 1600s when the slave-heavy state was first named. J. B. Scott, pp. 84-85. See also pp. 86-87.
2374. Civil War Society, ECW, s.v. "Stowe, Harriet Beecher."
2375. Nye, p. 161.
2376. Wiley, LJR, p. 162.
2377. Encyc. Brit., s.v. "slavery."

2378. W. Wilson, DR, pp. 126-127.
2379. W. Wilson, DR, p. 181.
2380. Chesnut, DD, p. 184.
2381. Chesnut, DD, p. 189.
2382. Chesnut, MCCW, pp. 583, 730. My paraphrasal.
2383. Boatner, s.v. "*Uncle Tom's Cabin*."
2384. Hedrick, p. 9.
2385. Garraty and McCaughey, p. 230.
2386. Thornton and Daugherty, p. 92.
2387. Hacker, p. 558.
2388. S. K. Taylor, p. 65.
2389. Hedrick, pp. 9, 10.
2390. L. Lewis, p. 292.
2391. Stowe named her lead character, the much-hated fanciful figure, Simon Legree, after a real slave owner in South Carolina with the surname Legare. Chesnut, MCCW, p. 168.
2392. Rosenbaum and Brinkley, s.v. "Uncle Tom's Cabin."
2393. Garraty and McCaughey, p. 230.
2394. Fox-Genovese, p. 360.
2395. Garraty and McCaughey, p. 230.
2396. Stowe admitted as much, which is why Henson later republished his autobiography under the title: *The Memoirs of Uncle Tom*.
2397. N. Adams, p. 97. Emphasis added.
2398. Martineau, SIA, Vol. 2, pp. 7-8. Emphasis added.
2399. Genovese, p. 556.
2400. Weintraub, p. 65.
2401. See Seabrook, L, pp. 584-633.
2402. Fogel, p. 254.
2403. During the time Garrison supported and "approved" of the ACS, he considered it a "praiseworthy association." W. L. Garrison, p. 3.
2404. Fox, p. 50.
2405. Ahlstrom, p. 651.
2406. According to Parker Pillsbury, Weld owned 42 slaves at the time he emancipated them. Birney, pp. 3-4.
2407. Burlingame, p. 50.
2408. Buckley, p. 71.
2409. Skidmore, p. 114; Isaacson, p. 154; McKissack and McKissack, p. 177; Fields, p. 269.
2410. Drescher and Engerman, p. 218.
2411. See Fogel and Engerman, pp. 49-54, 70, 79-84, 109-126, 128.
2412. C. Morris, s.v. "Slavery."
2413. Shillington, p. 236.
2414. Drescher and Engerman, p. 392.
2415. Lyell, Vol. 2, p. 93.
2416. A. J. Northrup, pp. 275-278; U. B. Phillips, ASN, pp. 469-472.
2417. C. Johnson, TPIGTTS, p. 239; Pollard, SHW, Vol. 1, p. 364.
2418. Rosenbaum and Brinkley, s.v. "Slave Revolts."
2419. There were fugitive slave laws meant to protect slave owners from such incidents, but in most cases they were essentially ineffectual: by the time local law enforcement found out about the servants' escape, they had usually disappeared into thin air.
2420. Bruford, p. 107.
2421. U. B. Phillips, ANS, pp. 341-342.
2422. Chesnut, MCCW, p. 716. My paraphrasal.
2423. Fogel and Engerman, p. 242.
2424. Buckley, p. 81.

2425. Seabrook, EYWTACWW, p. 158. Also see Stephenson, ALATU, p. 168; Cooper, JDA, p. 378; Quarles, TNITCW, p. xiii; Ransom, pp. 214-215.
2426. Katcher, CWSB, p. 225.
2427. Garraty and McCaughey, p. 159.
2428. M. M. Smith, p. 37.
2429. C. Johnson, TPIGTTS, p. 239.
2430. Garraty and McCaughey, p. 81.
2431. Hurst, p. 330.
2432. Seabrook, NBF, p. 67.
2433. Southern slavery lasted only from 1749 to 1865. See McKissack and McKissack, p. 3; Rutherford, FA, p. 38; Wallechinsky, Wallace, and Wallace, p. 11; Woods, p. 67.
2434. Rosenbaum and Brinkley, s.v. "Slave Revolts."
2435. Rosenbaum and Brinkley, s.v. "Slave Revolts."
2436. Furnas, p. 408; Rosenbaum and Brinkley, s.v. "Liberator, The."
2437. L. Abbott, p. 148. Emphasis added.
2438. Seabrook, L, pp. 345-346.
2439. Blassingame, p. 129.
2440. T. R. Gray, p. 13.
2441. Derry, p. 67; Kennedy, p. 91.
2442. Derry, p. 90.
2443. Current, TC, s.v. "Bleeding Kansas."
2444. Boatner, s.v. "Bleeding Kansas"; Rosenbaum, s.v. "Brown, John."
2445. Born Frederick Augustus Washington Bailey in Talbot County, Maryland, Douglass was the son of a white father and a black mother. After freedom he adopted the surname Douglass, which he borrowed from James Douglas, the hero of Sir Walter Scott's poem, *Lady of the Lake*. Douglass' two marriages, the first to a black woman (Anna Murray), the second to a white woman (Helen Pitts), caused considerable controversy at the time. After purchasing his freedom he went on to become the most famous black civil rights leader and orator in early American history. His impassioned antislavery lectures, books, and his newspaper, the *North Star*, aided the movement to finally abolish the "peculiar institution" that had begun years earlier in the North. However, unlike pacifist William Lloyd Garrison, feminist-abolitionist and former Northern slave Sojourner Truth, and many others, Douglass eventually began advocating violence as a means to end servitude, one of the few beliefs he had in common with his so-called "friend" President Lincoln. Wilson and Ferris, s.v. "Douglass, Frederick."
2446. One of Brown's more famous supporters was Allan Pinkerton (the man who arrested Southern heroine and "spy" Rose O'Neal Greenhow), who gave his moniker to the famous detective agency of the same name. Pinkerton donated $500 to Brown, the equivalent of about $13,000 dollars today. Shenkman and Reiger, p. 100.
2447. Boatner, s.v. "Brown, John."
2448. To their credit not all Yankees idolized Brown. Of the anti-South madman, Massachusettsian Nathaniel Hawthorne, author of *The Scarlet Letter* (1850), *The House of the Seven Gables* (1851), and *The Blithedale Romance* (1852), said: "Nobody was ever more justly hanged." N. Hawthorne, Vol. 12, p. 327.
2449. Estes, pp. 229-230.
2450. Not all Northerner's appreciated the macabre, overtly anti-South tone of *John Brown's Body*. One, U.S. General George B. McClellan, found it so offensive he tried to have it banned, unsuccessfully. It remained popular enough in the North, however, that the music from the song—by composer William Steffe—was later used to support the lyrics of the American patriotic anthem, *The Battle Hymn of the Republic*, written by Northern abolitionist Julia Ward Howe. McKissack and McKissack, p. 131.
2451. Nicolay and Hay, ALCW, Vol. 1, p. 609. Emphasis added.
2452. Rozwenc, p. 29; Rosenbaum and Brinkley, s.v. "Slave Revolts."
2453. Nicolay and Hay, ALCW, Vol. 1, p. 609.
2454. Wallechinsky and Wallace, p. 423.
2455. Ashe, p. 39.
2456. Seabrook, AL, pp. 212-215.
2457. Woods, pp. 58-59.

2458. Grissom, p. 129.
2459. J. M. McPherson, BCF, p. 205.
2460. Wiley, LJR, p. 15.
2461. J. M. McPherson, BCF, p. 210.
2462. Daugherty, p. 95.
2463. Rhodes, Vol. 2, p. 414.
2464. Shenkman and Reiger, p. 99. Brown was also called "Old Brown of Osawatomie." Neilson, s.v. "Brown, John."
2465. Farrow, Lang, and Frank, p. 176.
2466. L. H. Johnson, pp. 33, 34, 129; Farrow, Lang, and Frank, pp. 155-177; Chace, pp. 11-12.
2467. Kennedy and Kennedy, pp. 53-58.
2468. Catton, Vol. 1, p. 216; J. M. McPherson, BCF, p. 209.
2469. J. M. McPherson, MFO, pp. 14-15. My paraphrasals.
2470. See J. M. McPherson, MFO, pp. 16-18.
2471. Sword, SI, p. 23.
2472. Daugherty, p. 95. My paraphrasal.
2473. Stanford, p. 76.
2474. Carpenter, p. 69.
2475. All six of these men, Brown's primary financial backers, were in fact Northerners, individuals completely ignorant of both Southern culture and Southern slavery. The names of the Secret Six are listed here in infamy so that they will never be forgotten: Gerrit Smith, Thomas Wentworth Higginson, Theodore Parker, Samuel Gridley Howe, George L. Stearns, and Franklin B. Sanborn. It was the money from these six Northerners that helped fund Brown's insane murder spree across the country, which in turn fanned the flames that led to the War for Southern Independence. Not the flames of the South's small proslavery movement, as Yankee myth teaches, but the flames of the South's massive states' rights movement.
2476. J. M. McPherson, BCF, p. 204.
2477. Sanborn eventually fled to Canada, ostensibly to avoid appearing at Brown's trial, then returned after the abolitionist's one-way trip to the gallows on December 2, 1859. When an investigative committee was formed to look into the Secret Six, Sanborn again escaped northward to avoid testifying, even resisting arrest in the interim. He was only spared the pain and humiliation of imprisonment because Massachusetts Chief Justice Lemuel Shaw canceled the criminal's arrest warrant. Emerson would have supported the various illicit shenanigans of his student Sanborn, a talented writer who would later go on to write biographies of not only his abolitionist mentor (in 1901) and of Thoreau (in 1882), but also of Brown himself (in 1885). Neilson, s.v. "Sanborn, Franklin Benjamin."
2478. L. H. Johnson, p. 58.
2479. Neilson, s.v. "Howe, Samuel Gridley."
2480. Parry, s.v. "Brown, John." The original words and music for *John Brown's Body Lies A-mouldering in the Grave* are traditionally attributed to Thomas B. Bishop, who penned the song to commemorate Brown's raid on Harper's Ferry. Parry, s.v. "Brown, John."
2481. R. W. Emerson, TCWORWE, Vol. 11, pp. 279, 280.
2482. Neilson, s.v. "Parker, Theodore."
2483. *The Liberator*, February 3, 1860.
2484. Rhodes, Vol. 2, p. 410.
2485. Nevins, TEP, p. 258.
2486. *The Great Issue*, p. 14.
2487. Rodriguez, THEOWS, Vol. 1, s.v. "Higginson, Thomas Wentworth."
2488. Page Smith, Vol. 5, pp. 308-309.
2489. O. J. Scott, p. 302.
2490. Neilson, s.v. "Higginson, Thomas Wentworth Storrow."
2491. Eaton, HSC, p. 263.
2492. L. H. Johnson, pp. 59, 60. My paraphrasal.
2493. Boatner, s.v. "Brown, John."
2494. Warren, JB, pp. 428-429.

2495. It is exceedingly strange and contradictory that Emerson, an abolitionist and racist, a staunch individualist, a rebel toward authority, imitation, and conformance, the author of the famed essay "Self Reliance," and the man who admonished 19th-Century Americans to buck conformity (see D. H. Donald, LR, p. 226), would be so violently against the independent-thinking South, which was attempting to follow this very advice. It is tempting to think that if Emerson had been born in the South, and was still living there in the mid 1800s, he would have been a pro-secessionist *and* an abolitionist, like so many other "rebellious" and individualistic Southerners. (The same could be said for the South-hating Yankee Thoreau, who was what we would today call a libertarian.)
2496. Chesnut, MCCW, p. 245. My paraphrasal.
2497. DiLorenzo, LU, pp. 40-41; Current, LNK, p. 234.
2498. Eaton, HSC, p. 13.
2499. Shenkman and Reiger, p. 100.
2500. D. H. Donald, L, p. 385.
2501. Shenkman and Reiger, p. 100.
2502. Lincoln is said to have given Brown $100, today's equivalent of about $2,500. Oates, AL, p. 19.
2503. Shenkman and Reiger, p. 100.
2504. Van Deusen, p. 214. My paraphrasal.
2505. W. B. Garrison, CWTFB, p. 76.
2506. Daugherty, p. 246. See also Oates, AL, pp. 8-9.
2507. Whitman, LOG, pp. 278, 286.
2508. Oates, AL, p. 118.
2509. Meltzer, Vol. 2, p. 139. Also see Cartmell, p. 26; Norwood, p. 31.
2510. G. H. Moore, pp. 5, 11, 17-19; Blake, p. 370.
2511. U. B. Phillips, ANS, p. 439.
2512. Rosenbaum and Brinkley, s.v. "Jim Crow Laws."
2513. C. Johnson, TPIGTTS, pp. 206-207.
2514. Rosenbaum and Brinkley, s.v. "Free Blacks."
2515. Lincoln conceded that the Emancipation Proclamation had "no constitutional or legal justification, except as a military measure." D. Donald, LR, p. 203.
2516. H. C. Bailey, p. 155; DiLorenzo, RL, pp. 26-27, 257-258.
2517. Thornton and Ekelund, pp. 95-98.
2518. D. H. Donald, L, pp. 261-267.
2519. See e.g., Litwack, NS, pp. 70-72.
2520. Seabrook, L, p. 421.
2521. Woodard, p. 15.
2522. Nye, p. 49.
2523. Fox, pp. 36-37.
2524. Fox, p. 36. Emphasis added.
2525. M. Hall, p. 140. Emphasis added.
2526. Fox, p. 37. Emphasis added.
2527. Kennedy, p. 165.
2528. Berwanger, pp. 4-5.
2529. Seaman, p. 4; Wilson and Ferris, s.v. "Miscegenation." The names of the three men who invented the word miscegenation are David G. Croly (from New York), George Wakeman (also from New York), and Samuel S. Cox (a congressman from Ohio).
2530. Nicolay and Hay, ALCW, Vol. 1, p. 273.
2531. Nicolay and Hay, ALCW, Vol. 1, p. 234. Emphasis added.
2532. Lincoln was indeed wrong: later scientific studies, such as those done by Edward Byron Reuter, revealed that the percentage of mulattos went up only *after* slavery ended. Reuter, pp. 120-122. Thus there was almost no connection between slavery and "amalgamation" (race mixing), as Lincoln derogatorily referred to it. See Fogel and Engerman, pp. 130-136.
2533. Curry, p. 79. Emphasis added.
2534. Woods, p. 81.
2535. Greene, pp. 208-209.

2536. E. J. McManus, BBITN, pp. 65, 85.
2537. U. B. Phillips, ASN, p. 103.
2538. E. J. McManus, BBITN, p. 65.
2539. A. M. Grant, p. 38. Emphasis added.
2540. Berwanger, pp. 32, 33.
2541. Garraty and McCaughey, p. 253.
2542. O. Williams, pp. 48, 70.
2543. U. B. Phillips, ANS, pp. 438-439.
2544. U. B. Phillips, ANS, p. 111.
2545. E. A. Andrews, p. 51.
2546. M. Hall, pp. 137, 138.
2547. E. A. Andrews, p. 167.
2548. See e.g., Fox, p. 36.
2549. Nicolay and Hay, ALCW, Vol. 2, p. 597. Emphasis added.
2550. Berwanger, p. 4-5.
2551. DeCaro, p. 17.
2552. Berwanger, p. 30. My paraphrasal. Note that Illinois was considered a Western state at the time.
2553. N. D. Harris, pp. 233-234. Emphasis added.
2554. Litwack, NS, p. 70.
2555. W. B. Garrison, CWTFB, p. 179.
2556. Litwack, NS, p. 71.
2557. J. M. McPherson, NCW, p. 252.
2558. *Anglo-African*, January 14, 1865. My paraphrasal. Emphasis added.
2559. J. M. Burns, p. 393.
2560. U. B. Phillips, ANS, p. 112.
2561. Commissioners of Statutory Revision, pp. 520, 762.
2562. E. A. Andrews, p. 35.
2563. J. M. Burns, p. 393.
2564. Wilson and Ferris, s.v. "Miscegenation"; K. C. Davis, p. 9.
2565. U. B. Phillips, ASN, p. 103.
2566. Drescher and Engerman, pp. 350-351.
2567. Lyell, Vol. 2, p. 57.
2568. *The North British Review*, p. 240.
2569. See Nicolay and Hay, ALCW, Vol. 2, pp. 237-238.
2570. Tocqueville, Vol. 1, pp. 357-358. Emphasis added.
2571. Lyell, Vol. 2, p. 162.
2572. L. Abbott, p. 157.
2573. Lyell, Vol. 2, pp. 98-99.
2574. Buckingham, TSSOA, Vol. 2, p. 112.
2575. Hawthorne, Vol. 2, pp. 109-110. Emphasis added.
2576. Martineau, ROWT, Vol. 1, p. 191. Emphasis added.
2577. E. K. Barnard, p. 111.
2578. Sturge, p. 40. Emphasis added.
2579. Dicey, Vol. 1, pp. 70-72. Emphasis added.
2580. Lyell, Vol. 2, p. 99.
2581. Lyell, Vol. 2, pp. 100-101. Emphasis added.
2582. See Fogel and Engerman, pp. 179-180.
2583. Olmsted, CK, Vol. 1, p. 39. Emphasis added.
2584. Chesnut, DD, p. 226.
2585. Sewall later recognized his error in helping to condemn dozens of innocent people to death as "witches," and spent the rest of his life repenting.
2586. Sewall, Vol. 2, pp. 17-18. Emphasis added.
2587. McKissack and McKissack, p. 56.

2588. U. B. Phillips, ANS, pp. 419-420.
2589. J. T. Wilson, p. 99.
2590. LeVert, s.v. "New York Draft Riots."
2591. Simmons, s.v. "Draft Riots."
2592. Thomson, pp. 160-161.
2593. Kemble, p. 11. Emphasis added.
2594. M. Hall, p. 17. Emphasis added.
2595. Olmsted, AJITSSS, p. 636. Emphasis added.
2596. Olmsted, AJITSSS, pp. 103-104. Emphasis added.
2597. Quillin, p. 29. Emphasis added.
2598. Crandall's Connecticut school for colored girls was eventually torched by the townspeople, but not before Yankees harassed, arrested, and imprisoned her. Eventually, under continuing threats of violence, she was driven from the state. C. Adams, pp. 130-131; Nye, p. 63; Buckley, p. 62; G. W. Williams, HOTNR, Vol. 2, p. 151; Garrison and Garrison, Vol. 1, p. 323.
2599. U. B. Phillips, ANS, pp. 439-440. Emphasis added.
2600. *The Liberator*, August 15, 1862. Emphasis added. For more on the thoughts and writings of 18th- and 19th-Century Northern blacks, see Sterling, passim.
2601. F. Douglass, LTFD, p.186.
2602. Website: www.nps.gov/archive/frdo/fdlife.htm.
2603. F. Douglass, NLFD, p. xiv; K. C. Davis, p. 439.
2604. F. Douglass, NLFD, p. 116.
2605. J. M. Burns, p. 393.
2606. J. T. Adams, p. 254.
2607. See Nicolay and Hay, CWAL, Vol. 11, pp. 105-106; Nicolay and Hay, ALCW, Vol. 1, p. 483; Holzer, pp. 22-23, 67, 318, 361.
2608. Litwack, NS, p. 226.
2609. Garrison and Garrison, Vol. 1, p. 327.
2610. Latham, p. 158.
2611. Litwack, NS, pp. 205-208.
2612. Litwack, NS, p. 227.
2613. *The Congressional Globe*, Vol. 13, p. 239.
2614. See J. M. McPherson, NCW, pp. 245-270; Litwack, NS, pp. 104-112.
2615. Greenberg and Waugh, p. 152.
2616. Seabrook, ARB, pp. 12, 26.
2617. Wiley, SN, pp. 64-66.
2618. Barrow, Segars, and Rosenburg, BC, p. 4.
2619. Drescher and Engerman, p. 175.
2620. Wiley, LJR, p. 328.
2621. Barrow, Segars, and Rosenburg, BC, pp. 155-156.
2622. Bedford and Colbourn, p. 177.
2623. Stampp, pp. 147, 279, 406-407; Fogel, p. 191.
2624. Gates, p. 375.
2625. U. B. Phillips, ANS, p. 429.
2626. Garraty and McCaughey, p. 254
2627. Nicolay and Hay, ALCW, Vol. 1, p. 241.
2628. Nicolay and Hay, ALCW, Vol. 1, p. 556. Emphasis added.
2629. Seabrook, TMOCP, p. 96.
2630. Blake, p. 450. Emphasis added
2631. Weeks, p. 232. Emphasis added.
2632. Weeks, pp. 232-233. Emphasis added.
2633. Weeks, pp. 233-234. Emphasis added.
2634. Devine, p. 1.
2635. McFeely, G, p. 127.

2636. Nicolay and Hay, ALCW, Vol. 1, p. 556.
2637. J. M. Burns, p. 329.
2638. Knowles and Prewitt, p. 137.
2639. M. Hall, p. 57. Emphasis added.
2640. DiLorenzo, RL, pp. 26-27, 257-258.
2641. Knowles and Prewitt, p. 80.
2642. W. C. Wade, pp. 151, 343.
2643. Website: www.foxnews.com/story/0,2933,301403,00.html.
2644. Blassingame, p. 25.
2645. Garraty and McCaughey, p. 145.
2646. Fox, p. 36. Emphasis added.
2647. Adams and Sanders, p. 228.
2648. Easton, TWH, p. 684.
2649. Rosenbaum, s.v. "Garvey, Marcus Moziah."
2650. Rosenbaum, s.v. "Delaney, Martin Robinson."
2651. Rosenbaum and Brinkley, s.v. "Back to Africa"; "Colonization." Also see Horton, passim.
2652. For more on the black nationalist and back-to-Africa movements, see Redkey, passim.
2653. H. Howe, p. 472. The Travis surname is also sometimes spelled Travers.
2654. H. Howe, p. 472.
2655. The names of the individuals killed by Turner and his men on August 21 and 22, 1831, are as follows: Joseph Travers and wife and three children; Mrs. Elizabeth Turner; Hartwell Prebles; Sarah Newsome; Mrs. P. Reese and son William; Trajan Doyle; Henry Bryant and wife and child, and wife's mother; Mrs. Catherine Whitehead, son Richard and four daughters and grandchild; Salathiel Francis; Nathaniel Francis' overseer and two children; John T. Barrow; George Vaughan; Mrs. Levi Waller and ten children; William Williams, wife and two boys; Mrs. Caswell Worrell and child; Mrs. Rebecca Vaughan; Ann Eliza Vaughan, and son Arthur; Mrs. John K. Williams and child; Mrs. Jacob Williams and three children; Edwin Drury.
2656. For the complete factual story of the Nat Turner rebellion, see T. R. Gray, passim.
2657. Wallechinsky and Wallace, p. 80.
2658. Derry, p. 67.
2659. Bennett, BTM, p. 33.
2660. Bedford and Colbourn, p. 181.
2661. U. B. Phillips, ANS, pp. 415-416. Emphasis added.
2662. U. B. Phillips, ANS, p. 451.
2663. Drescher and Engerman, p. 214.
2664. Website: www.blackpast.org/aah/brown-fellowship-society-1790-1945; Rodriguez, SITUS, pp. 27, 203-204.
2665. Long and Long, s.v. "February 25, 1862."
2666. Boller and Story, p. 180.
2667. R. S. Phillips, s.v. "Emancipation Proclamation."
2668. Encyc. Brit., s.v. "slavery."
2669. Woods, p. 67; Rutherford, FA, p. 38; Wallechinsky, Wallace, and Wallace, p. 11. Grant did not free his slaves until he was forced to by the passage of the Thirteenth Amendment on December 6, 1865, eight months after Lincoln's War ended.
2670. Seabrook, AL, p. 315; Nicolay and Hay, ALCW, Vol. 2, pp. 287-288.
2671. T. A. Baily, p. 341.
2672. Nicolay and Hay, ALCW, Vol. 2, pp. 287-288.
2673. Sandburg, SOL, p. 152.
2674. In reality, Lincoln waged war on the South neither to preserve the Union *or* end slavery. It was solely to install Henry Clay's big government "American System" in Washington. Rosenbaum and Brinkley, s.v. "American System"; DeGregorio, s.v. "John Quincy Adams"; Simpson, p. 75; Weintraub, pp. 48-49.
2675. Nicolay and Hay, ALCW, Vol. 2, p. 302.

2676. Seabrook, EYWTATCWIW, pp. 191-195; Owsley, pp. 65-66, 187-190, 538-541; E. M. Thomas, pp. 293-294; J. D. Richardson, ACOTMAPOTC, Vol. 2, pp. 709, 713; Durden, pp. 149-150; W. J. Cooper, JDA, pp. 552-553; Eaton, HSC, p. 81.
2677. Ashe, p. 35.
2678. Nicolay and Hay, ALCW, Vol. 2, p. 237.
2679. Sandburg, SOL, p. 154.
2680. Eaton, HSC, pp. 74-75.
2681. C. Johnson, TPIGTTS, p. 239.
2682. Nicolay and Hay, ALCW, Vol. 2, p. 454.
2683. W. J. Cooper, JDA, p. 378; Quarles, TNITCW, p. xiii.
2684. Berkin and Wood, p. 31.
2685. Current, LNK, p. 228. See also Barney, p. 141.
2686. Gragg, p. 88.
2687. Current, LNK, p. 228.
2688. B. F. Riley, pp. 63-64. Emphasis added.
2689. L. H. Johnson, p. 180.
2690. Seabrook, AL, p. 330; Quarles, TNITCW, p. 37; Greenberg and Waugh, pp. 372-373.
2691. Barrow, Segars, and Rosenburg, BC, pp. 8, 25.
2692. E. M. Thomas, p. 236; Fleming, p. 208; Quarles, TNITCW, pp. xiii, 48.
2693. Genovese, p. 541.
2694. There were some 182,000 free blacks in the eleven states of the Confederacy (Quarles, TNITCW, p. 35), nearly all who sided with Dixie. In addition, most traditional Southern historians believe that between 100,000 and 300,000 Southern slaves fought for Dixie. See Barrow, Segars, and Rosenburg, BC, p. 97; *The United Daughters of the Confederacy Magazine*, Vols. 54-55, 1991, p. 32; Hinkle, p. 106; R. M. Brown, p. xiv; Shenkman and Reiger, p. 106.
2695. See e.g., Barrow, Segars, and Rosenburg, BC, p. 19; Greenberg and Waugh, p. 385.
2696. See Kautz, p. 11.
2697. These numbers do not include the other three "races," yellow, brown, and red, that sided with and fought for the Confederacy. See C. Johnson, TPIGTTS, pp. 169-197.
2698. Using Kautz' definition and these numbers, 200,000 blacks fought for the Union, 1 million blacks for the Confederacy. Thus, five times, or 500 percent, more blacks wore Rebel gray than wore Yankee blue.
2699. Derry, p. 114. Emphasis added.
2700. Seabrook, L, p. 647.
2701. Nicolay and Hay, ALCW, Vol. 2, p. 318. Emphasis added.
2702. Nicolay and Hay, ALCW, Vol. 2, p. 398. Emphasis added.
2703. See e.g., C. Adams, p. 135; DiLorenzo, GC, p. 255; Johannsen, p. 55; Boller and Story, p. 167.
2704. Kinder and Hilgemann, Vol. 2, p. 117.
2705. C. Johnson, TPIGTTS, p. 170; Eaton, HSC, p. 93; Hinkle, p. 125.
2706. Wiley, SN, pp. 241, 309-310, 317.
2707. Kane, p. 167.
2708. Simmons, s.v. "Lincoln, Abraham."
2709. See Seabrook, L, pp. 584-633.
2710. R. S. Phillips, s.v. "Emancipation Proclamation."
2711. W. Phillips, p. 457.
2712. H. W. Wilbur, p. 70.
2713. Nicolay and Hay, ALCW, Vol. 2, p. 234.
2714. See e.g., Nicolay and Hay, ALCW, Vol. 2, p. 674.
2715. Buckley, p. 65. See also Greenberg and Waugh, pp. 351-358.
2716. Greenberg and Waugh, p. 353; Coffin, p. 457; Current, LNK, p. 225.
2717. For estimates on the number of Northern slaves in 1776, see Rutherford, FA, p. 61. For the early 1860s, see Eaton, HSC, p. 93; Hinkle, p. 125.
2718. Quarles, TNITCW, p. 133.
2719. Seabrook, L, p. 327; W. Phillips, p. 456.

2720. G. W. Williams, HOTNR, Vol. 2, p. 257.
2721. Nicolay and Hay, ALCW, Vol. 2, pp. 287-288, 508.
2722. Meriwether, p. 16. Emphasis added.
2723. Current, TC, p. 189. My paraphrasal.
2724. Garrison, CWTFB, p. 93. My paraphrasals.
2725. Hinkle, p. 125; Eaton, HSC, p. 93.
2726. See J. M. McPherson, NCW, pp. 245-270; Litwack, pp. 104-112; Greenberg and Waugh, p. 152.
2727. L. H. Johnson, p. 129; Donald, L, p. 315; C. Adams, pp. 134-135; S. Foote, Vol. 1, pp. 95-97. When Frémont's wife, Jessie Ann (Benton) Frémont, later visited Lincoln in an attempt to defend her husband's actions, he gave her this acid reply: "The General should have never bothered with the Negro in the first place. This is a war for a momentous national purpose, and the black man has nothing whatsoever to do with it." (My paraphrasal.) See Nevins, F, p. 517; Herr and Spence, pp. 264-267; Carwardine, p. 179. For more on Jessie's confrontation with Lincoln, see Nicolay and Hay, ALCW, Vol. 4, p. 415; Rhodes, Vol. 3, p. 478. Note: Jessie Ann's family married into one of my families, the McDowells of Virginia: Jessie's father was noted U.S. senator and onetime Franklin, Tennessee, resident Thomas Hart Benton. Thomas' wife was Elizabeth Preston McDowell, a descendant of one of my European lines through my 12th great-grandfather, Scotsman Utrecht McDowell, whose wife, Euphemia Dunbar, descended from the royal Bruce and the Stewart families. King of Scotland Robert the Bruce is my 22nd great-grandfather. See Seabrook, TMOCP, p. 42.
2728. S. Foote, Vol. 1, pp. 242-243.
2729. Quarles, TNITCW, pp. 115-116.
2730. Quarles, TNITCW, pp. 113-114.
2731. W. B. Garrison, LNOK, 136-141; S. Foote, Vol. 1, p. 535.
2732. Katcher, CWSB, p. 158.
2733. Neely, p. 35.
2734. Lincoln admitted that he nullified the emancipation proclamations of his officers because, as he put it, there was no "indispensable necessity." Nicolay and Hay, ALCW, Vol. 2, p. 508. The nation's 4,500,000 slaves (North and South) must have wondered what he meant by this.
2735. Lester, pp. 359-360.
2736. W. B. Garrison, LNOK, p. 192.
2737. McGehee, p. 81; Meriwether, p. 159.
2738. My paraphrasal. Dawson was related to Lincoln through marriage: Dawson's wife, Elodie Todd, was the half-sister of Lincoln's wife Mary Todd, making Elodie Lincoln's sister-in-law. Dawson then, was Lincoln's brother-in-law.
2739. D. H. Donald, LR, pp. 19-20. My paraphrasal.
2740. This is a patent lie, or at least, a misrepresentation of the facts. Confederate forces did not "enslave" blacks that they came across during battle. Such men were either impressed into military service to serve as laborers, or enlisted on the spot to serve as armed soldiers.
2741. Nicolay and Hay, ALCW, Vol. 2, pp. 234-236. Emphasis added.
2742. Nicolay and Hay, ALCW, Vol. 1, p. 531. Emphasis added.
2743. For more on Lincoln's anti-Christian atheism, see Seabrook, L, pp. 918-938.
2744. Seabrook, L, pp. 31-32.
2745. Guelzo, p. 90; Nye, p. 169. My paraphrasal.
2746. Minor, p. 49; DeGregorio, s.v. "Abraham Lincoln"; Beschloss, p. 113; K. C. Davis, p. 219; Flood, p. 37; D. H. Donald, L, p. 319.
2747. Fogel, p. 207.
2748. In other words, it cost Americans ten times more to fight and kill each other for four years than if they would have simply ended slavery (more proof that Lincoln's War was not over slavery). Rutland, p. 226. See also C. Johnson, TPIGTTS, p. 200.
2749. On March 9, 1862, Lincoln wrote to Henry Jarvis Raymond: "Have you noticed the facts that less than one half day's cost of this war would pay for all the slaves in Delaware at $400 per head—that eighty-seven days' cost of this war would pay for all in Delaware, Maryland, District of Columbia, Kentucky, and Missouri at the same price? Were those States to take the step, do you doubt that it would shorten the war more than eighty-seven days, and thus be an actual saving of expense?" Nicolay and Hay,

ALCW, Vol. 2, p. 132. See also pp. 137-138.
2750. Nicolay and Hay, ALCW, Vol. 2, p. 270.
2751. Nicolay and Hay, ALCW, Vol. 2, p. 272.
2752. Current, LNK, pp. 242-246; W. C. Davis, AHD, p. 164; Garrison, LNOK, p. 181; Weintraub, p. 73.
2753. Nicolay and Hay, ALCW, Vol. 2, pp. 237, 615.
2754. See e.g., Lincoln's Preliminary Emancipation Proclamation, Nicolay and Hay, ALCW, Vol. 2, p. 237.
2755. Nicolay and Hay, ALCW, Vol. 2, p. 550; E. McPherson, PHUSADGR, p. 301.
2756. Nicolay and Hay, ALH, Vol. 9, pp. 215, 217.
2757. Seabrook, AL, pp. 371-373.
2758. Nicolay and Hay, ALH, Vol. 10, p. 123.
2759. Seabrook, GTBTAY, p. 48.
2760. DiLorenzo, LU, pp. 24, 25.
2761. Nicolay and Hay, ALCW, Vol. 2, p. 6.
2762. Beard and Beard, Vol. 2, p. 65.
2763. W. S. Powell, p. 144.
2764. Unger, Vol. 2, p. 438.
2765. Simmons, s.v. "One-Tenth Plan, Lincoln's."
2766. Current, LNK, pp. 223, 239, 240, 241. For Lincoln's actual wording, see Nicolay and Hay, ALCW, Vol. 2, pp. 443-444.
2767. Oats, AL, pp. 115-116.
2768. Dimont, p. 360.
2769. Burne, p. 862.
2770. Harwell, p. 307.
2771. Charles Dickens, "American Disunion," *All the Year Round*, December 21, 1861, p. 299.
2772. Quarles, TNITCW, p. 68.
2773. Hacker, p. 580.
2774. That Lincoln did not consider himself an abolitionist, that he in fact intentionally distinguished and separated himself from the entire group, is clearly evidenced by a statement he made during a speech at Chicago, Illinois, on July 10, 1858: "I have always hated slavery, I think, as much as any Abolitionist." Nicolay and Hay, ALCW, Vol. 3, p. 33.
2775. W. B. Garrison, CWC, p. 97; DiLorenzo, LU, pp. 52-61.
2776. Seabrook, TUAL, p. 44; C. Adams, p. 135; DiLorenzo, GC, p. 255; Johannsen, p. 55.
2777. Seabrook, L, pp. 325-326; Nicolay and Hay, CWAL, Vol. 1, p. 15.
2778. Seabrook, L, p. 326; Stephenson, p. 69.
2779. Nicolay and Hay, ALCW, Vol. 1, p. 174.
2780. Trexler, p. 232.
2781. W. B. Garrison, LNOK, pp. 136-138. As noted, Frémont's wife, my cousin Jessie Ann Benton, was the daughter of the illustrious Democratic (then Conservative) senator and Southern slave owner, "Old Bullion," Thomas Hart Benton, who once owned land in Leiper's Fork, near Franklin, Tennessee.
2782. R. W. Black, p. 165; Wiley, SN, pp. 296-298; Leech, pp. 305-306.
2783. Confederate leaders, including President Jefferson Davis, were outraged at Hunter's unlawful activities, and sent out an order stating that he was a "felon to be executed if captured."
2784. Greeley, TAC, Vol. 2, p. 246.
2785. Donald, L, p. 363; Leech, p. 155.
2786. Quarles, TNITCW, pp. 113-116.
2787. McKissack and McKissack, pp. 134, 135.
2788. Seabrook, TUAL, p. 48; W. Phillips, p. 456.
2789. Stephenson, p. 70.
2790. See e.g., Boller and Story, p. 167.
2791. See Seabrook, L, pp. 312-352.
2792. Lincoln and Douglas, p. 187. Emphasis added.
2793. Sandburg, SOL, p. 418.

2794. Faust, s.v. "slavery." For examples of the many black contributions to American culture, see Wilson and Ferris, s.v. "Black life." See also M. M. Smith, p. 30; Rogers, AGA, passim.
2795. Seabrook, L, p. 710.
2796. See Napolitano, p. 8.
2797. Thornton and Ekelund, pp. 98-99.
2798. Website: www.lewrockwell.com/orig/mencken2.html. Emphasis added. See also C. Adams, pp. 198-199; Woods, p. 75.
2799. A. Cooke, ACA, p. 214. My paraphrasal.
2800. One writer has gone so far as to name his book, *Lincoln's Gettysburg Address: Echoes of the Bible and Book of Common Prayer*; this despite the fact that Lincoln was a proven lifelong, unwavering, anti-Christian and a devout atheist who despised the Bible and never prayed.
2801. Seabrook, L, p. 712.
2802. Seabrook, TUAL, p. 72.
2803. Mullen, p. 33; Rosenbaum and Brinkley, s.v. "Forty Acres and a Mule."
2804. J. H. Franklin, RATCW, p. 37.
2805. Grissom, p. 162.
2806. Foner, R, pp. 70-71.
2807. Thornton and Ekelund, p. 96.
2808. Seabrook, AL, p. 468; K. C. Davis, p. 427. For more on Lincoln's broken promises to "emancipated slaves," see McFeely, YS, passim.
2809. Norton, Katzman, Escott, Chudacoff, Paterson, and Tuttle, Vol. 2, p. 440.
2810. W. Reid, Vol. 1, p. 470.
2811. Page, p. 38.
2812. See Nicolay and Hay, ALCW, Vol. 2, pp. 287-288.
2813. Seabrook, L, p. 647.
2814. Rosenbaum and Brinkley, s.v. "Lincoln and Douglas."
2815. Thornton and Ekelund, p. 96.
2816. Stephens, RAHS, pp. 83, 137; Stephens, CV, Vol. 2, p. 615.
2817. Bailyn, Dallek, Davis, Donald, Thomas, and Wood, p. 16.
2818. K. C. Davis, p. 426.
2819. Latham, p. 66.
2820. Muzzey, Vol. 2, p. 10.
2821. Lyell, Vol. 2, pp. 94-95. Emphasis added.
2822. Latham, p. 144.
2823. B. F. Riley, pp. 66-67. Emphasis added.
2824. Smedes, MOASP, p. 3. Emphasis added.
2825. Buckley, p. 116. My paraphrasal.
2826. Website: www.archives.gov/nae/news/featured-programs/lincoln/080920Lincoln02Transcript.pdf. Emphasis added.
2827. Fogel and Engerman, p. 261.
2828. Billingsley, p. 69.
2829. Hurmence, p. 102. My paraphrasal.
2830. To his credit, Lincoln had at first crusaded for gradual compensated emancipation. But the Radicals (that is, abolitionists) in his party wanted complete, immediate, unconditional, and non-compensated emancipation. Under pressure to secure votes for his 1864 reelection campaign, Lincoln caved into the abolitionists and issued his disastrous and illegal Final Emancipation Proclamation on January 1, 1863.
2831. Foner, R, pp. 70-71.
2832. Thornton and Ekelund, p. 96.
2833. Stephens, RAHS, pp. 83, 137; Stephens, CV, Vol. 2, p. 615.
2834. Seabrook, L, pp. 689-690.
2835. Seabrook, L, p. 690.
2836. Bailyn, Dallek, Davis, Donald, Thomas, and Wood, p. 11. My paraphrasal.
2837. Thornton and Ekelund, p. 96.

2838. Wilson and Ferris, s.v. "Cotton Culture."
2839. Gragg, pp. 87-88. My paraphrasal.
2840. Chesnut, MCCW, p. 834. My paraphrasal.
2841. Latham, pp. 269-270. Emphasis added.
2842. Harper, Hammond, Simms, and Dew, p. 133.
2843. M. M. Smith, p. 33.
2844. C. Johnson, TPIGTTS, pp. 14-15. In a 1977 interview for *Newsweek* magazine (November 28), President Jimmy Carter said that his favorite film was *Gone With the Wind*. His, however, was a "different version" from the one normally seen. In Carter's rendition his favorite scenes were "the burning of Schenectady, New York, and President Grant surrendering to Robert E. Lee." Website: http://muendy.tripod.com/quotes.html.
2845. Gragg, p. 88.
2846. Current, LNK, p. 228.
2847. Shenkman, p. 124. One other overly generous estimate puts the number of slaves aided by the Underground Railroad at an unlikely 4,000 individuals—even if accurate, still a fraction of the total. See Rosenbaum and Brinkley, s.v. "Underground Railroad."
2848. Gragg, pp. 191-192.
2849. S. M. Dawson, pp. 211-212.
2850. N. Adams, p. 92.
2851. See e.g., Nicolay and Hay, ALCW, Vol. 2, pp. 473-474.
2852. White, Foscue, and McKnight, p. 212. It should be pointed out that there were also white sharecroppers. Wilson and Ferris, s.v. "Plantations."
2853. Fogel and Engerman, pp. 23-24.
2854. Scott and Stowe, p. 321. After his passing, Dr. Washington was indeed buried at Tuskegee, Alabama.
2855. S. Andrews, pp. 128-129, 130. Emphasis added.
2856. W. J. Cooper, JDA, p. 690.
2857. R. S. Phillips, s.v. "Lincoln, Abraham."
2858. Davenport, p. 25.
2859. L. Lewis, pp. 92-93, 325.
2860. Weintraub, p. 74.
2861. Nicolay and Hay, ALCW, Vol. 1, p. 533.
2862. See e.g., Nicolay and Hay, CWAL, Vol. 11, pp. 105-106; Nicolay and Hay, ALCW, Vol. 1, p. 483; Nicolay and Hay, ALCW, Vol. 2, p. 237; Holzer, pp. 22-23, 67, 318, 361.
2863. *Douglass' Monthly*, September 1862, Vol. 5, pp. 707-708.
2864. Schwartz, p. 86. My paraphrasal.
2865. F. Douglass, LTFD, p. 872. Emphasis added.
2866. C. Adams, p. 135; DiLorenzo, GC, p. 255; Johannsen, p. 55.
2867. Nicolay and Hay, ALCW, Vol. 3, p. 33.
2868. Nicolay and Hay, CWAL, Vol. 1, p. 15.
2869. McKissack and McKissack, pp. 134, 135.
2870. Seabrook, L, p. 647.
2871. W. B. Garrison, LNOK, p. 186; DiLorenzo, LU, p. 28.
2872. De Angelis, pp. 12-18; Lott, p. 65; J. J. Holland, passim.
2873. Garrison, LNOK, p. 176; J. M. McPherson, BCF, pp. 788-789.
2874. See Spooner, NT, No. 6, p. 54; Pollard, LC, p. 154; Graham, BM, passim.
2875. See Nicolay and Hay, CWAL, Vol. 11, pp. 105-106; Nicolay and Hay, ALCW, Vol. 1, p. 483; Holzer, pp. 22-23, 67, 318, 361.
2876. Current, LNK, pp. 242-246; W. C. Davis, AHD, p. 164; Garrison, LNOK, p. 181; Weintraub, p. 73.
2877. B. F. Butler, p. 903. See also W. P. Pickett, pp. 326-327.
2878. Current, LNK, p. 218-219; W. B. Garrison, LNOK, pp. 35-37; Greenberg and Waugh, p. 355.
2879. Seabrook, GTBTAY, p. 48; Nicolay and Hay, ALCW, Vol. 2, p. 6; Beard and Beard, Vol. 2, p. 65; DiLorenzo, LU, pp. 24, 25.

2880. M. Davis, p. 83. See also Seabrook, AL, passim.
2881. A. Cooke, ACA, p. 216.
2882. January 10, 2011, *U.S. Grant: Warrior*, PBS.
2883. See e.g., Oates, AL, p. 17.
2884. See e.g., Tagg, passim.
2885. Seabrook, L, p. 336.
2886. Nicolay and Hay, ALCW, Vol. 2, p. 271.
2887. Lincoln's colonization experiments in Panama, Belize, and Haiti all failed miserably, with death rates of over 50 percent in some cases. C. Johnson, TPIGTTS, p. 182.
2888. Nicolay and Hay, ALCW, Vol. 2, pp. 274-275.
2889. Seabrook, TUAL, p. 81.
2890. Seabrook, TUAL, p. 91.
2891. Nicolay and Hay, ALCW, Vol. 1, p. 257.
2892. Thomson, p. 192.
2893. Foley, pp. 811-812.
2894. Nicolay and Hay, ALCW, Vol. 1, p. 288.
2895. The issuance of Lincoln's several emancipations proceeded this way: the first, a draft submitted privately to his cabinet on July 22, 1862; the second, the Preliminary one released publicly on September 22, 1862; the third, a draft of the Final proclamation submitted to his cabinet on December 30, 1862; and the fourth, the Final version issued on January 1, 1863. See Nicolay and Hay, ALCW, Vol. 2, p. 213; Nicolay and Hay, ALCW, Vol. 2, pp. 237-238; Nicolay and Hay, ALCW, Vol. 2, p. 285; Nicolay and Hay, ALCW, Vol. 2, pp. 287-288.
2896. D. H. Donald, L, p. 374.
2897. Nicolay and Hay, ALCW, Vol. 2, p. 237.
2898. Seabrook, L, p. 642.
2899. Political expediency was one of the few forms of pressure that could motivate Lincoln to act against his own personal wishes. See Foote, Vol. 1, pp. 536-537.
2900. Nicolay and Hay, ALCW, Vol. 2, p. 274.
2901. Cornish, p. 95.
2902. G. Alexander, p. 557.
2903. Nicolay and Hay, ALCW, Vol. 2, p. 271.
2904. D. H. Donald, L, p. 355.
2905. See e.g., Tocqueville, Vol. 1, pp. 357-358.
2906. Unger, Vol. 2, p. 442. See also Brodie, passim.
2907. *Report of the Select Committee on Emancipation and Colonization*, pp. 14, 15, 16. Emphasis added.
2908. *Report of the Select Committee on Emancipation and Colonization*, p. ii.
2909. Long and Long, pp. 240-241.
2910. Ahlstrom, p. 655.
2911. Seabrook, AL, pp. 124-125; Drescher and Engerman, p. 324.
2912. Rhodes, Vol. 1, pp. 307, 309.
2913. Shufeldt, p. 115. Emphasis added.
2914. McManus BBITN, p. 66.
2915. Seligmann, p. 9.
2916. See Darwin, p. 91.
2917. Bailyn, Dallek, Davis, Donald, Thomas, and Wood, p. 29.
2918. By "authentic abolitionists" I mean antislavery advocates who were both for abolition *and* for welcoming blacks into American society as full-fledged citizens with complete equal rights. Very few individuals, even the so-called most vociferous abolitionists, fell into this category. In fact, authentic abolitionists were so rare at the time that they could almost be counted on one hand. Even William Lloyd Garrison (the founder of the *Northern* abolition movement), Horace Greeley (abolitionist founder of the New York *Tribune*), and Harriet Beecher Stowe (abolitionist author of *Uncle Tom's Cabin*), at one time supported black colonization: the deportation of all free African-Americans. Fogel, p. 254; Burlingame, p. 50.
2919. Nicolay and Hay, ALCW, Vol. 1, p. 539. Emphasis added.

2920. Seabrook, TUAL, p. 94; E. McPherson, PHUSADGR, 134.
2921. Nicolay and Hay, ALAH, Vol. 6, p. 356. See also pp. 357-358.
2922. Quarles, TNITCW, p. 146.
2923. For more on the history of the black colonization movement, see Staudenraus, passim.
2924. Fogel, p. 252; Blake, p. 359; Fox, p. 43.
2925. Nye, pp. 30, 49.
2926. Bedford and Colbourn, p. 187.
2927. Ahlstrom, p. 650.
2928. Nicolay and Hay, ALCW, Vol. 1, p. 288. See also H. U. Faulkner, p. 318.
2929. Fox, p. 52.
2930. Fox, p. 54.
2931. Blake, p. 359.
2932. Fox, p. 42.
2933. Blake, p. 361.
2934. Fox, p. 51.
2935. Website: www.slavenorth.com/colonize.htm.
2936. Fox, p. 43.
2937. Fox, p. 43.
2938. Fox, p. 51.
2939. Fox, pp. 92, 106.
2940. For more on Garrison's views on black colonization, see W. L. Garrison, passim.
2941. Blake, p. 451.
2942. Fogel, p. 254; Burlingame, p. 50.
2943. Fox, p. 50.
2944. Fox, p. 87.
2945. Fox, pp. 9-10.
2946. Fox, pp. 79-80. Emphasis added.
2947. E. A. Andrews, pp. 36-37. As well as possessing chapters of the ACS, Maryland, like the other Northern states, had its own black deportation organization called the "Maryland Colonization Society." See e.g., E. A. Andrews, p. 84.
2948. Seabrook, GTBTAY, p. 31.
2949. Nye, p. 20.
2950. Blake, p. 438.
2951. Fox, p. 41. Emphasis added.
2952. Fifth Annual Report, p. 5.
2953. Emerson once wrote of the typical Southerner that he is a "spoiled child . . . [and] very good to be spoiled more, but good for nothing else—a mere parader," who "in civil, educated company, where anything human is going forward, is dumb and unhappy, like an Indian in church. . . . [Southerners] are mere bladders of conceit. . . . They are more civilized than the Seminoles, however, in my opinion; a little more." Seabrook, ARB, p. 41.
2954. See e.g., Carpenter, p. 69.
2955. Fifth Annual Report, p. 4.
2956. Fifth Annual Report, pp. 17-18.
2957. Fifth Annual Report, p. 18.
2958. Fifth Annual Report, p. 15.
2959. See Bennett, FIG, passim.
2960. Nicolay and Hay, ALCW, Vol. 2, p. 274.
2961. Nicolay and Hay, ALCW, Vol. 1, p. 299.
2962. W. B. Garrison, LNOK, p. 186.
2963. DiLorenzo, LU, p. 28. For more on the history of Illinois' massive slavery system, see N. D. Harris, passim.
2964. See Foley, p. 816.
2965. Nicolay and Hay, ALCW, Vol. 1, p. 608. Emphasis added.
2966. Seabrook, AL, pp. 254-255.

2967. We will note here that like racism itself, those who are against interracial relationships can be found among all races, creeds, and colors.
2968. Seabrook, L, p. 576; Nicolay and Hay, ALCW, Vol. 1, p. 234. Emphasis added.
2969. For more on the early American white view of miscegenation or race mixing, see Helper, M, passim.
2970. J. G. de R. Hamilton, pp. 156-157. Emphasis added.
2971. See e.g., Nicolay and Hay, ALCW, Vol. 1, p. 449; Lincoln and Douglas, p. 221.
2972. Nicolay and Hay, ALCW, Vol. 1, p. 175. Emphasis added.
2973. Nicolay and Hay, ALCW, Vol. 1, p. 176.
2974. Nicolay and Hay, ALCW, Vol. 1, p. 176.
2975. Seabrook, L, p. 597; Nicolay and Hay, ALCW, Vol. 1, pp. 175-176. Emphasis added.
2976. Goodwyn, p. 6.
2977. Billingsley, p. 65.
2978. M. Davis, pp. 146-153.
2979. Seabrook, AL, p. 252.
2980. Nicolay and Hay, ALCW, Vol. 1, pp. 175-176.
2981. See E. J. McManus, BBITN, p. 197.
2982. *The National Almanac* (1863), p. 250. For the exact wording of Lincoln's District of Columbia Emancipation Act, see Seabrook, L, pp. 600-601. Though the sentiment was often unspoken or merely tacitly referred to in his speeches and writings, in reality Lincoln was deeply obsessed with what he called the "*immediate* separation" of the races. See e.g., Seabrook, L, pp. 576, 594.
2983. See Nicolay and Hay, ALCW, Vol. 2, p. 144.
2984. Latham, p. 112.
2985. Scott and Stowe, p. 321.
2986. Seabrook, AL, pp. 523-524.
2987. Drescher and Engerman, p. 165.
2988. Hacker, p. 584.
2989. See e.g., Nicolay and Hay, ALCW, Vol. 2, p. 126.
2990. Quarles, TNITCW, pp. 146-147.
2991. Nicolay and Hay, ALCW, Vol. 2, pp. 222-225. Emphasis added.
2992. R. L. Riley, p. 109.
2993. Quarles, TNITCW, p. 148.
2994. Oates, AL, p. 103. See also Janessa Hoyte, "Taking Another Look at Abraham Lincoln," *The Crisis*, November/December 2000, pp. 52-54.
2995. *Douglass' Monthly*, September, 1862, Vol. 5, pp. 707-708. Emphasis added.
2996. See the *National Anti-Slavery Standard*, September 6, 1862.
2997. See Seabrook, AL, pp. 478-485; Remsburg, passim; Christian, p. 7; Meriwether, pp. 54-55; Oates, AL, pp. 5, 40, 53; Current, LNK, pp. 58, 60-61; Kane, p. 163; *Southern Review*, January 1873, Vol. 12, No. 25, p. 364; Lamon, LAL, pp. 488, 489, 493; W. B. Garrison, LNOK, p. 265; Barton, p. 146; DeGregorio, s.v. "Abraham Lincoln."
2998. E. A. Andrews, p. 57.
2999. Fogel, pp. 31-32; Remsburg, passim.
3000. Meltzer, Vol. 2, p. 127.
3001. Fogel and Engerman, pp. 23-24. Contrary to Northern mythology, of the South's 3.5 million black servants, only 14 percent (or about 500,000 individuals) were brought from Africa by Yankees between the settling of Jamestown, Virginia, and 1861. The other 3 million (86 percent), all American-born, were the result of natural reproduction. Garraty and McCaughey, p. 214.
3002. Blight, p. 141.
3003. *An Appeal*, pp. 4, 7-8.
3004. W. W. Brown, pp. 258-259. Emphasis added.
3005. Melden, pp. 30-32. Emphasis added.
3006. Nicolay and Hay, ALCW, Vol. 2, p. 495. Emphasis added.
3007. Nicolay and Hay, ALCW, Vol. 2, p. 605. Emphasis added.

3008. B. F. Butler, p. 903. See also W. P. Pickett, p. 326; M. Davis, pp. 147-148; Adams and Sanders, p. 192.
3009. Seabrook, AL, p. 256; B. F. Butler, p. 903. See also W. P. Pickett, pp. 326-327; Woodson, p. 20.
3010. Seabrook, AL, p. 256; B. F. Butler, p. 907.
3011. J. G. de R. Hamilton, p. 157. Emphasis added.
3012. Woodson, p. 21.
3013. W. P. Pickett, pp. 328, 330.
3014. Lincoln's death in April 1865, at Booth's hands, allowed the Radicals (abolitionists) in his party to take over the government, after which they pushed through the Thirteenth Amendment in December 1865. It was this bill, not Lincoln's Emancipation Proclamation, that finally ended slavery across the entire U.S. In this sense then Booth was the "Great Emancipator," not Lincoln.
3015. Blake, p. 366.
3016. Bedford and Colbourn, p. 188.
3017. Ahlstrom, p. 651.
3018. Fox, p. 89.
3019. M. Perry, p. 49.
3020. E. A. Andrews, p. 96; Fox, p. 49.
3021. Seabrook, ARB, p. 213.
3022. Rodriguez, THEOWS, Vol. 1, s.v. "American Colonization Society."
3023. See Foote, Vol. 1, pp. 536-537.
3024. See Nicolay and Hay, ALCW, Vol. 1, pp. 433, 451, 468.
3025. Nicolay and Hay, ALCW, Vol. 1, p. 659. For Stephens' response, see Seabrook, TQAHS, pp. 98-101.
3026. Nicolay and Hay, ALCW, Vol. 2, p. 268.
3027. Nicolay and Hay, ALCW, Vol. 1, p. 197. Emphasis added.
3028. Seabrook, L, pp. 420-421; Nicolay and Hay, ALCW, Vol. 1, p. 508. Emphasis added.
3029. Nicolay and Hay, ALCW, Vol. 1, p. 234. Emphasis added.
3030. Nicolay and Hay, ALCW, Vol. 1, p. 556.
3031. Seabrook, L, pp. 353-475; Ransom, p. 173.
3032. Nicolay and Hay, ALCW, Vol. 1, p. 257.
3033. W. Wilson, DR, pp. 130-131.
3034. DiLorenzo, LU, p. 101.
3035. *The Congressional Globe*, 36th Congress, 1st Session, p. 58; Carey, p. 181.
3036. Woods, p. 45.
3037. DiLorenzo, LU, p. 101.
3038. Ransom, p. 173.
3039. Bedford and Colbourn, p. 188.
3040. *Appendix to the Congressional Globe*, 29th Congress, 2nd Session, February 8, 1847, p. 317. Emphasis added.
3041. Ransom, p. 97.
3042. Klinkner and Smith, p. 42.
3043. Seabrook, TUAL, p. 81.
3044. Melden, pp. 33-34.
3045. Seabrook, TUAL, p. 80. Emphasis added.
3046. Seabrook, TUAL, p. 80. Emphasis added.
3047. Seabrook, TUAL, p. 81. Emphasis added.
3048. Seabrook, TUAL, p. 80. Emphasis added.
3049. Seabrook, TUAL, pp. 77-78. Emphasis added.
3050. For more on contemporary black support of the Confederacy, see Hervey, passim. Especially see H. K. Edgerton's Website: www.southernheritage411.com.
3051. J. T. Wilson, pp. 482-483.
3052. J. T. Wilson, pp. 491-492. Emphasis added.
3053. J. T. Wilson, pp. 491-492.

3054. Barrow, Segars, and Rosenburg, BC, p. 97; *The United Daughters of the Confederacy Magazine*, Vols. 54-55, 1991, p. 32. Though the exact number is not known, estimates of the number of Southern blacks who fought for the Confederacy range from 30,000 to 93,000, from 100,000 to 300,000. See e.g., Hinkle, p. 106; R. M. Brown, p. xiv; Shenkman and Reiger, p. 106. I have chosen to go with the largest figure for reasons that I discuss. Skewing the already confusing figures were the thousands of blacks who posed as whites (presumably the lighter skinned blacks), eager to join the Confederate army or navy. See e.g., E. L. Jordan, p. 217. Since these particular men were never counted, the number 300,000 is almost certainly quite conservative.
3055. Seabrook, L, p. 909; E. M. Thomas, p. 236. As Yankees cruelly and unnecessarily bombed Southern courthouses where records were stored (see e.g., Henry, ATSF, p. 188), there is no documentation of the exact number of blacks that served on the Confederate side. But reliable estimates are still possible.
3056. The exact number of Yanks and Rebels, by some estimates, was 2,898,304 of the former, 1,234,000 of the latter. Livermore, pp. 1, 22, 63. These are *Yankee* estimates, however, and as such hold little value for Southern historians.
3057. Barrow, Segars, and Rosenburg, BC, p. 97; *The United Daughters of the Confederacy Magazine*, Vols. 54-55, 1991, p. 32. See also Hinkle, p. 106.
3058. Kautz, p. 11. Emphasis added.
3059. Seabrook, AL, pp. 335-336.
3060. Smedes, ASP, pp. 194-195. Emphasis added.
3061. For a European's view of the severity of Northern white racism (as compared to Southern white racism) in the early 1800s, see Tocqueville, Vol. 1, pp. 357-358. See also Seabrook, AL, pp. 189-240.
3062. Greenberg and Waugh, p. 385.
3063. Seabrook, TMOCP, p. 109.
3064. L. H. Steiner, pp. 19-20.
3065. ORA, Ser. 2, Vol. 8, p. 324.
3066. See Seabrook, L, pp. 883-917.
3067. *Douglass' Monthly*, September, 1861, Vol. 4, p. 516. Emphasis added.
3068. Seabrook, AL, p. 201.
3069. ORA, Ser. 4, Vol. 3, p. 1161. Emphasis added.
3070. J. T. Wilson, p. 491.
3071. J. T. Wilson, pp. 493-494. Emphasis added.
3072. L. H. Johnson, p. 135.
3073. Seabrook, L, p. 64; Nicolay and Hay, ALCW, Vol. 1, p. 556.
3074. Litwack, NS, pp. 113-152; Quarles, TNITCW, pp. 235-238; Garraty and McCaughey, p. 254.
3075. Gragg, p. 88.
3076. Current, LNK, p. 228.
3077. Smedes, ASP, p. 197.
3078. See Smedes, MOASP, frontispiece, and pp. 52, 246.
3079. Quarles, TNITCW, p. 273.
3080. E. M. Thomas, p. 236.
3081. See Barrow, Segars, and Rosenburg, BC and FC, passim; also see Segars and Barrow, BSCA, passim.
3082. Kennedy and Kennedy, SWR, p. 89.
3083. Gragg, pp. 191-192.
3084. L. W. Hopkins, pp. 203-205. Emphasis added.
3085. Leech, p. 293.
3086. Long and Wright, pp. 319-320. Emphasis added.
3087. Seabrook, L, p. 916; Nicolay and Hay, ALCW, Vol. 2, p. 662. Emphasis added.
3088. ORA, Ser. 3, Vol. 2, p. 809. Emphasis added.
3089. ORA, Ser. 3, Vol. 2, p. 809.
3090. White, Foscue, and McKnight, p. 212. Note: there were also white sharecroppers. See Wilson and Ferris, s.v. "Plantations."
3091. Estes, pp. 162-163. Emphasis added.
3092. L. W. Hopkins, pp. 136-137. Emphasis added.

3093. The "Civil War" did not technically end until President Andrew Johnson issued his *second* Peace Proclamation on August 20, 1866. He had issued his *first* on April 2, 1866. Muzzey, Vol. 2, p. 3.
3094. Chesnut, DD, p. 403.
3095. Seabrook, ARB, p. 259.
3096. Eaton, HSC, p. 93.
3097. Barrow, Segars, and Rosenburg, BC, p. 97; Hinkle, p. 106; *The United Daughters of the Confederacy Magazine*, Vols. 54-55, 1991, p. 32. If we utilize Yankee General August Valentine Kautz's definition of a "soldier," then as many as 1 million Southern blacks served in one capacity or another in the Confederate military. See Kautz, p. 11.
3098. Hinkle, p. 108. See also Quintero, Gonzales, and Velazquez, passim.
3099. Lonn, p. 218.
3100. Rosen, p. 161. Southern Jews were urged by their rabbis to join the Confederate army, resulting in a number of Confederate Jewish generals and hundreds of Jewish field officers. Dimont, p. 360. Many other Jews worked as Confederate blockade runners out of Southern ports like Mobile, Alabama. Latham, p. 146.
3101. Hinkle, p. 108; Blackerby, passim.
3102. Seabrook, AL, p. 343.
3103. The real reason racism-phobes engage in this behavior is to shut down dialog, and also to distract others from seeing their own bigotry and intolerance. Actually they only end up drawing more attention to it. For more on American racism, among all races, see Min, passim.
3104. See Rutherford, FA, p. 38; Wallechinsky, Wallace, and Wallace, p. 11; Woods, p. 67.
3105. For more on the "slaves" of the Lee household, see Seabrook, TOR, passim, and Seabrook TQREL, passim.
3106. Seabrook, TQREL, p. 106.
3107. Kennedy, p. 91.
3108. Smelser, DR, p. 42; Buckley, p. 37.
3109. Foley, p. 970.
3110. Farrow, Lang, and Frank, pp. 82-90, 179-191; Meltzer, Vol. 2, pp. 139, 145, 148; E. J. McManus, BBITN, pp. 6-7, 9, 10, 11; Bowen, p. 217; C. Johnson, TPIGTTS, pp. 125-126.
3111. Seabrook, TQREL, pp. 113-114. Emphasis added.
3112. Durden, pp. 245, 215; Quarles, TNITCW, p. 280.
3113. Derry, p. 428.
3114. ORA, Ser. 4, Vol. 1, p. 1020.
3115. J. T. Wilson, p. 481. Emphasis added.
3116. ORA, Ser. 4, Vol. 2, p. 767.
3117. ORA, Ser. 4, Vol. 2, pp. 947-948.
3118. Quarles, TNITCW, pp. 278-279.
3119. Seabrook, CPGS, p. 56; McDonough and Connelly, pp. 137-138.
3120. Warner, GG, s.v. "Patrick Ronayne Cleburne."
3121. Seabrook, EBF, s.v. "Cleburne, Patrick Ronayne"; Seabrook, CPGS, pp. 55-57.
3122. See ORA, Ser. 1, Vol. 52, Pt. 2, pp. 586-592. Emphasis added.
3123. Seabrook, TMOCP, p. 160; Kennedy and Kennedy, p. 112.
3124. Barrow, Segars, and Rosenburg, BC, pp. 12-13, 94.
3125. B. T. Washington, pp. 13-14. Emphasis added.
3126. Bennett, BTM, 466.
3127. Cornish, p. 15.
3128. E. L. Jordan, pp. 218, 266.
3129. ORA, Ser. 4, Vol. 1, p. 409.
3130. Greeley, AC, Vol. 2, p. 522.
3131. Seabrook, AL, pp. 335-336.
3132. ORA, Ser. 1, Vol. 15, pp. 556-557.
3133. J. M. McPherson, NCW, p. 165. See also Seabrook, AL, p. 376.
3134. Tocqueville, Vol. 1, pp. 357-358.

3135. For more on Lincoln's lifelong blatant racism, particularly toward black U.S. soldiers, see Seabrook, L, pp. 883-917, and passim.
3136. Seabrook, AL, pp. 437-438.
3137. At first Lincoln also refused to allow Native-Americans to serve in the Union army. Secretary of War Cameron was speaking for Lincoln when he said that the conflict "forbids the use of savages." ORA, Ser. 3, Vol. 1, p. 184.
3138. ORA, Ser. 3, Vol. 1, p. 107.
3139. W. Reid, Vol. 1, p. 489.
3140. J. M. McPherson, TSFE, p. 195.
3141. ORA, Ser. 3, Vol. 1, p. 133. Emphasis added.
3142. Nicolay and Hay, ALCW, Vol. 2, p. 235.
3143. Seabrook, TMOCP, p. 292; Page Smith, Vol. 5, p. 308.
3144. Henderson, Vol. 2, p. 411; C. Adams, p. 134.
3145. Page Smith, Vol. 5, p. 308. My paraphrasal.
3146. Quarles, TNITCW, p. 31.
3147. Norton, Katzman, Escott, Chudacoff, Paterson, and Tuttle, Vol. 2, p. 439.
3148. Quarles, TNITCW, p. 31.
3149. See W. Reid, Vol. 1, p. 468.
3150. J. T. Wilson, pp. 141-142. Emphasis added.
3151. E. J. McManus, BBITN, p. 156.
3152. Bennett, BTM, pp. 447, 449.
3153. See Quarles, TNITAR, passim.
3154. Mullen, pp. 9-15.
3155. Nell, pp. 236-237. Emphasis added.
3156. ORA, Ser. 3, Vol. 1, p. 184. The Union opinion of America's "savages" was aptly expressed by Yankee General Philip H. Sheridan, who said of them, "they are bound to be exterminated." Latham, p. 155.
3157. Quarles, TNITCW, p. 132.
3158. Mullen, p. 18.
3159. M. A. D. Howe, HLOGS, pp. 252-253. Emphasis added.
3160. Nicolay and Hay, ALCW, Vol. 2, p. 235.
3161. W. Reid, Vol. 1, p. 468. Note: the statement, "left to the cruelty of the Rebel cavalry and of the enraged masters whom they had been encouraged to desert," is obviously nothing more than a piece of the North's massive catalog of anti-South Civil War mythology.
3162. S. Foote, Vol. 2, p. 393; Katcher, CWSB, p. 159.
3163. Eaton, HSC, p. 263.
3164. Voegeli, p. 102; L. H. Johnson, p. 134; Jimerson, p. 96.
3165. L. H. Johnson, p. 134.
3166. Durden, p. 133. My paraphrasal.
3167. Durden, pp. 76, 83-84. My paraphrasal.
3168. Cornish, p. 318.
3169. Quarles, p. 193.
3170. ORA, Ser. 3, Vol. 5, p. 662.
3171. L. H. Johnson, p. 134.
3172. Pollard, SHW, Vol. 2, pp. 196-198.
3173. Wiley, SN, pp. 241, 309-310, 317.
3174. L. H. Johnson, p. 134.
3175. Henry, ATSF, p. 248.
3176. L. H. Johnson, p. 134.
3177. ORA, Ser. 3, Vol. 4, p. 1029.
3178. J. M. McPherson, NCW, p. 170. My paraphrasal.
3179. F. Moore, pp. 278-279. Emphasis added.
3180. J. T. Wilson, p. 132.
3181. Wiley, SN, pp. 12-14.

3182. Gragg, p. 85.
3183. H. C. Dean, p. 83.
3184. Barrow, Segars, and Rosenburg, BC, p. 15. My paraphrasal.
3185. Keckley, p. 140. Emphasis added.
3186. J. T. Wilson, p. 129.
3187. Norton, Katzman, Escott, Chudacoff, Paterson, and Tuttle, Vol. 2, p. 439.
3188. Nicolay and Hay, ALCW, Vol. 2, p. 288.
3189. Cartmell, p. 141.
3190. Shenkman and Reiger, p. 105.
3191. Leech, p. 310.
3192. L. H. Johnson, p. 131.
3193. A. D. Richardson, pp. 267-268. Emphasis added.
3194. Pollard, SHW, Vol. 2, p. 198; L. H. Johnson, p. 135; McFeely, G, p. 126. For official reference to Lincoln's "government plantations," see, for example, ORA, Ser. 1, Vol. 26, Pt. 1, p. 764. See also Nicolay and Hay, ALCW, Vol. 2, pp. 471-472.
3195. ORA, Ser. 1, Vol. 15, p. 595. See also pp. 593-594.
3196. Quarles, p. 94.
3197. Wiley, SN, pp. 200-201.
3198. See ORA, Ser. 1, Vol. 24, Pt. 3, pp. 156-157.
3199. Woodward, p. 279.
3200. Cornish, p. xv.
3201. Nicolay and Hay, ALCW, Vol. 2, p. 288.
3202. Cornish, p. 240.
3203. Quarles, p. 205.
3204. Buckley, p. 82; Barney, p. 128.
3205. See Chesnut, MCCW, p. 829. My paraphrasal.
3206. *The Congressional Globe*, 37th Congress, 2nd Session, p. 3203.
3207. Barrow, Segars, and Rosenburg, BC, p. 4; Mullen, p. 31.
3208. L. H. Johnson, p. 134.
3209. Horn, DBN, p. 74. Thanks, in great part to Lincoln, neither the U.S. military or the federal civil service were desegregated until 1948. It was President Harry Truman's Executive Order 9981 that finally put an official end to Lincoln's institutionalized white military racism. Adams and Sanders, p. 269. Truman's integration policy was not implemented immediately, however. It was not until half way through the Korean War (1950-1953) that American forces became officially integrated for the first time since the Revolutionary War. Thus the Vietnam War (1959-1975) became the first conflict in which whites and blacks served as equals from beginning to end. Buckley, p. xx. This is the pitiful legacy of the so-called "Great Emancipator," a man who failed to do a single thing during his presidency to promote, create, or maintain racial equality within his military.
3210. Simmons, s.v. "Negro troops"; L. H. Johnson, p. 135.
3211. Hansen, p. 168.
3212. See Nicolay and Hay, ALCW, Vol. 2, p. 398.
3213. McFeely, G, pp. 126, 127.
3214. Faust, s.v. "black soldiers."
3215. Barrow, Segars, and Rosenburg, BC, p. 97; Hinkle, p. 106; *The United Daughters of the Confederacy Magazine*, Vols. 54-55, 1991, p. 32.
3216. C. Eaton, HSC, p. 93.
3217. Hinkle, p. 108. See also Quintero, Gonzales, and Velazquez, passim.
3218. Lonn, p. 218.
3219. Rosen, p. 161.
3220. Hinkle, 108; Blackerby, passim.
3221. C. Johnson, TPIGTTS, pp. 206-207.
3222. L. H. Johnson, p. 134.
3223. See Nicolay and Hay, ALCW, Vol. 1, p. 284; Basler, ALSW, pp. 400, 402, 403-404; Stern, pp. 492-493; Holzer, pp. 189, 251.

3224. Owing to his voluminous muttonchops, Burnside—who was relieved of his command after the disastrous Battle of the Crater—went on to give his name to the male facial hair style, sideburns.
3225. For more on the Battle of the Crater, see Slotkin, passim.
3226. Cornish, p. 276.
3227. B. F. Butler, p. 721.
3228. Buckley, pp. 105-106.
3229. Current, TC, s.v. "Petersburg Campaign."
3230. S. A. Channing, p. 129; Page Smith, Vol. 5, p. 387. My paraphrasal.
3231. E. L. Jordan, p. 142.
3232. G. W. Williams, HNTWR, p. 143.
3233. Sterling, pp. 333-334.
3234. Quarles, pp. 203-204.
3235. Buckley, p. 93.
3236. A. D. Richardson, p. 516. Emphasis added.
3237. A. D. Richardson, pp. 205-206, 208-210, 267.
3238. ORA, Ser. 3, Vol. 3, p. 252.
3239. Cornish, p. 46.
3240. Wiley, SN, pp. 322-323; Mullen, p. 25.
3241. See Cornish, pp. 181-196.
3242. F. Douglass, LTFD, p. 303.
3243. Barney, pp. 146-147.
3244. S. K. Taylor, p. 51.
3245. Quarles, pp. 200-201.
3246. Page Smith, Vol. 5, p. 308.
3247. Though 5,000 noncommissioned white Union officers (from volunteer regiments) eventually commanded all-black troops, only "about one hundred" blacks ever held Union officer commissions during Lincoln's War, and this despite the apathy, protests, and even outright opposition of Lincoln and his War Department. Cornish, pp. 201, 214-215.
3248. Alotta, p. 27. Lincoln paid his black soldiers $7 a month; he paid his white soldiers $13 a month. Quarles, p. 200.
3249. E. M. Thomas, p. 297.
3250. Cornish, p. 214.
3251. Wiley, LBY, p. 313; J. M. McPherson, NCW, pp. 238-239.
3252. ORA, Ser. 3, Vol. 3, p. 46. Emphasis added.
3253. J. T. Wilson, p. 103.
3254. Buckley, p. 83.
3255. Pearson, Vol. 2, pp. 70-74.
3256. See W. C. Davis, JDMH, p. 599; Quarles, p. 279; Durden, pp. 203, 269, 272.
3257. E. M. Thomas, pp. 296-297.
3258. See Cornish, pp. 184, 192, 195.
3259. *The Liberator*, May 22, 1863.
3260. *Douglass' Monthly*, March 1863, Vol. 5, p. 802.
3261. *Charlotte Daily Bulletin*, November 13, 1862. Emphasis added.
3262. Catton, Vol. 3, p. 24. My paraphrasal.
3263. Garrison, CWC, p. 105.
3264. Simmons, s.v. "Negro Troops."
3265. Seabrook, AL, p. 365; Page Smith, Vol. 5, p. 309.
3266. ORA, Ser. 3, Vol. 4, p. 1029; Katcher, CWSB, pp. 128, 158-159.
3267. Gragg, p. 192.
3268. Seabrook, AL, p. 294; Pollard, SHW, Vol. 2, pp. 196-198.
3269. Eaton, HSC, p. 30.
3270. Cornish, pp. 87, 269.
3271. Latham, p. 55.

3272. Nicolay and Hay, ALCW, Vol. 2, p. 398.
3273. Seabrook, L, p. 656.
3274. ORA, Ser. 1, Vol. 38, Pt. 5, p. 792. Emphasis added.
3275. Furnas, p. 750.
3276. Simmons, s.v. "Negro Troops."
3277. Wiley, SN, pp. 201-202, 212-213.
3278. Leech, p. 293.
3279. Quarles, TNITCW, p. 60.
3280. Wiley, SN, p. 175.
3281. Rhodes, Vol. 3, p. 466.
3282. See e.g., Nicolay and Hay, ALCW, Vol. 1, p. 539; Nicolay and Hay, ALCW, Vol. 2, pp. 257, 289, 369-370, 433.
3283. See e.g., Nicolay and Hay, ALCW, Vol. 2, pp. 257, 449, 469.
3284. M. Hall, p. 56.
3285. E. A. Andrews, pp. 21-23.
3286. Estes, p. 232. Emphasis added.
3287. Garrison, LNOK, p. 176.
3288. J. M. McPherson, BCF, pp. 788-789.
3289. Mullen, p. 25; Bennett, BTM, p. 466.
3290. S. A. Channing, p. 23.
3291. Seabrook, AL, p. 225; Wiley, SN, pp. 322-323. See also McFeely, G, p. 127.
3292. Drescher and Engerman, p. 351.
3293. Leech, p. 312.
3294. Current, TC, s.v. "African-Americans in the Confederacy."
3295. Quarles, pp. 204-205.
3296. Cartmell, pp. 144, 145.
3297. Cartmell, pp. 144, 145.
3298. Wiley, SN, pp. 323-324.
3299. Seabrook, AL, p. 361.
3300. Alotta, pp. 26-28.
3301. Seabrook, L, pp. 918-938; Christian, p. 7; Meriwether, pp. 54-55; Oates, AL, pp. 5, 40, 53; Current, LNK, pp. 58, 60-61; Kane, p. 163; *Southern Review*, January 1873, Vol. 12, No. 25, p. 364; Lamon, LAL, pp. 488, 489, 493; W. B. Garrison, LNOK, p. 265; Barton, p. 146; DeGregorio, s.v. "Abraham Lincoln."
3302. Seabrook, TMOCP, p. 297.
3303. Jimerson, p. 81; Swint, p. 61; Jaquette, p. 37.
3304. Simmons, s.v. "Negro Troops."
3305. Garraty and McCaughey, p. 254.
3306. Current, TC, s.v. "African-Americans in the Confederacy."
3307. Nicolay and Hay, ALCW, Vol. 2, p. 398.
3308. Durden, p. 269.
3309. McKissack and McKissack, pp. 138-139.
3310. My paraphrasal. See N. A. Hamilton, p. 120; Förster and Nagler, p. 207; Masur, p. 110; J. M. McPherson, NCW, p. 163.
3311. Nicolay and Hay, ALCW, Vol. 2, p. 1.
3312. DiLorenzo, RL, p. 21.
3313. L. H. Johnson, p. 135.
3314. McFeely, G, p. 126.
3315. Pollard, SHW, Vol. 2, p. 198.
3316. Wiley, SN, p. 202.
3317. Page Smith, Vol. 5, pp. 362-363.
3318. Quarles, TNITCW, pp. 46-47. See also Seabrook, TMOCP, pp. 289-290, 300.
3319. Seabrook, TMOCP, pp. 289, 300.

3320. Chesnut, DD, p. 227.
3321. Faust, s.v. "black soldiers."
3322. Simmons, s.v. "Negro troops"; Quarles, p. 64.
3323. Chesnut, MCCW, p. 798. My paraphrasal.
3324. G. H. Moore, pp. 5, 11, 17-19; Blake, p. 370.
3325. S. Foote, Vol. 1, p. 537. Note that the abolition of the American slave trade in July 1862 was separate and distinct from the abolition of American slavery, which did not occur until December 1865.
3326. Seabrook, L, p. 281; Truth, p. 254.
3327. De Angelis, pp. 12-18; Lott, p. 65.
3328. De Angelis, p. 49.
3329. McKissack and McKissack, pp. 142, 143, 144.
3330. See Nicolay and Hay, CWAL, Vol. 11, pp. 105-106; Nicolay and Hay, ALCW, Vol. 1, p. 483; Holzer, pp. 22-23, 67, 318, 361.
3331. See e.g., Nicolay and Hay, ALCW, Vol. 1, pp. 257, 259, 449, 469.
3332. Horwitz, p. 204.
3333. See e.g., Woodward, p. 279.
3334. Meriwether, p. 219.
3335. C. Johnson, TPIGTTS, p. 167. Emphasis added.
3336. W. Reid, Vol. 1, p. 493. Emphasis added.
3337. Tragically, refugeeing slaves sometimes meant the breakup of black families as well as plantation communities themselves, a rich social network of white and black relationships, many of them tender, loving, and lifelong. E. M. Thomas, p. 240. In this way, among many others, Lincoln actually damaged race relations in the South, one of his goals to begin with.
3338. C. Adams, p. 134.
3339. Henderson, Vol. 2, p. 411. Emphasis added.
3340. D. Donald, LR, p. 203.
3341. Leech, p. 291.
3342. Lincoln formally dismissed Porter from military service in January 1863, over problems at the Battle of Second Manassas, on August 29, 1862. As usual, Lincoln acted incorrectly. In 1879, 14 years after his death, more intelligent individuals prevailed: Porter's dismissal was revoked and he was reinstated in the Federal army. J. S. Bowman, CWDD, s.v. "10 January 1863"; "21 January 1863."
3343. D. H. Donald, L, p. 385.
3344. B. Thornton, p.176. My paraphrasal.
3345. Murphy, p. 86.
3346. Barrow, Segars, and Rosenburg, BC, p. 45. My paraphrasal.
3347. E. L. Jordan, p. 141. My paraphrasal.
3348. Wiley, LBY, p. 281. My paraphrasal.
3349. Barrow, Segars, and Rosenburg, BC, p. 45. My paraphrasal.
3350. D. H. Donald, L, p. 385.
3351. Nye, p. 140.
3352. S. Foote, Vol. 1, p. 538.
3353. Page Smith, Vol. 5, p. 309.
3354. Cornish, pp. 118-119.
3355. ORA, Ser. 1, Vol. 24, Pt. 3, p. 220. Emphasis added.
3356. Charlottesville, Virginia, *Daily Chronicle*, March 30, 1864. My paraphrasal.
3357. J. M. McPherson, NCW, p. 195.
3358. Simmons, s.v. "Negro troops."
3359. W. B. Garrison, CWC, p. 105; Quarles, p. 197.
3360. Greeley, AC, Vol. 2, p. 527.
3361. Cornish, p. 101.
3362. ORA, Ser. 3, Vol. 3, pp. 1126-1128. Emphasis added.
3363. Nicolay and Hay, ALCW, Vol. 2, pp. 396-399.
3364. See e.g., Nicolay and Hay, ALCW, Vol. 2, p. 126.
3365. Quarles, p. 60.

3366. Nicolay and Hay, ALCW, Vol. 1, p. 539.
3367. Wiley, SN, p. 175.
3368. K. C. Davis, p. 276. My paraphrasal.
3369. See E. J. McManus, BBITN, p. 197.
3370. Seabrook, L, p. 421.
3371. Nicolay and Hay, ALCW, Vol. 2, p. 287.
3372. Seabrook, L, p. 647.
3373. D. Donald, LR, p. 203.
3374. Weintraub, p. 73.
3375. See e.g., Wiley, SN, pp. 241, 309-310, 317.
3376. C. Johnson, TPIGTTS, p. 170.
3377. Eaton, HSC, p. 93; Hinkle, p. 125.
3378. J. Davis, RFCG, Vol. 1, p. 80.
3379. Seabrook, TUAL, p. 40.
3380. Meriwether, p. 219.
3381. Eaton, HSC, p. 93.
3382. Hinkle, p. 125.
3383. For the Northern white population in 1860, see Katcher, CWSB, p. 46.
3384. Johnston, p. 19; E. J. McManus, BBITN, pp. 196, 199.
3385. McElroy, p. 357.
3386. McFeely, G, p. 71.
3387. A. D. Richardson, p. 95.
3388. A. D. Richardson, p. 152.
3389. McFeely, G, pp. 22, 62, 69.
3390. Website: www.understandingprejudice.org/slavery/presinfo.php?president=18.
3391. Cramer, p. 85.
3392. S. Foote, Vol. 2, p. 638. Grant uttered this remark in a letter to Elihu B. Washburne, August 30, 1863.
3393. U. S. Grant, Vol. 1, p. 215.
3394. As Daugherty writes of the Emancipation Proclamation: Lincoln "had played his trump card, and nothing had happened." Daugherty, p. 169.
3395. Rutherford, FA, p. 38; Wallechinsky, Wallace, and Wallace, p. 11; Woods, p. 67.
3396. T. N. Page, p. 57; R. H. McKim, p. 31.
3397. Rutherford, FA, p. 38.
3398. McFeely, G, p. 439.
3399. Confederate, p. 83.
3400. R. E. Lee, Jr., p. 100.
3401. Latham, pp. 263-267. Emphasis added.
3402. U. B. Phillips, ANS, p. 514. Emphasis added.
3403. For more on the brutality of ancient and Medieval slavery, see e.g., Blake, Chapters 1-8.
3404. Blake, p. 479. Emphasis added.
3405. A. Barnes, pp. 9-10. Emphasis added.
3406. Estes, pp. 83-84. Emphasis added.
3407. E. C. Holland, p. 10.

BIBLIOGRAPHY

NOTE: While my work discusses and illustrates the positive aspects of Southern society, culture, tradition, history, and heritage—particularly as they relate to slavery—the vast majority of the books listed in my bibliography are anti-South, many in the extreme. This is especially true of nearly all of those titles published by university presses, most which openly and proudly specialize in liberal, socialist, anti-American, anti-capitalist, even racist anti-white material. Why then do I include such works in my research? Not only are at least 99 percent of *all* history books leftist *and* anti-South in tone, but a great deal of revealing information and even important facts may be garnered from studying the writings of the unenlightened, the uninformed, the uneducated, and especially the South-ignorant. And in fact, I recommend this practice to all earnest students of history, whatever their historical, regional, or political viewpoints may be.

Abbott, John Stevens Cabot. *The Life of General Ulysses S. Grant*. Boston, MA: B. B. Russell, 1868.

Abbott, Lyman. *Henry Ward Beecher*. Boston, MA: Houghton, Mifflin and Co., 1903.

Abel, Annie Heloise. *The American Indian as Slaveholder and Secessionist*. Cleveland, OH: Arthur H. Clarke Co., 1915.

——. *The American Indian as Participant in the Civil War*. Cleveland, Ohio: Arthur H. Clark, 1919.

Adams, Charles. *When in the Course of Human Events: Arguing the Case for Southern Secession*. Lanham, MD: Rowman and Littlefield, 2000.

Adams, Charles Francis (ed.). *Memoirs of John Quincy Adams, Comprising Portions of His Diary From 1795 to 1848*. 4 vols. Philadelphia, PA: J. B. Lippincott and Co., 1875.

Adams, Francis D., and Barry Sanders. *Alienable Rights: The Exclusion of African Americans in a White Man's Land, 1619-2000*. 2003. New York, NY: Perennial, 2004 ed.

Adams, H. (ed.). *South Africa: Sociological Perspectives*. New York, NY: Oxford University press, 1971.

Adams, Henry (ed.). *Documents Relating to New-England Federalism, 1800-1815*. Boston, MA: Little, Brown, and Co., 1877.

Adams, Herbert Baxter. *Baltimore, Slavery, and Constitutional History* (Vol. 14). Baltimore, MD: Johns Hopkins Press, 1896.

Adams, James Truslow. *The Epic of America*. Boston, MA: Little, Brown, and Co., 1931.

Adams, Nehemiah. *A South-side View of Slavery: Three Months at the South in 1854*. Boston, MA: T. R. Marvin, 1855.

Adams, William Henry Davenport. *Shore and Sea; Or, Stories of Great Vikings and Sea Captains*. London, UK: Hodder and Stoughton, 1883.

Adeuyan, Jacob Oluwatayo. *The Return of the Tidal Flow of the Middle Passage*. Bloomington, IN: AuthorHouse, 2011.

Agorsah, E. Kofi (ed.). *Maroon Heritage: Archaeological, Ethnographic and Historical Perspectives*. Kingston, Jamaica: Canoe Press, 1994.

Ahlstrom, Sydney E. *A Religious History of the American People*. New Haven, CT: Yale University Press, 1972.

Albrecht-Carrié, René. *Europe, 1500-1848*. 1953. Patterson, NJ: Littlefield, Adams, and Co., 1962 ed.

Alexander, Gross (ed.). *The Methodist Review Quarterly*, July 1909. Nashville, TN: Methodist Episcopal Church, 1909.

Alexander, William T. *History of the Colored Race in America*. Kansas City, MO: Palmetto Publishing Co., 1899.

Alfriend, Frank H. *The Life of Jefferson Davis*. Cincinnati, OH: Caxton Publishing House, 1868.

Alland, Alexander, Jr. *Human Diversity*. Garden City, NY: Anchor Books, 1973.

Allen, Gardner Weld. *Our Navy and the Barbary Corsairs*. Boston, MA: Houghton, Mifflin and Co., 1905.

Alotta, Robert I. *Civil War Justice: Union Army Executions Under Lincoln*. Shippensburg, PA: White Mane, 1989.

Amann, Peter (ed.). *The Eighteenth-Century Revolution: French or Western?* Lexington, MA: D. C. Heath and Co., 1963.

American Colonization Society. *Forty-fourth Annual Report of the American Colonization Society*. Washington, D.C.: American Colonization Society, 1861.

Ames, Mary. *From a New England Woman's Diary in Dixie in 1865*. Norwood, MA: The Plimpton Press, 1906.

An Appeal From the Colored Men of Philadelphia to the President of the United States. Philadelphia, PA, 1862.

Anderson, John Q. (ed.). *Brokenburn: The Journal of Kate Stone, 1861-1868*. 1955. Baton Rouge, LA: Louisiana

State University Press, 1995 ed.

Andrewes, Antony. *The Greeks.* 1967. New York, NY: W. W. Norton and Co., 1978 ed.

Andrews, E. Benjamin. *History of the United States: From the Earliest Discovery of America to the End of 1902.* 2 vols. New York, NY: Charles Scribner's Sons, 1904.

Andrews, Ethan Allen. *Slavery and the Domestic Slave Trade in the United States.* Boston, MA: Light and Stearns, 1836.

Andrews, Sidney. *The South Since the War: As Shown by Fourteen Weeks of Travel and Observation.* Boston, MA: Ticknor and Fields, 1866.

Angle, Paul M. (ed.). *The Complete Lincoln-Douglas Debates of 1858.* Chicago, IL: University of Chicago Press, 1991.

Annunzio, Frank (chairman). *The Capitol: A Pictorial History of the Capitol and of the Congress.* Washington, D.C.: U.S. Joint Committee on Printing, 1983.

Anonymous. *Life of John C. Calhoun: Presenting a Condensed History of Political Events, From 1811 to 1843.* New York, NY: Harper and Brothers, 1843.

Appleman, Roy Edgar (ed.). *Abraham Lincoln: From His Own Words and Contemporary Accounts.* Washington, D.C.: U.S. Department of the Interior, National Park Service, 1942.

Aptheker, Herbert. *American Negro Slave Revolts.* New York, NY: Columbia University Press, 1943.

Araujo, Ana Lucia. *Public Memory of Slavery: Victims and Perpetrators in the South Atlantic.* Amherst, NY: Cambria Press, 2010.

Archer, Léonie (ed.). *Slavery and Other Forms of Unfree Labor.* London, UK: Routledge, 1988.

Ariès, Philippe, and George Duby (eds.). *A History of Private Life: From Pagan Rome to Byzantium.* Cambridge, MA: Belknap Press, 1987.

Armstrong, George Dodd. *The Christian Doctrine of Slavery.* New York, NY: Charles Scribner, 1857.

Arnold, Isaac Newton. *The History of Abraham Lincoln, and the Overthrow of Slavery.* Chicago, IL: Clarke and Co., 1866.

Aron, Raymond. *Progress and Disillusion: The Dialectics of Modern Society.* New York, NY: Mentor, 1969.

Ashdown Paul, and Edward Caudill. *The Myth of Nathan Bedford Forrest.* 2005. Lanham, MD: Rowman and Littlefield, 2006 ed.

Ashe, Captain Samuel A'Court. *A Southern View of the Invasion of the Southern States and War of 1861-1865.* 1935. Crawfordville, GA: Ruffin Flag Co., 1938 ed.

Ashworth, John. *Slavery, Capitalism, and Politics in the Antebellum Republic.* 2 vols. New York, NY: Cambridge University Press, 2007.

Astor, Gerald. *The Right to Fight: A History of African Americans in the Military.* Cambridge, MA: Da Capo, 2001.

Ayers, Edward. *The Promise of the New South.* Oxford, UK: Oxford University Press, 1992.

Baepler, Paul (ed.). *White Slaves, African Masters: An Anthology of American Barbary Captivity Narratives.* Chicago, IL: University of Chicago Press, 1999.

Baigent, Michael, Richard Leigh, and Henry Lincoln. *Holy Blood, Holy Grail.* New York, NY: Dell, 1983.

——. *The Messianic Legacy.* New York, NY: Dell, 1986.

Bailey, Anne C. *African Voices of the Atlantic Slave Trade: Beyond the Silence and the Shame.* Boston, MA: Beacon Press, 2005.

Bailey, Hugh C. *Hinton Rowan Helper: Abolitionist-Racist.* Tuscaloosa, AL: University of Alabama Press, 1965.

Bailey, Thomas A. *A Diplomatic History of the American People.* 1940. New York, NY: Appleton-Century-Crofts, 1970 ed.

Bailyn, Bernard, Robert Dallek, David Brion Davis, David Herbert Donald, John L. Thomas, and Gordon S. Wood. *The Great Republic: A History of the American People.* 1977. Lexington, MA: D. C. Heath and Co., 1992 ed.

Baker, George E. (ed.). *The Works of William H. Seward.* 5 vols. 1861. Boston, MA: Houghton, Mifflin and Co., 1888 ed.

Baker, Ray Stannard. *Following the Color Line: An Account of Negro Citizenship in the American Democracy.* New York, NY: Doubleday, Page and Co., 1908.

Baldwin, James. *The Fire Next Time.* New York, NY: The Dial Press, 1963.

Ball, Charles. *Slavery in the United States: A Narrative of the Life and Adventures of Charles Ball, a Black Man.* New York, NY: John S. Taylor, 1837.

Ballagh, James Curtis. *White Servitude in the Colony of Virginia: A Study of the System of Indentured Servitude in the American Colonies.* Whitefish, MT: Kessinger Publishing, 2004.

Bancroft, Frederic. *The Life of William H. Seward.* 2 vols. New York, NY: Harper and Brothers, 1900.

——. *Slave-Trading in the Old South.* Baltimore, MD: J. H. Furst, 1931.

Bancroft, Frederic, and William A. Dunning (eds.). *The Reminiscences of Carl Schurz*. 3 vols. New York, NY: McClure Co., 1909.

Bancroft, George. *History of the United States of America, From the Discovery of the Continent*. 10 vols. New York, NY: D. Appleton and Co., 1886.

Banks, Noreen. *Early American Almanac*. New York, NY: Bantam, 1975.

Banton, Michael. *Racial Consciousness*. London, UK: Longmans, 1988.

Barclay, Alexander. *A Practical View of the Present State of Slavery in the West Indies*. London, UK: Smith, Elder and Co., 1828.

Bark, William Carroll. *Origins of the Medieval World*. Garden City, NY: Anchor, 1958.

Barnard, Alan, and Jonathan Spencer. *Encyclopedia of Social and Cultural Anthropology*. 1996. London, UK: Routledge, 2002 ed.

Barnard, Ella Kent. *Dorothy Payne, Quakeress: A Side-light Upon the Career of "Dolly" Madison*. Philadelphia, PA: Ferris and Leach, 1909.

Barnes, Albert. *An Inquiry into the Scriptural Views of Slavery*. 1846. Philadelphia, PA: Parry and McMillan, 1855 ed.

Barnes, Gilbert H. *The Antislavery Impulse, 1830-1844*. New York, NY: Harbinger, 1964.

Barnes, Gilbert H., and Dwight L. Dumond (eds.). *Letters of Theodore Dwight Weld, Angelina Grimké Weld and Sarah Grimké, 1822-1844*. 2 vols. New York, NY: D. Appleton-Century Co., 1934.

Barney, William L. *Flawed Victory: A New Perspective on the Civil War*. New York, NY: Praeger Publishers, 1975.

Barraclough, Geoffrey. *The Times Atlas of World History*. 1978. Maplewood, NJ: Hammond, 1989 ed.

Barringer, Paul Brandon. *The American Negro: His Past and Future*. Raleigh, NC: Edwards and Broughton, 1900.

Barrow, Charles Kelly, J. H. Segars, and R. B. Rosenburg (eds.). *Black Confederates*. 1995. Gretna, LA: Pelican Publishing Co., 2001 ed.

——. *Forgotten Confederates: An Anthology About Black Southerners*. Saint Petersburg, FL: Southern Heritage Press, 1997.

Bartlett, Irving H. *John C. Calhoun: A Biography*. New York, NY: W. W. Norton, 1994.

——. *Wendell Phillips: Brahmin Radical*. Boston, MA: Beacon Press, 1961.

Barton, William E. *The Soul of Abraham Lincoln*. New York, NY: George H. Doran, 1920.

Bascom, Henry Bidleman. *Methodism and Slavery: With Other Matters in Controversy Between the North and the South*. Frankfort, KY: Henry Bidleman Bascom, 1845.

Basler, Roy Prentice (ed.). *Abraham Lincoln: His Speeches and Writings*. 1946. New York, NY: Da Capo Press, 2001 ed.

—— (ed.). *The Collected Works of Abraham Lincoln*. 9 vols. New Brunswick, NJ: Rutgers University Press, 1953.

Bateman, William O. *Political and Constitutional Law of the United States of America*. St. Louis, MO: G. I. Jones and Co., 1876.

Baughman, Emmett E. *Black Americans: A Psychological Analysis*. New York, NY: Academic Press, 1971.

Baxter, Maurice G. *Henry Clay and the American System*. Lexington, KY: University Press of Kentucky, 2004.

Beard, Charles A. (ed.). *Whither Mankind: A Panorama of Modern Civilization*. New York, NY: Longmans, Green and Co., 1928.

Beard, Charles A., and Birl E. Schultz. *Documents on the State-Wide Initiative, Referendum and Recall*. New York, NY: Macmillan, 1912.

Beard, Charles A., and Mary R. Beard. *The Rise of American Civilization*. 1927. New York, NY: MacMillan, 1930 ed.

Beaumont, Alexander. *The History of Spain, From the Earliest Authentic Accounts to the Present Times*. London, UK: S. A. and H. Oddy, 1809.

Beck, Glenn. *Glenn Beck's Common Sense: The Case Against an Out-of-Control Government, Inspired by Thomas Paine*. New York, NY: Threshold, 2009.

Becker, Carl L., and Frederic Duncalf. *Story of Civilization*. 1938. New York, NY: Silver Burdett Co., 1944 ed.

Beckles, Hilary, and Verene Shepherd. *Caribbean Slave Society and Economy: A Student Reader*. Kingston, Jamaica: Ian Randle, 1994.

Bede, Saint. *A History of the English Church and People*. (Original work written in 731.) 1955. Harmondsworth, UK: Penguin, 1974 ed.

Bedford, Henry F., and Trevor Colbourn. *The Americans: A Brief History*. 1972. New York, NY: Harcourt Brace Jovanovich, 1980 ed.

Behrens, C. B. A. *The Ancien Régime*. New York, NY: Harcourt, Brace and World, 1967.

Bekkaoui, Khalid. *White Women Captives in North Africa: Narratives of Enslavement, 1735-1830*. New York, NY:

Macmillan, 2011.

Bellagamba, Alice, Sandra E. Greene, and Martin A. Klein (eds). *African Voices on Slavery and the Slave Trade*. Cambridge, UK: Cambridge University Press, 2013.

Belloc, Hilaire. *Characters of the Reformation*. 1958. Garden City, NY: Image Books, 1961 ed.

Benedict, Ruth. *Patterns of Culture*. 1934. New York, NY: Mentor, 1960 ed.

Benedict, S. W., and Isaac Knapp (eds.). *The American Anti-Slavery Almanac for 1839 and 1840*. New York, NY: American Anti-Slavery Society, 1840.

Bennett, Lerone, Jr. *Before the Mayflower: A History of Black America*. 1961. Harmondsworth, UK: Penguin, 1993 ed.

——. *Forced Into Glory: Abraham Lincoln's White Dream*. Chicago, IL: Johnson Publishing Co., 2000.

Benson, Al, Jr., and Walter Donald Kennedy. *Lincoln's Marxists*. Gretna, LA: Pelican Publishing, 2011.

Benton, Thomas Hart. *Thirty Years View; or A History of the Working of the American Government for Thirty Years, From 1820 to 1850*. 2 vols. New York, NY: D. Appleton and Co., 1854.

Bergh, Albert Ellery (ed.). *The Writings of Thomas Jefferson*. 20 vols. Washington, D.C.: Thomas Jefferson Memorial Association of the U.S., 1905.

Berkin, Carol, and Leonard Wood. *Land of Promise: A History of the United States From 1865*. Glenview, IL: Scott, Foresman and Co., 1983.

Berlin, Ira, and Philip D. Morgan (eds.). *The Slaves' Economy: Independent Production by Slaves in the Americas*. London, UK: Frank Cass, 1991.

Bernard, Jessie. *Marriage and Family Among Negroes*. Englewood Cliffs, NJ: Prentice-Hall, 1966.

Bernhard, Winfred E. A. (ed.). *Political Parties in American History* (Vol. 1, 1789-1828). New York, NY: G. P. Putnams' Sons, 1973.

Berry, Wendell. *The Unsettling of America: Culture and Agriculture*. San Francisco, CA: Sierra Club Books, 1996.

Bertrand, Louis. *The History of Spain*. New York, NY: Collier, 1971.

Berwanger, Eugene H. *The Frontier Against Slavery: Western Anti-Negro Prejudice and the Slavery Extension Controversy*. 1967. Urbana, IL: University of Illinois Press, 1971 ed.

Beschloss, Michael R. *Presidential Courage: Brave Leaders and How They Changed America, 1789-1989*. New York, NY: Simon and Schuster, 2007.

Bevan, William Latham. *The Student's Manual of Ancient Geography*. London, UK: John Murray, 1875.

Billingsley, Andrew. *Black Families in White America*. Englewood Cliffs, NJ: Prentice-Hall, 1968.

Birney, James Gillespie. *The American Churches, the Bulwarks of American Slavery*. Concord, NH: Parker Pillsbury, 1885.

Birney, William. *James G. Birney and His Times: The Genesis of the Republican Party With Some Account of Abolition Movements in the South Before 1828*. New York, NY: D. Appleton and Co., 1890.

Black, Chauncey F. *Essays and Speeches of Jeremiah S. Black*. New York, NY: D. Appleton and Co., 1886.

Black, Robert W., Col. *Cavalry Raids of the Civil War*. Mechanicsburg, PA: Stackpole, 2004.

Blackburn, George A. (ed.). *The Life Work of John L. Girardeau, D.D., LL.D.* Columbia, SC: The State Company, 1916.

Blackburn, Robin. *The Overthrow of Colonial Slavery, 1776-1848*. London, UK: Verso, 1988.

Blackerby, Hubert R. *Blacks in Blue and Gray*. New Orleans, LA: Portals Press, 1979.

Blackford, Charles Minor. *The Trials and Trial of Jefferson Davis*. Lynchburg, VA: J. P. Bell Co., 1901.

Blackmon, Douglas A. *Slavery By Another Name: The Re-Enslavement of Black Americans From the Civil War to World War II*. New York, NY: Doubleday, 2008.

Blair, William A. (ed.). *Journal of the Civil War Era*. Spring 2014 Issue (ebook). Chapel Hill, NC: University of North Carolina Press, 2014.

Blake, William O. *The History of Slavery and the Slave Trade, Ancient and Modern*. Columbus, OH: H. Miller, 1861.

Blakeman, A. Noel. *Personal Recollections of the War of Rebellion*. New York, NY: G. P. Putnam's Son, 1912.

Blanchard, Jonathan, and Nathan Lewis Rice. *A Debate on Slavery: Held in the City of Cincinnati, on the First, Second, Third, and Sixth Days of October, 1845*. Cincinnati, OH: William H. Moore, 1846.

Blanchard, Peter. *Slavery and Abolition in Early Republican Peru*. Wilmington, DE: Scholarly Resources, 1992.

Blassingame, John W. *The Slave Community: Plantation Life in the Antebellum South*. 1972. New York, NY: Oxford University Press, 1974 ed.

Bledsoe, Albert Taylor. *An Essay on Liberty and Slavery*. Philadelphia, PA: J. B. Lippincott and Co., 1856.

——. *A Theodicy; or a Vindication of the Divine Glory, as Manifested in the Constitution and Government of the Moral World*. New York, NY: Carlton and Porter, 1856.

——. *Is Davis a Traitor; or Was Secession a Constitutional Right Previous to the War of 1861?* Richmond, VA:

Hermitage Press, 1907.

Blee, Kathleen M. *Women of the Klan: Racism and Gender in the 1920s.* 1991. Berkeley, CA: University of California Press, 1992 ed.

Blight, David W. *Frederick Douglass' Civil War: Keeping Faith in Jubilee.* 1989. Baton Rouge, LA: Louisiana State University Press, 1991 ed.

Bliss, William Dwight Porter (ed.). *The Encyclopedia of Social Reform.* New York, NY: Funk and Wagnalls, 1897.

Blitzer, Charles. *Age of Kings.* New York, NY: Time-Life, 1967.

Bloch, Marc. *Slavery and Serfdom in the Middle Ages: Selected Papers.* Berkeley, CA: University of California Press, 1975.

Blum, Jerome. *The End of the Old Order in Rural Europe.* Princeton, NJ: Princeton University Press, 1978.

Blyth, Stephen Cleveland. *History of the War Between the United States and Tripoli, and other Barbary Powers: To Which is Prefixed a Geographical, Religious, and Political History of the Barbary States in General.* Salem, MA: Salem Gazette, 1806.

Boardman, John, Jasper Griffin, and Oswyn Murray. *The Roman World.* 1986. Oxford, UK: Oxford University Press, 1988 ed.

Boas, Franz. *The Mind of Primitive Man.* New York, NY: Macmillan Co., 1911.

Boatner, Mark Mayo. *The Civil War Dictionary.* 1959. New York, NY: David McKay Co., 1988 ed.

Bode, Carl, and Malcolm Cowley (eds.). *The Portable Emerson.* 1941. Harmondsworth, UK: Penguin, 1981 ed.

Boller, Paul F., Jr., and Ronald Story. *A More Perfect Union: Documents in U.S. History - Vol. 1: to 1877.* Boston, MA: Houghton Mifflin Co., 1984.

Bone, Robert Gehlmann. *Ancient History.* Ames, IA: Littlefield, Adams and Co., 1955.

Bonhoeffer, Dietrich. *Ethics.* 1949. New York, NY: Macmillan, 1975 ed.

Bonnassie, Pierre. *From Slavery to Feudalism in South-Western Europe.* Cambridge, UK: Cambridge University Press, 1991.

Boren, Henry C. *The Roman Republic.* Princeton, NJ: D. Van Nostrand Co., 1965.

Boorstin, Daniel J. *The Discoverers: A History of Man's Search to Know His World and Himself.* 1983. New York, NY: Vintage, 1985 ed.

Booth, Mary Louise. *History of the City of New York, From its Earliest Settlement to the Present Time.* New York, NY: W. R. C. Clark and Co., 1860.

Boston Female Anti-Slavery Society. *Annual Report of the Boston Female Anti-Slavery Society.* Boston, MA: Isaac Knapp, 1837.

Botkin, Benjamin Albert (ed.). *Lay My Burden Down: A Folk History of Slavery.* 1945. Chicago, IL: University of Chicago Press, 1969 ed.

Botume, Elizabeth Hyde. *First Days Amongst the Contrabands.* Boston, MA: Lee and Shepard, 1893.

Bourne, George. *Picture of Slavery in the United States of America.* Middletown, CT: Edwin Hunt, 1834.

Bourne, Theodore. *Rev. George Bourne: The Pioneer of American Antislavery.* Methodist Church (article from the *Methodist Quarterly Review*, January 1882).

Boxer, Charles R. *Race Relations in the Portuguese Colonial Empire, 1415-1825.* Oxford, UK: Clarendon Press, 1963.

Bowen, Catherine Drinker. *John Adams and the American Revolution.* 1949. New York, NY: Grosset and Dunlap, 1977 ed.

Bowers, John. *Chickamauga and Chattanooga: The Battles that Doomed the Confederacy.* New York, NY: HarperCollins, 1994.

Bowman, John S. (ed.). *The Civil War Day by Day: An Illustrated Almanac of America's Bloodiest War.* 1989. New York, NY: Dorset Press, 1990 ed.

——. *Encyclopedia of the Civil War* (ed.). 1992. North Dighton, MA: JG Press, 2001 ed.

Bowser, Frederick P. *The African Slave in Colonial Peru, 1524-1650.* Stanford, CA: Stanford University Press, 1974.

Boyde, Henry. *Several Voyages to Barbary: Containing an Historical and Geographical Account of the Country, With the Hardships, Sufferings, and Manner of Redeeming Christian Slaves.* London, UK: Olive Payne, 1736.

Brackett, Jeffrey Richardson. *The Negro in Maryland: A Study of the Institution of Slavery.* Baltimore, MD: Johns Hopkins University, 1889.

Braddy, Nella (ed.). *The New Concise Illustrated Encyclopedia.* 1934. Cleveland, OH: World Publishing Co., 1943 ed.

Bradford, James C. (ed.). *Atlas of American Military History.* New York, NY: Oxford University Press, 2003.

Bradford, Ned (ed.). *Battles and Leaders of the Civil War*. 1-vol. ed. New York, NY: Appleton-Century-Crofts, 1956.

Bradley, K. R. *Slaves and Masters in the Roman Empire: A Study in Social Control*. New York, NY: Oxford University Press, 1987.

——. *Slavery and Rebellion in the Roman World 140 B.C.-70 B.C.* Bloomington, IN: Indiana University Press, 1989.

——. *Slavery and Society at Rome*. Cambridge, UK: Cambridge University Press, 1994.

Bradley, Michael R. *Nathan Bedford Forrest's Escort and Staff*. Gretna, LA: Pelican Publishing Co., 2006.

Brady, Cyrus Townsend. *Three Daughters of the Confederacy*. New York, NY: G. W. Dillingham, 1905.

Brady, James S. (ed.). *Ronald Reagan: A Man True to His Word - A Portrait of the 40th President of the United States In His Own Words*. Washington D.C.: National Federation of Republican Women, 1984.

Breasted, James Henry. *Ancient Times: A History of the Early World*. 1916. Boston, MA: Ginn and Co., 1944 ed.

——. *The Conquest of Civilization*. New York, NY: Harper and Brothers, 1926.

Breman, Jan. *Patronage and Exploitation: Changing Agrarian Relations in South Gujarat, India*. Berkeley, CA: University of California Press, 1974.

Bremer, Fredrika. *The Homes of the New World; Impressions of America*. 2 vols. New York, NY: Harper and Brothers, 1858.

Bridgwater, William (ed.). *The Columbia Viking Desk Encyclopedia*. New York, NY: Viking Press, 1953.

Brigham, Clarence S. (ed.). *The Early Records of Portsmouth*. Providence, RI: E. L. Freeman, 1901.

Briggs, Katherine Mary. *The Vanishing People: Fairy Lore and Legends*. New York, NY: Pantheon, 1978.

Brigs, Robin. *The Scientific Revolution of the Seventeenth Century*. 1969. London, UK: Longman, 1973 ed.

Brinkley, Alan. *The Unfinished Nation: A Concise History of the American People*. 1993. Boston, MA: McGraw-Hill, 2000 ed.

Brinton, Crane, John B. Christopher, and Robert Lee Wolff. *A History of Civilization - Vol. 2: 1715 to the Present*. Englewood Cliffs, NJ: Prentice Hall, 1955. (For Vol. 1, see Robin W. Winks, et al.)

British and Foreign Anti-Slavery Society. *Slavery and the Slave Trade in British India; With Notices of the Existence of These Evils in the Islands of Ceylon, Malacca, and Penang, Drawn from Official Documents*. London, UK: Thomas Ward, 1841.

Brockett, Linus Pierpont. *The Life and Times of Abraham Lincoln, Sixteenth President of the United States*. Philadelphia, PA: Bradley and Co., 1865.

Brodie, Fawn McKay. *Thaddeus Stevens: Scourge of the South*. New York, NY: W. W. Norton, 1966.

Brodnax, William H. *The Speech of William H. Brodnax, in the House of Delegates of Virginia, on the Policy of the State With Respect to its Colored Population*. Richmond, VA: William H. Brodnax, 1832.

Bronowski, J., and Bruce Mazlish. *The Western Intellectual Tradition: From Leonardo to Hegel*. 1960. New York, NY: Harper and Row, 1975 ed.

Brooks, Gertrude Zeth. *First Ladies of the White House*. Chicago, IL: Charles Hallberg and Co., 1969.

Brooksher, William R., and David K. Snider. *Glory at a Gallop: Tales of the Confederate Cavalry*. 1993. Gretna, LA: Pelican Publishing Co., 2002 ed.

Brown, Dee. *Bury My Heart at Wounded Knee: An Indian History of the American West*. 1970. New York, NY: Owl Books, 1991 ed.

Brown, James. *American Slavery in its Moral and Political Aspects, Comprehensively Examined*. New York, NY: James Brown, 1840.

Brown, Rita Mae. *High Hearts*. New York, NY: Bantam, 1987.

Brown, William Montgomery. *The Crucial Question, or Where and How Shall the Color Line Be Drawn*. Little Rock, AR: The Arkansas Churchman's Publishing Co., 1907.

Brown, William Wells. *The Black Man: His Antecedents, His Genius, and His Achievements*. New York, NY: Thomas Hamilton, 1863.

Browne, Ray B., and Lawrence A. Kreiser, Jr. *The Civil War and Reconstruction*. Westport, CT: Greenwood Publishing, 2003.

Bruce, Henry Clay. *The New Man: Twenty-nine Years a Slave, Twenty-nine Years a Free Man*. York, PA: P. Anstadt and Sons, 1895.

Bruce, Philip Alexander. *The Plantation Negro As a Freeman*. New York, NY: G. P. Putnam's Sons, 1889.

Bruford, W. H. *Germany in the Eighteenth Century: The Social Background of the Literary Revival*. 1935. Cambridge, UK: Cambridge University Press, 1965 ed.

Brunner, Borgna (ed.). *The Time Almanac* (1999 ed.). Boston, MA: Information Please, 1998.

Bruns, Roger (ed.). *Am I Not a Man and a Brother: The Antislavery Crusade of Revolutionary America 1688-1788*. New York, NY: Chelsea House, 1977.

Bryan, William Jennings. *The Commoner Condensed*. New York, NY: Abbey Press, 1902.
Bryant, Sophie. *Celtic Ireland*. London, UK: Kegan Paul, 1889.
Buchanan, James. *The Works of James Buchanan*. 12 vols. Philadelphia, PA: J. B. Lippincott Co., 1911.
Buchanan, Patrick J. *A Republic, Not an Empire: Reclaiming America's Destiny*. Washington, D.C.: Regenry, 1999.
Buckingham, James Silk. *Travels in Mesopotamia*. 2 vols. London, UK: Henry Colburn, 1827.
——. *The Slave States of America*. 2 vols. London, UK: Fisher, Son, and Co., 1842.
Buckland, William Warwick. *The Roman Law of Slavery: The Condition of the Slave in Private Law From Augustus to Justinian*. Cambridge, UK: Cambridge University Press, 1908.
Buckley, Gail. *American Patriots: The Story of Blacks in the Military From the Revolution to Desert Storm*. New York, NY: Random House, 2001.
Bullock, Alan. *Hitler: A Study in Tyranny*. 1962. New York, NY: Perennial Library, 1971 abridged ed.
Bultman, Bethany. *Redneck Heaven: Portrait of a Vanishing Culture*. New York, NY: Bantam, 1996.
Bunson, Matthew. *Encyclopedia of the Roman Empire*. New York, NY: Facts On File, 1994.
Burckhardt, John Lewis. *Travels in Nubia*. London, UK: John Murray, 1819.
Burin, Eric. *Slavery and the Peculiar Solution: A History of the American Colonization Society*. Gainesville, FL: University of Florida Press, 2008.
Burke, James. *Connections*. Boston, MA: Little, Brown and Co., 1978.
Burlingame, Michael. *The Inner World of Abraham Lincoln*. Champaign, IL: University of Illinois Press, 1997.
Burn, Andrew Robert. *The Pelican History of Greece*. 1965. Harmondsworth, UK: Penguin, 1968 ed.
Burne, Jerome (ed.). *Chronicle of the World*. 1989. Mount Kisco, NY: Ecam, 1990 ed.
Burns, James MacGregor. *The Vineyard of Liberty*. New York, NY: Knopf, 1982.
Burns, James MacGregor, and Jack Walter Peltason. *Government by the People: The Dynamics of American National, State, and Local Government*. 1952. Englewood Cliffs, NJ: Prentice-Hall, 1964 ed.
Burns, James MacGregor, Jack Walter Peltason, Thomas E. Cronin, David B. Magleby, and David M. O'Brien. *Government by the People* (National Version). 1952. Upper Saddle River, NJ: Prentice Hall, 2001-2002 ed.
Burrell, Sidney A. *Handbook of Western Civilization: Beginnings to 1700*. 1965. New York, NY: John Wiley and Sons, 1972 ed.
Burton, Robert. *The Anatomy of Melancholy*. 3 vols. 1621. London, UK: George Bell and Sons, 1896 ed.
Bush, Barbara. *Slave Women in Caribbean Society, 1650-1838*. Kingston, Jamaica: Heinemann Caribbean, 1990.
Bushnell, Horace. *The Census and Slavery, Thanksgiving Discourse, Delivered in the Chapel at Clifton Springs, New York, November 29, 1860*. Hartford, CT: L. E. Hunt, 1860.
Butler, Benjamin Franklin. *Butler's Book (Autobiography and Personal Reminiscences of Major-General Benjamin F. Butler: A Review of His Legal, Political, and Military Career)*. Boston, MA: A. M. Thayer and Co., 1892.
Butler, Lindley S., and Alan D. Watson (eds.). *The North Carolina Experience: An Interpretive and Documentary History*. Chapel Hill, NC: University of North Carolina Press, 1984.
Butler, Trent C. (ed.). *Holman Bible Dictionary*. Nashville, TN: Holman Bible Publishers,1991.
Buxton, Thomas Fowell. *The African Slave Trade and the Remedy For It*. Edinburgh, Scotland: Ballantine and Co., 1840.
Cahill, Thomas. *How the Irish Saved Civilization: The Untold Story of Ireland's Heroic Role From the Fall of Rome to the Rise of Medieval Europe*. New York, NY: Doubleday, 1995.
Caldwell, Arthur Bunyan (ed.). *History of the American Negro and His Institutions*. Atlanta, GA: A. B. Caldwell, 1917.
Calvert, Thomas H. *The Federal Statutes Annotated*. 10 vols. Northport, NY: Edward Thompson, 1905.
Cameron, Rondo. *A Concise Economic History of the World: From Paleolithic Times to the Present*. 1989. Oxford, UK: Oxford University Press, 2003 ed.
Campbell, Bernard G. (ed.). *Humankind Emerging*. Boston, MA: Little, Brown and Co., 1976.
Campbell, Gwyn, Suzanne Miers, and Joseph C. Miller (eds.). *Women and Slavery*. 2 vols. Athens, OH: Ohio University Press, 2007.
Campbell, Joseph. *The Masks of God: Primitive Mythology*. 1959. New York, NY: Arkana, 1991 ed.
Cannon, Devereaux D., Jr. *The Flags of the Confederacy: An Illustrated History*. Memphis, TN: St. Lukes Press, 1988.
Cantor, Milton (ed.). *Black Labor in America*. Westport, CT: Negro Universities Press, 1969.
Cantor, Norman F. *Inventing the Middle Ages: The Lives, Works, and Ideas of the Great Medievalists of the Twentieth Century*. New York, NY: William Morrow and Co., 1991.
Cappelluti, Frank J., and Ruth H. Grossman. *The Human Adventure: A History of Our World*. San Francisco, CA:

Field Educational Publications, 1970.

Carey, Anthony Gene. *Parties, Slavery, and the Union in Antebellum Georgia*. Athens, GA: University of Georgia Press, 1997.

Carey, Matthew, Jr. (ed.). *The Democratic Speaker's Hand-Book*. Cincinnati, OH: Miami Print and Publishing Co., 1868.

Carlton, Frank Tracy. *Organized Labor in America*. New York, NY: D. Appleton and Co., 1920.

Carman, Harry J., and Harold C. Syrett. *A History of the American People - Vol. 1: To 1865*. 1952. New York, NY: Knopf, 1958 ed.

Carney, Judith A. *Black Rice: The African Origins of Rice Cultivation in the Americas*. Cambridge, MA: Harvard University Press, 2009.

Carpenter, Stephen D. *Logic of History: Five Hundred Political Texts, Being Concentrated Extracts of Abolitionism*. Madison, WI: Stephen D. Carpenter, 1864.

Carroll, Joseph C. *Slave Insurrections in the United States, 1800-1865*. Boston, MA: Chapman and Grimes, 1938.

Carruth, Gorton (ed.). *The Volume Library: A Modern, Authoritative Reference for Home and School Use*. 1917. Nashville, TN: The Southwestern Co., 1988 ed.

Cartmell, Donald. *Civil War 101*. New York, NY: Gramercy, 2001.

Carwardine, Richard. *Lincoln: A Life of Purpose and Power*. New York, NY: Vintage, 2007.

Cash, W. J. *The Mind of the South*. 1941. New York, NY: Vintage, 1969 ed.

Catterall, Helen T. (ed.). *Judicial Cases Concerning American Slavery and the Negro*. 5 vols. Washington, D.C.: Carnegie Institute, 1926-1937.

Catton, Bruce. *The Coming Fury* (Vol. 1). 1961. New York, NY: Washington Square Press, 1967 ed.

——. *Terrible Swift Sword* (Vol. 2). 1963. New York, NY: Pocket Books, 1967 ed.

——. *A Stillness at Appomattox* (Vol. 3). 1953. New York, NY: Pocket Books, 1966 ed.

Celeste, Sister Mary. *The Old World's Gifts to the New*. 1932. Long Prairie, MN: Neumann Press, 1999 ed.

Chace, Elizabeth Buffum. *Anti-Slavery Reminiscences*. Central Falls, RI: E. L. Freeman and Son, 1891.

Chadwick, Owen. *A History of Christianity*. New York, NY: St. Martin's Griffin, 1998.

Chamberlain, Nathan Henry. *Samuel Sewall and the World He Lived In*. Boston, MA: De Wolfe, Fiske and Co., 1898.

Chambers, Mortimer, Raymond Grew, David Herily, Theodore K. Rabb, and Isser Woloch. *The Western Experience - Vol. 2: the Early Modern Period*. 1974. New York, NY: Knopf, 1987 ed.

Chambers, Robert (ed.). *The Book of Days: A Miscellany of Popular Antiquities in Connection with the Calender*. 2 vols. London, UK: W. and R. Chambers, 1883.

Chambers, William. *Things as They Are in America*. London, UK: William and Robert Chambers, 1854.

Chan, Alexandra. *Slavery in the Age of Reason: Archaeology at a New England Farm*. Knoxville, TN: University of Tennessee Press, 2007.

Channing, Edward. *The Narragansett Planters: A Study of Causes*. Baltimore, MD: Johns Hopkins University, 1886.

Channing, Steven A. *Confederate Ordeal: The Southern Home Front*. 1984. Morristown, NJ: Time-Life Books, 1989 ed.

Channing, William Ellery. *Slavery*. Boston, MA: James Munroe and Co., 1835.

Chayanov, A. V. *The Theory of Peasant Economy*. Madison, WI: University of Wisconsin Press, 1986.

Chesnut, Mary. *A Diary From Dixie: As Written by Mary Boykin Chesnut, Wife of James Chesnut, Jr., United States Senator from South Carolina, 1859-1861, and Afterward an Aide to Jefferson Davis and a Brigadier-General in the Confederate Army*. (Isabella D. Martin and Myrta Lockett Avary, eds.). New York, NY: D. Appleton and Co., 1905 ed.

——. *Mary Chesnut's Civil War*. 1860-1865 (Woodward, Comer Vann, ed.). New Haven, CT: Yale University Press, 1981 ed.

Child, Lydia Maria. *The Evils of Slavery, and the Cure of Slavery. The First Proved by Southerners Themselves, the Last Shown by Historical Evidence*. Newburyport, MA: Charles Whipple, 1836.

Childe, Gordon. *What Happened in History*. 1942. Harmondsworth, UK: Penguin, 1964 ed.

Chirichigno, Gregory C. *Debt-Slavery in Israel and the Ancient Near East*. Sheffield, UK: JSOT Press, 1993.

Chodes, John. *Destroying the Republic: Jabez Curry and the Re-Education of the Old South*. New York, NY: Algora, 2005.

Christian, George L. *Abraham Lincoln: An Address Delivered Before R. E. Lee Camp, No. 1 Confederate Veterans at Richmond, VA, October 29, 1909*. Richmond, VA: L. H. Jenkins, 1909.

Church, Thomas. *The History of the Great Indian War of 1675 and 1676, Commonly Called Philip's War*. New York, NY: H. Dayton, 1845.

Cimprich, John. *Fort Pillow, a Civil War Massacre, and Public Memory*. Baton Rouge, LA: Louisiana State University Press, 2005.

Cisco, Walter Brian. *War Crimes Against Southern Civilians.* Gretna, LA: Pelican Publishing Co., 2007.

Civil War Book of Lists. 1993. Edison, NJ: Castle Books, 2004 ed.

Civil War Society, The. *Civil War Battles: An Illustrated Encyclopedia*. 1997. New York, NY: Gramercy, 1999 ed.

——. *The Civil War Society's Encyclopedia of the Civil War*. New York, NY: Wings Books, 1997.

Clare, Israel Smith. *Modern History*. 15 vols. New York, NY: Union Book Co., 1906.

Clarence-Smith, William Gervase (ed.). *The Economics of the Indian Ocean Slave Trade in the Nineteenth Century*. London, UK: Frank Cass, 1989.

Clark, Arthur Hamilton. *The Clipper Ship Era: An Epitome of Famous American and British Clipper Ships, Their Owners, Builders, Commanders, and Crews, 1843-1869*. New York, NY: G. P. Putnam's Sons, 1912.

Clark, Kenneth. *Civilisation: A Personal View*. New York, NY: Harper and Row, 1969.

Clarke, James W. *The Lineaments of Wrath: Race, Violent Crime, and American Culture*. 1998. New Brunswick, NJ: Transaction, 2001 ed.

Clarkson, Thomas. *An Essay on the Slavery and Commerce of the Human Species, Particularly the African*. London, UK: Thomas Clarkson, 1787.

Clough, Ethlyn T. (ed.). *Africa: An Account of Past and Contemporary Conditions and Progress*. Detroit, MI: Bay View Reading Club, 1911.

Clough, Shepard B. *The Rise and Fall of Civilization: An Inquiry Into the Relationship Between Economic Development and Civilization*. 1951. New York, NY: Columbia University Press, 1957 ed.

Clough, Shepard B., Nina G. Garsoian, and David L. Hicks. *A History of the Western World: Ancient and Medieval*. Boston, MA: D. C. Heath and Co., 1964.

Cmiel, Kenneth. *Democratic Eloquence: The Fight Over Popular Speech in Nineteenth-Century America*. Berkeley, CA: University of California Press, 1990.

Cobb, Thomas Read Rootes. *An Inquiry into the Law of Negro Slavery in the United States of America*. 2 vols. Savannah, GA: W. Thorne Williams, 1858.

——. *An Historical Sketch of Slavery, From the Earliest Periods*. Savannah, GA: W. Thorne Williams, 1858.

Cobden, John C. *The White Slaves of England*. New York, NY: C. M. Saxton, Barker and Co., 1860.

Coe, Joseph. *The True American*. Concord, NH: I. S. Boyd, 1840.

Coffin, Charles Carleton. *Abraham Lincoln*. New York, NY: Harper and Brothers, 1893.

Cohen, David W., and Jack P. Greene (eds.). *Neither Slave nor Free: The Freedman of African Descent in the Slave Societies of the New World*. Baltimore, MD: Johns Hopkins University Press, 1972.

Coit, Margaret L. *John C. Calhoun: American Portrait*. Boston, MA: Sentry, 1950.

Coldham, Peter Wilson. *Emigrants in Chains, 1607-1776*. Baltimore, MD: Genealogical Publishing Co., 1992.

Collections of the Massachusetts Historical Society. Boston, MA: Massachusetts Historical Society, 1877.

Collier, Christopher, and James Lincoln Collier. *Decision in Philadelphia: The Constitutional Convention of 1787*. 1986. New York, NY: Ballantine, 1987 ed.

Collins, Elizabeth. *Memories of the Southern States*. Taunton, UK: J. Barnicott, 1865.

Collins, John A. (ed.). *The Anti-Slavery Picknick: A Collection of Speeches, Poems, Dialogues and Songs Intended for Use in Schools and Anti-Slavery Meetings*. Boston, MA: H. W. Williams, 1842.

Collins, Winfield Hazlitt. *The Domestic Slave Trade of the Southern States*. New York, NY: Broadway Publishing, 1904.

Commager, Henry Steele, and Erik Bruun (eds.). *The Civil War Archive: The History of the Civil War in Documents*. 1950. New York, NY: Black Dog and Leventhal, 1973 ed.

Commissioners of Statutory Revision. *The Colonial Laws of New York From the Year 1664 to the Revolution*. 2 vols. Albany, NY: New York State, 1894.

Compton's Encyclopedia. 1922. Chicago, IL: William Benton, 1969 ed.

Confederate [no name]. *The Grayjackets and How They Lived, Fought, and Died For Dixie*. Richmond, VA: Jones Brothers and Co., 1867.

Confer, Clarissa W. *The Cherokee Nation in the Civil War*. Norman, OK: University of Oklahoma Press, 2012.

Conner, Frank. *The South Under Siege, 1830-2000: A History of the Relations Between the North and the South*. Newnan, GA: Collards Publishing Co., 2002.

Conquest, Robert. *The Great Terror: Stalin's Purge of the Thirties*. 1968. New York, NY: Macmillan, 1973 ed.

Conrad, Robert. *The Destruction of Brazilian Slavery, 1850-1888*. Berkeley, CA: University of California Press, 1972.

Conway, Moncure Daniel. *Testimonies Concerning Slavery*. London, UK: Chapman and Hall, 1865.

Cooke, Alistair. *Alistair Cooke's America*. 1973. New York, NY: Knopf, 1984 ed.
Cooke, John Esten. *A Life of General Robert E. Lee*. New York, NY: D. Appleton and Co., 1871.
Cooley, Henry S. *A Study of Slavery in New Jersey*. Baltimore, MD: Johns Hopkins University Press, 1896.
Cooper, Frederick. *Plantation Slavery on the East Coast of Africa*. New Haven, CT: Yale University Press, 1977.
Cooper, William J., Jr. *Jefferson Davis, American*. New York, NY: Vintage, 2000.
——. (ed.). *Jefferson Davis: The Essential Writings*. New York, NY: Random House, 2003.
Copley, Esther. *A History of Slavery, and its Abolition*. London, UK: Houlston and Stoneman, 1839.
Cornford, Francis MacDonald. *The Republic of Plato*. 1941. New York, NY: Oxford University Press, 1964 ed.
Cornish, Dudley Taylor. *The Sable Arm: Black Troops in the Union Army, 1861-1865*. 1956. Lawrence, KS: University Press of Kansas, 1987 ed.
Costello, Peter. *In Search of Lake Monsters*. New York, NY: Berkley Medallion, 1975.
Cottrol, Robert J. (ed.). *From African to Yankee: Narratives of Slavery and Freedom in Antebellum New England*. Armonk, NY: M. E. Sharpe, 1998.
Coughlan, Robert. *Tropical Africa*. New York, NY: Time, 1962.
Coughtry, Jay. *The Notorious Triangle: Rhode Island and the African Slave Trade, 1700-1807*. Philadelphia, PA: Temple Press, 1981.
Coulter, Ann. *Guilty: Liberal "Victims" and Their Assault on America*. New York, NY: Three Rivers Press, 2009.
Countryman, Edward. *The American Revolution*. 1985. New York, NY: Hill and Wang, 1993 ed.
Cox, Earnest Sevier. *White America: The American Racial Problem As Seen in a Worldwide Perspective and Lincoln's Negro Policy*. Richmond, VA: White America Society, 1923.
Craig, Albert M., William A. Graham, Donald Kagan, Steven Ozment, and Frank M. Turner. *The Heritage of World Civilizations - Vol. 1: To 1600*. 1986. New York, NY: Macmillan College Publishing Co., 1994 ed.
Crallé, Richard Kenner. (ed.). *The Works of John C. Calhoun*. 6 vols. New York: NY: D. Appleton and Co., 1853-1888.
Cramer, Jesse Grant (ed.). *Letters of Ulysses S. Grant to His Father and His Youngest Sister, 1857-78*. New York, NY: G. P. Putnam's Sons, 1912.
Crane, Louise, Harvey Feinberg, Eleanor Berman, and Susan Hall. *Africa: History, Culture, Geography*. Englewood Cliffs, NJ: Globe Book Co., 1989.
Craven, John J. *Prison Life of Jefferson Davis*. New York: NY: Carelton, 1866.
Crawford, Samuel Wylie. *The Genesis of the Civil War: The Story of Sumter, 1860-1861*. New York, NY: Charles L. Webster and Co., 1887.
Crocker, H. W., III. *The Politically Incorrect Guide to the Civil War*. Washington, D.C.: Regnery, 2008.
Cromie, Alice Hamilton. *A Tour Guide to the Civil War: The Complete State-by-State Guide to Battlegrounds, Landmarks, Museums, Relics, and Sites*. 1964. Nashville, TN: Rutledge Hill Press, 1990 ed.
Cromwell, John Wesley. *The Negro in American History: Men and Women Eminent in the Evolution of the American of African Descent*. Washington, D.C.: American Negro Academy, 1914.
Cross, F. L., and F. A. Livingston (eds.). *The Oxford Dictionary of the Christian Church*. 1957. London, UK: Oxford University Press, 1974 ed.
Crothers, William L. *The Masting of American Merchant Sail in the 1850s: An Illustrated Study*. Jefferson, NC: McFarland and Co., 2014.
Crutchfield, James A. *Franklin: A Photographic Recollection*. 2 vols. Franklin, TN: Canaday Enterprises, 1996.
Crutchfield, James A., and Robert Holladay. *Franklin: Tennessee's Handsomest Town*. Franklin, TN: Hillsboro Press, 1999.
Cummins, Joseph. *Anything For a Vote: Dirty Tricks, Cheap Shots, and October Surprises in U.S. Presidential Campaigns*. Philadelphia, PA: Quirk, 2007.
Current, Richard N. *The Lincoln Nobody Knows*. 1958. New York, NY: Hill and Wang, 1963 ed.
——. (ed.) *The Confederacy (Information Now Encyclopedia)*. 1993. New York, NY: Macmillan, 1998 ed.
Curry, Leonard P. *Blueprint for Modern America: Nonmilitary Legislation of the First Civil War Congress*. Nashville, TN: Vanderbilt University Press, 1968.
Curti, Merle, Willard Thorpe, and Carlos Baker (eds.). *American Issues: The Social Record*. 1941. Chicago, IL: J. B. Lippincott, 1960 ed.
Curtin, Philip D. *The Atlantic Slave Trade: A Census*. Madison, WI: University of Wisconsin Press, 1969.
——. *The Rise and Fall of the Plantation Complex: Essays in Atlantic History*. 1990. Cambridge, UK: Cambridge University Press, 1999 ed.
Curtis, George Ticknor. *Life of James Buchanan: Fifteenth President of the United States*. 2 vols. New York, NY:

Harper and Brothers, 1883.
Curtis, William Eleroy. *Abraham Lincoln*. Philadelphia, PA: J. B. Lippincott Co., 1902.
Cushman, Horatio Bardwell. *History of the Choctaw, Chickasaw and Natchez Indians*. Greenville, TX: Headlight Printing House, 1899.
Custer, George Armstrong. *Wild Life on the Plains and Horrors of Indian Warfare*. St. Louis, MO: Excelsior Publishing, 1891.
Dabbs, James M. *The Southern Heritage*. New York, NY: Knopf, 1958.
Dabney, Robert Lewis. *A Defense of Virginia and the South*. Dahlonega, GA: Confederate Reprint Co., 1999.
Dahlberg, Gunnar. *Race, Reason and Rubbish: A Primer of Race Biology*. New York, NY: Columbia University Press, 1942.
Daniel, John M. *The Richmond Examiner During the War*. New York, NY: John M. Daniel, 1868.
Daniel, John W. *Life and Reminiscences of Jefferson Davis by Distinguished Men of His Time*. Baltimore, MD: R. H. Woodward and Co., 1890.
Darwin, Charles. *On the Origin of Species By Means of Natural Selection*. London, UK: John Murray, 1866.
Daugherty, James. *Abraham Lincoln*. 1943. New York, NY: Scholastic Book Services, 1966 ed.
d' Auvergne, Edmund B. *Human Livestock: An Account of the Share of the English-speaking Peoples in the Development, Maintenance and Suppression of Slavery and the Slave Trade*. London, UK: Grayson and Grayson, 1933.
Davenport, Robert R. *Roots of the Rich and Famous: Real Cases of Unlikely Lineage*. Dallas, TX: Taylor Publishing Co., 1998.
Davidson, Basil. *The African Slave Trade*. 1961. Boston, MA: Back Bay Books, 1980 ed.
——. *The Black Man's Burden: Africa and the Curse of the Nation-State*. New York, NY: Times Books, 1992.
Davidson, James Woods. *The Living Writers of the South*. New York, NY: Carleton, 1869.
Davidson, Marshall B. *Life in America*. 2 vols. Boston, MA: Houghton Mifflin, 1974.
Davis, Charles S. *The Cotton Kingdom in Alabama*. Montgomery, AL: Alabama State Dept. of Archives and History, 1939.
Davis, Darién J. (ed.). *Slavery and Beyond: The African Impact on Latin America and the Caribbean*. Lanham, MD: SR Books, 1995.
Davis, David Brion. *The Problem of Slavery in Western Culture*. 1966. Ithaca, NY: Cornell University Press, 1969 ed.
Davis, Jefferson. *The Rise and Fall of the Confederate Government*. 2 vols. New York, NY: D. Appleton and Co., 1881.
——. *A Short History of the Confederate States of America*. New York, NY: Belford, 1890.
——. *Andersonville and Other War-Prisons*. New York, NY: Belford Co., 1890.
Davis, Kenneth C. *Don't Know Much About the Civil War: Everything You Need to Know About America's Greatest Conflict But Never Learned*. 1996. New York, NY: HarperCollins, 1997 ed.
Davis, Michael. *The Image of Lincoln in the South*. Knoxville, TN: University of Tennessee Press, 1971.
Davis, Robert C. *Christian Slaves, Muslim Masters: White Slavery in the Mediterranean, the Barbary Coast and Italy, 1500-1800*. New York, NY: Macmillan, 2004.
Davis, Simon. *Race Relations in Ancient Egypt: Greek, Egyptian, Hebrew, Roman*. London, UK: Methuen, 1953.
Davis, Varina. *Jefferson Davis: Ex-President of the Confederate States of America - A Memoir by His Wife*. 2 vols. New York, NY: Belford Co., 1890.
Davis, William C. *Jefferson Davis: The Man and His Hour*. New York, NY: HarperCollins, 1991.
——. *An Honorable Defeat: The Last Days of the Confederate Government*. New York, NY: Harcourt, 2001.
——. *Look Away: A History of the Confederate States of America*. 2002. New York, NY: Free Press, 2003 ed.
Dawood, N. J. (trans.). *The Koran*. 1956. New York, NY: Penguin, 1990 ed.
Dawson, Christopher. *Understanding Europe*. Garden City, NY: Image, 1960.
Dawson, Sarah Morgan. *A Confederate Girl's Diary*. London, UK: William Heinemann, 1913.
Dean, Henry Clay. *Crimes of the Civil War, and Curse of the Funding System*. Baltimore, MD: William T. Smithson, 1869.
Dean, Vera Micheles. *The Nature of the Non-Western World*. 1957. New York, NY: Mentor, 1962 ed.
De Angelis, Gina. *It Happened in Washington, D.C.* Guilford, CT: Globe Pequot Press, 2004.
De Bow, James Dunwoody Brownson (ed.). *The Industrial Resources, Etc., of the Southern and Western States*. Vol. 4. New Orleans, LA: *De Bow's Review*, 1853.
DeCaro, Louis A., Jr. *Fire From the Midst of You: A Religious Life of John Brown*. New York, NY: New York University Press, 2002.
Deems, Edward Mark. *Holy-Days and Holidays: A Treasury of Historical Material, Sermons in Full and Brief,*

Suggestive Thoughts, and Poetry. New York, NY: Funk and Wagnalls, 1902.

DeFord, Deborah H. *Life Under Slavery*. New York, NY: Chelsea House, 2006.

De Forest, John William. *A Volunteer's Adventures: A Union Captain's Record of the Civil War*. 1946. North Haven, CT: Archon, 1970 ed.

Degler, Carl N. *Neither Black Nor White: Slavery and Race Relations in Brazil and the United States*. New York, NY: Macmillan, 1971.

DeGregorio, William A. *The Complete Book of U.S. Presidents*. 1984. New York, NY: Barricade, 1993 ed.

De Kock, Victor. *Those in Bondage*. London, UK: George Allen and Unwin, 1950.

de la Rochefoucauld Liancourt, Duke. *Travels Through the United States of North America, the Country of the Iroquois, and Upper Canada, in the Years 1795, 1796, and 1797*. 2 vols. London, UK: R. Phillips, 1800.

de las Casas, Bartolomé. *The Tears of the Indians: Being an Historical and True Account of the Cruel Massacres and Slaughters of Above Twenty Millions of Innocent People; Committed by the Spaniards in the Islands of Hispaniola, Cuba, Jamaica, etc.; As also, in the Continent of Mexico, Peru, and Other Places of the West Indies, to the Total Destruction of Those Countries*. London, UK: Nathaniel Brook, 1656.

de la Vega, Garcilaso. *The Incas*. New York, NY: Avon, 1961.

Delbanco, Andrew. *The Portable Abraham Lincoln*. New York, NY: Penguin, 1992.

Deloria, Vine, Jr. *Custer Died for Your Sins: An Indian Manifesto*. 1969. New York, NY: Avon, 1973 ed.

Denney, Robert E. *The Civil War Years: A Day-by-Day Chronicle of the Life of a Nation*. 1992. New York, NY: Sterling Publishing, 1994 ed.

Denson, John V. (ed.). *Reassessing the Presidency: The Rise of the Executive System and the Decline of Freedom*. Auburn, AL: Mises Institute, 2001.

DeRosa, Marshall L. *The Confederate Constitution of 1861: An Inquiry into American Constitutionalism*. Columbia, MO: University of Missouri Press, 1991.

De Rosa, Peter. *Vicars of Christ: The Dark Side of the Papacy*. New York, NY: Crown, 1988.

Derry, Joseph Tyrone. *Story of the Confederate States; or, History of the War for Southern Independence*. Richmond, VA: B. F. Johnson, 1895.

de Saint Croix, G. E. M. *The Class Struggle in the Ancient Greek World: From the Archaic Age to the Arab Conquests*. Ithaca, NY: Cornell University Press, 1980.

Devine, Edward T. (ed.). *The Negro in the Cities of the North*. New York, NY: The Charity Organization Society, 1905.

Dew, Charles B. *Bond of Iron: Master and Slave at Buffalo Forge*. New York, NY: W. W. Norton, 1994.

Diamond, Jared. *Guns, Germs, and Steel: The Fate of Human Societies*. 1997. New York, NY: W. W. Norton, 1999 ed.

Di Bonaventura, Allegro. *For Adam's Sake: A Family Saga in Colonial New England*. New York, NY: W. W. Norton, 2013.

Dicey, Edward. *Six Months in the Federal States*. 2 vols. London, UK: Macmillan and Co., 1863.

Dick, Everett Newfon. *The Dixie Frontier: A Social History*. New York, NY: Knopf, 1948.

Diller, Daniel C. (ed.). *The Middle East*. 1979. Washington, D.C.: Congressional Quarterly, 1991 ed.

DiLorenzo, Thomas J. "The Great Centralizer: Abraham Lincoln and the War Between the States." *The Independent Review*, Vol. 3, No. 2, Fall 1998, pp. 243-271.

——. *The Real Lincoln: A New Look at Abraham Lincoln, His Agenda, and an Unnecessary War*. Three Rivers, MI: Three Rivers Press, 2003.

——. *Lincoln Unmasked: What You're Not Supposed to Know About Dishonest Abe*. New York, NY: Crown Forum, 2006.

——. *Hamilton's Curse: How Jefferson's Archenemy Betrayed the American Revolution—and What It Means for America Today*. New York, NY: Crown Forum, 2008.

Dimont, Max I. *Jews, God and History*. New York, NY: Signet, 1962.

Dinkins, James. *1861 to 1865: Personal Recollections and Experiences in the Confederate Army, by an "Old Johnnie."* Cincinnati, OH: Robert Clarke, 1897.

Diouf, Sylviane A. *Servants of Allah: African Muslims Enslaved in the Americas*. New York, NY: New York University Press, 1998.

Dixon, Mrs. Archibald. *History of Missouri Compromise and Slavery in American Politics*. Cincinnati, OH: Robert Clarke, Co., 1903.

Dockés, Pierre. *Medieval Slavery and Liberation*. Chicago, IL: University of Chicago Press, 1982.

Dodd, William E. *Jefferson Davis*. Philadelphia, PA: George W. Jacobs and Co., 1907.

——. *The Cotton Kingdom: A Chronicle of the Old South*. New Haven, CT: Yale University Press, 1920.

Doddridge, Joseph. *Notes on the Settlement and Indian Wars of the Western Parts of Virginia and Pennsylvania, From 1763 to 1783, Inclusive*. Albany, NY: Joel Munsell, 1876.

Dodson, Howard. *Jubilee: The Emergence of African-American Culture*. New York, NY: National Geographic, 2003.

Donald, David Herbert. *Lincoln Reconsidered: Essays on the Civil War Era*. 1947. New York, NY: Vintage Press, 1989 ed.

——. (ed.). *Why the North Won the Civil War*. 1960. New York, NY: Collier, 1962 ed.

——. *Lincoln's Herndon*. New York, NY: Knopf, 1989.

——. *Lincoln*. New York, NY: Simon and Schuster, 1995.

Donald, Leland. *Aboriginal Slavery on the Northwest Coast of North America*. Berkeley, CA: University of California Press, 1997.

Donnan, Elizabeth (ed.). *Documents Illustrative of the History of the Slave Trade to America*. 3 vols. Washington, D.C.: Carnegie Institute, 1930-1935.

Dormon, James H., and Robert R. Jones. *The Afro-American Experience: A Cultural History Through Emancipation*. New York, NY: John Wiley and Sons, 1974.

Doubleday's Encyclopedia. 1931. New York, NY: Doubleday, Doran and Co., 1939 ed.

Douglas, Henry Kyd. *I Rode With Stonewall: The War Experiences of the Youngest Member of Jackson's Staff*. 1940. Chapel Hill, NC: University of North Carolina Press, 1968 ed.

Douglass, Frederick. *Narrative of the Life of Frederick Douglass: An American Slave*. 1845. New York, NY: Signet, 1997 ed.

——. *The Life and Times of Frederick Douglass, From 1817 to 1882*. London, UK: Christian Age Office, 1882.

Douglass, Harlan Paul. *Christian Reconstruction in the South*. Cambridge, MA: The University Press, 1909.

Dowd, Jerome. *The Negro in American Life*. New York, NY: Century, 1926.

Dowley, Tim (ed.). *The History of Christianity*. 1977. Oxford, UK: Lion, 1990 ed.

Doyle, Bertram W. *The Etiquette of Race Relations in the South: A Study in Social Control*. Chicago, IL: University of Chicago Press, 1937.

Drake, Raleigh M. *Abnormal Psychology*. 1954. Paterson, NJ: Littlefield, Adams and Co., 1959 ed.

Drake, St. Clair, and Horace Clayton. *Black Metropolis: A Study of Negro Life in a Northern City*. New York, NY: Harcourt, Brace and Co., 1945.

Draper, John William. *History of the American Civil War*. 3 vols. New York, NY: Harper and Brothers, 1870.

Drescher, Seymour. *The Mighty Experiment: Free Labor Versus Slavery in British Emancipation*. New York, NY: Oxford University Press, 2002.

Drescher, Seymour, and Stanley L. Engerman (eds.). *A Historical Guide to World Slavery*. New York, NY: Oxford University Press, 1998.

Drew, Benjamin. *The Refugee: Or the Narratives of Fugitive Slaves in Canada*. Boston, MA: John P. Jewett and Co., 1856.

Driscoll, Mark, and Gerry Breshears. *Vintage Jesus: Timeless Answers to Timely Questions*. Wheaton, IL: Crossway, 2007.

Du Bois, William Edward Burghardt. *The Suppression of the African Slave Trade to the United States of America, 1638-1870*. New York, NY: Longmans, Green, and Co., 1896.

——. *Darkwater: Voices From Within the Veil*. New York, NY: Harcourt, Brace and Howe, 1920.

——. *The Gift of Black Folk: The Negroes in the Making of America*. Boston, MA: Stratford, 1924.

——. *Black Reconstruction*. New York, NY: Harcourt, Brace, 1935.

Du Bois, William Edward Burghardt, and Augustus Granville Dill (eds.). *The Negro American Artisan*. Atlanta, GA: Atlanta University Press, 1912.

DuBose, John Witherspoon. *General Joseph Wheeler and the Army of Tennessee*. New York, NY: Neale Publishing Co., 1912.

Duby, George. *Rural Economy and Country Life in the Medieval West*. Columbia, SC: University of South Carolina Press, 1968.

——. *The Early Growth of European Economy: Warriors and Peasants From the Seventeenth to the Twelfth Century*. London, UK: Weidenfeld and Nicolson, 1974.

Duff, Mountstuart E. Grant. *Notes From a Diary, 1851-1872*. 2 vols. London, UK: John Murray, 1897.

Duke, Basil W. *Reminiscences of General Basil W. Duke, C.S.A.* New York, NY: Doubleday, Page and Co., 1911.

Dumond, Dwight Lowell. *Antislavery Origins of the Civil War in the United States*. 1939. Ann Arbor, MI: University of Michigan Press, 1960 ed.

Dunn, L. C., and Theodosius Dobzhansky. *Heredity, Race and Society: A Scientific Explanation of Human Differences*. 1946. New York, NY: Mentor, 1949 ed.

Dunn, Mary M., and Richard S. Dunn (eds.). *The Papers of William Penn*. 2 vols. Philadelphia, PA: University of Pennsylvania Press, 1986.

Dunn, Richard S. *Sugar and Slaves: The Rise of the Planter Class in the English West Indies*. Chapel Hill, NC: University of North Carolina Press, 1972.

Dunner, Joseph (ed.). *Handbook of World History: Concepts and Issues*. New York, NY: Philosophical Library, 1967.

Durant, Will. *Our Oriental Heritage*. 1935. New York, NY: Simon and Schuster, 1954 ed.

Durant, Will, and Ariel Durant. *The Age of Reason Begins: A History of European Civilization in the Period of Shakespeare, Bacon, Montaigne, Rembrandt, Galileo, and Descartes, 1558-1648*. New York, NY: Simon and Schuster, 1961.

Durden, Robert F. *The Gray and the Black: The Confederate Debate on Emancipation*. Baton Rouge, LA: Louisiana State University Press, 1972.

Earle, Thomas (ed.). *The Life, Travels and Opinions of Benjamin Lundy*. Philadelphia, PA: William D. Parrish, 1847.

Early, Jubal A. *A Memoir of the Last Year of the War for Independence in the Confederate States of America*. Lynchburg, VA: Charles W. Button, 1867.

Easton, Stewart C. *The Heritage of the Past: From the Earliest Times to the Close of the Middle Ages*. 1955. New York, NY: Rinehart and Co., 1957 ed.

——. *The Western Heritage*. New York, NY: Holt, Rinehart and Winston, 1961.

Eaton, Clement. *A History of the Southern Confederacy*. 1945. New York, NY: Free Press, 1966 ed.

——. *Henry Clay and the Art of American Politics*. Chicago, IL: Scott Foresman and Co., 1957.

——. *Jefferson Davis*. New York, NY: Free Press, 1977.

Eaton, John, and Ethel Osgood Mason. *Grant, Lincoln and the Freedmen: Reminiscences of the Civil War, With Special Reference to the Work of the Contrabands and Freedmen of the Mississippi Valley*. New York, NY: Longmans, Green, and Co., 1907.

Eban, Abba. *Heritage: Civilization and the Jews*. New York, NY: Summit, 1984.

Edmonds, Franklin Spencer. *Ulysses S. Grant*. Philadelphia, PA: George W. Jacobs and Co., 1915.

Edwards, I. E. S. *The Pyramids of Egypt*. 1947. Harmondsworth, UK: Penguin, 1967 ed.

Eggleston, Edward. *The Ultimate Solution of the American Negro Problem*. Boston, MA: The Gorham Press, 1913.

Ekirch, A. Roger. *Bound for America: The Transportation of British Convicts to the Colonies, 1718-1775*. New York, NY: Oxford University Press, 1987.

Eldredge, Elizabeth, and Fred Morton (eds.). *Slavery in South Africa: Captive Labor on the Dutch Frontier*. Boulder, CO: Westview Press, 1994.

El Hamel, Chouki. *Black Morocco: A History of Slavery, Race, and Islam*. Cambridge, UK: Cambridge University Press, 2013.

Elkins, Stanley. *Slavery: A Problem in American Institutional and Intellectual Life*. Chicago, IL: University of Chicago Press, 1959.

Elliot, Jonathan. *The Debates in the Several State Conventions on the Adoption of the Federal Constitution, As Recommended by the General Convention at Philadelphia in 1787*. 5 vols. Philadelphia, PA: J. B. Lippincott, 1891.

Elliott, E. N. *Cotton is King, and Pro-Slavery Arguments: Comprising the Writings of Hammond, Harper, Christy, Stringfellow, Hodge, Bledsoe, and Cartwright, on this Important Subject*. Augusta, GA: Pritchard, Abbott and Loomis, 1860.

Elliott, Stephen P. (ed.). *The New Illustrated Encyclopedia of Knowledge*. 1970. New York, NY: Portland House, 1986 ed.

Ellis, Joseph J. *American Sphinx: The Character of Thomas Jefferson*. 1996. New York, NY: Vintage, 1998 ed.

——. *Founding Brothers: The Revolutionary Generation*. 2000. New York, NY: Vintage, 2002 ed.

Ellison, Ralph. *Shadow and Act*. New York, NY: Random House, 1964.

Eltis, David. *Economic Growth and the Ending of the Transatlantic Slave Trade*. New York, NY: Oxford University Press, 1987.

——. *The Rise of African Slavery in the Americas*. Cambridge, UK: Cambridge University Press, 2000.

Eltis, David, and Stanley L. Engerman (eds.). *The Cambridge World History of Slavery: Vol. 3 - AD 1420-AD 1804*. Cambridge, UK: Cambridge University Press, 2011.

Eltis, David, and David Richardson (eds.). *Routes to Slavery: Direction, Ethnicity and Mortality in the Atlantic Slave Trade*. Abingdon, UK: Routledge, 1997.

Emerson, Bettie Alder Calhoun. *Historic Southern Monuments: Representative Memorials of the Heroic Dead of the Southern Confederacy*. New York, NY: Neale Publishing Co., 1911.

Emerson, Ralph Waldo. *The Complete Works of Ralph Waldo Emerson*. 12 vols. 1878. Boston, MA: Houghton, Mifflin and Co., 1904 ed.

——. *Journals of Ralph Waldo Emerson*. 10 vols. Edward Waldo Emerson and Waldo Emerson Forbes, eds. Boston, MA: Houghton, Mifflin and Co., 1910.

——. *The Journals and Miscellaneous Notebooks of Ralph Waldo Emerson*. 16 vols. Cambridge, MA: Belknap Press, 1975.

Emison, John Avery. *Lincoln Über Alles: Dictatorship Comes to America*. Gretna, LA: Pelican Publishing Co., 2009.

Emmer, P. C. (ed.). *Colonialism and Migration: Indentured Labour Before and After Slavery*. Dordrecht, The Netherlands: Martinus Nijhoff, 1986.

Encyclopedia Britannica: A New Survey of Universal Knowledge. 1768. Chicago, IL/London, UK: Encyclopedia Britannica, 1955 ed.

Escott, Paul D. (ed.). *North Carolinians in the Era of the Civil War and Reconstruction*. Chapel Hill, NC: University of North Carolina Press, 2008.

Esposito, Barbara, and Lee Wood. *Prison Slavery*. Washington, D.C.: Committee to Abolish Prison Slavery, 1982.

Essah, Patience. *A House Divided: Slavery and Emancipation in Delaware, 1638-1865*. Charlottesville, VA: University Press of Virginia, 1996.

Essig, James D. *The Bonds of Wickedness: American Evangelicals Against Slavery, 1770-1808*. Philadelphia, PA: Temple University Press, 1982.

Estes, Matthew. *A Defence of Negro Slavery, as it Exists in the United States*. Montgomery, AL: Press of the *Alabama Journal*, 1846.

Evans, Clement Anselm (ed.). *Confederate Military History: A Library of Confederate States History, in Twelve Volumes, Written By Distinguished Men of the South*. 12 vols. Atlanta, GA: Confederate Publishing Co., 1899.

Evans, Eli N. *Judah P. Benjamin: The Jewish Confederate*. 1988. New York, NY: Free Press, 1989 ed.

Evans, Lawrence B. (ed.). *Writings of George Washington*. New York, NY: G. P. Putnam's Sons, 1908.

Ewald, Janet J. *Soldiers, Traders, and Slaves: State Formation and Economic Transformation in the Greater Nile Valley, 1700-1885*. Madison, WI: University of Wisconsin Press, 1990.

Fadiman, Clifton (ed.). *The Treasury of the Encyclopedia Britannic*. Harmondsworth, UK: Viking, 1992.

Fallows, Samuel. *Story of the American Flag With Patriotic Selections and Incidents*. Boston, MA: Educational Publishing Co., 1903.

Falola, Toyin, and Paul E. Lovejoy (eds.). *Pawnship in Africa: Debt Bondage in Historical Perspective*. Boulder, CO: Westview Press, 1994.

Faragher, John Mack. *Sugar Creek: Life on the Illinois Prairie*. New Haven, CT: Yale University Press, 1986.

Farrar, Victor John. *The Annexation of Russian America to the United States*. Washington D.C.: W. F. Roberts, 1937.

Farrow, Anne, Joel Lang, and Jennifer Frank. *Complicity: How the North Promoted, Prolonged, and Profited From Slavery*. New York, NY: Ballantine, 2005.

Faulkner, Harold Underwood. *American Political and Social History*. 1937. New York, NY: Appleton-Century-Crofts, 1948 ed.

Faulkner, William. *The Unvanquished*. 1934. New York, NY: Vintage, 1966 ed.

Faust, Patricia L. (ed.). *Historical Times Illustrated Encyclopedia of the Civil War*. New York, NY: Harper and Row, 1986.

Faux, William. *Memorable Days in America: Being a Journal of a Tour to the United States, Principally Undertaken to Ascertain, by Positive Evidence, the Condition and Probable Prospects of British Emigrants*. London, UK: W. Simpkin and R. Marshall, 1823.

Fay, Edwin Hedge. *This Infernal War: The Confederate Letters of Edwin H. Fay*. Austin, TX: University of Texas Press, 1958.

Featherstonhaugh, George William. *Excursion Through the Slave States*. 2 vols. London, UK: John Murray, 1844.

Fehrenbacher, Don E. (ed.). *Abraham Lincoln: A Documentary Portrait Through His Speeches and Writings*. New York, NY: Signet, 1964.

——. *Lincoln in Text and Context: Collected Essays*. Stanford, CA: Stanford University Press, 1987.

——. (ed.) *Abraham Lincoln: Speeches and Writings, 1859-1865*. New York, NY: Library of America, 1989.

——. *The Slaveholding Republic: An Account of the United States Government's Relations to Slavery*. New York, NY: Oxford University Press, 2002.

Ferguson, Wallace K., and Geoffrey Bruun. *A Survey of European Civilization - Part 1: To 1660*. 1936. Boston, MA: Houghton Mifflin Co., 1947 ed.

——. *A Survey of European Civilization - Part 2: Since 1660*. 1936. Boston, MA: Houghton Mifflin Co., 1947 ed.

Ferris, Marcie Cohen, and Mark I. Greenberg (eds.). *Jewish Roots in Southern Soil: A New History*. Waltham, MA: Brandeis University Press, 2006.

Ferris, William Henry. *The African Abroad, or His Evolution in Western Civilization*. 2 vols. New Haven CT: The Tuttle, Morehouse and Taylor Press, 1913.

Fields, Annie (ed.) *Life and Letters of Harriet Beecher Stowe*. Cambridge, MA: Riverside Press, 1897.

Fifth Annual Report of the Boards of Managers of the Massachusetts Colonization Society. Presented May 27, 1846. Boston, MA: self-published, 1846.

Findlay, Bruce, and Esther Findlay. *Your Rugged Constitution: How America's House of Freedom is Planned and Built*. 1950. Stanford, CA: Stanford University Press, 1951 ed.

Finger, Ben, Jr. *Concise World History*. New York, NY: Philosophical Library, 1959.

Finkelman, Paul (ed.). *Slavery and the Law*. Lanham, MD: Rowman and Littlefield, 2002.

Finley, Moses I. *Ancient Slavery and Modern Ideology*. New York, NY: Viking Press, 1980.

——. *The Legacy of Greece: A New Appraisal*. Oxford, UK: Oxford University Press, 1984.

Fisher, Allan G. B., and Humphrey J. Fisher. *Slavery and Muslim Society in Africa*. London, UK: C. Hurst, 1970.

Fisher, N. R. E. *Slavery in Classical Greece*. London, UK: Bristol Classical Press, 1993.

Fisk University. *Unwritten History of Slavery: Autobiographical Accounts of Negro Ex-slaves*. Nashville, TN: Fisk University, 1968.

Fite, Emerson David. *The Presidential Election of 1860*. New York, NY: MacMillan, 1911.

Fitts, Robert. K. *Inventing New England's Slave Paradise: Master/Slave Relations in Eighteenth-Century Narragansett, Rhode Island*. New York, NY: Garland, 1998.

Fleming, Walter Lynwood. *Civil War and Reconstruction in Alabama*. New York, NY: Macmillan, 1905.

Flint, Timothy. *The History and Geography of the Mississippi Valley*. 2 vols. Cincinnati, OH: E. H. Flint, 1833.

Flood, Charles Bracelen. *1864: Lincoln At the Gates of History*. New York, NY: Simon and Schuster, 2009.

Fogel, Robert William. *Without Consent or Contract: The Rise and Fall of American Slavery*. New York, NY: W. W. Norton, 1989.

Fogel, Robert William, and Stanley L. Engerman. *Time On the Cross: The Economics of American Negro Slavery*. Boston, MA: Little, Brown, and Co., 1974.

Foley, John P. (ed.). *The Jeffersonian Cyclopedia*. New York, NY: Funk and Wagnalls, 1900.

Foner, Eric. *Free Soil, Free Labor, Free Men: The Ideology of the Republican Party Before the Civil War*. New York, NY: Oxford University Press, 1970.

——. *Reconstruction: America's Unfinished Revolution, 1863-1877*. 1988. New York, NY: Harper and Row, 1989 ed.

——. *Gateway to Freedom: The Hidden History of the Underground Railroad*. New York, NY: W. W. Norton and Co., 2015.

Foote, Shelby. *The Civil War: A Narrative, Fort Sumter to Perryville, Vol. 1*. 1958. New York, NY: Vintage, 1986 ed.

——. *The Civil War: A Narrative, Fredericksburg to Meridian, Vol. 2*. 1963. New York, NY: Vintage, 1986 ed.

——. *The Civil War: A Narrative, Red River to Appomattox, Vol. 3*. 1974. New York, NY: Vintage, 1986 ed.

Foote, Thelma Wills. *Black and White Manhattan: The History of Racial Formation in Colonial New York City*. New York, NY: Oxford University Press, 2004.

Ford, Paul Leicester (ed.). *The Works of Thomas Jefferson*. 12 vols. New York, NY: G. P. Putnam's Sons, 1904.

Ford, Worthington Chauncey (ed.). *A Cycle of Adams Letters*. 2 vols. Boston, MA: Houghton Mifflin, 1920.

Forman, S. E. *The Life and Writings of Thomas Jefferson*. Indianapolis, IN: Bowen-Merrill, 1900.

Förster, Stig, and Jörg Nagler (eds.). *On the Road to Total War: The American Civil War and the German Wars of Unification, 1861-1871*. 1997. Cambridge, UK: Cambridge University Press, 2002 ed.

Fortune, Timothy T. *Black and White: Land, Labor, and Politics in the South*. New York, NY: Arno, 1968.

Foster, John W. *A Century of American Diplomacy*. Boston, MA: Houghton, Mifflin and Co., 1901.

Fowler, John D. *The Confederate Experience Reader: Selected Documents and Essays*. New York, NY: Routledge, 2007.

Fowler, William Chauncey. *The Sectional Controversy; or Passages in the Political History of the United States, Including the Causes of the War Between the Sections*. New York, NY: Charles Scribner, 1864.

Fox, Early Lee. *The American Colonization Society, 1817-1840*. Baltimore, MD: Johns Hopkins Press, 1919.

Fox-Genovese, Elizabeth. *Within the Plantation Household: Black and White Women of the Old South (Gender and American Culture)*. Chapel Hill, NC: University of North Carolina Press, 1988.

Franklin, Benjamin. *The Life and Writings of Benjamin Franklin*. 2 vols. Philadelphia, PA: McCarty and Davis, 1834.

——. *The Complete Works of Benjamin Franklin*. 10 vols. New York, NY: G. P. Putnam's Sons, 1887.

Franklin, John Hope. *The Free Negro in North Carolina, 1790-1860*. Chapel Hill, NC: University of North Carolina Press, 1943.

——. *Reconstruction After the Civil War*. Chicago, IL: University of Chicago Press, 1961.

Frazier, James George. *The Golden Bough: A Study in Magic and Religion*. London, UK: Macmillan and Co., 1913.

Fredrickson, George M. *The Black Image in the White Mind: The Debate on Afro-American Character and Destiny, 1817-1914*. New York, NY: Harper and Row, 1971.

Fremantle, Arthur James. *Three Months in the Southern States, April-June, 1863*. New York, NY: John Bradburn, 1864.

Fremont-Barnes, Gregory. *The Wars of the Barbary Pirates: To the Shores of Tripoli - The Rise of the US Navy and Marines*. Oxford, UK: Osprey, 2006.

French, A. M. *Slavery in South Carolina and the Ex-Slaves; Or the Port Royal Mission*. New York, NY: Winchell M. French, 1862.

Freyre, Gilberto. *The Masters and the Slaves*. New York, NY: Knopf, 1956.

Friedenwald, Herbert. *The Declaration of Independence: An Interpretation and an Analysis*. New York, NY: The Macmillan Co., 1904.

Friedman, Saul S. *Jews and the American Slave Trade*. New Brunswick, NJ: Transaction, 2000.

Frost, Frank J. *Greek Society*. 1971. Lexington, MA: D. C. Heath, 1980 ed.

Furguson, Ernest B. *Freedom Rising: Washington in the Civil War*. 2004. New York, NY: Vintage, 2005 ed.

Furnas, J. C. *The Americans: A Social History of the United States, 1587-1914*. New York, NY: G. P. Putnam's Sons, 1969.

Galenson, David W. *White Servitude in Colonial America*. New York, NY: Cambridge University Press, 1981.

Gallay, Alan (ed.). *Indian Slavery in Colonial America*. Lincoln, NE: University of Nebraska, 2009.

Gamoran, Mamie G. *The New Jewish History: From the Discovery of America to Our Own Day*. 1957. New York, NY: The Union of American Hebrew Congregations, 1959 ed.

Ganshof, F. L. *Feudalism*. 1957. New York, NY: Harper Torchbooks, 1961 ed.

Gardner, Joseph L. (ed.). *Mysteries of the Ancient Americas: The New World Before Columbus*. 1986. Pleasantville, NY: Reader's Digest, 1992 ed.

Garlan, Yvon. *Slavery in Ancient Greece*. Ithaca, NY: Cornell University Press, 1988.

Garland, Hugh A. *The Life of John Randolph of Roanoke*. New York, NY: D. Appleton and Co., 1874.

Garraty, John A. *The American Nation: A History of the United States to 1877*. 1966. New York, NY: Harper and Row, 1971 ed.

——. (ed.) *Historical Viewpoints: Notable Articles From American Heritage, Vol. One to 1877*. 1970. New York, NY: Harper and Row, 1979 ed.

Garraty, John A., and Robert A. McCaughey. *A Short History of the American Nation*. 1966. New York, NY: HarperCollins, 1989 ed.

Garrison, Webb B. *Civil War Trivia and Fact Book*. Nashville, TN: Rutledge Hill Press, 1992.

——. *The Lincoln No One Knows: The Mysterious Man Who Ran the Civil War*. Nashville, TN: Rutledge Hill Press, 1993.

——. *Civil War Curiosities: Strange Stories, Oddities, Events, and Coincidences*. Nashville, TN: Rutledge Hill Press, 1994.

——. *The Amazing Civil War*. Nashville, TN: Rutledge Hill Press, 1998.

Garrison, Wendell Phillips, and Francis Jackson Garrison. *William Lloyd Garrison, 1805-1879*. 4 vols. New York, NY: Century Co., 1889.

Garrison, William Lloyd. *Thoughts on African Colonization*. Boston, MA: Garrison and Knapp, 1832.

Gaspar, David Barry, and Darlene Clark Hine (eds.). *More Than Chattel: Black Women and Slavery in the Americas*. Bloomington, IN: Indiana University Press, 1996.

Gates, Henry Louis, Jr. (ed.) *The Classic Slave Narratives*. New York, NY: Mentor, 1987.

Gellman, David N. *Emancipating New York: The Politics of Slavery and Freedom 1777-1827*. Baton Rouge, LA: Louisiana State University Press, 2006.

Gemery, Henry A., and Jan S. Hogendorn (eds.). *The Uncommon Market: Essays in the Economic History of the Atlantic Slave Trade*. New York, NY: Academic Press, 1979.

Genovese, Eugene D. *Roll, Jordan, Roll: The World the Slaves Made*. New York, NY: Pantheon, 1974.

Gerster, Patrick, and Nicholas Cords (eds.). *Myth and Southern History*. 2 vols. 1974. Champaign, IL:

University of Illinois Press, 1989 ed.

Gibbon, Edward. *The History of the Decline and Fall of the Roman Empire.* 6 vols. New York, NY: Harper and Brothers, 1850.

Gilbert, J. T. *The Celtic Records and Historic Literature of Ireland.* Dublin, Ireland: W. B. Kelly, 1861.

Gilliam, Edward Winslow. *Uncle Sam and the Negro in 1920.* Lynchburg, VA: J. P. Bell Co., 1906.

Gimbutas, Marija. *The Civilization of the Goddess: The World of Old Europe.* New York, NY: Harper Collins, 1991.

Golay, Michael. *A Ruined Land: The End of the Civil War.* New York, NY: John Wiley and Sons, 1999.

Goldschmidt, Arthur, Jr. *A Concise History of the Middle East.* 1979. Boulder, CO: Westview Press, 1988 ed.

Goodell, William. *The American Slave Code in Theory and Practice.* New York, NY: The American and Foreign Anti-Slavery Society, 1853.

Goodloe, Daniel Reaves. *Inquiry Into the Causes Which Have Retarded the Accumulation of Wealth and Increase of Population in the Southern States: In Which the Question of Slavery is Considered in a Politico-Economical Point of View.* Washington, D.C.: W. Blanchard (printer), 1846.

Goodman, Nathan G. (ed.). *A Benjamin Franklin Reader.* New York, NY: Thomas Y. Crowell Co., 1945.

Goodwyn, Lawrence. *The Populist Moment: A Short History of the Agrarian Revolt in America.* 1976. Oxford, UK: Oxford University Press, 1978 ed.

Gordon, Armistead Churchill. *Figures From American History: Jefferson Davis.* New York, NY: Charles Scribner's Sons, 1918.

Gordon, Irving L. *World History: Review Text.* 1965. New York, NY: Amsco School Publications, 1969 ed.

Goubert, Pierre. *Louis XIV and Twenty Million Frenchman.* 1966. New York, NY: Vintage, 1972 ed.

Gower, Herschel, and Jack Allen (eds.). *Pen and Sword: The Life and Journals of Randal W. McGavock.* Nashville, TN: Tennessee Historical Commission, 1959.

Gragg, Rod. *The Illustrated Confederate Reader: Extraordinary Eyewitness Accounts by the Civil War's Southern Soldiers and Civilians.* New York, NY: Gramercy Books, 1989.

Graham, John Remington. *A Constitutional History of Secession.* Gretna, LA: Pelican Publishing Co., 2003.

——. *Blood Money: The Civil War and the Federal Reserve.* Gretna, LA: Pelican Publishing Co., 2006.

Graham, Lloyd M. *Deceptions and Myths of the Bible.* 1975. New York, NY: Citadel Press, 1991 ed.

Graham, Stephen. *Children of the Slaves.* London, UK: Macmillan and Co., 1920.

Grant, Anne MacVicar. *Memoirs of an American Lady, With Sketches of Manners and Scenery in America as They Existed Previous to the Revolution.* 2 vols in 1. New York, NY: D. Appleton and Co., 1846.

Grant, Arthur James. *Greece in the Age of Pericles.* London, UK: John Murray, 1893.

Grant, Michael. *The World of Rome.* 1960. New York, NY: Mentor, 1964 ed.

——. *Constantine the Great: The Man and His Times.* New York, NY: Charles Scribner's Sons, 1993.

Grant, Ulysses Simpson. *Personal Memoirs of U. S. Grant.* 2 vols. 1885-1886. New York, NY: Charles L. Webster and Co., 1886.

Gray, Louis Herbert (ed.). *The Mythology of All Races.* 13 vols. Boston, MA: Marshall Jones, 1918.

Gray, Robert, Rev. (compiler). *The McGavock Family: A Genealogical History of James McGavock and His Descendants, from 1760 to 1903.* Richmond, VA: W. E. Jones, 1903.

Gray, Thomas R. *The Confessions of Nat Turner: The Leader of the Late Insurrection in Southampton, Virginia.* Richmond, VA: Thomas R. Gray, 1831.

Greeley, Horace (ed.). *The Writings of Cassius Marcellus Clay.* New York, NY: Harper and Brothers, 1848.

——. *A History of the Struggle for Slavery Extension or Restriction in the United States From the Declaration of Independence to the Present Day.* New York, NY: Dix, Edwards and Co., 1856.

——. *The American Conflict: A History of the Great Rebellion in the United States, 1861-1865.* 2 vols. Hartford, CT: O. D. Case and Co., 1867.

Green, Constance McLaughlin. *Eli Whitney and the Birth of American Technology.* Boston, MA: Little, Brown, and Co., 1956.

——. *Washington: A History of the Capital, 1800-1950.* 1962. Princeton, NJ: Princeton University Press, 1976 ed.

Green, John Richard. *A Short History of the English People.* 2 vols. London, UK: Macmillan and Co., 1892.

Green, William A. *British Slave Emancipation: The Sugar Colonies and the Great Experiment, 1830-1865.* Oxford, UK: Clarendon Press, 1976.

Greenberg, Martin H., and Charles G. Waugh (eds.). *The Price of Freedom: Slavery and the Civil War—Vol. 1, The Demise of Slavery.* Nashville, TN: Cumberland House, 2000.

Greene, Lorenzo Johnston. *The Negro in Colonial New England, 1620-1776.* New York, NY: Columbia University Press, 1942.

Greene, Sandra E. *West African Narratives of Slavery: Texts From Late Nineteenth- and Early Twentieth-Century Ghana.* Bloomington, IN: Indiana University Press, 2011.

Greenhow, Rose O'Neal. *My Imprisonment and the First Year of Abolition Rule at Washington.* London, UK: Richard Bentley, 1863.

Greer, Thomas H. *A Brief History of Western Man: To 1650.* New York, NY: Harcourt Brace Jovanovich, 1972.

Grey, Lewis Cecil. *History of Agriculture in the Southern United States to 1860.* 2 vols. Washington, DC: Carnegie Institution of Washington, 1933.

Grimké, Angelina Emily. *Letters to Catherine E. Beecher, in Reply to an Essay on Slavery and Abolitionism, Addressed to A. E. Grimké.* Boston, MA: Angelina Emily Grimké, 1838.

Grimsley, Mark. *The Hard Hand of War: Union Military Policy Toward Southern Civilians, 1861-1865.* 1995. Cambridge, UK: Cambridge University Press, 1997 ed.

Grissom, Michael Andrew. *Southern By the Grace of God.* 1988. Gretna, LA: Pelican Publishing Co., 1995 ed.

Groom, Winston. *Shrouds of Glory - From Atlanta to Nashville: The Last Great Campaign of the Civil War.* New York, NY: Grove Press, 1995.

Grun, Bernard. *The Timetables of History: A Horizontal Linkage of People and Events.* 1946. New York, NY: Touchstone, 1982 ed.

Guelzo, Allen C. *Abraham Lincoln As a Man of Ideas.* Carbondale, IL: Southern Illinois University Press, 2009.

Gutman, Herbert G. *The Black Family in Slavery and Freedom, 1750-1925.* New York, NY: Pantheon, 1976.

Gwatkin, H. M., and J. P. Whitney (eds.). *The Cambridge Medieval History, Vol. 2: The Rise of the Saracens and the Foundation of the Western Empire.* New York, NY: Macmillan, 1913.

Hacker, Louis Morton. *The Shaping of the American Tradition.* New York, NY: Columbia University Press, 1947.

Hadas, Moses (ed.). *A History of Rome: From Its Origins to 259 A.D. as Told by Roman Historians.* Garden City, NY: Doubleday Anchor, 1956.

Haines, C. Grove, and Warren B. Walsh. *The Development of Western Civilization.* 2 vols. 1941. New York, NY: Henry Holt and Co., 1947 ed.

Hale, John. *The Civilization of Europe in the Renaissance.* New York, NY: Atheneum, 1994.

Hale, Will Thomas, and Dixon Lanier Merritt. *A History of Tennessee and Tennesseans.* 8 vols. Chicago, IL: Lewis Publishing Co., 1913.

Hall, B. C., and C. T. Wood. *The South: A Two-step Odyssey on the Backroads of the Enchanted Land.* New York, NY: Touchstone, 1996.

Hall, Basil. *Travels in North America, in the Years 1827 and 1828.* 3 vols. Edinburgh, Scotland: Cadell and Co., 1829.

Hall, Francis. *Travels in Canada, and the United States, in 1816 and 1817.* London, UK: Longman, Hurst, Rees, Orme, and Brown, 1818.

Hall, Gwendolyn M. *Africans in Colonial Louisiana: The Development of Afro-Creole Culture in the Eighteenth Century.* Baton Rouge, LA: Louisiana State University Press, 1992.

Hall, John (ed.). *Forty Years' Familiar Letters of James W. Alexander, D.D.* 2 vols. New York, NY: Charles Scribner, 1860.

Hall, Kermit L. (ed). *The Oxford Companion to the Supreme Court of the United States.* New York, NY: Oxford University Press, 1992.

Hall, Marshall. *The Two-Fold Slavery of the United States; With a Project of Self-Emancipation.* London, UK: Adam Scott, 1854.

Hall, Walter Phelps, Robert Greenhalgh Albion, and Jennie Barnes Pope. *A History of England and the Empire-Commonwealth.* 1937. Waltham, MA: Blaisdell, 1965 ed.

Hamblin, Ken. *Pick a Better Country: An Unassuming Colored Guy Speaks His Mind About America.* New York, NY: Touchstone, 1997.

Hamilton, Alexander, James Madison, and John Jay. *The Federalist: A Collection of Essays by Alexander Hamilton, James Madison, and John Jay.* New York, NY: The Co-operative Publication Society, 1901.

Hamilton, Edith. *The Greek Way to Western Civilization.* 1930. New York, NY: Mentor, 1959 ed.

——. *The Roman Way to Western Civilization.* 1932. New York, NY: Mentor, 1961 ed.

Hamilton, Holman. *Zachary Taylor: Soldier in the White House.* Indianapolis, IN: Bobbs-Merrill, 1951.

Hamilton, J. G. de Roulhac (ed.). *Selections From the Writings of Abraham Lincoln.* Chicago, IL: Scott, Foresman and Co., 1922.

Hamilton, Neil A. *Rebels and Renegades: A Chronology of Social and Political Dissent in the United States.* New York, NY: Routledge, 2002.

Handler, Jerome S. *The Unappropriated People: Freedmen in the Slave Society of Barbados.* Baltimore, MD: Johns

Hopkins University Press, 1974.

Handlin, Oscar (ed.). *Readings in American History: Vol. 1 - From Settlement to Reconstruction.* 1957. New York, NY: Knopf, 1970 ed.

Hannity, Sean. *Let Freedom Ring: Winning the War of Liberty Over Liberalism.* New York, NY: HarperCollins, 2002.

Hansen, Harry. *The Civil War: A History.* 1961. Harmondsworth, UK: Mentor, 1991 ed.

Harden, Edward J. *The Life of George M. Troup.* Savannah, GA: E. J. Purse, 1859.

Harding, Samuel Bannister. *The Contest Over the Ratification of the Federal Constitution in the State of Massachusetts.* New York, NY: Longmans, Green, and Co., 1896.

Harnden, Henry. *The Capture of Jefferson Davis - Part Taken by Wisconsin Troops.* Madison, WI: n.p., 1898.

Harper, William. *Memoir of Slavery, Read Before the Society for the Advancement of Learning, of South Carolina, at its Annual Meeting at Columbia.* Charleston, SC: James S. Burges, 1838.

Harper, William, James Henry Hammond, William Gilmore Simms, and Thomas Roderick Dew. *The Pro-Slavery Argument, As Maintained by the Most Distinguished Writers of the Southern States.* Charleston, SC: Walker, Richards and Co., 1852.

Harrell, David Edwin, Jr., Edwin S. Gaustad, John B. Boles, Sally Foreman Griffith, Randall M. Miller, and Randall B. Woods. *Unto a Good Land: A History of the American People.* Grand Rapids, MI: William B. Eerdmans, 2005.

Harris, Joel Chandler. *Stories of Georgia.* New York, NY: American Book Co., 1896.

Harris, Joseph E., Alusine Jalloh, Joseph E. Inikori, Colin A. Palmer, Douglas B. Chambers, and Dale T. Graden. *The African Diaspora.* Arlington, TX: Texas A&M University Press, 1996.

Harris, Leslie M. *In the Shadow of Slavery: African Americans in New York City, 1626-1863.* Chicago, IL: University of Chicago Press, 2004.

Harris, Marvin. *Our Kind: Who We Are, Where We Came From, Where We Are Going.* New York, NY: Harper and Row, 1989.

Harris, Norman Dwight. *The History of Negro Servitude in Illinois.* Chicago, IL: A. C. McClurg and Co., 1904.

Harrison, Peleg D. *The Stars and Stripes and Other American Flags.* 1906. Boston, MA: Little, Brown, and Co., 1908 ed.

Hart, Albert Busnell. *Slavery and Abolition.* New York, NY: Haskell House, 1906.

——. *The Southern South.* New York, NY: D. Appleton and Co., 1912.

Hartman, Gertrude, and Lucy S. Saunders. *Builders of the Old World.* 1946. Boston, MA: Little, Brown and Co., 1959 ed.

Hartzell, Josiah. *The Genesis of the Republican Party.* Canton, OH: n.p., 1890.

Harwell, Richard B. (ed.). *The Confederate Reader: How the South Saw the War.* 1957. Mineola, NY: Dover, 1989 ed.

Hattaway, Herman, and Archer Jones. *How the North Won: A Military History of the Civil War.* 1983. Champaign, IL: University of Illinois Press, 1991 ed.

Hawkins, Ernest. *Historical Notices of the Church of England in the American Colonies.* London, UK: Fellowes, 1845.

Hawthorne, Julian (ed.). *Orations of American Orators.* 2 vols. New York, NY: Colonial Press, 1900.

Hawthorne, Julian, James Schouler, and Elisha Benjamin Andrews. *United States, From the Discovery of the North American Continent Up to the Present Time.* 9 vols. New York, NY: Co-operative Publication Society, 1894.

Hawthorne, Nathaniel. *The Works of Nathaniel Hawthorne.* 15 vols. 1850. Boston, MA: Houghton, Mifflin and Co., 1888 ed.

Hay, John H. Drummond. *Western Barbary: Its Wild Tribes and Savage Animals.* London, UK: John Murray, 1891.

Hayes, Carlton J. H., Marshall Whited Baldwin, and Charles Woolsey Cole. *History of Europe.* 1949. New York, NY: Macmillan Co., 1950 ed.

Haygood, Atticus G. *Our Brother in Black: His Freedom and His Future.* Nashville, TN: M. E. Church, 1896.

Hedrick, Joan D. (ed.). *The Oxford Harriet Beecher Stowe Reader.* New York, NY: Oxford University Press, 1999.

Heer, Friedrich. *The Medieval World - Europe: 1100-1350.* 1961. New York, NY: Mentor, 1962 ed.

Heimert, Alan, and Perry Miller (eds.). *The Great Awakening: Documents Illustrating the Crisis and Its Consequences.* 1967. Indianapolis, IN: Bobbs-Merrill, 1977 ed.

Hellie, Richard. *Slavery in Russia, 1450-1725.* Chicago, IL: University of Chicago Press, 1982.

Helper, Hinton Rowan. *Compendium of the Impending Crisis of the South.* New York, NY: A. B. Burdick, 1860.

——. *Miscegenation: The Theory of Blending of the Races, Applied to the American White Man and Negro.* Hamilton, NY: H. Dexter, 1864.

——. *Nojoque: A Question for a Continent.* New York, NY: George W. Carleton, 1867.

——. *The Negroes in Negroland: The Negroes in America; and Negroes Generally.* New York, NY: George W. Carlton, 1868.

——. *Oddments of Andean Diplomacy and Other Oddments.* St. Louis, MO: W. S. Bryan, 1879.

Hendelson, William H. (ed). *Funk and Wagnalls New Encyclopedia.* New York, NY: Funk and Wagnalls, 1973 ed.

Henderson, George Francis Robert. *Stonewall Jackson and the American Civil War.* 2 vols. London, UK: Longmans, Green, and Co., 1919.

Henry, Robert Selph (ed.). *The Story of the Confederacy.* 1931. New York, NY: Konecky and Konecky, 1999 ed.

——. *As They Saw Forrest: Some Recollections and Comments of Contemporaries.* 1956. Wilmington, NC: Broadfoot Publishing Co., 1991 ed.

——. *First With the Most: Forrest.* New York, NY: Konecky and Konecky, 1992.

Henson, Josiah. *Father Henson's Story of His Own Life.* Boston, MA: John P. Jewett and Co., 1858.

Herm, Gerhard. *The Celts: The People Who Came Out of the Darkness.* New York, NY: St. Martin's Press, 1975.

Herndon, William H., and Jesse W. Weik. *Abraham Lincoln: The True Story of a Great Life.* New York, NY: D. Appleton and Co., 1909.

Herr, Pamela, and Mary Lee Spence (eds.). *The Letters of Jessie Benton Frémont.* Urbana, IL: University of Illinois Press, 1993.

Herring, Hubert. *A History of Latin America: From the Beginnings to the Present.* 1955. New York, NY: Knopf, 1968 ed.

Herskovits, Melville J. *The Myth of the Negro Past.* 1941. Boston, MA: Beacon Press, 1969 ed.

Hertz, Emanuel. *The Hidden Lincoln.* New York, NY: Blue Ribbon Works, 1940.

Hervey, Anthony. *Why I Wave the Confederate Flag, Written By a Black Man: The End of Niggerism and the Welfare State.* Oxford, UK: Trafford Publishing, 2006.

Heston, Alfred Miller. *Story of the Slave: Slavery and Servitude in New Jersey.* Camden, NJ: Sinnickson Chew and Sons Co., 1903.

Heuman, Gad J. *Between Black and White: Race, Politics, and the Free Coloreds in Jamaica, 1792-1865.* Westport, CT: Greenwood Press, 1981.

——. *Out of the House of Bondage, Runaways, Resistance and Maroonage in Africa and the New World.* London, UK: Frank Cass, 1986.

Hey, David. *The Oxford Guide to Family History.* Oxford, UK: Oxford University Press, 1993.

Heyward, Duncan Clinch. *Seed From Madagascar.* Columbia, SC: University of South Carolina, 1972.

Hickey, William. *The Constitution of the United States.* Philadelphia, PA: T. K. and P. G. Collins, 1853.

Highsmith, Carol M. and Ted Landphair. *Civil War Battlefields and Landmarks: A Photographic Tour.* New York, NY: Random House, 2003.

Higman, Barry W. *Slave Populations of the British Caribbean, 1807-1834.* Baltimore, MD: Johns Hopkins University Press, 1984.

Hildreth, Richard. *The White Slave: Another Picture of Slave Life in America.* London, UK: George Rutledge and Co., 1852.

——. *The History of the United States.* 6 vols. New York, NY: Harper and Brothers, 1882.

Hill, George Birkbeck (ed.). *Colonel Gordon in Central Africa 1874-1879.* London, UK: Thomas de la Rue, 1881.

Hill, Shirley, A. *Families: A Social Class Perspective.* Thousand Oaks, CA: Sage, 2012.

Hilton, Rodney. *Class Conflict and the Crisis of Feudalism: Essays in Medieval Social History.* London, UK: Hambledon Press, 1985.

Hinkle, Don. *Embattled Banner: A Reasonable Defense of the Confederate Battle Flag.* Paducah, KY: Turner Publishing Co., 1997.

Hinnells, John R. *Dictionary of Religions: From Abraham to Zoroaster.* 1984. Harmondsworth, UK: Penguin, 1986.

Hinsie, Leland E., and Robert Jean Campbell. *Psychiatric Dictionary.* 1940. New York, NY: Oxford University Press, 1970 ed.

Hirshon, Stanley P. *Farewell to the Bloody Shirt: Northern Republicans and the Southern Negro.* Bloomington, IN: Indiana University Press, 1962.

Hitler, Adolf. *Mein Kampf.* 2 vols. 1925, 1926. New York: NY: Reynal and Hitchcock, 1941 English translation ed.

Hobsbawm, Eric. *The Age of Revolution, 1789-1898*. London, UK: Weidenfeld and Nicolson, 1962.

Hodgson, Adam. *Letters From North America, Written During a Tour in the United States and Canada*. 2 vols. London, UK: Hurst, Robinson, and Co., 1824.

Hoffman, Michael A., II. *They Were White and They Were Slaves: The Untold History of the Enslavement of Whites in Early America*. Dresden, NY: Wiswell Ruffin House, 1993.

Hofstadter, Richard. *The American Political Tradition, and the Men Who Made It*. New York, NY: Knopf, 1948.

Holland, Edwin Clifford. *A Refutation of the Calumnies Circulated Against the Southern and Western States, Respecting the Institution and Existence of Slavery Among Them*. Charleston, SC: A. E. Miller (printer), 1822.

Holland, Jesse J. *Black Men Built the Capitol: Discovering African-American History in and Around Washington, D.C.* Guilford, CT: The Globe Pequot Press, 2007.

Holland, Rupert Sargent (ed.). *Letters and Diary of Laura M. Towne: Written From the Sea Islands of South Carolina, 1862-1884*. Cambridge, MA: Riverside Press, 1912.

Holmes, Burton. *Burton Holmes Travelogues: Cities of the Barbary Coast, Vol. 4*. New York, NY: McClure Co., 1908.

Holmes, Thomas Rice. *Caesar's Conquest of Gaul: An Historical Narrative*. London, UK: Macmillan and Co., 1903.

Holzer, Harold (ed.). *The Lincoln-Douglas Debates: The First Complete, Unexpurgated Text*. 1993. Bronx, NY: Fordham University Press, 2004 ed.

Homans, Isaac Smith. *Sketches of Boston, Past and Present, and of Some Few Places in its Vicinity*. Boston, MA: Phillips, Samson, and Co., 1851.

Hood, John Bell. *Advance and Retreat: Personal Experiences in the United States and Confederate States Armies*. New Orleans, LA: G. T. Beauregard, 1880.

Hopkins, John Henry. *The Bible View of American Slavery: A Letter From the Bishop of Vermont to the Bishop of Pennsylvania*. London, UK: Saunders, Otley, and Co., 1863.

Hopkins, Keith. *Conquerors and Slaves*. Cambridge, UK: Cambridge University Press, 1978.

Hopkins, Luther W. *From Bull Run to Appomattox: A Boy's View*. Baltimore, MD: Fleet-McGinley Co., 1908.

Horn, Stanley F. *Invisible Empire: The Story of the Ku Klux Klan, 1866-1871*. 1939. Montclair, NJ: Patterson Smith, 1969 ed.

——. *The Decisive Battle of Nashville*. 1956. Baton Rouge, LA: Louisiana State University Press, 1991 ed.

Horton, James A. B. (ed.). *Black Nationalism in Africa, 1867*. New York, NY: Africana Publishing, 1969.

Horwitz, Tony. *Confederates in the Attic: Dispatches From the Unfinished Civil War*. 1998. New York, NY: Vintage, 1999 ed.

Howard, Warren S. *American Slavers and the Federal Law, 1837-1862*. Berkeley, CA: University of California Press, 1963.

Howe, Daniel Wait. *Political History of Secession*. New York, NY: G. P. Putnam's Sons, 1914.

Howe, George L. *Mount Hope: A New England Chronicle*. New York, NY: Viking Press, 1959.

Howe, Henry. *Historical Collections of Virginia*. Charleston, SC: William R. Babcock, 1852.

Howe, M. A. DeWolfe (ed.). *Home Letters of General Sherman*. New York, NY: Charles Scribner's Sons, 1909.

——. *Bristol, Rhode Island: A Town Biography*. Cambridge, MA: Harvard University Press, 1930.

Howells, William. *Back of History: The Story of Our Own Origins*. 1954. Garden City, NY: Doubleday, 1963 ed.

Hubbard, John Milton. *Notes of a Private*. St. Louis, MO: Nixon-Jones, 1911.

Hubbard, William. *A Narrative of the Indian Wars in New England, From the First Planting Thereof in the Year 1607, to the Year 1677*. Stockbridge, MA: Heman Willard, 1803.

Hudson, Larry E., Jr. *To Have and to Hold: Slave Work and Family Life in Antebellum South Carolina*. Athens, GA: University of Georgia Press, 1997.

Humphreys, Mary Gay. *Catherine Schuyler*. New York, NY: Charles Scribner's Sons, 1897.

Hundley, Daniel Robinson. *Social Relations in Our Southern States*. New York, NY: Henry B. Price, 1860.

Hunt, John Gabriel (ed.). *The Essential Abraham Lincoln*. Avenel, NJ: Portland House, 1993.

Hurd, John Codman. *The Law of Freedom and Bondage in the United States*. 2 vols. Boston, MA: Little, Brown and Co., 1862.

Hurmence, Belinda (ed.). *Before Freedom, When I Can Just Remember: Twenty-seven Oral Histories of Former South Carolina Slaves*. 1989. Winston-Salem, NC: John F. Blair, 2002 ed.

Hurst, Jack. *Nathan Bedford Forrest: A Biography*. 1993. New York, NY: Vintage, 1994 ed.

Illinois State Historical Society. *Transactions of the Illinois State Historical Society for the Year 1908*. (Pub. 13, Ninth Annual Meeting of the Society.) Springfield, IL: Illinois State Historical Society, 1909.

Ingersoll, Charles Jared. *African Slavery in America*. Philadelphia, PA: Charles Jared Ingersoll, 1856.

Ingersoll, Thomas G., and Robert E. O'Connor. *Politics and Structure: Essential of American National Government.* North Scituate, MA: Duxbury Press, 1979.

Ingraham, Joseph Holt. *The South-West.* 2 vols. New York, NY: Harper and Brothers, 1835.

Inikori, Joseph E., and Stanley L. Engerman (eds.). *The Atlantic Slave Trade: Effects on Economics, Societies, and Peoples in Africa, the Americas, and Europe.* Durham, NC: Duke University Press, 1992.

Isaacman, Allen F. *Mozambique: The Africanization of a European Institution: The Zambezi Prazos, 1750-1902.* Madison, WI: University of Wisconsin Press, 1972.

Isichei, Elizabeth. *A History of African Societies to 1870.* 1997. Cambridge, UK: Cambridge University Press, 2000 ed.

Jackson, G. A. *Algiers: Being a Complete Picture of the Barbary States; Their Government, Laws, Religion, and Natural Productions.* London, UK: R. Edwards, 1817.

Jacobs, Harriet Ann ("Linda Brent"). *Incidents in the Life of a Slave Girl.* Boston, MA: the author, 1861.

Jameson, J. Franklin (ed.). *Narratives of New Netherland, 1609-1664.* New York, NY: Charles Scribner's Sons, 1909.

Jamieson, Alan G. *Lords of the Sea: A History of the Barbary Corsairs.* London, UK: Reaktion, 2012.

Jaquette, Henrietta Stratton (ed.). *South After Gettysburg: Letters of Cornelia Hancock, 1863-1868.* Philadelphia, PA: University of Pennsylvania Press, 1937.

Jahoda, Gloria. *The Trail of Tears: The Story of the American Indian Removals, 1813-1855.* 1975. New York, NY: Wings Book, 1995 ed.

Jayyusi, Salma Khadra (ed.). *The Legacy of Muslim Spain.* 1992. Leiden, The Netherlands: E. J. Brill, 1994 ed.

Jefferson, Thomas. *Notes on the State of Virginia.* Boston, MA: H. Sprague, 1802.

——. *Thomas Jefferson's Farm Book.* (Edwin Morris Betts, ed.). Charlottesville, VA: Thomas Jefferson Memorial Foundation, 1999.

Jensen, De Lamar. *Reformation Europe: Age of Reform and Revolution.* 1981. Lexington, MA: D. C. Heath and Co., 1992 ed.

Jensen, Merrill. *The New Nation: A History of the United States During the Confederation, 1781-1789.* New York, NY: Vintage, 1950.

——. *The Articles of Confederation: An Interpretation of the Social-Constitutional History of the American Revolution, 1774-1781.* Madison, WI: University of Wisconsin Press, 1959.

Jernegan, Marcus W. *Laboring and Dependent Classes in Colonial America.* Chicago, IL: University of Chicago Press, 1931.

Jervey, Theodore D. *Robert Y. Hayne and His Times.* New York, NY: Macmillan, 1909.

Jimerson, Randall C. *The Private Civil War: Popular Thought During the Sectional Conflict.* Baton Rouge, LA: Louisiana State University Press, 1988.

Johannsen, Robert Walter. *Lincoln, the South, and Slavery: The Political Dimension.* Baton Rouge, LA: Louisiana State University Press, 1991.

Johnsen, Julie E. *The Negro Problem.* New York, NY: H. W. Wilson Co., 1921.

Johnson, Adam Rankin. *The Partisan Rangers of the Confederate States Army.* Louisville, KY: George G. Fetter, 1904.

Johnson, Allen W., and Timothy Earle. *The Evolution of Human Societies: From Foraging Group to Agrarian State.* Stanford, CA: Stanford University Press, 1987.

Johnson, Benjamin Heber. *Making of the American West: People and Perspectives.* Santa Barbara, CA: ABC-Clio, 2007.

Johnson, Clint. *The Politically Incorrect Guide to the South (and Why It Will Rise Again).* Washington, D.C.: Regnery, 2006.

——. *A Vast and Fiendish Plot: The Confederate Attack on New York City.* New York, NY: Kensington, 2010.

Johnson, Ludwell H. *North Against South: The American Iliad, 1848-1877.* 1978. Columbia, SC: Foundation for American Education, 1993 ed.

Johnson, Michael, and James L. Roark. *Black Masters: A Free Family of Color in the Old South.* New York, NY: W.W. Norton, 1984.

Johnson, Oliver. *William Lloyd Garrison and His Times.* 1879. Boston, MA: Houghton Mifflin and Co., 1881 ed.

Johnson, Robert Underwood (ed.). *Battles and Leaders of the Civil War.* 4 vols. New York, NY: The Century Co., 1884-1888.

Johnson, Thomas Cary. *The Life and Letters of Robert Lewis Dabney.* Richmond, VA: Presbyterian Committee of Publication, 1903.

Johnston, William D. *Slavery in Rhode Island, 1755-1776.* Providence, RI: Rhode Island Historical Society,

1894.

Jones, Charles Colcock. *The Religious Instruction of the Negroes in the United States.* Savannah, GA: Thomas Purse, 1842.

Jones, Gwyn. *A History of the Vikings.* 1968. Oxford, UK: Oxford University Press, 1984 ed.

Jones, Jacqueline. *Labor of Love, Labor of Sorrow: Black Women and the Family From Slavery to the Present.* New York, NY: Basic Books, 1985.

Jones, John Beauchamp. *A Rebel War Clerk's Diary at the Confederate States Capital.* 2 vols. in 1. Philadelphia, PA: J. B. Lippincott and Co., 1866.

Jones, John William. *Personal Reminiscences, Anecdotes, and Letters of Gen. Robert E. Lee.* New York, NY: D. Appleton and Co., 1874.

——. *The Davis Memorial Volume; Or Our Dead President, Jefferson Davis and the World's Tribute to His Memory.* Atlanta, GA: B. F. Johnson and Co., 1889.

Jones, Norrece T., Jr. *Born a Child of Freedom, Yet a Slave: Mechanisms of Control and Strategies of Resistance in Antebellum South Carolina.* Hanover, NH: Wesleyan University Press, 1990.

Jones, Prudence, and Nigel Pennick. *A History of Pagan Europe.* London, UK: Routledge, 1995.

Jones, Wilmer L. *Generals in Blue and Gray.* 2 vols. Westport, CT: Praeger, 2004.

Jordan, Don, and Michael Walsh. *White Cargo: The Forgotten History of Britain's White Slaves in America.* New York, NY: New York University Press, 2008.

Jordan, Ervin L. *Black Confederates and Afro-Yankees in Civil War Virginia.* Charlottesville, VA: University Press of Virginia, 1995.

Jordan, Thomas, and John P. Pryor. *The Campaigns of General Nathan Bedford Forrest and of Forrest's Cavalry.* New Orleans, LA: Blelock and Co., 1868.

Jordan, Winthrop D. *White Over Black: American Attitudes Toward the Negro 1550-1812.* Chapel Hill, NC: University of North Carolina Press, 1968.

Josephus, Flavius. *Josephus: Complete Works.* Circa AD 75-94. (William Whiston, trans.) 1960. Grand Rapids, MI: Kregel Publications, 1980 ed.

Joshel, Sandra R. *Work, Identity, and Legal Status at Rome: A Study of the Occupational Inscriptions.* Norman, OK: University of Oklahoma Press, 1992.

Joyner, Charles. *Down by the Riverside: A South Carolina Slave Community.* Urbana, IL: University of Illinois Press, 1984.

Julian, George Washington. *Speeches on Political Questions.* New York, NY: Hurd and Houghton, 1872.

Kagan, Donald. *Problems in Ancient History - Vol. 1: The Ancient Near East and Greece.* 1966. New York, NY: Macmillan, 1975 ed.

Kamble, N. D. *Bonded Labor in India.* New Delhi, India: Uppal, 1982.

Kane, Joseph Nathan. *Facts About the Presidents: A Compilation of Biographical and Historical Data.* 1959. New York, NY: Ace, 1976 ed.

Karasch, Mary. *Slave Life in Rio de Janeiro.* Princeton, NJ: Princeton University Press, 1987.

Katcher, Philip. *The Civil War Source Book.* 1992. New York, NY: Facts on File, 1995 ed.

——. *Brassey's Almanac: The American Civil War.* London, UK: Brassey's, 2003.

Katz, William Loren. *Black Indians: A Hidden Heritage.* New York, NY: Simon and Schuster, 2012.

Kautz, August Valentine. *Customs of Service for Non-Commissioned Officers and Soldiers (as Derived from Law and Regulations and Practised in the Army of the United States).* Philadelphia, PA: J. B. Lippincott and Co., 1864.

Keckley, Elizabeth. *Behind the Scenes, or Thirty Years a Slave, and Four Years in the White House.* New York, NY: G. W. Carlton and Co., 1868.

Kelly, Alfred H., Winfred A. Harbison, and Herman Belz. *The American Constitution: Its Origins and Development* (Vol. 2). 1965. New York, NY: W.W. Norton, 1991 ed.

Kemble, Frances Anne. *Journal of a Residence on a Georgian Plantation in 1838-1839.* New York, NY: Harper and Brothers, 1864.

Kennedy, James Ronald, and Walter Donald Kennedy. *The South Was Right!* Gretna, LA: Pelican Publishing Co., 1994.

——. *Why Not Freedom!: America's Revolt Against Big Government.* Gretna, LA: Pelican Publishing Co., 2005.

——. *Nullifying Tyranny: Creating Moral Communities in an Immoral Society.* Gretna, LA: Pelican Publishing Co., 2010.

Kennedy, Walter Donald. *Myths of American Slavery.* Gretna, LA: Pelican Publishing Co., 2003.

Kennett, Lee B. *Sherman: A Soldier's Life.* 2001. New York, NY: HarperCollins, 2002 ed.

Kettell, Thomas Prentice. *History of the Great Rebellion.* Hartford, CT: L. Stebbins, 1865.

Kinder, Hermann, and Werner Hilgemann. *The Anchor Atlas of World History: From the French Revolution to the American Bicentennial.* 2 vols. Garden City, NY: Anchor, 1978.

King, Charles R. (ed.). *The Life and Correspondence of Rufus King.* 6 vols. New York, NY: G. P. Putnam's Sons, 1897.

King, Edward. *The Great South: A Record of Journeys.* Hartford, CT: American Publishing Co., 1875.

King, Moses. *King's Handbook of New York City: An Outline History and Description of the American Metropolis.* Boston, MA: Moses King, 1892.

Kingsley, Vine Wright. *Reconstruction in America.* New York, NY: W. I. Pooley, 1865.

Kinloch, Graham C. *The Dynamics of Race Relations: A Sociological Analysis.* New York, NY: McGraw-Hill, 1974.

Kinshasa, Kwando Mbiassi. *Black Resistance to the Ku Klux Klan in the Wake of the Civil War.* Jefferson, NC: McFarland and Co., 2006.

Kirkland, Edward Chase. *The Peacemakers of 1864.* New York, NY: Macmillan, 1927.

Kishlansky, Mark, Patrick Geary, and Patricia O'Brien. *Civilization in the West - Vol. 2: Since 1555.* New York, NY: Harper Collins, 1995.

Klein, Herbert S. *Slavery in the Americas: A Comparative Study of Virginia and Cuba.* Chicago, IL: University of Chicago Press, 1967.

——. *The Middle Passage: Comparative Studies in the Atlantic Slave Trade.* Princeton, NJ: Princeton University Press, 1978.

——. *African Slavery in Latin America and the Caribbean.* New York, NY: Oxford University Press, 1986.

Klein, Martin A. (ed.). *Breaking the Chains: Slavery, Bondage and Emancipation in Africa and Asia.* Madison, WI: University of Wisconsin Press, 1993.

——. *Historical Dictionary of Slavery and Abolition.* Lanham, MD: Scarecrow Press, 2002.

Klingaman, William K. *Abraham Lincoln and the Road to Emancipation, 1861-1865.* 2001. New York, NY: Penguin, 2002 ed.

Klinkner, Philip A., and Rogers M. Smith. *The Unsteady March: The Rise and Decline of Racial Equality in America.* 1999. Chicago, IL: University of Chicago Press, 2002 ed.

Knight, Charles. *The Popular History of England: An Illustrated History of Society and Government From the Earliest Period to Our Own Times.* 8 vols. London, UK: Bradbury and Evans, 1862.

Knoblock, Glenn A. *The American Clipper Ship, 1845-1920: A Comprehensive History, With a Listing of Builders and their Ships.* Jefferson, NC: Mcfarland and Co., 2014.

Knowles, Louis L., and Kenneth Prewitt (eds.). *Institutional Racism in America.* Englewood Cliffs, NJ: Prentice-Hall, 1969.

Knox, Thomas Wallace. *Camp-Fire and Cotton-Field: Southern Adventure in Time of War - Life With the Union Armies, and Residence on a Louisiana Plantation.* New York, NY: Blelock and Co., 1865.

Koger, Larry. *Black Slaveowners: Free Black Slave Masters in South Carolina, 1790-1860.* Columbia, SC: University of South Carolina Press, 1995.

Kolchin, Peter. *American Slavery, 1619-1877.* 1993. New York, NY: Hill and Wang, 2003 ed.

Kousser, J. Morgan. *The Shaping of Southern Politics.* New Haven, CT: Yale University Press, 1974.

Kramer, Samuel Noah. *Cradle of Civilization.* New York, NY: Time-Life Books, 1967.

Kramnick, Isaac. *James Madison, Alexander Hamilton, and John Jay: The Federalist Papers.* 1788. London, UK: Penguin, 1987 ed.

Krauthamer, Barbara. *Black Slaves, Indian Masters: Slavery, Emancipation, and Citizenship in the Native American South.* Chapel Hill, NC: University of North Carolina Press, 2013.

Kuczynski, Jürgen. *The Rise of the Working Class.* 1968. New York, NY: McGraw-Hill, 1971 ed.

Lai, Walton Look. *Indentured Labor, Caribbean Sugar: Chinese and Indian Migrants to the British West Indies, 1838-1918.* Baltimore, MD: Johns Hopkins University Press, 1993.

Lamb, Daniel Smith. *Howard University Medical Department, Washington, D.C.: A Historical, Biographical and Statistical Souvenir.* Washington, D.C.: R. Beresford, 1900.

Lamon, Ward Hill. *The Life of Abraham Lincoln: From His Birth to His Inauguration as President.* Boston, MA: James R. Osgood and Co., 1872.

——. *Recollections of Abraham Lincoln: 1847-1865.* Chicago, IL: A. C. McClurg and Co., 1895.

Lancaster, Bruce, and J. H. Plumb. *The American Heritage Book of the Revolution.* 1958. New York, NY: Dell, 1975 ed.

Lang, J. Stephen. *The Complete Book of Confederate Trivia.* Shippensburg, PA: Burd Street Press, 1996.

Langer, William L. (ed.). *Perspectives in Western Civilization.* New York, NY: American Heritage, 1972.

Lanier, Robert S. (ed.). *The Photographic History of the Civil War.* 10 vols. Springfield, MA: Patriot Publishing Co., 1911.

Lanning, Michael Lee. *The African-American Soldier: From Crispus Attucks to Colin Powell.* 1997. New York, NY: Citadel Press, 2004 ed.

Latham, Henry. *Black and White: A Journal of a Three Months' Tour in the United States.* Philadelphia, PA: Lippincott, 1867.

Lauber, Almon Wheeler. *Indian Slavery in Colonial Times Within the Present Limits of the United States.* 1913. New York, NY: AMS Press, 1969 ed.

Lawrence, William. *Life of Amos A. Lawrence.* Boston, MA: Houghton, Mifflin, and Co., 1899.

Lee, Robert E., Jr. *Recollections and Letters of General Robert E. Lee.* New York, NY: Doubleday, Page and Co., 1904.

Leech, Margaret. *Reveille in Washington, 1860-1865.* 1941. Alexandria, VA: Time-Life Books, 1980 ed.

Leigh, Frances Butler. *Ten Years on a Georgia Plantation Since the War.* London, UK: Richard Bentley and Son, 1883.

Lemay, J. A. Leo, and P. M. Zall (eds.). *Benjamin Franklin's Autobiography: An Authoritative Text, Backgrounds, Criticism.* 1791. New York, NY: W. W. Norton and Co., 1986 ed.

Lemire, Elise. *Black Walden: Slavery and Its Aftermath in Concord, Massachusetts.* Philadelphia, PA: University of Pennsylvania Press, 2009.

Leonard, Jonathan Norton. *Ancient America.* New York, NY: Time, 1967.

Lerner, Gerda. *The Creation of Patriarchy.* New York, NY: Oxford University Press, 1986.

Lerner, Max. *America as a Civilization: Vol. 2 - Culture and Personality.* 1957. New York, NY: Simon and Schuster, 1961 ed.

Lester, Charles Edwards. *Life and Public Services of Charles Sumner.* New York, NY: U.S. Publishing Co., 1874.

Lester, John C., and D. L. Wilson. *Ku Klux Klan: Its Origin, Growth, and Disbandment.* 1884. New York, NY: Neale Publishing, 1905 ed.

Levine, Lawrence. *Black Culture and Black Consciousness: Afro-American Folk Thought From Slavery to Freedom.* New York, NY: Oxford University Press, 1977.

Lewis, Bernard. *Race and Slavery in the Middle-East.* New York, NY: Oxford University Press, 1990.

Lewis, Lloyd. *Myths After Lincoln.* 1929. New York, NY: The Press of the Reader's Club, 1941 ed.

Lewis, Ronald L. *Coal, Iron, and Slaves: Industrial Slavery in Maryland and Virginia, 1715-1865.* Westport, CT: Greenwood Press, 1979.

LeVert, Suzanne (ed.). *The Civil War Society's Encyclopedia of the Civil War.* New York, NY: Wings Books, 1997.

Levin, Mark R. *Liberty and Tyranny: A Conservative Manifesto.* New York, NY: Threshold, 2009.

Levy, Andrew. *The First Emancipator: Slavery, Religion, and the Quiet Revolution of Robert Carter.* New York, NY: Random House, 2005.

Libby, David J. *Slavery and Frontier Mississippi, 1720-1835.* Jackson, MS: University of Mississippi Press, 2004.

Liddell, Henry George. *A History of Rome: From the Earliest Times to the Establishment of the Empire.* 2 vols. London, UK: John Murray, 1855.

Lincoln, Abraham. *The Autobiography of Abraham Lincoln* (selected from the *Complete Works of Abraham Lincoln*, 1894, by John G. Nicolay and John Hay). New York, NY: Francis D. Tandy Co., 1905.

Lincoln, Abraham, and Stephen A. Douglas. *Political Debates Between Abraham Lincoln and Stephen A. Douglas.* Cleveland, OH: Burrows Brothers Co., 1894.

Lindsey, Benjamin J. *Old Marblehead Sea Captains and the Ships in Which They Sailed.* Marblehead, MA: Marblehead Historical Society, 1915.

Linton, Ralph. *The Study of Man: An Introduction.* New York, NY: Appleton-Century-Crofts, 1936.

Littell, Eliakim (ed.). *The Living Age.* Seventh Series, Vol. 30. Boston, MA: The Living Age Co., 1906.

Litwack, Leon F. *North of Slavery: The Negro in the Free States, 1790-1860.* Chicago, IL: University of Chicago Press, 1961.

——. *Been in the Storm So Long: The Aftermath of Slavery.* New York, NY: Vintage, 1980.

Livermore, Thomas L. *Numbers and Losses in the Civil War in America, 1861-65.* 1900. Carlisle, PA: John Kallmann, 1996 ed.

Livingstone, E. A. *The Concise Oxford Dictionary of the Christian Church.* 1977. Oxford, UK: Oxford University Press, 1980 ed.

Livingstone, William. *Livingstone's History of the Republican Party.* 2 vols. Detroit, MI: William Livingstone, 1900.

Locke, John. *Two Treatises of Government* (Mark Goldie, ed.). 1924. London, UK: Everyman, 1998 ed.

Lodge, Henry Cabot (ed.). *The Works of Alexander Hamilton.* 12 vols. New York, NY: G. P. Putnam's Sons, 1904.

Logan, John Alexander. *The Great Conspiracy: Its Origin and History.* New York, NY: A. R. Hart, 1886.

Logsdon, David R. (ed.). *Eyewitnesses at the Battle of Franklin.* 1988. Nashville, TN: Kettle Mills Press, 2000 ed.

——. *Tennessee Antebellum Trail Guidebook.* Nashville, TN: Kettle Mills Press, 1995.

Long, Armistead Lindsay, and Marcus J. Wright. *Memoirs of Robert E. Lee: His Military and Personal History.* New York, NY: J. M. Stoddart and Co., 1887.

Long, Everette Beach, and Barbara Long. *The Civil War Day by Day: An Almanac, 1861-1865.* 1971. New York, NY: Da Capo Press, 1985 ed.

Lonn, Ella. *Foreigners in the Confederacy.* 1940. Chapel Hill, NC: University of North Carolina Press, 2002 ed.

Lott, Stanley K. *The Truth About American Slavery.* 2004. Clearwater, SC: Eastern Digital Resources, 2005 ed.

Lovejoy, Paul E. *Transformations in Slavery: A History of Slavery in Africa.* Cambridge, UK: Cambridge University Press, 1983.

Lovejoy, Paul E., and Jan S. Hogendorn. *Slow Death for Slavery: The Course of Abolition in Northern Nigeria, 1897-1936.* Cambridge, UK: Cambridge University Press, 1993.

Löwenheim, Oded. *Predators and Parasites: Persistent Agents of Transnational Harm and Great Power Authority.* Ann Arbor, MI: University of Michigan Press, 2007.

Lubasz, Heinz (ed.). *Revolutions in Modern European History.* New York, NY: Macmillan, 1966.

Lubbock, Francis Richard. *Six Decades in Texas, or Memoirs of Francis Richard Lubbock, Governor of Texas in War-Time, 1861-1863.* 1899. Austin, TX: Ben C. Jones, 1900 ed.

Ludlow, Daniel H. (ed.). *Encyclopedia of Mormonism: The History, Scripture, Doctrine, and Procedure of the Church of Jesus Christ of Latter-Day Saints.* New York, NY: Macmillan, 1992.

Luna, Francisco Vidal, and Herbert S. Klein. *Slavery and the Economy of São Paulo, 1750-1850.* Stanford, CA: Stanford University Press, 2003.

Lyell, Charles. *A Second Visit to the United States of North America.* 2 vols. London, UK: John Murray, 1850.

Lytle, Andrew Nelson. *Bedford Forrest and His Critter Company.* New York, NY: G. P. Putnam's Sons, 1931.

Macaulay, Zachary. *Negro Slavery; Or a View of Some of the More Prominent Features of That State of Society, as it Exists in the United States of America and in the Colonies of the West Indies, Especially in Jamaica.* London, UK: Hatchard and Son, 1823.

MacDonald, William. *Select Documents Illustrative of the History of the United States 1776-1861.* New York, NY: Macmillan, 1897.

Macionis, John J. *Society: The Basics.* 1992. Saddle River, NJ: Prentice Hall, 1996 ed.

Mackay, Charles. *Life and Liberty in America, or Sketches of a Tour in the United States and Canada in 1857-58.* New York, NY: Harper and Brothers, 1859.

MacQuarrie, Kim. *The Last Days of the Incas.* New York, NY: Simon and Schuster, 2007.

Madden, Richard Robert. *Egypt and Mohammed Ali, Illustrative of the Condition of His Slaves and Subjects.* London, UK: Hamilton, Adams and Co., 1841.

——. *The Island of Cuba: Its Resources, Progress, and Prospects.* London, UK: Charles Gilpin, 1849.

Madison, James. *Letters and Other Writings of James Madison, Fourth President of the United States.* 4 vols. Philadelphia, PA: J. B. Lippincott and Co., 1865.

Magoffin, Ralph V. D., and Frederic Duncalf. *Ancient and Medieval History: The Rise of Classical Culture and the Development of Medieval Civilization.* Morristown, NJ: Silver Burdett Co., 1959.

Maihafer, Harry J. *War of Words: Abraham Lincoln and the Civil War Press.* Dulles, VA: Brassey's, 2001.

Main, Jackson Turner. *The Anti-Federalists: Critics of the Constitution, 1781-1788.* 1961. New York, NY: W. W. Norton and Co., 1974 ed.

Mallard, Robert Q. *Plantation Life Before Emancipation.* Richmond, VA: Whittet and Shepperson, 1892.

Malone, Ann Patton. *Sweet Chariot: Slave Family and Household Structure in Nineteenth-Century Louisiana.* Chapel Hill, NC: University of North Carolina Press, 1992.

Mancall, Peter C. (ed.). *The Atlantic World and Virginia, 1550-1624.* Chapel Hill, NC: University of North Carolina Press, 2007.

Mandel, Bernard. *Labor, Free and Slave: Workingmen and the Anti-Slavery Movement in the United States.* New York, NY: Associated Authors, 1955.

Manegold, C. S. *Ten Hills Farm: The Forgotten History of Slavery in the North.* Princeton, NJ: Princeton University Press, 2010.

Mann, Horace. *Slavery and the Slave-Trade in the District of Columbia.* Speech delivered in the House of Representatives of the United States, February 23, 1849. Philadelphia, PA: Merrihew and Thompson (printers), 1849.

Mann, Kristin. *Slavery and the Birth of an African City: Lagos, 1760-1900.* Bloomington, IN: Indiana University Press, 2007.

Manning, Patrick. *Slavery and African Life: Occidental, Oriental, and African Slave Traders.* Cambridge, UK: Cambridge University Press, 1990.

Manning, Timothy D., Sr. (ed.) *Lincoln Reconsidered: Conference Reader.* High Point, NC: Heritage Foundation Press, 2006.

Mannix, Daniel Pratt. *Black Cargoes: A History of the Atlantic Slave Trade, 1518-1865.* New York, NY: Viking, 1962.

Marsh, Edward G. (ed.). *Account of the Slavery of Friends in the Barbary States, Towards the Close of the Seventeenth Century.* London, UK: Edward G. Marsh, 1848.

Marshack, Alexander. *The Roots of Civilization: The Cognitive Beginnings of Man's First Art, Symbol, and Notation.* New York, NY: McGraw-Hill, 1972.

Marten, James. *The Children's Civil War.* Chapel Hill, NC: University of North Carolina Press, 1998.

Martin, Iain C. *The Quotable American Civil War.* Guilford, CT: Lyons Press, 2008.

Martin, Kingsley. *French Liberal Thought in the Eighteenth Century: A Study of Political Ideas From Bayle to Condorcet.* 1929. New York, NY: Harper and Row, 1963 ed.

Martineau, Harriet. *Society in America.* 3 vols. London, UK: Saunders and Otley, 1837.

——. *Retrospect of Western Travel.* 2 vols. London, UK: Saunders and Otley, 1838.

Martinez, James Michael. *Carpetbaggers, Cavalry, and the Ku Klux Klan: Exposing the Invisible Empire During Reconstruction.* Lanham, MD: Rowman and Littlefield, 2007.

Mason, Robert C. *George Mason of Virginia: Citizen, Statesman, Philosopher.* New York, NY: Oscar Aurelius Morgner, 1919.

Masur, Louis P. *The Real War Will Never Get In the Books: Selections From Writers During the Civil War.* New York, NY: Oxford University Press, 1993.

Mathes, Capt. J. Harvey. *General Forrest.* New York, NY: D. Appleton and Co., 1902.

Maude, H. E. *Slavers in Paradise: The Peruvian Slave Trade in Polynesia, 1862-1864.* Stanford, CT: Stanford University Press, 1981.

Maury, Dabney Herndon. *Recollections of a Virginian in the Mexican, Indian, and Civil Wars.* New York, NY: Charles Scribner's Sons, 1894.

Mayer, Brantz (ed.). *Captain Canot; or, Twenty Years of an African Slaver.* New York, NY: D. Appleton and Co., 1854.

Mayer, David N. *The Constitutional Thought of Thomas Jefferson.* Charlottesville, VA: University of Virginia Press, 1995.

Mayer, Henry. *All on Fire: William Lloyd Garrison and the Abolition of Slavery.* New York, NY: St. Martin's Press, 1998.

Mbiti, John S. *African Religions and Philosophy.* 1969. Nairobi, Kenya: Heinemann Kenya Limited, 1988 ed.

McAfee, Ward M. *Citizen Lincoln.* Hauppauge, NY: Nova History Publications, 2004.

McCabe, James Dabney. *Our Martyred President: The Life and Public Services of Gen. James A. Garfield, Twentieth President of the United States.* Philadelphia, PA: National Publishing Co., 1881.

McCallen, Robert Seth (pseudonym Dick Maple). *Master and Slave.* St. Louis, MO: National Book Concern, 1907.

McCarty, Burke (ed.). *Little Sermons In Socialism by Abraham Lincoln.* Chicago, IL: The Chicago Daily Socialist, 1910.

McClure, Alexander Kelly. *Abraham Lincoln and Men of War-Times: Some Personal Recollections of War and Politics During the Lincoln Administration.* Philadelphia, PA: Times Publishing Co., 1892.

——. *Our Presidents and How We Make Them.* New York, NY: Harper and Brothers, 1900.

McCulloch, James Ramsay. *A Dictionary of Geographical, Statistical, and Historical, of the Various Countries, Places, and Principal Natural Objects in the World.* 2 vols. London, UK: Longman, Orme, Brown, Green, and Longmans, 1841.

McCullough, David. *John Adams.* New York, NY: Touchstone, 2001.

McCusker, John J., and Russell R. Menard. *The Economy of British America, 1607-1789.* Chapel Hill, NC: University of North Carolina Press, 1985.

McDannald, A. H. (ed.). *The Modern Encyclopedia.* 1 vol. New York, NY: William H. Wise and Co., 1933.

McDonald, Forrest. *States' Rights and the Union: Imperium in Imperio, 1776-1876.* Lawrence, KS: University Press of Kansas, 2000.

McDonough, James Lee, and Thomas L. Connelly. *Five Tragic Hours: The Battle of Franklin.* 1983. Knoxville, TN: University of Tennessee Press, 2001 ed.

McElroy, Robert. *Jefferson Davis: The Unreal and the Real.* 1937. New York, NY: Smithmark, 1995 ed.

McEnnis, John T. *The White Slaves of Free America: Being an Account of the Sufferings, Privations and Hardships of the*

Weary Toilers in Our Great Cities. Chicago, IL: R. S. Peale and Co., 1888.
McFeely, William S. *Yankee Stepfather: General O. O. Howard and the Freedmen - The Story of a Civil War Promise to Former Slaves Made—and Broken*. 1968. New York, NY: W. W. Norton, 1994 ed.
——. *Grant: A Biography*. 1981. New York, NY: W. W. Norton, 1982 ed.
McGarry, Daniel D., and Clarence L. Hohl, Jr. (eds.). *Sources of Western Civilization: Vol. 1 - From the Ancient World to the Reformation Era*. Boston, MA: Houghton Mifflin Co., 1962.
McGehee, Jacob Owen. *Causes That Led to the War Between the States*. Atlanta, GA: A. B. Caldwell, 1915.
McGlynn, Frank, and Seymour Drescher (eds.). *The Meaning of Freedom: Economics, Politics and Culture After Slavery*. Pittsburgh, PA: University of Pittsburgh Press, 1992.
McGuire, Hunter, and George L. Christian. *The Confederate Cause and Conduct in the War Between the States*. Richmond, VA: L. H. Jenkins, 1907.
McHenry, George. *The Cotton Trade: Its Bearing Upon the Prosperity of Great Britain and Commerce of the American Republics, Considered in Connection with the System of Negro Slavery in the Confederate States*. London, UK: Saunders, Otley, and Co., 1863.
McIlwaine, Shields. *Memphis Down in Dixie*. New York, NY: E. P. Dutton, 1848.
McKay, John P., Bennett D. Hill, and John Buckler. *A History of Western Society - Vol. 1: From Antiquity to the Enlightenment*. Boston, MA: Houghton Mifflin, 1987.
——. *A History of Western Society - Vol. 2: Since 1500*. Boston, MA: Houghton Mifflin, 1988.
McKenzie, John L. *Dictionary of the Bible*. New York, NY: Collier, 1965.
McKim, Randolph H. *The Soul of Lee*. New York, NY: Longmans, Green and Co., 1918.
McKissack, Patricia C., and Frederick McKissack. *Sojourner Truth: Ain't I a Woman?* New York: NY: Scholastic, 1992.
McKitrick, Eric (ed.). *Slavery Defended: The Views of the Old South*. Englewood Cliffs, NJ: Prentice-Hall, 1963.
McLoughlin, William G. *Isaac Backus and the American Pietistic Tradition*. Boston, MA: Little, Brown and Co., 1967.
McManus, Edgar J. *A History of Negro Slavery in New York*. Syracuse, NY: Syracuse University Press, 1966.
——. *Black Bondage in the North*. Syracuse, NY: Syracuse University Press, 1973.
McManus, Jason (ed.). *The Divine Campaigns: Timeframe AD 1100-1200*. Alexandria, VA: Time-Life, 1988.
McMaster, John Bach. *Our House Divided: A History of the People of the United States During Lincoln's Administration*. 1927. New York, NY: Premier, 1961 ed.
McNeese, Tim. *The American Colonies*. Dayton, OH: Milliken, 2002.
McNeill, William H. *The Rise of the West: A History of the Human Community*. 1963. New York, NY: Mentor, 1965 ed.
McPherson, Edward. *The Political History of the United States of America, During the Great Rebellion (from November 6, 1860, to July 4, 1864)*. Washington, D.C.: Philp and Solomons, 1864.
——. *The Political History of the United States of America, During the Period of Reconstruction, (from April 15, 1865, to July 15, 1870,) Including a Classified Summary of the Legislation of the Thirty-ninth, Fortieth, and Forty-first Congresses*. Washington, D.C.: Solomons and Chapman, 1875.
McPherson, James M. *The Struggle for Equality: Abolitionists and the Negro in the Civil War and Reconstruction*. 1964. Princeton, NJ: Princeton University Press, 1992 ed.
——. *The Negro's Civil War: How American Negroes Felt and Acted During the War for the Union*. 1965. Chicago, IL: University of Illinois Press, 1982 ed.
——. *Battle Cry of Freedom: The Civil War Era*. Oxford, UK: Oxford University Press, 2003.
——. *The Atlas of the Civil War*. Philadelphia, PA: Courage Books, 2005.
McPherson, James M., and the staff of the *New York Times*. *The Most Fearful Ordeal: Original Coverage of the Civil War by Writers and Reporters of the New York Times*. New York, NY: St. Martin's Press, 2004.
McWhiney, Grady, and Judith Lee Hallock. *Braxton Bragg and Confederate Defeat*. 2 vols. Tuscaloosa, AL: University of Alabama Press, 1991.
McWhiney, Grady, and Perry D. Jamieson. *Attack and Die: Civil War Military Tactics and the Southern Heritage*. Tuscaloosa, AL: University of Alabama Press, 1982.
Mead, Margaret. *Male and Female: A Study of the Sexes in a Changing World*. 1949. New York, NY: Mentor, 1959 ed.
——. *Science and the Concept of Race*. New York, NY: Columbia University Press, 1968.
Meine, Franklin J. (ed.). *The Consolidated-Webster Encyclopedic Reference Dictionary*. 1940. Chicago, IL: Consolidated Book Publishers, 1947 ed.
Meillassoux, Claude. *The Anthropology of Slavery: The Womb of Iron and Gold*. Chicago, IL: University of Chicago Press, 1991.

Melden, Charles Manly. *From Slave to Citizen*. New York, NY: Methodist Book Concern, 1921.

Melick, Charles Wesley. *Some Phases of the Negro Question*. Mt. Rainier, MD: David H. Deloe, 1908.

Melish, Joanne Pope. *Disowning Slavery: Gradual Emancipation and "Race" in New England 1780-1860*. Ithaca, NY: Cornell University Press, 1998.

Mellafe, Rolando. *Negro Slavery in Latin America*. Berkeley, CA: University of California Press, 1975.

Meltzer, Milton. *Slavery: A World History*. 2 vols. in 1. 1971. New York, NY: Da Capo Press, 1993 ed.

Mendelsohn, I. *Slavery in the Ancient Near East: A Comparative Study of Slavery in Babylonia, Assyria, Syria, Palestine, from the Middle of the Third Millennium*. New York, NY: Oxford University Press, 1949.

Mendelssohn, Kurt. *The Riddle of the Pyramids*. 1974. London, UK: Thames and Hudson, 1986 ed.

Meriwether, Elizabeth Avery. *Facts and Falsehoods Concerning the War on the South, 1861-1865*. (Originally written under the pseudonym "George Edmonds.") Memphis, TN: A. R. Taylor, 1904.

Message of the President of the United States and Accompanying Documents to the Two Houses of Congress at the Commencement of the Third Session of the 40th Congress. Washington, D.C.: Government Printing Office, 1868.

Metzger, Bruce M., and Michael D. Coogan (eds.). *The Oxford Companion to the Bible*. New York, NY: Oxford University Press, 1993.

Miers, Suzanne. *Britain and the Ending of the Slave Trade*. London, UK: Longmans, 1975.

Miers, Suzanne, and Igor Kopytoff (eds.). *Slavery in Africa: Historical and Anthropological Perspectives*. Madison, WI: University of Wisconsin Press, 1977.

Miers, Suzanne, and Martin A. Klein (eds.). *Slavery and Colonial Rule in Africa*. Abingdon, UK: Frank Cass, 1999.

Miers, Suzanne, and Richard Roberts (eds.). *The End of Slavery in Africa*. Madison, WI: University of Wisconsin Press, 1988.

Miles, Tiya. *Ties That Bind: The Story of an Afro-Cherokee Family in Slavery and Freedom*. Berkeley, CA: University of California Press, 2005.

Miller, Francis Trevelyan. *Portrait Life of Lincoln*. Springfield, MA: Patriot Publishing Co., 1910.

Miller, John Chester. *The Wolf By the Ears: Thomas Jefferson and Slavery*. 1977. Charlottesville, VA: University Press of Virginia, 1994 ed.

Miller, Joseph C. *Way of Death: Merchant Capitalism and the Angolan Slave Trade, 1730-1830*. Madison, WI: University of Wisconsin Press, 1988.

Miller, Marion Mills (ed.). *Great Debates in American History*. 14 vols. New York, NY: Current Literature, 1913.

Miller, Nathan. *Star-Spangled Men: America's Ten Worst Presidents*. New York, NY: Touchstone, 1998.

Mills, Dorothy. *The Middle Ages*. New York, NY: G. P. Putnam's Sons, 1935.

Milton, Giles. *White Gold: The Extraordinary Story of Thomas Pellow and Islam's One Million White Slaves*. New York, NY: Farrar, Straus, and Giroux, 2005.

Min, Pyong Gap (ed.). *Encyclopedia of Racism in the United States*. 3 vols. Westport, CT: Greenwood Press, 2005.

Minges, Patrick N. *Slavery in the Cherokee Nation: The Keetoowah Society and the Defining of a People, 1855-1867*. New York, NY: Routledge, 2003.

Minor, Charles Landon Carter. *The Real Lincoln: From the Testimony of His Contemporaries*. Richmond, VA: Everett Waddey Co., 1904.

Mirabello, Mark. *Handbook for Rebels and Outlaws*. Oxford, UK: Mandrake of Oxford, 2009.

Mish, Frederick C. (ed.). *Webster's Ninth New Collegiate Dictionary*. 1984. Springfield, MA: Merriam-Webster.

Mitchell, J. (ed.). *Race Riots in Black and White*. Englewood Cliffs, NJ: Prentice-Hall, 1970.

Mitchell, James T., and Henry Flanders (eds.). *The Statutes at Large of Pennsylvania From 1682-1801*. 16 vols. Harrisburg, PA: State Printer, 1896-1911.

Mitchell, Margaret. *Gone With the Wind*. 1936. New York, NY: Avon, 1973 ed.

Mitgang, Herbert (ed.). *Lincoln As They Saw Him*. 1956. New York, NY: Collier, 1962 ed.

Mode, Peter George. *Source Book and Bibliographical Guide for American Church History*. Menasha, WI: Collegiate Press, 1921.

Montague, Ashley. *Man's Most Dangerous Myth: The Fallacy of Race*. 1942. Walnut Creek, CA: AltaMira Press, 1997 ed.

——. *Statement on Race*. 1951. New York, NY: Oxford University Press, 1972 ed.

——. (ed.) *The Concept of Race*. 1964. London, UK: Collier Books, 1969 ed.

Montefiore, Simon Sebag. *Stalin: The Court of the Red Star*. 2003. New York, NY: Vintage, 2004 ed.

Montgomery, David Henry. *The Leading Facts of English History*. 1896. Boston, MA: Ginn and Co., 1900 ed.

——. *The Student's American History*. 1897. Boston, MA: Ginn and Co., 1905 ed.

Mooney, Charles C. *Slavery in Tennessee*. Bloomington, IN: Indiana University Press, 1957.

Moore, Clark D., and Ann Dunbar (eds.). *Africa Yesterday and Today*. 1968. New York, NY: 1970 ed.

Moore, Frank (ed.). *The Rebellion Record: A Diary of American Events*. 12 vols. New York, NY: G. P. Putnam, 1861.

Moore, George Henry. *Notes on the History of Slavery in Massachusetts*. New York, NY: D. Appleton and Co., 1866.

Moorhead, James H. *American Apocalypse: Yankee Protestants and the Civil War, 1860-1869*. New Haven, CT: Yale University Press, 1971.

Morel, Edmund D. *The Congo Slave State: A Protest Against the New African Slavery*. Liverpool, UK: John Richardson and Sons, 1903.

Morey, William Carey. *Outlines of Greek History With a Survey of Ancient Oriental Nations*. New York, NY: American Book Co., 1903.

Morgan, Edmund. *American Slavery, American Freedom: The Ordeal of Colonial Virginia*. New York, NY: W. W. Norton, 1975.

Morgan, Joseph. *A Compleat History of the Piratical States of Barbary*. London, UK: R. Griffiths, 1750.

Morison, Samuel Eliot, and Henry Steele Commager. *The Growth of the American Republic*. 2 vols. 1930. New York, NY: Oxford University Press, 1965 ed.

Morel, Edmund Dene. *Affairs of West Africa*. London, UK: William Heinemann, 1902.

——. *The Congo Slave State*. Liverpool, UK: William Heinemann, 1903.

Mörner, Magnus. *Race Mixture in the History of Latin America*. Boston, MA: Little, Brown and Co., 1967.

Morrall, John B. *Political Thought in Medieval Times*. 1958. New York, NY: Harper Torchbooks, 1962 ed.

Morris, Benjamin Franklin (ed.). *The Life of Thomas Morris: Pioneer and Long a Legislator of Ohio, and U.S. Senator from 1833 to 1839*. Cincinnati, OH: Moore, Wilstach, Keys and Overend, 1856.

Morris, Charles (ed.). *Winston's Cumulative Encyclopedia*. Philadelphia, PA: John C. Winston Co., 1912.

Morris, Richard B. *Government and Labor in Early America*. New York, NY: Columbia University Press, 1947.

Morris, Thomas D. *Free Men All: The Personal Liberty Laws of the North, 1780-1861*. Baltimore, MD: Johns Hopkins University Press, 1974.

——. *Southern Slavery and the Law, 1619-1860*. Chapel Hill, NC: University of North Carolina Press, 1996.

Morrissey, Marietta. *Slave Women in the New World: Gender Stratification in the Caribbean*. Lawrence, KS: University Press of Kansas, 1989.

Morton, Fred. *Children of Ham: Freed Slaves and Fugitive Slaves on the Kenya Coast, 1873 to 1907*. Boulder, CO: Westview, 1990.

Morton, John Watson. *The Artillery of Nathan Bedford Forrest's Cavalry*. Nashville, TN: The M. E. Church, 1909.

Morton, Louis. *Robert Carter of Nomini Hall: A Virginia Tobacco Planter of the Eighteenth Century*. Charlottesville, VA: University Press of Virginia, 1969.

Morton, Patricia. *Disfigured Images: The Historical Assault on Afro-American Women*. New York, NY: Greenwood Press, 1991.

Moses, John. *Illinois: Historical and Statistical, Comprising the Essential Facts of Its Planting and Growth as a Province, County, Territory, and State* (Vol. 2). Chicago, IL: Fergus Printing Co., 1892.

Moss, Richard Shannon. *Slavery on Long Island: A Study in Local Institutional and Early African-American Communal Life*. New York, NY: Garland, 1993.

Mostert, Noel. *The Line Upon the Wind: The Great War at Sea, 1793-1815*. New York, NY: W. W. Norton, 2008.

Muehlbauer, Matthew S., and David J. Ulbrich. *Ways of War: American Military History From the Colonial Era to the Twenty-First Century*. New York, NY: Routledge, 2014.

Mullen, Robert W. *Blacks in America's Wars: The Shift in Attitudes From the Revolutionary War to Vietnam*. 1973. New York, NY: Pathfinder, 1991 ed.

Muller, Herbert J. *The Uses of the Past: Profiles of Former Societies*. 1954. New York, NY: Mentor, 1960 ed.

Munford, Beverly Bland. *Virginia's Attitude Toward Slavery and Secession*. 1909. Richmond, VA: L. H. Jenkins, 1914 ed.

Murnane, William J. *The Penguin Guide to Ancient Egypt*. 1983. Harmondsworth, UK: Penguin, 1984 ed.

Murphy, Jim. *A Savage Thunder: Antietam and the Bloody Road to Freedom*. New York, NY: Margaret K. McElderry, 2009.

Muzzey, David Saville. *The American Adventure*. 2 vols. 1924. New York, NY: Harper and Brothers, 1927 ed.

Myers, Philip Van Ness. *Ancient History*. 1904. Boston, MA: Ginn and Co., 1916 ed.

Nall, John Thomas. *God Save the South: A Treasure Chest of Forbidden Information*. Bloomington, IN:

AuthorHouse, 2013.

Napolitano, Andrew P. *The Constitution in Exile: How the Federal Government Has Seized Power by Rewriting the Supreme Law of the Land.* Nashville, TN: Nelson Current, 2006.

Nash, Gary B. *The Urban Crucible: The Northern Seaports and the Origins of the American Revolution.* Cambridge, MA: Harvard University Press, 1986.

Nash, Gary B., and Jean R. Soderlund. *Freedom By Degrees: Emancipation in Pennsylvania and Its Aftermath.* Oxford, UK: Oxford University Press, 1991.

Naylor, Celia E. *African Cherokees in Indian Territory: From Chattel to Citizens.* Chapel Hill, NC: University of North Carolina Press, 2008.

Neely, Mark E., Jr. *The Fate of Liberty: Abraham Lincoln and Civil Liberties.* New York, NY: Oxford University Press, 1991.

Neilson, William Allan (ed.). *Webster's Biographical Dictionary.* Springfield, MA: G. and C. Merriam Co., 1943.

Nell, William Cooper. *The Colored Patriots of the American Revolution, With Sketches of Several Distinguished Colored Persons to Which is Added a Brief Survey of the Condition and Prospects of Colored Americas.* Boston, MA: Robert F. Wallcut, 1855.

Nellis, Eric G. *Shaping the New World: African Slavery in the Americas, 1500-1888.* North York, Canada: University of Toronto Press, 2013.

Neufeldt, Victoria (ed.). *Webster's New World Dictionary of American English* (3rd college ed.). 1970. New York, NY: Prentice Hall, 1994 ed.

Nevins, Allan. *The Evening Post: A Century of Journalism.* New York, NY: Boni and Liveright, 1922.

——. *Frémont: Pathmarker of the West.* New York, NY: D. Appleton-Century Co., 1939.

Nevins, Allan, and Henry Steele Commager. *A Pocket History of the United States.* 1942. New York, NY: Pocket Books, 1981 ed.

Nevinson, Henry W. *A Modern Slavery.* London, UK: Harper and Brothers, 1906.

Nichols, James Lawrence, and William Henry Crogman. *Progress of a Race, or the Remarkable Advancement of the American Negro.* Naperville, IL: J. L. Nichols and Co., 1920.

Nicolay, John G., and John Hay (eds.). *Abraham Lincoln: A History.* 10 vols. New York, NY: The Century Co., 1890.

——. *Complete Works of Abraham Lincoln.* 12 vols. 1894. New York, NY: Francis D. Tandy Co., 1905 ed.

——. *Abraham Lincoln: Complete Works.* 12 vols. 1894. New York, NY: The Century Co., 1907 ed.

Nieboer, Herman Jeremias. *Slavery as an Industrial System: Ethnological Researches.* The Hague, Netherlands: Martinus Nijhoff, 1900.

Nivola, Pietro S., and David H. Rosenbloom (eds.). *Classic Readings in American Politics.* New York, NY: St. Martin's Press, 1986.

Noah, Mordecai M. *Travels in England, France, Spain, and the Barbary States: In the years 1813-1814 and 1815.* New York, NY: Kirk and Mercein, 1819.

Noble, Frederic Perry. *The Redemption of Africa: A Story of Civilization.* 2 vols. Chicago, IL: Fleming H. Revell Co., 1899.

Noel, Donald L. (ed.). *The Origins of American Slavery and Racism.* Columbus, OH: Charles E. Merrill, 1972.

Nolen, Claude H. *African American Southerners in Slavery, Civil War and Reconstruction.* Jefferson, NC: McFarland and Co., 2001.

Norris, Robert. *A Short Account of the African Slave Trade.* London, UK: W. Lowndes, 1789.

Northrup, Ansel Judd. *Slavery in New York.* (Article from the *State Library Bulletin*, "History," No. 4, May 1900.) New York, NY: University of the State of New York, 1900.

Northrup, David. *Indentured Labor in the Age of Imperialism, 1834-1922.* Cambridge, UK: Cambridge University Press, 1995.

Northup, Solomon. *Twelve Years a Slave: Narrative of Solomon Northup, a Citizen of New-York, Kidnapped in Washington City in 1841, and Rescued in 1853, From a Cotton Plantation Near the Red River, in Louisiana.* New York, NY: Miller, Orton, and Mulligan, 1855.

Norton, Charles Eliot. *Letters of Charles Eliot Norton.* 2 vols. Boston, MA: Houghton Mifflin Co., 1913.

Norton, Mary Beth, David M. Katzman, Paul D. Escott, Howard P. Chudacoff, Thomas G. Paterson, and William M. Tuttle, Jr. *A People and a Nation: A History of the United States - Vol. 2: Since 1865.* Boston, MA: Houghton Mifflin Co., 1990.

Norwood, Thomas Manson. *A True Vindication of the South.* Savannah, GA: Citizens and Southern Bank, 1917.

Nuñez, Benjamin. *Dictionary of Afro-Latin American Civilization.* Westport, CT: Greenwood Press, 1980.

Nye, Russel B. *William Lloyd Garrison and the Humanitarian Reformers.* Boston, MA: Little, Brown and Co.,

1955.
Oakes, James. *The Ruling Race: A History of American Slaveholders.* New York, NY: Knopf, 1982.
——. *Slavery and Freedom: An Interpretation of the Old South.* New York, NY: Knopf, 1990.
Oates, Stephen B. *Abraham Lincoln: The Man Behind the Myths.* New York, NY: Meridian, 1984.
——. *The Approaching Fury: Voices of the Storm, 1820-1861.* New York, NY: Harper Perennial, 1998.
O'Brien, Arthur. *Europe Before Modern Times: An Ancient and Mediaeval History.* Chicago, IL: Loyola University Press, 1943.
O'Brien, Cormac. *Secret Lives of the U.S. Presidents: What Your Teachers Never Told You About the Men of the White House.* Philadelphia, PA: Quirk, 2004.
——. *Secret Lives of the Civil War: What Your Teachers Never Told You About the War Between the States.* Philadelphia, PA: Quirk, 2007.
O'Callaghan, Edward Bailey. *Voyage of the Slavers St. John and Arms of Amsterdam.* Albany, NY: Munsell, 1967.
Oglesby, Thaddeus K. *Some Truths of History: A Vindication of the South Against the Encyclopedia Britannica and Other Maligners.* Atlanta, GA: Byrd Printing, 1903.
Ohaegbulam, Festus Ugboaja. *Towards an Understanding of the African Experience From Historical and Contemporary Perspectives.* Lanham, MD: University Press of America, 1990.
Oliver, Edmund Henry. *Roman Economic Conditions to the Close of the Republic.* Toronto, CAN: University of Toronto Library, 1907.
Olmsted, Frederick Law. *A Journey in the Seaboard Slave States, With Remarks on Their Economy.* New York, NY: Dix and Edwards, 1856.
——. *A Journey Through Texas; or a Saddle-Trip on the Western Frontier.* New York, NY: Dix and Edwards, 1857.
——. *A Journey in the Back Country.* New York, NY: Mason Brothers, 1860.
——. *The Cotton Kingdom: A Traveler's Observations on Cotton and Slavery in the American Slave States.* 2 vols. London, UK: Sampson Low, Son, and Co., 1862.
Olson, Ted (ed.). *CrossRoads: A Southern Culture Annual.* Macon, GA: Mercer University Press, 2004.
Oostindie, Gert (ed.). *Fifty Years Later: Antislavery, Capitalism and Modernity in the Dutch Orbit.* Pittsburgh, PA: University of Pittsburgh Press, 1996.
ORA (full title: *The War of the Rebellion: A Compilation of the Official Records of the Union and Confederate Armies.* (Multiple volumes.) Washington, D.C.: Government Printing Office, 1880.
ORN (full title: *Official Records of the Union and Confederate Navies in the War of the Rebellion*). (Multiple volumes.) Washington, D.C.: Government Printing Office, 1894.
Osler, Edward. *The Life of Admiral Viscount Exmouth.* London, UK: Smith, Elder and Co., 1841.
Owsley, Frank Lawrence. *King Cotton Diplomacy: Foreign Relations of the Confederate States of America.* 1931. Chicago, IL: University of Chicago Press, 1959 ed.
Page, Thomas Nelson. *Robert E. Lee: Man and Soldier.* New York, NY: Charles Scribner's Sons, 1911.
Palin, Sarah. *Going Rogue: An American Life.* New York, NY: HarperCollins, 2009.
Palmer, Colin. *Human Cargoes: The British Slave Trade to Spanish America, 1700-1739.* Urbana, IL: University of Illinois Press, 1981.
Palmer, R. R., and Joel Colton. *A History of the Modern World.* 1950. New York, NY: Knopf, 1965 ed.
Palmié, Stephan (ed.). *Slave Cultures and the Cultures of Slavery.* Knoxville, TN: University of Tennessee Press, 1995.
Paquette, Robert L., and Mark M. Smith (eds.). *The Oxford Handbook of Slavery in the Americas.* Oxford, UK: Oxford University Press, 2010.
Park, Mungo. *Travels in the Interior Districts of Africa, Performed in the Years 1795, 1796, and 1797.* 2 vols. London, UK: William Griffin, 1816.
Parker, Bowdoin S. (ed.). *What One Grand Army Post Has Accomplished: History of Edward W. Kinsley Post, No. 113.* Norwood, MA: Norwood Press, 1913.
Parkes, James. *A History of the Jewish People.* 1962. Harmondsworth, UK: Penguin, 1964 ed.
Parrinder, Edward Geoffrey. *African Traditional Religion.* London, UK: Hutchinson's University Library, 1954.
Parrish, Peter J. *Slavery, History and Historians.* New York, NY: Harper and Row, 1989.
Parry, J. H. *The Establishment of the European Hegemony, 1415-1715: Trade and Exploration in the Age of the Renaissance.* 1949. New York, NY: Harper Torchbooks, 1966 ed.
Parry, Melanie (ed.). *Chambers Biographical Dictionary.* 1897. Edinburgh, Scotland: Chambers Harrap, 1998 ed.
Parsons, Theophilus. *Slavery: Its Origin, Influence, and Destiny.* Boston, MA: William Carter and Brother, 1863.
Patnaik, U., and M. Dingwaney (eds.). *Chains of Servitude: Bondage and Slavery in India.* Madras, India: Sangam Books, 1985.

Patrick, Rembert W. *Jefferson Davis and His Cabinet*. Baton Rouge, LA: Louisiana State University Press, 1944.

Patterson, Caleb Perry. *The Negro in Tennessee, 1790-1865: A Study in Southern Politics*. Austin, TX: University of Texas, 1922.

Patterson, James. *The Old School Presbyterian Church on Slavery*. New Wilmington, PA: Vincent, Ferguson and Co., 1857.

Patterson, Orlando. *Slavery and Social Death*. Cambridge, MA: Harvard University Press, 1982.

Paul, Ron. *The Revolution: A Manifesto*. New York, NY: Grand Central Publishing, 2008.

Paulding, James Kirke. *Slavery in the United States*. New York, NY: Harper and Brothers, 1836.

Pearson, Henry Greenleaf. *The Life of John A. Andrew, Governor of Massachusetts, 1861-1865*. 2 vols. Boston, MA: Houghton, Mifflin and Co., 1904.

Pendleton, Louis Beauregard. *Alexander H. Stephens*. Philadelphia, PA: George W. Jacobs and Co., 1907.

Penney, Norman (ed.). *The Journal of George Fox*. 2 vols. Cambridge, UK: Cambridge University Press, 1911.

Penrose, Boies. *Travel and Discovery in the Renaissance, 1420-1620*. 1952. New York, NY: Atheneum, 1962 ed.

Perbi, Akosua Adoma. *A History of Indigenous Slavery in Ghana: From the 15th to the 19th Century*. Legon-Accra Ghana, West Africa: Sub-Saharan Publishers, 2004.

Perkins, Henry C. *Northern Editorials on Secession*. 2 vols. D. Appleton and Co., 1942.

Perlman, Alan M. *What Went Wrong?* Bloomington, IN: CrossBooks, 2013.

Perry, James M. *Touched With Fire: Five Presidents and the Civil War Battles That Made Them*. New York, NY: Public Affairs, 2003.

Perry, John C. *Myths and Realities of American Slavery: The True History of Slavery in America*. Shippenburg, PA: Burd Street Press, 2002.

Perry, Mark. *Lift Up Thy Voice: The Grimké Family's Journey From Slaveholders to Civil Rights Leaders*. New York, NY: Penguin, 2001.

Perry, Marvin. *Western Civilization: A Brief Survey - Vol. 1: to 1789*. Boston, MA: Houghton Mifflin, 1990.

Peter, Laurence J., and Raymond Hull *The Peter Principle: Why Things Always Go Wrong*. New York, NY: William Morrow and Co., 1969.

Peters, F. E. *The Harvest of Hellenism: A History of the Near East From Alexander the Great to the Triumph of Christianity*. New York, NY: Touchstone, 1970.

Peterson, Derek R. (ed.). *Abolitionism and Imperialism in Britain, Africa, and the Atlantic*. Athens, OH: Ohio University Press, 2010.

Peterson, Merrill D. (ed.). *James Madison, A Biography in His Own Words*. (First published posthumously in 1840.) New York, NY: Harper and Row, 1974 ed.

——. (ed.). *Thomas Jefferson: Writings, Autobiography, A Summary View of the Rights of British America, Notes on the State of Virginia, Public Papers, Addresses, Messages and Replies, Miscellany, Letters*. New York, NY: Literary Classics, 1984.

Peterson, Paul R. *Quantrill of Missouri: The Making of a Guerilla Warrior, The Man, the Myth, the Soldier*. Nashville, TN: Cumberland House, 2003.

Petherick, John. *Egypt, the Soudan and Central Africa—With Explorations From Khartoum on the White Nile to the Regions of the Equator*. Edinburgh, Scotland: William Blackwood and Sons, 1861.

Pettigrew, William A. *Freedom's Debt: The Royal African Company and the Politics of the Atlantic Slave Trade, 1672-1752*. Chapel Hill, NC: University of North Carolina Press, 2013.

Phillips, Michael. *White Metropolis: Race, Ethnicity, and Religion in Dallas, 1841-2001*. Austin, TX: University of Texas Press, 2006.

Phillips, Robert S. (ed.). *Funk and Wagnalls New Encyclopedia*. 1971. New York, NY: Funk and Wagnalls, 1979 ed.

Phillips, Ulrich Bonnell. *Plantation and Frontier Documents: 1649-1863 - Illustrative of Industrial History in the Colonial and Ante-Bellum South*. 2 vols. Cleveland, OH: Arthur H. Clark Co., 1909.

——. *American Negro Slavery: A Survey of the Supply, Employment and Control of Negro Labor as Determined by the Plantation Régime*. New York, NY: D. Appleton and Co., 1929.

——. *Life and Labor in the Old South*. Boston, MA: Little, Brown and Co., 1929.

Phillips, Wendell. *Speeches, Letters, and Lectures*. Boston, MA: Lee and Shepard, 1894.

Phillips, William D. *Slavery From Roman Times to the Early Transatlantic Trade*. Minneapolis, MN: University of Minnesota Press, 1985.

Piatt, Donn. *Memories of the Men Who Saved the Union*. New York, NY: Belford, Clarke, and Co., 1887.

Piatt, Donn, and Henry V. Boynton. *General George H. Thomas: A Critical Biography*. Cincinnati, OH: Robert Clarke and Co., 1893.

Pickett, George E. *The Heart of a Soldier: As Revealed in the Intimate Letters of General George E. Pickett, CSA*. 1908. New York, NY: Seth Moyle, 1913 ed.

Pickett, William Passmore. *The Negro Problem: Abraham Lincoln's Solution*. New York, NY: G. P. Putnam's Sons, 1909.

Pierson, Donald. *Negroes in Brazil*. Carbondale, IL: Southern Illinois University Press, 1942.

Pike, James Shepherd. *The Prostrate State: South Carolina Under Negro Government*. New York, NY: D. Appleton and Co., 1874.

Pinkerton, John. *An Inquiry Into the History of Scotland Preceding the Reign of Malcolm III, or the Year 1056*. 2 vols. London, UK: George Nicol, 1789.

Pitman, Frank Wesley. *The Development of the British West Indies, 1700-1763*. 4 vols. New Haven, CT: Yale University Press, 1917.

Planter, Professional (pseudonym). *Practical Rules for the Management and Medical Treatment of Negro Slaves, in the Sugar Colonies*. London, UK: Vernor and Hood, 1803.

Plumb, J. H. *The Italian Renaissance: A Concise Survey of Its History and Culture*. 1961. New York, NY: Harper and Row, 1965 ed.

Polk, William Mecklenburg. *Leonidas Polk, Bishop and General*. 2 vols. London, UK: Longman's Green, and Co., 1893.

Pollard, Edward A. *Black Diamonds Gathered in the Darkey Homes of the South*. New York, NY: Pudney and Russell, 1859.

——. *Southern History of the War*. 2 vols. in 1. New York, NY: Charles B. Richardson, 1866.

——. *The Lost Cause*. 1867. Chicago, IL: E. B. Treat, 1890 ed.

——. *The Lost Cause Regained*. New York, NY: G. W. Carlton and Co., 1868.

——. *Life of Jefferson Davis, With a Secret History of the Southern Confederacy, Gathered "Behind the Scenes in Richmond."* Philadelphia, PA: National Publishing Co., 1869.

Post, Lydia Minturn (ed.). *Soldiers' Letters, From Camp, Battlefield and Prison*. New York, NY: Bunce and Huntington, 1865.

Postma, Johannes. *The Dutch in the Atlantic Slave Trade, 1600-1815*. Cambridge, UK: Cambridge University Press, 1990.

Potter, David M. *The Impending Crisis: 1848-1861*. New York, NY: Harper and Row, 1976.

Powdermaker, Hortence. *After Freedom: A Cultural Study in the Deep South*. New York, NY: Atheneum, 1968.

Powell, Edward Payson. *Nullification and Secession in the United States: A History of the Six Attempts During the First Century of the Republic*. New York, NY: G. P. Putnam's Sons, 1897.

Powell, William S. *North Carolina: A History*. 1977. Chapel Hill, NC: University of North Carolina Press, 1988 ed.

Power, Tyrone. *Impressions of America; During the Years 1833, 1834, and 1835*. 2 vols. Philadelphia, PA: Carey, Lea, and Blanchard, 1836.

Prakash, Gyan. *Bonded Histories: Genealogies of Labour Servitude in Colonial India*. Cambridge, UK: Cambridge University Press, 1990.

Price, Richard (ed.). *Maroon Societies: Rebel Slave Communities in the Americas*. Baltimore, MD: Johns Hopksin University Press, 1979.

Priest, Josiah. *Slavery, As it Relates to the Negro, or African Race, Examined in the Light of Circumstances, History and the Holy Scriptures*. Albany, NY: Josiah Priest, 1843.

——. *Bible Defence of Slavery; and Origin, Fortunes, and History of the Negro Race*. Glasgow, KY: W. S. Brown, 1852.

Pritchard, Russ A., Jr. *Civil War Weapons and Equipment*. Guilford, CT: Lyons Press, 2003.

Providence Institution for Savings. *Ships and Shipmasters of Old Providence: A Brief Account of Some of the Famous Merchants, Sea Captains, and Ships of the Past*. Providence, RI: Providence Institution for Savings, 1919.

Putnam, George P. (ed.). *Hand-book of Chronology and History*. New York, NY: George P. Putnam, 1852.

Putnam, Samuel Porter. *400 Years of Free Thought*. New York, NY: Truth Seeker Co., 1894.

Quaife, Milo Milton. *The Doctrine of Non-Intervention With Slavery in the Territories*. Chicago, IL: Mac C. Chamberlain Co., 1910.

Quaker Biographies. 5 vols. Philadelphia, PA: Representatives of the Religious Society of Friends for Pennsylvania, New Jersey and Delaware, 1916.

Quarles, Benjamin. *The Negro in the Civil War*. 1953. Cambridge, MA: Da Capo Press, 1988 ed.

——. *The Negro in the American Revolution*. Chapel Hill, NC: University of North Carolina Press, 1961.

——. *Black Abolitionists*. New York, NY: Oxford University Press, 1969.

Quillin, Frank Uriah. *The Color Line in Ohio: A History of Race Prejudice in a Typical Northern State*. Ann Arbor, MI: George Wahr, 1913.

Quintero, José Agustín, Ambrosio José Gonzales, and Loreta Janeta Velazquez (Phillip Thomas Tucker, ed.). *Cubans in the Confederacy*. Jefferson, NC: McFarland and Co., 2002.

Rabinowitz, Howard. *Race Relations in the Urban South, 1865-1890*. Urbana, IL: University of Illinois Press, 1980.

Rable, George C. *The Confederate Republic: A Revolution Against Politics*. Chapel Hill, NC: University of North Carolina Press, 1994.

Raboteau, Albert. *Slave Religion: The Invisible Institution in the Antebellum South*. New York, NY: Oxford University Press, 1978.

Radice, Betty (ed.). *Fall of the Roman Empire: Six Lives by Plutarch*. 1958. London, UK: Penguin, 1972 ed.

——. *Cassius Dio: The Roman History: The Reign of Augustus*. 1987. Harmondsworth, UK: Penguin, 1988 ed.

Radzinsky, Edvard. *Stalin: The First In-depth Biography Based on Explosive New Documents From Russia's Secret Archives*. New York, NY: Anchor, 1996.

Ramage, James A. *Rebel Raider: The Life of General John Hunt Morgan*. Lexington, KY: University Press of Kentucky, 1986.

Randall, James Garfield. *Lincoln: The Liberal Statesman*. New York, NY: Dodd, Mead and Co., 1947.

Randall, James Garfield, and Richard N. Current. *Lincoln the President: Last Full Measure*. 1955. Urbana, IL: University of Illinois Press, 2000 ed.

Randolph, Thomas Jefferson (ed.). *Memoir, Correspondence, and Miscellanies, from the Papers of Thomas Jefferson*. 4 vols. Charlottesville, VA: F. Carr and Co., 1829.

Ransom, Roger L. *Conflict and Compromise: The Political Economy of Slavery, Emancipation, and the American Civil War*. Cambridge, UK: Cambridge University Press, 1989.

Ransom, Roger L., and Richard Sutch. *One Kind of Freedom: The Economic Consequences of Emancipation*. Cambridge, UK: Cambridge University Press, 1977.

Rawick, George P. *The American Slave: A Composite Autobiography*. 10 vols. 1941. Westport, CT: Greenwood Publishing Co., 1972 ed.

Rawle, William. *A View of the Constitution of the United States of America*. Philadelphia, PA: Philip H. Nicklin, 1829.

Rawley, James A. *The Transatlantic Slave Trade: A History*. New York, NY: W. W. Norton, 1981.

Rayfield, Donald. *Stalin and His Hangmen: The Tyrant and Those Who Killed For Him*. New York, NY: Random House, 2004.

Rayner, B. L. *Sketches of the Life, Writings, and Opinions of Thomas Jefferson*. New York, NY: Alfred Francis and William Boardman, 1832.

Redkey, Edwin S. *Black Exodus: Black Nationalist and Back-to-Africa Movements, 1890-1910*. New Haven, CT: Yale University Press, 1969.

Redpath, James. *The Roving Editor: Or, Talks With Slaves in the Southern States*. New York, NY: A. B. Burdick, 1859.

Reid, Anthony (ed.). *Slavery, Bondage and Dependency in Southeast Asia*. St. Lucia, Queensland, Australia: University of Queensland Press, 1983.

Reid, Richard M. *Freedom for Themselves: North Carolina's Black Soldiers in the Era of the Civil War*. Chapel Hill, NC: University of North Carolina Press, 2008.

Reid, Whitelaw. *Ohio in the War: Her Statesmen, Her Generals, and Soldiers*. 2 vols. Cincinnati, OH: Moore, Wilstach and Baldwin, 1868.

Remsburg, John B. *Abraham Lincoln: Was He a Christian?* New York, NY: The Truth Seeker Co., 1893.

Report From the Select Committee on the Extinction of Slavery Throughout the British Dominions. London, UK: J. Hadon, 1833.

Report of the Select Committee on Emancipation and Colonization (for the Thirty-seventh Congress, Second Session, Report No. 148). Washington, D.C.: Government Printing Office, 1862.

Reports of Committees of the Senate of the United States (for the Thirty-eighth Congress). Washington, D.C.: Government Printing Office, 1864.

Report of the Joint Committee on Reconstruction (at the First Session, Thirty-ninth Congress). Washington, D.C.: Government Printing Office, 1866.

Reports of Committees of the Senate of the United States (for the Second Session of the Forty-second Congress). Washington, D.C.: Government Printing Office, 1872.

Report of the Joint Select Committee to Inquire into the Condition of Affairs in the Late Insurrectionary States. Washington, D.C.: Government Printing Office, 1872.

Reuter, Edward Byron. *The Mulatto in the United States.* Boston, MA: Gorham Press, 1918.

Reyes, E. Christopher. *In His Name.* Bloomington, IN: AuthorHouse, 2010.

Rhodes, James Ford. *History of the United States from the Compromise of 1850 to the Final Restoration of Home Rule at the South in 1877.* 7 vols. 1895. New York, NY: Macmillan Co., 1907 ed.

Rhys, John. *Celtic Folklore: Welsh and Manx.* 2 vols. Oxford, UK: Clarendon Press, 1901.

——. *Celtic Britain.* London, UK: Society for Promoting Christian Knowledge, 1908.

Rice, Allen Thorndike (ed.). *The North American Review*, Vol. 227. New York, NY: D. Appleton and Co., 1879.

——. (ed.). *Reminiscences of Abraham Lincoln, by Distinguished Men of His Time.* New York, NY: North American Review, 1888.

Rice, David. *A Kentucky Protest Against Slavery.* New York, NY: The Rebellion Record, 1812.

Richardson, Albert Deane. *A Personal History of Ulysses S. Grant.* Hartford, CT: American Publishing Co., 1868.

Richardson, James Daniel (ed.). *A Compilation of the Messages and Papers of the Confederacy.* 2 vols. Nashville, TN: United States Publishing Co., 1905.

——. *A Compilation of the Messages and Papers of the Presidents, 1789-1908.* 11 vols. New York, NY: Bureau of National Literature and Art, 1909.

Richardson, John Anderson. *Richardson's Defense of the South.* Atlanta, GA: A. B. Caldwell, 1914.

Richburg, Keith B. *Out of America: A Black Man Confronts Africa.* New York, NY: Basic Books, 2009.

Riedel, Eunice, Thomas Tracy, and Barbara D. Moskowitz. *The Book of the Bible.* New York, NY: William Morrow and Co., 1979.

Rickard, J. A. *History of England.* 1933. New York, NY: Barnes and Noble, 1957 ed.

Riley, Benjamin F. *The White Man's Burden: A Discussion of the Interracial Question With Special Reference to the Responsibility of the White Race to the Negro Problem.* Birmingham, AL: B. F. Riley, 1910.

Riley, Franklin Lafayette (ed.). *Publications of the Mississippi Historical Society.* Oxford, MS: The Mississippi Historical Society, 1902.

——. *General Robert E. Lee After Appomattox.* New York, NY: MacMillan Co., 1922.

Riley, Russell Lowell. *The Presidency and the Politics of Racial Inequality.* New York, NY: Columbia University Press, 1999.

Ripley, George, and Charles Anderson Dana (eds.). *The American Cyclopedia: A Popular Dictionary of General Knowledge.* New York, NY: D. Appleton and Co., 1881.

Rives, John (ed.). *Abridgement of the Debates of Congress: From 1789 to 1856* (Vol. 13). New York, NY: D. Appleton and Co., 1860.

Roberts, Andrew. *A History of the Bemba: Political Growth and Change in North-eastern Zambia Before 1900.* Madison, WI: University of Wisconsin Press, 1973.

Roberts, Paul M. *United States History: Review Text.* 1966. New York, NY: Amsco School Publications, Inc., 1970 ed.

Roberts, R. Philip. *Mormonism Unmasked: Confronting the Contradictions Between Mormon Beliefs and True Christianity.* Nashville, TN: Broadman and Holman, 1998.

Roberts, Sam. *Who We Are: A Portrait of America Based on the Latest U.S. Census.* New York, NY: Time, 1994.

Robertson, Claire, and Martin A. Klein (eds.). *Women and Slavery in Africa.* Madison, WI: University of Wisconsin Press, 1983.

Robertson, James I., Jr. *Soldiers Blue and Gray.* 1988. Columbia, SC: University of South Carolina Press, 1998 ed.

Robinson, Thomas H., and Others. *Men, Groups, and the Community: A Survey in the Social Sciences.* New York, NY: Harper and Brothers, 1940.

Roche, Emma Langdon. *Historic Sketches of the South.* New York, NY: The Knickerbocker Press, 1914.

Rockwell, Llewellyn H., Jr. "Genesis of the Civil War." Website: www.lewrockwell.com/rockwell/civilwar.html.

Rodney, Walter. *West Africa and the Atlantic Slave-Trade.* Dar es Salaam, Tanzania: Historical Society of Tanzania, 1967.

Rodriguez, Junius P. (ed.). *The Historical Encyclopedia of World Slavery.* 2 vols. Santa Barbara, CA: ABC-CLIO, 1997.

——. (ed.) *Slavery in the United States: A Social, Political, and Historical Encyclopedia.* Santa Barbara, CA: ABC-CLIO, 2007.

——. (ed.) *Encyclopedia of Slave Resistance and Rebellion.* 2 vols. Westport, CT: Greenwood Press, 2007.

Rogers, Joel Augustus. *The Ku Klux Spirit.* 1923. Baltimore, MD: Black Classic Press, 1980 ed.

——. *Africa's Gift to America: The Afro-American in the Making and Saving of the United States.* St. Petersburg, FL:

Helga M. Rogers, 1961.

Rolleston, Thomas William. *Myths and Legends of the Celtic Race*. London, UK: Constable and Co., 1911.

Roman, Charles Victor. *American Civilization and the Negro: The Afro-American in Relation to National Progress*. Philadelphia, PA: F. A. Davis Co., 1916.

Rose, Willie Lee. *Rehearsal for Reconstruction: The Port Royal Experiment*. Indianapolis, IN: Bobbs-Merrill, 1964.

——. *A Documentary History of Slavery in North America*. New York, NY: Oxford University Press, 1976.

Rosen, Robert N. *The Jewish Confederates*. Columbia, SC: University of South Carolina Press, 2000.

Rosenbaum, Robert A. (ed). *The New American Desk Encyclopedia*. 1977. New York, NY: Signet, 1989 ed.

Rosenbaum, Robert A., and Douglas Brinkley (eds.). *The Penguin Encyclopedia of American History*. New York, NY: Viking, 2003.

Ross, Fitzgerald. *A Visit to the Cities and Camps of the Confederate States*. Edinburgh, Scotland: William Blackwood and Sons, 1865.

Ross, Frederick Augustus. *Slavery Ordained of God*. Philadelphia, PA: J. B. Lippincott and Co., 1857.

Rothenberg, Paula S. *Race, Class and Gender in the United States: An Integrated Study*. New York, NY: St. Martin's Press, 1992.

Rothschild, Alonzo. *"Honest Abe": A Study in Integrity Based on the Early Life of Abraham Lincoln*. Boston, MA: Houghton Mifflin Co., 1917.

Rouse, Adelaide Louise (ed.). *National Documents: State Papers So Arranged as to Illustrate the Growth of Our Country From 1606 to the Present Day*. New York, NY: Unit Book Publishing Co., 1906.

Rowland, Dunbar (ed.). *Jefferson Davis, Constitutionalist: His Letters, Papers, and Speeches*. 10 vols. Jackson, MS: Mississippi Department of Archives and History,1923.

Rozwenc, Edwin Charles (ed.). *The Causes of the American Civil War*. 1961. Lexington, MA: D. C. Heath and Co., 1972 ed.

Rubenzer, Steven J., and Thomas R. Faschingbauer. *Personality, Character, and Leadership in the White House: Psychologists Assess the Presidents*. Dulles, VA: Brassey's, 2004.

Rubin, Morton. *Plantation County*. Chapel Hill, NC: University of North Carolina Press, 1951.

Ruby, Robert. H. *Indian Slavery in the Pacific Northwest*. Glendale, CA: Arthur H. Clark, 1993.

Ruffin, Edmund. *The Diary of Edmund Ruffin: Toward Independence: October 1856-April 1861*. Baton Rouge, LA: Louisiana State University Press, 1972.

Runciman, Steven. *A History of the Crusades*. 3 vols. 1951. New York, NY: Harper Torchbook, 1964 ed.

Ruoff, Henry Woldmar (ed.). *The Standard Dictionary of Facts*. 1908. Buffalo, NY: Frontier Press Co., 1914 ed.

Russell, Bertrand. *A History of Western Philosophy*. 1945. New York, NY: Touchstone, 1972 ed.

Russell, John Henderson. *The Free Negro in Virginia, 1619-1865*. Baltimore, MD: Johns Hopkins Press, 1913.

Russell, Michael. *History and Present Condition of the Barbary States*. New York, NY: Harper and Brothers, 1854.

Russell, Robert. *North America, Its Agriculture and Culture*. Edinburgh, Scotland: Adam and Charles Black, 1857.

Russell, William Howard. *My Diary North and South*. 2 vols. London, UK: Bradbury and Evans, 1863.

Rutherford, Mildred Lewis. *Four Addresses*. Birmingham, AL: The Mildred Rutherford Historical Circle, 1916.

——. *A True Estimate of Abraham Lincoln and Vindication of the South*. N.p., n.d.

——. *Truths of History: A Historical Perspective of the Civil War From the Southern Viewpoint*. Confederate Reprint Co., 1920.

——. *The South Must Have Her Rightful Place In History*. Athens, GA, 1923.

Rutland, Robert Allen. *The Birth of the Bill of Rights, 1776-1791*. 1955. Boston, MA: Northeastern University Press, 1991 ed.

Sachsman, David B., S. Kittrell Rushing, and Roy Morris, Jr. (eds.). *Words at War: The Civil War and American Journalism*. West Lafayette, IN: Purdue University Press, 2008.

Salley, Alexander Samuel, Jr. *South Carolina Troops in Confederate Service*. 2 vols. Columbia, SC: R. L. Bryan, 1913 and 1914.

Salzberger, Ronald P., and Mary C. Turck (eds.). *Reparations For Slavery: A Reader*. Lanham, MD: Rowman and Littlefield, 2004.

Sam, Dickey. *Liverpool and Slavery: An Historical Account of the Liverpool-Africa Slave Trade*. Liverpool, UK: A. Bowker and Son, 1884.

Samuel, Bunford. *Secession and Constitutional Liberty*. 2 vols. New York, NY: Neale Publishing, 1920.

Sancho, Ignatius. *Letters of the Late Ignatius Sancho, an African*. 1782. New York, NY: Cosimo Classics, 2005 ed.

Sandburg, Carl. *Abraham Lincoln: The War Years*. 4 vols. New York, NY: Harcourt, Brace and World, 1939.

——. *Storm Over the Land: A Profile of the Civil War*. 1939. Old Saybrook, CT: Konecky and Konecky, 1942 ed.

Sanger, George P. (ed.). *Public Laws of the United States of America, Passed at the First Session of the Thirty-seventh Congress; 1861*. Boston, MA: Little, Brown and Co., 1861.

Sargent, F. W. *England, the United States, and the Southern Confederacy*. London, UK: Sampson Low, Son, and Co., 1863.

Saxon, Lyle, Edward Dreyer, and Robert Tallant. *Gumbo Ya-Ya: Folk Tales of Louisiana*. Boston, MA: Houghton Mifflin Co., 1945.

Scanzoni, John H. *The Black Family in Modern Society: Patterns of Stability and Security*. Boston, MA: Allyn and Bacon, 1971.

Scharf, John Thomas. *History of the Confederate Navy, From Its Organization to the Surrender of Its Last Vessel*. Albany, NY: Joseph McDonough, 1894.

Schauffler, Robert Haven. *Our American Holidays: Lincoln's Birthday - A Comprehensive View of Lincoln as Given in the Most Noteworthy Essays, Orations and Poems, in Fiction and in Lincoln's Own Writings*. 1909. New York, NY: Moffat, Yard and Co., 1916 ed.

Schlüter, Herman. *Lincoln, Labor and Slavery: A Chapter From the Social History of America*. New York, NY: Socialist Literature Co., 1913.

Schoepf, Johann David. *Travels in the Confederation, 1783-1784*. 2 vols. (Alfred J. Morrison, trans. and ed.) 1788. Philadelphia, PA: William J. Campbell, 1911 ed.

Schrier, Arnold, Harry J. Carroll, Jr., Ainslie T. Embree, Knox Mellon, Jr., and Alastair M. Taylor. *Modern European Civilization: A Documentary History of Politics, Society, and Thought From the Renaissance to the Present*. 1961. Chicago, IL: Scott, Foresman and Co., 1963 ed.

Schultz, Alfred P. *Race or Mongrel*. Boston, MA: L. C. Page and Co., 1908.

Schurz, Carl. *Life of Henry Clay*. 2 vols. 1887. Boston, MA: Houghton, Mifflin and Co., 1899 ed.

Schwartz, Barry. *Abraham Lincoln and the Forge of National Memory*. Chicago, IL: University of Chicago Press, 2000.

Schwartz, Philip J. *Slave Laws in Virginia*. Athens, GA: University of Georgia Press, 1996.

Scott, Alexander Maccallum. *Barbary: The Romance of the Nearest East*. New York, NY: Dodd, Mead and Co., 1921.

Scott, Emmett J., and Lyman Beecher Stowe. *Booker T. Washington: Builder of a Civilization*. Garden City, NY: Doubleday, Page, and Co., 1916.

Scott, James Brown. *James Madison's Notes of Debates in the Federal Convention of 1787, and Their Relation to a More Perfect Society of Nations*. New York, NY: Oxford University Press, 1918.

Scott, Otto J. *The Secret Six: John Brown and the Abolitionist Movement*. New York, NY: New York Times Books, 1979.

Scruggs, Leonard M. *The Un-Civil War: Truths Your Teacher Never Told You*. Hendersonville, NC: Tribune Papers, 2007.

Scully, Pamela. *Liberating the Family: Gender and British Slave Emancipation in the Rural Western Cape of Good Hope*. Portsmouth, NH: Heinemann, 1998.

Seabrook, Lochlainn. *Britannia Rules: Goddess-Worship in Ancient Anglo-Celtic Society - An Academic Look at the United Kingdom's Matricentric Spiritual Past*. 1999. Franklin, TN: Sea Raven Press, 2007 ed.

——. *The Caudills: An Etymological, Ethnological, and Genealogical Study - Exploring the Name and National Origins of a European-American Family*. 2003. Franklin, TN: Sea Raven Press, 2010 ed.

——. *Carnton Plantation Ghost Stories: True Tales of the Unexplained From Tennessee's Most Haunted Civil War House!* 2005. Franklin, TN: Sea Raven Press, 2010 ed.

——. *Nathan Bedford Forrest: Southern Hero, American Patriot: Honoring a Confederate Hero and the Old South*. 2007. Franklin, TN: Sea Raven Press, 2010 ed.

——. *Abraham Lincoln: The Southern View*. 2007. Franklin, TN: Sea Raven Press, 2013 ed.

——. *The McGavocks of Carnton Plantation: A Southern History - Celebrating One of Dixie's Most Noble Confederate Families and Their Tennessee Home*. 2008. Franklin, TN: Sea Raven Press, 2011 ed.

——. *A Rebel Born: A Defense of Nathan Bedford Forrest*. 2010. Franklin, TN: Sea Raven Press, 2011 ed.

——. *A Rebel Born: The Movie* (screenplay). Franklin, TN: Sea Raven Press, unpublished.

——. *Everything You Were Taught About the Civil War is Wrong, Ask a Southerner!* 2010. Franklin, TN: Sea Raven Press, revised 2014 ed.

——. *The Quotable Jefferson Davis: Selections From the Writings and Speeches of the Confederacy's First President*. Franklin, TN: Sea Raven Press, 2011.

——. *Lincolnology: The Real Abraham Lincoln Revealed In His Own Words*. Franklin, TN: Sea Raven Press, 2011.

——. *The Unquotable Abraham Lincoln: The President's Quotes They Don't Want You To Know!* Franklin, TN: Sea Raven Press, 2011.

——. *The Quotable Robert E. Lee: Selections From the Writings and Speeches of the South's Most Beloved Civil War General.* 2011. Franklin, TN: Sea Raven Press, 2014 ed.

——. *The Constitution of the Confederate States of America Explained: A Clause-by-Clause Study of the South's Magna Carta.* Franklin, TN: Sea Raven Press, 2012.

——. *The Old Rebel: Robert E. Lee As He Was Seen By His Contemporaries.* Franklin, TN: Sea Raven Press, 2012.

——. *The Quotable Stonewall Jackson: Selections From the Writings and Speeches of the South's Most Famous General.* Franklin, TN: Sea Raven Press, 2012.

——. *Honest Jeff and Dishonest Abe: A Southern Children's Guide to the Civil War.* Franklin, TN: Sea Raven Press, 2012.

——. *Give 'Em Hell Boys! The Complete Military Correspondence of Nathan Bedford Forrest.* Franklin, TN: Sea Raven Press, 2012 Sesquicentennial Civil War Edition.

——. *The Great Impersonator: 99 Reasons to Dislike Abraham Lincoln.* Franklin, TN: Sea Raven Press, 2012.

——. *Forrest! 99 Reasons to Love Nathan Bedford Forrest.* Franklin, TN: Sea Raven Press, 2012 Sesquicentennial Civil War Edition.

——. *The Quotable Nathan Bedford Forrest: Selections From the Writings and Speeches of the Confederacy's Most Brilliant Cavalryman.* Franklin, TN: Sea Raven Press, 2012 Sesquicentennial Civil War Edition.

——. *Encyclopedia of the Battle of Franklin: A Comprehensive Guide to the Conflict That Changed the Civil War.* Franklin, TN: Sea Raven Press, 2012 Sesquicentennial Civil War Edition.

——. *The Quotable Alexander H. Stephens: Selections From the Writings and Speeches of the Confederacy's First Vice President.* Franklin, TN: Sea Raven Press, 2013.

——. *The Alexander H. Stephens Reader: Excerpts From the Works of a Confederate Founding Father.* Franklin, TN: Sea Raven Press, 2013.

——. *Saddle, Sword, and Gun: A Biography of Nathan Bedford Forrest For Teens.* Franklin, TN: Sea Raven Press, 2013 Sesquicentennial Civil War Edition.

——. *Jesus and the Law of Attraction: The Bible-Based Guide to Creating Perfect Health, Wealth, and Happiness Following Christ's Simple Formula.* Franklin, TN: Sea Raven Press, 2013.

——. *The Articles of Confederation Explained: A Clause-by-Clause Study of America's First Constitution.* Franklin, TN: Sea Raven Press, 2014.

——. *Give This Book to a Yankee: A Southern Guide to the Civil War For Northerners.* Franklin, TN: Sea Raven Press, 2014.

——. *Confederacy 101: Amazing Facts You Never Knew About America's Oldest Political Tradition.* Franklin, TN: Sea Raven Press, 2015.

——. *The Great Yankee Coverup: What the North Doesn't Want You to Know About Lincoln's War!* Franklin, TN: Sea Raven Press, 2015.

Seaman, L. *What Miscegenation Is! And What We Are to Expect Now That Mr. Lincoln is Re-elected.* New York, NY: Waller and Willetts, 1864.

Searing, James F. *West African Slavery and Atlantic Commerce: The Senegal River Valley, 1700-1860.* Cambridge, UK: Cambridge University Press, 1993.

Segal, Charles M. (ed.). *Conversations with Lincoln.* 1961. New Brunswick, NJ: Transaction, 2002 ed.

Segal, Ronald. *Islam's Black Slaves: The Other Black Diaspora.* New York, NY: Farrar, Straus and Giroux, 2002.

Segars, J. H., and Charles Kelly Barrow. *Black Southerners in Confederate Armies: A Collection of Historical Accounts.* Atlanta, GA: Southern Lion Books, 2001.

Seligmann, Herbert J. *The Negro Faces America.* New York, NY: Harper and Brothers, 1920.

Sellers, James Benson. *Slavery in Alabama.* Tuscaloosa, AL: University of Alabama Press, 1950.

Semmes, Admiral Ralph. *Service Afloat, or the Remarkable Career of the Confederate Cruisers Sumter and Alabama During the War Between the States.* London, UK: Sampson Low, Marston, Searle, and Rivington, 1887.

SenGupta, Gunja. *From Slavery to Poverty: The Racial Origins of Welfare in New York, 1840-1918.* New York, NY: New York University, 2009.

Sewall, Samuel. *Diary of Samuel Sewall.* 3 vols. Boston, MA: The Society, 1879.

Sewell, Richard H. *John P. Hale and the Politics of Abolition.* Cambridge, MA: Harvard University Press, 1965.

Shannon, Joseph (comp.). *Manual of the Corporation of the City of New York.* New York, NY: n.p., 1869.

Sharp, Granville. *The Just Limitation of Slavery in the Laws of God, Compared With the Unbounded Claims of the African Traders and British American Slaveholders.* London, UK: B. White, 1776.

Shaw, A. G. L. *Convicts and the Colonies: A Study of Penal Transportation From Great Britain and Ireland to Australia and Other Parts of the British Empire.* London, UK: Faber, 1966.

Shaw, Wilfred B. *The Quarterly Review of the Michigan Alumnus.* Ann Arbor, MI: The Alumni Association of the

University of Michigan, October 1934.

Shea, George. *Jefferson Davis: A Statement Concerning the Imputed Special Causes of His Long Imprisonment by the Government of the United States, and His Tardy Release by Due Process of Law*. London, UK: Edward Stanford, 1877.

Shell, Robert Carl-Heinz. *Children of Bondage: A Social History of the Slave Society at the Cape of Good Hope, 1652-1838*. Hanover, NH: University Press of New England, 1994.

Shenkman, Richard. *Legends, Lies and Cherished Myths of American History*. New York, NY: Perennial, 1988.

Shenkman, Richard, and Kurt Edward Reiger. *One-Night Stands with American History: Odd, Amusing, and Little-Known Incidents*. 1980. New York, NY: Perennial, 2003 ed.

Sherman, William A. *Forced Native Labor in Sixteenth-Century Central America*. Lincoln, NE: University of Nebraska Press, 1979.

Sherman, William Tecumseh. *Memoirs of General William T. Sherman*. 2 vols. 1875. New York, NY: D. Appleton and Co., 1891 ed.

Sherwood, Marika. *After Abolition: Britain and the Slave Trade Since 1807*. London, UK: I. B. Tauris, 2007.

Shillington, Kevin. *History of Africa*. 1989. New York, NY: St. Martin's Press, 1994 ed.

Shirer, William L. *The Rise and Fall of the Third Reich: A History of Nazi Germany*. New York, NY: Simon and Schuster, 1960.

Shorto, Russell. *Thomas Jefferson and the American Ideal*. Hauppauge, NY: Barron's, 1987.

Shotwell, Walter G. *Life of Charles Sumner*. New York, NY: Thomas Y. Crowell and Co., 1910.

Shufeldt, Robert Wilson. *The Negro: A Menace to American Civilization*. Boston, MA: Richard G. Badger, 1907.

Shuffleton, Frank (ed.). *A Mixed Race: Ethnicity in America*. New York, NY: Oxford University Press, 1993.

Siebert, Wilbur H. *The Underground Railroad: From Slavery to Freedom*. New York, NY: Macmillan, 1898.

Siepel, Kevin H. *Rebel: The Life and Times of John Singleton Mosby*. New York, NY: St. Martin's Press, 1983.

Sikainga, Ahmad Alawad. *Slaves Into Workers: Emancipation and Labor in Colonial Sudan*. Austin, TX: University of Texas Press, 1996.

Simmons, Henry E. *A Concise Encyclopedia of the Civil War*. New York, NY: Bonanza Books, 1965.

Simons, Gerald. *Barbarian Europe*. 1968. New York, NY: Time-Life Books, 1975 ed.

Simpson, Lewis P. (ed.). *I'll Take My Stand: The South and the Agrarian Tradition*. 1930. Baton Rouge, LA: University of Louisiana Press, 1977 ed.

Sinha, Manisha. *The Counterrevolution of Slavery: Politics and Ideology in Antebellum South Carolina*. Chapel Hill, NC: University of North Carolina Press, 2000.

Sitterson, J. Carlyle. *Sugar Country: The Cane Sugar Industry in the South, 1753-1950*. Lexington, KY: University of Kentucky Press, 1953.

Sladen, Douglas. *The Secrets of the Vatican*. Philadelphia, PA: J. B. Lippencott Co., 1907.

Slotkin, Richard. *No Quarter: The Battle of the Crater, 1864*. New York, NY: Random House, 2009.

Smallwood, Stephanie E. *Saltwater Slavery: A Middle Passage from Africa to American Diaspora*. Cambridge, MA: Harvard University Press, 2009.

Smedes, Susan Dabney. *A Southern Planter: Social Life in the Old South*. 1887. New York, NY: James Pott and Co., 1900 ed.

——. *Memorials of a Southern Planter*. Baltimore, MD: Cushings and Bailey, 1888.

Smedley, Audrey. *Race in North America: Origin and Evolution of a World View*. Boulder, CO: Westview Press, 1993.

Smelser, Marshall. *American Colonial and Revolutionary History*. 1950. New York, NY: Barnes and Noble, 1966 ed.

——. *The Democratic Republic, 1801-1815*. New York, NY: Harper and Row, 1968.

Smith, Abbot Emerson. *Colonists in Bondage: White Servitude and Convict Labor in America, 1607-1776*. Chapel Hill, NC: University of North Carolina Press, 1947.

Smith, Emma Peters, David Saville Muzzey, and Minnie Lloyd. *World History: The Struggle for Civilization*. Boston, MA: Ginn and Co., 1946.

Smith, Hedrick. *Reagan: The Man, The President*. Oxford, UK: Pergamon Press, 1980.

Smith, John David (ed.). *Black Soldiers in Blue: African American Troops in the Civil War Era*. Chapel Hill, NC: University of North Carolina Press, 2002.

Smith, Joseph. *The Pearl of Great Price*. Salt Lake City, UT: George Q. Cannon and Sons, 1891.

Smith, Lacey Baldwin. *This Realm of England: 1399 to 1688*. 1966. Lexington, MA: D. C. Heath and Co., 1983 ed.

Smith, Mark M. (ed.). *The Old South*. Oxford, UK: Blackwell Publishers, 2001.

Smith, Page. *A People's History of the United States*. 8 vols. New York, NY: McGraw-Hill, 1976-1987.

Smith, Philip. *A History of the World: From the Creation to the Fall of the Western Roman Empire*. 3 vols. New York, NY: D. Appleton and Co., 1885.

Smith, Philip D., Jr. *Tartan for Me!: Suggested Tartan for 13,695 Scottish, Scotch-Irish, Irish and North American Names with Lists of Clan, Family, and District Tartans*. Bruceton, WV: Scotpress, 1990.

Smith, Robert Edwin. *Christianity and the Race Problem*. New York, NY: Fleming H. Revell Co., 1922.

Smucker, Samuel M. *The Life and Times of Thomas Jefferson*. Philadelphia, PA: J. W. Bradley, 1859.

Snay, Mitchell. *The Gospel of Disunion: Religion and Separatism in the Antebellum South*. Cambridge, UK: Cambridge University Press, 1993.

Sobel, Mechal. *The World They Made Together: Black and White Values in Eighteenth-Century Virginia*. Princeton, NJ: Princeton University Press, 1987.

Sobel, Robert (ed.). *Biographical Directory of the United States Executive Branch, 1774-1898*. Westport, CT: Greenwood Press, 1990.

Soderlund, Jean R. *Quakers and Slavery: A Divided Spirit*. Princeton, NJ: Princeton University Press, 1985.

Solow, Barbara L. (ed.). *Slavery and the Rise of the Atlantic System*. Cambridge, UK: Cambridge University Press, 1991.

Spaeth, Harold J., and Edward Conrad Smith. *The Constitution of the United States*. 1936. New York, NY: HarperCollins, 1991 ed.

Sparks, Jared. *The Works of Benjamin Franklin*. 10 vols. Chicago, IL: Townsend MacCoun, 1882.

Speer, Albert. *Inside the Third Reich*. 1969. New York, NY: Avon, 1971 ed.

Speight, Ernest Edwin, and Robert Morton Nance. *Britain's Sea Story, B.C. 55-A.D.1805*. London, UK: Hodder and Stoughton, 1906.

Spence, James. *On the Recognition of the Southern Confederation*. Ithaca, NY: Cornell University Library, 1862.

Spero, Sterling D., and Abram L. Harris. *The Black Worker: A Study of the Negro and the Labor Movement*. New York, NY: Columbia University Press, 1931.

Spooner, Lysander. *No Treason* (only Numbers 1, 2, and 6 were published). Boston, MA: Lysander Spooner, 1867-1870.

Stampp, Kenneth M. *The Peculiar Institution: Slavery in the Antebellum South*. New York, NY: Vintage, 1956.

Stanford, Peter Thomas. *The Tragedy of the Negro in America*. Boston, MA: Peter Thomas Stanford, 1898.

Stanley, Henry Morton. *The Autobiography of Sir Henry Morton Stanley*. Boston, MA: Houghton Mifflin Co., 1909.

Starobin, Robert S. *Industrial Slavery in the Old South*. New York, NY: Oxford University Press, 1970.

Starr, Chester G. *Civilization and the Caesars: The Intellectual Revolution in the Roman Empire*. 1954. New York, NY: W. W. Norton and Co., 1965 ed.

Staudenraus, P. J. *The African Colonization Movement, 1816-1865*. New York, NY: Columbia University Press, 1961.

Stavrianos, Leften Stavros. *The World Since 1500: A Global History*. 1966. Englewood Cliffs, NJ: Prentice Hall, 1991 ed.

Stealey, John E., III. *The Antebellum Kanawha Salt Business and Western Markets*. Lexington, KY: University Press of Kentucky, 1993.

Stebbins, Rufus Phineas. *An Historical Address Delivered At the Centennial Celebration of the Incorporation of the Town of Wilbraham, June 15, 1863*. Boston, MA: George C. Rand and Avery, 1864.

Stedman, Edmund Clarence, and Ellen Mackay Hutchinson (eds.). *A Library of American Literature From the Earliest Settlement to the Present Time*. 10 vols. New York, NY: Charles L. Webster and Co., 1888.

Steele, Shelby. *White Guilt: How Blacks and Whites Together Destroyed the Promise of the Civil Rights Era*. New York, NY: Harper Perennial, 2007.

Stein, Ben, and Phil DeMuth. *How To Ruin the United States of America*. Carlsbad, CA: New Beginnings Press, 2008.

Steiner, Bernard Christian. *History of Slavery in Connecticut*. Baltimore, MD: Johns Hopkins University Press, 1893.

Steiner, Lewis Henry. *Report of Lewis H. Steiner: Inspector of the Sanitary Commission, Containing a Diary Kept During the Rebel Occupation of Frederick, MD, September, 1862*. New York, NY: Anson D. F. Randolph, 1862.

Steinfeld, Robert J. *The Invention of Free Labor: The Employment Relation in English and American Law and Culture, 1350-1870*. Chapel Hill, NC: University of North Carolina Press, 1991.

Stephen, James. *The Slavery of the British West India Colonies Delineated, As it Exists in Both Law and Practice*. 2 vols. London, UK: Joseph Butterworth and Son, 1824.

Stephens, Alexander H. *A Constitutional View of the Late War Between the States; Its Causes, Character, Conduct and*

Results. 2 vols. Philadelphia, PA: National Publishing, Co., 1870.
——. *Recollections of Alexander H. Stephens: His Diary Kept When a Prisoner at Fort Warren, Boston Harbour, 1865.* New York, NY: Doubleday, Page, and Co., 1910.
Stephenson, Nathaniel Wright. *Lincoln: An Account of His Personal Life, Especially of Its Springs of Action as Revealed and Deepened by the Ordeal of War.* Indianapolis, IN: Bobbs-Merrill, 1922.
Sterling, Dorothy (ed.). *Speak Out in Thunder Tones: Letters and Other Writings by Black Northerners, 1787-1865.* 1973. Cambridge, MA: Da Capo, 1998 ed.
Stern, Philip Van Doren (ed.). *The Life and Writings of Abraham Lincoln.* 1940. New York, NY: Modern Library, 2000 ed.
Stevenson, Brenda E. *Life in Black and White: Family and Community in the Slave South.* New York, NY: Oxford University Press, 1996.
Steward, Austin. *Twenty-two Years a Slave, and Forty Years a Freeman.* Canandaigua, NY: the author, 1867.
Stewart, James Brewer. *Holy Warriors: The Abolitionists and American Slavery.* New York, NY: Hill and Wang, 1976.
Stewart, L. Lloyd. *A Far Cry From Freedom: Gradual Abolition (1799-1827): New York State's Crime Against Humanity.* Bloomington, IN: AuthorHouse, 2005.
Stiles, Robert. *Four Years Under Marse Robert.* New York, NY: Neal Publishing Co., 1910.
Still, William. *The Underground Railroad: A Record of Facts, Authentic Narratives, Letters, Etc.* Philadelphia, PA: Porter and Coates, 1872.
Stimpson, George. *A Book About American History.* 1956. New York, NY: Premier Books, 1960 ed.
Stirling, James. *Letters From the Slave States.* London, UK: John W. Parker and Son, 1857.
Stone, Alfred Holt. *Studies in the American Race Problem.* New York, NY: Doubleday, Page and Co., 1908.
Stone, Kate. *Brokenburn: The Journal of Kate Stone, 1861-1868.* (John Q. Anderson, ed.). Baton Rouge, LA: Louisiana State University Press, 1955.
Stonebraker, J. Clarence. *The Unwritten South: Cause, Progress and Results of the Civil War - Relics of Hidden Truth After Forty Years.* Seventh ed., n.p., 1908.
Storke, Elliot G., and Linus Pierpoint Brockett. *A Complete History of the Great Rebellion, Embracing Its Causes, Events and Consequences.* 3 vols. Auburn, NY: The Auburn Publishing Co., 1865.
Stovall, Pleasant A. *Robert Toombs: Statesman, Speaker, Soldier, Sage.* New York, NY: Cassell Publishing, 1892.
Stowe, Harriet Beecher. *Uncle Tom's Cabin.* London, UK: John Cassell, 1852.
Strain, John Paul. *Witness to the Civil War: The Art of John Paul Strain.* Philadelphia, PA: Courage, 2002.
Strode, Hudson. *Jefferson Davis: American Patriot.* 3 vols. New York, NY: Harcourt, Brace and World, 1955, 1959, 1964.
Stroud, George M. *A Sketch of the Laws in Relation to Slavery in the United States of America.* Philadelphia, PA: Kimber and Sharpless, 1827.
Stuckey, Sterling. *Slave Culture: Nationalist Theory and the Foundation of Black America.* Oxford, UK: Oxford University Press, 1987.
Sturge, Joseph. *A Visit to the United States in 1841.* London, UK: Hamilton, Adams, and Co., 1842.
Sumner, Charles. *White Slavery in the Barbary States: A Lecture Before the Boston Mercantile Library Association, Feb. 17, 1847.* Boston, MA: William D. Ticknor and Co., 1847.
——. *The Crime Against Kansas: The Apologies for the Crime - The True Remedy.* Boston, MA: John P. Jewett, 1856.
Supplement to the Encyclopedia Britannica (4th, 5th, and 6th editions, 1815-1824). Edinburgh, Scotland: Encyclopedia Britannica, 1824.
Swain, Joseph Ward. *The Harper History of Civilization.* New York, NY: Harper and Brothers, 1958.
Swint, Henry L. (ed.) *Dear Ones at Home: Letters From Contraband Camps.* Nashville, TN: Vanderbilt University Press, 1966.
Sword, Wiley. *The Confederacy's Last Hurrah: Spring Hill, Franklin, and Nashville.* New York, NY: HarperCollins, 1992.
——. *Southern Invincibility: A History of the Confederate Heart.* New York, NY: St. Martin's Press, 1999.
Sydnor, Charles Sackett. *Slavery in Mississippi.* 1933. Baton Rouge, LA: Louisiana State University Press, 1966 ed.
Tadman, Michael. *Speculators and Slaves: Masters, Traders, and Slaves in the Old South.* Madison, Wisconsin: University of Wisconsin Press, 1989.
Tagg, Larry. *The Unpopular Mr. Lincoln: The Story of America's Most Reviled President.* New York, NY: Savas Beatie, 2009.
Tannenbaum, Frank. *Slave and Citizen: The Negro in the Americas.* New York, NY: Vintage Books, 1947.
Tarbell, Ida Minerva. *The Life of Abraham Lincoln.* 4 vols. New York, NY: Lincoln History Society, 1895-1900.

Tatalovich, Raymond, and Byron W. Daynes. *Presidential Power in the United States.* Monterey, CA: Brooks/Cole, 1984.

Taylor, Joe Gray. *Negro Slavery in Louisiana.* New York, NY: Negro Universities Press, 1969.

Taylor, Richard. *Destruction and Reconstruction: Personal Experiences of the Late War in the United States.* New York, NY: D. Appleton, 1879.

Taylor, Susie King. *Reminiscences of My Life in Camp With the 33rd United States Colored Troops Late 1st S. C. Volunteers.* Boston, MA: Susie King Taylor, 1902.

Taylor, Walter Herron. *General Lee: His Campaigns in Virginia, 1861-1865, With Personal Reminiscences.* Norfolk, VA: Nusbaum Book and News Co., 1906.

Temperley, Howard. *British Antislavery, 1833-1870.* London, UK: Longmans, 1972.

—— (ed.). *After Slavery: Emancipation and its Discontents.* London, UK: Frank Cass, 2000.

Tenney, William Jewett. *The Military and Naval History of the Rebellion in the United States.* New York, NY: D. Appleton and Co., 1865.

Terkel, Studs. *Hard Times: An Oral History of the Great Depression.* New York, NY: Avon, 1970.

Testimony Taken By the Joint Select Committee to Inquire Into the Condition of Affairs in the Late Insurrectionary States. 13 vols. Washington, D.C.: Government Printing Office, 1872.

Thackeray, William Makepeace. *Roundabout Papers.* Boston, MA: Estes and Lauriat, 1883.

The American Annual Cyclopedia and Register of Important Events of the Year 1861. New York, NY: D. Appleton and Co., 1868.

The American Annual Cyclopedia and Register of Important Events of the Year 1862. New York, NY: D. Appleton and Co., 1869.

The Congressional Globe, Containing Sketches of the Debates and Proceedings of the First Session of the Twenty-Eighth Congress (Vol. 13). Washington, D.C.: The Globe, 1844.

The Great Issue to be Decided in November Next: Shall the Constitution and the Union Stand or Fall, Shall Sectionalism Triumph? Washington, D.C.: National Democratic Executive Committee, 1860.

The National Almanac and Annual Record for the Year 1863. Philadelphia, PA: George W. Childs, 1863.

The Outlook. September 4, 1909. New York, NY: The Outlook Company, 1909.

The Oxford English Dictionary. Compact edition, 2 vols. 1928. Oxford, UK: Oxford University Press, 1979 ed.

The Quarterly Review (Vol. 111). London, UK: John Murray, 1862.

The Southern Publication Society. *The South in the Building of the Nation.* Richmond, VA: The Southern Publication Society, 1909.

The World Book Encyclopedia. 1928. Chicago, IL: Field Enterprises Educational Corp., 1966 ed.

Thomas, Emory M. *The Confederate Nation: 1861-1865.* New York, NY: Harper and Row, 1979.

Thomas, Gabriel. *An Account of Pennsylvania and West New Jersey.* 1698. Cleveland, OH: Burrows Brothers Co., 1903 ed.

Thomas, Hugh. *The Slave Trade: The History of the Atlantic Slave Trade, 1440-1870.* New York, NY: Simon and Schuster, 1999.

Thomas, William Hannibal. *The American Negro: What He Was, What He Is, and What He May Become.* New York, NY: Macmillan Co., 1901.

Thome, James A., and J. Horace Kimball. *Emancipation in the West Indies: A Six Month's Tour in Antigua, Barbadoes, and Jamaica, in the Year 1837.* New York, NY: The American Anti-Slavery Society, 1838.

Thompson, Edward Palmer. *The Making of the English Working Class.* London, UK: Victor Gollancz, 1963.

Thompson, Frank Charles (ed.). *The Thompson Chain Reference Bible* (King James Version). 1908. Indianapolis, IN: B. B. Kirkbride Bible Co., 1964 ed.

Thompson, Jack H., and Robert D. Reischauer (eds.). *Modernization of the Arab World.* Princeton, NJ: D. Van Nostrand Co., 1966.

Thompson, James Westfall, and Edgar Nathaniel Johnson. *An Introduction to Medieval Europe: 300-1500.* New York, NY: W. W. Norton and Co., 1937.

Thompson, Neal. *Driving With the Devil: Southern Moonshine, Detroit Wheels, and the Birth of NASCAR.* Three Rivers, MI: Three Rivers Press, 2006.

Thompson, Robert Means, and Richard Wainwright (eds.). *Confidential Correspondence of Gustavus Vasa Fox, Assistant Secretary of the Navy, 1861-1865.* 2 vols. 1918. New York, NY: Naval History Society, 1920 ed.

Thomson, William. *A Tradesman's Travels in the United States and Canada, in the Year 1840, 40, and 42.* Edinburgh, Scotland: Oliver and Boyd, 1842.

Thoreau, Henry David. *Walden*. New York, NY: Thomas Y. Crowell and Co., 1910.
Thorndike, Rachel Sherman (ed.). *The Sherman Letters*. New York, NY: Charles Scribner's Sons, 1894.
Thornton, Brian. *101 Things You Didn't Know About Lincoln: Loves and Losses, Political Power Plays, White House Hauntings*. Avon, MA: Adams Media, 2006.
Thornton, Gordon. *The Southern Nation: The New Rise of the Old South*. Gretna, LA: Pelican Publishing Co., 2000.
Thornton, John. *Africa and Africans in the Making of the Atlantic World, 1400-1800*. 1992. Cambridge, UK: Cambridge University Press, 1999 ed.
Thornton, Mark, and Robert B. Ekelund, Jr. *Tariffs, Blockades, and Inflation: The Economics of the Civil War*. Wilmington, DE: Scholarly Resources, 2004.
Thornton, Willis, and James Daugherty. *Almanac for Americans*. 1941. New York, NY: Greenberg, 1954 ed.
Thwaites, Reuben Gold (ed.). *Early Western Travels, 1748-1846* (Vol. 12). Cleveland, OH: Arthur H. Clark Co., 1905.
Tibbles, Anthony (ed.). *Transatlantic Slavery: Against Human Dignity*. 1995. Liverpool, UK: Liverpool University Press, 2005 ed.
Tilley, John Shipley. *Lincoln Takes Command*. 1941. Nashville, TN: Bill Coats Limited, 1991 ed.
——. *Facts the Historians Leave Out: A Confederate Primer*. 1951. Nashville, TN: Bill Coats Limited, 1999 ed.
Tinker, Hugh. *A New System of Slavery: The Export of Indian Labour Overseas, 1830-1920*. London, UK: Oxford University Press, 1974.
Tocqueville, Alexis de. *Democracy in America*. 2 vols. (Translated by Henry Reeve.) New York, NY: George Adlard, 1839.
Toland, John. *Adolph Hitler*. 1976. New York, NY: Ballantine, 1987 ed.
Tomich, Dale W. *Slavery in the Circuit of Sugar: Martinique in the World Economy, 1830-1848*. Baltimore, MD: Johns Hopkins University Press, 1990.
Tomlins, Christopher L. *Law, Labor and Ideology in the Early American Republic*. Cambridge, UK: Cambridge University Press, 1993.
Torbett, David. *Theology and Slavery: Charles Hodge and Horace Bushnell*. Macon, GA: Mercer University Press, 2006.
Torrey, Bradford (ed.). *The Writings of Henry David Thoreau*. 20 vols. Boston, MA: Houghton Mifflin and Co., 1906.
Torrey, Jesse. *A Portraiture of Domestic Slavery, in the United States*. Philadelphia, PA: Jesse Torrey, 1817.
Tourgee, Albion W. *A Fool's Errand By One of the Fools*. London, UK: George Routledge and Sons, 1883.
Townsend, John. *The South Alone, Should Govern the South, and African Slavery Should be Controlled by Those Only Who Are Friendly to It*. Charleston, SC: n.p., 1860.
Toy, John. *Slavery Indispensable to the Civilization of Africa*. Baltimore, MD: John Toy, 1855.
Traboulay, David M. *Columbus and Las Casas: The Conquest and Christianization of America, 1492-1566*. Lanham, MD: University Press of America, 1994.
Trager, James. *The New York Chronology: The Ultimate Compendium of Events, People, and Anecdotes From the Dutch to the Present*. New York, NY: HarperCollins, 2003.
Traupman, John C. *The New College Latin and English Dictionary*. 1966. New York, NY: Bantam, 1988 ed.
Trevelyan, George Macaulay. *History of England*. 2 vols. 1926. Garden City, NY: Doubleday Anchor, 1952 ed.
Trexler, Harrison Anthony. *Slavery in Missouri, 1804-1865*. Baltimore, MD: Johns Hopkins Press, 1914.
Trumbull, Lyman. *Speech of Honorable Lyman Trumbull, of Illinois, at a Mass Meeting in Chicago, August 7, 1858*. Washington, D.C.: Buell and Blanchard, 1858.
Truth, Sojourner. *Sojourner Truth's Narrative and Book of Life*. 1850. Battle Creek, MI: Sojourner Truth, 1881 ed.
Tuchman, Barbara W. *A Distant Mirror: The Calamitous 14th Century*. New York, NY: Knopf, 1978.
Tucker, St. George. *On the State of Slavery in Virginia, in View of the Constitution of the United States, With Selected Writings*. Indianapolis, IN: Liberty Fund, 1999.
Turner, Edward Raymond. *The Negro in Pennsylvania: Slavery, Servitude, Freedom, 1639-1861*. Washington, D.C.: American Historical Association, 1911.
——. *Slavery in Pennsylvania: A Dissertation*. Baltimore, MD: The Lord Baltimore Press, 1911.
Tushnet, Mark. *The American Law of Slavery, 1810-1860*. Princeton, NJ: Princeton University Press, 1981.
Tyler, Lyon Gardiner. *The Letters and Times of the Tylers*. 3 vols. Williamsburg, VA: n.p., 1896.
——. *Propaganda in History*. Richmond, VA: Richmond Press, 1920.
——. *The Gray Book: A Confederate Catechism*. Columbia, TN: Gray Book Committee, SCV, 1935.

Unger, Irwin. *These United States: The Question of Our Past - Vol. 2: Since 1865*. 1978. Englewood Cliffs, NJ: Prentice Hall, 1992 ed.

Upshur, Abel Parker. *A Brief Enquiry Into the True Nature and Character of Our Federal Government*. Philadelphia, PA: John Campbell, 1863.

Vaillant, George C. *The Aztecs of Mexico: Origin, Rise and Fall of the Aztec Nation*. 1944. Harmondsworth, UK: Penguin, 1960 ed.

Vallandigham, Clement Laird. *Speeches, Arguments, Addresses, and Letters of Clement L. Vallandigham*. New York, NY: J. Walter and Co., 1864.

Vanauken, Sheldon. *The Glittering Illusion: English Sympathy for the Southern Confederacy*. Washington, D.C.: Regnery, 1989.

Van Buren, Anson De Puy. *Jottings of a Year's Sojourn in the South; or First Impressions of the Country and its People; With a Glimpse at School-Teaching in That Southern Land, and Reminiscences of Distinguished Men*. Battle Creek, MI: 1859.

Van Buren, G. M. *Abraham Lincoln's Pen and Voice: Being a Complete Compilation of His Letters, Civil, Political, and Military*. Cincinnati, OH: Robert Clarke and Co., 1890.

Van Deusen, Glyndon Garlock. *William Henry Seward*. New York, NY: Oxford University Press, 1967.

Van Evrie, John H. *Negroes and Negro "Slavery": The First an Inferior Race: The Latter Its Normal Condition*. New York, NY: Van Evrie, Horton, and Co., 1863.

Van Loon, Hendrik Willem. *The Story of America*. 1927. Cleveland, OH: The World Publishing Co., 1942 ed.

Van Nostrand, John J., and Paul Schaeffer. *Western Civilization: A Political, Social, and Cultural History - Vol. 1, to 1660*. 1949. Princeton, NJ: D. Van Nostrand Co., 1956 ed.

Varhola, Michael O. *Life in Civil War America*. Cincinnati, OH: Family Tree Books, 1999.

Vassa, Gustavus. *The Interesting Narrative of the Life of Olaudah Equiano, or Gustavus Vassa, the African*. London, UK: Gustavus Vassa, 1794.

Ver Steeg, Clarence Lester, and Richard Hofstadter. *A People and a Nation*. New York, NY: Harper and Row, 1977.

Villard, Henry. *Memoirs of Henry Villard, Journalist and Financier, 1835-1900*. 2 vols. Boston, MA: Houghton, Mifflin and Co., 1904.

Voegeli, Victor Jacque. *Free But Not Equal: The Midwest and the Negro During the Civil War*. Chicago, IL: University of Chicago Press, 1967.

Volk, Ernest. *The Archaeology of the Delaware Valley*. Cambridge, MA: Peabody Museum of American Archeology and Ethnology, 1911.

Wade, Richard C. *Slavery in the Cities: The South 1820-1860*. New York, NY: Oxford University Press, 1964.

Wade, Wyn Craig. *The Fiery Cross: The Ku Klux Klan in America*. 1987. New York, NY: Touchstone, 1988 ed.

Walker, Barbara G. *The Woman's Encyclopedia of Myths and Secrets*. New York, NY: Harper and Row, 1983.

——. *The Woman's Dictionary of Symbols and Sacred Objects*. New York, NY: Harper and Row, 1988.

Walker, Gary C. *A General History of the Civil War: The Southern Point of View*. 2004. Gretna, LA: Pelican Publishing, 2008 ed.

Walker, Moses Fleetwood. *Our Home Colony: A Treatise on the Past, Present and Future of the Negro Race in America*. Steubenville, OH: M. F. Walker, 1908.

Walker, Sheila S. (ed.). *African Roots/American Cultures: Africa in the Creation of the Americas*. Lanham, MD: Rowman and Littlefield, 2001.

Wallace, David Duncan. *The Life of Henry Laurens*. New York, NY: G. P. Putnam's Sons, 1915.

Wallcut, R. F. (pub.). *Southern Hatred of the American Government, the People of the North, and Free Institutions*. Boston, MA: R. F. Wallcut, 1862.

Wallechinsky, David, and Irving Wallace. *The People's Almanac #2*. New York, NY: William Morrow and Co., 1978.

Wallechinsky, David, Irving Wallace, and Amy Wallace. *The People's Almanac Presents The Book of Lists*. New York, NY: William Morrow and Co., 1977.

Walsh, George. *"Those Damn Horse Soldiers": True Tales of the Civil War Cavalry*. New York, NY: Forge, 2006.

Walsh, Robert. *An Appeal From the Judgments of Great Britain Respecting the United States of America*. London, UK: John Miller, 1819.

Ward, Adolphus William, and George Peabody Gooch (eds.). *The Cambridge History of British Foreign Policy, 1783-1919*. 3 vols. Cambridge, UK: Cambridge University Press, 1923.

Ward, John William. *Andrew Jackson: Symbol for an Age*. 1953. Oxford, UK: Oxford University Press, 1973 ed.

Ware, Camilla. *Slavery In Vermont, and in Other Parts of the United States*. Woodstock, VT: Davis and Greene,

1858.

Waring, George Edward, Jr. *Whip and Spur*. New York, NY: Doubleday and McClure, 1897.

Warner, Ezra J. *Generals in Gray: Lives of the Confederate Commanders*. 1959. Baton Rouge, LA: Louisiana State University Press, 1989 ed.

——. *Generals in Blue: Lives of the Union Commanders*. 1964. Baton Rouge, LA: Louisiana State University Press, 2006 ed.

Warnock, Robert, and George K. Anderson. *The Ancient Foundations*. 1950. Glenview, IL: Scott, Foresman and Co., 1967 ed.

Warren, Robert Penn. *John Brown: The Making of a Martyr*. New York, NY: Payson and Clarke, 1929.

——. *Who Speaks for the Negro?* New York, NY: Random House, 1965.

Washington, Booker T. *Up From Slavery: An Autobiography*. 1901. Garden City, NY: Doubleday, Page and Co., 1919 ed.

Washington, Henry Augustine. *The Writings of Thomas Jefferson*. 9 vols. New York, NY: H. W. Derby, 1861.

Watkins, Samuel Rush. *"Company Aytch," Maury Grays, First Tennessee Regiment; or, A Side Show of the Big Show*. 1882. Chattanooga, TN: Times Printing Co., 1900 ed.

Watson, Alan. *Roman Slave Law*. Baltimore, MD: Johns Hopkins University Press, 1987.

——. *Slave Law in the Americas*. Athens, GA: University of Georgia Press, 1989.

Watson, Harry L. *Andrew Jackson vs. Henry Clay: Democracy and Development in Antebellum America*. New York, NY: St. Martin's Press, 1998.

Watson, James L. (ed.). *Asian and African Systems of Slavery*. Oxford, UK: Basil Blackwood, 1980.

Watts, Peter. *A Dictionary of the Old West*. 1977. New York, NY: Promontory Press, 1987 ed.

Waugh, John C. *Surviving the Confederacy: Rebellion, Ruin, and Recovery - Roger and Sara Pryor During the Civil War*. New York, NY: Harcourt, 2002.

Weatherford, Willis D., and Charles S. Johnson. *Race Relations: Adjustment of Whites and Negroes in the United States*. Boston, MA: Heath, 1934.

Webster, Daniel. *Webster's Speeches: Reply to Hayne - The Constitution and the Union*. Boston, MA: Ginn and Co., 1897.

Weeks, Stephen Beauregard. *Southern Quakers and Slavery: A Study in Institutional History*. Baltimore, MD: Johns Hopkins Press, 1896.

Weiner, Marli F. *Mistresses and Slaves: Plantation Women in South Carolina, 1830-1880*. Urbana, IL: University of Illinois Press, 1997.

Weintraub, Max. *The Blue Book of American History*. New York, NY: Regents Publishing Co., 1960.

Welby, Adlard. *A Visit to North America and the English Settlements in Illinois, With a Winter Residence at Philadelphia*. London, UK: J. Drury, 1821.

Weld, Theodore D. (ed.). *American Slavery As It Is: Testimony of a Thousand Witnesses*. New York, NY: American Anti-Slavery Society, 1839.

Welles, Gideon. *Diary of Gideon Welles, Secretary of the Navy Under Lincoln and Johnson* (Vol. 1). Boston, MA: Houghton Mifflin, 1911.

Welling, James Clarke. *Slavery in the Territories*. Washington, D.C.: U.S. Government Printing Office, 1892.

Wells, H. G. *The Outline of History: Being a Plain History of Life and Mankind*. 2 vols. 1920. Garden City, NY: Garden City Books, 1961 ed.

Wertenbaker, Thomas Jefferson. *The Puritan Oligarchy: The Founding of American Civilization*. New York, NY: Grosset's Universal Library, 1947.

——. *The Shaping of Colonial Virginia: The Planters of Colonial Virginia*. New York, NY: Russell and Russell, 1958.

Westermann, William L. *The Story of Ancient Nations*. New York, NY: D. Appleton and Co., 1912.

Wheeler, Jacob D. *Practical Treatise on the Law of Slavery*. New York, NY: Allan Pollock, Jr., 1837.

White, Charles Langdon, Edwin Jay Foscue, and Tom Lee McKnight. *Regional Geography of Anglo-America*. 1943. Englewood Cliffs, NJ: Prentice-Hall, 1985 ed.

White, Deborah Gray. *Ar'n't I a Woman? Female Slaves in the Plantation South*. New York, NY: W. W. Norton, 1985.

White, Henry Alexander. *Robert E. Lee and the Southern Confederacy, 1807-1870*. 1897. New York, NY: G. P. Putnam's Sons, 1900 ed.

White, Jon Manchip. *Everyday Life in Ancient Egypt*. 1963. New York, NY: Perigee, 1980 ed.

White, Reginald Cedric. *A. Lincoln: A Biography*. New York, NY: Random House, 2009.

White, R. J. *The Horizon Concise History of England*. New York, NY: American Heritage Publishing Co., 1971.

White, Shane. *Somewhat More Independent: The End of Slavery in New York City, 1770-1810*. Athens, GA: University of Georgia Press, 1991.

Whitehead, Albert Carlton. *Two Great Southerners: Jefferson Davis and Robert E. Lee.* New York, NY: American Book Co., 1912.

Whitman, Walt. *Leaves of Grass.* 1855. New York, NY: Modern Library, 1921 ed.

——. *Complete Prose Works.* Boston, MA: Small, Maynard, and Co., 1901.

Whitmore, William H. (ed.). *The Colonial Laws of Massachusetts.* 1672. Boston, MA: Rockwell and Churchill, 1890.

Whitsitt, William Heth. *Genealogy of Jefferson Davis and of Samuel Davies.* New York, NY: The Neale Publishing Co., 1910.

Wiedemann, Thomas. *Greek and Roman Slavery.* Baltimore, MD: Johns Hopkins University Press, 1981.

Wilbur, C. M. *Slavery in China During the Former Han Dynasty.* Chicago, IL: Field Museum of Natural History, 1943.

Wilbur, Henry Watson. *President Lincoln's Attitude Towards Slavery and Emancipation: With a Review of Events Before and Since the Civil War.* Philadelphia, PA: W. H. Jenkins, 1914.

Wilbur, Sibyl. *The Life of Mary Baker Eddy.* 1907. Boston, MA: The Christian Science Publishing Society, 1976 ed.

Wilder, Craig Steven. *A Covenant With Color: Race and Social Power in Brooklyn.* New York, NY: Columbia University Press, 2000.

Wiley, Bell Irvin. *Southern Negroes: 1861-1865.* 1938. New Haven, CT: Yale University Press, 1969 ed.

——. *The Life of Johnny Reb: The Common Soldier of the Confederacy.* 1943. Baton Rouge, LA: Louisiana State University Press, 1978 ed.

——. *The Life of Billy Yank: The Common Soldier of the Union.* 1952. Baton Rouge, LA: Louisiana State University Press, 2001 ed.

Wilkens, J. Steven. *America: The First 350 Years.* Monroe, LA: Covenant Publications, 1998.

Williams, Charles Richard. *The Life of Rutherford Birchard Hayes, Nineteenth President of the United States.* 2 vols. Boston, MA: Houghton Mifflin Co., 1914.

Williams, Eric. *Capitalism and Slavery.* Chapel Hill, NC: University of North Carolina, 1944.

Williams, George Washington. *History of the Negro Race in America: From 1619 to 1880, Negroes as Slaves, as Soldiers, and as Citizens.* 2 vols. New York, NY: G. P. Putnam's Sons, 1883.

——. *A History of the Negro Troops in the War of the Rebellion 1861-1865.* New York, NY: Harper and Brothers, 1888.

Williams, Henry Smith (ed.). *The Historians' History of the World.* 25 vols. London, UK: Hooper and Jackson, 1908.

Williams, James. *The South Vindicated.* London, UK: Longman, Green, Longman, Roberts, and Green, 1862.

Williams-Meyers, A. J. *Long Hammering: Essays on the Forging of an African American Presence in the Hudson River Valley to the Early Twentieth Century.* Trenton, NJ: Africa World Press, 1994.

Williams, Oscar. *African Americans and Colonial Legislation in the Middle Colonies.* New York, NY: Garland Publishing, 1998.

Williams, William H. *Slavery and Freedom in Delaware, 1639-1865.* Wilmington, DE: Scholarly Resources, 1996.

Willis, F. Roy. *World Civilizations - Vol. 1: From Ancient Times Through the Sixteenth Century.* 1982. Lexington, MA: D. C. Heath and Co., 1986 ed.

Willis, J. L. M. (ed.). *Old Eliot: A Monthly Magazine of the History and Biography of the Upper Parish of Kittery, Now Eliot.* Vol. 2. Eliot, ME: J. L. M. Willis, 1898.

Wills, Brian Steel. *The Confederacy's Greatest Cavalryman: Nathan Bedford Forrest.* Lawrence, KS: University Press of Kansas, 1992.

Wilson, Charles Reagan, and William Ferris. *Encyclopedia of Southern Culture* (Vol. 1). New York, NY: Anchor, 1989.

Wilson, Clyde N. *Why the South Will Survive: Fifteen Southerners Look at Their Region a Half Century After I'll Take My Stand.* Athens, GA: University of Georgia Press, 1981.

——. *A Defender of Southern Conservatism: M.E. Bradford and His Achievements.* Columbia, MO: University of Missouri Press, 1999.

——. *From Union to Empire: Essays in the Jeffersonian Tradition.* Columbia, SC: The Foundation for American Education, 2003.

——. *Defending Dixie: Essays in Southern History and Culture.* Columbia, SC: The Foundation for American Education, 2005.

Wilson, E. O. *Sociobiology: The New Synthesis.* Cambridge, MA: Belknap Press, 1975.

Wilson, Henry. *History of the Rise and Fall of the Slave Power in America.* 3 vols. Boston, MA: James R. Osgood and Co., 1877.

Wilson, Joseph Thomas. *The Black Phalanx: A History of the Negro Soldiers of the United States in the Wars of 1775-1812, 1861-'65*. Hartford, CT: American Publishing Co., 1890.

Wilson, Theodore B. *The Black Codes of the South*. Tuscaloosa, AL: University of Alabama Press, 1965.

Wilson, Woodrow. *Division and Reunion: 1829-1889*. 1893. New York, NY: Longmans, Green, and Co., 1908 ed.

——. *A History of the American People*. 5 vols. 1902. New York, NY: Harper and Brothers, 1918 ed.

Winks, Robin W. *The Blacks in Canada: A History*. New Haven, CT: Yale University Press, 1971.

Winks, Robin W., Crane Brinton, John B. Christopher, and Robert Lee Wolff. *A History of Civilization - Vol. 1: Prehistory to 1715*. 1955. Englewood Cliffs, NJ: Prentice Hall, 1988 ed. (For Vol. 2, see Crane Brinton, et al.)

Wise, Jennings Cropper. *Ye Kingdome of Accawmacke or the Eastern Shore of Virginia in the Seventeenth Century*. Richmond, VA: The Bell Book Stationary Co., 1911.

Wish, Harvey (ed.). *The Negro Since Emancipation*. Englewood Cliffs, NJ: Prentice-Hall, 1964.

Wood, Betty. *The Origins of American Slavery: Freedom and Bondage in the English Colonies*. New York, NY: Hill and Wang, 1998.

Wood, W. J. *Civil War Generalship: The Art of Command*. 1997. New York, NY: Da Capo Press, 2000 ed.

Woodard, Komozi. *A Nation Within a Nation: Amiri Baraka (LeRoi Jones) and Black Power Politics*. Chapel Hill, NC: University of North Carolina Press, 1999.

Woods, Thomas E., Jr. *The Politically Incorrect Guide to American History*. Washington, D.C.: Regnery, 2004.

Woodson, Carter G. (ed.). *The Journal of Negro History* (Vol. 4). Lancaster, PA: Association for the Study of Negro Life and History, 1919.

Woodward, William E. *Meet General Grant*. 1928. New York, NY: Liveright Publishing, 1946 ed.

Woodworth, Steven E. *Jefferson Davis and His Generals: The Failure of Confederate Command in the West*. Lawrence, KS: University Press of Kansas, 1990.

Worden, Nigel. *Slavery in Dutch South Africa*. Cambridge, UK: Cambridge University Press, 1985.

Workman, William D. *The Case For the South*. New York, NY: Devin-Adair, 1960.

Wright, Elizur, Jr. *The Sin of Slavery and Its Remedy: Containing Some Reflections on the Moral Influence of African Colonization*. New York, NY: Elizur Wright, Jr., 1833.

Wright, Gavin. *The Political Economy of the Cotton South: Households, Markets and Wealth in the Nineteenth Century*. New York, NY: W. W. Norton, 1978.

——. *Old South, New South: Revolutions in the Southern Economy Since the Civil War*. New York, NY: Basic Books, 1986.

——. *Slavery and American Economic Development*. Baton Rouge, LA: Louisiana State University Press, 2006.

Wright, John D. *The Language of the Civil War*. Westport, CT: Oryx, 2001.

Wright, Marcia. *Strategies of Slaves and Women: Life-Stories From East/Central Africa*. New York, NY: Lilian Barber Press, 1993.

Wyatt-Brown, Bertram. *Yankee Saints and Southern Sinners*. Baton Rouge, LA: Louisiana State University Press, 1990.

Wyeth, John Allan. *Life of General Nathan Bedford Forrest*. 1899. New York, NY: Harper and Brothers, 1908 ed.

Yates, John, and Joseph Moulton. *History of the State of New York, Including Its Aboriginal and Colonial Annals*. 2 vols. New York, NY: Goodrich, 1824-1826.

Yetman, Norman R. *Life Under the "Peculiar Institution": Selections from the Slave Narrative Collection*. New York, NY: Holt McDougal, 1970.

Young, Arthur (ed.). *Annals of Agriculture and Other Useful Arts* (Vol. 18). London, UK: Bury St. Edmund's, 1792.

Young, Charles. *The Last of the Vikings: A Book For Boys*. London, UK: George Bell and Sons, 1895.

Yun, Lisa. *The Coolie Speaks: Chinese Indentured Laborers and African Slaves in Cuba*. Philadelphia, PA: Temple University Press, 2008.

Zaehner, R. C. (ed.) *Encyclopedia of the World's Religions*. 1959. New York, NY: Barnes and Noble, 1997 ed.

Zetterberg, H. L. *On Theory and Verification in Sociology*. Toronto, Canada: Bedminster Press, 1965.

Zilversmit, Arthur. *The First Emancipation: The Abolition of Slavery in the North*. Chicago, IL: University of Chicago Press, 1967.

Zimmerman, Stan. *A History of Smuggling in Florida: Rum Runners and Cocaine Cowboys*. 2006. Charleston, SC: History Press, 2008 ed.

Zinn, Howard. *A People's History of the United States: 1492-Present*. 1980. New York, NY: HarperCollins, 1995.

INDEX

"All the South has ever desired was that the Union as established by our forefathers should be preserved; and that the government as originally organized should be administered in purity and truth."

ROBERT E. LEE, JANUARY 6, 1866

MEET THE AUTHOR

LOCHLAINN SEABROOK, winner of the Jefferson Davis Historical Gold Medal for his "masterpiece," *A Rebel Born: A Defense of Nathan Bedford Forrest,* is an unreconstructed Southern historian, award-winning author, Civil War scholar, and traditional Southern Agrarian of Scottish, English, Irish, Welsh, German, and Italian extraction. An encyclopedist, lexicographer, musician, artist, graphic designer, genealogist, and photographer, as well as an award-winning poet, songwriter, and screenwriter, he has a forty year background in historical nonfiction writing and is a member of the Sons of Confederate Veterans, the Civil War Trust, and the National Grange.

Due to similarities in their writing styles, ideas, and literary works, Seabrook is often referred to as the "new SHELBY FOOTE," the "Southern JOSEPH CAMPBELL," and the "American ROBERT GRAVES" (his English cousin).

The grandson of an Appalachian coal-mining family, Seabrook is a seventh-generation Kentuckian, co-chair of the Jent/Gent Family Committee (Kentucky), founder and director of the Blakeney Family Tree Project, and a board member of the Friends of Colonel Benjamin E. Caudill. Seabrook's literary works have been endorsed by leading authorities, museum curators, award-winning historians, bestselling authors, celebrities, noted scientists, well respected educators, TV show hosts, renown military artists, esteemed Southern organizations, and distinguished academicians from around the world.

As a professional writer Seabrook has authored over forty popular adult books specializing in the following topics: the American Civil War, pro-South studies, Confederate biography and history, religion, (theology and thealogy), the law of Attraction, Jesus, the Bible, the Apocrypha, self-help, health, spirituality, ghost stories, the paranormal, genealogical monographs, family histories, military encyclopedias, etymological dictionaries, ufology, social issues, comparative analysis of the origins of Christmas, and cross-cultural studies of the family and marriage.

Seabrook's eight children's books include a Southern guide to the Civil War, a biography of Nathan Bedford Forrest, a dictionary of religion and myth, a rewriting of the King Arthur legend (which reinstates the original pre-Christian motifs), two bedtime stories for preschoolers, a naturalist's guidebook to owls, a worldwide look at the family, and an examination of the Near-Death Experience.

Of blue-blooded Southern stock through his Kentucky, Tennessee, Virginia, West Virginia, and North Carolina ancestors, he is a direct descendant of European royalty via his 6th great-grandfather, the EARL OF OXFORD, after which London's famous Harley Street is named. Among his celebrated male Celtic ancestors is ROBERT THE BRUCE, King of Scotland, Seabrook's 22nd great-grandfather. The 21st great-grandson of EDWARD I "LONGSHANKS" PLANTAGENET), King of England, Seabrook is a thirteenth-generation Southerner through his descent from the colonists of Jamestown, Virginia (1607).

The 2nd, 3rd, and 4th great-grandson of dozens of Confederate soldiers, one of his closest connections to the War for Southern Independence is through his 3rd great-grandfather, ELIAS JENT, SR., who fought for the Confederacy in the Thirteenth Cavalry Kentucky under Seabrook's 2nd cousin, Colonel BENJAMIN E. CAUDILL. The Thirteenth, also known as "Caudill's Army," fought in numerous conflicts, including the Battles of Saltville, Gladsville, Mill Cliff, Poor Fork, Whitesburg, and Leatherwood.

Seabrook is also related to the following Confederates and other 19th-Century luminaries: ALEXANDER H. STEPHENS, ROBERT E. LEE, STEPHEN DILL LEE, JOHN SINGLETON MOSBY, STONEWALL JACKSON, NATHAN BEDFORD FORREST, JAMES LONGSTREET, JOHN HUNT MORGAN, JEB STUART, P. G. T. BEAUREGARD (designed the Confederate Battle Flag), JOHN BELL HOOD, ALEXANDER PETER STEWART, ARTHUR M. MANIGAULT, JOSEPH MANIGAULT, CHARLES SCOTT VENABLE, THORNTON A. WASHINGTON, JOHN A. WASHINGTON, ABRAHAM BUFORD, EDMUND W. PETTUS, THEODRICK "TOD" CARTER, JOHN B. WOMACK, JOHN H. WINDER, GIDEON J. PILLOW, STATES RIGHTS GIST, EDMUND WINCHESTER RUCKER, HENRY R. JACKSON, JOHN C. BRECKINRIDGE, LEONIDAS POLK, ZACHARY TAYLOR, SARAH KNOX TAYLOR (the first wife of JEFFERSON DAVIS), RICHARD TAYLOR, DAVY CROCKETT, DANIEL BOONE, MERIWETHER LEWIS (of the Lewis and Clark

Expedition) ANDREW JACKSON, JAMES K. POLK, ABRAM POINDEXTER MAURY (founder of Franklin, TN), WILLIAM GILES HARDING, ZEBULON VANCE, THOMAS JEFFERSON, GEORGE WYTHE RANDOLPH (grandson of Jefferson), FELIX K. ZOLLICOFFER, FITZHUGH LEE, NATHANIEL F. CHEAIRS, JESSE JAMES, FRANK JAMES, ROBERT BRANK VANCE, CHARLES SIDNEY WINDER, JOHN W. MCGAVOCK, CARRIE (WINDER) MCGAVOCK, DAVID HARDING MCGAVOCK, LYSANDER MCGAVOCK, JAMES RANDAL MCGAVOCK, RANDAL WILLIAM MCGAVOCK, FRANCIS MCGAVOCK, EMILY MCGAVOCK, WILLIAM HENRY F. LEE, LUCIUS E. POLK, MINOR MERIWETHER (husband of noted pro-South author Elizabeth Avery Meriwether), ELLEN BOURNE TYNES (wife of Forrest's chief of artillery, Captain John W. Morton), South Carolina Senators PRESTON SMITH BROOKS and ANDREW PICKENS BUTLER, and famed South Carolina diarist MARY CHESNUT.

Seabrook's modern day cousins include: PATRICK J. BUCHANAN (conservative author), CINDY CRAWFORD (model), SHELBY LEE ADAMS (Letcher County, Kentucky, portrait photographer), BERTRAM THOMAS COMBS (Kentucky's fiftieth governor), EDITH BOLLING (wife of President Woodrow Wilson), and actors ROBERT DUVALL, REESE WITHERSPOON, LEE MARVIN, REBECCA GAYHEART, ANDY GRIFFITH, and TOM CRUISE.

Born with music in his blood, Seabrook is an award-winning, multi-genre, BMI-Nashville songwriter and lyricist who has composed some 3,000 songs (250 albums), and whose original music has been heard on TV and radio worldwide. A musician, producer, multi-instrumentalist, and renown performer—whose keyboard work has been variously compared to pianists from HARGUS ROBBINS and VINCE GUARALDI to ELTON JOHN and LEONARD BERNSTEIN—Seabrook has opened for groups such as the EARL SCRUGGS REVIEW, TED NUGENT, and BOB SEGER, and has performed privately for such public figures as President RONALD REAGAN, BURT REYNOLDS, and Senator EDWARD W. BROOKE.

(Photo © Lochlainn Seabrook)

Seabrook's cousins in the music business include: JOHNNY CASH, ELVIS PRESLEY, BILLY RAY and MILEY CYRUS, PATTY LOVELESS, TIM MCGRAW, LEE ANN WOMACK, DOLLY PARTON, PAT BOONE, NAOMI, WYNONNA, and ASHLEY JUDD, RICKY SKAGGS, the SUNSHINE SISTERS, MARTHA CARSON, and CHET ATKINS.

Seabrook lives with his wife and family in historic Middle Tennessee, the heart of Forrest country and the Confederacy, where his conservative Southern ancestors fought valiantly against Liberal Lincoln and the progressive North in defense of Jeffersonianism, constitutional government, and personal liberty.

LOCHLAINNSEABROOK.COM

MEET THE FOREWORD WRITER

BARBARA G. MARTHAL, B.A., M.ED., is owner and representative of SULI (Stories-U-Like, Inc.), providing seminars on the use of storytelling, literature and music in the classroom; grades K-12. She designs and conducts workshops that empower participants through the use of stories, music and creative movement. In addition to storytelling performances, she occasionally accepts speaking engagements. She earned her Bachelor of Arts from Fisk University, Nashville, Tennessee, with a major in Sociology and a minor in Anthropology. She also holds a Master of Education with a concentration in Reading and Story Arts from East Tennessee State University, Johnson City, Tennessee.

As a Civil War reenactor, "I share stories that are inspired by historical texts and family research in Tennessee, (Wilson and Davidson) counties. My intent is to give voice and face to Antebellum American people of African descent, particularly women both slave and free. The purpose of my stories is to provide a glimpse into the daily lives of slaves and free people of color that goes beyond the one dimensional image of victimization. Through these stories I focus on a people who had their own unique sense of self and shared with all humanity the same dreams of hope, love and community for themselves and their families." She is author of the children's book entitled *Fighting for Freedom: A Documented Story* which tells the historic account of Richard T. Davis, a young Confederate soldier and his servant, Handy Davis Crudup. The story tells why they fought, how the servant is freed and what happens to them after the war.

Barbara lives with her husband, Bill Harris, an active member of the Sons of Confederate Veterans. She is an active member of the Tennessee Society Order of Confederate Rose, a member of the Confederate Belles of Tennessee and member of the Civil War Roundtable of Nashville, Tennessee. Barbara and Bill enjoy attending events and sharing the history of their ancestors during the Civil War.

BGMARTHAL.COM